THE NAVARRE BIBLE

THE PENTATEUCH

VOLUMES IN THIS SERIES
Standard Edition
NEW TESTAMENT
St Matthew's Gospel
St Mark's Gospel
St Luke's Gospel
St John's Gospel
Acts of the Apostles
Romans and Galatians
Corinthians
Captivity Letters
Thessalonians and Pastoral Letters
Hebrews
Catholic Letters
Revelation

OLD TESTAMENT
The Pentateuch
Joshua–Kings [Historical Books 1]
Chronicles–Maccabees [Historical Books 2]
The Psalms and the Song of Solomon
Wisdom Books
Major Prophets
Minor Prophets

Reader's (Omnibus) Edition
The Gospels and Acts
The Letters of St Paul
Revelation, Hebrews and Catholic Letters

Single-volume, large-format New Testament

THE NAVARRE BIBLE

The Pentateuch

The Books of Genesis, Exodus, Leviticus,
Numbers and Deuteronomy
in the Revised Standard Version and New Vulgate
with a commentary by members of the
Faculty of Theology of the University of Navarre

FOUR COURTS PRESS • DUBLIN
SCEPTER PUBLISHERS • PRINCETON, NJ

Nihil obstat: Martin Hogan, LSS, PhD, *censor deputatus*.
Imprimi potest: Desmond, Archbishop of Dublin, 17 February 1999

Typeset by Carrigboy Typesetting Services for
FOUR COURTS PRESS
7 Malpas Street, Dublin 8, Ireland.
www.fourcourtspress.ie
and in North America for
SCEPTER PUBLISHERS, INC.
P.O. Box 211, New York, NY 10018–0004
www.scepterpublishers.org

© Text of the Pentateuch in English: The translation used in this book is
the Revised Standard Version, Catholic Edition, copyrighted
1965 and 1966 by the Division of Christian Education of the National
Council of the Churches of Christ in the U.S.A. and used by permission.

© Other material (origination and selection):
Ediciones Universidad de Navarra, SA 1997

© Translation and typography: Michael Adams 1999

A catalogue record for this title is available from the British Library.

ISBN 978-1-85182-498-4 (Four Courts Press)
ISBN 978-1-889334-21-9 (Scepter Publishers)
1st printing 1999; reprinted 2000, 2006, 2008, 2011, 2013, 2018.

Library of Congress Cataloging-in-Publication Data

Bible. O.T. English. Revised Standard. 1999.
 The Navarre Bible. – North American ed.
  p. cm
 "The Books of Genesis, Exodus, Leviticus, Numbers, Deuteronomy in the Revised Standard
  Version and New Vulgate with a commentary by members of the Faculty of Theology of the
  University of Navarre."
 Includes bibliographical references.
 Contents: [1] The Pentateuch.
 ISBN 1-889334-21-9 (hardback: alk. paper)
I. Title.
 BS891.A1 1999.P75   99-23033
 221.7'7—dc21   CIP

ACKNOWLEDGMENTS

Original title: *Sagrada Biblia: Pentateuco.*
Quotations from Vatican II documents are based on
the translation in *Vatican Council II:
The Conciliar and Post Conciliar Documents,*
ed. A. Flannery, OP (Dublin 1981).
Quotations from the following editions published by
the Catholic University Press of America are used with permission:
Origen, *Homilies on Genesis and Exodus*, trs. R. Heine;
St Augustine, *De civitate Dei*, trs. G. Walsh and G. Monaghan;
St John Chrysostom, *Homilies on Genesis*, ed. Robert Hill.

The English translation of the *Catechism of the Catholic Church* is copyright for Ireland
© 1994 Veritas Publishers and Libreria Editrice Vaticana. All rights reserved.

Printed and bound in England by TJ International, Padstow, Cornwall.

Contents

Preface and Preliminary Notes   7

List of Abbreviations   9

The Old Testament in the Context of the Bible   11
  1. Holy Scripture in the mystery of Christ and his Church   11
  2. The Old Testament and its interpretation   13

Introduction to the Pentateuch   17
  1. Structure and content   17
  2. Composition   19
  3. The five books form a unity   21
  4. Message   23
  5. The Pentateuch in the light of the New Testament   24
  6. Interpretation   25

GENESIS   27

Introduction   29
  1. Structure and content   29
  2. Historical background   32
  3. Composition   32
  4. Message   34
  5. Genesis in the light of the New Testament   34
Text and commentary   36

EXODUS   233

Introduction   235
  1. Structure and content   235
  2. Historical background   238
  3. Composition   240
  4. Message   241
  5. Exodus in the light of the Old and New Testament   243
Text and commentary   245

Contents

LEVITICUS   411

Introduction   413
1. Structure and content   413
2. Historical outline of the laws of the people of Israel   414
3. Composition   416
4. Message   417
5. Leviticus in the light of the New Testament   418
Text and commentary   421

NUMBERS   519

Introduction   521
1. Structure and content   521
2. Historical background: Israel in the desert   524
3. Composition   524
4. Message   525
5. Numbers in the light of the New Testament   527
Text and commentary   529

DEUTERONOMY   655

Introduction   657
1. Structure and content   657
2. The Deuteronomic tradition: a theology of history   659
3. Composition   661
4. Message   662
5. Deuteronomy in the light of the New Testament   663
Text and commentary   664

Explanatory Notes in the RSVCE   803

Sources Quoted in the Commentary   807

Headings Added to the Biblical Text   811

Maps   818

Preface and Preliminary Notes

The project of a new Spanish translation of the Bible, with commentary, was originally entrusted to the faculty of theology at the University of Navarre by St Josemaría Escrivá, the founder of Opus Dei and the university's first chancellor.

The main feature of the English edition, *The Navarre Bible*, is the commentary, that is, the notes and introductions provided by the editors; rarely very technical, these are designed to elucidate the spiritual and theological message of the Bible. Quotations from commentaries by the Fathers, and excerpts from other spiritual writers, not least St Josemaría, are provided to show how they read Scripture and made it meaningful in their lives. This edition also carries the Western Church's official Latin version of the Bible, the *editio typica altera* of the New Vulgate (1986).

For the English edition we consider ourselves fortunate in having the Revised Standard Version as the translation of Scripture and wish to record our appreciation for permission to use that text.[1]

PRELIMINARY NOTES

The headings in the biblical text have been provided by the editors (they are not taken from the RSV); this is true also of the cross references in the marginal notes. These headings are also listed together at the end of the book, to act as a sort of index.

References in the margin of the biblical text or its headings point to parallel passages or other passages which deal with the same theme. With the exception of the New Testament and Psalms, the marginal references are to the New Vulgate, that is, they are not normally adjusted to the RSV.

Some headings carry an asterisk; this means there is an asterisked note below, more general than the normal and one which examines the structure or content of an entire passage. To get an overview of each book, the reader may find it helpful to read the asterisked notes before reading the biblical text and the more specific notes. An asterisk *inside the RSV text* refers the reader to the Explanatory Notes at the end of the book.

---

1. Integral to which are the RSV footnotes, which are indicated by superior letters.

Abbreviations

1. BOOKS OF HOLY SCRIPTURE

Acts	Acts of the Apostles	1 Kings	1 Kings
Amos	Amon	2 Kings	2 Kings
Bar	Baruch	Lam	Lamentations
1 Chron	1 Chronicles	Lev	Leviticus
2 Chron	2 Chronicles	Lk	Luke
Col	Colossians	1 Mac	1 Maccabees
1 Cor	1 Corinthians	2 Mac	2 Maccabees
2 Cor	2 Corinthians	Mal	Malachi
Dan	Daniel	Mic	Micah
Deut	Deuteronomy	Mk	Mark
Eccles	Ecclesiastes (Qohelet)	Mt	Matthew
Esther	Esther	Nah	Nahum
Eph	Ephesians	Neh	Nehemiah
Ex	Exodus	Num	Number
Ezek	Ezekiel	Obad	Obadiah
Ezra	Ezra	1 Pet	1 Peter
Gal	Galatians	2 Pet	2 Peter
Gen	Genesis	Phil	Philippians
Hab	Habakkuk	Philem	Philemon
Hag	Haggai	Ps	Psalms
Heb	Hebrews	Prov	Proverbs
Hos	Hosea	Rev	Revelations (Apocalypse)
Is	Isaiah	Rom	Romans
Jas	James	Ruth	Ruth
Jer	Jeremiah	1 Sam	1 Samuel
Jn	John	2 Sam	2 Samuel
1 Jn	1 John	Sir	Sirach (Ecclesiasticus)
2 Jn	2 John	Song	Song of Solomon
3 Jn	3 John	I Thess	1 Thessalonians
Job	Job	2 Thess	2 Thessalonians
Joel	Joel	1 Tim	1 Timothy
Jon	Jonah	2 Tim	2 Timothy
Josh	Joshua	Tit	Titus
Jud	Judith	Wis	Wisdom
Jude	Jude	Zech	Zechariah
Judg	Judges	Zeph	Zephaniah

Abbreviations

2. RSV ABBREVIATIONS

In the notes indicated by superior *letters* in the RSV biblical text, the following abbreviations are used:

Cn   a correction made where the text has suffered in transmission and the versions provide no satisfactory restoration but the RSV Committee agrees with the judgment of competent scholars as to the most probable reconstruction of the original text

Heb   the Hebrew of the consonantal Masoretic Text of the Old Testament.

Gk   Septuagint, Greek Version of the Old Testament

Lat   Latin Version of Tobit, Judith, and 2 Maccabees

Ms   manuscript

Mss   Manuscripts

MT   the Hebrew of the pointed Masoretic Text of the Old Testament

Sam   Samaritan Hebrew text of Old Testament

Syr   Syriac Version of the Old Testament

Tg   Targum

Vg   Vulgate, Latin Version of Old Testament

N.B. See the explanation given in footnote **f** on p. 259 regarding the significance of the rendering of LORD in capital letters in the RSV text.

3. OTHER ABBREVIATIONS

ad loc.	*ad locum*, commentary on this passage	f	and following (*pl.* ff)
AAS	*Acta Apostolicae Sedis*	ibid.	*ibidem*, in the same place
Apost.	Apostolic	in loc.	*in locum,* commentary on this passage
can.	canon	loc.	*locum*, place or passage
chap.	chapter	par.	parallel passages
cf.	*confer*, compare	Past.	Pastoral
Const.	Constitution	RSV	Revised Standard Version
Decl.	Declaration	RSVCE	Revised Standard Version, Catholic Edition
Dz-Sch	Denzinger-Schönmetzer, *Enchiridion Biblicum* (4th edition, Naples-Rome, 1961)	SCDF	Sacred Congregation for the Doctrine of the Faith
Enc.	Encyclical	sess.	session
Exhort.	Exhortation	v.	verse (*pl.* vv.)

The Old Testament in the
Context of the Bible

1. HOLY SCRIPTURE IN THE MYSTERY OF
CHRIST AND HIS CHURCH

1. Analogy with the Word made flesh
Jesus Christ is the key to understanding the nature and message of the sacred books of the Bible. Through these books God has deigned to speak to us in a human language, in the same way as the Eternal Word of the Father condescended to take up our human nature and become one of us.[1] In Holy Scripture God speaks to us through the human authors of the various books (the hagiographers), using their words. The books of the Old Testament, containing the word of God that prepared the way for the coming of the Redeemer, were a first step towards the incarnation of the Eternal Word of the Father. The books of the New Testament bear witness to the zenith of God's revelation—Jesus Christ—and record his words and doings. Jesus Christ is, then, the goal towards which the entire Bible tends; he is its heart, the source of its life; he is its deepest meaning.

Because they are inspired by the Holy Spirit, the books of both Testaments are means whereby God (Father, Son and Holy Spirit) and man communicate. It was God's saving plan that those books should proclaim the new life that flows from the crucified and risen Jesus as from a spring, and that is spread abroad through the preaching of the Gospel and through the sacraments of the Church. The Holy Scriptures are not, then, the basis of Christianity, as if Christianity were a "religion of the book". Christianity is "the religion of the 'Word' of God, a word which is 'not a written and mute word, but the Word which is incarnate and living';"[2] it is the life which flows from the Son of God made man into the hearts of his followers. So, for us to understand the true scope of the Holy Scriptures, "Christ, the eternal Word of the living God, must, through the Holy Spirit, 'open [our] minds to understand them' (cf. Lk 24:45)".[3]

Like the mystery of Jesus Christ the words of the Bible have a divine dimension and yet at the same time are truly human; what is termed the "law

---

1. Cf. Vatican II, *Dei Verbum*, 13. **2.** *Catechism of the Catholic Church*, 108. **3.** Ibid.

of the Incarnation" applies to them: "To compose the sacred books, God chose certain men who, all the while he employed them in this task, made full use of their powers and faculties so that, though he acted in them and by them, it was as true authors that they consigned to writing whatever he wanted written, and no more."[4] Therefore, in order to understand the meaning of the sacred books one needs to call into play all available resources (linguistic, historical, literary, etc.), given the fact that these books were written in times and cultures different from our own. However, scholarship of this sort is inadequate on its own; we need to have the guidance of the Holy Spirit and for this, in turn, John Paul II pointed out, "one must first be guided by the Holy Spirit and it is necessary to pray for that, to pray much, to ask in prayer for the interior light of the Spirit and docilely accept that light, to ask for the love that alone enables one to understand the language of God, who is 'love' (1 Jn 4:8, 16)."[5]

2. God speaking to his Church

Being docile to the Holy Spirit implies being faithful to the Church, the community of salvation founded by Christ; the texts of Holy Scripture have been entrusted to the Church "in order to nourish faith and guide the life of charity [...]. Being faithful to the Church, in fact, means resolutely finding one's place in the mainstream of the great Tradition that, under the guidance of the Magisterium, assured of the Holy Spirit's assistance, has recognized the canonical writings as the word addressed by God to his people and has never ceased meditating on them and discovering their inexhaustible riches."[6] So, the Scriptures entrusted to the Church are a treasure that belongs to all believers: "Sacred Tradition and Sacred Scripture make up a single sacred deposit of the Word of God, which is entrusted to the Church. By adhering to it the entire holy people, united to its pastors, remains always faithful to the teaching of the apostles."[7]

Because of its essential link to the Church, Holy Scripture is part and parcel of the hierarchical and charismatic dimension of the Church. The Magisterium has a God-given charge to authentically interpret the word of God, whether oral or written, on behalf of Jesus; and when it propounds the teaching of Revelation it is interpreting and "actualizing" Scripture, that is, applying it to the cultural and historical circumstances in which the faithful find themselves. As successors of the apostles, bishops are the first witnesses to and guarantors of the living tradition in which the Scriptures are interpreted from age to age. And priests, as co-workers of bishops, have a special charism to interpret Scripture when, conveying not their own personal ideas but the Word of God, they apply the eternal truth of the Gospel to the concrete

---

4. Vatican II, *Dei Verbum*, 11. **5.** Cf. John Paul II, 'Address on the Interpretation of the Bible in the Church', *L'Osservatore Romano*, weekly edition in English, 28 April 1993, published in an edition of Pontifical Biblical Commission, *The Interpretation of the Bible in the Church* (1994). **6.** Ibid. **7.** Vatican II, *Dei Verbum*, 10; cf. 21.

circumstances of life.[8] The Spirit has also been given to individual Christians to enable them to burn with the love of God when, in a group or on their own, they prayerfully study the Scriptures.

However, there are two areas in the life of the Church where Holy Scripture is most directly interpreted and presented to us—the liturgy, and the *lectio divina* or spiritual reading of the biblical texts.

The Second Vatican Council teaches that, in the liturgy of the Church and especially the celebration of the Eucharist, all the baptized come to experience the presence of Christ in his word, "since it is he himself who speaks when the holy scriptures are read in the Church".[9] By the very fact of listening to the word, the people of God contribute to the supernatural meaning of faith. In principle, it is in the celebration of the Eucharist that the sacred texts are most vividly brought alive, for it is in the Mass that the Word of God is proclaimed among the community of believers gathered around Christ "to give glory to God and to effect the work of salvation which Holy Scripture proclaims".[10]

Lectio divina, or the spiritual reading of Scripture done in a group or on one's own, is another way to go deeper into its meaning and apply it to one's life, and thereby obtain a growing love for the Word of God, the source of interior life and apostolic fruitfulness.[11] This reading is never private, because the believer always reads and interprets in the context of the Church's faith—and this reading in turn enhances that faith's treasury.[12] That is why the Second Vatican Council called for the faithful to be given every facility to access the Scriptures.[13]

2. THE OLD TESTAMENT AND ITS INTERPRETATION

1. Books of the Old Testament
The Old Testament is an indispensable part of Holy Scripture. Its books are divinely inspired and "retain a permanent value, for the Old Covenant has never been revoked. In fact, the economy of the Old Testament was deliberately so oriented that it should prepare for and declare in prophecy the coming of Christ, redeemer of all men."[14]

The canon of the Old Testament comprises 46 texts (45, if Jeremiah and Lamentations are counted together), which in Catholic editions are grouped into three blocks:

(1) *Historical books*: the five that make up the Pentateuch (Genesis, Exodus, Leviticus, Numbers, Deuteronomy), plus Joshua, Judges, Ruth, 1 and 2

---

8. Cf. Vatican II, *Presbyterorum ordinis*, 4. **9.** Vatican II, *Sacrosanctum Concilium*, 7. **10.** Ibid., 6. **11.** Cf. Vatican II, *Dei Verbum*, 21. **12.** Cf. Pontifical Biblical Commission, *The Interpretation of the Bible in the Church*. **13.** Cf. Vatican II, *Dei Verbum*, 22 and 25. **14.** *Catechism of the Catholic Church*, 121-122, quoting *Dei Verbum*, 14–15.

Samuel, 1 and 2 Kings, 1 and 2 Chronicles, Ezra, Nehemiah, Tobit, Judith, Esther and 1 and 2 Maccabees.

(2) *Didactical, poetical or wisdom books*: Job, Psalms, Proverbs, Qoheleth (Ecclesiastes), Song of Songs, Wisdom and Sirach (Ecclesiasticus).

(3) *Prophetical books*: Isaiah, Jeremiah, Lamentations, Baruch, Ezekiel, Daniel, Hosea, Joel, Amos, Obadiah, Jonah, Micah, Nahum, Habakkuk, Zephaniah, Haggai, Zechariah, Malachi.

Being the word of God, the books of the Old Testament are timeless, they have an enduring value; yet they do reflect the times and circumstances in which they were written. Therefore, " 'even though they contain matters imperfect and provisional,' the books of the Old Testament bear witness to the whole divine pedagogy of God's saving love: these writings 'are a storehouse of sublime teaching on God and of sound wisdom on human life, as well as a wonderful treasury of prayers; in them, too, the mystery of our salvation is present in a hidden way' (*Dei Verbum*, 15)."[15]

2. Interpreting the Old Testament
The Church reads the Old Testament books for the testimony they bear to the history of salvation. But because that history found its fulfilment in Christ and is illuminated by Christ, the Church interprets these books in the light of the paschal event—the death and resurrection of the Lord; this light exposes a radically new meaning and a definitive one.[16] This new insight into the meaning of the ancient Scriptures is an integral part of the Christian faith. This means that reading the Old Testament in the light of the death and resurrection of Jesus does not change the original meaning of the texts—but it does enable us to go deeper and to reach its fullest meaning by the light of Christ's definitive revelation; so, not only does the Old Testament continue to be valid, but we are enabled to understand it better. Any attempt to set aside the Old Testament or to change its substance would deprive the New Testament of its roots in history.[17]

Two basic principles need to be borne in mind in order to interpret the books of the Old Testament properly:

(a) *Any biblical text has to be read first in the context and in the light of Scripture as a whole.*
"Attention must be devoted to the content and unity of the whole of Scripture, if we are to derive their true meaning from the sacred texts . . .".[18] At times the Bible, particularly the Old Testament, can look like an agglomerate of books rather than a single coherent work; however, all the biblical texts have, under

15. Ibid., 122. **16.** Cf. Vatican II, *Dei Verbum*, 4. **17.** Cf. *Catechism of the Catholic Church*, 123. **18.** Vatican II, *Dei Verbum*, 12.

God's inspiration, come into being from within the community of believers, and they have been passed on as something that is all of a piece. Each of these books, therefore, needs to be read and interpreted as part of the entire Bible, if we are to see the way that divine Revelation develops and the various ways it is communicated to man. But it is also the case that "the texts of the Bible are the expression of religious traditions which existed before them. The mode of their connexion with these traditions is different in each case, with the creativity of the authors shown in various degrees. In the course of time, multiple traditions have flowed together little by little to form one great common tradition. The Bible is a privileged expression of this process: it has itself contributed to the process and continues to have controlling influence upon it."[19]

These connexions between texts and traditions or between one text and another do occur within the Old Testament, but they really come into their own in the New Testament, containing as it does many explicit and interpreted quotations from the Old. This fact shows that the New Testament writers recognized that the Old Testament was divinely inspired and that the revelation it contained reached its fulfilment in the life, teaching and, particularly, the death and resurrection of Jesus. When they went to the Old Testament texts to obtain light on the salvific meaning of Jesus' words and deeds, they necessarily had to rely on the methods of interpretation and the skills available in their own time. It would have been anachronistic for them to use the methods of modern scholarship. By contrast, when we read the Old Testament we should indeed interpret it with the aid of what modern science has to tell us about the world and with the help also of modern scholarship and of what we now know about the methods of interpretations available to the ancient writers. But no matter how much light these new resources provide, the fact remains that the Old Testament and the New Testament are closely linked;[20] indeed, St Augustine's words are much easier to understand now than when they were first written: *Novum in Vetere latet et in Novo Vetus patet* (The New is hidden in the Old, and the Old is made manifest in the New).[21]

(b) *The Bible should be interpreted in the context of Church Tradition.*
Biblical tradition extends into the living Tradition of the Church. God entrusted the Bible not to any one individual, but to the Church.[22] It is only through the Church that we come to have the canon of Holy Scripture, that is, to know which books are inspired, which books form part of the Bible. "Guided by the Holy Spirit and in the light of the living tradition which it has received, the Church has discerned the writings which should be regarded as Sacred Scripture [...]. The discernment of a 'canon' of Sacred Scripture was the result of a long process."[23]

19. Pontifical Biblical Commission, *The Interpretation of the Bible in the Church.* **20.** Cf. Vatican II, *Dei Verbum*, 16. **21.** St Augustine, *Questiones in Heptateuchum*, 2, 73 (PL 34, 623). **22.** Cf. Vatican II, *Dei Verbum*, 11. **23.** Pontifical Biblical Commission, *The Interpretation of the Bible in the Church*, B. 1.

The Church identified which books are inspired (both the Old and the New Testaments), and by discerning the canon of Scripture she discerned her own identity: the Scriptures are, from then on, a mirror in which the Church is constantly enabled to see herself and to check, century after century, how she should be responding to the Gospel.[24] The Church is aware that it was the Holy Spirit himself who moved the hagiographers to write the sacred books—and it is he who guided her to recognize which books were inspired and who always helps her to correctly and authentically interpret them. Any interpretation of of Holy Scripture which wants to respect the nature of those books must, therefore, be done *in sinu Ecclesiae*, in the bosom of the Church.

There is, then, a close connexion between Tradition, Scripture and Magisterium. Tradition has been set down in writing in certain books, and these books have been recognized as sacred, as part of Scripture, by that same living Tradition which interprets them as being the genuine Word of God. Thus, the third element, interpretation, is part and parcel of Scripture itself, because Scripture is shaped by a series of actions taken by the Church which is, by virtue of its constitution, a community of tradition.

In the course of this great Tradition, the Fathers provided an exegesis which drew out of Scripture guidelines for the doctrinal tradition of the Church; their work has made a rich theological contribution to the instruction and spiritual nourishment of the faithful. The Fathers' reading and interpretation of Scripture are a treasury, from which the Church is forever drawing— this, despite the fact that the methods the Fathers used to explore the meaning of the texts were those of the times and cultures in which they lived, and in many instances have lost their scholarly validity.[25] Ever since the epoch of the Fathers, preaching and study have produced an enormous amount of commentary, providing further insights into the meaning of Scripture.

Be that as it may, the interpretation of Scripture should never be approached as a research exercise dependent on the researcher's technical skills. It is, rather, an encounter with the Word of God in the living Tradition of the Church, an encounter with an immense multitude of men and women who have rooted their lives in the Church and made their services available to her.

---

24. Cf. Vatican II, *Dei Verbum*, 18. **25.** Cf. ibid., 23.

Introduction to the Pentateuch

The "Pentateuch" is the name given to the first five books of the Bible—Genesis, Exodus, Leviticus, Numbers and Deuteronomy. Taken together, the sacred texts form something like a work in five parts. The name "Pentateuch", coming from the Greek *Pentateuchos*, means "a book composed of five rolls" and from the start of the Christian era it was applied to the case or container in which the rolls of these five books were stored. Jews, and often Christians too, call the Pentateuch the "Law", in Hebrew *ha-Toráh*.

1. STRUCTURE AND CONTENT

The general content of the Pentateuch can be seen from the titles given to the books that make it up. *Genesis* deals with the origin of the world, mankind and the people of Israel; *Exodus*, the Israelites' escape from Egypt; *Leviticus*, the levitical laws on holiness and worship; *Numbers*, censuses and lists of those who came out of Egypt and wandered about the desert; *Deuteronomy*, the second Law, laid down by Moses before the entry into the promised land.

However, when we look more closely at the content of the Pentateuch we see it as something quite complex. On the one hand, there is a line of narrative running from Adam to Moses; and on the other a series of laws and regulations which really have to do with various different circumstances experienced by the people of Israel. We have in the Pentateuch a mesh of narrative accounts and laws: there is no book like it. The events it narrates, from the creation of the world to the end of the people of Israel's pilgrimage in the desert, provide the setting for the laws; and the laws, in their turn, originate in, derive from, the events described. If we look at the Pentateuch as a whole, it is easy to see that God reveals himself by means of events and words which are intrinsically connected with one another, in such a way that the works performed by God bear out the doctrine signified by the words, and the words, for their part, throw light on the works.[1]

The division into five books does not exactly keep step with the historical narrative; in fact the narrative is interrupted at various points to take in blocks of laws. Here is an outline of the narrative:

---

1. Vatican II, *Dei Verbum*, 2.

The Pentateuch

1 Gen 1–11   The Creation and the history of humankind up to Abraham. Prehistory.

2 Gen 12–50   The history of the patriarchs: Abraham, Isaac, Jacob and his sons.

3 Ex 1–18   Sojourn in Egypt; deliverance from slavery and escape into Sinai.

4 Ex 19–40   The Covenant made in Sinai. A huge collection of laws: the Ten Commandments, the Code of the Covenant and ritual regulations.

5 Lev 1–27   Laws about sacrifices, priests, ritual purity and holiness.

6 Num 1–10   Preparations for leaving Sinai; some laws.

7 Num 11–36   Stages in the journey from Sinai to Moab, with a long intermediate stop at Kadesh; further laws about sacrifices and priests.

8 Deut 1–30   Three wide-ranging discourses given by Moses in Moab recalling the stages of the Israelites' pilgrimage in the desert and reminding them of the commandments.

9 Deut 31–34   Moses' last instructions. His death (in Moab).

The history narrated in the Pentateuch is clearly a selective one. The book of Genesis, in its early stages, covers humankind as a whole—creation, the drama of the first sin, the human race spreading across the earth, and the growth of evil which earns the punishment of the flood. With Noah, however, mankind gets a new start; but the text focuses on the descendants of Shem (one of Noah's sons), whose line continues right down to Abraham, the man to whom God promises the land of Canaan and countless offspring. The biblical narrative then follows the sons of Abraham, first Isaac's line and then that of Jacob, ignoring that of Ishmael and later that of Esau (these receive only a mention). It then concentrates on the twelve sons of Jacob, from whom will come the twelve tribes that go to make up the people of Israel; the most mention is given to Judah and Joseph. The book of Exodus focuses on Moses and Aaron, descendants of Levi. However, from this stage onwards the main protagonist is the people of Israel. So, by this process of selection the narrative moves from humankind as a whole to direct its attention to just one nation, God's chosen people.

2. COMPOSITION

The laws by which Israel was governed were known as the "Law of Moses" (cf. Deut 31:9; Josh 8:31–35; 23:6; 25:25). Thus, in Exodus 34:27–28 we are told that God commanded Moses to write the words of the Covenant on tablets of stone; and in the book of Nehemiah we hear that on the return from the Babylonian exile the book of the "law of Moses which the Lord had given to Israel" was read out in public (cf. Neh 8:1–8). Much later on, shortly before the time of Jesus Christ, these passages were taken to mean that Moses himself was the author of the Pentateuch. Statements to this effect (which are also to be found in the New Testament: cf. Mt 8:4; Mk 7:10; Luke 24:24; Jn 1:45; 5:46; Acts 3:22; Rom 10:5, 19; 1 Cor 9:9; 2 Cor 3:15) show the great authority these five books had as the word of God written down by the great prophet Moses and given to the people of Israel. From this time onwards, in both Jewish and Christian tradition, we find constant references to Moses' being the author of the Pentateuch.

From very early times, however, biblical scholars were aware that the Pentateuch as we now know it comes from the time of the return from exile in Babylon (6th–5th centuries).[2] But in more recent times, beginning in the eighteenth century, the sources of the Pentateuch have been the subject of careful scholarly research. What that research shows is that the final redaction used materials from many different periods, some of them very old indeed—materials which were rearranged and rewritten by the inspired writers; this edited text consists of the five sacred books as they reached the Jewish people—and later the Church. In them is revealed a core teaching which was particularly meaningful to the Jews after their experience of exile—that Israel is God's chosen people, who have received the gift of the Law, and they must keep that Law if they are to remain as a people and dwell in the promised land. God used certain men, at different times, to compose the sacred books "so that, though he acted in them and by them, it was as true authors that they consigned to writing whatever he wanted written, and no more."[3]

We have no reliable information as to what form this material took prior to its being incorporated in the Pentateuch or what the history of that material was; but there is good reason to suppose that ancient traditions about the patriarchs, Moses and the wilderness years, and the conquest of the promised land, were all collected and expanded in various ways at peak periods of religious and cultural activity among the Jewish people.

During the period of the monarchy stress was laid on religious traditions such as the Covenant with God in the wilderness, obedience to what that

---

2. St Jerome explained that the account of Moses' death (cf. Deut 34), and some other remarks, such as when it says "to this day" (Gen 26:33; 35:20), are attributable to Ezra when he copied out the Law of Moses (cf. *De perpetua virginitate B. Mariae*, 7; PL 23, 190). **3.** Vatican II, *Dei Verbum*, 11.

Covenant laid down, and the transcendence of God. In their preaching, prophets like Amos and Hosea went deeper into the religous meaning that these traditions had for the people. It may well be that when the Northern kingdom fell to the Assyrians (9th century), many Israelites fled south and brought with them their own interpreted traditions containing that theological content. This Northern tradition is called the "Elohistic" tradition (E), because in its accounts God is referred to by the name of "Elohim".

The 7th century BC, under Kings Hezekiah and Josiah, saw profound religious changes which helped towards a new understanding of the past and brought about a literary revival; this in turn, during and after the Exile, led to the writing of a history of Israel from the conquest of the promised land onwards (the books of Joshua, Judges, Samuel and Kings). This account is usually described as the "Deuteronomic" account (D), because it included Deuteronomy, or part of it, as an introduction to the history narrated in those books. It expounds the Law of Moses in a series of great discourses and it stresses the gratuitous nature of God's choice of Israel, and the need to faithfully obey his commandment. It also makes the case for centralizing religious worship in one shrine only—the temple of Jerusalem.

The literary activity of the Deuteronomic reform may well have extended beyond the writing of the history of the period from Joshua to Kings. It probably helped form certain traditional accounts (written and oral) into narrative cycles—the story of the origin of the world and of man, the patriarchs, Israel in Egypt, the Exodus, the years in the desert before entering the land of Canaan. This laid the foundations for the composition of an elaborate prologue to Deuteronomy and to the history of the subsequent years, a prologue which would weave into a harmonious whole ancient tradition about the history of salvation, from the origin of the world to the early days of Israel's settlement in the land of Canaan. In those narrative cycles God is sometimes referred to as "Yahweh"; that is why the tradition from which these passages derive is called the "Yahwistic" tradition (for which the abbreviation J is used, from the German *Jahwist*).

The Exile in Bablyon (6th century BC) led to a period of deep religious soul-searching. The priests among the exiles had to try to keep the people's faith alive and to protect them from the influences of Babylonian religion which was full of pagan myths and ritual practices. To do this they kept reminding the people of the traditions of their ancestors, pointing out that the entire history of mankind and particularly that of the people of Israel involved a series of covenants made by God with men. The literary activity of these priestly groups in Babylon (which was kept up after the return from exile) is to be seen in elaborate collections of laws about worship, priestly purity, and the purity of the people. In modern scholarship all this literary activity is described as belonging to the Priestly tradition (P, from *Priester*, the German for "priest"), a tradition which has left a profound impression on our text of the Pentateuch.

Recent scholarship has tried (though no consensus has yet emerged) to identify which parts of the content of the Pentateuch date from which of these historical periods. It seems fairly clear that the teaching contained in these five books did not develop all of a sudden at the time of their final redaction or in the period immediately before that; rather, the basic elements—God's choice of the people of Israel, the Covenant, the Law, the form of worship—were part of the earliest traditions of the people.

3. THE FIVE BOOKS FORM A UNITY

All the various traditions which must have existed prior to the final redaction, even though they each have their own literary and doctrinal characteristics, were brought together by divine inspiration to form the great masterpiece we call the "Pentateuch" and become the "Law of Moses". If we look at the opening words of each of the five books (the title, as it were, given them by their authors), we will see the line of continuity running through them.

Genesis provides the reply (uttered by belief in the Lord) to the question: When and how did the people of Israel come into being? But obviously attention had to be paid to the existence of other nations more numerous than Israel—and the whole matter of the origin of the world and of humankind had to be addressed. To answer these questions, the writers availed themselves of traditions that spoke about the beginnings—the creation of the world and of man, the origin of the various peoples, particularly the origin of Israel, that is, Abraham, who had come from Mestopotamia (cf. Josh 24:2; Is 51:2), and Jacob the Aramean nomad who travelled down into Egypt (cf. Deut 26:5). All this is dealt with in the same book, Genesis, whose content justifies the words with which the Hebrew text begins—*Bereshit* ("In the beginning": Gen 1:1). This opens the way to describing the first stage in the history of the people, the stage when they were chosen by God as his own.

The book of Genesis ends with the Israelites living in Egypt. However, that was only the beginning of their history: it continued when they left that country. At this stage in the story Moses is the central figure: the narrative concentrates on him and on those who, along with him, were rescued from Egypt and who made a solemn undertaking to obey the will of God who had made them his chosen people among whom he was going to pitch his tent. It was very important to identify who precisely were those people who formed the core of the reinvigorated people of God; therefore, this stage in the story of the chosen people (covered by the book of Exodus) begins with the words "These are the names of the sons of Israel who came to Egypt with Jacob" (Ex 1:1). The book of Exodus covers all the traditions about the departure from Egypt, the Covenant and the Lord's coming to dwell in the midst of his people.

If God is dwelling among his people, then they have to live in holiness. However, the history of the people was a succession of infidelities followed by punishment and pardon. Would they ever manage to obtain forgiveness once-and-for-all, and live in holiness from then on? How could they come to know the will of God? The answer to these questions is to be found in the Law and in worship. There were all kinds of detail regulations about divine worship (the product of priestly circles) and the third book (Leviticus) in this work made up of five rolls, the Pentateuch, was the natural place to spell out all these regulations. God himself tells his people, through Moses, how they are to serve him at all times. So, the book which gathers up all these laws begins with the words "The Lord called Moses, and spoke to him from the tent of meeting" (Lev 1:1), that is to say, he called the people to serve him and he gave them rules about how they should go about this.

The narrative was still incomplete, because in the previous book Israel was left at the foot of Sinai, whereas God had promised to give it the land of Canaan. So we are told about how the people set out marching across the desert again, in perfect formation, and we are told of all the trials they underwent. Some found it too much for them and they gave up. This explains why the Israelites spent forty years in the desert: that sinful generation needed to be purified and the new generation had to prove it was worthy to cross the Jordan and take possession of the land God had promised Abraham. This part of the work, the book of Numbers, is based on a mix of ancient accounts of the strife between Israel and the surrounding peoples. Its purpose is clearly to show the tension that exists between punishment and salvation. Punishment extends even to Moses and Aaron, who will not enter the promised land; salvation is detected in the name of the new hero, Joshua, meaning "Yahweh saves". Life in the desert has shaped the personality of this people which has been given the Word of God; so the book which covers all this material about the pilgrimage in Sinai opens with the words "The Lord spoke to Moses in the wilderness of Sinai" (Num 1:1).

When they reached the plains of Moab, before entering the promised land, the time was right for the great discourses given by Moses, in which the history of Israel is clearly interpreted as salvation history: Israel has been chosen by God, not because it is a big nation or is exceptional in some way: it is chosen by God's great love; love is what lies behind God's choice. These Mosaic discourses become the fifth roll, Deuteronomy, and the content of the book is heralded by its opening lines: "These are the words that Moses spoke to all Israel" (Deut 1:1)—words which show the meaning and purpose of Israel's long history, namely, the fact that it is an expression of the paternal love of God and of his people's filial response to that love.

From the religious point of view, all the material assembled in the Pentateuch constitutes teaching to which the people of Israel must subscribe. It has now all become part of the "Law" of the Lord. This combination of vari-

ous traditions has an enriching effect: they complement one another and in no sense conflict. Now that they are integrated in a single whole (the "Law"), they show how God acts towards his people and the response he expects.

4. MESSAGE

The message contained in the Pentateuch is basically a religious one: it shows God at work in human history and his creation of the people of Israel,[4] and it spells out the kind of response the people must make to God. It identifies, therefore, the basis of Israel's faith and religion: we see Israel acknowledging and proclaiming how God intervened in its past history (cf. Deut 26:5–10; Josh 24:2–13), doing things which are otherwise inexplicable. At the same time it tells us that God makes his will known through people who speak on his behalf. Hence the importance of the words placed on Moses' lips. So, events, and the words that interpret them, that show what God's will is, are intrinsically linked. Both things—events and words—come from God and form part of the history of salvation.

The history of God's revelation as narrated in the Pentateuch is also a history of man's knowledge of the true God. By means of significant historical events and words uttered by God's spokesmen, Israel came to know the one and only God, transcendent and almighty (cf. Ex 34:1–6). This is the image of God portrayed by the first five books of the Bible.

The Pentateuch teaches that God has acted in human history by choosing a particular nation to be the means by which all nations will attain salvation. This election or choice, which is unmerited and entirely the product of God's love, is the key to understanding the story that unfolds not only in the Pentateuch but right through the Bible. The Pentateuch really begins with the singling out of one man, Abraham, and it develops to the point where that election extends to the entire people of Israel through the mediation of another chosen man, Moses.

Each election is accompanied by a *promise*. The Pentateuch is also the book of the promises. God promises Abraham and the patriarchs the land of Canaan and many descendants; he renews this promise to the people of Israel, whom he has rescued from Egypt; and he promises liberation and victory over evil to all of Adam's line (cf. Gen 3:15).

Election and promise are ratified by the *Covenant*. The Covenant between God and his people (mediated by Moses) constitutes the centre of the Pentateuch. But this Covenant is really the climax of a series of covenants which begins with Noah and then continues with Abraham and the other patriarchs down to Moses' time. Israel is quite right to see itself as the people of the Covenant.

4. For a summary of the stages of Revelation, cf. *Catechism of the Catholic Church*, 54–63.

The Covenant brings with it the *Law*, which is a series of injunctions or regulations the people must obey in order to maintain their pact with God. So, the Law has a deep meaning: if one accepts it, that means one is gratefully accepting God's will; keeping the Law means that one really and truly wants to obtain the promised gift. As we have seen, Jewish tradition calls the Pentateuch the "Law"; this means not just law in the sense of regulation but law as "God's saving intervention" as reported in these books.

5. THE PENTATEUCH IN THE LIGHT OF THE NEW TESTAMENT

When read in the light of the Christian faith, the Pentateuch does not lose any of its sublime religious meaning: rather, we perceive that meaning better than before, because we are able to see it in the context of divine biblical revelation as a whole. We recognize the Pentateuch to be, as it were, a stage in a process, the first stage in salvation history, a history which is on-going and which attains its climax in Jesus Christ and in the Church, the new people of God.

The God whom himself in Jesus Christ reveals is the same God as made himself known to Moses and the patriarchs, the one and only God, transcendent and merciful, who is active in human history. The New Testament teaches that this action of God went further than we could have dreamed: God became man in order to save man (cf. Jn 1:14). And in this central event of history, God revealed himself to be Father, Son and Holy Spirit, a Trinity of Persons in one God.

The aim of God's choice of Israel (to be a means whereby all nations will be blessed) is fulfilled in the New Testament by its showing us that the Saviour has come from within the people of Israel. Christ represents Israel, for he is the Chosen One of God who is to bring salvation to all mankind; with him and through him the number of the elect has no limit to it (cf. Gen 3:15).

In the Pentateuch election is linked to promise; in the New Testament we are shown that the promises have been fulfilled through Christ. He is the affirmation of the promises (cf. Rev 7:12), promises which, over the course of Old Testament salvation history, go beyond the boundary of one nation and point to a Kingdom of God. This is the Kingdom Christ will establish; and God has made an irrevocable promise that it will come about and that it will endure.

The covenants that ratified the original election and the promises reach their climax in the new and definitive Covenant sealed with the blood of Christ. But that Covenant cannot be understood without reference to the earlier covenants, which had special features of their own but were nevertheless a preparation for the definitive Covenant. The New Covenant exists because there previously existed an Old Covenant. And together with the New

Covenant a New Law is revealed which, based likewise on the Old (cf. Mt 7:12), is now presented as the Law of Christ, written on man's heart by the Holy Spirit.

In all these ways, the Law, that is, the Pentateuch as a whole, was and continues to be, as St Paul teaches, the tutor that leads us to Christ (cf. Gal 3:24–25). The *Catechism of the Catholic Church* explains that "the Law remains the first stage on the way to the Kingdom. It prepares and disposes the chosen people and each Christian for conversion and faith in the Saviour God. It provides a teaching which endures for ever, like the Word of God. The Old Law is a *preparation for the Gospel*: 'The Law is a pedagogy and a prophecy of things to come (St Irenaeus, *Adv. Haer.* 4, 15, 1).' It prophesies and presages the work of liberation from sin which will be fulfilled in Christ: it provides the New Testament with images, 'types', and symbols for expressing the life according to the Spirit. Finally, the Law is completed by the teaching of the sapiential books and the prophets which set its course toward the New Covenant and the Kingdom of heaven."[5]

6. INTERPRETATION

The Pentateuch gives an account of a key stage in salvation history—the origins of the people of Israel and its establishment as the people of God founded on the Covenant and the Law. In the events it describes and also in the laws it presents, the Pentateuch allows us to glimpse God's plans for the salvation of mankind. It therefore seeks to be, and is, a predominantly historical work; and at the same time it seeks to offer, and does offer, a code of human behaviour. As we have seen, it recounts the history of the Israelites' ancestors from the viewpoint of a faith that is based on later revelation (that of the events of Sinai and the teachings of the prophets). It deals with Mosaic law from the perspective of the Israelites' experiences over the course of centuries, from the very start down to the time of the Exile in Babylon. The kind of history found in the Pentateuch is of a very special kind: it is a history in which the most important element is not that it allows the reader to check whether events took place in this way or in some other way: what matters is that he can identify the teaching that the book is trying to get across. As far as the laws are concerned, the essential thing quite often is not the regulations being made for a particular situation in the life of the chosen people but the spirit behind the laws and the degree of universal validity they have. As the Second Vatican Council put it, the important thing is to ascertain "the meaning which the sacred writers really had in mind, that meaning which God had thought well to manifest through the medium of their words".[6] It is this meaning—usually termed the

5. Nos. 1963f. 6. *Dei Verbum*, 12.

"historical" or "literal" meaning—that we try in the first instance to bring out in our commentary on the text.

In addition to an "historical" interpretation, the books of the Pentateuch, like any other writings (or more so), are also open to a theological or spiritual interpretation. The early chapters of Genesis particularly lend themselves to this type of interpretation. In addition to the meaning they may have had at the time when they were written, they are open to being better understood and to taking on greater relevance when viewed from other cultural and religious standpoints (that is why, for example, our commentary on Genesis 1–3 includes teachings given by Pope John Paul II apropos of them). Moreover, when concrete individuals make an appearance in the Pentateuch narratives, it is possible also to interpret them symbolically in the sense that we can see in them models for how we ought to behave and the kind of attitude we should have towards God, and lessons about spiritual values. There is a tendency towards this kind of interpretation towards the end of the Old Testament (cf. Sir 44) and it extends into the New (cf. Heb 11); it was particularly to the fore in the Patristic period. In accounts about concrete individuals or events, this style of interpretation is able to uncover a spiritual meaning (compatible with the historical meaning) which helps us to read the texts of the Pentateuch as a catechesis of Christian life. Our commentary includes some interpretations of this sort.

Finally, reading the Pentateuch in the light of Christ's revelation, one comes to see that it is not just a stage in salvation history but also a direct announcement of the final outcome of that history, that is, Christ and the Church. We can see certain persons and things in these books as standing for Christ and his Church. In these instances we find a latent presence of Christ and his Church. This typological interpretation of the Pentateuch occurs in the New Testament (as when St Paul sees Hagar as standing for the Old Covenant and Sarah for the New: cf. Gal 4:21), but it is particularly a feature of the Fathers. Its main value is that it helps to show how Christ is present right throughout the Bible. In the commentaries that follow, the reader will find some of this typological interpretation which discloses "the inexhaustible content of the Old Testament [... and] indicates the dynamic movement towards the fulfilment of the divine plan when 'God [will] be everything to everyone' (1 Cor 15:28)."[7]

---

7. *Catechism of the Catholic Church*, 129f.

GENESIS

Introduction

The opening words of the narrative ("In the beginning God created . . .") signal the purpose and even the content of the first book of the Bible—namely, to show how God acted in the early days of the world and of peoples and in particular the people of Israel. The author knows that the ultimate explanation for things and for history can be found only in God. He is not attempting to provide a scientific account of reality or of history. His focus is *religious*; this needs to be borne in mind if we are to understand the book properly. Its name—*Genesis* ("The origins")—was the Greek name given to it when it was translated into that language in the second century BC.

1. STRUCTURE AND CONTENT

There is a phrase which occurs ten times in the course of the book: "These are the generations [origins, line of descent] . . . "; this phrase divides the book into sections of unequal length and it gives a sense of development to the narrative. However, there are so many differences in the content of the first eleven chapters as compared with the rest of the book that Genesis is usually also divided into two big parts:

PART ONE: CREATION AND THE FIRST STAGE OF THE LIFE OF MAN (1:1—11:26). This part contains the creation account and what we might call "prehistory". It includes five of the sections which start with the words "These are the generations of . . .":

(1) Genesis 2:4, the point when the first account of the creation of the world and man finishes, and a new account begins—that of the creation of Adam and Eve and their first offspring. The book of Genesis began by teaching that God created the world, the heavens and the earth—and he created man on the earth and entered into dialogue with him from the very start (1:1—2:25). It goes on to tell how man was no sooner created than he disobeyed his Creator; thereby sin enters the picture (3:1—4:26).

(2) Genesis 5:1, where we are introduced to Adam's descendants down to Noah. Thanks to God's blessing, the human race of Man increases and spreads over the earth. But evil also abounds, to the point where God can tolerate no more (5:1—6:8).

29

(3) Genesis 6:9, where we are told about Noah's descendants at the time of the flood that God sent as a punishment, leaving only a remnant alive—Noah and his family (6:9—8:22)—with whom God immediately makes a covenant (9:1–17).

(4) Genesis 10:1, which is the point where the descendants of the sons of Noah (Shem, Ham, and Japheth) begin to be introduced; all the nations are descended from these people. Starting with the sons of Noah, the earth will be populated once more (10:1–32); however, human pride is still alive, as we can see from the attempt to build the tower of Babel; as a punishment for this the Lord scatters mankind over the face of the earth (11:1–9).

(5) Genesis 11:10 where the narrative focuses on Shem and his descendants as far as Terah, the father of Abraham.

PART TWO: THE ORIGIN AND DEVELOPMENT OF THE CHOSEN PEOPLE (11:27—50:26). This part covers the history of the patriarchs, that is, the history of the remote origins of Israel, linked to the first part of the book. We are also told, in passing, something about the origins of neighbouring peoples. The sacred writer introduces stages in this history by repeating (five times, again) the words "These are the generations of . . ." In this second part of the book the phrase occurs at:

(6) Genesis 11:27, where the descendants of Terah begin to be introduced—Abraham, Nahor and Haran. Some time after the scattering that took place at Babel, God decides to rebuild bridges and become friends with mankind again and pour out his blessings. With this end in view he calls Abraham (chap. 12), whom he will make the father of a great people through the patriarchs that follow him. This people will produce the Messiah, Jesus Christ, the Saviour of the world. Abraham is the protagonist of chapters 12–25 of Genesis. God tells him to leave his land in Mesopotamia and go to the land of Canaan; he promises to give him possession of this land, and promises too that he will have many descendants (12:1–9). Abraham travels south, to the Negeb desert; but famine in that zone forces him to go down to Egypt; from there he goes north again, and he and Lot separate (Lot had come with him from Mesopotamia): 12:10—13:18. Abraham settles at Hebron, from where he makes a foray to support Lot, defeating a coalition of four kings; and on his way back he meets Melchizedek, the king of Salem, who blesses him (14:1–24). After God ratifies his promises to Abraham by means of a covenant rite (15:1–21), Abraham has a son, Ishmael, by Hagar a slavegirl, because his wife Sarah was barren (16:1–16). Then, in a further ratification of the promises, God orders Abraham to apply the rite of circumcision to himself and his descendants, as a mark of the Covenant (17:1–27); God appears to Abraham again at Mamre, promises that he will have a son by Sarah (18:1–15) and tells him that Sodom and Gomorrah are going to be destroyed (Abraham pleads for

these cities, but to no avail: 18:16—19:38). Abraham moves south once more and gets as far as Gerar, where he meets its king, Abimilech (20:1–18). Sarah bears Abraham a son, Isaac, and then forces Abraham to expel Ishmael and Hagar from his household (21:1–21). In Beer-sheba Abraham makes a pact with Abimelech (19:23–33); but then God orders Abraham to go to the land of Moriah (Jerusalem) and there sacrifice his son Isaac, whom God, as it turns out, saves (22:1–14). Abraham then goes back to the region of Beer-sheba (22:19), and, as he passes through Hebron, buys land and a sepulchre in which to bury Sarah (23:1–20). In his great old age he sends one of his servants from Beer-sheba to his land of origin to seek a wife for Isaac (24:1–67). When he dies, he is buried with Sarah in Hebron (25:7–11).

(7) Genesis 25:12, giving the names of the descendants of Ishmael the son of Abraham and Hagar his slave.

(8) Genesis 25:19, where the narrative moves on to give the descendants of Isaac. From this point on, the focus is on the story of Isaac. We are told, firstly, about the birth of his two sons, Esau and Jacob, and how Jacob manages to get the rights of the first-born. Then Isaac moves to Gerar and Beer-sheba, as his father Abraham had done (26:1–35). In his old age Isaac gives his blessing for the first-born to Jacob, who had taken Esau's place (27:1–33), at the instigation of Rebekah his wife, who did not like the fact that Esau chose wives from among the women of the neighbourhood (27:46); Isaac then sends Jacob to look for a wife in the land of his forebears (28:11); from this point on the narrative centres on Jacob. After seeing a vision of God in Bethel (28:10–22), Jacob reaches the house of Laban where he takes to wife Leah and Rachel (29:15–30); eleven sons are born to him and he becomes exceedingly prosperous (29:30—30:43). He loses favour with Laban and, in obedience to God, he secretly makes off for Canaan; but Laban overtakes him and the two make an agreement (31:1—32:3). Jacob then prepares to meet his brother Esau; he crosses the ford of Jabbok and there is a mysterious episode in which he wrestles with God, who blesses him and changes his name from Jacob to Israel (32:2–32). Jacob's meeting with Esau proves peaceful and he settles down at Shehem (33:1–20), but he has to leave there due to the revenge taken by his sons Simeon and Levi over the rape of their sister Dinah (34:1–31). God tells Jacob to go to Bethel, and there he renews the promises he made to his forefather (35:11–12). He then goes to Hebron; on the way there, Benjamin, his youngest child, is born, and Rachel dies and is buried near Bethlehem. At Hebron he meets his elderly father, and Isaac dies; both Jacob and Esau are present at his burial (35:27–29).

(9) Genesis 36:1, which deals with the line of Esau, the eldest son of Isaac. Esau (identified with Edom) goes to settle in the land of Seir (36:1–43), whereas Jacob (Israel) stays in Canaan (37:2–36).

(10) Genesis 37:2. Here begins the account of the sons of Jacob, which takes up the rest of the book. It tells how Jacob's favourite son, Joseph, was

sold by his brothers (37:2–36), and narrates the story of Judah and Tamar (38:1–26). It describes how Joseph gets on in Egypt and becomes very influential (39:1—41:57). The other sons of Jacob are forced by famine to go down into Egypt; Joseph puts them through many tests and then makes himself known to them in a very touching scene (42:1—45:28). When Jacob himself comes down to Egypt with all his family he is received with all honours (46:1—47:3); he adopts as his own the children of Joseph (48:1–22), and blesses his sons one by one (49:1–28). When Jacob dies, his body is borne with all solemnity to be buried in Canaan, in the sepulchre Abraham purchased (49:29—50:14); but his family continues to live in Egypt under Joseph's protection (50:15–26). The book ends with the death of Joseph in Egypt.

2. HISTORICAL BACKGROUND

The *first part* is concerned with revealing religious truths; to do this, the sacred writer uses the kind of symbolic language in general use in ancient times. The first eleven chapters provide teaching about the origin of the world and of man, while also explaining present reality. What is said assumes a belief in one God who has revealed himself to man; it does not derive from religious intuitions underlying the mythology of nations neighbouring on Israel. Although at certain points one does find traces of the language of those myths, divine inspiration has seen to it that the polytheistic and magical elements have been filtered out; the whole text is imbued with faith in the one God; it conveys fundamental truths about the world and man which clearly have an historical rather than a mythological meaning—the creation of the world and of man by God, human dignity, and the existence of evil due to sin.

The *second part* has quite a different tone. The account of the story of the patriarchs provides definite geographical and historical information. Archeology confirms the socio-cultural context of the account. It takes place in the Middle East; to be more precise, in the crescent formed by Mesopotamia, Palestine and Egypt. The time-frame starts in the eighteenth century BC (which seems to be when Abraham arrives in Canaan), but it is not possible to say when exactly the sons of Jacob went down into Egypt. The Genesis accounts certainly cover events which occurred before the thirteenth century BC, the presumed time of the Exodus.

3. COMPOSITION

In order to make revelations about himself, God led the chosen people to reflect profoundly on the origin of man and the world. Many of Israel's neighbours had done the same, and, to explain things which were beyond the scope

of ordinary language, they devised all sorts of myths about the origins of the world and man and about the earliest times of man. The sacred writers of Genesis sifted through these myths and selected certain literary elements suited to the mentality of their contemporaries in order to convey the message of faith that they wanted to pass on, through their writings, to the people of Israel and, through Israel's religious experience, to all mankind.

In this "account of the origins" we can fairly easily distinguish passages whose literary features can be identified as belonging to the "Yahwistic" and "Priestly" traditions.[1] In addition to the symbolic language typical of the Middle East, we can find in this "account of the origins" other literary elements which derive from ancient local traditions (Mesopotamia, Canaan). We also find genealogical lists designed to show that the human race was populating the entire world. All this material is used to fill in the period of time from the creation of the world to the age of Abraham. Positioned as they now are, at the start of the Bible, the eleven first chapters of Genesis act as a kind of general introduction bringing us up as far as Abraham; with this man, according to the book, history takes a new turn when God calls and man obeys.

For their part the Genesis accounts of the patriarchs incorporate all sorts of diverse oral traditions. We meet up with epics and with poetical and family accounts which describe events whose historical accuracy cannot be checked by reference to other sources. However, they are in keeping with the atmosphere, customs and conditions of the second millennium BC (the period in which the patriarchs lived) and they certainly have considerable value for the historian. In other passages we find accounts which reflect a cultic context; that is to say, they narrate events which have connexions with places of religious cult in Canaan, such as Bethel, Hebron and Shechem. In these accounts the sacredness of a particular place is explained by reference to its association with a patriarch or with some name or manifestation of God. These and other literary materials taken from very ancient oral tradition are used to create a history of the patriarchs which also includes (suitably adapted) ancient pieces of poetry such as the blessings of Jacob (cf. Gen 49). All this material was shaped into cycles built round personalities and places; and then, at a later stage, when the final redaction of the Pentateuch took place, all this was included in the book of Genesis.

The place Genesis holds within the Pentateuch shows that the history it recounts, although it does have value as religious history, is all geared towards the events which will be covered in the book of Exodus. The history of the patriarchs takes place in the land of Canaan, which, because it is the promised land, will become a key element in the beliefs of Israel (cf. Josh 24; Deut 26); but this history also has to be seen as connected with another key event—the

1. Cf. "Introduction to the Pentateuch", pp 19–21, above.

escape from Egypt and the Covenant of Sinai. The story of Joseph acts as the link between the story of the patriarchs and those earlier events.

4. MESSAGE

The central idea in Genesis, as in the entire Pentateuch, is God's choice of Israel. Genesis teaches that that election begins with the call addressed to Abraham, and it is strengthened by Abraham's obedience, which goes so far that he is ready to sacrifice his son Isaac. Genesis also teaches other basic truths—the creation by God of the world and man, the oneness of the human race, the origin of evil in the sin of our first parents and sin's presence throughout history, and also hope of salvation. God is depicted as being the Creator; he transcends the world and man, and he looks after them with loving kindness. Once created, the world is liberated from its original chaos by the word of God; and by that same word Abraham and Israel with him become the firstfruits of a mankind set free from the chaos of idolatry and from the sort of confusion to be seen in Babel (cf. Gen 10–12). Throughout the account of the patriarchs God is seen to act in line with his choice of Israel and to reaffirm his promise to give it a land of its own and make it a great people.

5. GENESIS IN THE LIGHT OF THE NEW TESTAMENT

Read in the light of the New Testament, that is, in the light of the person and work of Christ, Genesis acquires a new dimension. Christ ratifies the enduring value of Genesis when, for example, he uses its teaching to ground the indissolubility of marriage (cf. Mt 19:4–6) and thereby invites us always to have recourse to these biblical passages which reveal the true dignity of man and of his experience.

Moreover, in the New Testament we see the ultimate outcome of the events reported in Genesis. We come to see that the promise God made to Abraham referred in the last analysis to Jesus Christ, and that Abraham already had prophetically seen its fulfilment in the coming of the Lord (cf. Jn 8:56). Christ is the true "offspring" of Abraham (cf. Gal 3:16), and those who believe in Christ are the true sons of Abraham (cf. Gal 3:7); in this way is fulfilled the announcement that in Abraham shall all the nations of the earth be blessed (cf. Gal 3:8–9).

The New Testament not only shows the full reach of the history of the patriarchs; it also adds greatly to our appreciation of the mystery of the creation of the world and of man: we now see that the creation of the world "in the beginning" as being the work of the Holy Trinity (cf. Jn 1:1–3); in the same way it is understood that Christ Jesus, the perfect Image of God, was

already foreshadowed and in some way present in the creation of the world and of man; we learn that on account of that Image, in which every human being participates, all things were brought into being (cf. Col 1:15–16). In the light of the New Testament, which depicts Christ as the new Adam (cf. 1 Cor 15:22), we appreciate also how every human being is involved in the sin of the first Adam (cf. Rom 5:17), and also the fact that sin affects all creation (cf. Rom 8:20). The Redemption wrought by Christ reveals the full scope of the promise of salvation which God gave our first parents. The New Testament also shows us that complete happiness means being with God and that earthly joy is only a symbol of that happiness (cf. Rev 22:14).

PART ONE

The Creation and the First Age of Mankind

Gen 2:4–25
Job 38-39
Ps 104
Heb 11:3
Prov 8:22–31
2 Mac 7:28
Jn 1:1–3
Col 1:15–17
Rev 21:1
2 Pet 3:5

1. THE ORIGIN OF HEAVEN AND EARTH

The Creation account*

1 ¹*In the beginning God created^a the heavens and the earth. ²The earth was without form and void, and darkness was upon the

---

*1:1—2:4a. Creation is the beginning of salvation history and the foundation on which are built God's salvific plans, which reach their climax in Jesus Christ. The biblical accounts of creation focus on the action of God; it is he who sets the scene and he is the creator, too, of those who will act out the drama and with whom he will enter into dialogue.

The sacred text incorporates ancient traditions about the origin of the world; scholars identify two separate accounts in the early chapters of Genesis. The first of these emphasizes God's transcendence over all created things, and is written in a very schematic style; this account (1:1—2:4a) is attributed to the "Priestly" tradition. The second, which also covers the fall and the expulsion from paradise, speaks of God in an anthropomorphic way; this more vivid, more popular account (2:4b—4:26) is considered to belong to the "Yahwistic" tradition. Here we have two different ways in which the Word of God (not intending to provide a scientific explanation of the origin of the world and of man) expounds the basic facts and truths on the subject in a way people can readily understand, inviting

us to see the greatness and love of God as manifested first in creation and then in the history of mankind. "Our faith teaches us," St Josemaría Escrivá writes, "that all creation, the movement of the earth and the other heavenly bodies, the good actions of creatures and all the good that has been achieved in history, in short everything, comes from God and is directed toward him" (*Christ Is Passing By*, 130).

In the first account the Bible offers us profound teaching about God, about man and about the world. About God, who is the only God, creator of all things and of man in particular; he transcends the created world and is its supreme master. About man, who is the image and likeness of God, above all other created beings and placed in the world to rule all creation. About the world, which is something good and is at the service of man.

1.1. "Three things are affirmed in these first words of Scripture: the eternal God gave a beginning to all that exists outside of himself; he alone is Creator (the verb 'create'—Hebrew *bara*—always has God for its subject). The totality of what

---

¹In principio creavit Deus caelum et terram. ²Terra autem erat inanis et vacua, et tenebrae super faciem

a. Or *When God began to create*

36

face of the deep; and the Spirit[b] of God was moving over the face
of the waters.

---

exists (expressed by the formula 'the heavens and the earth') depends on the One who gives it being" (*Catechism of the Catholic Church*, 290).

"In the beginning" means that creation marks the start of time and the course of history. Time and history have a beginning and they are headed towards a final goal, which the Bible will tell us more about, especially in its last book, Revelation. At the end, we are told: "Then I saw a new heaven and a new earth; for the first heaven and the first earth had passed away, and the sea was no more" (Rev 21:1).

God the Creator is the same God as will manifest himself to the patriarchs, to Moses and to the prophets and make himself known to us through Jesus Christ. In the light of the New Testament we know that God created all things through his eternal Word, his beloved Son (cf. Jn 1:1; Col 1:16–17). God the Creator is Father and Son and (the relationship of love between them) the Holy Spirit. Creation is the work of the Blessed Trinity, and all of creation (particularly man, created in the image and likeness of God) in some way bears their seal. Some Fathers of the Church (Augustine, Ambrose and Basil, for example), in the light of the New Testament, saw the words "in the beginning" as having a deeper meaning—namely, "in the Son".

The *action of creating* belongs exclusively to God; man cannot create; he can only "change" or "develop" something that already exists. In the creation accounts of other Near East religions the

world and gods developed out of pre-existent matter. The Bible, however, records gradual revelation of the mystery of creation interpreted in the light of God's choice of Israel and his Covenant with mankind; it roundly asserts that everything was made by God. Later on it will draw the conclusion that everything was created out of nothing: "I beseech you, my child, to look at the heavens and the earth and see everything that is in them, and to recognize that God did not make them out of things that existed" (2 Mac 7:28). This creative power of God is also able to give sinful man a pure heart (cf. Ps 51:10), to restore the dead to life and to give the light of faith to those who do not know him (cf. 2 Cor 4:6).

It was God's love and wisdom that moved him to create the world, thereby communicating his goodness and making his glory manifest. The world, therefore, "is not the product of any necessity whatever, nor of blind fate or chance. We believe that it proceeds from God's free will; he wanted to make his creatures share in his being, wisdom and goodness" (*Catechism of the Catholic Church*, 295).

The expression "the heavens and the earth" means everything that exists. The earth is the world of men; the sky (or the heavens) can mean the firmament or the divine world, God's own "place", his glory and all spiritual (non-material) creatures—the angels.

1:2. The Bible teaches not just that God created all things, but also that the separation and ordering of the elements of nature is something established by God

---

abyssi, et spiritus Dei ferebatur super aquas. ³Dixitque Deus: «Fiat lux». Et facta est lux. ⁴Et vidit Deus

b. Or *wind*

³And God said, "Let there be light"; and there was light. ⁴And God saw that the light was good; and God separated the light from the darkness. ⁵God called the light Day, and the darkness he called Night. And there was evening and there was morning, one day.

⁶And God said, "Let there be a firmament in the midst of the waters, and let it separate the waters from the waters." ⁷And God made the firmament and separated the waters which were under the firmament from the waters which were above the firmament. And it was so. ⁸And God called the firmament Heaven. And there was evening and there was morning, a second day.

---

once and for all. The presence of the loving power of God, symbolized by a gentle breeze or a breath (the text refers to it as a spirit; *ruah* in Hebrew) which hovers and keeps watch over the world when it is still in chaos, shows that, as the text will go on to say, the Word of God and his Breath are present in the origin of being and in the origin of every creature's life. That is why many Fathers of the Church (Jerome and Athanasius, for example) saw this passage as reflecting the presence of the Holy Spirit as a divine Person who, along with the Father and the Son, is at work in the creation of the world. "This biblical concept of creation", John Paul II explains, "includes not only the call to existence of the very being of the cosmos, that is to say, *the giving of existence*, but also the presence of the Spirit of God in creation, that is to say, the beginning of God's salvific self-communication to the things he creates. This is true *first of all concerning man*, who has been created in the image and likeness of God" (*Dominum et Vivificantem*, 12).

1:3–5. At this point strictly speaking begins the description of the creation, which, according to the literary plan of this account, is going to take place over six days. These six days are meant to indicate the orderliness with which God went about his work, and to show a rhythm of work and rest: the Jewish Law laid down Saturday, the sabbath, as a day of rest and a day dedicated to the Lord. In the Christian Church this day was shifted to Sunday, because Sunday was the day on which our Lord rose from the dead, thereby inaugurating the new Creation: Sunday, the *dies dominica* (Latin), the Lord's day.

On the first day God creates light and separates light from darkness (the latter, being something negative—the absence of light—cannot be created). Light is seen here as being a thing in its own right (without reference to the fact that daylight comes from the sun, which will not be created until the fourth day). The fact that God puts names on things (or in this case on situations caused by some elements being separated from others) indicates that

---

lucem quod esset bona et divisit Deus lucem ac tenebras. ⁵Appellavitque Deus lucem Diem et tenebras Noctem. Factumque est vespere et mane, dies unus. ⁶Dixit quoque Deus: «Fiat firmamentum in medio aquarum et dividat aquas ab aquis». ⁷Et fecit Deus firmamentum divisitque aquas, quae erant sub firmamento, ab his, quae erant super firmamentum. Et factum est ita. ⁸Vocavitque Deus firmamentum Caelum. Et factum est vespere et mane, dies secundus. ⁹Dixit vero Deus: «Congregentur aquae, quae sub caelo sunt, in locum unum, et appareat arida». Factumque est ita. ¹⁰Et vocavit Deus aridam Terram

⁹And God said, "Let the waters under the heavens be gathered together into one place, and let the dry land appear." And it was so. ¹⁰God called the dry land Earth, and the waters that were gathered together he called Seas. And God saw that it was good. ¹¹And God said, "Let the earth put forth vegetation, plants yielding seed, and fruit trees bearing fruit in which is their seed, each according to its kind, upon the earth." And it was so. ¹²The earth brought forth vegetation, plants yielding seed according to their own kinds, and trees bearing fruit in which is their seed, each according to its kind. And God saw that it was good. ¹³And there was evening and there was morning, a third day.

2 Pet 3:5

1 Cor 15:38
Heb 6:7

Is 40:26
Acts 17:26

---

he wields absolute power over them. God is in authority, whether it be day or night.

Here we meet for the first time a phrase which is going to be used seven times over the course of the narrative: "And God saw that it was good." This means that everything that God creates is good because in some way it bears his seal and shares in his own goodness, for it has come from divine goodness. The goodness of the world proclaimed here by Holy Scripture has important consequences for the Christian: "We must love the world and work and all human things. For the world is good. Adam's sin destroyed the divine balance of creation; but God the Father sent his only Son to re-establish peace, so that we, his children by adoption, might free creation from disorder and reconcile all things to God" (St Josemaría Escrivá, *Christ Is Passing By*, 112).

1:6–8. In line with the culture of their time, the early Hebrews thought that rain came from huge containers of water in the vault of heaven; when trapdoors were

opened, the rain poured down. When it says here that God separated the waters which were above the firmament from those below, what is really being taught is that God imposed order on the natural world and is responsible for the phenomenon of rain. It is also making it clear from the outset that the firmament must not be thought to involve any divinity (as was believed in the nations roundabout Israel); the firmament is part of the created world.

1:11. As the inspired author depicts it here, a distinction is made between God's action in separating and ordering the elements (creating the vast spaces of sky, sea and land) and his action of filling or adorning these spaces with different kinds of creatures. These creatures are introduced in an increasing order of dignity (in line with the thinking of the time)—first the vegetable kingdom, then the stellar kingdom, and, lastly, the animal kingdom. Everything is perfectly arranged; the world of Creation invites us to contemplate the Creator.

---

congregationesque aquarum appellavit Maria. Et vidit Deus quod esset bonum. ¹¹Et ait Deus: «Germinet terra herbam virentem et herbam facientem semen et lignum pomiferum faciens fructum iuxta genus suum, cuius semen in semetipso sit super terram». Et factum est ita. ¹²Et protulit terra herbam virentem et herbam afferentem semen iuxta genus suum lignumque faciens fructum, qui habet in semetipso sementem secundum speciem suam. Et vidit Deus quod esset bonum. ¹³Et factum est vespere et mane, dies tertius. ¹⁴Dixit autem Deus: «Fiant luminaria in firmamento caeli, ut dividant diem

¹⁴And God said, "Let there be lights in the firmament of the heavens to separate the day from the night; and let them be for signs and for seasons and for days and years, ¹⁵and let them be lights in the firmament of the heavens to give light upon the

Ps 136:7–9 earth." And it was so. ¹⁶And God made the two great lights, the greater light to rule the day, and the lesser light to rule the night; he made the stars also. ¹⁷And God set them in the firmament of the heavens to give light upon the earth, ¹⁸to rule over the day and over the night, and to separate the light from the darkness. And God saw that it was good. ¹⁹And there was evening and there was morning, a fourth day.

1 Cor 15:39 ²⁰And God said, "Let the waters bring forth swarms of living creatures, and let birds fly above the earth across the firmament of the heavens." ²¹So God created the great sea monsters and every living creature that moves, with which the waters swarm, accord-

---

1:14–17. Against the neighbouring religions, which regarded the heavenly bodies as divinities exerting influence over human life, the biblical author, enlightened by inspiration, teaches that the sun, moon and stars are simply created things; their purpose is to serve man by giving him light by day and night, and to be a way of measuring time. Put in their proper, natural place heavenly bodies (like all the rest of creation) lead man to appreciate the greatness of God, and to praise him for his awesome works: "The heavens are telling the glory of God; and the firmament proclaims his handiwork . . ." (Ps 19:1; cf. Ps 104). It follows that all forms of divination are to be rejected—consulting horoscopes, astrology, clairvoyance etc. (cf. *Catechism of the Catholic Church*, 2116).

1:26. The sacred text emphasizes the special significance of this moment: God seems to stop to reflect and plan every detail of his next creation—man. Ancient Jewish interpretation (followed also by some Christian writers) saw the use of the plural "Let *us* make . . ." as meaning that God deliberated with his heavenly court, that is, with the angels (implying that God had created them at the very start, when he "created the heavens and the earth"). But the use of the plural should rather be taken as reflecting the greatness and power of God. A considerable part of Christian tradition has seen the "Let *us* make" as reflecting the Holy Trinity, for New Testament revelation has made the Christian reader more aware of the unfathomable greatness of the divine mystery.

"Man" here has a collective meaning:

---

ac noctem et sint in signa et tempora et dies et annos, ¹⁵ut luceant in firmamento caeli et illuminent terram. Et factum est ita. ¹⁶Fecitque Deus duo magna luminaria: luminare maius, ut praeesset diei, et luminare minus, ut praeesset nocti, et stellas. ¹⁷Et posuit eas Deus in firmamento caeli, ut lucerent super terram ¹⁸et praeessent diei ac nocti et dividerent lucem ac tenebras. Et vidit Deus quod esset bonum. ¹⁹Et factum est vespere et mane, dies quartus. ²⁰Dixit etiam Deus: «Pullulent aquae reptile animae viventis, et volatile volet super terram sub firmamento caeli». ²¹Creavitque Deus cete grandia et omnem animam viventem atque motabilem, quam pullulant aquae secundum species suas, et omne volatile

ing to their kinds, and every winged bird according to its kind. And God saw that it was good. [22]And God blessed them, saying, "Be fruitful and multiply and fill the waters in the seas, and let birds multiply on the earth." [23]And there was evening and there was morning, a fifth day.

[24]And God said, "Let the earth bring forth living creatures according to their kinds: cattle and creeping things and beasts of the earth according to their kinds." And it was so. [25]And God made the beasts of the earth according to their kinds and the cattle according to their kinds, and everything that creeps upon the ground according to its kind. And God saw that it was good.

[26]Then God said, "Let us make man in our image, after our likeness; and let them have dominion over the fish of the sea, and over the birds of the air, and over the cattle, and over all the earth,

1 Cor 15:39
Acts 10:12; 11:6

Gen 5:1–3; 9:6
Ps 8:4–5
Sir 17:3–4
Wis 2:23; 9:2
Eph 4:24
Col 3:10
Jas 3:9

---

every human being, by his or her very nature, is in the image and likeness of God. The human being is intelligible not by reference to other created beings in the universe but by reference to God. The likeness between God and man is not a physical one, for God has no body; it is a spiritual likeness, lying in the human being's capacity for interiority. The Second Vatican Council teaches that "man is not deceived when he regards himself as superior to bodily things and as more than just a speck of nature or a nameless unit in the city of man. For by his power to know himself in the depths of his being he rises above the whole universe of mere objects. When he is drawn to think about his real self, he turns to those deep recesses of his being where God who probes the heart (1 Kings 16:7; Jer 17:10) awaits him, and where he himself decides his own destiny in the sight

of God. So when he recognizes in himself a spiritual and immortal soul, he is not being led astray by false imaginings that are due to merely physical or social causes. On the contrary, he grasps what is profoundly true in this matter" (*Gaudium et spes*, 14).

The fact that God creates man in his own image and likeness "means not only rationality and freedom as constitutive properties of human nature, but also, from the very beginning, the capacity of having a *personal relationship* with God, as 'I' and 'you' and therefore the *capacity of having a covenant*, which will take place in God's salvific communication with man" (John Paul II, *Dominum et Vivificantem*, 34). In the light of this communication, brought about in all its fullness by Jesus Christ, the Fathers of the Church read the words "image and likeness" as meaning, on the one hand,

---

secundum genus suum. Et vidit Deus quod esset bonum; [22]benedixitque eis Deus dicens: «Crescite et multiplicamini et replete aquas maris, avesque multiplicentur super terram». [23]Et factum est vespere et mane, dies quintus. [24]Dixit quoque Deus: «Producat terra animam viventem in genere suo, iumenta et reptilia et bestias terrae secundum species suas». Factumque est ita. [25]Et fecit Deus bestias terrae iuxta species suas et iumenta secundum species suas et omne reptile terrae in genere suo. Et vidit Deus quod esset bonum. [26]Et ait Deus: «Faciamus hominem ad imaginem et similitudinem nostram; et praesint

Gen 2:18–24
Mt 19:4
Mk 10:6
Acts 17:29
Rom 8:29
1 Cor 11:7

and over every creeping thing that creeps upon the earth." [27]So God created man in his own image, in the image of God he created him; male and female he created them. [28]And God blessed them, and

man's spiritual condition, and, on the other, his sharing in the divine nature through sanctifying grace. Even after the fall, man is still in the "image" of God; through sin, however, he lost his "likeness" but this was restored through Christ's redemption.

It is part of God's design that human beings should have dominion over other created things (represented here by the animals). This dominion makes man God's representative (everything really belongs to God) in the created world. Therefore, although man is going to be the lord of creation, he needs to recognize that God alone is the Creator; man has to respect and look after creation; he is responsible for it.

These words of Scripture show that "man is the only creature that God has loved for itself alone, because all others were created to be at the service of man. Here we can see, too, the basic equality of all human beings. For the Church, this equality, which has its roots in man's very being, takes on the very special dimension of brotherhood through the Incarnation of the Son of God. [. . .] Therefore, discrimination of any type [. . .] is absolutely unacceptable" (John Paul II, Address, 7 July 1984).

1:27. The creation of man marks the completion of God's plan. In presenting this final act of creation, the sacred writer offers us a summary of the things that go to make up the human being. As well as repeating that God created man in his image and likeness, he tells us that God created them man and woman, that is to

say, corporeal beings, endowed with sexuality, and designed to live in society. "Being in the image of God, the human individual possesses the dignity of a *person*, who is not just something, but someone. He is capable of self-knowledge, of self-possession and of freely giving himself and entering into communion with other persons. And he is called by grace to a covenant with his Creator, to offer him a response of faith and love that no other creature can give in his stead" (*Catechism of the Catholic Church*, 357).

"The fact that man 'created as man and woman' is the image of God means not only that each of them individually is like God, as a rational and free being. It also means that man and woman, created as a 'unity of the two' in their common humanity, are called to live in a communion of love, and in this way to mirror in the world the communion of love that is in God, through which the Three Persons love each other in the intimate mystery of the one divine life. This 'unity of the two', which is a sign of interpersonal communion, *shows that the creation of man* is also marked by a certain likeness to the divine communion ('*communio*'). This likeness is a quality of the personal being of both man and woman, and is also a call and a task" (John Paul II, *Mulieris dignitatem*, 7).

The fact that the Bible and everyday language speak of God as masculine is a the result of cultural influences and the great care taken in the Bible to avoid any hint of polytheism (which could arise if the godhead were described as feminine,

piscibus maris et volatilibus caeli et bestiis universaeque terrae omnique reptili, quod movetur in terra».

1 Tim 2:13
Ps 8:5–8
Sir 17:2–4
Wis 9:2; 10:2
Acts 17:26
Jas 3:7

God said to them, "Be fruitful and multiply, and fill the earth and subdue it; and have dominion over the fish of the sea and over the birds of the air and over every living thing that moves upon the

---

opening the way to generations of gods, as in other religions). God transcends the body and sexuality; therefore, both man (masc.) and woman (fem.) equally reflect his image and likeness. In these words of Genesis, for the very first time in history, the fundamental equality in dignity of man and woman is proclaimed—in marked contrast with the low esteem in which women were held in the ancient world.

According to the traditional Jewish and Christian interpretation, this verse is alluding to marriage, as if God had already created the first man and the first woman as a married couple—forming that human community which is the basis of every society. In the second Genesis account of the creation of man and woman (cf. 2:18–24), this will emerge even more clearly.

1:28. God has already created animals, endowing them with fruitfulness (v. 22). He now addresses these two human beings personally: "God said to them . . ."; this indicates that the reproductive power of human beings (and therefore their sexuality) are values for which they must assume responsibility before God, as a way of co-operating in God's plans. Thus, God, "wishing to associate them in a special way with his own creative work, blessed man and woman with the words: 'Be fruitful and multiply' (Gen 1:28). Without intending to underestimate the other ends of marriage, it must be said that true married love and the whole structure of family life which results from it is directed to disposing the

spouses to cooperate valiantly with the love of the Creator and Saviour, who through them will increase and enrich his family from day to day" (Vatican II, *Gaudium et spes*, 50).

God also commands man to make the earth serve him. Here divine Revelation is teaching us that human work is to be regarded as a way by which man co-operates in the plan God had when he created the world: "By the work of his hands and with the aid of technical means man tills the earth to bring forth fruit and to make it a dwelling place fit for all mankind; he also consciously plays his part in the life of social groups; in so doing he is realizing the design, which God revealed at the beginning of time, to subdue the earth and perfect the work of creation, and at the same time he is improving his own person" (Vatican II, *Gaudium et spes*, 57).

From this divine disposition we can see the importance a person's work has in his or her personal life: "Your human vocation is a part—and an important part—of your divine vocation. That is the reason why you must strive for holiness, giving a particular character to your human personality, a style to your life; contributing at the same time to the sanctification of others, your fellow men; sanctifying your work and your environment: the profession or job that fills your day, your home and family and the country where you were born and which you love [. . .]. Work, all work, bears witness to the dignity of man, to his dominion over creation. It is an opportunity to develop one's personality. It is a bond of

---

²⁷Et creavit Deus hominem ad imaginem suam; / ad imaginem Dei creavit illum; / masculum et femi-

earth." [29]And God said, "Behold, I have given you every plant yielding seed which is upon the face of all the earth, and every tree with seed in its fruit; you shall have them for food. [30]And to every beast of the earth, and to every bird of the air, and to everything that creeps on the earth, everything that has the breath of life, I have given every green plant for food." And it was so. [31]And God saw everything that he had made, and behold, it was very good. And there was evening and there was morning, a sixth day.

Acts 11:6

Sir 39:33–35
Eccles 3:11; 7:29
1 Tim 4:4

Heb 4:4–10
Ex 20:4; 20:8

2 [1]Thus the heavens and the earth were finished, and all the host of them. [2]And on the seventh day God finished his work which he had done, and he rested on the seventh day from all his

---

union with others, the way to support one's family, a means of aiding the improvement of the society in which we live and in the progress of all mankind" (St J. Escrivá, *Christ Is Passing By*, 46–47).

Man is charged by God with mastery over the earth; but he may not do whatever he likes with it or act despotically: he should respect the universe as being the work of the Creator. In this regard, Wisdom 9:3 says: "O God, [. . .] who hast formed man, to have dominion over the creatures thou hast made, and rule the world in holiness and righteousness, and pronounce judgment in uprightness of soul." "This holds good also for our daily work. When men and women provide for themselves and their families in such a way as to be of service to the community as well, they can rightly look upon their work as a prolongation of the work of the creator, a service to their fellow men, and their personal contribution to the fulfilment in history of the divine plan" (Vatican II, *Gaudium et spes*, 34).

1:31. These words bring to an end this first description of the work of Creation. It is as if God, after making man, stood back to see what he had done and was very pleased with the result. Whereas the wording previously used was "And God saw that it was good," now we are told that it was "very good". In this way, the goodness of the created world is being stressed, indicating that "this natural goodness of theirs receives an added dignity from their relation with the human person, for whose use they have been created" (Vatican II, *Apostolicam actuositatem*, 7). From this it follows that the human person and his/her dignity must be valued above all other created things, and all human endeavour should be geared to foster and defend these values.

2:1–3. From this point onwards, God will almost never intervene in creation directly. Now it is up to man to act in the created world through the work he does.

---

nam creavit eos. [28]Benedixitque illis Deus et ait illis Deus: «Crescite et multiplicamini et replete terram et subicite eam et dominamini piscibus maris et volatilibus caeli et universis animantibus, quae moventur super terram». [29]Dixitque Deus: «Ecce dedi vobis omnem herbam afferentem semen super terram et universa ligna, quae habent in semetipsis fructum ligni portantem sementem, ut sint vobis in escam [30]et cunctis animantibus terrae omnique volucri caeli et universis, quae moventur in terra et in quibus est anima vivens, omnem herbam virentem ad vescendum». Et factum est ita. [31]Viditque Deus cuncta, quae fecit, et ecce erant valde bona. Et factum est vespere et mane, dies sextus. [1] Igitur perfecti sunt

work which he had done. ³So God blessed the seventh day and hallowed it, because on it God rested from all his work which he had done in creation.

⁴These are the generations of the heavens and the earth when they were created.

Ex 20:8–11
Deut 5:12–14

The creation of Adam*

*In the day that the LORD God made the earth and the heavens, ⁵when no plant of the field was yet in the earth and no herb of the

Gen 1:1–2:4
Job 34:14–15
Ps 104:29–30
Eccles 3:20

God's "resting" sets an example for man. By resting, we are acknowledging that creation in the last analysis depends on and belongs to God, and that God is watching over it. Here rest is an example set by the Creator; we shall later find it as one of the Ten Commandments (cf. Ex 20:8–18; Deut 5:12–14). "The institution of the Lord's Day helps everyone enjoy adequate rest and leisure to cultivate their familial, cultural, social and religious lives" (*Catechism of the Catholic Church*, 2184; cf. also John Paul II, Apostolic Letter, *Dies Domini*, 31 May 1998).

Apropos of the sabbath, unlike the other days there is no mention of there being evening and morning. It is as if that rhythm of time were being broken by the sabbath—prefiguring the situation in which man, once he has accomplished his mission of mastering the earth, will enjoy an unending rest, at an eternal feast in God's presence (cf. Heb 4:1–10). In the language of the Bible "feast" or "festival" means three things—a) obligatory rest from everyday work; b) recognition of God as Lord of creation, and joyful contemplation of the created world; c) a foretaste of the enduring rest and joy that will be man's after he leaves this world.

*2:4b—4:26. At v. 2:4b begins a new

creation account which scholars identify with the "Yahwistic" tradition and which does indeed carry features which suggest it is older than the previous account. It runs to the end of chapter 4 and covers the creation of man and woman (chap. 2), the fall of our first parents and their expulsion from paradise (chap. 3) and the continuation of human life in a context of sin (chap. 4). All this is described in symbolic language and a very vivid style; here are matters of the highest historical importance, and anthropological, psychological and religious features of the human being in all epochs.

Once again the sacred book goes right back to the origins of the world and man and evil. The message here is that Yahweh alone, the God of Israel, is the master of life, because he gave life to man and to animals; that from the very start God looked after man most lovingly and established a covenant with him; that created man was a free being and transgressed that covenant, allowing pain, death and evil to enter the world; and, finally, that, in spite of everything, the Lord continued to watch over man and kept up his hope by promising him victory over evil.

2:5–6. These verses are designed to show that the first and most important thing on

---

Gen 3:19
Is 29:16
Jer 18:6
Ps 104:29f
Eccles 12:17
Lk 3:38
Jn 20:22
Rom 9:20–21
1 Cor 15:45, 47
1 Tim 2:13

field had yet sprung up—for the LORD God had not caused it to rain upon the earth, and there was no man to till the ground; 6but a mistᶜ went up from the earth and watered the whole face of the ground—7then the LORD God formed man of dust from the ground, and breathed into his nostrils the breath of life; and man became a living being.

earth is man, on whose behalf all other things were made. The text does not discuss whether any other types of vegetative or animal life existed on the planet prior to man's appearance on the scene—much less whether any type of evolution into higher forms could have taken place.

Giving due weight to the data of faith and to scientific discoveries about the evolution of species, Catholic theology is not opposed to the idea that God could have infused a soul into an already-existing being, having previously prepared a body to suit it, thereby making it a "man". This way of explaining things is called "moderate evolutionism". In this connexion, John Paul II, in his 22 October 1996 message to the Pontifical Academy of Sciences, after recalling the teachings of Pius XII's 1950 encyclical *Humani generis*, pointed out that recent advances in scholarship "lead one no longer to regard the theory of evolution as a mere hypothesis". But at the same time he said that there is not just one "theory of evolution" but a number of such theories, and he indicated which ones are contrary to faith: "The theories of evolution which, in line with the philosophies which inspire them, regard the spirit as something that emerges from the forces of living matter or as a mere epiphenomenon of that matter, are

incompatible with the truth about man" (ibid.).

So, it is not only "a question of knowing when and how the universe arose physically, or when man appeared, but rather of discovering the meaning of such an origin: is the universe governed by chance, blind fate, anonymous necessity, or by a transcendent, intelligent and good Being called 'God'?" (*Catechism of the Catholic Church*, 284).

2:7. As far as his body is concerned, man belongs to the earth. To affirm this, the sacred writer must have been always conscious of the fact that when a person dies, his/her body will turn into dust, as Genesis 3:19 will in due course tell us. Or it may be that this sort of account (a special one like the literary genre of all these chapters) is based on the similarity between the word *adam*, which means man in general, and *adamáh*, which means "reddish soil"; and given that the words look alike, the sacred writer may have drawn the conclusion that there is in fact a connexion between the two very things (unsophisticated etymology goes in for this sort of thing). But the fact that man belongs to the earth is not his most characteristic feature: as the author sees it, animals too are made up of the stuff of the earth. What makes man different is

gultum agri, antequam oriretur in terra, omnisque herba regionis, priusquam germinaret; non enim pluerat Dominus Deus super terram, et homo non erat, qui operaretur humum, 6sed fons ascendebat e terra irrigans universam superficiem terrae—7tunc formavit Dominus Deus hominem pulverem de

c. Or *flood*

Man in paradise

[8]And the LORD God planted a garden in Eden, in the east; and there he put the man whom he had formed. [9]And out of the ground the LORD God made to grow every tree that is pleasant to the sight and good for food, the tree of life also in the midst of the garden, and the tree of the knowledge of good and evil.

Gen 3:5
Rev 22:1–2
Rev 2:7

---

the fact that he receives his life from God. Life is depicted here in terms of breathing, because only living animals breathe. The fact that God infuses life into man in this way means that although man on account of his corporeal nature is material, his existence as a living being comes directly from God, that is, it is animated by a vital principle—the soul or the spirit—which does not derive from the earth. This principle of life received from God also endows man's body with its own dignity and puts it on a higher level than that of animals.

God is portrayed as a potter who models man's body in clay; this means that man is supposed to live in accordance with a source of life that is higher than that deriving from matter. The image of God as a potter shows that man (all of him) is in God's hands just like clay in a potter's hands; he should not resist or oppose God's will (cf. Is 29:16; Jer 18:6; Rom 9:20–21).

2:8–15. Here we have a scenario in which God and man are friends; there is no such thing as evil or death. The garden is described as being a leafy oasis, with the special feature of having two trees in the centre, the tree of life and the tree of the knowledge of good and evil—symbolizing the power to give life, and the ultimate reference-point for man's moral behaviour. Out of the garden flow the four rivers the author is most

familiar with; these water the entire earth and make it fertile. What the Bible is teaching here is that man was created to be happy, to enjoy the life and goodness which flow from God. "The Church, interpreting the symbolism of biblical language in an authentic way, in the light of the New Testament and Tradition, teaches that our first parents, Adam and Eve, were constituted in an original 'state of holiness and justice' (Council of Trent, *De peccato originali*). This grace of original holiness was 'to share in . . . divine life' (*Lumen gentium*, 2)" (*Catechism of the Catholic Church*, 375).

From the outset, man is charged with cultivating the garden—working it, protecting it and making it bear fruit. Here again we can see that work is a commission that God gives man for the start. "From the beginning of creation man has had to work," St J. Escrivá said. "This is not something that I have invented. It is enough to turn to the opening pages of the Bible. There you can read that, before sin entered the world, and in its wake death, punishment and misery (cf. Rom 5:12), God made Adam from the clay of the earth, and created for him and his descendants this beautiful world we live in, *ut operaretur et custodiret illum* (Gen 2:15), so that we might cultivate it and look after it" (*Friends of God*, 57). But man needs to recognize God's mastery over creation and over himself by obeying the commandment God gives him as

humo et inspiravit in nares eius spiraculum vitae, et factus est homo in animam viventem. [8]Et plantavit Dominus Deus paradisum in Eden ad orientem, in quo posuit hominem, quem formaverat. [9]Produxitque Dominus Deus de humo omne lignum pulchrum visu et ad vescendum suave, lignum

Rev 22:1   ¹⁰A river flowed out of Eden to water the garden, and there it divided and became four rivers. ¹¹The name of the first is Pishon; it is the one which flows around the whole land of Havilah, where there is gold; ¹²and the gold of that land is good; bdellium and onyx stone are there. ¹³The name of the second river is Gihon; it is the one which flows around the whole land of Cush. ¹⁴And the name of the third river is Tigris, which flows east of Assyria. And the fourth river is the Euphrates.

¹⁵The LORD God took the man and put him in the garden of Eden to till it and keep it. ¹⁶And the LORD God commanded the man, saying, "You may freely eat of every tree of the garden; ¹⁷but

Rom 5:12; 7:10
Heb 5:14   of the tree of the knowledge of good and evil you shall not eat, for in the day that you eat of it you shall die."

---

a kind of covenant, telling him not to eat the forbidden fruit. If man lost the original happiness he was created to enjoy (the writer will later explain), it was because he broke that covenant.

2:16–17. The fact that man had access to the "tree of the knowledge of good and evil" means that God left the way open to the possibility of evil in order to ensure a greater good—the freedom which is man's endowment. By using his reason and following his conscience, man is able to discern what is good and what is evil; but he himself cannot *make* something good or evil. So, God's command to our first parents implies that they have a duty to recognize that they are creatures and have a duty to reverence and respect goodness, as reflected in the laws of creation and in the dignity proper to man as a person. Were man to want to decide on good and evil for himself, ignoring the goodness God impressed on things when he created them, it would mean man

wanted to be like God. Man is always being tempted towards absolute moral autonomy—and he gives in to that temptation when he forgets that there exists a God who is the Creator and Lord of all, man included.

"The tree of the knowledge of good and evil," John Paul II comments, "was to express and constantly remind man of the 'limit' impassable for a created being" (*Dominum et Vivificantem*, 36).

2:18–25. God continues to take care of man, his creature. The sacred writer conveys this by means of a human metaphor, depicting God as a potter who realizes his creation is not yet perfect. The creation of the human being is not yet over: he needs to be able to live in a full and deep union with another of his kind. The animals were also created by God, but they cannot provide complete companionship. So God creates woman, giving her the same body as man. From now on it is possible for the human being to com-

---

etiam vitae in medio paradisi lignumque scientiae boni et mali. ¹⁰Et fluvius egrediebatur ex Eden ad irrigandum paradisum, qui inde dividitur in quattuor capita. ¹¹Nomen uni Phison: ipse est, qui circuit omnem terram Hevila, ubi est aurum; ¹²et aurum terrae illius optimum est; ibi invenitur bdellium et lapis onychinus. ¹³Et nomen fluvio secundo Geon: ipse est, qui circuit omnem terram Aethiopiae. ¹⁴Nomen vero fluminis tertii Tigris: ipse vadit ad orientem Assyriae. Fluvius autem quartus ipse est Euphrates. ¹⁵Tulit ergo Dominus Deus hominem et posuit eum in paradiso Eden, ut operaretur et custodiret illum; ¹⁶praecepitque Dominus Deus homini dicens: «Ex omni ligno paradisi comede; ¹⁷de ligno

The creation of Eve

[18]Then the LORD God said, "It is not good that the man should be alone; I will make him a helper fit for him." [19]So out of the ground the LORD God formed every beast of the field and every bird of the air, and brought them to the man to see what he would call them; and whatever the man called every living creature, that was its name. [20]The man gave names to all cattle, and to the birds of the air, and to every beast of the field; but for the man there was not found a helper fit for him. [21]So the LORD God caused a deep sleep to fall upon the man, and while he slept took one of his ribs and closed up its place with flesh; [22]and the rib which the LORD

Gen 1:27ff
1 Cor 11:8–9

1 Cor 11:8
1 Tim 2:13

---

municate. The creation of woman, therefore, marks the climax of God's love for the human being he created.

This passage also shows us man's interiority: he is aware of his own aloneness. Although here loneliness is more a possibility and a fear rather than a real situation, we are being told that it is through awareness of being alone that man can appreciate the benefit of communion with others.

2:19–20. Like man, animals are created out of matter, but they are not said to have received from God the breath of life. Only man is given the breath of life, and this is what makes him essentially different from animals: man has a form of life given him directly by God; that is to say, he is animated by a spiritual principle which enables him to converse with God and to have real communion with other human beings. We call this "soul" or "spirit". It makes man more akin to God than to animals, even though the human body is made from the earth and belongs to the earth just as an animal's body does (cf. the notes on 1:26 and 2:7).

"The unity of soul and body is so profound that one has to consider the soul to be the 'form' of the body (cf. Council of Vienne, *Fidei catholicae*): that is, it is because of its spiritual soul that the body made of matter becomes a living, human body; spirit and matter, in man, are not two natures united, but rather their union forms a single nature" (*Catechism of the Catholic Church*, 365).

2:21–22. This sleep is a kind of death; it is as if God suspended the life he gave man, in order to re-shape him so that he can begin to live again in another way— by being two, man and woman, and no longer alone. By describing the creation of woman as coming from one of Adam's ribs, the sacred writer is saying that, contrary to people's thinking at the time, man and woman have the same nature and the same dignity, for both have come from the same piece of clay that God shaped and made into a living being. The Bible is also explaining the mutual att-

---

autem scientiae boni et mali ne comedas; in quocumque enim die comederis ex eo, morte morieris». [18]Dixit quoque Dominus Deus: «Non est bonum esse hominem solum; faciam ei adiutorium simile sui». [19]Formatis igitur Dominus Deus de humo cunctis animantibus agri et universis volatilibus caeli, adduxit ea ad Adam, ut videret quid vocaret ea; omne enim, quod vocavit Adam animae viventis, ipsum est nomen eius. [20]Appellavitque Adam nominibus suis cuncta pecora et universa volatilia caeli et omnes bestias agrii Adae vero non inveniebatur adiutor similis eius. [21]Immisit ergo Dominus Deus soporem in Adam. Cumque obdormisset, tulit unam de costis eius et replevit carnem pro ea; [22]et aedificavit

God had taken from the man he made into a woman and brought
her to the man. [23]Then the man said,

> "This at last is bone of my bones and
> flesh of my flesh;

Mt 19:5
Mk 10:7
1 Cor 6:16

> she shall be called Woman,[d]
> because she was taken out of Man."[e]

raction man and woman have for one another.

2:23 When man—now in the sense of the male human being—recognizes woman as a person who is his equal, someone who has the same nature as himself, he discovers in her the fit "helper" God wanted him to have. Now indeed the creation of the human being is complete, having become "man becomes the image of God not so much in the moment of solitude as in the moment of communion" (John Paul II, General Audience, 14 November 1979).

The first man's acclaim for the first woman shows the capacity both have to associate intimately in marriage. Man's attitude to woman as it comes across here is that of husband to wife. "In his wife he sees the fulfilment of God's intention: 'It is not good that the man should be alone; I will make him a helper fit for him,' and he makes his own the cry of Adam, the first husband: 'This at last is bone of my bones and flesh of my flesh.' Authentic conjugal love presupposes and requires that a man have a profound respect for the equal dignity of his wife: 'You are not her master,' writes St Ambrose (*Hexaemeron*, 5, 7, 19) 'but her husband; she was not given to you to be your slave, but your wife [. . .]. Reciprocate her attentiveness to you and be grateful to her

for her love'" (John Paul II, *Familiaris consortio*, 25).

2:24. These words are a comment by the sacred writer in which, having told the story of the creation of woman, he depicts the institution of marriage as something established by God at the time when human life began. As John Paul II explains, "this conjugal communion sinks its roots in the natural complementarity that exists between man and woman, and is nurtured through the personal willingness of the spouses to share their entire life-project, what they have and what they are: for this reason such communion is the fruit and the sign of a profoundly human need" (*Familiaris consortio*, 19).

By joining in marriage, man and woman form a family. Even the earliest translations of the Bible (Greek and Aramaic), interpreted this passage as meaning "*the two* will become one flesh", thereby indicating that marriage as willed by God was monogamous. Jesus also referred to this passage about the origin of man to teach the indissolubility of marriage, drawing the conclusion that "what God has joined together, let no man put asunder" (Mt 19:5 and par.). The Church teaches the same: "The intimate partnership of life and the love which constitutes the married state has been established by the Creator and endowed by him with its

---

Dominus Deus costam, quam tulerat de Adam, in mulierem et adduxit eam ad Adam. [23]Dixitque Adam: «Haec nunc os ex ossibus meis / et caro de carne mea! / Haec vocabitur Virago, / quoniam de viro sumpta est haec». [24]Quam ob rem relinquet vir patrem suum et matrem et adhaerebit uxori suae;

d. Heb. *ishshah*   **e.** Heb *ish*

²⁴Therefore a man leaves his father and his mother and cleaves to *Eph 5:31*
his wife, and they become one flesh. ²⁵And the man and his wife
were both naked, and were not ashamed.

Rom 5:12–21
Rev 12:1–17
Mt 4:3

Temptation and the first sin*

Wis 2:24

3 ¹The serpent was more subtle than any other wild creature that
the LORD God had made. He said to the woman, "Did God say,

Jn 8:44
Mt 10:16
Rev 12:9

own proper laws: it is rooted in the contract of its partners, that is, in their irrevocable personal consent. It is an institution confirmed by the divine law and receiving its stability, even in the eyes of society, from the human act by which the partners mutually surrender themselves to each other; for the good of the partners, of the children, and of society this sacred bond no longer depends on human decision alone. For God himself is the author of marriage and has endowed it with various benefits and with various ends in view" (Vatican II, *Gaudium et spes*, 48).

2:25. Here we can see how man and his body were totally in harmony, as were man and woman; this harmony will be broken due to the sin the narrative goes on to report.

*3:1–24. "The account of the fall in Genesis 3 uses figurative language, but affirms a primeval event, a deed that took place *at the beginning of the history of man*. Revelation gives us the certainty of faith that the whole of human history is marked by the original fault freely committed by our first parents" (*Catechism of the Catholic Church*, 390). The Bible is teaching us here about the origin of evil—of all the evils mankind experiences, and particularly the evil of death. Evil does not come from God (he created man to live a happy life and to be his friend); it comes from sin, that is, from the fact that man broke the divine com-

mandment, thereby destroying the happiness he was created for, and his harmony with God, with himself, and with creation in general. "Man, tempted by the devil, let his trust in his Creator die in his heart and, abusing his freedom, *disobeyed* God's command. This is what man's first sin consisted of. All subsequent sin would be disobedience toward God and lack of trust in his goodness" (*Catechism of the Catholic Church*, 397).

In his description of that original sin and its consequences, the sacred writer uses symbolic language (garden, tree, serpent) in order to convey an important historical and religious truth—that no sooner did he walk the earth than man disobeyed God, and therein lies the cause of evil. We can also see here how every sin happens and what results from it: "The eyes of our soul grow dull. Reason proclaims itself sufficient to understand everything, without the aid of God. This is a subtle temptation, which hides behind the power of our intellect, given by our Father God to man so that he might know and love him freely. Seduced by this temptation, the human mind appoints itself the centre of the universe, being thrilled with the prospect that 'you shall be like gods' (Gen 3:15). So filled with love for itself, it turns its back on the love of God" (St Josemaría Escrivá, *Christ Is Passing By*, 6).

3:1. The serpent symbolizes the devil, a personal being who tries to frustrate

et erunt in carnem unam. ²⁵Erant autem uterque nudi, Adam scilicet et uxor eius, et non erubescebant.

51

'You shall not eat of any tree of the garden'?" ²And the woman said to the serpent, "We may eat of the fruit of the trees of the Rev 2:7 garden; ³but God said, 'You shall not eat of the fruit of the tree which is in the midst of the garden, neither shall you touch it, lest Gen 2:17; 3:22 you die.'" ⁴But the serpent said to the woman, "You will not die. Is 14:14 ⁵For God knows that when you eat of it your eyes will be opened, Heb 5:14 1 Tim 2:14 and you will be like God, knowing good and evil." ⁶So when the woman saw that the tree was good for food, and that it was a

---

God's plans and draw man to perdition. "Behind the disobedient choice of our first parents lurks a seductive voice, opposed to God, which makes them fall into death out of envy (cf. Wis 2:24). Scripture and the Church's Tradition see in this being a fallen angel, called 'Satan' or the 'devil'. The Church teaches that Satan was at first a good angel, made by God: 'The devil and the other demons were indeed created naturally good by God, but they became evil by their own doing' (Fourth Lateran Council)" (*Catechism of the Catholic Church*, 391).

3:2–5. The devil's temptation strategy is very realistically described here: he falsifies what God has said, raises suspicions about God's plans and intentions, and, finally, portrays God as man's enemy. "The analysis of sin in its original dimension indicates that, through the influence of the 'father of lies', *throughout the history of humanity there will be a constant pressure on man to reject God*, even to the point of hating him: '*Love of self to the point of contempt for God*,' as St Augustine puts it (cf. *De Civitate Dei*, 14, 28). Man will be inclined to see in God primarily a limitation of himself,

and not the source of his own freedom and the fullness of good. We see this confirmed in the modern age, when the atheistic ideologies seek *to root out religion* on the grounds that religion causes the radical '*alienation*' *of man*, as if man were dispossessed of his own humanity when, accepting the idea of God, he attributes to God what belongs to man, and exclusively to man! Hence a process of thought and historico-sociological practice in which the rejection of God has reached the point of declaring his 'death'. An absurdity, both in concept and expression!" (John Paul II, *Dominum et Vivificantem*, 38).

3:6 And so both of them, the man and the woman, disobeyed God's commandment. Genesis refers not to an apple but to a mysterious fruit: eating it symbolizes Adam and Eve's sin—one of disobedience.

The sacred writer leads us to the denouement by giving a masterly psychological description of temptation, dialogue with the tempter, doubt about God's truthfulness, and then yielding to one's sensual appetites. This sin, Pope John Paul II also commented, "consti-

---

¹Et serpens erat callidior cunctis animantibus agri, quae fecerat Dominus Deus. Qui dixit ad mulierem: «Verene praecepit vobis Deus, ut non comederetis de omni ligno paradisi?». ²Cui respondit mulier: «De fructu lignorum, quae sunt in paradiso, vescimur; ³de fructu vero ligni, quod est in medio paradisi, praecepit nobis Deus, ne comederemus et ne tangeremus illud, ne moriamur». ⁴Dixit autem serpens ad mulierem: «Nequaquam morte moriemini! ⁵Scit enim Deus quod in quocumque die comederitis ex eo, aperientur oculi vestri, et eritis sicut Deus scientes bonum et malum». ⁶Vidit igitur mulier quod bonum esset lignum ad vescendum et pulchrum oculis et desiderabile esset lignum ad intellegendum; et tulit

delight to the eyes, and that the tree was to be desired to make one wise, she took of its fruit and ate; and she also gave some to her husband, and he ate. [7]Then the eyes of both were opened, and they knew that they were naked; and they sewed fig leaves together and made themselves aprons.

[8]And they heard the sound of the LORD God walking in the garden in the cool of the day, and the man and his wife hid themselves from the presence of the LORD God among the trees of the

---

tutes *the principle and root of all the others*. We find ourselves faced with the original reality of sin in human history and at the same time in the whole of the economy of salvation. [. . .] This original disobedience presupposes *a rejection*, or at least *a turning away from the truth contained in the Word of God*, who creates the world. [. . .] 'Disobedience' means precisely going beyond that limit, which remains impassable to the will and the freedom of man as a created being. For God the Creator is the one definitive source of the moral order in the world created by him. Man cannot decide by himself what is good and what is evil— cannot 'know good and evil, like God'. In the created world *God* indeed remains the first and sovereign source *for deciding about good and evil*, through the intimate truth of being, which is the reflection *of the Word*, the eternal Son, consubstantial with the Father. To man, created to the image of God, the Holy Spirit gives the gift of *conscience*, so that in this conscience the image may faithfully reflect its model, which is both Wisdom and eternal Law, the source of the moral order in man and in the world. 'Disobedience', as the original dimension of sin, means the *rejection of this source*, through man's claim to become an independent and exclusive source for deciding about good and evil" (*Dominum et Vivificantem*, 33–36).

3:7–13. This passage begins the description of the effects of the original sin. Man and woman have come to know evil, and it shows, initially, in a most direct way— in their own bodies. The inner harmony described in Genesis 2:25 is broken, and concupiscence rears its head. Their friendship with God is also broken, and they flee from his presence, to avoid their nakedness being seen. As if their Creator could not see them! The harmony between man and woman is also fractured: he puts the blame on her, and she puts it on the serpent. But all three share in the responsibility, and therefore all three are going to pay the penalty.

"The harmony in which they found themselves, thanks to original justice, is now destroyed: the control of the soul's spiritual faculties over the body is shattered; the union of man and woman becomes subject to tensions (cf. Gen 3:7–16), their relations henceforth marked by lust and domination. Harmony with creation is broken: visible creation has become alien and hostile to man (cf. Gen 3:17, 19). Because of man, creation is now subject 'to its bondage to decay' (Rom 8:21). Finally, the consequence explicitly foretold for this disobedience will come true: man will 'return to the ground' (Gen 3:19), for out of it he was taken. *Death makes its entrance into human history* (cf. Rom 5:12)" (*Catechism of the Catholic Church*, 400).

---

de fructu illius et comedit deditque etiam viro suo secum, qui comedit. [7]Et aperti sunt oculi amborum.

53

garden. [9]But the LORD God called to the man, and said to him, "Where are you?" [10]And he said, "I heard the sound of thee in the garden, and I was afraid, because I was naked; and I hid myself." [11]He said, "Who told you that you were naked? Have you eaten of the tree of which I commanded you not to eat?" [12]The man said, "The woman whom thou gavest to be with me, she gave me fruit of the tree, and I ate." [13]Then the LORD God said to the woman, "What is this that you have done?" The woman said, "The serpent beguiled me, and I ate." [14]The LORD God said to the serpent,

Rom 7:11
2 Cor 11:3
1 Tim 2:14
Rev 12:9

3:14–15. The punishment God imposes on the serpent includes confrontation between woman and the serpent, between mankind and evil, with the promise that man will come out on top. That is why this passage is called the "Proto-gospel": it is the first announcement to mankind of the good news of the Redeemer-Messiah. Clearly, a bruise to the head is deadly, whereas a bruise to the heel is curable.

As the Second Vatican Council teaches, "God, who creates and conserves all things by his Word (cf. Jn 1:3), provides men with constant evidence of himself in created realities (cf. Rom 1:19–20). And furthermore, wishing to open up the way to heavenly salvation, by promising redemption (cf. Gen 3:15); and he has never ceased to take care of the human race. For he wishes to give eternal life to all those who seek salvation by patience in well-doing (cf. Rom 2:6–7)" (*Dei Verbum*, 3).

Victory over the devil will be brought about by a descendant of the woman, the Messiah. The Church has always read these verses as being messianic, referring to Jesus Christ; and it has seen in the woman the mother of the promised Saviour; the Virgin Mary is the new Eve. "The earliest documents, as they are read in the Church and are understood in the light of a further and full revelation, bring the figure of a woman, Mother of the Redeemer, into a gradually clearer light. Considered in this light, she is already prophetically foreshadowed in the promise of victory over the serpent which was given to our first parents after their fall into sin (cf. Gen 3:15) [. . .]. Hence not a few of the early Fathers gladly assert with Irenaeus in their preaching: 'the knot of Eve's disobedience was untied by Mary's obedience: what the virgin Eve bound through her disbelief, Mary loosened by her faith' (St Irenaeus, *Adv. haer.* 3, 22, 4) Comparing Mary with Eve, they call her 'Mother of the living' (St Epiphanius, *Adv. haer. Panarium* 78, 18) and frequently claim: 'death through Eve, life through Mary' (St Jerome, *Epistula* 22, 21; etc.)" (Vatican II, *Lumen gentium*, 55–56).

So, woman is going to have a key role in that victory over the devil. In his Latin translation of the Bible, the

---

Cumque cognovissent esse se nudos, consuerunt folia ficus et fecerunt sibi perizomata. [8]Et cum audissent vocem Domini Dei deambulantis in paradiso ad auram post meridiem, abscondit se Adam et uxor eius a facie Domini Dei in medio ligni paradisi. [9]Vocavitque Dominus Deus Adam et dixit ei: «Ubi es?». [10]Qui ait: «Vocem tuam audivi in paradiso et timui eo quod nudus essem et abscondi me». [11]Cui dixit: «Quis enim indicavit tibi quod nudus esses, nisi quod ex ligno, de quo tibi praeceperam, ne comederes, comedisti?». [12]Dixitque Adam: «Mulier, quam dedisti sociam mihi, ipsa dedit mihi de ligno, et comedi». [13]Et dixit Dominus Deus ad mulierem: «Quid hoc fecisti?». Quae respondit:

"Because you have done this,
cursed are you above all cattle,
and above all wild animals;
upon your belly you shall go,
and dust you shall eat
all the days of your life.
[15]I will put enmity between you and the woman,
and between your seed and her seed;
he shall bruise your head,*
and you shall bruise his heel."
[16]To the woman he said,

Lk 10:19
Rev 12:17

Gen 2:22
1 Cor 11:3; 14:34

Vulgate, St Jerome in fact reads the relevant passage as "she [the woman] shall bruise your head". That woman is the Blessed Virgin, the new Eve and the mother of the Redeemer, who shares (by anticipation and pre-eminently) in the victory of her Son. Sin never left its mark on her, and the Church proclaims her as the Immaculate Conception.

St Thomas explains that the reason why God did not prevent the first man from sinning was because "God allows evils to be done in order to draw forth some greater good. Thus St Paul says, 'Where sin increased, grace abounded all the more' (Rom 5:20); and the *Exultet* sings, 'O happy fault, . . . which gained for us so great a Redeemer'" (*Summa theologiae*, 3, 1, 3 ad 3; cf. *Catechism of the Catholic Church*, 412).

3:16. Turning to the woman, God tells her what effects sin is going to have on her, as a mother and a wife. The pain of childbirth also points to the presence of physical pain in mankind, as a consequence of sin. Sin is also the cause of disorder in family life, especially between husband and wife: the text expressly instances a husband's despotic

behaviour towards his wife. Discrimination against women is here seen as the outcome of sin; it is something, therefore, that the Bible regards as evil. Sin is also the reason why people fail to appreciate the dignity of marriage and the family—a widespread failing denounced by the Second Vatican Council: "the dignity of these partnerships is not reflected everywhere, but is overshadowed by polygamy, the plague of divorce, so-called free love, and similar blemishes; furthermore, married love is too often dishonoured by selfishness, hedonism, and unlawful contraceptive practices. Besides, the economic, social, psychological, and civil climate of today has a severely disturbing effect on family life" (*Gaudium et spes*, 47).

3:17–19 The effects of sin that man is warned about are closely connected with his God-given mission—to till and keep the garden, or, to put it another way, to master the earth by means of his activity, work. The harmony between man and nature has been shattered through sin: from now on man is going to find work burdensome and it will cause him much distress. Thus, the effects of sin are all

---

«Serpens decepit me, et comedi». [14]Et ait Dominus Deus ad serpentem: «Quia fecisti hoc, maledictus es / inter omnia pecora / et omnes bestias agri! / Super pectus tuum gradieris / et pulverem comedes cunctis diebus vitae tuae. / [15]Inimicitias ponam inter te et mulierem / et semen tuum et semen illius; /

1 Tim 2:12
Rev 12:2
"I will greatly multiply your pain in childbearing;
in pain you shall bring forth children,
yet your desire shall be for your husband,
and he shall rule over you."

Hos 4:3
Is 11:16
Rom 8:20
1 Cor 15:21
17And to Adam he said,
"Because you have listened to the voice of your wife,
and have eaten of the tree
of which I commanded you,
'You shall not eat of it,'
cursed is the ground because of you;
in toil you shall eat of it all the days of your life;

Heb 6:8
18thorns and thistles it shall bring forth to you;
and you shall eat the plants of the field.

Gen 2:7
Heb 9:27
19In the sweat of your face
you shall eat bread
till you return to the ground,
for out of it you were taken;
you are dust,
and to dust you shall return."

---

the various kinds of injustice which are to be found in the world of work and in man's control over the goods of the earth. God meant the earth and all that it contains to benefit all mankind, but what in fact happens is that "in the midst of huge numbers deprived of the absolute necessities of life there are some who live in riches and squander their wealth; and this happens in less developed areas as well. Luxury and misery exist side by side. While a few individuals enjoy an almost unlimited opportunity to choose for themselves, the vast majority have no chance whatever of exercising personal initiative and responsibility, and quite often have to live and work in conditions unworthy of human beings" (Vatican II, *Gaudium et spes*, 63).

The consequences of sin will stay with man until he returns to the earth, that is, until he dies. However, God does not immediately put into effect what he threatened in Genesis 2:17; man continues to live on earth, but he is destined to die. It is in this sense that St Paul explains human existence, in the light of the work of Christ whom he sees as being the second Adam: "Therefore as sin came into the world through one man and death through sin, [. . .] so death spread to all men because all men sinned. [. . .] If, because of one man's trespass death reigned through that one man, much more will those who receive the abundance of grace and the free gift of righteousness reign in life through the one man Jesus Christ" (Rom 5:12, 17).

---

ipsum conteret caput tuum, / et tu conteres calcaneum eius». 16Mulieri dixit: «Multiplicabo aerumnas tuas / et conceptus tuos: / in dolore paries filios, / et ad virum tuum erit appetitus tuus, / ipse autem dominabitur tui». 17Adae vero dixit: «Quia audisti vocem uxoris tuae et comedisti de ligno, ex quo praeceperam tibi, ne comederes, / maledicta humus propter te! / In laboribus comedes ex ea / cunctis diebus vitae tuae. / 18Spinas et tribulos germinabit tibi, / et comedes herbas terrae; / 19in sudore vultus

²⁰The man called his wife's name Eve,ᶠ because she was the mother of all living.

Rom 5:12
Ex 25:18–22
Rev 22:2.14

Adam and Eve are expelled from paradise

²¹And the LORD God made for Adam and for his wife garments of skins, and clothed them.

²²Then the LORD God said, "Behold, the man has become like one of us, knowing good and evil; and now, lest he put forth his hand and take also of the tree of life, and eat, and live for ever"— ²³therefore the LORD God sent him forth from the garden of Eden, to till the ground from which he was taken. ²⁴He drove out the man; and at the east of the garden of Eden he placed the cherubim, and a flaming sword which turned every way, to guard the way to the tree of life.

Gen 2:17
Rev 2:7

The first children of Adam and Eve*

4 ¹*Now Adam knew Eve his wife, and she conceived and bore Cain, saying, "I have gottenᵍ a man with the help of the

---

3:21–24. Even after the fall, God still takes care of man. Man will continue to populate the earth, in spite of death, thanks to woman's role as mother. God comes to the rescue of man's nakedness, which made him feel so afraid and ashamed. Man's place in history emerges with his expulsion from paradise. He now knows good and evil; he is deprived of the happiness for which he was created and, with death as his fate, he yearns for the immortality which in fact belongs to God alone. This is the human condition; it affects everyone and its cause lies in sin. Thus, "we do know by Revelation that Adam had received original holiness and justice not for himself alone, but for all

human nature. By yielding to the tempter, Adam and Eve committed a personal sin, but this sin affected *the human nature* that they would then transmit *in a fallen state* (cf. Council of Trent, *De peccato originali*). It is a sin which will be transmitted by propagation to all mankind, that is, by the transmission of a human nature deprived of original holiness and justice. And that is why original sin is called 'sin' only in an analogical sense: it is a sin 'contracted' and not 'committed'—a state and not an act" (*Catechism of the Catholic Church*, 404).

*4:1–26. The sacred writer goes on to show how human life was transmitted,

---

tui vesceris pane, / donec revertaris ad humum, / de qua sumptus es, / quia pulvis es et in pulverem reverteris». ²⁰Et vocavit Adam nomen uxoris suae Eva, eo quod mater esset cunctorum viventium. ²¹Fecit quoque Dominus Deus Adae et uxori eius tunicas pelliceas et induit eos. ²²Et ait Dominus Deus: «Ecce homo factus est quasi unus ex nobis, ut sciat bonum et malum; nunc ergo, ne mittat manum suam et sumat etiam de ligno vitae et comedat et vivat in aeternum!». ²³Emisit eum Dominus Deus de paradiso Eden, ut operaretur humum, de qua sumptus est. ²⁴Eiecitque hominem et collocavit ad orientem paradisi Eden cherubim et flammeum gladium atque versatilem ad custodiendam viam ligni vitae.

f. The name in Hebrew resembles the word for *living* **g.** Heb *qanah*, get

Wis 10:3
Mt 23:35
Heb 11:4;
12:24
1 Jn 3:12–15

Ex 34:19
Lev 3:16
Heb 11:4

LORD." ²And again, she bore his brother Abel. Now Abel was a keeper of sheep, and Cain a tiller of the ground.

Cain and Abel

³In the course of time Cain brought to the LORD an offering of the fruit of the ground, ⁴and Abel brought of the firstlings of his flock and of their fat portions. And the LORD had regard for Abel and his offering, ⁵but for Cain and his offering he had no regard. So Cain was very angry, and his countenance fell. ⁶The LORD said to Cain,

---

starting with the first human parents, and how, at the same time, man's life on earth continues to bear the mark of evil and sin. "Man has become the enemy of his fellow man" (*Catechism of the Catholic Church*, 2259). Scripture shows this by the episode of Cain and Abel, which uses ancient traditions to teach that from the very beginning of mankind evil gained ground by violence and injustice; nothing could better show this than the murder of an innocent brother.

St Augustine reads a deeper meaning into the fact that Cain was born before Abel: "In regard to mankind," he writes, "I have made a division. On the one side are those who live according to man; on the other, those who live according to God. And I have said that, in a deeper sense, we may speak of two cities or two human societies [. . .]. The first child born of the two parents of the human race was Cain. He belonged to the city of man. The next born was Abel, and he was of the City of God. Notice here a parallel between the individual man and the whole race. We all experience as individuals what the Apostle says: 'It is not the spiritual that comes first, but the physical, and then the spiritual' (1 Cor 15:46). The fact is that every individual springs from a condemned stock and, because of

Adam, must be first cankered and carnal, only later to become sound and spiritual by the process of rebirth in Christ" (*De civitate Dei*, 15,1).

4:1. To refer to sexual intercourse between man and woman, the Bible uses the term "to know", thereby signalling the human depth of that relationship: although it takes place via the body, it does so in a context of mind and will.

The name of Cain has an explanation in the biblical text: it echoes Eve's exclamation, "I have gotten . . ." (in Hebrew, *qaniti*). This shows God's part in the generation of her child. The Bible will keep on teaching that children are a gift from God, and that it is God who gives or witholds fertility. Consequently the Church reminds married couples of their duty "to transmit human life and to educate their children; they should realize that they are thereby cooperating with the love of God the Creator and are, in a certain sense, its interpreters" (Vatican II, *Gaudium et spes*, 50).

4:3–8. We can see here how from the start God picks out particular people (without any merit on their part), sometimes giving preference to the youngest or the weakest: Jacob is preferred to Esau,

---

¹Adam vero cognovit Evam uxorem suam, quae concepit et peperit Cain dicens: «Acquisivi virum per Dominum». ²Rursusque peperit fratrem eius Abel. Et fuit Abel pastor ovium et Cain agricola. ³Factum

"Why are you angry, and why has your countenance fallen? ⁷If you do well, will you not be accepted? And if you do not do well, sin is couching at the door; its desire is for you, but you must master it." ⁸Cain said to Abel his brother, "Let us go out to the field."ʰ And when they were in the field, Cain rose up against his brother Abel, and killed him. ⁹Then the LORD said to Cain, "Where is Abel your brother?" He said, "I do not know; am I my brother's keeper?" ¹⁰And the LORD said, "What have you done? The voice of your brother's blood is crying to me from the ground. ¹¹And

Jn 8:34

Wis 10:3
Mt 23:35
Lk 11:51

1 Jn 3:12
Jude 11

Mt 23:35
Lk 11:51
Heb 11:4; 12:24

for example; David to his brothers. The origin of Cain's sin lies in the fact that he does not accept God's preference for his younger brother, and he gives way to anger, envy (cf. Wis 10:3) and gloominess. Despite that, God loves Cain too and he invites him to master temptation (v. 7) by acting rightly; but Cain killed his brother Abel.

Cain is the prototype of the perverse and murderous man; Abel, of the just man who blamelessly suffers violent death. For this reason Abel is seen as a figure of Jesus Christ, whose blood spilt on the cross speaks even more eloquently than the blood of Abel: "But you have come [. . .] to Jesus, the mediator of a new covenant, and to the spiritual blood that speaks more graciously than the blood of Abel" (Heb 12:24). Cain, on the other hand, symbolizes every man who hates his neighbour, for hatred implies desiring that the other person should not exist. St John interprets the story of Cain in this sense when he writes: "This is the message which you have heard from the beginning, that we should love one another, and not be like Cain who was of the evil one and murdered his brother. And why did he murder him? Because his own deeds were evil and his brother's righteous. [. . .] Any one who hates his brother is a murderer, and we know that no murderer has eternal life abiding in him" (1 Jn 3:11–12, 15).

Assuming that Cain was ill-intentioned in his offerings, St Bede the Venerable comments that "men often are placated by gifts from those who have offended them; but God, who 'discerns the thoughts and intentions of the heart' (Heb 4:12), lets himself be placated by no gift as much as by the pious devotion of the offerer. Once he has seen the purity of our heart, he will then also accept our prayers and our works" (*Hexaemeron 2: in Gen*, 4:4–5).

4:9–16. The question God puts to Cain is one that is constantly being asked of all human beings as regards their fellows. And the death by violence of any innocent person cries for justice, a cry to which God is never indifferent. He bur-

est autem post aliquot dies ut offerret Cain de fructibus agri munus Domino. ⁴Abel quoque obtulit de primogenitis gregis sui et de adipibus eorum. Et respexit Dominus ad Abel et ad munus eius, ⁵ad Cain vero et ad munus illius non respexit. Iratusque est Cain vehementer, et concidit vultus eius. ⁶Dixitque Dominus ad eum: «Quare iratus es, et cur concidit facies tua? ⁷Nonne si bene egeris, vultum attolles? Sin autem male, in foribus peccatum insidiabitur, et ad te erit appetitus eius, tu autem dominaberis illius». ⁸Dixitque Cain ad Abel fratrem suum: «Egrediamur foras». Cumque essent in agro, consurrexit Cain adversus Abel fratrem suum et interfecit eum. ⁹Et ait Dominus ad Cain: «Ubi est Abel frater

h. Sam Gk Syr Compare Vg: Heb lacks *Let us go out to the field*

now you are cursed from the ground, which has opened its mouth to receive your brother's blood from your hand. [12]When you till the ground, it shall no longer yield to you its strength; you shall be a fugitive and a wanderer on the earth." [13]Cain said to the LORD, "My punishment is greater than I can bear. [14]Behold, thou hast driven me this day away from the ground; and from thy face I shall be hidden; and I shall be a fugitive and a wanderer on the earth, and whoever finds me will slay me." [15]Then the LORD said to him, "Not so![i] If any one slays Cain, vengeance shall be taken on him sevenfold." And the LORD put a mark on Cain, lest any who came upon him should kill him. [16]Then Cain went away from the presence of the LORD, and dwelt in the land of Nod,[j] east of Eden.

The descendants of Cain

[17]Cain knew his wife, and she conceived and bore Enoch; and he built a city, and called the name of the city after the name of his son, Enoch. [18]To Enoch was born Irad; and Irad was the father of Me-huja-el, and Me-huja-el the father of Me-thusha-el, and

dens Cain's conscience with the weight of his crime, even though he protects his life by putting a mark on him to prevent anyone taking revenge. In the context of this account, the mark is meant as a protection, not a sign of infamy. The fact that Cain, on account of what he has done, is sent out of God's presence and has to wander on the earth symbolizes the break with God that sin causes.

"Human life is sacred," the Church teaches, "because from its beginning it involves the creative action of God and it remains for ever in a special relationship with the Creator, who is its sole end. God alone is the Lord of life from its beginning until its end: no one can under any circumstance claim for himself the right directly to destroy an innocent human being" (*Catechism of the Catholic Church*, 2258).

*4:17–24. By giving the names of Cain's descendants the sacred writer is saying that a part of mankind (that which traces its line back to Adam's first-born son)

tuus?». Qui respondit: «Nescio. Num custos fratris mei sum ego?». [10]Dixitque ad eum: «Quid fecisti? Vox sanguinis fratris tui clamat ad me de agro. [11]Nunc igitur maledictus eris procul ab agro, qui aperuit os suum et suscepit sanguinem fratris tui de manu tua! [12]Cum operatus fueris eum, amplius non dabit tibi fructus suos; vagus et profugus eris super terram». [13]Dixitque Cain ad Dominum: «Maior est poena mea quam ut portem eam. [14]Ecce eicis me hodie a facie agri, et a facie tua abscondar et ero vagus et profugus in terra; omnis igitur, qui invenerit me, occidet me». [15]Dixitque ei Dominus: «Nequaquam ita fiet, sed omnis qui occiderit Cain, septuplum punietur!». Posuitque Dominus Cain signum, ut non eum interficeret omnis qui invenisset eum. [16]Egressusque Cain a facie Domini habitavit in terra Nod ad orientalem plagam Eden. [17]Cognovit autem Cain uxorem suam, quae concepit et peperit Henoch. Et aedificavit civitatem vocavitque nomen eius ex nomine filii sui Henoch. [18]Porro Henoch

i. Gk Syr Vg: Heb *Therefore*   j. That is *Wandering*

Me-thusha-el the father of Lamech. [19]And Lamech took two wives; the name of the one was Adah, and the name of the other Zillah. [20]Adah bore Jabal; he was the father of those who dwell in tents and have cattle. [21]His brother's name was Jubal; he was the father of all those who play the lyre and pipe. [22]Zillah bore Tubal-cain; he was the forger of all instruments of bronze and iron. The sister of Tubal-cain was Naamah.

[23]Lamech said to his wives:

"Adah and Zillah, hear my voice;
you wives of Lamech, hearken to what I say:
I have slain a man for wounding me,
a young man for striking me.
[24]If Cain is avenged sevenfold,   Mt 18:22
Lamech seventy-seven-fold."

The birth of Seth

[25]And Adam knew his wife again, and she bore a son and called   Lk 3:38
his name Seth, for she said, "God has appointed for me another
child instead of Abel, for Cain slew him." [26]To Seth* also a son   Ex 3:14

---

lived separated from God. He attributes to them the building of cities and the invention of trades, and also the start of polygamy and rampant vengeance (v. 24). Material progress, imbued with idolatry, was always a temptation for the Israelites.

The names of Cain's descendants are connected etymologically with those of the cities they built or the skills they developed. But it is worth remembering that it is not the Bible's intention to provide a history lesson chronicling human progress; the point it is making is that the earth is being populated in line with God's commandment; it is outlining how,

after the creation of man, the human race conducted itself in relation to God.

4:25–26. This is the part of mankind which retained its knowledge of the true God, who in due course will reveal himself to Abraham (cf. chap. 12) and Moses (cf. Ex 3:14). Seth's name is given an etymological explanation, but now one connected not with cities and skills (cf. the note on 4:17–24) but with God: Seth gets his name because God gave him to Eve to take the place of Abel. This will be the line of descendants of Adam and Eve from which will come the chosen people, through the calling of Abraham.

genuit Irad, et Irad genuit Maviael, et Maviael genuit Mathusael, et Mathusael genuit Lamech. [19]Qui accepit uxores duas: nomen uni Ada et nomen alteri Sella. [20]Genuitque Ada Iabel, qui fuit pater habitantium in tentoriis atque pastorum. [21]Et nomen fratris eius Iubal; ipse fuit pater omnium canentium cithara et organo. [22]Sella quoque genuit Tubalcain, qui fuit malleator et faber in cuncta opera aeris et ferri. Soror vero Tubalcain Noema. [23]Dixitque Lamech uxoribus suis: «Ada et Sella, audite vocem meam; / uxores Lamech, auscultate sermonem meum: / occidi virum pro vulnere meo / et adulescentulum pro livore meo; / [24]septuplum ultio dabitur de Cain, / de Lamech vero septuagies septies». [25]Cognovit quoque Adam uxorem suam, et peperit filium vocavitque nomen eius Seth dicens: «Posuit mihi Deus semen aliud pro Abel, quem occidit Cain». [26]Sed et Seth natus est filius, quem vocavit Enos.

was born, and he called his name Enosh. At that time men began to call upon the name of the LORD.

2. ADAM'S DESCENDANTS. FROM SETH TO NOAH

1 Chron 1:1–4

Gen 1:26
Mt 1:1
1 Cor 11:7
Mt 19:4
Mk 10:6
1 Cor 15:49

The increase of the human race*

5 ¹This is the book of the generations* of Adam. When God created man, he made him in the likeness of God. ²Male and female he created them, and he blessed them and named them Man when they were created. ³When Adam had lived a hundred and thirty years, he became the father of a son in his own likeness, after his image, and named him Seth. ⁴The days of Adam after he became the father of Seth were eight hundred years; and he had other sons and daughters. ⁵Thus all the days that Adam lived were nine hundred and thirty years; and he died.

The fact that there is no mention of Seth's descendants devoting themselves to trades may be designed to show that their specific contribution to mankind was their keeping the knowledge of the true God—a greater contribution than that made by others.

"In a figurative manner," St Bede explains, "Enoch, the son of Seth, stands for the Christian people who, through faith and the sacrament of the passion and resurrection of the Lord, is born every day, the world over, of water and the Holy Spirit. This people [. . .] in all that it does is always invoking the name of the Lord, saying, Our Father, who are in heaven, hallowed by thy name" (*Hexaemeron* 2: *in Gen*, 4:25–26).

***5:1–32** This "book of the generations of Adam" collects names of famous

ancestors and traditions about them; according to biblical scholars, this material may have reached the text via the "Priestly" tradition. The aim is to show that mankind was increasing in number in line with God's commandment as recorded in Genesis 1:28. There is no mention of Cain, because the text is giving only the descendants of Seth, from whom will eventually come the chosen people.

The ages given for the patriarchs are symbolic, not exact. We can see that the ages of the people reduce, the further away they get from the earliest time of human life, that is, the further they get from God; there is a process of degeneration at work due to the presence of evil. In a way there is the same sort of outlook here as in Proverbs 10:27: "The fear of the Lord prolongs life, but the years of

---

Tunc coeperunt invocare nomen Domini. ¹ Hic est liber generationis Adam. In die qua creavit Deus hominem, ad similitudinem Dei fecit illum. ²Masculum et feminam creavit eos et benedixit illis; et vocavit nomen eorum Adam in die, quo creati sunt. ³Vixit autem Adam centum triginta annis et genuit ad similitudinem et imaginem suam vocavitque nomen eius Seth. ⁴Et facti sunt dies Adam, postquam genuit Seth, octingenti anni, genuitque filios et filias. ⁵Et factum est omne tempus, quod vixit Adam,

6When Seth had lived a hundred and five years, he became the father of Enosh. 7Seth lived after the birth of Enosh eight hundred and seven years, and had other sons and daughters. 8Thus all the days of Seth were nine hundred and twelve years; and he died.

9When Enosh had lived ninety years, he became the father of Lk 3:36 Kenan. 10Enosh lived after the birth of Kenan eight hundred and fifteen years, and had other sons and daughters. 11Thus all the days of Enosh were nine hundred and five years; and he died.

12When Kenan had lived seventy years, he became the father of Gen 4:17 Ma-halalel. 13Kenan lived after the birth of Ma-halalel eight hundred and forty years, and had other sons and daughters. 14Thus all the days of Kenan were nine hundred and ten years; and he died.

15When Ma-halalel had lived sixty-five years, he became the father of Jared. 16Ma-halalel lived after the birth of Jared eight hundred and thirty years, and had other sons and daughters. 17Thus all the days of Ma-halalel were eight hundred and ninety-five years; and he died.

---

the wicked will be short." Mankind becomes more debased, so God reduces the allotted span to one hundred and twenty years (cf. Gen 6:3).

Like the other ones given in the Bible, this genealogy shows the benefits of human reproduction. By it man fulfils the commandment God gave him when he created him, to increase and multiply and subdue the earth; in this way, too, man co-operates with the saving plans of God, for these will come about through his choosing a people stemming from one of these genealogical lines; and from that people Jesus Christ will be born. To underline the universal scope of the redemption brought about by Christ, St Luke in his Gospel links Christ right back to Adam,

the father of the Jews and Gentiles (cf. Lk 3:23–38).

5:3. The divine image and likeness in which Adam, the first man, was created is passed on by reproduction to all his descendants. They are the image and likeness of the first man, just as he is in the image of God. This image and likeness is therefore stamped on every human being, whatever his or her race, independently of how they conduct themselves. From this it follows that one's primary attitude towards others should be "to respect and understand each person for what he is, in his intrinsic dignity as a man and child of God" (St Josemaría Escrivá, *Christ Is Passing By*, 72). Cf. the note on Gen 1:2.

---

anni nongenti triginta, et mortuus est. 6Vixit quoque Seth centum quinque annos et genuit Enos. 7Vixitque Seth, postquam genuit Enos, octingentis septem annis genuitque filios et filias. 8Et facti sunt omnes dies Seth nongentorum duodecim annorum, et mortuus est. 9Vixit vero Enos nonaginta annis et genuit Cainan. 10Et vixit Enos, postquam genuit Cainan, octingentis quindecim annis et genuit filios et filias. 11Factique sunt omnes dies Enos nongentorum quinque annorum, et mortuus est. 12Vixit quoque Cainan septuaginta annis et genuit Malaleel. 13Et vixit Cainan, postquam genuit Malaleel, octingentos quadraginta annos genuitque filios et filias. 14Et facti sunt omnes dies Cainan nongenti decem anni, et mortuus est. 15Vixit autem Malaleel sexaginta quinque annos et genuit Iared. 16Et vixit Malaleel,

¹⁸When Jared had lived a hundred and sixty-two years he became the father of Enoch. ¹⁹Jared lived after the birth of Enoch eight hundred years, and had other sons and daughters. ²⁰Thus all the days of Jared were nine hundred and sixty-two years; and he died.

Sir 44:16; 49:14
Jude 14–15

²¹When Enoch had lived sixty-five years, he became the father of Methuselah. ²²Enoch walked with God after the birth of Methuselah three hundred years, and had other sons and daughters. ²³Thus all the days of Enoch were three hundred and sixty-

Wis 4:10–11
Heb 11:5

five years. ²⁴Enoch walked with God; and he was not, for God took him.

²⁵When Methuselah had lived a hundred and eighty-seven years, he became the father of Lamech. ²⁶Methuselah lived after the birth of Lamech seven hundred and eighty-two years, and had other sons and daughters. ²⁷Thus all the days of Methuselah were nine hundred and sixty-nine years; and he died.

²⁸When Lamech had lived a hundred and eighty-two years, he became the father of a son, ²⁹and called his name Noah, saying,

---

5:21–24. Enoch is different from the other patriarchs in three ways: he lives for only 365 years (a perfect number, being the same as the number of days in a year); we are told he "walked with God", that is, he was particularly holy; and, finally, he did not die, because God "took him" to himself. On this account Jewish tradition held him in high regard (cf. Sir 44:16; 49:14; Heb 11:5), and books of revelation were attributed to him. The Letter of St Jude describes him as a prophet who denounces the sins of mankind (cf. Jude 14–15).

5:29. The tradition of the Church has often regarded Noah as a figure of Christ.

Thus, Origen in his commentary on this verse, observes that these words find their true fulfilment in our Saviour: "If you look to our Lord Jesus Christ of whom it is said: 'Behold the Lamb of God, behold him who takes away the sin of the world' (Jn 1:29) and of whom it is said again: 'Being made a curse for us that he might redeem us from the curse of the law' (Gal 3:13), and again when Scripture says, 'Come to me all who labour and are burdened and I will refresh you and you shall find rest for your souls' (Mt 11:28–29), you will find him to be the one who truly has given rest to men and has freed the earth from

---

postquam genuit Iared, octingentis triginta annis et genuit filios et filias. ¹⁷Et facti sunt omnes dies Malaleel octingenti nonaginta quinque anni, et mortuus est. ¹⁸Vixitque Iared centum sexaginta duobus annis et genuit Henoch. ¹⁹Et vixit Iared, postquam genuit Henoch, octingentos annos et genuit filios et filias. ²⁰Et facti sunt omnes dies Iared nongenti sexaginta duo anni, et mortuus est. ²¹Porro Henoch vixit sexaginta quinque annis et genuit Mathusalam. ²²Et ambulavit Henoch cum Deo, postquam genuit Mathusalam, trecentis annis et genuit filios et filias. ²³Et facti sunt omnes dies Henoch trecenti sexaginta quinque anni, ²⁴ambulavitque cum Deo et non apparuit, quia tulit eum Deus. ²⁵Vixit quoque Mathusala centum octoginta septem annos et genuit Lamech. ²⁶Et vixit Mathusala, postquam genuit Lamech, septingentos octoginta duos annos et genuit filios et filias. ²⁷Et facti sunt omnes dies Mathusalae nongenti sexaginta novem anni, et mortuus est. ²⁸Vixit autem Lamech centum octoginta

"Out of the ground which the Lord has cursed this one shall bring us relief from our work and from the toil of our hands." ³⁰Lamech lived after the birth of Noah five hundred and ninety-five years, and had other sons and daughters. ³¹Thus all the days of Lamech were seven hundred and seventy-seven years; and he died.

³²After Noah was five hundred years old, Noah became the father of Shem, Ham, and Japheth. Gen 10:1–32

The spread of wickedness*

6 ¹When men began to multiply on the face of the ground, and daughters were born to them, ²the sons of God* saw that the daughters of men were fair; and they took to wife such of them as they chose. ³Then the LORD said, "My spirit shall not abide in man for ever, for he is flesh, but his days shall be a hundred and twenty years." ⁴The Nephilim were on the earth in those days, and also afterward, when the sons of God came in to the daughters of men, 2 Pet 2:4
Jude 6
Lk 20:36
1 Cor 11:10
Gen 2:7
Jn 3:5–6
Num 13:34
Deut 2:10
Bar 3:26–28

---

the curse with which the Lord God cursed it" (*Homiliae in Genesim*, 2,3).

5:32. Three lines will come from Noah; the sacred writer sees mankind as fitting into one or other of these three—Semites, Hamites and Japhethites. The division of nations according to race and which ones stem from which of these three is given in Genesis 10:1–32.

*6:1–8. From the very beginning, evil and sin spread in tandem with the growth of mankind. We can see this in the episode of Cain and Abel and the same point is being made, somewhat obscurely, in this account, which bears traces of the ancient Yahwistic tradition.

6:1–4. Alluding perhaps to a myth in vogue in ancient times, to the effect that

giants were the offspring of women who mated with beings of a higher order, the sacred writer is stressing here the headway that sin and disorder have made. In this passage we are told that God put a limit on man's lifespan as a punishment for sin.

We cannot quite work out what the expression "sons of God" means here. Jewish tradition and some ancient Christian writers read it as meaning fallen angels; but that explanation does not fit in with the spiritual nature of angels. Therefore, it has been interpreted as meaning good men, the descendants of Seth who indiscriminately took as wives descendants of Cain, here called "daughters of men". This is the explanation given by St Augustine (*De civitate Dei*, 15, 23), St John Chrysostom (*Homiliae in Genesim*, 22, 4), St Cyril of Alex-

---

duobus annis et genuit filium ²⁹vocavitque nomen eius Noe dicens: «Iste consolabitur nos ab operibus nostris et labore manuum nostrarum in agro, cui maledixit Dominus». ³⁰Vixitque Lamech, postquam genuit Noe, quingentos nonaginta quinque annos et genuit filios et filias. ³¹Et facti sunt omnes dies Lamech septingenti septuaginta septem anni, et mortuus est. ³²Noe vero, cum quingentorum esset annorum, genuit Sem, Cham et Iapheth. ¹ Cumque coepissent homines multiplicari super terram et filias procreassent, ²videntes filii Dei filias hominum quod essent pulchrae, acceperunt sibi uxores ex omnibus, quas elegerant. ³Dixitque Deus: «Non permanebit spiritus meus in homine in aeternum, quia caro est; eruntque dies illius centum viginti annorum». ⁴Gigantes erant super terram in diebus illis et

and they bore children to them. These were the mighty men that were of old, the men of renown.

[5]The LORD saw that the wickedness of man was great in the earth, and that every imagination of the thoughts of his heart was only evil continually. [6]And the Lord was sorry that he had made man on the earth, and it grieved him to his heart. [7]So the LORD said, "I will blot out man whom I have created from the face of the ground, man and beast and creeping things and birds of the air, for I am sorry that I have made them." [8]But Noah found favour in the eyes of the LORD.

Sir 16:7

Lk 1:30
Heb 11:7

3. THE STORY OF NOAH. HIS DESCENDANTS*

Gen 5:22
Sir 44:17

[9]These are the generations of Noah. Noah was a righteous man, blameless in his generation; Noah walked with God. [10]And Noah had three sons, Shem, Ham, and Japheth.

---

andria (*Glaphyra in Genesim*, 2, 2) and other Fathers. Mankind's moral decline on account of pride and abuses of marriage prepares the way for the upcoming account of the flood.

6:5–8. The severity of these words shows just how corrupt mankind had become. There is also a lesson here about the absolute sovereignty of God, who has power to wipe mankind off the face of the earth.

God's original plan when he created man seems to have been a failure—hence his decision (couched in very human terms) to destroy what he has made. But that is not going to happen: mankind will be saved through the fidelity of one man, Noah; and the earth will be populated again after the flood. We see two themes coming in here which have a high profile

in the Bible: the first is that God loves everything he creates, and his interventions (even in the form of punishment) are always aimed at man's salvation; the second is that the righteous man, or a small remnant of faithful people, brings about the salvation of all mankind. It is in this sense that the Fathers also see in Noah a figure of Christ, because through Christ's obedience God's mercy reaches every human being.

Jesus recalled this episode of Genesis to warn us that we need to be always vigilant and ready to receive him at his second coming: "As were the days of Noah, so will be the coming of the Son of man. For as in those days before the flood they were eating and drinking, marrying and giving in marriage, until the day when Noah entered the ark, and they did not know until the flood came and swept

---

etiam, postquam ingressi sunt filii Dei ad filias hominum, illaeque eis genuerunt: isti sunt potentes a saeculo viri famosi. ⁵Videns autem Dominus quod multa malitia hominum esset in terra, et cuncta cogitatio cordis eorum non intenta esset nisi ad malum omni tempore, ⁶paenituit Dominum quod hominem fecisset in terra. Et tactus dolore cordis intrinsecus: ⁷«Delebo, inquit, hominem, quem creavi, a facie terrae, ab homine usque ad pecus, usque ad reptile et usque ad volucres caeli; paenitet enim me fecisse eos». ⁸Noe vero invenit gratiam coram Domino. ⁹Hae sunt generationes Noe: Noe vir iustus atque per-

[11]*Now the earth was corrupt in God's sight, and the earth was filled with violence. [12]And God saw the earth, and behold, it was corrupt; for all flesh had corrupted their way upon the earth.

Mt 24:37–39
Lk 17:27
Rom 3:20
Gal 2:16

The announcement of the flood

[13]And God said to Noah, "I have determined to make an end of all flesh; for the earth is filled with violence through them; behold, I will destroy them with the earth. [14]Make yourself an ark of gopher wood; make rooms in the ark, and cover it inside and out with pitch. [15]This is how you are to make it: the length of the ark three hundred cubits, its breadth fifty cubits, and its height thirty cubits. [16]Make a roof[k] for the ark, and finish it to a cubit above; and set the door of the ark in its side; make it with lower, second, and third decks. [17]For behold, I will bring a flood of waters upon the earth, to destroy all flesh in which is the breath of life from under heaven; everything that is on the earth shall die. [18]But I will estab-

Ps 14:2–3

Wis 14:6–7

2 Pet 2:5

Gen 9:9ff

---

them all away, so will be the coming of the Son of man" (Mt 24:37–39).

*6:9—8:22. The flood happens because man rejected the law of God (this process began with Adam and Eve). God punishes man's disobedience by undoing the order of nature that he himself had established for man's benefit. Thus, the waters above and below, which God had wisely separated from the earth (cf. 1:7), now invade the land in full force (cf. 7:11). The result is a return to chaos, and mankind is on the point of disappearing. The situation calls for a new beginning following on a severe purification. The Bible is offering us here an impressive lesson about the destiny of mankind when it turns its back

on God and rejects the laws that are stamped on creation itself.

In many religions, not only those of the Near East, we can find stories to do with the destruction of mankind (or a large part of it) in pre-history—be it by water or fire or some cataclysm. Most of these stories tie in with belief in malevolent gods and man's fear of them, or with his sense of a need for purification. For example, certain Sumerian and Babylonian legends had features very like those in the Bible account of the flood. But there is a fundamental difference: the Bible depicts the flood as a consequence of mankind's sin, and as a new starting-point from which the true God, the Creator of the world and of man, can

fectus fuit in generatione sua; cum Deo ambulavit. [10]Et genuit tres filios: Sem, Cham et Iapheth. [11]Corrupta est autem terra coram Deo et repleta est iniquitate. [12]Cumque vidisset Deus terram esse corruptam —omnis quippe caro corruperat viam suam super terram— [13]dixit ad Noe: «Finis universae carnis venit coram me; repleta est enim terra iniquitate a facie eorum, et ecce ego disperdam eos de terra. [14]Fac tibi arcam de lignis cupressinis; mansiunculas in arca facies et bitumine linies eam intrinsecus et extrinsecus. [15]Et sic facies eam: trecentorum cubitorum erit longitudo arcae, quinquaginta cubitorum latitudo et triginta cubitorum altitudo illius. [16]Fenestram in arca facies et cubito consummabis summitatem eius. Ostium autem arcae pones ex latere; tabulatum inferius, medium et superius facies in ea. [17]Ecce ego adducam diluvii aquas super terram, ut interficiam omnem carnem, in qua spi-

k Or *window*

lish my covenant with you; and you shall come into the ark, you, your sons, your wife, and your sons' wives with you. [19]And of every living thing of all flesh, you shall bring two of every sort into the ark, to keep them alive with you; they shall be male and female. [20]Of the birds according to their kinds, and of the animals according to their kinds, of every creeping thing of the ground according to its kind, two of every sort shall come in to you, to keep them alive. [21]Also take with you every sort of food that is eaten, and store it up; and it shall serve as food for you and for them." [22]Noah did this; he did all that God commanded him.

7 [1]Then the LORD said to Noah, "Go into the ark, you and all your household, for I have seen that you are righteous before me in this generation. [2]Take with you seven pairs of all clean animals, the male and his mate; and a pair of the animals that are not clean, the male and his mate; [3]and seven pairs of the birds of the air also, male and female, to keep their kind alive upon the face of all the earth. [4]For in seven days I will send rain upon the earth forty days and forty nights; and every living thing that I have made I will blot out from the face of the ground."

Lev 11

Ezek 14:14
Heb 11:7

Boarding the ark

[5]And Noah did all that the LORD had commanded him.

---

advance his plans of salvation through a remnant; from that remnant will later emerge Abraham, the father of the chosen people.

6:19. The fate of the animal world is closely linked to that of man, in terms of both punishment and salvation. This verse is a way of reminding us that all creation is designed for man's benefit and has a share in man's destiny. In the light of Christ's redemption, St Paul expresses the same truth when he says that "for the creation was subjected to futility, not of its own will but by the will of him who subjected it in hope; because the creation itself will be set free from its bondage to decay and obtain the glorious liberty of the children of God" (Rom 8:20–21).

ritus vitae est subter caelum: universa, quae in terra sunt, consumentur. [18]Ponamque foedus meum tecum; et ingredieris arcam tu et filii tui, uxor tua et uxores filiorum tuorum tecum. [19]Et ex cunctis animantibus universae carnis bina induces in arcam, ut vivant tecum, masculini sexus et feminini. [20]De volucribus iuxta genus suum et de iumentis in genere suo et ex omni reptili terrae secundum genus suum: bina de omnibus ingredientur ad te, ut possint vivere. [21]Tu autem tolle tecum ex omnibus escis, quae mandi possunt, et comportabis apud te; et erunt tam tibi quam illis in cibum». [22]Fecit ergo Noe omnia, quae praeceperat illi Deus; sic fecit. [1]Dixitque Dominus ad Noe: «Ingredere tu et omnis domus tua arcam; te enim vidi iustum coram me in generatione hac. [2]Ex omnibus pecoribus mundis tolle septena septena, masculum et feminam; de pecoribus vero non mundis duo duo, masculum et feminam. [3]Sed et de volatilibus caeli septena septena, masculum et feminam, ut salvetur semen super faciem universae terrae. [4]Adhuc enim et post dies septem ego pluam super terram quadraginta diebus et quadraginta noctibus et delebo omnem substantiam, quam feci, de superficie terrae». [5]Fecit ergo Noe

⁶Noah was six hundred years old when the flood of waters came upon the earth. ⁷And Noah and his sons and his wife and his sons' wives with him went into the ark, to escape the waters of the flood. ⁸Of clean animals, and of animals that are not clean, and of birds, and of everything that creeps on the ground, ⁹two and two, male and female, went into the ark with Noah, as God had commanded Noah. ¹⁰And after seven days the waters of the flood came upon the earth.

The flood

¹¹In the six hundredth year of Noah's life, in the second month, on the seventeenth day of the month, on that day all the fountains of the great deep burst forth, and the windows of the heavens were opened. ¹²And rain fell upon the earth forty days and forty nights. ¹³On the very same day Noah and his sons, Shem and Ham and Japheth, and Noah's wife and the three wives of his sons with them entered the ark, ¹⁴they and every beast according to its kind, and all the cattle according to their kinds, and every creeping thing that creeps on the earth according to its kind, and every bird according to its kind, every bird of every sort. ¹⁵They went into the ark with Noah, two and two of all flesh in which there was the breath of life. ¹⁶And they that entered, male and female of all flesh, went in as God had commanded him; and the LORD shut him in.

Wis 10:4
Mt 24:38
Lk 17:27
Gen 1:7
1 Pet 3:20
2 Pet 2:4–5

7:4. On the seven days' downpour St Ambrose, following 1 Peter 3:20, which speaks of God's patience at that time, explaining that "the Lord made available a time for penance, because he prefers pardon to punishment" (*De Noe et arca,* 13, 42).

7:5. In contrast with Adam's disobedience, which was the source of all evil in the world, Noah followed the Lord's instructions exactly, even in the smallest details (cf. 6:22). For his obedience Noah will be exalted as one who put his faith in God into practice: "By faith Noah, being warned by God of events as yet unseen, took hold and constructed an ark for the saving of his household; by this he condemned the world and became an heir of the righteousness which comes by faith" (Heb 11:7).

7:7. The ark is built to the design given personally by God to Noah (cf. 6:14–16);

omnia, quae mandaverat ei Dominus. ⁶Eratque Noe sexcentorum annorum, quando diluvii aquae inundaverunt super terram. ⁷Et ingressus est Noe et filii eius, uxor eius et uxores filiorum eius cum eo in arcam propter aquas diluvii. ⁸De pecoribus mundis et immundis et de volucribus et ex omni, quod movetur super terram, ⁹duo et duo ingressa sunt ad Noe in arcam, masculus et femina, sicut praeceperat Deus Noe. ¹⁰Cumque transissent septem dies, aquae diluvii inundaverunt super terram. ¹¹Anno sexcentesimo vitae Noe, mense secundo, septimo decimo die mensis rupti sunt omnes fontes abyssi magnae, et cataractae caeli apertae sunt; ¹²et facta est pluvia super terram quadraginta diebus et quadraginta noctibus. ¹³In articulo diei illius ingressus est Noe et Sem et Cham et Iapheth filii eius, uxor illius et tres uxores filiorum eius cum eis in arcam. ¹⁴Ipsi et omne animal secundum genus suum,

Lk 17:27
1 Pet 3:20
¹⁷The flood continued forty days upon the earth; and the waters increased, and bore up the ark, and it rose high above the earth. ¹⁸The waters prevailed and increased greatly upon the earth; and the ark floated on the face of the waters. ¹⁹And the waters prevailed so mightily upon the earth that all the high mountains under the whole heaven were covered; ²⁰the waters prevailed

2 Pet 3:6
Lk 17:27
above the mountains, covering them fifteen cubits deep. ²¹And all flesh died that moved upon the earth, birds, cattle, beasts, all swarming creatures that swarm upon the earth, and every man; ²²everything on the dry land in whose nostrils was the breath of

1 Pet 3:20
life died. ²³He blotted out every living thing that was upon the face of the ground, man and animals and creeping things and birds of the air; they were blotted out from the earth. Only Noah was left, and those that were with him in the ark. ²⁴And the waters prevailed upon the earth a hundred and fifty days.

Ps 104:5–9 **The flood subsides**

8 ¹But God remembered Noah and all the beasts and all the cattle that were with him in the ark. And God made a wind blow over the earth, and the waters subsided; ²the fountains of the

---

those who enter it are saved; everything that remains outside will perish. That is why the Fathers saw the ark as a figure of the Church. "God ordered Noah to build an ark in which he and his family would escape from the devastation of the flood. Undoubtedly the ark is a symbol of the City of God on pilgrimage in this world, that is, a symbol of the Church which was saved by the wood on which there hung the Mediator between God and men—

Christ Jesus, himself a man. Even the measurements of length, height and breadth of the ark are a symbol of the human body in which He came. [. . .] The door opened in the side of the ark surely symbolizes the open wound made by the lance in the side of the Crucified—the door by which those who come to him enter in the sense that believers enter the Church by means of the sacraments which issued from that wound" (*De civitate Dei*, 15, 26).

universaque iumenta in genere suo, et omne reptile, quod movetur super terram in genere suo, cunctumque volatile secundum genus suum, universae aves omnesque volucres ¹⁵ingressae sunt ad Noe in arcam, bina et bina ex omni carne, in qua erat spiritus vitae. ¹⁶Et quae ingressa sunt, masculus et femina ex omni carne introierunt, sicut praeceperat ei Deus; et inclusit eum Dominus de foris. ¹⁷Factumque est diluvium quadraginta diebus super terram, et multiplicatae sunt aquae et elevaverunt arcam in sublime a terra. ¹⁸Vehementer enim inundaverunt et omnia repleverunt in superficie terrae; porro arca ferebatur super aquas. ¹⁹Et aquae praevaluerunt nimis super terram, opertique sunt omnes montes excelsi sub universo caelo. ²⁰Quindecim cubitis altior fuit aqua super montes, quos operuerat. ²¹Consumptaque est omnis caro, quae movebatur super terram, volucrum, pecorum, bestiarum omniumque reptilium, quae reptant super terram, et universi homines: ²²cuncta, in quibus spiraculum vitae in terra, mortua sunt. ²³Et delevit omnem substantiam, quae erat super terram, ab homine usque ad pecus, usque ad reptile et usque ad volucres caeli; et deleta sunt de terra. Remansit autem solus Noe et qui cum eo erant in arca. ²⁴Obtinueruntque aquae terram centum quinquaginta diebus. ¹Recordatus autem Deus Noe cunctorumque animantium et omnium iumentorum, quae erant cum eo in arca, adduxit spiritum super terram,

deep and the windows of the heavens were closed, the rain from the heavens was restrained, ³and the waters receded from the earth continually. At the end of a hundred and fifty days the waters had abated; ⁴and in the seventh month, on the seventeenth day of the month, the ark came to rest upon the mountains of Ararat. ⁵And the waters continued to abate until the tenth month; in the tenth month, on the first day of the month, the tops of the mountains were seen.

⁶At the end of forty days Noah opened the window of the ark which he had made, ⁷and sent forth a raven; and it went to and fro until the waters were dried up from the earth. ⁸Then he sent forth

---

8:6–12. The sending of the raven and the dove shows how anxious and how hopeful of salvation those in the Ark are; it also shows Noah's wisdom and, yet again, the harmony there should be between man and the animal world for things to go well. This episode has led to the dove and the olive-branch becoming symbols of peace and co-operation.

In Christian tradition the dove became a symbol of the Holy Spirit. On the basis of this image Rupert of Deutz offers a spiritual application of this entire passage: "The dove that Noah sent out from the ark means the Holy Spirit, and he sent it three times because every faithful soul draws from the sacraments of Christ or of the Church a triple grace of the Holy Spirit. The first grace is remission of sins; the second, distribution of the various gifts; the third, re-compense in the resurrection of the dead [. . .]. Therefore, the first sending of the dove means the remission of sins which Christ, the true Noah, sent immediately after his resurrection when he said:

'Receive the Holy Spirit. If you forgive the sins of any, they are forgiven; if you retain the sins of any, they are retained' (Jn 20:23) [. . .]. After it was sent the second time, the dove came back in the evening bearing in its beak a small olive leaf, because the apostles were given the Holy Spirit a second time on the day of the Pentecost, and at the end of the life of each of them he called them to the rest enjoyed by the heavenly Church with the eternal reward of perfect peace. After the dove was sent the third time it did not return, because after the resurrection of the dead (which will be the third out-pouring of the Holy Spirit) they will not be sent out to return once more, for they will go out not to work but to reign for ever. So too as regards the elect: this same dove comes to them three times: first when they are baptized, for the remission of sins: second, to receive the imposition of hands from the bishops; third (as I have said) in the resurrection of the dead" (*Commentarium in Genesim*, 4:23).

---

et imminutae sunt aquae. ²Et clausi sunt fontes abyssi et cataractae caeli, et prohibitae sunt pluviae de caelo. ³Reversaeque sunt aquae de terra euntes et redeuntes et coeperunt minui post centum quinquaginta dies. ⁴Requievitque arca mense septimo, de cima septima die mensis super montes Ararat. ⁵At vero aquae ibant et decrescebant usque ad decimum mensem; decimo enim mense, prima die mensis, apparuerunt cacumina montium. ⁶Cumque transissent quadraginta dies, aperiens Noe fenestram arcae, quam fecerat, dimisit corvum; ⁷qui egrediebatur exiens et rediens, donec siccarentur aquae super terram. ⁸Emisit quoque columbam a se, ut videret si iam cessassent aquae super faciem terrae. ⁹Quae,

a dove from him, to see if the waters had subsided from the face of the ground; [9]but the dove found no place to set her foot, and she returned to him to the ark, for the waters were still on the face of the whole earth. So he put forth his hand and took her and brought her into the ark with him. [10]He waited another seven days, and again he sent forth the dove out of the ark; [11]and the dove came back to him in the evening, and lo, in her mouth a freshly plucked olive leaf; so Noah knew that the waters had subsided from the earth. [12]Then he waited another seven days, and sent forth the dove; and she did not return to him any more.

[13]In the six hundred and first year, in the first month, the first day of the month, the waters were dried from off the earth; and Noah removed the covering of the ark, and looked, and behold, the face of the ground was dry. [14]In the second month, on the twenty-seventh day of the month, the earth was dry.

8:13. The year "six hundred and one" in the life of Noah.

8:15–19. God gives the order (v. 15), to come out of the ark, which makes it clear that it is not man who is taking the initiative: God himself is presenting man and the animals with a rejuvenated and renewed earth. From now on the Lord will never abandon man. The earth has been purified of sinful men and women, and it is embarking on a new stage, populated by Noah and his children. The waters of the flood were the means of purification through which Noah was saved in the ark. The water is doubly symbolic: it stands for destruction and purification from evil, on the one hand; and for a means of salvation and the start of a new stage, on the other. This symbolism of the water will be heightened by the passage of the Red Sea, whose waters were a cause of death for the Egyptians and of salvation for the Israelites (cf. Ex 14:15–31). The same symbolism is to be found in the sacrament of Baptism, in which, through water, God blots out sin and causes a man to be born again to a new life. The analogy between the flood and Baptism is to be found in the New Testament itself, when it says that "a few, that is, eight persons, were saved through water. Baptism, which corresponds to this, now saves you, not as a removal of dirt from the body but as an appeal to God for a clear conscience, through the resurrection of Jesus Christ" (1 Pet 3:20–21).

Christian tradition did a lot of work along these lines on the typology of the flood and the ark. St Bede writes: "The ark stands for the Church; the flood, for

---

cum non invenisset, ubi requiesceret pes eius, reversa est ad eum in arcam; aquae enim erant super universam terram. Extenditque manum et apprehensam intulit in arcam. [10]Exspectatis autem ultra septem diebus aliis, rursum dimisit columbam ex arca. [11]At illa venit ad eum ad vesperam portans ramum olivae virentibus foliis in ore suo. Intellexit ergo Noe quod cessassent aquae super terram. [12]Exspectavitque nihilominus septem alios dies; et emisit columbam, quae non est reversa ultra ad eum. [13]Igitur sexcentesimo primo anno, primo mense, prima die mensis, siccatae sunt aquae super terram; et aperiens Noe tectum arcae, et ecce aspexit viditque quod exsiccata erat superficies terrae. [14]Mense

Leaving the ark

Wis 10:4

¹⁵Then God said to Noah, ¹⁶"Go forth from the ark, you and your
wife, and your sons and your sons' wives with you. ¹⁷Bring forth 1 Cor 15:39
with you every living thing that is with you of all flesh—birds and
animals and every creeping thing that creeps on the earth —that
they may breed abundantly on the earth, and be fruitful and mul-
tiply upon the earth." ¹⁸So Noah went forth, and his sons and his 2 Pet 2:5
wife and his sons' wives with him. ¹⁹And every beast, every creeping thing, and every bird, everything that moves upon the earth,
went forth by families out of the ark.

²⁰Then Noah built an altar to the LORD, and took of every clean Gen 9:8–17
animal and of every clean bird, and offered burnt offerings on the
altar. ²¹And when the LORD smelled the pleasing odour, the LORD Ex 29:18

the water of baptism, whereby the
Church, in all its members, is washed and
sanctified" (*Hexaemeron*, 2: *in Gen*
6:13–14). In the blessing of baptismal
water during the Easter Vigil, the liturgy
invokes God, recalling the flood: "The
waters of the great flood you made a sign
of the waters of baptism, that make an
end to sin and a new beginning of goodness" (*Roman Missal, Easter Vigil*, 42).
Cf. *Catechism of the Catholic Church*,
1219.

8:20–22. The sacred writer highlights
this first sacrifice that mankind offered
God after emerging from the flood. Here
man is acknowledging God, and God is
pleased to accept man's gesture. God's
contentment (described in very human
terms) is to be seen particularly in his
decision not to punish man any further:
man's very nature (which he gets from

Adam) inclines him towards evil, so in
view of his weakness, God undertakes
never again to disturb the order of the
cosmos.

Rendering God due worship (both
interiorly and externally) is a duty man
has by his very nature. Thus, through
religious cult and specifically through
some form of sacrifice, man recognizes
God as his Creator and Lord, to whom he
owes everything that he is and everything
he has, even his own life. Acknowledging
God in this way is a form of prayer, for,
as the *Catechism of the Catholic Church*
says, "prayer is lived in the first place
beginning with the realities of *creation*.
The first nine chapters of Genesis
describe this relationship with God as an
offering of the first-born of Abel's flock,
as the invocation of the divine name at
the time of Enoch, and as 'walking with
God' (cf. Gen 4:4, 26; 5:24). Noah's

secundo, septima et vicesima die mensis, arefacta est terra. ¹⁵Locutus est autem Deus ad Noe dicens:
¹⁶«Egredere de arca tu et uxor tua, filii tui et uxores filiorum tuorum tecum. ¹⁷Cuncta animantia, quae
sunt apud te ex omni carne, tam in volatilibus quam in pecoribus et in universis reptilibus, quae reptant super terram, educ tecum, ut pullulent super terram et crescant et multiplicentur super eam».
¹⁸Egressus est ergo Noe et filii eius, uxor illius et uxores filiorum eius cum eo. ¹⁹Sed et omnia ani-
mantia, iumenta, volatilia et reptilia, quae reptant super terram, secundum genus suum egressa sunt de
arca. ²⁰Aedificavit autem Noe altare Domino; et tollens de cunctis pecoribus mundis et volucribus
mundis obtulit holocausta super altare. ²¹Odoratusque est Dominus odorem suavitatis et locutus est
Dominus ad cor suum: «Nequaquam ultra maledicam terrae propter homines, quia cogitatio humani
cordis in malum prona est ab adulescentia sua. Non igitur ultra percutiam omnem animam viventem,

Num 28:2
Phil 4:18

said in his heart, "I will never again curse the ground because of man, for the imagination of man's heart is evil from his youth; neither will I ever again destroy every living creature as I have done. ²²While the earth remains, seed time and harvest, cold and heat, summer and winter, day and night, shall not cease."

God's Covenant with Noah

Gen 1:26, 28
Jas 3:7

9 ¹And God blessed Noah and his sons, and said to them, "Be fruitful and multiply, and fill the earth. ²The fear of you and the dread of you shall be upon every beast of the earth, and upon every bird of the air, upon everything that creeps on the ground

---

offering is pleasing to God, who blesses him and through him all creation (cf. Gen 8:20—9:17), because his heart was upright and undivided; Noah, like Enoch before him, 'walks with God' (cf. Gen 6:9). This kind of prayer is lived by many righteous people in all religions. In his indefectible covenant with every living creature (cf. Gen 9:8–16), God has always called people to prayer. But it is above all beginning with our father Abraham that prayer is revealed in the Old Testament" (no. 2569).

Seen from a Christian perspective, the different kinds of sacrifices mentioned in the course of Old Testament salvation history point to the perfect and enduring sacrifice which Christ offered on the cross and which is perpetuated century after century in the holy sacrifice of the Mass. Commenting on the present passage, St Bede observes: "Just as Abel consecrated the start of the first age of the world by means of a sacrifice to God, so Noah began the second age"; and (after recalling the sacrifices offered by Abraham, Melchizedek, and the patriarchs, kings and priests of the Old Testament) he goes on to say that "All those sacrifices were figures of our

supreme King and true priest who on the altar of the holy cross offered God the host of his body and his blood" (*Hexaemeron*, 2: *in Gen* 8:21).

9:1–7. The sacred text now describes the new order of things that emerged after the flood. Noah and his sons receive from God, in the first place, the same blessings as Adam and Eve were given after they were created—fruitfulness and dominion over the earth; and then God makes another disposition, to the effect that the beasts will serve them as food, for, according to the biblical narrative, prior to the fall, in paradise (cf. 1:29), they only had plants available to them; now, in the new situation of mankind, after the first sin, the original harmony of the world has been shattered and violence has come on the scene. Finally, God makes two prohibitions—eating meat with blood in it, and murder. The first of these reflects the culture of a period when blood was regarded as the source of life; therefore, even in the case of animals, that life was to be respected in some way, by avoiding the eating of flesh which had blood in it, thereby acknowledging that life comes from God.

---

sicut feci. ²²Cunctis diebus terrae, sementis et messis, frigus et aestus, aestas et hiems, dies et nox non requiescent». ¹Benedixitque Deus Noe et filiis eius et dixit ad eos: «Crescite et multiplicamini et implete terram. ²Et terror vester ac tremor sit super cuncta animalia terrae et super omnes volucres caeli

and all the fish of the sea; into your hand they are delivered. ³Every moving thing that lives shall be food for you; and as I gave you the green plants, I give you everything. ⁴Only you shall not eat flesh with its life, that is, its blood. ⁵For your lifeblood I will surely require a reckoning; of every beast I will require it and of man; of every man's brother I will require the life of man. ⁶Whoever sheds the blood of man, by man shall his blood be shed; for God made man in his own image. ⁷And you, be fruitful and multiply, bring forth abundantly on the earth and multiply in it."

⁸Then God said to Noah and to his sons with him, ⁹"Behold, I establish my covenant with you and your descendants after you, ¹⁰and with every living creature that is with you, the birds, the

Gen 1:29
Deut 12:15–16
1 Tim 4:3
Lev 17:10–14
Acts 15:20
Ex 20:15
Lev 1:5
Gen 1:26
Mt 26:52
Gen 8:20–22
Gen 6:18

The second prohibition refers to human life, which is always sacred because every human being (we are reminded) is God's image and likeness. As in the case of Cain and Abel, God is never indifferent to the taking of human life, no matter who the victim is.

9:8–17. To show that he was pleased by Noah's sacrifice, God promised that he would never again flood the earth (cf. 8:20–22); now he renews that promise in the context of a covenant that covers all creation and which is ratified by a sign—the rainbow.

This marks the start of a series of covenants which God will freely establish with men. The first covenant (with Noah) takes in all creation, now purified and renewed by the flood. Later there will be the covenant with Abraham, which will affect only himself and his descendants (cf. chap. 17). Finally, under Moses, he will establish the covenant of

Sinai (cf. Ex 19), also confined to the people of Israel. But because man proved unable to keep these successive covenants, God promised, through the prophets, to establish a new covenant in the messianic age: "I will put my law within them and I will write it upon their hearts; and I will be their God, and they shall be my people" (Jer 31:33). This promise found its fulfilment in Christ, as he himself said when he instituted the eucharistic sacrifice of his body and blood: "This cup which is poured out for you is the new covenant in my blood" (Lk 22:20).

The Fathers and ecclesiastical writers saw this rainbow as the first proclamation of this new covenant. Rupert of Deutz, for example, writes: "In it God established a covenant with men through his son Jesus Christ; by the death (of Christ) on the cross God reconciled us to himself, cleansing us of our sins in his blood, and he gave us through (Christ)

cum universis, quae moventur super terram; omnes pisces maris manui vestrae traditi sunt. ³Omne, quod movetur et vivit, erit vobis in cibum; quasi holera virentia tradidi vobis omnia, ⁴excepto quod carnem cum anima, quae est in sanguine, non comedetis. ⁵Sanguinem enim animarum vestrarum requiram de manu cunctarum bestiarum; et de manu hominis, de manu viri fratris eius requiram animam hominis. ⁶Quicumque effuderit humanum sanguinem, / per hominem fundetur sanguis illius; / ad imaginem quippe Dei / factus est homo. ⁷Vos autem crescite et multiplicamini et pullulate super terram et dominamini ei». ⁸Haec quoque dixit Deus ad Noe et ad filios eius cum eo: ⁹«Ecce ego statuam pactum meum vobiscum et cum semine vestro post vos ¹⁰et ad omnem animam viventem, quae

cattle, and every beast of the earth with you, as many as came out
of the ark.[l] [11]I establish my covenant with you, that never again
shall all flesh be cut off by the waters of a flood, and never again
shall there be a flood to destroy the earth." [12]And God said, "This
is the sign of the covenant which I make between me and you and
every living creature that is with you, for all future generations: [13]I
set my bow in the cloud, and it shall be a sign of the covenant
between me and the earth. [14]When I bring clouds over the earth
and the bow is seen in the clouds, [15]I will remember my covenant
which is between me and you and every living creature of all
flesh; and the waters shall never again become a flood to destroy
all flesh. [16]When the bow is in the clouds, I will look upon it
and remember the everlasting covenant between God and every
living creature of all flesh that is upon the earth." [17]God said to
Noah, "This is the sign of the covenant which I have established
between me and all flesh that is upon the earth."

Is 54:9–10
Sir 44:18

Gen 17
Ex 19
Jer 31:33–34
Lk 22:20

Ezek 1:28
Rev 4:3

---

the Holy Spirit of his love, instituting the baptism of water and the Holy Spirit by which we are reborn. Therefore, that rainbow which appears in the clouds is a sign of the Son of God. [. . .] It is the sign that God will never again destroy all flesh by the waters of the flood; the Son of God himself, who was taken out of sight by a cloud, and who is lifted up beyond the clouds, above all the heavens, is forever a sign which reminds God the Father; he is an eternal memorial of our peace: now that he in his flesh has destroyed the old enmity, friendship between God and men is secure: men are no longer servants but friends and chil-

dren of God" (*Commentarium in Genesim*, 4, 36).

9:18–28. From the sons of Noah new peoples and nations will arise, as described in detail in the following chapter. At this point we are given an overview of the destiny of these peoples and their interrelationships, via the prophetic blessings Noah addressed to his sons.

Two other features of this passage are worth noting. First, the confirmation that, after the flood, man continues to be inclined towards evil, which flourishes anew. We see Noah's abuse of wine, and

---

est vobiscum tam in volucribus quam in iumentis et in omnibus bestiis terrae, quae sunt vobiscum, cunctis, quae egressa sunt de arca, universis bestiis terrae. [11]Statuam pactum meum vobiscum; et nequaquam ultra interficietur omnis caro aquis diluvii, neque erit deinceps diluvium dissipans terram». [12]Dixitque Deus: «Hoc signum foederis, quod do inter me et vos et ad omnem animam viventem, quae est vobiscum, in generationes sempiternas: [13]arcum meum ponam in nubibus, et erit signum foederis inter me et inter terram. [14]Cumque obduxero nubibus caelum, apparebit arcus meus in nubibus, [15]et recordabor foederis mei vobiscum et cum omni anima vivente, quae carnem vegetat; et non erunt ultra aquae diluvii ad delendum universam carnem. [16]Eritque arcus in nubibus, et videbo illum et recordabor foederis sempiterni, quod pactum est inter Deum et omnem animam viventem universae carnis, quae est super terram». [17]Dixitque Deus ad Noe: «Hoc erit signum foederis, quod constitui inter me et omnem carnem super terram». [18]Erant ergo filii Noe, qui egressi sunt de arca, Sem, Cham et Iapheth.

l. Gk: Heb repeats *every beast of the earth*

A curse on Canaan, a blessing on Shem

[18]The sons of Noah who went forth from the ark were Shem, Gen 10:6
Ham, and Japheth. Ham was the father of Canaan. [19]These three
were the sons of Noah; and from these the whole earth was peo-
pled.

[20]Noah was the first tiller of the soil. He planted a vineyard; Eccles 3:12–13
[21]and he drank of the wine, and became drunk, and lay uncovered
in his tent. [22]And Ham, the father of Canaan, saw the nakedness
of his father, and told his two brothers outside. [23]Then Shem and Eph 6:1–3
Japheth took a garment, laid it upon both their shoulders, and
walked backward and covered the nakedness of their father; their
faces were turned away, and they did not see their father's nakedness. [24]When Noah awoke from his wine and knew what his
youngest son had done to him, [25]he said,

"Cursed be Canaan;
    a slave of slaves shall he be to his brothers."

[26]He also said,
    "Blessed by the LORD my God be Shem;[m]
    and let Canaan be his slave."

[27]God enlarge Japheth,
    and let him dwell in the tents of Shem;
    and let Canaan be his slave."

[28]After the flood Noah lived three hundred and fifty years. [29]All
the days of Noah were nine hundred and fifty years; and he
died.

---

discord in family relationships—Ham's
disrespect towards his father, and disputes among the brothers. This discord
marks the start of strife between the
nations, which will reach a climax in the
pride which precedes the building of the
tower of Babel. The second feature is the
way it explains the predominance of the

Israelites (the descendants of Shem) over
the Canaanites. The latter were cursed in
their ancestor (Ham or Canaan): they
were to be subject to their brothers
(Shem and Japheth, that is, the Israelites
and the peoples who descended from
Japheth).

Porro Cham ipse est pater Chanaan. [19]Tres isti filii sunt Noe, et ab his disseminatum est omne
hominum genus super universam terram. [20]Coepitque Noe agricola plantare vineam; [21]bibensque vinum
inebriatus est et nudatus in tabernaculo suo. [22]Quod cum vidisset Cham pater Chanaan, verenda scilicet patris sui esse nudata, nuntiavit duobus fratribus suis foras. [23]At vero Sem et Iapheth pallium imposuerunt umeris suis et incedentes retrorsum operuerunt verecunda patris sui, faciesque eorum aversae
erant, et patris virilia non viderunt. [24]Evigilans autem Noe ex vino, cum didicisset, quae fecerat ei filius
suus minor, [25]ait: «Maledictus Chanaan! / Servus servorum erit fratribus suis». [26]Dixitque: «Benedictus
Dominus Deus Sem! / Sitque Chanaan servus eius. / [27]Dilatet Deus Iapheth, / et habitet in tabernaculis
Sem, / sitque Chanaan servus eius». [28]Vixit autem Noe post diluvium trecentis quinquaginta annis. [29]Et

m. Or *Blessed be the* LORD, *the God of Shem*

4. THE ORIGIN OF PEOPLES. THE TOWER OF BABEL

Acts 17:26

10 [1]These are the generations* of the sons of Noah, Shem, Ham, and Japheth; sons were born to them after the flood.

1 Chron 1:5-7 **The descendants of Japheth**
[2]The sons of Japheth: Gomer, Magog, Madai, Javan, Tubal, Meshech, and Tiras. [3]The sons of Gomer: Ashkenaz, Riphath, and Togarmah. [4]The sons of Javan: Elishah, Tarshish, Kittim, and Dodanim.[n] [5]From these the coastland peoples spread. These are the sons of Japheth in their lands, each with his own language, by their families, in their nations.

1 Chron 1:8-16 **The descendants of Ham**
1 Kings 10:1 [6]The sons of Ham: Cush, Egypt, Put, and Canaan. [7]The sons of Cush: Seba, Havilah, Sabtah, Raamah, and Sabteca. The sons of Raamah: Sheba and Dedan. [8]Cush became the father of Nimrod; he was the first on earth to be a mighty man. [9]He was a mighty hunter before the Lord; therefore it is said, "Like Nimrod a mighty hunter before the Lord." [10]The beginning of his kingdom was Babel, Erech, and Accad, all of them in the land of Shinar. [11]From that land he went into Assyria, and built Nineveh, Rehoboth-Ir, Calah, and [12]Resen between Nineveh and Calah; that is the great city. [13]Egypt became the father of Ludim, Anamim, Lehabim, Naph-tuhim, [14]Pathrusim, Casluhim (whence came the Philistines), and Caphtorim.

10:1-32. According to this genealogical list, all nations are descended from the sons of Noah; in this way the Bible once more teaches that the whole human race is of the same stock. The peoples of Mesopotamia and Assyria are regarded, like Hebrews, as descendants of Shem. The peoples of the South, such as Egypt and Ethiopia (Cush), are seen as descendants of Ham: these include the Canaan-

impleti sunt omnes dies eius nongentorum quinquaginta annorum, et mortuus est. [1]Hae sunt generationes filiorum Noe, Sem, Cham et Iapheth; natique sunt eis filii post diluvium. [2]Filii Iapheth: Gomer et Magog et Madai et Iavan et Thubal et Mosoch et Thiras. [3]Porro filii Gomer: Aschenez et Riphath et Thogorma. [4]Filii autem Iavan: Elisa et Tharsis, Cetthim et Rodanim. [5]Ab his divisae sunt insulae gentium in regionibus suis, unusquisque secundum linguam suam et familias suas in nationibus suis. [6]Filii autem Cham: Chus et Mesraim et Phut et Chanaan. [7]Filii Chus: Saba et Hevila et Sabatha et Regma et Sabathacha. Filii Regma: Saba et Dedan. [8]Porro Chus genuit Nemrod: ipse coepit esse potens in terra [9]et erat robustus venator coram Domino. Ob hoc exivit proverbium: «Quasi Nemrod robustus venator coram Domino». [10]Fuit autem principium regni eius Babylon et Arach et Achad et Chalanne in terra Sennaar. [11]De terra illa egressus est in Assyriam et aedificavit Nineven et Rohobothir et Chale, [12]Resen quoque inter Nineven et Chale; haec est civitas magna. [13]At vero Mesraim genuit Ludim et Anamim et

n. Compare verses 20, 31. Heb lacks *These are the sons of Japheth*

¹⁵Canaan became the father of Sidon his first-born, and Heth,
¹⁶and the Jebusites, the Amorites, the Girgashites, ¹⁷the Hivites,
the Arkites, the Sinites, ¹⁸the Arvadites, the Zemarites, and the
Hamathites. Afterward the families of the Canaanites spread
abroad. ¹⁹And the territory of the Canaanites extended from
Sidon, in the direction of Gerar, as far as Gaza, and in the direction of Sodom, Gomorrah, Admah, and Zeboiim, as far as
Lasha.²⁰ These are the sons of Ham, by their families, their languages, their lands, and their nations.

The descendants of Shem

1 Chron 1:17–23
Lk 3:36

²¹To Shem also, the father of all the children of Eber, the elder
brother of Japheth, children were born. ²²The sons of Shem: Elam,
Asshur, Arpachshad, Lud, and Aram. ²³The sons of Aram: Uz,
Hul, Gether, and Mash. ²⁴Arpachshad became the father of Shelah;
and Shelah became the father of Eber. ²⁵To Eber were born two
sons: the name of the one was Peleg,° for in his days the earth was
divided, and his brother's name was Joktan. ²⁶Joktan became the
father of Almodad, Sheleph, Hazarmaveth, Jerah, ²⁷Hadoram,
Uzal, Diklah, ²⁸Obal, Abima-el, Sheba, ²⁹Ophir, Havilah, and
Jobab; all these were the sons of Joktan. ³⁰The territory in which
they lived extended from Mesha in the direction of Sephar to the
hill country of the east. ³¹These are the sons of Shem, by their
families, their languages, their lands, and their nations.

³²These are the families of the sons of Noah, according to
their genealogies, in their nations; and from these the nations
spread abroad on the earth after the flood.

---

ites, because although they are certainly
Semitic by race, their name looks like that
of Ham and moreover they are seen as
being enemies of Israel. Finally, the peoples of Asia Minor and the Mediterranean are taken as descendants of
Japheth. Here we are offered the most
complete ethnographic map to come from
the ancient world. Family connexions and
connexions between peoples reflect the

Laabim, Nephthuim ¹⁴et Phetrusim et Chasluim et Caphtorim, de quibus egressi sunt Philisthim.
¹⁵Chanaan autem genuit Sidonem primogenitum suum, Hetthaeum ¹⁶et Iebusaeum et Amorraeum,
Gergesaeum, ¹⁷Hevaeum et Aracaeum, Sinaeum ¹⁸et Aradium, Samaraeum et Emathaeum; et post haec
disseminati sunt populi Chananaeorum. ¹⁹Factique sunt termini Chanaan venientibus a Sidone Geraram
usque Gazam, donec ingrediaris Sodomam et Gomorram et Adamam et Seboim usque Lesa. ²⁰Hi sunt
filii Cham in cognationibus et linguis terrisque et gentibus suis. ²¹De Sem quoque nati sunt, patre
omnium filiorum Heber, fratre Iapheth maiore. ²²Filii Sem: Elam et Assur et Arphaxad et Lud et Aram.
²³Filii Aram: Us et Hul et Gether et Mes. ²⁴At vero Arphaxad genuit Sala, de quo ortus est Heber.
²⁵Natique sunt Heber filii duo: nomen uni Phaleg, eo quod in diebus eius divisa sit terra, et nomen
fratris eius Iectan.²⁶Qui Iectan genuit Elmodadet Saleph et Asarmoth, Iare²⁷ et Adoram et Uzal et Decla
²⁸et Ebal et Abimael, Saba ²⁹et Ophir et Hevila et Iobab. Omnes isti filii Iectan; ³⁰et facta est habitatio

o. That is *Division*

Wis 10:5
Acts 2:5–12
Rev 7:9–10
Gen 10:10
Lk 14:28

Sir 40:19

Babel: the confusion of language

11 [1]*Now the whole earth had one language and few words. [2]And as men migrated from the east, they found a plain in the land of Shinar and settled there. [3]And they said to one another, "Come, let us make bricks, and burn them thoroughly." And they had brick for stone, and bitumen for mortar. [4]Then they said, "Come, let us build ourselves a city, and a tower with its top in the heavens, and let us make a name for ourselves, lest we be scattered abroad upon the face of the whole earth." [5]And the LORD

---

conviction that all should live together in peace as members of one family.

These genealogies were worked out by reference to the geographical positions of the various nations, similarity of names, and popular traditions about certain heroes (as in the case of Nimrod in v. 8). However, the main thing about this list is that it is a way of showing how God's blessing on Noah has come true: "Be fruitful and multiply, and fill the earth" (9:1); also, it shows the gratuitous nature of the Lord's choice of Israel from among the large number of nations on the earth.

11:1–9. The text goes on to describe the growth of evil (cf. 8:21; 9:20–27), and, as one of its results, the fact that mankind is scattered and its God-given unity is fragmented. Thus, the text begins by talking about mankind when it was still together; it came from the east, where it originated and settled in the plains of Mesopotamia (in Shinar; cf. 10:10). But the people are filled with pride, and want to make a name for themselves, and to guarantee their own security by reaching heaven by their own efforts. This attitude is epitomized by the project of building a massive tower (we can get some idea of it

from the tower-temples of Mesopotamia, the ziggurats, on whose high terraces the Babylonians thought they could gain access to the Godhead and thus dominate God).

The text also offers an explanation for why there are so many languages; it sees languages as a sign of division and misunderstanding between individuals and nations. It is based on the popular meaning of the word "babel", connecting it with the Hebrew *balbaláh*, confusion; but in fact Babel means "gate of God". We have here an instance of literary devices being used to expound deep convictions—in this case the view that disunion in mankind is the outcome of men's pride and sinfulness.

Babel thus becomes the opposite of Jerusalem, the city to which, the prophets say, all the nations will flock (cf. Is 2:2–3). And it will be in the Church, the new Jerusalem, that men of all nations, races and tongues will join in faith and love, as will be seen in the Pentecost event (cf. Acts 2:1–13). There the phenomenon of Babel will be reversed: all will understand the same language. In the history of mankind, in effect, the Church is a kind of sign or sacrament of the

---

eorum de Messa pergentibus usque Sephar montem orientalem. [31]Isti filii Sem secundum cognationes et linguas et regiones in gentibus suis. [32]Hae familiae filiorum Noe iuxta generationes et nationes suas. Ab his divisae sunt gentes in terra post diluvium. [1]Erat autem universa terra labii unius et sermonum eorundem. [2]Cumque proficiscerentur de oriente, invenerunt campum in terra Sennaar et habitaverunt in eo. [3]Dixitque alter ad proximum suum: «Venite, faciamus lateres et coquamus eos igni». Habueruntque lateres pro saxis et bitumen pro caemento. [4]Et dixerunt: «Venite, faciamus nobis civi-

came down to see the city and the tower, which the sons of men had built. [6]And the LORD said, "Behold, they are one people, and Gen 3:22 they have all one language; and this is only the beginning of what they will do; and nothing that they propose to do will now be impossible for them. [7]Come, let us go down, and there confuse their language, that they may not understand one another's speech." [8]So the LORD scattered them abroad from there over the face of all the earth, and they left off building the city. [9]Therefore its name was called Babel, because there the LORD confused[p] the

union of God and men, and of the unity of the whole human race (cf. Vatican II, *Lumen gentium*, 1).

11:4. St Augustine explains the frustration of man's designs against God in this way: "Where would man's vain presumption have ended if it succeeded in rearing a building of such size and height, even to the sky in the face of God—since that would have been higher than any mountain and would have reached beyond the limits of our atmosphere? In any case, no harm could have come to God from any straining after spiritual or physical elevation" (*De civitate Dei*, 16, 4).

This new sin of mankind is basically the same sort of sin as was committed in paradise; it is a kind of continuation of it. It is the sin of pride to which man is always prone and it has been well described in the following words of St Josemaría Escrivá when he comments on 1 John 2:16: "The eyes of our soul grow dull. Reason proclaims itself sufficient to understand everything, without the aid of God. This is a subtle tempta-

tion, which hides behind the power of our intellect, given by our Father God to man so that he might know and love him freely. Seduced by this temptation, the human mind appoints itself the centre of the universe, being thrilled with the prospect that 'you shall be like gods' (cf. Gen 3:5). So, filled with love for itself, it turns its back on the love of God. In this way does our existence fall prey unconditionally to the third enemy: pride of life. It's not merely a question of passing thoughts of vanity or self-love, it's a state of general conceit. Let's not deceive ourselves, for this is the worst of all evils, the root of every false step. The fight against pride has to be a constant battle, to such an extent that someone once said that pride only disappears twenty-four hours after a person dies. It is the arrogance of the Pharisee whom God cannot transform because he finds in him the obstacle of self-sufficiency. It is the haughtiness which leads to despising other people, to lording it over them, and so mistreating them. For 'when pride comes, then comes disgrace' (Prov 11:2)" (*Christ Is Passing By*, 6).

tatem et turrim, cuius culmen pertingat ad caelum, et faciamus nobis nomen, ne dividamur super faciem universae terrae». [5]Descendit autem Dominus, ut videret civitatem et turrim, quam aedificaverunt filii hominum, [6]et dixit Dominus: «Ecce unus est populus et unum labium omnibus; et hoc est initium operationis eorum, nec eis erit deinceps difficile, quidquid cogitaverint facere. [7]Venite igitur, descendamus et confundamus ibi linguam eorum, ut non intellegat unusquisque vocem proximi sui». [8]Atque ita divisit eos Dominus ex illo loco super faciem universae terrae, et cessaverunt aedificare ci-

p. Compare Heb *balal*, confuse

81

language of all the earth; and from there the LORD scattered them abroad over the face of all the earth.

1 Chron 1:17–27
Lk 3:34–36

5. THE SEMITES

[10]These are the descendants of Shem. When Shem was a hundred years old, he became the father of Arpachshad two years after the flood; [11]and Shem lived after the birth of Arpachshad five hundred years, and had other sons and daughters.

[12]When Arpachshad had lived thirty-five years, he became the father of Shelah; [13]and Arpachshad lived after the birth of Shelah four hundred and three years, and had other sons and daughters.

[14]When Shelah had lived thirty years, he became the father of Eber; [15]and Shelah lived after the birth of Eber four hundred and three years, and had other sons and daughters.

[16]When Eber had lived thirty-four years, he became the father of Peleg; [17]and Eber lived after the birth of Peleg four hundred and thirty years, and had other sons and daughters.

[18]When Peleg had lived thirty years, he became the father of Reu; [19]and Peleg lived after the birth of Reu two hundred and nine years, and had other sons and daughters.

[20]When Reu had lived thirty-two years, he became the father of Serug; [21]and Reu lived after the birth of Serug two hundred and seven years, and had other sons and daughters.

11:10–26. This new list of Shem's descendants introduces the narrative of God's calling of Abraham; it sets the origin of the people of Israel, descended from Abraham, in the context of world history. Some of the names given here coincide exactly (according to archeology) with those of cities or regions of Mesopotamia around the start of the second millennium BC.

These patriarchs are ten in number, just as ten were named for the period prior to the flood (cf. chap. 5); and they are given remarkable lifespans (though not as long as the earlier patriarchs). The sacred author seems to see no contradiction with what is said in Genesis 6:3 where a limit of one hundred and twenty years is put on man's lifespan; perhaps he means that these patriarchs did not come

---

vitatem. [9]Et idcirco vocatum est nomen eius Babel, quia ibi confusum est labium universae terrae, et inde dispersit eos Dominus super faciem universae terrae. [10]Hae sunt generationes Sem. Sem centum erat annorum, quando genuit Arphaxad biennio post diluvium; [11]vixitque Sem, postquam genuit Arphaxad, quingentos annos et genuit filios et filias. [12]Porro Arphaxad vixit triginta quinque annos et genuit Sala. [13]Vixitque Arphaxad, postquam genuit Sala, quadringentis tribus annis et genuit filios et filias. [14]Sala quoque vixit triginta annis et genuit Heber. [15]Vixitque Sala, postquam genuit Heber, quadringentis tribus annis et genuit filios et filias. [16]Vixit autem Heber triginta quattuor annis et genuit Phaleg. [17]Et vixit Heber, postquam genuit Phaleg, quadringentis triginta annis et genuit filios et filias. [18]Vixit quoque Phaleg triginta annis et genuit Reu. [19]Vixitque Phaleg, postquam genuit Reu, ducentis

²²When Serug had lived thirty years, he became the father of Nahor; ²³and Serug lived after the birth of Nahor two hundred years, and had other sons and daughters. ²⁴When Nahor had lived twenty-nine years, he became the father of Terah; ²⁵and Nahor lived after the birth of Terah a hundred and nineteen years, and had other sons and daughters. ²⁶When Terah had lived seventy years, he became the father of Abram, Nahor, and Haran.

PART TWO

The Origin and Formation of the Chosen People*

6. THE STORY OF ABRAHAM

²⁷Now these are the descendants of Terah. Terah was the father of Abram, Nahor, and Haran; and Haran was the father of Lot.

---

under that divine sentence because, as descendants of Noah, they were not involved in the sins which provoked it.

*11:27—50:26 We now come to the story of the patriarchs, the fathers of the people of Israel; it is a story of clans and tribes, set in a chronological framework with references to geographical places in the Middle East—Mesopotamia, Palestine and Egypt—which when seen on a map have a half-moon shape referred to as the "fertile crescent". Abraham emerges as the father of Ishmael and Isaac. Ishmael is the ancestor of the Ishmaelites (or Arabs); Isaac, the father of the chosen people. Isaac is the father of Esau and Jacob. Esau is identified with Edom; Jacob (or Israel) will be the father of twelve sons, who go down to Egypt and whose descendants came back from there, forming the twelve tribes, the people of Israel. The people of Israel form the subject of the book of Exodus.

Traditions about the patriarchs must have been preserved over a long space of time in oral form, as the history of families and clans, or connected to sacred

novem annis et genuit filios et filias. ²⁰Vixit autem Reu triginta duobus annis et genuit Seruch. ²¹Vixitque Reu, postquam genuit Seruch, ducentis septem annis et genuit filios et filias. ²²Vixit vero Seruch triginta annis et genuit Nachor. ²³Vixit Seruch, postquam genuit Nachor, ducentos annos et genuit filios et filias. ²⁴Vixit autem Nachor viginti novem annis et genuit Thare. ²⁵Vixitque Nachor, postquam genuit Thare, centum decem et novem annos et genuit filios et filias. ²⁶Vixitque Thare septuaginta annis et genuit Abram, Nachor et Aran. ²⁷Hae sunt autem generationes Thare. Thare genuit

²⁸Haran died before his father Terah in the land of his birth, in Ur
Gen 22:20–23 of the Chaldeans. ²⁹And Abram and Nahor took wives; the name
of Abram's wife was Sarai, and the name of Nahor's wife, Milcah,
Gen 16:1–2; the daughter of Haran the father of Milcah and Iscah. ³⁰Now Sarai
17:19–22 was barren; she had no child.
Acts 7:2   ³¹Terah took Abram his son and Lot the son of Haran, his
grandson, and Sarai his daughter-in-law, his son Abram's wife,

---

places in Canaan. These histories are designed to show the origin of the twelve tribes and of other neighbouring peoples—their characteristic features, their relationship with God and with the places where they lived. On being gathered together later to produce the biblical text, these traditions were couched basically in religious terms and integrated into an over-view of the history of Israel; yet they do retain features connected with the time in which they first arose and also traces of the form they acquired as they were passed on. This can be seen in the fact that they contain evidences of customs and circumstances pertaining to those ancient times (archeology provides a yardstick), although it is only in Genesis 14 that definite names are given of kings of the region of Canaan with whom the patriarchs had contact.

In the final redaction of the book of Genesis these traditions about the patriarchs are grouped around the personalities to which they refer; so we can distinguish an Abraham cycle (chaps. 12–25); an Isaac cycle (chap. 26); a Jacob cycle (chaps. 27–35) and the history of Joseph (chaps. 37–50).

In this patriarchal history the main thing the Bible wants to show is that God's plan is being put into effect—his plan to chose one people so as to make a covenant with it, the covenant of Sinai; it is prepared for by means of earlier covenants that God makes with the patriarchs. God's saving plan begins to take concrete form with Abraham. As the Second Vatican Council teaches, "in his own time God called Abraham, and made him into a great nation (cf. Gen 12:2). After the era of the patriarchs, he taught this nation, by Moses and the prophets, to recognize him as the only living and true God, as a provident Father and just judge. He taught them, too, to look for the promised Saviour. And so, throughout the ages, he prepared the way for the Gospel" (*Dei Verbum*, 3).

11:27–30. The other branches of Seth's line have been left to one side, and attention is now focused on the family of Terah, from which will come Abraham, the central character of the narrative. Here the text gives the names of the ancestors of Israel, Abraham and Sarah, the family to which they belonged, their place of origin and the circumstances which led to their settling in Canaan. All will become part of the history and faith of the people of Israel, as we read in Joshua 24:2–4: "Thus says the Lord, the God of Israel, 'Your fathers lived of old beyond the Euphrates, Terah, the father of Abraham and of Nahor; and they served other gods. Then I took your father Abraham from beyond the river . . .'" (cf. Deut 26:5).

Abram, Nachor et Aran. Porro Aran genuit Lot; ²⁸mortuusque est Aran ante Thare patrem suum in terra nativitatis suae in Ur Chaldaeorum. ²⁹Duxerunt autem Abram et Nachor uxores: nomen uxoris Abram Sarai, et nomen uxoris Nachor Melcha, filia Aran patris Melchae et patris Ieschae. ³⁰Erat autem Sarai

and they went forth together from Ur of the Chaldeans to go into
the land of Canaan; but when they came to Haran, they settled
there. ³²The days of Terah were two hundred and five years; and   Acts 7:4
Terah died in Haran.

The call of Abram and God's promise to him

Wis 10:5
Acts 7:3
Heb 11:8

12 ¹*Now the LORD said to Abram, "Go from your country and
your kindred and your father's house to the land that I will

In presenting the figure of Abraham,
the Bible sets him squarely in the real
history of the peoples and events of the
ancient Near East. In chaps. 1–11 what is
provided is more of a pre-history, covering a vast period of time—from the
creation of the world up to the start of
the second millennium before Christ,
the time when the patriarchs lived. Also,
we have come to an historical context
when we can truly say that mankind has
attained a substantial degree of cultural
development, as can be seen from the
great civilizations of Mesopotamia and
Egypt. This is the period when, through
God's call to Abraham, his plan for the
salvation of mankind begins to be put
into effect.

11:31. The city of Ur, where Abraham's
people came from, was in the south of
Mesopotamia, on the banks of the
Euphrates, near the Persian Gulf. Haran,
the final destination of the first migration,
was in the north east, between the upper
reaches of the Tigris and the Euphrates.
This is the place Abraham leaves from.
We do not know exactly when he lived or
which Semitic group he belonged to.
The description "a wandering Aramaean"
in Deuteronomy 26:5 is really a reference

to Jacob, and it is too general to allow us
to identify the patriarchs. Scholars usually place Abraham among the *amurru*
(Amorites) or north-western Semites, of
whom some semi-nomadic groups roved
around Syria and Palestine, reaching
even as far as Egypt (cf. the note on
14:13).

The most probable time for Abraham's
move into Canaan seems to be between
1800 and 1600 BC, perhaps coinciding
with the time the Hurrites moved there
(these people, of Indo-European race,
came from the north, in the area of Haran).
Some scholars say that it was a couple of
centuries later that Abraham migrated—
that he moved at the same time as the
Hyksos, a Semitic race which eventually
established itself in Egypt (cf. the note on
37:2—50:26).

12:1–6. God's call to Abraham (the name
he would give him instead of Abram: cf.
17:5) marks the start of a new stage in his
dealings with mankind, because his
covenant with Abraham will prove a
blessing to all nations. It means that
Abraham has to break earthly ties, ties
with family and place, and put his trust
entirely in God's promise—an unknown
country, many descendants (even though

---

sterilis nec habebat liberos. ³¹Tulitque Thare Abram filium suum et Lot filium Aran filium filii sui et
Sarai nurum suam, uxorem Abram filii sui, et eduxit eos de Ur Chaldaeorum, ut irent in terram
Chanaan. Veneruntque usque Charran et habitaverunt ibi. ³²Et facti sunt dies Thare ducentorum quinque
annorum. et mortuus est in Charran. ¹ Dixit autem Dominus ad Abram: «Egredere de terra tua et de
cognatione tua / et de domo patris tui / in terram, quam monstrabo tibi. / ²Faciamque te in gentem

Jer 4:2
Neh 9:7–8 show you. [2]And I will make of you a great nation, and I will bless
Sir 44:21 you, and make your name great, so that you will be a blessing. [3]I
Acts 3:25
Gal 3:8, 13–16 will bless those who bless you, and him who curses you I will
Rev 1:7 curse; and by you all the families of the earth shall bless them-
selves."[q]
Heb 11:8   [4]So Abram went, as the LORD had told him; and Lot went with
him. Abram was seventy-five years old when he departed from
Acts 7:4 Haran. [5]And Abram took Sarai his wife, and Lot his brother's son,
and all their possessions which they had gathered, and the persons
that they had gotten in Haran; and they set forth to go to the land

---

his wife is barren: cf. 11:30) and God's constant protection. This divine calling also involves a break with the idolatrous cult followed by Abraham's family in the city of Haran (apparently a moon cult) so as to worship the true God.

Abraham responds to God's call; believing and trusting totally in the divine word, he leaves his country and heads for Canaan. Abraham's attitude is in sharp contrast with the human pride described earlier in connexion with the tower of Babel (cf. 11:1–9), and even more so with the disobedience of Adam and Eve which was the cause of mankind's break with God.

The divine plan of salvation begins to operate by requiring man to make an act of obedience: in Abraham's case, he is asked to set out on a journey. The plan will reach its goal with the perfect obedience shown by Jesus "made obedient unto death, even death on a cross" (Phil 2:8), whereby all mankind will obtain the mercy of God (cf. Rom 5:19). Everyone who listens and obeys the voice of the Lord, all believers, can therefore be regarded as children of

Abraham. "Thus Abraham 'believed God, and it was reckoned to him as righteousness.' So you see that it is men of faith who are the sons of Abraham. And the scripture foreseeing that God would justify the Gentiles by faith, preached the gospel beforehand to Abraham, saying, 'In you shall all the nations be blessed.' So then, those who are men of faith are blessed with Abraham who had faith" (Gal 3:6–9).

Jewish and Christian tradition sees the three things God requires Abram to give up as epitomizing the demands of faith: "Through these three departures— from country, kindred and father's house," according to Alcuin's interpretation, "is meant that we have to leave behind the earthly man, the ties of our vices, and the world under the devil's power" (*Interrogationes in Genesim*, 154).

Abraham's response also involves an attitude of prayer, an intimate relationship with God. Although prayer makes its appearance at the very start of the Old Testament (cf. Gen 4:4, 26; 5:24; etc.), it really comes into its own with our father

---

magnam / et benedicam tibi / et magnificabo nomen tuum, / erisque in benedictionem. / [3]Benedicam benedicentibus tibi / et maledicentibus tibi maledicam, / atque in te benedicentur / universae cognationes terrae!». [4]Egressus est itaque Abram, sicut praeceperat ei Dominus, et ivit cum eo Lot. Septuaginta quinque annorum erat Abram, cum egrederetur de Charran. [5]Tulitque Sarai uxorem suam et Lot filium fratris sui universamque substantiam, quam acquisiverant, et animas, quas fecerant in

q. Or *in you all the families of the earth shall be blessed*

of Canaan. When they had come to the land of Canaan, ⁶Abram Gen 33:18–20
passed through the land to the place at Shechem, to the oakʳ of
Moreh. At that time the Canaanites were in the land. ⁷Then the Gen 13:15;
LORD appeared to Abram, and said, "To your descendants I will 15:18; 17:8; 26:4
Acts 7:5
give this land." So he built there an altar to the LORD, who had Gal 3:16
appeared to him. ⁸Thence he removed to the mountain on the east Heb 11:9
of Bethel, and pitched his tent, with Bethel on the west and Ai on
the east; and there he built an altar to the LORD and called on the
name of the LORD. ⁹And Abram journeyed on, still going toward
the Negeb.

Abraham, as the *Catechism of the Catholic Church* teaches: "When God calls him, Abraham goes forth 'as the Lord had told him' (Gen 12:4). Abraham's heart is entirely submissive to the Word and so he obeys. Such attentiveness of the heart, whose decisions are made according to God's will, is essential to prayer, while the words used count only in relation to it. Abraham's prayer is expressed first by deeds: a man of silence, he constructs an altar to the Lord at each stage of his journey. Only later does Abraham's first prayer in words appear: a veiled complaint reminding God of his promises which seem unfulfilled (cf. Gen 15:2–3). Thus one aspect of the drama of prayer appears from the beginning: the test of faith in the fidelity of God" (no. 2570).

Abraham gets as far as the central part of Palestine, from where he moves south, building as he goes altars to the Lord, to the true God, in places which will become important shrines in later periods. The biblical text shows that Yahweh accompanies Abraham and that

the latter renders him acceptable worship, in contrast with the idolatrous cult practised by the inhabitants of the country (given the generic name of "Canaanites"). God, for his part, in all his appearances to the patriarch, promises to give this land to his descendants (cf. Gen 13:15; 15:18; 17:8; 26:4). In this way the text is showing the radical source of the legitimacy of Israel's possession of the land of Canaan. However, this promise of a land to the descendants of Abraham goes beyond the empirical fact of acquiring territory, and becomes a symbol of the blessings and the divine gifts in which all mankind will share.

Speaking about Abraham's faith in the word of God, St Paul interprets Abraham's "descendants" in the singular, as referring to one descendant only, Jesus Christ, because only he, being the Son of God and making himself obedient unto death, possesses all the divine goods and communicates them to man: "Christ redeemed us [. . .] that in Christ Jesus the blessing of Abraham might come upon the Gentiles, that we might receive the

---

Charran, et egressi sunt, ut irent in terram Chanaan; et venerunt in terram Chanaan. ⁶Pertransivit Abram terram usque ad locum Sichem, usque ad Quercum Moreh. Chananaeus autem tunc erat in terra. ⁷Apparuit autem Dominus Abram et dixit ei: «Semini tuo dabo terram hanc». Qui aedificavit ibi altare Domino, qui apparuerat ei. ⁸Et inde transgrediens ad montem, qui erat contra orientem Bethel, tetendit ibi tabernaculum suum ab occidente habens Bethel et ab oriente Hai; aedificavit quoque ibi altare Domino et invocavit nomen Domini. ⁹Perrexitque Abram de mansione in mansionem usque ad Nageb.

r. Or *terebinth*

Gen 20:1–18;
26:1–11

Abram in Egypt

[10]Now there was a famine in the land. So Abram went down to Egypt to sojourn there, for the famine was severe in the land. [11]When he was about to enter Egypt, he said to Sarai his wife, "I know that you are a woman beautiful to behold; [12]and when the Egyptians see you, they will say, 'This is his wife'; then they will kill me, but they will let you live. [13]Say you are my sister, that it may go well with me because of you, and that my life may be spared on your account." [14]When Abram entered Egypt the Egyptians saw that the woman was very beautiful. [15]And when the princes of Pharaoh saw her, they praised her to Pharaoh. And the woman was taken into Pharaoh's house. [16]And for her sake he dealt well with Abram; and he had sheep, oxen, he-asses, menservants, maidservants, she-asses, and camels.

---

promise of the Spirit. [. . .] Now the promises were made to Abraham and to his offspring. It does not say, 'And to offsprings,' referring to many; but, referring to one, 'And to your offspring,' which is Christ" (Gal 3:13–16).

12:10–20. A similar episode, with slight variations, will later be recounted about Abraham himself (cf. 20:1–8) and later still about Isaac (cf. 26:1–13). These accounts highlight the beauty of their wives (mothers of the chosen people), the difficulties they experience and their resourcefulness in solving them, and most especially the way God protects them.

Abraham's going down into Egypt is in keeping with the semi-nomadic lifestyle attributed to him and with the relocations typical of such people. In the book of Genesis, however, it has a special meaning. Famine in the land of Canaan is as it were the first test Abraham has to

undergo, and it leads him to seek another country, Egypt, whose wealth is legendary (cf. 13:10). But that is not where he should settle: he has to return to the place where he built an altar and called on the name of Yahweh (cf. 13:4).

It is important to note how God comes to Abraham's aid in Egypt, and how he defends his marriage with Sarah, despite the patriarch's attitude; through fear, Abraham is on the point of giving up his wife, the woman God chose to be the mother of his line. The point is that the Lord is not like a local God, tied to a particular shrine, but a personal God, who protects his servant no matter where he is. This passage teaches us, therefore, to trust in God in all circumstances, even when weakness and fear lead us to opt out of the plans God has for us: "Trust always in your God. He does not lose battles" (St Josemaría Escrivá, *The Way*, 733). In the later version of the event (cf. 20:1–18),

---

[10]Facta est autem fames in terra; descenditque Abram in Aegyptum, ut peregrinaretur ibi; praevaluerat enim fames in terra. [11]Cumque prope esset, ut ingrederetur Aegyptum, dixit Sarai uxori suae: «Novi quod pulchra sis mulier [12]et quod, cum viderint te Aegyptii, dicturi sunt: 'Uxor ipsius est'; et interficient me et te reservabunt. [13]Dic ergo, obsecro te, quod soror mea sis, ut bene sit mihi propter te, et vivat anima mea ob gratiam tui». [14]Cum itaque ingressus esset Abram Aegyptum, viderunt Aegyptii mulierem quod esset pulchra nimis, [15]et viderunt eam principes pharaonis et laudaverunt eam apud illum; et sublata est mulier in domum pharaonis. [16]Abram vero bene usus est propter illam; fueruntque

¹⁷But the LORD afflicted Pharaoh and his house with great plagues because of Sarai, Abram's wife. ¹⁸So Pharaoh called Abram, and said, "What is this you have done to me? Why did you not tell me that she was your wife? ¹⁹Why did you say, 'She is my sister,' so that I took her for my wife? Now then, here is your wife, take her, and be gone." ²⁰And Pharaoh gave men orders concerning him; and they set him on the way, with his wife and all that he had.

Abram in Bethel
Gen 12:8

13 ¹So Abram went up from Egypt, he and his wife, and all that he had, and Lot with him, into the Negeb.

²Now Abram was very rich in cattle, in silver, and in gold. ³And he journeyed on from the Negeb as far as Bethel, to the place where his tent had been at the beginning, between Bethel and Ai, ⁴to the place where he had made an altar at the first; and there Abram called on the name of the LORD. ⁵And Lot, who went with Abram, also had flocks and herds and tents, ⁶so that the land Gen 36:7 could not support both of them dwelling together; for their possessions were so great that they could not dwell together, ⁷and there was strife between the herdsmen of Abram's cattle and the herdsmen of Lot's cattle. At that time the Canaanites and the Perizzites dwelt in the land.

Abram and Lot separate
Gen 19:23–29

⁸Then Abram said to Lot, "Let there be no strife between you and me, and between your herdsmen and my herdsmen; for we are

---

what the patriarch says is justified by the fact that Sarah, his wife, was also his half-sister (they shared the same father).

13:1–18. Abraham prospers in the land God has promised will be his; this is an

early confirmation of God's blessing. But he still has to undergo another test—family rows over pastures. The patriarch comes across as a peaceable person; he lets Lot have first choice. Abraham's behaviour is a kind of new act of faith in

---

ei oves et boves et asini et servi et famulae et asinae et cameli. ¹⁷Flagellavit autem Dominus pharaonem plagis maximis et domum eius propter Sarai uxorem Abram. ¹⁸Vocavitque pharao Abram et dixit ei: «Quidnam est hoc quod fecisti mihi? Quare non indicasti mihi quod uxor tua esset? ¹⁹Quam ob causam dixisti esse sororem tuam, ut tollerem eam mihi in uxorem? Nunc igitur, ecce coniux tua: accipe eam et vade!». ²⁰Praecepitque pharao super Abram viris; et deduxerunt eum et uxorem illius et omnia, quae habebat. ¹Ascendit ergo Abram de Aegypto ipse et uxor eius et omnia, quae habebat, et Lot cum eo ad Nageb. ²Abram autem erat dives valde in pecoribus, argento et auro. ³Et profectus est de mansione in mansionem a Nageb in Bethel usque ad locum, ubi prius fixerat tabernaculum inter Bethel et Hai, ⁴in loco altaris, quod fecerat prius, et invocavit ibi nomen Domini. ⁵Sed et Lot, qui ibat cum Abram, fuerunt greges ovium et armenta et tabernacula; ⁶nec poterat eos capere terra, ut habitarent simul: erat

kinsmen. ⁹Is not the whole land before you? Separate yourself from me. If you take the left hand, then I will go to the right; or if you take the right hand, then I will go to the left." ¹⁰And Lot lifted up his eyes, and saw that the Jordan valley was well watered everywhere like the garden of the LORD, like the land of Egypt, in the direction of Zoar; this was before the LORD destroyed Sodom and Gomorrah. ¹¹So Lot chose for himself all the Jordan valley, and Lot journeyed east; thus they separated from each other.

Heb 11:9 ¹²Abram dwelt in the land of Canaan, while Lot dwelt among the cities of the valley and moved his tent as far as Sodom. ¹³Now the men of Sodom were wicked, great sinners against the LORD.

Gen 12:7
Acts 7:5
Gal 3:16

A new promise to Abram

¹⁴The LORD said to Abram, after Lot had separated from him, "Lift up your eyes, and look from the place where you are, northward and southward and eastward and westward; ¹⁵for all the land

---

the divine promise, accepting as he does that God gives the land to whomever he chooses. Once Lot has gone off, God emphatically reaffirms his promise of descendants and land, and Abraham will progress across the country, taking possession of it, as it were. He eventually settles at Hebron, in the south of Palestine, on the edge of the Negeb desert.

Lot has chosen the rich lands, the Jordan plains; but the sacred writer points out how near he is to Sodom, the city of sin. Lot will later regret his decision to settle there (cf. chap. 19). The account seems to imply a geography with no Dead Sea, at least not as we know it today.

Apropos of this passage, St John Chrysostom points out how family peace was being undermined by prosperity: "Their flocks grew bigger, great wealth accrued to them, and immediately harmony between them was disrupted— where there had been peace and the bonds of affection, now there was trouble and hostility. You see, whenever it is a question of mine and yours, there are grounds for the utmost trouble and a basis for hostility: by contrast, where this isn't the case, habits of peace and harmony exist together without any confusion" (*Homiliae in Genesim,* 33, 3).

---

quippe substantia eorum multa, et nequibant habitare communiter. ⁷Unde et facta est rixa inter pastores gregum Abram et pastores gregum Lot. Eo autem tempore Chananaeus et Pherezaeus habitabant in illa terra. ⁸Dixit ergo Abram ad Lot: «Ne, quaeso, sit iurgium inter me et te et inter pastores meos et pastores tuos: fratres enim sumus. ⁹Nonne universa terra coram te est? Recede a me, obsecro: si ad sinistram ieris, ego dexteram tenebo; si tu dexteram elegeris, ego ad sinistram pergam». ¹⁰Elevatis itaque Lot oculis, vidit omnem circa regionem Iordanis, quae universa irrigabatur, antequam subverteret Dominus Sodomam et Gomorram, sicut paradisus Domini et sicut Aegyptus usque in Segor. ¹¹Elegitque sibi Lot omnem regionem circa Iordanem et recessit ad orientem; divisique sunt alterutrum a fratre suo. ¹²Abram habitavit in terra Chanaan; Lot vero moratus est in oppidis, quae erant circa Iordanem, et tabernacula movit usque ad Sodomam. ¹³Homines autem Sodomitae pessimi erant et peccatores coram Domino nimis. ¹⁴Dixitque Dominus ad Abram, postquam divisus est Lot ab eo: «Leva oculos tuos et vide a loco, in quo nunc es, ad aquilonem et ad meridiem, ad orientem et ad occidentem: ¹⁵omnem terram, quam conspicis, tibi dabo et semini tuo usque in sempiternum ¹⁶faciamque semen

which you see I will give to you and to your descendants for ever. ¹⁶I will make your descendants as the dust of the earth; so that if one can count the dust of the earth, your descendants also can be counted. ¹⁷Arise, walk through the length and the breadth of the land, for I will give it to you." ¹⁸So Abram moved his tent, and came and dwelt by the oaks of Mamre, which are at Hebron; and there he built an altar to the LORD.

Lot is captured

14 ¹In the days of Amraphel king of Shinar, Arioch king of Ellasar, Ched-or-laomer king of Elam, and Tidal king of Goiim, ²these kings made war with Bera king of Sodom, Birsha king of Gomorrah, Shinab king of Admah, Shemeber king of Zeboiim, and the king of Bela (that is, Zoar). ³And all these joined forces in the Valley of Siddim (that is, the Salt Sea). ⁴Twelve years they had served Ched-or-laomer, but in the thir-

14:1–16. This episode fits in pretty well with the unsettled history of Syria and Palestine in the 19th to 18th centuries BC—frequent local wars between petty kings. This particular episode seems to deal with an incursion from northern kings who laid waste Transjordan and the Jordan valley. The names given do not coincide with any available from other sources of the period, though they look quite like Hurrite and Elamite names. In recording this tradition the text highlights Abraham's valour as also his family loyalty and generosity, in coming to Lot's aid.

As for Lot, he is now paying the price for settling near Sodom, but he and his property are saved thanks to Abraham's intervention. We can also see from this episode that even after God's

call to Abraham, life goes on as before; violence and war are still there.

Focusing on the figure of Abraham (particularly in this passage) we learn from Holy Scripture that responding to God's plan involves being concerned about other people: "Magnanimity means greatness of spirit, a largeness of heart wherein many can find refuge. Magnanimity gives us the energy to break out of ourselves and be prepared to undertake generous tasks which will be of benefit to all. Small-mindedness has no home in the magnanimous heart, nor has meanness, nor egoistic calculation, nor self-interested trickery. The magnanimous person devotes all his strength, unstintingly, to what is worthwhile. As a result he is capable of giving himself. He is not content with merely giving. He gives *his*

tuum sicut pulverem terrae: si quis potest hominum numerare pulverem terrae, semen quoque tuum numerare poterit. ¹⁷Surge et perambula terram in longitudine et in latitudine sua, quia tibi daturus sum eam». ¹⁸Movens igitur tabernaculum suum, Abram venit et habitavit iuxta Quercus Mambre, quae sunt in Hebron, aedificavitque ibi altare Domino. ¹Factum est autem in illo tempore, ut Amraphel rex Sennaar et Arioch rex Ellasar et Chodorlahomor rex Elam et Thadal rex gentium ²inirent bellum contra Bara regem Sodomae et contra Bersa regem Gomorrae et contra Sennaab regem Adamae et contra Semeber regem Seboim contraque regem Belae; ipsa est Segor. ³Omnes hi convenerunt in vallem Siddim, quae nunc est mare Salis. ⁴Duodecim annis servierant Chodorlahomor et tertio decimo anno

Deut 2:10 teenth year they rebelled. [5]In the fourteenth year Ched-or-laomer and the kings who were with him came and subdued the Rephaim in Ashteroth-karnaim, the Zuzim in Ham, the Emim in Shaveh-kiriathaim, [6]and the Horites in their Mount Seir as far as Ex 17:8 El-paran on the border of the wilderness; [7]then they turned back Deut 7:1 and came to Enmishpat (that is, Kadesh), and subdued all the country of the Amalekites, and also the Amorites who dwelt in Hazazon-tamar. [8]Then the king of Sodom, the king of Gomorrah, the king of Admah, the king of Zeboiim, and the king of Bela (that is, Zoar) went out, and they joined battle in the Valley of Siddim [9]with Ched-or-laomer king of Elam, Tidal king of Goiim, Amraphel king of Shinar, and Arioch king of Ellasar, four kings against five. [10]Now the Valley of Siddim was full of bitumen pits; and as the kings of Sodom and Gomorrah fled, some fell into them, and the rest fled to the mountain. [11]So the enemy took all the goods of Sodom and Gomorrah, and all their provisions, and went their way; [12]they also took Lot, the son of Abram's brother, who dwelt in Sodom, and his goods, and departed.

Lot is set free

Gen 13:18 [13]Then one who had escaped came, and told Abram the Hebrew, who was living by the oaks[s] of Mamre the Amorite, brother of

---

very self. He thus comes to understand that the greatest expression of magnanimity consists in giving oneself to God" (St Josemaría Escrivá, *Friends of God*, 80).

14:13. "The Hebrew": the first time this term occurs in the Old Testament. The Greek tradition is that it means "he from

the other side", that is, he who came over from the other side of the Euphrates. But current scholarship tends to link the word "Hebrew" with *hapiru*, a word which occurs in the letters of Tell-el-Amarna (Egypt, 14th century BC), in Babylonian documents from the time of Hammurabi (18th century BC) and in other documents of the period. The *hapiru* seems to have

---

recesserunt ab eo. [5]Igitur anno quarto decimo venit Chodorlahomor et reges, qui erant cum eo, percusseruntque Raphaim in Astharothcarnaim et Zuzim in Ham et Emim in Savecariathaim [6]et Chorraeos in montibus Seir usque ad Elpharan, quae est in deserto. [7]Reversique sunt et venerunt ad fontem Mesphat; ipsa est Cades. Et percusserunt omnem regionem Amalecitarum et etiam Amorraeum, qui habitabat in Asasonthamar. [8]Et egressi sunt rex Sodomae et rex Gomorrae rexque Adamae et rex Seboim necnon et rex Belae, quae est Segor; et direxerunt contra eos aciem in valle Siddim, [9]scilicet adversus Chodorlahomor regem Elam et Thadal regem gentium et Amraphel regem Sennaar et Arioch regem Ellasar: quattuor reges adversus quinque. [10]Vallis autem Siddim habebat puteos multos bituminis. Itaque rex Sodomae et Gomorrae terga verterunt cecideruntque illuc; et qui remanserant, fugerunt ad montem. [11]Tulerunt autem omnem substantiam Sodomae et Gomorrae et universa, quae ad

s. Or *terebinths*

Eshcol and of Aner; these were allies of Abram. [14]When Abram heard that his kinsman had been taken captive, he led forth his trained men, born in his house, three hundred and eighteen of them, and went in pursuit as far as Dan. [15]And he divided his forces against them by night, he and his servants, and routed them and pursued them to Hobah, north of Damascus. [16]Then he brought back all the goods, and also brought back his kinsman Lot with his goods, and the women and the people.

Melchizedek blesses Abram

Ps 110:4
Heb 7:1f

[17]After his return from the defeat of Ched-or-laomer and the kings who were with him, the king of Sodom went out to meet him at the Valley of Shaveh (that is, the King's Valley). [18]And Melchizedek* king of Salem brought out bread and wine; he was priest of God Most High. [19]And he blessed him and said,

Mk 5:7
Lk 8:28

Heb 7:6
Rev 10:6

> "Blessed be Abram by God Most High,
>   maker of heaven and earth;
> [20]and blessed be God Most High,
>   who has delivered your enemies into your hand!"

Heb 7:4

---

been a social class very actively involved in caravan arrangements. The word "Hebrew" may also be connected with Eber, a descendant of Shem according to 11:16.

14:18–20. After the account of Abraham's victory over the kings of the North, there is this little insertion, apparently, that records a piece of tradition which shows Abraham's connexion with Jerusalem and its king. In the context of the story of the patriarchs, this episode implies recognition by the local nations (Salem, Sodom) of the blessing they

receive through Abraham (cf. 12:3). In the specific case of Salem, we get a glimpse of the fact that the true God, the Creator of heaven and earth, was worshipped there, under the name of El-Elyón, or God Most High, and also that he is acknowledged by Abraham as the Lord himself, "maker of heaven and earth" (cf. 14:22). The bread and wine are first-fruits of the land, offered in sacrifice as a sign of recognition of the Creator. In the name of El-Elyón Abraham receives Melchizedek's blessing, thereby making Jerusalem the place from where the Lord imparts his blessing (cf. Ps

cibum pertinent, et abierunt; [12]ceperunt et Lot et substantiam eius, filium fratris Abram, qui habitabat in Sodoma. [13]Et ecce unus, qui evaserat, nuntiavit Abram Hebraeo, qui habitabat iuxta Quercus Mambre Amorraei fratris Eschol et fratris Aner; hi enim pepigerant foedus cum Abram. [14]Quod cum audisset Abram, captum videlicet Lot fratrem suum, numeravit expeditos vernaculos suos trecentos decem et octo et persecutus est usque Dan; [15]et, divisis sociis, irruit super eos nocte percussitque eos et persecutus est eos usque Hoba, quae est ad laevam Damasci; [16]reduxitque omnem substantiam, necnon et Lot fratrem suum cum substantia illius, mulieres quoque et populum. [17]Egressus est autem rex Sodomae in occursum eius, postquam reversus est a caede Chodorlahomor et regum, qui cum eo erant, in vallem Save, quae est vallis Regis. [18]At vero Melchisedech rex Salem proferens panem et vinum —erat enim sacerdos Dei altissimi— [19]benedixit ei et ait: «Benedictus Abram a Deo excelso, /

And Abram gave him a tenth of everything. [21]And the king of Sodom said to Abram, "Give me the persons, but take the goods for yourself." [22]But Abram said to the king of Sodom, "I have sworn to the LORD God Most High, maker of heaven and earth, [23]that I would not take a thread or a sandal-thong or anything that is yours, lest you should say, 'I have made Abram rich.' [24]I will take nothing but what the young men have eaten, and the share of the men who went with me; let Aner, Eshcol, and Mamre take their share."

Rev 10:6

Gen 13:14–17; 17:1–22

God's Covenant with Abram*

Mt 15:12

15 [1]After these things the word of the LORD came to Abram in a vision, "Fear not, Abram, I am your shield; your reward

---

134:3). It is also significant that Abraham gives the king of Jerusalem a tenth of everything, implying that he had a right to receive it.

In Jewish tradition the city of Salem and the figure of Melchizedek acquired a special meaning. It identifies Salem with Jerusalem or Zion, where the Lord dwells: "His abode has been established in Salem, his dwelling place in Zion," Psalm 76:3 acclaims. Melchizedek is regarded as having a priesthood earlier and greater than that of Aaron; cf. when the King Messiah is praised: "You are a priest for ever, after the order of Melchizedek" (Ps 110:4). In the New Testament, the mysterious priestly figure of Melchizedek is portrayed as a type of the priesthood of Christ, for Christ is truly the eternal priest even though he (like Melchizedek) does not belong to the priesthood of Aaron. "For this Melchizedek, king of Salem, priest of the Most High God, met Abraham returning from the slaughter of the kings and blessed him; and to him apportioned a tenth part of everything. He is first, by translation of his name, king of righteousness, and then he is also king of Salem, that is, king of peace. He is without father or mother or genealogy, and has neither beginning of days nor end of life, but resembling the Son of God he continues a priest forever" (Heb 7:1–3).

In the light of all this, Christian liturgy has seen a prefiguring of the Eucharist in the bread and wine offered by Melchizedek (cf. *Roman Missal*, Eucharistic Prayer I); tradition sees him as a figure of priests of the New Law.

*15:1–21. God rewards Abraham for his generosity towards Mechizedek and for his renouncing of the riches offered him by the king of Sodom. He appears to him in a vision and promises his help, many descendants and the land of Canaan. Here all that is required of Abraham is that he

---

qui creavit caelum et terram; / [20]et benedictus Deus excelsus, / qui tradidit hostes tuos in manus tuas». Et dedit ei decimas ex omnibus. [21]Dixit autem rex Sodomae ad Abram: «Da mihi animas; substantiam tolle tibi». [22]Qui respondit ei: «Levo manum meam ad Dominum Deum excelsum, creatorem caeli et terrae, [23]a filo subteminis usque ad corrigiam caligae non accipiam ex omnibus, quae tua sunt, ne dicas: 'Ego ditavi Abram'; [24]exceptis his, quae comederunt iuvenes, et partibus virorum, qui venerunt mecum, Aner, Eschol et Mambre: isti accipient partes suas». [1] His itaque transactis, factus est sermo Domini ad Abram per visionem dicens: «Noli timere, Abram! Ego protector tuus sum, et merces tua magna erit

shall be very great."* ²But Abram said, "O Lord GOD, what wilt thou give me, for I continue childless, and the heir of my house is Eliezer of Damascus?" ³And Abram said, "Behold, thou hast given me no offspring; and a slave born in my house will be my heir." ⁴And behold, the word of the LORD came to him, "This man shall not be your heir; your own son shall be your heir." ⁵And he brought him outside and said, "Look toward heaven, and number the stars, if you are able to number them." Then he said to him, "So shall your descendants be." ⁶And he believed the LORD; and he reckoned it to him as righteousness.

Deut 1:10
1 Mac 2:52
Rom 4:18
Heb 11:12

Rom 4:3, 9
Gal 3:6
Jas 2:23

---

believe in the promise that God himself, through a rite of covenant, undertakes to fulfil. This passage emphasizes the gravity of God's promise and speaks of the faithfulness of God, who will keep his word.

15:2–3. Abraham does not understand how God can keep the promise he made to him in Haran (cf. chap. 12). The fact that he has no children is a severe test of his faith; and anything else God may give him means little by comparison. This is the first time Abraham speaks to God, and their conversation shows the deep intimacy between them. He makes his concerns known to God: because Lot has left him and Abraham has no son of his own, he needs to appoint an heir who will take over leadership of the clan in return for serving Abraham in his lifetime. This is the first friendly dialogue the Bible records between God and a man since the dialogue God had with Adam in paradise (cf. 3:9–12). It is a conversation between friends and the first example, therefore, of a prayer of friendship and filiation, for to pray is to speak to God.

"Of Damascus": this is the translation most frequently given for a word which is very unclear (the original text is unrecoverably corrupt). It does not seem to mean that Eliezer was a native of Damascus, for he was a slave or servant born in Abraham's house (v. 3); therefore, it must be some other sort of title whose meaning escapes us.

15:4–6. Once more Abraham is asked to make an act of faith in the word of God, and he does so. This pleases God and is reckoned righteous. This makes Abraham the father of all those who believe in God and his saving word.

In the light of this passage St Paul sees Abraham as the model of how a person becomes righteous in God's eyes—through faith in his word, the definitive word being the announcement that God saves us through the death and resurrection of Jesus. In this way, Abraham not only becomes the father of the Jewish people according to the flesh, but also the father of those who without being Jews have become members of the new people of God through faith in Jesus: "We say that faith was reckoned to Abraham

nimis». ²Dixitque Abram: «Domine Deus, quid dabis mihi? Ego vadam absque liberis, et heres domus meae erit Damascenus Eliezer». ³Addiditque Abram: «En mihi non dedisti semen, et ecce vernaculus meus heres meus erit». ⁴Sed ecce sermo Domini factus est ad eum: «Non erit hic heres tuus, sed qui egredietur de visceribus tuis, ipsum habebis heredem». ⁵Eduxitque eum foras et ait illi: «Suspice caelum et numera stellas, si potes». Et dixit ei: «Sic erit semen tuum». ⁶Credidit Domino, et reputatum

Gen 11:31
Acts 7:2
Heb 11:8

Lk 1:18
⁷And he said to him, "I am the Lord who brought you from Ur of the Chaldeans, to give you this land to possess." ⁸But he said, "O Lord GOD, how am I to know that I shall possess it?" ⁹He said to him, "Bring me a heifer three years old, a she-goat three years old, a ram three years old, a turtledove, and a young pigeon." ¹⁰And he brought him all these, cut them in two, and laid each half over against the other; but he did not cut the birds in two. ¹¹And when birds of prey came down upon the carcasses, Abram drove them away.

Acts 10:10
Rev 11:11

Acts 7:6f
¹²As the sun was going down, a deep sleep fell on Abram; and lo, a dread and great darkness fell upon him. ¹³Then the Lord said to Abram, "Know of a surety that your descendants will be sojourners in a land that is not theirs, and will be slaves there, and Ex 12:40
Jud 5:9ff
Acts 13:20
Gal 3:17 they will be oppressed for four hundred years; ¹⁴but I will bring judgment on the nation which they serve, and afterward they shall

as righteousness. How then was it reckoned to him? Was it before or after he was circumcised? It was not after, but before he was circumcised. He received circumcision as a sign or seal of the righteousness which he had by faith while he was still uncircumcised. The purpose was to make him the father of all who believe without being circumcised and who thus have righteousness reckoned to them, and likewise the father of the circumcised who are not merely circumcised but also follow the example of the faith which our father Abraham had before he was circumcised" (Rom 4:9–12).

Abraham's faith revealed itself in his obedience to God when he left his homeland (cf. 12:4), and later on when he was ready to sacrifice his son (cf. 22:1–4). This is the aspect of Abraham's obedience which is given special emphasis in

the Letter of St James, inviting Christians to prove the genuineness of their faith with obedience to God and good works: "Was not Abraham our father justified by works, when he offered his son Isaac upon the altar? You see that faith was active along with his works, and faith was completed by works, and scripture was fulfilled which says, 'Abraham believed God, and it was reckoned to him as righteousness'; and he was called the friend of God" (Jas 2:21–23).

15:7–21. The strength of God's resolve to give the land of Canaan is vividly demonstrated by his ordaining a rite of covenant to externalize the commitment undertaken by both parties. According to this ancient rite (cf. Jer 34:18), the action of the two parties—*passing between* the pieces of the victims—indicated a readi-

est ei ad iustitiam. ⁷Dixitque ad eum: «Ego Dominus, qui eduxi te de Ur Chaldaeorum, ut darem tibi terram istam, et possideres eam». ⁸Et ille ait: «Domine Deus, unde scire possum quod possessurus sim eam?». ⁹Respondens Dominus: «Sume, inquit, mihi vitulam triennem et capram trimam et arietem annorum trium, turturem quoque et columbam». ¹⁰Qui tollens universa haec divisit ea per medium et utrasque partes contra se altrinsecus posuit; aves autem non divisit. ¹¹Descenderuntque volucres super cadavera, et abigebat eas Abram. ¹²Cumque sol occumberet, sopor irruit super Abram, et ecce horror magnus et tenebrosus invasit eum. ¹³Dictumque est ad eum: «Scito praenoscens quod peregrinum futurum sit semen tuum in terra non sua, et subicient eos servituti et affligent quadringentis annis. ¹⁴Verumtamen et gentem, cui servituri sunt, ego iudicabo, et post haec egredientur cum magna sub-

come out with great possessions. [15]As for yourself, you shall go to   Lk 2:29
your fathers in peace; you shall be buried in a good old age. [16]And   1 Thess 2:16
they shall come back here in the fourth generation; for the iniquity
of the Amorites is not yet complete."
[17]When the sun had gone down and it was dark, behold, a   Jer 34:18
smoking firepot and a flaming torch passed between these pieces.   Gen 12:7;
[18]On that day the LORD made a covenant with Abram, saying, "To   17:8; 26:4
your descendants I give this land, from the river of Egypt to the   Neh 9:7–8
great river, the river Euphrates, [19]the land of the Kenites, the   Rev 9:14
Kenizzites, the Kadmonites, [20]the Hittites, the Perizzites, the   Num 24:21
Rephaim, [21]the Amorites, the Canaanites, the Girgashites and the   Deut 7:1
Jebusites."

Gen 25:12–18
The birth of Ishmael   Gal 4:22–26

16 [1]Now Sarai, Abram's wife, bore him no children. She had an   Acts 7:5
Egyptian maid whose name was Hagar; [2]and Sarai said

---

ness to be similarly cut in pieces if one were guilty of breaking the pact. The text makes the point that God (represented by the flaming torch: cf. Ex 3:2; 13:21; 19:18) *passes between* the bloody limbs of the victims, to ratify his promise.

This is how the book of Genesis portrays the people of Israel's right to the land of Canaan and explains how the land came to belong to it only in recent times, after the Exodus. During the ceremony Abraham is given advance information about the afflictions the people will suffer before the promise is fulfilled. An explanation is also given as to why God will take the land away from the Canaanites (here described as Amorites):

their evil-doing will have gone too far. God emerges here as the Lord of the earth and of nations. On the sojourn of the people of Israel in Egypt, cf. the note on 37:2—50:25.

16:1–6. Sarah, too, seems to be impatient about the delay in the fulfilment of the divine promise to give Abraham descendants. Therefore, she resorts to a custom of the time designed to increase the number of children. It was not strictly speaking polygamy but rather a means the lawful wife used in order to give her husband children. From what we know of Babylonian laws of the time, if the slave-girl became pregnant and then

---

stantia. [15]Tu autem ibis ad patres tuos in pace, sepultus in senectute bona. [16]Generatione autem quarta revertentur huc; necdum enim completae sunt iniquitates Amorraeorum usque ad praesens tempus». [17]Cum ergo occubuisset sol, facta est caligo tenebrosa, et apparuit clibanus fumans et lampas ignis transiens inter divisiones illas. [18]In illo die pepigit Dominus cum Abram foedus dicens: «Semini tuo dabo terram hanc a fluvio Aegypti usque ad magnum fluvium Euphraten, [19]Cinaeos et Cenezaeos, Cedmonaeos [20]et Hetthaeos et Pherezaeos, Raphaim quoque [21]et Amorraeos et Chananaeos et Gergesaeos et Iebusaeos». [1] Sarai autem uxor Abram non genuerat ei liberos; sed habens ancillam Aegyptiam nomine Agar, [2]dixit marito suo: «Ecce conclusit me Dominus, ne parerem; ingredere ad ancillam meam, si forte saltem ex illa suscipiam filios». Cumque ille acquiesceret deprecanti, [3]tulit Agar Aegyptiam ancillam suam post annos decem quam habitare coeperant in terra Chanaan, et dedit eam viro suo uxorem. [4]Qui ingressus est ad eam. At illa concepisse se videns despexit dominam suam. [5]Dixitque Sarai ad Abram: «Inique agis contra me; ego dedi ancillam meam in sinum tuum, quae

to Abram, "Behold now, the LORD has prevented me from bearing children; go in to my maid; it may be that I shall obtain children by her." And Abram hearkened to the voice of Sarai. ³So, after Abram had dwelt ten years in the land of Canaan, Sarai, Abram's wife, took Hagar the Egyptian, her maid, and gave her to Abram her husband as a wife. ⁴And he went in to Hagar, and she conceived;* and when she saw that she had conceived, she looked with contempt on her mistress. ⁵And Sarai said to Abram, "May the wrong done to me be on you! I gave my maid to your embrace, and when she saw that she had conceived, she looked on me with contempt. May the LORD judge between you and me!" ⁶But Abram said to Sarai, "Behold, your maid is in your power; do to her as you please." Then Sarai dealt harshly with her, and she fled from her.

⁷The angel of the LORD found her by a spring of water in the wilderness, the spring on the way to Shur. ⁸And he said, "Hagar, maid of Sarai, where have you come from and where are you going?" She said, "I am fleeing from my mistress Sarai." ⁹The angel of the LORD said to her, "Return to your mistress, and

Gen 21: 8–19

Ex 15:22

---

began to look down on her mistress, she could be punished and revert to being treated as a slave. That is what Hagar fears will happen, so she runs away.

The patriarchs follow the customs of their time; some of which (as in this case) were morally defective. In the light of the teaching of the Bible taken as a whole, we can see that behaviour of this sort was a consequence of man's original sin, and we can also see that God gradually led man back to a morality that was fully in keeping with human dignity as reflected in the Creation accounts. Consider, for example, what Jesus has to say on the subject of marriage (Mt 5:31–32). However, prior to that, God educates mankind bit by bit and to do so he tolerates imperfect customs and types of behaviour *in order to* lead mankind towards those higher goals. "The books of the Old Testament provide an

understanding of God and man and make clear to all men how a just and merciful God deals with mankind. These books, even though they contain matters imperfect and provisional, nevertheless show us authentic divine teaching" (*De Verbum*, 15).

16:7–16. This is the first appearance in the Bible of the "angel of the Lord"; here it means God himself coming out to meet man by making himself visible in some way. Also, the passage includes a tradition which explains the name of a place in the Negeb desert linked to stories about the patriarchs. According to 25:11 Beer-lahai-roi was where Isaac was based. Both this place-name (Lahai-roi in Hebrew sounds like "the living one who sees me") and Ishmael's name ("God heard") are given an etymological explanation.

---

videns quod conceperit, despectui me habet. Iudicet Dominus inter me et te». ⁶Cui respondens Abram: «Ecce, ait, ancilla tua in manu tua est; utere ea, ut libet». Affligente igitur eam Sarai, aufugit ab ea. ⁷Cumque invenisset illam angelus Domini iuxta fontem aquae in deserto, ad fontem in via Sur, ⁸dixit: «Agar, ancilla Sarai, unde venis et quo vadis?». Quae respondit: «A facie Sarai dominae meae ego

submit to her." ¹⁰The angel of the LORD also said to her, "I will so greatly multiply your descendants that they cannot be numbered for multitude." ¹¹And the angel of the LORD said to her, "Behold, you are with child, and shall bear a son; you shall call his name Ishmael;ᵗ because the LORD has given heed to your affliction. ¹²He shall be a wild ass of a man, his hand against every man and everyman's hand against him; and he shall dwell over against all his kinsmen." ¹³So she called the name of the LORD who spoke to her, "Thou art a God of seeing"; for she said, "Have I really seen God and remained alive after seeing him?"ᵘ ¹⁴Therefore the well was called Beer-lahai-roi;ᵛ it lies between Kadeshand Bered.

¹⁵And Hagar bore Abram a son; and Abram called the name of his son, whom Hagar bore, Ishmael. ¹⁶Abram was eighty-six years old when Hagar bore Ishmael to Abram.

Lk 1:31

Gen 24:62; 25:11

Gal 4:22

The renewal of the Covenant: Abram's name is changed

Gen 9:9; 15:1–21

17 ¹When Abram was ninety-nine years old the Lord appeared to Abram, and said to him, "I am God Al-

---

Ishmael is the ancestor of the desert Arabs who live on the fringes of cultivated lands. By stressing the link between Abraham and Ishmael the text wants to show the connexions (sometimes tense, yet always familial) between the Jews and these Arabs. The main thing the biblical account shows us is that God loves and protects this people too and he has compassion towards anyone who suffers—in this case, the Egyptian slave.

*17:1–27. If previously, in chapter 15, the text stressed the way the promise was

linked to God's covenant with Abraham, it now shows the duties it placed on the patriarchs and their descendants—to be holy, to acknowledge the one true God and to practise the rite of circumcision. The covenant, as we have seen, had its origin in an initiative on God's part, but it also commits man. In Abraham's case this commitment involves in accepting circumcision as a commandment from God to himself and his descendants.

17:1. "El-Shaddai" is the name the patriarchs often gave to God (cf. 28:3; 35:11; 43:14; 48:3; 49:25), because the name

---

fugio». ⁹Dixitque ei angelus Domini: «Revertere ad dominam tuam et humiliare sub manibus ipsius». ¹⁰Et dixit ei angelus Domini: «Multiplicans multiplicabo semen tuum, et non numerabitur prae multitudine». ¹¹Et dixit ei angelus Domini: «Ecce, concepisti et paries filium / vocabisque nomen eius Ismael, / eo quod audierit Dominus afflictionem tuam. / ¹²Hic erit homo onagro similis; / manus eius contra omnes, / et manus omnium contra eum; / et e regione universorum fratrum suorum figet tabernacula». ¹³Vocavit autem nomen Domini, qui loquebatur ad eam: «Tu Deus, qui vidisti me». Dixit enim: «Profecto hic vidi posteriora videntis me». ¹⁴Propterea appellatur puteus ille Lahairoi (*id est Viventis et Videntis me*); ipse est inter Cades et Barad. ¹⁵Peperitque Agar Abrae filium; qui vocavit nomen filii sui, quem pepererat Agar, Ismael. ¹⁶Octoginta et sex annorum erat Abram, quando peperit

---

t. That is *God hears* **u.** Cn: Heb *have I even here seen after him who sees me?* **v.** That is *the well of one who sees and lives*

mighty;[w] walk before me, and be blameless. [2]And I will make my covenant between me and you, and will multiply you exceedingly." [3]Then Abram fell on his face; and God said to him, [4]"Behold, my covenant is with you, and you shall be the father of a multitude of nations. [5]No longer shall your name be Abram,[x] but your name shall be Abraham;[y] for I have made you the father of a multitude of nations. [6]I will make you exceedingly fruitful; and I will make nations of you, and kings shall come forth from you. [7]And I will establish my covenant between me and you and your descendants after you throughout their generations for an everlasting covenant, to be God to you and to your descendants after you. [8]And I will give to you, and to your descendants after you, the land of your sojournings, all the land of Canaan, for an everlasting possession; and I will be their God."

Neh 9:7–8
Rom 4:17

Gen 12:7;
15:18; 26:4
Acts 7:5, 45
Gal 3:16

"Yahweh" had not yet been revealed (cf. Ex 3:13–14). Following the earliest Greek version (the Septuagint) it is usually translated as "God Almighty" (which is the RSV practice), although it could also mean "God of the mountains" or "God of abundance". By recording the names the patriarchs used when referring to God or invoking him, the Bible is, on the one hand, identifying the God the patriarchs worshipped with Yahweh, the God of the Sinai Covenant; and on the other hand, it is showing the way God reveals himself gradually over the course of time.

God asks Abraham to live in his presence and to be perfect. The two things are closely connected: "This is the only way to avoid falling," Clement of Alexandria points out; "being conscious that God is always at our side" (*Paeda-*

gogus, 3, 33, 3). This is the first time in the Bible that God tells a human being to be perfect, "blameless". This call, here addressed to Abraham, will be extended by Jesus to all mankind (cf. Mt 5:48).

17:5. Abraham is the first person in biblical history to have his name changed by God. By doing this God is conferring a new personality and a new mission, as can be seen from the meaning of his new name, "father of a multitude of nations". This name, therefore, is linked to the promise attached to the Covenant; from now on, the entire personality of the patriarch stems from the Covenant and is subservient to it. Abraham is the "father of the Covenant"; in the light of New Testament revelation St Paul will interpret this new name of Abraham as having a connexion with Gentiles converted to

---

ei Agar Ismaelem. [1]Postquam Abram nonaginta et novem annorum factus est, apparuit ei Dominus dixitque ad eum: «Ego Deus omnipotens, ambula coram me et esto perfectus. [2]Ponamque foedus meum inter me et te et multiplicabo te vehementer nimis». [3]Cecidit Abram pronus in faciem. [4]Dixitque ei Deus: «Ecce, pactum meum tecum. Erisque pater multarum gentium, [5]nec ultra vocabitur nomen tuum Abram, sed Abraham erit nomen tuum, quia patrem multarum gentium constitui te. [6]Faciamque te crescere vehementissime et ponam te in gentes; regesque ex te egredientur. [7]Et statuam pactum meum inter me et te et inter semen tuum post te in generationibus suis foedere sempiterno, ut sim Deus tuus

---

w. Heb *El Shaddai*   **x.** That is *exalted father*   **y.** Here taken to mean *father of a multitude*

The commandment of circumcision

⁹And God said to Abraham, "As for you, you shall keep my covenant, you and your descendants after you throughout their generations. ¹⁰This is my covenant, which you shall keep, between me and you and your descendants after you: Every male among you shall be circumcised. ¹¹You shall be circumcised in the flesh of your foreskins, and it shall be a sign of the covenant between me and you. ¹²He that is eight days old among you shall be circumcised; every male throughout your generations, whether born in your house, or bought with your money from any foreigner who is not of your offspring, ¹³both he that is born in your house and he that is bought with your money, shall be circumcised. So shall my covenant be in your flesh an everlasting covenant. ¹⁴Any uncircumcised male who is not circumcised in the flesh of his foreskin shall be cut off from his people; he has broken my covenant."

Jn 7:22
Rom 4:10–12
Acts 7:8
Gal 4:4; 5:6
Col 2:11–13

Lev 12:3
Lk 1:59

Acts 7:8

Christianity (cf. Rom 4:17). This name, "father of a multitude of nations" becomes, therefore, a prophetic announcement of the fact that the non-Jewish world will in due course become part of the people of the New Covenant, the Church.

17:10–14. Circumcision, which consists in a circular cutting of part of the foreskin, may originally have been a sexual and marriage initiation rite of a type widespread in the ancient Near East. Reasons of hygiene may have played a part in its use. The people of Israel regarded it as a divine commandment involved in the Covenant, and as a distinguishing mark to show membership of the people of God. It is easy to see why

Christian tradition regards circumcision as prefiguring Baptism. "Jesus' *circumcision*, on the eighth day after his birth (cf. Lk 2:21), is the sign of his incorporation into Abraham's descendants, into the people of the covenant. It is the sign of his submission to the Law (cf. Gal 4:4) and his deputation to Israel's worship, in which he will participate throughout his life. This sign prefigures that 'circumcision of Christ' which is Baptism (Col 2:11–13)" (*Catechism of the Catholic Church*, 527). In the new economy of salvation that sign would no longer serve any purpose: "For in Christ Jesus neither circumcision nor uncircumcision is of any avail, but faith working through love" (Gal 5:6).

---

et seminis tui post te. ⁸Daboque tibi et semini tuo post te terram peregrinationis tuae, omnem terram Chanaan in possessionem aeternam; eroque Deus eorum». ⁹Dixit iterum Deus ad Abraham: «Tu autem pactum meum custodies, et semen tuum post te in generationibus suis. ¹⁰Hoc est pactum meum, quod observabitis, inter me et vos et semen tuum post te. Circumcidetur ex vobis omne masculinum, ¹¹et circumcidetis carnem praeputii vestri, ut sit in signum foederis inter me et vos. ¹²Infans octo dierum circumcidetur in vobis: omne masculinum in generationibus vestris, tam vernaculus quam empticius ex omnibus alienigenis, quicumque non fuerit de stirpe vestra. ¹³Circumcidetur vernaculus et empticius, eritque pactum meum in carne vestra in foedus aeternum. ¹⁴Masculus, cuius praeputii caro circumcisa non fuerit, delebitur anima illa de populo suo; pactum meum irritum fecit». ¹⁵Dixit quoque Deus ad Abraham: «Sarai uxorem tuam non vocabis nomen eius Sarai, sed Sara erit nomen eius. ¹⁶Et benedicam

Gen 18:9–15
Heb 11:11–12 **Sarai's name is changed and Abraham is promised a son**

¹⁵And God said to Abraham, "As for Sarai your wife, you shall
Gal 4:23 not call her name Sarai, but Sarah shall be her name. ¹⁶I will
bless her, and moreover I will give you a son by her; I will bless
her, and she shall be a mother of nations; kings of peoples shall
Gen 18:12; 21:6–9
Lk 1:18 come from her." ¹⁷Then Abraham fell on his face and laughed,
Jn 8:56 and said to himself, "Shall a child be born to a man who is a
Rom 4:19 hundred years old? Shall Sarah, who is ninety years old, bear a
child?" ¹⁸And Abraham said to God, "O that Ishmael might live
Mt 1:21
Lk 1:13 in thy sight!" ¹⁹God said, "No, but Sarah your wife shall bear
Heb 11:11 you a son, and you shall call his name Isaac.ᶻ I will establish my
Gen 25:13–16 covenant with him as an everlasting covenant for his descendants
after him. ²⁰As for Ishmael, I have heard you; behold, I will bless
him and make him fruitful and multiply him exceedingly; he
shall be the father of twelve princes, and I will make him a great
nation. ²¹But I will establish my covenant with Isaac, whom
Sarah shall bear to you at this season next year."
²²When he had finished talking with him, God went up from
Abraham.

17:15–22. The carrying into effect of
God's plan (cf. the promise in chap. 15)
is going to exceed Abraham's expectations. True, he already does have a son,
Ishmael, by the slave-girl Hagar according to the customs of the time, that is, in
accord with human laws and recourses.
But it is not through this son that God is
going to keep his promise, but through a
son to be born of Sarah, and whose birth
will clearly reveal the power of God.

Sarah, Abraham's wife, is also going
to have a direct involvement in the way
the promise is fulfilled. And so she too is
going to be given a new name, to show
the new personality she acquires by shar-

ing directly in God's designs through her
motherhood. This is what Abraham is
now told.

Abraham's laugh (as also Sarah's in
the next chapter: cf. 18:12–14) conveys
the astonishment the announcement
causes (it seems unbelievable); it is also
connected with the name of the child
who will be born—Isaac (cf. the note on
21:1–7). However, Abraham keeps on
thinking in terms of the son he already
has, Ishmael. He too will be the recipient
of divine blessings; he will become the
father of a great nation, the Ishmaelites,
or Arabs. But the patriarch is now asked
for a new act of faith in God—despite the

---

ei; et ex illa quoque dabo tibi filium. Benedicturus sum eam, eritque in nationes; reges populorum ori-
entur ex ea». ¹⁷Cecidit Abraham in faciem suam et risit dicens in corde suo: «Putasne centenario nasce-
tur filius? Et Sara nonagenaria pariet?». ¹⁸Dixitque ad Deum: «Utinam Ismael vivat coram te». ¹⁹Et ait
Deus: «Sara uxor tua pariet tibi filium, vocabisque nomen eius Isaac; et constituam pactum meum illi
in foedus sempiternum et semini eius posteum. ²⁰Super Ismael quoque exaudivi te: ecce benedicam ei
et crescere faciam et multiplicabo eum vehementissime; duodecim duces generabit, et faciam illum in
gentem magnam. ²¹Pactum vero meum statuam ad Isaac, quem pariet tibi Sara tempore isto in anno
altero». ²²Cumque cessasset loqui cum eo, ascendit Deus ab Abraham. ²³Tulit ergo Abraham Ismael

z. That is *he laughs*

Circumcision

²³Then Abraham took Ishmael his son and all the slaves born in his house or bought with his money, every male among the men of Abraham's house, and he circumcised the flesh of their foreskins that very day, as God had said to him. ²⁴Abraham was ninety-nine years old when he was circumcised in the flesh of his foreskin. ²⁵And Ishmael his son was thirteen years old when he was circumcised in the flesh of his foreskin. ²⁶That very day Abraham and his son Ishmael were circumcised; ²⁷and all the men of his house, those born in the house and those bought with money from a foreigner, were circumcised with him.

The apparition of God at Mamre*

Heb 12:3

18 ¹And the LORD appeared to him by the oaksᵃ of Mamre, as he sat at the door of his tent in the heat of the day. ²He lifted

---

fact that they are both old, to expect Sarah to give birth to a son, who will be the protagonist in the Covenant, just like his father. God's actions, in effect, surpass man's expectations.

17:23–27. The promptness and exactness with which Abraham obeys God's commandment is an invitation addressed to the Israelites to practise circumcision and thereby feel involved in that Covenant. But at the same time Abraham's obedience is an example of faithfulness to God by readily fulfilling his commandments. "He who faithfully obeys," St Bernard says, "knows no delay, avoids leaving things for the morrow, does not know what postponement means, gives priority to what is commanded. He is always on the look-out, his ears open, his tongue ready to speak, his hands to work, his feet to be on the move. Everything is done to carry out the wishes of the person in charge" (*Sermones de diversis*, 41, 7).

*18:1—19:38. These two episodes—God's appearance to Abraham at Mamre and the destruction of Sodom—form a single account. Once again we can see the sort of relationship that obtains between God and Abraham; this time, what is emphasized is not just the promise of a son for Sarah, but also the patriarch's intercession on behalf of Sodom and Gomorrah. This intercession saves Lot and his family (cf. 19:29). Thus, Abraham is already a blessing for all the descendants of Lot. This narrative is quite colourful, and includes some curious little details—making it one of the most popular passages in the story of the patriarchs.

18:1–15. This new appearance of God to Abraham is somewhat mysterious: the

---

filium suum et omnes vernaculos domus suae universosque, quos emerat: cunctos mares ex omnibus viris domus suae; et circumcidit carnem praeputii eorum statim in ipsa die, sicut praeceperat ei Deus. ²⁴Abraham nonaginta novem erat annorum, quando circumcisus est in carne praeputii sui; ²⁵et Ismael filius eius tredecim annos impleverat tempore circumcisionis suae. ²⁶Eadem die circumcisus est Abraham et Ismael filius eius; ²⁷et omnes viri domus illius, tam vernaculi quam empticii ex alienigenis, circumcisi sunt cum eo. ¹Apparuit autem ei Dominus iuxta Quercus Mambre sedenti in ostio taber-

a. Or *terebinths*

up his eyes and looked, and behold, three men stood in front of him. When he saw them, he ran from the tent door to meet them, and bowed himself to the earth, ³and said, "My lord, if I have

Lk 7:44 found favour in your sight, do not pass by your servant. ⁴Let a little water be brought, and wash your feet, and rest yourselves under the tree, ⁵while I fetch a morsel of bread, that you may refresh yourselves, and after that you may pass on—since you have come

Mt 13:33 to your servant." So they said, "Do as you have said." ⁶And Abraham hastened into the tent to Sarah, and said, "Make ready quickly three measures^b of fine meal, knead it, and make cakes." ⁷And Abraham ran to the herd, and took a calf, tender and good, and gave it to the servant, who hastened to prepare it. ⁸Then he took curds, and milk, and the calf which he had prepared, and set it before them; and he stood by them under the tree while they ate.

---

three men stand for God. When Abraham speaks to them, sometimes he addresses them in the singular (as if there were only one person there: cf. v. 3), and sometimes in the plural (as if there were three: cf. v. 4). That is why some Fathers interpreted this appearance as an early announcement of the mystery of the Holy Trinity; others, following Jewish tradition (cf. Heb 13:2) take these personages to be angels. The sacred text says that one of the three men (Yahweh, apparently) stays with Abraham (cf. v. 22), while the other two, who are referred to as angels, go to Sodom (cf. 19:1). Although the early chapters of Genesis do not expressly talk about the creation of angels, that creation can be read into the word "heavens" in Genesis 1:1: "at the beginning of time, God created out of nothing both types of creatures, spiritual and corporeal, that is, angelic and earthly," says Lateran Council IV (*De fide catolica*). In Holy Scripture angels are mentioned as being servants and messengers of God, and, despite the way they are sometimes described, such as in this passage, they should be understood as being purely spiritual, personal and immortal creatures, endowed with intelligence and will. "Angels have been present since creation (cf. Job 38:7, where the angels are called 'sons of God') and throughout the history of salvation, announcing this salvation from afar or near and serving the accomplishment of the divine plan: they closed the earthly paradise (cf. Gen 3:24); protected Lot (cf. Gen 19); saved Hagar and her child (cf. Gen 21:17); stayed Abraham's hand (cf. Gen 22.11); communicated the law by their ministry (cf. Acts 7:53); led the people of God (cf. Ex 23:20–23); announced births (cf. Judg 13) and callings (cf. Judg 6:11–24; Is 6:6); and assisted the prophets (cf. 1 Kings 19:5), just to cite a few examples. Finally, the angel Gabriel announced the birth of the Precursor and that of Jesus himself (cf. Lk 1:11–26)" (*Catechism of the Catholic Church*, 332).

---

naculi sui in ipso fervore diei. ²Cumque elevasset oculos, apparuerunt ei tres viri stantes prope eum. Quo cum vidisset, cucurrit in occursum eorum de ostio tabernaculi et adoravit in terram ³et dixit: «Domine mi, si inveni gratiam in oculis tuis, ne transeas servum tuum; ⁴afferatur pauxillum aquae, et lavate pedes vestros et requiescite sub arbore. ⁵Ponamque buccellam panis, et confortate cor vestrum,

Isaac's birth is promised

Gen 15:2–4;
17:15–21; 21:1–7

⁹They said to him, "Where is Sarah your wife?" And he said, "She is in the tent." ¹⁰The LORD said, "I will surely return to you in the Rom 9:9 spring, and Sarah your wife shall have a son." And Sarah was listening at the tent door behind him. ¹¹Now Abraham and Sarah were Lk 1:7, 18 old, advanced in age; it had ceased to be with Sarah after the manner of women. ¹²So Sarah laughed to herself, saying, "After I have grown old, and my husband is old, shall I have pleasure?" ¹³The LORD said to Abraham, "Why did Sarah laugh, and say, 'Shall Mt 19:26 I indeed bear a child, now that I am old?' ¹⁴Is anything too hard^c for Mk 10:27 the LORD? At the appointed time I will return to you, in the spring, Lk 1:37
Rom 9:9 and Sarah shall have a son." ¹⁵But Sarah denied, saying, "I did not laugh"; for she was afraid. He said, "No, but you did laugh." Amos 3:7
Jn 15:15
Rom 3:5–6
Jas 6:16

Abraham intercedes for Sodom

¹⁶Then the men set out from there, and they looked toward Sodom; Acts 3:25 and Abraham went with them to set them on their way. ¹⁷The LORD Rom 4:13
Gal 3:8

In the general context of Genesis, this episode points up the new situation created by the Covenant. God speaks to Abraham directly, as he spoke to Adam before he committed sin. Abraham, for his part, receives God through his hospitality, and God again promises that Sarah will have a son (now specifying when the child will be born). "Because Abraham believed in God and walked in his presence and in covenant with him (cf. Gen 15:6; 17:1–2), the patriarch is ready to welcome a mysterious Guest into his tent. Abraham's remarkable hospitality at Mamre foreshadows the annunciation of the true Son of the promise (cf. Gen 18:1–15; Lk 1:26–38). After that, once God has confided his plan, Abraham's

heart is attuned to his Lord's compassion for men and he dares to intercede for them with bold confidence (cf. Gen 18:16–33)" (ibid., 2571).

18:6. The measure mentioned here, a *seah* (pl. *seim*) is a measure of dry grain (cf. 1 Sam 25:18; 2 Kings 7:1, 16, 18) which was probably a third of an ephah, that is, about seven litres or two gallons.

18:10. "In the spring"; this could also be translated as "next year". Literally, "the time of life", which some interpret as "the time of a woman's pregnancy", that is, nine months.

18:16–33. When interceding for Sodom

postea transibitis; idcirco enim declinastis ad servum vestrum». Qui dixerunt: «Fac ut locutus es». ⁶Festinavit Abraham in tabernaculum ad Saram dixitque: «Accelera, tria sata similae commisce et fac subcinericios panes». ⁷Ipse vero ad armentum cucurrit et tulit inde vitulum tenerrimum et optimum deditque puero; qui festinavit et coxit illum. ⁸Tulit quoque butyrum et lac et vitulum, quem coxerat, et posuit coram eis. Ipse vero stabat iuxta eos sub arbore; et comederunt. ⁹Dixeruntque ad eum: «Ubi est Sara uxor tua?». Ille respondit: «Ecce in tabernaculo est». ¹⁰Cui dixit: «Revertens veniam ad te tempore isto, et habebit filium Sara uxor tua». Quo audito, Sara risit ad ostium tabernaculi, quod erat post eum. ¹¹Erant autem ambo senes provectaeque aetatis, et desierant Sarae fieri muliebria. ¹²Quae risit

b. Heb *seim*   **c.** Or *wonderful*

said, "Shall I hide from Abraham what I am about to do, [18]seeing that Abraham shall become a great and mighty nation, and all the

Mt 22:16 nations of the earth shall bless themselves by him?[d] [19]No, for I have chosen[e] him, that he may charge his children and his household after him to keep the way of the LORD by doing righteousness and justice; so that the Lord may bring to Abraham what he has

Rev 18:5
Lk 17:28 promised him." [20]Then the LORD said, "Because the outcry against Sodom and Gomorrah is great and their sin is very grave, [21]I will go down to see whether they have done altogether according to the outcry which has come to me; and if not, I will know."

[22]So the men turned from there, and went toward Sodom; but Abraham still stood before the LORD. [23]Then Abraham drew near, and said, "Wilt thou indeed destroy the righteous with the wicked? [24]Suppose there are fifty righteous within the city; wilt thou then destroy the place and not spare it for the fifty righteous who are in it? [25]Far be it from thee to do such a thing, to slay the righteous with the wicked, so that the righteous fare as the wicked! Far be that from thee! Shall not the Judge of all the earth do right?" [26]And the LORD said, "If I find at Sodom fifty righteous in the city, I will spare the whole place for their sake." [27]Abraham answered, "Behold, I have taken upon myself to speak to the LORD, I who am

---

and Gomorrah, Abraham argues in terms of collective responsibility, as understood in ancient times in Israel: the entire people shared the same fate even though not all of them sinned, for the sin of some affected all. According to that way of looking at things, if there were enough just people in the city (Abraham did not dare go below ten) God would not have destroyed it. This way of thinking also shows how the salvation of many (even if they are sinners) can come through the faithfulness of a few, thereby preparing the way to see how the salvation of all mankind is brought about by the obedience of one man alone, Jesus Christ.

occulte dicens: «Postquam consenui, et dominus meus vetulus est, voluptas mihi erit?». [13]Dixit autem Dominus ad Abraham: «Quare risit Sara dicens: 'Num vere paritura sum anus?'. [14]Numquid Domino est quidquam difficile? Revertar ad te hoc eodem tempore, et habebit Sara filium». [15]Negavit Sara dicens: «Non risi», timore perterrita. Ille autem dixit: «Non; sed risisti». [16]Cum ergo surrexissent inde viri, direxerunt oculos contra Sodomam; et Abraham simul gradiebatur deducens eos. [17]Dixitque Dominus: «Num celare potero Abraham, quae gesturus sum, [18]cum futurus sit in gentem magnam ac robustissimam, et benedicendae sint in illo omnes nationes terrae? [19]Nam elegi eum, ut praecipiat filiis suis et domui suae post se, ut custodiant viam Domini et faciant iustitiam et iudicium, ut adducat Dominus super Abraham omnia, quae locutus est ad eum». [20]Dixit itaque Dominus: «Clamor contra Sodomam et Gomorram multiplicatus est, et peccatum eorum aggravatum est nimis. [21]Descendam et videbo utrum clamorem, qui venit ad me, opere compleverint an non; sciam». [22]Converteruntque se inde viri et abierunt Sodomam; Abraham vero adhuc stabat coram Domino. [23]Et appropinquans ait: «Numquid vere perdes iustum cum impio? [24]Si forte fuerint quinquaginta iusti in civitate, vere perdes et non parces loco illi propter quinquaginta iustos, si fuerint in eo? [25]Absit a te, ut rem hanc facias et

d. Or *in him all the nations of the earth shall be blessed*   **e.** Heb *known*

but dust and ashes. [28]Suppose five of the fifty righteous are lacking? Wilt thou destroy the whole city for lack of five?" And he said, "I will not destroy it if I find forty-five there." [29]Again he spoke to him, and said, "Suppose forty are found there." He answered, "For the sake of forty I will not do it." [30]Then he said, "Oh let not the LORD be angry, and I will speak. Suppose thirty are found there." He answered, "I will not do it, if I find thirty there." [31]He said, "Behold, I have taken upon myself to speak to the LORD. Suppose twenty are found there." He answered, "For the sake of twenty I will not destroy it." [32]Then he said, "Oh let not the LORD be angry, and I will speak again but this once. Suppose ten are found there." He answered, "For the sake of ten I will not destroy it." [33]And the LORD went his way, when he had finished speaking to Abraham; and Abraham returned to his place.

Jer 5:1
Ezek 22:30

The sin of the inhabitants of Sodom*

19 [1]*The two angels came to Sodom in the evening; and Lot was sitting in the gate of Sodom. When Lot saw them, he rose to meet them, and bowed himself with his face to the earth, [2]and said, "My lords, turn aside, I pray you, to your servant's house and spend the night, and wash your feet; then you may rise up early and go on your way." They said, "No; we will spend the

Heb 13:2

The final outcome of this episode shows that, even though he destroys these cities, God saves the righteous who live in them. God does not punish the just man along with the sinner (as Abraham thought); a person is allowed to perish or is saved depending on his personal behaviour. This truth, which is to be found in the Bible from the start, will be given special emphasis in the teaching of the prophets, particularly Jeremiah and Ezekiel (cf. Jer 31:29–30; Ezek 18), who stress individual and personal responsibility before God.

*19:1–38. The fate of Lot, who, having separated from Abraham, settles down in a city of sinful people, is in contrast with that of Abraham, who continues to live a nomadic life and pitches his tent in

occidas iustum cum impio, fiatque iustus sicut impius; absit a te. Nonne iudex universae terrae faciet iudicium?». [26]Dixitque Dominus: «Si invenero Sodomae quinquaginta iustos in medio civitatis, dimittam omni loco propter eos». [27]Respondensque Abraham ait: «Ecce coepi loqui ad Dominum meum, cum sim pulvis et cinis. [28]Quid, si forte minus quinquaginta iustis quinque fuerint? Delebis propter quinque universam urbem?». Et ait: «Non delebo, si invenero ibi quadraginta quinque». [29]Rursumque locutus est ad eum: «Si forte inventi fuerint ibi quadraginta?». Ait: «Non percutiam propter quadraginta». [30]«Ne quaeso, inquit, indignetur Dominus meus, si loquar. Si forte ibi inventi fuerint triginta?». Respondit: «Non faciam, si invenero ibi triginta». [31]«Ecce, ait, coepi loqui ad Dominum meum. Si forte inventi fuerint ibi viginti?». Dixit: «Non interficiam propter viginti». [32]«Obsecro, inquit, ne irascatur Dominus meus, si loquar adhuc semel. Si forte inventi fuerint ibi decem?». Dixit: «Non delebo propter decem». [33]Abiit Dominus, postquam cessavit loqui ad Abraham; et ille reversus est in locum suum. [1]Veneruntque duo angeli Sodomam vespere, sedente Lot in foribus civitatis. Qui cum vidisset eos, surrexit et ivit obviam eis adoravitque pronus in terram [2]et dixit: «Obsecro, domini mei, declinate in

night in the street." ³But he urged them strongly; so they turned aside to him and entered his house; and he made them a feast, and baked unleavened bread, and they ate. ⁴But before they lay down, the men of the city, the men of Sodom, both young and old, all the people to the last man, surrounded the house; ⁵and they called to Lot, "Where are the men who came to you tonight? Bring them out to us, that we may know them." ⁶Lot went out of the door to the men, shut the door after him, ⁷and said, "I beg you, my brothers, do not act so wickedly. ⁸Behold, I have two daughters who have not known man; let me bring them out to you, and do to them as you please; only do nothing to these men, for they have come under the shelter of my roof." ⁹But they said, "Stand back!" And they said, "This fellow came to sojourn, and he would play the judge! Now we will deal worse with you than with them." Then they pressed hard against the man Lot, and drew near to break the door. ¹⁰But the men put forth their hands and brought Lot into the house to them, and shut the door. ¹¹And they struck with blindness the men who were at the door of the house, both small and great, so that they wearied themselves groping for the door.

Judg 19:22–23
Jude 7
Lev 20:13
Rom 1:26–27
1 Cor 6:9
1 Tim 1:10

2 Pet 2:7

2 Kings 6:18

Mamre. Lot is the victim of his own decision to go and live in a fertile area, yet one which turns out to be populated by wicked men (cf. 13:10–13). Lot acts like a just man; he is hospitable, as Abraham was (cf. 18:1–8); but, due to the wickedness of the local inhabitants he is going to find himself in a tragic situation, from which he is saved thanks to the Lord's compassion and Abraham's intercession (cf. v. 29).

19:4–5. This biblical account has led to homosexual relationships being referred to as "sodomy". The gravity of this sin is underlined here and it is compounded, in this case, by the fact that it does violence to the right of asylum which Lot's hospitality included. In Holy Scripture sins of homosexuality are portrayed as being very depraved: the Law of Moses punished them with death (cf. Lev 20:13), and, in the New Testament, they are seen as the height of depravity when men do not want to live according to the law of God (cf. Rom 1:26–27; 1 Cor 6:9; 1 Tim 1:10).

domum pueri vestri et pernoctate; lavate pedes vestros et mane proficiscemini in viam vestram». Qui dixerunt: «Minime, sed in platea pernoctabimus». ³Compulit illos oppido, et diverterunt ad eum. Ingressisque domum illius fecit convivium et coxit azyma, et comederunt. ⁴Prius autem quam irent cubitum, viri civitatis, viri Sodomae, vallaverunt domum a iuvene usque ad senem, omnis populus simul. ⁵Vocaveruntque Lot et dixerunt ei: «Ubi sunt viri, qui introierunt ad te nocte? Educ illos ad nos, ut cognoscamus eos». ⁶Egressus ad eos Lot post tergum occludens ostium ait: ⁷«Nolite, quaeso, fratres mei, nolite malum hoc facere. ⁸Ecce, habeo duas filias, quae necdum cognoverunt virum; educam eas ad vos, et facite eis sicut placuerit vobis, dummodo viris istis nihil faciatis ideo enim ingressi sunt sub umbra tecti mei». ⁹At illi dixerunt: «Recede illuc». Et rursus: «Unus ingressus est, inquiunt, ut advena et vult iudicare? Te ergo ipsum magis quam hos affligemus». Vimque faciebant Lot vehementissime, iamque prope erat, ut effringerent fores. ¹⁰Et ecce miserunt manum viri et introduxerunt ad se Lot clauseruntque ostium; ¹¹et eos, qui foris erant, percusserunt caecitate a minimo usque ad maximum, ita

[12]Then the men said to Lot, "Have you any one else here? Jude 7
Sons-in-law, sons, daughters, or any one you have in the city,
bring them out of the place; [13]for we are about to destroy this
place, because the outcry against its people has become great
before the LORD, and the LORD has sent us to destroy it." [14]So Lot
went out and said to his sons-in-law, who were to marry his
daughters, "Up, get out of this place; for the Lord is about to
destroy the city." But he seemed to his sons-in-law to be jesting.

The flight of Lot and his family

[15]When morning dawned, the angels urged Lot, saying, "Arise, Lk 17:29
take your wife and your two daughters who are here, lest you be
consumed in the punishment of the city." [16]But he lingered; so the 2 Pet 2:7
men seized him and his wife and his two daughters by the hand,
the LORD being merciful to him, and they brought him forth and
set him outside the city. [17]And when they had brought them forth, Mt 24:15ff
Lk 9:62; 17:31
they[f] said, "Flee for your life; do not look back or stop anywhere
in the valley; flee to the hills, lest you be consumed." [18]And Lot
said to them, "Oh, no, my lords; [19]behold, your servant has found Lk 1:58
favour in your sight, and you have shown me great kindness in

---

Basing itself on Holy Scripture, Tradition has always declared that "homosexual acts are intrinsically evil" (Congregation for the Doctrine of the Faith, *Persona humana*, 8). "They are contrary to the natural law. They close the sexual act to the gift of life. They do not proceed from a genuine affective and sexual complementarity. Under no circumstances can they be approved" (*Catechism of the Catholic Church*, 2357).

In our own time, the *Catechism of the Catholic Church* also teaches, "the num-ber of men and women who have deep-seated homosexual tendencies is not negligible. This inclination, which is objectively disordered, constitutes for most of them a trial. They must be accepted with respect, compassion and sensitivity. Every sign of unjust discrimination in their regard should be avoided. These persons are called to fulfil God's will in their lives and, if they are Christians, to unite to the sacrifice of the Lord's Cross the difficulties they may encounter from their condition" (no. 2358).

---

ut ostium invenire non possent. [12]Dixerunt autem viri ad Lot: «Habes hic quempiam tuorum? Generum et filios et filias et omnes, qui tui sunt in urbe, educ de loco hoc: [13]delebimus enim locum istum, eo quod increverit clamor contra eos coram Domino, qui misit nos, ut perdamus eam». [14]Egressus itaque Lot locutus est ad generos suos, qui accepturi erant filias eius, et dixit: «Surgite, egredimini de loco isto, quia delebit Dominus civitatem». Et visus est eis quasi ludens loqui. [15]Cumque esset mane, cogebant eum angeli dicentes: «Surge, tolle uxorem tuam et duas filias, quas habes hic, ne pereas in scelere civitatis». [16]Tardante illo, apprehenderunt viri manum eius et manum uxoris ac duarum filiarum eius, eo quod parceret Dominus illi. [17]Et eduxerunt eum posueruntque extra civitatem. Ibi locutus est: «Salvare, agitur de vita tua; noli respicere post tergum, nec stes in omni circa regione; sed in monte salvum te fac, ne pereas». [18]Dixitque Lot ad eos: «Non, quaeso, Domine. [19]Ecce invenit servus tuus

f. Gk Syr Vg: Heb *he*

saving my life; but I cannot flee to the hills, lest the disaster over-take me, and I die. [20]Behold, yonder city is near enough to flee to, and it is a little one. Let me escape there—is it not a little one?— and my life will be saved!" [21]He said to him, "Behold, I grant you this favour also, that I will not overthrow the city of which you have spoken. [22]Make haste, escape there; for I can do nothing till you arrive there." Therefore the name of the city was called Zoar.[g]

The destruction of Sodom and Gomorrah

[23]The sun had risen on the earth when Lot came to Zoar. [24]Then the LORD rained on Sodom and Gomorrah brimstone and fire from the LORD out of heaven; [25]and he overthrew those cities, and all the valley, and all the inhabitants of the cities, and what grew on the ground. [26]But Lot's wife behind him looked back, and she became a pillar of salt. [27]And Abraham went early in the morning to the place where he had stood before the LORD;

Deut 29:22
Is 1:9
Amos 4:11
Mt 11:23–24

Mt 10:15
Lk 17:29
2 Pet 2:6
Rev 14:10–11
Wis 10:7
Lk 9:62; 17:32

19:24 The ruins of Sodom and Gomorrah probably lie under the waters of the Dead Sea, to the south. The biblical account interprets the disappearance of these cities as being the result of some terrible cataclysm, which God sent as a punishment for the sins of their inhabitants.

Throughout the Bible one meets many references to the dramatic destruction of these two cities and the land round about (now desolate) as an instance of the rigour of divine punishment (cf. Deut 29:22; Is 13–19; Jer 49:18; etc.) from which Israel is preserved in spite of its sins, thanks to the faithfulness of a small remnant (cf. Is 1:9) and from which righteous men are also preserved (cf. Wis 10:6–7). Our Lord Jesus Christ compares the punishment inflicted on Sodom and Gomorrah to that which will come on the day of

Judgment and which will be even greater (cf. Mt 10:15; 11:23–24), and he invites us to bear that cataclysm in mind, so as always to be on the watch (cf. Lk 17:28–30).

As happened at the time of the flood from which Noah was saved (cf. Gen 6:8–12), God "by turning the cities of Sodom and Gomorrah to ashes condemned them to extinction and made of them an example to those who were to be ungodly; and if he rescued righteous Lot, greatly distressed by the licentiousness of the wicked (for by what that righteous man saw and heard as he lived among them, he was vexed in his righteous soul day after day with their lawless deeds), then the Lord knows how to rescue the godly from trial, and to keep the unrighteous under punishment until the day of judgment, and especially those who

---

gratiam coram te, et magnificasti misericordiam tuam, quam fecisti mecum, ut salvares animam meam; nec possum in monte salvari, ne forte apprehendat me malum et moriar. [20]Ecce, civitas haec iuxta, ad quam possum fugere, parva, et salvabor in ea—numquid non modica est?—et vivet anima mea». [21]Dixitque ad eum: «Ecce, etiam in hoc suscepi preces tuas, ut non subvertam urbem, pro qua locutus es. [22]Festina et salvare ibi, quia non potero facere quidquam, donec ingrediaris illuc». Idcirco vocatum

g. That is *Little*

²⁸and he looked down toward Sodom and Gomorrah and toward all the land of the valley, and beheld, and lo, the smoke of the land went up like the smoke of a furnace. ²⁹So it was that, when God destroyed the cities of the valley, God remembered Abraham, and sent Lot out of the midst of the overthrow, when he overthrew the cities in which Lot dwelt.

Is 34:9–10
Rev 9:2;
14:10–11

2 Pet 2:7

The children of Lot: the origin of the Moabites and Ammonites
³⁰Now Lot went up out of Zoar, and dwelt in the hills with his two daughters, for he was afraid to dwell in Zoar; so he dwelt in a cave with his two daughters. ³¹And the first-born said to the younger, "Our father is old, and there is not a man on earth to come in to us after the manner of all the earth. ³²Come, let us make our father drink wine, and we will lie with him, that we may preserve offspring through our father." ³³So they made their father drink wine that night; and the first-born went in, and lay with her father; he did not know when she lay down or when she arose.

---

indulge in the lust of defiling passion and despise authority" (2 Pet 2:6–10).

19:26. The story of Lot's wife is a warning not to turn back once one has set out on one's way. Our Lord reminds us about it, applying it to the fact that we cannot foresee the day of Judgment (cf. Lk 17:32). Christian tradition has applied it to the need to persevere in one's good resolutions. Here is what one ancient writer says: "Lot's wife, who was turned into a pillar of salt, is an example to the simple, that they should not look back with sick curiosity when they are advancing to a holy resolution" (Quodvultdeus, *De promissionibus*, 1). And, applying the same image to the Christian vocation, St Josemaría Escrivá exhorts: "You have

seen very clearly that you are a child of God. Even if you were never again to see it—it won't happen!—you should continue along your way forever, out of a sense of faithfulness, without ever looking back" (*The Forge*, 420).

19:30–38. Moab and Ammon were two of Israel's neighbours, on the eastern bank of the Jordan (cf. Num 21:11, 24). In this short account the sacred writer's intention may have been to show the superiority of the people of Israel, a people created by a very special divine plan, over the other peoples of the region. The Moabites and the Ammonites are portrayed as something inferior on account of their incestuous origin.

est nomen urbis illius Segor. ²³Sol egressus est super terram, et Lot ingressus est Segor. ²⁴Igitur Dominus pluit super Sodomam et Gomorram sulphur et ignem a Domino de caelo ²⁵et subvertit civitates has et omnem circa regionem, universos habitatores urbium et cuncta terrae virentia. ²⁶Respiciensque uxor eius post se versa est in statuam salis. ²⁷Abraham autem consurgens mane venit ad locum, ubi steterat prius cum Domino, ²⁸intuitus est Sodomam et Gomorram et universam terram regionis illius; viditque ascendentem favillam de terra quasi fornacis fumum. ²⁹Cum enim subverteret Deus civitates regionis illius, recordatus Abrahae liberavit Lot de subversione urbium, in quibus habitaverat. ³⁰Ascenditque Lot de Segor et mansit in monte, duae quoque filiae eius cum eo; timuerat enim manere in Segor. Et mansit in spelunca ipse et duae filiae eius. ³¹Dixitque maior ad minorem: «Pater noster senex est, et nullus virorum remansit in terra, qui possit ingredi ad nos iuxta morem uni-

³⁴And on the next day, the first-born said to the younger, "Behold, I lay last night with my father; let us make him drink wine tonight also; then you go in and lie with him, that we may preserve offspring through our father." ³⁵So they made their father drink wine that night also; and the younger arose, and lay with him; and he did not know when she lay down or when she arose. ³⁶Thus both the daughters of Lot were with child by their father. ³⁷The first-born bore a son, and called his name Moab; he is the father of the Moabites to this day. ³⁸The younger also bore a son, and called his name Ben-ammi; he is the father of the Ammonites to this day.

Gen 12:10–20;
26:1–11   **Abraham and Sarah in Gerar: the meeting with Abimelech**

20 ¹From there Abraham journeyed toward the territory of the Negeb, and dwelt between Kadesh and Shur; and he sojourned in Gerar. ²And Abraham said of Sarah his wife, "She is my sister." And Abimelech king of Gerar sent and took Sarah. ³But God came to Abimelech in a dream by night, and said to him, "Behold, you are a dead man, because of the woman whom you have taken; for she is a man's wife." ⁴Now Abimelech had not approached her; so he said, "Lord, wilt thou slay an innocent

Mt 5:8   people? ⁵Did he not himself say to me, 'She is my sister'? And she herself said, 'He is my brother.' In the integrity of my heart and the innocence of my hands I have done this." ⁶Then God said to him in the dream, "Yes, I know that you have done this in the integrity of your heart, and it was I who kept you from sinning

---

20:1–18. In keeping with the movements of a semi-nomadic tribe, Abraham travels as far as Gerar, which is in the northern part of the Negeb desert. Concerning this journey, the biblical text recalls an episode similar to that narrated in chapter 12, but with some variants: for one thing, the patriarch's behaviour is justified by pointing out that Sarah really was his sister through his father (cf. v. 12); for another,

versae terrae. ³²Veni, inebriemus patrem nostrum vino dormiamusque cum eo, ut servare possimus ex patre nostro semen». ³³Dederunt itaque patri suo bibere vinum nocte illa, et ingressa est maior dormivitque cum patre; at ille non sensit, nec quando accubuit filia, nec quando surrexit. ³⁴Altera quoque die dixit maior ad minorem: «Ecce, dormivi heri cum patre meo; demus ei bibere vinum etiam hac nocte, et ingressa dormies cum eo, ut salvemus semen de patre nostro». ³⁵Dederunt et illa nocte patri suo bibere vinum, ingressaque minor filia dormivit cum eo; et ne tunc quidem sensit, quando illa concubuerit vel quando surrexerit. ³⁶Conceperunt ergo duae filiae Lot de patre suo. ³⁷Peperitque maior filium et vocavit nomen eius Moab; ipse est pater Moabitarum usque in praesentem diem. ³⁸Minor quoque peperit filium et vocavit nomen eius Benammi (*id est Filius populi mei*); ipse est pater Ammonitarum usque hodie. ¹Profectus inde Abraham in terram Nageb, habitavit inter Cades et Sur et peregrinatus est in Geraris. ²Dixitque de Sara uxore sua: «Soror mea est». Misit ergo Abimelech rex Gerarae et tulit eam. ³Venit autem Deus ad Abimelech per somnium nocte et ait illi: «En morieris propter mulierem, quam tulisti; habet enim virum». ⁴Abimelech vero non tetigerat eam. Et ait: «Domine, num gentem etiam iustam interficies? ⁵Nonne ipse dixit mihi: 'Soror mea est', et ipsa quoque ait: 'Frater meus est'? In simplicitate cordis mei et munditia manuum mearum feci hoc».

against me; therefore I did not let you touch her. ⁷Now then restore the man's wife; for he is a prophet, and he will pray for you, and you shall live. But if you do not restore her, know that you shall surely die, you, and all that are yours."

⁸So Abimelech rose early in the morning, and called all his servants, and told them all these things; and the men were very much afraid. ⁹Then Abimelech called Abraham, and said to him, "What have you done to us? And how have I sinned against you, that you have brought on me and my kingdom a great sin? You have done to me things that ought not to be done." ¹⁰And Abimelech said to Abraham, "What were you thinking of, that you did this thing?" ¹¹Abraham said, "I did it because I thought, There is no fear of God at all in this place, and they will kill me because of my wife. ¹²Besides she is indeed my sister, the daughter of my father but not the daughter of my mother; and she became my wife. ¹³And when God caused me to wander from my father's house, I said to her, 'This is the kindness you must do me: at every place to which we come, say of me, He is my brother.'" ¹⁴Then Abimelech took sheep and oxen, and male and female slaves, and gave them to Abraham, and restored Sarah his wife to him. ¹⁵And Abimelech said, "Behold, my land is before you; dwell where it pleases you." ¹⁶To Sarah he said, "Behold, I have given your brother a thousand pieces of silver; it is your vindication in the eyes of all who are with you; and before every one you are righted." ¹⁷Then Abraham prayed to God; and God healed

we again see the power of Abraham's intercession (cf. v. 7), and how God's providence protects Abimelech from committing a great sin even though he acted in good faith. The account as a whole shows how God protects Abraham's marriage when his wife is in danger of being taken from him. Once again divine intervention makes it possible for Abraham and Sarah to have a child.

⁶Dixitque ad eum Deus per somnium: «Et ego scio quod simplici corde feceris; et ideo custodivi te, ne peccares in me, et non dimisi, ut tangeres eam. ⁷Nunc igitur redde viro suo uxorem, quia propheta est; et orabit pro te, et vives. Si autem nolueris reddere, scito quod morte morieris tu et omnia, quae tua sunt». ⁸Statimque de nocte consurgens Abimelech vocavit omnes servos suos et locutus est universa verba haec in auribus eorum; timueruntque viri valde. ⁹Vocavit autem Abimelech etiam Abraham et dixit ei: «Quid fecisti nobis? Quid peccavi in te, quia induxisti super me et super regnum meum peccatum grande? Quae non debuisti facere, fecisti mihi». ¹⁰Rursusque ait: «Quid vidisti, ut hoc faceres?». ¹¹Respondit Abraham: «Cogitavi mecum: Certe non est timor Dei in loco isto, et interficient me propter uxorem meam. ¹²Alias autem et vere soror mea est, filia patris mei et non filia matris meae, et duxi eam in uxorem. ¹³Cum autem vagari me faceret Deus de domo patris mei, dixi ad eam: Hanc misericordiam facies mecum: in omni loco, ad quem ingrediemur, dices quod frater tuus sim». ¹⁴Tulit igitur Abimelech oves et boves et servos et ancillas et dedit Abraham; reddiditque illi Saram uxorem suam ¹⁵et ait: «Ecce terra mea coram te; ubicumque tibi placuerit, habita». ¹⁶Sarae autem dixit: «Ecce mille argenteos dedi fratri tuo; ecce hoc erit tibi in velamen oculorum ad omnes, qui tecum sunt, et apud omnes iustificaberis». ¹⁷Orante autem Abraham, sanavit Deus Abimelech et uxorem ancillasque eius et pepererunt;

Abimelech, and also healed his wife and female slaves so that they bore children. [18]For the LORD had closed all the wombs of the house of Abimelech because of Sarah, Abraham's wife.

The birth and circumcision of Isaac

Lk 3:34
Gal 4:22
Heb 11:11

21 [1]The LORD visited Sarah as he had said, and the LORD did to Sarah as he had promised. [2]And Sarah conceived, and bore Abraham a son in his old age at the time of which God had spoken to him. [3]Abraham called the name of his son who was born to him, whom Sarah bore him, Isaac. [4]And Abraham cir-

Acts 7:8

cumcised his son Isaac when he was eight days old, as God had

Gen 17:17

commanded him. [5]Abraham was a hundred years old when his son Isaac was born to him. [6]And Sarah said, "God has made laughter for me; every one who hears will laugh over me." [7]And she said, "Who would have said to Abraham that Sarah would suckle children? Yet I have borne him a son in his old age."

Gen 16:6–14
Jn 8:31–37
Gal 4:22–31

Hagar and Ismael are sent away

[8]And the child grew, and was weaned; and Abraham made a great feast on the day that Isaac was weaned. [9]But Sarah saw the son of

---

21:1–7. The promise recounted in 15:18 and 17:19–21 now begins to be fulfilled. The patriarch's age serves to show the special intervention by God in the birth of Isaac; as does the etymological explanation of the child's name, "she began to laugh", which is now interpreted as "God has made laughter for me", that is, has made me happy (cf. 18:15). And Abraham's obedience is very clear: he strictly fulfils the commandment of circumcision.

This is perhaps the most joyful moment in the patriarch's life: up to now it has been very much marked by trials and tribulations. With the birth of Isaac Abraham's trust in God grows, as can be seen now by his prompt obedience to his Law. The

Lord is strengthening the patriarch for the final test which he will make him undergo later. This event in Abraham's life helps us to see that in moments of darkness in the course of our life we need to put our trust in God: "The time has come to cry to him, Remember, Lord, the promises you made, filling me with hope; they console me in my nothingness and fill my life with strength (Ps 119:49–50). Our Lord wants us to rely on him for everything: it is now glaringly evident to us that without him we can do nothing (cf. Jn 15:5), whereas with him we can do all things (cf. Phil 4:13). We confirm our decision to walk always in his presence (cf. Ps 119:168)" (St J. Escrivá, *Friends of God*, 305).

---

[18]concluserat enim Dominus omnem vulvam domus Abimelech propter Saram uxorem Abraham. [1]Visitavit autem Dominus Saram, sicut promiserat, et implevit Sarae, quae locutus est; [2]concepitque et peperit Abrahae filium in senectute eius tempore, quo praedixerat ei Deus. [3]Vocavitque Abraham nomen filii sui, quem genuit ei Sara, Isaac [4]et circumcidit eum octavo die, sicut praeceperat ei Deus. [5]Cum Abraham centum esset annorum, natus est ei Isaac filius eius. [6]Dixitque Sara: «Risum fecit mihi Deus; / quicumque audierit, corridebit mihi». [7]Rursumque ait: «Quis auditurum crederet Abraham / quod Sara lactaret filios, / quia peperit ei filium / iam seni?». [8]Crevit igitur puer et ablactatus est.

Hagar the Egyptian, whom she had borne to Abraham, playing
with her son Isaac.[h] [10]So she said to Abraham, "Cast out this slave *Gal 4:30*
woman with her son; for the son of this slave woman shall not be
heir with my son Isaac." [11]And the thing was very displeasing to
Abraham on account of his son. [12]But God said to Abraham, "Be *Rom 9:7*
not displeased because of the lad and because of your slave *Heb 11:18*
woman; whatever Sarah says to you, do as she tells you, for
through Isaac shall your descendants be named. [13]And I will make
a nation of the son of the slave woman also, because he is your
offspring." [14]So Abraham rose early in the morning, and took
bread and a skin of water, and gave it to Hagar, putting it on her
shoulder, along with the child, and sent her away. And she
departed, and wandered in the wilderness of Beer-sheba.

[15]When the water in the skin was gone, she cast the child
under one of the bushes. [16]Then she went, and sat down over
against him a good way off, about the distance of a bowshot; for
she said, "Let me not look upon the death of the child." And as
she sat over against him, the child lifted up his voice[i] and wept.
[17]And God heard the voice of the lad; and the angel of God called *Gen 16:7*
to Hagar from heaven, and said to her, "What troubles you, *Jn 12:29*

21:8–21. This second expulsion of Hagar
and Ishmael from the house of Abraham
completes the story given in chapter 16.
We now see the reason for it, given that
expulsion went against the established
law. Sarah's attitude was a decisive factor
in ensuring that Isaac alone would be
Abraham's heir. Acting against the succession laws of the time, Sarah seconds
God's plan to have Abraham's true descent come through Isaac, the son according to the promise, and not through
Ishmael, his son according to nature

alone. In this way the role of woman is
highlighted, particularly the role of
mother, in the fulfilment of the divine
designs. For St Paul, Hagar and Sarah
and the circumstances surrounding them
are a type of the two Covenants (cf. Gal
4:21–31)—the first, that of Mount Sinai,
represented by the slave-girl Hagar who
gives birth according to the flesh; the
second, referring to the new Covenant in
Christ, represented by Sarah, the free
wife, who gives birth according to the
promise. Writing to the Christians of

Fecitque Abraham grande convivium in die ablactationis eius. [9]Cumque vidisset Sara filium Agar
Aegyptiae iocantem cum Isaac filio suo, dixit ad Abraham: [10]«Eice ancillam hanc et filium eius; non
enim erit heres filius ancillae cum filio meo Isaac». [11]Dure accepit hoc Abraham propter filium suum.
[12]Cui dixit Deus: «Non tibi videatur asperum super puero et super ancilla tua; omnia, quae dixerit tibi
Sara, audi vocem eius, quia in Isaac vocabitur tibi semen. [13]Sed et filium ancillae faciam in gentem
magnam, quia semen tuum est». [14]Surrexit itaque Abraham mane et tollens panem et utrem aquae
imposuit scapulae eius tradiditque puerum et dimisit eam. Quae, cum abisset, errabat in deserto
Bersabee. [15]Cumque consumpta esset aqua in utre, abiecit puerum subter unum arbustum [16]et abiit; se-
ditque e regione procul, quantum potest arcus iacere. Dixit enim: «Non videbo morientem puerum».
Et sedens contra levavit vocem suam et flevit. [17]Exaudivit autem Deus vocem pueri; vocavitque angelus

h. Gk Vg: Heb lacks *with her son Isaac* **i.** Gk: Heb *she lifted up her voice*

Hagar? Fear not; for God has heard the voice of the lad where he is. ¹⁸Arise, lift up the lad, and hold him fast with your hand; for I will make him a great nation." ¹⁹Then God opened her eyes, and she saw a well of water; and she went, and filled the skin with water, and gave the lad a drink. ²⁰And God was with the lad, and he grew up; he lived in the wilderness, and became an expert with the bow. ²¹He lived in the wilderness of Paran; and his mother took a wife for him from the land of Egypt.

Jn 4:11

Gen 26:15–33

Abraham and Abimelech make a pact
²²At that time Abimelech and Phicol the commander of his army said to Abraham, "God is with you in all that you do; ²³now therefore swear to me here by God that you will not deal falsely with me or with my offspring or with my posterity, but as I have dealt loyally with you, you will deal with me and with the land where you have sojourned." ²⁴And Abraham said, "I will swear."

²⁵When Abraham complained to Abimelech about a well of water which Abimelech's servants had seized, ²⁶Abimelech said, "I do not know who has done this thing; you did not tell me, and

---

Galatia, and in the light of this typology, St Paul exclaims: "So, brethren, we are not children of the slave but of the free woman" (Gal 4:31).

The scene of Hagar in the wilderness is itself an example of the mercy of God for, as St John Chrysostom teaches, "whenever God wishes, even if we are utterly alone, even if we are in desperate trouble, even if we have no hope of survival, we need no other assistance, since God's grace is all we require. You see, if we win favour from him, no one will get the better of us, but rather we will prevail against anyone" (*Homiliae in Genesim*, 46, 2).

21:22–33. This episode describes a dispute over rights to a watering-hole—typical of the sort of clash which can happen between desert shepherds. The name of the place, Beer-sheba, is given two different etymologies—by references to the "seven lambs" (vv. 28–29) and "the well of the oath" (vv. 23–31). This episode may have been used to justify the rights of the Israelites over the desert area and the strip of land occupied by the Philistines.

It is interesting to note Abraham's benevolent attitude and the peaceable way he goes about solving a dispute, first by dialogue and then by a mutual pact

---

Dei Agar de caelo dicens: «Quid tibi, Agar? Noli timere; exaudivit enim Deus vocem pueri de loco, in quo est. ¹⁸Surge, tolle puerum et tene illum manu tua, quia in gentem magnam faciam eum». ¹⁹Aperuitque Deus oculos eius; quae videns puteum aquae abiit et implevit utrem deditque puero bibere. ²⁰Et fuit Deus cum eo; qui crevit et moratus est in solitudine factusque est iuvenis sagittarius. ²¹Habitavitque in deserto Pharan; et accepit illi mater sua uxorem de terra Aegypti. ²²Eodem tempore dixit Abimelech et Phicol princeps exercitus eius ad Abraham: «Deus tecum est in universis, quae agis. ²³Iura ergo per Deum, ne noceas mihi et posteris meis stirpique meae; sed iuxta fidem, quam feci tibi, facies mihi et terrae, in qua versatus es advena». ²⁴Dixitque Abraham: «Ego iurabo». ²⁵Et increpavit Abraham Abimelech propter puteum aquae, quem vi abstulerant servi eius. ²⁶Responditque Abimelech:

I have not heard of it until today." ²⁷So Abraham took sheep and oxen and gave them to Abimelech, and the two men made a covenant. ²⁸Abraham set seven ewe lambs of the flock apart. ²⁹And Abimelech said to Abraham, "What is the meaning of these seven ewe lambs which you have set apart?" ³⁰He said, "These seven ewe lambs you will take from my hand, that you may be a witness for me that I dug this well." ³¹Therefore that place was called Beer-sheba;ʲ because there both of them swore an oath. ³²So they made a covenant at Beer-sheba. Then Abimelech and Phicol the commander of his army rose up and returned to the land of the Philistines. ³³Abraham planted a tamarisk tree in Beer-sheba, and called there on the name of the LORD, the Everlasting God. ³⁴And Abraham sojourned many days in the land of the Philistines.

Gen 4:26

Wis 10:5
Sir 44:20
Rom 8:31–32
Heb 11:17–19
Jas 2:21–22
Gen 31:11; 46:2
Ex 3:4
1 Sam 3:4f

The sacrifice of Isaac and the renewal of the promise*

22 ¹After these things God tested Abraham, and said to him, "Abraham!" And he said, "Here am I." ²He said, "Take your son, your only son Isaac, whom you love, and go to the land

(Abraham's generous spirit is clear to see). It may be that the tradition about this incident is designed to stress that this peaceful way of solving disputes between shepherds is much better than the violent rows which were typical of the time (cf. 26:19–22). In any event, this biblical scene sets an example which is valid for all times. "We cannot but express our admiration," the Second Vatican Council says, "for all who forgo the use of violence to vindicate their rights and resort to those other means of defence which are available to weaker parties, provided it

can be done without harm to the rights and duties of others and of the community" (*Gaudium et spes*, 78).

*22:1–19. God has been true to his promise: he has given Abraham a son by Sarah. Now it is Abraham who should show his fidelity to God by being ready to sacrifice his son in recognition that the boy belongs to God. The divine command seems to be senseless: Abraham has already lost Ishmael, when he and Hagar were sent away; now he is being asked to sacrifice his remaining son.

«Nescivi quis fecerit hanc rem; sed et tu non indicasti mihi, et ego non audivi praeter hodie». ²⁷Tulit itaque Abraham oves et boves et dedit Abimelech; percusseruntque ambo foedus. ²⁸Et statuit Abraham septem agnas gregis seorsum. ²⁹Cui dixit Abimelech: «Quid sibi volunt septem agnae istae, quas stare fecisti seorsum?». ³⁰At ille: «Septem, inquit, agnas accipies de manu mea, ut sint in testimonium mihi, quoniam ego fodi puteum istum». ³¹Idcirco vocatus est locus ille Bersabee, quia ibi uterque iuraverunt. ³²Et inierunt foedus in Bersabee. ³³Surrexit autem Abimelech et Phicol princeps militiae eius reversique sunt in terram Philisthim. Abraham vero plantavit nemus in Bersabee et invocavit ibi nomen Domini Dei aeterni. ³⁴Et fuit colonus in terra Philisthim diebus multis. ¹Quae postquam gesta sunt, tentavit Deus Abraham et dixit ad eum: «Abraham». Ille respondit: «Adsum». ²Ait: «Tolle filium tuum unigenitum, quem diligis, Isaac et vade in terram Moria; atque offer eum ibi in holocaustum super unum

j. That is *Well of seven* or *well of the oath*

117

2 Chron 3:1
Mt 3:17 of Moriah, and offer him there as a burnt offering upon one of the
Lk 3:22 mountains of which I shall tell you." ³So Abraham rose early in the
morning, saddled his ass, and took two of his young men with him,
and his son Isaac; and he cut the wood for the burnt offering, and
arose and went to the place of which God had told him. ⁴On the
third day Abraham lifted up his eyes and saw the place afar off.
⁵Then Abraham said to his young men, "Stay here with the ass; I
and the lad will go yonder and worship, and come again to you."
Jn 19:17 ⁶And Abraham took the wood of the burnt offering, and laid it on
Isaac his son;* and he took in his hand the fire and the knife. So
they went both of them together. ⁷And Isaac said to his father
Abraham, "My father!" And he said, "Here am I, my son." He said,

---

Disposing of his son meant detaching himself even from the fulfilment of the promise which Isaac represented. In spite of all this, Abraham obeys.

"As a final stage in the purification of his faith, Abraham 'who had received the promises' (Heb 11:17) is asked to sacrifice the son God had given him. Abraham's faith does not weaken ('God himself will provide the lamb for a burnt offering'), for he 'considered that God was able to raise men even from the dead' (Heb 11:19). And so the father of believers is conformed to the likeness of the Father who will not spare his own son but will deliver him up for us all (cf. Rom 8:32). Prayer restores man to God's likeness and enables him to share in the power of God's love that saves the multitude (cf. Rom 4:16–21)" (*Catechism of the Catholic Church*, 2572).

By undergoing the test which God set, Abraham attains perfection (cf. Jas 2:21) and he is now in a position for God to reaffirm in a solemn way the promise he made previously (cf. Gen 12:3).

The sacrifice of Isaac has features which make it a figure of the redemptive sacrifice of Christ. Thus, there is the father giving up his son; the son who surrenders himself to his father's will; and the tools of sacrifice such as the wood, the knife and the altar. The account reaches its climax by showing that through Abraham's obedience and Isaac's non-resistance, God's blessing will reach all the nations of the earth (cf. v. 18). So, it is not surprising that Jewish tradition should attribute a certain redemptive value to Isaac's submissiveness, and that the Fathers should see this episode as prefiguring the passion of Christ, the only Son of the Father.

22:2. "The land of Moriah": according to the Syrian version of Genesis this is the "land of the Ammorites". We do not in fact know where this place was, although in 2 Chronicles 3:1 it is identified with the mountain on which the temple of Jerusalem was built, to stress the holiness of that site.

---

montium, quem monstravero tibi». ³Igitur Abraham de nocte consurgens stravit asinum suum ducens secum duos iuvenes suos et Isaac filium suum. Cumque concidisset ligna in holocaustum, surrexit et abiit ad locum, quem praeceperat ei Deus. ⁴Die autem tertio, elevatis oculis, vidit locum procul ⁵dixitque ad pueros suos: «Exspectate hic cum asino. Ego et puer illuc usque properantes, postquam adoraverimus, revertemur ad vos». ⁶Tulit quoque ligna holocausti et imposuit super Isaac filium suum; ipse vero portabat in manibus ignem et cultrum. Cumque duo pergerent simul, ⁷dixit Isaac Abrahae patri

"Behold, the fire and the wood; but where is the lamb for a burnt offering?" [8]Abraham said, "God will provide himself the lamb for a burnt offering, my son." So they went both of them together.

[9]When they came to the place of which God had told him, Abraham built an altar there, and laid the wood in order, and bound Isaac his son, and laid him on the altar, upon the wood. [10]Then Abraham put forth his hand, and took the knife to slay his son. [11]But the angel of the LORD called to him from heaven, and said, "Abraham, Abraham!" And he said, "Here am I." [12]He said, "Do not lay your hand on the lad or do anything to him; for now I know that you fear God, seeing you have not withheld your son, your only son, from me." [13]And Abraham lifted up his eyes and

Jas 2:21

Jn 3:16
Rom 8:32
Heb 11:17
1 Jn 4:9

22:12. God is satisfied just by Abraham's sincere intention to do what he asked of him. It is as good as if he had actually done the deed. "The patriarch turned sacrificer of his son for the love of God; he stained his right hand with blood in intention and offered sacrifice. But owing to God's loving kindness beyond telling he received his son back safe and sound and went off with him; the patriarch was commended for his intention and bedecked with a crown; he had engaged in the ultimate struggle and at every stage proved his godly attitude" (Chrysostom, *Homiliae in Genesim*, 48, 1).

Making an implicit comparison between Isaac and Jesus, St Paul sees in the death of Christ the culmination of God's love; he writes: "He who did not spare his own Son but gave him up for us all, will he not also give us all things with him?" (Rom 8:32).

If staying Abraham's hand was really a sign of God's love, an even greater one was the fact that he allowed Jesus to die

as an expiatory sacrifice on behalf of all mankind. In that later sacrifice, because "God is love" (1 Jn 4:8), "the abyss of malice which sin opens wide has been bridged by his infinite charity. God did not abandon men. His plans foresaw that the sacrifices of the Old Law would be insufficient to repair our faults and re-establish the unity which had been lost. A man who was God would have to offer himself up" (St Josemaría Escrivá, *Christ Is Passing By*, 95).

22: 13–14. Some Fathers see this ram as a prefiguration of Jesus Christ, insofar as, like Christ, the ram was immolated in order to save man. In this sense, St Ambrose wrote: "Whom does the ram represent, if not him of whom it is written, 'He has raised up a horn for his people' (Ps 148:14)? [. . .] Christ: It is He whom Abraham saw in that sacrifice; it was his passion he saw. Thus, our Lord himself says of Abraham: 'Your father Abraham rejoiced that he was to see my

---

suo: «Pater mi». Ille respondit: «Quid vis, fili?». «Ecce, inquit, ignis et ligna; ubi est victima holocausti?». [8]Dixit Abraham: «Deus providebit sibi victimam holocausti, fili mi». Pergebant ambo pariter; [9]et venerunt ad locum, quem ostenderat ei Deus, in quo aedificavit Abraham altare et desuper ligna composuit. Cumque colligasset Isaac filium suum, posuit eum in altari super struem lignorum [10]extenditque Abraham manum et arripuit cultrum, ut immolaret filium suum. [11]Et ecce angelus Domini de caelo clamavit: «Abraham, Abraham». Qui respondit: «Adsum». [12]Dixitque: «Non extendas manum tuam super puerum neque facias illi quidquam. Nunc cognovi quod times Deum et non pepercisti filio

looked, and behold, behind him was a ram, caught in a thicket by his horns; and Abraham went and took the ram, and offered it up as a burnt offering instead of his son. [14]So Abraham called the name of that place The LORD will provide;[k] as it is said to this day, "On the mount of the LORD it shall be provided."[l]

[15]And the angel of the LORD called to Abraham a second time from heaven, [16]and said, "By myself I have sworn, says the LORD, because you have done this, and have not withheld your son, your only son, [17]I will indeed bless you, and I will multiply your descendants as the stars of heaven and as the sand which is on the seashore. And your descendants shall possess the gate of their enemies, [18]and by your descendants shall all the nations of the earth bless themselves, because you have obeyed my voice." [19]So Abraham returned to his young men, and they arose and went together to Beer-sheba; and Abraham dwelt at Beer-sheba.*

Rom 8:32
Heb 6:13

Gen 12:2; 15:5;
16:10; 32:13
Heb 6:14;
11:12

Gen 12:3
Rom 4:13
Mt 1:1
Acts 3:25

Gen 24:15; **The descendants of Nahor**
25:20; 28:2 [20]Now after these things it was told Abraham, "Behold, Milcah also has borne children to your brother Nahor: [21]Uz the first-born,

day; he saw it and was glad' (Jn 8:56). Therefore Scripture says: 'Abraham called the name of that place "The Lord will provide",' so that today one can say: the Lord appeared on the mount, that is, he appeared to Abraham revealing his future passion in his body, whereby he redeemed the world; and sharing, at the same time, the nature of his passion when he caused him to see the ram suspended by his horns. The thicket stands for the scaffold of the cross" (*De Abraham*, 1, 8, 77–78).

22:20–24. We are here told about the line of Nahor, Abraham's brother, which includes the Aramean tribes of Syria as a whole. This shows the blood relationship these tribes have with the Israelites, preparing the way for the later episode of Isaac's marriage with Rebekah. Like the descendants of Ishmael (cf. 25:12–16) and those of Jacob (cf. 35:22–26), Nahor has twelve descendants also. In the New Testament also the number twelve will mark the constitution of the new people of God, the Church.

tuo unigenito propter me». [13]Levavit Abraham oculos suos viditque arietem unum inter vepres haerentem cornibus; quem assumens obtulit holocaustum pro filio. [14]Appellavitque nomen loci illius: «Dominus videt». Unde usque hodie dicitur: «In monte Dominus videtur». [15]Vocavit autem angelus Domini Abraham secundo de caelo et dixit: [16]«Per memetipsum iuravi, dicit Dominus: quia fecisti hanc rem et non pepercisti filio tuo unigenito, [17]benedicam tibi et multiplicabo semen tuum sicut stellas caeli et velut arenam, quae est in litore maris. Possidebit semen tuum portas inimicorum suorum, [18]et benedicentur in semine tuo omnes gentes terrae, quia oboedisti voci meae». [19]Reversus est Abraham ad pueros suos, et surrexerunt abieruntque Bersabee simul, et habitavit Abraham in Bersabee. [20]His ita gestis, nuntiatum est Abrahae quod Melcha quoque genuisset filios Nachor fratri suo: [21]Us primogenitum et

k. Or *see* **l.** Or *he will be seen*

Buz his brother, Kemuel the father of Aram, ²²Chesed, Hazo, Pildash, Jidlaph, and Bethuel." ²³Bethuel became the father of Rebekah. These eight Milcah bore to Nahor, Abraham's brother. ²⁴Moreover, his concubine, whose name was Reumah, bore Tebah, Gaham, Tahash, and Maacah.

Abraham buys the cave of Mach-pelah*

Gen 33:19–20; 49:30–31

23 ¹Sarah lived a hundred and twenty-seven years; these were the years of the life of Sarah. ²And Sarah died at Kiriath-arba (that is, Hebron) in the land of Canaan; and Abraham went in to mourn for Sarah and to weep for her. ³And Abraham rose up from before his dead, and said to the Hittites, ⁴"I am a stranger and a sojourner among you; give me property among you for a burying place, that I may bury my dead out of my sight." ⁵The Hittites answered Abraham, ⁶"Hear us, my lord; you are a mighty prince among us. Bury your dead in the choicest of our sepulchres; none of us will withhold from you his sepulchre, or hinder you from burying your dead." ⁷Abraham rose and bowed to the Hittites, the people of the land. ⁸And he said to them, "If you are willing that I should bury my dead out of my sight, hear me, and entreat for me Ephron the son of Zohar, ⁹that he may give me the cave of Mach-pelah, which he owns; it is at the end of his field.

Heb 11:9
1 Pet 2:11

---

*23:1–20. The story of Abraham ends, strictly speaking, with the episode, which shows the initial fulfilment of God's promise of the land to Abraham. By acquiring a sepulchre and a small plot, he ceases to be a mere resident alien and acquires rights over this country.

The style of the account and the courtesy conventions used, as well as the contract of sale, indicate, by their similarity to Hittite customs, the antiquity of this event. The Hittites, or sons of Heth, carved out a huge empire in Asia Minor in the second millennium BC. It is not easy to explain their presence in Canaan in Abraham's time, unless it was that small isolated groups of Hittites lived there. Or it could be that all non-Semites living in the country were loosely referred to as "Hittites". In any event, what the passage does show is that even during Abraham's lifetime the promise begins to be fulfilled, though by purchase and scarcely more than in a symbolic way. This is very much in contrast with God's later outright gift of the entire land to Abraham's descendants.

Buz fratrem eius et Camuel patrem Aram ²²et Cased et Azau, Pheldas quoque et Iedlaph ²³ac Bathuel, de quo nata est Rebecca. Octo istos genuit Melcha Nachor fratri Abrahae. ²⁴Concubina vero illius, nomine Reuma, peperit Tabee et Gaham et Tahas et Maacha. ¹Vixit autem Sara centum viginti septem annis ²et mortua est in Cariatharbe, quae est Hebron, in terra Chanaan; venitque Abraham, ut plangeret et fleret eam. ³Cumque surrexisset ab officio funeris, locutus est ad filios Heth dicens: ⁴«Advena sum et inquilinus apud vos; date mihi possessionem sepulcri vobiscum, ut sepeliam mortuum meum». ⁵Responderunt filii Heth dicentes: ⁶«Audi nos, domine, princeps Dei es apud nos: in nobilissimo sepulcrorum nostrorum sepeli mortuum tuum; nullusque te prohibebit, quin in sepulcro eius sepelias mortuum tuum». ⁷Surrexit Abraham et adoravit populum terrae, filios videlicet Heth, ⁸dixitque ad eos: «Si

For the full price let him give it to me in your presence as a possession for a burying place." ¹⁰Now Ephron was sitting among the Hittites; and Ephron the Hittite answered Abraham in the hearing of the Hittites, of all who went in at the gate of his city, ¹¹"No, my lord, hear me; I give you the field, and I give you the cave that is in it; in the presence of the sons of my people I give it to you; bury your dead." ¹²Then Abraham bowed down before the people of the land. ¹³And he said to Ephron in the hearing of the people of the land, "But if you will, hear me; I will give the price of the field; accept it from me, that I may bury my dead there." ¹⁴Ephron answered Abraham, ¹⁵"My lord, listen to me; a piece of land worth four hundred shekels of silver, what is that between you and me? Bury your dead." ¹⁶Abraham agreed with Ephron; and Abraham weighed out for Ephron the silver which he had named in the hearing of the Hittites, four hundred shekels of silver, according to the weights current among the merchants.

¹⁷So the field of Ephron in Mach-pelah, which was to the east of Mamre, the field with the cave which was in it and all the trees that were in the field, throughout its whole area, was made over ¹⁸to Abraham as a possession in the presence of the Hittites, before all who went in at the gate of his city. ¹⁹After this, Abraham buried Sarah his wife in the cave of the field of Machpelah east of Mamre (that is, Hebron) in the land of Canaan. ²⁰The field and the cave that is in it were made over to Abraham as a possession for a burying place by the Hittites.

23:11. Abraham wanted to buy only the cave, but Ephron makes him buy the cave and the whole field. This apparently brought with it a duty to render some sort of feudal service. If one remembers that Abraham, as a semi-nomadic resident, had no right to acquire any property at all, it is easier to see how important this purchase was to Abraham and therefore why he was the one who gave in and agreed to buy the whole field.

23:19. In this same spot were buried Abraham, Isaac, Rebekah, Leah and Jacob, so it became as it were a symbol to the Israelites of the fact that this was

placet animae vestrae, ut sepeliam mortuum meum, audite me et intercedite pro me apud Ephron filium Seor, ⁹ut det mihi speluncam Machpela, quam habet in extrema parte agri sui. Pecunia digna tradat eam mihi coram vobis in possessionem sepulcri». ¹⁰Sedebat autem Ephron in medio filiorum Heth. Responditque Ephron Hetthaeus ad Abraham, filiis Heth audientibus cunctis, qui ingrediebantur portam civitatis illius, dicens: ¹¹«Nequaquam ita fiat, domine mi, ausculta me. Agrum do tibi et speluncam, quae in eo est, praesentibus filiis populi mei; sepeli mortuum tuum». ¹²Adoravit Abraham coram populo terrae ¹³et locutus est ad Ephron, audiente populo terrae: «Quaeso, ut audias me. Dabo pecuniam pro agro; suscipe eam, et sic sepeliam mortuum meum in eo». ¹⁴Respondit Ephron ad Abraham dicens ei: ¹⁵«Domine mi, audi me. Terra quadringentorum siclorum argenti inter me et te, quid est hoc? Sepeli mortuum tuum». ¹⁶Auscultavit Abraham Ephron et appendit pecuniam, quam Ephron postulaverat, audientibus filiis Heth, quadringentos siclos argenti, sicut mos erat apud negotiatores.

The marriage of Isaac*

24 [1]Now Abraham was old, well advanced in years; and the LORD had blessed Abraham in all things. [2]And Abraham said to his servant, the oldest of his house, who had charge of all that he had, "Put your hand under my thigh, [3]and I will make you swear by the LORD, the God of heaven and of the earth, that you will not take a wife for my son from the daughters of the Canaanites, among whom I dwell, [4]but will go to my country and to my kindred, and take a wife for my son Isaac." [5]The servant said to him, "Perhaps the woman may not be willing to follow me to this land; must I then take your son back to the land from which you came?" [6]Abraham said to him, "See to it that you do not take my son back there. [7]The LORD, the God of heaven, who took me from my father's house and from the land of my birth,

Gen 47:29

Mk 5:7

Gen 28:2

Gen 12:7
Gal 3:16

---

their land, even during their time in Egypt. A mosque today stands on the spot which tradition assigns to the tomb of the patriarchs, venerated by Jews, Christians and Moslems.

***24:1–67.** Isaac's marriage is narrated before Abraham's death to underline the continuity between the story of Abraham and that of Isaac. The next stage of the history of the patriarchs will focus on the sons of Rebekah—Esau and Jacob (cf. 25:19ff). Apparently Isaac and Abraham are no longer based at Mamre (cf. 23:19), but more to the south, in the Negeb desert (cf. 24:62).

This account is very much in line with the context and customs of the patriarchal period, but its style is more artistic and it has a particularly discreet way of

describing God's intervention. The story is told in five scenes and five dialogues, interleaved with short narrative notes. In the first scene Abraham and his servant appear (vv. 1–9); in the second, the servant and Rebekah (vv. 10–28); in the third, in Rebekah's house, the servant and Laban (vv. 29–53); in the fourth, at the moment of parting, Rebekah and her family (54–61); and in the fifth, Rebekah, the servant and Isaac (vv. 62–67). The narrator seems to savour these vignettes and dialogues. As regards God's intervention, it should be noted that, although it is never obvious, he is still really the protagonist, because he is providentially steering the course of events.

24:1–9. The tone of this passage suggests that Abraham feels he is nearing his end

---

[17]Confirmatusque est ager Ephronis, qui erat in Machpela respiciens Mambre, tam ipse quam spelunca in eo et omnes arbores eius in cunctis terminis eius per circuitum, [18]Abrahae in possessionem, videntibus filiis Heth cunctis, qui intrabant portam civitatis illius. [19]Deinde sepelivit Abraham Saram uxorem suam in spelunca agri Machpela, qui respiciebat Mambre—haec est Hebron—in terra Chanaan. [20]Et confirmatus est ager et antrum, quod erat in eo, Abrahae in possessionem sepulcri a filiis Heth. [1]Erat autem Abraham senex dierumque multorum; et Dominus in cunctis benedixerat ei. [2]Dixitque Abraham ad servum seniorem domus suae, qui praeerat omnibus, quae habebat: «Pone manum tuam subter femur meum, [3]ut adiurem te per Dominum Deum caeli et Deum terrae, ut non accipias uxorem filio meo de filiabus Chananaeorum, inter quos habito; [4]sed ad terram et cognationem meam proficiscaris et inde accipias uxorem filio meo Isaac». [5]Respondit servus: «Si noluerit mulier venire mecum in terram hanc, num reducere debeo filium tuum ad terram, a quo tu egressus es?». [6]Dixit Abraham:

and who spoke to me and swore to me, 'To your descendants I will give this land,' he will send his angel before you, and you shall take a wife for my son from there. ⁸But if the woman is not willing to follow you, then you will be free from this oath of mine; only you must not take my son back there." ⁹So the servant put his hand under the thigh of Abraham his master, and swore to him concerning this matter.

Gen 11:31
¹⁰Then the servant took ten of his master's camels and departed, taking all sorts of choice gifts from his master; and he arose, and went to Mesopotamia, to the city of Nahor. ¹¹And he made the camels kneel down outside the city by the well of water at the time of evening, the time when women go out to draw water. ¹²And he said, "O LORD, God of my master Abraham, grant me success today, I pray thee, and show steadfast love to my master Abraham. ¹³Behold, I am standing by the spring of water, and the daughters of the men of the city are coming out to draw

1 Sam 14:10
water. ¹⁴Let the maiden to whom I shall say, 'Pray let down your jar that I may drink,' and who shall say, 'Drink, and I will water your camels'—let her be the one whom thou hast appointed for thy servant Isaac. By this I shall know that thou hast shown steadfast love to my master."

---

and he can see that God's promise with regard to his descendants and the land is being kept. Therefore the patriarch is concerned to find a wife for his son from among his own family, in line with the customs of semi-nomadic peoples of that time. However, Abraham is clearly adamant that Isaac shall not give up living where he is. The form of oath, with the hand under the thigh (cf. 47:29), which Abraham makes his servant take, is an exceptionally strong one: it obliges the servant, whose faithfulness is evident, to do exactly what he swears to do. Here,

once again, Abraham's faith copes with all the difficulties his servant foresees. He is fully confident that God in his providence will sweep away all these obstacles, which is what happens, as one can gather from the end of the account.

Abraham's decision about the wife Isaac should take points to the importance a wife has in sustaining her husband's faith and that of her family. St Ambrose comments that "often a woman's seduction deceives even the strongest of husbands and causes them to give up religion. [. . .] For the first thing

---

«Cave, ne quando reducas illuc filium meum. ⁷Dominus, Deus caeli, qui tulit me de domo patris mei et de terra nativitatis meae, qui locutus est mihi et iuravit mihi dicens: 'Semini tuo dabo terram hanc', ipse mittet angelum suum coram te, et accipies inde uxorem filio meo. ⁸Sin autem noluerit mulier sequi te, non teneberis iuramento; filium tantum meum ne reducas illuc». ⁹Posuit ergo servus manum sub femore Abraham domini sui et iuravit illi super hac re. ¹⁰Tulitque servus decem camelos de grege domini sui et abiit ex omnibus bonis eius portans secum; profectusque perrexit in Aram Naharaim ad urbem Nachor. ¹¹Cumque camelos fecisset accumbere extra oppidum iuxta puteum aquae vespere, tempore quo solent mulieres egredi ad hauriendam aquam, dixit: ¹²«Domine Deus domini mei Abraham, occurre obsecro mihi hodie et fac misericordiam cum domino meo Abraham. ¹³Ecce ego sto prope

Rebekah at the well

[15]Before he had done speaking, behold, Rebekah, who was born to Bethuel the son of Milcah, the wife of Nahor, Abraham's brother, came out with her water jar upon her shoulder. [16]The maiden was very fair to look upon, a virgin, whom no man had known. She went down to the spring, and filled her jar, and came up. [17]Then the servant ran to meet her, and said, "Pray give me a little water to drink from your jar." [18]She said, "Drink, my lord"; and she quickly let down her jar upon her hand, and gave him a drink. [19]When she had finished giving him a drink, she said, "I will draw for your camels also, until they have done drinking." [20]So she quickly emptied her jar into the trough and ran again to the well to draw, and she drew for all his camels. [21]The man gazed at her in silence to learn whether the LORD had prospered his journey or not.

[22]When the camels had done drinking, the man took a gold ring weighing a half shekel, and two bracelets for her arms weighing ten gold shekels, [23]and said, "Tell me whose daughter you are. Is there room in your father's house for us to lodge in?" [24]She said to him, "I am the daughter of Bethuel the son of Milcah, whom

---

that should be sought in conjugal life is religion. [. . .] Learn, therefore, what to seek in a woman: Abraham sought not gold or silver or property, but the gift of a good heart" (*De Abraham*, 1, 9, 84-85).

24:10. "Mesopotamia": literally "Aram-Naharaim" or "Syria of the two rivers", a reference to the region in Upper Meso-

potamia (where the city of Haran was) where Abraham's family lived, according to Genesis 11:31. The mention of the ten camels shows how wealthy Abraham was, for semi-nomadic tribes used a breed of very hardy donkeys.

This episode clearly shows how faithful Abraham's servant was in carrying out his mission.

---

fontem aquae, et filiae habitatorum huius civitatis egredientur ad hauriendam aquam. [14]Igitur puella, cui ego dixero: 'Inclina hydriam tuam, ut bibam', et illa responderit: 'Bibe, quin et camelis tuis dabo potum', ipsa est, quam praeparasti servo tuo Isaac, et per hoc intellegam quod feceris misericordiam cum domino meo». [15]Necdum intra se verba compleverat, et ecce Rebecca egrediebatur filia Bathuel filii Melchae uxoris Nachor fratris Abraham habens hydriam in scapula: [16]puella decora nimis, virgo et incognita viro. Descendit ad fontem et implevit hydriam ac revertebatur. [17]Occurritque ei servus et ait: «Pauxillum mihi ad sorbendum praebe aquae de hydria tua». [18]Quae respondit: «Bibe, domine mi». Celeriterque deposuit hydriam super ulnam suam et dedit ei potum. [19]Cumque ille bibisset, adiecit: «Quin et camelis tuis hauriam aquam, donec cuncti bibant». [20]Effundensque hydriam in canalibus recurrit ad puteum, ut hauriret aquam; et haustam omnibus camelis dedit. [21]Ille autem contemplabatur eam tacitus, scire volens utrum prosperum fecisset iter suum Dominus an non. [22]Postquam ergo biberunt cameli, protulit vir anulum aureum pondo dimidii sicli pro naribus et duas armillas pro manibus eius pondo siclorum decem; [23]dixitque: «Cuius es filia? Indica mihi. Est in domo patris tui locus nobis ad pernoctandum?». [24]Quae respondit: «Filia Bathuelis sum filii Melchae, quem peperit

she bore to Nahor." 25She added, "We have both straw and provender enough, and room to lodge in." 26The man bowed his head and worshiped the LORD, 27and said, "Blessed be the LORD, the God of my master Abraham, who has not forsaken his steadfast love and his faithfulness toward my master. As for me, the LORD has led me in the way to the house of my master's kinsmen."

28Then the maiden ran and told her mother's household about these things.

Abraham's servant is welcomed to Rebekah's home

29Rebekah had a brother whose name was Laban; and Laban ran out to the man, to the spring. 30When he saw the ring, and the bracelets on his sister's arms, and when he heard the words of Rebekah his sister, "Thus the man spoke to me," he went to the man; and behold, he was standing by the camels at the spring. 31He said, "Come in, O blessed of the LORD; why do you stand outside? For I have prepared the house and a place for the camels." 32So the man came into the house; and Laban ungirded the camels, and gave him straw and provender for the camels, and water to wash his feet and the feet of the men who were with him. 33Then food was set before him to eat; but he said, "I will not eat until I have told my errand." He said, "Speak on."

34So he said, "I am Abraham's servant. 35The LORD has greatly blessed my master, and he has become great; he has given him flocks and herds, silver and gold, menservants and maidservants, camels and asses. 36And Sarah my master's wife bore a son to my master when she was old; and to him he has given all that he has.

Heb 11:13 37My master made me swear, saying, 'You shall not take a wife for my son from the daughters of the Canaanites, in whose land I dwell; 38but you shall go to my father's house and to my kindred, and take a wife for my son.' 39I said to my master, 'Perhaps the

Nachor». 25Et addidit dicens: «Palearum quoque et pabuli plurimum est apud nos et locus ad pernoctandum». 26Inclinavit se homo et adoravit Dominum 27dicens: «Benedictus Dominus, Deus domini mei Abraham, qui non abstulit misericordiam et veritatem suam a domino meo et recto itinere me perduxit in domum fratris domini mei». 28Cucurrit itaque puella et nuntiavit in domum matris suae omnia, quae evenerant. 29Habebat autem Rebecca fratrem nomine Laban, qui festinus egressus est ad hominem, ubi erat fons. 30Cumque vidisset anulum in naribus et armillas in manibus sororis suae et audisset cuncta verba referentis: «Haec locutus est mihi homo», venit ad virum, qui stabat iuxta camelos et prope fontem aquae, 31dixitque ad eum: «Ingredere, benedicte Domini, cur foris stas? Praeparavi domum et locum camelis». 32Et introduxit eum in hospitium ac destravit camelos; deditque paleas et pabulum camelis et aquam ad lavandos pedes eius et virorum, qui venerant cum eo. 33Et apposuit in conspectu eius panem. Qui ait: «Non comedam, donec loquar sermones meos». Respondit: «Loquere». 34At ille: «Servus, inquit, Abraham sum; 35et Dominus benedixit domino meo valde magnificatusque est; et dedit ei oves et boves, argentum et aurum, servos et ancillas, camelos et asinos. 36Et peperit Sara uxor domini mei filium domino meo in senectute sua; deditque illi omnia, quae habuerat. 37Et adiuravit me dominus meus dicens: 'Non accipies uxorem filio meo de filiabus Chananaeorum, in quorum terra habito;

woman will not follow me.' ⁴⁰But he said to me, 'The LORD, before whom I walk, will send his angel with you and prosper your way; and you shall take a wife for my son from my kindred and from my father's house; ⁴¹then you will be free from my oath, when you come to my kindred; and if they will not give her to you, you will be free from my oath.'

⁴²"I came today to the spring, and said, 'O LORD, the God of my master Abraham, if now thou wilt prosper the way which I go, ⁴³behold, I am standing by the spring of water; let the young woman who comes out to draw, to whom I shall say, "Pray give me a little water from your jar to drink," ⁴⁴and who will say to me, "Drink, and I will draw for your camels also," let her be the woman whom the Lord has appointed for my master's son.'

⁴⁵"Before I had done speaking in my heart, behold, Rebekah came out with her water jar on her shoulder; and she went down to the spring, and drew. I said to her, 'Pray let me drink.' ⁴⁶She quickly let down her jar from her shoulder, and said, 'Drink, and I will give your camels drink also.' So I drank, and she gave the camels drink also. ⁴⁷Then I asked her, 'Whose daughter are you?' She said, The daughter of Bethuel, Nahor's son, whom Milcah bore to him.' So I put the ring on her nose, and the bracelets on her arms. ⁴⁸Then I bowed my head and worshiped the LORD, and blessed the LORD, the God of my master Abraham, who had led me by the right way to take the daughter of my master's kinsman for his son. ⁴⁹Now then, if you will deal loyally and truly with my master, tell me; and if not, tell me; that I may turn to the right hand or to the left."

⁵⁰Then Laban and Bethuel answered, "The thing comes from the LORD; we cannot speak to you bad or good. ⁵¹Behold,

---

³⁸sed ad domum patris mei perges et de cognatione mea accipies uxorem filio meo'. ³⁹Ego vero respondi domino meo: Quid si noluerit venire mecum mulier? ⁴⁰Dominus, ait, in cuius conspectu ambulo, mittet angelum suum tecum et diriget viam tuam; accipiesque uxorem filio meo de cognatione mea et de domo patris mei. ⁴¹Innocens eris a maledictione mea, cum veneris ad propinquos meos, et non dederint tibi; tunc innocens eris a maledictione mea». ⁴²Veni ergo hodie ad fontem et dixi: Domine Deus domini mei Abraham, si direxisti viam meam, in qua nunc ambulo, ⁴³ecce sto iuxta fontem aquae; et virgo, quae egredietur ad hauriendam aquam, audierit a me: 'Da mihi pauxillum aquae ad bibendum ex hydria tua'; ⁴⁴et dixerit mihi: 'Et tu bibe, et camelis tuis hauriam', ipsa est mulier, quam praeparavit Dominus filio domini mei. ⁴⁵Dum haec tacitus mecum volverem, apparuit Rebecca veniens cum hydria, quam portabat in scapula; descenditque ad fontem et hausit aquam. Et aio ad eam: Da mihi paululum bibere. ⁴⁶Quae festina deposuit hydriam de umero et dixit mihi: 'Et tu bibe, et camelis tuis potum tribuam'. Bibi, et adaquavit camelos. ⁴⁷Interrogavique eam et dixi: Cuius es filia? Quae respondit: 'Filia Bathuelis sum filii Nachor, quem peperit illi Melcha'. Suspendi itaque anulum in naribus eius et armillas posui in manibus eius. ⁴⁸Pronusque adoravi Dominum benedicens Domino, Deo domini mei Abraham, qui perduxit me recto itinere, ut sumerem filiam fratris domini mei filio eius. ⁴⁹Quam ob rem, si facitis misericordiam et veritatem cum domino meo, indicate mihi; sin autem aliud placet, et hoc dicite mihi, ut vadam ad dexteram sive ad sinistram». ⁵⁰Responderunt Laban et Bathuel: «A

Rebekah is before you, take her and go, and let her be the wife of your master's son, as the LORD has spoken."

⁵²When Abraham's servant heard their words, he bowed himself to the earth before the LORD. ⁵³And the servant brought forth jewelry of silver and of gold, and raiment, and gave them to Rebekah; he also gave to her brother and to her mother costly ornaments. ⁵⁴And he and the men who were with him ate and drank, and they spent the night there.

Gen 22:17–18 **The meeting between Rebekah and Isaac**

When they arose in the morning, he said, "Send me back to my master." ⁵⁵Her brother and her mother said, "Let the maiden remain with us awhile, at least ten days; after that she may go." ⁵⁶But he said to them, "Do not delay me, since the LORD has prospered my way; let me go that I may go to my master." ⁵⁷They said, "We will call the maiden, and ask her." ⁵⁸And they called Rebekah, and said to her, "Will you go with this man?" She said, "I will go." ⁵⁹So they sent away Rebekah their sister and her nurse, and Abraham's servant and his men. ⁶⁰And they blessed Rebekah, and said to her, "Our sister, be the mother of thousands of ten thousands; and may your descendants possess the gate of those who hate them!" ⁶¹Then Rebekah and her maids arose, and rode upon the camels and followed the man; thus the servant took Rebekah, and went his way.

24:57–58. Rebekah is consulted as regards the time of her leaving, not about the marriage itself which, according to the customs of the time, it was for the head of the house to arrange (cf. vv. 50–51). However, according to that ancient law, it seems that the young woman could remain for a while in her father's house. Rebekah's firm decision suggests that God has already disposed her to love her future husband, Isaac.

Domino egressus est sermo; non possumus extra placitum eius quidquam aliud loqui tecum. ⁵¹En Rebecca coram te est; tolle eam et proficiscere, et sit uxor filii domini tui, sicut locutus est Dominus». ⁵²Quod cum audisset puer Abraham, procidens adoravit in terram Dominum. ⁵³Prolatisque vasis argenteis et aureis ac vestibus, dedit ea Rebeccae; res pretiosas dedit fratri eius et matri. ⁵⁴Tunc comederunt et biberunt ipse et viri, qui erant cum eo, et pernoctaverunt ibi. Surgens autem mane locutus est puer: «Dimittite me, ut vadam ad dominum meum». ⁵⁵Responderuntque frater eius et mater: «Maneat puella saltem decem dies apud nos et postea proficiscetur». ⁵⁶«Nolite, ait, me retinere, quia Dominus direxit viam meam; dimittite me, ut pergam ad dominum meum». ⁵⁷Dixerunt: «Vocemus puellam et quaeramus ipsius voluntatem». ⁵⁸Cumque vocata venisset, sciscitati sunt: «Vis ire cum homine isto?». Quae ait: «Vadam». ⁵⁹Dimiserunt ergo Rebeccam sororem eorum et nutricem illius servumque Abraham et comites eius, ⁶⁰imprecantes prospera sorori suae atque dicentes: «Soror nostra es, / crescas in mille milia, / et possideat semen tuum / portas inimicorum suorum!». ⁶¹Igitur surrexit Rebecca et puellae illius et, ascensis camelis, secutae sunt virum; sumpsitque servus Rebeccam et abiit. ⁶²Isaac autem venerat a regione putei Lahairoi et habitabat in terra Nageb. ⁶³Et egressus est Isaac ad lamentandum in

[62]Now Isaac had come from[n] Beer-lahai-roi, and was dwelling Gen 16:13–14
in the Negeb. [63]And Isaac went out to meditate in the field in the
evening; and he lifted up his eyes and looked, and behold, there
were camels coming. [64]And Rebekah lifted up her eyes, and when
she saw Isaac, she alighted from the camel, [65]and said to the ser- 1 Cor 11:10
vant, "Who is the man yonder, walking in the field to meet us?"
The servant said, "It is my master." So she took her veil and covered herself. [66]And the servant told Isaac all the things that he had
done. [67]Then Isaac brought her into the tent,[o] and took Rebekah,
and she became his wife; and he loved her. So Isaac was comforted after his mother's death.

Other descendants of Abraham*

1 Chron 1:32–33

25 [1]Abraham took another wife, whose name was Keturah.
[2]She bore him Zimran, Jokshan, Medan, Midian, Ishbak, Ex 2:15–20
Gen 10:7
and Shuah. [3]Jokshan was the father of Sheba and Dedan. The sons 1 Kings 10:1
of Dedan were Asshurim, Letushim, and Le-ummim. [4]The sons Is 21:13
of Midian were Ephah, Epher, Hanoch, Abida, and Eldaah. All Jer 6:20
these were the children of Keturah. [5]Abraham gave all he had to
Isaac. [6]But to the sons of his concubines Abraham gave gifts, and

---

24:66–67. In the beautiful conclusion to
the story ("He loved her and so was comforted after his mother's death") we see
borne out the words of Genesis 2:24
about the creation of Eve: "A man leaves
his father and his mother and cleaves to
his wife, and they become one flesh."
Jewish and Christian tradition see the
marriage of Isaac and Rebekah as a
model of conjugal love.

*25:1–18. Before going on to deal with
the history of Isaac's descendants (cf.
25:19), three short items dealing with

Abraham are recorded—children of the
patriarch other than the son of the
promise (vv. 1–6), his death (vv. 7–11),
and the descendants of Ishmael (vv.
12–18). Here we see fulfilled the promise
that Abraham would be the father of a
multitude of nations (cf. 17:4).

25:1–6. Mention is made of some Arab
peoples with whom Israel had a connexion at some point in its history. Some of
them are mentioned elsewhere in the
Bible, like the Midianites (cf. Gen 37:28;
Ex 2:15–22), the Sabeans (Gen 10:7; 1

---

agro, inclinata iam die. Cumque levasset oculos, vidit camelos venientes. [64] Rebecca quoque levavit
oculos et vidit Isaac; descenditque de camelo [65] et ait ad puerum: «Quis est ille homo, qui venit per
agrum in occursum nobis?». Dixitque ei: «Ipse est dominus meus». At illa tollens cito velum operuit
se. [66] Servus autem cuncta, quae gesserat, narravit Isaac; [67] qui introduxit eam in tabernaculum Sarae
matris suae et accepit Rebeccam uxorem; et dilexit eam et consolatus est a morte matris suae.
[1]Abraham vero aliam duxit uxorem nomine Ceturam, [2] quae peperit ei Zamran et Iecsan et Madan et
Madian et Iesboc et Sue. [3]Iecsan quoque genuit Saba et Dedan. Filii Dedan fuerunt Assurim et Latusim
et Loommim. [4]At vero ex Madian ortus est Epha et Opher et Henoch et Abida et Eldaa. Omnes hi filii

---

n. Syr Tg: Heb *from coming to* **o.** Heb adds *Sarah his mother*

while he was still living he sent them away from his son Isaac, eastward to the east country.

Gen 16:13–14;
23:1–20 **The death and burial of Abraham**

⁷These are the days of the years of Abraham's life, a hundred and seventy-five years. ⁸Abraham breathed his last and died in a good old age, an old man and full of years, and was gathered to his people. ⁹Isaac and Ishmael his sons buried him in the cave of Mach-pelah, in the field of Ephron the son of Zohar the Hittite, east of Mamre, ¹⁰the field which Abraham purchased from the

Gen 16:14;
24:62 Hittites. There Abraham was buried, with Sarah his wife. ¹¹After the death of Abraham God blessed Isaac his son. And Isaac dwelt at Beer-lahai-roi.

Gen 16:12; 17:20
1 Chron 1:29–31

7. THE DESCENDANTS OF ISHMAEL

¹²These are the descendants of Ishmael, Abraham's son, whom Hagar the Egyptian, Sarah's maid, bore to Abraham. ¹³These are

---

Kings 10:1; Jer 6:20) and the Dedanites (cf. Gen 10:7; Is 21:13). Of some of these nothing at all is known. The purpose of this short genealogical list is to show the historical connexion between these peoples and Israel, pointing out that they all come from Abraham; but, at the same time, to stress how exceptional Isaac (and therefore the chosen people) was among all the other peoples of the same race: we are told very clearly in v. 5 that Isaac is Abraham's true heir and that his other sons had already been given what was due to them.

25:7–11. By saying that Abraham "was gathered to his people" (v. 8), that is, to his ancestors, the text is referring in some

way to life after death, although there is no suggestion yet that this is a point when one is rewarded or punished. The reward for Abraham's faithfulness mentioned here is his longevity and the fact that his sons are at his bedside when he dies—Isaac, who was living with him, and Ishmael, who suddenly appears on the scene. The divine blessing, which included the promise of many descendants and of the land of Canaan, now passes to Isaac by God's free choice.

25:12–18. The account of the twelve descendants of Ishmael must include ancient traditions about the Ishmaelites; even the symbolism of the number twelve confirms that God has kept his

---

Ceturae. ⁵Deditque Abraham cuncta, quae possederat, Isaac; ⁶filiis autem concubinarum suarum largitus est munera et separavit eos ab Isaac filio suo, dum adhuc ipse viveret, ad plagam orientalem. ⁷Fuerunt autem dies vitae Abrahae centum septuaginta quinque anni. ⁸Et deficiens mortuus est Abraham in senectute bona provectaeque aetatis et plenus dierum congregatusque est ad populum suum. ⁹Et sepelierunt eum Isaac et Ismael filii sui in spelunca Machpela, quae sita est in agro Ephron filii Seor Hetthaei e regione Mambre, ¹⁰quem emerat a filiis Heth. Ibi sepultus est ipse et Sara uxor eius. ¹¹Et post obitum illius benedixit Deus Isaac filio eius, qui habitabat iuxta puteum Lahairoi. ¹²Hae

the names of the sons of Ishmael, named in the order of their birth: Nebaioth, the first-born of Ishmael; and Kedar, Adbeel, Mibsam, [14]Mishma, Dumah, Massa, [15]Hadad, Tema, Jetur, Naphish, and Kedemah. [16]These are the sons of Ishmael and these are their names, by their villages and by their encampments, twelve princes according to their tribes. [17](These are the years of the life of Ishmael, a hundred and thirty-seven years; he breathed his last and died, and was gathered to his kindred.) [18]They dwelt from Havilah to Shur, which is opposite Egypt in the direction of Assyria; he settled[p] over against all his people.

8. THE DESCENDANTS OF ISAAC.
THE STORY OF JACOB*

The birth of Esau and Jacob

[19]*These are the descendants of Isaac, Abraham's son: Abraham was the father of Isaac, [20]and Isaac was forty years old when he

---

promise—to make Ishmael, too, a great people (cf. 17:20). It is not easy to work out what tribe each of these names refers to. Nebaioth may be the father of the Nabatheans, whose capital, in Roman times, was at Petra. Little or nothing is known of the others. The passage does, however, set the limits of where these peoples lived—from the north-east of Arabia (which is where Havilah is) to the border with Egypt, which at that time was protected by a huge wall along the edge of the desert.

Once it has shown that God's promise with respect to Ishmael has been kept, the Bible will concern itself no longer with him, to concentrate on Isaac and his descendants.

*25:19—37:1. The story of Isaac really begins here and it will go on up to his death in 35:29. However, Jacob is in fact the patriarch who is centre-stage in these chapters (except chap. 26). Everything to do with Isaac has been linked to the story of Jacob or else given previously in the story of Abraham. Isaac's main importance is that he is a link through whom the promise passes from Abraham to Jacob.

The story of Jacob in Genesis is a blending of two traditional cycles—one about Jacob and Esau, the other about Jacob and Laban. The first provides the framework more or less for the story of Jacob, which is as follows: 1) accounts about how Jacob acquired the birthright

---

sunt generationes Ismael filii Abrahae, quem peperit ei Agar Aegyptia famula Sarae. [13]Et haec nomina filiorum Ismael in vocabulis et generationibus suis: primogenitus Ismaelis Nabaioth, dein Cedar et Adbeel et Mabsam, [14]Masma quoque et Duma et Massa, [15]Hadad et Thema, Iethur et Naphis et Cedma. [16]Isti sunt filii Ismaelis, et haec nomina eorum per vicos et mansiones eorum: duodecim principes tribuum suarum. [17]Et facti sunt anni vitae Ismaelis centum triginta septem; deficiens mortuus est et appositus ad populum suum. [18]Habitaverunt autem ab Hevila usque Sur, quae respicit Aegyptum introe-

p. Heb *fell*

131

took to wife Rebekah, the daughter of Bethuel the Aramean of
Paddan-aram, the sister of Laban the Aramean. [21]And Isaac
prayed to the LORD for his wife, because she was barren; and the
_{Lk 1:41} LORD granted his prayer, and Rebekah his wife conceived. [22]The
children struggled together within her; and she said, "If it is thus,
_{Mal 1:2–5} why do I live?"[q] So she went to inquire of the LORD. [23]And the
_{2 Sam 8:13–14}
_{Rom 9:12} LORD said to her,

> "Two nations are in your womb,
>   and two peoples, born of you, shall be divided;
> the one shall be stronger than the other,
>   the elder shall serve the younger."

(cf. 25:19–34; 27:1–45); 2) his flight
from his brother and from the promised
land (cf. 27:46—32:3; 3) his return and
his meeting with Esau; he settles in
Canaan, Esau in Edom (cf. 32:4—37:1).

Jacob (Israel) and Esau (Edom) stand
for the two nations descended from
them—Israelites and Edomites (cf. 36:8).
In the relations between the brothers we
can see in broad outline the relationship
between Israel and Edom. Thus, Edom
was already established in Canaan when
the Israelites arrived (cf. Num 20:14–21),
so they could be regarded as having a
right to that land, in the same sort of way
as Esau was the first-born and therefore
the natural heir of the rights of primogen-
iture. However, it was Israel who would
dwell in the land of Canaan and who
even came to dominate Edom in the
times of the monarchy (cf. 2 Sam
8:13–14), as God planned would happen
(cf. Gen 25:23). In the persons of their
ancestors, each people is assigned its territory—to Israel Canaan, to Edom the
mountains of Seir in the desert region to
the south of the Dead Sea. Thus the his-

tory of Israel will see the divine promises
fulfilled. The stories about the birthright,
then, allow us to see that the Land is
going to be a gratuitous gift from God,
and that God chooses the one of less
account, someone who had no chance of
inheriting according to human laws.

25:21–23. Sarah was barren; now
Rebekah is barren—and in both cases
God is going to intervene in order to keep
his promise. The ultimate destiny of
Rebekah's two sons is also highlighted—
two peoples who will fight with one
another until eventually the lesser one
wins; God foresaw this from the start.

Here word of the Lord takes the form
of an oracle, predicting what will happen
and identifying the route the Lord will
take to put his plan of salvation into
effect. This route is different from the
one Isaac envisaged; he thought it would
happen through his elder son, his first-
born, the heir to the blessing and therefore to the divine promise. But God
chooses whomever he wishes, with total
freedom, and in this case, as he had done

---

untibus Assyriam. In faciem cunctorum fratrum suorum obiit. [19]Hae sunt generationes Isaac filii
Abraham: Abraham genuit Isaac; [20]qui, cum quadraginta esset annorum, duxit uxorem Rebeccam
filiam Bathuelis Aramaei de Paddanaram, sororem Laban Aramaei. [21]Deprecatusque est Isaac
Dominum pro uxore sua, eo quod esset sterilis. Qui exaudivit eum et dedit conceptum Rebeccae. [22]Sed

q. Syr: Heb obscure

[24]When her days to be delivered were fulfilled, behold, there were twins in her womb. [25]The first came forth red, all his body like a hairy mantle; so they called his name Esau. [26]Afterward his brother came forth, and his hand had taken hold of Esau's heel; so his name was called Jacob.[r] Isaac was sixty years old when she bore them.

Lk 2:6

Hos 12:4
Mt 1:2
Lk 3:34
Acts 7:8

Esau sells his birthright

[27]When the boys grew up, Esau was a skilful hunter, a man of the field, while Jacob was a quiet man, dwelling in tents. [28]Isaac loved Esau, because he ate of his game; but Rebekah loved Jacob.

---

with Abel and Isaac, his choice falls on the younger son. "This is interpreted by the Apostle Paul," Augustine says, "as an obvious proof of the working of grace: 'For though they [Rebekah's children] were not yet born and had done nothing either good or bad,' the younger was chosen, through no merits of his own, and the older rejected (Rom 9:11–12). So far as original sin goes, both were equal; as for personal sins, neither had any" (*De civitate Dei*, 16, 35).

God acts in this way in the calling of Christians, too. Reflecting on the call of the disciples chosen by our Lord, St Josemaría Escrivá comments: "Something similar has happened to us. With little effort we could find among our family, friends and acquaintances—not to mention the crowds of the world—so many worthier persons that Christ could have called, yes, persons who are simpler and wiser, more influential and important, more grateful and generous. [. . .] But I also realize that human logic

cannot possibly explain the world of grace. God usually seeks out deficient instruments so that the work can more clearly be seen to be his" (*Christ Is Passing By*, 3).

25:24–26. As frequently happens in stories about births, the names of the children are explained by recourse to popular etymologies. Here the name Esau is supposed to have come from the colour red (but Edom would be a closer link with red) and from the sheepskin with hair (wool) signified by the name Seir, a place where Esau would later live. The name of Jacob is said to have to do with the word "heel" due to the circumstance of his birth.

In v. 26 we read that Isaac was sixty years old when Esau and Jacob were born, whereas in v. 20 it says that he was forty when he married and began to pray for his wife, who was barren. So, he spent twenty years praying. St John Chrysostom uses this nugget of informa-

---

collidebantur in utero eius parvuli. Quae ait: «Si sic est, cur mihi?». Perrexitque, ut consuleret Dominum. [23]Qui respondens ait: «Duae gentes sunt in utero tuo, / et duo populi ex ventre tuo dividentur; / populusque populum superabit, / et maior serviet minori». [24]Iam tempus pariendi venerat, et ecce gemini in utero eius. [25]Qui primus egressus est rufus erat et totus quasi pallium pilo sum; vocatumque est nomen eius Esau. Postea frater eius egrediens plantam Esau tenebat manu, et idcirco appellatum est nomen eius Iacob. [26]Sexagenarius erat Isaac, quando nati sunt parvuli. [27]Quibus adultis, factus est Esau

r. That is *He takes by the heel* or *He supplants*

²⁹Once when Jacob was boiling pottage, Esau came in from the field, and he was famished. ³⁰And Esau said to Jacob, "Let me eat some of that red pottage, for I am famished!" (Therefore his name was called Edom.ˢ) ³¹Jacob said, "First sell me your birthright." ³²Esau said, "I am about to die; of what use is a birthright to me?" ³³Jacob said, "Swear to me first."ᵗ So he swore to him, and sold his birthright to Jacob. ³⁴Then Jacob gave Esau bread and pottage of lentils, and he ate and drank, and rose and went his way. Thus Esau despised his birthright.

Deut 21:17

Heb 12:16

*Gen 12:11–20;
20:2–18*

Heb 12:16

Isaac at Gerar: his meeting with Abimelech

26 ¹Now there was a famine in the land, besides the former famine that was in the days of Abraham. And Isaac went to Gerar, to Abimelech king of the Philistines. ²And the Lord

---

tion to comment that "we, too, should imitate the good man and implore God with supplication when seeking something from him. If this good man, you see, being virtuous and enjoying so much favour with God, gave evidence of such a degree of zeal and enthusiasm in beseeching God constantly as to relieve Rebecca's sterility, what could we plead, carrying as we do such a heavy load of sins and yet giving evidence of not the smallest fraction of the good man's virtue? Rather, even if we do show some little zeal, we lose heart and fall away if the response to prayer is not immediate" (*Homiliae in Genesim*, 49, 1).

25:29–34 Once again the text uses etymology to explain a name, Edom (Esau), but this time it associates it with the stew made by Jacob. The sacred text also

emphasizes Jacob's astuteness and the way he manages to get the birthright; whereas it criticizes Esau's failure to appreciate the value of his rights. "Listening to this," St John Chrysostom says, "let us learn the lesson never to neglect the gifts from God, nor forfeit important things for worthless trifles. I mean, why, tell me, should we be obsessed with a desire for money when the kingdom of heaven and those ineffable blessings are within our grasp, and why prefer to those that endure forever and ever others that are passing and scarcely last until evening?" (*Homiliae in Genesim*, 50, 2).

*26:1–35. This chapter records a number of episodes to do with Isaac, and they are very similar to stories told about Abraham—making his wife out to be his

---

vir gnarus venandi et homo agrestis; Iacob autem vir compositus et habitans in tabernaculis. ²⁸Isaac amabat Esau, eo quod de venationibus illius libenter vesceretur; et Rebecca diligebat Iacob. ²⁹Coxit autem Iacob pulmentum; ad quem, cum venisset Esau de agro lassus, ³⁰ait: «Da mihi de coctione hac rufa, quia oppido lassus sum». Quam ob causam vocatum est nomen eius Edom (*id est Rufus*). ³¹Cui dixit Iacob: «Vende mihi prius primogenita tua». ³²Ille respondit: «En morior; quid mihi proderunt primogenita?». ³³Ait Iacob: «Iura ergo mihi». Iuravit et vendidit primogenita. ³⁴Et sic, accepto pane et lentis edulio, comedit et bibit; surrexit et abiit parvipendens quod primogenita vendidisset. ¹Orta autem fame super terram, post eam sterilitatem, quae acciderat in diebus Abraham, abiit Isaac ad Abimelech regem Philisthim in Gerara. ²Apparuitque ei Dominus et ait: «Ne descendas in Aegyptum, sed habita

s. That is *Red*   **t.** Heb *today*

appeared to him, and said, "Do not go down to Egypt; dwell in the land of which I shall tell you. ³Sojourn in this land, and I will be with you, and will bless you; for to you and to your descendants I will give all these lands, and I will fulfil the oath which I swore to Abraham your father. ⁴I will multiply your descendants as the stars of heaven, and will give to your descendants all these lands; and by your descendants all the nations of the earth shall bless themselves: ⁵because Abraham obeyed my voice and kept my charge, my commandments, my statutes, and my laws."

⁶So Isaac dwelt in Gerar. ⁷When the men of the place asked him about his wife, he said, "She is my sister"; for he feared to say, "My wife," thinking, "lest the men of the place should kill me for the sake of Rebekah"; because she was fair to look upon. ⁸When he had been there a long time, Abimelech king of the Philistines looked out of a window and saw Isaac fondling Rebekah his wife. ⁹So Abimelech called Isaac, and said, "Behold, she is your wife; how then could you say, 'She is my sister'?" Isaac said to him, "Because I thought, 'Lest I die because of her.'"

---

sister (cf. 12:11–20; 20:2–18); disputes over wells (cf. 21:25–34); appearances of Yahweh, and building an altar (cf. 12:8; 15:1–21; etc.). Isaac behaves very much as Abraham has done. The main idea is that Isaac is the bearer of the divine promise, the link between Abraham and Jacob. God in fact repeats his promise to Isaac in view of the oath he swore to Abraham (cf. v. 3) and in view of Abraham's fidelity (cf. v. 5). The great importance of Isaac in the history of salvation is that he marks the continuity of the promise and the blessing God gave Abraham. The figure of Isaac teaches us that every man or woman, being the heir

of gifts that God gave to previous generations, advances God's salvific plans through his or her own fidelity. "No human life is ever isolated. It is bound up with other lives. No man or woman is a single verse; we all make up one divine poem which God writes with the cooperation of our freedom" (St Josemaría Escrivá, *Christ Is Passing By*, 111).

26:7–11. This episode is very like these told in chapters 12 and 20 in connexion with Abraham. Here again it is easy to see how prudently the patriarch acts in a difficult situation, and the seriousness of the sin of adultery (had it been committed).

---

in terra, quam dixero tibi, ³et peregrinare in ea; eroque tecum et benedicam tibi. Tibi enim et semini tuo dabo universas regiones has complens iuramentum, quod spopondi Abraham patri tuo, ⁴et multiplicabo semen tuum sicut stellas caeli daboque posteris tuis universas regiones has; et benedicentur in semine tuo omnes gentes terrae, ⁵eo quod oboedierit Abraham voci meae et custodierit praecepta et mandata mea et iustificationes legesque servaverit». ⁶Mansit itaque Isaac in Geraris. ⁷Qui cum interrogaretur a viris loci illius super uxore sua, respondit: «Soror mea est». Timuerat enim confiteri quod sibi esset sociata coniugio, reputans ne forte interficerent eum propter illius pulchritudinem. ⁸Cumque pertransissent dies plurimi et ibidem moraretur, prospiciens Abimelech rex Philisthim per fenestram vidit eum iocantem cum Rebecca uxore sua. ⁹Et, accersito eo, ait: «Perspicuum est quod uxor tua sit; cur mentitus es eam sororem tuam esse?». Respondit: «Timui, ne morerer propter eam». ¹⁰Dixitque

[10]Abimelech said, "What is this you have done to us? One of the people might easily have lain with your wife, and you would have brought guilt upon us." [11]So Abimelech warned all the people, saying, "Whoever touches this man or his wife shall be put to death."

Gen 13:2   [12]And Isaac sowed in that land, and reaped in the same year a hundredfold. The LORD blessed him, [13]and the man became rich, and gained more and more until he became very wealthy. [14]He had possessions of flocks and herds, and a great household, so that the Philistines envied him.

Gen 21:25–34   **Disputes over wells**

[15](Now the Philistines had stopped and filled with earth all the wells which his father's servants had dug in the days of Abraham his father.) [16]And Abimelech said to Isaac, "Go away from us; for you are much mightier than we."

26:12–14 God blesses Isaac's work in the land of Canaan, giving him rich harvests and great wealth, as he had done to Abraham too (cf. 13:2). Here, wealth is the product of work and also a sign of God's blessing. Holy Scripture does not condemn wealth as such, or its possession; but it does condemn being attached to things and putting our trust in them (cf. Lk 12:13–21). Apropos of material goods, the Church teaches that "in his use of things man should regard the external goods he legitimately owns not merely as exclusive to himself but common to others also, in the sense that they can benefit others as well as himself" (Vatican II, *Gaudium et spes*, 69).

26:15–33 Isaac experiences the same sort of difficulties as his father (cf. 21:25–34), and, like Abraham, he adopts a concilia-tory attitude to the local people. First he makes his way south, even at the cost of giving up rights; later he will accept the pact that Abimelech offers him (vv. 26–30). God rewards him for this by giving him new finds of water and making him prosperous (cf. vv. 22 and 32), and, above all, by revealing himself at Beer-sheba.

The wells get their names from an incident that goes back to the time they were dug. On the etymology of Beer-sheba, cf. 21:28–31.

God reveals himself to Isaac as the God of his father Abraham (v. 24), and therefore as a personal God who wants to be on friendly terms with man. Later on God will reveal himself to Moses as "I am the God of your fathers, the God of Abraham, the God of Isaac, and the God of Jacob" (Ex 3:6), thus making it clear

Abimelech: «Quare hoc fecisti nobis? Potuit coire quispiam de populo cum uxore tua, et induxeras super nos grande peccatum». Praecepitque omni populo dicens: [11]«Qui tetigerit hominem hunc et uxorem eius, morte morietur». [12]Sevit autem Isaac in terra illa et invenit in ipso anno centuplum; benedixitque ei Dominus. [13]Et locupletatus est homo et ibat proficiens atque succrescens, donec magnus vehementer effectus est; [14]habuitque possessionem ovium et armentorum et familiae plurimum. Ob haec invidentes ei Philisthim [15]omnes puteos, quos foderant servi patris illius in diebus Abraham, obstruxerunt implentes humo, [16]in tantum ut ipse Abimelech diceret ad Isaac: «Recede a

[17]So Isaac departed from there, and encamped in the valley of Gerar and dwelt there. [18]And Isaac dug again the wells of water which had been dug in the days of Abraham his father; for the Philistines had stopped them after the death of Abraham; and he gave them the names which his father had given them. [19]But when Isaac's servants dug in the valley and found there a well of springing water, [20]the herdsmen of Gerar quarreled with Isaac's herdsmen, saying, "The water is ours." So he called the name of the well Esek,[u] because they contended with him. [21]Then they dug another well, and they quarreled over that also; so he called its name Sitnah.[v] [22]And he moved from there and dug another well, and over that they did not quarrel; so he called its name Rehoboth,[w] saying, "For now the LORD has made room for us, and we shall be fruitful in the land."

Jn 4:10

God appears to Isaac

*Gen 12:8;
15:1–21*

[23]From there he went up to Beer-sheba. [24]And the LORD appeared to him the same night and said, "I am the God of Abraham your father; fear not, for I am with you and will bless you and multiply your descendants for my servant Abraham's sake." [25]So he built an altar there and called upon the name of the LORD, and pitched his tent there. And there Isaac's servants dug a well.

Gen 4:26

---

that the God the patriarchs worship is the same as the God who made the Covenant on Sinai; and, at the same time, showing how closely linked he is to the people of Israel. The description of God as the God of a particular individual and specifically as the God of the patriarchs and later on as the God of our Lord Jesus Christ (cf. Eph 1:3) leads us to regard him as our personal God insofar as we are linked to

that person with whom God entered into a special relationship.

"I am with you," the Lord says to Isaac (v. 23), and he says the same thing to those who believe in him—Abraham, for example. "We've got to be convinced," St Josemaría Escrivá teaches, "that God is always near to us. We live as though he were far away, in the heavens high above, and we forget that he is also con-

---

nobis, quoniam potentior nostri factus es valde». [17]Et ille discedens tentoria fixit ad torrentem Gerarae habitavitque ibi. [18]Rursum fodit puteos, quos foderant in diebus patris sui Abraham et quos, illo mortuo, obstruxerant Philisthim. Appellavitque eos eisdem nominibus, quibus ante pater vocaverat. [19]Foderunt servi Isaac in torrente et reppererunt ibi puteum aquae vivae. [20]Sed et ibi iurgium fuit pastorum Gerarae adversus pastores Isaac dicentium: «Nostra est aqua!». Quam ob rem nomen putei vocavit Esec (*id est Iurgium*), quia iurgati sunt cum eo. [21]Foderunt autem et alium puteum, et pro illo quoque rixati sunt; appellavitque eum Sitna (*id est Inimicitias*). [22]Profectus inde fodit alium puteum, pro quo non contenderunt; itaque vocavit nomen eius Rehoboth (*id est Latitudinem*) dicens: «Nunc dilatavit nos Dominus, et crescemus in terra». [23]Ascendit autem ex illo loco in Bersabee, [24]ubi apparuit ei Dominus in ipsa nocte dicens: «Ego sum Deus Abraham patris tui. / Noli timere, quia tecum sum; / benedicam tibi / et multiplicabo semen tuum / propter servum meum Abraham». [25]Itaque aedificavit

u. That is *Contention*   **v.** That is *Enmity*   **w.** That is *Broad places* or *Room*

Gen 12:22–23,
28–31 **Isaac's pact with the inhabitants of Canaan**

²⁶Then Abimelech went to him from Gerar with Ahuzzath his adviser and Phicol the commander of his army. ²⁷Isaac said to them, "Why have you come to me, seeing that you hate me and have sent me away from you?" ²⁸They said, "We see plainly that the LORD is with you; so we say, let there be an oath between you and us, and let us make a covenant with you, ²⁹that you will do us no harm, just as we have not touched you and have done to you nothing but good and have sent you away in peace. You are now the blessed of the LORD." ³⁰So he made them a feast, and they ate and drank. ³¹In the morning they rose early and took oath with one another; and Isaac set them on their way, and they departed from him in peace. ³²That same day Isaac's servants came and told him about the well which they had dug, and said to him, "We have found water." ³³He called it Shibah; therefore the name of the city is Beer-sheba to this day.

Gen 27:46;
36:1–5
Heb 12:16 ³⁴When Esau was forty years old, he took to wife Judith the daughter of Be-eri the Hittite, and Basemath the daughter of Elon the Hittite; ³⁵and they made life bitter for Isaac and Rebekah.

Jacob obtains Isaac's blessing by cunning*

27 ¹When Isaac was old and his eyes were dim so that he could not see, he called Esau his older son, and said to him, "My son"; and he answered, "Here I am." ²He said, "Behold,

---

tinually by our side. He is there like a loving Father. He loves each one of us more than all the mothers in the world can love their children—helping us, inspiring us, blessing . . . and forgiving. [. . .] We've got to be filled, to be imbued with the idea that our Father, and very much our Father, is God who is both near us and in heaven" (*The Way*, 267).

*27:1–45. Jacob managed to get the birthright; now he is going to get the blessing his father intended for his first-born son. Seemingly, this blessing meant

---

ibi altare et, invocato nomine Domini, extendit tabernaculum, et servi Isaac foderunt ibi puteum. ²⁶Abimelech autem venit ad eum de Geraris et Ochozath amicus illius et Phicol dux militum, ²⁷et locutus est eis Isaac: «Quid venistis ad me hominem, quem odistis et expulistis a vobis?». ²⁸Qui responderunt: «Vidimus tecum esse Dominum et idcirco diximus: Sit iuramentum inter nos et te, et ineamus tecum foedus, ²⁹ut non facias nobis quidquam mali, sicut et nos non attigimus te et nihil fecimus tibi nisi bonum et cum pace dimisimus te. Tu es enim benedictus Domini». ³⁰Fecit ergo eis convivium, et comederunt et biberunt. ³¹Surgentesque mane iuraverunt sibi mutuo. Dimisitque eos Isaac, et profecti sunt ab eo cum pace. ³²Ecce autem venerunt in ipso die servi Isaac annuntiantes ei de puteo, quem foderant, atque dicentes: «Invenimus aquam». ³³Unde appellavit eum Sabee (*quod significat Abundantiam*); et nomen urbi impositum est Bersabee usque in praesentem diem. ³⁴Esau vero quadragenarius duxit uxores Iudith filiam Beeri Hetthaei, et Basemath filiam Elon Hetthaei. ³⁵Quae ambae offenderant animum Isaac et Rebeccae. ¹ Senuit autem Isaac, et caligaverunt oculi eius, et videre non poterat. Vocavitque Esau filium suum maiorem et dixit ei: «Fili mi». Qui respondit: «Adsum». ²Cui

I am old; I do not know the day of my death. ³Now then, take your weapons, your quiver and your bow, and go out to the field, and hunt game for me, ⁴and prepare for me savoury food, such as I love, and bring it to me that I may eat; that I may bless you before I die."

⁵Now Rebekah was listening when Isaac spoke to his son Esau. So when Esau went to the field to hunt for game and bring it, ⁶Rebekah said to her son Jacob, "I heard your father speak to your brother Esau, ⁷'Bring me game, and prepare for me savoury food, that I may eat it, and bless you before the Lord before I die.' ⁸Now therefore, my son, obey my word as I command you. ⁹Go to the flock, and fetch me two good kids, that I may prepare from them savoury food for your father, such as he loves; ¹⁰and you shall

---

he acquired a right to the inheritance he had already bought from Esau and it meant he would be the head of the family (cf. v. 29). Moreover, by getting his father's blessing he also received God's blessing. The Bible does not make a judgment about the methods Jacob used to deflect his father's blessing to himself; but it does make it clear, once again, that he had no right to it as far as human laws were concerned; no, he received both the birthright and the blessing as a gratuitous gift from God, who chose the younger son (cf. 25:23). Here too, as in the case of Isaac (cf. 21:8–13), the part played by the mother is stressed; she ignores custom, and plays an active part in the furthering of God's plans. The passage also stresses how shrewd the patriarch is by comparison with Esau. Jacob's action is justified in the overall context of the narrative, given that he bought the

birthright previously from his brother. However, the prophet Hosea was of the opinion that Jacob had done something he should be sorry for; in which case Jacob prefigures the people of Israel, whom the prophet calls to repentance (cf. Hos 12:37).

This account is in a style similar to what we saw in chapter 24: the action unfolds over five scenes, each of which includes a dialogue between two people (their psychology is captured very well); dramatic tension is maintained by curiosity as to who will end up winning the blessing; the story is well told, and rather amusing.

27:5–17. Rebekah apparently acts out of human motives, impelled by her love for her favourite (younger) son (cf. 25:28). God will use this favouritism to guide events so that his plans for the two sons

---

pater: «Vides, inquit, quod senuerim et ignorem diem mortis meae; ³sume arma tua, pharetram et arcum, et egredere in agrum. Cumque venatu aliquid apprehenderis, ⁴fac mihi inde pulmentum, sicut velle me nosti, et affer, ut comedam; et benedicat tibi anima mea, antequam moriar». ⁵Rebecca autem audierat Isaac loquentem cum Esau filio suo. Esau ergo abiit in agrum, ut venationem caperet et offerret eam. ⁶Rebecca autem dixit filio suo Iacob: «Ecce, audivi patrem tuum loquentem cum Esau fratre tuo et dicentem ei: ⁷'Affer mihi venationem tuam et fac cibos, ut comedam et benedicam tibi coram Domino, antequam moriar'. ⁸Nunc ergo, fili mi, audi vocem meam in eo, quod praecipio tibi. ⁹Pergens ad gregem affer mihi duos haedos optimos, ut faciam ex eis escas patri tuo, quibus libenter vescitur. ¹⁰Quas cum intuleris patri tuo, et comederit, benedicat tibi, priusquam moriatur». ¹¹Cui ille respondit:

bring it to your father to eat, so that he may bless you before he dies." [11]But Jacob said to Rebekah his mother, "Behold, my brother Esau is a hairy man, and I am a smooth man. [12]Perhaps my father will feel me, and I shall seem to be mocking him, and bring a curse upon myself and not a blessing." [13]His mother said to him, "Upon me be your curse, my son; only obey my word, and go, fetch them to me." [14]So he went and took them and brought them to his mother; and his mother prepared savoury food, such as his father loved. [15]Then Rebekah took the best garments of Esau her older son, which were with her in the house, and put them on Jacob her younger son; [16]and the skins of the kids she put upon his hands and upon the smooth part of his neck; [17]and she gave the savoury food and the bread, which she had prepared, into the hand of her son Jacob.

[18]So he went in to his father, and said, "My father"; and he said, "Here I am; who are you, my son?" [19]Jacob said to his father, "I am Esau your first-born. I have done as you told me; now sit up and eat of my game, that you may bless me." [20]But Isaac said to his son, "How is it that you have found it so quickly, my son?" He answered, "Because the Lord your God granted me success." [21]Then Isaac said to Jacob, "Come near, that I may feel you, my son, to know whether you are really my son Esau or not." [22]So Jacob went near to Isaac his father, who felt him and said, "The voice is Jacob's voice, but the hands are the hands of Esau." [23]And he did not recognize him, because his hands were hairy like his brother Esau's hands; so he blessed him. [24]He said, "Are you really my son Esau?" He answered, "I am." [25]Then he said,

---

take effect (cf. 25:23). Holy Scripture does not justify Rebekah's action, but God draws great good from it: the promises made to Abraham pass, through Jacob, to the people of Israel, his descendants.

27:20. Jacob's reply, invoking the name

«Nosti quod Esau frater meus homo pilosus sit, et ego lenis. [12]Si attrectaverit me pater meus et senserit, timeo, ne putet me sibi voluisse illudere; et inducam super me maledictionem pro benedictione». [13]Ad quem mater: «In me sit, ait, ista maledictio, fili mi; tantum audi vocem meam et perge afferque, quae dixi». [14]Abiit et attulit deditque matri. Paravit illa cibos, sicut noverat velle patrem illius. [15]Et vestibus Esau valde bonis, quas apud se habebat domi, induit eum [16]pelliculasque haedorum circumdedit manibus et colli nuda protexit; [17]dedit pulmentum optimum et panes, quos coxerat, in manus filii sui Iacob. [18]Qui ingressus ad patrem suum dixit: «Pater mi». At ille respondit: «Audio. Quis es tu, fili mi?». [19]Dixitque Iacob ad patrem suum: «Ego sum Esau primogenitus tuus. Feci sicut praecepisti mihi; surge, sede et comede de venatione mea, ut benedicat mihi anima tua». [20]Rursum Isaac ad filium suum: «Quomodo, inquit, tam cito invenire potuisti, fili mi?». Qui respondit: «Voluntas Domini Dei tui fuit, ut occurreret mihi». [21]Dixitque Isaac ad Iacob: «Accede huc, ut tangam te, fili mi, et probem, utrum tu sis filius meus Esau an non». [22]Accessit ille ad patrem et, palpato eo, dixit Isaac: «Vox quidem, vox Iacob est, sed manus, manus sunt Esau». [23]Et non cognovit eum, quia pilosae manus similitudinem

"Bring it to me, that I may eat of my son's game and bless you."
So he brought it to him, and he ate; and he brought him wine, and
he drank. ²⁶Then his father Isaac said to him, "Come near and kiss
me, my son." ²⁷So he came near and kissed him; and he smelled   Heb 11:20
the smell of his garments, and blessed him, and said,

> "See, the smell of my son
> > is as the smell of a field which the LORD has blessed!
> ²⁸May God give you of the dew of heaven,
> > and of the fatness of the earth,
> > and plenty of grain and wine.
> ²⁹Let peoples serve you,   Gen 25:23
> > and nations bow down to you.

---

of God as it does, is not a little astute: he
does not explain how he obtained the
game, but the reader is led to believe that
it was Rebekah's doing.

27:26–29. The blessing Isaac gives Jacob
evokes the fine qualities of this son, the
fruitfulness of the land and lordship over
the nations—three things connected with
the call to Abraham and the promise of
land and descendants, as will be pointed
out later on when Isaac reaffirms his
blessing after he discovers he has been
deceived (cf. 28:3–4). The Letter to the
Hebrews (cf. Heb 11:20) teaches that this
blessing and also that received by Esau
(cf. Gen 27:39–40), are inspired by faith
and are given with a view to the future,
that is, to the fullness of time. And so St
Augustine interprets that "what the blessing of Jacob typifies is, then, the preaching of Christ to all nations. [. . .] Isaac is
the law and prophecy by which Christ is
blessed by means of the mouth of the
Jews. But, since law and prophecy was

not understood, it was as though it came
from one who spoke in ignorance. It is
with the aroma of Christ's name that the
world, like a field, is filled. His is the
blessing of the dew from heaven (meaning
the shower of His divine words) and of
the fruitfulness of the earth (in the sense
of the gathering in of the peoples of the
earth). His is the harvest of grain and of
wine (interpreted as the multitude of those
who gather the grain and wine in the
sacrament of his Body and Blood. [. . .]
His Father's sons, in the sense of the sons
of Abraham according to faith, adore Him
who is, in turn, a son of Abraham according to the flesh. Anyone who curses Him
is cursed, and anyone who blesses Him is
blessed. What I mean is that it is our
Christ who is blessed (in the sense of
being truly announced) even by the Jews
themselves, who, for all their errors of
hoping for some other Messiah and of
thinking that it is he who is being blessed,
still sing in their synagogues the Laws and
the Prophets" (*De civitate Dei,* 16, 37).

---

maioris expresserant. Benedixit ergo illi. ²⁴Ait: «Tu es filius meus Esau?». Respondit: «Ego sum». ²⁵At
ille: «Affer, inquit, mihi, et comedam de venatione tua, fili mi, ut benedicat tibi anima mea». Quos cum
oblatos comedisset, obtulit ei etiam vinum. Quo hausto, ²⁶dixit ad eum Isaac pater eius: «Accede ad me
et da mihi osculum, fili mi». ²⁷Accessit et osculatus est eum. Statimque, ut sensit vestimentorum illius
fragrantiam, benedicens illi ait: «Ecce odor filii mei / sicut odor agri pleni, / cui benedixit Dominus. /
²⁸Det tibi Deus de rore caeli / et de pinguedine terrae / et abundantiam frumenti et vini. / ²⁹Et serviant
tibi populi, / et adorent te nationes; / esto dominus fratrum tuorum, / et incur ventur ante te filii matris
tuae. / Qui maledixerit tibi, sit maledictus; / et, qui benedixerit tibi, sit benedictus!». ³⁰Vix Isaac bene-

> Be lord over your brothers,
> and may your mother's sons bow down to you.
> Cursed be every one who curses you,
> and blessed be every one who blesses you!"

^{Heb 12:17} is rendered as:

Heb 12:17 ³⁰As soon as Isaac had finished blessing Jacob, when Jacob had scarcely gone out from the presence of Isaac his father, Esau his brother came in from his hunting. ³¹He also prepared savoury food, and brought it to his father. And he said to his father, "Let my father arise, and eat of his son's game, that you may bless me." ³²His father Isaac said to him, "Who are you?" He answered, "I am your son, your first-born, Esau." ³³Then Isaac trembled violently, and said, "Who was it then that hunted game and brought it to me, and I ate it all[x] before you came, and I have blessed him?—yes, and he shall be blessed."

Esau's reaction

³⁴When Esau heard the words of his father, he cried out with an exceedingly great and bitter cry, and said to his father, "Bless me, even me also, O my father!" ³⁵But he said, "Your brother came with guile, and he has taken away your blessing." ³⁶Esau said, "Is he not rightly named Jacob? For he has supplanted me these two times. He took away my birthright; and behold, now he has taken away my blessing." Then he said, "Have you not reserved a bless-

Gen 25:29–34
Jer 9:3
Hos 12:4

27:33. Whether they come directly from God or from one who has authority to represent him, blessings (like curses) once given cannot be revoked, and they are effective irrespective of the circumstances which led to their being given. This conviction which we find in the Bible does not mean that ritual blessings carry some sort of magic; it simply stresses the strength and power of words when spoken by those who have authority to speak.

The blessings of the patriarchs are in this category. As St Ambrose comments, "they show us what reverence we should show our parents, because, as we read here, when someone is blessed by his father, that blessing stays in place. Therefore, God gives parents this grace in order to sustain the devotion of their children, for (blessing) is the prerogative of parents, obedience, that of children" (*De benedictionibus patriarcharum*, 1,1).

dictionem Iacob finierat, et Iacob egressus erat a patre suo Isaac, venit Esau frater eius ³¹coctosque de venatione cibos intulit patri dicens: «Surge, pater mi, et comede de venatione filii tui, ut benedicat mihi anima tua». ³²Dixitque illi Isaac pater eius: «Quis enim es tu?». Qui respondit: «Ego sum filius tuus primogenitus Esau». ³³Expavit Isaac stupore vehementi ultra modum et ait: «Quis igitur ille est, qui dudum captam venationem attulit mihi, et comedi ex omnibus, priusquam tu venires? Benedixique ei, et erit benedictus!». ³⁴Auditis Esau sermonibus patris, irrugiit clamore magno et amaro ultra modum et ait patri suo: «Benedic etiam mihi, pater mi!». ³⁵Qui ait: «Venit germanus tuus fraudulenter et accepit

x. Cn: Heb *of all*

ing for me?" [37]Isaac answered Esau, "Behold, I have made him your lord, and all his brothers I have given to him for servants, and with grain and wine I have sustained him. What then can I do for you, my son?" [38]Esau said to his father, "Have you but one blessing, my father? Bless me, even me also, O my father." And Esau lifted up his voice and wept. Heb 11:20

[39]Then Isaac his father answered him:

> "Behold, away from[y] the fatness of the earth shall your
> dwelling be,
> and away from[y] the dew of heaven on high.
> [40]By your sword you shall live,
> and you shall serve your brother;
> but when you break loose
> you shall break his yoke from your neck."

[41]Now Esau hated Jacob because of the blessing with which his father had blessed him, and Esau said to himself, "The days of mourning for my father are approaching; then I will kill my brother Jacob." [42]But the words of Esau her older son were told to Rebekah; so she sent and called Jacob her younger son, and said to him, "Behold, your brother Esau comforts himself by planning to kill you. [43]Now therefore, my son, obey my voice; arise, flee to Laban my brother in Haran, [44]and stay with him a while, until your brother's fury turns away; [45]until your brother's anger turns Wis 10:10 Gen 24:29

27:45. Rebekah's intervention saves not only Jacob but also Esau, for if Esau had killed Jacob he would have had to become a fugitive or else die under the law of retaliation. Rebekah shows she is a sensible person: she sees that time and patience will sort things out. However, as the narrative will go on to tell us, she will never again see Jacob.

"Let us learn, then, from Rebekah, how to ensure that envy does not give rise to anger, or anger to parricide. Imitate Rebekah, that is, her patience, the good guardian of innocence; let her persuade us by her example not to give anger an outlet. Let us keep our distance from whomever it may be, until time tones down our indignation and we gradually manage to forget the offence" (St Ambrose, *De Jacob et vita beata*, 2, 4, 14).

benedictionem tuam». [36]At ille subiunxit: «Iuste vocatum est nomen eius Iacob; supplantavit enim me en altera vice: primogenita mea ante tulit et nunc secundo surripuit benedictionem meam». Rursumque ait: «Numquid non reservasti mihi benedictionem?». [37]Respondit Isaac: «Ecce, dominum tuum illum constitui et omnes fratres eius servituti illius subiugavi; frumento et vino stabilivi eum. Et tibi post haec, fili mi, ultra quid faciam?». [38]Dixitque Esau ad patrem suum: «Num unam tantum benedictionem habes, pater mi? Mihi quoque obsecro, ut benedicas!». Cumque eiulatu magno fleret, [39]motus Isaac dixit ad eum: «Ecce, procul a pinguedine terrae / erit habitatio tua / et procul a rore caeli desuper. / [40]De gladio tuo vives / et fratri tuo servies. / Tempusque veniet, cum excutias / et solvas iugum eius de cervicibus tuis». [41]Oderat ergo Esau Iacob pro benedictione, qua benedixerat ei pater, dixitque in corde

y. Or *of*

away, and he forgets what you have done to him; then I will send, and fetch you from there. Why should I be bereft of you both in one day?"

Jacob leaves for Haran*

Gen 23:3; 24:3–4; 26:34–35; 36:1–5 ⁴⁶Then Rebekah said to Isaac, "I am weary of my life because of the Hittite women. If Jacob marries one of the Hittite women such as these, one of the women of the land, what good will my life be to me?"

---

*27:46—28:9. After telling us how Jacob managed to obtain the birthright and also his father's blessing, and the consequences which he had to face from Esau, the book of Genesis now provides a kind of summary in which it leaves aside the tensions within the family and concentrates on the marriages of Jacob and Esau—the former keeping to the traditions of his ancestors (cf. chap. 24), the latter going against them.

The sacred text makes two things clear—one, the fact that Jacob obeys his parents in a matter of such importance as the choice of a wife; the other, the passing on to Jacob of the blessing and promises God made to Abraham. The reason why Jacob has to leave the promised land this time is Rebekah's aversion towards the women of the area (she was displeased by the way they had treated her: cf. 26:34–35). Isaac, following his wife's wishes, sends Jacob to the country of his ancestors, which was where Rebekah was from too; but first he passes on to him the blessing God gave Abraham. The reason which is implicitly

given here for why the blessing should fall on Jacob and not to Esau is that Esau had contracted marriage with women of Canaan, against what Abraham told Isaac to do (cf. chap. 24). Marriage with Canaanite women will always be very much frowned on in Israel because it brought with it idolatry and the worship of Baal.

This concludes Rebekah's intervention. She has obtained the birthright and Isaac's blessing for her son Jacob—and now he has been given the divine blessing and promises made to Abraham and his descendants.

Esau's gesture of taking a wife from Abraham's family (cf. v. 9) in addition to the wives he already has, seems to come too late and does not fully meet Isaac's wishes. This detail indicates the relationship between the Edomites (descendants of Esau) and the Arabs (descendants of Ishmael), distinguishing them both more clearly from the future chosen people. On Heth and the Hittites, cf. the note on 23:1–20.

suo: «Appropinquabunt dies luctus patris mei, et occidam Iacob fratrem meum». ⁴²Nuntiata sunt Rebeccae verba Esau filii eius maioris, quae mittens et vocans Iacob filium suum minorem dixit ad eum: «Ecce, Esau frater tuus minatur, ut occidat te. ⁴³Nunc ergo, fili mi, audi vocem meam et consurgens fuge ad Laban fratrem meum in Charran; ⁴⁴habitabisque cum eo dies paucos, donec requiescat furor fratris tui, ⁴⁵et cesset indignatio eius, obliviscaturque eorum, quae fecisti in eum. Postea mittam et adducam te inde huc. Cur utroque orbabor filio in uno die?». ⁴⁶Dixit quoque Rebecca ad Isaac: «Taedet me vitae meae propter filias Heth; si acceperit Iacob uxorem de filiabus Heth sicut istis de filiabus terrae, nolo vivere». ¹ Vocavit itaque Isaac Iacob et benedixit eum praecepitque ei dicens: «Noli accipere coniugem de filiabus Chanaan; ²surge, vade in Paddanaram ad domum Bathuel patris matris

28 ¹Then Isaac called Jacob and blessed him, and charged him, "You shall not marry one of the Canaanite women. ²Arise, go to Paddan-aram to the house of Bethuel your mother's father; and take as wife from there one of the daughters of Laban your mother's brother. ³God Almighty^z bless you and make you Gen 17:1 fruitful and multiply you, that you may become a company of peoples. ⁴May he give the blessing of Abraham to you and to your descendants with you, that you may take possession of the land of your sojournings which God gave to Abraham!" ⁵Thus Isaac sent Jacob away; and he went to Paddan-aram to Laban, the son of Bethuel the Aramean, the brother of Rebekah, Jacob's and Esau's mother.

⁶Now Esau saw that Isaac had blessed Jacob and sent him away to Paddan-aram to take a wife from there, and that as he blessed him he charged him, "You shall not marry one of the Canaanite women," ⁷and that Jacob had obeyed his father and his mother and gone to Paddan-aram. ⁸So when Esau saw that the

---

*28:10–22 The narrative continues with this scene which deals with the first appearance of God to Jacob, when he confirms to him the promise he made to Abraham; it also recalls the foundation of the shrine at Bethel.

It is significant that these events occur in Canaan, the land of the promise and the land to which Jacob and his sons will later have reason to return. After the exodus from Egypt and the conquest of the land, the Israelites consulted Yahweh at Bethel (cf. Judg 20:18, 26–28); and after the division of the country into two kingdoms, on the death of Solomon, Bethel became one of the main religious shrines of the Northern kingdom (cf. 1 Kings 12:26–33).

In the context in which it appears here, the account of Jacob's dream shows how the patriarch, strengthened by God who has revealed to him his plan, is now able to face the long years which he will have to spend away from the promised land. The Lord will not appear to him again until he returns (cf. 32:22–32). The Lord does the same thing with us, sometimes allowing quite a time to go by when we do not feel his presence. "You told me that God sometimes fills you with light for a while and sometimes does not. I reminded you, firmly, that the Lord is always infinitely good. That is why those moments of light are enough to help you carry on; but the times when you see no light are good for you too, and make you more faithful" (St Josemaría Escrivá, *Furrow*, 341).

tuae et accipe tibi inde uxorem de filiabus Laban avunculi tui. ³Deus autem omnipotens benedicat tibi et crescere te faciat atque multiplicet, ut sis in multitudinem populorum; ⁴et det tibi benedictiones Abraham tibi et semini tuo tecum, ut possideas terram peregrinationis tuae, quam pollicitus est Deus avo tuo». ⁵Cumque dimisisset eum Isaac, profectus est in Paddanaram ad Laban filium Bathuel Aramaei fratrem Rebeccae matris Iacob et Esau. ⁶Videns autem Esau quod benedixisset pater suus Iacob et misisset eum in Paddanaram, ut inde uxorem duceret, et quod post benedictionem praecepisset ei dicens: «Non accipies uxorem de filiabus Chanaan», ⁷quodque oboediens Iacob parentibus suis

z. Heb *El Shaddai*

Canaanite women did not please Isaac his father, [9]Esau went to Ishmael and took to wife, besides the wives he had, Mahalath the daughter of Ishmael Abraham's son, the sister of Nebaioth.

Gen 12:3;
32:22–32;
35:6–8; 48:3–4
Hos 12:5
Wis 10:10–12

Jn 1:51

Rev 1:7
Gen 12:3

Jacob's dream

[10]Jacob left Beer-sheba, and went toward Haran. [11]And he came to a certain place, and stayed there that night, because the sun had set. Taking one of the stones of the place, he put it under his head and lay down in that place to sleep. [12]And he dreamed that there was a ladder set up on the earth, and the top of it reached to heaven; and behold, the angels of God were ascending and descending on it! [13]And behold, the Lord stood above it[a] and said, "I am the LORD, the God of Abraham your father and the God of Isaac; the land on which you lie I will give to you and to your descendants; [14]and your descendants shall be like the dust of the earth, and you shall spread abroad to the west and to the east and to the north and to the south; and by you and your descendants shall all the families of the

---

28:12. As described in the biblical text, the ladder which Jacob sees in his dream (which might have been like the staircases in Mesopotamian or Egyptian temples, copied in turn in the shrines of Canaan) is filled with deep symbolism: it is the link between heaven and earth. Some Fathers of the Church interpret this ladder as being divine providence, which reaches earth through the ministry of angels; others see it as a sign of the Incarnation of Christ (who is of the line of Jacob), for the Incarnation is truly the time when divine and human join, since Christ is true God and true man.

In St John's Gospel we see Jacob's dream fulfilled in the glorification of Jesus through his death on the cross:

"Truly, truly, I say to you, you will see heaven opened, and the angels of God ascending and descending upon the Son of man" (Jn 1:51). And so other prominent interpreters see Jacob's ladder as representing the cross, whereby Christ and Christians attain the glory of heaven. St Bernard applied the symbolism of the ladder to the Blessed Virgin: "She is the ladder of Jacob, which has twelve rungs, counting the two sides. The right-hand side is disdain for oneself out of love for God; the left-hand side is disdain for the world, for love for the Kingdom. The ascent up its twelve rungs represents the degrees of humility. [. . .] By these rungs angels ascend and men are raised up . . ." (*Sermo ad Beatam Virginem*, 4).

---

isset in Paddanaram; [8]probans quoque quod non libenter aspiceret filias Chanaan pater suus, [9]ivit ad Ismaelem et duxit uxorem, absque iis, quas habebat, Mahalath filiam Ismael filii Abraham sororem Nabaioth. [10]Igitur egressus Iacob de Bersabee pergebat Charran. [11]Cumque venisset ad quendam locum et vellet in eo requiescere post solis occubitum, tulit de lapidibus, qui iacebant, et supponens capiti suo dormivit in eodem loco. [12]Viditque in somnio scalam stantem super terram et cacumen illius tangens caelum, angelos quoque Dei ascendentes et descendentes per eam [13]et Dominum innixum scalae dicentem sibi: «Ego sum Dominus, Deus Abraham patris tui et Deus Isaac. Terram, in qua dormis, tibi dabo et semini tuo. [14]Eritque semen tuum quasi pulvis terrae; dilataberis ad occidentem et orientem et

a. Or *beside him*

earth bless themselves.ᵇ ¹⁵Behold, I am with you and will keep Heb 13:5
you wherever you go, and will bring you back to this land; for I
will not leave you until I have done that of which I have spoken to
you." ¹⁶Then Jacob awoke from his sleep and said, "Surely the
LORD is in this place; and I did not know it." ¹⁷And he was afraid, Ex 19:12
and said, "How awesome is this place! This is none other than the
house of God, and this is the gate of heaven."

¹⁸So Jacob rose early in the morning, and he took the stone Judg 20:18, 26–28
which he had put under his head and set it up for a pillar and
poured oil on the top of it. ¹⁹He called the name of that place Judg 1:23
Bethel;ᶜ but the name of the city was Luz at the first. ²⁰Then
Jacob made a vow, saying, "If God will be with me, and will
keep me in this way that I go, and will give me bread to eat and
clothing to wear, ²¹so that I come again to my father's house in
peace, then the LORD shall be my God, ²²and this stone, which I
have set up for a pillar, shall be God's house; and of all that thou
givest me I will give the tenth to thee."*

28:14. Once more, divine revelation makes it clear that the reason for choosing the people of Israel (a choice now confirmed to Jacob) is to have the blessing of God reach all nations (cf. 12:3), and to let all men, created as they are in God's image and likeness (cf. 1:26), benefit from that choice. The fact that God chose one people does not mean that he has put a limit on his goodness; it is simply the way that he, the Creator of all, chose to make his fatherly call reach the ears of all. "Connected with the mystery of creation is the *mystery of the election*, which in a special way shaped the history of the people whose spiritual father is Abraham by virtue of his faith. Nevertheless, through this people which journeys forward through the history both of the Old Covenant and of the New, that mystery of election refers to every man and woman, to the whole great human family. 'I have loved you with an everlasting love, therefore I have continued my faithfulness to you' (Jer 31:3)" (John Paul II, *Dives in misericordiae*, 4).

28:20. St John Chrysostom comments that the words "will give me bread to eat" were endorsed by Jesus in the Our Father: "Give us this day our daily bread": "Let us request of him no mater-

septentrionem et meridiem; et benedicentur in te et in semine tuo cunctae tribus terrae. ¹⁵Et ecce, ego tecum sum et custodiam te, quocumque perrexeris, et reducam te in terram hanc; nec dimittam te, nisi complevero quae dixi tibi». ¹⁶Cumque evigilasset Iacob de somno, ait: «Vere Dominus est in loco isto, et ego nesciebam». ¹⁷Pavensque: «Quam terribilis est, inquit, locus iste! Non est hic aliud nisi domus Dei et porta caeli». ¹⁸Surgens ergo Iacob mane tulit lapidem, quem supposuerat capiti suo, et erexit in titulum fundens oleum desuper. ¹⁹Appellavitque nomen loci illius Bethel; prius autem urbs vocabatur Luza. ²⁰Vovit Iacob etiam votum dicens: «Si fuerit Deus mecum et custodierit me in via hac, per quam ambulo, et dederit mihi panem ad vescendum et vestimentum ad induendum, ²¹reversusque fuero prospere ad domum patris mei, erit mihi Dominus in Deum, ²²et lapis iste, quem erexi in titulum, erit domus Dei; cunctorumque, quae dederis mihi, decimas offeram tibi». ¹Profectus ergo Iacob venit in

b. Or *be blessed*   **c.** That is *The house of God*

Jacob and Laban meet*

Gen 24:11–12
Ex 2:16–17

29 [1]Then Jacob went on his journey, and came to the land of the people of the east. [2]As he looked, he saw a well in the field, and lo, three flocks of sheep lying beside it; for out of that well the flocks were watered. The stone on the well's mouth was large, [3]and when all the flocks were gathered there, the shepherds would roll the stone from the mouth of the well, and water the sheep, and put the stone back in its place upon the mouth of the well.

[4]Jacob said to them, "My brothers, where do you come from?" They said, "We are from Haran." [5]He said to them, "Do you know Laban the son of Nahor?" They said, "We know him." [6]He said to them, "Is it well with him?" They said, "It is well; and see, Rachel his daughter is coming with the sheep!" [7]He said, "Behold, it is still high day, it is not time for the animals to be gathered together; water the sheep, and go, pasture them." [8]But they said, "We cannot until all the flocks are gathered together, and the stone is rolled from the mouth of the well; then we water the sheep."

---

ial things beyond this. I mean, it would be quite inappropriate to ask of such a generous giver, who enjoys such an abundance of power, things that will dissolve with this present life and undergo great transformation and decay. All such things are, in fact, human, whether you refer to wealth, or power, or human glory. Let us instead ask for what lasts forever, for what is permanent' (*Homiliae in Genesim,* 54, 5).

*29:1—32:3. This section tells about Jacob's sojourn away from the promised land, in the house of Laban, who stands here for continuity with Abraham's forebears (cf. chap. 24). Here Jacob will marry (cf. 29:1–30), have children (cf. 29:31—30:24), and prosper (cf. 30:25–43); and rather as Abraham did, he will return from here to settle in the land of Canaan (cf. 31:1—32:3).

The sacred text shows how God continues arranging things to suit his plan of salvation. In the relationship between Jacob and Laban, we can see how the young man gets gradually richer and his relative gets poorer. Jacob is being constantly blessed by God with prosperity; Laban eventually finds his livestock sadly depleted and he has to bow to circumstances when, at God's orders, Jacob and his wives (Laban's daughters) leave him.

29:1–14. Jacob's arrival at Laban's house and his meeting with Rachel are somewhat similar to the episode about Abraham's servant and Rebekah (cf. chap. 24). However, here the designation of the place is very vague—"the land of the

---

terram orientalium. [2]Et vidit puteum in agro, tres quoque greges ovium accubantes iuxta eum; nam ex illo adaquabantur pecora, et os eius grandi lapide claudebatur. [3]Morisque erat, ut, cunctis ovibus congregatis, devolverent lapidem et, refectis gregibus, rursum super os putei ponerent. [4]Dixitque ad pastores: «Fratres, unde estis?». Qui responderunt: «De Charran». [5]Quos interrogans: «Numquid, ait, nostis Laban filium Nachor?». Dixerunt: «Novimus». [6]«Sanusne est?», inquit. «Valet, inquiunt, et ecce Rachel filia eius venit cum grege». [7]Dixitque: «Adhuc multum diei superest, nec est tempus, ut congregentur greges; date potum ovibus et sic ad pastum eas reducite». [8]Qui responderunt: «Non pos-

⁹While he was still speaking with them, Rachel came with her father's sheep; for she kept them. ¹⁰Now when Jacob saw Rachel the daughter of Laban his mother's brother, and the sheep of Laban his mother's brother, Jacob went up and rolled the stone from the well's mouth, and watered the flock of Laban his mother's brother. ¹¹Then Jacob kissed Rachel, and wept aloud. ¹²And Jacob told Rachel that he was her father's kinsman, and that he was Rebekah's son; and she ran and told her father.

¹³When Laban heard the tidings of Jacob his sister's son, he ran to meet him, and embraced him and kissed him, and brought him to his house. Jacob told Laban all these things, ¹⁴and Laban said to him, "Surely you are my bone and my flesh!" And he stayed with him a month.

Jacob marries Leah and Rachel

¹⁵Then Laban said to Jacob, "Because you are my kinsman, should you therefore serve me for nothing? Tell me, what shall

people of the east", which would really suggest the north-east of the Arabian desert, an extensive area used by semi-nomadic shepherds (Aram-Naharim in the case of Abraham, or "the land of the people of the east" in the case of Jacob). Of course, tribes of this type did move around, and sometimes settled down for a while, so even though Rebekah and Rachel came from the same family there is no reason why they need have been from the same place.

Although events seem to happen in an unplanned way, the context does show the providence of God at work (Jacob had implored God to help him when he met him at Bethel: cf. 28:20).

29:12. The text literally says that Jacob told her he was her father's *brother*; but it must be read (as the RSV does) as *kinsman* (he was really her second cousin, according to what Genesis 24 says: Laban was Rebeka's brother and the son of Bethuel, the son of Nahor, the brother of Abraham, who was Jacob's grandfather). Here, however, Laban is called the son of Nahor (cf. v. 5), jumping over Bethuel, which does not seem important here or in the previous account of Rebekah's marriage (cf. Gen 24).

29:15–30. Jacob's marriage has special importance because from it will come the twelve tribes of Israel; the sacred writer identifies who is the mother of each son; the story is full of significant detail, odd nuances and little ironies.

sumus, donec omnia pecora congregentur et amoveamus lapidem de ore putei, ut adaquemus greges». ⁹Adhuc loquebatur cum eis, et ecce Rachel veniebat cum ovibus patris sui; nam gregem ipsa pascebat. ¹⁰Cum vidisset Iacob Rachel filiam Laban avunculi sui ovesque Laban avunculi sui, accedens amovit lapidem de ore putei ¹¹et adaquavit gregem Laban avunculi sui. Tunc Iacob osculatus est Rachel et elevata voce flevit; ¹²et indicavit ei quod frater esset patris eius et filius Rebeccae. At illa festinans nuntiavit patri suo. ¹³Qui cum audisset venisse Iacob filium sororis suae, cucurrit obviam ei; complexusque eum et in oscula ruens duxit in domum suam. Auditis autem omnibus, quae evenerant, ¹⁴respondit: «Vere os meum es et caro mea!». Et, postquam Iacob habitavit apud eum per dies mensis unius, ¹⁵dixit

149

your wages be?" [16]Now Laban had two daughters; the name of the older was Leah, and the name of the younger was Rachel. [17]Leah's eyes were weak, but Rachel was beautiful and lovely. [18]Jacob loved Rachel; and he said, "I will serve you seven years for your younger daughter Rachel." [19]Laban said, "It is better that I give her to you than that I should give her to any other man; stay with me." [20]So Jacob served seven years for Rachel, and they seemed to him but a few days because of the love he had for her.

[21]Then Jacob said to Laban, "Give me my wife that I may go in to her, for my time is completed." [22]So Laban gathered together all the men of the place, and made a feast. [23]But in the evening he took his daughter Leah and brought her to Jacob; and he went in to her. [24](Laban gave his maid Zilpah to his daughter Leah to be her maid.) [25]And in the morning, behold, it was Leah; and Jacob

---

Laban, who previously seemed to be a warm, hospitable man (vv. 13–14), is now being portrayed as very defensive of his own interests (v. 15) and his daughters' future. He moves from being a friend to being a rival of Jacob, who shrewdly tries to get the better of him.

Jacob is showing his qualities and his limitations: he is so passionately in love with Rachel that he agrees to two seven-year spells of unpaid service as a bride-price (*mohar*)—prefiguring the two great periods Israel will later have to spend in slavery. He accepts with resignation the deception played on him when Laban switches Leah for Rachel, because he knows that legal right is on the side of the elder sister (v. 26)—even though he himself, though the younger of two brothers, managed to get the privileges which should have been Esau's. Accepting the

trick played on him, he manages to combine his love for Rachel with his new responsibility toward Leah. He will be a good husband to each of them, and they for their part will both play important roles.

Leah, who will be the mother of Judah and therefore, the ancestor of David, is portrayed as a woman of remarkable dignity: she does not have great natural charm but she has all the rights due her as the eldest daughter of Laban and Jacob's first wife.

Rachel, who will be the mother of the tribes of Joseph and Benjamin, is Jacob's favourite and also the wife who will cause him most suffering.

And over and above these protagonists there is God, who uses the circumstances, qualities and limitations of each of them to advance his plan of shaping a

---

ei Laban: «Num, quia frater meus es, gratis servies mihi? Dic quid mercedis accipias». [16]Habebat vero filias duas: nomen maioris Lia, minor vero appellabatur Rachel; [17]sed Lia lippis erat oculis, Rachel decora et venusto aspectu. [18]Quam diligens Iacob ait: «Serviam tibi pro Rachel filia tua minore septem annis». [19]Respondit Laban: «Melius est, ut tibi eam dem quam alteri viro; mane apud me». [20]Servivit igitur Iacob pro Rachel septem annis, et videbantur illi pauci dies prae amoris magnitudine. [21]Dixitque ad Laban: «Da mihi uxorem meam, quia iam tempus expletum est, ut ingrediar ad eam». [22]Qui, vocatis omnibus viris loci ad convivium, fecit nuptias. [23]Et vespere sumpsit Liam filiam suam et introduxit ad eum, et venit ad eam. [24]Et dedit Laban ancillam filiae Zelpham nomine. Facto mane, vidit, et ecce erat Lia. [25]Et dixit ad socerum suum: «Quid hoc fecisti mihi? Nonne pro Rachel servivi tibi? Quare imposuisti mihi?». [26]Respondit Laban: «Non est in loco nostro consuetudinis, ut minorem ante maiorem

said to Laban, "What is this you have done to me? Did I not serve
with you for Rachel? Why then have you deceived me?" ²⁶Laban
said, "It is not so done in our country, to give the younger before
the first-born. ²⁷Complete the week of this one, and we will give
you the other also in return for serving me another seven years."
²⁸Jacob did so, and completed her week; then Laban gave him his
daughter Rachel to wife. ²⁹(Laban gave his maid Bilhah to his
daughter Rachel to be her maid.) ³⁰So Jacob went in to Rachel
also, and he loved Rachel more than Leah, and served Laban for
another seven years.

The sons of Jacob in Paddan-aram*
Acts 7:8

³¹When the LORD saw that Leah was hated, he opened her womb;
but Rachel was barren. ³²And Leah conceived and bore a son, and   Lk 1:48

---

people who will be the channel of salvation. He who chose Jacob also chooses (by different routes) the women who will be the progenitors of his people.

It is not surprising to find that certain moral shortcomings in this beautiful story, such as trickery, prejudice and polygamy, are overlooked; the sacred writer is not trying to base the effectiveness of God's plan on the perfection of the human characters involved but rather on God's personal initiative. So the original reader and the modern reader are well aware that although each personality has his or her limitations and defects, each is called to co-operate usefully in the plan of salvation.

*29:31—30:24. In this context the account of the birth of the sons of Jacob shows the connexion between the patriarchs and the tribes which will later make up the people of God. The only one not here is Benjamin, who will be born in

Canaan (cf. 35:16); all the others come to the promised land from outside. The names of the sons are given popular (non-scientific) etymological explanations. These explanations refer to the circumstances in which each was born, under divine providence, in the context of rivalry between Jacob's two wives. The writer wants to show that the birth of each son and therefore the existence of each tribe is in line with God's plans.

29:31. Jacob's love for Rachel is such that Leah feels inferior in her husband's eyes. But God comes to the help of the weaker (as the text stresses) and gives Leah, not Rachel, fertility, with the result that Leah wins Jacob's favour. Through the passage we are shown the rivalry between the two wives to win their husband's affection by bearing him children, and consciousness that in the last analysis it is God who gives them to her (cf. the note on 4:1).

---

tradamus ad nuptias. ²⁷Imple hebdomadam hanc, et alteram quoque dabo tibi pro opere, quo serviturus es mihi septem annis aliis». ²⁸Acquievit placito et, hebdomada transacta, dedit ei Laban filiam suam Rachel uxorem, ²⁹cui servam Bilham tradidit. ³⁰Et ingressus etiam ad Rachel amavit eam plus quam Liam serviens apud eum septem annis aliis. ³¹Videns autem Dominus quod despiceret Liam, aperuit vulvam eius, Rachel sterili permanente. ³²Et concepit Lia et genuit filium vocavitque nomen eius Ruben dicens: «Vidit Dominus humilitatem meam; nunc amabit me vir meus». ³³Rursumque concepit

she called his name Reuben;[d] for she said, "Because the LORD has looked upon my affliction; surely now my husband will love me." [33]She conceived again and bore a son, and said, "Because the LORD has heard[e] that I am hated, he has given me this son also"; and she called his name Simeon. [34]Again she conceived and bore a son, and said, "Now this time my husband will be joined[f] to me, because I have borne him three sons"; therefore his name was called Levi. [35]And she conceived again and bore a son, and said, "This time I will praise[g] the LORD"; therefore she called his name Judah; then she ceased bearing.

Mt 1:2
Lk 3:33

30 [1]When Rachel saw that she bore Jacob no children, she envied her sister; and she said to Jacob, "Give me children, or I shall die!" [2]Jacob's anger was kindled against Rachel, and he said, "Am I in the place of God, who has withheld from you the fruit of the womb?" [3]Then she said, "Here is my maid Bilhah; go in to her, that she may bear upon my knees, and even I may have children through her." [4]So she gave him her maid Bilhah as a wife; and Jacob went in to her. [5]And Bilhah conceived

Gen 16:2

30:1–13. In order to give her husband sons, Rachel has recourse to the same method as we saw Sarah use (cf. 16:1–2). This sort of custom is explicable in a social context in which the slave-girl belonged to her mistress and therefore could be used by the mistress even as a surrogate mother. And so the son whom the slave-girl had by her mistress' husband was regarded as being the son of the wife herself because she had given her husband the slave for that very purpose and took the child (when born) on her knees. Just like other customs from the period (such as polygamy), the using of the maid as a surrogate mother is out of keeping with personal dignity and, specifically, the dignity of women, as that dignity is depicted in the Creation accounts (chaps. 1–2). The Bible clearly teaches that all human beings, male or female, are of equal dignity; all are created in the image and likeness of God (cf. 1:26), and it also teaches that God's plan for marriage is that it is monogamous (cf. Gen 2:24; Mt 19:5).

The fact that the patriarchs followed customs which were not in keeping with God's original plan simply shows the presence in mankind of the disorder resulting from sin (cf. chap. 3), and it also shows God's condescension and his teaching method; he starts off by taking things as he finds them and then gradually trains the

---

et peperit filium et ait: «Quoniam audivit me Dominus haberi contemptui, dedit etiam istum mihi»; vocavitque nomen illius Simeon. [34]Concepit tertio et genuit alium filium dixitque: «Nunc quoque copulabitur mihi maritus meus, eo quod pepererim ei tres filios»; et idcirco appellavit nomen eius Levi. [35]Quarto concepit et peperit filium et ait: «Modo confitebor Domino»; et ob hoc vocavit eum Iudam. Cessavitque parere. [1]Cernens autem Rachel quod infecunda esset, invidit sorori et ait marito suo: «Da mihi liberos, alioquin moriar». [2]Cui iratus respondit Iacob: «Num pro Deo ego sum, qui privavit te

---

d. That is *See, a son*   **e.** Heb *shama'*   **f.** Heb *lawah*   **g.** Heb *'odeh*

and bore Jacob a son. [6]Then Rachel said, "God has judged me, and has also heard my voice and given me a son"; therefore she called his name Dan.[h] [7]Rachel's maid Bilhah conceived again and bore Jacob a second son. [8]Then Rachel said, "With mighty wrestlings I have wrestled[i] with my sister, and have prevailed"; so she called his name Naphtali.

[9]When Leah saw that she had ceased bearing children, she took her maid Zilpah and gave her to Jacob as a wife. [10]Then Leah's maid Zilpah bore Jacob a son. [11]And Leah said, "Good fortune!" so she called his name Gad.[j] [12]Leah's maid Zilpah bore Jacob a second son. [13]And Leah said, "Happy am I! For the women will call me happy"; so she called his name Asher.[k]

[14]In the days of wheat harvest Reuben went and found mandrakes in the field, and brought them to his mother Leah. Then Rachel said to Leah, "Give me, I pray, some of your son's mandrakes." [15]But she said to her, "Is it a small matter that you have taken away my husband? Would you take away my son's mandrakes also?" Rachel said, "Then he may lie with you tonight for

Lk 1:48

---

chosen people to appreciate human dignity and the true nature of marriage and the family (cf. the note on 16:1–6).

30:14–24. In Hebrew the word for "mandrake" comes from the same root "love", and the ancients attributed aphrodisiacal and fertility powers to the plant. However, one can see a break in the thread of in the text, for Rachel's fertility is not caused by the mandrakes; it is due to God, who "opened her womb" (v. 22). We can see Jacob's preference for Rachel despite the fact that she has borne him no

children, and how she does everything humanly possible to try to be a mother; but in the last analysis (the point the passage is making) motherhood is a gift from God.

The name "Joseph", like the previous names, is connected with two divine actions—taking away ("God has taken away my reproach") and adding ("May the Lord add to me another son").

These words spoken by Rachel show how a woman could lose face in those times if she did not have children. Jacob, however, continues to be in love with

---

fructu ventris?». [3]At illa: «Ecce, inquit, famula mea Bilha; ingredere ad illam, ut pariat super genua mea, et habeam ex illa et ego filios». [4]Deditque illi Bilham famulam suam in coniugium. Quae, [5]ingresso ad se Iacob, concepit et peperit filium. [6]Dixitque Rachel: «Iudicavit mihi Deus et exaudivit vocem quoque meam dans mihi filium»; et idcirco appellavit nomen illius Dan. [7]Rursumque Bilha famula Rachel concepit et peperit Iacob alterum filium, et [8]ait Rachel: «Certamina Dei certavi cum sorore mea et invalui»; vocavitque eum Nephthali. [9]Sentiens Lia quod parere desisset, sumpsit Zelpham ancillam suam et tradidit eam Iacob in uxorem. [10]Quae peperit Iacob filium. [11] Dixitque Lia: «Feliciter!»; et idcirco vocavit nomen eius Gad. [12]Peperit quoque Zelpha ancilla Liae Iacob alterum filium. [13]Dixitque Lia: «Pro beatitudine mea! Beatam quippe me dicent mulieres»; propterea appellavit eum Aser. [14]Egressus autem Ruben tempore messis triticeae, repperit in agro mandragoras, quas Liae matri suae detulit. Dixitque Rachel: «Da mihi partem de mandragoris filii tui». [15]Illa respondit:

h. That is *He judged* **i.** Heb *niphtal* **j.** That is *Fortune* **k.** That is *Happy*

your son's mandrakes." [16]When Jacob came from the field in the evening, Leah went out to meet him, and said, "You must come in to me; for I have hired you with my son's mandrakes." So he lay with her that night. [17]And God hearkened to Leah, and she conceived and bore Jacob a fifth son. [18]Leah said, "God has given me my hire[l] because I gave my maid to my husband"; so she called his name Issachar. [19]And Leah conceived again, and she bore Jacob a sixth son. [20]Then Leah said, "God has endowed me with a good dowry; now my husband will honour[m] me, because I have borne him six sons"; so she called his name Zebulun. [21]Afterwards she bore a daughter, and called her name Dinah. [22]Then God remembered Rachel, and God hearkened to her and opened her womb. [23]She conceived and bore a son, and said, "God has taken away my reproach"; [24]and she called his name Joseph,[n] saying, "May the LORD add to me another son!"

Lk 1:25

Jacob plans to leave Laban

[25]When Rachel had borne Joseph, Jacob said to Laban, "Send me away, that I may go to my own home and country. [26]Give me my wives and my children for whom I have served you, and let me go; for you know the service which I have given you." [27]But Laban said to him, "If you will allow me to say so, I have learned

---

Rachel, preferring her to Leah. Here we can see that even with the imperfection of that polygamous marriage, the institution of marriage was not regarded as being designed only for procreation but included communion of life and love between the spouses. Nowadays, it is easier for us to see that "even in cases where despite the intense desire of the spouses there are no children, marriage still retains its character of being a whole manner and communion of life and preserves its value and indissolubility" (Vatican II, *Gaudium et spes*, 50). A married couple who are childless without wanting to be are also called to follow their matrimonial vocation and to give their paternity and maternity a wider pro-

«Parumne tibi videtur, quod praeripueris maritum mihi, ut etiam mandragoras filii mei auferas?». Ait Rachel: «Dormiat ergo tecum hac nocte pro mandragoris filii tui». [16]Redeuntique ad vesperam Iacob de agro egressa est in occursum eius Lia et: «Ad me, inquit, intra bis, quia mercede conduxi te pro mandragoris filii mei». Dormivitque cum ea nocte illa. [17]Et exaudivit Deus Liam, concepitque et peperit Iacob filium quintum [18]et ait: «Dedit Deus mercedem mihi, quia dedi ancillam meam viro meo»; appellavitque nomen illius Issachar. [19]Rursum Lia concepit et peperit Iacob sextum filium [20]et ait: «Donavit me Deus dono bono; hac vice honorabit me maritus meus, eo quod genuerim ei sex filios»; et idcirco appellavit nomen eius Zabulon. [21]Post quem peperit filiam nomine Dinam. [22]Recordatus quoque Deus Rachelis exaudivit eam Deus et aperuit vulvam illius. [23]Quae concepit et peperit filium dicens: «Abstulit Deus opprobrium meum»; [24]et vocavit nomen illius Ioseph dicens: «Addat mihi Dominus filium alterum!». [25]Nato autem Ioseph, dixit Iacob ad Laban: «Dimitte me, ut revertar in patriam et ad terram meam. [26]Da mihi uxores et liberos meos, pro quibus servivi tibi, ut

l. Heb *sakar*   **m.** Heb *zabal*   **n.** That is *He adds*

by divination that the Lord has blessed me because of you; [28]name your wages, and I will give it." [29]Jacob said to him, "You yourself know how I have served you, and how your cattle have fared with me. [30]For you had little before I came, and it has increased abundantly; and the LORD has blessed you wherever I turned. But now when shall I provide for my own household also?" [31]He said, "What shall I give you?" Jacob said, "You shall not give me anything; if you will do this for me, I will again feed your flock and keep it: [32]let me pass through all your flock today, removing from it every speckled and spotted sheep and every black lamb, and the spotted and speckled among the goats; and such shall be my wages. [33]So my honesty will answer for me later, when you come to look into my wages with you. Every one that is not speckled and spotted among the goats and black among the lambs, if found with me, shall be counted stolen." [34]Laban said, "Good! Let it be as you have said." [35]But that day Laban removed the he-goats that were striped and spotted, and all the she-goats that were speckled and spotted, every one that had white on it, and every lamb that was black, and put them in charge of his sons; [36]and he set a distance of three days' journey between himself and Jacob; and Jacob fed the rest of Laban's flock.

jection than to offspring of their own. "Of course, there are couples to whom our Lord does not grant any children. If this happens, it is a sign that he is asking them to go on loving each other with the same affection and to put their efforts, if they can, into serving and working for the good of other souls" (St Josemaría Escrivá, *Christ Is Passing By*, 27).

30:25–43. This passage shows how God blesses Jacob by giving him wealth and prosperity. The first thing we see is that, through a kind of deal between Laban and Jacob, God has blessed Laban by enriching him at the expense of Jacob; then it goes on to tell us how Jacob cleverly manages to enrich himself. The scheme used by Jacob is clearly in line with the sort of skills shepherds had (and it shows the antiquity of the story). It takes for granted the fact that in those latitudes sheep were white and goats were black or dark; anything that did not fit into that

abeam; tu nosti servitutem, qua servivi tibi». [27]Ait illi Laban: «Inveniam gratiam in conspectu tuo; augurio didici, quia benedixerit mihi Deus propter te. [28]Constitue mercedem tuam, quam dem tibi». [29]At ille respondit: «Tu nosti quomodo servierim tibi et quanti in manibus meis facti sint greges tui. [30]Modicum habuisti, antequam venirem ad te, et nunc multiplicatum est vehementer, benedixitque tibi Dominus ad introitum meum. Nunc autem quando providebo etiam domui meae?». [31]Dixitque Laban: «Quid tibi dabo?». At ille ait: «Nihil mihi dabis; si feceris, quod postulo, iterum pascam et custodiam pecora tua. [32]Gyrabo omnes greges tuos hodie; separa cuncta pecora varia et maculosa et, quodcumque furvum in ovibus et maculosum variumque in capris fuerit, erit merces mea. [33]Respondebitque mihi cras iustitia mea; quando veneris, ut inspicias mercedem meam, omnia, quae non fuerint varia et maculosa in capris et furva in ovibus, furti me arguent». [34]Dixit Laban: «Gratum habeo, quod petis!». [35]Et

Gen 24:35;
26:12–14 **How Jacob becomes rich**

[37]Then Jacob took fresh rods of poplar and almond and plane, and peeled white streaks in them, exposing the white of the rods. [38]He set the rods which he had peeled in front of the flocks in the runnels, that is, the watering troughs, where the flocks came to drink. And since they bred when they came to drink, [39]the flocks bred in front of the rods and so the flocks brought forth striped, speckled, and spotted. [40]And Jacob separated the lambs, and set the faces of the flocks toward the striped and all the black in the flock of Laban; and he put his own droves apart, and did not put them with Laban's flock. [41]Whenever the stronger of the flock were breeding Jacob laid the rods in the runnels before the eyes of the flock, that they might breed among the rods, [42]but for the feebler of the flock he did not lay them there; so the feebler were Laban's, and the stronger Jacob's. [43]Thus the man grew exceedingly rich, and had large flocks, maidservants and menservants, and camels and asses.

Jacob's flight*

31 [1]Now Jacob heard that the sons of Laban were saying, "Jacob has taken all that was our father's; and from what

---

scheme was regarded as likely to happen very rarely. So, Laban thinks that he is a sure winner, but he is beaten by Jacob's shrewdness and his skill as a shepherd.

***31:1—32:3.** Jacob has become sufficiently rich and strong to provoke the envy of Laban's clan, and to feel up to returning to Canaan and facing his brother Esau. In this way the blessing that Isaac gave Jacob (cf. 28:1–5) has worked out (in fact it forms the back-

ground to this whole story). But Jacob is not going to find it easy to get away from Laban; the sacred writer is going to tell us exactly what happened, to show God's express will and direct help in action (in previous chapters God was, so to speak, in the background). Jacob's prosperity, previously seen from a human and natural perspective, we now discover to have been due to God's direct intervention on the patriarch's behalf and not the result of Jacob's astuteness.

---

separavit in die illo hircos striatos atque maculosos et omnes capras varias et maculosas, omne, in quo album erat, et omne furvum in ovibus, et tradidit in manu filiorum suorum. [36]Et posuit spatium itineris trium dierum inter se et Iacob, qui pascebat reliquos greges Laban. [37]Tollens ergo Iacob virgas virides populeas et amygdalinas et ex platanis, ex parte ita decorticavit eas, ut in his, quae spoliata fuerant, candor appareret. [38]Posuitque virgas, quas ex parte decorticaverat, in canalibus, ubi effundebatur aqua, ut, cum venissent greges ad bibendum, ante oculos haberent virgas et in aspectu earum conciperent. [39]Factumque est ut in ipso calore coitus greges intuerentur virgas et parerent striata et varia et maculosa. [40]Agnos autem segregavit Iacob et posuit gregem ex adverso striatorum et omnium furvorum in grege Laban et constituit sibi greges seorsum neque statuit eos cum grege Laban. [41]Quotiescumque igitur calefiebant pecora robusta, ponebat Iacob virgas in canalibus aquarum ante oculos pecorum, ut in earum contemplatione conciperent. [42]Quando vero pecora debilia erant, non ponebat eas. Factaque sunt debilia Laban et robusta Iacob; [43]ditatusque est homo ultra modum et habuit greges multos, ancillas et servos, camelos et asinos. [1] Postquam autem audivit verba filiorum Laban dicentium: «Tulit

was our father's he has gained all this wealth." ²And Jacob saw that Laban did not regard him with favour as before. ³Then the LORD said to Jacob, "Return to the land of your fathers and to your kindred, and I will be with you." ⁴So Jacob sent and called Rachel and Leah into the field where his flock was, ⁵and said to them, "I see that your father does not regard me with favor as he did before. But the God of my father has been with me. ⁶You know that I have served your father with all my strength; ⁷yet your father has cheated me and changed my wages ten times, but God did not permit him to harm me. ⁸If he said, 'The spotted shall be your wages,' then all the flock bore spotted; and if he said, 'The striped shall be your wages,' then all the flock bore striped. ⁹Thus God has taken away the cattle of your father, and given them to me. ¹⁰In the mating season of the flock I lifted up my eyes, and saw in a dream that the he-goats which leaped upon the flock were striped, spotted, and mottled. ¹¹Then the angel of God said to me in the dream, 'Jacob,' and I said, 'Here I am!' ¹²And he said, 'Lift up your eyes and see, all the goats that leap upon the flock are striped, spotted, and mottled; for I have seen all that

---

As the story develops we are told first about the preparations for Jacob's departure (cf. 31:1–16); then, his flight (cf. 31:17–21), and Laban giving chase (cf. 3:22–25), and finally the discussions between Jacob and Laban and the pact they arrive at (cf. 31:26—32:3).

31:1–16. Firstly, Jacob explains to his wives that God has intervened on his behalf; once they have this explanation they freely agree to leave with him (cf. v. 16). By this device the text reveals the true causes of what has happened: the

strategies used by Jacob worked because God, who had appeared to him when he was setting out to go to Laban (cf. 28:10–22), was with him and was helping him dodge the traps Laban was setting for him.

In vv. 11–13 "the angel of God", that is, his messenger or envoy, is in some way identified with God himself; but despite this we can detect a certain difference between "the angel of God" and the "God of Bethel"—like a distinction between a divine presence (even if experienced in a dream) and God himself in

---

Iacob omnia, quae fuerunt patris nostri, et de patris nostri facultate acquisivit has divitias», ²animadvertit quoque faciem Laban quod non esset erga se sicut heri et nudiustertius. ³Et dixit Dominus ad Iacob: «Revertere in terram patrum tuorum et ad cognationem tuam, eroque tecum». ⁴Misit Iacob et vocavit Rachel et Liam in agrum, ubi pascebat greges, ⁵dixitque eis: «Video faciem patris vestri quod non sit erga me sicut heri et nudiustertius; Deus autem patris mei fuit mecum, ⁶et ipsae nostis quod totis viribus meis servierim patri vestro. ⁷Sed pater vester circumvenit me et mutavit mercedem meam decem vicibus; et tamen non dimisit eum Deus, ut noceret mihi. ⁸Si quando dixit: 'Variae erunt mercedes tuae', pariebant omnes oves varios fetus. Quando vero e contrario ait: 'Striata quaeque accipies pro mercede', omnes greges striata pepererunt. ⁹Tulitque Deus substantiam patris vestri et dedit mihi. ¹⁰Postquam enim conceptus gregis tempus advenerat, levavi oculos meos et vidi in somnis ascendentes mares super feminas, striatos et varios et respersos. ¹¹Dixitque angelus Dei ad me in somnis: 'Iacob'. Et ego respondi: Adsum. ¹²Qui ait: 'Leva oculos tuos et vide universos masculos ascendentes super

Gen 28:18–22 Laban is doing to you. ¹³I am the God of Bethel, where you anointed a pillar and made a vow to me. Now arise, go forth from this land, and return to the land of your birth.'" ¹⁴Then Rachel and Leah answered him, "Is there any portion or inheritance left to us in our father's house? ¹⁵Are we not regarded by him as foreigners? For he has sold us, and he has been using up the money given for us. ¹⁶All the property which God has taken away from our father belongs to us and to our children; now then, whatever God has said to you, do."

¹⁷So Jacob arose, and set his sons and his wives on camels; ¹⁸and he drove away all his cattle, all his livestock which he had gained, the cattle in his possession which he had acquired in Paddan-aram, to go to the land of Canaan to his father Isaac.

Judg 17:5
1 Sam 19:13–16 ¹⁹Laban had gone to shear his sheep, and Rachel stole her

---

his inaccessible mystery. Over the course of the Bible the distinction between God and his heavenly messengers, the angels, will gradually become more explicit. That differentiation is not detectable here; the sacred writer may be trying to avoid speaking about God in too anthropomorphic a way (which he would do if he were to say that God himself appeared to someone in a physical form).

31:13. God now speaks to Jacob in the same sort of way as he once called Abraham (cf. 12:1): "Go from your country . . ."; but in Jacob's case it is a matter of returning to his own land (which God had given Abraham and where Jacob had been born). The background to the episodes is similar: Abraham as the first recipient of the promises and Jacob as the father of the people of the twelve tribes—both these

patriarchs have to leave the place where they are and travel to the promised land. However, there is an important difference: Abraham is given the land as a totally gratuitous gift, whereas Jacob, who more closely represents the chosen people, has to recover the land as something which belongs to him by virtue of the original gift. Called by God to return to his native country, Jacob can symbolize the attitude of the Christian who is called once and again to conversion, to return to that gift he was once given (the gift of grace), to come back to his Father's house. "Human life is in some way a constant returning to our Father's house. We return through contrition, through the conversion of heart which means a desire to change, a firm decision to improve our life and which, therefore, is expressed in sacrifice and self-giving" (St J. Escrivá, *Christ Is Passing By*, 64).

feminas, striatos et varios atque respersos. Vidi enim omnia, quae fecit tibi Laban. ¹³Ego sum Deus Bethel, ubi unxisti lapidem et votum vovisti mihi. Nunc ergo surge et egredere de terra hac revertens in terram nativitatis tuae'». ¹⁴Responderunt ei Rachel et Lia: «Numquid habemus adhuc partem et hereditatem in domo patris nostri? ¹⁵Nonne quasi alienas reputavit nos et vendidit nos comeditque pretium nostrum? ¹⁶Sed omnes opes, quas tulit Deus patri nostro, nobis abstulit ac filiis nostris; unde omnia, quae praecepit tibi Deus, fac». ¹⁷Surrexit itaque Iacob et imposuit liberos suos ac coniuges suas super camelos. ¹⁸Tulitque omnes greges suos et omnem substantiam suam, quidquid in Paddanaram acquisierat, ut iret ad Isaac patrem suum in terram Chanaan. ¹⁹Eo tempore Laban ierat ad tondendas

father's household gods. [20]And Jacob outwitted Laban the Aramean, in that he did not tell him that he intended to flee. [21]He fled with all that he had, and arose and crossed the Euphrates, and set his face toward the hill country of Gilead.

Laban overtakes Jacob*

[22]When it was told Laban on the third day that Jacob had fled, [23]he took his kinsmen with him and pursued him for seven days and followed close after him into the hill country of Gilead. [24]But God came to Laban the Aramean in a dream by night, and said to him, "Take heed that you say not a word to Jacob, either good or bad."

[25]And Laban overtook Jacob. Now Jacob had pitched his tent in the hill country, and Laban with his kinsmen encamped in the hill country of Gilead. [26]And Laban said to Jacob, "What have

---

31:14–16. Rachel and Leah both acknowledge their father's greed. Laban had made Jacob pay a high price for his daughters—not just presents, as was the case with Rebekah (cf. 24:22). Moreover, he had kept the *mohar* or bride-price for himself (the price was the years of work Jacob put in) instead of giving it back to his daughters and their children as an endowment, as contemporary custom dictated. So, the two daughters could accuse their father of using their money (literally, "eating our dinner"); in this sense, the text makes it quite clear that God was justified in doing what he did, because what Jacob took from Laban's flock really belonged to his wives. As they (and the reader) see it, Jacob is fully within his rights.

31:19. The "household gods" stolen by Rachel were probably statuettes (in human form: cf. 1 Sam 19:13–16) of gods who protected the house and its people. It is possible that possession of these idols had some inheritance rights attaching to

it; but Rachel seems to have wanted them for superstitious reasons. Anyway, the passage shows that a polytheistic cult was practised in Laban's house. For a long time, Israelites continued to have attachment to idols of this sort, as we can see from the warnings issued by the prophets (cf. Hos 2:7–15; Jer 2:5–13, 27–28; Is 40:19–20; 44:9–20).

*31:22–54. This last confrontation between Jacob and Laban first shows them locked in a legal dispute (cf. 31:26–30), which is interrupted by Laban's search of Jacob's tent (cf. 31:31–42) and settled by a pact (cf. 31:43–54). The text makes it clear that if it went no further than words, that was due to God's intervening on Jacob's behalf, this time by appearing to Laban (cf. v. 24). It is God who gives judgment, finding Laban to be at fault (cf. v. 42).

31:26–30. Although he cleverly comes up with an excuse to justify his hot pur-

---

oves, et Rachel furata est theraphim patris sui. [20]Iacob autem decepit cor Laban, non indicans ei quod fugeret. [21]Cumque fugisset cum omnibus, quae possidebat, et, amne transmisso, pergeret contra montem Galaad, [22]nuntiatum est Laban die tertio quod fugisset Iacob. [23]Qui, assumptis fratribus suis, persecutus est eum diebus septem et comprehendit eum in monte Galaad. [24]Venit autem Deus ad Laban Aramaeum per somnium noctis dixitque ei: «Cave, ne quidquam loquaris contra Iacob!». [25]Iamque Iacob extenderat in monte tabernaculum, cum Laban, consecutus eum cum fratribus suis, in eodem

you done, that you have cheated me, and carried away my daughters like captives of the sword? [27]Why did you flee secretly, and cheat me, and did not tell me, so that I might have sent you away with mirth and songs, with tambourine and lyre? [28]And why did you not permit me to kiss my sons and my daughters farewell? Now you have done foolishly. [29]It is in my power to do you harm; but the God of your father spoke to me last night, saying, 'Take heed that you speak to Jacob neither good nor bad.' [30]And now you have gone away because you longed greatly for your father's house, but why did you steal my gods?" [31]Jacob answered Laban, "Because I was afraid, for I thought that you would take your daughters from me by force. [32]Any one with whom you find your gods shall not live. In the presence of our kinsmen point out what I have that is yours, and take it." Now Jacob did not know that Rachel had stolen them.

[33]So Laban went into Jacob's tent, and into Leah's tent, and into the tent of the two maidservants, but he did not find them.

Lev 15:19–20 And he went out of Leah's tent, and entered Rachel's. [34]Now Rachel had taken the household gods and put them in the camel's saddle, and sat upon them. Laban felt all about the tent, but did not find them. [35]And she said to her father, "Let not my lord be

---

suit of Jacob, the tone of Laban's remarks shows that his attitude has changed, due to God's intervention. So, God continues to watch over Jacob and, as St John Chrysostom comments, "The hand of God is the strongest of all and it protects us and makes us invincible at all times. This can clearly be seen in the case of this just man (Jacob). For the one who pursues him so relentlessly and who seeks to inflict on him the punishment of flight, not only has no scathing criticism

to make but in fact addresses to him mildly as father to son: 'What have you done? Why did you flee secretly?' What a change you can see: he had been wild with anger, but now he is as gentle as a lamb" (*Homiliae in Genesim*, 57, 5).

31:35. "The way of women is upon me": a reference to menstruation. A woman was regarded as being in a state of uncleanness during this period, so that she contaminated anything she touched (cf.

---

monte Galaad fixit tentorium. [26]Et dixit ad Iacob: «Quare ita egisti et decepisti cor meum, abigens filias meas quasi captivas gladio? [27]Cur clam fugisti et decepisti me, non indicans mihi, ut prosequerer te cum gaudio et canticis et tympanis et citharis? [28]Non es passus, ut oscularer filios meos ac filias; stulte operatus es. Et nunc [29]valet quidem manus mea reddere tibi malum, sed Deus patris vestri heri dixit mihi: 'Cave, ne loquaris contra Iacob quidquam!'. [30]Esto, profectus es, quia desiderio tibi erat domus patris tui; cur furatus es deos meos?». [31]Respondit Iacob: «Quia timui. Dixi enim, ne forte violenter auferres filias tuas a me. [32]Apud quemcumque inveneris deos tuos, non vivat! Coram fratribus nostris scrutare, quidquid tuorum apud me inveneris, et aufer». Ignorabat enim Iacob quod Rachel furata esset theraphim. [33]Ingressus itaque Laban tabernacula Iacob et Liae et utriusque famulae, non invenit. Egressus de tentorio Liae intravit tentorium Rachelis. [34]Illa autem absconderat theraphim in stramento cameli et sedit desuper. Scrutantique omne tentorium et nihil invenienti [35]ait: «Ne irascatur dominus

angry that I cannot rise before you, for the way of women is upon me." So he searched, but did not find the household gods.

³⁶Then Jacob became angry, and upbraided Laban; Jacob said to Laban, "What is my offence? What is my sin, that you have hotly pursued me? ³⁷Although you have felt through all my goods, what have you found of all your household goods? Set it here before my kinsmen and your kinsmen, that they may decide between us two. ³⁸These twenty years I have been with you; your ewes and your she-goats have not miscarried, and I have not eaten the rams of your flocks. ³⁹That which was torn by wild beasts I did not bring to you; I bore the loss of it myself; of my hand you required it, whether stolen by day or stolen by night. ⁴⁰Thus I was; by day the heat consumed me, and the cold by night, and my sleep fled from my eyes. ⁴¹These twenty years I have been in your house; I served you fourteen years for your two daughters, and six years for your flock, and you have changed my wages ten times. ⁴²If the God of my father, the God of Abraham and the Fear of Isaac, had not been on my side, surely now you would have sent me away empty-handed. God saw my affliction and the labour of my hands, and rebuked you last night."

Ex 22:12

Lev 15:19–20). This attitude probably can be traced back to a feeling of fear before the presence of bleeding when no one knew exactly its cause. That a woman in that state should sit on sacred objects such as idols would never even enter Laban's mind; but the sacred writer may well be poking fun at such objects, too.

31:42. Jacob, and Laban earlier (cf. 31:29), declare that the God who has intervened on Jacob's behalf is the God of his fathers, that is, the God of Abraham and the God of Isaac. This same God is recognized and called as witness to the subsequent pact, both by Laban and by Jacob (cf. 31:53). However, Jacob on both occasions invokes him by giving him a special, rather mysterious, title, which can mean "kinsman" or "godfather" and which is normally translated as "fear" or "the terrible", a reference to his power and his justice when he punishes (cf. Ps 76). Here we can see that the various names used all refer to the one God, who revealed himself to Abraham; but we can also glimpse the fact that the patriarchs worshipped him, above all, as the "God of my father", that is, a personal God who had spoken to their ancestors

---

meus, quod coram te assurgere nequeo, quia iuxta consuetudinem feminarum nunc accidit mihi». Quaesivit ergo et non invenit theraphim. ³⁶Tumensque Iacob cum iurgio ait: «Quam ob culpam meam et ob quod peccatum meum sic persecutus es me, ³⁷quia scrutatus es omnem supellectilem meam? Quid invenisti de cuncta substantia domus tuae? Pone hic coram fratribus meis et fratribus tuis, et iudicent inter me et te. ³⁸Ecce, viginti annis fui tecum. Oves tuae et caprae non abortiverunt, arietes gregis tui non comedi; ³⁹nec dilaceratum a bestia ostendi tibi: ego damnum omne reddebam: quidquid die noctuque furto perierat, a me exigebas. ⁴⁰Die aestu consumebar et nocte gelu, fugiebatque somnus ab oculis meis. ⁴¹Sic per viginti annos in domo tua servivi tibi: quattuordecim pro filiabus et sex pro gregibus tuis; immutasti quoque mercedem meam decem vicibus. ⁴²Nisi Deus patris mei, Deus Abraham et

A pact between Laban and Jacob

[43]Then Laban answered and said to Jacob, "The daughters are my daughters, the children are my children, the flocks are my flocks, and all that you see is mine. But what can I do this day to these my daughters, or to their children whom they have borne? [44]Come now, let us make a covenant, you and I; and let it be a witness between you and me." [45]So Jacob took a stone, and set it up as a pillar. [46]And Jacob said to his kinsmen, "Gather stones," and they took stones, and made a heap; and they ate there by the heap. [47]Laban called it Jegar-sahadutha:[o] but Jacob called it Galeed. [48]Laban said, "This heap is a witness between you and me today." Therefore he named it Galeed,[p] [49]and the pillar[q] Mizpah,[r] for he said, "The LORD watch between you and me, when we are absent one from the other. [50]If you ill-treat my daughters, or if you take wives besides my daughters, although no man is with us, remember, God is witness between you and me."

---

and now spoke to them. The patriarchs, therefore, did not see God as a reflection of the forces of nature, or as being linked to certain sacred places and no more; they referred to him primarily as to a personal God, who revealed himself to persons in different generations, wherever they happened to be at the time (cf. the note on 26:15–33).

31:43–54. The pact between Jacob and Laban has two aspects to it—the first, dealing with Jacob's behaviour towards Laban's daughters (vv. 49–50); the second, designed to fix the border between their respective territories (cf. vv. 51–52).

The first aspect is connected with the name "Mizpah" which means "watchtower" or "place of vigilance"; the second, with the Aramaean name "Jegar-sahadutha" or the Hebrew Galeed, for both names mean the same ("witness"). Thus, the story of the pact explains the names given to this particular place; and the name of this particular mound will serve as a reminder and help to reconstruct the history and basis of the relations between Israel and the Aramaeans.

The pact as described has features typical of alliance treaties in antiquity—an enduring sign, such as a heap of stones; a feast; various clauses; and invo-

---

Timor Isaac, affuisset mihi, certe modo nudum me dimisisses; afflictionem meam et laborem manuum mearum respexit Deus et iudicavit heri». [43]Respondit ei Laban: «Filiae filiae meae et filii filii mei et greges greges mei et omnia, quae cernis, mea sunt; et filiabus meis quid possum facere illis hodie et filiis earum, quos genuerunt? [44]Veni ergo, et ineamus foedus ego et tu, ut sit in testimonium inter me et te». [45]Tulit itaque Iacob lapidem et erexit illum in titulum; [46]dixitque fratribus suis: «Afferte lapides». Qui congregantes fecerunt tumulum comederuntque ibi super eum. [47]Quem vocavit Laban Iegarsahadutha (*id est Tumulus testimonii*), et Iacob Galed (*uterque iuxta proprietatem linguae suae*). [48]Dixitque Laban: «Tumulus iste testis erit inter me et te hodie»; et idcirco appellatum est nomen eius Galed (*id est Tumulus testis*) [49]et etiam Maspha (*id est Specula*), quia dixit: «Speculetur Dominus inter me et te, quando absconditi erimus ab invicem. [50]Si afflixeris filias meas et si introduxeris uxores alias

---

o. In Aramaic *The heap of witnesses*   **p.** In Hebrew *The heap of witness*   **q.** Compare Sam: Heb lacks *the pillar*   **r.** That is *Watchpost*

⁵¹Then Laban said to Jacob, "See this heap and the pillar, which I have set between you and me. ⁵²This heap is a witness, and the pillar is a witness, that I will not pass over this heap to you, and you will not pass over this heap and this pillar to me, for harm. ⁵³The God of Abraham and the God of Nahor, the God of their father, judge between us." So Jacob swore by the Fear of his father Isaac, ⁵⁴and Jacob offered a sacrifice on the mountain and called his kinsmen to eat bread; and they ate bread and tarried all night on the mountain.

⁵⁵ˢEarly in the morning Laban arose, and kissed his grandchildren and his daughters and blessed them; then he departed and returned home.

32 ¹Jacob went on his way and the angels of God met him; ²and when Jacob saw them he said, "This is God's army!" So he called the name of that place Mahanaim.ᵗ

Gen 19:15; 21:17
Ps 91:11

---

cation of the parties' gods. These human pacts are serious and worthy things; they serve as a model for expressing the relationship between God and his people as a bilateral covenant.

32:1–2. God continues to be present to Jacob after he leaves Laban. This is what is meant by "the angels of God met him". This conviction is also connected with the name of a place—"Mahanaim", which means "camps". Jacob does not travel alone; beside his camp is the camp of the angels of God. This story, and others about the patriarchs (cf. Gen 19:15; 21:17; etc.), must have inspired the words of Psalm 91:11, "for he will give his angels charge of you, to guard you in all your ways"—words which find perfect fulfilment in the life of our Lord, when angels serve him after he is tempted in the wilderness (cf. Mt 4:11) and when an angel comforts him during his passion (cf. Lk 22:43). In the light of all this, we can appreciate the role angels have in the life of the Church, which benefits from "the mysterious and powerful help of angels (cf. Acts 5:18–20; 8:26–29; 10:3–8; 12:6–11; 27:23–25)" (*Catechism of the Catholic Church*, 334), and in our own lives, as St Josemaría Escrivá asks us to consider: "Let us look for a moment at this appearance of angels in Jesus' life, for it will help us to better understand their role—their angelic mission—in all human life. Christian tradition describes the guardian angels as powerful friends, placed by God alongside each one of us, to accompany us on our way. And that is why he invites us to make friends with them and get them to help us" (*Christ Is Passing By*, 63).

---

super eas, cum nemo nobiscum sit, vide, Deus est testis inter me et te». ⁵¹Dixitque Laban ad Iacob: «En tumulus hic et lapis, quem erexi inter me et te. ⁵²Testis erit tumulus iste et lapis quod ego non transibo tumulum hunc pergens ad te, neque tu transibis tumulum hunc et lapidem hunc ad malum. ⁵³Deus Abraham et Deus Nachor iudicent inter nos». Iuravit Iacob per Timorem patris sui Isaac; ⁵⁴immolatisque victimis in monte, vocavit fratres suos, ut ederent panem. Qui cum comedissent, pernoctaverunt in monte. ¹ Laban vero de nocte consurgens osculatus est filios et filias suas et benedixit illis reversusque est in locum suum. ²Iacob quoque abiit itinere, quo coeperat, fueruntque ei obviam angeli

s. Ch 32:1 in Heb [and New Vulgate] **t.** Here taken to mean *two armies*

Jacob prepares for his meeting with Esau

³And Jacob sent messengers before him to Esau his brother in the land of Seir, the country of Edom, ⁴instructing them, "Thus you shall say to my lord Esau: Thus says your servant Jacob, 'I have sojourned with Laban, and stayed until now; ⁵and I have oxen, asses, flocks, menservants, and maidservants; and I have sent to tell my lord, in order that I may find favour in your sight.'"

⁶And the messengers returned to Jacob, saying, "We came to your brother Esau, and he is coming to meet you, and four hundred men with him." ⁷Then Jacob was greatly afraid and distressed; and he divided the people that were with him, and the flocks and herds and camels, into two companies, ⁸thinking, "If Esau comes to the one company and destroys it, then the company which is left will escape."

⁹And Jacob said, "O God of my father Abraham and God of

---

*32:3—33:20. Esau and Jacob were out of touch while Jacob was working for Laban; the brothers now meet again. Esau, the ancestor of Edom (cf. 25:19–30) is portrayed as already living in his own territory, Seir, the mountainous area extending from the south-east of the Dead Sea to the gulf of Akabah.

The biblical narrative of these episodes contains an important aspect of salvation history—the formation of the people of Israel, fulfilling the promise God made to Abraham. The figure of Jacob, returning with his sons to the promised land, shows that God wants to give this land to his people, Israel. It is significant that Jacob's return to Canaan is sketched in a way reminiscent of the exodus from Egypt—departure, laden with riches, from a pagan and hostile country; the crossing of the river; a

chase; night being the time when God passes by; and journeying to the promised land.

Jacob is now the recipient and bearer of the divine promise, and he personally must make a journey of faith and fellowship with God, like that made by Abraham. One notices, however, that God models these two patriarchs in different ways: Abraham through tests which he accepts with faith and radical obedience to the divine will; Jacob, however, through natural events of life which the patriarch has to alter or overcome, in a constant struggle—remember, for example, how Jacob acquired the birthright or how he managed to marry Rachel and become prosperous. We see this difference also in the wrestling described in 32:23–30, whereby Jacob obtains the divine bless-

Dei. ³Quos cum vidisset, ait: «Castra Dei sunt haec »; et appellavit nomen loci illius Mahanaim (*id est Castra*). ⁴Misit autem nuntios ante se ad Esau fratrem suum in terram Seir, in regionem Edom. ⁵Praecepitque eis dicens: «Sic loquimini domino meo Esau: Haec dicit servus tuus Iacob: Apud Laban peregrinatus sum et fui usque in praesentem diem. ⁶Habeo boves et asinos, oves et servos atque ancillas; mittoque nunc legationem ad dominum meum, ut inveniam gratiam in conspectu tuo». ⁷Reversique sunt nuntii ad Iacob dicentes: «Venimus ad Esau fratrem tuum, et ecce properat in occursum tibi cum quadringentis viris». ⁸Timuit Iacob valde et perterritus divisit populum, qui secum erat, greges quoque et oves et boves et camelos in duas turmas ⁹dicens: «Si venerit Esau ad unam turmam et percusserit

my father Isaac, O LORD who didst say to me, 'Return to your country and to your kindred, and I will do you good,' [10]I am not worthy of the least of all the steadfast love and all the faithfulness which thou hast shown to thy servant, for with only my staff I crossed this Jordan; and now I have become two companies. [11]Deliver me, I pray thee, from the hand of my brother, from the hand of Esau, for I fear him, lest he come and slay us all, the mothers with the children. [12]But thou didst say, 'I will do you good, and make your descendants as the sand of the sea, which cannot be numbered for multitude.'"

Heb 11:12

[13]So he lodged there that night, and took from what he had with him a present for his brother Esau, [14]two hundred she-goats and twenty he-goats, two hundred ewes and twenty rams, [15]thirty milch camels and their colts, forty cows and ten bulls, twenty she-asses and ten he-asses. [16]These he delivered into the hand of his

---

ing. If the key moment in the story of Abraham is his obedience to God when he is asked to sacrifice his son, in the case of Jacob it is when he wrestles with God to obtain the blessing. Once this is over, Jacob, whose name has significantly been changed to Israel, will be qualified to enter the promised land.

32:3–21. Jacob suspects that his brother is hostile to him: he sent a small embassy to Esau, but Esau comes back with four hundred men. So Jacob makes detailed preparations for the meeting: first, he divides up his people; second, he prays—giving thanks to God and also asking for his help; third, he sends gifts, in waves as it were, to placate Esau's anger. In this way he shows his brother his peaceful intentions and his desire for reconciliation.

Here is what St Ambrose has to say

on the little piece of information about Jacob lodging in the camp overnight: "Perfect virtue has the serenity and stability of rest. Therefore the Lord reserves his gift to the perfect, saying: 'My peace I leave you, my peace I give you.' Typically, people who are perfect do not easily become restless on account of worldly things, or let themselves be disturbed by fear, or haunted by suspicion, or allow terror to get the better of them, or give way to fear; rather, they retain their peace and keep a serene spirit, they are confident, the way a wide beach is against the tides of worldly disturbances.[. . .] The wicked, on the contrary, do themselves more damage by their suspicion of others than they get from blows from outside, and they have more wounds in their spirit than those have whose bodies are beaten by others" (*De Jacob et vita beata*, 2, 6, 28).

---

eam, alia turma, quae reliqua est, salvabitur». [10]Dixitque Iacob: «Deus patris mei Abraham et Deus patris mei Isaac, Domine, qui dixisti mihi: 'Revertere in terram tuam et in locum nativitatis tuae, et benefaciam tibi',[11] minor sum cunctis miserationibus et cuncta veritate, quam explesti servo tuo. In baculo meo transivi Iordanem istum et nunc cum duabus turmis regredior. [12]Erue me de manu fratris mei, de manu Esau, quia valde eum timeo; ne forte veniens percutiat matrem cum filiis. [13]Tu locutus es quod bene mihi faceres et dilatares semen meum sicut arenam maris, quae prae multitudine numerari non potest». [14]Mansit ibi nocte illa et sumpsit de his, quae habebat, munera Esau fratri suo: [15]capras

servants, every drove by itself, and said to his servants, "Pass on before me, and put a space between drove and drove." [17]He instructed the foremost, "When Esau my brother meets you, and asks you, 'To whom do you belong? Where are you going? And whose are these before you?' [18]then you shall say, 'They belong to your servant Jacob; they are a present sent to my lord Esau; and moreover he is behind us.'" [19]He likewise instructed the second and the third and all who followed the droves, "You shall say the same thing to Esau when you meet him, [20]and you shall say, 'Moreover your servant Jacob is behind us.'" For he thought, "I may appease him with the present that goes before me, and afterwards I shall see his face; perhaps he will accept me."

Ex 4:24–26
Judg 13:17–22
Hos 12:5
Wis 10:12

Jacob wrestles with the angel of the Lord

[21]So the present passed on before him; and he himself lodged that night in the camp. [22]The same night he arose and took his two wives, his two maids, and his eleven children, and crossed the ford of the Jabbok. [23]He took them and sent them across the

---

32:22–29. In spite of the danger and even though he feels afraid, Jacob takes an important decision on his journey towards the land of Canaan—to cross the river, bringing his nearest and dearest with him. From the text we do not know which side of the river Jacob himself was on after that decision, but he was clearly alone when God mysteriously came out to meet him and transformed him. The account tells us that God revealed himself to Jacob and made him Israel and gave him a blessing which extended to all his people. The concept of God in this passage has clearly anthropomorphic features. Jacob's strength is highlighted: God fails to defeat him in this struggle

and he dislocates his thigh. This fact and the fact that God wants to leave before daybreak allow Jacob to recognize God in the person he is wrestling; taking advantage of his strength and the time constraint, he asks for a blessing. First, however, Jacob has to identify himself; then God changes his name: now he is Israel.

In the context of the narrative the sacred writer explains what the name Israel means—"he who has striven with God". This shows one of the key features of the personality of the father of the chosen people—his struggle to hold on to God, trying to discover his name and obtain his blessing. This is also a defin-

---

ducentas, hircos viginti, oves ducentas et arietes viginti, [16]camelos fetas cum pullis suis triginta, vaccas quadraginta et tauros decem, asinas viginti et pullos earum decem. [17]Et misit per manus servorum suorum singulos seorsum greges dixitque pueris suis: «Antecedite me, et sit spatium inter gregem et gregem». [18]Et praecepit priori dicens: «Si obvium habueris Esau fratrem meum, et interrogaverit te: 'Cuius es?' et 'Quo vadis?' et 'Cuius sunt ista, quae sequeris?', [19]respondebis: Servi tui Iacob; munera misit domino meo Esau. Ipse quoque post nos venit». [20]Similiter mandata dedit secundo ac tertio et cunctis, qui sequebantur greges, dicens: «Iisdem verbis loquimini ad Esau, cum inveneritis eum, [21]et addetis: Ipse quoque servus tuus Iacob iter nostrum insequitur. Dixit enim: Placabo illum muneribus, quae praecedunt, et postea videbo faciem eius: forsitan propitiabitur mihi». [22]Praecesserunt itaque

stream, and likewise everything that he had. ²⁴And Jacob was left alone; and a man wrestled with him until the breaking of the day. ²⁵When the man saw that he did not prevail against Jacob, he touched the hollow of his thigh; and Jacob's thigh was put out of joint as he wrestled with him. ²⁶Then he said, "Let me go, for the day is breaking." But Jacob said, "I will not let you go, unless you bless me." ²⁷And he said to him, "What is your name?" And he said, "Jacob." ²⁸Then he said, "Your name shall no more be called Jacob, but Israel,ᵘ for you have striven with God and with men, and have prevailed." ²⁹Then Jacob asked him, "Tell me, I pray, your name." But he said, "Why is it that you ask my name?" And there he blessed him. ³⁰So Jacob called the name of the place Peniel,ᵛ saying, "For I have seen God face to face, and yet my life

Ex 33:20
1 Cor 13:12

ing feature of the religious nature of the people of God. We discover the significance of Jacob's attempt to discover the name of his "rival", and all that that implied as regards having some power over him. But God does not identify himself. He remains shrouded in mystery, yet he does give Jacob his blessing. This will also be a feature which should define Israel—the continuous search for the name of God, that is, for his innermost Being and his Mystery, yet realizing that God can never be encompassed within the meaning of any name.

The features whereby the patriarch Jacob-Israel is described also apply to the people that bears his name. The prophet Hosea will apply this episode to the way Israel resists God over the course of its history (Hos 12:4-6). This aspect can also be seen in the patriarch's life: in spite of his resistance, God advances his

salvific plans for his people through him and through his life. We can see this in what Hosea has to say about the people of Israel and about Jacob himself.

The mysterious nature of the one who wrestles with Jacob has been interpreted in many different ways in Christian tradition. Some Fathers, such as St Jerome and St Augustine, were of the view that he was a good angel, given that that was how God most often revealed himself in the Old Testament. Origen, however, thought that he was a bad angel, the demon. Others, such as St Justin and St Ambrose, suggested that he was the Son of God, the Word, who would later become man; or an angel who prefigured Christ.

The struggle depicted here can also be taken in a spiritual sense, as standing for the interior struggle and the efficacy of prayer, which overpowers even God (cf.

munera ante eum, ipse vero mansit nocte illa in castris. ²³Cumque nocte surrexisset, tulit duas uxores suas et totidem famulas cum undecim filiis et transivit vadum Iaboc; ²⁴sumptis ergo traductisque illis et omnibus, quae ad se pertinebant, per torrentem, ²⁵mansit solus. Et ecce vir luctabatur cum eo usque mane. ²⁶Qui cum videret quod eum superare non posset, tetigit acetabulum femoris eius, et statim luxatum est acetabulum femoris Iacob, cum luctaretur cum illo. ²⁷Dixitque: «Dimitte me, iam enim ascendit aurora». Respondit: «Non dimittam te, nisi benedixeris mihi». ²⁸Ait ad eum: «Quod nomen est tibi?». Respondit: «Iacob». ²⁹At ille: «Nequaquam, inquit, Iacob amplius appellabitur nomen tuum, sed

u. That is *He who strives with God* or *God strives* **v.** That is *the face of God*

167

is preserved." [31]The sun rose upon him as he passed Penuel, limping because of his thigh. [32]Therefore to this day the Israelites do not eat the sinew of the hip which is upon the hollow of the thigh, because he touched the hollow of Jacob's thigh on the sinew of the hip.*

Jacob's meeting with Esau

33 [1]And Jacob lifted up his eyes and looked, and behold, Esau was coming, and four hundred men with him. So he divided the children among Leah and Rachel and the two maids. [2]And he put the maids with their children in front, then Leah with her children, and Rachel and Joseph last of all. [3]He himself went on before them, bowing himself to the ground seven times, until Acts 20:37 he came near to his brother.

[4]But Esau ran to meet him, and embraced him, and fell on his neck and kissed him, and they wept. [5]And when Esau raised his eyes and saw the women and children, he said, "Who are these

---

Wis 10:12). "From this account, the spiritual tradition of the Church has retained the symbol of prayer as a battle of faith and as the triumph of perseverance (cf. Gen 32:25–31; Lk 18:1–8)" (*Catechism of the Catholic Church*, 2573).

Along these lines St Ambrose writes: "What does fighting with God mean if not engaging in the combat of virtue and aspiring to the highest, making oneself, above all, an imitator of God? And because his faith and his devotion could not be overpowered, the Lord revealed to him the secret mysteries" (*De Jacob et vita beata*, 2, 7, 30).

32:31. After the explanation of the mean-

ing of the name of the place (Penuel) and the name of the person or people (Israel), we are now told about the origin of a dietary law. The hagiographer uses this tradition to confirm the truthfulness of the foregoing account, offering a proof taken from the customs of the people and also providing an explanation for that custom. Although this use of groundless folk explanation is a common device, it does not take from the point the writer is making: he wants to show that what he is teaching is true.

33:1–20. Jacob does not know what Esau's intentions are, so he has recourse to one last way of winning his favour—

Israel: quoniam certasti cum Deo et cum hominibus et praevaluisti!». [30]In terrogavit eum Iacob: «Dic mihi, quo appellaris nomine?». Respondit: «Cur quaeris nomen meum?». Et benedixit ei in eodem loco. [31]Vocavitque Iacob nomen loci illius Phanuel dicens: «Vidi Deum facie ad faciem, et salva facta est anima mea». [32]Ortusque est ei sol, cum transgrederetur Phanuel; ipse vero claudicabat propter femur. [33]Quam ob causam non comedunt filii Israel nervum, qui est in femore, usque in praesentem diem, eo quod tetigerit nervum femoris Iacob. [1] Elevans autem Iacob oculos suos vidit venientem Esau et cum eo quadringentos viros; divisitque filios Liae et Rachel ambarumque famularum. [2]Et posuit utramque ancillam et liberos earum in principio, Liam vero et filios eius in secundo loco, Rachel autem et Ioseph novissimos. [3]Et ipse praegrediens adoravit pronus in terram septies, donec appropinquaret ad fratrem suum. [4]Currens itaque Esau obviam fratri suo amplexatus est eum; stringensque collum eius osculatus est eum, et fleverunt. [5]Levatisque oculis, vidit mulieres et liberos earum et ait: «Qui sunt isti

with you?" Jacob said, "The children whom God has graciously given your servant." ⁶Then the maids drew near, they and their children, and bowed down; ⁷Leah likewise and her children drew near and bowed down; and last Joseph and Rachel drew near, and they bowed down. ⁸Esau said, "What do you mean by all this company which I met?" Jacob answered, "To find favour in the sight of my lord." ⁹But Esau said, "I have enough, my brother; keep what you have for yourself." ¹⁰Jacob said, "No, I pray you, if I have found favour in your sight, then accept my present from my hand; for truly to see your face is like seeing the face of God, with such favour have you received me. ¹¹Accept, I pray you, my gift that is brought to you, because God has dealt graciously with me, and because I have enough." Thus he urged him, and he took it.

¹²Then Esau said, "Let us journey on our way, and I will go before you." ¹³But Jacob said to him, "My lord knows that the children are frail, and that the flocks and herds giving suck are a

---

bowing to the ground seven times, which is equivalent to acknowledging someone to be a king or emperor. Then, when he sees the kind look on his brother's face, it seems to remind him of the benevolence of the face of God who appeared to him the previous night. Despite this, Jacob still takes precautions and he manages to convince Esau to go on ahead of him, and then he takes another route. This brings him through the Jordan valley, where Succoth is, to the promised land, to the city of Shechem, which Abraham also reached when he entered Canaan (cf. 12:6). Here Jacob acquires some land where he builds an altar: in a way he somewhat formally takes possession of the land even before he reaches Bethel, which will be where the patriarch settles

down to live until he goes into Egypt. The name given to the altar, El-Elohe-Israel, is a kind of confession of faith: "God is the God of Israel."

Jacob shows very brotherly feelings towards Esau (as can be seen from his emotional embrace: v. 4) but he also behaves with great prudence. This is one of the patriarch's prominent virtues: he always manages to act circumspectly in the difficult situations he often encounters. "*Prudence* is the virtue that disposes practical reason to discern our true good in every circumstance and to choose the right means of achieving it; 'the prudent man looks where he is going' (Prov 14:15). [. . .] Prudence is 'right reason in action', writes St Thomas Aquinas, following Aristotle (*S. Th.*, 2–2, 47, 2). It is

---

tibi?». Respondit: «Liberi sunt, quos donavit mihi Deus servo tuo». ⁶Et appropinquantes ancillae et filii earum incurvati sunt. ⁷Accessit quoque Lia cum liberis suis et, cum similiter adorassent, extremi Ioseph et Rachel adoraverunt. ⁸«Quaenam sunt, inquit, istae turmae, quas obvias habui?». Respondit: «Ut invenirem gratiam coram domino meo». ⁹At ille: «Habeo, ait, plurima, frater mi; sint tua tibi». ¹⁰Dixit Iacob: «Noli ita, obsecro; sed, si inveni gratiam in oculis tuis, accipe munusculum de manibus meis; sic enim vidi faciem tuam quasi viderim vultum Dei, et mihi propitius fuisti. ¹¹Suscipe, quaeso, benedictionem, quae allata est tibi; quia Deus misertus est mihi, et habeo omnia». Et, cum compelleret illum, suscepit ¹²et ait: «Gradiamur simul, eroque socius itineris tui». ¹³Dixit Iacob: «Nosti, domine mi,

care to me; and if they are overdriven for one day, all the flocks will die. [14]Let my lord pass on before his servant, and I will lead on slowly, according to the pace of the cattle which are before me and according to the pace of the children, until I come to my lord in Seir."

[15]So Esau said, "Let me leave with you some of the men who are with me." But he said, "What need is there? Let me find favour in the sight of my lord."

Jacob in Shechem

[16]So Esau returned that day on his way to Seir. [17]But Jacob journeyed to Succoth,[w] and built himself a house, and made booths for his cattle; therefore the name of the place is called Succoth.

Gen 12:6–7

[18]And Jacob came safely to the city of Shechem, which is in the land of Canaan, on his way from Paddan-aram; and he

Acts 7:16
Josh 24:32

camped before the city. [19]And from the sons of Hamor, Shechem's father, he bought for a hundred pieces of money[x] the piece of land on which he had pitched his tent. [20]There he erected an altar and called it El-Elohe-Israel.[y]

---

not to be confused with timidity or fear, nor with duplicity or dissimulation. It is called *auriga virtutum* (the charioteer of the virtues); it guides the other virtues by setting rule and measure. It is prudence that immediately guides the judgment of conscience. The prudent man determines and directs his conduct in accordance with this judgment. With the help of this virtue we apply moral principles to particular cases without error and overcome doubts about the good to achieve and the evil to avoid" (*Catechism of the Catholic Church*, 1806).

St John Chrysostom has this to say about Jacob's attitude to Esau: "Nothing is more potent than meekness: just as throwing water on a fiercely blazing fire usually puts it out, so too a word spoken with meekness quenches a rage flaring more fiercely than a furnace. It also brings us double advantage—for showing meekness on our part, and for putting an end to our brother's anger and thus freeing his mind from disturbance. Why, in fact, tell me? Do you not blame and accuse your brother who is angry with you and hostile in intent? So, why do you

quod parvulos habeam teneros et oves et boves fetas mecum; quas si plus in ambulando fecero laborare vel una die, morientur cuncti greges. [14]Praecedat dominus meus ante servum suum; et ego sequar paulatim secundum gressum pecorum ante me et secundum gressum parvulorum, donec veniam ad dominum meum in Seir». [15]Respondit Esau: «Oro te, ut de populo, qui mecum est, saltem socii remaneant viae tuae». «Non est, inquit, necesse; hoc uno indigeo, ut inveniam gratiam in conspectu domini mei». [16]Reversus est itaque illo die Esau itinere suo in Seir. [17]Et Iacob venit in Succoth, ubi, aedificata sibi domo et fixis tentoriis pro gregibus suis, appellavit nomen loci illius Succoth (*id est Tabernacula*). [18]Transivitque Iacob incolumis ad urbem Sichem, quae est in terra Chanaan, cum veniret de Paddanaram; et habitavit iuxta oppidum. [19]Emitque partem agri, in qua fixerat tabernaculum suum, a filiis Hemmor patris Sichem centum argenteis. [20]Et erexit ibi altare et vocavit illud: «Deus est Deus

w. That is *Booths* **x.** Heb *a hundred qesitah* **y.** That is *God, the God of Israel*

Dinah is dishonoured by Shechem

34 ¹Now Dinah the daughter of Leah, whom she had borne to Jacob, went out to visit the women of the land; ²and when Shechem the son of Hamor the Hivite, the prince of the land, saw her, he seized her and lay with her and humbled her. ³And his soul was drawn to Dinah the daughter of Jacob; he loved the maiden and spoke tenderly to her. ⁴So Shechem spoke to his father Ex 22:15–16 Hamor, saying, "Get me this maiden for my wife." ⁵Now Jacob heard that he had defiled his daughter Dinah; but his sons were with his cattle in the field, so Jacob held his peace until they came. ⁶And Hamor the father of Shechem went out to Jacob to speak with him. ⁷The sons of Jacob came in from the field when they heard of it; and the men were indignant and very angry,

---

not take the opposite approach to the problem instead of insisting on getting more and more angry? After all, surely fire cannot quench fire? This is contrary to nature. In the same way, it could never happen that anger would suppress anger: I mean, what water does to fire, meekness and gentleness do to anger" (*Homiliae in Genesim*, 58, 5).

34:1–31. Shechem is both the name of the city opposite which Jacob camped and the name of a particular individual. And Hamor is both the name of the people to which the inhabitants of Shechem belong, and the name of an individual. In the present narrative it is sometimes not clear whether it is the city or the person that is being referred to.

Given the place this story occupies in the overall context of Genesis, it looks as if the sacred writer wants to draw a parallel between Jacob and Abraham. Abraham was also in Shechem and there

he received the promise of the land (cf. 12:6–7). Now that Jacob has arrived, that promise seems in a sense to be fulfilled; but the violent behaviour of his sons cuts it short. So, Jacob, like Abraham, heads for Bethel, to the hill country. This account also provides a justification for the future fortunes of the tribes of Simeon and Levi—the former being practically absorbed into the tribe of Judah, the latter having no right to a territory of its own (a situation which will also be described in chapter 49, and one for which this account is preparing us).

We should notice the explicit rejection of sexual assault, aggravated here by the fact that it is a young Jewish woman being violated by a non-Jew; and also the implied condemnation of the bloody vengeance and treachery done by the sons of Jacob (v. 30).

34:2. "The Hivite": the Hivites were a people who lived in Canaan before the

Israel». ¹Egressa est autem Dina filia, quam Lia pepererat Iacob, ut videret filias regionis illius. ²Quam cum vidisset Sichem filius Hemmor Hevaei principis terrae illius, adamavit eam et rapuit; et dormivit cum illa, vi opprimens illam. ³Et conglutinata est anima eius cum ea, et amavit puellam et locutus est ad cor eius. ⁴Dixitque ad Hemmor patrem suum: «Accipe mihi puellam hanc coniugem». ⁵Cum audisset Iacob quod violasset Dinam filiam suam, absentibus filiis et in pastu pecorum occupatis, siluit, donec redirent. ⁶Egresso autem Hemmor patre Sichem, ut loqueretur ad Iacob, ⁷ecce filii Iacob veniebant de agro, auditoque, quod acciderat, contristati et irati sunt valde, eo quod foedam rem esset

because he had wrought folly in Israel by lying with Jacob's daughter, for such a thing ought not to be done.

[8]But Hamor spoke with them, saying, "The soul of my son Shechem longs for your daughter; I pray you, give her to him in marriage. [9]Make marriages with us; give your daughters to us, and take our daughters for yourselves. [10]You shall dwell with us; and the land shall be open to you; dwell and trade in it, and get property in it." [11]Shechem also said to her father and to her brothers, "Let me find favour in your eyes, and whatever you say to me I will give. [12]Ask of me ever so much as marriage present and gift, and I will give according as you say to me; only give me the maiden to be my wife."

The sons of Jacob take revenge

[13]The sons of Jacob answered Shechem and his father Hamor deceitfully, because he had defiled their sister Dinah. [14]They said to them, "We cannot do this thing, to give our sister to one who is uncircumcised, for that would be a disgrace to us. [15]Only on this condition will we consent to you: that you will become as we are and every male of you be circumcised. [16]Then we will give our daughters to you, and we will take your daughters to ourselves, and we will dwell with you and become one people. [17]But if you will not listen to us and be circumcised, then we will take our daughter, and we will be gone."

[18]Their words pleased Hamor and Hamor's son Shechem. [19]And the young man did not delay to do the thing, because he

arrival of the Israelites (cf. Num 13:29; Josh 11:3; Judg 3:3); we do not know much about where they came from or what they were like. Instead of "Hivite" the ancient Greek translation, the Septuagint, reads "Hurrite", another people, of non-Semitic origin, who were spread over the Middle East. The fact that the inhabitants of Shechem did not practise circumcision leads one to think that its inhabitants were Hurrites.

operatus in Israel et, violata filia Iacob, rem illicitam perpetrasset. [8]Locutus est itaque Hemmor ad eos: «Sichem filii mei adhaesit anima filiae vestrae; date eam illi uxorem, [9]et iungamus vicissim conubia: filias vestras tradite nobis et filias nostras accipite vobis. [10]Et habitate nobiscum; terra in potestate vestra est: manete, perambulate et possidete eam». [11]Sed et Sichem ad patrem et ad fratres eius ait: «Inveniam gratiam coram vobis et, quaecumque statueritis, dabo. [12]Augete mihi valde dotem et munera; libens tribuam, quod petieritis. Tantum date mihi puellam hanc uxorem». [13]Responderunt filii Iacob Sichem et Hemmor patri eius in dolo ob stuprum sororis: [14]«Non possumus facere, quod petitis, dare sororem nostram homini incircumciso, opprobrium enim esset nobis. [15]In hoc tantum valebimus acquiescere vobis: si esse volueritis similes nostri, circumcidatur in vobis omne masculini sexus; [16]tunc dabimus et accipiemus mutuo filias nostras ac vestras et habitabimus vobiscum erimusque unus populus. [17]Si autem circumcidi nolueritis, tollemus filiam nostram et recedemus». [18]Placuit oblatio eorum Hemmor et Sichem filio eius, [19]nec distulit adulescens quin statim, quod petebatur, expleret; amabat

had delight in Jacob's daughter. Now he was the most honoured of all his family. ²⁰So Hamor and his son Shechem came to the gate of their city and spoke to the men of their city, saying, ²¹"These men are friendly with us; let them dwell in the land and trade in it, for behold, the land is large enough for them; let us take their daughters in marriage, and let us give them our daughters. ²²Only on this condition will the men agree to dwell with us, to become one people: that every male among us be circumcised as they are circumcised. ²³Will not their cattle, their property and all their beasts be ours? Only let us agree with them, and they will dwell with us." ²⁴And all who went out of the gate of his city hearkened to Hamor and his son Shechem; and every male was circumcised, all who went out of the gate of his city.

²⁵On the third day, when they were sore, two of the sons of Jacob, Simeon and Levi, Dinah's brothers, took their swords and came upon the city unawares, and killed all the males. ²⁶They slew Hamor and his son Shechem with the sword, and took Dinah out of Shechem's house, and went away. ²⁷And the sons of Jacob came upon the slain, and plundered the city, because their sister had been defiled; ²⁸they took their flocks and their herds, their asses, and whatever was in the city and in the field; ²⁹all their wealth, all their little ones and their wives, all that was in the houses, they captured and made their prey. ³⁰Then Jacob said to Simeon and Levi, "You have brought trouble on me by making me odious to the inhabitants of the land, the Canaanites and the Perizzites; my numbers are few, and if they gather themselves against me and attack me, I shall be destroyed, both I and my household." ³¹But they said, "Should he treat our sister as a harlot?"

Gen 49:5–7

Lk 21:24

enim filiam Iacob valde, et ipse erat inclitus in omni domo patris sui. ²⁰Ingressique portam urbis, Hemmor et Sichem filius eius locuti sunt ad viros civitatis suae: ²¹«Viri isti pacifici sunt erga nos; maneant in terra et perambulent eam, quae spatiosa et lata est eis; filias eorum accipiemus uxores et nostras illis dabimus. ²²Tantum in hoc valebunt viri acquiescere nobis, ut maneant nobiscum et efficiamur unus populus, si circumcidamus masculos nostros ritum gentis imitantes; ²³et pecora et substantia et armenta eorum nostra erunt. Tantum in hoc acquiescamus, et habitabunt nobiscum». ²⁴Assensique sunt omnes, circumcisis cunctis maribus, qui egrediebantur e porta civitatis suae. ²⁵Et ecce, die tertio, quando gravissimus vulnerum dolor est, arreptis duo filii Iacob Simeon et Levi fratres Dinae gladiis, ingressi sunt urbem securi; interfectisque omnibus masculis, ²⁶Hemmor et Sichem pariter necaverunt, tollentes Dinam de domo Sichem sororem suam. ²⁷Filii Iacob irruerunt super occisos, et depopulati sunt urbem in ultionem stupri. ²⁸Oves eorum et armenta et asinos cunctaque, quae in civitate et in agris erant, tulerunt. ²⁹Omnes opes eorum, parvulos quoque et uxores duxerunt captivas et diripuerunt omnia, quae in domibus erant. ³⁰Iacob autem dixit ad Simeon et Levi: «Turbastis me et odiosum fecistis me Chananaeis et Pherezaeis habitatoribus terrae huius. Nos pauci sumus; illi congregati percutient me, et delebor ego et domus mea». ³¹Responderunt: «Numquid ut scorto abuti debuere sorore nostra?». ¹Locutus est Deus ad Iacob: «Surge et ascende Bethel et habita ibi; facque altare Deo,

Gen 28:10–22 **Jacob returns to Bethel**

35 ¹God said to Jacob, "Arise, go up to Bethel, and dwell there; and make there an altar to the God who appeared to you when you fled from your brother Esau." ²So Jacob said to his household and to all who were with him, "Put away the foreign gods that are among you, and purify yourselves, and change your garments; ³then let us arise and go up to Bethel, that I may make there an altar to the God who answered me in the day of my distress and has been with me wherever I have gone." ⁴So they gave to Jacob all the foreign gods that they had, and the rings that were in their ears; and Jacob hid them under the oak which was near Shechem.

Gen 12:6 ⁵And as they journeyed, a terror from God fell upon the cities that were round about them, so that they did not pursue the sons of Jacob. ⁶And Jacob came to Luz (that is, Bethel), which is in Tit 2:11 the land of Canaan, he and all the people who were with him, ⁷and there he built an altar, and called the place El-bethel,^z because there God had revealed himself to him when he fled from his brother. ⁸And Deborah, Rebekah's nurse, died, and she

---

35:1–15. Jacob's trek from Shechem to Bethel is given all the features of a religious pilgrimage—a divine command, purification before setting out, God's mysterious protection, arrival at the place and the building of an altar, and a divine apparition which confirms Jacob's new personality as Israel and reaffirms the promises made to Abraham and Isaac. Allon-bacuth means "oak of weeping". The change of Jacob's name to Israel (v. 10) was already reported in 32:23–32, so it looks as though various traditional accounts are being drawn on. One cannot

fail to notice how frequently God now speaks to Jacob (cf. vv. 1, 9, 11). Obviously the sacred writer wants to stress that God accompanies Jacob and that they are on familiar terms, now that the patriarch is once again in the promised land; even though God did not leave him unprotected when he was abroad. God's way of acting towards Jacob teaches us that he also keeps company with everyone whom he has brought into his Church through Baptism. "Just think about the wonder of God's love. Our Lord comes out to meet

---

qui apparuit tibi, quando fugiebas Esau fratrem tuum». ²Iacob vero, convocata omni domo sua, ait: «Abigite deos alienos, qui in medio vestri sunt, et mundamini ac mutate vestimenta vestra. ³Surgamus et ascendamus in Bethel, ut faciamus ibi altare Deo, qui exaudivit me in die tribulationis meae et socius fuit itineris mei». ⁴Dederunt ergo ei omnes deos alienos, quos habebant, et inaures, quae erant in auribus eorum; at ille infodit ea subter Quercum, quae est prope urbem Sichem. ⁵Cumque profecti essent, terror Dei invasit omnes per circuitum civitates, et non sunt ausi persequi filios Iacob. ⁶Venit igitur Iacob Luzam, quae est in terra Chanaan, id est Bethel, ipse et omnis populus cum eo. ⁷Aedificavitque ibi altare et appellavit nomen loci illius Deus Bethel; ibi enim apparuit ei Deus, cum fugeret fratrem suum. ⁸Eodem tempore mortua est Debora nutrix Rebeccae et sepulta est ad radices

z. That is *God of Bethel*

174

was buried under an oak below Bethel; so the name of it was called Allon-bacuth.[a]

[9]God appeared to Jacob again, when he came from Paddan-aram, and blessed him. [10]And God said to him, "Your name is Jacob; no longer shall your name be called Jacob, but Israel shall be your name." So his name was called Israel. [11]And God said to him, "I am God Almighty:[b] be fruitful and multiply; a nation and a company of nations shall come from you, and kings shall spring from you. [12]The land which I gave to Abraham and Isaac I will give to you, and I will give the land to your descendants after you." [13]Then God went up from him in the place where he had spoken with him. [14]And Jacob set up a pillar in the place where he had spoken with him, a pillar of stone; and he poured out a drink offering on it, and poured oil on it. [15]So Jacob called the name of the place where God had spoken with him, Bethel.

Gen 32:23–32

Gen 17:1
Heb 7:5

Gen 12:7

The birth of Benjamin and the death of Rachel

[16]Then they journeyed from Bethel; and when they were still some distance from Ephrath, Rachel travailed, and she had hard labour. [17]And when she was in her hard labour, the midwife said to

Acts 7:8

---

us, he waits for us, he's by the roadside where we cannot but see him, and he calls each of us personally, speaking to us about our own things—which are also his. He stirs us to sorrow, opens our conscience to be generous; he encourages us to want to be faithful, so that we can be called his disciples. When we hear these intimate words of grace, which are by way of an affectionate reproach, we realize at once that our Lord has not forgotten us during all the time in which,

through our fault, we did not see him" (St J. Escrivá, *Christ Is Passing By*, 59).

35:16–29. Jacob's trek ends in Hebron, where Abraham and Isaac also lived. At this stage the narrative loses the tone of a religious pilgrimage which it had earlier, and draws on various traditions—that of the birth of Benjamin (with an explanation of what his name means); that of Reuben's sin, which causes him to lose his leading role as the firstborn

---

Bethel subter quercum; vocatumque est nomen loci illius Quercus fletus. [9]Apparuit iterum Deus Iacob, postquam reversus est de Paddanaram, benedixitque ei [10]dicens: «Non vocaberis ultra Iacob, sed Israel erit nomen tuum», et appellavit eum Israel. [11]Dixitque ei: «Ego Deus omnipotens. Cresce et multiplicare; gens et congregatio nationum erunt ex te, reges de lumbis tuis egredientur. [12]Terramque, quam dedi Abraham et Isaac, dabo tibi; et semini tuo post te dabo terram hanc». [13]Et ascendit ab eo Deus. [14]Ille vero erexit titulum lapideum in loco, quo locutus ei fuerat Deus, libans super eum libamina et effundens oleum [15]vocansque nomen loci illius Bethel. [16]Egressi sunt de Bethel. Et adhuc spatium quoddam erat usque ad Ephratham, cum parturiret Rachel; [17]ob dificultatem partus periclitari coepit, dixitque ei obstetrix: «Noli timere, quia et hac vice habes filium». [18]Egrediente autem anima et immi-

a. That is *Oak of weeping*   **b.** Heb *El Shaddai*

Gen 48:7 her, "Fear not; for now you will have another son." [18]And as her soul was departing (for she died), she called his name Ben-oni;[c] Mic 5:1 but his father called his name Benjamin.[d] [19]So Rachel died, and Mt 2:18 she was buried on the way to Ephrath (that is, Bethlehem), [20]and Jacob set up a pillar upon her grave; it is the pillar of Rachel's tomb, which is there to this day.

Gen 49:34 **Reuben's sin**

[21]Israel journeyed on, and pitched his tent beyond the tower of Eder.

[22]While Israel dwelt in that land Reuben went and lay with Bilhah his father's concubine; and Israel heard of it.

Gen 29:31;
30:24 **Jacob reaches Hebron. The death of Isaac**
Lk 3:33–34 Now the sons of Jacob were twelve. [23]The sons of Leah: Reuben (Jacob's first-born), Simeon, Levi, Judah, Issachar, and Zebulun. [24]The sons of Rachel: Joseph and Benjamin. [25]The sons of Bilhah, Rachel's maid: Dan and Naphtali. [26]The sons of Zilpah, Leah's maid: Gad and Asher. These were the sons of Jacob who were born to him in Paddan-aram.

Heb 11:9 [27]And Jacob came to his father Isaac at Mamre, or Kiriath-arba (that is, Hebron), where Abraham and Isaac had sojourned. [28]Now the days of Isaac were a hundred and eighty years. [29]And Isaac breathed his last; and he died and was gathered to his people, old and full of days; and his sons Esau and Jacob buried him.

---

among the tribes, with this prerogative now given to Judah (cf. chap. 49); the list of the sons of Jacob; and the death of Isaac.

35:17–18. The name Benjamin means "son of the right hand", that is, "of happy omen", and is a kind of counterpoint to Benoni, "son of my sorrow".

nente iam morte, vocavit nomen filii sui Benoni (*id est Filius doloris mei*) pater vero appellavit eum Beniamin (*id est Filius dextrae*). [19]Mortua est ergo Rachel et sepulta est in via, quae ducit Ephratham; haec est Bethlehem. [20]Erexitque Iacob titulum super sepulcrum eius; hic est titulus monumenti Rachel usque in praesentem diem. [21]Egressus inde Israel, fixit tabernaculum trans Magdaleder (*id est Turris gregis*). [22]Cumque habitaret in illa regione, abiit Ruben et dormivit cum Bilha concubina patris sui; quod illum minime latuit. Erant autem filii Iacob duodecim. [23]Filii Liae: primogenitus Ruben et Simeon et Levi et Iudas et Issachar et Zabulon. [24]Filii Rachel: Ioseph et Beniamin. [25]Filii Bilhae ancillae Rachelis: Dan et Nephthali. [26]Filii Zelphae ancillae Liae: Gad et Aser. Hi sunt filii Iacob, qui nati sunt ei in Paddanaram. [27] Venit Iacob ad Isaac patrem suum in Mambre Cariatharbe, id est Hebron, ubi peregrinatus est Abraham et Isaac. [28]Et completi sunt dies Isaac centum octoginta annorum; [29]consumptusque aetate mortuus est et appositus est populo suo senex et plenus dierum. Et sepelierunt eum Esau et Iacob filii sui. [1]Hae sunt autem generationes Esau. Ipse est Edom. [2]Esau accepit uxores de filiabus

c. That is *Son of my sorrow*   **d.** That is *Son of the right hand* or *Son of the South*

9. THE DESCENDANTS OF ESAU*

I Chron 1:35–54

36 ¹These are the descendants of Esau (that is, Edom). ²Esau took his wives from the Canaanites: Adah the daughter of Elon the Hittite, Oholibamah the daughter of Anah the son^e of Zibeon the Hivite, ³and Basemath, Ishmael's daughter, the sister of Nebaioth. ⁴And Adah bore to Esau, Eliphaz; Basemath bore Reuel; ⁵and Oholibamah bore Jeush, Jalam, and Korah. These are the sons of Esau who were born to him in the land of Canaan.

Gen 26:34–35; 28:6–9

⁶Then Esau took his wives, his sons, his daughters, and all the members of his household, his cattle, all his beasts, and all his property which he had acquired in the land of Canaan; and he went into a land away from his brother Jacob. ⁷For their possessions were too great for them to dwell together; the land of their sojournings could not support them because of their cattle. ⁸So Esau dwelt in the hill country of Seir; Esau is Edom.

Rev 18:13

⁹These are the descendants of Esau the father of the Edomites in the hill country of Seir. ¹⁰These are the names of Esau's sons: Eliphaz the son of Adah the wife of Esau, Reuel the son of Basemath the wife of Esau. ¹¹The sons of Eliphaz were Teman, Omar, Zepho, Gatam, and Kenaz. ¹²(Timna was a concubine of

---

*36:1–43 Using various sources of a genealogical type, possibly drawn from a tradition of Edom or of Israel itself, the sacred author wants to show, in effect, how the promise is being fulfilled: the older son cedes to the younger his right to the land. The sacred text makes no mention now of the disputes between the two brothers; what we have here, rather, is the sort of peaceful separation that we already saw in the case of Abraham and Lot (cf. chap. 13). Also, the fruitfulness

of Esau's line confirms the blessing given him by Isaac (cf. 26:4).

36:1–5 The divergencies in the names of Esau's wives between 36:1–5 and 26:34–35 may be due to the fact that the final editor of the text was using various traditions and did not try to reconcile them. The same may apply to the lists of Esau's descendants (vv. 9–14) and the list of the chiefs of the tribes of Edom which follows it (vv. 15–18).

Chanaan: Ada filiam Elon Hetthaei et Oolibama filiam Ana filii Sebeon Horraei; ³Basemath quoque filiam Ismael sororem Nabaioth. ⁴ Peperit autem Ada Eliphaz, Basemath genuit Rahuel, ⁵Oolibama genuit Iehus et Ialam et Core. Hi filii Esau, qui nati sunt ei in terra Chanaan. ⁶Tulit autem Esau uxores suas et filios et filias et omnes animas domus suae et pecora armenta et cuncta, quae acquisierat in terra Chanaan, et abiit in terram Seir; recessitque a fratre suo Iacob. ⁷Divites enim erant valde et simul habitare non poterant; nec sustinebat eos terra peregrinationis eorum prae multitudine gregum. ⁸Habitavitque Esau in monte Seir. Ipse est Edom. ⁹Hae autem sunt generationes Esau patris Edom in monte Seir, ¹⁰et haec nomina filiorum eius: Eliphaz filius Ada uxoris Esau, Rahuel quoque filius Basemath uxoris eius. ¹¹Fueruntque Eliphaz filii: Theman, Omar, Sepho et Gatham et Cenez. ¹²Erat

---

e. Sam Gk Syr: Heb *daughter*

Eliphaz, Esau's son; she bore Amalek to Eliphaz.) These are the sons of Adah, Esau's wife. [13]These are the sons of Reuel: Nahath, Zerah, Shammah, and Mizzah. These are the sons of Basemath, Esau's wife. [14]These are the sons of Oholibamah the daughter of Anah the son[f] of Zibeon, Esau's wife: she bore to Esau Jeush, Jalam, and Korah.

[15]These are the chiefs of the sons of Esau. The sons of Eliphaz the first-born of Esau: the chiefs Teman, Omar, Zepho, Kenaz, [16]Korah, Gatam, and Amalek; these are the chiefs of Eliphaz in the landof Edom; they are the sons of Adah. [17]These are the sons of Reuel, Esau's son: the chiefs Nahath, Zerah, Shammah, and Mizzah; these are the chiefs of Reuel in the land of Edom; they are the sons of Basemath, Esau's wife. [18]These are the sons of Oholibamah, Esau's wife: the chiefs Jeush, Jalam, and Korah; these are the chiefs born of Oholibamah the daughter of Anah, Esau's wife. [19]These are the sons of Esau (that is, Edom), and these are their chiefs.

[20]These are the sons of Seir the Horite, the inhabitants of the land: Lotan, Shobal, Zibeon, Anah, [21]Dishon, Ezer, and Dishan; these are the chiefs of the Horites, the sons of Seir in the land of Edom. [22]The sons of Lotan were Hori and Heman; and Lotan's sister was Timna. [23]These are the sons of Shobal: Alvan, Manahath, Ebal, Shepho, and Onam. [24]These are the sons of Zibeon: Aiah and Anah; he is the Anah who found the hot springs in the wilderness, as he pastured the asses of Zibeon his father. [25]These are the children of Anah: Dishon and Oholibamah the daughter of Anah. [26]These are the sons of Dishon: Hemdan, Eshban, Ithran, and Cheran. [27]These are the sons of Ezer: Bilhan, Zaavan, and Akan. [28]These are the sons of Dishan: Uz and Aran. [29]These are the chiefs of the Horites: the chiefs Lotan, Shobal,

---

autem Thamna concubina Eliphaz filii Esau, quae peperit ei Amalec. Hi sunt filii Ada uxoris Esau. [13]Filii autem Rahuel: Nahath et Zara, Samma et Meza; hi filii Basemath uxoris Esau. [14]Isti erant filii Oolibama filiae Ana filii Sebeon uxoris Esau, quos genuit ei: Iehus et Ialam et Core. [15]Hi duces filiorum Esau. Filii Eliphaz primogeniti Esau: dux Theman, dux Omar, dux Sepho, dux Cenez, [16]dux Core, dux Gatham, dux Amalec. Hi duces Eliphaz in terra Edom; hi filii Ada. [17]Hi filii Rahuel filii Esau: dux Nahath, dux Zara, dux Samma, dux Meza. Hi duces Rahuel in terra Edom; isti filii Basemath uxoris Esau. [18]Hi filii Oolibama uxoris Esau: dux Iehus, dux Ialam, dux Core. Hi duces Oolibama filiae Ana uxoris Esau. [19]Isti sunt filii Esau et hi duces eorum. Ipse est Edom. [20]Isti sunt filii Seir Horraei habitatores terrae: Lotan et Sobal et Sebeon et Ana [21]et Dison et Eser et Disan; hi duces Horraei filii Seir in terra Edom. [22]Facti sunt autem filii Lotan: Hori et Hemam; erat autem soror Lotan Thamna. [23]Et isti filii Sobal: Alvan et Manahath et Ebal, Sepho et Onam. [24]Et hi filii Sebeon: Aia et Ana. Iste est Ana, qui invenit aquas calidas in solitudine, cum pasceret asinos Sebeon patris sui. [25]Habuitque filium Dison et filiam Oolibama. [26]Et isti filii Dison: Hemdan et Eseban et Iethran et Charran. [27]Hi filii Eser: Bilhan et Zavan et Iacan. [28]Habuit autem filios Disan: Us et Aran. [29]Isti duces Horraeorum: dux Lotan, dux

f. Gk Syr: Heb *daughter*

Zibeon, Anah, [30]Dishon, Ezer, and Dishan; these are the chiefs of the Horites, according to their clans in the land of Seir.

[31]These are the kings who reigned in the land of Edom, before any king reigned over the Israelites. [32]Bela the son of Beor reigned in Edom, the name of his city being Dinhabah. [33]Bela died, and Jobab the son of Zerah of Bozrah reigned in his stead. [34]Jobab died, and Husham of the land of the Temanites reigned in his stead. [35]Husham died, and Hadad the son of Bedad, who defeated Midian in the country of Moab, reigned in his stead, the name of his city being Avith. [36]Hadad died, and Samlah of Masrekah reigned in his stead. [37]Samlah died, and Shaul of Rehoboth on the Euphrates reigned in his stead. [38]Shaul died, and Baal-hanan the son of Achbor reigned in his stead. [39]Baal-hanan the son of Achbor died, and Hadar reigned in his stead, the name of his city being Pau; his wife's name was Mehetabel, the daughter of Matred, daughter of Mezahab.

[40]These are the names of the chiefs of Esau, according to their families and their dwelling places, by their names: the chiefs Timna, Alvah, Jetheth, [41]Oholibamah, Elah, Pinon, [42]Kenaz, Teman, Mibzar, [43]Magdiel, and Iram; these are the chiefs of Edom (that is, Esau, the father of Edom), according to their dwelling places in the land of their possession.

37 [1]Jacob dwelt in the land of his father's sojournings, in the land of Canaan.

10. THE DESCENDANTS OF JACOB.
THE STORY OF JOSEPH*

Joseph and his brothers

[2]This is the history of the family of Jacob.

*Joseph, being seventeen years old, was shepherding the flock with his brothers; he was a lad with the sons of Bilhah and Zilpah,

Sobal, dux Sebeon, dux Ana, [30]dux Dison, dux Eser, dux Disan; isti duces Horraeorum secundum tribus eorum in terra Seir. [31]Reges autem, qui regnaverunt in terra Edom, antequam haberent regem filii Israel, fuerunt hi. [32]Regnavit in Edom Bela filius Beor, nomenque urbis eius Denaba. [33]Mortuus est autem Bela, et regnavit pro eo Iobab filius Zarae de Bosra. [34]Cumque mortuus esset Iobab, regnavit pro eo Husam de terra Themanorum. [35]Hoc quoque mortuo, regnavit pro eo Adad filius Badad, qui percussit Madian in regione Moab; et nomen urbis eius Avith. [36]Cumque mortuus esset Adad, regnavit pro eo Semla de Masreca. [37]Hoc quoque mortuo, regnavit pro eo Saul de Rohoboth iuxta fluvium. [38]Cumque et hic obiisset, successit in regnum Baalhanan filius Achobor. [39]Isto quoque mortuo, regnavit pro eo Adad, nomenque urbis eius Phau; et appellabatur uxor eius Meetabel filia Matred filiae Mezaab. [40]Haec ergo nomina ducum Esau in cognationibus et locis et vocabulis suis: dux Thamna, dux Alva, dux Ietheth, [41]dux Oolibama, dux Ela, dux Phinon, [42]dux Cenez, dux Theman, dux Mabsar, [43]dux Magdiel, dux Iram. Hi duces Edom habitantes in terra imperii sui. Ipse est Esau pater Idumaeorum. [1]Habitavit autem Iacob in terra Chanaan, in qua peregrinatus est pater suus. [2]Hae sunt generationes

Gen 30:22–24

his father's wives; and Joseph brought an ill report of them to their father. ³Now Israel loved Joseph more than any other of his children, because he was the son of his old age; and he made him a long robe with sleeves. ⁴But when his brothers saw that their father loved him more than all his brothers, they hated him, and could not speak peaceably to him.

---

*37:2—50:26. From here to the end of the book of Genesis, with the exception of chapters 38 and 49, we have the story of Joseph. This concludes the "history of the patriarchs", leaving them not in the promised land, Canaan, but in Egypt. This sets the scene for the narrative of the great Exodus. The story of Joseph is, thus, the link between patriarchal history and the departure from Egypt, and it therefore constitutes an important stage in the development of salvation history as recorded in the Old Testament.

In the story of Joseph we can see, on the one hand, the testimony borne by ancient accounts about the Israelites going down into Egypt and, on the other, the skill of the narrator who describes the acts of a drama full of emotion, which comes to a happy ending and from which the reader can draw one fundamental lesson: God is guiding everything that happens (even events which seem negative) towards good, towards salvation. *Omnia in bonum* (cf. Rom 8:28) might well be the title of the story of Joseph (cf. 50:20).

The original source of this section may have been quite different from the patriarchal traditions we have seen so far: there is no reference to places of worship, no explanations as to the meaning of names of places and people, no direct divine interventions (except in the case of Jacob in 46:2–4); it assumes that

Joseph's mother is still living (cf. 37:10) and shows Jacob to have a number of daughters (cf. 37:35).

From the information provided in the story of Joseph and from other biblical traditions (cf. for example, Gen 15:16; Ex 12:40–41), it is not possible to say exactly when the Israelites went down into Egypt. The most likely period is when Egypt was under the control of the Hyksos (1720–1580 BC), invaders who were partly Semitic. The Hyksos had their capital in Avaris, in the Nile delta, and this is where the capital is in the biblical account. The account reminds us of past events and their significance. The whole story of Joseph, as told in the Bible, is very instructive about how God guided the steps of Israel's ancestors, to work wonders among them, redeeming them from slavery and making them into a people, the chosen people of God. The literary skill with which this last part of the story is told, not only does not take from the historical value of the account: it helps us to grasp the true meaning of all that happened to the "fathers" of Israel, and shows us how the Word of God is able to express itself in language which it knows will hold the reader's attention.

37:2. "This is the history of . . .": ten times over the course of Genesis the final

---

Iacob. Ioseph, cum decem et septem esset annorum, pascebat gregem cum fratribus suis adhuc puer; et erat cum filiis Bilhae et Zelphae uxorum patris sui; detulitque patri malam eorum famam. ³Israel autem diligebat Ioseph super omnes filios suos, eo quod in senectute genuisset eum; fecitque ei tunicam talarem. ⁴Videntes autem fratres eius quod a patre plus cunctis filiis amaretur, oderant eum, nec

Joseph's dreams

⁵Now Joseph had a dream, and when he told it to his brothers they only hated him the more. ⁶He said to them, "Hear this dream which I have dreamed: ⁷behold, we were binding sheaves in the field, and lo, my sheaf arose and stood upright; and behold, your sheaves gathered round it, and bowed down to my sheaf." ⁸His

---

redactor of the book uses this formal phrase to impose order on its content, dividing it into a number of genealogical sections (cf. "Introduction", p. 29 above). Here he uses it for the last time, to notify the reader that he has reached the last section, the story of how Jacob-Israel went down into Egypt: one of his sons, Joseph, was sold by his brothers and taken to Egypt (chap. 37); Joseph prospered in that country and became very important (cf. chaps. 39–41); Jacob and his other sons went to Egypt where they met Joseph and, through his good offices, received special treatment from the pharaoh; finally, the patriarch Jacob died in Egypt but was brought back to the land of Canaan to be buried (cf. chaps. 49–50).

37:3–4. The tunic with long sleeves made Joseph look like a prince, in some way foretelling his glorious future. Although Jacob's preferential love for Joseph is due to human causes, behind it we can see something which occurs throughout the Bible—how some people, gratuitously, enjoy special favour, including special divine favour and love, without this meaning that the love shown to others is diminished. Joseph, the object of Jacob's special love, thereby becomes a figure of Jesus Christ, the Beloved of the Father (cf. Mt 1:11). The sin of Jacob's sons, like Cain's in some way (cf.

Gen 4:5), begins with their reacting against God's preferential love; it then turns into hatred and envy (cf. vv. 8–11) and ends up with their getting rid of their brother (cf. v. 20).

37:5–11. Dreams play an important role in the story of Joseph (cf. chaps. 40–41). These (unlike those in previous chapters) are not a vehicle for divine revelations, but simply a way of foretelling the future. However, in them one can see the providence of God guiding events.

Even Jacob is surprised when he realizes the meaning of his son's dreams, and he rebukes Joseph because he thinks he may be getting ideas above his station. However, Jacob does not forget the incident and he is open to the possibility of what may happen even though he doesn't yet understand it. Joseph's brothers have a different reaction: they don't want the dream to come true, so they begin to plot against him. But God will draw great good for them all out of their wickedness.

St Ambrose sees, underlying the dreams reported in this passage, "the future resurrection of Christ, whom, when they saw him in Jerusalem, the eleven disciples worshipped, and whom all the saints will adore when they rise again bearing the fruits of their good works, as it is written, 'They come with joy, bearing their sheaves'" (Ps 126:6)" (*De Joseph*, 2,7).

poterant ei quidquam pacifice loqui. ⁵Accidit quoque ut visum somnium referret fratribus suis; quae causa maioris odii seminarium fuit. ⁶Dixitque ad eos: «Audite somnium meum, quod vidi. ⁷Putabam ligare nos manipulos in agro, et quasi consurgere manipulum meum et stare, vestrosque manipulos cir-

brothers said to him, "Are you indeed to reign over us? Or are you indeed to have dominion over us?" So they hated him yet more

Rev 12:1 for his dreams and for his words. [9]Then he dreamed another dream, and told it to his brothers, and said, "Behold, I have dreamed another dream; and behold, the sun, the moon, and eleven stars were bowing down to me." [10]But when he told it to his father and to his brothers, his father rebuked him, and said to him, "What is this dream that you have dreamed? Shall I and your mother and your brothers indeed come to bow ourselves to the

Dan 7:28
Lk 2:19–51 ground before you?" [11]And his brothers were jealous of him, but

Acts 7–9 his father kept the saying in mind.

Ps 105:17–19
Wis 10:13
Mt 26:15

Joseph is sold to Egyptians as a slave

[12]Now his brothers went to pasture their father's flock near Shechem. [13]And Israel said to Joseph, "Are not your brothers pasturing the flock at Shechem? Come, I will send you to them." And he said to him, "Here I am." [14]So he said to him, "Go now, see if it is well with your brothers, and with the flock; and bring me word again." So he sent him from the valley of Hebron, and he came to Shechem. [15]And a man found him wandering in the fields; and the man asked him, "What are you seeking?" [16]"I am seeking my brothers," he said, "tell me, I pray you, where they are pasturing the flock." [17]And the man said, "They have gone away, for I heard them say, 'Let us go to Dothan.'" So Joseph went after his broth-

---

37:12–36. This episode deals with the horrible crime of disposing of their brother and the providential events which take Joseph to Egypt. We can see that the narrative is drawing on two sources: one emphasizes the intervention of Judah (v. 26), the other that of Reuben. The true key to what is happening will emerge at the

end of the story: "You meant evil against me," Joseph tells his brothers, "but God meant it for good" (50:20). In the light of the whole narrative we can see the way God's plan is being put into operation: "Joseph," comments St Gregory the Great, "was sold by his brothers because they did not want to do him honour; but that is

---

cumstantes adorare manipulum meum». [8]Responderunt fratres eius: «Numquid rex noster eris? Aut subiciemur dicioni tuae?». Haec ergo causa somniorum atque sermonum, invidiae et odii fomitem ministravit. [9]Aliud quoque vidit somnium, quod narrans fratribus ait: «Vidi per somnium quasi solem et lunam et stellas undecim adorare me». [10]Quod cum patri suo et fratribus retulisset, increpavit eum pater suus et dixit: «Quid sibi vult hoc somnium, quod vidisti? Num ego et mater tua et fratres tui adorabimus te proni in terram?». [11]Invidebant igitur ei fratres sui; pater vero rem tacitus considerabat. [12]Cumque fratres illius in pascendis gregibus patris morarentur in Sichem, [13]dixit Israel ad Ioseph: «Fratres tui pascunt oves in Sichimis; veni, mittam te ad eos». Quo respondente: [14]«Praesto sum», ait ei: «Vade et vide, si cuncta prospera sint erga fratres tuos et pecora, et renuntia mihi quid agatur». Missus de valle Hebron venit in Sichem; [15]invenitque eum vir errantem in agro et interrogavit quid quaereret. [16]At ille respondit: «Fratres meos quaero; indica mihi, ubi pascant greges». [17]Dixitque ei vir: «Recesserunt de loco isto; audivi autem eos dicentes: 'Eamus in Dothain'». Perrexit ergo Ioseph post fratres suos et invenit eos in Dothain. [18]Qui cum vidissent eum procul, antequam accederet ad eos, co-

ers, and found them at Dothan. ¹⁸They saw him afar off, and
before he came near to them they conspired against him to kill
him. ¹⁹They said to one another, "Here comes this dreamer.
²⁰Come now, let us kill him and throw him into one of the pits; Mk 12:7
then we shall say that a wild beast has devoured him, and we shall
see what will become of his dreams." ²¹But when Reuben heard it,
he delivered him out of their hands, saying, "Let us not take his
life." ²²And Reuben said to them, "Shed no blood; cast him into
this pit here in the wilderness, but lay no hand upon him"—that he
might rescue him out of their hand, to restore him to his father.
²³So when Joseph came to his brothers, they stripped him of his
robe, the long robe with sleeves that he wore; ²⁴and they took him
and cast him into a pit. The pit was empty, there was no water in
it.

²⁵Then they sat down to eat; and looking up they saw a cara-
van of Ishmaelites coming from Gilead, with their camels bearing
gum, balm, and myrrh, on their way to carry it down to Egypt. Gen 4:10
²⁶Then Judah said to his brothers, "What profit is it if we slay our Job 16:18
brother and conceal his blood? ²⁷Come, let us sell him to the Is 26:21
Ishmaelites, and let not our hand be upon him, for he is our Ezek 24:7
brother, our own flesh." And his brothers heeded him. ²⁸Then Acts 7:9
Midianite traders passed by; and they drew Joseph up and lifted
him out of the pit, and sold him to the Ishmaelites for twenty
shekels of silver; and they took Joseph to Egypt.

²⁹When Reuben returned to the pit and saw that Joseph was
not in the pit, he rent his clothes ³⁰and returned to his brothers,

---

exactly what they do do, by the very fact
of selling him. [. . .] So too, when one
wants to avoid the divine will, then is
when it is fulfilled" (*Moralia*, 6, 18, 20).

37:36. Potiphar is the same name as is

given in 41:45, 50 and 46:20 to a priest
of the sun god at Heliopolis whose
daughter will marry Joseph. It certainly is
an Egyptian name, as can be seen from
a stele of the 11th century BC (21st
dynasty).

gitaverunt illum occidere. ¹⁹Et mutuo loquebantur: «Ecce somniator venit; ²⁰venite, occidamus eum et
mittamus in unam cisternarum dicemusque: Fera pessima devoravit eum. Et tunc apparebit quid illi
prosint somnia sua». ²¹Audiens autem hoc Ruben nitebatur liberare eum de manibus eorum et dixit:
²²«Non interficiamus animam eius». Et dixit ad eos: «Non effundatis sanguinem; sed proicite eum in
cisternam hanc, quae est in solitudine, manusque vestras servate innoxias». Hoc autem dicebat volens
eripere eum de manibus eorum et reddere patri suo. ²³Confestim igitur, ut pervenit ad fratres suos,
nudaverunt eum tunica talari ²⁴miseruntque eum in cisternam, quae non habebat aquam. ²⁵Et sederunt,
ut comederent panem. Attollentes autem oculos viderunt Ismaelitas viatores venire de Galaad et camelos eorum portantes tragacanthum et masticem et ladanum in Aegyptum. ²⁶Dixit ergo Iudas fratribus
suis: «Quid nobis prodest, si occiderimus fratrem nostrum et celaverimus sanguinem ipsius? ²⁷Melius
est ut vendatur Ismaelitis, et manus nostrae non polluantur; frater enim et caro nostra est».
Acquieverunt fratres sermonibus illius. ²⁸Et praetereuntibus Madianitis negotiatoribus, extrahentes

and said, "The lad is gone; and I, where shall I go?" [31]Then they took Joseph's robe, and killed a goat, and dipped the robe in the blood; [32]and they sent the long robe with sleeves and brought it to their father, and said, "This we have found; see now whether it is your son's robe or not." [33]And he recognized it, and said, "It is my son's robe; a wild beast has devoured him; Joseph is without doubt torn to pieces." [34]Then Jacob rent his garments, and put sackcloth upon his loins, and mourned for his son many days. [35]All his sons and all his daughters rose up to comfort him; but he refused to be comforted, and said, "No, I shall go down to Sheol to my son, mourning." Thus his father wept for him. [36]Meanwhile the Midianites had sold him in Egypt to Poti-phar, an officer of Pharaoh, the captain of the guard.

The story of Judah and Tamar*

38 [1]It happened at that time that Judah went down from his brothers, and turned in to a certain Adullamite, whose name was Hirah. [2]There Judah saw the daughter of a certain

*38:1–30. After telling about the sin Jacob's sons commit against Joseph, the sacred text provides another sketch of the sort of life they have in Canaan, this time focussing on Judah and his family. Although what we have here is an episode about Judah himself, it does tell us about the origin of the tribe he began.

It may well be that the insertion of the "story of Judah" here is due to a certain parallelism it has with the "story of Joseph", in the sense that the tribes that both began became the leading ones. It could also be that the writer wants to draw a contrast between the behaviour of Judah who takes Tamar thinking she is a prostitute, and the chastity of Joseph in the face of the temptation set him by Potiphar's wife (cf. next chapter). At any event, the account as a whole is of special interest because it deals with the tribe from which will come first king David and later the Messiah. This tribe, Judah, was separated from the rest of the tribes, but in God's plans it was to have a key role in the life of the chosen people.

The protagonist of this account is Tamar, a poor widow who defends her rights very cleverly and decisively. On the other hand, Judah, who has gone away from his brothers and acted self-

Ioseph de cisterna, vendiderunt eum Ismaelitis viginti argenteis. Qui duxerunt eum in Aegyptum. [29]Reversusque Ruben ad cisternam non invenit puerum [30]et, scissis vestibus, pergens ad fratres suos ait: «Puer non comparet, et ego quo ibo?». [31]Tulerunt autem tunicam eius et in sanguinem haedi, quem occiderant, tinxerunt [32]mittentes, qui ferrent ad patrem et dicerent: «Hanc invenimus; vide, utrum tunica talaris filii tui sit an non?». [33]Quam cum agnovisset pater, ait: «Tunica filii mei est; fera pessima comedit eum, bestia devoravit Ioseph». [34]Scissisque vestibus, indutus est cilicio lugens filium suum multo tempore. [35]Congregatis autem cunctis liberis eius, ut lenirent dolorem patris, noluit consolationem accipere et ait: «Descendam ad filium meum lugens in infernum». Et flevit super eo pater eius. [36]Madianitae autem vendiderunt Ioseph in Aegypto Putiphari eunucho pharaonis, magistro satellitum. [1]Eo tempore descendens Iudas a fratribus suis divertit ad virum Odollamitem nomine Hiram. [2]Viditque ibi filiam hominis Chananaei vocabulo Sue et, accepta uxore, ingressus est ad eam. [3]Quae concepit et

Canaanite whose name was Shua; he married her and went in to her, ³and she conceived and bore a son, and he called his name Er. ⁴Again she conceived and bore a son, and she called his name Onan. ⁵Yet again she bore a son, and she called his name Shelah. She[g] was in Chezib when she bore him. ⁶And Judah took a wife for Er his first-born, and her name was Tamar. ⁷But Er, Judah's first-born, was wicked in the sight of the LORD; and the LORD slew him. ⁸Then Judah said to Onan, "Go in to your brother's wife, and perform the duty of a brother-in-law to her, and raise up offspring for your brother."

Deut 25:5–10
Ruth 1:11–13
Mt 22:24
Mk 12:19
Lk 20:28

The sin of Onan

⁹But Onan knew that the offspring would not be his; so when he went into his brother's wife he spilled the semen on the ground, lest he should give offspring to his brother. ¹⁰And what he did was displeasing in the sight of the LORD, and he slew him also. ¹¹Then Judah said to Tamar his daughter-in-law, "Remain a widow in your father's house, till Shelah my son grows up"—for he feared

---

ishly against the established law, is trapped by his fault and eventually has to recognize that woman's right. She manages to obtain her objective (to have children of the same blood as her dead husband's—indeed directly by his father). Tamar thereby becomes the means by which Judah's line will be continued—the line from which David will be born. In this sense she has an influence on salvation history in the same sort of way as Sarah and Rebekah had earlier and as other women will later have. In the light of Holy Scripture in its totality, a person reading this passage can see how, through very ordinary circum-

stances like this, but, above all, through this woman's Tamar's valour, God guided history to fulfil his plan to make David king and to make him an ancestor of the Messiah. Tamar is mentioned in the genealogy of our Lord Jesus Christ given by St Matthew (cf. Mt 1:3).

38:8–10. According to the levirate law (cf. Deut 25:5), if a married man died without children, his brother or nearest relative was obliged to marry his widow in order to give the dead man descendants, because the first male child of this marriage was legally considered to be the son and heir of the dead man and so his

---

peperit filium vocavitque nomen eius Her. ⁴Rursumque concepto fetu, natum filium nominavit Onan. ⁵Tertium quoque peperit, quem appellavit Sela. Ipsa autem erat in Chasib, quando peperit illum. ⁶Dedit autem Iudas uxorem primogenito suo Her nomine Thamar. ⁷Fuit quoque Her primogenitus Iudae nequam in conspectu Domini, et ab eo occisus est. ⁸Dixit ergo Iudas ad Onan: «Ingredere ad uxorem fratris tui et sociare illi, ut suscites semen fratri tuo». ⁹Ille, sciens non sibi nasci hunc filium, introiens ad uxorem fratris sui semen fundebat in terram, ne proles fratris nomine nasceretur. ¹⁰Et idcirco occidit et eum Dominus, quod rem detestabilem fecerat. ¹¹Quam ob rem dixit Iudas Thamar nurui suae: «Esto vidua in domo patris tui, donec crescat Sela filius meus». Timebat enim, ne et ipse moreretur sicut

g. Gk: Heb *He*

that he would die, like his brothers. So Tamar went and dwelt in her father's house.

Tamar deceives Judah

[12]In course of time the wife of Judah, Shua's daughter, died; and when Judah was comforted, he went up to Timnah to his sheep shearers, he and his friend Hirah the Adullamite. [13]And when Tamar was told, "Your father-in-law is going up to Timnah to shear his sheep," [14]she put off her widow's garments, and put on a veil, wrapping herself up, and sat at the entrance to Enaim, which is on the road to Timnah; for she saw that Shelah was grown up, and she had not been given to him in marriage. [15]When Judah saw her, he thought her to be a harlot, for she had covered her face. [16]He went over to her at the road side, and said, "Come, let me come into you," for he did not know that she was his daughter-in-law. She said, "What will you give me, that you may come in to me?" [17]He answered, "I will send you a kid from the flock." And she said, "Will you give me a pledge, till you send

property could pass to that son. But by taking the dead man's wife as his own, the new husband became the administrator of the dead man's property. The same law underlies the plot of the book of Ruth (cf. Ruth 1:11–13) and the hypothetical cases the Sadducees put to Jesus about the resurrection from the dead (cf. Mt 22:24).

Onan's sin (from which comes the word "onanism") consists in interrupting sexual intercourse to prevent procreation. In the actual case of Onan, we can see how selfish he was: by marrying his sister-in-law he gets control over his dead brother's property—control which he can retain because he avoids having children by the woman. The gravity of Onan's sin is that it distorts the meaning of marriage

and married love; hence his punishment. The Church has seen this passage of the Bible as establishing that such an act is gravely sinful and is opposed to natural law and to the will of God. The *Catechism of the Catholic Church*, repeating what the Church has previously had to say, teaches that "'every action which, whether in anticipation of the conjugal act, or in its accomplishment, or in the development of its natural consequences, proposes, whether as an end or as a means, to render procreation impossible' (*Humanae vitae*, 14) is intrinsically evil" (no. 2370).

38:14. Although Tamar's behaviour is not entirely blameless, she is praised, not

fratres eius. Quae abiit et habitavit in domo patris sui. [12]Evolutis autem multis diebus, mortua est filia Sue uxor Iudae. Qui, post luctum consolatione suscepta, ascendebat ad tonsores ovium suarum ipse et Hiras amicus suus Odollamites in Thamnam. [13]Nuntiatumque est Thamar quod socer illius ascenderet in Thamnam ad tondendas oves. [14]Quae, depositis viduitatis vestibus, cooperuit se velo et, mutato habitu, sedit in porta Enaim in via, quae ducit Thamnam; eo quod crevisset Sela, et non eum accepisset maritum. [15]Quam cum vidisset Iudas, suspicatus est esse meretricem; operuerat enim vultum suum. [16]Declinansque ad eam in via ait: «Veni, coeam tecum»; nesciebat enim quod nurus sua esset. Qua respondente: «Quid mihi dabis, ut fruaris concubitu meo?», [17]dixit: «Mittam tibi haedum de gregibus».

it?" [18]He said, "What pledge shall I give you?" She replied, "Your signet and your cord, and your staff that is in your hand." So he gave them to her, and went in to her, and she conceived by him. [19]Then she arose and went away, and taking off her veil she put on the garments of her widowhood.

[20]When Judah sent the kid by his friend the Adullamite, to receive the pledge from the woman's hand, he could not find her. [21]And he asked the men of the place, "Where is the harlot[h] who was at Enaim by the wayside?" And they said, "No harlot has been here." [22]So he returned to Judah, and said, "I have not found her; and also the men of the place said, 'No harlot has been here.'" [23]And Judah replied, "Let her keep the things as her own, lest we be laughed at; you see, I sent this kid, and you could not find her."

[24]About three months later Judah was told, "Tamar your daughter-in-law has played the harlot; and moreover she is with child by harlotry." And Judah said, "Bring her out, and let her be

Lev 20:10; 21:9
Jn 8:41

---

only here but also in Ruth 4:12, because what she really wants is not to prostitute herself but to obtain through shrewd action what Judah (by his delaying tactic) was refusing to give her—the right to have children who are descendants of the family of Judah; in doing what she does she is taking a big risk. It is not clear from the text whether Tamar disguised herself as a sacred prostitute (of the sort who worked at places of Canaanite worship) or as an ordinary prostitute (a profession sometimes practised by foreign women in Israel). The account focusses its attention on Tamar's boldness and Judah's ingenuousness rather than on a moral evaluation of prostitution which elsewhere in the Old Testament is fre-

quently condemned, particularly in the prophetical and wisdom books.

38:24. The harsh sentence Judah lays down applies to the sin of adultery which he thinks Tamar has committed, for he regards her as being bound by the levirate law to his own son Shelah (cf. v. 11), even though they have not yet married. It was up to Judah, as head of the house, to decide the issue. According to the Law (which came later), only in the case of the daughter of a priest was the woman punished by burning (cf. Lev 21:9). In all other cases, people who committed adultery (whether men or women) were punished by death (cf. Lev 20:10) through stoning, not at the stake.

Rursum illa dicente: «Si dederis mihi arrabonem, donec mittas illum», [18]ait Iudas: «Quid vis tibi pro arrabone dari?». Respondit: «Sigillum tuum et funiculum et baculum, quem manu tenes». Et dedit ei. In coitu cum eo mulier concepit [19]et surgens abiit; depositoque velo, induta est viduitatis vestibus. [20]Misit autem Iudas haedum per amicum suum Odollamitem, ut reciperet pignus, quod dederat mulieri. Qui cum non invenisset eam, [21]interrogavit homines loci illius: «Ubi est meretrix, quae sedebat in Enaim in via?». Respondentibus cunctis: «Non fuit in loco isto meretrix», [22]reversus est ad Iudam et dixit ei: «Non inveni eam; sed et homines loci illius dixerunt mihi numquam ibi sedisse scortum». [23]Ait

h. Or *cult prostitute*

burned." [25]As she was being brought out, she sent word to her father-in-law, "By the man to whom these belong, I am with child." And she said, "Mark, I pray you, whose these are, the signet and the cord and the staff." [26]Then Judah acknowledged them and said, "She is more righteous than I, inasmuch as I did not give her to my son Shelah." And he did not lie with her again.

The birth of Perez, David's ancestor

[27]When the time of her delivery came, there were twins in her womb. [28]And when she was in labour, one put out a hand; and the midwife took and bound on his hand a scarlet thread, saying,

Ruth 4:12
Mt 1:3
Lk 3:33 "This came out first." [29]But as he drew back his hand, behold, his brother came out; and she said, "What a breach you have made for yourself!" Therefore his name was called Perez.[i] [30]Afterward his brother came out with the scarlet thread upon his hand; and his name was called Zerah.

Joseph in Egypt, in the house of Potiphar*

39 [1]Now Joseph was taken down to Egypt, and Poti-phar, an officer of Pharaoh, the captain of the guard, an Egyptian, bought him from the Ishmaelites who had brought him down

---

38:27–30. Once again the children's names are explained by reference to the circumstances of the birth. Perez was the ancestor of David, and in the amusing anecdote about his birth we can see that Perez would be the first-born not by the natural order of events but by an odd twist in which the reader can see God's providence at work in deciding who will in fact be the heir to the promises.

*39:1–23. The history of Joseph is picked up again after the insertion of chapter 38. This is the second act, as it were. Here attention is focussed on the Lord's presence alongside Joseph and on his professional competence. Joseph managed his master's affairs wisely; he holds out against temptation because keeping the law is more important to him even than life itself; and he is a model of the virtue of chastity.

Iudas: «Habeat sibi; ne simus in ludibrium. Ego misi haedum, quem promiseram, et tu non invenisti eam». [24]Ecce autem post tres menses nuntiaverunt Iudae dicentes: «Fornicata est Thamar nurus tua et gravida est ex fornicatione». Dixitque Iudas: «Producite eam, ut comburatur». [25]Quae cum educeretur ad poenam, misit ad socerum suum dicens: «De viro, cuius haec sunt, concepi; cognosce cuius sit sigillum et funiculus et baculus». [26]Qui, agnitis pignoribus, ait: «Iustior me est, quia non tradidi eam Sela filio meo». Attamen ultra non cognovit illam. [27]Instante autem partu, apparuerunt gemini in utero; atque in ipsa effusione infantium unus protulit manum, in qua obstetrix ligavit coccinum dicens: [28]«Iste egressus est prior». [29]Illo vero retrahente manum, egressus est frater eius; dixitque mulier: «Qualem rupisti tibi rupturam?». Et ob hanc causam vocatum est nomen eius Phares (*id est Ruptura*). [30]Postea egressus est frater eius, in cuius manu erat coccinum; qui appellatus est Zara (*id est Ortus solis*). [1]Igitur Ioseph ductus est in Aegyptum; emitque eum Putiphar eunuchus pharaonis, princeps satellitum, vir

---

i. That is *A breach*

there. ²The LORD was with Joseph, and he became a successful Acts 7:9
man; and he was in the house of his master the Egyptian, ³and his
master saw that the LORD was with him, and that the LORD caused
all that he did to prosper in his hands. ⁴So Joseph found favour in Mt 24:45
his sight and attended him, and he made him overseer of his
house and put him in charge of all that he had. ⁵From the time that
he made him overseer in his house and over all that he had the
LORD blessed the Egyptian's house for Joseph's sake; the blessing
of the LORD was upon all that he had, in house and field. ⁶So he
left all that he had in Joseph's charge; and having him he had no
concern for anything but the food which he ate.

Now Joseph was handsome and good-looking. ⁷And after a
time his master's wife cast her eyes upon Joseph, and said, "Lie
with me." ⁸But he refused and said to his master's wife, "Lo,
having me my master has no concern about anything in the house,
and he has put everything that he has in my hand; ⁹he is not
greater in this house than I am; nor has he kept back anything
from me except yourself, because you are his wife; how then can
I do this great wickedness, and sin against God?" ¹⁰And although
she spoke to Joseph day after day, he would not listen to her, to lie
with her or to be with her. ¹¹But one day, when he went into the

Those familiar with the genre will
know that the theme of temptation by a
woman is to be found in Egyptian
wisdom literature; we find it in the
"Story of the Two Brothers", a tale contained in a manuscript of the 21st dynasty
(13th century BC). But although there is a
similarity in subject-matter between the
Egyptian story and the history of Joseph,
the latter has an originality of its own: it
is designed to highlight the great wisdom

of Joseph, and the providence of God
who stays with him and makes him successful.

The book of Genesis depicts each of
the patriarchs as a model of some virtue.
Here we see one of the virtues that
Joseph stands for. St Ambrose comments:
"Learn from Abraham firm obedience of
faith; from Isaac the genuineness of a
sincere heart; from Jacob perseverance
in the midst of trials. [. . .] And so the

Aegyptius, de manu Ismaelitarum, a quibus perductus erat. ²Fuitque Dominus cum eo, et erat vir in
cunctis prospere agens habitabatque in domo domini sui. ³Qui optime noverat esse Dominum cum eo
et omnia, quae gereret, ab eo dirigi in manu illius. ⁴Invenitque Ioseph gratiam coram domino suo et
ministrabat ei. Et factum est, postquam prae posuit eum domui suae et omnia, quae possidebat, tradidit
in manum eius, ⁵benedixit Dominus domui Aegyptii propter Ioseph, et benedictio Domini erat in omni
possessione eius tam in aedibus quam in agris. ⁶Et reliquit omnia, quae possidebat, in manu Ioseph,
nec cum eo quidquam aliud noverat nisi panem, quo vescebatur. Erat autem Ioseph pulchra facie et
decorus aspectu. ⁷Post haec ergo iniecit uxor domini eius oculos suos in Ioseph et ait: «Dormi mecum».
⁸Qui nequaquam acquiescens dixit ad eam: «Ecce dominus meus, omnibus mihi traditis, non curat de
ulla re in domo sua, ⁹nec quisquam maior est in domo hac quam ego, et nihil mihi subtraxit praeter te,
quae uxor eius es. Quomodo ergo possum malum hoc magnum facere et peccare in Deum?».
¹⁰Huiuscemodi verbis per singulos dies et mulier molesta erat adulescenti, et ille recusabat stuprum.
¹¹Accidit autem quadam die, ut intraret Ioseph domum et opus suum absque arbitris faceret; ¹²illa,

house to do his work and none of the men of the house was there in the house, [12]she caught him by his garment, saying, "Lie with me." But he left his garment in her hand, and fled and got out of the house. [13]And when she saw that he had left his garment in her hand, and had fled out of the house, [14]she called to the men of her household and said to them, "See, he has brought among us a Hebrew to insult us; he came in to me to lie with me, and I cried out with a loud voice; [15]and when he heard that I lifted up my voice and cried, he left his garment with me, and fled and got out of the house." [16]Then she laid up his garment by her until his master came home, [17]and she told him the same story, saying, "The Hebrew servant, whom you have brought among us, came in to me to insult me; [18]but as soon as I lifted up my voice and cried, he left his garment with me, and fled out of the house."

[19]When his master heard the words which his wife spoke to him, "This is the way your servant treated me," his anger was kin-

Ps 105:18–19 dled. [20]And Joseph's master took him and put him into the prison, the place where the king's prisoners were confined, and he was there in prison.

Joseph in prison

Wis 10:13–14 [21]But the LORD was with Joseph and showed him steadfast love, and gave him favour in the sight of the keeper of the prison. [22]And

---

saintly Joseph has been set as an example of chastity" (*De Ioseph*, 1,1).

39:12. This is what St Caesarius of Arles has to say about Joseph's example in this passage: "Joseph flees in order to escape from that shameless woman. Learn, therefore, to flee if you want to win out against the attack made by lust. Do not be ashamed to flee if you want to attain the palm of chastity. [. . .] Among all the fights a Christian has to engage in, the most difficult are those of chastity; here

the struggle is a daily one, and victory is difficult. In this a Christian cannot but have daily acts of martyrdom. For if Christ is chastity, truth and justice, anyone who puts obstacles on the way of these virtues is a persecutor (of Christ), and anyone who tries to defend them in others or protect them in himself will be a martyr" (*Sermones*, 41, 1–3). *The Way* is very much to the point here: "Don't show the cowardice of being 'brave'; take to your heels!" (St Josemaría Escrivá, *The Way*, 132).

---

apprehensa lacinia vestimenti eius, dixit: «Dormi mecum». Qui, relicto in manu illius pallio, fugit et egressus est foras. [13]Cumque vidisset illum mulier vestem reliquisse in manibus suis et fugisse foras, [14]vocavit homines domus suae et ait ad eos: «En introduxit virum Hebraeum, ut illuderet nobis; ingressus est ad me, ut coiret mecum. Cumque ego succla massem, [15]et audisset vocem meam, reliquit pallium, quod tenebam, et fugit foras». [16]Retentum pallium ostendit marito revertenti domum [17]et secundum verba haec locuta est: «Ingressus est ad me servus Hebraeus, quem adduxisti, ut illuderet mihi; [18]cumque audisset me clamare, reliquit pallium, quod tenebam, et fugit foras». [19]Dominus, auditis his verbis coniugis, iratus est valde; [20]tradiditque Ioseph in carcerem, ubi vincti regis custodieban-

the keeper of the prison committed to Joseph's care all the prisoners who were in the prison; and whatever was done there, he was the doer of it; ²³the keeper of the prison paid no heed to anything that was in Joseph's care, because the LORD was with him; and whatever he did, the Lord made it prosper.   Acts 7:9

Joseph, the interpreter of dreams

40 ¹Some time after this, the butler of the king of Egypt and his baker offended their lord the king of Egypt. ²And Pharaoh was angry with his two officers, the chief butler and the chief baker, ³and he put them in custody in the house of the captain of the guard, in the prison where Joseph was confined. ⁴The captain of the guard charged Joseph with them, and he waited on them; and they continued for some time in custody. ⁵And one night they both dreamed—the butler and the baker of the king of Egypt, who were confined in the prison—each his own dream, and each dream with its own meaning. ⁶When Joseph came to them in the morning and saw them, they were troubled. ⁷So he

---

39:21–23. If one bears in mind that events, institutions and people in the Old Testament prefigure those of the New, one can see in Joseph not just a figure of Christ, but also (perhaps due to his name) of St Joseph, the husband of the Blessed Virgin. St Bernard comments: "That Joseph sold due to his brothers' envy and led into Egypt, prefigured Christ, who would be sold; this other Joseph, fleeing the envy of Herod, brought Christ to Egypt. That Joseph, out of faithfulness to his master did not lie with the woman; this Joseph, recognizing his wife to be a virgin, the mother of his Lord, and staying continent himself, guarded her faithfully. It was given to the first Joseph to understand the secrets of dreams; the second has been granted a knowledge of and share in the heavenly sacraments. The first Joseph stored grain, not for himself but for all the people; the second receives the charge of tending to the living bread that comes down from heaven, both for himself and for the whole world" (*Homiliae super Missus est*, 2, 16).

40:1–23. The account of the time Joseph spends in prison shows that the Lord was with him (cf. 39:21). As against Egyptian magical practices of divination, v. 8 teaches that interpretation of dreams is a gift from God, which has been given to Joseph, who finds himself not only a prisoner in a foreign country but a servant of two prominent prisoners.

---

tur. Et erat ibi clausus. ²¹Fuit autem Dominus cum Ioseph et misertus illius dedit ei gratiam in conspectu principis carceris. ²²Qui tradidit in manu Ioseph universos vinctos, qui in custodia tenebantur, et, quidquid ibi faciendum erat, ipse faciebat, ²³nec princeps carceris spectabat quidquid in manu eius erat: Dominus enim erat cum illo et omnia opera eius dirigebat. ¹His ita gestis, accidit ut peccarent pincerna regis Aegypti et pistor domino suo. ²Iratusque pharao contra duos eunuchos, praepositum pincernarum et praepositum pistorum, ³misit eos in carcerem principis satellitum, in quo erat vinctus et Ioseph. ⁴Et princeps satellitum tradidit eos Ioseph, qui ministrabat eis. Aliquantulum temporis illi in custodia tenebantur. ⁵Videruntque ambo somnium nocte una iuxta interpretationem congruam sibi. ⁶Ad

asked Pharaoh's officers who were with him in custody in his

Gen 41:15–16 master's house, "Why are your faces downcast today?" [8]They said to him, "We have had dreams, and there is no one to interpret them." And Joseph said to them, "Do not interpretations belong to God? Tell them to me, I pray you."

[9]So the chief butler told his dream to Joseph, and said to him, "In my dream there was a vine before me, [10]and on the vine there were three branches; as soon as it budded, its blossoms shot forth, and the clusters ripened into grapes. [11]Pharaoh's cup was in my hand; and I took the grapes and pressed them into Pharaoh's cup, and placed the cup in Pharaoh's hand." [12]Then Joseph said to him, "This is its interpretation: the three branches are three days; [13]within three days Pharaoh will lift up your head and restore you to your office; and you shall place Pharaoh's cup in his hand as

Lk 23:42 formerly, when you were his butler. [14]But remember me, when it is well with you, and do me the kindness, I pray you, to make mention of me to Pharaoh, and so get me out of this house. [15]For I was indeed stolen out of the land of the Hebrews; and here also I have done nothing that they should put me into the dungeon."

[16]When the chief baker saw that the interpretation was favourable, he said to Joseph, "I also had a dream: there were three cake baskets on my head, [17]and in the uppermost basket there were all sorts of baked food for Pharaoh, but the birds were eating it out of the basket on my head." [18]And Joseph answered, "This is its interpretation: the three baskets are three days; [19]within three days Pharaoh will lift up your head—from you!—and hang you on a tree; and the birds will eat the flesh from you."

[20]On the third day, which was Pharaoh's birthday, he made a feast for all his servants, and lifted up the head of the chief butler

---

quos cum introisset Ioseph mane et vidisset eos tristes, [7]sciscitatus est eos dicens: «Cur tristior est hodie solito facies vestra?». [8]Qui responderunt: «Somnium vidimus, et non est qui interpretetur nobis». Dixitque ad eos Ioseph: «Numquid non Dei est interpretatio? Referte mihi quid videritis». [9]Narravit praepositus pincernarum somnium suum: «Videbam coram me vitem, [10]in qua erant tres propagines, crescere paulatim in gemmas et post flores uvas maturescere; [11]calicemque pharaonis in manu mea. Tuli ergo uvas et expressi in calicem, quem tenebam, et tradidi poculum pharaoni». [12]Respondit Ioseph: «Haec est interpretatio somnii: tres propagines, tres adhuc dies sunt, [13]post quos elevabit pharao caput tuum et restituet te in gradum pristinum; dabisque ei calicem iuxta officium tuum, sicut facere ante consueveras. [14]Tantum memento mei, cum tibi bene fuerit, et facias mecum misericordiam, ut suggeras pharaoni, ut educat me de isto carcere; [15]quia furto sublatus sum de terra Hebraeorum et hic innocens in lacum missus sum». [16]Videns pistorum magister quod somnium in bonum dissolvisset, ait: «Et ego vidi somnium, quod tria canistra farinae haberem super caput meum; [17]et in uno canistro, quod erat excelsius, portare me ex omnibus cibis pharaonis, qui fiunt arte pistoria, avesque comedere eos». [18]Respondit Ioseph: «Haec est interpretatio somnii: tria canistra, tres adhuc dies sunt, [19]post quos auferet pharao caput tuum ac suspendet te in patibulo, et comedent volucres carnes tuas». [20]Exinde dies tertius natalicius pharaonis erat; qui faciens grande convivium pueris suis elevavit caput magistri pincernarum et caput pistorum principis in medio puerorum suorum; [21]restituitque alterum in locum suum,

and the head of the chief baker among his servants. [21]He restored the chief butler to his butlership, and he placed the cup in Pharaoh's hand; [22]but he hanged the chief baker, as Joseph had interpreted to them. [23]Yet the chief butler did not remember Joseph, but forgot him.

The pharaoh's dreams*

41 [1]After two whole years, Pharaoh dreamed that he was standing by the Nile, [2]and behold, there came up out of the Nile seven cows sleek and fat, and they fed in the reed grass. [3]And behold, seven other cows, gaunt and thin, came up out of the Nile after them, and stood by the other cows on the bank of the Nile. [4]And the gaunt and thin cows ate up the seven sleek and fat cows. And Pharaoh awoke. [5]And he fell asleep and dreamed a second time; and behold, seven ears of grain, plump and good, were growing on one stalk. [6]And behold, after them sprouted seven ears, thin and blighted by the east wind. [7]And the thin ears swallowed up the seven plump and full ears. And Pharaoh awoke, and behold, it was a dream. [8]So in the morning his spirit was troubled; and he sent and called for all the magicians of Egypt and all its wise men; and Pharaoh told them his dream, but there was none who could interpret[j] it to Pharaoh.

Ex 7:11–22;
8:1–3
Deut 2:1–13

---

*41:1–57. The chief butler forgot about Joseph, but God did not: he continues to steer events to give him high status in Egypt. The general tone of these dreams, as also their interpretation and the whole narrative, reflect the atmosphere of that land of wise men and magicians (cf. Ex 7–8). But what the author wants us to see here is that all that apparatus of Egyptian wisdom was nothing compared with the wisdom God gives Joseph. As Joseph himself openly declares, he has not merited this skill; it is a gift from God (cf. v. 16).

The history of Egypt, we know, was one long series of periods of plenty followed by periods of scarcity; there was even one in a much later period (around the 3rd century BC) which was described as a famine lasting seven years.

---

ut porrigeret ei poculum, [22]alterum suspendit in patibulo, sicut interpretatus erat eis Ioseph. [23]Attamen praepositus pincernarum non est recordatus Ioseph, sed oblitus est interpretis sui. [1]Post duos annos vidit pharao somnium. Putabat se stare super fluvium, [2]de quo ascendebant septem boves pulchrae et crassae et pascebantur in locis palustribus. [3]Aliae quoque septem emergebant post illas de flumine foedae confectaeque macie et stabant in ipsa amnis ripa; [4]devoraveruntque septem boves pulchras et crassas. Expergefactus pharao [5]rursum dormivit et vidit alterum somnium. Septem spicae pullulabant in culmo uno plenae atque formosae. [6]Aliae quoque totidem spicae tenues et percussae vento urente oriebantur [7]devorantes omnem priorum pulchritudinem. Evigilavit pharao, et ecce erat somnium! [8]Et, facto mane, pavore perterritus misit ad omnes coniectores Aegypti cunctosque sapientes suos; et accersitis narravit somnium, nec erat qui interpretaretur. [9]Tunc demum reminiscens pincernarum magister

j. Gk: Heb *them*

⁹Then the chief butler said to Pharaoh, "I remember my faults today. ¹⁰When Pharaoh was angry with his servants, and put me and the chief baker in custody in the house of the captain of the guard, ¹¹we dreamed on the same night, he and I, each having a dream with its own meaning. ¹²A young Hebrew was there with us, a servant of the captain of the guard; and when we told him, he interpreted our dreams to us, giving an interpretation to each man according to his dream. ¹³And as he interpreted to us, so it came to pass; I was restored to my office, and the baker was hanged."

¹⁴Then Pharaoh sent and called Joseph, and they brought him hastily out of the dungeon; and when he had shaved himself and changed his clothes, he came in before Pharaoh. ¹⁵And Pharaoh said to Joseph, "I have had a dream, and there is no one who can interpret it; and I have heard it said of you that when you hear a dream you can interpret it." ¹⁶Joseph answered Pharaoh, "It is not in me; God will give Pharaoh a favourable answer." ¹⁷Then Pharaoh said to Joseph, "Behold, in my dream I was standing on the banks of the Nile; ¹⁸and seven cows, fat and sleek, came up out of the Nile and fed in the reed grass; ¹⁹and seven other cows came up after them, poor and very gaunt and thin, such as I had never seen in all the land of Egypt. ²⁰And the thin and gaunt cows ate up the first seven fat cows, ²¹but when they had eaten them no one would have known that they had eaten them, for they were still as gaunt as at the beginning. Then I awoke. ²²I also saw in my dream seven ears growing on one stalk, full and good; ²³and seven ears, withered, thin, and blighted by the east wind, sprouted after them, ²⁴and the thin ears swallowed up the seven good ears. And I told it to the magicians, but there was no one who could explain it to me."

²⁵Then Joseph said to Pharaoh, "The dream of Pharaoh is one; God has revealed to Pharaoh what he is about to do. ²⁶The seven

---

ait: «Confiteor peccatum meum. ¹⁰Iratus rex servis suis me et magistrum pistorum retrudi iussit in carcerem principis satellitum, ¹¹ubi una nocte uterque vidimus somnium praesagum futurorum. ¹²Erat ibi puer Hebraeus eiusdem ducis satellitum famulus, cui narrantes somnia ¹³audivimus quidquid postea rei probavit eventus. Ego enim redditus sum officio meo, et ille suspensus est in patibulo». ¹⁴Protinus ad regis imperium eductum de carcere Ioseph totonderunt ac, veste mutata, obtulerunt ei. ¹⁵Cui ille ait: «Vidi somnia, nec est qui edisserat; quae audivi te sapientissime conicere». ¹⁶Respondit Ioseph: «Absque me Deus respondebit prospera pharaoni!». ¹⁷Narravit ergo pharao, quod viderat: «Putabam me stare super ripam fluminis ¹⁸et septem boves de amne conscendere pulchras nimis et obesis carnibus, quae in pastu paludis virecta carpebant. ¹⁹Et ecce has sequebantur aliae septem boves in tantum deformes et macilentae, ut numquam tales in terra Aegypti viderim; ²⁰quae, devoratis et consumptis prioribus, ²¹nullum saturitatis dedere vestigium; sed simili macie et squalore torpebant. Evigilans, rursus sopore depressus, ²²vidi somnium: Septem spicae pullulabant in culmo uno plenae atque pulcherrimae. ²³Aliae quoque septem tenues et percussae vento urente oriebantur e stipula; ²⁴quae

good cows are seven years, and the seven good ears are seven years; the dream is one. ²⁷The seven lean and gaunt cows that came up after them are seven years, and the seven empty ears blighted by the east wind are also seven years of famine. ²⁸It is as I told Pharaoh, God has shown to Pharaoh what he is about to do. ²⁹There will come seven years of great plenty throughout all the land of Egypt, ³⁰but after them there will arise seven years of famine, and all the plenty will be forgotten in the land of Egypt; the famine will consume the land, ³¹and the plenty will be unknown in the land by reason of that famine which will follow, for it will be very grievous. ³²And the doubling of Pharaoh's dream means that the thing is fixed by God, and God will shortly bring it to pass. ³³Now therefore let Pharaoh select a man discreet and wise, and set him over the land of Egypt. ³⁴Let Pharaoh proceed to appoint overseers over the land, and take the fifth part of

41:33-36. Joseph not only responds to the pharaoh's request that he interpret the dreams; he offers him practical advice about how to deal with the upcoming situation. The point being made here is that even though one aspect of the future is already fixed as the dream says and as God makes known, God also wants people to have initiative and foresight to control the future as much as possible. In fact, God counts on people acting in this way in order to carry out his salvific plans which, in the present context, include the Israelites' travelling down to Egypt and the survival of Jacob and his sons.

Man's efforts to control earthly affairs are taken into account in God's plans; and it is part of man's very nature that he should make such efforts. In the light of what has been revealed in Holy Scripture from the beginning, the Second Vatican Council says that "Individual and collective activity, that monumental effort of man through the centuries to improve the circumstances of the world, presents no problem to believers: considered in itself, it corresponds to the plan of God. Man was created in God's image and was commanded to conquer the earth with all it contains and to rule the world in justice and holiness (cf. Gen 1:26-27; Wis 9:2-3): he was to acknowledge God as maker of all things and relate himself and the totality of creation to him, so that through the dominion of all things by man the name of God would be majestic in all the earth (cf. Ps 8:6, 9)" (*Gaudium et spes*, 34).

priorum pulchritudinem devoraverunt. Narravi coniectoribus somnium, et nemo est qui edisserat». ²⁵Respondit Ioseph: «Somnium regis unum est: quae facturus est, Deus ostendit pharaoni. ²⁶Septem boves pulchrae et septem spicae plenae septem ubertatis anni sunt; eandemque vim somnii comprehendunt. ²⁷Septem quoque boves tenues atque macilentae, quae ascenderunt post eas, et septem spicae tenues et vento urente percussae septem anni sunt venturae famis, ²⁸qui hoc ordine complebuntur: ²⁹ecce septem anni venient fertilitatis magnae in universa terra Aegypti; ³⁰quos sequentur septem anni alii tantae sterilitatis, ut oblivioni tradatur cuncta retro abundantia. Consumptura est enim fames omnem terram, ³¹et ubertatis magnitudinem perditura est inopiae magnitudo. ³²Quod autem vidisti secundo ad eandem rem pertinens somnium, firmitatis indicium est, eo quod fiat sermo Dei et velocius a Deo impleatur. ³³Nunc ergo provideat rex virum intellegentem et sapientem et praeficiat eum terrae Aegypti ³⁴constituatque praepositos per cunctas regiones et quintam partem fructuum per septem annos

the produce of the land of Egypt during the seven plenteous years. [35]And let them gather all the food of these good years that are coming, and lay up grain under the authority of Pharaoh for food in the cities, and let them keep it. [36]That food shall be a reserve for the land against the seven years of famine which are to befall the land of Egypt, so that the land may not perish through the famine."

Joseph's promotion

[37]This proposal seemed good to Pharaoh and to all his servants. [38]And Pharaoh said to his servants, "Can we find such a man as this, in whom is the Spirit of God?" [39]So Pharaoh said to Joseph, "Since God has shown you all this, there is none so discreet and wise as you are; [40]you shall be over my house, and all my people shall order themselves as you command; only as regards the throne will I be greater than you." [41]And Pharaoh said to Joseph, "Behold, I have set you over all the land of Egypt." [42]Then Pharaoh took his signet ring from his hand and put it on Joseph's hand, and arrayed him in garments of fine linen, and put a gold chain about his neck; [43]and he made him to ride in his second chariot; and they cried before him, "Bow the knee!"[k] Thus he set him over all the land of Egypt. [44]Moreover Pharaoh said to Joseph, "I am Pharaoh, and without your consent no man shall lift up hand or foot in all the land of Egypt." [45]And Pharaoh called

Ps 105:20–22

Lk 15:22

Acts 7:10

41:37–45. The narrative does contain (very sketchy) details which are in line with Egyptian customs. To show the high status Joseph has attained, he is portrayed as vizier, or second in command after the pharaoh. The religious teaching that comes across is, on the one hand, that God was with Joseph and was going to save Israel from famine through him; and, on the other, that Joseph's dreams in Canaan about his brothers and his father were going to come true, as we are told in the chapters that follow.

---

fertilitatis, [35]qui iam nunc futuri sunt, congreget in horrea; et omne frumen tum sub pharaonis potestate condatur serveturque in urbibus; [36]et paretur futurae septem annorum fami, quae pressura est Aegyptum, et non consumetur terra inopia». [37]Placuit pharaoni consilium et cunctis ministris eius. [38]Locutusque est ad eos: «Num invenire poterimus talem virum, qui spiritu Dei plenus sit?». [39]Dixit ergo ad Ioseph: «Quia ostendit tibi Deus omnia, quae locutus es, numquid sapientiorem et consimilem tui invenire potero? [40]Tu eris super domum meam, et ad tui oris imperium cunctus populus meus oboediet; uno tantum regni solio te praecedam». [41]Dixitque rursus pharao ad Ioseph: «Ecce, constitui te super universam terram Aegypti». [42]Tulitque anulum de manu sua et dedit eum in manu eius; vestivitque eum stola byssina et collo torquem auream circumposuit. [43]Fecitque eum ascendere super currum suum secundum, clamante praecone: «Abrech!», ut omnes coram eo genuflecterent et praepositum esse scirent universae terrae Aegypti. [44]Dixit quoque rex ad Ioseph: «Ego sum pharao; absque tuo imperio non movebit quisquam manum aut pedem in omni terra Aegypti». [45]Vertitque nomen eius

k. *abrek*, probably an Egyptian word similar in sound to the Hebrew word meaning *to kneel*

Joseph's name Zaphenath-paneah; and he gave him in marriage
Asenath, the daughter of Potiphera priest of On.

Joseph, the pharaoh's administrator
So Joseph went out over the land of Egypt.

[46]Joseph was thirty years old when he entered the service of
Pharaoh king of Egypt. And Joseph went out from the presence of
Pharaoh, and went through all the land of Egypt. [47]During the
seven plenteous years the earth brought forth abundantly, [48]and he
gathered up all the food of the seven years when there was plenty[l]
in the land of Egypt, and stored up food in the cities; he stored up
in every city the food from the fields around it. [49]And Joseph
stored up grain in great abundance, like the sand of the sea, until
he ceased to measure it, for it could not be measured.

[50]Before the year of famine came, Joseph had two sons, whom
Asenath, the daughter of Potiphera priest of On, bore to him.
[51]Joseph called the name of the first-born Manasseh,[m] "For," he
said, "God has made me forget all my hardship and all my
father's house." [52]The name of the second he called Ephraim,[n]
"For God has made me fruitful in the land of my affliction."

[53]The seven years of plenty that prevailed in the land of Egypt
came to an end; [54]and the seven years of famine began to come, as

Lk 3:23
Acts 7:10

Acts 7:11
Ps 105:16

41:50–52. Not only is Joseph a successful administrator; he has the children he
so much yearned for—a clear sign of
God's blessing, although that is not said
in as many words. Joseph's sons have
Hebrew, not Egyptian names—and ones
belonging to the Israelite tribes which
later occupied central Palestine. Joseph's
descendants, therefore, are linked to the
promised land from the very start, even
though they were born outside it.

41:53–57. Egypt had an elaborate irriga-
tion system, which allowed it to protect
its food supply in periods of famine
caused, no doubt, by periodic droughts in
the Middle East. Thanks to Joseph's man-
agement at that time, the country was
able not only to relieve famine at home
when the need arose but also to relieve
"all the earth" scourged by that plague.
Here we see how divine providence came
to the rescue of all nations through a

---

et vocavit eum lingua Aegyptiaca Saphaneth Phanec (*quod interpretatur Salvator mundi*) deditque illi
uxorem Aseneth filiam Putiphare sacerdotis Heliopoleos. Egressus est itaque Ioseph ad terram Aegypti
[46]—triginta autem annorum erat quando stetit in conspectu regis pharaonis—et circuivit omnes
regiones Aegypti. [47]Venitque fertilitas septem annorum, et segetes congregavit in horrea Aegypti [48]con-
dens in singulis urbibus frumentum camporum in circuitu. [49]Tantaque fuit abundantia tritici, ut arenae
maris coaequaretur, et copia mensuram excederet. [50]Nati sunt autem Ioseph filii duo, antequam veniret
fames, quos ei peperit Aseneth filia Putiphare sacerdotis Heliopoleos. [51]Vocavitque nomen primogeniti Manasses dicens: «Oblivisci me fecit Deus omnium laborum meorum et domus patris mei».
[52]Nomen quoque secundi appellavit Ephraim dicens: «Crescere me fecit Deus in terra paupertatis

---

l. Sam Gk: Heb *which were*   **m.** That is *Making to forget*   **n.** From a Hebrew word meaning *to be
fruitfu*

197

Joseph had said. There was famine in all lands; but in all the land
Jn 2:5 of Egypt there was bread. [55]When all the land of Egypt was famished, the people cried to Pharaoh for bread; and Pharaoh said to all the Egyptians, "Go to Joseph; what he says to you, do." [56]So when the famine had spread over all the land, Joseph opened all the storehouses,[o] and sold to the Egyptians, for the famine was severe in the land of Egypt. [57]Moreover, all the earth came to Egypt to Joseph to buy grain, because the famine was severe over all the earth.

Acts 7:11–14 **The sons of Jacob go down to Egypt***

42 [1]When Jacob learned that there was grain in Egypt, he said
Acts 7:12–13 to his sons, "Why do you look at one another?" [2]And he

descendant of Abraham (cf. 12:3). Yet, despite all the progress mankind has made, the plague of hunger continues to ravage areas of the world even in our own time. And so, "faced with a world today where so many people are suffering from want, the [Second Vatican] Council asks individuals and governments to remember the saying of the Fathers: 'Feed the man dying of hunger, because if you do not feed him you are killing him,' and it urges them according to their ability to share and dispose of their goods to help others, above all by giving them aid which will enable them to help and develop themselves" (Vatican II, *Gaudium et spes*, 69).

The pharaoh himself tells the Egyptians where to find food—by having recourse to Joseph. He is the one providentially placed by God at that time not only to save the Egyptians but also to help Jacob and his sons, the ancestors of

the chosen people of the Old Testament. There is a profound analogy between this Joseph who provides nourishment to Egypt and Israel, and that other Joseph, the husband of Mary, whom God chose to care for and nourish the Holy Family, who also had to move to Egypt (cf. the note on 39:21–23). So the words spoken by the pharaoh, "Go to Joseph," can also be applied to recourse to St Joseph as an intercessor to bring us to Jesus: "Who could be a better teacher for us? If you want my advice, which I have never tired of repeating these many years, *Ite ad Ioseph*: 'Go to Joseph.' He will show us definite ways, both human and divine, to approach Jesus" (St Josemaría Escrivá, *Christ Is Passing By*, 38).

***42:1—47:12.** Here begins what we might call the second part of the history of Joseph. This does not end with his own prosperity and happiness after his many

meae». [53]Igitur, transactis septem annis ubertatis, qui fuerant in Aegypto, [54]coeperunt venire septem anni inopiae, quos praedixerat Ioseph, et in universo orbe fames praevaluit; in cuncta autem terra Aegypti erat panis. [55]Qua esuriente, clamavit populus ad pharaonem alimenta petens. Quibus ille respondit: «Ite ad Ioseph et, quidquid vobis dixerit, facite». [56]Et invaluit fames in omni terra Aegypti; aperuitque Ioseph universa horrea et vendebat Aegyptiis; nam et illos oppresserat fames. [57]Omnesque provinciae veniebant in Aegyptum, ut emerent escas apud Ioseph, quia inopia invaluerat in universa terra. [1] Audiens autem Iacob quod alimenta venderentur in Aegypto, dixit filiis suis: «Quare aspicitis

o. Gk Vg Compare Syr: Heb *all that was in them*

said, "Behold, I have heard that there is grain in Egypt; go down and buy grain for us there, that we may live, and not die." ³So ten of Joseph's brothers went down to buy grain in Egypt. ⁴But Jacob did not send Benjamin, Joseph's brother, with his brothers, for he feared that harm might befall him. ⁵Thus the sons of Israel came   Acts 7:11 to buy among the others who came, for the famine was in the land of Canaan.

⁶Now Joseph was governor over the land; he it was who sold to all the people of the land. And Joseph's brothers came, and bowed

---

trials; it opens the way to the salvation of all his people, thereby giving effect to God's design. This part reaches its climax with the descent of Jacob and his whole family into Egypt, and their settling there. The sons of Jacob travel into Egypt twice to buy grain (cf. chap. 42 and chaps 44–45). It may be that the writer has drawn on two separate traditions, but still the narrative has an extraordinary unity about it, evidencing the literary skill of the editor. It is a stirring account, with events and emotions building up to a climax at the end, when all Jacob's sons are gathered around him in Egypt.

As the story develops, we see come true the dreams Joseph had in Canaan about his brothers and his father; initially some and eventually all of them bow down before him. Meanwhile, due to the strategies Joseph uses, his brothers (though not realizing what is happening) come to acknowledge and gradually confess the sin they committed against him, to the point where they sincerely repent it. We also see a sense of brotherhood and solidarity develop among them all, to the point where they are all ready to become

slaves rather than abandon Benjamin (cf. 44:16); and one of them, Judah, is ready to give himself up on Benjamin's behalf. It is only then, at this point of brotherly union, that they are able to find again their lost brother, Joseph, and reconstitute the family of Jacob.

42:1–7. Jacob acts as a responsible family man concerned about his children's welfare. He is not resigned to see his family die of hunger; he thinks hard about the situation and decides to take a risky but necessary course of action—to send his sons to Egypt in search of food. Jacob's sons probably joined some caravan travelling there for the same reason. The account starts with this action on Jacob's part to explain why the Israelites went down into Egypt, leaving the land God had promised to Abraham. It rounds off this explanation when it tells how Jacob himself and all his family travelled to Egypt at God's bidding (cf. 46:1–5).

The dreams Joseph told his brothers about (cf. 37:5–9) now begin to come true. Joseph's harshness towards them does not stem from a spirit of vengeance; it is designed to give more dramatic

---

vos invicem?». ²Audivi quod triticum venumdetur in Aegypto; descendite et emite nobis necessaria, ut possimus vivere et non consumamur inopia. ³Descenderunt igitur fratres Ioseph decem, ut emerent frumenta in Aegypto, ⁴Beniamin fratre Ioseph domi retento a Iacob, qui dixerat fratribus eius: «Ne forte in itinere quidquam patiatur mali». ⁵Et ingressi sunt filii Israel terram Aegypti cum aliis, qui pergebant ad emendum. Erat autem fames in terra Chanaan. ⁶Et Ioseph erat princeps in terra Aegypti, atque ad eius nutum frumenta populis vendebantur. Cumque venissent et adorassent eum fratres sui proni in

themselves before him with their faces to the ground. [7]Joseph saw his brothers, and knew them, but he treated them like strangers and spoke roughly to them. "Where do you come from?" he said. They said, "From the land of Canaan, to buy food."

Joseph tests his brothers by keeping Simeon in Egypt

Gen 37:5–11   [8]Thus Joseph knew his brothers, but they did not know him. [9]And Joseph remembered the dreams which he had dreamed of them; and he said to them, "You are spies, you have come to see the weakness of the land." [10]They said to him, "No, my lord, but to buy food have your servants come. [11]We are all sons of one man, we are honest men, your servants are not spies." [12]He said to them, "No, it is the weakness of the land that you have come to see." [13]And they said, "We, your servants, are twelve brothers, the sons of one man in the land of Canaan; and behold, the youngest is this day with our father, and one is no more." [14]But Joseph said

---

interest to the story and to prepare for the eventual reunion, once all his brothers have admitted their fault.

42:8–24. Joseph's accusation against his brothers looks like a ruse to get them to identify what family they belong to. It is plain to see that for them Joseph "does not exist". It is possible that Joseph fears for what will happen to his mother's son, his brother Benjamin, and that that is why he insists that they bring him to him. Maybe Joseph is conscious of his father's pain and for that reason keeps Simeon rather than Reuben; or, now that he knows what Reuben did when the others wanted to kill him (cf. 37:21), maybe his decision not to detain Reuben is a form of recognition for that action. In any event, the whole story is told in a masterly way, and the reader's interest is unabated. When they see one of their brothers being taken from them by force, they begin to reflect on what they themselves did long before—consciously disposing of a brother (they thought that he was dead). They admit their fault and that it merits this sort of punishment from God. Their process of conversion has started: their conscience is beginning to accuse them. "Just as a drunkard who once he has drunk a lot of wine is not conscious of doing damage, but later on realizes how much evil he has done, so, too, sin, when it is being committed, darkens the mind and is like a dense cloud that corrupts it; but, later, one's conscience beings to wake up and it accuses one's mind vigorously, showing it how stupidly one has acted" (St John Chrysostom, *Homiliae in Genesim*, 54, 2).

---

terram, [7]et agnovisset eos, quasi ad alienos durius loquebatur interrogans eos: «Unde venistis?». Qui responderunt: «De terra Chanaan, ut emamus victui necessaria». [8]Et tamen fratres ipse cognoscens non est cognitus ab eis. [9]Recordatusque somniorum, quae aliquando viderat, ait ad eos: «Exploratores estis; ut videatis infirmiora terrae, venistis!». [10]Qui dixerunt: «Non est ita, domine; sed servi tui venerunt, ut emerent cibos. [11]Omnes filii unius viri sumus; sinceri sumus, nec quidquam famuli tui machinantur mali». [12]Quibus ille respondit: «Aliter est; immunita terrae huius considerare venistis!». [13]At illi: «Duodecim, inquiunt, servi tui fratres sumus filii viri unius in terra Chanaan; minimus cum patre nostro

to them, "It is as I said to you, you are spies. ¹⁵By this you shall
be tested: by the life of Pharaoh, you shall not go from this place
unless your youngest brother comes here. ¹⁶Send one of you, and
let him bring your brother, while you remain in prison, that your
words may be tested, whether there is truth in you; or else, by the
life of Pharaoh, surely you are spies." ¹⁷And he put them all
together in prison for three days.

Acts 7:13

¹⁸On the third day Joseph said to them, "Do this and you will
live, for I fear God: ¹⁹if you are honest men, let one of your brothers remain confined in your prison, and let the rest go and carry
grain for the famine of your households, ²⁰and bring your
youngest brother to me; so your words will be verified, and you
shall not die." And they did so. ²¹Then they said to one another,
"In truth we are guilty concerning our brother, in that we saw the
distress of his soul, when he besought us and we would not listen;
therefore is this distress come upon us." ²²And Reuben answered
them, "Did I not tell you not to sin against the lad? But you would
not listen. So now there comes a reckoning for his blood." ²³They
did not know that Joseph understood them, for there was an interpreter between them. ²⁴Then he turned away from them and wept;
and he returned to them and spoke to them. And he took Simeon
from them and bound him before their eyes. ²⁵And Joseph gave

Gen 37:21–22

42:25–28. On top of their grief at having
to leave Simeon in Egypt comes this surprise which leaves them disconcerted.
They cannot possibly imagine that the
man who treated them so harshly should
have given them this present out of generosity. They cannot help thinking that
something mysterious is going on—that
the hand of God is at work—and,
because of the fault that is now on their
conscience, they interpret the money in
their bags as a premonition of some new
punishment that will befall them: maybe
the Egyptians will pursue them and
accuse them, not just of being spies, but
of being thieves as well. Thus, Joseph's
well-meaning gesture becomes a reason
for them to feel even more fearful (cf. v.
35); it also makes the narrative more
exciting, contrasting Joseph's goodness
with the earlier wickedness of the brothers towards him.

est, alius non est super». ¹⁴«Hoc est, ait, quod locutus sum: exploratores estis! ¹⁵Iam nunc experimen-
tum vestri capiam: per salutem pharaonis, non egrediemini hinc, donec veniat frater vester minimus!
¹⁶Mittite ex vobis unum, et adducat eum; vos autem eritis in vinculis, donec probentur, quae dixistis,
utrum vera an falsa sint. Alioquin, per salutem pharaonis, exploratores estis!». ¹⁷Tradidit ergo illos custodiae tribus diebus. ¹⁸Die autem tertio eductis de carcere, ait: «Facite, quae dixi, et vivetis, Deum enim
timeo. ¹⁹Si sinceri estis, frater vester unus ligetur in carcere; vos autem abite et ferte frumenta, quae
emistis, in domos vestras, ²⁰et fratrem vestrum minimum ad me adducite, ut possim vestros probare
sermones, et non moriamini». Fecerunt, ut dixerat, ²¹et locuti sunt ad invicem: «Merito haec patimur,
quia peccavimus in fratrem nostrum videntes angustiam animae illius, cum deprecaretur nos, et non
audivimus. Idcirco venit super nos ista tribulatio». ²²Et Ruben ait: «Numquid non dixi vobis: Nolite
peccare in puerum? Et non audistis me. En sanguis eius exquiritur». ²³Nesciebant autem quod intel-
legeret Ioseph, eo quod per interpretem loquebatur ad eos. ²⁴Avertitque se parumper et flevit; et rever-

orders to fill their bags with grain, and to replace every man's money in his sack, and to give them provisions for the journey. This was done for them.

²⁶Then they loaded their asses with their grain, and departed. ²⁷And as one of them opened his sack to give his ass provender at the lodging place, he saw his money in the mouth of his sack; ²⁸and he said to his brothers, "My money has been put back; here it is in the mouth of my sack!" At this their hearts failed them, and they turned trembling to one another, saying, "What is this that God has done to us?"

²⁹When they came to Jacob their father in the land of Canaan, they told him all that had befallen them, saying, ³⁰"The man, the lord of the land, spoke roughly to us, and took us to be spies of the land. ³¹But we said to him, 'We are honest men, we are not spies; ³²we are twelve brothers, sons of our father; one is no more, and the youngest is this day with our father in the land of Canaan.' ³³Then the man, the lord of the land, said to us, 'By this I shall know that you are honest men: leave one of your brothers with me, and take grain for the famine of your households, and go your way. ³⁴Bring your youngest brother to me; then I shall know that you are not spies but honest men, and I will deliver to you your brother, and you shall trade in the land.'"

³⁵As they emptied their sacks, behold, every man's bundle of money was in his sack; and when they and their father saw their bundles of money, they were dismayed. ³⁶And Jacob their father said to them, "You have bereaved me of my children: Joseph is no more, and Simeon is no more, and now you would take Benjamin; all this has come upon me." ³⁷Then Reuben said to his father, "Slay my two sons if I do not bring him back to you; put him in my hands, and I will bring him back to you." ³⁸But he said, "My son shall not go down with you, for his brother is dead, and he only is left. If harm should befall him on the journey that you are to make, you would bring down my gray hairs with sorrow to Sheol."

---

sus locutus est ad eos. ²⁵Tollensque Simeon et ligans, illis praesentibus, iussit ministris, ut implerent eorum saccos tritico et reponerent pecunias singulorum in sacculis suis, datis supra cibariis in viam. Qui fecerunt ita. ²⁶At illi portantes frumenta in asinis suis profecti sunt. ²⁷Apertoque unus sacco, ut daret iumento pabulum in deversorio, contemplatus pecuniam in ore sacculi ²⁸dixit fratribus suis: «Reddita est mihi pecunia: en habetur in sacco!». Et obstupefacti turbatique mutuo dixerunt: «Quidnam est hoc, quod fecit nobis Deus?». ²⁹Veneruntque ad Iacob patrem suum in terram Chanaan; et narraverunt ei omnia, quae accidissent sibi, dicentes: ³⁰«Locutus est nobis dominus terrae dure et putavit nos exploratores esse provinciae». ³¹Cui respondimus: «Sinceri sumus, nec ullas molimur insidias; ³²duodecim fratres uno patre geniti sumus, unus non est super, minimus cum patre nostro est in terra Chanaan. ³³Et dixit nobis vir, dominus terrae: 'Sic probabo quod sinceri sitis: fratrem vestrum unum dimittite apud me et cibaria domibus vestris necessaria sumite et abite; ³⁴fratremque vestrum minimum adducite ad me, ut sciam quod non sitis exploratores et istum, qui tenetur in vinculis, recipere possitis ac deinceps peragrandi terram habeatis licentiam'». ³⁵His dictis, cum frumenta effunderent, singuli rep-

The sons of Jacob return to Egypt, bringing Benjamin with them

43 [1]Now the famine was severe in the land. [2]And when they had eaten the grain which they had brought from Egypt, their father said to them, "Go again, buy us a little food." [3]But Judah said to him, "The man solemnly warned us, saying, 'You shall not see my face, unless your brother is with you.' [4]If you will send our brother with us, we will go down and buy you food; [5]but if you will not send him, we will not go down, for the man said to us, 'You shall not see my face, unless your brother is with you.'" [6]Israel said, "Why did you treat me so ill as to tell the man that you had another brother?" [7]They replied, "The man questioned us carefully about ourselves and our kindred, saying, 'Is your father still alive? Have you another brother?' What we told him was in answer to these questions; could we in any way know that he would say, 'Bring your brother down'?" [8]And Judah said to Israel his father, "Send the lad with me, and we will arise and go, that we may live and not die, both we and you and also our little ones. [9]I will be surety for him; of my hand you shall require him. If I do not bring him back to you and set him before you, then let me bear the blame for ever; [10]for if we had not delayed, we would now have returned twice."

Gen 42:2, 37

43:1-10. Faced with the unhappy outcome of the first journey, Jacob, who thinks he has lost another son, is against any further action; but famine begins to press again, worse than before, and now the only surviving son of Rachel, the woman he loves, is the one most at risk.

Here, as elsewhere throughout this journey, it is Judah, instead of Reuben the first born, who intervenes and takes the initiative: he stands out among his brothers, just as the tribe whose ancestor he is, will later stand out, the tribe from which will come King David and the Messiah.

---

pererunt in ore saccorum ligatas pecunias; exterritisque simul omnibus, [36]dixit pater Iacob: «Absque liberis me esse fecistis: Ioseph non est super, Simeon tenetur in vinculis, et Beniamin auferetis. In me haec omnia mala reciderunt». [37]Cui respondit Ruben: «Duos filios meos interfice, si non reduxero illum tibi; trade illum in manu mea, et ego eum tibi restituam». [38]At ille: «Non descendet, inquit, filius meus vobiscum. Frater mortuus est, et ipse solus remansit; si quid ei adversi acciderit in via, deducetis canos meos cum dolore ad inferos». [1]Interim fames omnem terram vehementer premebat; [2]consumptisque cibis, quos ex Aegypto detulerant, dixit Iacob ad filios suos: «Revertimini et emite nobis pauxillum escarum». [3]Respondit Iudas: «Denuntiavit nobis vir ille sub attestatione iurisiurandi dicens: 'Non videbitis faciem meam, nisi fratrem vestrum minimum adduxeritis vobiscum'. [4]Si ergo vis eum mittere nobiscum, pergemus pariter et ememus tibi necessaria; [5]sin autem non vis, non ibimus. Vir enim, ut saepe diximus, denuntiavit nobis dicens: 'Non videbitis faciem meam absque fratre vestro minimo'». [6]Dixit eis Israel: «Cur in meam hoc fecistis miseriam, ut indicaretis ei et alium habere vos fratrem?». [7]At illi responderunt: «Interrogavit nos homo per ordinem nostram progeniem: si pater viveret, si haberemus fratrem; et nos respondimus ei consequenter iuxta id, quod fuerat sciscitatus. Numquid scire poteramus quod dicturus esset: 'Adducite fratrem vestrum vobiscum'?». [8]Iudas quoque dixit patri suo Israel: «Mitte puerum mecum, ut proficiscamur et possimus vivere, ne moriamur nos et tu et parvuli

[Gen 17:1]

¹¹Then their father Israel said to them, "If it must be so, then do this: take some of the choice fruits of the land in your bags, and carry down to the man a present, a little balm and a little honey, gum, myrrh, pistachio nuts, and almonds. ¹²Take double the money with you; carry back with you the money that was returned in the mouth of your sacks; perhaps it was an oversight. ¹³Take also your brother, and arise, go again to the man; ¹⁴may God Almighty[p] grant you mercy before the man, that he may send back your other brother and Benjamin. If I am bereaved of my children, I am bereaved." ¹⁵So the men took the present, and they took double the money with them, and Benjamin; and they arose and went down to Egypt, and stood before Joseph.

¹⁶When Joseph saw Benjamin with them, he said to the steward of his house, "Bring the men into the house, and slaughter an animal and make ready, for the men are to dine with me at noon." ¹⁷The man did as Joseph bade him, and brought the men to Joseph's house. ¹⁸And the men were afraid because they were

---

Judah goes guarantor for Benjamin, in order to save the whole family from death by hunger.

43:11–14. Jacob has to give in eventually and accept the pain of being parted from Benjamin and his other sons. But he does not despair. He acts as a responsible father should: he gives detailed instructions to ensure that the journey has a successful outcome; he calls on God to move the heart of that man in Egypt; and he accepts with resignation whatever may

ultimately happen to his sons and himself.

The fact that the reader already knows why the patriarch has been put in this anguished position does not lessen the dramatic effect of the account, or the greatness of soul that Jacob displays throughout. On the contrary: Jacob is an example of fortitude in the midst of trials.

43:18–23. As the events unfold (for example, the money being found in the sack and their being brought into Joseph's house) we see the contrast

---

nostri. ⁹Ego spondeo pro puero; de manu mea require illum. Nisi reduxero et reddidero eum tibi, ero peccati reus in te omni tempore. ¹⁰Si non intercessisset dilatio, iam vice altera venissemus». ¹¹Igitur Israel pater eorum dixit ad eos: «Si sic necesse est, facite, quod vultis; sumite de optimis terrae fructibus in vasis vestris et deferte viro munera: modicum resinae et mellis et tragacanthum et ladanum, pistacias terebinthi et amygdalas. ¹²Pecuniam quoque duplicem ferte vobiscum et illam, quam invenistis in sacculis, reportate, ne forte errore factum sit; ¹³sed et fratrem vestrum tollite et ite ad virum. ¹⁴Deus autem meus omnipotens faciat vobis eum placabilem et remittat vobiscum fratrem vestrum, quem tenet, et hunc Beniamin. Ego autem quasi orbatus absque liberis ero». ¹⁵Tulerunt ergo viri munera et pecuniam duplicem et Beniamin descenderuntque in Aegyptum; et steterunt coram Ioseph. ¹⁶Quos cum ille vidisset et Beniamin simul, praecepit dispensatori domus suae dicens: «Introduc viros domum et occide victimas et instrue convivium, quoniam mecum sunt comesturi meridie». ¹⁷Fecit ille, quod sibi fuerat imperatum, et introduxit viros in domum Ioseph. ¹⁸Ibique exterriti dixerunt mutuo: «Propter pecuniam, quam rettulimus prius in saccis nostris, introducti sumus, ut irruant in nos et violenter subiciant servituti et nos et asinos nostros». ¹⁹Quam ob rem in ipsis foribus accedentes ad dis-

p. Heb *El Shaddai*

brought to Joseph's house, and they said, "It is because of the money, which was replaced in our sacks the first time, that we are brought in, so that he may seek occasion against us and fall upon us, to make slaves of us and seize our asses." [19]So they went up to the steward of Joseph's house, and spoke with him at the door of the house, [20]and said, "Oh, my lord, we came down the first time to buy food; [21]and when we came to the lodging place we opened our sacks, and there was every man's money in the mouth of his sack, our money in full weight; so we have brought it again with us, [22]and we have brought other money down in our hand to buy food. We do not know who put our money in our sacks." [23]He replied, "Rest assured, do not be afraid; your God and the God of your father must have put treasure in your sacks for you; I received your money." Then he brought Simeon out to them. [24]And when the man had brought the men into Joseph's house, and given them water, and they had washed their feet, and when he had given their asses provender, [25]they made ready the present for Joseph's coming at noon, for they heard that they should eat bread there.

Gen 42:27–28

[26]When Joseph came home, they brought into the house to him the present which they had with them, and bowed down to him to the ground. [27]And he inquired about their welfare, and said, "Is your father well, the old man of whom you spoke? Is he still alive?" [28]They said, "Your servant our father is well, he is still alive." And they bowed their heads and made obeisance. [29]And he

Gen 37:5–9; 42:6

---

between the negative interpretation put on the situation by the conscience-stricken brothers, and the real intention of Joseph, which the reader is well aware of. The fact is that these events are gifts from God (and that is how Joseph's steward explains them: 43:23), but for the time being the brothers do not realize this and they think that events augur ill.

43:26–27. Once again (cf. 42:6) we are told that his brothers bow down to Joseph—stressing that the dreams he dreamt in Canaan are coming true.

---

pensatorem domus [20]ocuti sunt: «Oramus, domine, ut audias nos. Iam ante descendimus, ut emeremus escas; [21]quibus emptis, cum venissemus ad deversorium, aperuimus saccos nostros et invenimus pecuniam in ore saccorum; quam nunc eodem pondere reportavimus. [22]Sed et aliud attulimus argentum, ut emamus, quae nobis necessaria sunt. Non est in nostra conscientia, quis posuerit argentum in marsupiis nostris». [23]At ille respondit: «Pax vobiscum, nolite timere. Deus vester et Deus patris vestri dedit vobis thesauros in saccis vestris; nam pecuniam, quam dedistis mihi, probatam ego habeo». Eduxitque ad eos Simeon. [24]Et introductis domum attulit aquam, et laverunt pedes suos; deditque pabulum asinis eorum. [25]Illi vero parabant munera, donec ingrederetur Ioseph meridie; audierant enim quod ibi comesturi essent panem. [26]Igitur ingressus est Ioseph domum suam, obtuleruntque ei munera tenentes in manibus suis; et adoraverunt proni in terram. [27]At ille, clementer resalutatis eis, interrogavit eos dicens: «Salvusne est pater vester senex, de quo dixeratis mihi? Adhuc vivit?». [28]Qui responderunt: «Sospes est servus tuus pater noster, adhuc vivit». Et incurvati adoraverunt eum. [29]Attollens autem Ioseph

lifted up his eyes, and saw his brother Benjamin, his mother's son, and said, "Is this your youngest brother, of whom you spoke to me? God be gracious to you, my son!" ³⁰Then Joseph made haste, for his heart yearned for his brother, and he sought a place to weep. And he entered his chamber and wept there. ³¹Then he washed his face and came out; and controlling himself he said, "Let food be served." ³²They served him by himself, and them by themselves, and the Egyptians who ate with him by themselves, because the Egyptians might not eat bread with the Hebrews, for that is an abomination to the Egyptians. ³³And they sat before him, the first-born according to his birthright and the youngest according to his youth; and the men looked at one another in amazement. ³⁴Portions were taken to them from Joseph's table, but Benjamin's portion was five times as much as any of theirs. So they drank and were merry with him.

Gen 42:24

Joseph puts his brothers to the test again*

44 ¹Then he commanded the steward of his house, "Fill the men's sacks with food, as much as they can carry, and put each man's money in the mouth of his sack, ²and put my cup, the

---

43:30–31. Joseph does not find it easy to chide his brothers. St Gregory the Great comments: "Mercy takes over Joseph when he sees his innocent brother; but he contrives to keep a stern face, in order to cleanse them of their evil. He hides the cup in the sack belonging to the youngest [. . .]. Benjamin is arrested, and all the brothers follow him grieving. What sufferings does mercy not bring with it! It punishes yet it loves. That holy man pardons and punishes his brothers' crime: clemency is contained in the punishment;

though he has mercy, his brothers who have sinned do not go unpunished; and though he is just, they are not left without mercy. This is a good example of how to exercise authority: it shows how to pardon faults and yet punish them mercifully" (*Homiliae in Ezechielem*, 2, 9, 19).

***44:1–34.** The drama of the last test Joseph makes his brothers undergo is accentuated by the cordial, even familial, relationship they had just before. The scene reaches its climax with their con-

---

oculos vidit Beniamin fratrem suum uterinum et ait: «Iste est frater vester parvulus, de quo dixeratis mihi?». Et rursum: «Deus, inquit, misereatur tui, fili mi». ³⁰Festinavitque, quia commota fuerant viscera eius super fratre suo, et erumpebant lacrimae; et introiens cubiculum flevit. ³¹Rursumque, lota facie, egressus continuit se et ait: «Ponite panes». ³²Quibus appositis, seorsum Ioseph et seorsum fratribus, Aegyptiis quoque, qui vescebantur simul, seorsum —illicitum est enim Aegyptiis comedere cum Hebraeis, et profanum putant huiusce modi convivium—³³sederunt coram eo, primogenitus iuxta primogenita sua et minimus iuxta aetatem suam. Et mirabantur nimis, ³⁴sumptis partibus, quas ab eo acceperant; maiorque pars venit Beniamin, ita ut quinque partibus excederet. Biberuntque et inebriati sunt cum eo. ¹ Praecepit autem Ioseph dispensatori domus suae dicens: «Imple saccos eorum frumento, quantum possunt capere, et pone pecuniam singulorum in summitate sacci. ²Scyphum autem meum argenteum et pretium, quod dedit tritici, pone in ore sacci iunioris». Factumque est ita. ³Et, orto mane,

silver cup, in the mouth of the sack of the youngest, with his
money for the grain." And he did as Joseph told him. 3As soon as
the morning was light, the men were sent away with their asses.
4When they had gone but a short distance from the city, Joseph
said to his steward, "Up, follow after the men; and when you
overtake them, say to them, 'Why have you returned evil for
good? Why have you stolen my silver cup?[q] 5Is it not from this
that my lord drinks, and by this that he divines? You have done
wrong in so doing.'"
6When he overtook them, he spoke to them these words. 7They
said to him, "Why does my lord speak such words as these? Far
be it from your servants that they should do such a thing! 8Behold,
the money which we found in the mouth of our sacks, we brought
back to you from the land of Canaan; how then should we steal
silver or gold from your lord's house? 9With whomever of your

---

fession that they are sinners before God (cf. v. 16) and with Judah's very moving and winning speech (vv. 18–34). The sin they acknowledge is not that of stealing the cup (which they did not do) but their earlier treatment of Joseph in Canaan which, although they say nothing about it, they feel God is judging them for. Judah's final speech in which he tells about his father's feelings and shows that he is ready to atone for the sin they all committed, reveals how his brotherly love has come back in full force. Judah thereby manages to save them all, in the same way as the tribe which bears his name will save, through King David, the whole people of Israel.

44:5. This was a sacred cup used to divine the future by studying the sound, configuration and movement of the liquid, perhaps after some object or some drops of oil had been added.

44:9–17. The sons of Jacob reply in a rush (as happened during their first visit: cf. chap. 42) and they will have to pay for not being circumspect: their words have condemned Benjamin, without their realizing it. But at the same time they are all ready to pay, by staying as slaves. Joseph, however, pronounces a much more benign sentence—but it is a further test to see how far they will go in their loyalty to Benjamin and their father. Joseph will receive their reply from the lips of Judah, who will offer himself in order to save his brothers and their father. After such an offer, Joseph will not be able to keep his secret to himself much longer.

dimissi sunt cum asinis suis. 4Iamque urbem exierant et processerant paululum, tunc Ioseph, arcessito
dispensatore domus: «Surge, inquit, et persequere viros; et apprehensis dicito: 'Quare reddidistis
malum pro bono? Cur furati estis mihi scyphum argenteum? 5Nonne ipse est, in quo bibit dominus
meus et in quo augurari solet? Pessimam rem fecistis!'». 6Fecit ille, ut iusserat, et apprehensis per
ordinem locutus est. 7Qui responderunt: «Quare sic loquitur dominus noster? Absit a servis tuis, ut
tantum flagitii commiserimus. 8Pecuniam, quam invenimus in summitate saccorum, reportavimus ad
te de terra Chanaan; et quomodo consequens est, ut furati simus de domo domini tui aurum vel argentum? 9Apud quemcumque fuerit inventum servorum tuorum, quod quaeris, moriatur; et nos erimus

q. Gk Compare Vg: Heb lacks *Why have you stolen my silver cup?*

servants it be found, let him die, and we also will be my lord's slaves." [10]He said, "Let it be as you say: he with whom it is found shall be my slave, and the rest of you shall be blameless." [11]Then every man quickly lowered his sack to the ground, and every man opened his sack. [12]And he searched, beginning with the eldest and ending with the youngest; and the cup was found in Benjamin's sack. [13]Then they rent their clothes, and every man loaded his ass, and they returned to the city.

[14]When Judah and his brothers came to Joseph's house, he was still there; and they fell before him to the ground. [15]Joseph said to them, "What deed is this that you have done? Do you not know that such a man as I can indeed divine?" [16]And Judah said, "What shall we say to my lord? What shall we speak? Or how can we clear ourselves? God has found out the guilt of your servants; behold, we are my lord's slaves, both we and he also in whose hand the cup has been found." [17]But he said, "Far be it from me that I should do so! Only the man in whose hand the cup was found shall be my slave; but as for you, go up in peace to your father."

Judah's reaction

[18]Then Judah went up to him and said, "O my lord, let your servant, I pray you, speak a word in my lord's ears, and let not your anger burn against your servant; for you are like Pharaoh himself. [19]My lord asked his servants, saying, 'Have you a father, or a brother?' [20]And we said to my lord, 'We have a father, an old man, and a young brother, the child of his old age; and his brother is dead, and he alone is left of his mother's children; and his father loves him.' [21]Then you said to your servants, 'Bring him down to me, that I may set my eyes upon him.' [22]We said to my lord, 'The lad cannot

---

servi domini nostri». [10]Qui dixit eis: «Fiat iuxta vestram sententiam: apud quemcumque fuerit inventum, ipse sit servus meus; vos autem eritis innoxii». [11]Itaque festinato deponentes in terram saccos aperuerunt singuli. [12]Quos scrutatus incipiens a maiore usque ad minimum invenit scyphum in sacco Beniamin. [13]At illi, scissis vestibus, oneratisque rursum asinis, reversi sunt in oppidum. [14]Et Iudas cum fratribus ingressus est ad Ioseph —necdum enim de loco abierat— omnesque ante eum pariter in terram corruerunt. [15]Quibus ille ait: «Cur sic agere voluistis? An ignoratis quod non sit similis mei in augurandi scientia?». [16]Cui Iudas: «Quid respondebimus, inquit, domino meo? Vel quid loquemur aut iuste poterimus obtendere? Deus invenit iniquitatem servorum tuorum; en omnes servi sumus domini mei, et nos et apud quem inventus est scyphus». [17]Respondit Ioseph: «Absit a me, ut sic agam! Qui furatus est scyphum, ipse sit servus meus; vos autem abite liberi ad patrem vestrum». [18]Accedens autem propius Iudas confidenter ait: «Oro, domine mi, loquatur servus tuus verbum in auribus tuis, et ne irascaris famulo tuo; tu es enim sicut pharao! [19]Dominus meus interrogavit prius servos suos: 'Habetis patrem aut fratrem?'. [20]Et nos respondimus domino meo: 'Est nobis pater senex et puer parvulus, qui in senectute illius natus est, cuius uterinus frater mortuus est; et ipse solus superest a matre sua, pater vero tenere diligit eum'. [21]Dixistique servis tuis: 'Adducite eum ad me, et ponam oculos meos super illum'. [22]Suggessimus domino meo: 'Non potest puer relinquere patrem suum; si enim illum

leave his father, for if he should leave his father, his father would die.' ²³Then you said to your servants, 'Unless your youngest brother comes down with you, you shall see my face no more.' ²⁴When we went back to your servant my father we told him the words of my lord. ²⁵And when our father said, 'Go again, buy us a little food,' ²⁶we said, 'We cannot go down. If our youngest brother goes with us, then we will go down; for we cannot see the man's face unless our youngest brother is with us.' ²⁷Then your servant my father said to us, 'You know that my wife bore me two sons; ²⁸one left me, and I said, Surely he has been torn to pieces; and I Gen 37:31–34 have never seen him since. ²⁹If you take this one also from me, and harm befalls him, you will bring down my gray hairs in sorrow to Sheol.' ³⁰Now therefore, when I come to your servant my father, and the lad is not with us, then, as his life is bound up in the lad's life, ³¹when he sees that the lad is not with us, he will die; and your servants will bring down the gray hairs of your servant our father with sorrow to Sheol. ³²For your servant became surety for the lad to my father, saying, 'If I do not bring him back to you, then I shall bear the blame in the sight of my father all my life.' ³³Now therefore, let your servant, I pray you, remain instead of the lad as a slave to my lord; and let the lad go back with his brothers. ³⁴ For how can I go back to my father if the lad is not with me? I fear to see the evil that would come upon my father."

Joseph makes himself known* Acts 7:13–14

45

¹Then Joseph could not control himself before all those who stood by him; and he cried, "Make every one go out from

---

*45:1–28. The dénouement maintains the dramatic tone typical of the story so far. And now we are given the real reasons behind everything that Joseph, the wise man, has done. Once he makes himself known to his brothers, they interpret his behaviour from their own, human, point of view—their fear of his vengeance (cf.

dimiserit, morietur'. ²³Et dixisti servis tuis: 'Nisi venerit frater vester minimus vobiscum, non vide-bitis amplius faciem meam'. ²⁴Cum ergo ascendissemus ad famulum tuum patrem nostrum, narravimus ei omnia, quae locutus est dominus meus, ²⁵et dixit pater noster: 'Revertimini et emite nobis parum trit-ici'. ²⁶Cui diximus: 'Ire non possumus. Si frater noster minimus descenderit nobiscum, proficiscemur simul; alioquin, illo absente, non poterimus videre faciem viri'. ²⁷Ad quae servus tuus pater meus respondit: 'Vos scitis quod duos genuerit mihi uxor mea. ²⁸Egressus est unus a me, et dixi: Bestia devo-ravit eum! Et hucusque non comparet. ²⁹Si tuleritis et istum a facie mea, et aliquid ei in via contigerit, deducetis canos meos cum maerore ad inferos'. ³⁰Igitur, si intravero ad servum tuum patrem meum, et puer defuerit —cum anima illius ex huius anima pendeat—³¹videritque eum non esse nobiscum, mori-etur; et deducent famuli tui canos eius cum dolore ad inferos. ³²Servus tuus pro puero patri meo spo-pondit: Nisi reduxero eum, peccati reus ero in patrem meum omni tempore. ³³Manebo itaque servus tuus pro puero in ministerio domini mei, et puer ascendat cum fratribus suis. ³⁴Non enim possum redire

me." So no one stayed with him when Joseph made himself known to his brothers. [2]And he wept aloud, so that the Egyptians heard it, and the household of Pharaoh heard it. [3]And Joseph said to his brothers, "I am Joseph; is my father still alive?" But his brothers could not answer him, for they were dismayed at his presence.

[4]So Joseph said to his brothers, "Come near to me, I pray you." And they came near. And he said, "I am your brother, Joseph, whom you sold into Egypt. [5]And now do not be distressed, or angry with yourselves, because you sold me here; for God sent me before you to preserve life. [6]For the famine has been in the land these two years; and there are yet five years in which there will be neither plowing nor harvest. [7]And God sent me before you to preserve for you a remnant on earth, and to keep alive for you many survivors. [8]So it was not you who sent me here, but God; and he has made me a father to Pharaoh, and lord of all his house and ruler over all the land of Egypt. [9]Make haste and go up to my father and say to him, 'Thus says your son

Margin references: Gen 50:15 · Acts 7:9 · Gen 50:20–21 · Acts 7:10 · Acts 7:14

---

v. 3 and later 50:15). Joseph explains that everything was part of God's plan (cf. vv. 5–13). The generosity of the pharaoh was also a mark of divine mercy, but the greatest mercy of all is that Jacob has found the son he thought he lost (cf. v. 28).

As well as revealing God's mercy, this history shows forth the greatness of Joseph, who, far from harbouring rancour or even thinking of vengeance, directs all his actions to getting back his brothers, leading them gradually to repent the sin they committed, forgiving them from the very start and treating them as the brothers they are. Joseph's behaviour is a model of how we should treat one another; forgiveness should be ever-present in our relationship with others. Pope John Paul II has written that

"Society can become 'ever more human' only when we introduce into all the mutual relationships which form its moral aspect the moment of forgiveness, which is so much of the essence of the Gospel. Forgiveness demonstrates the presence in the world of *the love which is more powerful than sin*. Forgiveness is also the fundamental condition for reconciliation, not only in the relationship of God with man, but also in relationships between people. A world from which forgiveness was eliminated would be nothing but a world of cold and unfeeling justice, in the name of which each person would claim his or her own rights *vis-à-vis* others; the various kinds of selfishness latent in man would transform life and human society into a system of

---

ad patrem meum, absente puero, ne calamitatis, quae oppressura est patrem meum, testis assistam». [1]Non se poterat ultra cohibere Ioseph omnibus coram astantibus, unde clamavit: «Egredimini cuncti foras!». Et nemo aderat cum eo, quando manifestavit se fratribus suis. [2]Elevavitque vocem cum fletu, quam audierunt Aegyptii omnisque domus pharaonis. [3]Et dixit Ioseph fratribus suis: «Ego sum Ioseph! Adhuc pater meus vivit?». Nec poterant respondere fratres nimio terrore perterriti. [4]Ad quos ille clementer: «Accedite, inquit, ad me». Et cum accessissent prope: «Ego sum, ait, Ioseph frater vester, quem vendidistis in Aegyptum. [5]Nolite contristari, neque vobis durum esse videatur quod vendidistis me in his regionibus. Pro salute enim vestra misit me Deus ante vos in Aegyptum. [6]Biennium est enim

Joseph, God has made me lord of all Egypt; come down to me, do not tarry; [10]you shall dwell in the land of Goshen, and you shall be near me, you and your children and your children's children, and your flocks, your herds, and all that you have; [11]and there I will provide for you, for there are yet five years of famine to come; lest you and your household, and all that you have, come to poverty.' [12]And now your eyes see, and the eyes of my brother Benjamin see, that it is my mouth that speaks to you. [13]You must tell my father of all my splendour in Egypt, and of all that you have seen. Make haste and bring my father down here." [14]Then he fell upon his brother Benjamin's neck and wept; and Benjamin wept upon his neck. [15]And he kissed all his brothers and wept upon them; and after that his brothers talked with him.

[16]When the report was heard in Pharaoh's house, "Joseph's brothers have come," it pleased Pharaoh and his servants well. [17]And Pharaoh said to Joseph, "Say to your brothers, 'Do this:

Josh 10:41; 11:16; 15:51

Acts 20:37

---

oppression of the weak by the strong, or into an arena of permanent strife between one group and another" (*Dives in misericordia*, 14).

45:7. A veiled reference, given the context of the account, to the departure from Egypt narrated in the book of Exodus.

45:10. "The land of Goshen". Although the word Goshen seems to be Semitic, and not Egyptian (cf. Josh 15:51; 10:41; 11:16), in the light of other biblical passages such as Genesis 47:11 and Exodus 1:11, and from other indicators it is pos-

sible to situate the area where the Hebrews settled as Wadi Tumilat in the north-east of Egypt, on the eastern side of the Nile.

45:14–15. Joseph's gesture makes it plain that all the previous evil done has been drowned by the love he feels towards his brothers. St Caesarius of Arles comments: "He kissed each of them and wept for each of them, so that the shedding of his tears levelled the mountains of their fears, and with his tears of love he cleansed the hatred of his brothers" (*Sermons*, 90, 5).

---

quod coepit fames esse in terra, et adhuc quinque anni restant, quibus nec arari poterit nec meti. [7]Praemisitque me Deus, ut reservemini super terram, et servetur vita vestra in salvationem magnam. [8]Non vestro consilio, sed Dei voluntate huc missus sum, qui fecit me quasi patrem pharaonis et dominum universae domus eius ac principem in omni terra Aegypti. [9]Festinate et ascendite ad patrem meum et dicetis ei: 'Haec mandat filius tuus Ioseph: Deus fecit me dominum universae terrae Aegypti; descende ad me, ne moreris. [10]Et habitabis in terra Gessen; erisque iuxta me tu et filii tui et filii filiorum tuorum, oves tuae et armenta tua et universa, quae possides. [11]Ibique te pascam —adhuc enim quinque anni residui sunt famis— ne et tu pereas et domus tua et omnia, quae possides'. [12]En oculi vestri et oculi fratris mei Beniamin vident quia os meum est, quod loquitur ad vos. [13]Nuntiate patri meo universam gloriam meam in Aegypto et cuncta, quae vidistis. Festinate et adducite eum ad me». [14]Cumque amplexatus recidisset in collum Beniamin fratris sui, flevit, illo quoque similiter flente, super collum eius. [15]Osculatusque est Ioseph omnes fratres suos et ploravit super singulos. Post quae ausi sunt loqui ad eum. [16]Auditumque est et celebri sermone vulgatum in aula regis: «Venerunt fratres Ioseph!». Et gavisus est pharao atque omnis familia eius. [17]Dixitque ad Ioseph, ut imperaret fratribus suis dicens: «Onerantes iumenta ite in terram Chanaan [18]et tollite inde patrem vestrum et cognationem et venite ad

load your beasts and go back to the land of Canaan; [18]and take your father and your households, and come to me, and I will give you the best of the land of Egypt, and you shall eat the fat of the land.' [19]Command them[r] also, 'Do this: take wagons from the land of Egypt for your little ones and for your wives, and bring your father, and come. [20]Give no thought to your goods, for the best of all the land of Egypt is yours.'"

[21]The sons of Israel did so; and Joseph gave them wagons, according to the command of Pharaoh, and gave them provisions for the journey. [22]To each and all of them he gave festal garments; but to Benjamin he gave three hundred shekels of silver and five

Acts 7:14 festal garments. [23]To his father he sent as follows: ten asses loaded with the good things of Egypt, and ten she-asses loaded with grain, bread, and provision for his father on the journey. [24]Then he sent his brothers away, and as they departed, he said to them, "Do not quarrel on the way." [25]So they went up out of Egypt, and came to

Lk 24:11 the land of Canaan to their father Jacob. [26]And they told him, "Joseph is still alive, and he is ruler over all the land of Egypt." And his heart fainted, for he did not believe them. [27]But when they

---

*46:1—47:12. The narrative now focuses again on the family of Jacob in Canaan. The figure and position of Joseph act as the backdrop against which to explain the establishment of Israel in Egypt; it is the result of a divine command.

Jacob goes down to Egypt forced by the famine which is ravaging the land of Canaan (cf. 47:4). The Lord has prepared the way for him by means of a series of painful events and a series of tests whose meaning is now plain to see. This is a common human experience: "The test, I don't deny it, proves to be very hard: you have to go uphill, 'against the grain'. What is my advice? That you must say: *omnia in bonum*, everything that happens, 'everything that happens to me is for my own good . . .' Therefore the right conclusion is to accept, as a pleasant reality, what seems so hard to you" (St Josemaría Escrivá, *Furrow*, 127).

46:1–5. This movement to Egypt could have put a question-mark against God's promise to give the descendants of

---

me; et ego dabo vobis omnia bona Aegypti, ut comedatis medullam terrae. [19]Praecipe etiam: tollite plaustra de terra Aegypti ad subvectionem parvulorum vestrorum ac coniugum et tollite patrem vestrum et properate quantocius venientes. [20]Nec doleatis super supellectilem vestram, quia omnes opes Aegypti vestrae erunt». [21]Feceruntque filii Israel, ut eis mandatum fuerat. Quibus dedit Ioseph plaustra secundum pharaonis imperium et cibaria in itinere. [22]Singulis quoque proferri iussit vestimentum mutatorium; Beniamin vero dedit trecentos argenteos cum quinque [23]vestimentis mutatoriis. Patri suo misit similiter asinos decem, qui subveherent ex omnibus divitiis Aegypti, et totidem asinas triticum et panem et cibum pro itinere portantes. [24]Dimisit ergo fratres suos et proficiscentibus ait: «Ne irascamini in via!». [25]Qui ascendentes ex Aegypto venerunt in terram Chanaan ad patrem suum Iacob [26]et nuntiaverunt ei dicentes: «Ioseph vivit et ipse dominatur in omni terra Aegypti!». At cor eius frigidum mansit; non enim credebat eis. [27]Tunc referebant omnia verba Ioseph, quae dixerat eis.

r. Compare Gk Vg: Heb *You are commanded*

told him all the words of Joseph, which he had said to them, and when he saw the wagons which Joseph had sent to carry him, the spirit of their father Jacob revived; [28]and Israel said, "It is enough; Joseph my son is still alive; I will go and see him before I die."

Jacob journeys to Egypt*

Gen 12:1–4
Acts 7:15

46 [1]So Israel took his journey with all that he had, and came to Beer-sheba, and offered sacrifices to the God of his father Isaac. [2]And God spoke to Israel in visions of the night, and said, "Jacob, Jacob." And he said, "Here am I." [3]Then he said, "I am God, the God of your father; do not be afraid to go down to Egypt; for I will there make of you a great nation. [4]I will go down with you to Egypt, and I will also bring you up again; and Joseph's hand shall close your eyes." [5]Then Jacob set out from Beer-sheba; and the sons of Israel carried Jacob their father, their little ones, and their wives, in the wagons which Pharaoh had sent to carry him. [6]They also took their cattle and their goods, which they had gained in the land of Canaan, and came into Egypt, Jacob and all his offspring with him, [7]his sons, and his sons' sons

Acts 9:4

Gen 26:2;
26:23–25
Acts 7:15

Gen 50:1–14

Acts 7:14

Abraham and Isaac the land of Canaan. God's intervention convinces Jacob that this is all part of God's providential plans. In fact, Jacob's move to Egypt is the outcome of an express command from God. In Genesis 26:2 God forbade Isaac to go to Egypt: this was a sign that his land was Canaan. Now a similar command is needed to make Israel leave the country. Like everything in the patriarchal period this command is given in a night-time vision, the last such vision the patriarchs are to receive. The command does not however cancel God's promise about Canaan: God himself will go with

Jacob to Egypt, and he will take him out of there. The reference to this is not just to the fact that Jacob will be buried in Canaan (cf. 50:1–14) but to the ultimate liberation, the Exodus.

Jacob's status is not reduced by his going into Egypt; on the contrary, it is enhanced and underlined: "For, what does he need if God goes with him? [. . .] Who is as powerful in his homeland as Jacob was in a strange country? Who had such abundance of wealth, as he had in a time of famine? Who was as strong in his youth, as this man was in his old age? [. . .] Who was as rich in his kingdom, as

---

Cumque vidisset plaustra et universa, quae miserat ad adducendum eum, revixit spiritus eius, [28]et ait: «Sufficit mihi, si adhuc Ioseph filius meus vivit. Vadam et videbo illum, antequam moriar». [1]Profectusque Israel cum omnibus, quae habebat, venit Bersabee et, mactatis ibi victimis Deo patris sui Isaac, [2]audivit eum per visionem noctis vocantem se: «Iacob, Iacob!». Cui respondit: «Ecce adsum!». [3]Ait illi: «Ego sum Deus, Deus patris tui. Noli timere descendere in Aegyptum, quia in gentem magnam faciam te ibi. [4]Ego descendam tecum illuc et ego inde adducam te revertentem; Ioseph quoque ponet manus suas super oculos tuos». [5]Surrexit igitur Iacob a Bersabee, tuleruntque eum filii cum parvulis et uxoribus suis in plaustris, quae miserat pharao ad portandum senem, [6]sumpserunt quoque omnia, quae possederant in terra Chanaan; veneruntque in Aegyptum Iacob et omne semen eius, [7]filii eius et nepotes, filiae et cuncta simul progenies. [8]Haec sunt autem nomina filiorum Israel, qui ingressi

with him, his daughters, and his sons' daughters; all his offspring he brought with him into Egypt.

Num 26:5–51
Mt 2:13–15

⁸Now these are the names of the descendants of Israel, who came into Egypt, Jacob and his sons. Reuben, Jacob's first-born, ⁹and the sons of Reuben: Hanoch, Pallu, Hezron, and Carmi. ¹⁰The sons of Simeon: Jemuel, Jamin, Ohad, Jachin, Zohar, and Shaul, the son of a Canaanitish woman. ¹¹The sons of Levi:

Gen 38:3–10

Gershon, Kohath, and Merari. ¹²The sons of Judah: Er, Onan, Shelah, Perez, and Zerah (but Er and Onan died in the land of Canaan); and the sons of Perez were Hezron and Hamul. ¹³The sons of Issachar: Tola, Puvah, Iob, and Shimron. ¹⁴The sons of Zebulun: Sered, Elon, and Jahleel ¹⁵(these are the sons of Leah, whom she bore to Jacob in Paddan-aram, together with his daughter Dinah; altogether his sons and his daughters numbered thirty-three). ¹⁶The sons of Gad: Ziphion, Haggi, Shuni, Ezbon, Eri, Arodi, and Areli. ¹⁷The sons of Asher: Imnah, Ishvah, Ishvi, Beriah, with Serah their sister. And the sons of Beriah: Heber and Malchi-el ¹⁸(these are the sons of Zilpah, whom Laban gave to Leah his daughter; and these she bore to Jacob—sixteen persons). ¹⁹The sons of Rachel, Jacob's wife: Joseph and Benjamin.

Gen 41:45

²⁰And to Joseph in the land of Egypt were born Manasseh and

---

this man on his pilgrimage? He even blessed kings [. . .], and who will call him poor whom the world was not worthy to know? For his company was in heaven" (St Ambrose, *De Iacob et vita beata,* 2, 9, 38).

46:8–27. Interrupting the thread of his story, the sacred writer brings in here a detailed list of those who went down into Egypt; it is arranged according to mothers. It is a list of Jacob's descendants, included among whom are Joseph and his descendants (who did not come from Canaan). However, the expression "came into Egypt" can certainly be applied to Jacob's

descendants as a whole. The totals given differ in vv. 26 and 27 but this may have to do with the way the final redactor did his addition. Thus, if one excludes from the list Er and Onan, sons of Judah who died in Canaan (cf. v. 12), and Joseph and his two sons who were in Egypt already, and on the other hand includes Dinah (cf. v. 15) who was not counted in the total number of Leah's children (cf. v. 15), one gets the total figure of sixty-six which appears in v. 26. But if, on the other hand, Jacob is also taken into the count and also the group of Joseph and his two sons, the total is seventy, a traditional and symbolic figure. The

sunt in Aegyptum, ipse cum liberis suis. Primogenitus Ruben. ⁹Filii Ruben: Henoch et Phallu et Hesron et Charmi. ¹⁰Filii Simeon: Iamuel et Iamin et Ahod et Iachin et Sohar et Saul filius Chananitidis. ¹¹Filii Levi: Gerson et Caath et Merari. ¹²Filii Iudae: Her et Onan et Sela et Phares et Zara. Mortui sunt autem Her et Onan in terra Chanaan. Natique sunt filii Phares: Esrom et Hamul. ¹³Filii Issachar: Thola et Phua et Iasub et Semron. ¹⁴Filii Zabulon: Sared et Elon et Iahelel. ¹⁵Hi filii Liae, quos genuit in Paddanaram, cum Dina filia sua. Omnes animae filiorum eius et filiarum triginta tres. ¹⁶Filii Gad: Sephon et Haggi, Suni et Esebon, Heri et Arodi et Areli. ¹⁷Filii Aser: Iemna et Iesua et Isui et Beria, Sara quoque soror eorum. Filii Beria: Heber et Melchiel. ¹⁸Hi filii Zelphae, quam dedit Laban Liae filiae suae; et hos

Ephraim, whom Asenath, the daughter of Potiphera the priest of On, bore to him. [21]And the sons of Benjamin: Bela, Becher, Ashbel, Gera, Naaman, Ehi, Rosh, Muppim, Huppim, and Ard [22](these are the sons of Rachel, who were born to Jacob—fourteen persons in all). [23]The sons of Dan: Hushim. [24]The sons of Naphtali: Jahzeel, Guni, Jezer, and Shillem [25](these are the sons of Bilhah, whom Laban gave to Rachel his daughter, and these she bore to Jacob—seven persons in all). [26]All the persons belonging to Jacob who came into Egypt, who were his own offspring, not including Jacob's sons' wives, were sixty-six persons in all; [27]and the sons of Joseph, who were born to him in Egypt, were two; all the persons of the house of Jacob, that came into Egypt, were seventy.

Ex 1:1–5
Deut 10:22
Acts 7:14

[28]He sent Judah before him to Joseph, to appear[s] before him in Goshen; and they came into the land of Goshen. [29]Then Joseph made ready his chariot and went up to meet Israel his father in Goshen; and he presented himself to him, and fell on his neck, and wept on his neck a good while. [30]Israel said to Joseph, "Now let me die, since I have seen your face and know that you are still alive." [31]Joseph said to his brothers and to his father's household,

Lk 2:29

Greek version of the Old Testament gives a total of seventy-five, because to the previous list it has added five descendants of Ephraim and Manasseh. In this as in other passages of the Bible we can clearly see that the Word of God is being expressed in human language and with the forms and devices that people normally use, sometimes overlooking numerical exactness.

46:28–34. Joseph does not wait for Jacob to visit him as would be his due, given his high social position and the fact that the patriarch has immigrant status. His filial feelings and the honour owed to his father lead him to go to meet him without delay and throw himself into his arms.

Jacob sees all his sons gathered around him. Now he knows that his mission as Israel, the father of the people, is accomplished; he can die in peace. Because the Israelites are shepherds, they keep a certain distance from the Egyptians; this also ensures they do not lose their identity as a people. As regards Goshen, see the note on 45:10.

---

genuit Iacob: sedecim animas. [19]Filii Rachel uxoris Iacob: Ioseph et Beniamin. [20]Natique sunt Ioseph filii in terra Aegypti, quos genuit ei Aseneth filia Putiphare sacerdotis Heliopoleos: Manasses et Ephraim. [21]Filii Beniamin: Bela et Bochor et Asbel, Gera et Naaman et Echi et Ros, Mophim et Huphim et Ared. [22]Hi filii Rachel, quos genuit Iacob: omnes animae quattuordecim. [23]Filii Dan: Husim. [24]Filii Nephthali: Iasiel et Guni et Ieser et Sellem. [25]Hi filii Bilhae, quam dedit Laban Racheli filiae suae; et hos genuit Iacob: omnes animae septem. [26]Cunctae animae, quae ingressae sunt cum Iacob in Aegyptum et egressae de femore illius, absque uxoribus filiorum eius, sexaginta sex. [27]Filii autem Ioseph, qui nati sunt ei in terra Aegypti, animae duae. Omnes animae domus Iacob, quae ingressae sunt in Aegyptum, fuere septuaginta. [28]Misit autem Iudam ante se ad Ioseph, ut nuntiaret et occurreret in

s. Sam Syr Compare Gk Vg: Heb *to show the way*

"I will go up and tell Pharaoh, and will say to him, 'My brothers and my father's household, who were in the land of Canaan, have come to me; [32]and the men are shepherds, for they have been keepers of cattle; and they have brought their flocks, and their herds, and all that they have.' [33]When Pharaoh calls you, and says, 'What is your occupation?' [34]you shall say, 'Your servants have been keepers of cattle from our youth even until now, both we and our fathers,' in order that you may dwell in the land of Goshen; for every shepherd is an abomination to the Egyptians."

Israel settles in the land of Goshen

47 [1]So Joseph went in and told Pharaoh, "My father and my brothers, with their flocks and herds and all that they possess, have come from the land of Canaan; they are now in the land of Goshen." [2]And from among his brothers he took five men and presented them to Pharaoh. [3]Pharaoh said to his brothers, "What is your occupation?" And they said to Pharaoh, "Your servants are shepherds, as our fathers were." [4]They said to Pharaoh, "We have come to sojourn in the land; for there is no pasture for your servants' flocks, for the famine is severe in the land of Canaan; and now, we pray you, let your servants dwell in the land of Goshen." [5]Then Pharaoh said to Joseph, "Your father and your brothers have come to you. [6]The land of Egypt is before you; settle your

Ex 1:11;
8:18;12:37

47:5–12. The fact that Jacob blesses the pharaoh in this way underlines the dignity of the patriarch. This dignity is his not only on account of his advanced age, as the text points out, but also because he is the one chosen by God to be the father of the people of Israel and the bearer of the divine blessing and the promises God made to Abraham. Being God's elect meant that he had to undergo many trials and sufferings; but it has made him a person worthy of veneration, who now sees his mission accomplished. Jacob went down to Egypt as a united family; he will leave Egypt as a people.

Gessen. [29]Et venerunt in terram Gessen. Iunctoque Ioseph curru suo, ascendit obviam patri suo in Gessen; vidensque eum irruit super collum eius et inter amplexus diu flevit. [30]Dixitque Israel ad Ioseph: «Iam laetus moriar, quia vidi faciem tuam et superstitem te relinquo». [31]Et ille locutus est ad fratres suos et ad omnem domum patris sui: «Ascendam et nuntiabo pharaoni dicamque ei: Fratres mei et domus patris mei, qui erant in terra Chanaan, venerunt ad me. [32]Et sunt viri pastores ovium curamque habent alendorum gregum; pecora sua et armenta et omnia, quae habere potuerunt, adduxerunt secum. [33]Cumque vocaverit vos et dixerit: 'Quod est opus vestrum?'. [34]Respondebitis: 'Viri pastores sumus servi tui ab infantia nostra usque in praesens et nos et patres nostri'. Haec autem dicetis, ut habitare possitis in terra Gessen, quia detestantur Aegyptii omnes pastores ovium». [1]Ingressus ergo Ioseph nuntiavit pharaoni dicens: «Pater meus et fratres, oves eorum et armenta et cuncta, quae possident, venerunt de terra Chanaan; et ecce consistunt in terra Gessen». [2]Ex omnibus fratribus suis quinque viros statuit coram rege, [3]quos ille interrogavit: «Quid habetis operis?». Responderunt: «Pastores ovium sumus servi tui et nos et patres nostri». [4]Dixeruntque ad pharaonem: «Ad peregrinandum in terra

216

father and your brothers in the best of the land; let them dwell in the land of Goshen; and if you know any able men among them, put them in charge of my cattle."

⁷Then Joseph brought in Jacob his father, and set him before Pharaoh, and Jacob blessed Pharaoh. ⁸And Pharaoh said to Jacob, "How many are the days of the years of your life?" ⁹And Jacob said to Pharaoh, "The days of the years of my sojourning are a hundred and thirty years; few and evil have been the days of the years of my life, and they have not attained to the days of the years of the life of my fathers in the days of their sojourning." ¹⁰And Jacob blessed Pharaoh, and went out from the presence of Pharaoh. ¹¹Then Joseph settled his father and his brothers, and gave them a possession in the land of Egypt, in the best of the land, in the land of Rameses, as Pharaoh had commanded. ¹²And Joseph provided his father, his brothers, and all his father's household with food, according to the number of their dependents.

Gen 25:7; 35:38

Joseph administers Egypt to the pharaoh's advantage

¹³Now there was no food in all the land; for the famine was very severe, so that the land of Egypt and the land of Canaan languished by reason of the famine. ¹⁴And Joseph gathered up all the money that was found in the land of Egypt and in the land of

Gen 41:53–57

47:13–26. This passage describes how Joseph operated in Egypt as the pharaoh's administrator. It repeats in some way what we were told in chapter 41. Social conditions in Egypt, especially from the 16th century BC onwards, after the Hyksos were expelled, are known to have been very much as described in this passage: the entire land belonged to the pharaoh, except for some properties of priests. We do not know, however, about any tribute of a fifth.

This section is designed to highlight Joseph's wise administration on the pharaoh's behalf, and perhaps to contrast the freedom enjoyed by the sons of Jacob as shepherds with the servile life (cf. v. 21) to which the Egyptians were subject.

---

venimus, quoniam non est herba gregibus servorum tuorum, ingravescente fame, in terra Chanaan petimusque, ut esse nos iubeas servos tuos in terra Gessen». ⁵Dixit itaque rex ad Ioseph: «Pater tuus et fratres tui venerunt ad te. ⁶Terra Aegypti in conspectu tuo est; in optimo loco fac eos habitare et trade eis terram Gessen. Quod si nosti in eis esse viros industrios, constitue illos magistros pecorum meorum». ⁷Post haec introduxit Ioseph patrem suum ad regem et statuit eum coram eo, qui benedicens illi ⁸et interrogatus ab eo: «Quot sunt dies annorum vitae tuae?», ⁹respondit: «Dies peregrinationis meae centum triginta annorum sunt, parvi et mali; et non pervenerunt usque ad dies patrum meorum, quibus peregrinati sunt». ¹⁰Et benedicto rege, egressus est foras. ¹¹Ioseph vero patri et fratribus suis dedit possessionem in Aegypto in optimo terrae loco, in terra Ramesses, ut praeceperat pharao; ¹²et alebat eos omnemque domum patris sui praebens cibaria singulis. ¹³In tota terra panis deerat, et oppresserat fames terram valde, defecitque terra Aegypti et terra Chanaan prae fame. ¹⁴E quibus omnem pecuniam congregavit pro venditione frumenti et intulit eam in aerarium regis. ¹⁵Cumque defecisset emptoribus

Canaan, for the grain which they bought; and Joseph brought the money into Pharaoh's house. [15]And when the money was all spent in the land of Egypt and in the land of Canaan, all the Egyptians came to Joseph, and said, "Give us food; why should we die before your eyes? For our money is gone." [16]And Joseph answered, "Give your cattle, and I will give you food in exchange for your cattle, if your money is gone." [17]So they brought their cattle to Joseph; and Joseph gave them food in exchange for the horses, the flocks, the herds, and the asses: and he supplied them with food in exchange for all their cattle that year. [18]And when that year was ended, they came to him the following year, and said to him, "We will not hide from my lord that our money is all spent; and the herds of cattle are my lord's; there is nothing left in the sight of my lord but our bodies and our lands. [19]Why should we die before your eyes, both we and our land? Buy us and our land for food, and we with our land will be slaves to Pharaoh; and give us seed, that we may live, and not die, and that the land may not be desolate."

[20]So Joseph bought all the land of Egypt for Pharaoh; for all the Egyptians sold their fields, because the famine was severe upon them. The land became Pharaoh's; [21]and as for the people, he made slaves of them[t] from one end of Egypt to the other. [22]Only the land of the priests he did not buy; for the priests had a fixed allowance from Pharaoh, and lived on the allowance which Pharaoh gave them; therefore they did not sell their land. [23]Then Joseph said to the people, "Behold, I have this day bought you and your land for Pharaoh. Now here is seed for you, and you shall sow the land. [24]And at the harvests you shall give a fifth to Pharaoh, and four fifths shall be your own, as seed for the field and as food for yourselves and your households, and as food for

pretium, venit cuncta Aegyptus ad Ioseph dicens: «Da nobis panes! Quare morimur coram te, deficiente pecunia?». [16]Quibus ille respondit: «Adducite pecora vestra, et dabo vobis pro eis cibos, si pretium non habetis». [17]Quae cum adduxissent, dedit eis alimenta pro equis et ovibus et bobus et asinis; sustentavitque eos illo anno pro commutatione pecorum. [18]Venerunt quoque anno secundo et dixerunt ei: «Non celamus dominum nostrum quod, deficiente pecunia, pecora transierunt ad dominum nostrum; nec clam te est quod absque corporibus et terra nihil habeamus. [19]Cur ergo moriemur, te vidente, et nos et terra nostra? Eme nos et terram nostram in servitutem regiam et praebe semina, ne, pereunte cultore, redigatur terra in solitudinem». [20]Emit igitur Ioseph omnem terram Aegypti, vendentibus singulis possessiones suas prae magnitudine famis. Subiecitque eam pharaoni [21]et cunctos populos eius redegit ei in servitutem, a novissimis terminis Aegypti usque ad extremos fines eius. [22]Terram autem sacerdotum non emit, qui cibariis a rege statutis fruebantur, et idcirco non sunt compulsi vendere possessiones suas. [23]Dixit ergo Ioseph ad populos: «En, ut cernitis, et vos et terram vestram pharao possidet; accipite semina et serite agros, [24]ut fruges habere possitis. Quintam partem regi dabitis; quattuor reliquas permitto vobis in sementem et in cibum familiis et liberis vestris» [25]Qui responderunt: «Tu sal-

t. Sam Gk Compare Vg: Heb *he removed them to the cities*

your little ones." ²⁵And they said, "You have saved our lives; may it please my lord, we will be slaves to Pharaoh." ²⁶So Joseph made it a statute concerning the land of Egypt, and it stands to this day, that Pharaoh should have the fifth; the land of the priests alone did not become Pharaoh's.

Jacob blesses Joseph's sons

Gen 41:50–52; 50:6

²⁷Thus Israel dwelt in the land of Egypt, in the land of Goshen; and they gained possessions in it, and were fruitful and multiplied exceedingly. ²⁸And Jacob lived in the land of Egypt seventeen years; so the days of Jacob, the years of his life, were a hundred and forty-seven years.

Acts 7:17

²⁹And when the time drew near that Israel must die, he called his son Joseph and said to him, "If now I have found favour in your sight, put your hand under my thigh, and promise to deal loyally and truly with me. Do not bury me in Egypt, ³⁰but let me lie with my fathers; carry me out of Egypt and bury me in their burying place." He answered, "I will do as you have said." ³¹And he said, "Swear to me"; and he swore to him. Then Israel bowed himself upon the head of his bed.

Gen 24:2

Gen 25:9f; 49:29–32

Heb 11:21

47:27–31. Jacob's advanced age highlights the fact that he was blessed by God. As regards the form of the promise, cf. 24:3. In the Greek version the final phrase reads, instead, "on his ruler's staff", possibly due to a mis-reading.

In the stories about the patriarchs, death is referred to as being "gathered to his people" (Gen 25:8; 35:29)—a phrase which reflects some sort of conviction that man survives after death, though the truth of the immortality of the soul, and the resurrection of the dead, had not yet

been revealed. "God revealed the resurrection of the dead to his people progressively. Hope in the bodily resurrection of the dead established itself as a consequence intrinsic to faith in God as creator of the whole man, soul and body. The creator of heaven and earth is also the one who faithfully maintains his covenant with Abraham and his posterity. It was in this double perspective that faith in the resurrection came to be expressed" (*Catechism of the Catholic Church*, 992).

---

vasti nos! Respiciat nos tantum dominus noster, et laeti serviemus regi». ²⁶Ex eo tempore usque in praesentem diem in universa terra Aegypti regibus quinta pars solvitur; et factum est a Ioseph in legem absque terra sacerdotali, quae libera ab hac condicione est. ²⁷Habitavit ergo Israel in Aegypto, id est in terra Gessen, et possedit eam; auctusque est et multiplicatus nimis. ²⁸Et vixit Iacob in terra Aegypti decem et septem annis; factique sunt omnes dies vitae illius centum quadraginta septem annorum. ²⁹Cumque appropinquare cerneret diem mortis suae, vocavit filium suum Ioseph et dixit ad eum: «Si inveni gratiam in conspectu tuo, pone manum tuam sub femore meo et facies mihi misericordiam et veritatem, ut non sepelias me in Aegypto, ³⁰sed dormiam cum patribus meis, et auferas me de terra hac condasque in sepulcro maiorum meorum». Cui respondit Ioseph: «Ego faciam, quod iussisti». ³¹Et ille: «Iura ergo, inquit, mihi!». Quo iurante, adoravit Israel conversus ad lectuli caput. ¹His ita transactis,

Jacob adopts and blesses Manasseh and Ephraim

Rev 7:6

48 [1]After this Joseph was told, "Behold, your father is ill"; so he took with him his two sons, Manasseh and Ephraim. [2]And it was told to Jacob, "Your son Joseph has come to you";

Gen 17:1; 35:6, 11–12

then Israel summoned his strength, and sat up in bed. [3]And Jacob said to Joseph, "God Almighty[u] appeared to me at Luz in the land

Acts 7:5; 7:45

of Canaan and blessed me, [4]and said to me, 'Behold, I will make you fruitful, and multiply you, and I will make of you a company of peoples, and will give this land to your descendants after you for an everlasting possession.' [5]And now your two sons, who were born to you in the land of Egypt before I came to you in Egypt, are mine; Ephraim and Manasseh shall be mine, as Reuben and Simeon are. [6]And the offspring born to you after them shall be yours; they shall be called by the name of their brothers in their

Gen 35:16–20

inheritance. [7]For when I came from Paddan, Rachel to my sorrow died in the land of Canaan on the way, when there was still some distance to go to Ephrath; and I buried her there on the way to Ephrath (that is, Bethlehem)."

---

*48:1–22. Now the focus moves from Joseph to his sons, the ancestors of the tribes of Ephraim and Manasseh who occupied the central part of Palestine. The account acts as an explanation of where those two tribes came from—for these men do not figure among the sons of Jacob (Israel)—and why *two* tribes should descend from Joseph. There are also indications here as to why the tribe of Ephraim should come to be the stronger, even though Manasseh was the first-born. So, the subject of the chapter ties in with the possession of lands and therefore with the fulfilment of the promise God made to the patriarchs; that is why it goes into such detail.

48:5–6. Ephraim and Manasseh are being put on a par with the two oldest sons of Jacob. The importance of the tribes that will descend from them is explained by the fact that they were adopted by Jacob: it was he who put them on the same level as his eldest sons. None of Joseph's other sons became founders of tribes; the sacred writer makes mention of them only to show that Joseph too was blessed with a large family. The fact that traditionally twelve tribes are spoken about whereas in fact there were thirteen is because Jacob had twelve sons and territory was assigned to twelve tribes (no territory was given to Levi).

---

nuntiatum est Ioseph quod aegrotaret pater suus. Et assumpsit secum duos filios Manasse et Ephraim. [2]Dictumque est seni: «Ecce filius tuus Ioseph venit ad te». Qui confortatus sedit in lectulo [3]et ingresso ad se ait: «Deus omnipotens apparuit mihi in Luza, quae est in terra Chanaan, benedixitque mihi [4]et ait: 'Ego te augebo et multiplicabo et faciam te in multitudinem populorum; daboque tibi terram hanc et semini tuo post te in possessionem sempiternam'. [5]Duo ergo filii tui, qui nati sunt tibi in terra Aegypti, antequam huc venirem ad te, mei erunt: Ephraim et Manasses sicut Ruben et Simeon reputabuntur mihi. [6]Reliquos autem, quos genueris post eos, tui erunt et nomine fratrum suorum vocabun-

u. Heb *El Shaddai*

⁸When Israel saw Joseph's sons, he said, "Who are these?" ⁹Joseph said to his father, "They are my sons, whom God has given me here." And he said, "Bring them to me, I pray you, that I may bless them." ¹⁰Now the eyes of Israel were dim with age, so that he could not see. So Joseph brought them near him; and he kissed them and embraced them. ¹¹And Israel said to Joseph, "I had not thought to see your face; and lo, God has let me see your children also." ¹²Then Joseph removed them from his knees, and he bowed himself with his face to the earth. ¹³And Joseph took them both, Ephraim in his right hand toward Israel's left hand, and Manasseh in his left hand toward Israel's right hand, and brought them near him. ¹⁴And Israel stretched out his right hand and laid it upon the head of Ephraim, who was the younger, and his left hand upon the head of Manasseh, crossing his hands, for Manasseh was the first-born. ¹⁵And he blessed Joseph, and said,

Gen 49:24
Ps 23:1; 80:1-2

48:12–20. This seems to be a rite of adoption involving putting the children on or between the knees of the adopter. Joseph then removes them from Jacob's knees so that they can receive along with him the patriarch's blessing; he places them in such a way that when Jacob stretches out his hands his right hand rests on the head of Mannaseh, the first-born, and his left on Ephraim. But Jacob crosses his arms and puts his right hand on the head of Ephraim, which means that he gets the greater blessing: hence the superiority of the tribe of Ephraim over that of Mannaseh. Here is another instance of the lesser being given preference. In Jacob's action we can see how God uses human intermediaries (in this case Jacob, who does not do what Joseph wants) to make his will, his plans, known.

48:15. In pronouncing his blessing on Joseph and his sons, Jacob solemnly invokes God, identifying him as the God whom his ancestors Abraham and Isaac worshipped, and also as his own God, who has led and protected him all his life long. Here for the first time in the Bible we see God being described as a shepherd: "who has led me [literally, "been my shepherd"] all my life"; this image will come across strongly later in the Old Testament (cf., e.g., Ps 23:1) and in the New (cf. Jn 10:1). As well as invoking God, Jacob also invokes the angel who has protected and saved him, who has come to his aid in times of danger: God has protected Jacob through the angel.

As described here the angel has features of Jacob's guardian angel; and the fact that Jacob invokes him in such a formal and important blessing invites us

tur in possessionibus suis. ⁷Mihi enim, quando veniebam de Paddanaram, mortua est Rachel mater tua in terra Chanaan in ipso itinere, cum adhuc esset spatium aliquod usque ad Ephratham, et sepelivi eam iuxta viam Ephrathae, quae alio nomine appellatur Bethlehem». ⁸Videns autem filios eius dixit ad eum: «Qui sunt isti?». ⁹Respondit: «Filii mei sunt, quos donavit mihi Deus in hoc loco». «Adduc, inquit, eos ad me, ut benedicam illis!». ¹⁰Oculi enim Israel caligabant prae nimia senectute, et clare videre non poterat. Applicitosque ad se deosculatus et circumplexus eos ¹¹dixit ad filium suum: «Non sum fraudatus aspectu tuo; insuper ostendit mihi Deus semen tuum». ¹²Cumque tulisset eos Ioseph de gremio patris, adoravit pronus in terram. ¹³Et posuit Ephraim ad dexteram suam, id est ad sinistram Israel, Manassen vero in sinistra sua, ad dexteram scilicet patris; applicuitque ambos ad eum. ¹⁴Qui extendens

221

Jn 10:11
Heb 11:21
"The God before whom my fathers Abraham and Isaac walked, the God who has led me all my life long to this day, [16]the angel who has redeemed me from all evil, bless the lads; and in them let my name be perpetuated, and the name of my fathers Abraham and Isaac; and let them grow into a multitude in the midst of the earth." [17]When Joseph saw that his father laid his right hand upon the head of Ephraim, it displeased him; and he took his father's hand, to remove it from Ephraim's head to Manasseh's head. [18]And Joseph said to his father, "Not so, my father; for this one is the

Deut 33:17
first-born; put your right hand upon his head." [19]But his father refused, and said, "I know, my son, I know; he also shall become a people, and he also shall be great; nevertheless his younger brother shall be greater than he, and his descendants shall become

Gen 12:3
a multitude of nations." [20]So he blessed them that day, saying,

"By you Israel will pronounce blessings, saying,
'God make you as Ephraim and as Manasseh' ";

and thus he put Ephraim before Manasseh. [21]Then Israel said to Joseph, "Behold, I am about to die, but God will be with you, and

Jn 4:5
will bring you again to the land of your fathers. [22]Moreover I have given to you rather than to your brothers one mountain slope[v] which I took from the hand of the Amorites with my sword and with my bow."

---

to consider the role of the guardian angel in the life of every human being. "The Guardian Angel always accompanies us as a leading witness. It is he who, at your particular judgment, will recall the kind deeds you performed for our Lord over the course of your life. Furthermore, when the enemy's terrible accusations make you feel lost, your Angel will bring up those intimations of your heart (which maybe you yourself have forgotten), those proofs of your love for God the Father, God the Son and God the Holy Spirit. So, don't ever forget your Guardian Angel, and the Prince of Heaven will not abandon you now, or at that decisive moment" (St Josemaría Escrivá, *Furrow*, 693).

manum dexteram, posuit super caput Ephraim minoris fratris, sinistram autem super caput Manasse, qui maior natu erat, commutans manus. [15]Benedixitque Iacob Ioseph et ait: «Deus, in cuius conspectu ambulaverunt / patres mei Abraham et Isaac, / Deus, qui pascit me ab adulescentia mea / usque in praesentem diem, / [16]Angelus, qui eruit me de cunctis malis, / benedicat pueris istis! / Et invocetur super eos nomen meum, / nomina quoque patrum meorum Abraham et Isaac, / et crescant in multitudinem / super terram!». [17]Videns autem Ioseph quod posuisset pater suus dexteram manum super caput Ephraim, graviter accepit et apprehensam manum patris levare conatus est de capite Ephraim et transferre super caput Manasse. [18]Dixitque ad patrem: «Non ita convenit, pater, quia hic est primogenitus; pone dexteram tuam super caput eius!». [19]Qui renuens ait: «Scio, fili mi, scio; et iste quidem erit in populos et multiplicabitur, sed frater eius minor maior erit illo, et semen illius crescet in plenitudinem gentium». [20]Benedixitque eis in die illo dicens: «In te benedicet Israel atque dicet: / 'Faciat te Deus

v. Heb *shekem*, shoulder

Jacob's blessings on his twelve sons*

Deut 33:1–29
Judg 5:1–31

49 ¹*Then Jacob called his sons, and said, "Gather yourselves together, that I may tell you what shall befall you in days to come.

²Assemble and hear, O sons of Jacob,
   and hearken to Israel your father.

³Reuben, you are my first-born,
   my might, and the first fruits of my strength,
   pre-eminent in pride and pre-eminent in power.
⁴Unstable as water, you shall not have pre-eminence
   because you went up to your father's bed;
   then you defiled it—you^w went up to my couch!

Gen 35:22

⁵Simeon and Levi are brothers;
   weapons of violence are their swords.

---

*49:1–28. Although this passage is traditionally described as the "Blessings of Jacob" in the light of what it says in v. 28, it is in fact more like a series of prophetic oracles (cf. v. 1) which encapsulate and evaluate the history of each of the tribes by making predictions about the future. If we compare this with other passages which provide historical-prophetical summaries about the tribes (such as the "Blessings of Moses" in Deuteronomy 33 and the "canticle of Deborah" in Judges 5), we can see that what is described here reflects the situation of the tribes of Israel after the conquest of Canaan. The "Blessings of Jacob" show the tribe of Judah's pride of place, refer to its connexion with the Messiah and highlight the importance of the tribes descended from Joseph.

49:3–4. As regards Reuben, the episode described in 35:22 is recalled, as the reason why he loses the primacy due to him as first-born. In Deuteronomy 33:6 we are told that the tribe is already small in size.

49:5–7. The tribe of Simeon was virtually absorbed by that of Judah, and the tribe of Levi will not acquire a territory of its own; there is no mention here of the priestly character of the tribe of Levi (this will be seen, though, in Deuteronomy 33:8–11), but the "curse" put on both these tribes because of their violent character is mentioned (recalling Genesis 34:25–30), as also the consequences flowing from it: they were scattered throughout Israel.

---

sicut Ephraim et sicut Manasse!'». Constituitque Ephraim ante Manassen. ²¹Et ait ad Ioseph filium suum: «Ego morior, et erit Deus vobiscum reducetque vos ad terram patrum vestrorum. ²²Do tibi partem unam extra fratres tuos, quam tuli de manu Amorraei in gladio et arcu meo». ¹Vocavit autem Iacob filios suos et ait eis: «Congregamini, ut annuntiem, quae ventura sunt vobis in diebus novissimis. / ²Congregamini et audite, filii Iacob, / audite Israel patrem vestrum! / ³Ruben primogenitus meus, / tu fortitudo mea et principium roboris mei; / prior in dignitate, maior in robore! / ⁴Ebulliens sicut aqua non excellas, / quia ascendisti cubile patris tui / et maculasti stratum meum. / ⁵Simeon et Levi fratres, / vasa violentiae arma eorum. / ⁶In consilium eorum ne veniat anima mea, / et in coetu illorum non sit

w. Gk Syr Tg: Heb *he*

Gen 34:25–31

⁶O my soul, come not into their council;
O my spirit,ˣ be not joined to their company;
for in their anger they slay men,
and in their wantonness they hamstring oxen.
⁷Cursed be their anger, for it is fierce;
and their wrath, for it is cruel!
I will divide them in Jacob
and scatter them in Israel.

Deut 33:1

⁸Judah, your brothers shall praise you;
your hand shall be on the neck of your enemies;
your father's sons shall bow down before you.

49:8–12. The disqualification of the first three tribes has opened the way to the advancement of the tribe of Judah. Although Judah was not the first-born, he is going to be given primacy, because his three older brothers have lost it on account of their sins. The oracle about Judah not only acclaims Judah's strength as like that of a lion, but announces that the royal sceptre will be held by this tribe until one comes whom the peoples will obey and who will bring peace and prosperity. This may contain an immediate reference to David and his successors, but the text itself points to a descendant of Judah who will be universal king.

The Hebrew term used to describe this descendant (*siloh*) has been interpreted by Jewish and Christian tradition in a messianic sense, linking it to other oracles about the dynasty of David (cf. 2 Sam 7:14; Is 9:5ff; Mic 5:1–3; Zech 9:9). In the light of the New Testament we can see what the oracle means: with David royalty in Israel will emerge from the tribe of Judah and will extend until the coming of the "Son of David", Jesus

Christ, in whom all the prophecies find fulfilment (cf. Mt 21:9).

In the words of v. 11, "he washes his garments in wine and his vesture in the blood of grapes," some Fathers saw an allusion to the passion of Christ. St Ambrose, for example, interprets the wine as being the blood of Christ and the "garments" as his sacred humanity: "garments are the flesh of Christ, who covers up the sins of all, who bears the crimes of all, who takes on the faults of all. The garments clothe everyone in an outfit of joy. He washed these garments in wine when, on being baptized in the Jordan, the Holy Spirit came down on him in the shape of a dove and stayed over him. [. . .] For Jesus washed his garments not to clean away any filth of his own (for he had none) but to clean away our filth. And in the blood of grapes he washed his tunic, that is, he cleansed men with his blood in the passion of his body. [. . .] And it is right to speak of grapes because he was hung like a bunch of them on the wood [of the cross]. He is the vine and he is the grape: the vine because he is fixed

---

gloria mea; / quia in furore suo occiderunt virum / et in voluntate sua subnervaverunt tauros. / ⁷Maledictus furor eorum, quia pertinax, / et indignatio eorum, quia dura! / Dividam eos in Iacob / et dispergam eos in Israel. / ⁸Iuda, te laudabunt fratres tui; / manus tua in cervicibus inimicorum tuorum; / adorabunt te filii patris tui. / ⁹Catulus leonis Iuda: / a praeda, fili mi, ascendisti; / requiescens accubuit

x. Or *glory*

⁹Judah is a lion's whelp;
from the prey, my son, you have gone up.
He stooped down, he couched as a lion,
and as a lioness; who dares rouse him up?
¹⁰The scepter shall not depart from Judah,
nor the ruler's staff from between his feet,
until he comes to whom it belongs;ʸ
and to him shall be the obedience of the peoples.
¹¹Binding his foal to the vine
and his ass's colt to the choice vine,
he washes his garments in wine
and his vesture in the blood of grapes;
¹²his eyes shall be red with wine,
and his teeth white with milk.

¹³Zebulun shall dwell at the shore of the sea;
he shall become a haven for ships,
and his border shall be at Sidon.

¹⁴Issachar is a strong ass,
crouching between the sheepfolds;
¹⁵he saw that a resting place was good,
and that the land was pleasant;
so he bowed his shoulder to bear,
and became a slave at forced labour.

Rev 5:5
Num 24:17
2 Sam 7:11–16
Is 9:5f; 11:1
Ezek 21:32
Mic 5:1–3
Zech 9:9
Heb 7:14

Mk 11:2
Rev 7:14; 19:13

to the wood; the grape because when his side was pierced by the lance, blood and water flowed out. Water as purification, blood as the ransom price. Through the water he washed us clean; through the blood he redeemed us" (*De benedictionem Patriarcharum*, 4, 24).

49:13. A reference to the fact that Zebulun settled on the coast, near Sidon (Phoenicia).

49:14–15. The tribe of Issachat will occupy the rich plain of Esdraelon in the valley of Jezreel. "The sheepfolds" may be a reference to the geography of that region between the hills of Galilee and those of Gilboa. The oracle may refer to the fact that this tribe was a vassal of the Canaanites prior to the conquest, because they preferred working for them in the rich plains to being shepherds in the hill country.

ut leo / et quasi leaena; quis suscitabit eum? / ¹⁰Non auferetur sceptrum de Iuda / et baculus ducis de pedibus eius, / donec veniat ille, cuius est, / et cui erit oboedientia gentium; / ¹¹ligans ad vineam pullum suum / et ad vitem filium asinae suae / lavabit in vino stolam suam / et in sanguine uvae pallium suum; / ¹²nigriores sunt oculi eius vino / et dentes eius lacte candidiores. / ¹³Zabulon in litore mari habitabit / et in statione navium, / pertingens usque ad Sidonem. / ¹⁴Issachar asinus fortis, / accubans inter caulas / ¹⁵vidit requiem quod esset bona, / et terram quod optima; / et supposuit umerum suum ad portandum / factusque est tributis serviens. / ¹⁶Dan iudicabit populum suum / sicut una tribuum Israel. / ¹⁷Fiat Dan

y. Syr Compare Tg: Heb *until Shiloh comes* or *until he comes to Shiloh*

2 Sam 20:18

¹⁶Dan shall judge his people
as one of the tribes of Israel.
¹⁷Dan shall be a serpent in the way,
a viper by the path,
that bites the horse's heels
so that his rider falls backward.

Is 25:9

¹⁸I wait for thy salvation, O LORD.

¹⁹Raiders^z shall raid Gad,
but he shall raid at their heels.

Deut 44:24

²⁰Asher's food shall be rich,
and he shall yield royal dainties.

²¹Naphtali is a hind let loose,
that bears comely fawns.^a

Deut 33:13–17

²²Joseph is a fruitful bough,
a fruitful bough by a spring;
his branches run over the wall.

The comparison with an ass is in no way disrespectful; on the contrary, it is meant to show his strength and constancy in work. Because of this and drawing on the fact that the name Issachar is connected with "hire, payment" (cf. 30:40), some Fathers see in this patriarch a prefigurement of Christ; others see him as standing for the good Christian. "Issachar means recompense," St Ambrose comments, "and therefore it refers to Christ who is our recompense, and through whom we merit the hope of eternal life not by means of gold or silver but by faith and devotion. [. . .] In order to call all nations to the grace of their resurrection (symbolized by the rich and fertile land), Christ offered his shoulders to the task, submitting to the cross in order to bear our sins" (*De benedictionibus Patriarcharum*, 6, 30–31).

49:16–21. The special features of each of these tribes is indicated by playing with the names of ancestors. The Fathers saw in these tribes features which likened them to Christ: Gad, because he was attacked, recalls Christ in his passion; Asher, with his abundance of bread, prefigures Christ in the Eucharist; Naphtali, who produces beautiful offspring, represents Christ preaching the Gospel.

49:22–26. One cannot help noticing how much is said about Joseph, presumably on account of the preceding chapters and the importance of the tribes of Ephraim and Manasseh, who occupied the central

---

coluber in via, / cerastes in semita, / mordens calcanea equi, / ut cadat ascensor eius retro. / ¹⁸Salutare tuum exspectabo, Domine! / ¹⁹Gad, latrones aggredientur eum, / ipse autem aggredietur calcaneum eorum. / ²⁰Aser, pinguis panis eius, / et praebebit delicias regales. / ²¹Nephthali cerva emissa, / dans cornua pulchra. / ²²Arbor fructifera Ioseph, / arbor fructifera super fontem: / rami transcendunt murum. / ²³Sed exasperaverunt eum et iurgati sunt, / et adversati sunt illi habentes iacula. / ²⁴Et con-

z. Heb *gedud*, a raiding troop   **a.** Or *who gives beautiful words*

²³The archers fiercely attacked him,
  shot at him, and harassed him sorely;
²⁴yet his bow remained unmoved,
  his arms[b] were made agile
  by the hands of the Mighty One of Jacob
  (by the name of the Shepherd, the Rock of Israel),

²⁵by the God of your father who will help you,   Gen 17:1
  by God Almighty[u] who will bless you
  with blessings of heaven above,
blessings of the deep that couches beneath,
  blessings of the breasts and of the womb.
²⁶The blessings of your father
  are mighty beyond the blessings of the eternal mountains,[c]
  the bounties of the everlasting hills;
may they be on the head of Joseph,
  and on the brow of him who was separate from his brothers.

²⁷Benjamin is a ravenous wolf,
  in the morning devouring the prey,
  and at even dividing the spoil."

²⁸All these are the twelve tribes of Israel; and this is what their
father said to them as he blessed them, blessing each with the
blessing suitable to him.

---

part of Palestine. On El-Shaddai (cf. RSV note **u**) as the name of God, cf. the note on 17:1. On Joseph as a figure of Jesus Christ, cf. the note on 37:5–11.

49:27. The warlike and wild character of the tribe of Benjamin can be seen from the history of that tribe as recounted in Judges 3:15ff; 5:14; 19–20.

49:29–32. This repeats, in different words, the information given in 47:29–31,

but now with express reference to the life and burial of the previous patriarchs, Abraham (cf. 23:1–20; 25:9) and Isaac (cf. 25:27-29). This is the only place where it is mentioned that Abraham, Rebekah and Leah were buried here. The passage acts as a reminder that they belong where their ancestors are, and that they must return there. The scene is set for the theme of the book of Exodus. Verse 32 is missing from the Vulgate Latin version.

fractus est arcus eorum, / et dissoluti sunt nervi brachiorum eorum / per manus Potentis Iacob, / per nomen Pastoris, Lapidis Israel. / ²⁵Deus patris tui erit adiutor tuus, / et Omnipotens benedicet tibi / benedictionibus caeli desuper, / benedictionibus abyssi iacentis deorsum, / benedictionibus uberum et vulvae. / ²⁶Benedictiones patris tui confortatae sunt / super benedictiones montium aeternorum, / desiderium collium antiquorum; / fiant in capite Ioseph / et in vertice nazaraei inter fratres suos. / ²⁷Beniamin lupus rapax; / mane comedet praedam / et vespere dividet spolia». / ²⁸Omnes hi in tribubus

b. Heb *the arms of his hands* **u.** Heb *El Shaddai* **c.** Compare Gk: Heb *of my progenitors to*

The death of Jacob

29Then he charged them, and said to them, "I am to be gathered to my people; bury me with my fathers in the cave that is in the field of Ephron the Hittite, 30in the cave that is in the field at Machpelah, to the east of Mamre, in the land of Canaan, which Abraham bought with the field from Ephron the Hittite to possess as a burying place. 31There they buried Abraham and Sarah his wife; there they buried Isaac and Rebekah his wife; and there I buried Leah—32the field and the cave that is in it were purchased from the Hittites." 33When Jacob finished charging his sons, he drew up his feet into the bed, and breathed his last, and was gathered to his people.

Gen 23:1–20;
25:9; 35:27–29

Gen 48:2
Acts 7:15

Jacob's funeral*

Gen 46:4

50 1Then Joseph fell on his father's face, and wept over him, and kissed him. 2And Joseph commanded his servants the

---

*50:1–26. In this final chapter further stress is put on the greatness of the figure of Jacob by the account of that great mourning (vv. 1–14); and the meaning is clearly revealed of the entire story of Joseph and his brothers in the context of God's plans (vv. 15–26).

50:1–14. The description of the burial of Jacob includes aspects of Egyptian customs such as mummification (necessary, given the fact that the body had to travel a distance); also an explanation is provided of the names of some places which cannot nowadays be identified, such as "Abel-mizraim", which means "mourning of Egypt". The passage prefigures the later ascent of Israel, as a people, from Egypt to the promised land.

Joseph, and his brothers with him, appear as models of obedience and filial devotion to their father. Joseph has already shown himself to be a son full of love and reverence towards Jacob and of concern for his brothers. Now he spares no effort, no expense, to fulfil his father's last wish and to render him the honours due him as Joseph's father and the father of the whole people of Israel. Joseph's behaviour anticipates, in a natural way, what will later be laid down in the fourth commandment of the Law of God. In this connexion St Josemaría Escrivá, reminds us: "The commandment to love our parents belongs to both natural law and divine positive law, and I have always called it a 'most sweet precept'. Do not neglect your obligation to love your parents more each day, to mortify yourself for them, to pray for them and to be grateful to them for all the good you owe them" (*The Forge*, 21).

Israel duodecim. Haec locutus est eis pater suus benedixitque singulis benedictionibus propriis. 29Et praecepit eis dicens: «Ego congregor ad populum meum; sepelite me cum patribus meis in spelunca Machpela, quae est in agro Ephron Hetthaei 30contra Mambre in terra Chanaan, quam emit Abraham cum agro ab Ephron Hetthaeo in possessionem sepulcri; 31ibi sepelierunt eum et Saram uxorem eius, ibi sepultus est Isaac cum Rebecca coniuge sua, ibi et Lia condita iacet». 32Finitisque mandatis, quibus filios instruebat, collegit pedes suos super lectulum et obiit; appositusque est ad populum suum. 1Ioseph ruit super faciem patris flens et deosculans eum. 2Praecepitque servis suis medicis, ut aromatibus condirent patrem. 3Quibus iussa explentibus, transierunt quadraginta dies; iste quippe mos erat

physicians to embalm his father. So the physicians embalmed Israel; [3]forty days were required for it, for so many are required for embalming. And the Egyptians wept for him seventy days.

[4]And when the days of weeping for him were past, Joseph spoke to the household of Pharaoh, saying, "If now I have found favor in your eyes, speak, I pray you, in the ears of Pharaoh, saying, [5]My father made me swear, saying, 'I am about to die: in my tomb which I hewed out for myself in the land of Canaan, there shall you bury me.' Now therefore let me go up, I pray you, and bury my father; then I will return." [6]And Pharaoh answered, Gen 47:29–31 "Go up, and bury your father, as he made you swear." [7]So Joseph went up to bury his father; and with him went up all the servants of Pharaoh, the elders of his household, and all the elders of the land of Egypt, [8]as well as all the household of Joseph, his brothers, and his father's household; only their children, their flocks, and their herds were left in the land of Goshen. [9]And there went up with him both chariots and horsemen; it was a very great company. [10]When they came to the threshing floor of Atad, which is beyond the Jordan, they lamented there with a very great and sorrowful lamentation; and he made a mourning for his father seven days. [11]When the inhabitants of the land, the Canaanites, saw the mourning on the threshing floor of Atad, they said, "This is a grievous mourning to the Egyptians." Therefore the place was named Abel-mizraim;[d] it is beyond the Jordan. [12]Thus his sons did for him as he had commanded them; [13]for his sons carried him to Acts 7:16 the land of Canaan, and buried him in the cave of the field at Mach-pelah, to the east of Mamre, which Abraham bought with the field from Ephron the Hittite, to possess as a burying place. [14]After he had buried his father, Joseph returned to Egypt with his brothers and all who had gone up with him to bury his father.

---

cadaverum conditorum. Flevitque eum Aegyptus septuaginta diebus. [4]Et, expleto planctus tempore, locutus est Ioseph ad familiam pharaonis: «Si inveni gratiam in conspectu vestro, loquimini in auribus pharaonis, [5]eo quod pater meus adiuraverit me dicens: 'En morior; in sepulcro meo, quod fodi mihi in terra Chanaan, sepelies me'; ascendam nunc et sepeliam patrem meum ac revertar». [6]Dixitque ei pharao: «Ascende et sepeli patrem tuum, sicut adiuratus es». [7]Quo ascendente, ierunt cum eo omnes servi pharaonis, senes domus eius cunctique maiores natu terrae Aegypti, [8]domus Ioseph cum fratribus suis, absque parvulis et gregibus atque armentis, quae dereliquerant in terra Gessen. [9]Habuit quoque in comitatu currus et equites; et facta est turba non modica. [10]Veneruntque ad Gorenatad (*id est Aream rhamni*), quae sita est trans Iordanem; ubi celebrantes exsequias planctu magno atque vehementi impleverunt septem dies. [11]Quod cum vidissent habitatores terrae Chanaan, dixerunt: «Planctus magnus est iste Aegyptiis»; et idcirco vocatum est nomen loci illius Abelmesraim (*id est Planctus Aegypti*). [12]Fecerunt ergo filii Iacob, sicut praeceperat eis; [13]et portantes eum in terram Chanaan sepelierunt eum in spelunca Machpela, quam emerat Abraham cum agro in possessionem sepulcri ab Ephron Hetthaeo contra faciem Mambre. [14]Reversusque est Ioseph in Aegyptum cum fratribus suis et omni comitatu,

d. That is *meadow* (or *mourning*) *of Egypt*

After the death of Jacob

Gen 37:12–30; 45:3 [15]When Joseph's brothers saw that their father was dead, they said, "It may be that Joseph will hate us and pay us back for all the evil which we did to him." [16]So they sent a message to Joseph, saying, "Your father gave this command before he died, [17]'Say to Joseph, Forgive, I pray you, the transgression of your brothers and their sin, because they did evil to you.' And now, we pray you, forgive the transgression of the servants of the God of your father." Joseph wept when they spoke to him. [18]His brothers also came and fell down before him, and said, "Behold, we are your servants." [19]But Joseph said to them, "Fear not, for am I in the place Rom 8:28 of God? [20]As for you, you meant evil against me; but God meant it for good, to bring it about that many people should be kept alive, as they are today. [21]So do not fear; I will provide for you and your little ones." Thus he reassured them and comforted them.

[22]So Joseph dwelt in Egypt, he and his father's house; and Joseph lived a hundred and ten years. [23]And Joseph saw

---

50:15–21. In spite of the marks of fraternity Joseph has shown his brothers, when they lose their common father they also seem to lose their sense of fraternity. They continue to see things from a very human perspective; whereas Joseph has a more supernatural outlook, which also extends to his hope in the future (cf. v. 24). In this way the book of Genesis concludes its account of the origins of the world, of mankind and of the people of God, leaving the way open to a new and decisive intervention by God—the great deliverance from Egypt, which the book of Exodus will recount.

50:22–26. The Lord has blessed Joseph with a long life and the joy of seeing his great-grandchildren. Even as he dies, Joseph continues to think about his people, whose destiny (he reminds them) is the fulfilment of the promise God made to his ancestors. Joseph reaffirms that that promise will be kept, and he feels that he has a part in it. Therefore, he makes them swear that his bones will be taken up from Egypt to the promised land. And so the book of Genesis comes to an end, by showing Joseph's faith in the divine promises and inviting the reader, no matter what happens, to keep alive his or her hope in God's active help.

---

sepulto patre. [15]Quo mortuo, timentes fratres eius et mutuo colloquentes: «Ne forte memor sit iniuriae, quam passus est, et reddat nobis omne malum, quod fecimus», [16]mandaverunt ei dicentes: «Pater tuus praecepit nobis, antequam moreretur, [17]ut haec tibi verbis illius diceremus: 'Obsecro, ut obliviscaris sceleris fratrum tuorum et peccati atque malitiae, quam exercuerunt in te'. Nos quoque oramus, ut servis Dei patris tui dimittas iniquitatem hanc». Quibus auditis, flevit Ioseph. [18]Veneruntque ad eum fratres sui et proni coram eo dixerunt: «Servi tui sumus». [19]Quibus ille respondit: «Nolite timere. Num Dei possumus resistere voluntati? [20]Vos cogitastis de malum; sed Deus vertit illud in bonum, ut exaltaret me, sicut in praesentiarum cernitis, et salvos faceret multos populos. [21]Nolite timere: ego pascam vos et parvulos vestros». Consolatusque est eos et blande ac leniter est locutus. [22]Et habitavit in Aegypto cum omni domo patris sui; vixitque centum decem annis [23]et vidit Ephraim filios usque ad

Ephraim's children of the third generation; the children also of Machir the son of Manasseh were born upon Joseph's knees.

The death of Joseph

[24]And Joseph said to his brothers, "I am about to die; but God will visit you, and bring you up out of this land to the land which he swore to Abraham, to Isaac, and to Jacob." [25]Then Joseph took an oath of the sons of Israel, saying, "God will visit you, and you shall carry up my bones from here." [26]So Joseph died, being a hundred and ten years old; and they embalmed him, and he was put in a coffin in Egypt.

Gen 12:7
Ex 13:19
Josh 24:32
Heb 11:22

tertiam generationem; filii quoque Machir filii Manasse nati sunt in genibus Ioseph. [24]Quibus transactis, locutus est fratribus suis: «Post mortem meam Deus visitabit vos et ascendere vos faciet de terra ista ad terram, quam iuravit Abraham, Isaac et Iacob». [25]Cumque adiurasset eos atque dixisset: «Deus visitabit vos; asportate ossa mea vobiscum de loco isto», [26]mortuus est, expletis centum decem vitae suae annis. Et conditus aromatibus repositus est in loculo in Aegypto.

231

EXODUS

Introduction

"Exodus" is the title the Greek translators gave to the second book of the Pentateuch, a title later adopted by the Latin version and by translations into modern languages. The Jews, who usually call the books of the Bible by their opening words, call this book *"We'elleh shemot"* ("These are the names") or simply *"Shemot"* ("The Names"). "Exodus" means "leaving", "going out"; it applies particularly to the content of the first fifteen chapters of the book which tell how the Israelites managed to get out of Egypt; however, the word is perfectly suitable for the whole book, because it tells about how the Israelites escaped from slavery and gained their freedom, ceasing to be subject to Egypt and accepting the Covenant established on Sinai.

1. STRUCTURE AND CONTENT

The book of Exodus is made up of a number of interlinked accounts and lists of regulations which record most of the history of the children of Israel—from the time the incipient tribes settled in Egypt (thus it dovetails with the end of Genesis: cf. Ex 1:1–22) to their extended sojourn at the foot of Mount Sinai (which is where the book of Numbers finds them). The accounts cover the most important events in the history of Israel—its slavery in Egypt, the birth of Moses its leader, the signs God worked to release them from repression, the institution of the Passover, the making of the Covenant, the first apostasy and the establishment of religious worship. The laws assembled in the book of Exodus constitute the main corpus of law in the Pentateuch, and they cover the religious, moral and social life of Israel.

The book is usually divided into two main parts in line with the two key events it covers:

PART ONE: THE DEPARTURE FROM EGYPT (1:1—18:27) This is the epic account of the Exodus; it begins with the children of Israel in Egypt and follows them until they reach the foot of Mount Sinai (chaps. 1–18).

(1) The narrative begins with a short summary of the life of the tribes in Egypt—how they prospered (1:1–7) and their first setbacks (1:8–22).

(2) The following chapters contain an account of the calling of Moses, which goes from his infancy in the court of Egypt to his first interview with

235

the pharaoh on behalf of his people. It begins with his birth and rescue from the Nile by the pharaoh's daughter, and his upbringing at court (2:1–10). After killing an Egyptian and trying to make peace between two of his countrymen, Moses flees to Midian (2:11–25); there God reveals himself to him in the burning bush and tells him his name (3:1–22). In charging Moses with a mission to save his people, God gives him the power to work wonders (4:1–9) and designates Aaron as his spokesman (4:10–17). On his way back from Midian to Egypt, Moses and his son undergo circumcision, and Aaron and Moses meet in the desert (4:18–31). After this, the first interview with the pharaoh takes place; the pharaoh rejects Moses' request to let the people go into the desert for a religious feast: in fact, instead of his letting them off work for the occasion, he makes their work even heavier (5:1–18). Moses then pleads with God to come to the people's aid (5:19—16:1). The text then returns to the subject of the calling of Moses, and his mission (6:2–13). After giving details of the genealogy of Aaron and Moses we come to a new account of the interview with the pharaoh, in which the plagues are announced (6:14—7:7).

(3) The next five chapters deal with the plagues. In the course of the narrative, the theological meaning of each plague is underlined: thus, the magicians appear only in the account of the first three plagues (the waters of the Nile turning red, the frogs, and the gnats: 7:14—8:15); the next three (the flies, the cattle epidemic and the plague of ulcers prepare the way for the great storm which is recounted as a theophany of God in the face of which the pharaoh acknowledges God's sovereignty for the first time (9:13–35); and with the last three (the locusts, the darkness, and the death of the first-born) the pharaoh gradually comes round until eventually (after the death of the first-born) he gives in (10:1—11:10).

(4) In connexion with the last plague the rules for the Passover are spelled out. These rules deal with its institution (12:1–14), the celebration of the days of the unleavened bread (12:15–20), and various other instructions (12:21–28). We are then told about the death of the first-born (12:29–32) and the preparations for leaving Egypt (12:33–42), as well as new regulations about the Passover, the unleavened bread and the first born (12:43—13:16).

(5) The departure from Egypt is described with all due formality. It is all depicted as something planned by the Lord (13:17—14:4). Even though the Egyptians are in hot pursuit, the people of Israel manage to cross the Red Sea with the aid of divine marvels (15:1–21). The triumphal Hymn or Canticle of Miriam celebrates the wondrous deeds of the Lord (15:1–21).

(6) This part of Exodus reaches its climax with an account of the stages prior to their reaching the wilderness of Sinai—the episode of the bitter waters of Marah (15:22–27), the prodigy of the manna and the quails (16:1–36), the water from the rock (17:1–7), and the first battle and victory over the Amalekites (17:8–15). It ends with Jethro's visit to Moses and appointment of the judges (18:1–27).

PART TWO. THE PEOPLE OF ISRAEL IN THE SINAI (19:1—40:38) This deals with the main events that take place at Sinai—the making of the Covenant, the promulgation of the laws and precepts, and the building of the sanctuary:

(7) The theophany of the Lord is recounted in a solemn fashion which stresses its drama, and sets the scene for the Covenant and the promulgation of the Ten Commandments (19:1—20:21).

(8) The Code of the Covenant is then recorded as being part of the corpus of laws that God gives to Moses. The first section covers ordinances about worship (20:22–26), slaves, and penalties for injuries (21:1—22:16). These are followed by other regulations about social morality, trials, and treatment of enemies (22:17—23:9). Finally, it deals with sabbatical years, the sabbath and other cultic matters (23:10–19). It ends with a number of warnings and promises (23:20–33).

(9) The account of the theophany at Sinai concludes with the Ritual of the Covenant, which includes the rite of ratification (24:1–11) and Moses going up the sacred mountain again and staying there forty days and forty nights (24:12–18),

(10) There follows a section about rules to do with the Sanctuary. The first of these cover its construction and sacred objects (25:1—27:21); the section then goes on to deal with ministers and their roles in worship (28:1—31:18).

(11) Then comes an account of the most serious instance of apostasy to take place in the desert. This aberration consisted in the people adoring a golden calf, and it brought down the wrath of God (32:1–10). Moses intercedes for the people, but he fails to deflect God's punishment. The calf is destroyed (32:11–24), and the guilty die at the hands of the Levites (32:25–29). Moses again intercedes with the Lord, who, as a punishment for the sin, decides that only his angel and not He himself will accompany the people on their journey (32:30–35). After this episode the order is given to break camp and the Tent of Meeting is described (33:1–11). Finally, after Moses intercedes with God once more, He agrees to accompany the people personally (33:12–17). The section ends with the account of Moses' vision of the glory of the Lord (33:18–23).

(12) After the apostasy, everything had to be done all over again, as can be seen from the account of the renewing of the Covenant. This consisted of the handing over of the new tables of the Law (34:1–9), the so-called Ritual of the Covenant (34:10–28) and the appearance of Moses before the people, his face shining (34:29–35).

(13) The book ends with an account about how the rules for the construction of the sanctuary were followed in exact detail (35:1—36:38), as also those about the sacred objects (37:1—38:31) and the ministers (39:1–43). Once the construction and furnishing are completed, the sanctuary is consecrated (40:1–15); Moses does things exactly as the Lord directed him (40:16–33). By

way of epilogue, there is a short recapitulation about the protective function of the cloud that covered the tent of meeting: it is a sign that God is with his people and it is he who is leading them on their pilgrimage through the desert.

2. HISTORICAL BACKGROUND

The history recounted in Exodus should not be regarded as an exact, detailed chronicle. It is more a history of salvation which tells how the Lord made the "sons of Jacob" into the "people of God", that is, a people who have become part of the salvific mystery: he has chosen them to be the first fruits of salvation; he has established a Covenant of love with them and in his providence takes special care of them. The sacred writer has expounded this supernatural truth dressing events in a language of worship, theology and epic poetry. It is not always easy therefore to work out what the exact chain of events is.

What is certainly true (as even a non-religious historian will acknowledge) is that this book is telling us about key stages in the history of the people of Israel—(1) that the descendants of the patriarchs suffered ignominious oppression during the time they spent in the Nile delta; (2) that they managed to escape from there in very remarkable circumstances; (3) that during their lengthy stay in the desert region they developed a "national self-consciousness" with the help of Yahweh ("the Lord"), whom they acknowledged as the one true God; and (4) in the course of this remarkable adventure one figure stood out, that of Moses, who gave them cohesion and leadership and who was their great teacher.

(a) *Dating the Exodus*
The Israelites most probably left Egypt in the 13th century BC, the time when the main buildings of ancient Egypt were being constructed. In recent times historians and archeologists have added greatly to our knowledge of that culture; they tell us that there were thirty-one dynasties of pharaohs, divided over three empires: the Old Empire (2800–2300 BC) which was at its zenith in the third and fourth dynasties; the Middle Empire (2300–1500 BC) whose high point was in the eleventh to seventeenth dynasties; and the New Empire (1500–1000 BC). It was in this last period that Egypt reached the zenith of its power and prestige. Pharaohs Seti I (1291–1279) and Rameses II (1279–1212) came to the throne at a time of peace and stability and were responsible for important religious and cultural initiatives, the most outstanding of which included monumental buildings; in the construction of these, resident foreigners were used, Semites in particular.

One needs to remember that in the 18th–16th centuries BC the Hyksos, who were probably Canaanites and Ammorites from the general region of Syria and Palestine, invaded Egypt and then dominated it for over one hundred years.

The Egyptians maintained a resistance against them until around 1500 BC, when they managed to expel or suppress them. It may have been during these centuries that the descendants of the patriarchs arrived from Canaan and settled down in Egypt in very favourable circumstances.

From this date on (1550 BC) the enslavement of the Israelites probably began. The statement in Exodus 1:8 (to the effect that "There arose a new king over Egypt, who did not know Joseph") may be a reference to the early years of the New Empire.

The book of Exodus, which makes no reference to dates, likewise gives no names of pharaohs. The only reference which may give a guide is in 1 Kings 6:1, which speaks about four hundred and eighty years as being the length of time between when the people of Israel came out of Egypt and the building of Solomon's temple. Since Solomon's reign began in 960 BC, this means the Exodus would have taken place around 1440 BC. However, the figure given in 1 Kings rather looks as though it is saying that there were twelve generations (each of forty years) in the span; in other words, there is nothing exact about it.

However, in Exodus 1:11 there is mention of the store-cities, in the building of which Israelites were involved; this seems to be a firmer piece of information and it leads one to suppose that it was in the thirteenth century that the people of Israel left Egypt. The kind of building programme promoted by Seti I and Rameses II had no parallels in previous centuries.

On the other hand, if one accepts that the Exodus began early in the thirteenth century, the conquest of Palestine must be set some forty years later, that is, in the second half of the same century, the date archeologists give for the destruction of many cities of Canaan, such as Lachish, and Jazer.

(b) *The figure of Moses*

The structure of Israelite religion and the socio-political organization of the people stem from and hinge on Moses. There was once a time (when rationalism and positivism were very much in vogue) when a question-mark was put against whether there was ever any such person as Moses. The accepted opinion nowadays is that there is sufficient archeological and historical evidence for saying that he did exist. The source of our knowledge of this distinguished personality is the book of Exodus. That book, written from the standpoint of faith, portrays him as a leader and guide, a prophet and teacher, and the prototype of Israel, since his own life was marked by the same ups and downs as the people had to cope with.

As a leader and guide, Moses—always at the Lord's bidding and under his protection—manages to overcome, firstly, opposition from the Israelites themselves, and then the stubbornness of the pharaoh, and later still the forces of nature. As regards his leadership, the best example is his struggle to keep up the people's spirits and to counter their lack of faith. This begins when Moses is still living in the court of the pharaoh (cf. 2:14), it springs up again when he

puts the Exodus project to the people (5:21), and it crops up again when they start complaining in the wilderness (cf. 15:22–24; 17:1–17). Gradually Moses manages to get them to follow him and to accept the Covenant of the Lord willingly and to take on board the requirements it lays down (on a number of occasions they make a promise to this effect: "All the words which the Lord has spoken we will do": 24:3, 7; 19:8; 25:9).

Future generations will acknowledge Moses as prophet and teacher (cf. Deut 18:18; Hos 12:14), because the Law reached them through him. The sacred writers place on Moses' lips all the rules and regulations to do with the moral, religious and social life of the people. In the book of Exodus three codes or groups of important laws are included. These codes may have been redacted before the book was composed; from very early on, the various traditions attributed them to Moses. They are the moral Decalogue or ten commandments (20:1–17), the Code of the Covenant (20:22—23:33) and the Ritual Code (34:14–26). The books of Numbers and Leviticus attribute to Moses the laws that they contain; and Deuteronomy takes the form of a long discourse spoken by Moses.

But, first and foremost Moses is regarded and projected as a model for his people, its paradigm. His life is an image of the life of Israel: his remarkable birth, "drawn out of the water" (2:10), prefigures the birth of the people in the waters of the Red Sea; his pleasant childhood in the pharaoh's court (2:10) is like the easy years the sons of Israel spent in Egypt (1:6); his flight, which brought him to live as a stranger in Midian (2:11–22) is also an image of the persecution of the people. Consequently, Moses' faith in God's design (4:1–17) will be the basis of the faith of the entire people.

In this sort of way the sacred writer points up how closely Moses is linked to his people. He is not just an intermediary: he is their representative before God. From this angle, too, he is a figure of Jesus Christ who, having taken on human nature, opened the way of salvation to all mankind through the waters of Baptism.

3. COMPOSITION

The basic facts recounted in the book of Exodus were retained in the folk-memory of the people and celebrated on the great feast-days; they were sung about in hymns and generally passed on as being an essential element of their faith. By recalling, as they did, the history of the origins of the nation, those who eventually settled down in Israel (around the 13th century BC) gave religious meaning to the institutions, laws and customs that they practised, gradually linking them to the original events of the Exodus and the desert years. This process, which took place by a special providence of God, is all consolidated in Exodus. To explain how it (and the rest of the Pentateuch) came to be written, exegetes over the past hundred years talk about there being a number of known sources or traditions. As regards this book, there seems to be more evi-

dence of the presence of the "Yahwistic" and "Priestly" traditions.[1] But we should also bear in mind that "codes" of law probably existed from much earlier on and were passed on quite independently of the traditions just mentioned.

Even though the book draws on a diversity of sources, there is a marked unity about it: there are repetitions (as we shall point out), but the narrative thread is maintained throughout. Undoubtedly the last editor was skilled at collecting old traditions and blending them skilfully into a harmonious whole, which, without betraying the facts, focuses on the key theological truths—the saving intervention by God, the election of the people of Israel, the doctrinal and moral implications of the Covenant, and the purpose and meaning of worship.

4. MESSAGE

The whole book is designed to exalt the greatness of God who has done so many wondrous deeds, and to stress the special nature of the people of Israel, the beneficiary of so many blessings. The choice of Israel, the Covenant and worship are the three things which constitute the structure of the people's faith and religious life.

(a) *The choice of Israel*
The greatest salvific act in the history of Israel, and the necessary point of reference for explaining God's other salvific interventions, is the deliverance of Israel from bondage in Egypt. Through this act, God—entirely on his own initiative—made the descendants of Jacob into a free people. In the light of this great event future generations will come to see that their existence as a people was the outcome of a very special divine intervention, comparable to the act of creation. This is why, in the Old Testament, creation is depicted as an act of election-salvation (cf. Is 45:12–13) and why, in turn, every salvific act can be described as a creational act: God chose to produce out of chaos such things as are created; from among these, he chose man; from among men, he chose the people of Israel.

The narrative of the salvific events God brought about in Exodus is interwoven with an account of the people's acts of infidelity: first, there is their failure to believe what Moses says; then there is the murmuring against Moses and Aaron in the wilderness; later on, the worshipping of the golden calf, etc. These sins provoke the Lord's anger so much that he is on the point of wiping the entire people out. However, time and again he forgives them and confines himself to punishing them—with punishments which are also salvific actions because they show that it is sin that leads the people back into a situation of slavery and subjection. Election-salvation is the way the living and true God behaves towards his people, and it prepares the way for complete revelation, when all mankind is called in Christ to form part of the New People of God.

1. Cf. "Introduction to the Pentateuch", pp 19–21, above.

(b) *The Covenant*

The choosing of Israel from among the nations was equivalent to establishing it as the people of God by means of the Covenant. Already in chapter 6 it is spelled out that their liberation from slavery and oppression has this as its aim: "I will take you for my people, and I will be your God" (6:7). In the rite of the Covenant as described in chapters 19–24 (and in its renewal in chapter 34) we find phrases like "keeping the covenant" (19:5), "the blood of the covenant" (24:7), "the words of the covenant" (34:28), etc. The Covenant does not just mean the imposition of certain rules by God, which would mean a unilateral requirement to obey certain laws coming from outside, designed to regulate the religious and moral life of the people. Nor is it just the commitment the Israelites made to God to put certain basic laws into practice. It is first and foremost a bilateral pact whereby God, who is the one who takes the initiative, proposes to the people that they and he commit themselves to carry out certain obligations; for his part, God will protect Israel in a special way (it will be his people); and Israel, for its part, will acknowledge him as its God, the one God, and will obey all his commandments. The Covenant, therefore, is an event which regulates the religious, moral and social life of the members of the people, but it affects, above all, their innermost heart and it is what makes them the people of God, because it shows the special relationship the Lord has with them.

The term "covenant", in Hebrew *berit*, seems to mean "between-two", that is, a mutual agreement between two persons. It is likely that the way the establishment of the Covenant at Sinai is described is inspired not so much by private pacts such as those described in the book of Genesis between Jacob and Laban (cf. Gen 31:41) or between Abraham and his neighbours (Gen 14:13), as by the vassalage pacts which sealed the peace between peoples. The (extant) wording of some pacts from the second millennium BC has many similarities with the wording recorded in Exodus and in other books of the Bible. However, it is worth pointing out that the Covenant of Sinai is different in this respect: the Sinai Covenant includes the moral Decalogue (20:1–17), the Code of the Covenant (20:22—23:19) and the Ritual of the Code (34:17–26), that is, it regulates all aspects of the people's life, and its essence is that, by that Covenant, God made Israel "a kingdom of priests and a holy nation" (19:6). It is not just a peace pact or a vassalage agreement that is being sealed, but a pact which makes it a people of the utmost dignity.

The Covenant will be constantly renewed in Israel's liturgy, and the prophets are always reminding the people about it; when they break it, God himself will restore it (cf. Jer 31:31–35). In the fullness of time, Jesus Christ will seal with his blood the new and eternal Covenant (cf. Heb 8:6–13).

(c) *Worship*

Religious organization and religious worship had immense importance in Israel. The main body of prescriptions about worship is to be found in the

book of Exodus. Like the rest of the laws, these were regarded as having Moses as their author, even though many of them seem to reflect the splendour of the liturgy in the temple of Jerusalem during the period of the monarchy. These laws fall into three main groups—Passover, the festivals or feasts, and the sanctuary and its institutions.

The *Passover*, which is mentioned in the Ritual Code (cf. 34:25) and in the Code of the Covenant (cf. 23:13–19 and 34:17–26) is fully described in chapter 12 where the institution, ritual and meaning of this sacrifice are attributed to Moses. The immolation of the lamb and family participation in the feast are indicative of the simplicity of a sacrifice typical of nomadic peoples; but for generation after generation it constituted a vivid memorial of the liberation from Egypt. As time went by ceremonies grew up, giving the people a deep appreciation of the Passover, and these also are recorded in the Exodus account; they made the Passover the most typical of all Israel's sacrifices.

The *feasts* and the other rules to do with worship (cf. 23:13–19 and 34:17–26) are described in fairly simple language—which is indicative of their antiquity. Although some of these rites and even some of the feasts existed in Canaan before the Israelites came back from Egypt, only in Israel did they acquire their specific religious character. They all acknowledge the Lord as the only God and they recall and re-enact the wondrous events of the Exodus.

The *sanctuary*, its institutions and its ministers are regulated by prescriptions recorded in chapters 25–31. Here again elements from the desert period are mixed up with other much later ones—some even from after the Babylonian exile (6th century BC). But all are treated as ordinances from the Lord or from Moses, to show their obligatory and sacred character.

These brief remarks, which will be expanded upon in the notes, help to show how elaborate the religious life of Israel was; and they are also the things that the book of Exodus gives pride of place to, over and above exactness in dating or topography.

5. EXODUS IN THE OLD AND THE NEW TESTAMENT

The salvific events recounted in the book of Exodus constitute the foundation of Israelite history and religion; they are things which the people will keep alive in their memory. Phrases like "God brought Israel out of Egypt" or "God brought Israel out of Egypt with his powerful hand and his outstretched arm" occur more than seventy-five times in the Old Testament.

When the Bible wants to draw a contrast between the blessings of God and the sins of the people, it always evokes the Exodus and the desert as a sign of God's special love: "I brought you up out of the land of Egypt, and led you forty years in the wilderness [. . .]. But you commanded the prophets, saying, 'You shall not prophesy' " (Amos 2:10–12; cf. Amos 3:1–2). The biblical texts

also reflect the fact that God's choice of Israel is enduring: "When Israel was a child, I loved him, and out of Egypt I called my son" (cf. Hos 11:1). The memory of the Exodus stirs them to repentance: "O my people, what have I done to you? In what have I wearied you? Answer me! For I brought you up from the land of Egypt, and redeemed you from the house of bondage" (Mic 6:3–4; cf. Jer 2:5–6). The Exodus is, therefore, the point of departure for praising the greatness and powerful love of the Lord: "He smote the first-born of Egypt. [. . .] and brought Israel out from among them, for his steadfast love endures for ever" (Ps 136:10–11; cf. Ps 78; 105; 106; 114; Wis 16–19; etc.).

When it comes to describing the dire consequences of the Assyrian invasion (721 BC) and the deportation to Babylon (587 BC), bondage in Egypt is the benchmark: "They shall return to the land of Egypt, and Assyria shall be their king because they have refused to return to me" (Hos 11:5). But the Exodus is above all, the ground of their hope, for God, who did such wonders in bringing them out of Egypt, is ready to do them again in order to bring about a new and more enduring deliverance. Therefore, the return from exile in Babylon will be described as a glorious new exodus: "Thus says the Lord, who makes a way in the sea, [. . .] 'Remember not the former things. [. . .] Behold, I am doing a new thing. [. . .] I will make a way in the wilderness and rivers in the desert. [. . .] The people whom I formed for myself (will) declare my praises" (Is 43:16–21; cf. 48:24; 52:10–12; etc.). Since the Exodus is seen as being like creation, the return from the Babylonian captivity, described as a new exodus, is also equated to a new creation (cf. Is 44:24–28; 45:12–13; 51:9–11).

The New Testament, too, contains many references to the Exodus. In St Matthew's Gospel Jesus is portrayed as a new Moses: to him are applied the words of Hosea: "Out of Egypt have I called my son" (Mt 2:15). Christ will spend forty days in the wilderness (cf. Mt 4:2), which is evocative of the forty years the people spent in the desert and the forty days Moses spent on Mount Sinai (cf. Ex 24:18). The beatitudes are enunciated on the Mount (cf. Mt 5:1) in the same sort of way as the Law of Moses was promulgated on Sinai; and the transfiguration will take place on a mountain (cf. Mt 17:1–8).

St Paul, for his part, will recall many of the wonders of the Exodus, seeing them as a figure of things in the new economy of salvation: the manna is a figure of the Eucharist, and the rock from which Moses caused water to spring is a figure of Christ (cf. 1 Cor 11:1–5). The Covenant of Sinai prefigured the Covenant established by Christ in his blood (cf. 1 Cor 11:24–25); the sanctuary and the form of worship used in the wilderness are a pale shadow of what obtains in heaven (cf. Heb 8:5). Many other events will later be evoked as figures of the new economy, in line with the words of St Paul who has this to say about Exodus events: "Now these things happened to them as a warning, but they were written down for our instruction, upon whom the end of the ages has come" (1 Cor 10:11).

PART ONE

The Departure from Egypt

1. THE SONS OF ISRAEL IN EGYPT

The prosperity of the sons of Israel in Egypt

Gen 46:1–27
Acts 7:14–17

1 ¹These are the names of the sons of Israel who came to Egypt with Jacob, each with his household: ²Reuben, Simeon, Levi, and Judah, ³Issachar, Zebulun, and Benjamin, ⁴Dan and Naphtali, Gad and Asher. ⁵All the offspring of Jacob were seventy persons; Joseph was already in Egypt. ⁶Then Joseph died, and all his brothers, and all that generation. ⁷But the descendants of Israel were fruitful and increased greatly; they multiplied and grew exceedingly strong; so that the land was filled with them.

Gen 46:27
Deut 10:22
Acts 7:15
Gen 1:27
Ps 105:24
Acts 13:17

1:1–7. The book of Genesis (cf. Gen 46:8–27) already provided a list of the descendants of Jacob who went down into Egypt; these are now mentioned in a summary form here. Thus, in his opening verses the sacred writer makes it clear that the events of the Exodus are a continuation of those recounted in Genesis, and that the members of the people of Israel which is going to be established are in direct line of descent from the patriarchs. The number of seventy (cf. Gen 46:27) conveys the idea of completeness: that is, all Jacob's descendants moved to Egypt. But it is also a small number, showing that only God could turn them into the sizeable people of Israel.

"They increased greatly; they multiplied and grew exceedingly strong"

(v. 7)—language identical to that used in the first account of creation, recalling the divine blessing which guaranteed that the first human couple would be fruitful (cf. Gen 1:27), as would those who are now the first links in the people of Israel.

*1:8–14. The situation of the children of Israel is dramatically portrayed: the more they are oppressed, the stronger they become (v. 12). The frequent contrasts in the account and the fact that no names are supplied give the impression that God himself (even though he is yet not named) is on the Israelites' side and is against the pharaoh and his people. From the very beginning, over and above the comings and goings of men, God is at work; a religious event is taking shape.

For the first time the Bible here

---

¹Haec sunt nomina filiorum Israel, qui ingressi sunt Aegyptum cum Iacob; singuli cum domibus suis introierunt: ²Ruben, Simeon, Levi, Iuda, ³Issachar, Zabulon et Beniamin, ⁴Dan et Nephthali, Gad et Aser. ⁵Erant igitur omnes animae eorum, qui egressi sunt de femore Iacob, septuaginta; Ioseph autem in Aegypto erat. ⁶Quo mortuo et universis fratribus eius omnique cognatione illa, ⁷filii Israel creverunt et pullulantes multiplicati sunt ac roborati nimis impleverunt terram. ⁸Surrexit interea rex novus super

245

Jud 5:11 **The sons of Israel are oppressed***

Acts 7:18–19 ⁸Now there arose a new king over Egypt, who did not know Joseph. ⁹And he said to his people, "Behold, the people of Israel are too many and too mighty for us. ¹⁰Come, let us deal shrewdly with them, lest they multiply, and, if war befall us, they join our enemies and fight against us and escape from the land." Gen 47:11 ¹¹Therefore they set taskmasters over them to afflict them with heavy burdens; and they built for Pharaoh store-cities, Pithom and

---

speaks of the "people [of the sons] of Israel" (v. 9). The sacred book counterposes two peoples—the people of the pharaoh, cruel and oppressive, and the people of Israel, the victims of oppression. Over the course of their struggle to leave Egypt, the children of Israel will gradually become conscious of this—that they form a people chosen by God and released from bondage in order to fulfil an important historical mission. They are not a motley collection of tribes or families, but a people. "God, with loving concern contemplating, and making preparation for, the salvation of the whole human race, in a singular undertaking chose for himself a people to whom he would entrust his promises" (Vatican II, *Dei Verbum*, 14). At the same time the religious framework of this inspired book is established: on one side stand the enemies of God, on the other the people of the children of the Covenant (cf. Acts 3:25; *Catechism of the Catholic Church*, 527).

1:8. We do not know who exactly this "new king" was. He was probably Rameses II (early 13th century BC), who belonged to the nineteenth dynasty. This pharaoh sought to restore imperial control over foreigners and invaders. The

phrase "did not know Joseph" indicates how helpless and alone the "sons of Israel" were. The people of Israel never did count for very much politically, and yet God wills them to have an essential place in his plans.

Many Fathers of the Church saw in this pharaoh a personification of those who are opposed to the establishment of the Kingdom of Christ. St Bede, for example, reminds the Christian that if, having been baptized and having listened to the teachings of the faith, he goes back to living in a worldly way, "another king who knows not Joseph" will come to birth in him, that is, the selfishness which opposes the plans of God (cf. *Commentaria in Pentateuchum*, 2,1).

1:11. Pithom and Raamses are called "store-cities" because provisions for the frontier garrisons were stored in the silos of their temples. Reliable archeological studies identify Pithom (which in Egyptian means "dwelling of Athon") with some ruins a few kilometres from present-day Ishmailia, not far from the Suez canal. A temple of Athon has been discovered there, and huge stores of bricks. It is more difficult to say where Raamses was. The balance of probability

---

Aegyptum, qui ignorabat Ioseph; ⁹et ait ad populum suum: «Ecce, populus filiorum Israel multus et fortior nobis est: ¹⁰venite, prudenter agamus cum eo, ne forte multiplicetur et, si ingruerit contra nos bellum, addatur inimicis nostris, expugnatisque nobis, egrediatur de terra». ¹¹Praeposuit itaque eis magistros operum, ut affligerent eos oneribus; aedificaveruntque urbes promptuarias pharaoni, Phithom et

Raamses. [12]But the more they were oppressed, the more they mul- Deut 11:10
tiplied and the more they spread abroad. And the Egyptians were
in dread of the people of Israel. [13]So they made the people of
Israel serve with rigour, [14]and made their lives bitter with hard service, in mortar and brick, and in all kinds of work in the field; in
all their work they made them serve with rigour.

[15]Then the king of Egypt said to the Hebrew midwives, one of
whom was named Shiphrah and the other Puah, [16]"When you Mt 2:16

---

is that it was the earlier city of Avaris, a
capital during the dynasties of invader
pharaohs. It would later be called Tanis,
and nowadays it is just a series of big
ruins near a fishing village, San el-
Hagar, near Port Said, on the eastern part
of the Nile delta. Archeologists have discovered there the remains of an elaborate
temple built by Rameses II (1279–1212
BC), probably the pharaoh mentioned
here.

1:14. In ancient Egypt it was normal for
people, particularly foreigners, to work
for the pharaoh. This was not regarded as
a form of slavery or "oppression"; we
know, for example, there were towns or
entire cities which accommodated the
workers engaged in building the tombs
or temples of the pharaohs. The oppression the sacred writer refers to lay in the
fact that the Egyptians imposed particularly hard tasks on the Israelites—such
as brick-making, building and agricultural labour—and treated them cru-
elly.

St Isidore of Seville, commenting on
this passage, compares it with the situation of mankind which, after original sin,
is subject to the tyranny of the devil, who
often manages to turn work into slavery.

Just as the pharaoh imposed the hard
labour of mortar and brick, so too the
devil forces sinful man to engage in
"earthly, dusty tasks which are moreover
mixed with straw, that is to say, with friv-
olous and irrational acts" (cf. *Quaestiones in Exodum,* 3).

1:15–21. The situation of the Israelites
was worse than slavery. The most serious
thing was that they saw no future before
them because the pharaoh had ordered all
male children to be killed. As a kind of
echo of this, the evangelists point out that
Herod "sent and killed all the male children who were two years old or under"
(Mt 2:16).

God shows his revulsion towards
infanticide by protecting the midwives
and making the chosen people fruitful.
The brave action of the midwives has
been praised by commentators in every
age. The Targum, an Aramaic version
which reflects ancient Hebrew oral traditions, translates v. 21 by saying that God
gave them houses (descendants), the
royal house and the house of the high
priest. Apropos of this episode, Christian
writers comment that God always
rewards good actions. St Thomas says
that the midwives were rewarded not

Ramesses. [12]Quantoque opprimebant eos, tanto magis multiplicabantur et crescebant. [13]Formida-
veruntque filios Israel Aegyptii et in servitutem redegerunt eos [14]atque ad amaritudinem perducebant
vitam eorum operibus duris luti et lateris omnique famulatu, quo in terrae operibus premebantur. [15]Dixit
autem rex Aegypti obstetricibus Hebraeorum, quarum una vocabatur Sephra, altera Phua, [16]praecipi-
ens eis: «Quando obstetricabitis Hebraeas, et partus tempus advenerit, si masculus fuerit, interficite

serve as midwife to the Hebrew women, and see them upon the birthstool, if it is a son, you shall kill him; but if it is a daughter,

Acts 7:19 she shall live." [17]But the midwives feared God, and did not do as the king of Egypt commanded them, but let the male children live. [18]So the king of Egypt called the midwives, and said to them, "Why have you done this, and let the male children live?" [19]The midwives said to Pharaoh, "Because the Hebrew women are not like the Egyptian women; for they are vigorous and are delivered before the midwife comes to them." [20]So God dealt well with the midwives; and the people multiplied and grew very strong. [21]And

Acts 7:19 because the midwives feared God he gave them families. [22]Then Pharaoh commanded all his people, "Every son that is born to the Hebrews[a] you shall cast into the Nile, but you shall let every daughter live."

---

because they lied to the pharaoh but because they showed reverence to God (cf. *Summa theologiae*, 2–2, 110, 3 ad 2).

1:16. The Hebrew text says literally "see the two stones" for "see them upon the birthstool". Apparently, Hebrew women, when about to give birth, used to sit on two stones; the Targum translates it as "see the chairs". In any event, the point is that the midwives were told to be alert at the moment of childbirth, to see if it was a girl or a boy.

1:20. The people of Israel multiplied and grew strong despite difficulties and persecution, thanks to God's favour. The helpful part played by the midwives (who were probably Egyptians) serves to show God's great love. Women, Israelite and Egyptian, play a key role in the early stages of Israel's salvation.

St Cyril of Alexandria, applying this episode generally, comments that our situation is like that of the Israelites: "we were overwhelmed, by sin from the very beginning, from our first parents onwards; we were oppressed by a lack of good things, and in our unhappiness we found ourselves also, against our will, subject to the yoke of Satan, the prince of all evil. [. . .] There was no pain or suffering that we did not have, when God had mercy on us, set us free from the position we were in, and saved us" (*Glaphyra in Exodum*, 1, 3).

1:22. The original text always refers to "the River" because the entire life of ancient Egypt depended on it. Obviously it is referring to the Nile.

---

eum; si femina, reservate». [17]Timuerunt autem obstetrices Deum et non fecerunt iuxta praeceptum regis Aegypti, sed conservabant mares. [18]Quibus ad se accersitis rex ait: «Quidnam est hoc, quod facere voluistis, ut pueros servaretis?». [19]Quae responderunt: «Non sunt Hebraeae sicut Aegyptiae mulieres; ipsae enim robustae sunt et, priusquam veniamus ad eas, pariunt». [20]Bene ergo fecit Deus obstetricibus, et crevit populus confortatusque est nimis; [21]et, quia timuerunt obstetrices Deum, aedificavit illis domos. [22]Praecepit ergo pharao omni populo suo dicens: «Quidquid masculini sexus natum fuerit, in flumen proicite; quidquid feminei, reservate». [1]Egressus est vir de domo Levi et accepit uxorem stir-

---

a. Sam Gk Tg: Heb lacks *to the Hebrews*

2. THE CALL OF MOSES

The birth and early years of Moses*

2 ¹Now a man from the house of Levi went and took to wife a daughter of Levi. ²The woman conceived and bore a son; and when she saw that he was a goodly child, she hid him three months. ³And when she could hide him no longer she took for him a basket made of bulrushes, and daubed it with bitumen and pitch; and she put the child in it and placed it among the reeds at the river's brink. ⁴And his sister stood at a distance, to know what would be done to him. ⁵Now the daughter of Pharaoh came down to bathe at the river, and her maidens walked beside the river; she saw the basket among the reeds and sent her maid to fetch it. ⁶When she opened it she saw the child; and lo, the babe was crying. She took pity on him and said, "This is one of the Hebrews' children." ⁷Then his sister said to Pharaoh's daughter,

Ex 6:20
Acts 7:30
Heb 11:23
Gen 6:14
Acts 7:21
Acts 7:21

***2:1–10.** With lots of detail and good psychological insight, the sacred text recounts the birth and upbringing of Moses, the man whom divine providence had chosen to be the liberator and leader of the chosen people. What we have here is not so much chronological or topographical data as information which profiles the religious personality of the man who was both the guide and the prototype of the people.

In a masterly way the sacred writer highlights those aspects of his life and personality which most clearly show Moses to resemble the people and show divine intervention to be at work. Moses grew up during a period of severe persecution, but thanks to the good offices of three women (his mother, his sister and the pharaoh's daughter) he is received

into the Egyptian court and shown every honour. His tranquil childhood reflects the pleasant lifestyle of the sons of Israel in Egypt prior to the onset of oppression and persecution.

In this entire account of Moses' birth there is no mention of the names of his parents (Amram, according to Ex 6:20 his father, and Jochebed, his mother: Num 26:59) or his sister, Miriam (Ex 15:20). The sacred writer prefers to concentrate on Moses, making it clear that God takes care of him in birth and infancy, as he will also do of the people. Even the popular etymology of Moses' name ("taken from the waters") is an indication of God's intervention. The name in fact is Egyptian, meaning "son" or "born", as can be deduced from the names of some pharaohs Tut-mosis (son

pis suae; ²quae concepit et peperit filium et videns eum elegantem abscondit tribus mensibus. ³Cumque iam celare non posset, sumpsit fiscellam scirpeam et linivit eam bitumine ac pice; posuitque intus infantulum et exposuit eum in carecto ripae fluminis, ⁴stante procul sorore eius et considerante eventum rei. ⁵Ecce autem descendebat filia pharaonis, ut lavaretur in flumine, et puellae eius gradiebantur per crepidinem alvei. Quae cum vidisset fiscellam in papyrione, misit unam e famulabus suis; et allatam ⁶aperiens cernensque in ea parvulum vagientem, miserta eius ait: «De infantibus Hebraeorum est hic». ⁷Cui soror pueri: «Vis, inquit, ut vadam et vocem tibi mulierem Hebraeam, quae nutrire possit tibi infantulum?». ⁸Respondit: «Vade». Perrexit puella et vocavit matrem infantis. ⁹Ad quam locuta filia

"Shall I go and call you a nurse from the Hebrew women to nurse the child for you?" [8]And Pharaoh's daughter said to her, "Go." So the girl went and called the child's mother. [9]And Pharaoh's daughter said to her, "Take this child away, and nurse him for me, and I will give you your wages." So the woman took the child and nursed him. [10]And the child grew, and she brought him to Pharaoh's daughter, and he became her son; and she named him Moses,[b] for she said, "Because I drew him out[c] of the water."

Acts 7:21

---

of the god Tut) or Ra-mses (son of the god Ra)—but that does not matter: the important thing is that Moses is "the first to be saved", just as the Hebrew people is the first people to be saved, and that God is taking great care of him with a view to the important mission he has planned for him.

2:1–3. The Hebrew term translated here as "basket" is the same one as used for the Noah's "ark" (cf. Gen 6:14–9, 18, where it occurs 27 times). What we are told about the basket links Moses to Noah and his salvation from the waves of the flood which occurred so much earlier and in such dramatic circumstances. After the flood, mankind was reborn; now a new people is being born.

2:10. According to Egyptian law an adopted son had the same status as any other son. The text stresses that the pharaoh's daughter made him her son. In this paradox we can once again see God's providence at work: the child whom the Egyptians should have put to death is raised to great dignity, given the best of educations and thereby groomed for his future mission. Extra-biblical documents show that during this period the

pharaohs trained select foreign youths for posts in their civil service. However, although Moses spent his early years in the pharaoh's palace, he received from his true mother not only physical nourishment but also the faith of his ancestors and love for his people.

Origen, whom many Fathers follow, interprets this wonderful story in an allegorical sense: Moses is the law of the Old Testament, the pharaoh's daughter is the Church of Gentile background, because her father was wicked and unjust; the water of the Nile is Baptism. The Church of the pagans leaves her father's house, that is, leaves sin behind, to receive cleansing water, that is Baptism, and in the water she finds the law of Moses, that is, the Commandments. Only in the Church, in the royal palace of Wisdom, does the Law acquire complete maturity. "So," the ancient Christian writer concludes, "even if the pharaoh were our father, even if the prince of this world had begotten us in works of evil, by coming to the waters we receive the divine law. [. . .] We have a Moses great and strong. Let us not see anything mean in him . . . , for everything in him is greatness, sublimity and beauty. [. . .] And let us ask our Lord Jesus Christ to

---

pharaonis: «Accipe, ait, puerum istum et nutri mihi; ego dabo tibi mercedem tuam». Suscepit mulier et nutrivit puerum adultumque tradidit filiae pharaonis. [10]Quem illa adoptavit in locum filii vocatque nomen eius Moysen dicens: «Quia de aqua tuli eum». [11]In diebus illis, postquam creverat, Moyses

b. Heb *Mosheh* **c.** Heb *mashah*

Moses in Midian

Acts 7:23–29
Heb 11:24–27

[11]One day, when Moses had grown up, he went out to his people and looked on their burdens; and he saw an Egyptian beating a Hebrew, one of his people. [12]He looked this way and that, and seeing no one he killed the Egyptian and hid him in the sand. [13]When he went out the next day, behold, two Hebrews were struggling together; and he said to the man that did the wrong, "Why do you strike your fellow?" [14]He answered, "Who made Acts 7:27f, 35

---

show us and make known to us this greatness and sublimity of Moses" (*Homiliae in Exodum*, 2,4).

2:11–15. This is Act One in the calling of Moses. Because he carries out God's will he has to leave the pharaoh's palace, where he had a comfortable and easy life, and go out into the unknown. In this he is doing what the patriarchs did: first Abraham and then his descendants had to leave their homeland and their family (cf. Gen 12:1ff). The leader-to-be of Israel kills an Egyptian who is beating a Hebrew; and later he tries to make peace between two Hebrews. Freeing his people from oppression and slavery, and bringing about peace and unity among them are two of the goals of Moses' mission. Here again the sacred writer, over and above the details of events (about which he makes no moral judgments) is building up his theological profile of Moses and indicating the scope of his mission.

The same points are made when Moses is referred to in the New Testament. For example, according to St Stephen's reconstruction of these events in the Acts of the Apostles, Moses was forty years of age at this time and "mighty in his words and deeds"; his intervention on behalf of a member of his

people was, presumably, inspired by high ideals: "He supposed that his brethren understood that God was giving them deliverance by his hand" (Heb 7:25). The Letter to the Hebrews adds that "by faith Moses [. . .] refused to be called the son of Pharaoh's daughter, choosing rather to share ill-treatment with the people of God than to enjoy the fleeting pleasures of sin. He considered abuse suffered for the Christ greater wealth than the treasures of Egypt, for he looked to the reward" (Heb 11:24–26). However, his own people rejected him, and the pharaoh condemned him to death, furious at the killing of one of his overseers and fearful lest it signal an uprising of Hebrew slaves. Another forty years had to pass before Moses was actually given his mission (cf. Acts 7:30). On the basis of all these testimonies, St Cyril of Alexandria goes as far as to compare this episode of Moses' life with the Incarnation of Christ: "Do we not say that the Word of God the Father, who took on our condition, that is, became man, in some way went away from himself and became anonymous?[. . .] He left therefore to see his brothers, that is, the sons of Israel. For to them belong the promises and the patriarchs to whom the promises were made. And so he said, 'I have been sent only to the lost sheep of

---

egressus est ad fratres suos; viditque afflictionem eorum et virum Aegyptium percutientem quendam de Hebraeis fratribus suis. [12]Cumque circumspexisset huc atque illuc et nullum adesse vidisset, percussum Aegyptium abscondit sabulo. [13]Et egressus die altero conspexit duos Hebraeos rixantes dix-

Gen 24:11; 25:1–4;
29:2; 37:36
Num 10:29–32
Is 60:6
Mt 2:13
Acts 7:29
Heb 11:27

you a prince and a judge over us? Do you mean to kill me as you killed the Egyptian?" Then Moses was afraid, and thought, "Surely the thing is known." ¹⁵When Pharaoh heard of it, he sought to kill Moses.

But Moses fled from Pharaoh, and stayed in the land of Midian; and he sat down by a well. ¹⁶Now the priest of Midian had seven daughters; and they came and drew water, and filled the troughs to water their father's flock. ¹⁷The shepherds came and drove them away; but Moses stood up and helped them, and

---

Israel.' But, on seeing that they were subject to a heavy and intolerable tyranny, he chose to set them free and to make them see that they could hope for deliverance from pain of any kind" (*Glaphyra in Exodum,* 1, 7).

2:15 It is not at all clear where Midian was. The Bible often refers to Midianites, who were descendants of Abraham (cf. Gen 25:1–4) and were therefore related to the Israelites; we meet them as traders who used to travel from one place to another (cf. Gen 37:36; Num 10:29–32); who engage the Hebrews in battle (Num 25:6–18; 31:1–9) and are roundly defeated by Gideon (Judg 6–8). At the end of time, as the third part of the book of Isaiah announces, they will come to do homage before the Lord (Is 60:6). But none of this information tells us where exactly this place Midian was. Modern scholars are inclined to situate it somewhere in the Sinai peninsula, a desert region where people sought refuge who wanted to evade the Egyptian authorities.

Moses' flight into the wilderness is also part of his God-given mission,

according to the interpretation in the Letter to the Hebrews: "By faith he left Egypt, not being afraid of the anger of the king; for he endured as seeing him who is invisible" (Heb 11:27).

2:16–22. The ownership of wells and the right to use them caused frequent disputes. Moses' clear sense of justice leads him to take the part of the weaker side— once again showing him to be a liberator who "helps" (="saves", according to the Hebrew etymology of the word: v. 17) and "delivers" (v. 19) the daughters of the priest of Midian. The sacred writer stresses the religious dimension of the incident: the daughters of Reuel are *seven* in number; Reuel is a priest; and it is Moses who delivers them. Moses will eventually marry and have a family; but there is very little mention of it later.

In the years when Moses lived among the Midianites, he must have learned a lot about their customs and how they managed to cope with the great difficulties desert life involved; but there is no hard evidence that this Midianite priest taught Moses anything about their religious cult.

---

itque ei, qui faciebat iniuriam: «Quare percutis proximum tuum?». ¹⁴Qui respondit: «Quis te constituit principem et iudicem super nos? Num occidere me tu vis, sicut occidisti Aegyptium?». Timuit Moyses et ait: «Quomodo palam factum est verbum istud?». ¹⁵Audivitque pharao sermonem hunc et quaerebat occidere Moysen. Qui fugiens de conspectu eius moratus est in terra Madian; venit ergo in terram Madian et sedit iuxta puteum. ¹⁶Erant autem sacerdoti Madian septem filiae, quae venerunt ad hauriendam aquam; et impletis canalibus adaquare cupiebant greges patris sui. ¹⁷Supervenere pastores et

watered their flock. [18]When they came to their father Reuel, he said, "How is it that you have come so soon today?" [19]They said, "An Egyptian delivered us out of the hand of the shepherds, and even drew water for us and watered the flock." [20]He said to his daughters, "And where is he? Why have you left the man? Call him, that he may eat bread." [21]And Moses was content to dwell with the man, and he gave Moses his daughter Zipporah. [22]She bore a son, and he called his name Gershom; for he said, "I have been a sojourner[d] in a foreign land."

[23]In the course of those many days the king of Egypt died. And the people of Israel groaned under their bondage, and cried out for

Num 10:29
Judg 1:16;
4:11
Ex 3:1; 4:18;
18:1f

I Chron 23:15
Acts 7:6, 29

2:18. The priest of Midian (v. 16) and Moses' father-in-law have different names in different places: here he is called Reuel, and in Numbers 10:29 Moses' father-in-law is called Hobab the son of Reuel. In Judges 1:16 and 4:11, his father-in-law is not considered a Midianite: he is referred to as Heber the Kenite. In the book of Exodus, from chapter 3 on, he is called Jethro (cf. 3:1; 4:18; 18:1f). It may be that the sacred writer is using various traditions which he does not feel he should tamper with.

2:22. He called his son Gershom to show his gratitude towards a foreign land which accepted him as a guest and a sojourner (*ger*). The popular etymology given this name here and in 18:3 links Moses to Abraham and Jacob, who also had to live as exiles in a strange land (Deut 26:5): "A wandering Aramaean was my father; and he went down into Egypt and sojourned there, few in number" (cf. Gen 12:10). The term "sojourner" or "resident" is used in the sense of someone who settles down in a country that is not his own, with the

intention of staying there permanently or for a long time.

The sacred writer normally gives the meaning of certain proper names either because they are important figures in the history of salvation (Eve, Abraham, Jacob, Moses, etc.) or because the name is relevant to some point he wants to make (as is the case here). However, it is always a matter of popular, rather than scholarly, etymology. Here the text is emphasizing that Moses realized he was a stranger abroad and that he had a mission to lead his people into their own land; that people will itself spend time as a sojourner prior to settling down in its final home in Canaan.

2:23–25. The chapter ends by summing up the background to the time of Moses' youth, linking up with what it says at the start of the book (1:1–5). Both passages probably come from the Priestly tradition, which tends to focus on the logic of events over and above anecdotal details or concrete facts. Thus, these verses give the history of those years in telegraphic

---

eiecerunt eas; surrexitque Moyses et, defensis puellis, adaquavit oves earum. [18]Quae cum revertissent ad Raguel patrem suum, dixit ad eas: «Cur velocius venistis solito?». [19]Responderunt: «Vir Aegyptius liberavit nos de manu pastorum; insuper et hausit aquam nobis potumque dedit ovibus». [20]At ille: «Ubi est?», inquit. «Quare dimisistis hominem? Vocate eum, ut comedat panem». [21]Consensit ergo Moyses habitare cum eo accepitque Sephoram filiam eius uxorem. [22]Quae peperit ei filium, quem vocavit

d. Heb *ger*

Lk 1:72 help, and their cry under bondage came up to God. ²⁴And God
heard their groaning, and God remembered his covenant with
Abraham, with Isaac, and with Jacob. ²⁵And God saw the people
Ex 6:2–13; of Israel, and God knew their condition.
6:28–7:7
Acts 7:30–35
Acts 13:17 **God appears to Moses in the burning bush***

Ex 19 **3** ¹Now Moses was keeping the flock of his father-in-law,
1 Kings 19:8–19 Jethro, the priest of Midian; and he led his flock to the west
Mk 12:26

---

form: the death of the pharaoh who killed
the Hebrew male children might be
expected to augur improved conditions
but in fact bondage remains the order of
the day; the people petition God, and he
cannot ignore them.

God's action is summed up with four
characteristic verbs: he *heard* their cries,
he *remembered* the Covenant, he *saw*
them and *knew* their condition (vv. 24–25:
see the next note). It is an excellent outline of what divine providence does, and it
serves as an overture to the chapters that
follow, in which God's direct intervention
is going to be recounted. "the Lord saw
the affliction of his people reduced to
slavery, heard their cry, knew their sufferings and decided to deliver them (cf. Ex
3:7f). In this act of salvation by the Lord,
the prophet perceived his love and compassion (cf. Is 63:9). This is precisely the
grounds upon which the people and each
of its members based their certainty of the
mercy of God, which can be invoked
whenever tragedy strikes" (John Paul II,
Dives in misericordia, 4).

2:25. In the original Hebrew this verse is
unfinished: "And God saw the people of
Israel, and God knew. . ." The Greek and

New Vulgate read the last verb as being
passive: "And God saw the people of
Israel and he made himself known to
them". These are matters of different
nuances; really the original could be
translated literally, because the action of
"knowing" implies that God is listening
and looking after the people known (as
can be seen from Psalm 31:7–8).

***3:1—4:17.** This account of the calling
of Moses is charged with theological
content; it gives the features of the two
protagonists (Moses and God) and the
bases of the liberation of the people by
means of wondrous divine intervention.

In the dialogue between God and
Moses after the theophany of the burning
bush (vv. 1–10), the Lord endows Moses
with all the gifts he needs to carry out his
mission: he promises him help and protection (vv. 11–12), he makes his name
known to him (vv. 13–22), he gives him
the power to work wonders (4:1–9),
and he designates his brother Aaron as
his aide, who will be his spokesman
(4:10–17).

This section shows how God brings
about salvation by relying on the docility
of a mediator whom he calls and trains

Gersam dicens: «Advena sum in terra aliena». ²³Post multum vero temporis mortuus est rex Aegypti;
et ingemiscentes filii Israel propter opera vociferati sunt, ascenditque clamor eorum ad Deum ab
operibus. ²⁴Et audivit gemitum eorum ac recordatus est foederis, quod pepigit cum Abraham, Isaac et
Iacob; ²⁵et respexit Dominus filios Israel et apparuit eis. ¹Moyses autem pascebat oves Iethro soceri sui
sacerdotis Madian; cumque minasset gregem ultra desertum, venit ad montem Dei Horeb.
²Apparuitque ei angelus Domini in flamma ignis de medio rubi; et videbat quod rubus arderet et non

Gen 16:7; 2:11,
14; 31:11, 13
Ex 24:7
Lev 9:23–24
Ezra 1:17
Deut 33:16
Lk 20:37
Acts 7:30
Acts 7:31

side of the wilderness, and came to Horeb, the mountain of God. ²And the angel of the Lord appeared to him in a flame of fire out of the midst of a bush; and he looked, and lo, the bush was burning, yet it was not consumed. ³And Moses said, "I will turn aside and see this great sight, why the bush is not burnt." ⁴When the Lord saw that he turned aside to see, God called to him out of

---

for the purpose. But the initiative always stays with God. Thus, God himself designs the smallest details of the most important undertaking the Israelites will embark on—their establishment as a people and their passing from bondage to freedom and the possession of the promised land.

3:1–3. The mountain of God, Horeb, called in other traditions Sinai, probably lies in the south-east part of the Sinai peninsula. Even today shepherds in that region will leave the valleys scorched by the sun in search of better pasture in the mountains. Although we do not yet know exactly where Mount Horeb is, it still had primordial importance in salvation history. On this same mountain the Law will later be promulgated (chap. 19), in the context of another dramatic theophany. Elijah will come back here to meet God (1 Kings 19:8–19). It is the mountain of God *par excellence*.

The "angel of the Lord" is probably an expression meaning "God". In the most ancient accounts (cf., e.g., Gen 16:7; 22:11, 14; 31:11, 13), immediately after the angel comes on the scene it is God himself who speaks: since God is invisible he is discovered to be present and to be acting in "the angel of the Lord", who usually does not appear in human form. Later, in the period of the monarchy, the existence of heavenly

messengers distinct from God will begin to be recognized (cf. 2 Sam 19:28; 24:16; 1 Kings 19:5, 7; etc.).

Fire is often a feature of theophanies (cf., e.g., Ex 19:18; 24:17; Lev 9:23–24; Ezek 1:17), perhaps because it is the best symbol to convey the presence of things spiritual and the divine transcendence. The bush mentioned here would be one of the many thorny shrubs that grow in desert uplands in that region. Some Christian writers have seen in the burning bush an image of the Church which endures despite the persecutions and trials it undergoes. It is also seen as a figure of the Blessed Virgin, in whom the divinity always burned (cf. St Bede, *Commentaria in Pentateuchum*, 2,3).

All the details given in the passage help to bring out the simplicity and at the same time the drama of God's action; the scene is quite ordinary (grazing, a mountain, a bush . . .), but extraordinary things happen (the angel of the Lord, a flame which does not burn, a voice).

3:4–10. The calling of Moses is described in this powerful dialogue in four stages: God calls him by his name (v. 4); he introduces himself as the God of Moses' ancestors (v. 9); he makes his plan of deliverance known in a most moving way (vv. 7–9); and, finally, he imperiously gives Moses his mission (v. 10).

---

comburreretur. ³Dixit ergo Moyses: «Vadam et videbo visionem hanc magnam, quare non comburatur rubus». ⁴Cernens autem Dominus quod pergeret ad videndum, vocavit eum Deus de medio rubi et ait: «Moyses, Moyses». Qui respondit: «Adsum». ⁵At ille: «Ne appropies, inquit, huc; solve calceamen-

Gen 28:16–17
Josh 5:5
Acts 7:33
Ex 19:12; 33:20
Mt 22:32
Mk 12:26
Lk 20:37
Acts 3:13; 7:32
Heb 11:16

the bush, "Moses, Moses!" And he said, "Here am I." ⁵Then he said, "Do not come near; put off your shoes from your feet, for the place on which you are standing is holy ground." ⁶And he said, "I am the God of your father, the God of Abraham, the God of Isaac, and the God of Jacob." And Moses hid his face, for he was afraid to look at God.

Acts 7:34
Lev 20:24
Num 13:27
Deut 7:1; 26:9, 15
Jer 11:5; 32:22
Ezra 20:15
Gen 15:19–21
Ex 3:17; 13:5;
22:23, 28; 32:2;
34:11

⁷Then the Lord said, "I have seen the affliction of my people who are in Egypt, and have heard their cry because of their taskmasters; I know their sufferings, ⁸and I have come down to deliver them out of the hand of the Egyptians, and to bring them up out of that land to a good and broad land, a land flowing with milk and honey, to the place of the Canaanites, the Hittites, the

---

The repetition of his name ("Moses, Moses!") stresses how important this event is (cf. Gen 22:11; Lk 22:31). Taking one's shoes off is a way of showing veneration in a holy place. In some Byzantine communities there was a custom for a long time of celebrating the liturgy barefoot or wearing different footwear from normal. Christian writers have seen this gesture as being an act of humility and detachment in the face of the presence of God: "no one can gain access to God or see him unless first he has shed every earthly attachment" (*Glossa ordinaria in Exodum*, 3,4).

The sacred writer makes it clear that the God of Sinai is the same as the God of Moses' ancestors; Moses, then, is not a founder of a new religion; he carries on the religious tradition of the patriarchs, confirming the election of Israel as people of God. Four very expressive verbs are used to describe this election, this choice of Israel by God: I have seen . . . , I have heard . . . , I know . . . , I have come down to deliver (v. 8). This sequence of action includes no human action: the people are oppressed, they

cry, theirs is a sorry plight. But God has a clear aim in sight—"to deliver them and to bring them up [. . .] to a good and broad land" (v. 8). These two terms will become keynotes of God's saving action. To bring up to the promised land will come to mean, not only a geographical ascent but also a journey towards plenitude. St Luke's Gospel will take up the same idea. God's imperative command is clear in the original text (v. 10): ". . . bring forth my people, the sons of Israel, out of Egypt". This is another way of referring to the salvific event which gives its name to this book; according to Greek and Latin traditions "exodus" means "going out".

3:8. This description of the promised land is meant to show that it is extensive and fertile. Its fertility can be seen from its basic products—milk and honey (Lev 20:24; Num 13:27; Deut 26:9, 15; Jer 11:5; 32:22; Ezek 20:15)—the ideal desert food; a land which produces them in abundance is a veritable paradise.

The number of nations inhabiting the

---

tum de pedibus tuis; locus enim, in quo stas, terra sancta est». ⁶Et ait: «Ego sum Deus patris tui, Deus Abraham, Deus Isaac et Deus Iacob». Abscondit Moyses faciem suam; non enim audebat aspicere contra Deum. ⁷Cui ait Dominus: «Vidi afflictionem populi mei in Aegypto et clamorem eius audivi propter duritiam exactorum eorum. ⁸Et sciens dolorem eius descendi, ut liberem eum de manibus

Amorites, the Perizzites, the Hivites, and the Jebusites. ⁹And now, behold, the cry of the people of Israel has come to me, and I have seen the oppression with which the Egyptians oppress them. ¹⁰Come, I will send you to Pharaoh that you may bring forth my people, the sons of Israel, out of Egypt." Acts 7:34

The divine name is revealed

¹¹But Moses said to God, "Who am I that I should go to Pharaoh, and bring the sons of Israel out of Egypt?" ¹²He said, "But I will be with you; and this shall be the sign for you, that I have sent you: when you have brought forth the people out of Egypt, you shall serve God upon this mountain."

Gen 28:15
Josh 1:5
1 Sam 14:10
Jer 1:6
Lk 2:27
Acts 7:7

---

promised land and disputing over it gives an indication as to its extent and desirability. The Pentateuch often lists the pre-Israelite peoples (with small variations from one list to the other): cf. Gen 15:19–20; Ex 3:17; 13:5; 23:23, 28; 32:2; 34:11. Mentions like this probably act as a reminder of the difficulties the Israelites had in settling the land, and the countless ways in which God intervened on their behalf.

3:11–12. In reply to Moses' first objection about his sheer inability to do what God is asking of him, God assures him that he will be at his side and will protect him—as he will help all who have a difficult mission of salvation (cf. Gen 28:15; Josh 1:5; Jer 1:8). The Blessed Virgin will hear the same words at the Annunciation: "The Lord is with you" (Lk 1:27).

The sign which God gives Moses is linked to his faith, because it involves both a promise and a command: when they come out of Egypt, Moses and the

people will worship God on this very mountain. When this actually happens, Moses will acknowledge the supernatural nature of his mission but, meanwhile, he has to obey faithfully the charge given him by God.

Moses' conversation with the Lord is a beautiful prayer and one worth imitating. By following his example, a Christian can dialogue personally and intimately with the Lord: "We ought to be seriously committed to dealing with God. We cannot take refuge in the anonymous crowd. If interior life doesn't involve personal encounter with God, it doesn't exist—it's as simple as that. There are few things more at odds with Christianity than superficiality. To settle down to routine in our Christian life is to dismiss the possibility of becoming a contemplative soul. God seeks us out, one by one. And we ought to answer him, one by one: 'Here I am, Lord, because you have called me' (1 Kings 3:5)" (St Josemaría Escrivá, *Christ Is Passing By*, 174; cf. *Catechism of the Catholic Church*, 2574–5).

Aegyptiorum et educam de terra illa in terram bonam et spatiosam, in terram, quae fluit lacte et melle, ad loca Chananaei et Hetthaei et Amorraei et Pherezaei et Hevaei et Iebusaei. ⁹Clamor ergo filiorum Israel venit ad me, vidique afflictionem eorum, qua ab Aegyptiis opprimuntur; ¹⁰sed veni, mittam te ad pharaonem, ut educas populum meum, filios Israel, de Aegypto». ¹¹Dixitque Moyses ad Deum: «Quis sum ego, ut vadam ad pharaonem et educam filios Israel de Aegypto?». ¹²Qui dixit ei: «Ego ero tecum; et hoc habebis signum quod miserim te: cum eduxeris populum de Aegypto, servietis Deo super

Is 42:8
Jn 8:24;
17:6, 26
Heb 11:6
Rev 1:4
Acts 5:30
Mt 22:32
Mk 12:26
Lk 20:37
Acts 3:13;
7:32; 22:14

[13]Then Moses said to God, "If I come to the people of Israel and say to them, 'The God of your fathers has sent me to you,' and they ask me, 'What is his name?' what shall I say to them?" [14]God said to Moses, "I AM WHO I AM."[e]* And he said, "Say this to the people of Israel, 'I AM has sent me to you.'" [15]God also said to Moses, "Say this to the people of Israel, 'The Lord, the God of your fathers, the God of Abraham, the God of Isaac, and the God of Jacob, has sent me to you': this is my name for ever, and thus I am to be remembered throughout all generations.

3:13-15. Moses now raises another difficulty: he does not know the name of the God who is commissioning him. This gives rise to the revelation of the name "Yahweh" and the explanation of what it means—"I am who I am".

According to the tradition recorded in Genesis 4:26, a grandson of Adam, Enosh, was the first to call upon the name of the Lord (Yahweh). Thus, the biblical text is stating that a part of mankind knew the true God, whose name was revealed to Moses in this solemn way (Ex 35:15 and 6:2). The patriarchs invoked God under other names, to do with the divine attributes, such as the Almighty ("El-Shaddai": Gen 17:1; Ex 6:2-3). Other proper names of God which appear in very ancient documents lead one to think that the name Yahweh had been known from a long time back. The revelation of the divine name is important in salvation history because by that name God will be invoked over the course of the centuries.

All kinds of suggestions have been put forward as to the meaning of Yahweh; not all are mutually exclusive.

Here are some of the main ones: (a) God is giving an evasive answer here because he does not want those in ancient times, contaminated as they were by magical rites, to think that because they knew the name they would have power over the god. According to this theory, "I am who I am" would be equivalent to "I am he whom you cannot know", "I am the unnameable". This solution stresses the transcendence of God. (b) What God is revealing is his nature—that he is subsistent being; in which case "I am who I am" means I am he who exists *per sibi*, absolute be-ing. The divine name refers to what he is by essence; it refers to him whose essence it is to be. God is saying that he *is*, and he is giving the name by which he is to be called. This explanation is often to be found in Christian interpretation. (c) On the basis of the fact that Yahweh is a causative form of the ancient Hebrew verb *hwh* (to be), God is revealing himself as "he who causes to be", the creator, not so much in the fullest sense of the word (as creator of the universe) but above all the creator of the present situation—the one who gives

montem istum». [13]Ait Moyses ad Deum: «Ecce, ego vadam ad filios Israel et dicam eis: Deus patrum vestrorum misit me ad vos. Si dixerint mihi: 'Quod est nomen eius?', quid dicam eis?». [14]Dixit Deus ad Moysen: «Ego sum qui sum». Ait: «Sic dices filiis Israel: Qui sum misit me ad vos». [15]Dixitque iterum Deus ad Moysen: «Haec dices filiis Israel: Dominus, Deus patrum vestrorum, Deus Abraham, Deus Isaac et Deus Iacob, misit me ad vos; hoc nomen mihi est in aeternum, et hoc memoriale meum in generationem et generationem. [16]Vade et congrega seniores Israel et dices ad eos: Dominus, Deus

e. Or I AM WHAT I AM or I WILL BE WHAT I WILL BE

The mission of Moses

¹⁶Go and gather the elders of Israel together, and say to them,
'The LORD^f the God of your fathers, the God of Abraham, of
Isaac, and of Jacob, has appeared to me, saying, "I have observed
you and what has been done to you in Egypt; ¹⁷and I promise that
I will bring you up out of the affliction of Egypt, to the land of the
Canaanites, the Hittites, the Amorites, the Perizzites, the Hivites,
and the Jebusites, a land flowing with milk and honey."' ¹⁸And
they will hearken to your voice; and you and the elders of Israel

Deut 7:1

---

the people its being and who always stays with it. Thus, calling upon Yahweh will always remind the good Israelite of his reason-for-being, as an individual and as a member of a chosen people.

None of these explanations is entirely satisfactory. "This divine name is mysterious just as God is mystery. It is at once a name revealed and something like the refusal of a name, and hence it better expresses God as what he is—infinitely above everything that we can understand or say: he is the 'hidden God' (Is 45:15), his name is ineffable, and he is the God who makes himself close to men (cf. Judg 13:18)" (*Catechism of the Catholic Church*, 206).

At a later time, around the 4th century BC, out of reverence for the name of Yahweh the use of the word was avoided; when it occurred in the sacred text it was read as "Adonai", my Lord. In the Greek version it is translated as "Kyrios" and in the Latin as "Dominus". "It is under this title that the divinity of Jesus will be acclaimed: 'Jesus is Lord'" (ibid., 209). The RSV always renders "Yahweh" as "the Lord". The medieval form *Jehovah* was the result of a misreading of the

Hebrew text into which vowels were inserted by the Massoretes; it is simply a mistake and there is no justification for the use of "Jehovah" nowadays (cf. ibid., 446).

3:16–22. The Lord comes back again to the subject of Moses' mission; despite all the obstacles, it will be a success. "The elders of Israel" (v. 16), that is, the chiefs of clans, representing the whole community, will be happy to hear what Moses has to say. The words "I have observed you" (v. 16: literally, "I have carried out an inspection among you") are significant because they indicate the key thing—God's is a friendly presence; but it is also a demanding presence which expects an account of the use we make of gifts received (cf. 32:34; Jer 9:24; Hos 4:14). The three days' journey (v. 18) would not take them to Sinai but it was enough to get them away from Egypt. Later, three days will become a number symbolizing divine action. See the note on 6:10–13.

The pharaoh, unlike the elders, will refuse to let the people go—making it clearer that the Israelites will attain their

---

patrum vestrorum, apparuit mihi, Deus Abraham, Deus Isaac et Deus Iacob, dicens: Visitans visitavi vos et vidi omnia, quae acciderunt vobis in Aegypto; ¹⁷et dixi: Educam vos de afflictione Aegypti in terram Chananaei et Hetthaei et Amorraei et Pherezaei et Hevaei et Iebusaei, ad terram fluentem lacte et melle. ¹⁸ Et audient vocem tuam, ingredierisque tu et seniores Israel ad regem Aegypti, et dicetis ad

---

f. The word LORD, when spelled with capital letters, stands for the divine name, *YHWH*, which is here connected with the verb *hayah*, to be

shall go to the king of Egypt and say to him, 'The LORD, the God of the Hebrews, has met with us; and now, we pray you, let us go a three days' journey into the wilderness, that we may sacrifice to the LORD our God.' [19]I know that the king of Egypt will not let you go unless compelled by a mighty hand.[g] [20]So I will stretch out my hand and smite Egypt with all the wonders which I will do in it; after that he will let you go. [21]And I will give this people favor in the sight of the Egyptians; and when you go, you shall not go empty, [22]but each woman shall ask of her neighbour, and of her who sojourns in her house, jewelry of silver and of gold, and clothing, and you shall put them on your sons and on your daughters; thus you shall despoil the Egyptians."

Gen 15:14
Ex 11:2–3;
12:35–36
Wis 10:17

Moses is granted miraculous powers

Mt 13:57

4 [1]Then Moses answered, "But behold, they will not believe me or listen to my voice, for they will say, 'The LORD did not appear to you.'" [2]The LORD said to him, "What is that in your hand?" He said, "A rod." [3]And he said, "Cast it on the ground." So he cast it on the ground, and it became a serpent; and Moses fled from it. [4]But the LORD said to Moses, "Put out your hand, and take it by the tail"—so he put out his hand and caught it, and it became

Ex 7:9

---

freedom only if God comes to their rescue.

The "despoiling" of the Egyptians (v. 22) is by way of compensation for the years they have spent with nothing to show for it (cf. Gen 15:14; Wis 10:17) and also as a sort of booty of war (cf. Ex 11:2–3; 12:35–36): God comes out the victor in the struggle against the pharaoh, and he gives the sons of Israel a share in the booty. It may also be meant to signal festive joy: the Israelites are to dress up to celebrate the victory God has given them.

4:1–9. God replies to a new objection from Moses by working miracles; these are designed more to prove that God is intervening, not just to provide a spectacle: they are done that "they may believe that the Lord has appeared to you" (v. 5).

It is worth noting that the wonders worked here are tailor-made for the Egyptians, who were used to snake-charming or thought that only their own wise men knew how to cure leprosy. If Moses is more powerful than the wise men of Egypt, it is because he has been given divine power.

---

eum: Dominus, Deus Hebraeorum, occurrit nobis; et nunc eamus viam trium dierum in solitudinem, ut immolemus Domino Deo nostro. [19]Sed ego scio quod non dimittet vos rex Aegypti, ut eatis, nisi per manum validam. [20]Extendam enim manum meam et percutiam Aegyptum in cunctis mirabilibus meis, quae facturus sum in medio eius; post haec dimittet vos. [21]Daboque gratiam populo huic coram Aegyptiis, et, cum egrediemini, non exibitis vacui. [22]Sed postulabit mulier a vicina sua et ab hospita sua vasa argentea et aurea ac vestes; ponetisque eas super filios et filias vestras et spoliabitis Aegyptum». [1]Respondens Moyses ait: «Quid autem, si non credent mihi neque audient vocem meam,

g. Gk Vg: Heb *no, not by a mighty hand*

a rod in his hand—⁵"that they may believe that the LORD, the God of their fathers, the God of Abraham, the God of Isaac, and the God of Jacob, has appeared to you." ⁶Again, the LORD said to him, Lev 13:1 "Put your hand into your bosom." And he put his hand into his bosom; and when he took it out, behold, his hand was leprous, as white as snow. ⁷Then God said, "Put your hand back into your bosom." So he put his hand back into his bosom; and when he took it out, behold, it was restored like the rest of his flesh. ⁸"If they will not believe you," God said, "or heed the first sign, they may believe the latter sign. ⁹If they will not believe even these two signs or heed your voice, you shall take some water from the Nile and pour it upon the dry ground; and the water which you shall take from the Nile will become blood upon the dry ground."

Aaron, the mouthpiece of Moses

¹⁰But Moses said to the LORD, "Oh, my Lord, I am not eloquent, Jer 1:6 either heretofore or since thou hast spoken to thy servant; but I am slow of speech and of tongue." ¹¹Then the LORD said to him, "Who has made man's mouth? Who makes him dumb, or deaf, or seeing, or blind? Is it not I, the LORD? ¹²Now therefore go, and I Deut 18:18 will be with your mouth and teach you what you shall speak." Mt 10:19–20

4:10–17. Moses' last objection succeeds in irritating God. The sacred writer uses a nice anthropomorphism to show how patient God is and how determined he is to set the people free.

"He shall speak for you to the people; and he shall be a mouth for you, and you shall be to him as God" (v. 16). To speak in the name of God is the role of a prophet, quite independently of his qualities, whether he has or has not oratorical

skills (cf. Jer 1:6). Moses is the prototype of the prophet (cf. Deut 18:9–22); all future prophets should look up to him and try to copy him (cf. Acts 7:22).

By associating Aaron with Moses as his spokesman, the sacred text is making the point that there should never be disputes between temple priests and prophets; the mission of teaching the people belongs also to those in charge of divine worship (cf. Lev 10:11; Deut 33:10).

sed dicent: 'Non apparuit tibi Dominus'?». ²Dixit ergo ad eum: «Quid est quod tenes in manu tua?». Respondit: «Virga». ³Dixitque Dominus: «Proice eam in terram!». Proiecit, et versa est in serpentem, ita ut fugeret Moyses. ⁴Dixitque Dominus: «Extende manum tuam et apprehende caudam eius!». Extendit et tenuit, versaque est in virgam. ⁵«Ut credant, inquit, quod apparuerit tibi Dominus, Deus patrum suorum, Deus Abraham, Deus Isaac et Deus Iacob». ⁶Dixitque Dominus rursum: «Mitte manum tuam in sinum tuum!». Quam cum misisset in sinum, protulit leprosam instar nivis. ⁷«Retrahe, ait, manum tuam in sinum tuum!». Retraxit et protulit iterum, et erat similis carni reliquae. ⁸«Si non crediderint, inquit, tibi, neque audierint sermonem signi prioris, credent verbo signi sequentis. ⁹Quod si nec duobus quidem his signis crediderint neque audierint vocem tuam, sume aquam fluminis et effunde eam super aridam, et, quidquid hauseris de fluvio, vertetur in sanguinem». ¹⁰Ait Moyses: «Obsecro, Domine, non sum eloquens ab heri et nudiustertius et ex quo locutus es ad servum tuum, nam impeditioris et tardioris linguae sum». ¹¹Dixit Dominus ad eum: «Quis fecit os hominis? Aut quis fabricatus est mutum vel surdum vel videntem vel caecum? Nonne ego? ¹²Perge igitur, et ego ero in

¹³But he said, "Oh, my Lord, send, I pray, some other person."
¹⁴Then the anger of the LORD was kindled against Moses and he said, "Is there not Aaron, your brother, the Levite? I know that he can speak well; and behold, he is coming out to meet you, and

Ex 7:12 when he sees you he will be glad in his heart. ¹⁵And you shall speak to him and put the words in his mouth; and I will be with your mouth and with his mouth, and will teach you what you shall

Heb 2:17 do. ¹⁶He shall speak for you to the people; and he shall be a mouth for you, and you shall be to him as God. ¹⁷And you shall take in your hand this rod, with which you shall do the signs."

Moses returns to Egypt

Ex 2:18 ¹⁸Moses went back to Jethro his father-in-law and said to him, "Let me go back, I pray, to my kinsmen in Egypt and see whether they are still alive." And Jethro said to Moses, "Go in peace."

Mt 2:20 ¹⁹And the LORD said to Moses in Midian, "Go back to Egypt; for all the men who were seeking your life are dead." ²⁰So Moses took his wife and his sons and set them on an ass, and went back

Ex 7:3; 9:12; 10:1, 20, 27; 14:4, 8.17 Rom 9:18 to the land of Egypt; and in his hand Moses took the rod of God.
²¹And the LORD said to Moses, "When you go back to Egypt, see that you do before Pharaoh all the miracles which I have put

---

4:18–20. Moses' decision to return to Egypt immediately is recorded in two different ways—as something permitted by Jethro, the head of the clan (v. 18) and as something commanded by God (vv. 19–20). This may mean that there are two redactional sources, Elohistic and Yahwistic respectively, although it could also be that the sacred writer wants to put it on record that Moses is fulfilling a divine command without contravening family custom of the time, which required the permission of the chief of the tribe before one left like this. It is

worth noticing that Moses hid from Jethro his real motives for returning to Egypt; this is an indication that Moses did not learn the cult of Yahweh from the Midianites but that the initiative behind all these events is divine.

4:21–23. "I will harden his heart". This phrase comes up often (7:3; 9:12; 10:1, 20, 27; 9:12; 14:4, 8, 17) but it does not mean that the pharaoh is any less responsible for his actions (that, indeed, is specifically stated in the context: 8:11, 28; 9:34); rather, it emphasizes the man's

---

ore tuo; doceboque te quid loquaris». ¹³At ille: «Obsecro, inquit, Domine, mitte quem missurus es». ¹⁴Iratus Dominus in Moysen ait: «Aaron, frater tuus Levites, scio quod eloquens sit; ecce ipse egreditur in occursum tuum vidensque te laetabitur corde. ¹⁵Loquere ad eum et pone verba mea in ore eius; et ego ero in ore tuo et in ore illius et ostendam vobis quid agere debeatis. ¹⁶Ipse loquetur pro te ad populum et erit os tuum; tu autem eris ei ut Deus. ¹⁷Virgam quoque hanc sume in manu tua, in qua facturus es signa». ¹⁸Abiit Moyses et reversus est ad Iethro socerum suum dixitque ei: «Vadam, quaeso, et revertar ad fratres meos in Aegyptum, ut videam, si adhuc vivant». Cui ait Iethro: «Vade in pace». ¹⁹Dixit ergo Dominus ad Moysen in Madian: «Vade, revertere in Aegyptum; mortui sunt enim omnes, qui quaerebant animam tuam». ²⁰Tulit Moyses uxorem suam et filios suos et imposuit eos super asinum; reversusque est in Aegyptum portans virgam Dei in manu sua. ²¹Dixitque ei Dominus revertenti in

in your power; but I will harden his heart, so that he will not let
the people go. ²²And you shall say to Pharaoh, 'Thus says the
LORD, Israel is my first-born son, ²³and I say to you, "Let my son
go that he may serve me"; if you refuse to let him go, behold, I
will slay your first-born son.'"

Rom 9:4
Is 63:16; 64:8
Hos 11:1–4

Moses' son is circumcised

Gen 32:25–33

²⁴At a lodging place on the way the LORD met him and sought to
kill him. ²⁵Then Zipporah took a flint and cut off her son's foreskin, and touched Moses' feet with it, and said, "Surely you are a
bridegroom of blood to me!" ²⁶So he let him alone. Then it was
that she said, "You are a bridegroom of blood," because of the circumcision.

Josh 5:2–3

---

obstinacy and blindness. It needs to be borne in mind that the Semitic mind attributes directly to God (the first cause) the actions of creatures (secondary causes). Moreover, by being contrasted against the intransigent Egyptian king, God's love stands out more; God uses the pharaoh's increasing hardness of heart to show by ever more amazing deeds his special love for the people of Israel.

"Israel is my first-born son" (v. 22). God's confrontation with the pharaoh will end up in the death of the Egyptian first-born. God has a greater love for Israel than the pharaoh has for his first-born. One of the most consoling things that God has revealed is his fatherhood (cf. Hos 11:1–4); this revelation is a sign of his special favour (cf. Is 63:16; 64:8) "In Israel, God is called 'Father' inasmuch as he is Creator of the world (cf. Deut 32:6; Mal 2:10). Even more, God is Father because of the covenant and the gift of the law to Israel 'his first-born son' (Ex 4:22). God is also called the Father of the

king of Israel. Most especially he is 'the Father of the poor', of the orphaned and the widowed, who are under his loving protection (cf. Sam 7:14; Ps 68:5)" (*Catechism of the Catholic Church*, 238). Divine fatherhood, which in the Old Testament simply meant that there was a particularly close relationship between God and his people, prepared the way for the consoling fact that Jesus revealed: "Jesus revealed that God is Father in an unheard-of sense: he is Father not only in being Creator; he is eternally Father by his relationship to his only Son who, reciprocally, is Son only in relation to his Father: 'No one knows the Son except the Father, and no one knows the Father except the Son and any one to whom the Son chooses to reveal him' (Mt 11:27)" (ibid., 240; cf. nos. 2778–2782).

4:24–26. This is a puzzling episode because it concerns superstitious healing practices which are unknown nowadays: Moses falls gravely ill (this is what it

Aegyptum: «Vide, ut omnia ostenta, quae posui in manu tua, facias coram pharaone; ego indurabo cor eius, et non dimittet populum. ²²Dicesque ad eum: Haec dicit Dominus: Filius meus primogenitus Israel. ²³Dico tibi: Dimitte filium meum, ut serviat mihi; si autem non vis dimittere eum, ecce ego interficiam filium tuum primogenitum». ²⁴Cumque esset in itinere, in deversorio, occurrit ei Dominus et volebat occidere eum. ²⁵Tulit ilico Sephora acutissimam petram et circumcidit praeputium filii sui; tetigitque pedes eius et ait: «Sponsus sanguinum tu mihi es». ²⁶Et dimisit eum, postquam dixerat:

Moses meets Aaron

[27]The LORD said to Aaron, "Go into the wilderness to meet Moses." So he went, and met him at the mountain of God and kissed him. [28]And Moses told Aaron all the words of the LORD with which he had sent him, and all the signs which he had charged him to do. [29]Then Moses and Aaron went and gathered together all the elders of the people of Israel. [30]And Aaron spoke all the words which the LORD had spoken to Moses, and did the signs in the sight of the people. [31]And the people believed; and when they heard that the LORD had visited the people of Israel and that he had seen their affliction, they bowed their heads and worshipped.

Ex 14:31
Lk 1:68

Moses' first audience with the pharaoh

Ex 23:14–17

5 [1]Afterward Moses and Aaron went to Pharaoh and said, "Thus says the LORD, the God of Israel, 'Let my people go, that they

---

means when it says the Lord "met him and sought to kill him") and Zipporah interprets this as meaning that he has committed some fault. So she proceeds to circumcise the boy and also Moses himself (the mention of Moses' "feet" seems an obvious euphemism). So, this circumcision seems to be a religious rite, propiatory in character and somehow connected with marital relations, since his wife refers to him as "a bridegroom of blood". Many theories based on what circumcision meant to the Midianites have been put forward to explain this expression and the whole ritual; but so far none of them is very satisfactory. The Fathers tended to comment on the passage allegorically, saying that Moses blessed his wife and children by means of this rite, to give them a share in the fruits of his salvific mission. Anyway, it does seem as though the sacred writer included this episode in order to show

that Moses, the leader and lawgiver of the people, himself underwent circumcision before all the sons of Israel had to.

4:27–31. Moses meets no opposition from his brother Aaron, the elders or the people themselves. This docility is in sharp contrast to the pharaoh's reaction (v. 21). Whereas the Egyptians proved obstinate, "the people believed" (v. 21): God's plan for their deliverance can be put into action only if men are ready to believe in it; this first act of faith on the part of the people will suffer many ups and downs.

"The mountain of God" (v. 27) is Mount Horeb. The mention of the holy mountain in this context underlines the sacred character of Aaron's mission (cf. the note on 3:1–3). The Bible often reports important events as having happened on a mountain; this has led many writers to reflect on the spiritual meaning of mountain. Origen, for example, says:

«Sponsus sanguinum», ob circumcisionem. [27]Dixit autem Dominus ad Aaron: «Vade in occursum Moysi in desertum». Qui perrexit obviam ei in montem Dei et osculatus est eum. [28]Narravitque Moyses Aaron omnia verba Domini, quibus miserat eum, et signa, quae mandaverat. [29]Veneruntque simul et congregaverunt cunctos seniores filiorum Israel. [30]Locutusque est Aaron omnia verba, quae dixerat Dominus ad Moysen, et fecit signa coram populo. [31]Et credidit populus, audieruntque quod visitasset Dominus filios Israel et quod respexisset afflictionem eorum; et proni adoraverunt. [1]Post haec ingressi

may hold a feast to me in the wilderness.'" ²But Pharaoh said, "Who is the Lord, that I should heed his voice and let Israel go? I do not know the Lord, and moreover I will not let Israel go." ³Then they said, "The God of the Hebrews has met with us; let us go, we pray, a three days' journey into the wilderness, and sacrifice to the Lord our God, lest he fall upon us with pestilence or with the sword." ⁴But the king of Egypt said to them, "Moses and Aaron, why do you take the people away from their work? Get to your burdens." ⁵And Pharaoh said, "Behold, the people of the land are now many and you make them rest from their burdens!"

The Hebrews' work is made heavier
⁶The same day Pharaoh commanded the taskmasters of the people and their foremen, ⁷"You shall no longer give the people straw to

---

"Peter, James and John also went up the mountain of God to merit the vision of Jesus when he was transfigured and to see him talking to Moses and Elijah in heaven. And you too: if you do not climb the mountain of God, that is, if you do not attain the heights of spiritual knowledge, the Lord will be unable to open your mouth " (*Homiliae in Exodum*, 3,2).

5:1–5. This first confrontation with the pharaoh lets us see the difference between God's plans for salvation and the pharaoh's elaborate projects, whose only purpose is to immortalize his name. The pharaoh does not yet go directly against the Lord (whom he does not know: v. 2); he does not give any anti-religious reasons for not acceding to Moses' request. The objections he raises are social and economic: there is work to be done and it must not be delayed (v. 5). But his new commands are very hard on the Hebrews:

their bondage will worsen and the chance of deliverance will seem to diminish.

"To hold a feast" (v. 1)—a religious pilgrimage ending in a popular celebration. The three great pilgrimages to Jerusalem which Israelites were obliged to attend in later times (cf. 23:14–17) were called "feasts". The Israelites later came to appreciate the importance of this divine command, as also their duty to take part in the prescribed "feasts".

"The people of the land" (v. 5): in this context a reference to the fact that the Israelites belonged to the lower classes. Elsewhere in the Old Testament it is used with other meanings such as "autonomous grouping" or even freemen with a say in the election of a king (cf. 2 Kings 11:14, 18, 20).

5:6–9. "Taskmasters and foremen" (v. 6): the former must have been Egyptian officials overseeing the building work, while

---

sunt Moyses et Aaron et dixerunt pharaoni: «Haec dicit Dominus, Deus Israel: Dimitte populum meum, ut sacrificet mihi in deserto». ²At ille respondit: «Quis est Dominus, ut audiam vocem eius et dimittam Israel? Nescio Dominum et Israel non dimittam». ³Dixeruntque: «Deus Hebraeorum occurrit nobis; eamus, quaeso, viam trium dierum in solitudinem et sacrificemus Domino Deo nostro, ne forte accidat nobis pestis aut gladius». ⁴Ait ad eos rex Aegypti: «Quare, Moyses et Aaron, sollicitatis populum ab operibus suis? Ite ad onera vestra». ⁵Dixitque pharao: «Multus nimis iam est populus terrae; videtis quod turba succreverit; quanto magis si dederitis eis requiem ab operibus?». ⁶Praecepit ergo in die

make bricks, as heretofore; let them go and gather straw for themselves. [8]But the number of bricks which they made heretofore you shall lay upon them, you shall by no means lessen it; for they are idle; therefore they cry, 'Let us go and offer sacrifice to our God.' [9]Let heavier work be laid upon the men that they may labour at it and pay no regard to lying words."

[10]So the taskmasters and the foremen of the people went out and said to the people, "Thus says Pharaoh, 'I will not give you straw. [11]Go yourselves, get your straw wherever you can find it; but your work will not be lessened in the least.'" [12]So the people were scattered abroad throughout all the land of Egypt, to gather stubble for straw. [13]The taskmasters were urgent, saying, "Complete your work, your daily task, as when there was straw." [14]And the foremen of the people of Israel, whom Pharaoh's taskmasters had set over them, were beaten, and were asked, "Why have you not done all your task of making bricks today, as hitherto?"

[15]Then the foremen of the people of Israel came and cried to Pharaoh, "Why do you deal thus with your servants? [16]No straw is given to your servants, yet they say to us, 'Make bricks!' And behold, your servants are beaten; but the fault is in your own people." [17]But he said, "You are idle, you are idle; therefore you

---

the latter would have been Israelites in charge of a group of workers of their own ethnic background.

"Bricks" (v. 7): the usual building material in a region where stone was scarce; the Egyptians used the clay deposited by the Nile in flood, mixed it with straw and then left the bricks to harden in the heat of the sun.

5:10–18. This is a detailed account of the growing pressure on the sons of Israel; in addition to the physical demands being

made on them, the pharaoh was accusing them of being lazy. Perhaps there is a lesson here that those whom God chooses undergo all kinds of trials and misunderstanding but they should put their trust in God alone.

As Origen observes, history bears out that often "everything (they think) goes well for those who yield to the demands of the 'prince of this world', while the servants of God lack even modest means of subsistence" (*Homiliae in Exodum*, 3,3).

---

illo exactoribus populi et praefectis eius dicens: [7]«Nequaquam ultra dabitis paleas populo ad conficiendos lateres sicut prius, sed ipsi vadant et colligant stipulas. [8]Et mensuram laterum, quam prius faciebant, imponetis super eos; nec minuetis quidquam. Vacant enim et idcirco vociferantur dicentes: 'Eamus et sacrificemus Deo nostro'. [9]Opprimantur operibus et expleant ea, ut non acquiescant verbis mendacibus». [10]Igitur egressi exactores populi et praefecti eius dixerunt ad populum: «Sic dicit pharao: 'Non do vobis paleas. [11]Ite et colligite, sicubi invenire poteritis, nec minuetur quidquam de opere vestro'». [12]Dispersusque est populus per omnem terram Aegypti ad colligendas paleas. [13]Exactores quoque instabant dicentes: «Complete opus vestrum cotidie, ut prius facere solebatis, quando dabantur vobis paleae». [14]Flagellatique sunt praefecti filiorum Israel, quos constituerant super eos exactores pharaonis dicentes: «Quare non implestis mensuram laterum sicut prius, nec heri nec hodie?». [15]Veneruntque praefecti filiorum Israel et vociferati sunt ad pharaonem dicentes: «Cur ita agis contra

say, 'Let us go and sacrifice to the LORD.' ¹⁸Go now, and work; for no straw shall be given you, yet you shall deliver the same number of bricks."

Moses intercedes with the pharaoh

¹⁹The foremen of the people of Israel saw that they were in evil plight, when they said, "You shall by no means lessen your daily number of bricks." ²⁰They met Moses and Aaron, who were waiting for them, as they came forth from Pharaoh; ²¹and they said to them, "The LORD look upon you and judge, because you have made us offensive in the sight of Pharaoh and his servants, and have put a sword in their hand to kill us."

²²Then Moses turned again to the LORD and said, "O LORD, why hast thou done evil to this people? Why didst thou ever send me? ²³For since I came to Pharaoh to speak in thy name, he has done evil to this people, and thou hast not delivered thy people at all."

Ex 17:4;
32:11–13
Deut 9:26–29

6 ¹But the LORD said to Moses, "Now you shall see what I will do to Pharaoh; for with a strong hand he will send them out, yea, with a strong hand he will drive them out of his land."

Acts 13:17

5:19–23. Moses is the intermediary between God and the people. In this simple and tense exchange we see how the people feel, and the kind of obstacles Moses meets in performing his mission. By emphasizing the difficulties involved in leaving Egypt, the sacred writer is preparing the reader to appreciate how great God's intervention was. The people's obstinacy was one of the things that most tested Moses' faith.

Moses' prayer is sincere and simple; he is not being rebellious, but he is uneasy (cf. 17:4; 32:11–13; Deut 9:26–29), because he does not yet understand the ways of God. But it is a trusting prayer,

because he knows that only God can provide a lasting solution, as indeed he will (cf. Ex 6:1). The way Moses relates to the Lord is a fine example of mediatory prayer.

6:2–9. The narrative picks up again on the revelation of the divine name and the calling of Moses, an episode which was dealt with amply in chapter 3 (cf. 3:1—4:17). The Priestly tradition, from which this account is probably taken, usually concentrates more on doctrinal aspects than on the details of incidents. Here it is easy to see where the accent is being put—on the name of Yahweh (v.

---

servos tuos? ¹⁶Paleae non dantur nobis, et lateres similiter imperantur; en famuli tui flagellis caedimur, et populus tuus est in culpa». ¹⁷Qui ait: «Vacatis otio et idcirco dicitis: 'Eamus et sacrificemus Domino'. ¹⁸Ite ergo et operamini; paleae non dabuntur vobis, et reddetis consuetum numerum laterum». ¹⁹Videbantque se praefecti filiorum Israel in malo, eo quod diceretur eis: «Non minuetur quidquam de lateribus per singulos dies»; ²⁰occurreruntque Moysi et Aaron, qui stabant ex adverso egredientibus a pharaone, ²¹et dixerunt ad eos: «Videat Dominus et iudicet, quoniam foetere fecistis odorem nostrum coram pharaone et servis eius; et praebuistis ei gladium, ut occideret nos». ²²Reversusque est Moyses ad Dominum et ait: «Domine, cur afflixisti populum istum? Quare misisti me? ²³Ex eo enim quo ingressus sum ad pharaonem, ut loquerer in nomine tuo, afflixit populum tuum; et non liberasti eos». ¹Dixitque Dominus ad Moysen: «Nunc videbis quae facturus sim pharaoni; per

Ex 3:1-4, 23 **A new call to Moses**

Gen 17:1 ²And God said to Moses, "I am the LORD. ³I appeared to Abraham, to Isaac, and to Jacob, as God Almighty,ʰ but by my name the LORD I did not make myself known to them. ⁴I also established my covenant with them, to give them the land of Canaan, the land in which they dwelt as sojourners. ⁵Moreover I have heard the groaning of the people of Israel whom the Egyptians hold in bondage and I have remembered my covenant. Acts 13:17 ⁶Say therefore to the people of Israel, 'I am the LORD, and I will bring you out from under the burdens of the Egyptians, and I will deliver you from their bondage, and I will redeem you with an outstretched arm and with great acts of judgment, ⁷and I will take you for my people, and I will be your God; and you shall know that I am the LORD your God, who has brought you out from Gen 15; 24:7 under the burdens of the Egyptians. ⁸And I will bring you into the

---

2); on the fact that he is the same as the God of the patriarchs (v. 3); on the Covenant established in ancient times (v. 4); on the theological meaning of the Exodus ("I will bring you out", "I will deliver you": v. 6); on the profound wording of the Covenant ("I will take you for my people, and I will be your God": v. 7); and on his giving the Land to the patriarchs under oath (v. 8).

The doctrinal centre in the Priestly tradition is the Covenant, which God initially made with Noah (Gen 9:8ff) after the flood, and which he later ratified with Abraham (Gen 17:1ff) and definitively inaugurated with the entire chosen people (Ex 19:24). Pacts ensure peace when they are made between equals, as perhaps was the case with pacts between nomadic tribes in the desert; or else they formalize

a relationship between unequals when they are made, at the end of a war, between winner and loser (there are Hittite documents of that sort). In both cases the contracting parties come out as beneficiaries. In the divine Covenant things are different: God (and only he) is the one who takes the initiative; the people (and only they) derive benefit; God always does whatever he commits himself to do in the Covenant, even when the people break its main commandment—to follow him. The Covenant is, therefore, that act which best reveals God's unconditional love, first to the chosen people, and later to all men who in Christ share in the New and eternal Covenant.

6:6. "I will redeem you with an outstretched arm": here, for the first time a

---

manum enim fortem dimittet eos et in manu robusta eiciet illos de terra sua». ²Locutusque est Dominus ad Moysen dicens: «Ego Dominus, ³qui apparui Abraham, Isaac ut Iacob ut Deus omnipotens; et nomen meum Dominum non indicavi eis. ⁴Pepigique cum eis foedus, ut darem illis terram Chanaan, terram peregrinationis eorum, in qua fuerunt advenae. ⁵Ego audivi gemitum filiorum Israel, quia Aegyptii oppresserunt eos, et recordatus sum pacti mei. ⁶Ideo dic filiis Israel: Ego Dominus, qui educam vos de ergastulo Aegyptiorum; et eruam de servitute ac redimam in brachio excelso et iudiciis magnis. ⁷Et assumam vos mihi in populum et ero vester Deus; et scietis quod ego sum Dominus Deus vester, qui eduxerim vos de ergastulo Aegyptiorum ⁸et induxerim in terram, super quam levavi manum

h. Heb *El Shaddai*

land which I swore to give to Abraham, to Isaac, and to Jacob; I will give it to you for a possession. I am the LORD.'" [9]Moses spoke thus to the people of Israel; but they did not listen to Moses, because of their broken spirit and their cruel bondage.

[10]And the LORD said to Moses, [11]"Go in, tell Pharaoh king of Egypt to let the people of Israel go out of his land." [12]But Moses said to the LORD, "Behold, the people of Israel have not listened to me; how then shall Pharaoh listen to me, who am a man of uncircumcised lips?" [13]But the LORD spoke to Moses and Aaron, and gave them a charge to the people of Israel and to Pharaoh king of Egypt to bring the people of Israel out of the land of Egypt.

Ex 3:11; 4:10

The genealogy of Aaron and Moses

[14]These are the heads of their fathers' houses: the sons of Reuben, the first-born of Israel: Hanoch, Pallu, Hezron, and Carmi; these

Num 26:57–61; 3:1–10

Gen 46:9
Num 26:5–14

---

key word in salvation history is used—"redemption". A redeemer (in Hebrew, *go'el*) was the person or family who for reasons of blood-relationship had an obligation to re-assert the infringed rights of an offended family member, be it getting him out of bondage, recovering a field or some other piece of property unjustly taken from him, or ensuring that reprisals were taken against a murderer. By taking this role of redeemer, God is committing himself to wipe out any injustices against the people—in the first instance setting it free from the bondage of slavery, as a symbol of liberation from the deeper bondage of sin, devil and death (cf. the note on Lev 25:23–24).

The anthropomorphism of the "outstretched arm" occurs often in the Bible; it is used to show the power of God's action. It is a graphic image which anyone can understand; it is used nowadays, for example, in the phrase "the arm of the law".

6:10–13. This account about Moses' exchange with the Lord over his lack of eloquence covers the same ground as 3:11 and 4:10, but the style is more formal. According to this "Priestly tradition" account Moses has to win the total freedom of the people, not just get permission for a three-day pilgrimage (cf. 3:18; 5:1).

"Uncircumcised lips" (v. 12): using a religious metaphor to make it clear that his limited facility for speech got worse when it was things of God he had to deal with.

6:14–27. Genealogies (which usually come from the Priestly tradition) are not meant to be historically very accurate but are designed to show that there is continuity in the mission God entrusted to each of the tribes of Israel. The genealogy given here is important because it culminates in Aaron, the ancestor of the

---

meam, ut darem eam Abraham, Isaac et Iacob; daboque illam vobis possidendam, ego Dominus». [9]Narravit ergo Moyses omnia filiis Israel; qui non acquieverunt ei propter angustiam spiritus et opus durissimum. [10]Locutusque est Dominus ad Moysen dicens: [11]«Ingredere et loquere ad pharaonem regem Aegypti, ut dimittat filios Israel de terra sua». [12]Respondit Moyses coram Domino: «Ecce, filii Israel non audiunt me, et quomodo audiet me pharao, praesertim cum incircumcisus sim labiis?». [13]Locutusque est Dominus ad Moysen et Aaron et dedit mandatum ad filios Israel et ad pharaonem

are the families of Reuben. [15]The sons of Simeon: Jemuel, Jamin, Ohad, Jachin, Zohar, and Shaul, the son of a Canaanite woman; these are the families of Simeon. [16]These are the names of the sons of Levi according to their generations: Gershon, Kohath, and Merari, the years of the life of Levi being a hundred and thirty-seven years. [17]The sons of Gershon: Libni and Shime-i, by their families. [18]The sons of Kohath: Amram, Izhar, Hebron, and Uzziel, the years of the life of Kohath being a hundred and thirty-three years. [19]The sons of Merari: Mahli and Mushi. These are the families of the Levites according to their generations. [20]Amram took to wife Jochebed his father's sister and she bore him Aaron and Moses, the years of the life of Amram being one hundred and thirty-seven years. [21]The sons of Izhar: Korah, Nepheg, and Zichri. [22]And the sons of Uzziel: Misha-el, Elzaphan, and Sithri. [23]Aaron took to wife Elisheba, the daughter of Amminadab and the sister of Nahshon; and she bore him Nadab, Abihu, Eleazar, and Ithamar. [24]The sons of Korah: Assir, Elkanah, and Abiasaph; these are the families of the Korahites. [25]Eleazar, Aaron's son, took to wife one of the daughters of Puti-el; and she bore him Phinehas. These are the heads of the fathers' houses of the Levites by their families.

Gen 46:11
Num 3:17ff
1 Chron 6:1

Ex 2:1–2
Num 26:59

Lk 1:5

Num 25:6–13

---

priestly class; it is repeated word for word in Numbers 3:1–10 and 26:57–61.

6:28—7:7. In this new discourse of the Lord the first person singular is used in an emphatic way ("I make you as God", "all I command you", "I will harden Pharaoh's heart") to underline the religious character of the Exodus; it is not a human enterprise but rather the start of a key stage in salvation history, and the initiative always lies with God.

"Aaron your brother shall be your prophet" (v. 1): Moses as leader of the people enjoys an authority received from God, but Aaron has been given a charge to speak on Moses' behalf, which is the equivalent of speaking in God's name. A prophet is a man chosen by God to proclaim the will of God and his plans of salvation. Therefore, foretelling the future is not what typifies a prophet, except when that future plays a part in God's salvific plan.

---

regem Aegypti, ut educerent filios Israel de terra Aegypti. [14]Isti sunt principes domorum per familias suas. Filii Ruben primogeniti Israelis: Henoch et Phallu, Hesron et Charmi; hae cognationes Ruben. [15]Filii Simeon: Iamuel et Iamin et Ahod et Iachin et Sohar et Saul filius Chananitidis; hae progenies Simeon. [16]Et haec nomina filiorum Levi per cognationes suas: Gerson et Caath et Merari; anni autem vitae Levi fuerunt centum triginta septem. [17]Filii Gerson: Lobni et Semei per cognationes suas. [18]Filii Caath: Amram et Isaar et Hebron et Oziel; anni quoque vitae Caath centum triginta tres. [19]Filii Merari: Moholi et Musi; hae cognationes Levi per familias suas. [20]Accepit autem Amram uxorem Iochabed amitam suam, quae peperit ei Aaron et Moysen; fueruntque anni vitae Amram centum triginta septem. [21]Filii quoque Isaar: Core et Napheg et Zechri. [22]Filii quoque Oziel: Misael et Elisaphan et Sethri. [23]Accepit autem Aaron uxorem Elisabeth filiam Aminadab sororem Naasson, quae peperit ei Nadab et Abiu et Eleazar et Ithamar. [24]Filii quoque Core: Asir et Elcana et Abiasaph; hae sunt cognationes Coritarum. [25]At vero Eleazar filius Aaron accepit uxorem de filiabus Phutiel, quae peperit ei Phinees;

²⁶These are the Aaron and Moses to whom the LORD said: "Bring out the people of Israel from the land of Egypt by their hosts." ²⁷It was they who spoke to Pharaoh king of Egypt about bringing out the people Israel from Egypt, this Moses and this Aaron.

The announcement of the plagues

Ex 6:2–13

²⁸On the day when the LORD spoke to Moses in the land of Egypt, ²⁹the LORD said to Moses, "I am the LORD; tell Pharaoh king of Egypt all that I say to you." ³⁰But Moses said to the LORD, "Behold, I am of uncircumcised lips; how then shall Pharaoh listen to me?"

7 ¹And the LORD said to Moses, "See, I make you as God to Pharaoh; and Aaron your brother shall be your prophet. ²You shall speak all that I command you; and Aaron your brother shall tell Pharaoh to let the people of Israel go out of his land. ³But I will harden Pharaoh's heart, and though I multiply my signs and wonders in the land of Egypt, ⁴Pharaoh will not listen to you; then I will lay my hand upon Egypt and bring forth my hosts, my people the sons of Israel, out of the land of Egypt by great acts of judgment. ⁵And the Egyptians shall know that I am the LORD, when I stretch forth my hand upon Egypt and bring out the people of Israel from among them." ⁶And Moses and Aaron did so; they did as the LORD commanded them. ⁷Now Moses was eighty years old, and Aaron eighty-three years old, when they spoke to Pharaoh.

Ex 4:16
Jn 10:34

Ex 4:21
Ps 135:9
Acts 7:36
Rom 9:18

7:7. The ages given for Moses and Aaron are more symbolic than real. The sacred writer probably uses the figure forty to stand for a generation, and sees Moses' life as covering three stages or generations—the first spent at the pharaoh's court (cf. Acts 7:23), the second in Midian, and the third and most important leading the people to the promised land; his death comes then when he reaches one hundred and twenty. So even, in his chronology Moses is depicted as someone whom God takes perfect care of.

hi sunt principes familiarum Leviti carum per cognationes suas. ²⁶Iste est Aaron et Moyses, quibus praecepit Dominus, ut educerent filios Israel de terra Aegypti per turmas suas. ²⁷Hi sunt qui loquuntur ad pharaonem regem Aegypti, ut educant filios Israel de Aegypto; iste est Moyses et Aaron ²⁸in die, qua locutus est Dominus ad Moysen in terra Aegypti. ²⁹Et locutus est Dominus ad Moysen dicens: «Ego Dominus loquere ad pharaonem regem Aegypti omnia, quae ego loquor tibi». ³⁰Et ait Moyses coram Domino: «En incircumcisus labiis sum. Quomodo audiet me pharao?». ¹Dixitque Dominus ad Moysen: «Ecce constitui te deum pharaonis, et Aaron frater tuus erit propheta tuus. ²Tu loqueris omnia, quae mando tibi; et ille loquetur ad pharaonem, ut dimittat filios Israel de terra sua. ³Sed ego indurabo cor eius et multiplicabo signa et ostenta mea in terra Aegypti. ⁴Et non audiet vos; immittamque manum meam super Aegyptum et educam exercitum et populum meum, filios Israel, de terra Aegypti per iudicia maxima. ⁵Et scient Aegyptii quia ego sum Dominus, qui extenderim manum meam super Aegyptum et eduxerim filios Israel de medio eorum». ⁶Fecit itaque Moyses et Aaron, sicut praeceperat Dominus; ita egerunt. ⁷Erat autem Moyses octoginta annorum et Aaron octoginta trium, quando locuti

Ex 4:1–5
Ps 78; 105
Wis 11:14–20;
16–18

3. THE PLAGUES*

Moses' miraculous rod

[8]And the LORD said to Moses and Aaron, [9]"When Pharaoh says to you, 'Prove yourselves by working a miracle,' then you shall say to Aaron, 'Take your rod and cast it down before Pharaoh, that it may become a serpent.'" [10]So Moses and Aaron went to Pharaoh and did as the LORD commanded; Aaron cast down his rod before 2 Tim 3:8 Pharaoh and his servants, and it became a serpent. [11]Then Pharaoh

---

*7:8—11:10. The ten plagues are actions God takes to prepare the mind of the pharaoh and the heart of the people for the massive Exodus from Egypt.

The stylistic and doctrinal richness of this whole section indicates how deeply etched its content was on the social and religious memory of the people of Israel. The sacred writer has produced an account based on information in the old traditions, and he makes a point of spelling out the theological meaning of every event. Thus, he gives importance to order: there are ten plagues here, whereas Psalms 78:45–51 and 105:27–36 mention only seven. The magicians appear up to the third plague, when they are roundly defeated by Moses. The seventh plague, the storm, is something of a theophany (visible manifestation of God to man), given that it is explained in such detail and ends with the pharaoh admitting that he is at fault (9:27-28). In the three last plagues the pharaoh yields bit by bit until with the death of the first-born he gives in completely.

The plagues, as they come, do increasing damage: the first four are merely nuisances, though serious ones; the next four affect people and their property; the ninth plunges the Egyptians in a mysterious darkness which prevents all movement; the tenth inflicts terrible loss on families and forces the pharaoh to let the people of Israel go.

The narrative is written in an epic style which makes God's victory over the king even more pronounced: God begins by acting through Moses and Aaron who use the rod as a thaumaturgical tool, but he gradually uses them less and less until it is he alone who is involved in the final catastrophe affecting the first-born. Some of the plagues are rather like the natural phenomena which occur from time to time in Egypt; but their being reported as marvels serves to highlight profound basic teaching—that God, the Lord of nature and of history, is intervening in a supernatural way to save his people from bondage and lead them to a new state of freedom and well-being.

7:8–13. The miraculous rod (closely connected with the story told in 4:1–5) further emphasizes the importance of Aaron, who is the one who actually wields the thaumaturgical power.

---

sunt ad pharaonem. [8]Dixitque Dominus ad Moysen et Aaron: [9]«Cum dixerit vobis pharao: 'Ostendite signum', dices ad Aaron: Tolle virgam tuam et proice eam coram pharaone, ac vertetur in colubrum». [10]Ingressi ita que Moyses et Aaron ad pharaonem fecerunt, sicut praeceperat Dominus; proiecitque Aaron virgam coram pharaone et servis eius, quae versa est in colubrum. [11]Vocavit autem pharao sapientes et maleficos, et fecerunt etiam ipsi magi Aegypti per incantationes suas similiter. [12]Proieceruntque singuli virgas suas, quae versae sunt in colubros; sed devoravit virga Aaron virgas eorum.

summoned the wise men and the sorcerers; and they also, the magicians of Egypt, did the same by their secret arts. [12]For every man cast down his rod, and they became serpents. But Aaron's rod swallowed up their rods. [13]Still Pharaoh's heart was hardened, and he would not listen to them; as the LORD had said.

The first plague: the water turns to blood

Wis 11:68

[14]*Then the LORD said to Moses, "Pharaoh's heart is hardened, he refuses to let the people go. [15]Go to Pharaoh in the morning, as he

---

The "wise men", "sorcerers" and "magicians" (v. 11) were the pharaoh's circle of advisers. Magical rites and snake-charming were held in high regard in the cultural and religious life of Egypt (cf. Gen 41:8).

God is shown to be more powerful than the pharaoh and his magicians not so much by his ability to work wonders as by his sovereign power: God is the Lord, the only Lord; all other powers are subject to him. The Fathers saw the rod as a figure of the cross, for, as St Paul says, Christ on the cross is the "power of God and the wisdom of God" (1 Cor 1:24: cf. Origen, *Homiliae in Exodum*, 4, 6).

Jewish tradition has conserved the names of two of the magicians of Egypt; St Paul, making this tradition his own, mentions them as being the prototype of obstinate people who deny even the most obvious truth: "As Jannes and Jambres opposed Moses, so these men also oppose the truth, men of corrupt mind and counterfeit faith" (2 Tim 3:8).

7:13. The pharaoh's obstinacy is a refrain which is repeated up to the last plague (cf. 7;14; 8:11, 15, 28; 9:7, 12, 35). Insistence on this piece of information

helps the reader to see time and time again that God alone can overcome the huge obstacles being raised against the deliverance of the sons of Israel, as can be seen in the key statement in the plague account, "By this you shall know that I am the Lord" (cf. 7:17; 8:6, 18; 9:14; 10:2).

7:14–24. The first scourge used against the pharaoh is the water turned to blood. Being an epic account, it is not surprising that it should reflect a phenomenon with which the Egyptians were familiar: the Nile in springtime takes on a reddish, bloody colour, due to the mud which it brings down from Abyssinia; the natives call it the Red Nile. Nor should we be surprised to find small inconsistencies in this account: sometimes it is Moses who carries the rod, sometimes Aaron; the Egyptian magicians also turn water into blood even though *all* the water of Egypt has already become blood. In gathering together these ancient traditions the sacred writer's aim is to recount the pharaoh's direct confrontation with God, showing it as taking place on the Nile, which Egyptian literature mythologized as the country's source of life and wealth. The book of Wisdom interprets this first

---

[13]Induratumque est cor pharaonis, et non audivit eos, sicut dixerat Dominus. [14]Dixit autem Dominus ad Moysen: «Ingravatum est cor pharaonis: non vult dimittere populum. [15]Vade ad eum mane. Ecce egredietur ad aquas; et stabis in occursum eius super ripam fluminis. Et virgam, quae conversa est in serpentem, tolles in manu tua [16]dicesque ad eum: Dominus, Deus Hebraeorum, misit me ad te dicens:

is going out to the water; wait for him by the river's brink, and take in your hand the rod which was turned into a serpent. ¹⁶And you shall say to him, 'The LORD, the God of the Hebrews, sent me to you, saying, "Let my people go, that they may serve me in Rev 11:6; the wilderness; and behold, you have not yet obeyed." ¹⁷Thus 16:3–4 says the LORD, "By this you shall know that I am the LORD: behold, I will strike the water that is in the Nile with the rod that is in my hand, and it shall be turned to blood, ¹⁸and the fish in the Nile shall die, and the Nile shall become foul, and the Egyptians will loathe to drink water from the Nile."'" ¹⁹And the Rev 11:6; 16:4 LORD said to Moses, "Say to Aaron, 'Take your rod and stretch out your hand over the waters of Egypt, over their rivers, their canals, and their ponds, and all their pools of water, that they may become blood; and there shall be blood throughout all the land of Egypt, both in vessels of wood and in vessels of stone.'"

²⁰Moses and Aaron did as the LORD commanded; in the sight Ps 78:44; 105:29 of Pharaoh and in the sight of his servants, he lifted up the rod Rev 8:8 and struck the water that was in the Nile, and all the water that was in the Nile turned to blood. ²¹And the fish in the Nile died; and the Nile became foul, so that the Egyptians could not drink water from the Nile; and there was blood throughout all the land of Egypt. ²²But the magicians of Egypt did the same by their 2 Tim 3:8 secret arts; so Pharaoh's heart remained hardened, and he would not listen to them; as the LORD had said. ²³Pharaoh turned and went into his house, and he did not lay even this to heart. ²⁴And

---

plague as God's just response to the killing of Hebrew children by drowning in the Nile: "in rebuke for the decree to slay the infants" (Wis 11:7).

7:25—8:15. The second plague is desc-

ribed as an invasion by frogs and, probably, other types of amphibians. It is the immense quantity of these animals and the fact that they appear and disappear at Moses' say-so that shows the hand of God to be at work. The purpose of this

Dimitte populum meum, ut sacrificet mihi in deserto; et usque ad praesens audire noluisti. ¹⁷Haec igitur dicit Dominus: In hoc scies quod sim Dominus: ecce percutiam virga, quae in manu mea est, aquam fluminis; et vertetur in sanguinem. ¹⁸Pisces quoque, qui sunt in fluvio, morientur, et computrescent aquae, et taedebit Aegyptios bibere aquam fluminis». ¹⁹Dixit quoque Dominus ad Moysen: «Dic ad Aaron: Tolle virgam tuam et extende manum tuam super aquas Aegypti, super fluvios eorum et rivos ac paludes et omnes lacus aquarum, ut vertantur in sanguinem; et sit cruor in omni terra Aegypti, tam in ligneis vasis quam in saxeis». ²⁰Feceruntque ita Moyses et Aaron, sicut praeceperat Dominus. Et elevans virgam percussit aquam fluminis coram pharaone et servis eius; quae versa est in sanguinem. ²¹Et pisces, qui erant in flumine, mortui sunt, computruitque fluvius, et non poterant Aegyptii bibere aquam fluminis; et fuit sanguis in tota terra Aegypti. ²²Feceruntque similiter malefici Aegyptiorum incantationibus suis; et induratum est cor pharaonis, nec audivit eos, sicut dixerat Dominus. ²³Avertitque se et ingressus est domum suam nec ad hoc apposuit cor suum. ²⁴Foderunt autem omnes Aegyptii per circuitum fluminis aquam, ut biberent; non enim poterant bibere de aqua fluminis. ²⁵Impletique sunt

all the Egyptians dug round about the Nile for water to drink, for they could not drink the water of the Nile.

The second plague: the frogs

²⁵Seven days passed after the LORD had struck the Nile.

8 ¹ⁱThen the LORD said to Moses, "Go in to Pharaoh and say to him, 'Thus says the LORD "Let my people go, that they may serve me. ²But if you refuse to let them go, behold, I will plague all your country with frogs; ³the Nile shall swarm with frogs which shall come up into your house, and into your bedchamber and on your bed, and into the houses of your servants and of your people,ʲ and into your ovens and your kneading bowls; ⁴the frogs shall come up on you and on your people and on all your servants."'" ⁵ᵏAnd the LORD said to Moses, "Say to Aaron, 'Stretch out your hand with your rod over the rivers, over the canals, and over the pools, and cause frogs to come upon the land of Egypt!'" ⁶So Aaron stretched out his hand over the waters of Egypt; and the frogs came up and covered the land of Egypt. ⁷But the magicians did the same by their secret arts, and brought frogs upon the land of Egypt.

⁸Then Pharaoh called Moses and Aaron, and said, "Entreat the LORD to take away the frogs from me and from my people; and I will let the people go to sacrifice to the LORD." ⁹Moses said to Pharaoh, "Be pleased to command me when I am to entreat, for you and for your servants and for your people, that the frogs be

Ps 78:45; 105:30

Rev 16:13

Acts 8:24

wondrous phenomenon is to show that "there is no one like the Lord our God" (v. 10). Moreover, Moses' authority comes out enhanced, because he is seen to be the one who is able to intercede successfully with God (v. 9). It is worth noting also that the pharaoh for the first time entertains the idea of letting the people go, even though for selfish reasons, but he soon changes his mind (v. 8).

septem dies, postquam percussit Dominus fluvium. ²⁶Dixit quoque Dominus ad Moysen: «Ingredere ad pharaonem et dices ad eum: Haec dicit Dominus: Dimitte populum meum, ut sacrificet mihi. ²⁷Sin autem nolueris dimittere, ecce ego percutiam omnes terminos tuos ranis. ²⁸Et ebulliet fluvius ranas, quae ascendent et ingredientur domum tuam et cubiculum lectuli tui et super stratum tuum et in domos servorum tuorum et in populum tuum et in furnos tuos et in pistrina tua; ²⁹et ad te et ad populum tuum et ad omnes servos tuos intrabunt ranae». ¹Dixitque Dominus ad Moysen: «Dic ad Aaron: Extende manum tuam cum baculo tuo super fluvios, super rivos ac paludes et educ ranas super terram Aegypti». ²Et extendit Aaron manum super aquas Aegypti, et ascenderunt ranae operueruntque terram Aegypti. ³Fecerunt autem et malefici per incantationes suas similiter eduxeruntque ranas super terram Aegypti. ⁴Vocavit autem pharao Moysen et Aaron et dixit: «Orate Dominum, ut auferat ranas a me et a populo meo, et dimittam populum, ut sacrificet Domino». ⁵Dixitque Moyses ad pharaonem: «Constitue mihi, quando deprecer pro te et pro servis et pro populo tuo, ut abigantur ranae a te et a domo tua et tantum

i. Ch 7:26 in Heb [and in New Vulgate] **j.** Gk: Heb *upon your people* **k.** Ch 8:1 in Heb [and in New Vulgate]

destroyed from you and your houses and be left only in the Nile."
¹⁰And he said, "Tomorrow." Moses said, "Be it as you say, that
you may know that there is no one like the Lᴏʀᴅ our God. ¹¹The
frogs shall depart from you and your houses and your servants
and your people; they shall be left only in the Nile." ¹²So Moses
and Aaron went out from Pharaoh; and Moses cried to the Lᴏʀᴅ
concerning the frogs, as he had agreed with Pharaoh.ⁱ ¹³And the
Lᴏʀᴅ did according to the word of Moses; the frogs died out of
the houses and courtyards and out of the fields. ¹⁴And they gathered them together in heaps, and the land stank. ¹⁵But when
Pharaoh saw that there was a respite, he hardened his heart, and
would not listen to them; as the Lᴏʀᴅ had said.

The third plague: the gnats

¹⁶Then the Lᴏʀᴅ said to Moses, "Say to Aaron, 'Stretch out your
rod and strike the dust of the earth, that it may become gnats

Ps 105:31 throughout all the land of Egypt.'" ¹⁷And they did so; Aaron
stretched out his hand with his rod, and struck the dust of the
earth, and there came gnats on man and beast; all the dust of the

Wis 17:1 earth became gnats throughout all the land of Egypt. ¹⁸The magicians tried by their secret arts to bring forth gnats, but they could

Lk 11:20 not. So there were gnats on man and beast. ¹⁹And the magicians
said to Pharaoh, "This is the finger of God." But Pharaoh's heart

---

8:16–19. This account is usually attributed
to the Priestly tradition on the grounds that
the protagonist is Aaron. The climax of
this prodigy is the fact that the Egyptian
magicians cannot match it and they have
to admit that "the finger of God" (far more
powerful than their magical arts) is pre-

sent. Thus, the account of the plagues is
showing that people are gradually coming
to see the almighty power of God. With
the plague of gnats the magicians' defeat
is irreversible; no longer will they venture
to use their skills against the plagues. But
the pharaoh still refuses to yield.

---

in flumine remaneant». ⁶Qui respondit: «Cras». At ille: «Iuxta verbum, inquit, tuum faciam, ut scias
quoniam non est sicut Dominus Deus noster. ⁷Et recedent ranae a te et a domo tua et a servis tuis et a
populo tuo; tantum in flumine remanebunt». ⁸Egressique sunt Moyses et Aaron a pharaone; et clamavit
Moyses ad Dominum pro sponsione ranarum, quam condixerat pharaoni. ⁹Fecitque Dominus iuxta
verbum Moysi, et mortuae sunt ranae de domibus et de villis et de agris; ¹⁰Congregaveruntque eas in
immensos aggeres, et computruit terra. ¹¹Videns autem pharao quod data esset requies, ingravavit cor
suum et non audivit eos, sicut dixerat Dominus. ¹²Dixitque Dominus ad Moysen: «Loquere ad Aaron:
Extende virgam tuam et percute pulverem terrae, et sint scinifes in universa terra Aegypti».
¹³Feceruntque ita; et extendit Aaron manum virgam tenens percussitque pulverem terrae. Et facti sunt
scinifes in hominibus et in iumentis; omnis pulvis terrae versus est in scinifes per totam terram
Aegypti. ¹⁴Feceruntque similiter malefici incantationibus suis, ut educerent scinifes; et non potuerunt.
Erantque scinifes tam in hominibus quam in iumentis; ¹⁵et dixerunt malefici ad pharaonem: «Digitus
Dei est hic». Induratumque est cor pharaonis et non audivit eos, sicut praeceperat Dominus. ¹⁶Dixit

l. Or *which he had brought upon Pharaoh*

was hardened, and he would not listen to them; as the LORD had said.

The fourth plague: the flies

²⁰Then the LORD said to Moses, "Rise up early in the morning and wait for Pharaoh, as he goes out to the water, and say to him, 'Thus says the LORD, "Let my people go, that they may serve me. ²¹Else, if you will not let my people go, behold, I will send swarms of flies on you and your servants and your people, and into your houses; and the houses of the Egyptians shall be filled with swarms of flies, and also the ground on which they stand. ²²But on that day I will set apart the land of Goshen, where my people dwell, so that no swarms of flies shall be there; that you may know that I am the LORD in the midst of the earth. ²³Thus I will put a division^m between my people and your people. By tomorrow shall this sign be."'" ²⁴And the LORD did so; there came great swarms of flies into the house of Pharaoh and into his servants' houses, and in all the land of Egypt the land was ruined by reason of the flies.

²⁵Then Pharaoh called Moses and Aaron, and said, "Go, sacrifice to your God within the land." ²⁶But Moses said, "It would not be right to do so; for we shall sacrifice to the LORD our God offer-

Ps 78:45
Ex 7:15
Wis 16:9

Gen 47:1f

8:20–32. The description of the plague of the gadflies may come from the Yahwistic tradition (witness its colour and richness of detail); in fact, some authors think that this account may be a variant of the previous one (the gnats).

Moses has to meet the pharaoh again when the latter goes to the Nile in the early morning (cf. 7:15), either to bathe or to worship the God of the River. As in the previous plague, the insects obey Moses, this time to infest the houses of

the Egyptians. God's special protection of the people of Israel is underlined.

The conversation between Moses and the pharaoh is interesting. Moses cannot modify the plans of God; therefore he cannot agree to the restriction that the people's sacrifice take place within the boundaries of Egypt. The excuse Moses offers shows his astuteness: the Egyptians would be affronted if they saw the Israelites sacrificing lambs (cf. v. 26). Throughout this

quoque Dominus ad Moysen: «Consurge diluculo et sta coram pharaone. Egredietur enim ad aquas, et dices ad eum: Haec dicit Dominus: Dimitte populum meum, ut sacrificet mihi. ¹⁷Quod si non dimiseris eum, ecce ego immittam in te et in servos tuos et in populum tuum et in domos tuas omne genus muscarum; et implebuntur domus Aegyptiorum muscis et etiam humus, in qua fuerint. ¹⁸Et segregabo in die illa terram Gessen, in qua populus meus est, ut non sint ibi muscae, et scias quoniam ego Dominus in medio terrae; ¹⁹ponamque divisionem inter populum meum et populum tuum; cras erit signum istud». ²⁰Fecitque Dominus ita; et venit musca gravissima in domos pharaonis et servorum eius et in omnem terram Aegypti, corruptaque est terra ab huiuscemodi muscis. ²¹Vocavitque pharao Moysen et Aaron et ait eis: «Ite, sacrificate Deo vestro in terra». ²²Et ait Moyses: «Non potest ita fieri: abom-

m. Gk Vg: Heb *set redemption*

ings abominable to the Egyptians. If we sacrifice offerings abominable to the Egyptians before their eyes, will they not stone us? [27]We must go three days' journey into the wilderness and sacrifice to the LORD our God as he will command us." [28]So Pharaoh said, "I will let you go, to sacrifice to the LORD your God in the wilderness; only you shall not go very far away. Make entreaty for me." [29]Then Moses said, "Behold, I am going out from you and I will pray to the LORD that the swarms of flies may depart from Pharaoh, from his servants, and from his people, tomorrow; only let not Pharaoh deal falsely again by not letting the people go to sacrifice to the LORD." [30]So Moses went out from Pharaoh and prayed to the LORD. [31]And the LORD did as Moses asked, and removed the swarms of flies from Pharaoh, from his servants, and from his people; not one remained. [32]But Pharaoh hardened his heart this time also, and did not let the people go.

The fifth plague: the livestock epidemic

Ps 78:48

9 [1]Then the LORD said to Moses, "Go in to Pharaoh, and say to him, 'Thus says the LORD, the God of the Hebrews, "Let my people go, that they may serve me. [2]For if you refuse to let them go and still hold them, [3]behold, the hand of the LORD will fall with a very severe plague upon your cattle which are in the field, the horses, the asses, the camels, the herds, and the flocks. [4]But the

---

account the sacred writer emphasizes the separateness of the people of Israel: it is not like other peoples, for God has segregated it, has chosen it for a special mission (cf. 19:1–5). The pharaoh continues to refuse; but his obstinacy is weakening.

9:1–7. The cattle epidemic is a much more serious scourge than the previous plagues because it affects possessions necessary to people's livelihood. Brief though it is, the account has features which suggest it comes from the Yahwistic tradition, such as the listing of types of domestic animals

---

inationes enim Aegyptiorum immolabimus Domino Deo nostro; quod si mactaverimus ea, quae colunt Aegyptii, coram eis, lapidibus nos obruent. [23]Viam trium dierum pergemus in solitudinem et sacrificabimus Domino Deo nostro, sicut praecepit nobis». [24]Dixitque pharao: «Ego dimittam vos, ut sacrificetis Domino Deo vestro in deserto, verumtamen longius ne abeatis; rogate pro me». [25]Et ait Moyses: «Egressus a te, orabo Dominum, et recedet musca a pharaone et a servis suis et a populo eius cras; verumtamen noli ultra fallere, ut non dimittas populum sacrificare Domino». [26]Egressusque Moyses a pharaone oravit Dominum; [27]qui fecit iuxta verbum illius et abstulit muscas a pharaone et a servis suis et a populo eius; non superfuit ne una quidem. [28]Et ingravatum est cor pharaonis, ita ut ne hac quidem vice dimitteret populum. [1]Dixit autem Dominus ad Moysen: «Ingredere ad pharaonem et loquere ad eum: Haec dicit Dominus, Deus Hebraeorum: Dimitte populum meum, ut sacrificet mihi. [2]Quod si adhuc renuis et retines eos, [3]ecce manus Domini erit super possessionem tuam in agris, super equos et asinos et camelos et boves et oves, pestis valde gravis; [4]et distinguet Dominus inter possessiones Israel et possessiones Aegyptiorum, ut nihil omnino pereat ex his, quae pertinent ad filios Israel. [5]Constituitque Dominus tempus dicens: Cras faciet Dominus verbum istud in terra». [6]Fecit ergo Dominus verbum hoc altera die, mortuaque sunt omnia animantia Aegyptiorum; de animalibus vero

LORD will make a distinction between the cattle of Israel and the cattle of Egypt, so that nothing shall die of all that belongs to the people of Israel."'" ⁵And the LORD set a time, saying, "Tomorrow the LORD will do this thing in the land." ⁶And on the morrow the LORD did this thing; all the cattle of the Egyptians died, but of the cattle of the people of Israel not one died. ⁷And Pharaoh sent, and behold, not one of the cattle of the Israelites was dead. But the heart of Pharaoh was hardened, and he did not let the people go.

The sixth plague: the boils

⁸And the LORD said to Moses and Aaron, "Take handfuls of ashes from the kiln, and let Moses throw them toward heaven in the sight of Pharaoh. ⁹And it shall become fine dust over all the land of Egypt, and become boils breaking out in sores on man and beast throughout all the land of Egypt." ¹⁰So they took ashes from the kiln, and stood before Pharaoh, and Moses threw them toward heaven, and it became boils breaking out in sores on man and beast. ¹¹And the magicians could not stand before Moses because of the boils, for the boils were upon the magicians and upon all the Egyptians. ¹²But the LORD hardened the heart of Pharaoh, and he did not listen to them; as the LORD had spoken to Moses.

Rev 16:2

Mt 27:10

The seventh plague: the hail

¹³Then the LORD said to Moses, "Rise up early in the morning and stand before Pharaoh, and say to him, 'Thus says the LORD, the

Ps 78:47ff; 105:32 Rev 16:21

(v. 3) and the hyperbole that "all" the cattle succumbed. It stresses the distinction God makes between the Egyptians and the Israelites, and points out that God sets a time limit on the plague.

9:8–12. This plague, too, is narrated in few words; the account may come from the Priestly tradition. The severity of the scourge is worse again: it affects people as

well as livestock. Indeed, even the magicians (who have said and done nothing since the plague of gnats) are themselves affected. By showing the worsening plague, the sacred writer manages to make the reader feel increasing hostility towards the obstinate and foolish pharaoh, and to identify with the Lord, who does not impose himself by force but takes action to gradually bend the tyrant's will.

---

filiorum Israel nihil omnino periit. ⁷Et misit pharao ad videndum; nec erat quidquam mortuum de his, quae possidebat Israel. Ingravatumque est cor pharaonis, et non dimisit populum. ⁸Et dixit Dominus ad Moysen et Aaron: «Tollite plenas manus cineris de camino, et spargat illum Moyses in caelum coram pharaone; ⁹sitque pulvis super omnem terram Aegypti; erunt enim in hominibus et iumentis ulcera et vesicae turgentes in universa terra Aegypti». ¹⁰Tuleruntque cinerem de camino et steterunt coram pharaone, et sparsit illum Moyses in caelum; factaque sunt ulcera vesicarum turgentium in hominibus et iumentis. ¹¹Nec poterant malefici stare coram Moyse propter ulcera, quae in illis erant et in omni terra Aegypti. ¹²Induravitque Dominus cor pharaonis, et non audivit eos, sicut locutus est Dominus ad Moysen. ¹³Dixitque Dominus ad Moysen: «Mane consurge et sta coram pharaone et dices ad eum:

God of the Hebrews, "Let my people go, that they may serve me. [14]For this time I will send all my plagues upon your heart, and upon your servants and your people, that you may know that there is none like me in all the earth. [15]For by now I could have put forth my hand and struck you and your people with pestilence,

Rom 9:17 and you would have been cut off from the earth; [16]but for this purpose have I let you live, to show you my power, so that my name may be declared throughout all the earth. [17]You are still exalting

Mk 13:19 yourself against my people, and will not let them go. [18]Behold, tomorrow about this time I will cause very heavy hail to fall, such as never has been in Egypt from the day it was founded until now. [19]Now therefore send, get your cattle and all that you have in the field into safe shelter; for the hail shall come down upon every man and beast that is in the field and is not brought home, and they shall die."' " [20]Then he who feared the word of the LORD among the servants of Pharaoh made his slaves and his cattle flee into the houses; [21]but he who did not regard the word of the LORD left his slaves and his cattle in the field.

9:13–35. The seventh plague, the hailstorm, knows no limits: affects the entire land of Egypt—plants, animals and men.

In the Bible a storm accompanied by hail, thunder and lightning is a sign that God is making himself manifest (cf. 19:18; Ps 18:9–14; 29:3–9); this theophany is meant to show that there is none greater than God (vv. 14–16). St Paul refers to this passage of Exodus (cf. Rom 9:17), pointing out that the pharaoh himself had an important role in God's designs: his blindness made God's power and wisdom plainer to see.

All those living in Egypt were witnesses to God's intervention and they reacted by more or less acknowledging the Lord: the Israelites, who were living in Goshen, presumably realized the special protection they were enjoying; the pharaoh's ministers for the first time "feared the word of the Lord" (v. 20); the pharaoh himself began to admit his fault in his suit against God: "The Lord is in the right, and I and my people are in the wrong" (v. 27).

The sacred writer has seen in the scourge of hailstones a clearer manifestation of God's saving plan; this plague is recalled forcefully in Psalms 78:47f and 105:32, and, later on, the book of Revelation refers to it as an eschatological sign (Rev 16:21).

Haec dicit Dominus, Deus Hebraeorum: Dimitte populum meum, ut sacrificet mihi; [14]quia in hac vice mittam omnes plagas meas super cor tuum et super servos tuos et super populum tuum, ut scias quod non sit similis mei in omni terra. [15]Nunc enim extendens manum si percussissem te et populum tuum peste, perisses de terra. [16]Idcirco autem servavi te, ut ostendam in te fortitudinem meam, et narretur nomen meum in omni terra. [17]Adhuc retines populum meum et non vis dimittere eum? [18]En pluam cras, hac ipsa hora, grandinem multam nimis, qualis non fuit in Aegypto a die, qua fundata est, usque in praesens tempus. [19]Mitte ergo iam nunc et congrega iumenta tua et omnia, quae habes in agro; homines enim et iumenta universa, quae inventa fuerint foris nec congregata de agris, cadet super ea grando, et morientur». [20]Qui timuit verbum Domini de servis pharaonis, fecit confugere servos suos et iumenta in domos; [21]qui autem neglexit sermonem Domini, dimisit servos suos et iumenta in agris. [22]Et dixit Dominus ad Moysen: «Extende manum tuam in caelum, ut fiat grando in universa terra Aegypti super

²²And the Lord said to Moses, "Stretch forth your hand toward heaven, that there may be hail in all the land of Egypt, upon man and beast and every plant of the field, throughout the land of Egypt." ²³Then Moses stretched forth his rod toward heaven; and the Lord sent thunder and hail, and fire ran down to the earth. And the Lord rained hail upon the land of Egypt; ²⁴there was hail, and fire flashing continually in the midst of the hail, very heavy hail, such as had never been in all the land of Egypt since it became a nation. ²⁵The hail struck down everything that was in the field throughout all the land of Egypt, both man and beast; and the hail struck down every plant of the field, and shattered every tree of the field. ²⁶Only in the land of Goshen, where the people of Israel were, there was no hail.

²⁷Then Pharaoh sent, and called Moses and Aaron, and said to them, "I have sinned this time; the Lord is in the right, and I and my people are in the wrong. ²⁸Entreat the Lord; for there has been enough of this thunder and hail; I will let you go, and you shall stay no longer." ²⁹Moses said to him, "As soon as I have gone out of the city, I will stretch out my hands to the Lord; the thunder will cease, and there will be no more hail, that you may know that the earth is the Lord's. ³⁰But as for you and your servants, I know that you do not yet fear the Lord God." ³¹(The flax and the barley were ruined, for the barley was in the ear and the flax was in bud. ³²But the wheat and the spelt were not ruined, for they are late in coming up.) ³³So Moses went out of the city from Pharaoh, and stretched out his hands to the Lord; and the thunder and the hail ceased, and the rain no longer poured upon the earth. ³⁴But when Pharaoh saw that the rain and the hail and the thunder had ceased, he sinned yet again, and hardened his heart, he and his servants. ³⁵So the heart of Pharaoh was hardened, and he did not let the people of Israel go; as the Lord had spoken through Moses.

Ps 78:47; 105:32
Wis 16:6
Rev 16:21; 8:7
Rev 11:19; 16:18
Acts 8:24
Deut 10:14
Ps 24:1

The eighth plague: the locusts

Joel 1:2–10

10 ¹Then the LORD said to Moses, "Go in to Pharaoh; for I have hardened his heart and the heart of his servants, that I

Ex 12:26; 13:8
Deut 4:9;
6:20–25

may show these signs of mine among them, ²and that you may tell in the hearing of your son and of your son's son how I have made sport of the Egyptians and what signs I have done among them; that you may know that I am the LORD."

³So Moses and Aaron went in to Pharaoh, and said to him, "Thus says the LORD, the God of the Hebrews, 'How long will you refuse to humble yourself before me? Let my people go, that

Wis 16:9

they may serve me. ⁴For if you refuse to let my people go, behold, tomorrow I will bring locusts into your country, ⁵and they shall cover the face of the land, so that no one can see the land; and they shall eat what is left to you after the hail, and they shall eat every tree of yours which grows in the field, ⁶and they shall fill your houses, and the houses of all your servants and of all the Egyptians; as neither your fathers nor your grandfathers have seen, from the day they came on earth to this day.'" Then he turned and went out from Pharaoh.

⁷And Pharaoh's servants said to him, "How long shall this man be a snare to us? Let the men go, that they may serve the LORD

10:1–20. Plagues of locusts often affected north Africa, including Egypt; borne by the wind, they can descend on a region in vast numbers and leave farmland devastated. However, this particular plague is, we are told, a severe punishment sent by God (cf. Joel 1:2–10). The sacred writer once again says things which indicate the deep meaning of all the prodigies which preceded the

Exodus—particularly the religious meaning of the plagues (their main object is to make known that "I am the Lord": v. 2); the intervention of the pharaoh's servants who, although they do not know the Lord, are at least ready to let the Israelites go (v. 7); the pharaoh's readiness to let the men go, while holding the women and children hostage (vv. 8–11); and his admission of his sin.

---

vatum est cor eius et servorum illius et induratum nimis; nec dimisit filios Israel, sicut dixerat Dominus per manum Moysi. ¹Et dixit Dominus ad Moysen: «Ingredere ad pharaonem: ego enim induravi cor eius et servorum illius, ut faciam signa mea haec in medio eorum, ²et narres in auribus filii tui et nepotum tuorum, quotiens contriverim Aegyptios et signa mea fecerim in eis; et sciatis quia ego Dominus». ³Introierunt ergo Moyses et Aaron ad pharaonem et dixerunt ei: «Haec dicit Dominus, Deus Hebraeorum: Usquequo non vis subici mihi? Dimitte populum meum, ut sacrificet mihi. ⁴Sin autem resistis et non vis dimittere eum, ecce ego inducam cras locustam in fines tuos, ⁵quae operiat superficiem terrae, ne quidquam eius appareat, sed comedatur, quod residuum fuerit grandini; corrodet enim omnia ligna, quae germinant in agris. ⁶Et implebunt domos tuas et servorum tuorum et omnium Aegyptiorum, quantam non viderunt patres tui et avi, ex quo orti sunt super terram usque in praesentem diem». Avertitque se et egressus est a pharaone. ⁷Dixerunt autem servi pharaonis ad eum: «Usquequo patiemur hoc scandalum? Dimitte homines, ut sacrificent Domino Deo suo; nonne vides quod perierit Aegyptus?». ⁸Revocaveruntque Moysen et Aaron ad pharaonem, qui dixit eis: «Ite, sacrificate Domino Deo vestro. Quinam sunt qui ituri sunt?». ⁹Ait Moyses: «Cum parvulis nostris et

their God; do you not yet understand that Egypt is ruined?" [8]So Moses and Aaron were brought back to Pharaoh; and he said to them, "Go, serve the LORD your God; but who are to go?" [9]And Moses said, "We will go with our young and our old; we will go with our sons and daughters and with our flocks and herds, for we must hold a feast to the LORD." [10]And he said to them, "The LORD be with you, if ever I let you and your little ones go! Look, you have some evil purpose in mind.[n] [11]No! Go, the men among you, and serve the LORD, for that is what you desire." And they were driven out from Pharaoh's presence.

[12]Then the LORD said to Moses, "Stretch out your hand over the land of Egypt for the locusts, that they may come upon the land of Egypt, and eat every plant in the land, all that the hail has left." [13]So Moses stretched forth his rod over the land of Egypt, and the Lord brought an east wind upon the land all that day and all that night; and when it was morning the east wind had brought the locusts. [14]And the locusts came up over all the land of Egypt, and settled on the whole country of Egypt, such a dense swarm of locusts as had never been before, nor ever shall be again. [15]For they covered the face of the whole land, so that the land was darkened, and they ate all the plants in the land and all the fruit of the trees which the hail had left; not a green thing remained, neither tree nor plant of the field, through all the land of Egypt. [16]Then Pharaoh called Moses and Aaron in haste, and said, "I have sinned against the LORD your God, and against you. [17]Now therefore, forgive my sin, I pray you, only this once, and entreat the LORD your God only to remove this death from me." [18]So he went out from Pharaoh, and entreated the LORD. [19]And the LORD turned

Margin references: Ps 78:46; 105:34; Rev 9:3 (at v. 12); Lk 15:18 (at v. 16); Acts 8:24 (at v. 17)

senioribus pergemus, cum filiis et filiabus, cum ovibus et armentis; est enim sollemnitas Domini nobis». [10]Et respondit eis: «Sic Dominus sit vobiscum, quomodo ego dimittam vos et parvulos vestros. Cui dubium est quod pessime cogitetis? [11]Non fiet ita, sed ite tantum viri et sacrificate Domino; hoc enim et ipsi petistis». Statimque eiecti sunt de conspectu pharaonis. [12]Dixit autem Dominus ad Moysen: «Extende manum tuam super terram Aegypti, ut veniat locusta et ascendat super eam et devoret omnem herbam, quidquid residuum fuerit grandini». [13]Et extendit Moyses virgam super terram Aegypti, et Dominus induxit ventum urentem tota die illa et nocte. Et mane facto, ventus urens levavit locustas; [14]quae ascenderunt super universam terram Aegypti et sederunt in cunctis finibus Aegyptiorum innumerabiles, quales ante illud tempus non fuerant nec postea futurae sunt. [15]Operueruntque universam superficiem terrae, et obscurata est terra. Devoraverunt igitur omnem herbam terrae et, quidquid pomorum in arboribus fuit, quae grando dimiserat; nihilque omnino virens relictum est in lignis et in herbis terrae in cuncta Aegypto. [16]Quam ob rem festinus pharao vocavit Moysen et Aaron et dixit eis: «Peccavi in Dominum Deum vestrum et in vos. [17]Sed nunc dimittite peccatum mihi tantum hac vice et rogate Dominum Deum vestrum, ut auferat a me saltem mortem istam». [18]Egressusque Moyses de conspectu pharaonis oravit Dominum, [19]qui flare fecit ventum ab occidente vehementissimum et arreptam locustam proiecit in mare Rubrum; non remansit ne una quidem in cunc-

n. Heb *before your face*

a very strong west wind, which lifted the locusts and drove them into the Red Sea; not a single locust was left in all the country of Egypt. ²⁰But the LORD hardened Pharaoh's heart, and he did not let the children of Israel go.

Wis 17:1–18:4

The ninth plague: the darkness

Rev 8:12 ²¹Then the LORD said to Moses, "Stretch out your hand toward heaven that there may be darkness over the land of Egypt, a dark-
Ps 105:28 ness to be felt." ²²So Moses stretched out his hand toward heaven,
Rev 16:10 and there was thick darkness in all the land of Egypt three days; ²³they did not see one another, nor did any rise from his place for three days; but all the people of Israel had light where they dwelt. ²⁴Then Pharaoh called Moses, and said, "Go, serve the LORD; your children also may go with you; only let your flocks and your herds remain behind." ²⁵But Moses said, "You must also let us have sacrifices and burnt offerings, that we may sacrifice to the LORD our God. ²⁶Our cattle also must go with us; not a hoof shall be left behind, for we must take of them to serve the LORD our God, and we do not know with what we must serve the LORD until we arrive there." ²⁷But the LORD hardened Pharaoh's heart, and he

---

10:21–29. In springtime Egypt sometimes gets a warm desert wind so laden with sand particles as to produce a cloud that reduces visibility. Although there is a climatic basis to it, this ninth plague is particularly ominous. The book of Wisdom interprets darkness as a terrible abandonment of man by God. The sacred writer here points out that dialogue with the pharaoh has broken down: the other plagues were usually preceded by an announcement or a threat; not so this time, and after a tense interview the pharaoh and Moses regard their dealings as over.

Yet, we now glimpse that this is the beginning of the end: the pharaoh would allow the sons of Israel to leave, provided they left their flocks behind. But Moses will not accept this condition either; he openly talks about how they have to offer God sacrifices and burnt offerings—a clear allusion to the Passover sacrifice.

At the start of v. 24, in only a few Hebrew manuscripts, it says, "Then Pharaoh called Moses and Aaron"; but this reference to Aaron is found in all the Greek and Latin versions. His presence alongside Moses serves to emphasize how this plague is a figure of them all.

---

tis finibus Aegypti. ²⁰Et induravit Dominus cor pharaonis, nec dimisit filios Israel. ²¹Dixit autem Dominus ad Moysen: «Extende manum tuam in caelum, et sint tenebrae super terram Aegypti tam densae ut palpari queant». ²²Extenditque Moyses manum in caelum, et factae sunt tenebrae horribiles in universa terra Aegypti tribus diebus. ²³Nemo vidit fratrem suum nec movit se de loco, in quo erat. Ubi, cumque autem habitabant filii Israel, lux erat. ²⁴Vocavitque pharao Moysen et Aaron et dixit eis: «Ite, sacrificate Domino; oves tantum vestrae et armenta remaneant, parvuli vestri eant vobiscum». ²⁵Ait Moyses: «Etiamsi tu hostias et holocausta dares nobis, quae offeramus Domino Deo nostro, ²⁶tamen et greges nostri pergent nobiscum; non remanebit ex eis ungula, quoniam ex ipsis sumemus, quae necessaria sunt in cultum Domini Dei nostri; praesertim cum ignoremus quid debeat immolari,

would not let them go. ²⁸Then Pharaoh said to him, "Get away from me; take heed to yourself; never see my face again; for in the day you see my face you shall die." ²⁹Moses said, "As you say! I will not see your face again."

The tenth plague is announced

11 ¹The LORD said to Moses, "Yet one plague more I will bring upon Pharaoh and upon Egypt; afterwards he will let you go hence; when he lets you go, he will drive you away completely. ²Speak now in the hearing of the people, that they ask, every man of his neighbor and every woman of her neighbour, jewelry of silver and of gold." ³And the LORD gave the people favor in the sight of the Egyptians. Moreover, the man Moses was very great in the land of Egypt, in the sight of Pharaoh's servants and in the sight of the people.

⁴And Moses said, "Thus says the LORD: About midnight I will go forth in the midst of Egypt; ⁵and all the first-born in the land of Egypt shall die, from the first-born of Pharaoh who sits upon his throne, even to the first-born of the maidservant who is behind the mill; and all the first-born of the cattle. ⁶And there shall be a great

Ex 3:22
Ex 13:11ff

Ex 12:35

Sir 45:1
Acts 7:22

11:1–10. The account of the plagues ends with the announcement of the last one, the death of the first-born, whose fulfilment forms part of the institution of the Passover sacrifice described in the two chapters that follow. This chapter once again explains the reason behind all that has taken place so far. It is a preparation for the prodigies which will occur in the Passover and the departure from Egypt: *that* will be the most marvellous of the Lord's doings.

In the first place, we are told that there is "one plague more" (v. 1) to come—the first time the term "plague" appears—indicating that the previous ones were a sort of prelude to the definitive punishment. Then it tells us that Moses and the people gained the esteem of the Egyptians (v. 3), which serves to stress that the dispute is between the pharaoh alone, who regarded himself as a god, and the Lord, the only true God. Finally, the announcement of the slaying of the first-born sons (vv. 5–8) has profound significance: Israel alone is the first-born son and heir, in God's plan (cf. 4:23). Moreover, if Egypt loses its first-born, its survival is endangered; whereas Israel's

---

donec ad ipsum locum perveniamus». ²⁷Induravit autem Dominus cor pharaonis, et noluit dimittere eos. ²⁸Dixitque pharao ad eum: «Recede a me. Cave, ne ultra videas faciem meam; quocumque die apparueris mihi, morieris». ²⁹Respondit Moyses: «Ita fiet, ut locutus es; non videbo ultra faciem tuam». ¹Et dixit Dominus ad Moysen: «Adhuc una plaga tangam pharaonem et Aegyptum, et post haec dimittet vos utique, immo et exire compellet. ²Dices ergo omni plebi, ut postulet vir ab amico suo et mulier a vicina sua vasa argentea et aurea; ³dabit autem Dominus gratiam populo coram Aegyptiis». Fuitque Moyses vir magnus valde in terra Aegypti coram servis pharaonis et omni populo. ⁴Et ait Moyses: «Haec dicit Dominus: Media nocte egrediar in Aegyptum; ⁵et morietur omne primogenitum in terra Aegyptiorum, a primogenito pharaonis, qui sedet in solio eius, usque ad primogenitum ancillae, quae est ad molam, et omnia primogenita iumentorum. ⁶Eritque clamor magnus in universa terra Aegypti,

cry throughout all the land of Egypt, such as there has never been, nor ever shall be again. [7]But against any of the people of Israel, either man or beast, not a dog shall growl; that you may know that the LORD makes a distinction between the Egyptians and Israel. [8]And all these your servants shall come down to me, and bow down to me, saying, 'Get you out, and all the people who follow you.' And after that I will go out." And he went out from Pharaoh in hot anger. [9]Then the LORD said to Moses, "Pharaoh will not listen to you; that my wonders may be multiplied in the land of Egypt."

[10]Moses and Aaron did all these wonders before Pharaoh; and the LORD hardened Pharaoh's heart, and he did not let the people of Israel go out of his land.

Ex 12:21–28;
34:18
Lev 23:5–8
Num 28: 16–25
Deut 16:1–8
Ezek 45:21–24
Mt 26:17ff
Lk 22:15–16
1 Cor 5:7

4. THE PASSOVER

The institution of the Passover*

12 [1]*The Lord said to Moses and Aaron in the land of Egypt, [2]"This month shall be for you the beginning of months; it

---

survival and identity is assured. In Christ Jesus, the "first-born of all creation", the life of all believers is for ever assured (cf. Col 1:15–20).

***12:1–14.** This discourse of the Lord contains a number of rules for celebrating the Passover and the events commemorated in it; it is a kind of catechetical-liturgical text which admirably summarizes the profound meaning of that feast.

The Passover probably originated as a shepherds' feast held in springtime, when lambs are born and the migration to summer pastures was beginning; a new-born lamb was sacrificed and its

blood used to perform a special rite in petition for the protection and fertility of the flocks. But once this feast became connected with the history of the Exodus it acquired a much deeper meaning, as did the rites attaching to it.

Thus, the "congregation" (v. 3) comprises all the Israelites organized as a religious community to commemorate the most important event in their history, deliverance from bondage.

The victim will be a lamb, without blemish (v. 5) because it is to be offered to God. Smearing the doorposts and lintel with the blood of the victim (vv. 7, 13), an essential part of the rite, signifies protection from dangers. The Passover is

---

qualis nec ante fuit nec postea futurus est. [7]Apud omnes autem filios Israel non mutiet canis contra hominem et pecus, ut sciatis quanto miraculo dividat Dominus Aegyptios et Israel. [8]Descendentque omnes servi tui isti ad me et adorabunt me dicentes: 'Egredere tu et omnis populus, qui sequitur te'. Post haec egrediar». Et exivit a pharaone iratus nimis. [9]Dixit autem Dominus ad Moysen: «Non audiet vos pharao, ut multa signa fiant in terra Aegypti». [10]Moyses autem et Aaron fecerunt omnia ostenta haec coram pharaone; et induravit Dominus cor pharaonis, nec dimisit filios Israel de terra sua. [1]Dixit

shall be the first month of the year for you. ³Tell all the congregation of Israel that on the tenth day of this month they shall take every man a lamb according to their fathers' houses, a lamb for a household; ⁴and if the household is too small for a lamb, then a man and his neighbour next to his house shall take according to the number of persons; according to what each can eat you shall make your count for the lamb. ⁵Your lamb shall be without blemish, a male a year old; you shall take it from the sheep or from the goats; ⁶and you shall keep it until the fourteenth day of this month, when the whole assembly of the congregation of Israel shall kill their lambs in the evening.º ⁷Then they shall take some

Lev 22:19

---

essentially sacrificial from the very start.

The meal (v. 11) is also a necessary part, and the manner in which it is held is a very appropriate way of showing the urgency imposed by circumstances: there is no time to season it (v. 9); no other food is eaten with it, except for the bread and desert herbs (a sign of indigence); the dress and posture of those taking part (standing, wearing sandals and holding a staff) show that they are on a journey. In the later liturgical commemoration of the Passover, these things indicate that the Lord is passing among his people.

The rules laid down for the Passover are evocative of very ancient nomadic desert rites, where there was no priest or temple or altar. When the Israelites had settled in Palestine, the Passover continued to be celebrated at home, always retaining the features of a sacrifice, a family meal and, very especially, a memorial of the deliverance the Lord brought about on that night.

Our Lord chose the context of the Passover Supper to institute the Eucharist: "By celebrating the Last Supper with his apostles in the course of the Passover meal, Jesus gave the Jewish Passover its definitive meaning. Jesus' passing over to his Father by his death and Resurrection, the new Passover, is anticipated in the Supper and celebrated in the Eucharist, which fulfils the Jewish Passover and anticipates the final Passover of the Church in the glory of the kingdom" (*Catechism of the Catholic Church*, 1340).

12:2. This event is so important that it is going to mark the starting point in the reckoning of time. In the history of Israel there are two types of calendar, both based on the moon—one which begins the year in the autumn, after the feast of Weeks (cf. 23:16; 34:22), and the other beginning it in spring, between March and April. This second calendar probably

---

Dominus ad Moysen et Aaron in terra Aegypti: ²«Mensis iste vobis principium mensium, primus erit in mensibus anni. ³Loquimini ad universum coetum filiorum Israel et dicite eis: Decima die mensis huius tollat unusquisque agnum per familias et domos suas. ⁴Sin autem minor est numerus, ut sufficere possit ad vescendum agnum, assumet vicinum suum, qui iunctus est domui suae, iuxta numerum animarum, quae sufficere possunt ad esum agni. ⁵Erit autem vobis agnus absque macula, masculus, anniculus; quem de agnis vel haedis tolletis ⁶servabitis eum usque ad quartam decimam diem mensis huius; immolabitque eum universa congregatio filiorum Israel ad vesperam. ⁷Et sument de sanguine eius ac ponent super utrumque postem et in superliminaribus domorum, in quibus comedent illum; ⁸et

o. Heb *between the two evenings*

of the blood, and put it on the two doorposts and the lintel of the houses in which they eat them. ⁸They shall eat the flesh that night, roasted; with unleavened bread and bitter herbs they shall eat it. ⁹Do not eat any of it raw or boiled with water, but roasted, its head with its legs and its inner parts. ¹⁰And you shall let none of it remain until the morning, anything that remains until the morning *Lk 12:35* you shall burn. ¹¹In this manner you shall eat it: your loins girded, your sandals on your feet, and your staff in your hand; and you *Num 33:4* shall eat it in haste. It is the LORD's passover. ¹²For I will pass through the land of Egypt that night, and I will smite all the first-born in the land of Egypt, both man and beast; and on all the gods *Lev 1:5* of Egypt I will execute judgments: I am the LORD. ¹³The blood shall be a sign for you, upon the houses where you are; and when I see the blood, I will pass over you, and no plague shall fall upon you to destroy you, when I smite the land of Egypt.

---

held sway for quite a long time, for we know that the first month, known as Abib (spring)—cf. 13:4; 23:18; 34:18—was called, in the post-exilic period (from the 6th century BC onwards) by the Babylonian name of Nisan (Neh 2:1; Esther 3:7). Be that as it may, the fact that this month is called the first month is a way of highlighting the importance of the event which is going to be commemorated (the Passover).

12:11. Even now it is difficult to work out the etymology of the word "Passover".

In other Semitic languages it means "joy" or "festive joy" or also "ritual and festive leap". In the Bible the same root means "dancing or limping" in an idolatrous rite (cf. 1 Kings 18:21, 26) and

"protecting" (cf. Is 31:5), so it could mean "punishment, lash" and also "salvation, protection". In the present text the writer is providing a popular, non-scholarly etymology, and it is taken as meaning that "the Lord passes through", slaying Egyptians and sparing the Israelites.

In the New Testament it will be applied to Christ's passage to the Father by death and resurrection, and the Church's "passage" to the eternal Kingdom: "The Church will enter the glory of the kingdom only through this final Passover, when she will follow her Lord in his death and Resurrection" (*Catechism of the Catholic Church*, 677).

12:14. The formal tone of these words gives an idea of the importance the Pass-

---

edent carnes nocte illa assas igni et azymos panes cum lactucis amaris. ⁹Non comedetis ex eo crudum quid nec coctum aqua, sed tantum assum igni; caput cum pedibus eius et intestinis vorabitis. ¹⁰Nec remanebit quidquam ex eo usque mane; si quid residuum fuerit, igne comburetis. ¹¹Sic autem comedetis illum: renes vestros accingetis, calceamenta habebitis in pedibus, tenentes baculos in manibus, et comedetis festinanter; est enim Pascha (*id est Transitus*) Domini! ¹²Et transibo per terram Aegypti nocte illa percutiamque omne primogenitum in terra Aegypti ab homine usque ad pecus; et in cunctis diis Aegypti faciam iudicia, ego Dominus. ¹³Erit autem sanguis vobis in signum in aedibus, in quibus eritis; et videbo sanguinem et transibo vos, nec erit in vobis plaga disperdens, quando percussero terram Aegypti. ¹⁴Habebitis autem hanc diem in monumentum et celebrabitis eam sollemnem Domino

Exodus 12:18

¹⁴"This day shall be for you a memorial day, and you shall keep it as a feast to the LORD; throughout your generations you shall observe it as an ordinance for ever.

Ex 12:3–10;
23:15; 34:18
Deut 26:9
Lk 22:19
Mt 26:17
Mk 14:12

The feast of the unleavened bread

¹⁵Seven days you shall eat unleavened bread; on the first day you shall put away leaven out of your houses, for if any one eats what is leavened, from the first day until the seventh day, that person shall be cut off from Israel. ¹⁶On the first day you shall hold a holy assembly, and on the seventh day a holy assembly; no work shall be done on those days; but what everyone must eat, that only may be prepared by you. ¹⁷And you shall observe the feast of unleavened bread, for on this very day I brought your hosts out of the land of Egypt: therefore you shall observe this day, throughout your generations, as an ordinance for ever. ¹⁸In the first

1 Cor 5:7
Lk 2:43

Lk 23:56

Lk 22:7

over always had. If the historical books (Joshua, Judges, Samuel and Kings) hardly mention it, the reason is that they allude only to sacrifices in the temple, and the Passover was always celebrated in people's homes. When the temple ceased to be (6th century BC), the feast acquired more prominence, as can be seen from the post-exilic biblical texts (cf. Ezra 6:19–22; 2 Chron 30:1–27; 35:1–19) and extrabiblical texts such as the famous "Passover papyrus of Elephantine" (Egypt) of the 5th century BC. In Jesus' time a solemn passover sacrifice was celebrated in the temple and the passover meal was held at home.

12:15–20. The feast of the Azymes, or unleavened bread, seems to date back to earliest times in Canaan. It betokens an agricultural background (Deut 26:9) and it marked the start of the barley harvest.

Given that it is recorded here, it must have been celebrated from very early times along with the Passover. So, the feast of the unleavened bread, which would originally have simply been an offering of the first-fruits of the harvest, now acquires the same meaning as the Passover, that is, it commemorates the deliverance of the people of God, the "first-fruits", as it were, of the nations.

Unleavened bread was, and still is among the Bedouin, the norm in the desert. When the people eventually settled down in the promised land, the idea was kept that fermentation of any kind implied some impurity; which was why in the offering of sacrifices (cf. Lev 2:11; 6:10) and even more so in the passover meal, only unleavened bread was used. Jesus availed himself of this notion when he advised his disciples to "beware of the leaven of the Pharisees" (Mk 8:15), that

in generationibus vestris cultu sempiterno. ¹⁵Septem diebus azyma comedetis. Iam in die primo non erit fermentum in domibus vestris; quicumque comederit fermentatum, a primo die usque ad diem septimum, peribit anima illa de Israel. ¹⁶Dies prima erit sancta atque sollemnis, et dies septima eadem festivitate venerabilis. Nihil operis facietis in eis, exceptis his, quae ad vescendum pertinent. ¹⁷Et observabitis azyma, in eadem enim ipsa die eduxi exercitum vestrum de terra Aegypti; et custodietis diem istum in generationes vestras ritu perpetuo. ¹⁸Primo mense, quarta decima die mensis ad vesperam comedetis azyma; usque ad diem vicesimam primam eiusdem mensis ad vesperam. ¹⁹Septem

month, on the fourteenth day of the month at evening, you shall eat unleavened bread, and so until the twenty-first day of the month at evening. ¹⁹For seven days no leaven shall be found in your houses; for if any one eats what is leavened, that person shall be cut off from the congregation of Israel, whether he is a sojourner or a native of the land. ²⁰You shall eat nothing leavened; in all your dwellings you shall eat unleavened bread."

1 Cor 5:7

Ex 10:2; 12:1–14
1 Cor 5:7

Instructions relating to the Passover

²¹Then Moses called all the elders of Israel, and said to them, "Select lambs for yourselves according to your families, and kill the passover lamb. ²²Take a bunch of hyssop and dip it in the blood which is in the basin, and touch the lintel and the two doorposts with the blood which is in the basin; and none of you shall go out of the door of his house until the morning. ²³For the LORD will pass through to slay the Egyptians; and when he sees the blood on the lintel and on the two doorposts, the LORD will

Heb 11:28

---

is, of their evil dispositions. In the Latin rite the Church uses unleavened bread in the Eucharist, to imitate Jesus, who celebrated the Last Supper with this type of bread.

12:21–28. This section parallels 12:1–14 but, possibly because it comes from a different tradition, it omits many of the rites that appear there and instead adds some details not previously mentioned—like the hyssop, the basin for holding the blood, and the instruction that no one is to leave the house. But the most significant thing is the insistence on and details given about the rite of the blood, as if it were more important than the passover meal as such. This is another hint that the

Passover, in its origin, may have been a nomadic sacrifice designed very much to ward off every kind of evil.

The mention of the "destroyer" (v. 23) seems to come from an ancient tradition, because this unpleasant name is given to God or to an angel in order to enhance the drama of that night: God will be the cause of death for the Egyptians and of deliverance for the Hebrews.

The children's question about the meaning of the rite (v. 26) shows the importance that oral transmission of Tradition always had. Successive generations will learn the profound meaning of the Passover not from written documents but by word of mouth from their elders (cf. Rom 10:17).

---

diebus fermentum non invenietur in domibus vestris. Qui comederit fermentatum, peribit anima eius de coetu Israel, tam de advenis quam de indigenis terrae. ²⁰Omne fermentatum non comedetis; in cunctis habitaculis vestris edetis azyma». ²¹Vocavit autem Moyses omnes seniores filiorum Israel et dixit ad eos: «Ite tollentes animal per familias vestras et immolate Pascha. ²²Fasciculumque hyssopi tingite in sanguine, qui est in pelvi, et aspergite ex eo superliminare et utrumque postem. Nullus vestrum egrediatur ostium domus suae usque mane. ²³Transibit enim Dominus percutiens Aegyptios; cumque viderit sanguinem in super liminari et in utroque poste, transcendet ostium et non sinet percussorem ingredi domos vestras et laedere. ²⁴Custodite verbum istud legitimum tibi et filiis tuis usque in aeternum. ²⁵Cumque introieritis terram, quam Dominus daturus est vobis, ut pollicitus est, observabitis caeremo-

pass over the door, and will not allow the destroyer to enter your houses to slay you. [24]You shall observe this rite as an ordinance for you and for your sons for ever. [25]And when you come to the land which the LORD will give you, as he has promised, you shall keep this service. [26]And when your children say to you, 'What do you mean by this service?' [27]you shall say, 'It is the sacrifice of the LORD'S passover, for he passed over the houses of the people of Israel in Egypt, when he slew the Egyptians but spared our houses.'" And the people bowed their heads and worshiped.

[28]Then the people of Israel went and did so; as the LORD had commanded Moses and Aaron, so they did.

Ex 13:8–14

The tenth plague: death of the first-born

Ex 11:4–8; 13:11
Ps 78:51; 105:36;
135:8;136:10
Wis 18:6–19

[29]At midnight the LORD smote all the first-born in the land of Egypt, from the first-born of Pharaoh who sat on his throne to the first-born of the captive who was in the dungeon, and all the first-born of the cattle. [30]And Pharaoh rose up in the night, he, and all his servants, and all the Egyptians; and there was a great cry in Egypt, for there was not a house where one was not dead. [31]And he summoned Moses and Aaron by night, and said, "Rise up, go forth from among my people, both you and the people of Israel; and go, serve the LORD, as you have said. [32]Take your flocks and your herds, as you have said, and be gone; and bless me also!"

12:29–36. After this detailed description of the Passover, the narrative picks up the thread and recounts very quickly the death of the first-born of Egypt. The sacred text gives hardly any details about this tragedy that afflicts the Egyptians, whereas it gives much more detailed information about the long-awaited permission from the pharaoh for the Israelites to leave—giving the impression that their departure-deliverance is much more important than the last plague, however terrible we may find it today. The people leave in haste, but they leave victorious. The very Egyptians readily give them presents, to show that they acknowledge the dignity of Israel and of the God who gives them protection. Here is fulfilled to the letter the promise God made to Moses when he first entrusted him with his mission (cf. 3:21–22 and note).

---

nias istas; [26]et, cum dixerint vobis filii vestri: 'Quae est ista religio?', [27]dicetis eis: 'Victima Paschae Domino est, quando transivit super domos filiorum Israel in Aegypto percutiens Aegyptios et domos nostras liberans'». Incurvatusque populus adoravit; [28]egressi filii Israel fecerunt, sicut praeceperat Dominus Moysi et Aaron. [29]Factum est autem in noctis medio, percussit Dominus omne primogenitum in terra Aegypti, a primogenito pharaonis, qui in solio eius sedebat, usque ad primogenitum captivi, qui erat in carcere, et omne primogenitum iumentorum. [30]Surrexitque pharao nocte et omnes servi eius cunctaque Aegyptus, et ortus est clamor magnus in Aegypto, neque enim erat domus, in qua non iaceret mortuus. [31]Vocatisque pharao Moyse et Aaron nocte, ait: «Surgite, egredimini a populo meo, vos et filii Israel; ite, immolate Domino, sicut dicitis. [32]Oves vestras et armenta assumite, ut petieratis, et

Ex 3:21–22; 11:2
Wis 10:17 **Provisions for the Exodus**

³³And the Egyptians were urgent with the people, to send them out of the land in haste; for they said, "We are all dead men." ³⁴So the people took their dough before it was leavened, their kneading bowls being bound up in their mantles on their shoulders. ³⁵The people of Israel had also done as Moses told them, for they had asked of the Egyptians jewelry of silver and of gold, and clothing; ³⁶and the LORD had given the people favour in the sight of the Egyptians, so that they let them have what they asked. Thus they despoiled the Egyptians.

Num 33:3–5 **The sons of Israel leave Egypt**

Num 1:46;
26:51 ³⁷And the people of Israel journeyed from Rameses to Succoth, about six hundred thousand men on foot, besides women and children. ³⁸A mixed multitude also went up with them, and very many cattle, both flocks and herds. ³⁹And they baked unleavened cakes of the dough which they had brought out of Egypt, for it Gen 15:13 was not leavened, because they were thrust out of Egypt and

---

12:37–42. Here we are given concrete details about the departure from Egypt. They headed towards Succoth, a city which modern excavations locate some 15 kms (nine miles) south-east of Rameses, in the Nile delta. It seems to make sense that they should have avoided trade routes, which would have been quieter but busier and patrolled by Egyptian armies—the coast road to the country of the Philistines (cf. 13:17), the road through the southern desert, which led to Beer-sheba, or the trading route linking Egypt and Arabia. Even in this little thing one can see God's special providence at work: he has no need of beaten tracks to show his people where to go.

The figure of 600,000 is an idealized one (cf. Num 1:46; 26:51), for it would imply a total population of three million people, women and children included. Maybe for the hagiographer's contemporaries this figure had a significance which escapes us today; or perhaps it is just a way of indicating that there were very many people—part of the epic style of the account, to highlight the power of God.

The figure of 430 years for the time the sons of Israel had been in Egypt (v. 40) is slightly different from the 400 years which appears more often in the Bible (cf. Gen 15:13; Acts 7:6; Gal 3:16-17). In the Pentateuch numbers often

---

abeuntes benedicite mihi». ³³Urgebantque Aegyptii populum de terra exire velociter dicentes: «Omnes moriemur». ³⁴Tulit igitur populus conspersam farinam, antequam fermentaretur; et ligans pistrina in palliis suis posuit super umeros suos. ³⁵Feceruntque filii Israel, sicut praeceperat Moyses, et petierunt ab Aegyptiis vasa argentea et aurea vestemque plurimam. ³⁶Dominus autem dedit gratiam populo coram Aegyptiis, ut commodarent eis; et spoliaverunt Aegyptios. ³⁷Profectique sunt filii Israel de Ramesse in Succoth, sescenta fere milia peditum virorum absque parvulis. ³⁸Sed et vulgus promiscuum innumerabile ascendit cum eis, oves et armenta, animantia multa nimis. ³⁹Coxeruntque farinam, quam dudum de Aegypto conspersam tulerant, et fecerunt subcinericios panes azymos; neque enim poterant fermentari, cogentibus exire Aegyptiis et nullam facere sinentibus moram; nec pulmenti quidquam

could not tarry, neither had they prepared for themselves any provisions.

⁴⁰The time that the people of Israel dwelt in Egypt was four hundred and thirty years. ⁴¹And at the end of four hundred and thirty years, on that very day, all the hosts of the LORD went out from the land of Egypt. ⁴²It was a night of watching by the LORD, to bring them out of the land of Egypt; so this same night is a night of watching kept to the LORD by all the people of Israel throughout their generations. Gal 3:16–17

Acts 13:17

Further instructions about the Passover

⁴³And the LORD said to Moses and Aaron, "This is the ordinance of the passover: no foreigner shall eat of it; ⁴⁴but every slave that is bought for money may eat of it after you have circumcised him. ⁴⁵No sojourner or hired servant may eat of it. ⁴⁶In one house shall it be eaten; you shall not carry forth any of the flesh outside the house; and you shall not break a bone of it. ⁴⁷All the congregation of Israel shall keep it. ⁴⁸And when a stranger shall sojourn with Num 9:13
Jn 19:36
1 Cor 5:7

Num 9:14
Heb 11:28

---

have a more symbolic than chronological meaning (cf. the note on Gen 5:1–32). The 400 years would mean that the chosen people lived in Egypt for ten generations (forty years per generation: cf. the note on Ex 7:9), that is, a complete period of the history of Israel.

"Night of watching" (v. 42): if the darkness causes any misgiving, God will transform it into a time of salvation. Because God looks out for them, the Israelites will also commemorate the night of their deliverance by keeping watch. Christian liturgy celebrates the Lords' resurrection with a solemn vigil, commemorating the deliverance of the Israelites, the redemption of Christians, and Christ's

victory over death—three stages in God's intervention to save souls; as the Church sings: "This is the night when first you saved our fathers: you freed the people of Israel from their slavery. [. . .] This is the night when Christians everywhere (are) washed clean of sin and freed from all defilement. [. . .] This is the night when Jesus Christ broke the chains of death and rose triumphant from the grave" (*Roman Missal*, Exultet).

12:43–51. Here are new rules for the Passover which make its meaning more explicit. Only members of the people may eat it, for it will be the rite which marks the unity of the sons of Israel and

---

occurrerant praeparare. ⁴⁰Habitatio autem filiorum Israel, qua manserant in Aegypto, fuit quadringentorum triginta annorum. ⁴¹Quibus expletis, eadem die egressus est omnis exercitus Domini de terra Aegypti. ⁴²Nox ista vigiliarum Domino, quando eduxit eos de terra Aegypti: hanc observare debent Domino omnes filii Israel in generationibus suis. ⁴³Dixitque Dominus ad Moysen et Aaron: «Haec est religio Paschae: Omnis alienigena non comedet ex eo; ⁴⁴omnis autem servus empticius circumcidetur et sic comedet; ⁴⁵advena et mercennarius non edent ex eo. ⁴⁶In una domo comedetur, nec efferetis de carnibus eius foras nec os illius confringetis. ⁴⁷Omnis coetus filiorum Israel faciet illud. ⁴⁸Quod si quis peregrinorum in vestram voluerit transire coloniam et facere Pascha Domini, circumcidetur prius omne masculinum eius, et tunc rite celebrabit eritque sicut indigena terrae; si quis autem circumcisus non

you and would keep the passover to the LORD, let all his males be circumcised, then he may come near and keep it; he shall be as a native of the land. But no uncircumcised person shall eat of it. ⁴⁹There shall be one law for the native and for the stranger who sojourns among you."

Ex 13:11–16;
22:28–29; 34:19–20
Lev 27:26
Num 3:11–13,
40–51; 8:16–18;
18:15
Deut 15:19–23
Lk 2:22–24

⁵⁰Thus did all the people of Israel; as the LORD commanded Moses and Aaron, so they did. ⁵¹And on that very day the LORD brought the people of Israel out of the land of Egypt by their hosts.

The law about the first-born

Lk 2:23

13 ¹The LORD said to Moses, ²"Consecrate to me all the first-born; whatever is the first to open the womb among the people of Israel, both of man and of beast, is mine."

---

shows that they are special. It is the rite to be performed with maximum purity: those partaking must be circumcised and not a bone of the victim is to be broken (v. 46). This last requirement is used by St John to show that the passover lamb is a figure of Christ immolated on the cross (cf. Jn 19:36; cf. also 1 Cor 5:7).

13:1–2. The sacred text links to the events of the Exodus the ancient custom of consecrating all the first-born to God. Among the Phoenicians this custom went as far as immolating first-born children: but in Israel the sacrifice of infants was never permitted, as can be seen from the account of the sacrifice of Isaac (Gen 22:1–14), for whom a ram was substituted at the last minute. The legislation handed down in all the traditions recorded in the Pentateuch (Ex 22:28–29; Num 3:11–13; 3:40–45; Deut 15:19–23) commanded that every first-born should be sacrificed, but children were to be redeemed (Ex 13:13; 34:19–20; Num 18:15). Nor should unclean animals be

sacrificed; of domestic animals only the donkey was considered unclean and therefore its blood should not be shed (that is, it should not be sacrificed); instead it should have its neck broken or a lamb should be sacrificed instead of it. But the first-born child should always be redeemed. As the years went by, laws and rites developed concerning the consecration of the first-born to the Lord and about their redemption by means of an animal or even some payment (Ex 34:20; Num 3:40–51). We also know that later on Levites were consecrated to God as substitutes for the first-born (Num 3:12–13; 8:16–18).

This law, which is an acknowledgement that children are a gift from God and belong to him, stayed in place virtually unchanged up to the time of the New Testament. Jesus himself submitted to it in a profound act of humility (cf. Lk 2:22–24).

13:3–16. Just as more precise rules were given for the celebration of the Passover

---

fuerit, non vescetur ex eo. ⁴⁹Eadem lex erit indigenae et colono, qui peregrinatur apud vos». ⁵⁰Feceruntque omnes filii Israel, sicut praeceperat Dominus Moysi et Aaron; ⁵¹et in eadem die eduxit Dominus filios Israel de terra Aegypti per turmas suas. ¹Locutusque est Dominus ad Moysen dicens: ²«Sanctifica mihi omne primogenitum, quod aperit vulvam in filiis Israel, tam de hominibus quam de iumentis: mea sunt enim omnia». ³Et ait Moyses ad populum: «Mementote diei huius, in qua egressi

Instructions about the feast of the unleavened bread Ex 12:1; 12:
15–20; 34:18

³And Moses said to the people, "Remember this day, in which you came out from Egypt, out of the house of bondage, for by strength of hand the LORD brought you out from this place; no leavened bread shall be eaten. ⁴This day you are to go forth, in the month of Abib. ⁵And when the LORD brings you into the land of the Canaanites, the Hittites, the Amorites, the Hivites, and the Jebusites, which he swore to your fathers to give you, a land flowing with milk and honey, you shall keep this service in this month. ⁶Seven days you shall eat unleavened bread, and on the seventh day there shall be a feast to the LORD. ⁷Unleavened bread shall be 1 Cor 5:7
eaten for seven days; no leavened bread shall be seen with you, and no leaven shall be seen with you in all your territory. ⁸And Ex 12:26; 13:14
you shall tell your son on that day, 'It is because of what the LORD did for me when I came out of Egypt.' ⁹And it shall be to you as a Mt 23:5
sign on your hand and as a memorial between your eyes, that the law of the LORD may be in your mouth; for with a strong hand the LORD has brought you out of Egypt. ¹⁰You shall therefore keep this ordinance at its appointed time from year to year.

(12:44–51), the same is now done for the feast of the unleavened bread (vv. 3–10) and the consecration of the first-born (vv. 11–16). These are the three rites which the Israelites used to commemorate their deliverance from bondage.

The main feature of this new set of rules is its liturgical-catechetical character, involving the obligation to explain the rite to one's son (12:26; 13:8, 14), thereby keeping alive the memory of God's intervention. "In the sense of Sacred Scripture the *memorial* is not merely the recollection of past events but the proclamation of the mighty works wrought by God for men (cf. Ex 13:3). In

the liturgical celebration of these events, they become in a certain way present and real. This is how Israel understands its liberation from Egypt: every time Passover is celebrated the Exodus events are made present to the memory of believers so that they may conform their lives to them" (*Catechism of the Catholic Church*, 1363).

Verses 9 and 16 show that the two rites will be the distinguishing mark of the Israelite people. We do not know if they interpreted it as an external sign or whether this was the origin of the later custom of wearing phylacteries, that is, tiny rolls of parchment tied to the forehead

estis de Aegypto et de domo servitutis, quoniam in manu forti eduxit vos Dominus de loco isto, ut non comedatis fermentatum panem. ⁴Hodie egredimini, mense Abib (*id est novarum Frugum*). ⁵Cumque introduxerit te Dominus in terram Chananaei et Hetthaei et Amorraei et Hevaei et Iebusaei, quam iuravit patribus tuis, ut daret tibi, terram fluentem lacte et melle; celebrabis hunc morem sacrorum mense isto. ⁶Septem diebus vesceris azymis, et in die septimo erit sollemnitas Domini. ⁷Azyma comedetis septem diebus: non apparebit apud te aliquid fermentatum nec in cunctis finibus tuis. ⁸Narrabisque filio tuo in die illo dicens: 'Propter hoc, quod fecit mihi Dominus, quando egressus sum de Aegypto'. ⁹Et erit quasi signum in manu tua et quasi monumentum inter oculos tuos, ut lex Domini semper sit in ore tuo; in manu enim forti eduxit te Dominus de Aegypto. ¹⁰Custodies huiuscemodi

Ex 13:1–2 **Instructions about redeeming the first-born**

¹¹"And when the LORD brings you into the land of the Canaanites,
Gen 22:1 as he swore to you and your fathers, and shall give it to you, ¹²you
Lk 2:23 shall set apart to the LORD all that first opens the womb. All the
firstlings of your cattle that are males shall be the LORD'S. ¹³Every
firstling of an ass you shall redeem with a lamb, or if you will not
redeem it you shall break its neck. Every first-born of man among
Ex 12:26; 13:8 your sons you shall redeem. ¹⁴And when in time to come your son
asks you, 'What does this mean?' you shall say to him, 'By
strength of hand the LORD brought us out of Egypt, from the
Lk 2:23 house of bondage. ¹⁵For when Pharaoh stubbornly refused to let
us go, the LORD slew all the first-born in the land of Egypt, both
the first-born of man and the first-born of cattle. Therefore I sacrifice to the LORD all the males that first open the womb; but all
Deut 6:8; 11:18 the first-born of my sons I redeem.' ¹⁶It shall be as a mark on your
hand or frontlets between your eyes; for by a strong hand the
LORD brought us out of Egypt."

5. THE DEPARTURE FROM EGYPT

A roundabout way

¹⁷When Pharaoh let the people go, God did not lead them by way
Gen 50:25 of the land of the Philistines, although that was near; for God said,

---

and arm, on which were written the words
of Deuteronomy 6:4–9 and 11:13–21.

13:17–18. The geographical information
given in the book of Exodus is insufficient to enable us to say exactly what
route the Israelites took through the Sinai
peninsula. The sacred author probably
did not intend to give a detailed chronicle, but to describe the places and events

which help to show God's constant presence among his people. We do know that
they did not take any of the normal routes
but used a roundabout way through the
desert (v. 18), in the direction of the Red
Sea. This sea goes round the Sinai, forming the gulf of Akabah to the east and the
gulf of Suez to the west. The construction
of the Suez canal had a considerable
impact on the topography, but we do

---

cultum statuto tempore a diebus in dies. ¹¹Cumque introduxerit te Dominus in terram Chananaei, sicut
iuravit tibi et patribus tuis, et dederit tibi eam, ¹²separabis omne, quod aperit vulvam, Domino et quod
primitivum est in pecoribus tuis; quidquid habueris masculini sexus, consecrabis Domino.
¹³Primogenitum asini mutabis ove; quod, si non redemeris, interficies. Omne autem primogenitum
hominis de filiis tuis pretio redimes. ¹⁴Cumque interrogaverit te filius tuus cras dicens: 'Quid est hoc?',
respondebis ei: 'In manu forti eduxit nos Dominus de Aegypto, de domo servitutis. ¹⁵Nam, cum indura-
tus esset pharao et nollet nos dimittere, occidit Dominus omne primogenitum in terra Aegypti, a primogenito hominis usque ad primogenitum iumentorum; idcirco immolo Domino omne, quod aperit
vulvam, masculini sexus, et omnia primogenita filiorum meorum redimo'. ¹⁶Erit igitur quasi signum

"Lest the people repent when they see war, and return to Egypt." ^{Josh 24:32} ¹⁸But God led the people round by the way of the wilderness ^{Num 33:5–6} toward the Red Sea. And the people of Israel went up out of the land of Egypt equipped for battle. ¹⁹And Moses took the bones of Joseph with him; for Joseph had solemnly sworn the people of ^{Ex 40:36} Israel, saying, "God will visit you; then you must carry my bones ^{Num 14:14} with you from here." ²⁰And they moved on from Succoth, and ^{Deut 1:33}
^{Ps 78:14; 105:39} encamped at Etham, on the edge of the wilderness. ²¹And the ^{Neh 9:19} LORD went before them by day in a pillar of cloud to lead them ^{Wis 10:17–18; 18:3} along the way, and by night in a pillar of fire to give them light, ^{Is 4:5} that they might travel by day and by night; ²²the pillar of cloud by ^{Jn 8:12; 10:4}
^{1 Cor 10:1} day and the pillar of fire by night did not depart from before the ^{Rev 10:1} people.

---

know that, between the gulf of Suez and the Mediterranean there was a series of lakes and marshes which were affected by tides, which gave those waters a reddish hue; this is the reason why this whole area is also called the Red Sea; the Septuagint Greek (and with it the New Testament: Acts 7:36 and Heb 11:29) speaks here of the Eritrean Sea (*erythrós* means "red"). The Hebrew text, on the other hand, calls it the "Sea of Reeds" on account of the large amount of papyrus reeds on its banks. It is more than likely that the Israelites led by Moses crossed one of these marshy areas, and not the sea itself.

13:19. This piece of information is important because it serves to identify the Israelites who left Egypt with those of the patriarchal period.

Joseph made his brothers swear that they would not leave his bones in Egypt (cf. Gen 50:25). When they are leaving the country, the sons of Israel bring his remains with them and, according to the book of Joshua (24:32), those who settled in the land promised to the patriarchs buried them in Shechem. In this way, the memory of Joseph is a further link between the patriarchal traditions, those of the Exodus and those to do with taking possession of the Land.

13:21–22. The cloud and the fire are the sign that shows God is with them. The sacred writer gives all these details to make it clear that the entire people saw with their eyes that God himself had brought them out of Egypt, was leading them, was protecting them, and was making himself manifest to them.

in manu tua et quasi appensum quid ob recordationem inter oculos tuos, eo quod in manu forti eduxit nos Dominus de Aegypto». ¹⁷Igitur cum emisisset pharao populum, non eos duxit Deus per viam terrae Philisthim, quae vicina est, reputans ne forte paeniteret populum, si vidisset adversum se bella consurgere, et reverteretur in Aegyptum, ¹⁸sed circumduxit per viam deserti, quae est iuxta mare Rubrum. Et armati ascenderunt filii Israel de terra Aegypti. ¹⁹Tulit quoque Moyses ossa Ioseph secum, eo quod adiurasset filios Israel dicens: «Visitabit vos Deus; efferte ossa mea hinc vobiscum». ²⁰Profectique de Succoth castrametati sunt in Etham, in extremis finibus solitudinis. ²¹Dominus autem praecedebat eos ad ostendendam viam per diem in columna nubis et per noctem in columna ignis, ut dux esset itineris utroque tempore. ²²Nunquam defuit columna nubis per diem nec columna ignis per noctem coram populo. ¹Locutus est autem Dominus ad Moysen dicens: ²«Loquere filiis Israel: Reversi castrameten-

The Lord shapes events*

14 ¹Then the LORD said to Moses, ²"Tell the people of Israel to turn back and encamp in front of Pi-ha-hiroth, between Migdol and the sea, in front of Baal-zephon; you shall encamp over against it, by the sea. ³For Pharaoh will say of the people of Israel, 'They are entangled in the land; the wilderness has shut them in.' ⁴And I will harden Pharaoh's heart, and he will pursue them and I will get glory over Pharaoh and all his host; and the Egyptians shall know that I am the LORD." And they did so.

Ex 16:2–3; 17:3
Num 11:1–6;
14:1–4; 20:2;
21:4–5
Ps 78:40

The Egyptians in pursuit

⁵When the king of Egypt was told that the people had fled, the mind of Pharaoh and his servants was changed toward the

---

*14:1–31. The passage of the Red Sea, a great feat of God and his people against the pharaoh and his men, is something the Old Testament harks back to constantly. Just as the death of the first-born is the last of the prodigies prior to the Exodus, so the passage of the Red Sea is the first on the people's pilgrimage in the wilderness. But it is of such importance that it came to be seen as the zenith and obligatory reference-point of God's manifestation of his might and of his love for the people. To mention the passage of the Red Sea is to speak of God's deliverance of the Israelites from bondage. When they eventually enter the promised land, the crossing of the Jordan will be recounted in similar terms (cf. Josh 3–4) and both events will be sung in tribute to the liberating power of God (cf., e.g., Ps 66:6; 74:13–15; 78:15, 53; 114:1–4).

This account bears traces of the great Jewish traditions—which suggests that each of them kept these events very much in mind. One tradition depicts the cross-

ing of the sea as an epic event in which a series of natural elements combined spectacularly (strong winds, wheels sticking in the mud, etc.). Another puts the accent more on the miraculous side of things: the angel of God intervenes, the waters divide to form two walls through which the Israelites pass; the waters fall back into place to drown the pharaoh's chariots and cavalry, etc. Both traditions evidence the portentous action of God. Using all these elements, the writer has produced a masterly account, a veritable epic: he describes the geography of the place (v. 2); he includes God's speeches, which contain a command and an oracle (vv. 3–4, 15–18, 26); he inserts lively dialogues between Moses and the people (vv. 11–12) or Moses and God (v. 15); and above all he stresses the miraculous nature of the whole event: the pharaoh goes out with *all* his chariots (v. 7); the Lord himself gives *direct* help to the Israelites (v. 14); the Lord *looked down* on the Egyptians (v. 24)—which is

---

tur e regione Phihahiroth, quae est inte Magdolum et mare contra Beelsephon; in conspectu eius castra ponetis super mare. ³Dicturusque est pharao super filiis Israel: 'Errant in terra, conclusit eos desertum'. ⁴Et indurabo cor eius, ac persequetur eos, et glorificabor in pharaone et in omni exercitu eius; scientque Aegyptii quia ego sum Dominus». Feceruntque ita. ⁵Et nuntiatum est regi Aegyptiorum quod fugisset populus; immutatumque est cor pharaonis et servorum eius super populo, et dixerunt: «Quid hoc fecimus, ut dimitteremus Israel, ne servirent nobis?». ⁶Iunxit ergo currum et omnem populum

people, and they said, "What is this we have done, that we have let Israel go from serving us?" ⁶So he made ready his chariot and took his army with him, ⁷and took six hundred picked chariots and all the other chariots of Egypt with officers over all of them. ⁸And the LORD hardened the heart of Pharaoh king of Egypt and he pursued the people of Israel as they went forth defiantly. ⁹The Egyptians pursued them, all Pharaoh's horses and chariots and his horsemen and his army, and overtook them encamped at the sea, by Pi-ha-hiroth, in front of Baal-zephon.

¹⁰When Pharaoh drew near, the people of Israel lifted up their eyes, and behold, the Egyptians were marching after them; and they were in great fear. And the people of Israel cried out to the LORD; ¹¹and they said to Moses, "Is it because there are no graves

---

enough to frighten them (v. 24); etc. The end result is a real conviction that God has brought about the deliverance of his people. That is why, over the history of Israel, the Israelites will always look back to this event whenever they need to strengthen their hope of receiving further divine help at times of misfortune, or when they want to sing God's praises in times of prosperity. St Paul sees in the passage of the sea a figure of Christian Baptism. Baptism marks the start of salvation, and the start also of a persevering effort on the Christian's part to respond to it (cf. 1 Cor 10:1–5).

14:1–4. The positions of these cities has not yet been accurately established; it seems certain that they were situated in the marshy region north of the Bitter Lakes. They may have been small villages or even places of worship known to people when the book was first written.

In this dramatic salvation event the initiative lies with God: he planned it, he

gives the orders, he makes the Egyptians turn tail (v. 25) and see "the great work of the Lord" (v. 31). All these wondrous events have a theological purpose—to make known not only to the Israelites but even to the Gentiles, the Egyptians, the basic message: He is the Lord (vv 14–18).

14:10–14. The Eygptians get so close that the Israelites are terrified; this produces their first crisis of faith: the liberty they seek means giving up a quiet life in Egypt. Moses begins to reveal himself not just as a charismatic leader but as a mediator between the people and God. The words of v. 13 underlie the theological virtue of hope: God is the one who acts, man has to stand firm in faith; he has no reason to fear. As the Letter to the Hebrews teaches, Jesus is the model of faithfulness and hope: "Therefore [. . .] let us run with perseverance the race that is set before us, looking to Jesus the pioneer and perfecter of our faith, who for the joy that was set before him endured

---

suum assumpsit secum; ⁷tulitque sescentos currus electos et quidquid in Aegypto curruum fuit et bellatores in singulis curribus. ⁸Induravitque Dominus cor pharaonis regis Aegypti, et persecutus est filios Israel; at illi egressi erant in manu excelsa. ⁹Cumque persequerentur Aegyptii vestigia praecedentium, reppererunt eos in castris super mare; omnes equi et currus pharaonis, equites et exercitus eius erant in Phihahiroth contra Beelsephon. ¹⁰Cumque appropinquasset pharao, levantes filii Israel oculos viderunt

in Egypt that you have taken us away to die in the wilderness? What have you done to us, in bringing us out of Egypt? [12]Is not this what we said to you in Egypt, 'Let us alone and let us serve the Egyptians'? For it would have been better for us to serve the Egyptians than to die in the wilderness." [13]And Moses said to the people, "Fear not, stand firm, and see the salvation of the LORD, which he will work for you today; for the Egyptians whom you see today, you shall never see again. [14]The LORD will fight for you, and you have only to be still."

Josh 3–4
Ps 66:6; 74:
13–15; 78:15,
53; 105; 106;
114:1–4
Wis 10:18–19
1 Cor 10:1–5

Crossing the Red Sea

[15]The LORD said to Moses, "Why do you cry to me? Tell the people of Israel to go forward. [16]Lift up your rod, and stretch out your hand over the sea and divide it, that the people of Israel may go on dry ground through the sea. [17]And I will harden the hearts of the Egyptians so that they shall go in after them, and I will get glory over Pharaoh and all his host, his chariots, and his horsemen. [18]And the Egyptians shall know that I am the LORD, when I have gotten glory over Pharaoh, his chariots, and his horsemen."

Gen 16:7
Is 43:1–3
Wis 19:6–9

[19]Then the angel of God who went before the host of Israel moved and went behind them; and the pillar of cloud moved from

---

the cross, despising the shame, and is seated at the right hand of the throne of God" (Heb 12:12).

14:17–18. The military language and the depiction of God as a warrior should cause no surprise: it is a daring anthropomorphism which shows that God is almighty and therefore can deliver the elect from any danger that threatens: "You, too, if you distance yourself from the Egyptians and flee far from the power

of demons," Origen comments, "will see what great helps will be provided to you each day and what great protection is available to you. All that is asked of you is that you stand firm in the faith and do not let yourself be terrified by either the Egyptian cavalry or the noise of their chariots" (*Homiliae in Exodum*, 5, 4).

14:19–22. At the wonderful moment of the crossing of the sea, God, man and the forces of nature play the leading role. In

---

Aegyptios post se et timuerunt valde clamaveruntque ad Dominum [11]et dixerunt ad Moysen: «Forsitan non erant sepulcra in Aegypto? Ideo tulisti nos, ut moreremur in solitudine. Quid hoc fecisti, ut educeres nos ex Aegypto? [12]Nonne iste est sermo, quem loquebamur ad te in Aegypto, dicentes: Recede a nobis, ut serviamus Aegyptiis? Multo enim melius erat servire eis quam mori in solitudine». [13]Et ait Moyses ad populum: «Nolite timere; state et videte salutem Domini, quam facturus est vobis hodie; Aegyptios enim, quos nunc videtis, nequaquam ultra videbitis usque in sempiternum. [14]Dominus pugnabit pro vobis, et vos silebitis». [15]Dixitque Dominus ad Moysen: «Quid clamas ad me? Loquere filiis Israel, ut proficiscantur. [16]Tu autem eleva virgam tuam et extende manum tuam super mare et divide illud, ut gradiantur filii Israel in medio mari per siccum. [17]Ego autem indurabo cor Aegyptiorum, ut persequantur eos; et glorificabor in pharaone et in omni exercitu eius, in curribus et in equitibus illius. [18]Et scient Aegyptii quia ego sum Dominus, cum glorificatus fuero in pharaone, in curribus atque

before them and stood behind them, [20]coming between the host of Egypt and the host of Israel. And there was the cloud and the darkness; and the night passed[p] without one coming near the other all night.

[21]Then Moses stretched out his hand over the sea; and the LORD drove the sea back by a strong east wind all night, and made the sea dry land, and the waters were divided. [22]And the people of Israel went into the midst of the sea on dry ground, the waters being a wall to them on their right hand and on their left. [23]The Egyptians pursued, and went in after them into the midst of the sea, all Pharaoh's horses, his chariots, and his horsemen. [24]And in the morning watch the LORD in the pillar of fire and of cloud looked down upon the host of the Egyptians, and discomfited the host of the Egyptians, [25]clogging[q] their chariot wheels so that they drove heavily; and the Egyptians said, "Let us flee from before Israel; for the LORD fights for them against the Egyptians."

[26]Then the LORD said to Moses, "Stretch out your hand over the sea, that the water may come back upon the Egyptians, upon their chariots, and upon their horsemen." [27]So Moses stretched forth his hand over the sea, and the sea returned to its wonted flow when the morning appeared; and the Egyptians fled into it, and the LORD

Ps 77:16–19
Jn 14:1

1 Cor 10:1
Heb 11:29

Deut 11:4
Heb 11:29

---

the person of the angel of the Lord, God becomes more visible; he directs operations; he plays a direct part. Moses' part consists in doing as the Lord commands; he is his vicar. The sons of Israel have no active part; they benefit from what happens. Even the forces of nature come into play: the pillar of cloud which marked the route by day now blocks the Egyptians' way; night, the symbol of evil, has become, as in the Passover, the time of

God's visitation; the warm west wind, always feared for its harmful effects, now proves a great help; and the waters of the sea, so often the symbol of the abyss and of evil, allow the victorious passage of the sons of Israel.

The prophets see this event as an instance of the creative power of God (cf. Is 43:1–3), and Christian writers comment along the same lines. Thus, Origen will say: "See the goodness of God the

in equitibus eius». [19]Tollensque se angelus Dei, qui praecedebat castra Israel, abiit post eos; et cum eo pariter columna nubis, priora dimittens, post tergum. [20]Stetit inter castra Aegyptiorum et castra Israel; et erat nubes tenebrosa et illuminans noctem, ita ut ad se invicem toto noctis tempore accedere non valerent. [21]Cumque extendisset Moyses manum super mare, reppulit illud Dominus, flante vento vehementi et urente tota nocte, et vertit in siccum; divisaque est aqua. [22]Et ingressi sunt filii Israel per medium maris sicci; erat enim aqua quasi murus a dextra eorum et laeva. [23]Persequentesque Aegyptii ingressi sunt post eos, omnis equitatus pharaonis, currus eius et equites per medium maris. [24]Iamque advenerat vigilia matutina, et ecce respiciens Dominus super castra Aegyptiorum per columnam ignis et nubis perturbavit exercitum eorum; [25]et impedivit rotas curruum, ita ut difficile moverentur. Dixerunt ergo Aegyptii: «Fugiamus Israelem! Dominus enim pugnat pro eis contra nos». [26]Et ait Dominus ad Moysen: «Extende manum tuam super mare, ut revertantur aquae ad Aegyptios super currus et equi-

p. Gk: Heb *and it lit up the night*   **q.** Or *binding.* Sam Gk Syr: Heb *removing*

routed[r] the Egyptians in the midst of the sea. [28]The waters returned and covered the chariots and the horsemen and all the host[s] of Pharaoh that had followed them into the sea; not so much as one of them remained. [29]But the people of Israel walked on dry ground through the sea, the waters being a wall to them on their right hand and on their left.

[30]Thus the LORD saved Israel that day from the hand of the Egyptians; and Israel saw the Egyptians dead upon the seashore. [31]And Israel saw the great work which the LORD did against the Egyptians, and the people feared the LORD; and they believed in the LORD and in his servant Moses.

Ex 4:31

Song of victory*

Wis 10:20
Rev 15:3

15 [1]Then Moses and the people of Israel sang this song to the LORD, saying,

---

Creator: if you submit to his will and follow his Law, he will see to it that created things cooperate with you, against their own nature if necessary" (*Homiliae in Exodum*, 5,5).

The book of Wisdom turns the account of the crossing of the sea into a hymn of praise to the Lord who delivered Israel (cf. Wis 19:6–9), and St Paul sees the waters as a figure of baptismal water: "All were baptized into Moses in the cloud and in the sea" (1 Cor 10:2).

14:31. The main effect the miraculous crossing of the sea had on the Israelites was the faith it gave them in the power of God and in the authority of Moses. This section of the account of the escape from Egypt ends as it began—that is, showing that the people's faith (4:31) is now

strengthened. So, too, Christian faith is strengthened when we do what God desires: "Following Jesus on his way. You have understood what our Lord was asking from you and you have decided to accompany him on his way. You are trying to walk in his footsteps, to clothe yourself in Christ's clothing, to be Christ himself: well, your faith, your faith in the light our Lord is giving you, must be both operative and full of sacrifice" (St Josemaría Escrivá, *Friends of God*, 198).

***15:1–21.** This victory anthem, along with that of Deborah (Judg 5), is one of the oldest hymns of Israel. It probably goes as far back as the 13th century BC, long before the redactor of this book decided to include it as a colophon to his Exodus account. It is called the "Song of

---

tes eorum». [27]Cumque extendisset Moyses manum contra mare, reversum est primo diluculo ad priorem locum; fugientibusque Aegyptiis occurrerunt aquae, et involvit eos Dominus in mediis fluctibus. [28]Reversaeque sunt aquae et operuerunt currus et equites cuncti exercitus pharaonis, qui sequentes ingressi fuerant mare; ne unus quidem superfuit ex eis. [29]Filii autem Israel perrexerunt per medium sicci maris, et aquae eis erant quasi pro muro a dextris et a sinistris. [30]Liberavitque Dominus in die illo Israel de manu Aegyptiorum. Et viderunt Aegyptios mortuos super litus maris [31]et manum magnam, quam exercuerat Dominus contra eos; timuitque populus Dominum et crediderunt Domino et Moysi servo eius. [1]Tunc cecinit Moyses et filii Israel carmen hoc Domino, et dixerunt: «Cantemus Domino, / gloriose enim magnificatus est: / equum et ascensorem eius / deiecit in mare! / [2]Fortitudo mea et robur

---

r. Heb *shook off*　**s.** Gk Syr: Heb *to all the host*

"I will sing to the LORD, for he has triumphed gloriously;
   the horse and his rider[t] he has thrown into the sea.
²The LORD is my strength and my song,   Is 12:2
   and he has become my salvation;
this is my God, and I will praise him,
   my father's God, and I will exalt him.
³The LORD is a man of war;   Gen 3:14
   the LORD is his name.

⁴"Pharaoh's chariots and his host he cast into the sea;   Acts 7:36
   and his picked officers are sunk in the Red Sea.

Miriam" (v. 21) because, as we know from Ugarit poems of the period (13th–9th centuries BC) it was the practice to put at the end (not the start) the reason why the poem was written, the author's name and the poem's title (vv. 18–21). It is very likely that this canticle was recited in the liturgy and that the entire people said the response (vv. 1, 21) after each stanza was said or sung by the choir.

It is a hymn of praise and thanksgiving in which the three stages of the deliverance of Israel are remembered—the prodigies of the Red Sea (vv. 4–10), the triumphal pilgrimage in the desert (vv. 14–16) and the taking possession of the land of Canaan (vv. 17–18).

In this poetic re-creation of these events the divine attributes are extolled one by one (might, military power, redemption, etc); they reflect the theological implications of exodus, wilderness and land: it is God who has done all these wondrous things; he has done them because he has chosen the people to be his very own; he himself requires that they respond by acknowledging him to be God, Lord of all, the only deliverer.

15:1–3. Victory over the Egyptians has revealed the glory and might of God. Strength, power, salvation can be taken as meaning the same thing, for the sacred author does not regard the divine attributes as abstract qualities but as particular actions: only God could truly save the people.

"The Lord is a man of war": this daring description indicates that this is a very ancient poem. Some translations, possibly because they thought it might be misunderstood, toned it down a little: the Samaritan Pentateuch has "powerful in combat" and the Septuagint "he who breaks through battles". The Spanish version coincides with the RSV and the New Vulgate, retaining the blunt military imagery, which is very descriptive of the almighty power of God: "He is the Lord of the Universe [. . .]. He is master of history, governing hearts and events in keeping with his will" (*Catechism of the Catholic Church*, 269).

"The Lord is his name": literally, "his name is Yah", using an abbreviation of Yahweh which may have been customary in more ancient times. It may well be that there is an echo of this name in the "Alleluia" of the Psalms.

---

meum Dominus, / et factus est mihi in salutem. / Iste Deus meus, / et glorificabo eum; / Deus patris mei, / et exaltabo eum! / ³Dominus quasi vir pugnator; / Dominus nomen eius! / ⁴Currus pharaonis et exercitum eius / proiecit in mare, / electi bellatores eius / submersi sunt in mari Rubro. / ⁵Abyssi ope-

t. Or *its chariot*

⁵The floods cover them;
    they went down into the depths like a stone.

Jer 51:63
Rev 18:21
⁶Thy right hand, O LORD, glorious in power,
    thy right hand, O LORD, shatters the enemy.

Is 5:24
Obad 18
Nahum 1:10
⁷In the greatness of thy majesty thou overthrowest thy
    adversaries;
    thou sendest forth thy fury, it consumes them like stubble.

⁸At the blast of thy nostrils the waters piled up,
    the floods stood up in a heap;
    the deeps congealed in the heart of the sea.

⁹The enemy said, 'I will pursue, I will overtake,
    I will divide the spoil, my desire shall have its fill of them.
    I will draw my sword, my hand shall destroy them.'

¹⁰Thou didst blow with thy wind, the sea covered them;
    they sank as lead in the mighty waters.

Lev 19:2
Rev 13:4
¹¹"Who is like thee, O LORD, among the gods?
    Who is like thee, majestic in holiness,
    terrible in glorious deeds, doing wonders?

¹²Thou didst stretch out thy right hand,
    the earth swallowed them.

¹³"Thou hast led in thy steadfast love
    the people whom thou hast redeemed,

15:4–12. The crossing of the Red Sea is viewed as a sort of dyptich: on the one hand, the defeat of the Egyptians (vv. 4–5) leads to praise of God as the victor ("thy right hand", "thy majesty", "the blast of thy nostrils": vv. 6–8); on the other hand, the machinations of the enemy and God's intervening to punish them (vv. 9–10) leads to an act of faith in God: "Who is like thee, O Lord?" (vv. 11–13).

Faith in God, according to the Bible, is not something theoretical or based on philosophical reasoning; it is something practical and based on experience: one believes in God because one has experienced his powerful protection, one knows that he alone saves in a loving way.

15:8. "The deeps congealed in the heart of the sea": that is, the bottom of the sea was filled with the dead bodies of the enemy.

15:13–18. The image of the Red Sea is used to look ahead to the conquest of Canaan: the peoples there are so afraid

---

ruerunt eos, / descenderunt in profundum quasi lapis. / ⁶Dextera tua, Domine, / magnifice in fortitudine, / dextera tua, Domine, / percussit inimicum. / ⁷Et in multitudine gloriae tuae / deposuisti adversarios tuos; / misisti iram tuam, / quae devoravit eos sicut stipulam. / ⁸Et in spiritu furoris tui / congregatae sunt aquae; / stetit ut agger / unda fluens, / coagulatae sunt abyssi / in medio mari. / ⁹Dixit inimicus: / 'Persequar, comprehendam; / dividam spolia, / implebitur anima mea: / evaginabo gladium meum, / interficiet eos manus mea!'. / ¹⁰Flavit spiritus tuus, / et operuit eos mare; / submersi sunt quasi plumbum / in aquis vehementibus. / ¹¹Quis similis tui / in diis, Domine? / Quis similis tui, / magnificus in sanctitate, / terribilis atque laudabilis, / faciens mirabilia? / ¹²Extendisti manum tuam, / devoravit eos

thou hast guided them by thy strength to thy holy abode.

¹⁴The peoples have heard, they tremble; Rev 11:18
pangs have seized on the inhabitants of Philistia.

¹⁵Now are the chiefs of Edom dismayed; Num 20:21;
the leaders of Moab, trembling seizes them; 21:4–13
Deut 2:1–9
all the inhabitants of Canaan have melted away.

¹⁶Terror and dread fall upon them; Is 11:11
because of the greatness of thy arm, they are as still as a stone, Ps 74:2
I Kings 8:13
till thy people, O LORD, pass by, Rev 11:11
till the people pass by whom thou hast purchased. Eph 1:14

¹⁷Thou wilt bring them in, and plant them on thy own mountain,
the place, O LORD, which thou hast made for thy abode,
the sanctuary, LORD, which thy hands have established.

¹⁸The LORD will reign for ever and ever."

¹⁹For when the horses of Pharaoh with his chariots and his horsemen went into the sea, the LORD brought back the waters of the

---

that they act as the ways of the sea did: they become immobile, as if made of stone, while the Israelites pass through their lands in triumph.

Since this is a poetic recreation, the author does not want to limit himself to what exactly did happen when the Land was conquered: he just sketches in a few lines the peoples whom Israel will find there, on "thy own mountain", where the Lord's sanctuary is to be built. This does not mean that this part must necessarily have been written after the conquest of Palestine; it could be that the writer visualized that the Land would be conquered in this wonderful way, proving that it was the work of the Lord and showing his almighty power over all things, as the last verse puts it: "The Lord will reign for ever" (v. 18). The Vulgate translated

these words as "God reigns over all eternity and more", and some medieval philosophers used this to argue that it was not quite correct to say that God is eternal, for it would seem that some created things are also eternal. St Thomas replies, with his usual precision, saying that on the one hand God in his be-ing surpasses any imaginable duration, and on the other "even if something else were to exist forever, as certain philosophers believed the rotation of the heavens to do, the Lord would still reign beyond it, because his reign is instantaneously whole" (*Summa theologiae* 1, 10, 2 ad 2).

15:19–21. It was customary among the Israelites for women to celebrate victory in song and dance (cf. Judg 11:34; 1 Sam 18:6–7). This epilogue once more recalls

---

terra. / ¹³Dux fuisti in misericordia tua / populo, quem redemisti, / et portasti eum in fortitudine tua / ad habitaculum sanctum tuum. / ¹⁴Attenderunt populi et commoti sunt, / dolores obtinuerunt habitatores Philisthaeae. / ¹⁵Tunc conturbati sunt principes Edom, / potentes Moab obtinuit tremor, / obriguerunt omnes habitatores Chanaan. / ¹⁶Irruit super eos / formido et pavor; / in magnitudine brachii tui / fiunt immobiles quasi lapis, / donec pertranseat populus tuus, Domine, / donec pertranseat populus tuus iste, / quem possedisti. / ¹⁷Introduces eos et plantabis / in monte hereditatis tuae, / firmissimo habitaculo tuo, / quod operatus es, Domine, / sanctuario, Domine, / quod firmaverunt manus tuae. / ¹⁸Dominus regnabit / in aeternum et ultra!». ¹⁹Ingressi sunt enim equi pharaonis cum curribus et equi-

Num 26:59
Judg 11:34
1 Sam 18:6–7

sea upon them; but the people of Israel walked on dry ground in the midst of the sea. [20]Then Miriam, the prophetess, the sister of Aaron, took a timbrel in her hand; and all the women went out after her with timbrels and dancing. [21]And Miriam sang to them:

"Sing to the LORD, for he has triumphed gloriously;
the horse and his rider he has thrown into the sea."

6. ISRAEL IN THE DESERT*

The bitter water of Marah

Ex 17:5–6
Num 20:7–11;
33:8

[22]Then Moses led Israel onward from the Red Sea, and they went into the wilderness of Shur; they went three days in the wilderness

---

the epic crossing of the Red Sea, the festive dancing and the refrain of the canticle.

Miriam (*Miryam* in Hebrew) is described as a prophetess (v. 20) because, together with Aaron, she is portrayed as being a spokesperson of God (cf. Num 12:2) and, as we see here, the composer of this hymn. Deborah is also described as a prophetess (cf. Judg 4:4) and to her is attributed another of the most ancient canticles (cf. Judg 5:1–31). The prophets say that it will be a sign of the messianic age that "your sons and daughters shall prophesy" (Joel 2:28).

*15:22—18:27. During the first stage of their sojourn in the wilderness, the sons of Israel became gradually more aware of themselves as being a people, chosen by God to carry out a special mission. Their experiences in the desert (chaps. 16–18) and the promulgation of the laws (chaps 19–24) will give them a clear hierarchical structure and reassure them of God's special protection.

In this stage of consolidation of their national identity, God first puts them to

the test through the rigours of desert life—unvaried diet (chap. 16) and shortage of water (17:1–7). After a while Moses' leadership, already clear since the time they left Egypt, is strengthened and widened in scope: he is now their mediator (17:8–16) and a judge along with the elders (chap. 18).

15:22–27. Once they start to travel through the desert the first difficulty they meet is a shortage of water; this is going to happen more than once (cf. 17:5–6; Num 20:7–11). It is difficult to say where Marah and Elim were; most scholars accept that Marah is Ayun Mûsa (Fountain of Moses) a few kilometres/miles from where the crossing of the sea took place; Elim may be present-day Wadi Garandel, about 80 kilometers (50 miles) from Marah. Naturally, desert caravans encamped near wells or natural springs which gave rise to small leafy oases.

This episode contains a number of things which are reminiscent of important events or truths—the discovery that the water is undrinkable (the popular ety-

---

tibus eius in mare, et reduxit super eos Dominus aquas maris; filii autem Israel ambulaverunt per siccum in medio eius. [20]Sumpsit ergo Maria prophetissa soror Aaron tympanum in manu sua; egressaeque sunt omnes mulieres post eam cum tympanis et choris, [21]quibus praecinebat dicens: «Cantemus Domino, / gloriose enim magnificatus est: / equum et ascensorem eius / deiecit in mare!». [22]Tulit autem Moyses Israel de mari Rubro, et egressi sunt in desertum Sur; ambulaveruntque tribus diebus per soli-

and found no water. ²³When they came to Marah, they could not
drink the water of Marah because it was bitter; therefore it was
named Marah.ᵘ ²⁴And the people murmured against Moses,
saying, "What shall we drink?" ²⁵And he cried to the LORD; and
the LORD showed him a tree, and he threw it into the water, and
the water became sweet.

There the LORDᵛ made for them a statute and an ordinance and
there he proved them, ²⁶saying, "If you will diligently hearken to
the voice of the LORD your God, and do that which is right in his
eyes, and give heed to his commandments and keep all his
statutes, I will put none of the diseases upon you which I put upon
the Egyptians; for I am the LORD, your healer."

²⁷Then they came to Elim, where there were twelve springs of
water and seventy palm trees; and they encamped there by the
water.

Heb 38
Rev 8:11
Ex 14:11
Sir 38:5
Num 11
Deut 8:3, 16
Josh 5:10–12
Ps 78
Wis 16:20–29
Jn 6:26–58

The manna and the quails*

16 ¹They set out from Elim, and all the congregation of the
people of Israel came to the wilderness of Sin, which is

---

mology of Marah is "bitter" or "bitterness"), which recalls the first plague of
Egypt (v. 26); the people's complaints, so
often repeated (cf. 16:2; 17:3; Num 14:2;
20:3; etc.); Moses' intercession; the first
mention of a divine ordinance or law; the
promise of divine protection and the
description of God as "healer"; and the
arrival at Elim, a place where there were
trees and plenty of water. All this combines to convey an essential teaching:
because of the special love God has
shown his people, he will look after their
welfare, as long as they obey him.

The first Christian commentators saw
in this account symbols of things to do

with the New Covenant: in the tree that
Moses threw into the waters to purify
them, they see a prefiguration of the
cross by which we are all healed (St
Justin, Origen, St Cyril of Alexandria); in
the twelve springs and seventy palm
trees, the seventy disciples sent out by
our Lord, and the twelve Apostles
(Origen, St Gregory of Nyssa).

*16:1–36. The prodigy of the manna and
the quails was a very important sign of
God's special providence towards his
people while they were in the desert. It is
recounted here and in Numbers 11, but in
both accounts facts are interwoven with

---

tudinem et non inveniebant aquam. ²³Et venerunt in Mara, nec poterant bibere aquas de Mara, eo quod
essent amarae; unde vocatum est nomen eius Mara (*id est Amaritudo*). ²⁴Et murmuravit populus contra
Moysen dicens: «Quid bibemus?». ²⁵At ille clamavit ad Dominum, qui ostendit ei lignum; quod cum
misisset in aquas, in dulcedinem versae sunt. Ibi constituit ei praecepta atque iudicia et ibi tentavit eum
²⁶dicens: «Si audieris vocem Domini Dei tui et, quod rectum est coram eo, feceris et oboedieris mandatis eius custodierisque omnia praecepta illius, cunctum languorem, quem posui in Aegypto, non inducam super te: Ego enim Dominus sanator tuus». ²⁷Venerunt autem in Elim, ubi erant duodecim fontes
aquarum et septuaginta palmae; et castrametati sunt iuxta aquas. ¹Profectique sunt de Elim, et venit

u. That is *Bitterness* **v.** Heb *he*

between Elim and Sinai, on the fifteenth day of the second month

I Cor 10:10 after they had departed from the land of Egypt. [2]And the whole congregation of the people of Israel murmured against Moses and

Ex 14:11 Aaron in the wilderness, [3]and said to them, "Would that we had died by the hand of the LORD in the land of Egypt, when we sat by the fleshpots and ate bread to the full; for you have brought us out into this wilderness to kill this whole assembly with hunger."

---

interpretation of same and with things to do with worship and ethics.

Some scholars have argued that the manna is the same thing as a sweet secretion that comes from the tamarisk (*tamarix mannifera*) when punctured by a particular insect commonly found in the mountains of Sinai. The drops of this resin solidify in the coldness of the night and some fall to the ground. They have to be gathered up early in the morning because they deteriorate at twenty-four degrees temperature Celsius (almost seventy-five degrees Fahrenheit). Even today desert Arabs collect them and use them for sucking and as a sweetener in confectionery.

As we know, quails cross the Sinai peninsula on their migrations back and forth between Africa and Europe or Asia. In May or June, when they return from Africa they usually rest in Sinai, exhausted after a long sea crossing; they can be easily trapped at this point.

Although these phenomenon can show where the manna and the quail come from, the important thing is that the Israelites saw them as wonders worked by God. The sacred writer stops to describe the impact the manna had on the sons of Israel. They are puzzled by it, as can be seen from their remarks when it comes for the first time: "What is it?" they ask, which in Hebrew sounds

like "man hû", that is, manna (v. 15), which is how the Greek translation puts it. Indeed, the need to collect it every day gave rise to complaints about some people being greedy (v. 20) and who did not understand the scope of God's gift (v. 15). And just as manna is a divine gift to meet a basic human need (nourishment), so too the divine precepts, specifically that of the sabbath, are a free gift from the Lord (v. 28). So, obedience is not a heavy burden but the exercise of a capacity to receive the good things that God gives to those who obey him.

The prodigy of the manna will resound right through the Bible: in the "Deuteronomic" tradition it is a test that God gives his people to show them that "man does not live by bread alone, but [. . .] by everything that proceeds from the mouth of the Lord" (Deut 8:3). The psalmist discovers that manna is "the bread of the strong" ("of angels", says the Vulgate and the RSV), which God sent in abundance (Ps 78:23ff; cf. Ps 105:40). The book of Wisdom spells out the features of this bread from heaven "ready to eat, providing every pleasure and suited to every taste" (Wis 16:20–29). And the New Testament reveals the full depth of this "spiritual" food (1 Cor 10:3), for, as the *Catechism* teaches, "manna in the desert prefigured

---

omnis congregatio filiorum Israel in desertum Sin, quod est inter Elim et Sinai, quinto decimo die mensis secundi postquam egressi sunt de terra Aegypti. [2]Et murmuravit omnis congregatio filiorum Israel contra Moysen et Aaron in solitudine, [3]dixeruntque filii Israel ad eos: «Utinam mortui essemus

⁴Then the LORD said to Moses, "Behold, I will rain bread from heaven for you; and the people shall go out and gather a day's portion every day, that I may prove them, whether they will walk in my law or not. ⁵On the sixth day, when they prepare what they bring in, it will be twice as much as they gather daily." ⁶So Moses and Aaron said to all the people of Israel, "At evening you shall know that it was the LORD who brought you out of the land of Egypt, ⁷and in the morning you shall see the glory of the LORD, because he has heard your murmurings against the LORD. For what are we, that you murmur against us?" ⁸And Moses said,

Jn 6:32
1 Cor 10:3

2 Cor 3:18

---

the Eucharist, 'the true bread from heaven' (Jn 6:32)" (*Catechism of the Catholic Church*, 1094).

16:1. From the Byzantine period onwards, Christian tradition has identified Sinai with the range of mountains in the south of the Sinai peninsula; these mountains go as high as 2,500 metres (8,200 feet) above sea level.

The main mountains are Djébel Serbal, Djébel Katerina and Djébel Mûsa, the last mentioned of which tradition regards as Mount Sinai or Horeb. At the foot of this mountain lies the monastery of St Catherine. The desert of Sin (different from the desert of the same name running along the side of the Dead Sea: cf. the note on Num 20:1–19), is very near to this; people involved in mining the copper and turquoise that is found there used to camp there temporarily.

16:2–3. The complaining that usually precedes the desert prodigies (cf. 14:11; 15:24; 17:3; Num 11:1, 4; 14:2; 20:2; 21:4–5) brings into focus the chosen

people's lack of faith and hope, and (by contrast) the faithfulness of God, who time and again alleviates their needs even though they do not deserve it. At the same time, just as Moses and Aaron listened patiently to complaints, God too is always ready to dialogue with the sinner, sometimes listening to his complaints and sorting them out, and sometimes simply giving him a chance to repent: "Although God could inflict punishment on those whom he condemns without saying anything, he does not do so; on the contrary, up to the point when he does condemn, he speaks with the guilty person and lets him talk, so as to help him avoid condemnation" (Origen, *Homiliae in Ieremiam*, 1,1).

16:6–7. The manna and the quails not only alleviate the people's hunger; they are, above all, a sign of the triple presence of God: the Lord who brought them out of Egypt (v. 7) is not going to abandon them; he manifests his glory by dominating nature; he has not brought them out to die, but to make sure that they survive in spite of difficulties.

---

per manum Domini in terra Aegypti, quando sedebamus super ollas carnium et comedebamus panem in saturitate. Cur eduxisti nos in desertum istud, ut occideretis omnem coetum fame?». ⁴Dixit autem Dominus ad Moysen: «Ecce ego pluam vobis panes de caelo; egrediatur populus et colligat, quae sufficiunt per singulos dies, ut tentem eum, utrum ambulet in lege mea an non. ⁵Die autem sexta parabunt quod intulerint, et duplum erit quam colligere solebant per singulos dies». ⁶Dixeruntque Moyses et Aaron ad omnes filios Israel: «Vespere scietis / quod Dominus eduxerit vos / de terra Aegypti; / ⁷et

"When the LORD gives you in the evening flesh to eat and in the morning bread to the full, because the LORD has heard your murmurings which you murmur against him—what are we? Your murmurings are not against us but against the LORD."

⁹And Moses said to Aaron, "Say to the whole congregation of the people of Israel, 'Come near before the LORD, for he has heard your murmurings.'" ¹⁰And as Aaron spoke to the whole congregation of the people of Israel, they looked toward the wilderness, and behold, the glory of the LORD appeared in the cloud. ¹¹And the LORD said to Moses, ¹²"I have heard the murmurings of the people of Israel; say to them, 'At twilight you shall eat flesh, and in the morning you shall be filled with bread; then you shall know that I am the LORD your God.'"

¹³In the evening quails came up and covered the camp; and in the morning dew lay round about the camp. ¹⁴And when the dew had gone up, there was on the face of the wilderness a fine, flake-like thing, fine as hoar frost on the ground.* ¹⁵When the people of Israel saw it, they said to one another, "What is it?"ʷ For they did not know what it was. And Moses said to them, "It is the bread which the LORD has given you to eat. ¹⁶This is what the LORD has

Rom 9:4
2 Cor 3:18

Jn 6:32
1 Cor 10:2

16:16–20. The people of God are made up of members who enjoy equality of rights. From the very start, from the very constitution of the nation, there is a sense of social responsibility which imposes limits on the ownership of property. Greed is symptomatic of a grave mistrust in the Lord who "each day" provides sufficient to meet one's needs. The episode of the manna confirms the need to trust in God alone; so, when someone tries to gather up more than he needs, it rots (vv. 20–21). The Bible, and the Church later on, have tried to shed light on social questions and, specifically, the right to and limitations on private property. "Christian tradition", John Paul II writes, "has never upheld this right as absolute and untouchable. On the contrary, it has always understood this right within the broader context of the right common to all to use the goods of the whole of creation: *the right to private property is subordinated to the right to common use*, to the fact that goods are meant for everyone" (*Laborem exercens*, 14).

mane videbitis / gloriam Domini. Audivit enim murmur vestrum contra Dominum. Nos vero quid sumus, quia mussitatis contra nos?». ⁸Et ait Moyses: «Dabit Dominus vobis / vespere carnes edere / et mane panes in saturitate, / eo quod audierit murmurationes vestras, quibus murmurati estis contra eum. Nos enim quid sumus? Nec contra nos est murmur vestrum, sed contra Dominum». ⁹Dixitque Moyses ad Aaron: «Dic universae congregationi filiorum Israel: Accedite coram Domino; audivit enim murmur vestrum». ¹⁰Cumque loqueretur Aaron ad omnem coetum filiorum Israel, respexerunt ad solitudinem, et ecce gloria Domini apparuit in nube. ¹¹Locutus est autem Dominus ad Moysen dicens: ¹²«Audivi murmurationes filiorum Israel. Loquere ad eos: Vespere comedetis carnes et mane saturabimini panibus scietisque quod ego sum Dominus Deus vester». ¹³Factum est ergo vespere, et ascendens coturnix operuit castra; mane quoque ros iacuit per circuitum castrorum. ¹⁴Cumque operuisset superficiem deserti,

w. Or *"It is manna."* Heb *man hu*

commanded: 'Gather of it, every man of you, as much as he can eat; you shall take an omer apiece, according to the number of the persons whom each of you has in his tent.'" [17]And the people of Israel did so; they gathered, some more, some less. [18]But when they measured it with an omer, he that gathered much had nothing over, and he that gathered little had no lack; each gathered according to what he could eat. [19]And Moses said to them, "Let no man leave any of it till the morning." [20]But they did not listen to Moses; some left part of it till the morning, and it bred worms and became foul; and Moses was angry with them. [21]Morning by morning they gathered it, each as much as he could eat; but when the sun grew hot, it melted.

[22]On the sixth day they gathered twice as much bread, two omers apiece; and when all the leaders of the congregation came and told Moses, [23]he said to them, "This is what the LORD has commanded: 'Tomorrow is a day of solemn rest, a holy sabbath to the LORD; bake what you will bake and boil what you will boil, and all that is left over lay by to be kept till the morning.'" [24]So they laid it by till the morning, as Moses bade them; and it did not become foul, and there were no worms in it. [25]Moses said, "Eat it

2 Cor 8:15

Mt 6:34

Gen 12:1–3
Ex 20:11
Deut 5:15

16:22–30. The sabbath is the day consecrated entirely to God; therefore, it is unlawful to do the tasks one does on other days. There are social reasons for rest on the seventh day: the calendar is arranged by weeks and work is so organized as to allow all in the household, animals included, to be given a day of rest each week. But it is the religious side of the sabbath that Holy Scripture emphasizes most, and there are two aspects to it—imitation of God, and commemoration of the deliverance-salvation

obtained by the Exodus. To ground the idea that sabbath observance is an imitation of God (cf. the Ten Commandments in 20:11), the Priestly tradition's account of creation spans six days in such a way that God rested and blessed the seventh day (Gen 2:1–3). To show that each sabbath commemorated deliverance from Egypt (cf. Deut 5:15), the same tradition, when recounting the prodigy of the manna (in the passage we are discussing) stresses the observance of the sabbath rest.

---

apparuit minutum et squamatum in similitudinem pruinae super terram. [15]Quod cum vidissent filii Israel, dixerunt ad invicem: «Manhu?» (*quod significat: «Quid est hoc?»*). Ignorabant enim quid esset. Quibus ait Moyses: «Iste est panis, quem dedit Dominus vobis ad vescendum. [16]Hic est sermo, quem praecepit Dominus: 'Colligat ex eo unusquisque quantum sufficiat ad vescendum; gomor per singula capita iuxta numerum animarum vestrarum, quae habitant in tabernaculo, sic tolletis'». [17]Feceruntque ita filii Israel; et collegerunt alius plus, alius minus. [18]Et mensi sunt ad mensuram gomor; nec qui plus collegerat, habuit amplius, nec qui minus paraverat, repperit minus, sed singuli, iuxta id quod edere poterant, congregaverunt. [19]Dixitque Moyses ad eos: «Nullus relinquat ex eo in mane». [20]Qui non audierunt eum, sed dimiserunt quidam ex eis usque mane, et scatere coepit vermibus atque computruit; et iratus est contra eos Moyses. [21]Colligebant autem mane singuli, quantum sufficere poterat ad vescendum; cumque incaluisset sol, liquefiebat. [22]In die autem sexta collegerunt cibos duplices, id est duo

today, for today is a sabbath to the LORD; today you will not find it in the field. ²⁶Six days you shall gather it; but on the seventh day, which is a sabbath, there will be none." ²⁷On the seventh day some of the people went out to gather, and they found none. ²⁸And the LORD said to Moses, "How long do you refuse to keep my commandments and my laws? ²⁹See! The LORD has given you the sabbath, therefore on the sixth day he gives you bread for two days; remain every man of you in his place, let no man go out of his place on the seventh day." ³⁰So the people rested on the seventh day.

Num 11:7 ³¹Now the house of Israel called its name manna; it was like coriander seed, white, and the taste of it was like wafers made Rev 2:17 with honey. ³²And Moses said, "This is what the LORD has com-

---

Three basic ideas underlie this narrative. The main one is that, since the manna is the first wonder that God works for his people now that they have been established as a people, so too the sabbath is the first benefit and the first commandment that God gives them. Also, the precept specifies that the sabbath should be celebrated on the seventh day. And, no less important, its origin goes right back to Moses himself, who as God's spokesman explains the meaning of events (cf. 17:23–25, 28–29). As time goes by, the sons of Israel will become more aware of the sacred character of the sabbath and, particularly during the exile in Babylon, that day will acquire the importance we see reflected in the various biblical passages.

In New Testament times some Pharisees and adherents of other religious movements overburdened sabbath observance with many regulations, running the risk that its religious benefits would be lost sight of. Our Lord gives it back its true meaning when he says, "The sabbath was made for man, not man for the sabbath" (Mk 2:27).

From very early on, Christians realized that the sabbath, commemorating as it did God's role in creation and in delivering the Hebrew people from bondage, was a figure of God's supreme intervention in the resurrection of Jesus. And they began to celebrate the day on which Jesus rose as *dies dominica*, the day of the Lord. So, Sunday is not a transfer of the biblical sabbath; it is the great day which commemorates the definitive Redemption brought about by Christ, taking on the religious meaning which the sabbath had in the Old Testament (cf.

gomor per singulos homines. Venerunt autem omnes principes congregationis et narraverunt Moysi. ²³Qui ait eis: «Hoc est quod locutus est Dominus: Requies, sabbatum sanctum Domino cras; quodcumque torrendum est, torrete et, quae coquenda sunt, coquite; quidquid autem reliquum fuerit, reponite usque in mane». ²⁴Feceruntque ita, ut praeceperat Moyses, et non computruit, neque vermis inventus est in eo. ²⁵Dixitque Moyses: «Comedite illud hodie, quia sabbatum est Domino; non invenietur hodie in agro. ²⁶Sex diebus colligite; in die autem septimo sabbatum est Domino, idcirco non invenietur septima dies; et egressi de populo, ut colligerent, non invenerunt. ²⁸Dixit autem Dominus ad Moysen: «Usquequo non vultis custodire mandata mea et legem meam? ²⁹Videte quo Dominus dederit vobis sabbatum et propter hoc die sexta tribuit vobis cibos duplices; maneat unusquisque apud semetipsum, nullus egrediatur de loco suo die septimo». ³⁰Et sabbatizavit populus die septimo. ³¹Appellavitque domus Israel nomen eius Man: quod erat quasi semen coriandri album,

manded: 'Let an omer of it be kept throughout your generations, that they may see the bread with which I fed you in the wilderness, when I brought you out of the land of Egypt.'" [33]And Moses said to Aaron, "Take a jar, and put an omer of manna in it, and place it before the LORD, to be kept throughout your generations." [34]As the LORD commanded Moses, so Aaron placed it before the testimony, to be kept. [35]And the people of Israel ate the manna forty years, till they came to a habitable land; they ate the manna, till they came to the border of the land of Canaan. [36](An omer is the tenth part of an ephah.)

Heb 9:4

Num 21:5
Josh 5:10–12
Neh 9:21
Acts 13:18
1 Cor 10:3

The water from the rock

Num 20:1–13;
20:24

17 [1]All the congregation of the people of Israel moved on from the wilderness of Sin by stages, according to the command-

Num 33:12–14
Heb 3:16

Acts 20:7; 1 Cor 16:2; Rev 1:10). "In Christ's Passover, Sunday fulfils the spiritual truth of the Jewish sabbath and announces man's eternal rest in God" (*Catechism of the Catholic Church*, 2175). See also John Paul II, Apostolic Letter, *Dies Domini* (31 May 1998).

16:32–36. Later generations need to remember the importance of this event, by being able to see alongside the tables of the Decalogue (the Testimony v. 34) an urn containing manna (and probably made of gold: cf. Heb 9:4). The tradition about the manna being kept inside the ark may have been a later one, because when the ark was solemnly enthroned in the temple of Solomon (cf. 1 Kings 8:9) it contained only the tables of the Law. Be that as it may, the religious meaning of the manna was something never forgotten—this food which

God gave Israel in the desert for forty years (cf. Josh 5:10–11; Ps 78:24–25; Wis 16:20–21).

"Omer" means literally "sheaf". Here we are told it was a tenth of an ephah. An ephah was both a receptacle and the content of same, so it became a unit of volume; it was the equivalent of 21 litres (about five gallons).

17:1–7. The severity of desert life (notably hunger and thirst) leads God to help the Israelites in various ways, all of them full of theological implications. The miracle of the manna, which was preceded by that of the water which Moses made drinkable (15:22–25), is followed by a new work of wonder to do with water: Moses causes water to flow from a rock. This happened at Rephidim, probably what is now Wadi Refayid, some 13 km (8 miles) from Djébel Mûsa.

---

gustusque eius quasi similae cum melle. [32]Dixit autem Moyses: «Iste est sermo, quem praecepit Dominus: 'Imple gomor ex eo, et custodiatur in generationes vestras, ut noverint panem, quo alui vos in solitudine, quando educti estis de terra Aegypti'». [33]Dixitque Moyses ad Aaron: «Sume vas unum et mitte ibi man, quantum potest capere gomor; et repone coram Domino ad servandum in generationes vestras». [34]Sicut praecepit Dominus Moysi, posuit illud Aaron coram testimonio reservandum. [35]Filii autem Israel comederunt man quadraginta annis, donec venirent in terram habitabilem; hoc cibo aliti sunt, usquequo tangerent fines terrae Chanaan. [36]Gomor autem decima pars est ephi. [1]Igitur profecta omnis congregatio filiorum Israel de deserto Sin per mansiones suas iuxta sermonem Domini, cas-

ment of the LORD, and camped at Reph'idim; but there was no
water for the people to drink. ²Therefore the people found fault
with Moses, and said, "Give us water to drink." And Moses said
to them, "Why do you find fault with me? Why do you put the
LORD to the proof?" ³But the people thirsted there for water, and
the people murmured against Moses, and said, "Why did you
bring us up out of Egypt, to kill us and our children and our cattle
with thirst?" ⁴So Moses cried to the LORD, "What shall I do with
this people? They are almost ready to stone me." ⁵And the LORD
said to Moses, "Pass on before the people, taking with you some
of the elders of Israel; and take in your hand the rod with which
you struck the Nile, and go. ⁶Behold, I will stand before you
there on the rock at Horeb; and you shall strike the rock, and
water shall come out of it, that the people may drink." And
Moses did so, in the sight of the elders of Israel. ⁷And he called
the name of the place Massah[x] and Meribah,[y] because of the

Ex 14:11
Deut 16:6

1 Cor 10:4
Jn 7:38; 19:34
Deut 6:16; 9 22–
24; 32:51; 33:8
Ps 78: 15–16;
95: 8–9; 105:41;
106:32
Wis 11:4

The sons of Israel's faith in God and
Moses has been strengthening little by
little; but they often doubt whether God
is there at all (v. 7). They begin to murmur and to seek proofs of his presence:
have they been brought out of Egypt to
die, or to attain salvation? The water
which Moses causes to come out of the
rock is a further sign to bolster their faith.

This episode names two places—
Meribah, which in popular etymology
means "contention", "dispute", "lawsuit", and Massah, which is "proof",
"test", "temptation". Many biblical passages recall this sin (cf. Deut 6:16;
9:22–24; 33:8; Ps 95:8–9), even adding
that Moses himself lacked faith and
struck the rock twice (cf. Num 20:1–13;

Deut 32:51; Ps 106:32). Lack of trust in
the goodness and power of God means
tempting God and it is a grave sin against
faith—even more so in the case of
Moses, who had experienced God's special love and who ought to have given
good example. When man meets some
contradiction or some difficulty he
cannot immediately solve, his faith may
waver but he should never doubt, because
"if deliberately cultivated, doubt can lead
to spiritual blindness" (*Catechism of the
Catholic Church*, 2008).

There is a rabbinical tradition which
says that the rock stayed with the
Israelites throughout their sojourn in the
desert; St Paul refers to this legend when
he says "the Rock was Christ" (1 Cor

---

trametati sunt in Raphidim, ubi non erat aqua ad bibendum populo. ²Qui iurgatus contra Moysen ait:
«Da nobis aquam, ut bibamus». Quibus respondit Moyses: «Quid iurgamini contra me? Cur tentatis
Dominum?». ³Sitivit ergo ibi populus prae aquae penuria et murmuravit contra Moysen dicens: «Cur
fecisti nos exire de Aegypto, ut occideres nos et liberos nostros ac iumenta siti?». ⁴Clamavit autem
Moyses ad Dominum dicens: «Quid faciam populo huic? Adhuc paululum et lapidabunt me». ⁵Et ait
Dominus ad Moysen: «Antecede populum et sume tecum de senioribus Israel, et virgam, qua percus-
sisti fluvium, tolle in manu tua et vade. ⁶En ego stabo coram te ibi super petram Horeb; percutiesque
petram, et exibit ex ea aqua, ut bibat populus». Fecit Moyses ita coram senioribus Israel. ⁷Et vocavit
nomen loci illius Massa et Meriba, propter iurgium filiorum Israel et quia tentaverunt Dominum

x. That is *Proof*   **y.** That is *Contention*

faultfinding of the children of Israel, and because they put the Is 43:20
Heb 3:8
LORD to the proof by saying, "Is the LORD among us or not?" Gen 14:7;
36:12, 16
Num 24:20

A battle against the Amalekites
Judg 1:16
Josh 1:1
Wis 11:3
⁸Then came Amalek and fought with Israel at Rephidim. ⁹And
Moses said to Joshua, "Choose for us men, and go out, fight with
Amalek; tomorrow I will stand on the top of the hill with the rod
of God in my hand." ¹⁰So Joshua did as Moses told him, and
fought with Amalek; and Moses, Aaron, and Hur went up to the
top of the hill. ¹¹Whenever Moses held up his hand, Israel prevailed; and whenever he lowered his hand, Amalek prevailed.
¹²But Moses' hands grew weary; so they took a stone and put it
under him, and he sat upon it, and Aaron and Hur held up his
hands, one on one side, and the other on the other side; so his
hands were steady until the going down of the sun. ¹³And Joshua
mowed down Amalek and his people with the edge of the sword.

10:4). On the basis of biblical references
to the wondrous nature of waters (cf. Ps
78:15–16; 105:4; Wis 11:4–14) the
Fathers said this episode prefigures the
wonderful effects of Baptism: "See the
mystery: 'Moses' is the Prophet; the rod
is the word of God; the priest touches the
rock with the word of God, and water
flows, and the people of God drink" (St
Ambrose, *De sacramentis*, 8, 5, 1, 3).

17:8–16 In addition to shortages of food
and water the Israelites also had to cope
with attacks from other groups in the
desert over rights to wells and pastures.
Their confrontation with the Amalekites
shows that the same God as alleviated
their more pressing needs (hunger and
thirst) will protect them from enemy
attack.

The Amalekites were an ancient
people (cf. Num 24:20; Gen 14:7; 36:12,
16; Judg 1:16) who were spread all over
the north of the Sinai peninsula, the
Negeb, Seir and the south of Canaan;
they controlled the caravan routes
between Arabia and Egypt. In the Bible
they appear as a perennial enemy of
Israel (cf. Deut 25:17–18; 1 Sam 15:3;
27:8; 30) until in the time of Hezekiah (1
Chron 4:41–43) the oracle about blotting
out their memory finds fulfilment (v. 14).
The mention of Joshua leading the battle
and of Aaron and Hur helping Moses to
pray point to the fact that after Moses
political-military and religious authority
will be split, with the priests taking over
the latter.

With the rod in his hand, Moses
directs the battle from a distance, but his

---

dicentes: «Estne Dominus in nobis an non?». ⁸Venit autem Amalec et pugnabat contra Israel in
Raphidim. ⁹Dixitque Moyses ad Iosue: «Elige nobis viros et egressus pugna contra Amalec; cras ego
stabo in vertice collis habens virgam Dei in manu mea». ¹⁰Fecit Iosue, ut locutus erat ei Moyses, et
pugnavit contra Amalec; Moyses autem et Aaron et Hur ascenderunt super verticem collis. ¹¹Cumque
levaret Moyses manus, vincebat Israel; sin autem remisisset, superabat Amalec. ¹²Manus autem Moysi
erant graves; sumentes igitur lapidem posuerunt subter eum, in quo sedit; Aaron autem et Hur sus-
tentabant manus eius ex utraque parte. Et factum est ut manus eius non lassarentur usque ad occasum
solis. ¹³Vicitque Iosue Amalec et populum eius in ore gladii. ¹⁴Dixit autem Dominus ad Moysen:

1 Chron
4:41–43

¹⁴And the LORD said to Moses, "Write this as a memorial in a book and recite it in the ears of Joshua, that I will utterly blot out the remembrance of Amalek from under heaven." ¹⁵And Moses built an altar and called the name of it, The LORD is my banner, ¹⁶saying, "A hand upon the banner of the LORD!ᶻ The LORD will have war with Amalek from generation to generation."

Deut 25:17–18

1 Sam 15:3f;
27:8, 30

The meeting of Jethro and Moses*

Ex 2:18

18 ¹Jethro, the priest of Midian, Moses' father-in-law, heard of all that God had done for Moses and for Israel his people, how the LORD had brought Israel out of Egypt. ²Now Jethro, Moses' father-in-law, had taken Zipporah, Moses' wife, after he had sent her away, ³and her two sons, of whom the name of the one was Gershom (for he said, "I have been a sojournerᵃ in a for-

Ex 2:22

Acts 7:29

---

main involvement is by interceding for his people, asking God to give them victory. The Fathers read this episode as a figure of the action of Christ who, on the cross (symbolized by the rod), won victory over the devil and death (cf. Tertullian, *Adversus Marcionem*, 3, 18; St Cyprian, *Testimonia*, 2, 21).

17:14. This command given by Moses to record the battle in a book is one of the reasons for the traditional attribution of the Pentateuch to him. However, there are very strong motives for thinking that Moses did not write the five books (cf. "Introduction to the Pentateuch", pp 19f, above).

*18:1–27. Moses' meeting with his father-in-law Jethro and the institution of the Judges are the last two events in the

desert prior to the appearance of God on Sinai (chaps. 19–24). In the first, Jethro and the Midianites, who here stand for the Gentiles, celebrate with Israel its deliverance and share in a communion sacrifice. In the second, Moses, acting in the name of God, institutes the legal system. The book of Deuteronomy recounts this event after the Israelites leave Sinai (Deut 1:9–18). By situating it here, the sacred writer wants to show that God himself willed that the Israelites should have the structure of a people before the revelation on Sinai took place. The fact that the Israelites who came out of Egypt should form a people (with all that that meant in terms of authority, laws, common good etc.) is very important for seeing the way God chose to bring about man's salvation. "He has, however, willed to make men holy and

---

«Scribe hoc ob monumentum in libro et trade auribus Iosue; delebo enim memoriam Amalec sub caelo». ¹⁵Aedificavitque Moyses altare et vocavit nomen eius Dominus Nissi (*Dominus vexillum meum*) ¹⁶dicens: «Quia manus contra solium Domini: / bellum Domino erit contra Amalec / a generatione in generationem». ¹Cumque audisset Iethro sacerdos Madian socer Moysi omnia, quae fecerat Deus Moysi et Israel populo suo, eo quod eduxisset Dominus Israel de Aegypto, ²tulit Sephoram uxorem Moysi, quam remiserat, ³et duos filios eius, quorum unus vocabatur Gersam, dicente patre:

z. Cn: Heb obscure   **a.** Heb *ger*

eign land"), ⁴and the name of the other, Eliezerᵇ (for he said, Acts 12:11
"The God of my father was my help, and delivered me from the
sword of Pharaoh"). ⁵And Jethro, Moses' father-in-law, came Ex 19:1
with his sons and his wife to Moses in the wilderness where he
was encamped at the mountain of God. ⁶And when one told
Moses, "Lo,ᶜ your father-in-law Jethro is coming to you with
your wife and her two sons with her," ⁷Moses went out to meet
his father-in-law, and did obeisance and kissed him; and they
asked each other of their welfare, and went into the tent. ⁸Then
Moses told his father-in-law all that the LORD had done to
Pharaoh and to the Egyptians for Israel's sake, all the hardship
that had come upon them in the way, and how the LORD had
delivered them. ⁹And Jethro rejoiced for all the good which the
LORD had done to Israel, in that he had delivered them out of the
hand of the Egyptians.

---

save them, not as individuals without any bond or link between them, but rather to make them into a people who might acknowledge him and serve him in holiness. He therefore chose the Israelite race to be his own people and established a covenant with it. He gradually instructed this people—in its history manifesting both himself and the decree of his will—and made it holy unto himself" (Vatican II, *Lumen gentium*, 9).

18:1–12. In the first part of this book Moses' father-in-law was mentioned (under the name of Reuel: 2:18), as was his wife Zipporah (4:20, 24–26). The sacred writer seems to see in this episode many very significant details: the names of his two sons sum up the two last stages in Moses' life, first as a stranger among

the Midianites (*Gershom* means "guest": v. 3) and then later when he experiences God's protection in his leadership of the people (*Eliezer* means "God is my protection": v. 4). In this formal meeting (vv. 5–7) it is Jethro who is the visitor (thus acknowledging the superior status of Moses). At the centre of their conversation is the deliverance brought about by the Lord: this gives joy to all who hear it (vv. 8–11). The Midianites and in them all the Gentile nations will come to acknowledge the Lord as the true God and will share in his worship through appreciating the wonders that the Lord has worked (v. 12). Finally, the fact that the leaders of Israel partake of Jethro's sacrificial meal indicates that all the sacrifices and rites which are celebrated will have clear reference to the events of the Exodus.

«Advena fui in terra aliena», ⁴alter vero Eliezer: «Deus enim, ait, patris mei adiutor meus, et eruit me de gladio pharaonis». ⁵Venit ergo Iethro socer Moysi et filii eius et uxor eius ad Moysen in desertum, ubi erat castrametatus iuxta montem Dei; ⁶et mandavit Moysi dicens: «Ego socer tuus Iethro venio ad te et uxor tua et duo filii tui cum ea». ⁷Qui egressus in occursum soceri sui adoravit et osculatus est eum, salutaveruntque se mutuo verbis pacificis. Cumque intrasset tabernaculum, ⁸narravit Moyses socero suo cuncta, quae fecerat Dominus pharaoni et Aegyptiis propter Israel, universumque laborem, qui accidisset eis in itinere, et quod liberaverat eos Dominus. ⁹Laetatusque est Iethro super omnibus

b. Heb *Eli*, my god, *'eser*, help **c.** Sam Gk Syr: Heb *I*

¹⁰And Jethro said, "Blessed be the LORD, who has delivered you out of the hand of the Egyptians and out of the hand of Pharaoh. ¹¹Now I know that the LORD is greater than all gods, because he delivered the people from under the hand of the Egyptians,ᵈ when they dealt arrogantly with them." ¹²And Jethro, Moses' father-in-law, offeredᵉ a burnt offering and sacrifices to God; and Aaron came with all the elders of Israel to eat bread with Moses' father-in-law before God.

Deut 1:9–18 · **The appointment of judges**

¹³On the morrow Moses sat to judge the people, and the people stood about Moses from morning till evening. ¹⁴When Moses' father-in-law saw all that he was doing for the people, he said, "What is this that you are doing for the people? Why do you sit alone, and all the people stand about you from morning till evening?"

Ex 33:7 · ¹⁵And Moses said to his father-in-law, "Because the people come to me to inquire of God; ¹⁶when they have a dispute, they come to me and I decide between a man and his neighbor, and I make them know the statutes of God and his decisions."

Acts 6:2f · ¹⁷Moses' father-in-law said to him, "What you are doing is not

Num 11:14 · good. ¹⁸You and the people with you will wear yourselves out,

---

18:13–27. As the people's leader Moses personally held all authority, religious, legislative and legal. But the history of the Israelites shows that, although all authority had a sacred character, a separation gradually developed between strictly religious matters and political affairs. In various places in the Bible there are indications that the judicial arrangements of Israel were almost always copied from the neighbouring peoples. According to the present text, the institution of the judges was taken from the Midianites, who were governed along the lines of the people of Tyre, Carthage and many other places. Samuel's time saw the birth of the monarchy, with the Israelites themselves asking for "a king to govern us like all the nations" (1 Sam 8:5). The people of Israel were no different from the rest as far as their political structure was con-

---

bonis, quae fecerat Dominus Israel, eo quod eruisset eum de manu Aegyptiorum, ¹⁰et ait: «Benedictus Dominus, qui liberavit vos de manu Aegyptiorum et de manu pharaonis. ¹¹Nunc cognovi quia magnus Dominus super omnes deos, eo quod eruerit populum de manu Aegyptiorum, qui superbe egerunt contra illos». ¹²Obtulit ergo Iethro socer Moysi holocausta et hostias Deo; veneruntque Aaron et omnes seniores Israel, ut comederent panem cum eo coram Deo. ¹³Altero autem die sedit Moyses, ut iudicaret populum, qui assistebat Moysi de mane usque ad vesperam. ¹⁴Quod cum vidisset socer eius, omnia scilicet, quae agebat in populo, ait: «Quid est hoc, quod facis in plebe? Cur solus sedes, et omnis populus praestolatur de mane usque ad vesperam?». ¹⁵Cui respondit Moyses: «Venit ad me populus quaerens sententiam Dei. ¹⁶Cumque acciderit eis aliqua disceptatio, veniunt ad me, ut iudicem inter

d. Transposing the last clause of v. 10 to v. 11   **e.** Syr Tg Vg: Heb *took*

for the thing is too heavy for you; you are not able to perform it alone. ¹⁹Listen now to my voice; I will give you counsel, and God be with you! You shall represent the people before God, and bring their cases to God; ²⁰and you shall teach them the statutes and the decisions, and make them know the way in which they must walk and what they must do. ²¹Moreover choose able men from all the people, such as fear God, men who are trustworthy and who hate a bribe; and place such men over the people as rulers of thousands, of hundreds, of fifties, and of tens. ²²And let them judge the people at all times; every great matter they shall bring to you, but any small matter they shall decide themselves; so it will be easier for you, and they will bear the burden with you. ²³If you do this, and God so commands you, then you will be able to endure, and all this people also will go to their place in peace."

²⁴So Moses gave heed to the voice of his father-in-law and did all that he had said. ²⁵Moses chose able men out of all Israel, and made them heads over the people, rulers of thousands, of hundreds, of fifties, and of tens. ²⁶And they judged the people at all times; hard cases they brought to Moses, but any small matter they decided themselves. ²⁷Then Moses let his father-in-law depart, and he went his way to his own country.

Heb 5:1

Num 11:16–17

Num 10:30

---

cerned; its originality lay in their religious mission and in the fact that they were the chosen people; they would always have someone to "teach them the statutes and the decisions" and "make them know the way in which they must walk and what they must do" (v. 20).

This account sheds light on the human and at the same time transcendent extent of political authority: "It is clear that the political community and public authority are based on human nature, and therefore that they need belong to an order established by God; nevertheless, the choice of political régime and the appointment of rulers are left to the free decision of the citizens (cf. Rom 13:1–5)" (Vatican II, *Gaudium et spes*, 74).

---

eos et ostendam praecepta Dei et leges eius». ¹⁷At ille: «Non bonam, inquit, rem facis. ¹⁸Consumeris et tu et populus iste, qui tecum est. Ultra vires tuas est negotium; solus illud non poteris sustinere. ¹⁹Sed audi verba mea atque consilia, et erit Deus tecum: Esto tu populo in his, quae ad Deum pertinent, ut referas causas ad Deum ²⁰ostendasque populo praecepta et leges viamque, per quam ingredi debeant, et opus, quod facere debeant. ²¹Provide autem de omni plebe viros strenuos et timentes Deum, in quibus sit veritas et qui oderint avaritiam, et constitue ex eis tribunos et centuriones et quinquagenarios et decanos, ²²qui iudicent populum omni tempore. Quidquid autem maius fuerit, referant ad te, et ipsi minora tantummodo iudicent; leviusque sit tibi, partito cum aliis onere. ²³Si hoc feceris, implebis imperium Dei et praecepta eius poteris sustentare, et omnis hic populus revertetur ad loca sua cum pace». ²⁴Quibus auditis, Moyses fecit omnia, quae ille suggesserat; ²⁵et, electis viris strenuis de cuncto Israel, constituit eos principes populi, tribunos et centuriones et quinquagenarios et decanos, ²⁶qui iudicabant plebem omni tempore. Quidquid autem gravius erat, referebant ad eum, faciliora tantummodo iudicantes. ²⁷Dimisitque socerum suum, qui reversus abiit in terram suam. ¹Mense tertio egressionis

PART TWO

The People of Israel

7. IN THE DESERT OF SINAI*

The Israelites arrive in Sinai*

Num 33:15 **19** ¹On the third new moon after the people of Israel had gone forth out of the land of Egypt, on that day they came into

---

*19:1—24:18. These chapters deal with the central events of the book of Exodus—the encounter with the Lord, and the Covenant established between God and his people. They provide an excellent summary of the theological message of the Old Testament. On the one hand, there is God's revelation that in his plan for the salvation of men he has chosen a people from among all others and established a special relationship with it—the Covenant: "After the patriarchs, God formed Israel as his people by freeing them from slavery in Egypt. He established with them the covenant of Mount Sinai and, through Moses, gave them his law so that they would recognize him and serve him as the one living and true God, the provident Father and just judge, and so that they would look for the promised Saviour" (*Catechism of the Catholic Church*, 62). On the other hand, the events of Sinai clearly show Israel's destiny as the chosen people: "By this election, Israel is to be the sign of the future gathering of all nations" (ibid., 762). Thus, Israel is a figure of the new people of God, the Church.

This entire section has a degree of literary unity which binds together narratives and laws, all with much solemnity, because the sacred writer wants to emphasize that in the theophany at Sinai God offered Israel the Covenant and the Law. We could say the section breaks down as follows: (a) prologue (chap. 19); (b) legislative part, which includes the Ten Commandments (20:1–21) and the document of the Covenant (20:22—23:19); (c) exhortatory appendix (23:20–33); (d) the rite of the Covenant (24:1–18).

*19:1–25. This chapter is written as part of a magnificent liturgy in which the events of Sinai are re-enacted for the reader. The sacred author, then, does not seek to provide an exact, scholarly report on what happened there; what he is providing, rather, is a theological interpretation of the real contact which took place between God and his people.

As in other important sections of this book, it draws on the great traditions of Israel but combines them so skilfully that they have become inseparable; only now and then can one identify traces of particular traditions. The text as it now stands

---

Israel de terra Aegypti, in die hac venerunt in solitudinem Sinai. ²Nam profecti de Raphidim et pervenientes usque in desertum Sinai, castrametati sunt in eodem loco, ibique Israel fixit tentoria e regione

the wilderness of Sinai. ²And when they set out from Rephidim and came into the wilderness of Sinai, they encamped in the wilderness; and there Israel encamped before the mountain.

God promises a Covenant

³And Moses went up to God, and the LORD called to him out of the mountain, saying, "Thus you shall say to the house of Jacob, and tell the people of Israel:* ⁴You have seen what I did to the Egyptians, and how I bore you on eagles' wings and brought you to myself. ⁵Now therefore, if you will obey my voice and keep my covenant, you shall be my own possession among all peoples; for all the earth is mine, ⁶and you shall be to me a kingdom of priests

Acts 7:38
Deut 4:34;
29:2; 32:11
Rev 12:14
Deut 7:6: 10:14–
15; 26:17–19
Ps 135:4
Mal 3:17
Tit 2:14
Heb 8:9

---

is all of a piece. In this chapter there is a prologue (v. 9), summing up what follows, and the theophany proper (vv. 10–25).

19:1–2. This method of calculating time (v. 1) is one of the traces of the Priestly tradition, always keen to give dates a symbolic meaning (cf. 16:1 and 17:1). Three months is a very brief stage in the prolonged sojourn in the Sinai: in this way time becomes a sign of the religious importance of the events.

19:3–9. This passage summarizes the meaning of the Covenant that is going to be established. So, it contains the idea of *election*, though it does not use the term, and the idea of *demands* being made by God. Furthermore, we can see here the new status of the people (it is *God's own property*) and the basis of its *hope* (in the sense that Israel attains its dignity as a people to the extent that it is faithful to the divine will).

All the basic teachings are contained herein: (a) The basis of the Covenant is

Israel's deliverance from bondage (this has already happened: v. 4): the people are the object of God's preferential love; God made them a people by bringing about that deliverance. (b) If they keep the Covenant, they will become a very special kind of people. This offer will take effect the moment they take on their commitments, but Israel will develop towards its full maturity only to the extent that it listens to/obeys the will of God. (c) What God is offering the people is specified in three complementary expressions—"My own possession", "holy nation", "kingdom of priests".

The first of these expressions means private property, personally acquired and carefully conserved. Of all the nations of the earth Israel is to be "God's property" because he has chosen it and he protects it with special care. This new status is something which will be stressed frequently (cf. Deut 7:6; 26:17–19; Ps 135:4; Mal 3:17).

By being God's possession Israel shares in his holiness, it is a "holy nation", that is, a people separated out from among

montis. ³Moyses autem ascendit ad Deum, vocavitque eum Dominus de monte et ait: «Haec dices domui Iacob / et annuntiabis filiis Israel: / ⁴Vos ipsi vidistis, quae fecerim Aegyptiis, / quomodo portaverim vos super alas aquilarum / et adduxerim ad me. / ⁵Si ergo audieritis vocem meam / et custodieritis pactum meum, / eritis mihi in peculium de cunctis populis; / mea est enim omnis terra. / ⁶Et vos eritis mihi regnum sacerdotum / et gens sancta. / Haec sunt verba, quae loqueris ad filios Israel».

Lev 19:2
1 Pet 2:5, 9
Rev 1:6;
5:9–10; 20:6 and a holy nation. These are the words which you shall speak to the children of Israel."

⁷So Moses came and called the elders of the people, and set before them all these words which the LORD had commanded Josh 24:16–24
Deut 5:27 him. ⁸And all the people answered together and said, "All that the LORD has spoken we will do." And Moses reported the words of Ex 13:22;
14:31
Sir 45:5 the people to the LORD. ⁹And the LORD said to Moses, "Lo, I am coming to you in a thick cloud, that the people may hear when I speak with you, and may also believe you for ever."

Deut 4:10–12;
5:2–5, 25–32 Then Moses told the words of the people to the Lord.

Ps 18:7–8
29:3–4; **The theophany on Sinai**

77:16–17;
97:2ff
Rev 7:14 ¹⁰And the LORD said to Moses, "Go to the people and consecrate them today and tomorrow, and let them wash their garments, ¹¹and

---

the nations so as to keep a close relationship with God; in other passages we are told more—that this is the relationship of "a son of God" (cf. 4:22; Deut 14:1). This new way of being means that there is a moral demand on the members of the people to show by their lives what they are by God's election: "You shall be holy; for I the Lord your God am holy" (Lev 19:2).

And the expression "kingdom of priests" does not mean that that they will be ruled by priests, or that the entire people will exercise the role of priest (which is in fact reserved to the tribe of Levi); rather, it reflects the fact that God gives Israel the privilege of being the only nation in his service. Israel alone has been chosen to be a "kingdom for the Lord", that is, to be the sphere where he dwells and is recognized as the only Sovereign. Israel's acknowledgment of God is shown by the service the entire people renders to the Lord.

This section (vv. 7–8) ends with Moses' proposal of God's plans to the people and their acceptance of these plans by the elders and by all the people: "All that the Lord has spoken we will do" (v. 8). The same wording will be used twice again in the ceremony to ratify the Covenant (cf. 24:3, 7).

In the New Testament (1 Pet 2:5; Rev 1:6; 5:9–10) what happened here will be picked up again with the very same words, applying it to the new situation of the Christian in the Church, the new people of God and the true Israel (cf. Gal 3:29): every Christian shares in Christ's priesthood through his incorporation into Christ and is "called to serve God by his activity in the world, because of the common priesthood of the faithful, which makes him share in some way in the priesthood of Christ. This priesthood— though essentially distinct from the ministerial priesthood—gives him the

---

⁷Venit Moyses et, convocatis maioribus natu populi, exposuit omnes sermones, quos mandaverat Dominus. ⁸Responditque universus populus simul: «Cuncta, quae locutus est Dominus, faciemus». Cumque retulisset Moyses verba populi ad Dominum, ⁹ait ei Dominus: «Ecce ego veniam ad te in caligine nubis, ut audiat me populus loquentem ad te et tibi quoque credat in perpetuum». Nuntiavit ergo Moyses verba populi ad Dominum, ¹⁰qui dixit ei: «Vade ad populum et sanctifica illos hodie et cras; laventque vestimenta sua ¹¹et sint parati in diem tertium. In die enim tertio descendet Dominus coram omni plebe super montem Sinai. ¹²Constituesque terminos populo per circuitum et dices:

be ready by the third day; for on the third day the LORD will come
down upon Mount Sinai in the sight of all the people. [12]And you Heb 12:18:20
shall set bounds for the people round about, saying, 'Take heed
that you do not go up into the mountain or touch the border of it;
whoever touches the mountain shall be put to death; [13]no hand
shall touch him, but he shall be stoned or shot; whether beast or
man, he shall not live.' When the trumpet sounds a long blast, they
shall come up to the mountain." [14]So Moses went down from the Rev 7:14
mountain to the people, and consecrated the people; and they
washed their garments. [15]And he said to the people, "Be ready by Lev 15:16ff
the third day; do not go near a woman."

[16]On the morning of the third day there were thunders and Deut 4:10–12
lightnings, and a thick cloud upon the mountain, and a very loud Heb 12:19
Rev 1:10; 4:5
trumpet blast, so that all the people who were in the camp trem-

---

capacity to take part in the worship of the
Church and to help other men in their
journey to God, with the witness of his
word and his example, through his prayer
and work of atonement" (St Josemaría
Escrivá, *Christ Is Passing By*, 120).

19:10–25. This description of the
theophany on Sinai contains features of a
solemn liturgy in order to highlight the
majesty and transcendence of God.
Verses 10–15 cover as it were the preparation for the great event, and vv. 16–20
the event itself.

The preparation is very detailed: ritual
purification in the days previous, ablutions
and everything possible done to ensure
that the participants have the right dispositions, even a ban on sexual intercourse (cf.
Lev 15:16ff) as a sign of exclusive concentration on God who is coming to visit.
Also, the fact that the people have to keep
within bounds is a tangible way of show-

ing the transcendence of God. Once Jesus
Christ, God made man, comes, no barrier
will any longer be imposed.

The manifestation of God took place
on the third day. The smoke, the fire and
the earthquake are external signs of the
presence of God, who is the master of
nature. The two trumpet blasts (vv. 16,
19), the people's march to the foot of the
mountain and then standing to attention—all give a liturgical tone to their
acknowledgement of the Lord as their
only Sovereign. All these things and even
the voice of God in the thunder convey
the idea that this awesome storm was
something quite unique, for what was
happening, this special presence of God
on Sinai, could never happen again.

Israel will never forget this religious
experience, as we can see from the
Psalms (cf. Ps 18:7–8; 29:3–4; 77:16–17;
97:2ff). In the New Testament, extraordinary divine manifestations will carry

---

Cavete, ne ascendatis in montem nec tangatis fines illius; omnis, qui tetigerit montem, morte morietur.
[13]Manus non tanget eum, sed lapidibus opprimetur aut confodietur iaculis; sive iumentum fuerit, sive
homo, non vivet. Cum coeperit clangere bucina, tunc ascendant in montem». [14]Descenditque Moyses
de monte ad populum et sanctificavit eum; cumque lavissent vestimenta sua, [15]ait ad eos: «Estote parati
in diem tertium; ne appropinquetis uxoribus vestris». [16]Iamque advenerat tertius dies, et mane
inclaruerat; et ecce coeperunt audiri tonitrua ac micare fulgura et nubes densissima operire montem,
clangorque bucinae vehementis perstrepebat; et timuit populus, qui erat in castris. [17]Cumque eduxis-

bled. [17]Then Moses brought the people out of the camp to meet
Rev 9:2 God; and they took their stand at the foot of the mountain. [18]And
Mount Sinai was wrapped in smoke, because the LORD descended
upon it in fire; and the smoke of it went up like the smoke of a
Heb 12:19 kiln, and the whole mountain quaked greatly. [19]And as the sound
of the trumpet grew louder and louder, Moses spoke, and God
answered him in thunder. [20]And the LORD came down upon Mount
Sinai, to the top of the mountain; and the LORD called Moses to the
Ex 33:20 top of the mountain, and Moses went up. [21]And the LORD said to
Moses, "Go down and warn the people, lest they break through to
the LORD to gaze and many of them perish. [22]And also let the
priests who come near to the LORD consecrate themselves, lest the
LORD break out upon them." [23]And Moses said to the LORD, "The
people cannot come up to Mount Sinai; for thou thyself didst
charge us, saying, 'Set bounds about the mountain, and consecrate
Rev 4:1 it.'" [24]And the LORD said to him, "Go down, and come up bringing
Aaron with you; but do not let the priests and the people break
through to come up to the LORD, lest he break out against them."
[25]So Moses went down to the people and told them.

---

echoes of this theophany (cf. Mt 27:45;
51; Acts 2:2–4).

19:21–25. These verses, which repeat the
instructions about the people keeping
within fixed bounds, come from another
tradition, probably the Priestly tradition
given that priests are mentioned (and
their obligation to purify themselves
carefully: cf. 28:41). Verse 25 is an unfinished sentence; the redactor probably left
the phrase in the air to give more emphasis to the reading of the Decalogue, that
is, to make it appear as belonging to the
message Moses was given on the top of
the mountain.

*20:1–21. "Decalogue" comes from the
Greek, meaning "ten words" (cf. the literal sense of Deut 4:13). It consists of the
Ten Commandments or moral code,
recorded here and in Deuteronomy
5:6–21. The Decalogue is dealt with in a
very special way here: for one thing, it is
embedded in the account of the theophany, slotted in between 19:19 and
20:18; for another, attached to the concise commandments (identical in Exodus
and Deuteronomy) are other more elaborate commandments (giving reasons and
explanations) which differ as between the
two versions. The fact that the Decalogue
(and not any other legal code of the

---

set eos Moyses in occursum Dei de loco castrorum, steterunt ad radices montis. [18]Totus autem mons
Sinai fumabat, eo quod descendisset Dominus super eum in igne, et ascenderet fumus ex eo quasi de
fornace. Et tremuit omnis mons vehementer. [19]Et sonitus bucinae paulatim crescebat in maius; Moyses
loquebatur, et Deus respondebat ei cum voce. [20]Descenditque Dominus super montem Sinai in ipso
montis vertice et vocavit Moysen in cacumen eius. Quo cum ascendisset, [21]dixit ad eum: «Descende et
contestare populum, ne velit transcendere terminos ad videndum Dominum, et pereat ex eis plurima
multitudo. [22]Sacerdotes quoque, qui accedunt ad Dominum, sanctificentur, ne percutiat eos». [23]Dixitque
Moyses ad Dominum: «Non poterit vulgus ascendere in montem Sinai, tu enim testificatus es et iussisti dicens: 'Pone terminos circa montem et sanctifica illum'». [24]Cui ait Dominus: «Vade, descende;

The ten commandments*

Deut 5:6–22
Mt 5
Ex 34:10–27
Mt 9:16–22

20 [1]And God spoke all these words, saying,* [2]"I am the LORD your God, who brought you out of the land of Egypt, out of the house of bondage.

Pentateuch) is repeated practically verbatim in Exodus and Deuteronomy and has from ancient times been reproduced separately, as the Nash papyrus (2nd century BC) shows, indicates the importance the Decalogue always had among the people of Israel as a moral code.

On the supposition that the versions in Exodus and Deuteronomy can be reduced to a single original text, the variations between them can be explained in terms of the applications of the commandments to the circumstances of the period when each version was made; the final redaction, which we have here, is the one held to be inspired. The apodictic form (future imperative, second person: "You shall not kill") is that proper to biblical commandments and it differs from the casuistical type of wording that Israel shares with other Semitic people, as can be seen from the Code of the Covenant (chaps 21–23).

The ten commandments are the core of Old Testament ethics and they retain their value in the New Testament. Jesus often reminds people about them (cf. Lk 18:20) and he fills them out (cf. Mt 5:17ff). The Fathers and Doctors of the Church have commented on them at length because, as St Thomas points out, all the precepts of the natural law are contained in the Decalogue: the universal precepts, such as "Do good and avoid evil", "which are primary and general, are contained therein as principles in their proximate conclusions, while con-

versely, those which are mediated by the wise are contained in them as conclusions in their principles" (*Summa theologiae*, 1–2, 100, 3).

The commandments tend to be divided up in two different ways: thus, Jews and many Christian confessions divide the first commandment into two— the precept to adore only one God (vv. 2–3) and that of not making images (vv. 3–6); whereas Catholics and Lutherans (following St Augustine) make these commandments one and divide into two the last commandments (not to covet one's neighbour's wife: the ninth; and not to covet his goods: the tenth).

There is nothing sacrosanct about these divisions (their purpose is pedagogical); whichever way the commandments are divided, the Decalogue stands. In our commentary we follow St Augustine's division and make reference to the teaching of the Church, because the Ten Commandments contain the core of Christian morality (cf. the notes on Deut 5:1–22).

20:2. Hittite peoples (some of whose political and social documents have survived) used to begin peace treaties with an historical introduction, that is, by recounting the victory of a king over a vassal on whom specific obligations were being imposed. In a similar sort of way, the Decalogue begins by recalling the Exodus. However, what we have here is something radically different from a

---

ascendesque tu et Aaron tecum, sacerdotes autem et populus ne transeant terminos, nec ascendant ad Dominum, ne interficiat illos». [25]Descenditque Moyses ad populum et omnia narravit eis. [1]Locutusque est Deus cunctos sermones hos: [2]«Ego sum Dominus Deus tuus, qui eduxi te de terra Aegypti, de domo

Deut 6:4–5
Mk 12:28–31

Lev 19:4
Deut 14:15–20
Rev 5:3

Ex 34:7; 34:14
Jn 2:17; 9:2
Deut 4:24

Gen 2:2–3
Ex 16:22–30;
23:12; 31:12–17;
34:21; 35:1–3
Deut 5:15
Lev 19:3; 23:3
Lk 13:14

3"You shall have no other gods before me.[f]

4"You shall not make for yourself a graven image, or any likeness of anything that is in heaven above, or that is in the earth beneath, or that is in the water under the earth; 5you shall not bow down to them or serve them; for I the LORD your God am a jealous God, visiting the iniquity of the fathers upon the children to the third and the fourth generation of those who hate me, 6but showing steadfast love to thousands of those who love me and keep my commandments.

Hittite pact, because the obligation that the commandments imply is not based on a defeat but on a deliverance. God is offering the commandments to the people whom he has delivered from bondage, whereas human princes imposed their codes on peoples whom they had reduced to vassalage. The commandments are therefore an expression of the Covenant. Acceptance of them is a sign that man has attained maturity in his freedom. "Man becomes free when he enters into the Covenant of God" (Aphraates, *Demonstrationes*, 12). Jesus stressed the same idea: "My yoke is easy, and my burden is light" (Mt 11:30).

20:3–6 "You shall love God above all things" is the wording of the first commandment given in most catechisms (cf. *Catechism of the Catholic Church*, 2083) summarizing the teaching of Jesus (cf. Mk 12:28–31, which quotes the text of Deuteronomy 6:4–5). In the ten commandments this precept covers two aspects—monotheism (v. 3) and the obligation not to adore idols or images of the Lord (vv. 4–6).

Belief in the existence of only one

God is the backbone of the entire Bible message. The prophets will openly teach monotheism, holding that God is the sovereign Lord of the universe and of time; but this ban on other gods itself implies the sure conviction that there is only one true God. "You shall have no other Gods before [or, besides] me", implies a belief in one God, that is, monotheism.

The ban on images was something that marked Israel as different from other peoples. The ban not only covered idols or images of other gods, but also representations of the Lord.

The one true God is spiritual and transcendent: he cannot be controlled or manipulated (unlike the gods of Israel's neighbours). On the basis of the mystery of the incarnate Word, Christians began to depict scenes from the Gospel and in so doing they knew that this was not at odds with God's freedom nor did it make for idolatry. The Church venerates images because they are representations either of Jesus who, being truly man, had a body, or of saints, who as human beings were portrayable and worthy of veneration. The Second Vatican Council recommended the veneration of sacred

servitutis. ³Non habebis deos alienos coram me. ⁴Non facies tibi sculptile neque omnem similitudinem eorum, quae sunt in caelo desuper et quae in terra deorsum et quae in aquis sub terra. ⁵Non adorabis ea neque coles, quia ego sum Dominus Deus tuus, Deus zelotes visitans iniquitatem patrum in filiis in tertiam et quartam generationem eorum, qui oderunt me, ⁶et faciens misericordiam in milia his, qui dili-

f. Or *besides*

Deut 5:12–15
Mt 12:2
Mk 2:27
Lk 23:56
Acts 4:24; 14;
15; 17:24
Rev 10:6
Deut 27:16;
20:20; 23:22;
30:17
Mt 15:4; 19:18ff
Mk 7:10; 10:19
Lk 18:20
Dan 6:2–3

[7]"You shall not take the name of the Lord your God in vain; for the LORD will not hold him guiltless who takes his name in vain.

[8]"Remember the sabbath day, to keep it holy. [9]Six days you shall labour, and do all your work; [10]but the seventh day is a sabbath to the LORD your God; in it you shall not do any work, you, or your son, or your daughter, your manservant, or your maidservant, or your cattle, or the sojourner who is within your gates; [11]for in six days the LORD made heaven and earth, the sea, and all

---

images, while calling for sobriety and beauty: "The practice of placing sacred images in churches so that they be venerated by the faithful is to be maintained. Nevertheless their number should be moderate and their relative positions should reflect right order. For otherwise the Christian people may find them incongruous and they may foster devotion of doubtful orthodoxy" (*Sacrosanctum Concilium*, 125).

20:5–6. "A jealous God": an anthropomorphism emphasizing the uniqueness of God. Since he is the only true God, he cannot abide either the worship of other gods (cf. 34:14) or worship of idols. Idolatry is the gravest and most condemned sin in the Bible (cf. *Catechism of the Catholic Church*, 2113). Those in charge of worship in the temple are described as being "jealous" for the Lord (cf. Num 25:13; 1 Kings 19:10, 14), because they have to watch to ensure that no deviations occur. When expelling the money-changers from the temple (Jn 2:17), Jesus refers to this aspect of priests' responsibility: "Zeal for thy house has consumed me" (Ps 69:9).

On the Lord's merciful retribution, cf. the note on Ex 34:6–7.

20:7. Respect for God's name is respect for God himself. Hence this prohibition on invoking the name of the Lord to gain credence for evil, be it at a trial (by committing perjury), or by swearing to do something evil, or by blasphemy (cf. Sir 23:7–12). In ancient times, Israel's neighbours used the names of their gods in magical conjuration; in such a situation the invoking of the Lord's name is idolatrous. In general, this commandment forbids any abuse, any disrespect, any irreverent use of the name of God. And, to put it positively, "The second commandment *prescribes respect for the Lord's name*. Like the first commandment, it belongs to the virtue of religion and more particularly it governs our use of speech in sacred matters" (*Catechism of the Catholic Church*, 2142).

20:8–11 Israel's history evidently influenced the formulation of the sabbath precept, given that the usual apodictic mode is not used and that the prescriptions concerning this day are very well developed.

The commandment includes three ideas: the sabbath is a holy day, dedicated to the Lord; work is forbidden on it; one reason for it is to imitate God, who rested from creation on the seventh day.

---

gunt me et custodiunt praecepta mea. [7]Non assumes nomen Domini Dei tui in vanum, nec enim habebit insontem Dominus eum, qui assumpserit nomen Domini Dei sui frustra. [8]Memento, ut diem sabbati sanctifices. [9]Sex diebus operaberis et facies omnia opera tua; [10]septimus autem dies sabbatum Domino Deo tuo est; non facies omne opus tu et filius tuus et filia tua, servus tuus et ancilla tua, iumentum tuum

Lev 19:3
Eph 6:2
Gen 4:10; 9:6
Mt 5:21
Jas 2:11
Rom 13:9
Rev 9:21
that is in them, and rested the seventh day; therefore the LORD blessed the sabbath day and hallowed it.

12"Honour your father and your mother, that your days may be long in the land which the LORD your God gives you.

The sabbath is a holy day, that is, different from ordinary days (cf. Lev 23:3) because it is dedicated to God. No special rites are prescribed but the word "remember" (different from "observe" in Deuteronomy 5:10) is a word with cultic associations. Whatever the etymology or social origin of the sabbath was, in the Bible it is always something holy (cf. 16:22–30).

Sabbath rest implies that there is an obligation to work on the previous six days (v. 9). Work is the only justification for rest. The Hebrew word *shabbat* actually means "sabbath" and "rest". But on this day rest acquires a cultic value, for no special sacrifices or rites are prescribed for the sabbath: the whole community, and even animals, render homage to God by ceasing from their labours.

20:12 The fourth is the first commandment to do with inter-personal relationships (the subject of the second "table" as ancient Christian writers used to term these commandments: cf. *Catechism of the Catholic Church*, 2197). Like the sabbath precept, it is couched in a positive way; its direct reference is to family members. The fact that it comes immediately after the precepts that refer to God shows its importance. Parents, in effect, represent God within the family circle.

The commandment has to do not only with young children (cf. Prov 19:26; 20:20; 23:22; 30:17), who have a duty to remain subject to their parents (Deut

21:18–21), but to all children whatever their age, because it is offences committed by older children that incur a curse (cf. Deut 17:16).

The promise of a long life to those who keep this commandment shows how important it is for the individual, and also the importance the family has for society. The Second Vatican Council summed up the value of the family by calling it the "domestic church" (*Lumen gentium*, 11; cf. John Paul II, *Familiaris consortio*, 21).

20:13. The fifth commandment directly forbids vengeful killing of one's enemy, that is, murder; so it protects the sacredness of human life. The prohibition on murder already comes across in the account of the death of Abel (cf. Gen 4:10) and the precepts given to Noah (cf. Gen 9:6): life is something that belongs to God alone.

Revelation and the teaching of the Church tell us more about the scope of this precept: it is only in very specific circumstances (such as social or personal self-defence) that a person may be deprived of his or her life. Obviously, the killing of weaker members of society (abortion, direct euthanasia) is a particularly grave sin.

The encyclical *Evangelium vitae* spells out the Church's teaching on this commandment which "has absolute value when it refers to the *innocent person*. [. . .] Therefore, by the authority which Christ conferred upon Peter and

---

et advena, qui est intra portas tuas. 11Sex enim diebus fecit Dominus caelum et terram et mare et omnia, quae in eis sunt, et requievit in die septimo; idcirco benedixit Dominus diei sabbati et sanctificavit eum. 12Honora patrem tuum et matrem tuam, ut sis longaevus super terram, quam Dominus Deus tuus dabit

Lev 20:10
Deut 22:23ff
Prov 7:8–27;
23:27–28
Mt 5:27

¹³"You shall not kill.
¹⁴"You shall not commit adultery.
¹⁵"You shall not steal.

---

his Successors, and in communion with the Bishops of the Catholic Church, *I confirm that the direct and voluntary killing of an innocent human being is always gravely immoral"* (John Paul II, *Evangelium vitae*, 57).

Our Lord taught that the positive meaning of this commandment was the obligation to practise charity (cf. Mt 5:21-26): "In the Sermon on the Mount, the Lord recalls the commandment, 'You shall not kill' (Mt 5:21), and adds to it the proscription of anger, hatred and vengeance. Going further, Christ asks his disciples to turn the other cheek, to love their enemies (cf. Mt 5:22–28). He did not defend himself and told Peter to leave his sword in its sheath (cf. Mt 26:52)" (*Catechism of the Catholic Church*, 2262).

20:14. The sixth commandment is orientated to safeguarding the holiness of marriage. In the Old Testament there were very severe penalties for those who committed adultery (cf. Deut 22:23ff; Lev 20:10). As Revelation progresses, it will become clear that not only is adultery grave, because it damages the rights of the other spouse, but every sexual disorder degrades the dignity of the person and is an offence against God (cf., e.g., Prov 7:8–27; 23:27–28). Jesus Christ, by his life and teaching, showed the positive thrust of this precept (cf. Mt 5:27–32): "Jesus came to restore creation to the purity of its origins. In the Sermon on the Mount, he interprets God's plan strictly: 'You have heard that it was said, "You shall not commit adultery." But I say to

you that every one who looks at a woman lustfully has already committed adultery with her in his heart' (Mt 5:27–28). What God has joined together, let not man put asunder (cf. Mt 19:6). The tradition of the Church has understood the sixth commandment as encompassing the whole of human sexuality" (*Catechism of the Catholic Church*, 2336).

20:15. Because the Decalogue is regulating inter-personal relationships, this commandment condemns firstly the abducting of persons in order to sell them into slavery (cf. Deut 24:7) but obviously it covers unjust appropriation of another's goods. The Church continues to remind us that every violation of the right to property is unjust (cf. *Catechism of the Catholic Church*, 2409); but this is particularly true if actions of that type lead to the enslavement of human beings, or to depriving them of their dignity, as happens in traffic in children, trade in human embryos, the taking of hostages, arbitrary arrest or imprisonment, racial segregation, concentration camps, etc. "The seventh commandment forbids acts or enterprises that for any reason—selfish or ideological, commercial or totalitarian—lead to the *enslavement of human beings*, to their being bought, sold and exchanged like merchandise, in disregard for their personal dignity. It is a sin against the dignity of persons and their fundamental rights to reduce them by violence to their productive value or to a source of profit. St Paul directed a Christian master to treat his Christian slave 'no longer as a slave but more than

---

tibi. ¹³Non occides. ¹⁴Non moechaberis. ¹⁵Non furtum facies. ¹⁶Non loqueris contra proximum tuum

Sir 7:12–13
Jas 3:1–12
Lev 19:12
Acts 6:13
Mt 5:28
Rom 7:7
1 Jn 2:16
Mic 2:2
Deut 5:23–31
Heb 12:19
Ex 33:20

[16]"You shall not bear false witness against your neighbour. [17]"You shall not covet your neighbour's house; you shall not covet your neighbour's wife, or his manservant, or his maidservant, or his ox, or his ass, or anything that is your neighbour's." [18]Now when all the people perceived the thunderings and the lightnings and the sound of the trumpet and the mountain smoking, the people were afraid and trembled; and they stood afar off, [19]and said to Moses, "You speak to us, and we will hear; but let not God speak to us, lest we die." [20]And Moses said to the people, "Do not fear; for God has come to prove you, and that the fear of him may be before your eyes, that you may not sin."

---

a slave, as a beloved brother . . . both in the flesh and in the Lord' (Philem 16)" (*Catechism of the Catholic Church,* 2414).

20:16. Giving false testimony in court can cause one's neighbour irreparable damage because an innocent person may be found guilty. But, given that truth and fidelity in human relationships is the basis of social life (cf. Vatican II, *Gaudium et spes,* 26), this commandment prohibits lying, defamation (cf. Sir 7:12–13), calumny and the saying of anything that might detract from a neighbour's dignity (cf. Jas 3:1–12). "This moral prescription flows from the vocation of the holy people to bear witness to their God who is the truth and wills the truth. Offences against the truth express by word or deed a refusal to commit oneself to moral uprightness: they are fundamental infidelities to God and, in this sense, they undermine the foundations of the covenant" (*Catechism of the Catholic Church,* 2464).

20:17. The wording of this precept is different from that in Deuteronomy: there

the distinction is made between coveting one's neighbour's wife and coveting his goods (cf. Deut 5:21). "St John distinguishes three kinds of covetousness or concupiscence: lust of the flesh, lust of the eyes and pride of life (cf. 1 Jn 2:16). In the Catholic catechetical tradition, the ninth commandment forbids carnal concupiscence; the tenth forbids coveting another's goods" (*Catechism of the Catholic Church,* 2514).

20:18–21. The account of the theophany (interrupted at 19:24) continues here, at the end of the Decalogue. Once more attention is focused on the transcendence of God, so much so that the people are fearful not only of the physical presence of God but even of his words. They ask Moses to speak to them on God's behalf, rather than hear God himself speaking.

"Do not fear" (v. 20): Moses tells them that it is God that they should fear, not the storm that has made him present. The "holy fear of God" is acknowledgement of his transcendence and also the ready acceptance of the offer of his Covenant as spelled out in the command-

---

falsum testimonium. [17]Non concupisces domum proximi tui: non desiderabis uxorem eius, non servum, non ancillam, non bovem, non asinum nec omnia, quae illius sunt». [18]Cunctus autem populus videbat voces et lampades et sonitum bucinae montemque fumantem; et perterriti ac pavore concussi steterunt procul [19]dicentes Moysi: «Loquere tu nobis, et audiemus; non loquatur nobis Deus, ne moriamur». [20]Et ait Moyses ad populum: «Nolite timere; ut enim probaret vos, venit Deus, et ut timor illius esset in

²¹And the people stood afar off, while Moses drew near to the thick darkness where God was.

8. THE BOOK OF THE COVENANT*

Laws concerning worship

²²And the LORD said to Moses, "Thus you shall say to the people of Israel: 'You have seen for yourselves that I have talked with

---

ments. Fearing God means accepting the challenge of cooperating with him in the work of salvation, while being conscious of the fact that our weakness may prevent us from achieving what God expects of us. This explains the biblical proverb: "The fear of the Lord is the beginning of wisdom" (Prov 9:10). Within the sphere of the fear of God is to be found love for God, not only in the sense of feeling but particularly in the sense of doing, showing one's love with deeds and avoiding all evil (v. 20).

*20:22—23:19. This collection of laws is usually described as the "Book of the Covenant" on account of what is said in 24:7, or the "Code of the Covenant", because many of these laws are similar to those to be found in legal codes of Semitic peoples, such as the Sumerian code of Ur-Nammu (c.2050 BC), that of Esnunna (c.1950 BC), that of Lipit-Istar (c.1850 BC) and (the most famous) code of Hammurabi (c.1700 BC), which is conserved on a dioritic stone in the Louvre Museum, Paris.

The laws collected here probably existed earlier in a similar or even identical wording, but by being inserted into the Book of the Covenant in the context of the events of Sinai they acquire extra weight and authority. They become as it

were the "basic laws" of the people, ratified by God himself.

Within this corpus of law there are laws specific to Israel (such as the absolute or apodictic laws: e.g. 22:17, 27, 28), whereas others are casuistic laws, to be found in all the above-mentioned codes: they allow of different assumptions and reflect their own specific jurisprudence on particular cases (e.g. 21:2–11, 18–26). Also, the Code of the Covenant covers the various areas of social life: it contains laws about worship (20:22–26; 22:28–30; 23:10–19), moral laws (22:16–27; 23:1–9) and, mainly, civil and penal laws (21:1—22:14). Some clearly derive from nomadic life in the desert, where livestock is more important than land; others imply a settled life where agriculture is the more important.

The sacred text presents these regulations as something sanctioned by God himself and as part of the obligations of the Covenant. The point is thereby made that the people of Israel has to be seen, in all aspects of its life, to be the chosen people: politics, social and family life, worship and institutions generally—all have a religious character.

20:22–26. These are very early prescriptions concerning worship, because there is as yet no mention of temple (v. 25) or

---

vobis, ne peccaretis». ²¹Stetitque populus de longe; Moyses autem accessit ad caliginem, in qua erat Deus. ²²Dixit praeterea Dominus ad Moysen: «Haec dices filiis Israel: Vos vidistis quod de caelo locu-

you from heaven. ²³You shall not make gods of silver to be with me, nor shall you make for yourselves gods of gold. ²⁴An altar of earth you shall make for me and sacrifice on it your burnt offerings and your peace offerings, your sheep and your oxen; in every place where I cause my name to be remembered I will come to you and bless you. ²⁵And if you make me an altar of stone, you shall not build it of hewn stones; for if you wield your tool upon it you profane it. ²⁶And you shall not go up by steps to my altar, that your nakedness be not exposed on it.'

Lev 1:1–17; 3:1–17

Ex 27:1–8
Deut 27:5–6

Ex 28:43
2 Sam 6:20–23

Laws concerning slaves

Lev 25:39–46
Deut 15:12–18

Jer 34:8–18

21 ¹"Now these are the ordinances which you shall set before them. ²When you buy a Hebrew slave, he shall serve six years, and in the seventh he shall go out free, for nothing. ³If he comes in single, he shall go out single; if he comes in married,

---

altar (v. 24) or priests, or sacred vestments (v. 26). However, it is already possible to glimpse the theological background: the Lord is the only true God, who must not be confused with human idols; divine worship has to be conducted with special care (this applies both to the objects used in it and the people who take part in it).

The sacred altar has to be simple and natural, because if it were made of worked stone there would be a risk of impurity. Later (cf. 27:18) there came an instruction that the altar of sacrifice should be made of acacia wood. But at all times simplicity and sobriety will imbue everything to do with worship.

Only two types of offerings are mentioned (v. 24), the burnt offering in which the entire victim is burned (in recognition of the sovereignty of God), and the communion or peace offering (more specific to Israel) in which is burned the part

regarded as most noble (blood and fat), the rest being served as a sacrificial meal. The peace offering puts more stress on communion of the offerers with one another and with God. In Leviticus (cf. Lev 1–7) the ritual of offerings will be dealt with in full detail.

Since there is no mention of priests, one supposes that it was the father of the family who made the offering; but he has a religious character, as can be seen from the prescription that he should be modestly dressed (cf. 2 Sam 6:20). In that period men wore only a short wraparound, Egyptian style; this practice will change when the rules on priestly vestments come into force (28:40–42).

21:1–11. Slavery was part of the way society was organized at that time. The rules collected here are designed to avoid abuses regarding slaves. In the parallel text of Deuteronomy 15:12–18, Israel's

---

tus sim vobis. ²³Non facietis praeter me deos argenteos, nec deos aureos facietis vobis. ²⁴Altare de terra facietis mihi et offeretis super eo holocausta et pacifica vestra, oves vestras et boves; in omni loco, in quo memoriam fecero nominis mei, veniam ad te et benedicam tibi. ²⁵Quod si altare lapideum feceris mihi, non aedificabis illud de sectis lapidibus; si enim levaveris cultrum super eo, polluetur. ²⁶Non ascendes per gradus ad altare meum, ne reveletur turpitudo tua. ¹Haec sunt iudicia, quae propones eis: ²Si emeris servum Hebraeum, sex annis serviet tibi; in septimo egredietur liber gratis. ³Si solus

then his wife shall go out with him. [4]If his master gives him a wife and she bears him sons or daughters, the wife and her children shall be her master's and he shall go out alone. [5]But if the slave plainly says, 'I love my master, my wife, and my children; I will not go out free,' [6]then his master shall bring him to God, and he shall bring him to the door or the doorpost; and his master shall bore his ear through with an awl; and he shall serve him for life.

[7]"When a man sells his daughter as a slave, she shall not go out as the male slaves do. [8]If she does not please her master, who has designated her[g] for himself, then he shall let her be redeemed; he shall have no right to sell her to a foreign people, since he has dealt faithlessly with her. [9]If he designates her for his son, he shall deal with her as with a daughter. [10]If he takes another wife to himself, he shall not diminish her food, her clothing, or her marital rights. [11]And if he does not do these three things for her, she shall go out for nothing, without payment of money.

---

bondage in Egypt is recalled to justify kindly treatment of slaves.

"Hebrew" (v. 2): this is the second time this term appears in the Bible (cf. Gen 14:13); it may possibly refer to a particular social class, the disinherited; but it is almost certain that it is a word for a member of the people of God, the brothers (cf. Deut 15:12).

The rite of boring a hole in the ear (which might seem barbaric nowadays) was used to show that a person now had a right to share in all the privileges of the family. It needs to be remembered that slavery in Israel always took account of the dignity of the person; it cannot be equated to Roman slavery or the enslavement of Africans in the Americas.

"He shall deal with her as with a daughter" (v. 9): literally, "in accordance with the statute of daughters". It seems that women had certain rights of inheritance and honour within the family. The rules in vv. 7–11 clearly tend to favour the status of women, who were frequently disadvantaged in that part of the world.

The New Testament contains clear pointers to the abolition of slavery, such as St Paul's advice to Philemon to treat his slave "as a beloved brother" (Philem 16).

---

intraverit, solus exeat; si habens uxorem, et uxor egredietur simul. [4]Sin autem dominus dederit illi uxorem, et pepererit filios et filias, mulier et liberi eius erunt domini sui; ipse vero exibit solus. [5]Quod si dixerit servus: 'Diligo dominum meum et uxorem ac liberos, non egrediar liber', [6]afferet eum dominus ad Deum et applicabit eum ad ostium vel postes perforabitque aurem eius subula; et erit ei servus in saeculum. [7]Si quis vendiderit filiam suam in famulam, non egredietur sicut servi exire consueverunt. [8]Si displicuerit oculis domini sui, cui tradita fuerat, faciat eam redimi; populo autem alieno vendendi non habebit potestatem, quia fraudavit eam. [9]Sin autem filio suo desponderit eam, iuxta morem filiarum faciet illi. [10]Quod si alteram sibi acceperit, cibum et vestimentum et concubitum non negabit. [11]Si tria ista non fecerit ei, egredietur gratis absque pretio. [12]Qui percusserit hominem, et ille mortuus

g. Another reading is *so that he has not designated her*

Ex 10:12, 13, 15
Lev 24:17
Num 35:11–34
Deut 4:41–43;
19:1–3
Josh 20:1–9
Mt 5:21
1 Kings 2:28–34

Laws concerning homicide

¹²"Whoever strikes a man so that he dies shall be put to death. ¹³But if he did not lie in wait for him, but God let him fall into his hand, then I will appoint for you a place to which he may flee. ¹⁴But if a man willfully attacks another to kill him treacherously, you shall take him from my altar, that he may die.

¹⁵"Whoever strikes his father or his mother shall be put to death.

Lev 20:9
Deut 27:16
Sir 3:16
Mt 15:4
Mk 7:10

¹⁶"Whoever steals a man, whether he sells him or is found in possession of him, shall be put to death.

¹⁷"Whoever curses his father or his mother shall be put to death.

Laws concerning violence

¹⁸"When men quarrel and one strikes the other with a stone or with his fist and the man does not die but keeps his bed, ¹⁹then if

---

21:12–17. The very grave crimes condemned here (homicide, abduction, and cursing of parents) are punishable by death with no appeal. The wording of these laws, which are usually called apodictic, is specific to Israel and shows their special gravity: witness the way the delinquent is described ("he who strikes . . .") and the use of a very Semitic expression to indicate the penalty (literally, "he shall die the death").

By repeating so severely the fourth, fifth and seventh precepts of the moral Decalogue (cf. 20:12, 13, 15) the importance of these laws in the religious and social life of Israel is being underlined.

A person who killed another could obtain asylum only when he caused the death unintentionally, by accident and without fault (cf. Num 35:11–34; Deut 4:41–43; 19:1–3; Josh 20:1–9).

21:18–32. Less serious crimes against persons are regulated by the classic "law of vengeance" (the punishment to fit the crime exactly), formally enunciated in vv. 23–25 (cf. Lev 24:19–20; Deut 19:21). This marks a considerable development in the history of law among nomadic peoples, because family members' desire for revenge often led to abuses (cf. Gen 4:23–24): no one will be able to go too far, seeking twice or six or ten times more than the harm done; the punishment is to equal the offence. Jesus will correct this harsh and unsophisticated law by means of the precept of charity (cf. Mt 5:38–42).

In these laws a distinction is made between a free person and a slave. The law of vengeance applied more to the former; that is why the law goes into greater detail in regard to slaves, because

---

fuerit, morte moriatur. ¹³Qui autem non est insidiatus, sed Deus illum tradidit in manus eius, constituam tibi locum, in quem fugere debeat. ¹⁴Si quis de industria occiderit proximum suum et per insidias, ab altari meo evelles eum, ut moriatur. ¹⁵Qui percusserit patrem suum aut matrem, morte moriatur. ¹⁶Qui furatus fuerit hominem sive vendiderit eum sive inventus fuerit in manu eius, morte moriatur. ¹⁷Qui maledixerit patri suo vel matri, morte moriatur. ¹⁸Si rixati fuerint viri, et percusserit alter proximum suum lapide vel pugno, et ille mortuus non fuerit, sed iacuerit in lectulo, ¹⁹si surrexerit et ambulaverit foris super baculum suum, impunitus erit, qui percusserit, ita tamen, ut operas eius

the man rises again and walks abroad with his staff, he that struck him shall be clear; only he shall pay for the loss of his time, and shall have him thoroughly healed.

[20]"When a man strikes his slave, male or female, with a rod and the slave dies under his hand, he shall be punished. [21]But if the slave survives a day or two, he is not to be punished; for the slave is his money. *Mt 5:38*

[22]"When men strive together, and hurt a woman with child, so that there is a miscarriage, and yet no harm follows, the one who hurt her shall[h] be fined, according as the woman's husband shall lay upon him; and he shall pay as the judges determine. [23]If any harm follows, then you shall give life for life, [24]eye for eye, tooth for tooth, hand for hand, foot for foot, [25]burn for burn, wound for wound, stripe for stripe. *Lev 24:17ff* *Deut 19:21*

[26]"When a man strikes the eye of his slave, male or female, and destroys it, he shall let the slave go free for the eye's sake. [27]If

---

their rights were more open to abuse. In the Bible, more than in the codes of neighbouring peoples, the rights of slaves are defended: their status as persons is given more emphasis. In the context of God's gradual way of teaching, one could not expect much more, given the period in which this law was issued; one would have to wait until the New Testament to find clear condemnation of exploitation or marginalization (cf. Gal 3:28; Col 3:11), and open defence of the dignity of the person (cf. *Catechism of the Catholic Church*, 1929–1933).

Thirty coins, the payment for a slave (v. 32), was the price paid for the handing over of Jesus (cf. Mt 26:15).

21:22–23. This is the only passage in the Bible which mentions abortion caused indirectly. Although it is a very bald legal statement, it could be interpreted as meaning that someone should pay with his life if he has done (mortal) harm to the foetus or to the mother (v. 23); however, it seems that only when it was the mother who died was the death penalty enjoined; if it was the foetus that was killed, there was only a monetary fine. Although it cannot be deduced from this text that the foetus was regarded as a human person with all a person's rights, it is also true that the offence was severely punished if a blow provoked an abortion. What one may deduce is that, since there is no biblical law about directly provoked abortion, this never in fact happened, because the child was valued as such from the moment of conception. Moreover, spon-

---

deperditas et impensas pro medela restituat. [20]Qui percusserit servum suum vel ancillam virga, et mortui fuerint in manibus eius, ultioni subiacetur. [21]Sin autem uno die vel duobus supervixerit, non subiacebit poenae, quia pecunia illius est. [22]Si rixati fuerint viri, et percusserit quis mulierem praegnantem et abortivum quidem fecerit, sed aliud quid adversi non acciderit, subiacebit damno, quantum maritus mulieris expetierit, et arbitri iudicaverint. [23]Sin autem quid adversi acciderit, reddet animam pro anima, [24]oculum pro oculo, dentem pro dente, manum pro manu, pedem pro pede, [25]adustionem

h. Heb *he shall*

he knocks out the tooth of his slave, male or female, he shall let the slave go free for the tooth's sake.

28"When an ox gores a man or a woman to death, the ox shall be stoned, and its flesh shall not be eaten; but the owner of the ox shall be clear. 29But if the ox has been accustomed to gore in the past, and its owner has been warned but has not kept it in, and it kills a man or a woman, the ox shall be stoned, and its owner also shall be put to death. 30If a ransom is laid on him, then he shall give for the redemption of his life whatever is laid upon him. 31If it gores a man's son or daughter, he shall be dealt with according to this same rule. 32If the ox gores a slave, male or female, the owner shall give to their master thirty shekels of silver, and the ox shall be stoned.

Mt 26:15

Laws concerning restitution

33"When a man leaves a pit open, or when a man digs a pit and does not cover it, and an ox or an ass falls into it, 34the owner of the pit shall make it good; he shall give money to its owner, and the dead beast shall be his.

35"When one man's ox hurts another's, so that it dies, then they shall sell the live ox and divide the price of it; and the dead beast also they shall divide. 36Or if it is known that the ox has been accustomed to gore in the past, and its owner has not kept it in, he shall pay ox for ox, and the dead beast shall be his.

2 Sam 12:6
Lk 19:8

---

taneous abortion was regarded as a misfortune (cf. 23:26).

21:33–36. The rules about damage to property are couched as casuistical laws, that is in terms of concrete cases which frequently occurred. For the most part they are applications of the law of vengeance, specifying the compensation to be made by the person who did the damage. There is an obligation to compensate even if what happened was an accident; but if imprudence or negligence was involved, the compensation required is greater.

---

pro adustione, vulnus pro vulnere, livorem pro livore. 26Si percusserit quispiam oculum servi sui aut ancillae et luscos eos fecerit, dimittet eos liberos pro oculo. 27Dentem quoque si excusserit servo vel ancillae suae, dimittet eos liberos pro dente. 28Si bos cornu percusserit virum aut mulierem et mortui fuerint, lapidibus obruetur, et non comedentur carnes eius; dominus autem bovis innocens erit. 29Quod si bos cornupeta fuerit ab heri et nudiustertius, et contestati sunt dominum eius, nec recluserit eum, occideritque virum aut mulierem: et bos lapidibus obruetur, et dominum illius occident. 30Quod si pretium ei fuerit impositum, dabit pro anima sua, quidquid fuerit postulatus. 31Filium quoque vel filiam si cornu percusserit, simili sententiae subiacebit. 32Si servum vel ancillam invaserit, triginta siclos argenti dabit domino; bos vero lapidibus opprimetur. 33Si quis aperuerit cisternam vel foderit et non operuerit eam, cecideritque bos vel asinus in eam, 34dominus cisternae reddet pretium iumentorum; quod autem mortuum est, ipsius erit. 35Si bos alienus bovem alterius vulneraverit, et ille mortuus fuerit, vendent bovem vivum et dividet pretium; cadaver autem mortui inter se disperdient. 36Sin autem notum erat quod bos cornupeta esset ab heri et nudiustertius, et non custodivit eum dominus suus,

22 [1i]"If a man steals an ox or a sheep, and kills it or sells it, he shall pay five oxen for an ox, and four sheep for a sheep.[j] He shall make restitution; if he has nothing, then he shall be sold for his theft. [4]If the stolen beast is found alive in his possession, whether it is an ox or an ass or a sheep, he shall pay double.

[2k]"If a thief is found breaking in, and is struck so that he dies, there shall be no blood guilt for him; [3]but if the sun has risen upon him, there shall be blood guilt for him.

[5]"When a man causes a field or vineyard to be grazed over, or lets his beast loose and it feeds in another man's field, he shall make restitution from the best in his own field and in his own vineyard.

[6]"When fire breaks out and catches in thorns so that the stacked grain or the standing grain or the field is consumed, he that kindled the fire shall make full restitution.

[7]"If a man delivers to his neighbour money or goods to keep, Lev 5:21–26 and it is stolen out of the man's house, then, if the thief is found,

---

22:1–2. In these cases to do with theft, the law of vengeance is applied both to the thief and to anyone who tried to kill him. Thus, the thief always has to make restitution, either with his goods (22:1) or by being sold into slavery (22:2). On the other hand, if the thief is killed in the dark, so be it—perhaps because it is difficult to know whether the intruder intended simply to steal or also to kill. The principle of lawful defence underlies this precept. But if the thief is killed in the act of stealing in daylight, there is guilt on the person who kills him, because he could see the person was only a thief; stealing property and killing a person are different levels of crime. This law seeks to obviate the kind of excesses vengeance can lead to.

22:5–14. In all the cases mentioned here, the person who causes the damage has to compensate the owner. Even in that period it was common practice to leave money or objects of value on deposit. It was also common for lawsuits to be solved by recourse to religious methods (v. 7), although it is not said here whether

---

reddet bovem pro bove et cadaver integrum accipiet. [37]Si quis furatus fuerit bovem aut ovem et occiderit vel vendiderit, quinque boves pro uno bove restituet et quattuor oves pro una ove. [1]Si effringens fur domum sive suffodiens fuerit inventus et, accepto vulnere, mortuus fuerit, percussor non erit reus sanguinis. [2]Quod si orto sole hoc fecerit, erit reus sanguinis. Fur plene restituet. Si non habuerit, quod reddat, venumdabitur pro furto. [3]Si inventum fuerit apud eum, quod furatus est, vivens sive bos sive asinus sive ovis, duplum restituet. [4]Si quispiam depasci permiserit agrum vel vineam et dimiserit iumentum suum, ut depascatur agrum alienum, restituet plene ex agro suo secundum fruges eius; si autem totum agrum depastum fuerit, quidquid optimum habuerit in agro suo vel in vinea, restituet. [5]Si egressus ignis invenerit spinas et comprehenderit acervos frugum sive stantes segetes sive agrum, reddet damnum, qui ignem succenderit. [6]Si quis commendaverit amico pecuniam aut vasa in custo-

---

i. Ch 21:37 in Heb [and New Vulgate]   **j.** Restoring the second half of verse 3 and the whole of verse 4 to their place immediately following verse 1   **k.** Ch 22:1 in Heb [and New Vulgate]

he shall pay double. [8]If the thief is not found, the owner of the house shall come near to God, to show whether or not he has put his hand to his neighbour's goods.

[9]"For every breach of trust, whether it is for ox, for ass, for sheep, for clothing, or for any kind of lost thing, of which one says, 'This is it,' the case of both parties shall come before God; he whom God shall condemn shall pay double to his neighbour.

[10]"If a man delivers to his neighbour an ass or an ox or a

Heb 6:16 sheep or any beast to keep, and it dies or is hurt or is driven away, without anyone seeing it, [11]an oath by the LORD shall be between them both to see whether he has not put his hand to his neighbour's property; and the owner shall accept the oath, and he shall not make restitution. [12]But if it is stolen from him, he shall make restitution to its owner. [13]If it is torn by beasts, let him bring it as evidence; he shall not make restitution for what has been torn.

[14]"If a man borrows anything of his neighbour, and it is hurt or dies, the owner not being with it, he shall make full restitution. [15]If the owner was with it, he shall not make restitution; if it was hired, it came for its hire.[l]

---

this was done through oaths, oracles or rites of ordeal, or by means of the sacred lots of the Urim and Thummin, which the high priest used for consulting the Lord (cf. 28:20; Num 27:21).

22:16–17. An unmarried girl belongs to the family of her father. The case described could be regarded as a legitimate procedure, though not the normal way, for getting married. But the father has the right to withhold consent. This protected the rights of young women and their families. The payment of the *mohar*, money given to the bride's father (cf. Gen 34:12; 1 Sam 18:25), was in line with a marriage custom followed among Semitic peoples; it would be an anachronism to think that marriage at that time was a kind of buying-selling contract in

---

diam, et ab eo, qui susceperat, furto ablata fuerint, si invenitur fur, duplum reddet. [7]Si latet fur, dominus domus applicabitur ad Deum et iurabit quod non extenderit manum in rem proximi sui. [8]In omni causa fraudis tam de bove quam de asino et ove ac vestimento et, quidquid damnum inferre potest, si quis dixerit: «Hoc est!», ad Deum utriusque causa perveniet, et, quem Deus condemnaverit, duplum restituet proximo suo. [9]Si quis commendaverit proximo suo asinum, bovem, ovem vel omne iumentum ad custodiam, et mortuum fuerit aut fractum vel captum ab hostibus, nullusque hoc viderit, [10]iusiurandum per Dominum erit in medio quod non extenderit manum ad rem proximi sui; suscipietque dominus iuramentum, et ille reddere non cogetur. [11]Quod si furto ablatum fuerit, restituet damnum domino; [12]si dilaceratum a bestia, deferat, quod occisum est, in testimonium et non restituet. [13]Qui a proximo suo quidquam horum mutuo postulaverit, et fractum aut mortuum fuerit, domino non praesente, reddere compelletur. [14]Quod si impraesentiarum dominus fuerit, non restituet. Si mercennarius

---

l. Or *it is reckoned in* (Heb *comes into*) *its hire*

Gen 34:12
Deut 22:23–29
1 Sam 18:25

Violation of a virgin

¹⁶"If a man seduces a virgin who is not betrothed, and lies with her, he shall give the marriage present for her, and make her his wife.

¹⁷If her father utterly refuses to give her to him, he shall pay money equivalent to the marriage present for virgins.

Social laws

Lev 20:6, 27
Deut 18:10–14
Lev 18:23–25

¹⁸"You shall not permit a sorceress to live.

¹⁹"Whoever lies with a beast shall be put to death.

Deut 27:21

²⁰"Whoever sacrifices to any god, save to the LORD only, shall be utterly destroyed.

Deut 10:18–19;
24:17–18
Lev 19:33ff
Is 1:17
Jer 7:6
Mk 12:40
Lk 18:3
Jas 1:27
Deut 24:17ff; 27:19
Is 1:17

²¹"You shall not wrong a stranger or oppress him, for you were strangers in the land of Egypt. ²²You shall not afflict any widow or orphan. ²³If you do afflict them, and they cry out to me, I will surely hear their cry; ²⁴and my wrath will burn, and I will kill you with the sword, and your wives shall become widows and your children fatherless.

Lev 25:35–37
Deut 23:20–21

²⁵"If you lend money to any of my people with you who is poor, you shall not be to him as a creditor, and you shall not exact interest from him. ²⁶If ever you take your neighbour's garment in pledge,

---

which the woman was regarded as a "thing". Rather it seems clear that a marriage ceremony was a commitment made between families and that the family gaining this new couple in some way compensated the family which was deprived of it.

22:18–31 This passage contains a number of laws on social matters, in no particular order; some are apodictic, some religious, others are work-associated—but all deal with serious offences.

Sorcery, which only women used to engage in (v. 18) was punished by death (cf. Lev 20:6, 27; Deut 18:10–14), being a form of idolatry (cf. *Catechism of the Catholic Church*, 2117). It was also forbidden by Assyrian laws and by the Code of Hammurabi.

Bestiality (v. 19) was a perversion more often found in pastoral and nomadic life (cf. Lev 18:23–25); it too was punishable by death.

Sacrificing to false gods was a temptation ever-present to Israelites because they were surrounded by wealthy and powerful, but polytheistic, nations such

---

est, venit in mercedem operis sui. ¹⁵Si seduxerit quis virginem necdum desponsatam dormieritque cum ea, pretio acquiret eam sibi uxorem. ¹⁶Si pater virginis eam dare noluerit, appendet ei pecuniam iuxta pretium pro virginibus dandum. ¹⁷Maleficam non patieris vivere. ¹⁸Qui coierit cum iumento, morte moriatur. ¹⁹Qui immolat diis, occidetur, praeter Domino soli. ²⁰Advenam non opprimes neque affliges eum; advenae enim et ipsi fuistis in terra Aegypti. ²¹Viduae et pupillo non nocebitis. ²²Si laeseritis eos, vociferabuntur ad me, et ego audiam clamorem eorum; ²³et indignabitur furor meus, percutiamque vos gladio, et erunt uxores vestrae viduae et filii vestri pupilli. ²⁴Si pecuniam mutuam dederis in populo meo pauperi, qui habitat tecum, non eris ei quasi creditor; non imponetis ei usuram. ²⁵Si pignus a proximo tuo acceperis pallium, ante solis occasum reddes ei; ²⁶ipsum enim est solum, quo operitur, indumentum carnis eius, nec habet aliud, in quo dormiat; si clamaverit ad me, exaudiam eum, quia

Deut
24:10–13, 17
you shall restore it to him before the sun goes down; ²⁷for that is his only covering, it is his mantle for his body; in what else shall he sleep? And if he cries to me, I will hear, for I am compassionate.

Lev 24:15
Acts 23:5
Jn 10:34; 18:22
²⁸"You shall not revile God, nor curse a ruler of your people.

²⁹"You shall not delay to offer from the fulness of your harvest and from the outflow of your presses.

"The first-born of your sons you shall give to me. ³⁰You shall do likewise with your oxen and with your sheep: seven days it shall be with its dam; on the eighth day you shall give it to me.

Lev 17:15–16
Deut 14:21
³¹"You shall be men consecrated to me; therefore you shall not eat any flesh that is torn by beasts in the field; you shall cast it to the dogs.

Duties of justice

Lev 5:22; 19:16
Deut 19:15
Lev 19:15
Deut 16:18–20

23 ¹"You shall not utter a false report. You shall not join hands with a wicked man, to be a malicious witness. ²You shall not follow a multitude to do evil; nor shall you bear witness in a

---

as Egypt, Babylonia, Assyria and, especially, Canaan; ". . . shall be utterly destroyed" (v. 20): or "shall be put under the ban" or "shall be anathema".

Strangers who (due to war, disease or famine) found themselves forced to leave their country, widows without a family to support them, and orphans were typical marginalized or poor people in that tribal society. In its laws (e.g., Deut 10:17–18; 24:17) and in its prophetic message (e.g. Is 1:17; Jer 7;6), the Bible constantly speaks out on behalf of people most in need (cf. Jas 1:27). The oppression of the weak and of those on the margin of society is one of the sins that cry out to heaven (cf. *Catechism of Catholic Church*, 1867).

Blasphemy against God (v. 28) was punishable by death (cf. Lev 24:15); blasphemy against the person on sup-

reme authority in the nation was no less serious, because he was God's representative. In the time of St Paul this text was applied to offences against the high priest (cf. Acts 23:5).

On the law covering the first-born, cf. the note on 13:12. First-born sons had to be redeemed by means of an offering. Therefore, the very bald rule given in v. 29 needs to be interpreted in the light of others which describe how first-born sons were to be consecrated—for the sacrifice of human beings was never countenanced in Israel.

23:1–3. Offences against justice, especially if they occurred in the context of a lawsuit, were subject to severe penalties. Equity is to be the rule in lawsuits, which usually take place at the gates of the city. Verse 3 sounds rather shocking

---

misericors sum. ²⁷Deo non detrahes et principi populi tui non maledices. ²⁸Abundantiam areae tuae et torcularis tui non tardabis reddere. Primogenitum filiorum tuorum dabis mihi. ²⁹De bobus quoque et ovibus similiter facies: septem diebus sit cum matre sua, die octavo reddes illum mihi. ³⁰Viri sancti eritis mihi; carnem animalis in agro dilacerati non comedetis, sed proicietis canibus. ¹Non suscipies famam falsam nec iunges manum tuam cum impio, ut dicas falsum testimonium. ²Non sequeris turbam ad faciendum malum; nec in iudicio plurimorum acquiesces sententiae, ut a vero devies. ³Pauperis

suit, turning aside after a multitude, so as to pervert justice; ³nor shall you be partial to a poor man in his suit.

⁴"If you meet your enemy's ox or his ass going astray, you shall bring it back to him. ⁵If you see the ass of one who hates you lying under its burden, you shall refrain from leaving him with it, you shall help him to lift it up.ᵐ

⁶"You shall not pervert the justice due to your poor in his suit. ⁷Keep far from a false charge, and do not slay the innocent and righteous, for I will not acquit the wicked. ⁸And you shall take no bribe, for a bribe blinds the officials, and subverts the cause of those who are in the right.

⁹"You shall not oppress a stranger; you know the heart of a stranger, for you were strangers in the land of Egypt.

Deut 22:1-4

Deut 1:17;
16:19

Deut 16:19

Ex 22:20

The sabbatical year and the sabbath

¹⁰"For six years you shall sow your land and gather in its yield; ¹¹but the seventh year you shall let it rest and lie fallow, that the

Lev 25:1-7
Deut 15:1-3
Deut 24:19;
26:12-13

---

but it is really a call for judges to be impartial: they should not lean towards a rich man by accepting bribes, or towards a poor man on grounds of compassion (cf. Deut 16:19). Some commentators think that the original text said *gadol* (powerful), not *dal* (poor), in other words, that it should read "nor shall you be partial to a powerful man in his suit", similar to what Leviticus 19:15 says. But there is no Hebrew text or early translation that justifies changing the reading; therefore, it should be left as it is, even though it is difficult to explain.

St Augustine comments that this law does not lessen the value of mercy: "mercy is good, but never if it goes against justice" (*Quaestiones in Heptateuchum*, 2, 88).

23:4-9. Love of enemies is one of the new features in Christ's message (Mt 5:43-48), but the Old Testament prepared the ground for this great commandment by establishing laws which suppressed excesses of enmity (cf. Deut 22:1-4).

In v. 7 the New Vulgate translates this along these lines: "keep far away from lies". But the context in which this rule applies (trials: vv. 60-8) justifies the translation given ("a false charge"). For v. 8 also, the New Vulgate has a very literal translation: "bribery . . . corrupts the words of the just"; however, given the context (legal trials), the translation given is more correct.

23:10-13. The Code of the Covenant, which began with a set of laws dealing

quoque non misereberis in iudicio. ⁴Si occurreris bovi inimici tui aut asino erranti, reduc ad eum. ⁵Si videris asinum odientis te iacere sub onere suo, non pertransibis, sed sublevabis cum eo. ⁶Non pervertes iudicium pauperis in lite eius. ⁷Mendacium fugies. Insontem et iustum non occides, quia aversor impium. ⁸Nec accipies munera, quae excaecant etiam prudentes et sub vertunt verba iustorum. ⁹Peregrinum non opprimes; scitis enim advenarum animas, quia et ipsi peregrini fuistis in terra

m. Gk: Heb obscure

poor of your people may eat; and what they leave the wild beasts may eat. You shall do likewise with your vineyard, and with your olive orchard.

Ex 20:8
Mk 2:27
Josh 23:7

¹²"Six days you shall do your work, but on the seventh day you shall rest; that your ox and your ass may have rest, and the son of your bondmaid, and the alien, may be refreshed. ¹³Take heed to all that I have said to you; and make no mention of the names of other gods, nor let such be heard out of your mouth.

Ex 34:18–23
Lev 23
Deut 16:1–16
Lk 2:41

The great feasts

¹⁴"Three times in the year you shall keep a feast to me. ¹⁵You shall keep the feast of unleavened bread; as I commanded you, you shall eat unleavened bread for seven days at the appointed time in the month of Abib, for in it you came out of Egypt. None

---

with religious matters (20:22–26), now ends with laws—dealing with worship on the sabbath and on pilgrimage feasts.

In Leviticus 25:2–7 and Deuteronomy 15:1–3 there is more elaborate legislation to do with sabbatical years. The purpose of such laws is predominantly religious.

23:14–17. This is one of the oldest cycles of religious feasts; it is very like that included in the Ritual Code (Ex 34:18–23) and that of the Deuteronomic Code (Deut 16:1–6); Leviticus also has its version (cf. Lev 23). The Hebrew word used for these feasts means "dance" or "dance in a ring", a reference to the processional form taken by pilgrimages to sanctuaries.

The three great pilgrimage feasts are described here succinctly and accurately: the feast of the unleavened bread was

held in spring, starting on the day after the Passover, although originally it had no connexion with the latter. It lasted a week, during which no unleavened bread was eaten, to indicate divine blessing on the first fruits; in Israel it marked the birth of the people, when delivered from bondage.

The harvest feast, sometimes called the feast of Weeks (34:22) was held fifty days after the Passover (seven weeks after the feast of the unleavened bread); hence its Greek name of Pentecost (cf. Thess 2:1). It celebrated the end of the grain harvest. Later on, probably as early as the 1st century BC, it also commemorated the handing down of the Law on Sinai.

The harvest feast, celebrated in autumn at the end of September, was also called the feast of Tents (or booths) or Tabernacles (cf. Deut 16:13; Lev 23:34)

Aegypti. ¹⁰Sex annis seminabis terram tuam et congregabis fruges eius. ¹¹Anno autem septimo dimittes eam et requiescere facies, ut comedant pauperes populi tui; et quidquid reliquum fuerit, edant bestiae agri. Ita facies in vinea et in oliveto tuo. ¹²Sex diebus operaberis; septima die cessabis, ut requiescat bos et asinus tuus, et refrigeretur filius ancillae tuae et advena. ¹³Omnia, quae dixi vobis, custodite, et nomen externorum deorum non invocabitis, neque audietur ex ore tuo. ¹⁴Tribus vicibus per singulos annos mihi festa celebrabitis. ¹⁵Sollemnitatem Azymorum custodies: septem diebus comedes azyma, sicut praecepi tibi, tempore statuto mensis Abib, quando egressus es de Aegypto. Non apparebis in conspectu meo vacuus. ¹⁶Et sollemnitatem Messis primitivorum operis tui, quaecumque seminaveris in

shall appear before me empty-handed. [16]You shall keep the feast
of harvest, of the first fruits of your labor, of what you sow in the
field. You shall keep the feast of in gathering at the end of the
year, when you gather in from the field the fruit of your labour.
[17]Three times in the year shall all your males appear before the
LORD God.

[18]"You shall not offer the blood of my sacrifice with leavened
bread, or let the fat of my feast remain until the morning.

[19]"The first of the first fruits of your ground you shall bring
into the house of the LORD your God.

"You shall not boil a kid in its mother's milk.

Warnings and promises*

[20]"Behold, I send an angel before you, to guard you on the way
and to bring you to the place which I have prepared. [21]Give heed

1 Kings 8:2
Tob 2:1
Ezra 45:25

Ex 34:26

Deut 7:1–26

Ex 14:19; 33:2
Mal 3:1
Is 63:9

---

after the huts that were built for it (similar to those used during the grape harvest and the harvest of the last fruits). It was mainly a thanksgiving feast and it eventually became so popular that it was simply "the feast" (cf. 1 Kings 8:2; Ezek 45:25). In Israel it commemorated the years spent in the desert, when they had to live in tents because they had neither land nor houses of their own (cf. Lev 23:43).

In addition to these feasts there were other less important ones, many of which eventually disappeared. Those that lasted longest were the Day of Atonement (cf. Lev 16 and 23:27) and those which developed much later, such as Purim, to celebrate the lifting of judgments against the Jews in Persia (cf. Esther 9:24) and the Dedication of the Temple or the feast of Lights (cf. 1 Mac 4:59). There is no evidence that the New Year was celebrated in any very special way, despite the possible reference in Leviticus 23:34.

The feasts laid down in the Bible,

especially the three pilgrimage feasts, commemorate salvific actions of God in favour of his people, even though among the Canaanites they were linked to agricultural seasons. So we can see that salvation history and God's actions in the past were kept before people's minds by these liturgical celebrations.

23:19. We now know more than we used to about the religious background to this last prohibition, "You shall not boil a kid in its mother's milk". According to a Canaanite document called "The birth of the gods" this dish was often made as a fertility rite: the milk in which a kid had been cooked was sprinkled on fields or on animals in order to improve their fertility. Since this was a product of magic or sorcery, it was forbidden in Israel (cf. 34:26).

***23:20–33.** As an appendix and conclusion to the Code of the Covenant, the sacred writer put together these various

---

agro; sollemnitatem quoque Collectae in exitu anni, quando congregaveris omnes fruges tuas de agro. [17]Ter in anno apparebit omne masculinum tuum coram Domino Deo. [18]Non immolabis super fermento sanguinem victimae meae, nec remanebit adeps sollemnitatis meae usque mane. [19]Primitias primarum frugum terrae tuae deferes in domum Domini Dei tui. Non coques haedum in lacte matris suae. [20]Ecce

Mt 11:10
Mk 1:2
Lk 7:27 to him and hearken to his voice, do not rebel against him, for he will not pardon your transgression; for my name is in him.

²²"But if you hearken attentively to his voice and do all that I say, then I will be an enemy to your enemies and an adversary to your adversaries.

Deut 7:1
Ex 34:13
Deut 12:3;
16:22
2 Kings 17:10
Hos 4:10; 10:1
Mic 5:12–13 ²³"When my angel goes before you, and brings you in to the Amorites, and the Hittites, and the Perizzites, and the Canaanites, the Hivites, and the Jebusites, and I blot them out, ²⁴you shall not bow down to their gods, nor serve them, nor do according to their works, but you shall utterly overthrow them and break their pil-

---

warnings or promises. Strictly speaking, this is not a formal epilogue of the type usually attached to the end of codes of laws (cf. Lev 26 for the Code of the Holiness, and Deut 28 for the Deuteronomic Code) because it contains no blessings or curses, and makes no specific reference to the preceding laws. It is more a collection of instructions based on the fact that God is close to his people; it is designed to fortify Israel's hope and encourage it to be faithful.

"I send an angel before you" (v. 20). The word "angel", according to St Augustine, refers to his office, not his nature. "If you enquire as to his nature, I will tell you that he is a spirit; if you ask what it is he does, I will tell you that he is an angel" (*Enarrationes in Psalmos*, 103, 1, 15). The expression "angel of the Lord" is equivalent to the presence of God himself or his direct intervention (cf. 3:2; 14:19 and also Gen 16:7; 22:11, 14). However, when Scripture speaks of an "angel" or "my angel" (cf. Ex 33:2; Num 20:16) it seems to refer rather to those spiritual beings who are attentive to the Lord's commands and are faithful doers of his word (cf. Ps 103:20). The role

assigned to them is that of guarding the people in the name of the Lord, just as they protected Lot (cf. Gen 19) or Hagar and her son (cf. Gal 21:17). On the basis of this biblical teaching, the Church holds that angels continue to lend men the same mysterious and powerful help. "Each member of the faithful has at his side an angel as a protector and shepherd to lead him towards life" (St Basil, *Adversus Eunomium*, 3,1; cf. *Catechism of the Catholic Church*, 334–336).

Whereas he sends an angel to the Israelites, he sends two scourges against their enemies—terror (v. 27) and a plague of hornets (v. 28). As usual when the Bible tells us this, it does not mean that God is wicked, but rather that, since he is the only Supreme Being, all blessings and all misfortunes are attributable to him. Furthermore, it is very much in the style of Semitic literature to make a play of contrasts—the misfortunes of enemies are a way of showing how well one is being treated oneself.

23:24–25. "Break their pillars in pieces": in general stelae (in Hebrew, *massebot*) were stones commemorating some spe-

---

ego mittam angelum, qui praecedat te et custodiat in via et introducat ad locum, quem paravi. ²¹Observa eum et audi vocem eius, nec contemnendum putes; quia non dimittet, cum peccaveritis, quia est nomen meum in illo. ²²Quod si audieris vocem eius et feceris omnia, quae loquor, inimicus ero inimicis tuis et affligam affligentes te. ²³Praecedet enim te angelus meus et introducet te ad Amorraeum et Hetthaeum et Pherezaeum Chananaeumque et Hevaeum et Iebusaeum, quos ego conteram. ²⁴Non

lars in pieces. ^{25}You shall serve the LORD your God, and I^n will bless your bread and your water; and I will take sickness away from the midst of you. ^{26}None shall cast her young or be barren in your land; I will fulfil the number of your days. ^{27}I will send my terror before you, and will throw into confusion all the people against whom you shall come, and I will make all your enemies turn their backs to you. ^{28}And I will send hornets before you, which shall drive out Hivite, Canaanite, and Hittite from before you. ^{29}I will not drive them out from before you in one year, lest the land become desolate and the wild beasts multiply against you. ^{30}Little by little I will drive them out from before you, until you are increased and possess the land. ^{31}And I will set your bounds from the Red Sea to the sea of the Philistines, and from the wilderness to the Euphrates; for I will deliver the inhabitants of the land into your hand, and you shall drive them out before you. ^{32}You shall make no covenant with them or with their gods.

Lev 18:3
Num 33:52

Wis 12:3-10

Deut 7:20
Josh 24:12
Wis 12:8

Deut 7:22
Judg 2:6
Judg 20:1
1 Kings 5:1
Deut 11:24

---

cial event, erected as columns or obelisks (cf. Ex 24:4; 2 Kings 18:18). But in the Canaanite religion they were symbols of male gods (cf. Ex 34:13 and note). Both prophets (Hos 4:10; 10:1; Mic 5:12–13) and other books of the Bible (cf. Deut 16:22; 2 Kings 17:10; etc.) were severe in their condemnation of the idolatry implied in their presence in the holy land of Israel.

"I will bless" (v. 25): this is the translation also found in the Septuagint and the Vulgate. We prefer "He will bless".

23:27–30. This announcement that the conquest is going to take time is meant to be an explanation of what actually happened. For one thing, it would take time for the Israelites to settle down and cultivate the land: this is the most obvious reason for the delay. But there is a more theological reason, as the book of Wisdom implied (cf. Wis 12:3–10): God arranged to send a plague of hornets and other punishments in advance in order to give time to the pagan inhabitants of that land to repent, and to accept the true God.

23:31. The boundaries given here are those of the kingdom of Solomon (cf. 1 Kings 5:1; Judg 20:1), which ran from the Red Sea to the Mediterranean and from the Arabian desert to the Euphrates.

---

adorabis deos eorum, nec coles eos; non facies secundum opera eorum, sed destrues eos et confringes lapides eorum. ^{25}Servietisque Domino Deo vestro, ut benedicam panibus tuis et aquis et auferam infirmitatem de medio tui. ^{26}Non erit abortiens nec sterilis in terra tua; numerum dierum tuorum implebo. ^{27}Terrorem meum mittam in praecursum tuum et perturbabo omnem populum, ad quem ingredieris; cunctorumque inimicorum tuorum coram te terga vertam ^{28}emittens crabrones prius, qui fugabunt Hevaeum et Chananaeum et Hetthaeum, antequam introeas. ^{29}Non eiciam eos a facie tua anno uno, ne terra in solitudinem redigatur, et multiplicentur contra te bestiae agri. ^{30}Paulatim expellam eos de conspectu tuo, donec augearis et possideas terram. ^{31}Ponam autem terminos tuos a mari Rubro usque ad mare Palaestinorum et a deserto usque ad Fluvium. Tradam manibus vestris habitatores terrae et eiciam eos de conspectu vestro. ^{32}Non inibis cum eis foedus nec cum diis eorum. ^{33}Non habitent in terra tua,

n. Gk Vg: Heb *he*

³³They shall not dwell in your land, lest they make you sin against me; for if you serve their gods, it will surely be a snare to you."

9. THE COVENANT IS RATIFIED*

A sacred meal and sprinkling with blood

Ex 6:23; 18:21–26; 19:20; 28:1
Lev 10:1–2
Num 11:16
Lk 10:1

24 ¹And he said to Moses, "Come up to the LORD, you and Aaron, Nadab, and Abihu, and seventy of the elders of Israel, and worship afar off. ²Moses alone shall come near to the LORD; but the others shall not come near, and the people shall not come up with him."

---

*24:1–18. It was common practice for those peoples to ratify pacts by means of a rite or a meal. This section recounts a meal or rite whereby the Covenant was sealed. This event is very important for salvation history; it prefigures the sacrifice of Jesus Christ, which brought in the New Covenant.

The usual interpretation is that there were two stages in this ratification—first involving Moses and the elders, that is, the authorities (vv. 1–2, 9–11) and then the entire people (vv. 3–8). Other commentators think that there was only one ceremony, relayed by two different traditions. In both cases the final editor has tried to make it clear that both the leaders and the people themselves took part in and formally accepted the divine Covenant and all that it laid down.

24:1–11. Nabab and Abihu are priests of Aaron's line (cf. 6:33; 28:1; Lev 10:1–2); the elders represent the people on important matters. The ceremony takes place

on the top of the mountain, which all the leaders ascended—Moses; the priests, holders of religious authority; and the elders, that is, the civil and legal authorities (cf. 18:21–26).

Only Moses has direct access to God (v. 2), but all are able to see God without dying: what they see far outstrips in brilliance and luxury the great palaces and temples of the East (cf. the vision of Isaiah in Is 6:10). In fact, they all share the same table with God (v. 11): the description is reminiscent of a royal banquet, in which the guests are treated on a par with the host: thus, the king of Babylonia will show his benevolence to King Jehoiachin by having him as his dinner guest (cf. 2 Kings 25:27–30). But it is, above all, a ritual banquet in which sharing the same table shows the intimate relationship that exists between God and the leaders of the people, and shows too that both parties are mutually responsible for the Covenant now being sealed.

---

ne peccare te faciant in me, si servieris diis eorum; quod tibi certo erit in scandalum». ¹Moysi quoque dixit: «Ascende ad Dominum, tu et Aaron, Nadab et Abiu et septuaginta senes ex Israel, et adorabitis procul. ²Solusque Moyses ascendet ad Dominum, et illi non appropinquabunt, nec populus ascendet cum eo». ³Venit ergo Moyses et narravit plebi omnia verba Domini atque iudicia; responditque omnis populus una voce: «Omnia verba Domini, quae locutus est, faciemus». ⁴Scripsit autem Moyses universos sermones Domini; et mane consurgens aedificavit altare a radices montis et duodecim lapides

³Moses came and told the people all the words of the LORD and all the ordinances; and all the people answered with one voice, and said, "All the words which the LORD has spoken we will do." ⁴And Moses wrote all the words of the LORD. And he rose early in the morning, and built an altar at the foot of the mountain, and twelve pillars, according to the twelve tribes of Israel. ⁵And he sent young men of the people of Israel, who offered burnt offerings and sacrificed peace offerings of oxen to the LORD. ⁶And Moses took half of the blood and put it in basins, and half of the blood he threw against the altar. ⁷Then he took the book of the covenant, and read it in the hearing of the people; and they said, "All that the LORD has spoken we will do, and we will be obedient." ⁸And Moses took the blood and threw it upon the

Ex 19:8
Josh 24:16–24
Heb 9:19

Josh 4:3–9,
20–24;
24:26–27

1 Kings 18:31

Mt 26:28
Mk 14:24
Lk 22:20

24:3–8. The ceremony takes place on the slope of the mountain; Moses alone is the intermediary; but the protagonists are God and his people. The ceremony has two parts—the reading and accepting of the clauses of the Covenant (vv. 3–4), that is, the Words (Decalogue) and the laws (the so-called Code of the Covenant); then comes the offering which seals the pact.

The acceptance of the clauses is done with all due solemnity, using the ritual formula: "all the words which the Lord has spoken we will do". The people, who have already made this commitment (19:8), now repeat it after listening to Moses' address (v. 3) and just before being sprinkled with the blood of the offering. The binding force of the pact is thereby assured.

The offering has some very ancient features—the altar specially built for the occasion (v. 4; cf. 20:25); the twelve pillars, probably set around the altar; the young men, not priests, making the offerings; and particularly the sprinkling with

blood which is at the very core of the rite.

The dividing of the blood in two (one half for the altar which represents God, and the other for the people) means that both commit themselves to the requirements of the Covenant. There is evidence that nomadic peoples used to seal their pacts with the blood of sacrificed animals. But there are no traces in the Bible of blood being used in that way. This rite probably has deeper significance: given that blood, which stands for life (cf. Gen 4), belongs to God alone, it must only be poured on the altar or used to anoint people who are consecrated to God, such as priests (cf. Ex 29:19–22). When Moses sprinkled the blood of the offering on to the entire people, he was consecrating it, making it divine property and "a kingdom of priests" (cf. 19:3–6). The Covenant therefore is not only a commitment to obey its precepts but, particularly, the right to belong to the holy nation, which is God's possession. At the Last Supper, when instituting the

---

per duodecim tribus Israel. ⁵Misitque iuvenes de filiis Israel, et obtulerunt holocausta; immolaveruntque victimas pacificas Domino vitulos. ⁶Tulit itaque Moyses dimidiam partem sanguinis et misit in crateras; partem autem residuam respersit super altare. ⁷Assumensque volumen foederis legit, audiente populo, qui dixerunt: «Omnia, quae locutus est Dominus, faciemus et erimus oboedientes». ⁸Ille vero

347

1 Cor 11:25
Heb 9:20;
10:29; 13:20 people, and said, "Behold the blood of the covenant which the LORD has made with you in accordance with all these words."

⁹Then Moses and Aaron, Nadab, and Abihu, and seventy of the

Ex 33:20
Ezek 1–26
Rev 4:2–3 elders of Israel went up, ¹⁰and they saw the God of Israel; and there was under his feet as it were a pavement of sapphire stone, like the very heaven for clearness. ¹¹And he did not lay his hand on the chief men of the people of Israel; they beheld God, and ate and drank.

Ex 31:18;
32:15ff; 34:1,
28ff
Moses spends forty days on the mountain

Deut 4:13, 36;
5:22; 9:9, 15;
10:1–5 ¹²The LORD said to Moses, "Come up to me on the mountain, and wait there; and I will give you the tables of stone, with the law Josh 1:1 and the commandment, which I have written for their instruction."

Mt 17:1 ¹³So Moses rose with his servant Joshua, and Moses went up into

Ex 40:34–35
1 Kings 8:10 the mountain of God. ¹⁴And he said to the elders, "Tarry here for us, until we come to you again; and, behold, Aaron and Hur are Mt 17:1
Mk 9:2 with you; whoever has a cause, let him go to them."

Eucharist, Jesus uses the very same terms, "blood of the Covenant", thereby indicating the nature of the new people of God who, having been redeemed, is fully "the holy people of God" (cf. Mt 26:27 and par.; 1 Cor 11:23–25).

The Second Vatican Council has this to say about the connexion between the New and Old Covenants, pointing out that the Church is the true people of God: "God chose the Israelite race to be his own people and established a covenant with it. He gradually instructed this people—in its history manifesting both himself and the decree of his will—and made it holy unto himself. All these things, however, happened as a preparation and figure of that new and perfect covenant which was to be ratified in Christ, and of the fuller revelation which

was to be given through the Word of God made flesh. [. . .] Christ instituted this new covenant, namely the new covenant in his blood (cf. 1 Cor 11:25); he called a race made up of Jews and Gentiles which would be one, not according to the flesh, but in the Spirit, and this race would be the new People of God" (*Lumen gentium*, 4 and 9).

24:12–18. Once more Moses goes up the mountain; this time it has to do with the tragic episode of the golden calf (cf. Ex 32). Laws were normally written on stone, not on clay tablets, perhaps to convey the idea of their perennial nature (this, for example, was true of the Code of Hammurabi, which was carved on a huge dioritic stone). St Paul, on the other hand, in order to stress, rather, the interi-

---

sumptum sanguinem respersit in populum et ait: «Hic est sanguis foederis, quod pepigit Dominus vobiscum super cunctis sermonibus his». ⁹Ascenderuntque Moyses et Aaron, Nadab et Abiu et septuaginta de senioribus Israel. ¹⁰Et viderunt Deum Israel, et sub pedibus eius quasi opus lapidis sapphirini et quasi ipsum caelum, cum serenum est. ¹¹Nec in electos filiorum Israel misit manum suam; videruntque Deum et comederunt ac biberunt. ¹²Dixit autem Dominus ad Moysen: «Ascende ad me in montem et esto ibi; daboque tibi tabulas lapideas et legem ac mandata, quae scripsi, ut doceas eos». ¹³Surrexerunt Moyses et Iosue minister eius; ascendensque Moyses in montem Dei ¹⁴senioribus ait:

¹⁵Then Moses went up on the mountain, and the cloud covered the mountain. ¹⁶The glory of the LORD settled on Mount Sinai, and the cloud covered it six days; and on the seventh day he called to Moses out of the midst of the cloud. ¹⁷Now the appearance of the glory of the LORD was like a devouring fire on the top of the mountain in the sight of the people of Israel. ¹⁸And Moses entered the cloud, and went up on the mountain. And Moses was on the mountain forty days and forty nights.

Deut 4:36
2 Cor 3:18

Deut 9:9
Ex 34:28
Lk 9:34

10. INSTRUCTIONS FOR THE SANCTUARY*

Contributions for the sanctuary

25 ¹The LORD said to Moses, ²"Speak to the people of Israel, that they take for me an offering; from every man whose

Ex 35:4–29
Lev 7:14
Num 15:19–21

ority of the law, will say that the Gospel message is inscribed on our hearts (cf. 2 Cor 3:3). In this narrative the tables of stone are the symbol of the faithfulness that the people failed to maintain and which God's mercy reconstituted (cf. the note on 32:1–6).

Verses 15–18, which probably come from the Priestly tradition, describe the theophany by using the language of worship, speaking of the "glory of the Lord". This is the divine presence made visible in the form of a bright, yet opaque, cloud (v. 16), the same cloud as will later cover the ark (cf. 40:34–35) and, later still, the temple (cf. 1 Kings 8:10–11). It is also a devouring fire, which nothing can resist (cf. Deut 4:36). Both images symbolize the transcendence of God. The Holy Spirit, too, will come in the form of tongues of fire (cf. Acts 2:3–4). On the profound meaning of the cloud, cf. *Catechism of the Catholic Church*, 697.

God made Moses go through a week of preparation before making himself visible to him on the seventh day; then Moses stayed on the mountain for forty days, in close contact with the Lord. These periods of time are not meant to be exact but rather to show how intense Moses' relationship with God was; they will be evoked when important events are narrated later: thus, Elijah walked for forty days in search of God (cf. 1 Kings 19:8) and Jesus will spend forty days in the desert before beginning his public life (cf. Mt 4:2).

*25:1—31:18. These chapters cover the very detailed rules about the building of the ark and the tabernacle, rules which will be applied later, as we are told at the end of the book, when the Lord has re-established the order broken by the Israelites' adoration of the golden calf (cf. chaps. 35–40). The Priestly tradi-

«Exspectate hic, donec revertamur ad vos. Habetis Aaron et Hur vobiscum; si quid natum fuerit quaestionis, referetis ad eos». ¹⁵Cumque ascendisset Moyses in montem, operuit nubes montem; ¹⁶et habitavit gloria Domini super Sinai tegens illum nube sex diebus; septimo autem die vocavit eum de medio caliginis. ¹⁷Erat autem species gloriae Domini quasi ignis ardens super verticem montis in conspectu filiorum Israel. ¹⁸Ingressusque Moyses medium nebulae ascendit in montem; et fuit ibi quadraginta diebus et quadraginta noctibus. ¹Locutusque est Dominus ad Moysen dicens: ²«Loquere

heart makes him willing you shall receive the offering for me.
³And this is the offering which you shall receive from them: gold,
silver, and bronze, ⁴blue and purple and scarlet stuff and fine
twined linen, goats' hair, ⁵tanned rams' skins, goatskins, acacia
wood, ⁶oil for the lamps, spices for the anointing oil and for the
fragrant incense, ⁷onyx stones, and stones for setting, for the
ephod and for the breastpiece. ⁸And let them make me a sanctuary, that I may dwell in their midst. ⁹According to all that I show

Ex 25:40;
26:30; 27:8

---

tion, to whom both sections are attributed, has combined very ancient traditions about worship in the desert with
other more recent ones; the construction
of the temple of Zerubbabel (Ezek
40–48) will be built in line with the rules
given here.

Thus, it is historically probable that
the Israelite caravans in the desert set up
a special tent for the purposes of worship—the tabernacle—in which was set
the ark, a portable object which was specially venerated and in which were kept
the three symbols of Israel's deliverance—Moses' rod, the urn with the
manna (cf. Ex 16:33) and the tables of the
Law. All the details regarding sizes, materials and design reflect later buildings,
such as the temple of Shiloh and, particularly, Solomon's temple of Jerusalem.

The sacred writer has woven a
number of doctrinal themes into the narrative: firstly, he is making it clear that
the worship offered in the temple is perfectly orthodox, because everything
about the temple goes right back to
Moses; he is justifying the existence of a
temple, and the meaning thereof: the
tabernacle in the desert and, later on, the
temple are a visible sign of the presence
of God among his people; therefore, religious worship will always be an ack-

nowledgment of God's active presence
among mankind. Finally, the building of
the tabernacle is quite evocative of the
account of creation (cf. Gen 1:1–2:4):
there is a planned order, because God
himself stipulates how everything is to be
"made"; and, finally, Moses finishes his
great work (Ex 40:33; cf. Gen 2:2) and
blesses the craftsmen on that day (cf. Ex
39; 43; cf. Gen 2:3). In this way it is
shown that the temple and its worship
point to a new world.

With even more reason the Church is
very careful to ensure that its liturgy and
everything about it is done with dignity,
for it is celebrating the mystery of Christ
and prefiguring the heavenly liturgy: "In
the earthly liturgy we take part in a fore-
taste of that heavenly liturgy which is
celebrated in the Holy City of Jerusalem
toward which we journey as pilgrims,
where Christ is sitting at the right hand of
God, Minister of the holies and of the
true tabernacle. With all the warriors of
the heavenly army we sing a hymn of
glory to the Lord; venerating the memory
of the saints, we hope for some part and
fellowship with them; we eagerly await
the Saviour, Our Lord Jesus Christ, until
he, our life, shall appear and we too will
appear with him in glory" (Vatican II,
Sacrosanctum Concilium, 8).

---

filiis Israel, ut tollant mihi donaria; ab omni homine, qui offert ultroneus, accipietis ea. ³Haec sunt
autem, quae accipere debetis: aurum et argentum et aes, ⁴hyacinthum et purpuram coccumque et
byssum, pilos caprarum ⁵et pelles arietum rubricatas pellesque delphini et ligna acaciae, ⁶oleum ad
luminaria concinnanda, aromata in unguentum et in thymiama boni odoris, ⁷lapides onychinos et

you concerning the pattern of the tabernacle, and of all its furni- Num 8:4
ture, so you shall make it.

The ark

Ex 37:1–9

10"They shall make an ark of acacia wood; two cubits and a half
shall be its length, a cubit and a half its breadth, and a cubit and a
half its height. 11And you shall overlay it with pure gold, within
and without shall you overlay it, and you shall make upon it a

---

25:1–9. The sanctuary will be built from
things freely offered by the Israelites. The
Hebrew word *terumáh*, here translated as
"offering" (v. 2), is a sort of tribute in the
sense that each person has to decide in
conscience how much to give; basically it
is a religious matter, to do with sacrifice
or offering (cf. Lev 7:14; Num 15:19–21).

Worship is such a worthy thing that
only precious metals and valuable objects
should be used; some of the terms used
here make little sense today (cf.
"goatskins": v. 5; literally, "porpoise
skins" or the skin of a kind of badger, or
of an animal now extinct, perhaps a kind
of dolphin found in the Red Sea). The
Church too has taken a lot of care over
the aesthetics of places of worship and
the objects used for worship. "Holy
Mother Church has always been the
patron of the fine arts and has ever
sought their noble ministry, to the end
especially that all things set apart for use
in divine worship should be worthy,
becoming, and beautiful signs and symbols of things supernatural" (Vatican II,
Sacrosanctum Concilium, 122).

Sanctuary or tabernacle (vv. 8-9) are
two terms meaning the same thing; they
refer to the holy tent, that is, the tent in
which the ark was kept and where God
made himself present to the Hebrews.
The terminology helps to highlight the

fact that God is transcendent and at the
same time he is near his people: God
dwells in heaven, but he communicates
with his people in this *shekináh* (dwelling-
place). St Stephen recalls the true meaning of the sanctuary when he cites
Isaiah's words (66:1–2) to show that "the
Most High does not dwell in houses
made with hands" (Acts 7:48; cf. Heb
8:2; Rev 15:5).

25:10–22. The ark was a rectangular
chest, made of acacia wood and covered
with gold inside and out. A Hebrew cubit
was the distance between the elbow and
the tip of the middle finger; this means
the ark would have measured approximately 1.25 x .70 metres (4 x 2.3 feet).
The ark's accessories (rings and poles)
are designed to make it easier to carry
when moving from place to place in the
desert. The ark was of very great importance in the early history of Israel and
therefore it was given different names
according to where it was or the traditions which mention it. Thus, it is called
the Ark of God (in Joshua), the Ark of
the Lord (in 1 Samuel), the Ark of the
Law (in Deuteronomy), the Ark of
Witness. It was a memorial to the
Covenant between God and his people,
because it contained the tables of the
Covenant; but, first and foremost, it was

---

gemmas ad ornandum ephod ac pectorale. 8Facientque mihi sanctuarium, et habitabo in medio eorum.
9Iuxta omnem similitudinem habitaculi, quam ostendi tibi, et omnium vasorum in cultum eius:
sicque facietis illud. 10Arcam de lignis acaciae compingent; cuius longitudo habeat duos semis cubitos,

molding of gold round about. [12]And you shall cast four rings of gold for it and put them on its four feet, two rings on the one side of it, and two rings on the other side of it. [13]You shall make poles of acacia wood, and overlay them with gold. [14]And you shall put the poles into the rings on the sides of the ark, to carry the ark by them. [15]The poles shall remain in the rings of the ark; they shall not be taken from it. [16]And you shall put into the ark the testimony which I shall give you. [17]Then you shall make a mercy seat[o] of pure gold; two cubits and a half shall be its length, and a cubit and a half its breadth. [18]And you shall make two cherubim of gold; of hammered work shall you make them, on the two ends of the mercy seat. [19]Make one cherub on the one end, and one cherub on the other end; of one piece with the mercy seat shall you make the cherubim on its two ends. [20]The cherubim shall spread out their wings above, overshadowing the mercy seat with their wings, their faces one to another; toward the mercy seat shall the faces of the cherubim be. [21]And you shall put the mercy seat on the top of the ark; and in the ark you shall put the testimony that I shall give you. [22]There I will meet with you, and from above the mercy seat, from between the two cherubim that are upon the ark of the testimony, I will speak with you of all that I will give you in commandment for the people of Israel.

2 Sam 6:7
Ex 24:12
Heb 9:4
Lev 16:12–15
Rom 3:25
Heb 9:5

Heb 9:4

Ex 29:42
Num 7:89
1 Sam 4:4
2 Sam 6:2
2 Kings 19:15
Ps 99:1
Heb 9:5

---

a symbol of the presence of the Lord (v. 22; cf. 1 Sam 4:4; 2 Sam 6:2).

The ark was covered with a thick golden plate called the Mercy Seat, because on the Day of Atonement (cf. Lev 16:15–16) the priest used to sprinkle it with the blood of victims, imploring forgiveness of the people's sins. St Paul called Jesus Christ an "expiation" (from the same Hebrew word as "mercy seat")

because by Christ's blood man attains the remission of sins (cf. Rom 3:25).

On the two ends of the mercy seat were two cherubim, possibly two figures of winged animals which stood for the spiritual beings or angels who are ministers close to God. These figures, together with the mercy seat, formed a sort of majestic throne from which God would speak (v. 22; cf. Num 7: 89); hence the

---

latitudo cubitum et dimidium, altitudo cubitum similiter ac semissem. [11]Et deaurabis eam auro mundissimo intus et foris; faciesque supra coronam auream per circuitum [12]et conflabis ei quattuor circulos aureos, quos pones in quattuor arcae pedibus: duo circuli sint in latere uno et duo in altero. [13]Facies quoque vectes de lignis acaciae et operies eos auro; [14]inducesque per circulos, qui sunt in arcae lateribus, ut portetur in eis; [15]qui semper erunt in circulis nec umquam extrahentur ab eis. [16]Ponesque in arcam testimonium, quod dabo tibi. [17]Facies et propitiatorium de auro mundissimo; duos cubitos et dimidium tenebit longitudo eius, et cubitum ac semissem latitudo. [18]Duos quoque cherubim aureos et productiles facies ex utraque parte propitiatorii, [19]cherub unus sit in latere uno et alter in altero; ex propitiatorio facies cherubim in utraque parte eius. [20]Expandent alas sursum et operient alis suis propitiatorium; respicientque se mutuo, versis vultibus in propitiatorium, [21]quo operienda est arca, in qua pones

---

o. Or *cover*

The table for the offertory bread

Ex 37:10–16
Heb 9:2

²³"And you shall make a table of acacia wood; two cubits shall be its length, a cubit its breadth, and a cubit and a half its height. ²⁴You shall overlay it with pure gold, and make a molding of gold around it. ²⁵And you shall make around it a frame a handbreadth wide, and a molding of gold around the frame. ²⁶And you shall make for it four rings of gold, and fasten the rings to the four corners at its four legs. ²⁷Close to the frame the rings shall lie, as holders for the poles to carry the table. ²⁸You shall make the poles of acacia wood, and overlay them with gold, and the table shall be carried with these. ²⁹And you shall make its plates and dishes for incense, and its flagons and bowls with which to pour libations; of pure gold you shall make them. ³⁰And you shall set the bread of the Presence on the table before me always.

Lev 24:5–9
Num 4:7
1 Sam 21:4–7

Heb 9:2

The lampstand

Ex 37:17–24
Lev 24:2–4
Rev 1:12

³¹"And you shall make a lampstand of pure gold. The base and the shaft of the lampstand shall be made of hammered work; its cups, its capitals, and its flowers shall be of one piece with it; ³²and

form of words, "the Lord who is enthroned on the cherubim" (1 Sam 4:4; 2 Kings 19:15; Ps 99:1).

25:23–30. The table of the bread of the Presence (cf. 37:10–16) was also made of acacia wood and covered with gold. Every sabbath twelve cakes of bread had to be placed on it separated from each other by bowls of incense (cf. Lev 24:5–9). They served to show that the bread of each day originates in the goodness of the Lord (cf. the Our Father). They were given the name "bread of the Presence" (1 Sam 21:7)

because they were placed on this table in front of the ark, but they were also called "holy" or "consecrated" bread (cf. 1 Sam 21:4–6) and "perpetual" bread (Num 4:7; not reflected in RSV). Only priests could eat them, although David when he was an outlaw had no qualms about eating them (1 Sam 21:4–7), a fact which our Lord made use of to talk about freedom of spirit as against sticking to the letter of the law (cf. Mt 2:23–28).

25:31–40. The seven-branched lampstand or *menoráh* (cf. 37:17–24) had to

testimonium, quod dabo tibi. ²²Et conveniam te ibi et loquar ad te supra propitiatorium de medio duorum cherubim, qui erunt super arcam testimonii, cuncta, quae mandabo per te filiis Israel. ²³Facies et mensam de lignis acaciae habentem duos cubitos longitudinis et in latitudine cubitum et in altitudine cubitum ac semissem. ²⁴Et inaurabis eam auro purissimo; faciesque illi coronam auream per circuitum. ²⁵Facies quoque ei limbum altum quattuor digitis per circuitum et super illum coronam auream. ²⁶Quattuor quoque circulos aureos praeparabis et pones eos in quattuor angulis eiusdem mensae per singulos pedes. ²⁷Iuxta limbum erunt circuli aurei, ut mittantur vectes per eos, et possit mensa portari. ²⁸Ipsosque vectes facies de lignis acaciae et circumdabis auro, et per ipsos subvehitur mensa. ²⁹Parabis et acetabula ac phialas, vasa et cyathos, in quibus offerenda sunt libamina, ex auro purissimo. ³⁰Et pones super mensam panes propositionis in conspectu meo semper. ³¹Facies et candelabrum ductile de auro mundissimo: basis et hastile eius: scyphi ac sphaerulae ac flores in unum efformentur. ³²Sex calami

there shall be six branches going out of its sides, three branches of the lampstand out of one side of it and three branches of the lampstand out of the other side of it; ³³three cups made like almonds, each with capital and flower, on one branch, and three cups made like almonds, each with capital and flower, on the other branch—so for the six branches going out of the lampstand; ³⁴and on the lampstand itself four cups made like almonds, with their capitals and flowers, ³⁵and a capital of one piece with it under each pair of the six branches going out from the lampstand. ³⁶Their capitals and their branches shall be of one piece with it,

Rev 1:12 the whole of it one piece of hammered work of pure gold. ³⁷And you shall make the seven lamps for it; and the lamps shall be set up so as to give light upon the space in front of it. ³⁸Its snuffers

Heb 8:5 and their trays shall be of pure gold. ³⁹Of a talent of pure gold

Acts 7:44 shall it be made, with all these utensils. ⁴⁰And see that you make

Heb 8:5 them after the pattern for them, which is being shown you on the mountain.

Ex 33:7–11;
36:8–19
Heb 9:11–24 **The tabernacle**

26 ¹"Moreover you shall make the tabernacle with ten curtains of fine twined linen and blue and purple and scarlet stuff; with cherubim skilfully worked shall you make them. ²The length of each curtain shall be twenty-eight cubits, and the

---

be made of gold and weighed a talent (that is, about 32 kgs or 70 lbs). Its description is difficult to follow, but we can see that it was the item that involved most artistry. We do not know exactly what the seven branches symbolized; maybe the lampstand was meant to stand for a beautiful tree, another sign that the sanctuary was the place of the presence of God, who shel-

ters the faithful (see also the note on Num 8:1–4).

26:1–14. The sanctuary is described in minute detail, but it is not easy to visualize it exactly, due to the fact that it uses technical terms we are not familiar with nowadays. We can see that there were four curtains: the first, about 17 x 12 metres (56 x 40 feet), was made of linen

---

egredientur de lateribus, tres ex uno latere et tres ex altero. ³³Tres scyphi quasi in nucis modum in calamo uno sphaerulaeque simul et flores; et tres similiter scyphi instar nucis in calam altero sphaerulaeque simul et flores: hoc erit opus sex calamorum, qui producendi sunt de hastili. ³⁴In ipso autem hastili candelabri erunt quattuor scyphi in nucis modum sphaerulaeque et flores. ³⁵Singulae sphaerulae sub binis calamis per tria loca, qui simul sex fiunt, procedentes de hastili uno. ³⁶Sphaerulae igitur et calami unum cum ipso erunt, totum ductile de auro purissimo. ³⁷Facies et lucernas septem et pones eas super candelabrum, ut luceant in locum ex adverso. ³⁸Emunctoria quoque et vasa, in quibus emuncta condantur, fient de auro purissimo. ³⁹Omne pondus candelabri, cum universis vasis suis, habebit talentum auri purissimi. ⁴⁰Inspice et fac secundum exemplar, quod tibi in monte monstratum est. ¹Habitaculum vero ita facies: decem cortinas de bysso retorta et hyacintho ac purpura coccoque cum cherubim opere polymito facies. ²Longitudo cortinae unius habebit viginti octo cubitos, latitudo quat-

breadth of each curtain four cubits; all the curtains shall have one measure. ³Five curtains shall be coupled to one another; and the other five curtains shall be coupled to one another. ⁴And you shall make loops of blue on the edge of the outmost curtain in the first set; and likewise you shall make loops on the edge of the outmost curtain in the second set. ⁵Fifty loops you shall make on the one curtain, and fifty loops you shall make on the edge of the curtain that is in the second set; the loops shall be opposite one another. ⁶And you shall make fifty clasps of gold, and couple the curtains one to the other with the clasps, that the tabernacle may be one whole.

⁷"You shall also make curtains of goats' hair for a tent over the tabernacle; eleven curtains shall you make. ⁸The length of each curtain shall be thirty cubits, and the breadth of each curtain four cubits; the eleven curtains shall have the same measure. ⁹And you shall couple five curtains by themselves, and six curtains by themselves, and the sixth curtain you shall double over at the front of the tent. ¹⁰And you shall make fifty loops on the edge of the curtain that is outmost in one set, and fifty loops on the edge of the curtain which is outmost in the second set.

¹¹"And you shall make fifty clasps of bronze, and put the clasps into the loops, and couple the tent together that it may be one whole. ¹²And the part that remains of the curtains of the tent, the half curtain that remains, shall hang over the back of the taber-

---

and consisted of ten tapestries. The second (19 x 13 metres), was made of goatskin. Over these there were two further coverings, one made of goatskin, the other of fine leather, probably ramskin.

Although the sanctuary looked like the tents the Israelites used, it was clearly a very majestic sort of tent: the richness of the materials used in it highlighted the great regard in which the worship of God was held and the conviction that God always deserved the very best they could offer him.

---

tuor cubitorum erit. Unius mensurae fient universae cortinae. ³Quinque cortinae sibi iungentur mutuo, et aliae quinque nexu simili cohaerebunt. ⁴Ansulas hyacinthinas in latere facies cortinae unius in extremitate iuncturae et similiter facies in latere cortinae extremae in iunctura altera. ⁵Quinquaginta ansulas facies in cortina una et quinquaginta ansulas facies in summitate cortinae, quae est in iunctura altera, ita insertas, ut ansa contra ansam veniat. ⁶Facies et quinquaginta fibulas aureas, quibus cortinarum vela iungenda sunt, ut unum habitaculum fiat. ⁷Facies et saga cilicina undecim pro tabernaculo super habitaculum. ⁸Longitudo sagi unius habebit triginta cubitos et latitudo quattuor; aequa erit mensura sagorum omnium. ⁹E quibus quinque iunges seorsum et sex sibi mutuo copulabis, ita ut sextum sagum in fronte tecti duplices. ¹⁰Facies et quinquaginta ansas in ora sagi ultimi iuncturae unius et quinquaginta ansas in ora sagi iuncturae alterius. ¹¹Facies et quinquaginta fibulas aeneas, quibus iungantur ansae, ut unum ex omnibus tabernaculum fiat. ¹²Quod autem superfuerit in sagis, quae parantur tecto, id est unum sagum, quod amplius est, ex medietate eius operies posteriora habituli; ¹³et cubitus ex una parte pendebit, et alter ex altera, qui plus est in longitudine sagorum tabernaculi utrumque latus

nacle. [13]And the cubit on the one side, and the cubit on the other side, of what remains in the length of the curtains of the tent shall hang over the sides of the tabernacle, on this side and that side, to cover it. [14]And you shall make for the tent a covering of tanned rams' skins and goatskins.

Ex 25:40; 36:20–34

The framework for the tabernacle

[15]"And you shall make upright frames for the tabernacle of acacia wood. [16]Ten cubits shall be the length of a frame, and a cubit and a half the breadth of each frame. [17]There shall be two tenons in each frame, for fitting together; so shall you do for all the frames of the tabernacle. [18]You shall make the frames for the tabernacle: twenty frames for the south side; [19]and forty bases of silver you shall make under the twenty frames, two bases under one frame for its two tenons, and two bases under another frame for its two tenons; [20]and for the second side of the tabernacle, on the north side twenty frames, [21]and their forty bases of silver, two bases under one frame, and two bases under another frame; [22]and for the rear of the tabernacle westward you shall make six frames. [23]And you shall make two frames for corners of the tabernacle in the rear; [24]they shall be separate beneath, but joined at the top, at the first ring; thus shall it be with both of them; they shall form the two corners. [25]And there shall be eight frames, with their bases of silver, sixteen bases; two bases under one frame, and two bases under another frame.

26:15–30. The mounting for the sanctuary (cf. 36:20–34) was made up of huge planks (about 4.20 x .60 metres; or 12 feet x 2 feet). The whole thing would have been about 12 metres long by 5 metres wide by 4 metres high (40 x 16 x 13 feet). So, the structure was similar to the temple to be rebuilt in due course in Jerusalem, but with the difference that the desert sanctuary could be dismantled and moved from place to place.

---

habitaculi protegens. [14]Facies et operimentum aliud pro tabernaculo de pellibus arietum rubricatis et super hoc rursum aliud operimentum de pellibus delphini. [15]Facies et tabulas stantes habitaculi de lignis acaciae, [16]quae singulae denos cubitos in longitudine habeant et in latitudine singulos ac semissem. [17]In tabula una duo pedes fient, quibus tabula alteri tabulae conectatur; atque in hunc modum cunctae tabulae habitaculi parabuntur. [18]Quarum viginti erunt in latere meridiano, quod vergit ad austrum; [19]quibus quadraginta bases argenteas fundes, ut binae bases singulis pedibus singularum tabularum subiciantur. [20]In latere quoque secundo habitaculi, quod vergit ad aquilonem, viginti tabulae erunt, [21]quadraginta habentes bases argenteas; binae bases singulis tabulis supponentur. [22]Ad occidentalem vero plagam in tergo habitaculi facies sex tabulas; [23]et rursum alias duas, quae in angulis erigantur, post tergum habitaculi. [24]Eruntque geminae a deorsum usque sursum in compaginem unam; ita erit duabus istis, pro duabus angulis erunt. [25]Et erunt simul tabulae octo, bases earum argenteae sedecim, duabus basibus per unam tabulam supputatis. [26]Facies et vectes de lignis acaciae, quinque ad continendas tabulas in uno latere habitaculi [27]et quinque alios in altero et eiusdem numeri in tergo ad occidentalem plagam;

²⁶"And you shall make bars of acacia wood, five for the frames of the one side of the tabernacle, ²⁷and five bars for the frames of the other side of the tabernacle, and five bars for the frames of the side of the tabernacle at the rear westward. ²⁸The middle bar, halfway up the frames, shall pass through from end to end. ²⁹You shall overlay the frames with gold, and shall make their rings of gold for holders for the bars; and you shall overlay the bars with gold. ³⁰And you shall erect the tabernacle according to the plan for it which has been shown you on the mountain.

The veil

³¹"And you shall make a veil of blue and purple and scarlet stuff and fine twined linen; in skilled work shall it be made, with cherubim; ³²and you shall hang it upon four pillars of acacia overlaid with gold, with hooks of gold, upon four bases of silver. ³³And you shall hang the veil from the clasps, and bring the ark of the testimony in thither within the veil; and the veil shall separate for you the holy place from the most holy. ³⁴You shall put the

Ex 36:35–38
1 Kings 6:16
Mt 27:51
Mk 15:38
Lk 23:45
Heb 6:19; 9:1–14, 24; 10:19ff

26:31–37. The holy of holies (or the most holy), *Sancta sanctorum*, and the holy place or *sanctum* were the two parts into which the space formed by the mounting was divided. The first, a room 4 x 4 metres, was the holiest place of all; in it was kept the ark, and was considered to be the place where the Lord dwelt. Only the high priest was permitted to enter this space—and even then only once a year on the Day of Atonement (cf. Lev 16); the Letter to the Hebrews portrays Christ as the only priest, who brings about the redemption of all mankind, once for all, by his sacrifice on the cross and his glorious entry into heaven (cf. Heb 9:1–14).

This way of isolating the most holy

place helped to show the transcendence of God. The veil (v. 31) was retained in the temple of Solomon (cf. 1 Kings 6:15–16) and in that of Herod (this was the veil that was torn in two at the moment of Christ's death, as a sign that a new era of salvation was beginning (cf. Mt 27:51) in which all mankind has direct access to God).

In the area known as the "holy" (*hekal*), the table of the bread was kept, and in front of it the seven-branched lampstand. Ordinary Jews could not go in here either (as the entrance veil or screen positioned here showed). But the richly-worked screen or veil separating the most holy from the holy place was much the more important.

---

²⁸vectis autem medius transibit per medias tabulas a summo usque ad summum. ²⁹Ipsasque tabulas deaurabis et fundes eis anulos aureos, per quos vectes tabulata contineant, quos operies laminis aureis. ³⁰Et eriges habitaculum iuxta exemplar, quod tibi in monte monstratum est. ³¹Facies et velum de hyacintho et purpura coccoque et bysso retorta, opere polymito, cum cherubim intextis. ³²Quod appendes in quattuor columnis de lignis acaciae, quae ipsae quidem deauratae erunt et habebunt uncos aureos, sed bases argenteas. ³³Inseres autem velum subter fibulas, intra quod pones arcam testimonii et quo sanctum et sanctum sanctorum dividentur. ³⁴Pones et propitiatorium super arcam testimonii in

mercy seat upon the ark of the testimony in the most holy place. [35]And you shall set the table outside the veil, and the lampstand on the south side of the tabernacle opposite the table; and you shall put the table on the north side.

The screen at the entrance

[36]"And you shall make a screen for the door of the tent, of blue and purple and scarlet stuff and fine twined linen, embroidered with needlework. [37]And you shall make for the screen five pillars of acacia, and overlay them with gold; their hooks shall be of gold, and you shall cast five bases of bronze for them.

Ex 38:1–7
1 Kings 8:64
Ezra 43:13–17

The altar of holocaust

27 [1]"You shall make the altar of acacia wood, five cubits long and five cubits broad; the altar shall be square, and its height shall be three cubits. [2]And you shall make horns for it on its four corners; its horns shall be of one piece with it, and you shall overlay it with bronze. [3]You shall make pots for it to receive its ashes, and shovels and basins and forks and firepans; all its utensils you shall make of bronze. [4]You shall also make for it a grating, a network of bronze; and upon the net you shall make four bronze rings at its four corners. [5]And you shall set it under the ledge of the altar so that the net shall extend halfway down the altar. [6]And you shall make poles for the altar, poles of acacia wood, and overlay them with bronze; [7]and the poles shall be put

Ex 29:12
1 Kings 1:50;
2:28
Rev 9:13

27:1–8. The altar of offering (cf. 38:1–7) was a kind of altar of acacia wood measuring 2 metres wide by 2 metres long by 1.20 metres high. On the four corners there were four horns, which would be anointed with the blood of sacrificed victims (cf. 29:12); by clinging to these horns, fugitives could win the right to asylum (cf. 1 Kings 50; 2:28).

Apparently the victims were not burnt on the altar (because the altar was made of material which could not resist heat); so, probably the animals were burned elsewhere (in line with the system laid down in 20:24), and the flame on the altar was symbolic.

---

sancto sanctorum [35]mensamque extra velum et contra mensam candelabrum in latere habitaculi meridiano; mensa enim stabit in parte aquilonis. [36]Facies et velum in introitu tabernaculi de hyacintho et purpura coccoque et bysso retorta opere plumarii. [37]Et quinque columnas deaurabis lignorum acaciae, ante quas ducetur velum, quarum erunt unci aurei et bases aeneae. [1]Facies et altare de lignis acaciae, quod habebit quinque cubitos in longitudine et totidem in latitudine, id est quadrum, et tres cubitos in altitudine. [2]Cornua autem per quattuor angulos ex ipso erunt, et operies illud aere. [3]Faciesque in usus eius lebetes ad suscipiendos cineres et vatilla et pateras atque fuscinulas et ignium receptacula; omnia vasa ex aere fabricabis. [4]Craticulamque facies ei in modum retis aeneam, per cuius quattuor angulos erunt quattuor anuli aenei, [5]et pones eam subter marginem altaris; eritque craticula usque ad altaris medium. [6]Facies et vectes altaris de lignis acaciae duos, quos operies laminis aeneis, [7]et induces per anulos; eruntque ex utroque latere altaris ad portandum. [8]Cavum ex tabulis facies illud; sicut tibi in monte

through the rings, so that the poles shall be upon the two sides of the altar, when it is carried. [8]You shall make it hollow, with boards; as it has been shown you on the mountain, so shall it be made.

The court of the tabernacle

Ex 38:9–20
1 Kings 6:36
Ezek 40:17–49

[9]"You shall make the court of the tabernacle. On the south side the court shall have hangings of fine twined linen a hundred cubits long for one side; [10]their pillars shall be twenty and their bases twenty, of bronze, but the hooks of the pillars and their fillets shall be of silver. [11]And likewise for its length on the north side there shall be hangings a hundred cubits long, their pillars twenty and their bases twenty, of bronze, but the hooks of the pillars and their fillets shall be of silver. [12]And for the breadth of the court on the west side there shall be hangings for fifty cubits, with ten pillars and ten bases. [13]The breadth of the court on the front to the east shall be fifty cubits. [14]The hangings for the one side of the gate shall be fifteen cubits, with three pillars and three bases. [15]On the other side the hangings shall be fifteen cubits, with three pillars and three bases. [16]For the gate of the court there shall be a screen twenty cubits long, of blue and purple and scarlet stuff and fine twined linen, embroidered with needlework; it shall have four pillars and with them four bases. [17]All the pillars around the court shall be filleted with silver; their hooks shall be of silver, and their bases of bronze. [18]The length of the court shall be a hundred

---

27:9–21. The courtyard of the sanctuary (cf. 38:9–20) was an ample rectangular space some 42 metres (138 ft) long by 20 metres wide. There were curtains all round this sacred space hung from posts; they separated it from the rest of the encampment. In the temple of Solomon and in the second temple built after the Exile, this area formed the courtyards (cf. 1 Kings 6:36) out of which Jesus had to expel the money changers for profaning the holy place (Mt 21:12–17).

The use of pure olive oil (vv. 20–21) is a further small indication of the value and quality of all the items used in worship.

---

monstratum est, sic facient. [9]Facies et atrium habitaculi, in cuius plaga australi contra meridiem erunt tentoria de bysso retorta: centum cubitos unum latus tenebit in longitudine [10]et columnas viginti et bases totidem aeneas et uncos columnarum anulosque earum argenteos. [11]Similiter in latere aquilonis: per longum erunt tentoria centum cubitorum, columnae viginti et bases aeneae eiusdem numeri et unci columnarum anulique earum argenti. [12]In latitudine vero atrii, quae respicit ad occidentem, erunt tentoria per quinquaginta cubitos et columnae decem basesque totidem. [13]In ea quoque atrii latitudine, quae respicit ad orientem, quinquaginta cubiti erunt, [14]in quibus quindecim cubitorum tentoria lateri uno deputabuntur columnaeque tres et bases totidem; [15]et in latere altero erunt tentoria, cubitos obtinentia quindecim, columnae tres et bases totidem. [16]In introitu vero atrii fiet velum cubitorum viginti, ex hyacintho et purpura coccoque et bysso retorta opere plumarii; columnas habebit quattuor cum basibus totidem. [17]Omnes columnae atrii per circuitum cinctae erunt anulis argenteis et unci earum erunt

cubits, the breadth fifty, and the height five cubits, with hangings of fine twined linen and bases of bronze. ¹⁹All the utensils of the tabernacle for every use, and all its pegs and all the pegs of the court, shall be of bronze.

Lev 24:2–4 **The oil for the lamps**

²⁰"And you shall command the people of Israel that they bring to you pure beaten olive oil for the light, that a lamp may be set up Ex 30:7–8 to burn continually. ²¹In the tent of meeting, outside the veil which 1 Sam 3:3 is before the testimony, Aaron and his sons shall tend it from evening to morning before the LORD. It shall be a statute for ever to be observed throughout their generations by the people of Israel.

Lev 8:10
Heb 5:4 **The priests' vestments**

28 ¹"Then bring near to you Aaron your brother, and his sons with him, from among the people of Israel, to serve me as priests—Aaron and Aaron's sons, Nadab and Abihu, Eleazar and Ithamar. ²And you shall make holy garments for Aaron your brother, for glory and for beauty. ³And you shall speak to all who have ability, whom I have endowed with an able mind, that they make Aaron's garments to consecrate him for my priesthood.

28:1–5. After these regulations about the sanctuary and its content the text now gives us the rules about priests. Priesthood in Israel was hereditary; it was the province of the sons of Aaron, and later on of the tribe of Levi; but the latter always regarded Aaron as their model, because God himself had made him priest (cf. 29:4–7). The priestly class will perform an important role, not only as those who maintain and perform the liturgy but also as defenders of the faith and transmitters of doctrine, especially from the Babylonian exile onwards. And from the time of the Maccabees the priests will be prominent in political history too.

The vestments worn by the priests show the importance that worship has: they have to be made of rich material and by expert craftspeople.

argentei et bases aeneae. ¹⁸In longitudine occupabit atrium cubitos centum, in latitudine quinquaginta, altitudo quinque cubitorum erit; fietque de bysso retorta, et habebit bases aeneas. ¹⁹Cuncta vasa habitaculi in omnes usus eius et omnes paxillos eius et omnes paxillos atrii ex aere facies. ²⁰Praecipe filiis Israel, ut afferant tibi oleum de arboribus olivarum purissimum piloque contusum, ut ardeat lucerna semper ²¹in tabernaculo conventus, extra velum, quod oppansum est testimonio. Et parabunt eam Aaron et filii eius, ut a vespere usque mane luceat coram Domino. Perpetuus erit cultus per successiones eorum a filiis Israel. ¹Applica quoque ad te Aaron fratrem tuum cum filiis suis de medio filiorum Israel, ut sacerdotio fungantur mihi: Aaron, Nadab et Abiu, Eleazar et Ithamar. ²Faciesque vestes sanctas Aaron fratri tuo in gloriam et decorem; ³et loqueris cunctis sapientibus corde, quos replevi spiritu prudentiae, ut faciant vestes Aaron, in quibus sanctificatus ministret mihi. ⁴Haec autem erunt vestimenta, quae facient: pectorale et ephod, tunicam et subuculam textam, tiaram et balteum. Facient vestimenta sancta Aaron fratri tuo et filiis eius, ut sacerdotio fungantur mihi; ⁵accipientque aurum et hyacinthum

⁴These are the garments which they shall make: a breastpiece, an ephod, a robe, a coat of checker work, a turban, and a girdle; they shall make holy garments for Aaron your brother and his sons to serve me as priests.
⁵"They shall receive gold, blue and purple and scarlet stuff, and fine twined linen.

The ephod

⁶And they shall make the ephod of gold, of blue and purple and scarlet stuff, and of fine twined linen, skilfully worked. ⁷It shall have two shoulder-pieces attached to its two edges, that it may be joined together. ⁸And the skilfully woven band upon it, to gird it on, shall be of the same workmanship and materials, of gold, blue and purple and scarlet stuff, and fine twined linen. ⁹And you shall take two onyx stones, and engrave on them the names of the sons of Israel, ¹⁰six of their names on the one stone, and the names of the remaining six on the other stone, in the order of their birth. ¹¹As a jeweller engraves signets, so shall you engrave the two stones with the names of the sons of Israel; you shall enclose them in settings of gold filigree. ¹²And you shall set the two stones upon the shoulder-pieces of the ephod, as stones of remembrance for the sons of Israel; and Aaron shall bear their names

Ex 39:2–7
1 Sam 2:18
2 Sam 6:14

Ex 30:16
Num 31:54

28:6–30. The ephod (cf. 39:2–7) was the garment specific to priests (cf. 1 Kings 2:18) and those who had a direct role in divine worship (for example, David: cf. 2 Kings 6:14). The same word was used for a receptacle used in the early sanctuaries of the north to hold the lots for divining the will of God (cf. 1 Kings 2:28; 14:18–20); it even came to mean an idolatrous object (cf. Judg 8:26–27). As a priestly vestment the ephod was distinctive of the high priest; it was a kind of apron which was held in place by a belt and two shoulder-pads; these latter each

had on it an onyxstone engraved with the names of the tribes (six and six).

The breastpiece of judgment was a richly-embroidered square piece of fabric placed over the chest and fixed to the shoulder pads and the belt. At the time when the sacred author wrote this, priestly vestments had undergone many changes; so it is not easy to work out what form they originally took. However, it does seem that the breastpiece had a kind of bag inside it where the Urim and Tummim were kept; these were devices used for ascertaining the will of God and

---

et purpuram coccumque et byssum. ⁶Facient autem ephod de auro et hyacintho ac purpura coccoque bysso retorta opere polymito. ⁷Duas fascias umerales habebit et in utroque latere summitatum suarum copulabitur cum eis. ⁸Et balteus super ephod ad constringendum, eiusdem operis et unum cum eo, erit ex auro et hyacintho et purpura coccoque et bysso retorta. ⁹Sumesque duos lapides onychinos et sculpes in eis nomina filiorum Israel: ¹⁰sex nomina in lapide uno et sex reliqua in altero, iuxta ordinem nativitatis eorum. ¹¹Opere sculptoris et caelatura gemmarii sculpes eos nominibus filiorum Israel, inclusos textura aurea; ¹²et pones duos lapides super fascias umerales ephod, lapides memorialis filiorum

before the LORD upon his two shoulders for remembrance. [13]And you shall make settings of gold filigree, [14]and two chains of pure gold, twisted like cords; and you shall attach the corded chains to the settings.

Ex 39:8–21 **The breastpiece**

[15]"And you shall make a breastpiece of judgment, in skilled work; like the work of the ephod you shall make it; of gold, blue and purple and scarlet stuff, and fine twined linen shall you make it. [16]It shall be square and double, a span its length and a span its breadth. [17]And you shall set in it four rows of stones. A row of sardius, topaz, and carbuncle shall be the first row; [18]and the second row an emerald, a sapphire, and a diamond; [19]and the third row a jacinth, an agate, and an amethyst; [20]and the fourth row a beryl, an onyx, and a jasper; they shall be set in gold filigree.

Ex 39:10–13
Ezek 28:13
Rev 21:19

Rev 21:12, 19 [21]There shall be twelve stones with their names according to the names of the sons of Israel; they shall be like signets, each engraved with its name, for the twelve tribes. [22]And you shall make for the breastpiece twisted chains like cords, of pure gold; [23]and you shall make for the breastpiece two rings of gold, and put the two rings on the two edges of the breastpiece. [24]And you shall put the two cords of gold in the two rings at the edges of the breastpiece; [25]the two ends of the two cords you shall attach to the two settings of filigree, and so attach it in front to the shoulder-pieces of the ephod. [26]And you shall make two rings of gold, and put them at the two ends of the breastpiece, on its inside edge next to the ephod. [27]And you shall make two rings of gold, and attach them in front to the lower part of the two shoulder-pieces of the ephod, at its joining above the skilfully woven band of the ephod. [28]And they shall bind the breastpiece by its rings to the rings of

Israel. Portabitque Aaron nomina eorum coram Domino super utrumque umerum ob recordationem. [13]Facies ergo margines textas ex auro [14]et duas catenulas ex auro purissimo quasi funiculos opus tortile et inseres catenulas tortas marginibus. [15]Pectorale quoque iudicii facies opere polymito, iuxta texturam ephod, ex auro, hyacintho et purpura coccoque et bysso retorta. [16]Quadrangulum erit et duplex; mensuram palmi habebit tam in longitudine quam in latitudine. [17]Ponesque in eo quattuor ordines lapidum: in primo versu erit lapis sardius et topazius et smaragdus; [18]in secundo carbunculus, sapphirus et iaspis; [19]in tertio hyacinthus, achates et amethystus; [20]in quarto chrysolithus, onychinus et beryllus. Inclusi auro erunt per ordines suos. [21]Habebuntque nomina filiorum Israel: duodecim nominibus caelabuntur, singuli lapides nominibus singulorum per duodecim tribus. [22]Facies in pectorali catenas quasi funiculos, opus tortile, ex auro purissimo; [23]et duos anulos aureos, quos pones in utraque pectoralis summitate; [24]catenasque aureas iunges anulis, qui sunt in marginalibus eius; [25]et ipsarum catenarum extrema duobus copulabis marginibus in fasciis umeralibus ephod in parte eius anteriore. [26]Facies et duos anulos aureos, quos pones in summitatibus pectoralis in ora interiore, quae respicit ephod. [27]Necnon et alios duos anulos aureos, qui ponendi sunt in utraque fascia umerali ephod deorsum, versus partem anteriorem eius iuxta iuncturam eius supra balteum ephod, [28]et stringatur pectorale anulis suis

the ephod with a lace of blue, that it may lie upon the skilfully woven band of the ephod, and that the breastpiece shall not come loose from the ephod. [29]So Aaron shall bear the names of the sons of Israel in the breastpiece of judgment upon his heart, when he goes into the holy place, to bring them to continual remembrance before the LORD. [30]And in the breastpiece of judgment you shall Jn 11:51 put the Urim and the Thummim, and they shall be upon Aaron's heart, when he goes in before the LORD; thus Aaron shall bear the judgment of the people of Israel upon his heart before the LORD continually.

The robe Ex 39:22–26

[31]"And you shall make the robe of the ephod all of blue. [32]It shall have in it an opening for the head, with a woven binding around the opening, like the opening in a garment,[p] that it may not be torn. [33]On its skirts you shall make pomegranates of blue and Sir 45:9 purple and scarlet stuff, around its skirts, with bells of gold between them, [34]a golden bell and a pomegranate, a golden bell and a pomegranate, roundabout on the skirts of the robe. [35]And it shall be upon Aaron when he ministers, and its sound shall be heard when he goes into the holy place before the LORD, and when he comes out, lest he die.

---

the fate of the sons of Israel (v. 30). This garment too had twelve stones on it with the names of the tribes, to show that the high priest's main function was to represent the people before God at the most solemn liturgical ceremonies.

28:31–35 The robe of the ephod (cf. 39:22–26) was an ample garment rather like a dalmatic which reached as far as the knees; it was all one piece and had an opening for the head. It was very richly worked, with pomegranates embroidered on the edges, and bells. The tingling of these bells (we do not know their origin) was later to become "a reminder to the sons of his people" (Sir 45:9) of the splendour of the glory of the Lord.

cum anulis ephod vitta hyacinthina, ut maneat supra balteum ephod, et a se invicem pectorale et ephod nequeant separari. [29]Portabitque Aaron nomina filiorum Israel in pectorali iudicii super cor suum, quando ingredietur sanctuarium: memoriale coram Domino in aeternum. [30]Pones autem in pectorali iudicii Urim et Tummim, quae erunt super cor Aaron, quando ingredietur coram Domino; et gestabit iudicium filiorum Israel super cor suum in conspectu Domini semper. [31]Facies et pallium ephod totum hyacinthinum, [32]in cuius medio supra erit capitium et ora per gyrum eius textilis, sicut in capitio loricae, ne rumpatur. [33]Deorsum vero, ad pedes eiusdem pallii per circuitum, quasi mala punica facies ex hyacintho et purpura et cocco, mixtis in medio tintinnabulis aureis; [34]ita ut sit tintinnabulum aureum inter singula mala punica. [35]Et vestietur eo Aaron in officio ministerii, ut audiatur sonitus, quando ingreditur et egreditur sanctuarium in conspectu Domini, et non moriatur. [36]Facies et laminam de auro purissimo, in qua sculpes opere caelatoris: «Sanctum Domino». [37]Ligabisque eam vitta hyacinthina, et

p. The Hebrew word is of uncertain meaning

Ex 39:27–31 **The tiara or turban**

Rev 13:16 [36]"And you shall make a plate of pure gold, and engrave on it, like the engraving of a signet, 'Holy to the LORD.' [37]And you shall fasten it on the turban by a lace of blue; it shall be on the front of the turban. [38]It shall be upon Aaron's forehead, and Aaron shall take upon himself any guilt incurred in the holy offering which the people of Israel hallow as their holy gifts; it shall always be upon his forehead, that they may be accepted before the LORD.

[39]"And you shall weave the coat in checker work of fine linen, and you shall make a turban of fine linen, and you shall make a girdle embroidered with needlework.

Ex 20:26
2 Sam 6:20–23 **The vestments of the priests**

[40]"And for Aaron's sons you shall make coats and girdles and caps; you shall make them for glory and beauty. [41]And you shall put them upon Aaron your brother, and upon his sons with him, and shall anoint them and ordain them and consecrate them, that they may serve me as priests. [42]And you shall make for them linen breeches to cover their naked flesh; from the loins to the thighs they shall reach; [43]and they shall be upon Aaron, and upon his

---

28:36–39. The headpiece (cf. 39:27–31 and Lev 8:9) comprised of a magnificent turban or tiara at the centre of which was gold plate probably shaped like a flower (as the Hebrew root of the word suggests: cf. Num 17:23), symbol of life and health, inscribed with the words "Holy to the Lord", that is, separated out from others to attend to the things of God. This motto came to be understood by the people as meaning that involuntary ritual sins were expiated for in the person of the high priest. The expiatory role of the priest will receive increasing emphasis as time goes on, until eventu-

ally it is his main role: "He [the high priest] is bound to offer sacrifice for his own sins as well as for those of the people" (Heb 5:3).

28:40–43. The other priests will also wear suitably rich vestments but much less elaborate than the high priest's. The last stipulation (vv. 42–43) is connected to the precept of Exodus 20:26 and shows the importance given to the smallest details of cult, avoiding any trace of immodesty (cf. 2 Sam 6:20–23).

On the meaning of ordination (v. 21) see the note on Ex 29:9.

---

erit super tiaram [38]super frontem Aaron. Portabitque Aaron iniquitatem contra sancta, quae sanctificabunt filii Israel in cunctis muneribus et donariis suis. Eritque lamina semper in fronte eius, ut placatus eis sit Dominus. [39]Texesque tunicam bysso et tiaram byssinam facies et balteum opere plumarii. [40]Porro filiis Aaron tunicas lineas parabis et balteos ac mitras in gloriam et decorem; [41]vestiesque his omnibus Aaron fratrem tuum et filios eius cum eo. Et unges eos et implebis manus eorum sanctificabisque illos, ut sacerdotio fungantur mihi. [42]Facies eis et feminalia linea, ut operiant carnem turpitudinis suae a renibus usque ad femora; [43]et utentur eis Aaron et filii eius, quando ingredientur tabernaculum conventus, vel quando appropinquant ad altare, ut ministrent in sanctuario, ne iniquitatis

sons, when they go into the tent of meeting, or when they come near the altar to minister in the holy place; lest they bring guilt upon themselves and die. This shall be a perpetual statute for him and for his descendants after him.

The ordination of priests*

Lev 8
Heb 7:26–28

29 [1]"Now this is what you shall do to them to consecrate them, that they may serve me as priests. Take one young bull and two rams without blemish, [2]and unleavened bread, unleavened cakes mixed with oil, and unleavened wafers spread with oil. You shall make them of fine wheat flour. [3]And you shall put them in one basket and bring them in the basket, and bring the bull and the two rams. [4]You shall bring Aaron and his sons to the door of the tent of meeting, and wash them with water. [5]And you shall take the garments, and put on Aaron the coat and the robe of the ephod, and the ephod, and the breastpiece, and gird him with the skilfully woven band of the ephod; [6]and you shall set the

Lev 2:4

Ex 30:18–21
Heb 10:22

Ex 28:36ff;
39:30

---

*29:1–9. The rite of consecration of priests is described in great detail: more information on some of the ritual is given in Leviticus 8. This ceremony presupposes that the priesthood was exercised only by members of the tribe of Levi—which did not happen until after the exile in Babylon. Prior to that, priestly functions were on occasions performed by non-Levites such as Micah (cf. Judg 17:5), Eleazar (cf. 1 Sam 7:1), and David himself (cf. 2 Sam 8:18). So, this ritual includes ancient elements as well as others which did not come in until the temple of Zerubbabel was built.

There were two stages in the consecration—anointing and offering. The anointing with oil showed that the man was being dedicated exclusively to the service of the Lord.

It seems that only the high priest had to be anointed (cf. Lev 16:32; 21:10), despite the allusions to the anointing of all priests (cf. Ex 28:41; 30:30; 40:15). Before being anointed he had to be rewashed all over and carefully dressed in priestly garments. All this shows the complete ritual purity required of the high priest (cf. the note on 30:22–33).

29:4. Ritual washing symbolized the inner cleanliness of those officiating at the ceremony. Each time they approached the altar they had to wash hands and feet (cf. 30:18–21); but on the day of consecration they had to be washed all over.

In Christian liturgy there are simple ablutions, meant to symbolize interior contrition; for example, the *Lavabo* at

---

rei moriantur: legitimum sempiternum erit Aaron et semini eius post eum. [1]Sed et hoc facies eis, ut mihi in sacerdotio consecrentur: tolle vitulum unum de armento et arietes duos immaculatos [2]panesque azymos et crustulas absque fermento, quae conspersa sint oleo, lagana quoque azyma oleo lita; de simila triticea cuncta facies [3]et posita in canistro offeres, vitulum quoque et duos arietes. [4]Aaron ac filios eius applicabis ad ostium tabernaculi conventus. Cumque laveris patrem cum filiis suis aqua, [5]indues Aaron vestimentis suis, id est subucula et tunica ephod et ephod et pectorali, quod constringes ei cingulo ephod; [6]et pones tiaram in capite eius et diadema sanctum super tiaram [7]et oleum unctionis

^{Ex 28:41;}
^{30:22–23;}
^{30:30; 40:15}
^{Lev 8:1ff; 21:10}
turban on his head, and put the holy crown upon the turban. ⁷And you shall take the anointing oil, and pour it on his head and anoint him. ⁸Then you shall bring his sons, and put coats on them, ⁹and you shall gird them with girdles^q and bind caps on them; and the priesthood shall be theirs by a perpetual statute. Thus you shall ordain Aaron and his sons.

Sacrifices at ordination*

^{Lev 1:5; 4:1–12} ¹⁰"Then you shall bring the bull before the tent of meeting. Aaron and his sons shall lay their hands upon the head of the bull, ¹¹and you shall kill the bull before the LORD, at the door of the tent of ^{Lev 4:7} meeting, ¹²and shall take part of the blood of the bull and put it upon the horns of the altar with your finger, and the rest of^r the blood you shall pour out at the base of the altar. ¹³And you shall take all the fat that covers the entrails, and the appendage of the

---

Mass is, primarily, a sign of repentance, accompanied by some words taken from Psalm 51.

29:9. "Thus you shall ordain": literally, "you will fill their hands" (cf. 28:41; Lev 8:22-29; Judg 17:5, 12). This is a technical term which probably refers to the fact that they were being given for the first time part of the victims offered in the sacrifice. In the Christian rite of ordination of priests, the bishop gives the ordinand the chalice and paten as a sign of the ministry being conferred on him.

*29:10–37. The offerings or sacrifices at the consecration of priests were three in number—one expiatory (vv. 10–14), according to the ritual to be found in Leviticus 4:1–12); the second a burnt offering (vv. 14–18) in praise and thanksgiving to God (cf. Lev 1); the last a con-

secration sacrifice (vv. 19–37) which was a type of offering and which also involved the unleavened bread (v. 32); as well as having its own features, it was a communion offering (vv. 31–37).

The importance of the consecration of the high priest can be seen in the fact that it included the holding of the three most solemn kinds of sacrifice. In the Old Testament sacrifices were the key acts of worship, because they were an external expression of communion with God, his sovereignty over creation, and his mercy in forgiving sin. Communion with God is to be seen above all in the communion or peace offerings, probably the oldest sort of sacrifice, in which God accepts the victim offered and receives a part of it on the altar, while the rest is eaten by the offerers at a holy meal. God's sovereignty over creation is seen in the holocaust or burnt offering, in

---

fundes super caput eius; atque hoc ritu consecrabitur. ⁸Filios quoque illius applicabis et indues tunicis lineis cingesque balteo ⁹et impones eis mitras; eruntque sacerdotes mihi iure perpetuo. Postquam impleveris manus Aaron et filiorum eius, ¹⁰applicabis et vitulum coram tabernaculo conventus; imponentque Aaron et filii eius manus super caput illius, ¹¹et mactabis eum in conspectu Domini, iuxta ostium tabernaculi conventus. ¹²Sumptumque de sanguine vituli, pones super cornua altaris digito tuo,

q. Gk: Heb *girdles, Aaron and his sons* **r.** Heb *all*

liver, and the two kidneys with the fat that is on them, and burn them upon the altar. ¹⁴But the flesh of the bull, and its skin, and its dung, you shall burn with fire outside the camp; it is a sin offering.

Lev 4:1ff

¹⁵"Then you shall take one of the rams, and Aaron and his sons shall lay their hands upon the head of the ram, ¹⁶and you shall slaughter the ram, and shall take its blood and throw it against the altar round about. ¹⁷Then you shall cut the ram into pieces, and wash its entrails and its legs, and put them with its pieces and its head, ¹⁸and burn the whole ram upon the altar; it is a burnt offering to the LORD; it is a pleasing odour, an offering by fire to the LORD

Lev 1:1–17
Eph 5:2
Phil 4:18

¹⁹"You shall take the other ram; and Aaron and his sons shall lay their hands upon the head of the ram, ²⁰and you shall kill the

---

which God accepts the entire victim, itself a gift from the offerer showing that he acknowledges the supreme dominion of the Lord: "All things come from thee, and of thy own have we been given them" (1 Chron 29:14). Expiatory sacrifices, sin offerings, express faith in God's mercy: the ceremony involving the blood is essential because it symbolizes the purification which God is bringing about; however, these sacrifices were never magical rites which produced results irrespective of the attitude of the offerers. Hence the prophets' constant condemnation of those who try to get away with their depraved behaviour by going through the formality of ritual sacrifice (cf. Hos 2:3–15; Amos 4:4–5; etc.).

These three offerings are, like the Passover, a figure of the one, true sacrifice of Christ on the cross, which is at one and the same time atonement, holocaust and communion.

29:10. The imposition of hands on the victim's head is a rite that is frequently found in sacrifices. This gesture does not really mean that one is passing one's own sins onto the victim or that the victim is a substitute for the offerer; it is a sign of ownership, to show that *this* is the offerer's victim. Therefore, the gesture identifies who is the offerer making the sacrifice, even though it is others, the ministers, who perform the ceremonies.

29:18. This is an anthropomorphism frequently found in the Bible—describing the offering as smelling sweet to God. Far from implying a crass materialism, as if God were going to eat the tasty offering (cf. Deut 14:1–22), it is saying that God desires things to be offered up to him: that is why they are said to please him.

29:19–20. The most characteristic feature of the consecration offering is this ritual

---

reliquum autem sanguinem fundes iuxta basim eius. ¹³Sumes et adipem totum, qui operit intestina, et reticulum iecoris ac duos renes et adipem, qui super eos est, et offeres comburens super altare; ¹⁴carnes vero vituli et corium et fimum combures foris extra castra, eo quod pro peccato sit. ¹⁵Unum quoque arietem sumes, super cuius caput ponent Aaron et filii eius manus; ¹⁶quem cum mactaveris, tolles sanguinem eius et fundes super altare per circuitum. ¹⁷Ipsum autem arietem secabis in frusta lotaque intestina eius ac pedes pones super concisas carnes et super caput illius. ¹⁸Et adolebis totum arietem

ram, and take part of its blood and put it upon the tip of the right ear of Aaron and upon the tips of the right ears of his sons, and upon the thumbs of their right hands, and upon the great toes of their right feet, and throw the rest of the blood against the altar round about. ²¹Then you shall take part of the blood that is on the altar, and of the anointing oil, and sprinkle it upon Aaron and his garments, and upon his sons and his sons' garments with him; and he and his garments shall be holy, and his sons and his sons' garments with him.

²²"You shall also take the fat of the ram, and the fat tail, and the fat that covers the entrails, and the appendage of the liver, and the two kidneys with the fat that is on them, and the right thigh (for it is a ram of ordination), ²³and one loaf of bread, and one cake of bread with oil, and one wafer, out of the basket of unleav-

Lev 7:30ff ened bread that is before the LORD; ²⁴and you shall put all these in the hands of Aaron and in the hands of his sons, and wave them for a wave offering before the LORD. ²⁵Then you shall take them from their hands, and burn them on the altar in addition to the burnt offering, as a pleasing odour before the LORD; it is an offering by fire to the LORD.

²⁶"And you shall take the breast of the ram of Aaron's ordination and wave it for a wave offering before the LORD; and it shall

---

with the blood. The blood is put on the altar but also on the ears, hands and feet of the priest, who ought to be as far away from the people as the altar is from profane objects. The triple anointing spells out what his office entails: the priest ought always listen to the voice of God, devote himself to the work of the temple, and walk in holiness. That is what the consecration of priests is meant to imply.

29:26–28. This ceremony consisted in swinging in front of and behind oneself

that part of the victim which (now, after the offertory) belongs to the priests and is for their upkeep. The term *tenufáh* which is used for this waving and swinging passed into ordinary language; it can mean either the sacrifice in which the priests took part or the portion of the victim which was designated as theirs.

Another part of the offering (we do not now know what it was) was ceremoniously raised up and it too was kept as a stipend for the priests. The technical term *terumáh* became synonymous in ordinary

super altare: holocaustum est Domino, odor suavissimus, incensum est Domino. ¹⁹Tolles quoque arietem alterum, super cuius caput Aaron et filii eius ponent manus; ²⁰quem cum immolaveris, sumes de sanguine ipsius et pones super extremum auriculae dextrae Aaron et filiorum eius et super pollices manus eorum ac pedis dextri; fundesque sanguinem super altare per circuitum. ²¹Cumque tuleris de sanguine, qui est super altare, et de oleo unctionis, asperges Aaron et vestes eius, filios et vestimenta eorum cum ipso. Et sanctus erit ipse et vestimenta eius et filii eius et vestimenta eorum cum ipso. ²²Tollesque adipem de ariete et caudam et arvinam, quae operit intestina, ac reticulum iecoris et duos renes atque adipem, qui super eos est, armumque dextrum, eo quod sit aries consecrationis, ²³tortamque panis unam, crustulam unam conspersam oleo, laganum unum de canistro azymorum, quod positum

be your portion. ²⁷And you shall consecrate the breast of the wave offering, and the thigh of the priests' portion, which is waved, and which is offered from the ram of ordination, since it is for Aaron and for his sons. ²⁸It shall be for Aaron and his sons as a perpetual due from the people of Israel, for it is the priests' portion to be offered by the people of Israel from their peace offerings; it is their offering to the LORD.

²⁹"The holy garments of Aaron shall be for his sons after him, to be anointed in them and ordained in them. ³⁰The son who is priest in his place shall wear them seven days, when he comes into the tent of meeting to minister in the holy place.

The sacred meal

³¹"You shall take the ram of ordination, and boil its flesh in a holy place; ³²and Aaron and his sons shall eat the flesh of the ram and the bread that is in the basket, at the door of the tent of meeting. ³³They shall eat those things with which atonement was made, to Mt 7:6 ordain and consecrate them, but an outsider shall not eat of them, because they are holy. ³⁴And if any of the flesh for the ordination, or of the bread, remain until the morning, then you shall burn the remainder with fire; it shall not be eaten, because it is holy.

---

language with a religious offering or tribute (cf. 25:1).

29:31–37. The meal which follows the consecration was part of the whole ceremony and had a sacred character; no lay person could partake of it. Moreover, anything not eaten had to be burned. All the little details to do with the consecration offering serve to stress the transcendence and holiness of God. Everything to

do with the rite, be it the people or the things they use, should reflect the fact that it is all centred on God.

The consecration ceremonies lasted seven days (vv. 35–37), because they involved also the consecration of the altar and other items to do with worship. They were festive celebrations, expressing the joy of those who serve the Lord: "Serve the Lord with gladness! Come into his presence singing!" (Ps 100:2).

---

est in conspectu Domini; ²⁴ponesque omnia super manus Aaron et filiorum eius, ut agitent ea coram Domino. ²⁵Suscipiesque universa de manibus eorum et incendes in altari super holocausto in odorem suavissimum in conspectu Domini; quia incensum est Domino. ²⁶Sumes quoque pectusculum de ariete, quo initiatus est Aaron, elevabisque illud coram Domino; et cedet in partem tuam. ²⁷Sanctificabisque pectusculum elevatum et armum oblatum, quem de ariete separasti, ²⁸quo initiatus est Aaron et filii eius; cedentque in partem Aaron et filiorum eius iure perpetuo a filiis Israel; quia oblatio est et oblatio erit a filiis Israel de victimis eorum pacificis, oblatio eorum Domino. ²⁹Vestem autem sanctam, qua utetur Aaron, habebunt filii eius post eum, ut ungantur in ea, et impleantur in ea manus eorum. ³⁰Septem diebus utetur illa, qui pontifex pro eo fuerit constitutus de filiis eius, qui ingredietur tabernaculum conventus, ut ministret in sanctuario. ³¹Arietem autem consecrationis tolles et coques carnes eius in loco sancto. ³²Et vescetur Aaron et filii eius carnibus arietis et panibus, qui sunt in canistro, in vestibulo tabernaculi conventus. ³³Et comedent ea, quibus expiatio facta fuerit ad implendum manus

The consecration of the altar

[35]"Thus you shall do to Aaron and to his sons, according to all that I have commanded you; through seven days shall you ordain them, [36]and every day you shall offer a bull as a sin offering for atonement. Also you shall offer a sin offering for the altar, when you make atonement for it, and shall anoint it, to consecrate it.

Mt 23:19 [37]Seven days you shall make atonement for the altar, and consecrate it, and the altar shall be most holy; whatever touches the altar shall become holy.

Lev 6:2
Num 28:3–8
Ezek 46:13–15

The daily burnt offering

1 Kings 18:29
2 Kings 16:13
Heb 7:27

[38]"Now this is what you shall offer upon the altar: two lambs a year old day by day continually. [39]One lamb you shall offer in the morning, and the other lamb you shall offer in the evening; [40]and with the first lamb a tenth measure of fine flour mingled with a fourth of a hin of beaten oil, and a fourth of a hin of wine for a libation. [41]And the other lamb you shall offer in the evening, and shall offer with it a cereal offering and its libation, as in the morn-

Ex 25:22 ing, for a pleasing odour, an offering by fire to the LORD. [42]It shall be a continual burnt offering throughout your generations at the door of the tent of meeting before the LORD, where I will meet with you, to speak there to you. [43]There I will meet with the

---

29:38–46. Daily sacrifices were held in Israel from very early on, as we know from the story of Elijah (cf. 1 Kings 18:29) and from the offering made by Ahaz, king of Israel (2 Kings 16:13). But apparently it was not until after the Exile that they were conducted with all the detailed ritual described here (cf. Ezek 46:13–15; Lev 6:2–6).

In the language of worship a tenth-measure of flour is the equivalent to a tenth of an ephah of fine flour (cf. Lev

5:11; 6:13), that is, the tenth of the capacity of a receptacle that would hold 21 litres or five gallons (cf. the note on Ex 16:32–36). A hin (used for oil, wine or water) was about 3.6 litres.

Religious worship in Israel underwent many changes over the years, but despite the ever-present danger of falling into a mere external formalism it always held on to the idea that men can obtain access to God, who is present among his own people. The Christian liturgy makes

---

eorum, ad sanctificandum eos. Alienigena non vescetur ex eis, quia sancta sunt. [34]Quod si remanserit de carnibus consecrationis sive de panibus usque mane, combures reliquias igni; non comedentur, quia sancta sunt. [35]Omnia, quae praecepi tibi, facies super Aaron et filiis eius. Septem diebus consecrabis manus eorum [36]et vitulum pro peccato offeres per singulos dies ad expiandum. Mundabisque altare expians illud et unges illud in sanctificationem. [37]Septem diebus expiabis altare et sanctificabis; et erit sanctum sanctorum: omnis, qui tetigerit illud, sanctificabitur. [38]Hoc est quod facies in altari: agnos anniculos duos per singulos dies iugiter, [39]unum agnum mane et alterum vespere; [40]decimam partem similae conspersae oleo tunso, quod habeat mensuram quartam partem hin, et vinum ad libandum eiusdem mensurae in agno uno. [41]Alterum vero agnum offeres ad vesperam iuxta ritum matutinae oblationis et libationis in odorem suavitatis, incensum Domino, [42]holocaustum perpetuum in generationes

people of Israel, and it shall be sanctified by my glory; ⁴⁴I will consecrate the tent of meeting and the altar; Aaron also and his sons I will consecrate, to serve me as priests. ⁴⁵And I will dwell among the people of Israel, and will be their God. ⁴⁶And they shall know that I am the LORD their God, who brought them forth out of the land of Egypt that I might dwell among them; I am the LORD their God.

Ex 24:16; 40:34

The altar of incense

30 ¹"You shall make an altar to burn incense upon; of acacia wood shall you make it. ²A cubit shall be its length, and a cubit its breadth; it shall be square, and two cubits shall be its height; its horns shall be of one piece with it. ³And you shall overlay it with pure gold, its top and its sides round about and its horns; and you shall make for it a moulding of gold round about. ⁴And two golden rings shall you make for it; under its moulding on two opposite sides of it shall you make them, and they shall be holders for poles with which to carry it. ⁵You shall make the poles of acacia wood, and overlay them with gold. ⁶And you shall put it before the veil that is by the ark of the testimony, before the mercy seat that is over the testimony, where I will meet with you. ⁷And Aaron shall burn fragrant incense on it; every morning when

Ex 37:25–28; 40:26
1 Kings 6:20–22; 7:48
Num 4:11
Rev 8:3–5; 9:13

Lk 1:9

---

a reality of what was figure and symbol in the Old Testament: "Christ, indeed, always associates the Church with himself in this great work [the Liturgy] in which God is perfectly glorified and men are sanctified. The Church is his beloved Bride who calls to her Lord, and through him offers worship to the eternal Father" (Vatican II, *Sacrosanctum Concilium*, 7).

30:1–10. The altar of incense (cf. 37:25–28;

40:26) was a place in Solomon's temple in front of the Holy of Holies (cf. 1 Kings 6:20–22; 7:48). Incense was used in religious worship from very early on both in Mesopotamia and in Canaan. Being a sweet-smelling substance it is very good for conveying an atmosphere and for perfuming venues where big crowds gather for either religious or profane events; above all, it symbolizes praise making its way up to heaven.

---

vestras, ad ostium tabernaculi conventus coram Domino, ubi conveniam vos, ut loquar ad te. ⁴³Ibi conveniam filios Israel, et sanctificabitur locus in gloria mea. ⁴⁴Sanctificabo et tabernaculum conventus cum altari et Aaron cum filiis eius, ut sacerdotio fungantur mihi. ⁴⁵Et habitabo in medio filiorum Israel eroque eis Deus; ⁴⁶et scient quia ego Dominus Deus eorum, qui eduxi eos de terra Aegypti, ut manerem inter illos: ego Dominus Deus ipsorum. ¹Facies quoque altare ad adolendum thymiama de lignis acaciae ²habens cubitum longitudinis et alterum latitudinis, id est quadrangulum, et duos cubitos in altitudine; cornua ex ipso procedent. ³Vestiesque illud auro purissimo, tam craticulam eius quam parietes per circuitum et cornua. Faciesque ei coronam aureolam per gyrum ⁴et duos anulos aureos sub corona in duobus lateribus, ut mittantur in eos vectes, et altare portetur. ⁵Ipsos quoque vectes facies de lignis acaciae et inaurabis. ⁶Ponesque altare contra velum, quod ante arcam pendet testimonii, coram propitiatorio, quo tegitur testimonium, ubi conveniam ad te. ⁷Et adolebit incensum super eo Aaron suave fra-

he dresses the lamps he shall burn it, [8]and when Aaron sets up the lamps in the evening, he shall burn it, a perpetual incense before the LORD throughout your generations. [9]You shall offer no unholy incense thereon, nor burnt offering, nor cereal offering; and you

Heb 9:7 shall pour no libation thereon. [10]Aaron shall make atonement upon its horns once a year; with the blood of the sin offering of atonement he shall make atonement for it once in the year throughout your generations; it is most holy to the LORD."

Ex 38: 24–31 **The half-shekel tax**

2 Sam 24
Num 1 [11]The LORD said to Moses, [12]"When you take the census of the people of Israel, then each shall give a ransom for himself to the LORD when you number them, that there be no plague among them

Mt 17:24 when you number them. [13]Each who is numbered in the census shall give this: half a shekel according to the shekel of the sanctuary (the shekel is twenty gerahs), half a shekel as an offering to the LORD. [14]Every one who is numbered in the census, from twenty years old and upward, shall give the LORD's offering. [15]The rich shall not give more, and the poor shall not give less, than the half shekel, when you give the LORD's offering to make atonement for yourselves. [16]And you shall take the atonement money from the people of Israel, and shall appoint it for the service of the tent of meeting; that it may bring the people of Israel to remembrance before the LORD, so as to make atonement for yourselves."

30:11–16. In Israel tribute had a markedly religious character to it (cf. 38:24–31). Because each and every Israelite belonged to God, the authorities could not use them for their own advantage, nor could they extort taxes from them. Taking a census could cause temptation (cf. 2 Sam 24), because those in charge ran the risk of registering as belonging to them what in fact belonged to God alone; every census involved the risk of a plague or some other punishment (v. 12). To avoid anyone having that sort of twisted intention, every adult was given the *right* to help support divine worship; poor and rich are equal before God and have identical rights: that is the idea behind what it says in v. 15.

---

grans mane. Quando componet lucernas, incendet illud; [8]et quando collocabit eas ad vesperum, uret thymiama sempiternum coram Domino in generationes vestras. [9]Non offeretis super eo thymiama compositionis alterius nec holocaustum nec oblationem, nec libabitis libamina. [10]Et expiabit Aaron super cornua eius semel per annum in sanguine sacrificii pro peccato; et placabit super eo in generationibus vestris: sanctum sanctorum erit Domino». [11]Locutusque est Dominus ad Moysen dicens: [12]«Quando tuleris summam filiorum Israel iuxta numerum, dabunt singuli pretium expiationis pro animabus suis Domino; et non erit plaga in eis, cum fuerint recensiti. [13]Hoc autem dabit omnis, qui transit ad censum, dimidium sicli iuxta mensuram sanctuarii—siclus viginti obolos habet—; media pars sicli offeretur Domino. [14]Qui habetur in numero a viginti annis et supra, dabit pretium; [15]dives non addet ad medium sicli, et pauper nihil minuet, quando dabitis oblationem Domino in expiationem animarum vestrarum. [16]SuscepTamque expiationis pecuniam, quae collata est a filiis Israel, trades in usus tabernaculi con-

The bronze basin

Ex 38:8; 40:30
1 Kings 7:23-39

[17]The LORD said to Moses, [18]"You shall also make a laver of bronze, with its base of bronze, for washing. And you shall put it between the tent of meeting and the altar, and you shall put water in it, [19]with which Aaron and his sons shall wash their hands and their feet. [20]When they go into the tent of meeting, or when they come near the altar to minister, to burn an offering by fire to the LORD, they shall wash with water, lest they die. [21]They shall wash their hands and their feet, lest they die: it shall be a statute for ever to them, even to him and to his descendants throughout their generations."

The oil for anointing

Lev 8:10ff
Ex 37:29

[22]Moreover, the LORD said to Moses, [23]"Take the finest spices: of liquid myrrh five hundred shekels, and of sweet-smelling cinnamon half as much, that is, two hundred and fifty, and of aromatic cane two hundred and fifty, [24]and of cassia five hundred, according to the shekel of the sanctuary, and of olive oil a hin; [25]and you shall make of these a sacred anointing oil blended as by the perfumer; a holy anointing oil it shall be. [26]And you shall anoint with

---

30:17-21. The bronze basin or bath for the washings (cf. 38:8; 40:30) made it easier for the priests to do all the purifications their role involved. Unlike the other elements in the sanctuary, no great detail is laid down as regards the basin. We do not know its exact dimensions, although there is a reference to there being a huge receptacle in Solomon's temple (the "sea of bronze": cf. 1 Kings 7:23-26), upheld by twelve statues of bulls; there were other smaller containers as well (cf. 1 Kings 7:38-39).

30:22-33. The oil of unction (cf. 37:29) was a mixture of olive oil and various aromatic substances, many of them imported and very expensive. Given that oil was used both for personal embellishment (cf. Ruth 3:3; 2 Sam 12:20; Mt 6:17) and for healing wounds (cf. Is 1:6; Mk 6:13; Lk 10:34; etc.), the complicated mixture in the oil of unction is another indicator of the importance given to divine worship and of appreciation for the transcendence of God, who requires maximum moral perfection of his ministers.

---

ventus, ut sit monumentum eorum coram Domino et propitietur animabus illorum». [17]Locutusque est Dominus ad Moysen dicens: [18]«Facies et labrum aeneum cum basi aenea ad lavandum; ponesque illud inter tabernaculum conventus et altare. Et, missa aqua, [19]lavabunt in eo Aaron et filii eius manus suas ac pedes. [20]Quando ingressuri sunt tabernaculum conventus, lavabunt se aqua, ne moriantur; vel quando accessuri sunt ad altare, ut ministrent, ut adoleant victimam Domino. [21]Et lavabunt manus et pedes, ne moriantur: legitimum sempiternum erit, ipsi et semini eius per successiones». [22]Locutusque est Dominus ad Moysen [23]dicens: «Sume tibi aromata prima myrrhae electae quingentos siclos et cinnamomi boni odoris medium, id est ducentos quinquaginta siclos, calami suave olentis similiter ducentos quinquaginta, [24]casiae autem quingentos siclos, in pondere sanctuarii, olei de olivetis mensuram hin. [25]Faciesque unctionis oleum sanctum, unguentum compositum opere unguentarii; unctionis oleum sanctum erit. [26]Et unges ex eo tabernaculum conventus et arcam testamenti [27]mensamque cum vasis

it the tent of meeting and the ark of the testimony, [27]and the table and all its utensils, and the lampstand and its utensils, and the altar of incense, [28]and the altar of burnt offering with all its utensils and the laver and its base; [29]you shall consecrate them, that they may be most holy; whatever touches them will become holy. [30]And you shall anoint Aaron and his sons, and consecrate them, that they may serve me as priests. [31]And you shall say to the people of Israel, 'This shall be my holy anointing oil throughout your generations. [32]It shall not be poured upon the bodies of ordinary men, and you shall make no other like it in composition; it is holy, and it shall be holy to you. [33]Whoever compounds any like it or whoever puts any of it on an outsider shall be cut off from his people.'"

Ex 37:29 **The incense**

[34]And the LORD said to Moses, "Take sweet spices, stacte, and onycha, and galbanum, sweet spices with pure frankincense (of each shall there be an equal part), [35]and make an incense blended Ex 25:22 as by the perfumer, seasoned with salt, pure and holy; [36]and you shall beat some of it very small, and put part of it before the testimony in the tent of meeting where I shall meet with you; it shall

---

This oil was used to anoint the main items used in divine worship and also consecrated persons, specifically, priests, prophets and particularly, the king (vv. 25:30; 1 Sam 24:7; 26:9, 11, 23; 2 Sam 1:14, 16; 19:22). That is why the title of the "Anointed" is the one which most specifically identifies the future King-Messiah and which in the New Testament applies to Jesus, our Lord: "The word 'Christ' comes from the Greek translation of the Hebrew *Messiah*, which means 'anointed'. [. . .] Jesus fulfilled the messianic hope of Israel in his threefold office of priest, prophet and king" (*Catechism of the Catholic Church*, 436).

30:34–38. The recipe used for the incense (cf. 37:29) was quite complicated: some later rabbinical treatises describe an even more complex mixture, involving sixteen separate ingredients. All we can say is that many of the substances used for it were not native to Palestine, and that the use of incense was a further refinement in divine worship. It is therefore another indication that it is

---

suis, candelabrum et utensilia eius, altaria thymiamatis [28]et holocausti et universam supellectilem, quae ad cultum eorum pertinet, et labrum cum basi sua. [29]Sanctificabisque omnia, et erunt sancta sanctorum: qui tetigerit ea, sanctificabitur. [30]Aaron et filios eius unges sanctificabisque eos, ut sacerdotio fungantur mihi. [31]Filiis quoque Israel dices: Hoc oleum unctionis sanctum erit mihi in generationes vestras. [32]Caro hominis non ungetur ex eo, et iuxta compositionem eius non facietis aliud, quia sanctum est et sanctum erit vobis. [33]Homo quicumque tale composuerit et dederit ex eo super alienum, exterminabitur de populo suo». [34]Dixitque Dominus ad Moysen: «Sume tibi aromata, stacten et onycha, galbanum boni odoris et tus lucidissimum; aequalis ponderis erunt omnia. [35]Faciesque thymiama compositum opere unguentarii, sale conditum et purum et sanctum. [36]Cumque in tenuissimum pulverem ex parte

be for you most holy. ³⁷And the incense which you shall make according to its composition, you shall not make for yourselves; it shall be for you holy to the LORD. ³⁸Whoever makes any like it to use as perfume shall be cut off from his people."

The craftsmen for the sanctuary

Ex 35:30–35

31 ¹The LORD said to Moses, ²"See, I have called by name Acts 6:3 Bezalel the son of Uri, son of Hur, of the tribe of Judah: ³and I have filled him with the Spirit of God, with ability and intelligence, with knowledge and all craftsmanship, ⁴to devise artistic designs, to work in gold, silver, and bronze, ⁵in cutting stones for setting, and in carving wood, for work in every craft. ⁶And behold, I have appointed with him Oholiab, the son of Ahisamach, of the tribe of Dan; and I have given to all able men ability, that they may make all that I have commanded you: ⁷the tent of meeting, and the ark of the testimony, and the mercy seat that is thereon, and all the furnishings of the tent, ⁸the table and its utensils, and the pure lampstand with all its utensils, and the altar of incense, ⁹and the altar of burnt offering with all its utensils, and the laver and its base, ¹⁰and the finely worked garments, the holy garments for Aaron the priest and the garments of his sons, for

---

not good to be miserly when allocating resources whether material or personnel where divine worship is involved.

31:1–11. To ensure that the sanctuary is built with all due perfection, in line with the instructions given, God gives his spirit of wisdom to the craftsmen involved, that is, he gives them great skill.

Wisdom, so greatly appreciated among Eastern peoples, is according to the Bible a sharing in divine wisdom: God is the only Wise One; he has created the world with great skill and dexterity. Therefore, those men are wisest who best imitate God; the wise are not those who simply have theoretical knowledge or those who have greater intellectual ability or a better philosophy, but rather those who are endowed with a special skill that enables them to do what God wants. The craftsmen who make the sanctuary are equipped with the wisdom needed to

---

contuderis, pones ex eo coram testimonio in tabernaculo conventus, in quo conveniam ad te: sanctum sanctorum erit vobis thymiama. ³⁷Talem compositionem non facietis in usus vestros, quia tibi sanctum erit pro Domino; ³⁸homo quicumque fecerit simile, ut odore illius perfruatur, peribit de populis suis». ¹Locutusque est Dominus ad Moysen dicens: ²«Ecce vocavi ex nomine Beseleel filium Uri filii Hur de tribu Iudae ³et implevi eum spiritu Dei, sapientia et intelligentia et scientia in omni opere ⁴ad excogitandum, quidquid fabrefieri potest ex auro et argento et aere, ⁵ad scindendum et includendum gemmas et ad sculpendum ligna, ad faciendum omne opus; ⁶dedique ei socium Ooliab filium Achisamech de tribu Dan et in corde omnis eruditi posui sapientiam, ut faciant cuncta, quae praecepi tibi: ⁷tabernaculum conventus et arcam testimonii et propitiatorium, quod super eam est, et cuncta vasa tabernaculi ⁸mensamque et vasa eius, candelabrum purissimum cum vasis suis et altaria thymiamatis ⁹et holocausti et omnia vasa eorum, labrum cum basi sua ¹⁰et vestes textas et vestes sanctas Aaron sacerdoti et vestes

their service as priests, [11]and the anointing oil and the fragrant incense for the holy place. According to all that I have commanded you they shall do."

The sabbath rest

[12]And the LORD said to Moses, [13]"Say to the people of Israel, 'You shall keep my sabbaths, for this is a sign between me and you throughout your generations, that you may know that I, the LORD, sanctify you. [14]You shall keep the sabbath, because it is holy for you; every one who profanes it shall be put to death; whoever does any work on it, that soul shall be cut off from among his people. [15]Six days shall work be done, but the seventh day is a sabbath of solemn rest, holy to the LORD; whoever does any work on the sabbath day shall be put to death. [16]Therefore the people of Israel shall keep the sabbath, observing the sabbath throughout their generations, as a perpetual covenant. [17]It is a sign for ever between me and the people of Israel that in six days the LORD

Ex 20:8–11
Ezek 20:12
Mk 1:24
Heb 2:11
Num 15:32–36
Mk 3:6
Gen 2:2–3; 9:9
Ex 20:11

---

build it according to God's desire. Moreover, the Wisdom books will teach that the wise are not those who have most knowledge (even if that be religious knowledge) but those who live in keeping with that knowledge; that is, the wise person is the devout person.

Divine Wisdom is the attribute which is most fully described in the Old Testament, so much so that it becomes personified (cf. Prov 8:22–31). In the New Testament, for example in the Gospel of St John (Jn 1), features of the creative Wisdom of God are attributed to the Word.

31:12–17. By including here the rules about the sabbath, the sacred text wants

to show that sabbath observance is the key act of divine worship for the people of Israel. Perhaps because the rules contained in these final chapters (30–31) are later and more detailed, this section is usually seen as the one which has most to say about the sabbath.

Thus, three reasons are given (none of them social reasons) why sabbath rest is something to do with religion—the sovereignty of God (v. 13), the Covenant (vv. 16–17) and the fact that one is a member of the people of God (vv. 14–15). Christian Sunday rest means all these three things too; it commemorates the resurrection of the Lord, in which the new creation comes about, and the new Covenant and the new people of God.

---

filiorum eius, ut fungantur officio suo in sacris, [11]oleum unctionis et thymiama aromatum in sanctuario: omnia, quae praecepi tibi, facient». [12]Et locutus est Dominus ad Moysen dicens: [13]«Loquere filiis Israel et dices ad eos: Videte ut sabbatum meum custodiatis, quia signum est inter me et vos in generationibus vestris, ut sciatis quia ego Dominus, qui sanctifico vos. [14]Custodite sabbatum, sanctum est enim vobis. Qui polluerit illud, morte morietur; qui fecerit in eo opus, peribit anima illius de medio populi sui. [15]Sex diebus facietis opus; in die septimo sabbatum est, requies sancta Domino: omnis, qui fecerit opus in hac die, morietur. [16]Custodiant filii Israel sabbatum et celebrent illud in generationibus suis: pactum est sempiternum [17]inter me et filios Israel signumque perpetuum; sex enim diebus fecit Dominus caelum et terram et in septimo ab opere cessavit et respiravit». [18]Deditque Dominus Moysi,

made heaven and earth, and on the seventh day he rested, and was refreshed.'"

The tables of the Law

[18]And he gave to Moses, when he had made an end of speaking with him upon Mount Sinai, the two tables of the testimony, tables of stone, written with the finger of God.

Acts 7:38
2 Cor 3:3

11. ISRAEL'S APOSTASY*

The golden calf

32 [1]When the people saw that Moses delayed to come down from the mountain, the people gathered themselves together to Aaron, and said to him, "Up, make us gods, who shall go before us; as for this Moses, the man who brought us up out of the land of Egypt, we do not know what has become of him." [2]And Aaron said to them, "Take off the rings of gold which are in the ears of your wives, your sons, and your daughters, and bring

Acts 7:40–41
Ex 24:18

---

*32:1—34:35. After the account of the rules about how the sanctuary should be built, the narrative picks up where it left off in chapter 24. This last narrative section contains the account of the grave sin of apostasy committed in the desert (chap. 32) and the account of the renewal of the Covenant after that sin.

The first answer the people give to the love of God as expressed in the events of Sinai is a very grave sin of idolatry, one which merits severe punishment. But, through Moses' intercession, God stays true to his Covenant and continues to guide the course of Israelite history. In the events recounted here, the people take their sin to heart, and understand the punishment it deserves and the extent of God's forgiveness: he is "slow to anger, and abounding in steadfast love" (Ex 34:6).

Thus, we have here again the great teachings of Exodus: there is only one God, who wants to be the only God that is worshipped; he chose the Israelites to be his people, having delivered them from all kinds of danger but especially from inner wickedness; he made a Covenant time and again; and he has shown himself to be just and merciful and a close friend of men.

32:1–6. In the ancient East the bull or bull-calf was a symbol of divinity insofar as its strength symbolized divine omnipotence. King Jeroboam ordered golden calves to be put in the temples of Dan and Bethel (cf. 1 Kings 12:28) when the kingdom of the North broke away. Given that the image of a bull was being used to represent the true God, it was not so much a sin of idolatry as a sin against

---

completis huiuscemodi sermonibus in monte Sinai, duas tabulas testimonii lapideas scriptas digito Dei. [1]Videns autem populus quod moram faceret descendendi de monte Moyses, congregatus ad Aaron dixit: «Surge, fac nobis deos, qui nos praecedant; Moysi enim, huic viro, qui nos eduxit de terra Aegypti, ignoramus quid acciderit». [2]Dixitque ad eos Aaron: «Tollite inaures aureas de uxorum filiorumque et filiarum vestrarum auribus et afferte ad me». [3]Fecitque omnis populus, quae iusserat, de-

1 Kings 12:28
Neh 9:18
Ps 106:19ff
Acts 7:41 them to me." ³So all the people took off the rings of gold which were in their ears, and brought them to Aaron. ⁴And he received the gold at their hand, and fashioned it with a graving tool, and made a molten calf; and they said, "These are your gods, O Israel, who brought you up out of the land of Egypt!" ⁵When Aaron saw this, he built an altar before it; and Aaron made proclamation and Acts 7:41
1 Cor 10:7 said, "Tomorrow shall be a feast to the LORD." ⁶And they rose up early on the morrow, and offered burnt offerings and brought peace offerings; and the people sat down to eat and drink, and rose up to play.

Deut 9:7–14 **The Lord's ire**

⁷And the LORD said to Moses, "Go down; for your people, whom you brought up out of the land of Egypt, have corrupted them- Acts 7:41 selves; ⁸they have turned aside quickly out of the way which I

---

the ban on making images of the Lord; but it is also true that that commandment was aimed at avoiding any occasion of idolatry (cf. Acts 7:40–41).

While Moses was away up the mountain (cf. 24:18), Aaron proved unable to refuse the people when they pressed him to give them a god they could see and touch—the kind of god other peoples had. The contrast between Moses and Aaron in this account is intentional: Moses is in deep conversation with the Lord to equip himself to tell the people what God wants of them (cf. the note on 24:12–18); in his absence Aaron decides to act on his own initiative without taking the will of God into account. The teaching we can glimpse here is that the people must always take account of the word of God, over and above human interests or advantages. "Faith and love will be the guides of the blind, which will lead you, by a way you do not know, to

the hidden place of God. Faith is like the feet which bring the soul to God. Love is the guide that directs it" (St John of the Cross, *Spiritual Canticle*, 1,11).

The sacred writer emphasizes that the calf was made by human hands, from silver and gold, and it was made using techniques with which the people are familiar; this means it is just like any of those idols that have a mouth but say nothing, eyes but see nothing (cf. Ps 105:19–20; 115:5ff). The mention of a "feast" (v. 5) may imply idolatrous ceremonies and orgies, in imitation of what is done in other nations. So, it is perfectly clear that this was a very serious sin, a radical change of direction from the path marked out by the Lord (v. 8). The Covenant has been broken before it starts to operate.

32:7–14. The Lord's dialogue with Moses contains the doctrinal bases of sal-

---

ferens inaures ad Aaron. ⁴Quas cum ille accepisset, formavit stilo imaginem et fecit ex eis vitulum conflatilem. Dixeruntque: «Hi sunt dii tui, Israel, qui te eduxerunt de terra Aegypti!». ⁵Quod cum vidisset Aaron, aedificavit altare coram eo et praeconis voce clamavit dicens: «Cras sollemnitas Domini est». ⁶Surgentesque mane altero die obtulerunt holocausta et hostias pacificas; et sedit populus manducare et bibere et surrexerunt ludere. ⁷Locutus est autem Dominus ad Moysen: «Vade, descende; peccavit populus tuus, quem eduxisti de terra Aegypti. ⁸Recesserunt cito de via, quam praecepi eis, feceruntque

commanded them; they have made for themselves a molten calf, and have worshiped it and sacrificed to it, and said, 'These are your gods, O Israel, who brought you up out of the land of Egypt!'" ⁹And the LORD said to Moses, "I have seen this people, and behold, it is a stiff-necked people; ¹⁰now therefore let me alone, that my wrath may burn hot against them and I may consume them; but of you I will make a great nation."

Ex 33:3; 34:9
Deut 9:13
Num 14:12

Moses' prayer for Israel

Gen 18:22–23
Deut 9:26–29
Ps 106:23

¹¹But Moses besought the LORD his God, and said, "O LORD, why does thy wrath burn hot against thy people, whom thou hast brought forth out of the land of Egypt with great power and with a mighty hand? ¹²Why should the Egyptians say, 'With evil intent did he bring them forth, to slay them in the mountains, and to consume them from the face of the earth'? Turn from thy fierce

---

vation history—Covenant, sin, mercy. Only the Lord knows just how serious this sin is: by adoring the golden calf the people have taken the wrong road and have vitiated the whole meaning of the Exodus; but most of all, they have rebelled against God and turned their backs on him, breaking the Covenant (cf. Deut 9:7–14). God no longer calls them "my people" (cf. Hos 2:8) but "your people" (Moses') (v. 7). That is, he shows him that they have acted like anyone else, guided by human leaders.

The punishment that the sin deserves is their destruction (v. 10), for this is a stiff-necked nation (cf. 33:3; 34:9; Deut 9:13). The sin deserves death, as the first sin did (Gen 3:19) and the sin which gave rise to the flood (cf. Gen 6:6–7). However, mercy always prevails over the offence.

As Abraham did in another time on behalf of Sodom (Gen 18:22–23), Moses

intercedes with the Lord. But this time intercession proves successful, because Israel is the people that God has made his own; he chose it, bringing it out of Egypt in a mighty way; so, he cannot turn back now; in fact, he chose it ever since he swore his oath to Abraham (cf. Gen 15:5; 22:16–17; 35:11–12). He established the Covenant with Israel, as Moses reminds him when he refers to "thy people, whom thou has brought forth out of the land of Egypt" (v. 11). Thus, promise, election and Covenant form the foundation which guarantees that God's forgiveness will be forthcoming, even if they commit the gravest of sins.

God forgives *his* people (v. 14) not because they deserve to be forgiven, but out of pure mercy and moved by Moses' intercession. Thus God's forgiveness and the people's conversion are, both of them, a divine initiative.

---

sibi vitulum conflatilem et adoraverunt atque immolantes ei hostias dixerunt: 'Isti sunt dii tui, Israel, qui te eduxerunt de terra Aegypti!'». ⁹Rursumque ait Dominus ad Moysen: «Cerno quod populus iste durae cervicis sit; ¹⁰dimitte me, ut irascatur furor meus contra eos et deleam eos faciamque te in gentem magnam». ¹¹Moyses autem orabat Dominum Deum suum dicens: «Cur, Domine, irascitur furor tuus contra populum tuum, quem eduxisti de terra Aegypti in fortitudine magna et in manu robusta? ¹²Ne, quaeso, dicant Aegyptii: 'Callide eduxit eos, ut interficeret in montibus et deleret e terra'. Quiescat ira tua, et esto placabilis super nequitia populi tui. ¹³Recordare Abraham, Isaac et Israel servorum tuorum,

Gen 15:5; 22:
16–17;
35:11–12
Heb 11:12 wrath, and repent of this evil against thy people. [13]Remember
Abraham, Isaac, and Israel, thy servants, to whom thou didst
swear by thine own self, and didst say to them, 'I will multiply
your descendants as the stars of heaven, and all this land that I
have promised I will give to your descendants, and they shall
inherit it forever.'" [14]And the LORD repented of the evil which he
thought to do to his people.

The golden calf is destroyed

Ex 24:12
2 Cor 3:3 [15]And Moses turned, and went down from the mountain with the
two tables of the testimony in his hands, tables that were written
on both sides; on the one side and on the other were they written.
[16]And the tables were the work of God, and the writing was the
writing of God, graven upon the tables. [17]When Joshua heard the
noise of the people as they shouted, he said to Moses, "There is a
noise of war in the camp." [18]But he said, "It is not the sound of
shouting for victory, or the sound of the cry of defeat, but the
Amos 8:11–12 sound of singing that I hear." [19]And as soon as he came near the
camp and saw the calf and the dancing, Moses' anger burned hot,
and he threw the tables out of his hands and broke them at the

---

32:15–24. The punishment described in these verses is full of significance. In the first place, Moses breaks the tables on which God wrote the Law (vv. 16, 19), thereby showing that sin has broken the Covenant, and that the main effect of and punishment for sin is not to have the Law (cf. Amos 8:11–12), that is, what today we would call loss of the sense of sin.

Moses destroys the calf because of itself it has no power. The tables were "the work of God" (v. 16), whereas the calf was something made by men (v. 20). And he gives the people the residue of the calf to drink (v. 20), in a gesture which is reminiscent of trials by ordeal (cf. Num 5:23–24), but the main point he is making is that sin is personal: only those who have sinned are to be punished. And his reproach to Aaron, which echoes that which God made to Adam (cf. Gen 3:11), identifies the man who is truly to blame.

The mystery of sin affects even key figures chosen by God, and the Bible does not disguise this fact. Elsewhere Moses is reminded of his own sin (cf. Num 20:12; Deut 32:51), as is David (cf. 1 Sam 12:7–9); and in the New Testament Peter's denials are also recorded in detail (Mt 26:69–75). It is God who

---

quibus iurasti per temetipsum dicens: 'Multiplicabo semen vestrum sicut stellas caeli; et universam terram hanc, de qua locutus sum, dabo semini vestro, et possidebitis eam semper'». [14]Placatusque est Dominus, ne faceret malum, quod locutus fuerat adversus populum suum. [15]Et reversus est Moyses de monte portans duas tabulas testimonii in manu sua scriptas ex utraque parte [16]et factas opere Dei; scriptura quoque Dei erat sculpta in tabulis. [17]Audiens autem Iosue tumultum populi vociferantis dixit ad Moysen: «Ululatus pugnae auditur in castris». [18]Qui respondit: «Non est clamor vincentium / neque clamor fugientium, / sed clamorem cantantium / ego audio». [19]Cumque appropinquasset ad castra, vidit vitulum et choros; iratusque valde proiecit de manu tabulas et confregit eas ad radices montis.

380

foot of the mountain. [20]And he took the calf which they had made, Num 5:23-24
and burnt it with fire, and ground it to powder, and scattered it
upon the water, and made the people of Israel drink it. [21]And Gen 3:11
Moses said to Aaron, "What did this people do to you that you
have brought a great sin upon them?" [22]And Aaron said, "Let not
the anger of my lord burn hot; you know the people, that they are
set on evil. [23]For they said to me, 'Make us gods, who shall go Acts 7:40
before us; as for this Moses, the man who brought us up out of the
land of Egypt, we do not know what has become of him.' [24]And I
said to them, 'Let any who have gold take it off'; so they gave it
to me, and I threw it into the fire, and there came out this calf."

The zeal of the Levites
Deut 33:9

[25]And when Moses saw that the people had broken loose (for
Aaron had let them break loose, to their shame among their enemies), [26]then Moses stood in the gate of the camp, and said, "Who
is on the LORD's side? Come to me." And all the sons of Levi
gathered themselves together to him. [27]And he said to them, Deut 33:8–11
"Thus says the LORD God of Israel, 'Put every man his sword on Num 25:7–13
his side, and go to and fro from gate to gate throughout the camp,

---

shapes the history of salvation, and he
does this despite our infidelities.

32:25–29. To our modern minds the part
played by the Levites here seems rather
shocking. This account may be designed
to highlight the role which Levites would
play in future times: the sons of Levi are
praised for being obedient to the word of
God and to the Covenant (cf. Deut 33:9);
here they stay loyal to Moses and are able
to distinguish the guilty from the innocent. This whole section about the punish-

ment of the people's sin shows that, even
when sin is forgiven, punishment still
applies. The Church teaches that, in addition to being an offence against God, sin
"injures and weakens the sinner himself,
as well as his relationships with God and
neighbour. Absolution takes away sin, but
it does not remedy all the disorders
sin has caused. Raised up from sin, the
sinner must still recover his full spiritual
health by doing something more to make
amends for the sin [. . .]" (*Catechism of
the Catholic Church*, 1459).

---

[20]Arripiensque vitulum, quem fecerant, combussit et contrivit usque ad pulverem, quem sparsit in
aquam et dedit ex eo potum filiis Israel. [21]Dixitque ad Aaron: «Quid tibi fecit hic populus, ut induceres
super eum peccatum maximum?». [22]Cui ille respondit: «Ne indignetur dominus meus; tu enim nosti
populum istum, quod pronus sit ad malum. [23]Dixerunt mihi: 'Fac nobis deos, qui nos praecedant; huic
enim Moysi, qui nos eduxit de terra Aegypti, nescimus quid acciderit'. [24]Quibus ego dixi: Quis vestrum
habet aurum? Abstulerunt et dederunt mihi, et proieci illud in ignem; egressusque est hic vitulus».
[25]Vidit ergo Moyses populum quod esset effrenatus; relaxaverat enim ei Aaron frenum in ludibrium
hostium eorum. [26]Et stans in porta castrorum ait: «Si quis est Domini, iungatur mihi!». Congregatique
sunt ad eum omnes filii Levi. [27]Quibus ait: «Haec dicit Dominus, Deus Israel: Ponat unusquisque gladium super femur suum. Ite et redite de porta usque ad portam per medium castrorum, et occidat
unusquisque fratrem et amicum et proximum suum». [28]Fecerunt filii Levi iuxta sermonem Moysi;

and slay every man his brother, and every man his companion, and every man his neighbour.'" [28]And the sons of Levi did according to the word of Moses; and there fell of the people that day about three thousand men. [29]And Moses said, "Today you have ordained yourselves[s] for the service of the LORD, each one at the cost of his son and of his brother, that he may bestow a blessing upon you this day."

Ex 17:8–13
Num 12:13–14

Moses intercedes again

[30]On the morrow Moses said to the people, "You have sinned a great sin. And now I will go up to the LORD; perhaps I can make atonement for your sin." [31]So Moses returned to the LORD and said, "Alas, this people have sinned a great sin; they have made for themselves gods of gold. [32]But now, if thou wilt forgive their

Is 4:3
Lk 10:20

32:30–35. This new dialogue between Moses and God sums up the content of the whole chapter. Once again Moses plays intercessor, and the Lord shows himself to be merciful and forgiving. "From this intimacy with the faithful God, slow to anger and abounding in steadfast love, Moses drew strength and determination for his intercession (cf. Ex 34:6). He does not pray for himself but for the people whom God made his own. Moses already intercedes for them during the battle with the Amalekites (cf. Ex 17:8–13) and prays to obtain healing for Miriam (cf. Num 12:13–14). But it is chiefly after their apostasy that Moses 'stands in the breach' before God in order to save the people (Ps 106:23; cf. Ex 32:1—34:9). The arguments of his prayer—for intercession is also a mysterious battle—will inspire the boldness of the great intercessors among the Jewish

people and in the Church: God is love; he is therefore righteous and faithful; he cannot contradict himself; he must remember his marvellous deeds, since his glory is at stake, and he cannot forsake this people that bears his name" (*Catechism of the Catholic Church*, 2577).

But the people still has a penalty to pay for its offence (v. 34). Throughout the course of its history Israel continues to be aware that it deserves severe punishment for this and other sins that follow. The prophets say that Israel's debt is paid for by the exile in Babylon.

The reference to the book in which God writes the names of those whom he has chosen (in a kind of census, as it were: cf. Is 4:3; Rev 3:5, 12; 17:8), is a graphic way of showing that God has special love for those who have a mission to fulfil in the work of salvation.

---

cecideruntque de populo in die illa quasi tria milia hominum. [29]Et ait Moyses: «Implestis manus vestras hodie Domino unusquisque in filio et in fratre suo, ut detur vobis benedictio». [30]Facto autem altero die, locutus est Moyses ad populum: «Peccastis peccatum maximum; ascendam ad Dominum, si quo modo quivero eum deprecari pro scelere vestro». [31]Reversusque ad Dominum ait: «Obsecro, peccavit populus iste peccatum maximum, feceruntque sibi deos aureos; aut dimitte eis hanc noxam [32]aut, si non facis, dele me de libro tuo, quem scripsisti». [33]Cui respondit Dominus: «Qui peccaverit mihi, delebo

s. Gk Vg See Tg: Heb *ordain yourselves*

sin—and if not, blot me, I pray thee, out of thy book which thou hast written." ³³But the LORD said to Moses, "Whoever has sinned against me, him will I blot out of my book. ³⁴But now go, lead the people to the place of which I have spoken to you; behold, my angel shall go before you. Nevertheless, in the day when I visit, I will visit their sin upon them."

Rom 9:3
Rev 3:5, 12; 17:8

Dan 12:1
Ex 3:16; 23:20

³⁵And the LORD sent a plague upon the people, because they made the calf which Aaron made.

The order to pull out. An angel will lead the way*

33 ¹The LORD said to Moses, "Depart, go up hence, you and the people whom you have brought up out of the land of Egypt, to the land of which I swore to Abraham, Isaac, and Jacob, saying, 'To your descendants I will give it.' ²And I will send an

Num 10:11–13

Ex 23:20
Num 20:16
Deut 7:1

---

*33:1–23. The sacred writer explains how God is going to act in regard to his people from now on, given that they have sinned: his presence among them cannot be as it formerly was (vv. 1–6), when he worked wonders which filled them with joy; from now on there will be more to weep about and less celebration (v. 6); but he will continue to speak to Moses face to face (vv. 7–11). However, Moses pleads for God's presence to be more active (vv. 12–17) and he even manages to see the glory of the Lord (vv. 18–23).

33:1–6 The order to leave Sinai is based not so much on the exodus-covenant adjudged to Moses, but on the oath-promise which God made to the patri-archs. This means that the situation has changed radically due to the episode of the golden calf.

The Lord holds to his promise to lead the people to the promised land, but he is no longer going to help them directly.

The presence of the angel (v. 2), which had been seen as a sign of protection (cf. 23:20; Num 20:16), is now interpreted as a punishment, because it means that the Lord has decided to keep a certain distance away and send an intermediary. This decision makes the people very sad, and God will change his mind only after further intercession by Moses.

The punishment God is imposing on his people by refusing to remain among them is reminiscent of how Adam's sin was punished (cf. Gen 3:24). Adam's was the first sin man committed; this is the first sin the people commits, after it was constituted by the Covenant of Sinai. In the book of Genesis God sent Adam and Eve out of his presence; here he refuses to stay with the Israelites. There he ordered the angel to block their way and forced them out of paradise; here he again makes an angel his intermediary and forces the Israelites to take off their jewellery, which they probably had put

---

eum de libro meo. ³⁴Tu autem vade et duc populum istum, quo locutus sum tibi: angelus meus prae-cedet te; ego autem in die ultionis visitabo et hoc peccatum eorum». ³⁵Percussit ergo Dominus popu-lum pro reatu vituli, quem fecerat Aaron. ¹Locutusque est Dominus ad Moysen: «Vade, ascende de loco isto tu et populus tuus, quem eduxisti de terra Aegypti, in terram, quam iuravi Abraham, Isaac et Iacob dicens: Semini tuo dabo eam. ²Et mittam praecursorem tui angelum et eiciam Chananaeum et Amorraeum et Hetthaeum et Pherezaeum et Hevaeum et Iebusaeum, ³et intres in terram fluentem lacte

Gen 3:24;
32:9
Acts 7:51 angel before you, and I will drive out the Canaanites, the Amorites, the Hittites, the Perizzites, the Hivites, and the Jebusites. ³Go up to a land flowing with milk and honey; but I will not go up among you, lest I consume you in the way, for you are a stiff-necked people."

⁴When the people heard these evil tidings, they mourned; and no man put on his ornaments. ⁵For the LORD had said to Moses, "Say to the people of Israel, 'You are a stiff-necked people; if for a single moment I should go up among you, I would consume you. So now put off your ornaments from you, that I may know what to do with you.'" ⁶Therefore the people of Israel stripped themselves of their ornaments, from Mount Horeb onward.

The tent of meeting

Heb 13:13 ⁷Now Moses used to take the tent and pitch it outside the camp, far off from the camp; and he called it the tent of meeting. And every one who sought the LORD would go out to the tent of meeting, which was outside the camp. ⁸Whenever Moses went out to the tent, all the people rose up, and every man stood at his tent door, and looked after Moses, until he had gone into the tent.

---

on for the feast of the golden calf (vv. 5–6); he wants them to be detached from their valuables, to show the repentant attitude that should mark the rest of their pilgrimage through the desert.

33:7–11. The tent of meeting, sometimes called the tent of witness, and also the sanctuary, normally means the main tent in the sacred precinct (cf. chaps. 25–27). Here, however, it seems to be different from the sanctuary, because the sanctuary was located in the centre of the encampment and was a place of worship, whereas this tent is pitched away from the camp and is used for consultation.

This discrepancy may well be due to the fact that this passage belonged to an older tradition than the Priestly one. Whereas the Priestly tradition lays the stress on matters to do with worship, the earlier one would have focused more on social matters.

The sacred writer, through this account, is showing that God continues to be present but at a certain distance, and that only Moses has the privilege of speaking to him "face to face" (cf. 33:20). The people are simply the silent witnesses of the conversations which take place between God and Moses, but God still shows them special favour.

---

et melle. Non enim ascendam tecum, quia populus durae cervicis es, ne forte disperdam te in via». ⁴Audiens populus sermonem hunc pessimum luxit, et nullus ex more indutus est cultu suo. ⁵Dixitque Dominus ad Moysen: «Loquere filiis Israel: Populus durae cervicis es; uno momento, si ascendam in medio tui, delebo te. Nunc autem depone ornatum tuum, ut sciam quid faciam tibi». ⁶Deposuerunt ergo filii Israel ornatum suum a monte Horeb. ⁷Moyses autem tollens tabernaculum tetendit ei extra castra procul; vocavitque nomen eius Tabernaculum conventus. Et omnis, qui quaerebat Dominum, egrediebatur ad tabernaculum conventus extra castra. ⁸Cumque egrederetur Moyses ad tabernaculum, surgebat universa plebs, et stabat unusquisque in ostio papilionis sui; aspiciebantque tergum Moysi,

9When Moses entered the tent, the pillar of cloud would descend and stand at the door of the tent, and the LORD would speak with Moses. 10And when all the people saw the pillar of cloud standing at the door of the tent, all the people would rise up and worship, every man at his tent door. 11Thus the LORD used to speak to Moses face to face, as a man speaks to his friend. When Moses turned again into the camp, his servant Joshua the son of Nun, a young man, did not depart from the tent.

Ex 33:20
Num 12:8
Deut 34:10
Jn 15:15

God agrees to stay with his people

12Moses said to the LORD, "See, thou sayest to me, 'Bring up this people'; but thou hast not let me know whom thou wilt send with me. Yet thou hast said, 'I know you by name, and you have also found favour in my sight.' 13Now therefore, I pray thee, if I have found favour in thy sight, show me now thy ways, that I may know thee and find favour in thy sight. Consider too that this nation is thy people." 14And he said, "My presence will go with you, and I will give you rest." 15And he said to him, "If thy presence will not go with me, do not carry us up from here. 16For how shall it be known that I have found favour in thy sight, I and thy people? Is it

Mt 11:28
Heb 4:1

Lk 1:30

33:12–17. In this touching prayer Moses makes two requests: he asks God to show him his ways and to continue to stay with his people. What he is referring to is not the physical route through the desert (Moses and the Israelites were familiar with that) but rather the way to conduct themselves. Other biblical texts, especially the Psalms, uses "way", "ways" in this sense, as does Christian asceticism. "'Make me to know thy ways, O Lord; teach me thy paths' (Ps 25:4). We ask the Lord to guide us, to show us his footprints, so we can set out to attain the fullness of his commandments, which is charity"

(St J. Escrivá, *Christ Is Passing By*, 1).

The Lord also agrees to the second request—to stay with his people (vv. 15–17)—which means that he refrains from punishing them as he previously said he would (v. 3). So, his protective presence will still be the distinguishing mark of Israel: "After Israel's sin, when the people had turned away from God to worship the golden calf, God hears Moses' prayer of intercession and agrees to walk (cf. Ex 32) in the midst of an unfaithful people, thus demonstrating his love (cf. Ex 33:12–17)" (*Catechism of the Catholic Church*, 210).

---

donec ingrederetur tabernaculum. 9Ingresso autem illo tabernaculum, descendebat columna nubis et stabat ad ostium; loquebaturque cum Moyse, 10cernentibus universis quod columna nubis staret ad ostium tabernaculi. Stabantque ipsi et adorabant per fores tabernaculorum suorum. 11Loquebatur autem Dominus ad Moysen facie ad faciem, sicut solet loqui homo ad amicum suum. Cumque ille revertere- tur in castra, minister eius Iosue filius Nun puer non recedebat de medio tabernaculi. 12Dixit autem Moyses ad Dominum: «Praecipis, ut educam populum istum, et non indicas mihi, quem missurus es mecum; cum dixeris: 'Novi te ex nomine, et invenisti gratiam coram me'. 13Si ergo inveni gratiam in conspectu tuo, ostende mihi viam tuam, ut sciam te et inveniam gratiam ante oculos tuos; respice quia populus tuus est natio haec». 14Dixitque Dominus: «Facies mea ibit, et requiem dabo tibi». 15Et ait

not in thy going with us, so that we are distinct, I and thy people, from all other people that are upon the face of the earth?"

¹⁷And the LORD said to Moses, "This very thing that you have spoken I will do; for you have found favour in my sight, and I know you by name."

Moses sees the glory of God

¹⁸Moses said, "I pray thee, show me thy glory." ¹⁹And he said, "I will make all my goodness pass before you, and will proclaim before you my name 'The LORD'; and I will be gracious to whom I will be gracious, and will show mercy on whom I will show mercy. ²⁰But," he said, "you cannot see my face; for man shall not see me and live." ²¹And the LORD said, "Behold, there is a place by me where you shall stand upon the rock; ²²and while my glory passes by I will put you in a cleft of the rock, and I will cover you with my hand until I have passed by; ²³then I will take away my hand, and you shall see my back; but my face shall not be seen."

Ex 33:1
1 Kings 19:9–18
Jn 1:18
Rom 9:15
Gen 32:30
Ex 19:21
Deut 4:33
Judg 6:22–23
Is 6:2
Jn 1:18
1 Cor 12:12
1 Tim 6:16
1 Jn 3:2
1 Kings 19:9–13
Mt 17:1–7

God manifests his love to his people, by coming close to them. And he does so with every soul. "You were deeper than the most inward place of my heart and loftier than the highest" (St Augustine, *Confessions*, 3, 6–11). In the fullness of Revelation the Gospel of St John teaches that God's presence among men reaches its zenith in the Incarnation: "And the Word became flesh and dwelt among us" (Jn 1:14).

33:18–23. Moses asks for a more intimate knowledge of God—to see his glory, that is, to see him as he really is. But, because God is infinite, it is not possible for man, given his creaturely limitations, to fully comprehend God. The

Bible frequently refers to the fact that "no one can see the face of God and live" (cf. v. 20; Gen 32:30; Ex 19:21; Deut 4:33; Judg 6:22–23). To show the sublime greatness of God, Scripture says that even the Seraphim hide their face in the presence of the Lord (cf. Is 6:2).

The vision of God described so mysteriously here is a work of special favour to Moses, his special friend (cf. Num 12:7–8; Deut 34:10). But not even he is allowed to see God directly; he will see only the back of him, as if to say that man can only manage to see God in the tracks he leaves behind. This vision was a very special privilege, and it is one which will also be given to Elijah (cf. 1 Kings 19:9–13). And it is in fact these

---

Moyses: «Si non tu ipse eas, ne educas nos de loco isto; ¹⁶in quo enim scietur me et populum tuum invenisse gratiam in conspectu tuo, nisi ambulaveris nobiscum, ut glorificemur ego et populus tuus prae omnibus populis, qui habitant super terram?». ¹⁷Dixitque Dominus ad Moysen: «Et verbum istud, quod locutus es, faciam; invenisti enim gratiam coram me, et teipsum novi ex nomine». ¹⁸Qui ait: «Ostende mihi gloriam tuam». ¹⁹Respondit: «Ego ostendam omne bonum tibi et vocabo in nomine Domini coram te; et miserebor, cui voluero, et clemens ero, in quem mihi placuerit». ²⁰Rursumque ait: «Non poteris videre faciem meam; non enim videbit me homo et vivet». ²¹Et iterum: «Ecce, inquit, est locus apud me, stabis super petram; ²²cumque transibit gloria mea, ponam te in foramine petrae et protegam dextera mea, donec transeam; ²³tollamque manum meam, et videbis posteriora mea; faciem

12. THE COVENANT IS RENEWED*   Ex 19:14

34 ¹The LORD said to Moses, "Cut two tables of stone like the first; and I will write upon the tables the words that were on the first tables, which you broke. ²Be ready in the morning, and come up in the morning to Mount Sinai, and present yourself there to me on the top of the mountain. ³No man shall come up with you, and let no man be seen throughout all the mountain; let no flocks or herds feed before that mountain." ⁴So Moses cut two tables of stone like the first; and he rose early in the morning and went up on Mount Sinai, as the LORD had commanded him, and took in his hand two tables of stone. ⁵And the LORD descended in the cloud and stood with him there, and proclaimed the name of the LORD.

---

two men who appear in the Transfiguration on Mount Tabor (cf. Mt 17:1–7), where Christ's divinity is revealed. Only Christ has seen God and has made him known (cf. Jn 1:18). The blessed in heaven will attain the fullest vision of God (cf. 1 Cor 13:12; 1 Jn 3:2).

*34:1–28. This chapter narrating the renewal of the Covenant follows the same pattern as the account of its original establishment (cf. Ex 19–24); but it is shorter, concentrating on the two main protagonists, God and Moses. Thus, it begins with the preparations for the theophany and for the encounter with the Lord (vv. 1–5); then follows the revelation of God, and Moses' prayer (vv. 6–9); and it ends with the renewal of the Covenant and the so-called Rite of the Covenant (vv. 10–28). The account hinges on the remaking of the tables of

stone after the sin of the golden calf; the tables symbolize God's offer to keep to the pact and never to go back on it.

34:1–5. The theophany is described very soberly here, but it has exactly the same elements as given in chapter 19: very careful preparation by Moses (v. 2; cf. 19:10–11); the people forbidden to approach the mountain (v. 3; cf. 19:12–13); God appearing wrapped in the cloud (v. 5; cf. 19:16–20).

Comparing the two accounts, this one says less about the transcendence of God and puts more stress on his closeness to Moses: "he stood with him there" (v. 5). God's initiative in drawing close to man is clear to see; it lies at the very basis of the Covenant.

"He proclaimed the name of the Lord" (v. 6); the context would suggest that it is Moses who proclaims the name

autem meam videre non poteris». ¹Dixitque Dominus ad Moysen: «Praecide tibi duas tabulas lapideas instar priorum, et scribam super eas verba, quae habuerunt tabulae, quas fregisti. ²Esto paratus mane, ut ascendas statim in montem Sinai; stabisque mihi super verticem montis. ³Nullus ascendat tecum, nec videatur quispiam per totum montem; oves quoque et boves non pascantur e contra». ⁴Excidit ergo duas tabulas lapideas, quales antea fuerant; et de nocte consurgens ascendit in montem Sinai, sicut praeceperat ei Dominus, portans secum tabulas. ⁵Cumque descendisset Dominus per nubem, stetit cum eo vocans in nomine Domini. ⁶Et transiens coram eo clamavit: «Dominus, Dominus Deus, misericors

Ex 20:5-6
Num 14:18
Deut 5:9-18
Jn 1:17
Jas 5:11
Jn 1:14

Ex 32:11-14;
33:15-17
Ps 86:1-15;
103:8-10

God appears

[6]The LORD passed before him, and proclaimed, "The LORD, the LORD, a God merciful and gracious, slow to anger, and abounding in steadfast love and faithfulness, [7]keeping steadfast love for thousands, forgiving iniquity and transgression and sin, but who will by no means clear the guilty, visiting the iniquity of the fathers upon the children and the children's children, to the third and the fourth generation." [8]And Moses made haste to bow his head toward the earth, and worshiped. [9]And he said, "If now I have

---

of the Lord, but the Hebrew could indeed be as the RSV has it, "and he proclaimed his name, 'Lord' ". The same wording appears in v. 6 implying that it is the Lord who is "proclaiming", defining himself as he promised he would (cf. 33:19). The sacred writer may have intentionally left these words open to either interpretation; whether spoken by Moses or said directly by God, they are equal from the revelation point of view.

34:6-7. In response to Moses' pleading, the Lord makes himself manifest. The solemn repetition of the name of Yahweh (Lord) emphasizes that the Lord is introducing himself liturgically to the assembled Israelites. In the description of himself which follows (and which is repeated elsewhere, cf. 20:5-6; Num 14:18; Deut 5:9-18; etc.), two key attributes of God are underlined—justice and mercy. God cannot let sin go unpunished, nor does he; the prophets, too, will teach that sin is, first and foremost, something personal (cf. Jer 31:29; Ezek 18:2ff). But this ancient text refers only in a general way to the fact that God is just, and puts more stress on his mercy. A person who is conscious of his own sin has access to God only if he is sure that God can and

will forgive him. "The concept of 'mercy' in the Old Testament," John Paul II comments, "has a long and rich history. We have to refer back to it in order that the mercy revealed by Christ may shine forth more clearly. [. . .] [S]in too constitutes man's misery. The people of the Old Covenant experienced this misery from the time of the Exodus, when they set up the golden calf. The Lord himself triumphed over this act of breaking the covenant when he solemnly declared to Moses that he was a 'God merciful and gracious, slow to anger, and abounding in steadfast love and faithfulness' (Ex 34:6). It is in this central revelation that the chosen people, and each of its members, will find, every time that they have sinned, the strength and the motive for turning to the Lord to remind him of what he had exactly revealed about himself and to beseech his forgiveness" (*Dives in misericordia*, 4). On "God's jealousy", see the note on 20:5-6.

34:8-9. Moses once more implores the Lord on behalf of his people; he makes three requests, which sum up many earlier petitions: he begs God to stay with the people and protect them in their hazardous journeying in the desert (cf.

---

et clemens, patiens et multae miserationis ac verax, [7]qui custodit misericordiam in milia, qui aufert iniquitatem et scelera atque peccata, nihil autem impunitum sinit, qui reddit iniquitatem patrum in filiis ac nepotibus in tertiam et quartam progeniem». [8]Festinusque Moyses curvatus est pronus in terram et adorans [9]ait: «Si inveni gratiam in conspectu tuo, Domine, obsecro, ut gradiaris nobiscum; populus

found favour in thy sight, O Lord, let the Lord, I pray thee, go in the midst of us, although it is a stiff-necked people; and pardon our iniquity and our sin, and take us for thy inheritance."

The Covenant*

[10]And he said, "Behold, I make a covenant. Before all your people Jn 1:17
I will do marvels, such as have not been wrought in all the earth or Rev 15:3
in any nation; and all the people among whom you are shall see the
work of the LORD; for it is a terrible thing that I will do with you.

33:15–17), to forgive the very grave sin they have committed (cf. 32:11–14), and finally to make them his own property, thereby distinguishing them from all other peoples (cf. 33:16) and restoring them to their status as "his own possession" (cf. 19:5). These three requests are ones that were constantly on the lips of the people of Israel and in the hearts of everyone who acknowledges God (cf. Ps 86:1–15; 103:8–10; etc.).

*34:10–28. This section, which is considered to belong to the Yahwistic tradition, has a very ancient origin; it is probably older than the narrative into which it is set (just as other law sections of the book are). As in the text of the moral Decalogue (cf. 20:1–21), there is a preface which recalls the wondrous things God has done and which form the basis of the precepts and rules which will now be listed. This discourse of the Lord, begins in a solemn style, describing God's decision to establish a Covenant with his people.

The historical introduction (v. 10) does not confine itself to the marvels of the Exodus but covers all the wonderful things that God is doing all the time. God's initiative is the very origin and basis of the Covenant; Israel is to be a permanent wit-

ness to his protective presence.

If Israel were to make pacts and alliances with polytheistic nations, that would be equivalent to accepting their gods and exposing themselves to the danger of idolatry (vv. 12–13) or syncretism.

The establishing of the Covenant is followed by the so-called "Ritual Decalogue" (vv. 14–28). Although v. 28 refers to there being "ten commandments", it is not easy to reduce all these rules to ten. Most scholars agree that this "code" or codification of laws (cf. the note on 20:1–17), in its original form and as later modified, was not initially part of the book of Exodus. The regulations included here have basically to do with worship and they are so couched as to suggest that they belong to a people already settled and therefore able to organize the pilgrimage feasts (unleavened bread, Pentecost, Tabernacles), even though the rules given for them here are rather embryonic.

"You shall break their pillars and cut down their Asherim" (v. 13). The pillars were commemorative stones such as obelisks (cf. the note on 23:24–25). The Asherim were wooden monuments in the form of tree-stumps decorated in some way in honour of the fertility goddess Ashera (Astarte in Greek).

---

quidem durae cervicis est, sed tu auferes iniquitates nostras atque peccata nosque possidebis».
[10]Respondit Dominus: «Ego inibo pactum coram universo populo tuo; mirabilia faciam, quae numquam visa sunt super totam terram nec in ullis gentibus, ut cernat cunctus populus, in cuius es

Ex 23:20
Deut 7:1

¹¹"Observe what I command you this day. Behold, I will drive out before you the Amorites, the Canaanites, the Hittites, the Perizzites, the Hivites, and the Jebusites. ¹²Take heed to yourself, lest you make a covenant with the inhabitants of the land whither you go,

Ex 23:24–25

lest it become a snare in the midst of you. ¹³You shall tear down their altars, and break their pillars, and cut down their Asherim ¹⁴

The Ritual Decalogue

Ex 20:3–5
Deut 4:24

Acts 15:20

¹⁴(for you shall worship no other god, for the LORD, whose name is Jealous, is a jealous God), ¹⁵lest you make a covenant with the inhabitants of the land, and when they play the harlot after their gods and sacrifice to their gods and one invites you, you eat of his sacrifice, ¹⁶and you take of their daughters for your sons, and their daughters play the harlot after their gods and make your sons play the harlot after their gods.

Ex 20:4

¹⁷"You shall make for yourself no molten gods.

Ex 12:2; 23:14

¹⁸"The feast of unleavened bread you shall keep. Seven days you shall eat unleavened bread, as I commanded you, at the time appointed in the month Abib; for in the month Abib you came out

---

34:14–17. Verses 14 and 17 can be taken as a new wording of the first two commandments (cf. 20:3–5), centred on a ban on idolatry and the making of images. Verses 15 and 16 are prescriptions designed to prevent idolatry: they contain marriage imagery of the sort often found in the prophets from Hosea onwards (cf. Hos 2:4–25), meant to convey the idea of exclusive fidelity to God. Every idolatrous act is seen as prostitution or adultery against the Lord because the Covenant links man to God with the strength of the marriage bond. The image of married love continues into the New Testament, which applies it to Christ's love for his Church: "Husbands, love your wives, *as Christ loved the church"* (Eph 5:25). The Second Vatican Council repeats this teaching in these simple words: "Christ loves the Church as his bride, having been established as the model of a man loving his wife as his own body" (*Lumen gentium*, 7).

34:18–20. The keeping of the feast of the unleavened bread could be the third precept of this "Ritual Decalogue", and the rule about the first-born, the fourth. Here the month of Abib is given as the time the people came out of Egypt, but, unlike 12:2, it does not say it is the first month of the year. On the law about the first-born, see what is said in the note on 13:12.

---

medio, opus Domini terribile, quod facturus sum tecum. ¹¹Observa cuncta, quae hodie mando tibi: ego ipse eiciam ante faciem tuam Amorraeum et Chananaeum et Hetthaeum, Pherezaeum quoque et Hevaeum et Iebusaeum. ¹²Cave, ne umquam cum habitatoribus terrae, quam intraveris, iungas amicitias, quae tibi sint in ruinam; ¹³sed aras eorum destrue, confringe lapides palosque succide. ¹⁴Noli adorare deum alienum: Dominus Zelotes nomen eius, Deus est aemulator. ¹⁵Ne ineas pactum cum hominibus illarum regionum, ne, cum fornicati fuerint cum diis suis et sacrificaverint eis, vocet te quispiam, et comedas de immolatis. ¹⁶Nec uxorem de filiabus eorum accipies filiis tuis, ne, postquam ipsae fuerint fornicatae cum diis suis, fornicari faciant et filios tuos in deos suos. ¹⁷Deos conflatiles non facies tibi. ¹⁸Sollemnitatem Azymorum custodies: septem diebus vesceris azymis, sicut praecepi tibi, in tempore constituto mensis Abib mense enim verni temporis egressus es de Aegypto. ¹⁹Omne, quod

from Egypt. [19]All that opens the womb is mine, all your male[x] cattle, the firstlings of cow and sheep. [20]The firstling of an ass you shall redeem with a lamb, or if you will not redeem it you shall break its neck. All the first-born of your sons you shall redeem. And none shall appear before me empty.

[21]"Six days you shall work, but on the seventh day you shall rest; in plowing time and in harvest you shall rest. [22]And you shall observe the feast of weeks, the first fruits of wheat harvest, and the feast of ingathering at the year's end. [23]Three times in the year shall all your males appear before the LORD God, the God of Israel. [24]For I will cast out nations before you, and enlarge your borders; neither shall any man desire your land, when you go up to appear before the LORD your God three times in the year.

[25]"You shall not offer the blood of my sacrifice with leaven; neither shall the sacrifice of the feast of the passover be left until

Ex 13:1–3; 13:11

Ex 20:8

Ex 23:14–17

Ex 12:1–4; 23:18

34:21. The precept on sabbath rest, the first in this code, is oriented to an agricultural society (that is, not to the sort of circumstances that applied in the crossing of the desert: cf. the note on 20:8). No religious reasons for this rest are mentioned, whether because this is a very concise wording or because it comes from a very early source (from a time when the idea of the sabbath's being the day of the Lord had not yet come into its own). Divine revelation, even on commandments, was a gradual thing and would not reach its full development until the New Testament.

34:22–24. The annual feasts of Pentecost and Tabernacles are the subject of the sixth commandment in this code. The fact that there are three pilgrimages each year seems to imply that religious worship is already centralized in the temple of Jerusalem. For a detailed comment on the main feasts of the chosen people, see the note on 23:14–17.

34:25. The seventh and eighth precepts of this code have to do with the Passover. The Code of the Covenant (cf. 23:18) is worded similarly to this, but here the Passover is not linked to the feast of the unleavened bread, despite the fact that they were held at the same time from very early on. This passage gives grounds for thinking that they were originally two different celebrations, with different purposes and rituals. The Passover was much the older; it betokened God's special protection; and it was a true sacrifice, perhaps the only one held in the context of the home and not in the temple (cf. the note on 12:1–14).

---

aperit vulvam generis masculini, meum erit; de cuncto grege tuo tam de bobus quam de ovibus meum erit. [20]Primogenitum asini redimes ove, sin autem nec pretium pro eo dederis, franges cervicem eius. Primogenitum filiorum tuorum redimes, nec apparebis in conspectu meo vacuus. [21]Sex diebus operaberis, die septimo cessabis etiam arare et metere. [22]Sollemnitatem Hebdomadarum facies tibi in primitiis frugum messis tuae triticeae et sollemnitatem Collectae, quando, redeunte anni tempore, cuncta conduntur. [23]Tribus temporibus anni apparebit omne masculinum tuum in conspectu omnipotentis Domini Dei Israel. [24]Cum enim tulero gentes a facie tua et dilatavero terminos tuos, nullus insidiabitur

x. Gk Theodotion Vg Tg: Heb uncertain

Ex 23:19
Deut 26:1

the morning. [26]The first of the first fruits of your ground you shall bring to the house of the LORD your God. You shall not boil a kid in its mother's milk."

[27]And the LORD said to Moses, "Write these words; in accordance with these words I have made a covenant with you and

Ex 24:10, 18;
20:1
Mt 4:2

with Israel." [28]And he was there with the LORD forty days and forty nights; he neither ate bread nor drank water. And he wrote upon the tables the words of the covenant, the ten commandments.[t]

2 Cor 3:7–16
Mt 17:2
2 Cor 3:10

Moses' shining face

[29]When Moses came down from Mount Sinai, with the two tables of the testimony in his hand as he came down from the mountain, Moses did not know that the skin of his face shone because he had been talking with God. [30]And when Aaron and all the people of Israel saw Moses, behold, the skin of his face shone, and they were afraid to come near him. [31]But Moses called to them; and Aaron and all the leaders of the congregation returned to him, and Moses talked with them. [32]And afterward all the people of Israel

---

34:26. These last two precepts are also to be found in other lists of laws (cf. 23:19). They bring to a close this Ritual Code or Decalogue which contains a diverse series of laws, though all of them have to do with worship. For this reason, these precepts no longer apply, since Jesus Christ has come and it is he who renders true worship to the Father.

34:27–28. The conclusion of the Covenant is described as soberly as its introduction (v. 10). On the meaning of the forty days, see the note on 24:12–18.

34:29–35. The account of the events at

Sinai ends with Moses in sharp focus, his face reflecting the glory of God.

"His face shone" (vv. 29, 30, 35). The Hebrew word *qarán*, which means "to shine, to be radiant", is very similar to *qeren*, which means "horn". Hence St Jerome's translation in the Vulgate: "And his face turned with bright horns", which has had its influence on Christian tradition and art. Michelangelo, for example, gave his famous statue of Moses two bright lights, one on each side of his forehead. Anyway, the sacred author's point is that Moses was transformed due to the fact that he had been so near God. The veil covering his face emphasizes the

---

terrae tuae, ascendente te et apparente in conspectu Domini Dei tui ter in anno. [25]Non immolabis super fermento sanguinem hostiae meae; neque residebit mane de victima sollemnitatis Paschae. [26]Primitias frugum terrae tuae afferes in domum Domini Dei tui. Non coques haedum in lacte matris suae». [27]Dixitque Dominus ad Moysen: «Scribe tibi verba haec, quibus et tecum et cum Israel pepigi foedus». [28]Fuit ergo ibi cum Domino quadraginta dies et quadraginta noctes; panem non comedit et aquam non bibit et scripsit in tabulis verba foederis, decem verba. [29]Cumque descenderet Moyses de monte Sinai, tenebat duas tabulas testimonii et ignorabat quod resplenderet cutis faciei suae ex consortio sermonis Domini. [30]Videntes autem Aaron et filii Israel resplendere cutem faciei Moysi, timuerunt prope

t. Heb *words*

came near, and he gave them in commandment all that the LORD had spoken with him in Mount Sinai. [33]And when Moses had fin- ished speaking with them, he put a veil on his face; [34]but whenever Moses went in before the LORD to speak with him, he took the veil off, until he came out; and when he came out, and told the people of Israel what he was commanded, [35]the people of Israel saw the face of Moses, that the skin of Moses' face shone; and Moses would put the veil upon his face again, until he went in to speak with him.

2 Cor 3:16

13. BUILDING THE SANCTUARY*

The sabbath rest

35 [1]Moses assembled all the congregation of the people of Israel, and said to them, "These are the things which the LORD has commanded you to do. [2]Six days shall work be done, but on the seventh day you shall have a holy sabbath of solemn rest to the LORD; whoever does any work on it shall be put to death;

Ex 20:8; 31:12-17

Num 15:32ff

---

transcendence of God: not only can the Israelites not see God; they cannot even look at the face of Moses, his closest intermediary.

St Paul refers to this episode in order to show the radical superiority of the New Covenant and the meaning of apostolic ministry, for with the coming of Christ all has been revealed and man has direct access to the Father (cf. 2 Cor 3:7–18).

35:1—40:8. The last section of the book tells how the sanctuary and all its furnishings were made. In order to show how faithfully the Israelites obeyed, the sacred writer repeats even word for word the orders given in chapters 25–27 and 30. Even his little additions serve to show

how exactly those men carried out the Lord's instructions. It is a lesson on the quality a Christian's obedience should have.

35:1-3. The precept on sabbath rest came at the end of the instructions for building the sanctuary (31:12–17); here it is placed first, giving it all its due importance, for the day dedicated to the Lord should be kept even when the work being done is done at God's own bidding.

This is the only passage in the Old Testament to mention the ban on lighting fires on the sabbath (though that may be implied in 16:23). It is very much to the point, since metals would have had to be smelted to make much of the sanctuary fittings.

---

accedere; [31]vocatique ab eo reversi sunt tam Aaron quam principes synagogae. Et postquam locutus est ad eos, [32]venerunt ad eum etiam omnes filii Israel; quibus praecepit cuncta, quae audierat a Domino in monte Sinai. [33]Impletisque sermonibus, posuit velamen super faciem suam, [34]quod ingressus ad Dominum et loquens cum eo auferebat, donec exiret; et tunc loquebatur ad filios Israel omnia, quae sibi fuerant imperata. [35]Qui videbant cutem faciei Moysi resplendere, sed operiebat ille rursus faciem suam, donec ingressus loqueretur cum eo. [1]Igitur, congregato omni coetu filiorum Israel, dixit ad eos:

Ex 16:23 ³you shall kindle no fire in all your habitations on the sabbath day."

Ex 25:1–7 **Generous contributions**

⁴Moses said to all the congregation of the people of Israel, "This is the thing which the LORD has commanded. ⁵Take from among you an offering to the LORD; whoever is of a generous heart, let him bring the LORD's offering: gold, silver, and bronze; ⁶blue and purple and scarlet stuff and fine twined linen; goats' hair, ⁷tanned rams' skins, and goatskins; acacia wood, ⁸oil for the light, spices for the anointing oil and for the fragrant incense, ⁹and onyx stones and stones for setting, for the ephod and for the breastpiece.

¹⁰"And let every able man among you come and make all that the LORD has commanded: the tabernacle, ¹¹its tent and its covering, its hooks and its frames, its bars, its pillars, and its bases; ¹²the ark with its poles, the mercy seat, and the veil of the screen; ¹³the table with its poles and all its utensils, and the bread of the Presence; ¹⁴the lampstand also for the light, with its utensils and its lamps, and the oil for the light; ¹⁵and the altar of incense, with its poles, and the anointing oil and the fragrant incense, and the screen for the door, at the door of the tabernacle; ¹⁶the altar of burnt offering, with its grating of bronze, its poles, and all its utensils, the laver and its base; ¹⁷the hangings of the court, its pillars and its bases, and the screen for the gate of the court; ¹⁸the pegs of the tabernacle and the pegs of the court, and their cords; ¹⁹the finely wrought garments for ministering in the holy place, the holy garments for Aaron the priest, and the garments of his sons, for their service as priests."

²⁰Then all the congregation of the people of Israel departed from the presence of Moses. ²¹And they came, every one whose

---

«Haec sunt, quae iussit Dominus fieri: ²sex diebus facietis opus, septimus dies erit vobis sanctus, sabbatum et requies Domino; qui fecerit opus in eo, occidetur. ³Non succendetis ignem in omnibus habitaculis vestris per diem sabbati». ⁴Et ait Moyses ad omnem coetum filiorum Israel: «Iste est sermo, quem praecepit Dominus dicens: ⁵'Separate apud vos donaria Domino'. Omnis voluntarius et proni animi offerat ea Domino: aurum et argentum et aes, ⁶hyacinthum et purpuram coccumque et byssum, pilos caprarum ⁷et pelles arietum rubricatas et pelles delphini, ligna acaciae ⁸et oleum ad luminaria concinnanda et aromata, ut conficiatur unguentum et thymiama suavissimum, ⁹lapides onychinos et gemmas ad ornatum ephod et pectoralis. ¹⁰Quisquis vestrum sapiens est, veniat et faciat, quod Dominus imperavit, ¹¹habitaculum scilicet et tentorium eius atque operimentum, fibulas et tabulata cum vectibus, columnas et bases; ¹²arcam et vectes, propitiatorium et velum, quod ante illud oppanditur ¹³mensam cum vectibus et vasis et propositionis panibus; ¹⁴candelabrum ad luminaria sustentanda, vasa illius et lucernas et oleum ad nutrimenta luminarium; ¹⁵altare thymiamatis et vectes et oleum unctionis et thymiama ex aromatibus; velum ad ostium habitaculi; ¹⁶altare holocausti et craticulam eius aeneam cum vectibus et vasis suis, labrum et basim eius; ¹⁷cortinas atrii cum columnis et basibus, velum in foribus atrii; ¹⁸paxillos habitaculi et atrii cum funiculis suis; ¹⁹vestimenta texta, quorum usus est in ministerio sanctuarii, vestes sanctas Aaron pontificis ac vestes filiorum eius, ut sacerdotio fungantur mihi».

heart stirred him, and every one whose spirit moved him, and brought the LORD's offering to be used for the tent of meeting, and for all its service, and for the holy garments. ²²So they came, both men and women; all who were of a willing heart brought brooches and earrings and signet rings and armlets, all sorts of gold objects, every man dedicating an offering of gold to the LORD. ²³And every man with whom was found blue or purple or scarlet stuff or fine linen or goats' hair or tanned rams' skins or goatskins, brought them. ²⁴Every one who could make an offering of silver or bronze brought it as the LORD's offering; and every man with whom was found acacia wood of any use in the work, brought it. ²⁵And all women who had ability spun with their hands, and brought what they had spun in blue and purple and scarlet stuff and fine twined linen; ²⁶all the women whose hearts were moved with ability spun the goats' hair. ²⁷And the leaders brought onyx stones and stones to be set, for the ephod and for the breastpiece, ²⁸and spices and oil for the light, and for the anointing oil, and for the fragrant incense. ²⁹All the men and women, the people of Israel, whose heart moved them to bring anything for the work which the LORD had commanded by Moses to be done, brought it as their freewill offering to the LORD.

The craftsmen chosen

Ex 31:2–6

³⁰And Moses said to the people of Israel, "See, the LORD has called by name Bezalel the son of Uri, son of Hur, of the tribe of Judah; ³¹and he has filled him with the Spirit of God, with ability, with intelligence, with knowledge, and with all craftsmanship, ³²to devise artistic designs, to work in gold and silver and bronze, ³³in cutting stones for setting, and in carving wood, for work in every skilled craft. ³⁴And he has inspired him to teach, both him and

Acts 6:3

²⁰Egressus est omnis coetus filiorum Israel de conspectu Moysi, ²¹et venit, quisquis erat mentis promptissimae, et attulit sponte sua donaria Domino ad faciendum opus tabernaculi conventus et quidquid ad cultum et ad vestes sanctas necessarium erat. ²²Viri cum mulieribus, omnes voluntarii praebuerunt fibulas et inaures, anulos et dextralia; omne vas aureum in donaria Domini separatum est. ²³Si quis habebat hyacinthum et purpuram coccumque, byssum et pilos caprarum, pelles arietum rubricatas et pelles delphini, ²⁴argenti aerisque metalla, obtulerunt Domino lignaque acaciae in varios usus. ²⁵Sed et mulieres eruditae dederunt, quae neverant, hyacinthum, purpuram et coccum ac byssum ²⁶et pilos caprarum, sponte propria cuncta tribuentes. ²⁷Principes vero obtulerunt lapides onychinos et gemmas ad ephod et pectorale ²⁸aromataque et oleum ad luminaria concinnanda et ad praeparandum unguentum ac thymiama odoris suavissimi componendum. ²⁹Omnes viri et mulieres mente prompta obtulerunt donaria, ut fierent opera, quae iusserat Dominus per manum Moysi. Cuncti filii Israel voluntaria Domino dedicaverunt. ³⁰Dixitque Moyses ad filios Israel: «Ecce vocavit Dominus ex nomine Beseleel filium Uri filii Hur de tribu Iudae; ³¹implevitque eum spiritu Dei, sapientia et intellegentia et scientia ad omne opus, ³²ad excogitandum et faciendum opus in auro et argento et aere, ³³ad scindendum et includendum gemmas et ad sculpendum ligna, quidquid fabre adinveniri potest. ³⁴Dedit quoque in corde eius, ut alios doceret, ipsi et Ooliab filio Achisamech de tribu Dan. ³⁵Ambos implevit sapientia,

Ex 26:31–32 Oholiab the son of Ahisamach of the tribe of Dan. ³⁵He has filled them with ability to do every sort of work done by a craftsman or by a designer or by an embroiderer in blue and purple and scarlet stuff and fine twined linen, or by a weaver—by any sort of workman or skilled designer.

36 ¹Bezalel and Oholiab and every able man in whom the LORD has put ability and intelligence to know how to do any work in the construction of the sanctuary shall work in accordance with all that the LORD has commanded."

²And Moses called Bezalel and Oholiab and every able man in whose mind the LORD had put ability, every one whose heart stirred him up to come to do the work; ³and they received from Moses all the freewill offering which the people of Israel had brought for doing the work on the sanctuary. They still kept bringing him freewill offerings every morning, ⁴so that all the able men who were doing every sort of task on the sanctuary came, each from the task that he was doing, ⁵and said to Moses, "The people bring much more than enough for doing the work which the LORD has commanded us to do." ⁶So Moses gave command, and word was proclaimed throughout the camp, "Let neither man nor woman do anything more for the offering for the sanctuary." So the people were restrained from bringing; ⁷for the stuff they had was sufficient to do all the work, and more.

Ex 26:1–14 **Building the tabernacle**

⁸And all the able men among the workmen made the tabernacle with ten curtains; they were made of fine twined linen and blue

---

36:2–7. The Israelites were so generous that Moses had to call a halt to their offerings. In view of how well the sons of Israel acted, and mindful of all that God did for his people, the prophets and future generations looked back nostalgically on the journey in the desert as an ideal, a reference point, to encourage heartfelt conversion to God (cf., e.g., Hos 2:16–17; Jer 2:6).

---

ut faciant opera fabri polymitarii ac plumarii de hyacintho ac purpura coccoque et bysso et textoris, facientes omne opus ac nova quaeque reperientes». ¹Fecit ergo Beseleel et Ooliab et omnis vir sapiens, quibus dedit Dominus sapientiam et intellectum, ut scirent fabre operari, quae in usus sanctuarii necessaria sunt et quae praecepit Dominus. ²Cumque vocasset Moyses Beseleel et Ooliab et omnem eruditum virum, cui dederat Dominus sapientiam, omnes, qui sponte sua obtulerant se ad faciendum opus, ³acceperunt ab ipso universa donaria, quae attulerant filii Israel ad faciendum opus in cultum sanctuarii. Ipsi autem cotidie mane donaria ei offerebant. ⁴Unde omnes sapientes artifices venerunt singuli de opere suo pro sanctuario ⁵et dixerunt Moysi: «Plus offert populus quam necessarium est operi, quod Dominus iussit facere». ⁶Iussit ergo Moyses praeconis voce per castra clamari: «Nec vir nec mulier quidquam offerat ultra pro omni opere sanctuarii». Sicque cessatum est a muneribus offerendis, ⁷eo quod oblata sufficerent et superabundarent. ⁸Feceruntque omnes corde sapientes inter artifices habita-

and purple and scarlet stuff, with cherubim skilfully worked. ⁹The length of each curtain was twenty-eight cubits, and the breadth of each curtain four cubits; all the curtains had the same measure.

¹⁰And he coupled five curtains to one another, and the other five curtains he coupled to one another. ¹¹And he made loops of blue on the edge of the outmost curtain of the first set; likewise he made them on the edge of the outmost curtain of the second set; ¹²he made fifty loops on the one curtain, and he made fifty loops on the edge of the curtain that was in the second set; the loops were opposite one another. ¹³And he made fifty clasps of gold, and coupled the curtains one to the other with clasps; so the tabernacle was one whole.

¹⁴He also made curtains of goats' hair for a tent over the tabernacle; he made eleven curtains. ¹⁵The length of each curtain was thirty cubits, and the breadth of each curtain four cubits; the eleven curtains had the same measure. ¹⁶He coupled five curtains by themselves, and six curtains by themselves. ¹⁷And he made fifty loops on the edge of the outmost curtain of the one set, and fifty loops on the edge of the other connecting curtain. ¹⁸And he made fifty clasps of bronze to couple the tent together that it might be one whole. ¹⁹And he made for the tent a covering of tanned rams' skins and goatskins.

The framework for the tabernacle
Ex 26:15–30

²⁰Then he made the upright frames for the tabernacle of acacia wood. ²¹Ten cubits was the length of a frame, and a cubit and a half the breadth of each frame. ²²Each frame had two tenons, for fitting together; he did this for all the frames of the tabernacle. ²³The frames for the tabernacle he made thus: twenty frames for the southside; ²⁴and he made forty bases of silver under the twenty

culi cortinas decem de bysso retorta et hyacintho et purpura coccoque, cum cherubim intextis arte polymita; ⁹quarum una habebat in longitudine viginti octo cubitos et in latitudine quattuor: una mensura erat omnium cortinarum. ¹⁰Coniunxitque cortinas quinque alteram alteri et alias quinque sibi invicem copulavit. ¹¹Fecit et ansas hyacinthinas in ora cortinae unius in extremitate iuncturae et in ora cortinae extremae in iunctura altera similiter. ¹²Quinquagenas ansas fecit pro utraque cortina, ut contra se invicem venirent ansae et mutuo iungerentur. ¹³Unde et quinquaginta fudit fibulas aureas, quae morderent cortinarum ansas, et fieret unum habitaculum. ¹⁴Fecit et saga undecim de pilis caprarum pro tentorio super habitaculum; ¹⁵unum sagum in longitudine habebat cubitos triginta et in latitudine cubitos quattuor: unius mensurae erant omnia saga. ¹⁶Quorum quinque iunxit seorsum et sex alia separatim. ¹⁷Fecitque ansas quinquaginta in ora sagi ultimi iuncturae unius et quinquaginta in ora sagi iuncturae alterius, ut sibi invicem iungerentur; ¹⁸et fecit fibulas aeneas quinquaginta, quibus necteretur tentorium, ut esset unum. ¹⁹Fecit et opertorium tentorio de pellibus arietum rubricatis aliudque desuper velamentum de pellibus delphini. ²⁰Fecit et tabulas habitaculi de lignis acaciae stantes. ²¹Decem cubitorum erat longitudo tabulae unius, et unum ac semis cubitum latitudo retinebat. ²²Bini pedes erant per singulas tabulas, ut altera alteri iungeretur: sic fecit in omnibus tabulis habitaculi. ²³E quibus viginti ad plagam meridianam erant contra austrum ²⁴cum quadraginta basibus argenteis. Duae bases sub

frames, two bases under one frame for its two tenons, and two bases under another frame for its two tenons. ²⁵And for the second side of the tabernacle, on the north side, he made twenty frames ²⁶and their forty bases of silver, two bases under one frame and two bases under another frame. ²⁷And for the rear of the tabernacle westward he made six frames. ²⁸And he made two frames for corners of the tabernacle in the rear. ²⁹And they were separate beneath, but joined at the top, at the first ring; he made two of them thus, for the two corners. ³⁰There were eight frames with their bases of silver: sixteen bases, under every frame two bases.

³¹And he made bars of acacia wood, five for the frames of the one side of the tabernacle, ³²and five bars for the frames of the other side of the tabernacle, and five bars for the frames of the tabernacle at the rear westward. ³³And he made the middle bar to pass through from end to end halfway up the frames. ³⁴And he overlaid the frames with gold, and made their rings of gold for holders for the bars, and overlaid the bars with gold.

Ex 26:31–37 **The veil**

³⁵And he made the veil of blue and purple and scarlet stuff and fine twined linen; with cherubim skilfully worked he made it. ³⁶And for it he made four pillars of acacia, and overlaid them with gold; their hooks were of gold, and he cast for them four bases of silver. ³⁷He also made a screen for the door of the tent, of blue and purple and scarlet stuff and fine twined linen, embroidered with needlework; ³⁸and its five pillars with their hooks. He overlaid their capitals, and their fillets were of gold, but their five bases were of bronze.

Ex 25:10–20 **The ark**

37 ¹Bezalel made the ark of acacia wood; two cubits and a half was its length, a cubit and a half its breadth, and a

singulis tabulis ponebantur pro duabus pedibus. ²⁵Ad plagam quoque habitaculi, quae respicit ad aquilonem, fecit viginti tabulas ²⁶cum quadraginta basibus argenteis: duas bases per singulas tabulas. ²⁷Contra occidentem vero, id est ad eam partem habitaculi quae mare respicit, fecit sex tabulas ²⁸et duas alias per singulos angulos habitaculi retro; ²⁹quae gemellae erant a deorsum usque sursum in unam compaginem. Ita fecit duas tabulas in duobus angulis, ³⁰ut octo essent simul tabulae et haberent bases argenteas sedecim: binas scilicet bases sub singulis tabulis. ³¹Fecit et vectes de lignis acaciae quinque ad continendas tabulas unius lateris habitaculi ³²et quinque alios ad alterius lateris coaptandas tabulas; et extra hos quinque alios vectes ad occidentalem plagam habitaculi contra mare. ³³Fecit autem vectem medium, qui per medias tabulas ab una extremitate usque ad alteram perveniret. ³⁴Ipsa autem tabulata deauravit. Et anulos eorum fecit aureos, per quos vectes induci possent; quos et ipsos laminis aureis operuit. ³⁵Fecit et velum de hyacintho et purpura coccoque ac bysso retorta, opere polymitario, cum cherubim intextis; ³⁶et quattuor columnas de lignis acaciae, quas cum uncis suis deauravit, fusis basibus earum argenteis. ³⁷Fecit et velum in introitu tabernaculi ex hyacintho, purpura, cocco byssoque retorta opere plumarii; ³⁸et columnas quinque cum uncis suis. Et operuit auro capita et anulos earum

cubit and a half its height. ²And he overlaid it with pure gold within and without, and made a moulding of gold around it. ³And he cast for it four rings of gold for its four corners, two rings on its one side and two rings on its other side. ⁴And he made poles of acacia wood, and overlaid them with gold, ⁵and put the poles into the rings on the sides of the ark, to carry the ark. ⁶And he made a mercy seat of pure gold; two cubits and a half was its length, and a cubit and a half its breadth. ⁷And he made two cherubim of hammered gold; on the two ends of the mercy seat he made them, ⁸one cherub on the one end, and one cherub on the other end; of one piece with the mercy seat he made the cherubim on its two ends. ⁹The cherubim spread out their wings above, overshadowing the mercy seat with their wings, with their faces one to another; toward the mercy seat were the faces of the cherubim.

The table for the offertory bread

Ex 25:23–29

¹⁰He also made the table of acacia wood; two cubits was its length, a cubit its breadth, and a cubit and a half its height; ¹¹and he overlaid it with pure gold, and made a moulding of gold around it. ¹²And he made around it a frame a handbreadth wide, and made a molding of gold around the frame. ¹³He cast for it four rings of gold, and fastened the rings to the four corners at its four legs. ¹⁴Close to the frame were the rings, as holders for the poles to carry the table. ¹⁵He made the poles of acacia wood to carry the table, and overlaid them with gold. ¹⁶And he made the vessels of pure gold which were to be upon the table, its plates and dishes for incense, and its bowls and flagons with which to pour libations.

basesque earum fudit aeneas. ¹Fecit autem Beseleel et arcam de lignis acaciae habentem duos semis cubitos in longitudine et cubitum ac semissem in latitudine, altitudo quoque unius cubiti fuit et dimidii; vestivitque eam auro purissimo intus ac foris. ²Et fecit illi coronam auream per gyrum, ³conflans quattuor anulos aureos in quattuor pedibus eius; duos anulos in latere uno et duos in altero. ⁴Vectes quoque fecit de lignis acaciae, quos vestivit auro; ⁵et quos misit in anulos, qui erant in lateribus arcae, ad portandum eam. ⁶Fecit et propitiatorium de auro mundissimo: duorum cubitorum et dimidii in longitudine et cubiti ac semis in latitudine. ⁷Duos etiam cherubim ex auro ductili fecit ex utraque parte propitiatorii; ⁸cherub unum ex summitate unius partis et cherub alterum ex summitate partis alterius; duos cherubim ex singulis summitatibus propitiatorii ⁹extendentes alas sursum et tegentes alis suis propitiatorium seque mutuo et illud respicientes. ¹⁰Fecit et mensam de lignis acaciae in longitudine duorum cubitorum et in latitudine unius cubiti, quae habebat in altitudine cubitum ac semissem; ¹¹circumdeditque eam auro mundissimo et fecit illi coronam auream per gyrum. ¹²Fecit ei quoque limbum aureum quattuor digitorum per circuitum et super illum coronam auream. ¹³Fudit et quattuor circulos aureos, quos posuit in quattuor angulis per singulos pedes mensae ¹⁴iuxta limbum; misitque in eos vectes, ut possit mensa portari. ¹⁵Ipsos quoque vectes fecit de lignis acaciae et circumdedit eos auro; ¹⁶et vasa ad diversos usus mensae, acetabula, phialas et cyathos et crateras ex auro puro, in quibus offerenda sunt libamina. ¹⁷Fecit et candelabrum ductile de auro mundissimo, basim et hastile eius; scyphi sphaeru-

_{Ex 25:31–39} **The golden lampstand**

¹⁷He also made the lampstand of pure gold. The base and the shaft of the lampstand were made of hammered work; its cups, its capitals, and its flowers were of one piece with it. ¹⁸And there were six branches going out of its sides, three branches of the lampstand out of one side of it and three branches of the lampstand out of the other side of it; ¹⁹three cups made like almonds, each with capital and flower, on one branch, and three cups made like almonds, each with capital and flower, on the other branch—so for the six branches going out of the lampstand. ²⁰And on the lampstand itself were four cups made like almonds, with their capitals and flowers, ²¹and a capital of one piece with it under each pair of the six branches going out of it. ²²Their capitals and their branches were of one piece with it; the whole of it was one piece of hammered work of pure gold. ²³And he made its seven lamps and its snuffers and its trays of pure gold. ²⁴He made it and all its utensils of a talent of pure gold.

_{Ex 30:1–5} **The altar of incense**

²⁵He made the altar of incense of acacia wood; its length was a cubit, and its breadth was a cubit; it was square, and two cubits was its height; its horns were of one piece with it. ²⁶He overlaid it with pure gold, its top, and its sides round about, and its horns; and he made a moulding of gold round about it, ²⁷and made two rings of gold on it under its molding, on two opposite sides of it, as holders for the poles with which to carry it. ²⁸And he made the poles of acacia wood, and overlaid them with gold.

_{Ex 30:22–25; 34–35} ²⁹He made the holy anointing oil also, and the pure fragrant incense, blended as by the perfumer.

_{Ex 27:1–8} **The altar of holocaust**

38 ¹He made the altar of burnt offering also of acacia wood; five cubits was its length, and five cubits its breadth; it

---

laeque ac flores unum cum ipso erant: ¹⁸ sex in utroque latere, tres calami ex parte una et tres ex altera; ¹⁹tres scyphi in nucis modum in calamo uno sphaerulaeque simul et flores et tres scyphi instar nucis in calamo altero sphaerulaeque simul et flores. Aequum erat opus sex calamorum, qui procedebant de hastili candelabri. ²⁰In ipso autem hastili erant quattuor scyphi in nucis modum sphaerulaeque et flores; ²¹singulae sphaerulae sub binis calamis per loca tria, qui simul sex fiunt calami procedentes de hastili uno. ²²Sphaerulae igitur et calami unum cum ipso erant, totum ductile ex auro purissimo. ²³Fecit et lucernas septem cum emunctoriis suis et vasa, ubi emuncta condantur, de auro mundissimo. ²⁴Talentum auri purissimi appendebat candelabrum cum omnibus vasis suis. ²⁵Fecit et altare thymiamatis de lignis acaciae habens per quadrum singulos cubitos et in altitudine duos; e cuius angulis procedebant cornua. ²⁶Vestivitque illud auro purissimo cum craticula ac parietibus et cornibus. ²⁷ Fecitque ei coronam aureolam per gyrum et binos anulos aureos sub corona in duobus lateribus, ut mittantur in eos vectes, et possit altare portari. ²⁸Ipsos autem vectes fecit de lignis acaciae et operuit laminis aureis. ²⁹Composuit

was square, and three cubits was its height. [2]He made horns for it on its four corners; its horns were of one piece with it, and he overlaid it with bronze. [3]And he made all the utensils of the altar, the pots, the shovels, the basins, the forks, and the firepans: all its utensils he made of bronze. [4]And he made for the altar a grating, a network of bronze, under its ledge, extending halfway down. [5]He cast four rings on the four corners of the bronze grating as holders for the poles; [6]he made the poles of acacia wood, and overlaid them with bronze. [7]And he put the poles through the rings on the sides of the altar, to carry it with them; he made it hollow, with boards.

[8]And he made the laver of bronze and its base of bronze, from the mirrors of the ministering women who ministered at the door of the tent of meeting.

Ex 30:17–21
1 Sam 2:22

The court of the sanctuary

Ex 27:9–19

[9]And he made the court; for the south side the hangings of the court were of fine twined linen, a hundred cubits; [10]their pillars were twenty and their bases twenty, of bronze, but the hooks of the pillars and their fillets were of silver. [11]And for the north side a hundred cubits, their pillars twenty, their bases twenty, of bronze, but the hooks of the pillars and their fillets were of silver. [12]And for the west side were hangings of fifty cubits, their pillars ten, and their sockets ten; the hooks of the pillars and their fillets were of silver. [13]And for the front to the east, fifty cubits. [14]The hangings for one side of the gate were fifteen cubits, with three

---

38:8. It is not known what role these women had at the entrance to the tent of meeting (cf. 1 Sam 2:22). The Septuagint Greek says that they "fasted" and the Greek version of Onkelos says that they "prayed". This is the only Old Testament text that speaks of women taking part in temple activities.

pillars and three bases. [15]And so for the other side; on this hand and that hand by the gate of the court were hangings of fifteen cubits, with three pillars and three bases. [16]All the hangings round about the court were of fine twined linen. [17]And the bases for the pillars were of bronze, but the hooks of the pillars and their fillets were of silver; the overlaying of their capitals was also of silver, and all the pillars of the court were filleted with silver. [18]And the screen for the gate of the court was embroidered with needlework in blue and purple and scarlet stuff and fine twined linen; it was twenty cubits long and five cubits high in its breadth, corresponding to the hangings of the court. [19]And their pillars were four; their four bases were of bronze, their hooks of silver, and the overlaying of their capitals and their fillets of silver. [20]And all the pegs for the tabernacle and for the court round about were of bronze.

Materials used

Num 1:45–46 [21]This is the sum of the things for the tabernacle, the tabernacle of the testimony, as they were counted at the commandment of Moses, for the work of the Levites under the direction of Ithamar Ex 35:30–35 the son of Aaron the priest. [22]Bezalel the son of Uri, son of Hur, of the tribe of Judah, made all that the LORD commanded Moses; [23]and with him was Oholiab the son of Ahisamach, of the tribe of Dan, a craftsman and designer and embroiderer in blue and purple and scarlet stuff and fine twined linen.

[24]All the gold that was used for the work, in all the construction of the sanctuary, the gold from the offering, was twenty-nine

---

38:21–31. There is nothing in chapters 25–31 about an account having to be made up. This passage was probably added later because the Levites (v. 21) were not instituted until later (cf. Num 3:45–46) and Ithamar became their leader later still (cf. Num 4:33). But the passage does serve to show how generous the people were.

---

tentoria, [14]e quibus quindecim cubitos columnarum trium cum basibus suis unum tenebat latus; [15]et in parte alter —quia inter utraque introitum tabernaculi fecit— quindecim aeque cubitorum erant tentoria columnaeque tres et bases totidem. [16]Cuncta atrii tentoria in circuitu ex bysso retorta texuerat. [17]Bases columnarum fuere aeneae, unci autem earum et anuli earum argentei et capita earum vestivit argento et omnes columnas atrii cinxit anulis argenteis. [18]Et in introitu eius opere plumario fecit velum ex hyacintho, purpura, cocco ac bysso retorta; quod habebat viginti cubitos in longitudine, altitudo vero quinque cubitorum erat iuxta mensuram, quam cuncta atrii tentoria habebant. [19]Columnae autem in ingressu fuere quattuor cum basibus aeneis, uncis argenteis; capitaque et anulos earum vestivit argento. [20]Paxillos quoque habitaculi et atrii per gyrum fecit aeneos. [21]Hic est census habitaculi, habitaculi testimonii, qui recensitus est iuxta praeceptum Moysi ministerio Levitarum per manum Ithamar filii Aaron sacerdotis. [22]Beseleel filius Uri filii Hur de tribu Iudae fecit cuncta, quae praeceperat Dominus Moysi, [23]iuncto sibi socio Ooliab filio Achisamech de tribu Dan fabro et polymitario atque plumario

talents and seven hundred and thirty shekels, by the shekel of the sanctuary. ²⁵And the silver from those of the congregation who were numbered was a hundred talents and a thousand seven hundred and seventy-five shekels, by the shekel of the sanctuary: ²⁶a beka a head (that is, half a shekel, by the shekel of the sanctuary), for every one who was numbered in the census, from twenty years old and upward, for six hundred and three thousand, five hundred and fifty men. ²⁷The hundred talents of silver were for casting the bases of the sanctuary, and the bases of the veil; a hundred bases for the hundred talents, a talent for a base. ²⁸And of the thousand seven hundred and seventy-five shekels he made hooks for the pillars, and overlaid their capitals and made fillets for them. ²⁹And the bronze that was contributed was seventy talents, and two thousand and four hundred shekels; ³⁰with it he made the bases for the door of the tent of meeting, the bronze altar and the bronze grating for it and all the utensils of the altar, ³¹the bases round about the court, and the bases of the gate of the court, all the pegs of the tabernacle, and all the pegs round about the court.

The priestly vestments

39 ¹And of the blue and purple and scarlet stuff they made finely wrought garments, for ministering in the holy place; they made the holy garments for Aaron; as the LORD had commanded Moses.

39:1. "As the Lord had commanded Moses"—a phrase which is repeated throughout this chapter (vv. 1, 5, 7, 21, 29, 31) and the following one (vv. 16, 19, 21, 23, 25, 27, 29, 32). It serves to confirm that all this work was carried out perfectly: obedience is a sign of faithfulness and, as reported here, it is an encouragement to later generations to listen to the word of God and put it into practice.

---

ex hyacintho, purpura, cocco et bysso. ²⁴Omne aurum, quod expensum est in opere sanctuarii et quod oblatum est in donariis, viginti novem talentorum fuit et septingentorum triginta siclorum ad mensuram sicli sanctuarii. ²⁵Argentum autem eorum, qui in congregatione recensiti sunt, centum talentorum fuit et mille septingentorum et septuaginta quinque siclorum ad mensuram sicli sanctuarii. ²⁶Beca, id est dimidium sicli iuxta mensuram sicli sanctuarii, dedit quisquis transit ad censum a viginti annis et supra, de sescentis tribus milibus et quingentis quinquaginta armatorum. ²⁷De talentis centum argenti conflatae sunt bases sanctuarii et veli, singulis talentis per bases singulas supputatis. ²⁸De mille autem septingentis et septuaginta quinque siclis fecit uncos columnarum et vestivit capita earum et cinxit eas argento. ²⁹Aeris quoque oblata sunt septuaginta talenta et duo milia et quadringenti sicli, ³⁰ex quibus fecit bases in introitu tabernaculi conventus et altare aeneum cum craticula sua omniaque vasa, quae ad usum eius pertinent, ³¹et bases atrii tam in circuitu quam in ingressu eius et omnes paxillos habitaculi atque atrii per gyrum. ¹De hyacintho vero et purpura, cocco ac bysso fecerunt vestes textas pro ministerio sanctuarii. Et fecerunt vestes sacras Aaron, sicut praecepit Dominus Moysi. ²Fecerunt igitur ephod de auro, hyacintho et purpura coccoque et bysso retorta ³opere polymitario tundentes bratteas

Ex 28:6–13 **The ephod**

²And he made the ephod of gold, blue and purple and scarlet stuff, and fine twined linen. ³And gold leaf was hammered out and cut into threads to work into the blue and purple and the scarlet stuff, and into the fine twined linen, in skilled design. ⁴They made for the ephod shoulder-pieces, joined to it at its two edges. ⁵And the skilfully woven band upon it, to gird it on, was of the same materials and workmanship, of gold, blue and purple and scarlet stuff, and fine twined linen; as the Lord had commanded Moses.

⁶The onyx stones were prepared, enclosed in settings of gold filigree and engraved like the engravings of a signet, according to the names of the sons of Israel. ⁷And he set them on the shoulder-pieces of the ephod, to be stones of remembrance for the sons of Israel; as the Lord had commanded Moses.

Ex 28:15–30 **The breastpiece**

⁸He made the breastpiece, in skilled work, like the work of the ephod, of gold, blue and purple and scarlet stuff, and fine twined linen. ⁹It was square; the breastpiece was made double, a span its length and a span its breadth when doubled. ¹⁰And they set in it four rows of stones. A row of sardius, topaz, and carbuncle was the first row; ¹¹and the second row, an emerald, a sapphire, and a diamond; ¹²and the third row, a jacinth, an agate, and an amethyst; ¹³and the fourth row, a beryl, an onyx, and a jasper; they were

Rev 21:12 enclosed in settings of gold filigree. ¹⁴There were twelve stones with their names according to the names of the sons of Israel; they were like signets, each engraved with its name, for the twelve tribes. ¹⁵And they made on the breastpiece twisted chains like cords, of pure gold; ¹⁶and they made two settings of gold filigree and two gold rings, and put the two rings on the two edges of the breastpiece; ¹⁷and they put the two cords of gold in the two rings

---

aureas et extenuantes in fila, ut possent torqueri cum priorum colorum subtegmine. ⁴Fasciasque umerales fecerunt ei, cum quibus in utroque latere summitatum suarum copulabatur, ⁵et balteum, quo constringebatur ephod, eiusdem operis et unum cum eo ex auro, et hyacintho et purpura coccoque et bysso retorta, sicut praeceperat Dominus Moysi. ⁶Paraverunt et duos lapides onychinos, inclusos texturis aureis et sculptos arte gemmaria nominibus filiorum Israel; ⁷posueruntque eos in fasciis umeralibus ephod, lapides memorialis filiorum Israel, sicut praeceperat Dominus Moysi. ⁸Fecerunt et pectorale opere polymito iuxta opus ephod ex auro, hyacintho, purpura coccoque et bysso retorta, ⁹quadrangulum duplex mensurae palmi. ¹⁰Et posuerunt in eo gemmarum ordines quattuor: in primo versu erat sardius, topazius, smaragdus; ¹¹in secundo carbunculus, sapphirus et iaspis; ¹²in tertio hyacinthus, achates et amethystus; ¹³in quarto chrysolithus, onychinus et beryllus: inclusi textura aurea per ordines suos. ¹⁴Ipsique lapides duodecim sculpti erant nominibus duodecim tribuum Israel, singuli per nomina singulorum. ¹⁵Fecerunt in pectorali catenulas quasi funiculos opus tortile de auro purissimo ¹⁶et duos margines aureos totidemque anulos aureos. Porro duos anulos posuerunt in utraque summitate pectoralis; ¹⁷duos funiculos aureos inseruerunt anulis, qui in pectoralis angulis eminebant. ¹⁸Duas

at the edges of the breastpiece. ¹⁸Two ends of the two cords they had attached to the two settings of filigree; thus they attached it in front to the shoulder-pieces of the ephod. ¹⁹Then they made two rings of gold, and put them at the two ends of the breastpiece, on its inside edge next to the ephod. ²⁰And they made two rings of gold, and attached them in front to the lower part of the two shoulder-pieces of the ephod, at its joining above the skilfully woven band of the ephod. ²¹And they bound the breastpiece by its rings to the rings of the ephod with a lace of blue, so that it should lie upon the skilfully woven band of the ephod, and that the breastpiece should not come loose from the ephod; as the LORD had commanded Moses.

The robe   Ex 28:31–35

²²He also made the robe of the ephod woven all of blue; ²³and the opening of the robe in it was like the opening in a garment, with a binding around the opening, that it might not be torn. ²⁴On the skirts of the robe they made pomegranates of blue and purple and scarlet stuff and fine twined linen. ²⁵They also made bells of pure gold, and put the bells between the pomegranates upon the skirts of the robe round about, between the pomegranates; ²⁶a bell and a pomegranate, a bell and a pomegranate round about upon the skirts of the robe for ministering; as the LORD had commanded Moses.

Other vestments   Ex 28:38–42

²⁷They also made the coats, woven of fine linen, for Aaron and his sons, ²⁸and the turban of fine linen, and the caps of fine linen, and the linen breeches of fine twined linen, ²⁹and the girdle of fine twined linen and of blue and purple and scarlet stuff, embroidered with needlework; as the LORD had commanded Moses.

summitates amborum funiculorum colligaverunt duobus marginibus in fasciis umeralibus ephod in parte eius anteriore. ¹⁹Et fecerunt duos anulos aureos et posuerunt super duas summitates pectoralis in eius margine interiore contra ephod, sicut praecepit Dominus Moysi. ²⁰Feceruntque duos anulos aureos, quos posuerunt in duabus fasciis umeralibus ephod deorsum in latere eius anteriore secus iuncturam eius super balteum ephod. ²¹Et strinxerunt pectorale anulis eius ad anulos ephod vitta hyacinthina, ut esset super balteum ephod, ne amoveretur ab ephod, sicut praecepit Dominus Moysi. ²²Fecerunt quoque pallium ephod opere textili totum hyacinthinum ²³et capitium in medio eius supra oramque per gyrum sicut in capitio loricae ²⁴deorsum autem ad pedes mala punica ex hyacintho, purpura, cocco ac bysso retorta ²⁵et tintinnabula de auro purissimo, quae posuerunt inter malogranata in inferiore parte pallii per gyrum, ²⁶ut sit tintinnabulum inter singula mala punica, quibus ornatus incedebat pontifex, quando ministerio fungebatur, sicut praeceperat Dominus Moysi. ²⁷Fecerunt et tunicas byssinas opere textili Aaron et filiis eius ²⁸et tiaram et ornatum mitrarum ex bysso, feminalia quoque linea ex bysso retorta, ²⁹cingulum vero de bysso retorta, hyacintho, purpura ac cocco, arte plumaria, sicut praeceperat Dominus Moysi. ³⁰Fecerunt et laminam diadema sanctitatis de auro purissimo; scripseruntque in ea

Ex 28:36–37 **The tiara or turban**

³⁰And they made the plate of the holy crown of pure gold, and wrote upon it an inscription, like the engraving of a signet, "Holy to the LORD." ³¹And they tied to it a lace of blue, to fasten it on the turban above; as the LORD had commanded Moses.

³²Thus all the work of the tabernacle of the tent of meeting was finished; and the people of Israel had done according to all that the LORD had commanded Moses; so had they done.

The finished work is presented to Moses

³³And they brought the tabernacle to Moses, the tent and all its utensils, its hooks, its frames, its bars, its pillars, and its bases; ³⁴the covering of tanned rams' skins and goatskins, and the veil of the screen; ³⁵the ark of the testimony with its poles and the mercy seat; ³⁶the table with all its utensils, and the bread of the Presence; ³⁷the lampstand of pure gold and its lamps with the lamps set and all its utensils, and the oil for the light; ³⁸the golden altar, the anointing oil and the fragrant incense, and the screen for the door of the tent; ³⁹the bronze altar, and its grating of bronze, its poles, and all its utensils; the laver and its base; ⁴⁰the hangings of the court, its pillars, and its bases, and the screen for the gate of the court, its cords, and its pegs; and all the utensils for the service of the tabernacle, for the tent of meeting; ⁴¹the finely worked gar-

---

39:33–43. The importance of every item used in divine worship is stressed once again. One cannot fail to be impressed by the insistence on every little thing having to do with it. The Church, too, stresses how important everything laid down about the liturgy is, especially things having to do with the celebration of the Eucharist. "The Eucharist is a common possession of the whole Church as the sacrament of her unity. And thus the Church has the strict duty to specify everything which concerns participation in it and its celebration. We should therefore act according to the principles laid down [. . .]. [I]n *normal conditions* to ignore the liturgical directives can be interpreted as a lack of respect towards the Eucharist, dictated perhaps by individualism or by an absence of a critical sense concerning current opinions, or by a certain *lack of a spirit of faith*" (John Paul II, *Dominicae Cenae*, 12).

---

opere caelatoris: «Sanctum Domino»; ³¹et strinxerunt eam desuper cum tiara vitta hyacinthina, sicut praeceperat Dominus Moysi. ³²Perfectum est igitur omne opus habitaculi et tabernaculi conventus feceruntque filii Israel cuncta, quae praeceperat Dominus Moysi: sic fecerunt. ³³Et obtulerunt habitaculum et tabernaculum et universam supellectilem, fibulas, tabulas, vectes, columnas ac bases, ³⁴opertorium de pellibus arietum rubricatis et operimentum de pellibus delphini, velum, ³⁵arcam testimonii, vectes, propitiatorium, ³⁶mensam cum vasis suis et propositionis panibus, ³⁷candelabrum ex auro puro, lucernas in ordine earum et utensilia earum cum oleo candelabri, ³⁸altare aureum et unguentum et thymiama ex aromatibus et velum in introitu tabernaculi, ³⁹altare aeneum, craticulam aeneam, vectes et vasa eius omnia, labrum cum basi sua, ⁴⁰tentoria atrii et columnas cum basibus suis, velum in introitu

ments for ministering in the holy place, the holy garments for Aaron the priest, and the garments of his sons to serve as priests. ⁴²According to all that the LORD had commanded Moses, so the people of Israel had done all the work. ⁴³And Moses saw all the work, and behold, they had done it; as the LORD had commanded, so had they done it. And Moses blessed them.

The sanctuary is consecrated

40 ¹The LORD said to Moses, ²"On the first day of the first month you shall erect the tabernacle of the tent of meeting. ³And you shall put in it the ark of the testimony, and you shall screen the ark with the veil. ⁴And you shall bring in the table, and set its arrangements in order; and you shall bring in the lampstand, and set up its lamps. ⁵And you shall put the golden altar for incense before the ark of the testimony, and set up the screen for the door of the tabernacle. ⁶You shall set the altar of burnt offering before the door of the tabernacle of the tent of meeting, ⁷and place the laver between the tent of meeting and the altar, and put water in it. ⁸And you shall set up the court round about, and hang up the screen for the gate of the court. ⁹Then you shall take the anointing oil, and anoint the tabernacle and all that is in it, and consecrate it and all its furniture; and it shall become holy. ¹⁰You shall also anoint the altar of burnt offering and all its utensils, and consecrate the altar; and the altar shall be most holy. ¹¹You shall also anoint the laver and its base, and consecrate it. ¹²Then you shall bring Aaron and his sons to the door of the tent of meeting, and shall wash them with water, ¹³and put upon Aaron the holy garments, and you shall anoint him and consecrate him, that he may serve me as priest. ¹⁴You shall bring his sons also and put coats on them, ¹⁵and anoint them, as you anointed their father,

Rev 9:13

Heb 9:21

atrii funiculosque illius et paxillos. Nihil ex vasis defuit, quae in ministerium habitaculi in tabernaculo conventus iussa sunt fieri. ⁴¹Vestes quoque textas, quibus sacerdotes utuntur in sanctuario, et vestes sacras Aaron sacerdotis et vestes filiorum eius ⁴²obtulerunt filii Israel, sicut praeceperat Dominus Moysi. ⁴³Quae postquam Moyses cuncta vidit completa, benedixit eis. ¹Locutusque est Dominus ad Moysen dicens: ²Mense primo, die prima mensis eriges habitaculum, tabernaculum conventus, ³et pones in eo arcam testimonii, abscondes illam velo; ⁴et, illata mensa, pones super eam, quae rite praecepta sunt. Candelabrum stabit cum lucernis suis ⁵et altare aureum, in quo adoletur incensum, coram arca testimonii. Velum in introitu habitaculi pones, ⁶et ante tabernaculum conventus altare holocausti, ⁷et labrum inter altare et tabernaculum conventus et implebis illud aqua. ⁸Circumdabisque atrium tentoriis et pones velum in porta eius. ⁹Et, assumpto unctionis oleo, unges habitaculum et omnia, quae in eo sunt, et consecrabis illud cum vasis suis, et erit sanctum. ¹⁰Unges quoque altare holocausti et omnia vasa eius et consecrabis altare, et erit sanctum sanctorum. ¹¹Et unges labrum cum basi sua et consecrabis illud. ¹²Applicabisque Aaron et filios eius ad fores tabernaculi conventus et lotos aqua ¹³indues Aaron sanctis vestibus, unges et consecrabis eum, ut mihi sacerdotio fungatur; ¹⁴filios eius applicabis et vesties eos tunicis ¹⁵et unges eos, sicut unxisti patrem eorum, ut mihi sacerdotio fungantur, et unctio

that they may serve me as priests: and their anointing shall admit them to a perpetual priesthood throughout their generations."

Moses' obedience to God's commands

[16]Thus did Moses; according to all that the LORD commanded him, so he did. [17]And in the first month in the second year, on the first day of the month, the tabernacle was erected. [18]Moses erected the tabernacle; he laid its bases, and set up its frames, and put in its poles, and raised up its pillars; [19]and he spread the tent over the tabernacle, and put the covering of the tent over it, as the LORD had commanded Moses. [20]And he took the testimony and put it into the ark, and put the poles on the ark, and set the mercy seat above on the ark; [21]and he brought the ark into the tabernacle, and set up the veil of the screen, and screened the ark of the testimony; as the LORD had commanded Moses. [22]And he put the table in the tent of meeting, on the north side of the tabernacle, outside the veil, [23]and set the bread in order on it before the LORD; as the LORD had commanded Moses. [24]And he put the lampstand in the tent of meeting, opposite the table on the south side of the tabernacle, [25]and set up the lamps before the LORD; as the LORD had commanded Moses. [26]And he put the golden altar in the tent of meeting before the veil, [27]and burnt fragrant incense upon it; as the LORD had commanded Moses. [28]And he put in place the screen for the door of the tabernacle. [29]And he set the altar of burnt offering at the door of the tabernacle of the tent of meeting, and offered upon it the burnt offering and the cereal offering; as the LORD had commanded Moses. [30]And he set the laver between the tent of meeting and the altar, and put water in it for washing, [31]with which Moses and Aaron and his sons washed their hands and their feet; [32]when they went into the tent of meeting, and

Mt 12:4
Mk 2:26

---

eorum erit eis in sacerdotium sempiternum in generationibus eorum. [16]Fecitque Moyses omnia, quae praeceperat ei Dominus: sic fecit. [17]Igitur mense primo anni secundi, prima die mensis collocatum est habitaculum. [18]Erexitque Moyses illud et posuit bases ac tabulas et vectes statuitque columnas [19]et expandit tentorium super habitaculum, imposito desuper operimento, sicut Dominus imperaverat Moysi. [20]Sumpsit et posuit testimonium in arca et, subditis infra vectibus, posuit propitiatorium desuper. [21]Cumque intulisset arcam in habitaculum, appendit ante eam velum, sicut iusserat Dominus Moysi. [22]Posuit et mensam in tabernaculo conventus ad plagam septentrionalem extra velum, [23]ordinatis coram propositionis panibus, sicut praeceperat Dominus Moysi. [24]Posuit et candelabrum in tabernaculo conventus e regione mensae in parte australi, [25]locatis per ordinem lucernis, sicut praeceperat Dominus Moysi. [26]Posuit et altare aureum in tabernaculo conventus coram propitiatorio [27]et adolevit super eo incensum aromatum, sicut iusserat Dominus Moysi. [28]Posuit et velum in introitu habitaculi [29]et altare holocausti in vestibulo habitaculi, tabernaculi conventus, offerens in eo holocaustum et sacrificium, sicut Dominus imperaverat Moysi. [30]Labrum quoque statuit inter tabernaculum conventus et altare implens illud aqua; [31]laveruntque Moyses et Aaron ac filii eius manus suas et pedes, [32]cum ingrederentur tabernaculum conventus et accederent ad altare, sicut praeceperat Dominus Moysi.

when they approached the altar, they washed; as the LORD commanded Moses. ³³And he erected the court round the tabernacle and the altar, and set up the screen of the gate of the court. So Moses finished the work.

Num 9:15–33
1 Kings
8:10–11
Ezra 43:15

The glory of God fills the tabernacle

³⁴Then the cloud* covered the tent of meeting, and the glory of the LORD filled the tabernacle. ³⁵And Moses was not able to enter the tent of meeting, because the cloud abode upon it, and the glory of the LORD filled the tabernacle. ³⁶Throughout all their journeys, whenever the cloud was taken up from over the tabernacle, the people of Israel would go onward; ³⁷but if the cloud was not taken up, then they did not go onward till the day that it was taken up. ³⁸For throughout all their journeys the cloud of the LORD was upon the tabernacle by day, and fire was in it by night, in the sight of all the house of Israel.

Ex 13:21–22;
25:8
Mk 9:7
Rev 15:5, 8

Num 9:15–23

40:34–38. The book of Exodus ends by speaking once again about the Lord's presence among his people, mentioning the cloud and the glory of God (cf. Ex 13:21–22). The cloud will stay with the people throughout their journey in the desert (cf. Num 9:15ff), showing them the way to go. In Christian tradition the cloud is seen as an image of faith, which guides the Christian night and day as he makes his pilgrim way to the promised land. The Fathers also saw this cloud as a figure of Christ: "He is the pillar who, keeping himself upright and strong, cures our infirmity. By night he sheds light, by day he becomes opaque, so that those who do not see are enabled to see and those who see become blind" (St Isidore of Seville, *Quaestiones in Exodum*, 18, 1).

³³Erexit et atrium per gyrum habitaculi et altaris, ducto in introitu eius velo. Sic complevit opus. ³⁴Et operuit nubes tabernaculum conventus, et gloria Domini implevit habitaculum. ³⁵Nec poterat Moyses ingredi tabernaculum conventus, quia habitavit nubes super illud, et gloria Domini replevit habitaculum. ³⁶Si quando nubes de tabernaculo ascendebat, proficiscebantur filii Israel in omnibus stationibus suis; ³⁷si autem non ascendebat nubes, non proficiscebantur usque in diem, quo levabatur. ³⁸Nubes quippe Domini incubabat per diem habitaculo, et ignis in nocte, ante oculos universae domus Israel per cunctas mansiones suas.

LEVITICUS

Introduction

The Jewish name for this book (as for all Old Testament books) is taken from the first word in the text—*Wayiqrá* (= "And he called", from "And the Lord called Moses"). It is a name which fits in nicely with the content: when the people of Israel were in the desert, the Lord called them to himself, to make them a holy nation; and the rules and regulations contained in Leviticus are designed to show how to stay within the sphere of God (how to be holy) and what to do if one has strayed from him through sin.

In the Septuagint Greek translation, this book was called *Levitikon*, a name which passed into Latin versions as *Leviticus*: most of it in fact deals with matters to do with priests and Levites.

Leviticus is really a book about the rites of Jewish Liturgy; it contains laws about worship in general and rules about the ceremonies to be used in offerings and consecrations and about how feasts should be celebrated.

1. STRUCTURE AND CONTENT

The book of Leviticus can be divided into four main parts:

PART ONE: RULES CONCERNING SACRIFICE (1:1–7). This deals firstly with burnt offerings or holocausts (1:3–17), the main feature of which is that the animal was to be burned completely in acknowledgment of the Lord's absolute dominion. It then goes on to the cereal offering, *minjáh* (2:1–16); here what was offered was wheaten flour mixed with oil. It then comes to peace offerings or communion offerings, *shelamim* (3:1–17); in these sacrifices an animal's blood and fat (in which life was considered to reside) were burnt as an offering to the Lord, but the rest of the sacrificed animal was eaten at a sacred meal. This section is followed by ordinances on purification offerings, called "sin offerings" in the RSV (4:1—5:13) and reparation ("guilt offerings" in the RSV: 5:14–26). In the case of the former, distinctions are made depending on whether the sin was committed by the high priest, the whole congregation of Israel, a ruler, or a member of the ordinary people.

This first part finishes with two chapters which go over all these sacrifices again, but from the point of view of the priest (rules about how he is to perform the ceremony, and things to do with the "priests' portion" (6:1—7:38).

PART TWO: THE ORDINATION OR INSTITUTION OF PRIESTS (8:1—10:20). An account of the investiture of Aaron describes in effect the ceremony whereby priests are consecrated (8:1–36) and the sacrifices they are to offer at the start of their ministry (9:1–24). The last chapter in this part spells out rules that apply to priests when performing their duties.

PART THREE: RULES CONCERNING THE CLEAN AND THE UNCLEAN (11:1—16:34). This code specifies the circumstances or events which can give rise to legal uncleanness, and what purification needs to be done. First it spells out the criteria for an animal to be regarded as clean (11:1–47). This is followed by rules on purification after childbirth (12:1–8), and about identifying leprosy and other illnesses causing uncleanness in the sufferer (as also purification after cure) (13:1—15:33). The text then goes on to specify instances of sexual uncleanness (male and female) and purification of same. This third part ends with rules for celebrating the day of atonement or Yom Kippur.

PART FOUR: THE LAW OF HOLINESS (17:1—26:46). Moving on from the defects which make for uncleanness in human beings, animals and things (all covered in the previous part), the book now deals with the quality attaching to things and persons involved in worship: they have to be holy because the Lord is holy. The laws pertaining to this are to be found in this elaborate code. It begins with regulations about certain sacrifices and offerings (17:1–16), about conditions for holiness in marriage, and avoiding defilement (18:1–30), and about various moral and religious duties (19:1–37); and then it specifies penalties for offences against these rules (20:1–27). This is followed by rules to do with the holiness of priests and of those partaking in sacred meals (21:1—22:33), and a section on the celebration of feasts, and sabbatical and jubilee years (23:1—25:55). A short conclusion exhorting respect for the Lord and his commandments is followed by a list of blessings and curses on those who keep or fail to keep the laws in the code (26:1–46).

The last chapter is an appendix dealing with vows and their fulfilment or possible substitution by fee (27:1–34).

2. HISTORICAL OUTLINE OF THE LAWS OF THE PEOPLE OF ISRAEL

Like many Middle Eastern peoples, Israel had its own laws governing worship and social life. By examining these laws it is often possible to identify the historical circumstances in which particular laws were promulgated, and the ethical and religious values specific to the people God had chosen as his own and to which he revealed himself over time by means of deeds and words.

Introduction

No Canaanite legal document is extant from the period prior to Israel's settlement in Canaan. Ungarit texts, which are rich in mythological references, contain very little of legal interest. The oldest extant laws are those of Ur-Nammu, founder of the third dynasty of Ur (*c*.2000 BC); the laws of Bilalama, containing 60 articles, and those of Lipit-Istar, the fifth king of the dynasty of the city of Isin in Mesopotamia, which has 30 articles, are about a century later. The most famous early legal text is the so-called Code of Hammurabi, largely a compilation of earlier laws, was made in Babylonia in the first half of the 18th century BC. These legal texts consist of three distinct parts—a prologue, a collection of laws (the largest part of the document) and an epilogue containing blessings and curses.

Israel too had its own rules of legally binding custom, similar to those of its neighbours. It is quite possible that as soon as the Israelite tribes settled in the promised land (even before the monarchy) some of these were collected and written down. A considerable part of those legal texts are now to be found in the Code of the Covenant in the book of Exodus (Ex 20:22—23:19). That code still reflects the lifestyle of a society relying on grazing and livestock rather than agriculture; it is a society in which the family is all-important. But even this first Israelite code of laws is markedly different from other codes of the ancient East in that the sacred and the profane are inextricably mixed—a phenomenon which becomes even more pronounced as time goes on.

After the establishment of the monarchy and then the division into two kingdoms (10th century BC), the corpus of law continued to develop. The laws and customs of the ancients continued to be passed on to successive generations, and new circumstances led to new laws concerning worship and ordinary life. After a stable presence of some centuries in the promised land, the people's laws and rules concerning religious worship began to reflect an agricultural rather than a nomadic society: the liturgical cycle of feasts came to be more connected with the agricultural seasons.

That is probably the way the people of Israel gradually developed a basic core of legal arrangements which would in due course take the form of legal codes (in form the same as other peoples' codes of the time); these codes would regulate the nation's religious life in line with its traditional customs, enriched by experience and adapted to new historical situations as they arose. Using the heritage of the old Code of the Covenant, two collections of laws began to take shape, independently of one another—the Deuteronomic Code and the Law of Holiness.

The Deuteronomic Code, so-called because it is to be found in the book of Deuteronomy (Deut 12–25), is on many points the same as the Code of the Covenant, but there are also some differences; moreover, one can see that some primitive precepts have been reworded, and even some new ones included. The Deuteronomic Code still has a lot to say about many "humanitarian" aspects of ordinary life (particularly the protection of the weaker members of society) but

it puts the stress more on the rights of God. It is mainly concerned with stressing the unity of the people and the dedicated worship they should render to their one true God, who has given them the land and all its fruits.

For its part, the Law of Holiness, whose composition (by temple priests) began in the final years of the kingdom of Judah (6th century bc) and went on during the Exile, is much more clearly focused on matters to do with worship. It takes for granted a notion of God which transcends earthly matters; it sees worship as a way of accessing "holiness", a way of entering the sphere of the divine. This code, as it has come down to us, forms part of the book of Leviticus (Lev 17–26). It may well be that it includes the core of that great Priestly tradition which exerted such a great influence on the final edition of the Pentateuch (cf. pp 19–21 above).

3. COMPOSITION

The book of Leviticus, as it has come down to us, must have gone through various editions prior to receiving its present form via the Priestly tradition. Although it includes laws deriving from different periods, it is all very much of a piece. Its highpoint is the Law of Holiness, the great priestly legal code.

As already pointed out, the Law of Holiness is a code which includes very early laws of the people of Israel. To these were added other precepts and rules to do with worship until over time the code eventually took the shape it has today.

Specific regulations about worship must have been spelled out in more and more detail as time went by, thereby preparing the way for the rites which would eventually apply in the liturgy of the temple of Jerusalem—establishing the various rites of offering and a law about cleanness and uncleanness, providing criteria to ensure that persons, animals and things used in divine worship had no legal defects. All these regulations would eventually find the way into Leviticus.

Pride of place gradually came to be given to rites about the investiture ceremonies of priests and the rites that marked the start of their ministry.

The sacred writer used all this material to compose a book designed to include all the main legal regulations governing the life of the chosen people. Around his central theme, the worship of the thrice holy God (cf. Is 6:3), the hagiographer built up a series of steps of legislative material. First came the rites to be followed when offering sacrifices; then, on a higher level, those to do with the ordination of the men whose task it would be to offer these sacrifices, the priests; higher still, the rules which show priests and people how to be "pure", that is, to be worthy to take part in worship; finally, at the very top, the rules about divine worship itself, the rules about "holiness", which is what this Law covers.

Set as all this legal material is in the context of Sinai, after the book of Exodus and before the book of Numbers, great stress is laid on the fact that the Covenant of Sinai provides the basis for all Israel's legal superstructure.

The evidence suggests that this book took its final form during the Exile (6th century BC) and the years immediately after it.

4. MESSAGE

A superficial reading of Leviticus could give one the impression that this book is very difficult to understand and has no relevance to our own time. However, if one bears in mind that it was written very long ago, and reflects an outlook very different from ours, one can come to see that it does contain a religious meaning which is always valid.

Behind the various sacrifices or offerings it describes lies a deep conviction that God is the Lord of all creation. Man's physical needs are such that he has recourse to God by means of rites and offerings closely connected with the world on which he depends. Thus, when the people are leading a nomadic existence in the desert, their sacrifice consists of an animal taken from the flock. Later, when they are more typically tillers of the soil, they add further sacrifices and offer agricultural produce, the first-fruits. However, animal offerings continued to have pride of place, on account of the value attaching to animals and the symbolism involved (especially in the sheddings of blood). Sacrifice was the highest act of worship, the best way man could show his feelings towards God—adoration, recognition, gratitude and supplication.

Besides, in all ancient peoples man's religious sense always expressed itself in some form of ceremonial worship.

This explains why, albeit in a way peculiar to it, the chosen people had a system of worship in which it performed certain rites to show that it acknowledged and worshipped the God of Israel. The rules surrounding this worship took shape over time. Initially certain basic rites developed and, alongside them, the requirement that they be performed by a person with a certain authority, someone who would be the people's representative before God. In other words, the need for a priesthood emerged, and for persons to exercise that priesthood, that is, *priests*. In the early stages of the people of Israel it was the father of the family who performed the liturgy. Once the monarchy was established, this role passed to the king: his role was both royal and priestly. Later still, priestly functions became the preserve of people who had this special role—Eleazar and Zadok, for example, in David's time, and later on Zadok's descendants, the Zadokites, who exercised the high priesthood.

In the Levitical system, the laws concerning *cleanness* (purity) and *holiness* also contain profound teaching which extends much further than the formalism which is apparent at first sight. We need to see that anything unsuitable

for the worship of God was considered to be "unclean". God is pure, beautiful, the source of health and life; and nothing dirty, harmful or dead can gain access to him. "Purity" or cleanness, then, is something external and ritual, but it had very much to do with man's relationship with God. For its part, "holiness" is that inaccessible dwelling place of the mystery of God;[1] it is just possible to glimpse that holiness through the way God's majesty shines out in the things that he has created and in his interventions in history. Similarly, when Leviticus speaks about man's "holiness", it is referring to a quality which is both internal and external and has set the Israelites apart from the sphere of the merely profane; he wants them to belong to him and to order their lives in line with the teachings contained in his commandments. That person is "holy" who lives for God, in his inner life and in his external life. Hence God's call to the people of Israel: "You shall be holy, for I the Lord your God am holy" (Lev 19:2).

Thus, by carefully reading this sacred book in its entirety one discovers that Leviticus is not just a formal set of laws; it provides moral rules which contain teachings about God and about man, and about man's relationship with God. These rules often mention concrete aspects of ordinary life: there are rules, for example, about relationships within the family (cf. 19:3, 11, 35f; etc.) about duties to the elderly and the infirm (cf. 19:14), about kindness towards strangers or sojourners who are exiles from their own countries, and rules designed to counteract hatred and revenge (cf. 19:17ff). But in all these rules, and over and above the fact that some apply to particular cultural and historical circumstances, there is a religious message which is perennial and enduring.

5. LEVITICUS IN THE LIGHT OF THE NEW TESTAMENT

God's great loving-kindness and mercy is manifested in a sublime way through the Sacrifice of the New Law thanks to which man is enabled to offer the Lord a gift worthy of the divine Majesty. Because of this, the best way to read Leviticus is in the light of Christ's sacrifice on the cross. Its content prefigures what became a reality in the Redemption. Jesus has established a new form of worship in which true worshippers will worship the Father in union with Christ and moved by the Holy Spirit (cf. Jn 4:23).

Many passages in the New Testament, particularly the Letter to the Hebrews, use Leviticus as a reference point: it comes up every time there is a men-

---

1. Cf. *Cathechism of the Catholic Church*, 2809,

tion of sacrifices, feasts or liturgy. Hebrews contains an entire section devoted to showing that the sacrifice of Christ is greater than all the sacrifices of the Old Law (Heb 8:1—10:18). For example, it speaks about the excellence of Christ's sacrifice over the most solemn sacrifice of the day of atonement as prescribed in Leviticus: "These preparations having thus been made, the priests go continually into the outer tent, performing their ritual duties; but into the second only the high priest goes, and he but once a year, and not without taking blood which he offers for himself and for the errors of the people. By this the Holy Spirit indicates that the way into the sanctuary is not yet opened as long as the outer tent is still standing (which is symbolic for the present age). According to this arrangement, gifts and sacrifices are offered which cannot perfect the conscience of the worshipper, but deal only with food and drink and various ablutions, regulations for the body imposed until the time of reformation. But when Christ appeared as a high priest of the good things that have come, then through the greater and more perfect tent (not made with hands, that is, not of this creation) he entered once for all into the Holy Place, taking not the blood of goats and calves but his own blood, thus securing an eternal redemption" (Heb 9:6–12).

There is also a section in the Letter to the Hebrews aimed at showing that Christ is the high priest and is greater than the priests of the Mosaic Law (cf. Heb 4:14—7:28). And, particularly, the rules given in the Old Testament about priests very clearly portray the special features of the eternal priesthood of Christ: "It was fitting that we should have such a high priest, holy, blameless, unstained, separated from sinners, exalted above the heavens. He has no need, like those high priests, to offer sacrifices daily, for his own sins and then for those of the people; he did this once for all when he offered up himself" (Heb 7:26–27).

Among the features of Christ the priest which most clearly come across from this passage in Hebrews are purity and holiness—qualities to which Leviticus gives such importance and which never lose their validity. Indeed, it is in the New Testament that the need for purity comes into its own: the cleanness one needs to have to approach God is not confined, as in Leviticus, to a ritual purity; it is something that must come from inside man, from his heart, for "from out of the heart come evil thoughts, murder, adultery, fornication, theft, false witness, slander" (Mt 15:19). Thus, true cleanness calls for purification of the heart. Those who fit their mind, their will and their actions to what God's holiness requires will be happy, because that is how they will find their way to him: "Blessed are the pure in heart, for they shall see God" (Mt 5:8).

It is in the New Testament, too, that the meaning of holiness comes fully into its own. There we find that the Word became flesh in order to be our model of holiness. Jesus himself says so in the Gospel: "I am the way, the truth, and the life" (Jn 14:6). And it is plain to see that a person who orients his

Christian life towards identification with Christ, who is God and man, is entered on the way that has been opened up for man to gain access to full intimacy with God. Moreover, Christ's mission was that of opening the gates of holiness to all the members of the people of God: "Christ, the Son of God, who with the Father and the Spirit is hailed as 'alone holy', loved the Church as his Bride, giving himself up for her so as to sanctify her (cf. Eph 5:25–26); he joined her to himself as his body and endowed her with the gift of the Holy Spirit for the glory of God."[2]

The main teachings of the book of Leviticus find their climax and their marvellous synthesis in the teachings of Jesus: "In Jesus the name of the Holy God is revealed and given to us, in the flesh, as Saviour, revealed by what he is, by his word, and by his sacrifice. This is the heart of his priestly prayer: 'Holy Father, [. . .] for their sake I consecrate myself, that they also may be consecrated in truth' (Jn 17:19). Because he 'sanctifies' his own name, Jesus reveals to us the name of the Father. At the end of Christ's Passover, the Father gives him the name that is above all names: 'Jesus Christ is Lord, to the glory of God the Father'."[3]

---

2. Vatican II, *Lumen gentium*, 39. **3.** *Catechism of the Catholic Church*, 2812.

PART ONE

Rules concerning Sacrifice*

Ex 29:38–42
Lev 6:2
Num 28:3–8

Burnt offerings (holocaust)*

1 ¹The LORD called Moses, and spoke to him from the tent of Ex 25:22 meeting, saying, ²"Speak to the people of Israel, and say to them, When any man of you brings an offering to the LORD, you shall bring your offering of cattle from the herd or from the flock.

³"If his offering is a burnt offering from the herd, he shall offer Ex 12:5 / Deut 12:6 a male without blemish; he shall offer it at the door of the tent of Judg 6:19–21

---

*1:1—7:38. The book of Exodus ended with an account of the building of the sanctuary of the people of God (chaps. 35–40). The sanctuary was the central place for divine worship, so it was a good reference point for dealing with all the rules to do with the Lord's service (cf. Ex 25–31 and notes). At the start of the book of Leviticus, the Lord speaks to Moses from the tent of meeting and instructs him to pass on to the people the laws to do with the key act of worship—sacrifice, or offering. And so the book begins by listing all the rules concerning the different types of offering and the ceremonies to go with them. In the early chapters (1:1—5:26) it deals for the most part with sacrifices offered by ordinary individuals and then it goes on to give rules about sacrifices offered by priests (6:1—7:35).

*1:1–17. The first of the sacrifices mentioned is the burnt offering, sometimes translated as "holocaust", from the Greek

word meaning "burnt in its entirety". The main characteristic of this sacrifice lay in the fact that the victim was burned completely, in acknowledgement of the sovereignty and absolute dominion of the Lord. This type of sacrifice was unknown among the Assyrian-Babylonians, nor is it found among the Egyptians prior to the Hyksos (18th to 16th centuries BC). But it seems to have been offered in Israel from very early on and it held pride of place, especially from the time of the Judges onwards (cf. Judg 6:19–21; 13:19–20). It was offered as an act of thanksgiving, after God had made himself manifest. It was, therefore, a supplication expressing thanks to the Lord for a favour received, an offering that the angel of the Lord caused to ascend towards heaven amid the flames and smoke of the sacrifice. This fire flaming up into heaven symbolized man's desire to be one with God the Most High; the fact that the victim was entirely destroyed was a sign of one's recognition of God's dominion over all things.

---

¹Vocavit autem Moysen et locutus est ei Dominus de tabernaculo conventus dicens: ²«Loquere filiis Israel et dices ad eos: Homo, qui obtulerit ex vobis hostiam Domino de animalibus domesticis, de bobus et pecoribus offerens victimas, ³si holocaustum fuerit eius oblatio de armento, masculum immaculatum offeret ad ostium tabernaculi conventus ad placandum sibi Dominum; ⁴ponetque manum super

Ex 29:10
Lev 16:20–22
Gen 9:5
Ex 24:8; 29:10
Lev 17:11
Deut 12:16, 23
Ex 29:17–18

meeting, that he may be accepted before the LORD; ⁴he shall lay his hand upon the head of the burnt offering, and it shall be accepted for him to make atonement for him. ⁵Then he shall kill the bull before the LORD; and Aaron's sons the priests shall present the blood, and throw the blood round about against the altar that is at the door of the tent of meeting. ⁶And he shall flay the burnt offering and cut it into pieces; ⁷and the sons of Aaron the priest shall put fire on the altar, and lay wood in order upon the fire; ⁸and Aaron's sons the priests shall lay the pieces, the head, and the fat, in order upon the wood that is on the fire upon the altar; ⁹but its entrails and its legs he shall wash with water. And the priest shall burn the whole on the altar, as a burnt offering, an offering by fire, a pleasing odour to the LORD.

¹⁰"If his gift for a burnt offering is from the flock, from the sheep or goats, he shall offer a male without blemish; ¹¹and he

---

Once the people of Israel settled down in the promised land, a burnt offering took place in the temple every day, morning and evening (cf. Ez 29:28–42; Num 28:3–8), and on certain feast-days as well (cf. Lev 12:6–8; 16:3; etc.).

Leviticus 22:23–24 lists blemishes which make animals unsuitable as victims. The Hebrew word *tamim* is translated by the RSV as "without blemish". Other early translations give "perfect" (Aquila) or "whole/entire" (Symmachus). The requirement that the animal offered should have no blemish, no matter how small, reminds us that everyone should offer God the very best: unless one has no choice, nothing defective should be offered to the Lord.

1:4. The laying on of hands showed that the offering belonged to the person who presented it for sacrifice and that the offering was being made in his name

even though it was being done by ministers. However, it is also possible that this gesture signified that the animal was taking the place of the offerer. That certainly seems to be the case in the day of atonement ceremony: the imposition of hands by the priest on the head of the goat which was then let loose in the desert (16:20–22) probably symbolized that the people's faults were being transferred to the animal, to get rid of them.

1:5–9. The offerers did the necessary as regards preparing the animal for the offering—passing it over by means of the laying on of hands, killing it, skinning it, cutting it up into pieces and cleaning its entrails and feet of anything dirty or unclean. It was the priests who put the victim on the altar (their special consecration equipped them to perform the sacred actions of the liturgy: cf. the note on Ex 29:1–9; Ezek 44:11; Ezra 6:20; etc.).

---

caput hostiae, et acceptabilis erit atque in expiationem eius proficiens. ⁵Immolabitque vitulum coram Domino, et offerent filii Aaron sacerdotes sanguinem eius aspergentes per altaris circuitum, quod est ante ostium tabernaculi conventus. ⁶Detracta pelle, hostiam offerens in frusta concidet; ⁷et filii Aaron sacerdotis ponent in altari ignem, strueque lignorum super ignem composita, ⁸membra, quae caesa sunt, desuper ordinabunt, caput videlicet et adipem. ⁹Intestina autem et crura offerens lavabit aqua adolebitque ea sacerdos super altare in holocaustum, incensum suavissimi odoris Domino. ¹⁰Quod si

shall kill it on the north side of the altar before the LORD, and Aaron's sons the priests shall throw its blood against the altar round about. ¹²And he shall cut it into pieces, with its head and its fat, and the priest shall lay them in order upon the wood that is on the fire upon the altar; ¹³but the entrails and the legs he shall wash with water. And the priest shall offer the whole, and burn it on the altar; it is a burnt offering, an offering by fire, a pleasing odour to the LORD.

¹⁴"If his offering to the LORD is a burnt offering of birds, then he shall bring his offering of turtledoves or of young pigeons. ¹⁵And the priest shall bring it to the altar and wring off its head, and burn it on the altar; and its blood shall be drained out on the side of the altar; ¹⁶and he shall take away its crop with the feathers, and cast it beside the altar on the east side, in the place for ashes; ¹⁷he shall tear it by its wings, but shall not divide it asun-

Is 14:13
Ezek 1:4
Ps 48:2

Gen 15:9–10

Lev 4:12
1 Kings 13:5

The shedding of blood, a rite often used in Jewish religious ceremonies, was a way of acknowledging God's sovereignty, because the popular belief was that blood was the source and seat of life and that all life originated in God (cf. 17:11; Deut 12:16, 23). That was also the reason why it was forbidden to eat meat without its blood being first drained (cf. Gen 9:4; Lev 3:17; 17:12; Acts 15:29); and it is why the Old Testament makes it clear how evil the shedding of human blood is (cf. Gen 4:10; Ezek 24:7–8; etc.).

Blood plays a central role in these sacrificial rites and in those of the Covenant (cf. 24:8; Heb 9:18f). For example, in the Covenant of Sinai part of the blood was poured onto the altar and the rest was sprinkled on the people; this shows the union between God and people brought about by the Covenant, because the same blood as touched God (represented by the altar) touched the people. The role of the Eucharist is reminiscent of this in a way, though it uses sacramental signs and is on a higher level—mainly because it is no longer the blood of animals but that of Jesus himself which brings about the union (communion) of God and men.

1:10–13. Some scholars think that the fact that the killing of the animal took place on the north of the altar had to do with the idea that God dwelt away in the north (cf. Is 14:13; Ezek 1:4; Ps 48:2). However, it seems likely that the only reason the north is mentioned is that this was the only part of the altar that was

---

de pecoribus eius oblatio est, de ovibus sive de capris holocaustum, masculum absque macula offeret; ¹¹immolabitque ad latus altaris, quod respicit ad aquilonem, coram Domino. Sanguinem vero illius aspergent contra altare filii Aaron sacerdotes per circuitum; ¹²dividetque offerens membra, caput et adipem, et sacerdos imponet ea super ligna, quibus subest ignis in altari. ¹³Intestina vero et crura lavabit offerens aqua, et oblata omnia adolebit sacerdos super altare: holocaustum est et incensum odoris suavissimi Domino. ¹⁴Sin autem de avibus holocausti oblatio fuerit Domino, offeret de turturibus aut pullis columbae oblationem suam. ¹⁵Et sacerdos afferet eam ad altare; retortum ad collum caput adolebit in altari, sanguisque eius exprimetur contra parietem altaris. ¹⁶Vesiculam vero gutturis et plumas proiciet offerens prope altare ad orientalem plagam in loco, in quo cineres effundi solent; ¹⁷con-

der. And the priest shall burn it on the altar, upon the wood that is on the fire; it is a burnt offering, an offering by fire, a pleasing odour to the LORD.

Lev 6:7–16;
7:9–10
Num 15:1–16 **Cereal offerings***

2 [1]"When any one brings a cereal offering as an offering to the LORD, his offering shall be of fine flour; he shall pour oil upon it, and put frankincense on it, [2]and bring it to Aaron's sons the priests. And he shall take from it a handful of the fine flour and oil, with all of its frankincense; and the priest shall burn this as its memorial portion upon the altar, an offering by fire, a pleasing odor to the LORD [3]And what is left of the cereal offering shall be for Aaron and his sons; it is a most holy part of the offerings by fire to the LORD.

[4]"When you bring a cereal offering baked in the oven as an offering, it shall be unleavened cakes of fine flour mixed with oil, or unleavened wafers spread with oil. [5]And if your offering is a

---

free. The southern side was taken up by the staircase leading to the altar; on the west was the bronze basin containing the water for the washings (cf. Exod 30:18; 40:30), while the east was where the ashes were collected (cf. Lev 1:16).

***2:1–16.** This chapter deals with the various kinds of offerings to be done on the main altar of the sanctuary, the so-called altar of holocaust, the altar *par excellence* (in Hebrew *ha-mizbeaj*, etymologically the "place of immolation" or "place of sacrifice"). As regards the altar, cf. the note on Ex 27:1–8.

2:1–3. After dealing with the burnt offering rites, which involved the sacrifice of animals, the text now comes to oblation ceremonies, that is, ceremonies to do with *minjáh* (etymologically, "gift", "tribute"), in which agricultural produce was offered. This was an offering typical of an agricultural people; in other words, it implies that the Israelites were no longer nomads but had settled down. The offering consists of certain types of agricultural produce; only a part of the material offered was burnt, the flour being made into a shape with oil. This sort of offering is thought to be very ancient in origin: cf. offerings by Cain (Gen 4:3), Melchisedek (Gen 14:18) and Moses (Ex 29:40; Num 15:1–2).

The text specifies that these offerings should consist of wheaten flour, the best kind of flour—another reminder that only the best is good enough for God. In

---

fringetque eam inter alas, quas non secabit, et adolebit eam sacerdos super altare, lignis super ignem positis: holocaustum est et incensum suavissimi odoris Domino. [1]Anima cum obtulerit oblationem sacrificii farinae Domino, simila erit eius oblatio, fundetque super eam oleum et ponet tus [2]ac deferet ad filios Aaron sacerdotes, tolletque ex eo pugillum plenum similae et olei ac totum tus, et sacerdos adolebit memoriale super altare, incensum odoris suavissimi Domino. [3]Quod autem reliquum fuerit de sacrificio, erit Aaron et filiorum eius: sanctum sanctorum de incensis Domini. [4]Cum autem obtuleris sacrificium similae coctum in clibano: de simila erunt panes, scilicet absque fermento conspersi oleo et lagana azyma oleo lita; [5]Si oblatio tua fuerit de sartagine, simila erit, conspersa oleo et absque fer-

cereal offering baked on a griddle, it shall be of fine flour unleavened, mixed with oil; ⁶you shall break it in pieces, and pour oil on it; it is a cereal offering. ⁷And if your offering is a cereal offering cooked in a pan, it shall be made of fine flour with oil. ⁸And you shall bring the cereal offering that is made of these things to the LORD; and when it is presented to the priest, he shall bring it to the altar. ⁹And the priest shall take from the cereal offering its memorial portion and burn this on the altar, an offering by fire, a pleasing odour to the LORD. ¹⁰And what is left of the cereal offering shall be for Aaron and his sons; it is a most holy part of the offerings by fire to the LORD.

¹¹"No cereal offering which you bring to the LORD shall be made with leaven; for you shall burn no leaven nor any honey as an offering by fire to the LORD. ¹²As an offering of first fruits you may bring them to the LORD, but they shall not be offered on the altar for a pleasing odour. ¹³You shall season all your cereal offerings with salt; you shall not let the salt of the covenant with your

Lev 6:9

Num 18:19
2 Chron 13:5
Ezek 16:4

---

fact, on other occasions an offering of wheaten flour is made to personages of rank (cf. Gen 18:6). Along with the flour and the oil, incense was burned, to enhance the liturgical aura of the offering.

Since incense is a form of praise that wafts its way up to heaven, maybe the burning of the offering with incense symbolizes the submissive and supplicant attitude of the offerer, and the fact that God is pleased to accept it.

2:4–12. All the offerings mentioned in this chapter include "fine flour" (= wheaten flour), whether baked or fried. Leaven is prohibited out of a concern to avoid offering the Lord anything unclean, because leaven, being in a state of fer-

mentation, was seen as something rotting, something impure (cf. the note on Ex 12:15–20).

2:13. Salt was one of the necessary ingredients in certain kinds of sacrifice (cf. Ezra 6:9). It was used to add savour to the foodstuffs offered in sacrifice and then eaten in the sacred meal. But it was used mainly because of its quality of preserving things from corruption, thereby symbolizing the enduring, inviolable quality of the Covenant (cf. 2 Chron 13:5). "Eating salt with someone" meant making a pact, sometimes called a "covenant of salt", which established an enduring friendship (cf. Num 18:19). Thus, the Covenant between God and Israel, agreed to at Sinai, was not a pass-

---

mento; ⁶divides eam minutatim et fundes super eam oleum: oblatio similae est. ⁷Sin autem de frixorio fuerit sacrificium, aeque simila oleo conspergetur. ⁸Et deferes oblationem ex his Domino factam tradens manibus sacerdotis, ⁹qui afferet eam ad altare, tollet memoriale de sacrificio et adolebit super altare: incensum odoris suavissimi Domino. ¹⁰Quidquid autem reliquum est, erit Aaron et filiorum eius: sanctum sanctorum de incensis Domini. ¹¹Omnis oblatio similae, quam offeretis Domino, absque fermento fiet, quia nihil fermenti ac mellis adolebitis incensum Domino. ¹²Primitias tantum eorum offeretis tamquam munera Domino; super altare vero non ponentur in odorem suavitatis. ¹³Quidquid obtuleris sacrificii, similae sale condies nec auferes sal foederis Dei tui de sacrificio tuo: in omni obla-

Mk 9:49–50
Col 4:6

God be lacking from your cereal offering; with all your offerings you shall offer salt.

Deut 26:1–11   ¹⁴"If you offer a cereal offering of first fruits to the LORD, you shall offer for the cereal offering of your first fruits crushed new grain from fresh ears, parched with fire. ¹⁵And you shall put oil upon it, and lay frankincense on it; it is a cereal offering. ¹⁶And the priest shall burn as its memorial portion part of the crushed grain and of the oil with all of its frankincense; it is an offering by fire to the LORD.

Lev 7:11–16;
19:5–8; 22:21–
25; 23:19   **Peace offerings (communion offerings)***

1 Cor 10:16   **3** ¹"If a man's offering is a sacrifice of peace offering, if he offers an animal from the herd, male or female, he shall offer it without blemish before the LORD. ²And he shall lay his hand upon the head of his offering and kill it at the door of the tent of meeting; and Aaron's sons the priests shall throw the blood against the altar round about. ³And from the sacrifice of the peace

---

ing event but something on-going, something real for every generation. The salt used in sacrifices symbolized the perpetuity of the Covenant, and it was a reminder of that irrevocable commitment.

In the New Testament salt stands for wisdom and moral purity. The Gospel of St Mark makes mention of the salt of sacrifice, and of salt being a purifying element (Mt 9:49–50). In the Sermon on the Mount Jesus tells his disciples that they are the salt of the earth, that is, they are the ones who give a divine flavour to everything human and who prevent the world corrupting. St Paul also uses the symbol of salt when he tells the Christians of Colossae to season their speech "with salt, that you may know how you ought to answer every one"

(Col 4:6). There is also the use of salt in Baptism, though now it is only optional (it was an Israelite custom to rub a newborn baby with salt: cf. Ezek 16:4), whereby the neophyte is given a little taste of salt while the words are spoken, "Receive the salt of wisdom".

*3:1–17. This entire chapter deals with communion or peace offerings (*shelamin*). These were usually offered to keep a vow or as an act of thanksgiving; hence their also being called "eucharistic" sacrifices or offerings. These offerings could also be made as a rite of reconciliation with God, as a communion offering. They were normally private, freewill offerings, but later on they took on the nature of a public sacrifice (cf. 23:19). When a Nazirite vow was involv-

---

tione tua offeres sal. ¹⁴Sin autem obtuleris munus primarum frugum tuarum Domino, spicas tostas igni et grana fracta farris recentis offeres in sacrificium primarum frugum tuarum ¹⁵fundens supra oleum et tus imponens: similae oblatio est. ¹⁶De qua adolebit sacerdos tamquam memoriale partem farris fracti et olei ac totum tus. ¹Quod si hostia pacificorum fuerit eius oblatio et de bobus voluerit offerre marem sive feminam, immaculata offeret coram Domino. ²Ponetque manum super caput victimae suae, quam immolabit ad ostium tabernaculi conventus, fundentque filii Aaron sacerdotes sanguinem per circuitum altaris ³et offerent de hostia pacificorum tamquam incensum Domino adipem, qui operit vitalia, et

offering, as an offering by fire to the LORD, he shall offer the fat covering the entrails and all the fat that is on the entrails, ⁴and the two kidneys with the fat that is on them at the loins, and the appendage of the liver which he shall take away with the kidneys. ⁵Then Aaron's sons shall burn it on the altar upon the burnt offering, which is upon the wood on the fire; it is an offering by fire, a pleasing odour to the LORD.

⁶"If his offering for a sacrifice of peace offering to the LORD is an animal from the flock, male or female, he shall offer it without blemish. ⁷If he offers a lamb for his offering, then he shall offer it before the LORD, ⁸laying his hand upon the head of his offering and killing it before the tent of meeting; and Aaron's sons shall throw its blood against the altar round about. ⁹Then from the sacrifice of the peace offering as an offering by fire to the LORD he shall offer its fat, the fat tail entire, taking it away close by the backbone, and the fat that covers the entrails, and all the fat that is on the entrails, ¹⁰and the two kidneys with the fat that is on

---

ed, this type of sacrifice was obligatory (cf. Num 6:14, 17–18).

The text does not tell us everything about the rite for peace offerings. It seems to have been the same as that for a burnt offering except that the animal could be female, and it did not have to be burned entirely: only the fat and certain entrails needed to be burnt, that is, the best parts, which according to ancient thinking were the seat of the feelings (intestines and liver) or of the generative function (loins and kidneys). One of the features of peace offerings was the "swinging" or "waving" of the victim (cf. the note on Ex 30:11–16). The rite began in front of the sanctuary or tent of meeting. Only after that were certain parts of the victim offered by the priest on the altar of holocaust.

The rest of the animal (the portion not burned) was divided between the priest and the offerer(s), who had to eat it in a sacred place (cf. 7:11–21).

3:6–17. In addition to large livestock, small livestock could also be offered in sacrifice, always provided it was unblemished. The part burned in the fire was regarded as food for God. This anthropomorphism meant that both the Lord and those partaking in the offering were sharing in the same food, thereby establishing a communion similar to that which obtains when people sit and partake of the same meal.

All this, along with the fact that the peace offering often had the nature of thanksgiving, means that this sort of sacrifice was the one most like our Euchar-

---

quidquid pinguedinis eis adhaeret, ⁴duos renes cum adipe, quo teguntur iuxta ilia, et reticulum iecoris, quem iuxta renes, auferet. ⁵Adolebuntque ea filii Aaron in altari super holocausto, quod est super lignis et igne: incensum suavissimi odoris Domino. ⁶Si vero de pecoribus fuerit Domino eius oblatio, pacificorum scilicet hostia, sive masculum sive feminam obtulerit, immaculata erunt. ⁷Si agnum obtulerit coram Domino, ⁸ponet manum super caput victimae suae, quam immolabit coram tabernaculo conventus; fundentque filii Aaron sanguinem eius per altaris circuitum; ⁹et offeret de pacificorum hostia incensum Domino adipem et caudam totam, quam iuxta tergum, auferet, et pinguedinem, quae operit

them at the loins, and the appendage of the liver which he shall take away with the kidneys. [11]And the priest shall burn it on the altar as food offered by fire to the LORD.

[12]"If his offering is a goat, then he shall offer it before the LORD, [13]and lay his hand upon its head, and kill it before the tent of meeting; and the sons of Aaron shall throw its blood against the altar round about. [14]Then he shall offer from it, as his offering for an offering by fire to the LORD, the fat covering the entrails, and all the fat that is on the entrails, [15]and the two kidneys with the fat that is on them at the loins, and the appendage of the liver which he shall take away with the kidneys. [16]And the priest shall burn them on the altar as food offered by fire for a pleasing odour. All fat is the LORD's. [17]It shall be a perpetual statute throughout your generations, in all your dwelling places, that you eat neither fat nor blood."

Sin offerings*

Num 15:22–29
Eccles 5:5

4 [1]And the LORD said to Moses, [2]"Say to the people of Israel, If any one sins unwittingly in any of the things which the LORD has commanded not to be done, and does any one of them,

istic sacrifice, in which "because there is one bread, we who are many are one body, for we all partake of the one bread" (1 Cor 10:17).

*4:1—5:26. Chapters 4 and 5 deal with sin offerings and the kinds of animals to be sacrificed as guilt offerings. It covers four types of persons—priests, the entire community, rulers and ordinary people.

The sort of ideas we have today are far removed from those which held sway when the rules given here were assembled. We need to make an effort to grasp what those ancient texts mean. The main thing about these rules concerning sin offerings is that they denote great respect for the Sinai Covenant: any violation of it had to be expiated. Whether the offence being expiated was voluntary or unintentional was a secondary matter.

4:1–2. Unlike the sacrifices or offerings previously laid down (which were inspired mainly by recognition of God's sovereignty), these sacrifices all involve the idea of reparation and expiation.

Offerings of this sort seem to go back

ventrem, atque universum adipem, qui vitalibus adhaeret, [10]et utrumque renunculum cum adipe, qui est iuxta ilia, reticulumque iecoris, quem iuxta renunculos, auferet. [11]Et adolebit ea sacerdos super altare: panis et incensum Domino. [12]Si capra fuerit eius oblatio, offeret eam coram Domino, [13]ponet manum suam super caput eius immolabitque eam coram tabernaculo conventus. Et fundent filii Aaron sanguinem eius per altaris circuitum, [14]tolletque ex ea oblationem suam, incensum Domino, adipem scilicet, qui operit ventrem, et universum, qui vitalibus adhaeret, [15]duos renunculos cum adipe, qui est super eos iuxta ilia, et reticulum iecoris, quem iuxta renunculos, auferet; [16]adolebitque ea sacerdos super altare: panis et incensum suavissimi odoris omnis adeps Domino. [17]Iure perpetuo in generationibus et cunctis habitaculis vestris, nec adipem nec sanguinem omnino comedetis». [1]Locutusque est Dominus ad Moysen dicens: [2]«Loquere filiis Israel: Anima cum peccaverit per ignorantiam et de uni-

Offerings for sins of a priest

³if it is the anointed priest who sins, thus bringing guilt on the Ex 26:33;
people, then let him offer for the sin which he has committed a 27:2; 30:1–10
young bull without blemish to the LORD for a sin offering. ⁴He
shall bring the bull to the door of the tent of meeting before the
LORD, and lay his hand on the head of the bull, and kill the bull
before the LORD. ⁵And the anointed priest shall take some of the
blood of the bull and bring it to the tent of meeting; ⁶and the priest
shall dip his finger in the blood and sprinkle part of the blood
seven times before the LORD in front of the veil of the sanctuary.
⁷And the priest shall put some of the blood on the horns of the Ex 29:12
altar of fragrant incense before the LORD which is in the tent of
meeting, and the rest of the blood of the bull he shall pour out at
the base of the altar of burnt offering which is at the door of the
tent of meeting. ⁸And all the fat of the bull of the sin offering he
shall take from it, the fat that covers the entrails and all the fat that
is on the entrails, ⁹and the two kidneys with the fat that is on them
at the loins, and the appendage of the liver which he shall take
away with the kidneys ¹⁰(just as these are taken from the ox of the
sacrifice of the peace offerings), and the priest shall burn them

to very early times, as can be seen from
evidence about other Canaanite peoples
and from texts from Ras Shamra
(Ugarit), on the coast of Syria (15th to
14th centuries BC).

As regards things done unwittingly,
the matters mentioned here were not sins
strictly speaking: they were simply
"material sins" or ritual impurities.
However, there is an underlying idea that
some degree of imprudence is involved
(cf. Num 15:22–29; Eccles 5:5). We
prefer to translate it not as "ignorantia"
(New Vulgate) but by a word which (like

the Hebrew original) conveys the idea
that the ignorance was more the outcome
of human limitation than of lack of due
knowledge [so, the RSV "unwittingly"
seems fine].

4:3–12. At the start of the list of offerings
to be made for sins committed by a
priest, the point is made that his sin is
particularly serious because it brings
guilt on the people as well. Something
similar happened with the sin of a king
(cf. 2 Sam 24:10–15; 1 Kings 13:1–10).
The ceremony contains elements we

versis mandatis Domini, quae praecepit ut non fierent, quippiam fecerit, ³si sacerdos, qui est unctus,
peccaverit, delinquere faciens populum, offeret pro peccato suo vitulum immaculatum Domino sacrificium pro peccato; ⁴et adducet illum ad ostium tabernaculi conventus coram Domino ponetque manum
super caput eius et immolabit eum coram Domino. ⁵Hauriet quoque sacerdos unctus de sanguine vituli
inferens illum in tabernaculum conventus; ⁶cumque intinxerit digitum in sanguinem, asperget eo septies coram Domino contra velum sanctuarii; ⁷ponetque de eodem sanguine super cornua altaris
thymiamatis gratissimi coram Domino, quod est in tabernaculo conventus; omnem autem reliquum
sanguinem fundet in basim altaris holocausti in introitu tabernaculi. ⁸Et omnem adipem vituli pro peccato auferet tam eum, qui operit vitalia, quam omnem, qui vitalibus adhaeret, ⁹duos renunculos et
adipem, qui est super eos iuxta ilia, et reticulum iecoris, quem iuxta renunculos, auferet, ¹⁰sicut aufer-

upon the altar of burnt offering. ¹¹But the skin of the bull and all its flesh, with its head, its legs, its entrails, and its dung, ¹²the

Heb 13:13 whole bull he shall carry forth outside the camp to a clean place, where the ashes are poured out, and shall burn it on a fire of wood; where the ashes are poured out it shall be burned.

Offerings for sins of the people

¹³"If the whole congregation of Israel commits a sin unwittingly and the thing is hidden from the eyes of the assembly, and they do any one of the things which the LORD has commanded not to be

Heb 10:6 done and are guilty; ¹⁴when the sin which they have committed becomes known, the assembly shall offer a young bull for a sin offering and bring it before the tent of meeting; ¹⁵and the elders of

Ex 18:13–26 the congregation shall lay their hands upon the head of the bull before the LORD, and the bull shall be killed before the LORD. ¹⁶Then the anointed priest shall bring some of the blood of the bull to the tent of meeting, ¹⁷and the priest shall dip his finger in the blood and sprinkle it seven times before the LORD in front of the veil. ¹⁸And he shall put some of the blood on the horns of the altar which is in the tent of meeting before the LORD; and the rest of the blood he shall pour out at the base of the altar of burnt offering which is at the door of the tent of meeting. ¹⁹And all its

---

have seen in earlier sacrifices but there are new ones too. By burning the victim outside the camp (v. 12) the offerer was showing his sorrow for having sinned, for he renounced the possibility of eating the meat of the victim. This aspect of sin offerings is taken up in the Letter to the Hebrews, when it says that "Jesus also suffered outside the gate in order to sanctify the people through his own blood" (Heb 13:12).

4:13–21. Sins committed by the whole

people of Israel also had to be expiated. Because of their status as representatives of the people, it was the elders who laid their hands on the animal being offered. The Hebrew term (*kipper*), here translated as "forgiven" (v. 20), originally meant a supplication by the action of covering over or rubbing out something. In fact, the forgiveness of sins that the Old Testament talks about was no more than a plea for forgiveness; it was only when Christ died on the cross that the redemption of sins came about. "The

tur de vitulo hostiae pacificorum; et adolebit ea sacerdos super altare holocausti. ¹¹Pellem vero et omnes carnes cum capite et pedibus et intestinis et fimo, ¹²totum vitulum efferet extra castra in locum mundum, ubi cineres effundi solent; incendetque eum super lignorum struem igne: in loco effusorum cinerum cremabitur. ¹³Quod si omnis coetus Israel ignoraverit, et res abscondita fuerit ab oculis congregationis, feceritque quod contra mandatum Domini est et deliquerit, ¹⁴et postea intellexerit peccatum suum, offeret congregatio vitulum pro peccato adducetque eum ad ostium tabernaculi conventus. ¹⁵Et ponent seniores coetus populi manus super caput eius coram Domino, immolatoque vitulo in conspectu Domini, ¹⁶inferet sacerdos, qui unctus est, de sanguine eius in tabernaculum conventus, ¹⁷tincto digito aspergens septies contra velum; ¹⁸ponetque de eodem sanguine in cornibus altaris, quod est

fat he shall take from it and burn upon the altar. [20]Thus shall he do with the bull; as he did with the bull of the sin offering, so shall he do with this; and the priest shall make atonement for them, and they shall be forgiven. [21]And he shall carry forth the bull outside the camp, and burn it as he burned the first bull; it is the sin offering for the assembly.

Offerings for sins of a ruler

[22]"When a ruler sins, doing unwittingly any one of all the things which the LORD his God has commanded not to be done, and is guilty, [23]if the sin which he has committed is made known to him, he shall bring as his offering a goat, a male without blemish, [24]and shall lay his hand upon the head of the goat, and kill it in the place where they kill the burnt offering before the LORD; it is a sin offering. [25]Then the priest shall take some of the blood of the sin offering with his finger and put it on the horns of the altar of burnt offering, and pour out the rest of its blood at the base of the altar of burnt offering. [26]And all its fat he shall burn on the altar, like the fat of the sacrifice of peace offerings; so the priest shall make atonement for him for his sin, and he shall be forgiven.

Scriptures had foretold this divine plan of salvation through the putting to death of 'the righteous one, my Servant' (Is 53:11; cf. Acts 3:14) as a mystery of universal redemption, that is, as the ransom that would free men from the slavery of sin (cf. Is 53:11–12; Jn 8:34–36)": that is how the *Catechism of the Catholic Church*, 601, expounds the atonement for sin that our Lord's death brought about. It goes on to say that "Jesus did not experience reprobation as if he himself had sinned. But in the redeeming love that always united him to the Father, he assumed us in the state of our waywardness of sin, to the point that he could say in our name from the cross: 'My God, my God, why have your forsaken me?' (Mk 15:34; Ps 22:1). Having thus established him in solidarity with us sinners, God 'did not spare his own Son but gave him up for us all', so that we might be 'reconciled to God by the death of his Son' (Rom 5:10)" (ibid., 603).

4:22–35. Various Old Testaments pas-

coram Domino in tabernaculo conventus. Reliquum autem sanguinem fundet iuxta basim altaris holocaustorum, quod est in ostio tabernaculi conventus; [19]omnemque eius adipem tollet et adolebit super altare. [20]Sic faciens et de hoc vitulo quomodo fecit de vitulo pro peccato; sic faciet ei. Expiante eos sacerdote, propitius erit Dominus. [21]Ipsum autem vitulum efferet extra castra atque comburet sicut et priorem vitulum: sacrificium pro peccato est congregationis. [22]Si peccaverit princeps et fecerit unum ex omnibus per ignorantiam, quod Domini Dei sui lege prohibetur, deliqueritque, [23]aut indicatum ei fuerit peccatum suum, offeret hostiam Domino hircum de capris immaculatum [24]ponetque manum suam super caput eius et immolabit eum in loco, ubi solet mactari holocaustum coram Domino: sacrificium pro peccato est. [25]Et tinguat sacerdos digitum in sanguine hostiae pro peccato ponetque super cornua altaris holocausti et reliquum fundet ad basim eius. [26]Adipem vero adolebit supra, sicut in victimis

Offerings for sins of a private individual

[27]"If any one of the common people sins unwittingly in doing any one of the things which the LORD has commanded not to be done, and is guilty, [28]when the sin which he has committed is made known to him he shall bring for his offering a goat, a female without blemish, for his sin which he has committed. [29]And he shall lay his hand on the head of the sin offering, and kill the sin offering in the place of burnt offering. [30]And the priest shall take some of its blood with his finger and put it on the horns of the altar of burnt offering, and pour out the rest of its blood at the base of the altar. [31]And all its fat he shall remove, as the fat is removed from the peace offerings, and the priest shall burn it upon the altar for a pleasing odour to the LORD; and the priest shall make atonement for him, and he shall be forgiven.

[32]"If he brings a lamb as his offering for a sin offering, he shall bring a female without blemish, [33]and lay his hand upon the head of the sin offering, and kill it for as in offering in the place where they kill the burnt offering. [34]Then the priest shall take some of the blood of the sin offering with his finger and put it on the horns of the altar of burnt offering, and pour out the rest of its blood at the base of the altar. [35]And all its fat he shall remove as the fat of the lamb is removed from the sacrifice of peace offerings, and the priest shall burn it on the altar, upon the offerings by fire to the LORD; and the priest shall make atonement for him for the sin which he has committed, and he shall be forgiven.

---

sages refer to differences in status among members of the people of Israel—prince (cf. Ezek 44:3), high dignitary (cf. Ezra 1:8), ruler (cf. Ex 16:22; Num 1:16), the lowest status being that of the plain people (*'am ha-ares*, "the people of the land"). Therefore, the lower a person was on the social scale, the less valuable a victim was required.

Unlike the major sin offerings, an offering could be made by any priest; it was not necessary for the high priest to perform it. And the rite was simpler, when the high priest was not involved.

---

pacificorum fieri solet; expiabitque eum a peccato eius, ac dimittetur ei. [27]Quod si peccaverit anima per ignorantiam de populo terrae, ut faciat quidquam ex his, quae Domini lege prohibentur, atque delinquat, [28]aut indicatum ei fuerit peccatum suum, offeret capram immaculatam; [29]ponetque manum super caput hostiae pro peccato et immolabit eam in loco holocausti. [30]Tolletque sacerdos de sanguine in digito suo et ponet super cornua altaris holocausti et reliquum fundet ad basim eius. [31]Omnem autem auferens adipem, sicut auferri solet de victimis pacificorum, adolebit super altare in odorem suavitatis Domino, expiabitque eum, et propitius erit Dominus. [32]Sin autem de ovibus obtulerit victimam pro peccato, adducet agnam immaculatam; [33]ponet manum super caput eius et immolabit eam in loco, ubi solent holocaustorum caedi hostiae. [34]Sumetque sacerdos de sanguine eius digito suo et ponens super cornua altaris holocausti reliquum fundet ad basim eius. [35]Omnem quoque auferens adipem, sicut auferri solet adeps agni, qui immolatur pro pacificis, cremabit in altari super incensis Domini; expia-

Other sin offerings

5 [1]"If any one sins in that he hears a public adjuration to testify and though he is a witness, whether he has seen or come to know the matter, yet does not speak, he shall bear his iniquity. [2]Or if any one touches an unclean thing, whether the carcass of an unclean beast or a carcass of unclean cattle or a carcass of unclean swarming things, and it is hidden from him, and he has become unclean, he shall be guilty. [3]Or if he touches human uncleanness, of whatever sort the uncleanness may be with which one becomes unclean, and it is hidden from him, when he comes to know it he shall be guilty. [4]Or if any one utters with his lips a rash oath to do evil or to do good, any sort of rash oath that men swear, and it is hidden from him, when he comes to know it he shall in any of these be guilty. [5]When a man is guilty in any of these, he shall confess the sin he has committed, [6]and he shall bring his guilt offering to the LORD for the sin which he has committed, a female from the flock, a lamb or a goat, for a sin offering; and the priest shall make atonement for him for his sin.

Deut 19:15–20
Prov 29:24

Mt 5:36

Num 5:7
Mt 3:6

5:1–6. This chapter instances various sins, case by case. The first case is not very clear. Some think that it has to do with a cover-up on behalf of an offender by someone who was a witness to the offence (cf. Prov 29:24). Others think that it is about someone who refuses to give evidence about a crime he witnessed, despite being called on by a judge to do so. And others again think that it concerns a person refusing to give evidence about a crime of which he was the victim.

As regards contact with unclean things, be they persons or animals, this will be dealt with again in chapters 11–15.

The passage also refers to the Heb-

rews' bad habit of taking rash oaths. This was something that Jesus also criticized (cf. Mt 5:36); he, for his part, exhorted people to sincerity—to tell the truth at all times, avoiding any need to back up one's words by oath: "Let what you say be simply, 'Yes' or 'No'; anything more than this comes from evil" (Mt 5:37).

In order to atone for sins one first needed to declare oneself guilty of them (v. 5). This practice of humble acknowledgement of personal faults seems to have applied to all sin offerings (cf. Num 5:7). It was laid down that that form of acknowledgment of guilt should take place on Yom Kippur, the day of atonement. In later times this practice became

---

bitque eum et peccatum eius, et dimittetur illi. ¹Si peccaverit anima et audiverit vocem iurantis testisque fuerit, quod aut ipse vidit aut comperit, si non indicaverit, iniquitatem portabit; ²vel si anima tetigerit aliquid immundum, sive cadaver bestiae sit aut iumenti vel reptilis, et absconditum fuerit ab eo, ipse immundus et reus erit; ³aut si tetigerit quidquam de immunditia hominis iuxta omnem impuritatem, qua pollui solet, absconditumque fuerit ab eo, sed ipse cognoverit postea, subiacebit delicto; ⁴aut si anima temere iuraverit et protulerit labiis suis, ut vel male quid faceret vel bene iuxta omnia, quae homines temere iurant, absconditumque fuerit ab eo, sed ipse postea intellexerit, delicto subiacebit; ⁵si ergo reus factus fuerit uno ex istis, confiteatur peccatum suum ⁶et offerat Domino sacrificium delicti pro peccato suo agnam de gregibus sive capram ut sacrificium pro peccato; expiabitque

Leviticus 5:7

Lev 14:21; 27:8 **Offerings for sins of poor people**

⁷"But if he cannot afford a lamb, then he shall bring, as his guilt offering to the LORD for the sin which he has committed, two turtledoves or two young pigeons, one for a sin offering and the other for a burnt offering. ⁸He shall bring them to the priest, who shall offer first the one for the sin offering; he shall wring its head from its neck, but shall not sever it, ⁹and he shall sprinkle some of the blood of the sin offering on the side of the altar, while the rest of the blood shall be drained out at the base of the altar; it is a sin offering. ¹⁰Then he shall offer the second for a burnt offering according to the ordinance; and the priest shall make atonement for him for the sin which he has committed, and he shall be forgiven.

---

the typical penitential act. Thus, people who flocked to hear John the Baptist not only received baptism but also acknowledged themselves to be guilty of their sins (cf. Mt 3:6). That confession of sin was a kind of preparation for the later system of sacramental confession. That sacrament continued an ancient biblical practice, inspired by God for the benefit of his people. The sacrament of Penance, instituted by Christ, involving the confession of sins as a condition for their being forgiven, goes back to the Old Testament rites. However, there is a difference in form—and also a difference in effect: the Old Testament offerings were only a plea for forgiveness of sin, whereas the sacrament of Penance truly is an effective, sacramental forgiveness of sin. From the very start confession of sins was a practice held in high regard by the Church and a prerequisite for obtaining forgiveness.

5:7–13. The consideration shown towards the poor (cf. 14:21; 27:8) indicates that the value of an offering did not really lie in the value of the animal; it had more to do with the dispositions of the offerer. Contrition and sorrow for having sinned has always been basic to a good relationship with God: "You already have something you can offer," St Augustine comments. "Do not look to your flocks or fit out ships to go to far countries in search of spices. Seek within your heart what is pleasing to God. Make your heart contrite. Are you afraid that a contrite heart will perish? The psalm says, 'Create in me a clean heart, O God.' For God to be able to create a clean heart, the unclean heart has to be destroyed" (St Augustine, *Sermon*, 19, 3).

An ephah was a measure of dry grain equivalent to 21 litres (about five gallons): cf. the note on Ex 16:32–36. Unlike the cereal offerings no oil or incense was added, because these sacrifices were not joyful: they were made

eum sacerdos a peccato eius. ⁷Sin autem non potuerit offerre pecus, offerat ut sacrificium pro delicto duos turtures vel duos pullos columbarum Domino: unum in sacrificium pro peccato et alterum in holocaustum; ⁸dabitque eos sacerdoti, qui primum offerens ut sacrificium pro peccato retorquebit caput eius ad pennulas, ita ut collo haereat et non penitus abrumpatur; ⁹et asperget de sanguine eius parietem altaris; quidquid autem reliquum fuerit, faciet destillare ad fundamentum eius: sacrificium pro peccato est. ¹⁰Alterum vero adolebit holocaustum, ut fieri solet; expiabitque eum sacerdos a peccato eius, et dimittetur ei. ¹¹Quod si non quiverit manus eius offerre duos turtures aut duos pullos columbarum,

[11]"But if he cannot afford two turtledoves or two young Lk 2:24
pigeons, then he shall bring, as his offering for the sin which he
has committed, a tenth of an ephah of fine flour for a sin offering;
he shall put no oil upon it, and shall put no frankincense on it, for
it is a sin offering. [12]And he shall bring it to the priest, and the
priest shall take a handful of it as its memorial portion and burn
this on the altar, upon the offerings by fire to the LORD; it is a sin
offering. [13]Thus the priest shall make atonement for him for the sin
which he has committed in any one of these things, and he shall be
forgiven. And the remainder shall be for the priest, as in the cereal
offering."

Guilt offerings

[14]The LORD said to Moses, [15]"If any one commits a breach of faith
and sins unwittingly in any of the holy things of the LORD, he

---

out of sorrow for sin committed against
God.

5:7. This rule shows that Jesus was born
into a poor family, because, as we know,
Mary and Joseph offered a pair of doves
when the child was presented in the
temple (cf. Lk 2:22–24). It was an
instance of people who could not afford to
offer a "lamb"; still, they were not in
abject poverty, because (as one can see
from 5:11) a smaller offering was possible.

5:14—6:7. Offerings in atonement for
certain transgressions of the Law ("guilt
offerings") were different from those
dealt with so far ("sin offerings") and
from those for which atonement offerings were prescribed. The former transgressions were also unwitting, but the
cases now being discussed involved
unjust retention of sacred things (offer-

ings, first-fruits etc.) or else a violation
of divine rights (without specifying
which).

The *Anchor Bible Dictionary* prefers
to translate the Hebrew as "purification
offering" in place of the traditional "sin
offering", and "reparation offering" in
place of "guilt offering". It says, "in summary, one could say that the basic distinction between the purification and guilt
offerings is that the purification offering
deals with the issue of impurity while the
reparation offering deals with profanation
of sacred items." This does not always
apply, but it is generally the case.

There was guilt even if the person
was unaware that he was committing an
offence. So, it was a matter of a legal
fault, not a moral fault. However, on
occasion these rules were interpreted in
such a rigorous and legalistic way as to
make it almost impossible to keep the
Law (cf. Acts 15:10).

---

offeret pro peccato suo similae partem ephi decimam in sacrificium pro peccato; non mittet in eam
oleum, nec turis aliquid imponet, quia sacrificium pro peccato est. [12]Tradetque eam sacerdoti, qui,
plenum ex toto pugillum in memoriale hauriens, cremabit in altari super incensis Domini: sacrificium
pro peccato est. [13]Et expiabit eum sacerdos et peccatum eius in uno ex his casibus, et propitius erit
Dominus. Reliquam vero partem sacerdos habebit sicut in oblatione similae». [14]Locutus est Dominus
ad Moysen dicens: [15]«Anima, si praevaricans per errorem in his, quae Domino sunt sanctificata, pec-

shall bring, as his guilt offering to the LORD, a ram without blemish out of the flock, valued by you in shekels of silver, according to the shekel of the sanctuary; it is a guilt offering. [16]He shall also make restitution for what he has done amiss in the holy thing, and shall add a fifth to it and give it to the priest; and the priest shall make atonement for him with the ram of the guilt offering, and he shall be forgiven.

[17]"If any one sins, doing any of the things which the LORD has commanded not to be done, though he does not know it, yet he is guilty and shall bear his iniquity. [18]He shall bring to the priest a ram without blemish out of the flock, valued by you at the price for a guilt offering, and the priest shall make atonement for him for the error which he committed unwittingly, and he shall be forgiven. [19]It is a guilt offering; he is guilty before the LORD."

Ex 22:1–6
Num 5:5–10

6 [1a]The LORD said to Moses, [2]"If any one sins and commits a breach of faith against the LORD by deceiving his neighbour in a matter of deposit or security, or through robbery, or if he has oppressed his neighbour [3]or has found what was lost and lied about

---

6:1–7. Offences against property called for some form of restitution. It is assumed apparently that the person who committed the offences mentioned here was aware of the harm he was doing. It should be noted that the penalty being laid down is not the legal penalty, which was even heavier (cf. Ex 22:1–4), but a religious one. The fine levied is the same as before (Lev 5:16), but in these cases it goes to the injured party.

All these various rules are (distantly) reminiscent of the moral teaching of the Gospel, which the Church enunciates and interprets. So, for example, to obtain forgiveness of a sin committed against

someone else's property, it is not enough to be repentant and to confess the sin in the sacrament of Penance and to be resolved not to sin in the future: one also needs to restore what one stole or unjustly kept. Therefore, "in virtue of commutative justice, *reparation for injustice* committed requires the restitution of stolen goods to their owner: Jesus blesses Zacchaeus for his pledge: 'If I have defrauded anyone of anything, I restore it fourfold' (Lk 19:18). Those who, directly or indirectly, have taken possession of the goods of another are obliged to make restitution of them, or to return the equivalent in kind or in money, if the goods

---

caverit, offeret sacrificium pro delicto arietem immaculatum de gregibus iuxta aestimationem argenti siclorum pondere sanctuarii in paenitentiam; [16]ipsumque, quod intulit damni, restituet et quintam partem ponet supra tradens sacerdoti, qui expiabit eum offerens arietem, et dimittetur ei. [17]Anima, si peccaverit per ignorantiam feceritque unum ex his, quae Domini lege prohibentur, et peccati rea portaverit iniquitatem suam, [18]offeret arietem immaculatum de gregibus iuxta aestimationem sacerdoti, qui expiabit eum ab eo, quod nesciens fecerit, et dimittetur ei; [19]sacrificium pro delicto est, delinquens deliquit in Dominum». [20]Locutus est Dominus ad Moysen dicens: [21]«Anima, quae peccaverit et, con-

a. Ch 5:20 in Heb [and New Vulgate]

it, swearing falsely—in any of all the things which men do and sin therein, ⁴when one has sinned and become guilty, he shall restore what he took by robbery, or what he got by oppression, or the deposit which was committed to him, or the lost thing which he found, ⁵or anything about which he has sworn falsely; he shall restore it in full, and shall add a fifth to it, and give it to him to whom it belongs, on the day of his guilt offering. ⁶And he shall bring to the priest his guilt offering to the LORD, a ram without blemish out of the flock, valued by you at the price for a guilt offering; ⁷and the priest shall make atonement for him before the LORD, and he shall be forgiven for any of the things which one may do and thereby become guilty." Lk 19:8

The priest and burnt offerings*

⁸ᵇThe LORD said to Moses, ⁹"Command Aaron and his sons, saying, This is the law of the burnt offering. The burnt offering shall be on the hearth upon the altar all night until the morning, and the fire of the altar shall be kept burning on it. ¹⁰And the

Ex 29:38
Lev 9:24
2 Chron 7:1
2 Mac 1:19ff

---

have disappeared, as well as the profit or advantages their owner would have legitimately obtained from them. Likewise, all who in some manner have taken part in a theft or who have knowingly benefited from it —for example, those who ordered it, assisted in it or received the stolen goods—are obliged to make restitution in proportion to their responsibility and to their share of what was stolen" (*Catechism of the Catholic Church*, 2412).

*6:8—7:38. These verses contain rules about the rites or ceremonies for the sacrifices already listed in chapters 1–5. They apply to the priests involved, whereas the earlier chapters focused on the lay people, those making the offering.

6:8–13. Here it is laid down that the fire for burnt offerings is to burn continuously, night-time included. On certain occasions it was God himself who lit the holocaust fire (cf. 9:24; 2 Chron 7:1; 2 Mac 1:19ff). Keeping the fire burning day and night symbolized a desire to worship the Lord unceasingly.

It is interesting to see the stress being put on the sacredness of liturgical acts and on priests' dress. The Church, too, makes the same point; thus, the General Introduction to the Roman Missal reminds us that "in the Body of Christ not all members have the same function, and this diversity of ministries is shown externally in worship by the diversity of vestments. At the same time, the vest-

---

tempto Domino, negaverit proximo suo depositum, quod fidei eius creditum fuerat, vel vi aliquid extorserit aut calumniam fecerit, ²²sive rem perditam invenerit et infitians insuper peierarit in uno ex omnibus, in quibus peccare solent homines, ²³si quis sic peccaverit et deliquerit, reddet omnia, quae per rapinam vel calumniam abstulerit vel deposita retinuerit vel perdita invenerit ²⁴vel de quibus peierarit, et restituet integra et quintam insuper addet partem domino, cui damnum intulerat, in die sacrificii pro delicto. ²⁵Sacrificium pro delicto offeret Domino: arietem immaculatum de grege iuxta aestima-

b. Ch 6:1 in Heb [and New Vulgate]

priest shall put on his linen garment, and put his linen breeches upon his body, and he shall take up the ashes to which the fire has consumed the burnt offering on the altar, and put them beside the altar. [11]Then he shall put off his garments, and put on other garments, and carry forth the ashes outside the camp to a clean place. [12]The fire on the altar shall be kept burning on it, it shall not go out; the priest shall burn wood on it every morning, and he shall lay the burnt offering in order upon it, and shall burn on it the fat of the peace offerings. [13]Fire shall be kept burning upon the altar continually; it shall not go out.

The priest and cereal offerings

[14]"And this is the law of the cereal offering. The sons of Aaron shall offer it before the LORD, in front of the altar. [15]And one shall take from it a handful of the fine flour of the cereal offering with its oil and all the frankincense which is on the cereal offering, and burn this as its memorial portion on the altar, a pleasing odour to

ments should contribute to the appearance of the rite itself" (no. 297).

St Josemaría Escrivá, reflecting on the nobility of Old Testament worship and the reverence required of priests when offering the sacrifices of the people of Israel, commented: "Read the Scriptures. Go to the Old Testament and you will see how God our Lord describes point by point the way the Tabernacle is to be decorated, how the sacred vessels are to be made, how the priests are to dress, especially the High Priest, even down to his undergarments! Everything had to be of gold or other precious metals, and fine carefully fashioned fabrics. [. . .] The priesthood of the Old Law

was but a shadow of the true priesthood instituted by Christ. Nevertheless, the Holy Spirit said: *Nolite tangere Christos meos!* 'Do not ill-treat my Christs, do not profane holy things.' It is the voice of the Lord defending his majesty! For his priesthood transforms the one who receives it into another Christ: *alter Christus, ipse Christus*, and it turns everything which is used for the renewal of the Holy Sacrifice of the Mass into something sacred" (in Bernal, *Monsignor Josemaría Escrivá*, p. 330).

6:14–18. This repeats what is said in chapter 2 about the cereal offering. If someone who was not a priest touched

tionem; [26]qui expiabit eum coram Domino, et dimittetur illi pro singulis, quae faciendo peccaverit». [1]Locutus est Dominus ad Moysen dicens: [2]«Praecipe Aaron et filiis eius: Haec est lex holocausti: cremabitur in foco altaris tota nocte usque mane; ignis altaris in eo ardebit. [3]Vestietur sacerdos tunica et feminalibus lineis super verecunda sua, tolletque cineres, quos vorans ignis exussit, et ponet iuxta altare. [4]Porro spoliabitur prioribus vestimentis; indutusque aliis efferet cineres extra castra in locum mundum. [5]Ignis autem in altari semper ardebit, non exstinguetur, quem nutriet sacerdos subiciens ligna mane per singulos dies et, imposito holocausto, desuper adolebit adipes pacificorum. [6]Ignis est iste perpetuus, qui numquam deficiet in altari. [7]Haec est lex sacrificii similae, quod offerent filii Aaron coram Domino et coram altare: [8]tollet sacerdos ex eo pugillum similae, quae conspersa est oleo, et totum tus, quod super similam positum est; adolebitque illud in altari in odorem suavissimum, memoriale Domino. [9]Reliquam autem partem similae comedet Aaron cum filiis suis, et panis absque fermento

the LORD. [16]And the rest of it Aaron and his sons shall eat; it shall be eaten unleavened in a holy place; in the court of the tent of meeting they shall eat it. [17]It shall not be baked with leaven. I have given it as their portion of my offerings by fire; it is a thing most holy, like the sin offering and the guilt offering. [18]Every male among the children of Aaron may eat of it, as decreed forever throughout your generations, from the LORD's offerings by fire; whoever touches them shall become holy."

[19]The LORD said to Moses, [20]"This is the offering which Aaron and his sons shall offer to the LORD on the day when he is anointed: a tenth of an ephah of fine flour as a regular cereal offering, half of it in the morning and half in the evening. [21]It shall be made with oil on a griddle; you shall bring it well mixed, in baked[c] pieces like a cereal offering, and offer it for a pleasing odor to the LORD. [22]The priest from among Aaron's sons, who is anointed to succeed him, shall offer it to the LORD as decreed for ever; the whole of it shall be burned. [23]Every

Lev 2:11

Num 28:5
Sir 45:14
Ex 25:2

Ex 25:2

---

this offering, that person became holy or consecrated and had to be purified before he could go back to ordinary life: a "holy" person was not allowed to do ordinary things. Obviously, it is ritual, not moral, holiness that is being referred to. However, we can see a difference here from those who are sanctified and consecrated by the Baptism established by Christ. Ordinary everyday activity is not in any sense an obstacle for a Christian. In fact, it is precisely in everyday life that a Christian is supposed to try to attain holiness. Thus, the Second Vatican Council exhorts everyone to "rise to a higher sanctity, truly apostolic, by their everyday work itself" (*Lumen gentium*, 41).

St Josemaría Escrivá put it another way by saying that one needs to sanctify oneself in work, to sanctify that work, and to sanctify others by means of that work: "You must not forget that any worthy, noble and honest work at the human level can—and should!—be raised to the supernatural level, becoming a divine task" (*The Forge*, 687).

6:19–30. Apparently, this offering by the high priest, and not only the daily burnt offering (regulated by Exodus 29:38–42), was supposed to take place every day (cf. Num 28:5; Sir 45:14).

The holiness of the offering is stressed to the point of requiring that if any of

---

comedetur in loco sancto; in atrio tabernaculi conventus comedent illam. [10]Ideo autem non coquetur fermentata, quia ut partem eorum dedi illam ex incensis meis: sanctum sanctorum est, sicut sacrificium pro peccato atque pro delicto; [11]mares tantum stirpis Aaron comedent illud. Legitimum sempiternum est in generationibus vestris de incensis Domini; omnis, qui tetigerit illa, sanctificabitur». [12]Et locutus est Dominus ad Moysen dicens: [13]«Haec est oblatio Aaron et filiorum eius, quam offerre debent Domino in die unctionis ipsius: decimam partem ephi offerent similae in sacrificio sempiterno medium eius mane et medium vespere; [14]quae in sartagine oleo consparsa frigetur. Afferes eam calidam et offeres divisam minutatim, sacrificium in odorem suavissimum Domino. [15]Sacerdos unctus, qui patri iure successerit, faciet illud. Legitimum sempiternum: Domino tota cremabitur; [16]omne enim sacrifi-

c. Meaning of Hebrew is uncertain

cereal offering of a priest shall be wholly burned; it shall not be eaten."

The priest and sin offerings

[24]The LORD said to Moses, [25]"Say to Aaron and his sons, This is the law of the sin offering. In the place where the burnt offering is killed shall the sin offering be killed before the LORD; it is most holy. [26]The priest who offers it for sin shall eat it; in a holy place it shall be eaten, in the court of the tent of meeting. [27]Whatever[d] touches its flesh shall be holy; and when any of its blood is sprinkled on a garment, you shall wash that on which it was sprinkled in a holy place. [28]And the earthen vessel in which it is boiled shall be broken; but if it is boiled in a bronze vessel, that shall be scoured, and rinsed in water. [29]Every male among the priests may eat of it; it is most holy. [30]But no sin offering shall be eaten from which any blood is brought into the tent of meeting to make atonement in the holy place; it shall be burned with fire.

The priest and guilt offerings

Lev 5:14–25

7 [1]"This is the law of the guilt offering. It is most holy; [2]in the place where they kill the burnt offering they shall kill the guilt offering, and its blood shall be thrown on the altar round about. [3]And all its fat shall be offered, the fat tail, the fat that covers the

---

the victim's blood gets spattered on a garment, the garment needs to be cleaned in a holy place (v. 27).

7:1–10. Verses 1–6 are a "Semitic inclusion", a stylistic device for stressing an idea by opening and closing the passage with the idea one wants to emphasize: here it is stressing that the thing offered

as a guilt offering is something holy (cf. 5:14—6:7).

Then we are told that the priest who makes the offering keeps the unburnt part of the victim; and he also keeps the skin. But the other cereal offerings (v. 10), whether the flour is mixed with oil or not, were more communal and they were distributed equally among all the priests.

cium similae sacerdotum igne consumetur, nec quisquam comedet ex eo». [17]Locutus est Dominus ad Moysen dicens: [18]«Loquere Aaron et filiis eius: Ista est lex sacrificii pro peccato: in loco, ubi mactatur holocaustum, mactabitur coram Domino: sanctum sanctorum est. [19]Sacerdos, qui offert, comedet illud in loco sancto, in atrio tabernaculi conventus. [20]Quidquid tetigerit carnes eius, sanctificabitur: si de sanguine illius vestis fuerit aspersa, lavabitur in loco sancto; [21]vas autem fictile, in quo coctum est, confringetur; quod si vas aeneum fuerit, defricabitur et lavabitur aqua. [22]Omnis masculus de genere sacerdotali vescetur carnibus eius, quia sanctum sanctorum est. [23]omne autem sacrificium pro peccato, de cuius sanguine infertur in tabernaculum conventus ad expiandum in sanctuario, non comedetur, sed comburetur igni. [1]Haec quoque est lex sacrificii pro delicto: sanctum sanctorum est, [2]idcirco, ubi immolatur holocaustum, mactabitur et victima pro delicto; sanguis eius per gyrum fundetur altaris. [3]Omnemque adipem offeret ex ea, caudam scilicet et adipem, qui operit vitalia, [4]duos renunculos et

d. Or *Whoever*

440

entrails, [4]the two kidneys with the fat that is on them at the loins, and the appendage of the liver which he shall take away with the kidneys; [5]the priest shall burn them on the altar as an offering by fire to the LORD; it is a guilt offering. [6]Every male among the 1 Cor 10:18 priests may eat of it; it shall be eaten in a holy place; it is most holy. [7]The guilt offering is like the sin offering, there is one law for them; the priest who makes atonement with it shall have it. [8]And the priest who offers any man's burnt offering shall have for himself the skin of the burnt offering which he has offered. [9]And every cereal offering baked in the oven and all that is prepared on a pan or a griddle shall belong to the priest who offers it. [10]And every cereal offering, mixed with oil or dry, shall be for all the sons of Aaron, one as well as another.

The priest and peace offerings

[11]"And this is the law of the sacrifice of peace offerings which one Ps 50:14–23; may offer to the LORD. [12]If he offers it for a thanksgiving, then he $\frac{56:12}{\text{Heb 13:15}}$ shall offer with the thank offering unleavened cakes mixed with oil, unleavened wafers spread with oil, and cakes of fine flour well mixed with oil. [13]With the sacrifice of his peace offerings for thanksgiving he shall bring his offering with cakes of leavened bread. [14]And of such he shall offer one cake from each offering, as an offering to the LORD; it shall belong to the priest who throws the blood of the peace offerings. [15]And the flesh of the sacrifice of 1 Cor 10:18

7:11–18. Peace or communion offerings could be made as a praise in thanksgiving (cf. Ps 50:14, 23; 26:13; etc.), or in fulfilment of a vow, or simply out of devotion. The meat of the sacrifice had to be eaten on the same day; this ensured that there was no danger of its being profaned or becoming rotten.

"That person shall be cut from his people" (v. 21): this could mean death, but normally the sentence was commuted to exclusion from the community—involving loss of the privileges of a member of the chosen people, with no social protection and with the threat of death hanging over him (cf. Num 15:30–36).

pinguedinem, quae super eos iuxta ilia est, reticulumque iecoris, quem iuxta renunculos, auferet; [5]et adolebit ea sacerdos super altare ut incensum Domino: sacrificium pro delicto est. [6]Omnis masculus de sacerdotali genere in loco sancto vescetur his carnibus, quia sanctum sanctorum est. [7]Sicut sacrificium pro peccato, ita et sacrificium pro delicto, utriusque hostiae lex una est; ad sacerdotem, qui eam obtulerit, pertinebit. [8]Sacerdos, qui offert holocaustum cuiusdam viri, habebit pellem victimae, [9]et omne sacrificium similae, quod coquitur in clibano, et, quidquid in frixorio vel in sartagine praeparatur, eius erit sacerdotis, a quo offertur; [10]et omne sacrificium similae sive oleo conspersum sive aridum fuerit, cunctis filiis Aaron aequa mensura per singulos dividetur. [11]Haec est lex hostiae pacificorum quae offertur Domino; [12]si pro gratiarum actione fuerit oblatio, offeret panes absque fermento conspersos oleo et lagana azyma uncta oleo coctamque similam ut collyridas olei admixtione conspersas, [13]panes quoque fermentatos cum hostia pacificorum pro gratiarum actione, [14]ex quibus unus offeretur munus Domino et erit sacerdotis, qui fundet hostiae sanguinem. [15]Cuius carnes eadem comedentur die,

his peace offerings for thanksgiving shall be eaten on the day of his offering; he shall not leave any of it until the morning. [16]But if the sacrifice of his offering is a votive offering or a freewill offering, it shall be eaten on the day that he offers his sacrifice, and on the morrow what remains of it shall be eaten, [17]but what remains of the flesh of the sacrifice on the third day shall be burned with fire. [18]If any of the flesh of the sacrifice of his peace offering is eaten on the third day, he who offers it shall not be accepted, neither shall it be credited to him; it shall be an abomination, and he who eats of it shall bear his iniquity.

Rites concerning victims

[19]"Flesh that touches any unclean thing shall not be eaten; it shall be burned with fire. All who are clean may eat flesh, [20]but the person who eats of the flesh of the sacrifice of the LORD's peace offerings while an uncleanness is on him, that person shall be cut off from his people. [21]And if any one touches an unclean thing, whether the uncleanness of man or an unclean beast or any unclean abomination, and then eats of the flesh of the sacrifice of the LORD's peace offerings, that person shall be cut off from his people."

Lev 3:17   [22]The LORD said to Moses, [23]"Say to the people of Israel, You shall eat no fat, of ox, or sheep, or goat. [24]The fat of an animal that dies of itself, and the fat of one that is torn by beasts, may be put to any other use, but on no account shall you eat it. [25]For every person who eats of the fat of an animal of which an offering by

---

7:24–27. This passage repeats what was said earlier about the fat and blood of animals (cf. 3:17). Quite often such repetitions are due to the fact that laws have been copied into the text from different sources—sources which reflected the state of the law at a particular time. Concern to ensure that these legal traditions were not lost prevailed over the editor's aim of producing a synthesis. It is often not easy to find a reason for a repetition.

---

nec remanebit ex eis quidquam usque mane. [16]Si voto vel sponte quisquam obtulerit hostiam, eadem similiter edetur die; sed et si quid in crastinum remanserit, vesci licitum est; [17]quidquid autem tertius invenerit dies, ignis absumet. [18]Si quis de carnibus victimae pacificorum die tertio comederit, irrita fiet oblatio, nec proderit offerenti; quin potius, quaecumque anima tali se edulio contaminarit, praevaricationis rea erit. [19]Caro, quae aliquid tetigerit immundum, non comedetur, sed comburetur igni; ceterum carne, qui fuerit mundus, vescetur. [20]Anima polluta, quae ederit de carnibus hostiae pacificorum, quae oblata est Domino, peribit de populis suis; [21]et quae tetigerit immunditiam hominis vel iumenti, sive omnis rei abominabilis, quae polluere potest, et comederit de huiuscemodi carnibus, interibit de populis suis». [22]Locutusque est Dominus ad Moysen dicens: [23]«Loquere filiis Israel: Adipem bovis et ovis et caprae non comedetis. [24]Adipem cadaveris morticini et eius animalis, quod a bestia laceratum est, habebitis in usus varios, sed non comedetis. [25]Si quis adipem, qui offertur in incensum Domini, comederit, peribit de populo suo. [26]Sanguinem quoque omnis animalis non sumetis in cibo, tam de

fire is made to the Lord shall be cut off from his people. 26Moreover you shall eat no blood whatever, whether of fowl or of animal, in any of your dwellings. 27Whoever eats any blood, that person shall be cut off from his people."

The priest's portion

Ex 29:24
Deut 18:3

28The LORD said to Moses, 29"Say to the people of Israel, He that offers the sacrifice of his peace offerings to the LORD shall bring his offering to the LORD; from the sacrifice of his peace offerings 30he shall bring with his own hands the offerings by fire to the LORD; he shall bring the fat with the breast, that the breast may be waved as a wave offering before the LORD. 31The priest shall burn the fat on the altar, but the breast shall be for Aaron and his sons. 32And the right thigh you shall give to the priest as an offering from the sacrifice of your peace offerings; 33he among the sons of Aaron who offers the blood of the peace offerings and the fat shall have the right thigh for a portion. 34For the breast that is waved and the thigh that is offered I have taken from the people of Israel, out of the sacrifices of their peace offerings, and have given them to Aaron the priest and to his sons, as a perpetual due from the people of Israel. 35This is the portion of Aaron and of his sons from the offerings made by fire to the LORD, consecrated to them on the day they were presented to serve as priests of the LORD;

7:28–35. The text moves on to deal with the rights of priests—specifically as regards which parts of animals offered in sacrifice belonged to them (cf. Ex 29:26; Deut 18:3).

As one can see from v. 34, the first portion of the victim was waved in front of the altar; it was swung forward and back. This ritual waving is called *tenufáh* in Hebrew (see the notes on Ex 29:26–28

and Lev 3:1–17). The other portion was raised and then lowered, also in front of the altar. This ritual action of raising and lowering the offering was called *terumáh*. In both cases the action signified that the offering was being moved towards God and then He was returning it to the priest. There is a trace of this ritual in the Mass when the offering of the bread and wine is presented to the

---

avibus quam de pecoribus; 27omnis anima, quae ederit sanguinem, peribit de populis suis». 28Locutus est Dominus ad Moysen dicens: 29«Loquere filiis Israel: Qui offert victimam pacificorum Domino, afferat oblationem suam Domino de victima pacificorum. 30Tenebit manibus incensa Domini, adipem scilicet et pectusculum afferet; pectusculum, ut elevetur coram Domino. 31Et sacerdos adolebit adipem super altare; pectusculum autem erit Aaron et filiorum eius. 32Armus quoque dexter de pacificorum hostiis cedet in munus sacerdotis. 33Qui de filiis Aaron obtulerit sanguinem et adipem victimae pacificorum, ipse habebit armum dextrum in portione sua; 34pectusculum enim elationis et armum donationis tuli a filiis Israel de hostiis eorum pacificis et dedi Aaron sacerdoti ac filiis eius, lege perpetua, ab omni populo Israel». 35Haec est portio Aaron et filiorum eius de incensis Domini, die, qua applicavit eos, ut sacerdotio fungerentur; 36et quae praecepit dari eis Dominus a filiis Israel, die qua unxit eos,

Conclusion

Ex:30:32 ³⁶the LORD commanded this to be given them by the people of Israel, on the day that they were anointed; it is a perpetual due throughout their generations."

³⁷This is the law of the burnt offering, of the cereal offering, of the sin offering, of the guilt offering, of the consecration, and of the peace offerings, ³⁸which the LORD commanded Moses on Mount Sinai, on the day that he commanded the people of Israel to bring their offerings to the LORD, in the wilderness of Sinai.

PART TWO

The Ordination of Priests*

Ex 28:1–29, 35; 39:1–32; 40:12–15
Num 8:5–26
Heb 5:1, 3; 7:27; 10:1–4

Ordination rites*

8 ¹The LORD said to Moses, ²"Take Aaron and his sons with him, and the garments, and the anointing oil, and the bull of the sin offering, and the two rams, and the basket of unleavened bread;

Lord by being raised up during the offertory. And maybe, when the consecrated host and the chalice are raised up after the consecration the same symbolism is at work: the victim *par excellence* is presented by the priest to the Father, who gives it back to us for our nourishment and salvation.

*8:1—10:20. Chapter 8–10 form a kind of piece which is often called the "Priestly Code" and which constitutes the second of the two parts into which Leviticus can be divided (cf. "Introduction", pp 413–414

above). It has two sections—1) chapters 8–9, which deal with priestly investiture; 2) chapter 10, which contains a number of other regulations to do with priests.

*8:1—9:24. Chapters 8–9 continue the theme dealt with in Exodus 29 and 40. The book of Exodus gave rules for the consecration of Aaron and his sons as priests; Leviticus describes these rules being put into practice, adding the rule of anointing.

The *Catechism of the Catholic Church* explains the priesthood of the

---

religione perpetua in generationibus eorum. ³⁷Ista est lex holocausti et oblationis similae et sacrificii pro peccato atque delicto et pro consecratione et pacificorum victimis, ³⁸quam constituit Dominus Moysi in monte Sinai, quando mandavit filiis Israel, ut offerrent oblationes suas Domino in deserto Sinai. ¹Locutusque est Dominus ad Moysen dicens: ²«Tolle Aaron cum filiis suis, vestes eorum et unctionis oleum, vitulum pro peccato, duos arietes, canistrum cum azymis; ³et congregabis omnem coetum ad ostium tabernaculi conventus». ⁴Fecit Moyses, ut Dominus imperarat; congregatoque omni coetu

³and assemble all the congregation at the door of the tent of meeting." ⁴And Moses did as the LORD commanded him; and the congregation was assembled at the door of the tent of meeting. ⁵And Moses said to the congregation, "This is the thing which the LORD has commanded to be done." ⁶And Moses brought Aaron and his sons, and washed them with water. ⁷And he put on him the coat, and girded him with the girdle, and clothed him with the robe, and put the ephod upon him, and girded him with the skilfully woven band of the ephod, binding it to him therewith. ⁸And he placed the breastpiece on him, and in the breastpiece he put the Urim and the Thummim. ⁹And he set the turban upon his head, and on the turban, in front, he set the golden plate, the holy crown, as the LORD commanded Moses.

¹⁰Then Moses took the anointing oil, and anointed the tabernacle and all that was in it, and consecrated them. ¹¹And he sprinkled some of it on the altar seven times, and anointed the altar and

Ex 28:6

Num 27:21
Deut 33:8
1 Sam 14:41
Ezra 21:31

Ex 30:22

Old Covenant in this way: "The chosen people was constituted by God as 'a kingdom of priests and a holy nation' (Ex 19:6; cf. Is 61:6). But within the people of Israel, God chose one of the twelve tribes, that of Levi, and set it apart for liturgical service; God himself is its inheritance (cf. Num 1:48–53; Josh 13:33). A special rite consecrated the beginnings of the priesthood of the Old Covenant. The priests are 'appointed to act on behalf of men in relation to God, to offer gifts and sacrifices for sins' (Heb 5:1; cf. Ex 29:1–30; Lev 8). Instituted to proclaim the Word of God and to restore communion with God by sacrifices and prayer (cf. Mal 2:7–9), this priesthood nevertheless remains powerless to bring about salvation, needing to repeat its sacrifices ceaselessly and being unable to achieve a definitive sanctification, which only the sacrifice of Christ would accom-

plish' (cf. Heb 5:3; 7:27; 10:1–4). The liturgy of the Church, however, sees in the priesthood of Aaron and the service of the Levites, as in the institution of the seventy elders (cf. Num 11:24–25), a prefiguring of the ordained ministry of the New Covenant" (nos. 1539–1541).

The unction was usually made up of oil with various perfumes mixed in. By the rite of anointing, the person or thing anointed was consecrated to God for a particular role or function. In this passage, we find that, in addition to the priests, the tabernacle too is anointed and all that it contains. The pouring of the oil over the head of the high priest so that it flows down his beard (cf. Ps 133:2) showed that the fullness of priesthood was being conferred on him.

8:6–9. For a description of the priest's sacred vestments, cf. Ex 29:1–43;

---

ante fores tabernaculi conventus, ⁵ait: «Iste est sermo, quem iussit Dominus fieri». ⁶Statimque applicavit Aaron et filios eius. Cumque lavisset eos aqua, ⁷vestivit pontificem subucula linea accingens eum balteo et induens tunica hyacinthina et desuper ephod imposuit, ⁸quod astrinxit cingulo ephod firmiter; et imposuit ei pectorale, in quo dedit Urim et Tummim. ⁹Cidari quoque texit caput et super eam contra frontem posuit laminam auream, diadema sanctum, sicut praeceperat Dominus Moysi. ¹⁰Tulit et unctionis oleum, quo levit habitaculum cum omni supellectili sua et sanctificavit ea. ¹¹Cumque de eo asper-

all its utensils, and the laver and its base, to consecrate them. [12]And he poured some of the anointing oil on Aaron's head, and anointed him, to consecrate him. [13]And Moses brought Aaron's sons, and clothed them with coats, and girded them with girdles, and bound caps on them, as the LORD commanded Moses.

Lev 4:1–2   [14]Then he brought the bull of the sin offering; and Aaron and his sons laid their hands upon the head of the bull of the sin offer-

Heb 9:21   ing. [15]And Moses killed it, and took the blood, and with his finger put it on the horns of the altar round about, and purified the altar, and poured out the blood at the base of the altar, and consecrated it, to make atonement for it. [16]And he took all the fat that was on the entrails, and the appendage of the liver, and the two kidneys with their fat, and Moses burned them on the altar. [17]But the bull, and its skin, and its flesh, and its dung, he burned with fire outside the camp, as the LORD commanded Moses.

Lev 1:10–13   [18]Then he presented the ram of the burnt offering; and Aaron

Heb 9:21   and his sons laid their hands on the head of the ram. [19]And Moses killed it, and threw the blood upon the altar round about. [20]And when the ram was cut into pieces, Moses burned the head and the pieces and the fat. [21]And when the entrails and the legs were

---

39:1–32. In his interpretation of the high priest's vestments, St Thomas, echoing tradition, says that the high priest "ought, firstly, to be constantly remembering God in contemplation; and this was signified by the golden plate with the name of God on it, worn on the forehead; secondly, to bear the weaknesses of the people; this was denoted by the ephod he bore on his shoulders; thirdly, to keep the people in his heart and mind by his charitable concern, signified by the breastplate; fourthly, his manner of life should be heavenly in the perfection of his acts,

which is signified by the violet robe. Hence to the hem of this robe were fixed golden bells, signifying the teaching of divine things which ought to be conjoined to the heavenly mode of life of the priest. In addition to these there were the pomegranates, which signified unity of faith and harmony of conduct, because his teaching should be such as not to impair the unity of faith and peace" (*Summa theologiae*, 1–2, 102, 5).

8:14–32. Three sacrifices precede the rite of ordination strictly speaking (the rite

---

sisset altare septem vicibus, unxit illud et omnia vasa eius labrumque cum basi sua sanctificavit oleo. [12]Quod fundens super caput Aaron, unxit eum et consecravit; [13]filios quoque eius applicatos vestivit subuculis lineis et cinxit balteo imposuitque mitras, ut iusserat Dominus Moysi. [14]Adduxit et vitulum pro peccato; cumque super caput eius posuissent Aaron et filii eius manus suas, [15]immolavit eum; et hauriens Moyses sanguinem tincto digito tetigit cornua altaris per gyrum et mundavit illud; fuditque reliquum sanguinem ad fundamenta eius et sanctificavit illud expiando. [16]Adipem autem, qui erat super vitalia, et reticulum iecoris duosque renunculos cum arvinulis suis adolevit super altare; [17]vitulum cum pelle, carnibus et fimo cremans extra castra, sicut praeceperat Dominus Moysi. [18]Attulit et arietem in holocaustum, super cuius caput cum imposuissent Aaron et filii eius manus suas, [19]immolavit eum et fudit sanguinem eius per altaris circuitum. [20]Ipsumque arietem in frusta concidens, caput eius et artus

446

washed with water, Moses burned the whole ram on the altar, as a burnt offering, a pleasing odour, an offering by fire to the LORD, as the LORD commanded Moses.

²²Then he presented the other ram, the ram of ordination; and Aaron and his sons laid their hands on the head of the ram. ²³And Moses killed it, and took some of its blood and put it on the tip of Aaron's right ear and on the thumb of his right hand and on the great toe of his right foot. ²⁴And Aaron's sons were brought, and Moses put some of the blood on the tips of their right ears and on the thumbs of their right hands and on the great toes of their right feet; and Moses threw the blood upon the altar round about. ²⁵Then he took the fat, and the fat tail, and all the fat that was on the entrails, and the appendage of the liver, and the two kidneys with their fat, and the right thigh; ²⁶and out of the basket of unleavened bread which was before the LORD he took one unleavened cake, and one cake of bread with oil, and one wafer, and placed them on the fat and on the right thigh; ²⁷and he put all these in the hands of Aaron and in the hands of his sons, and waved them as a wave offering before the LORD. ²⁸Then Moses took them from their hands, and burned them on the altar with the

Lev 3

Ex 28:41

begins at v. 22). The first (vv. 14–17) is a sin offering, designed to purify Aaron and his sons from their sins and to sanctify the altar at the same time; we have already come across this rite (cf. 4:1–12). The second is a burnt offering performed according to the rite already explained (cf. 1:10–13). The last-mentioned sacrifice (vv. 22–32) is a consecration sacrifice in the strict sense, with rites similar to those of the communion sacrifice described in chapter 3. For example,

there are some variations in the blood ritual: the right ear, hand and toe are touched with the blood—thereby preparing the priest to listen carefully and docilely to the word of God, and disposing him to good works and upright conduct. The gesture of filling the hands of the priests (v. 27) symbolized handing over the sacred powers they would use in their liturgical actions. Their vestments, too, were consecrated by being sprinkled with oil and blood (v. 30).

et adipem adolevit igni; ²¹lotis prius intestinis et pedibus, totumque simul arietem adolevit super altare, eo quod esset holocaustum suavissimi odoris, incensum Domino, sicut praeceperat Dominus Moysi. ²²Attulit et arietem secundum in consecrationem sacerdotum; posueruntque super caput illius Aaron et filii eius manus suas. ²³Quem cum immolasset Moyses, sumens de sanguine tetigit extremum auriculae dextrae Aaron et pollicem manus eius dextrae, similiter et pedis. ²⁴Applicavit et filios Aaron; cumque de sanguine arietis immolati tetigisset extremum auriculae singulorum dextrae et pollices manus ac pedis dextri, reliquum fudit super altare per circuitum. ²⁵Tulitque adipem et caudam omnemque pinguedinem, quae operit intestina reticulumque iecoris, et duos renes cum adipibus suis et armo dextro. ²⁶Tollens autem de canistro azymorum, quod erat coram Domino, panem absque fermento et collyridam conspersam oleo laganumque posuit super adipes et armum dextrum, ²⁷tradens simul omnia super manus Aaron et filiorum eius. Qui, postquam levaverunt ea coram Domino, ²⁸rursum suscepta de manibus eorum adolevit in altari super holocausto, eo quod illa essent consecrationis

burnt offering, as an ordination offering, a pleasing odour, an offering by fire to the LORD. ²⁹And Moses took the breast, and waved it for a wave offering before the LORD; it was Moses' portion of the ram of ordination, as the LORD commanded Moses.

³⁰Then Moses took some of the anointing oil and of the blood which was on the altar, and sprinkled it upon Aaron and his garments, and also upon his sons and his sons' garments; so he consecrated Aaron and his garments, and his sons and his sons' garments with him.

³¹And Moses said to Aaron and his sons, "Boil the flesh at the door of the tent of meeting, and there eat it and the bread that is in the basket of ordination offerings, as I commanded, saying, 'Aaron and his sons shall eat it'; ³²and what remains of the flesh Sir 45:15 and the bread you shall burn with fire. ³³And you shall not go out Mal 2:5 from the door of the tent of meeting for seven days, until the days of your ordination are completed, for it will take seven days to ordain you. ³⁴As has been done today, the LORD has commanded to be done to make atonement for you. ³⁵At the door of the tent of meeting you shall remain day and night for seven days, performing what the LORD has charged, lest you die; for so I am commanded." ³⁶And Aaron and his sons did all the things which the LORD commanded by Moses.

8:33–36. The fact that the ceremony went on for a week shows how important it was, and also its very sacred character (the number seven has a special religious meaning in the Bible). On occasions these ceremonies will be recalled to the minds of the people and indeed the priests. Thus the book of Sirach says that this "was an everlasting covenant for him [Aaron] and for his descendants all the days of heaven, to minister to the Lord and serve as priest and bless his people in his [the Lord's] name" (Sir 45:15). And the prophet Malachi, upbraiding priests for their misconduct, warns them that that pact (consecration) was one of life and peace and also one of fear (cf. Mal 2:5).

---

oblatio, in odorem suavitatis: incensum erat Domino. ²⁹Tulit et pectusculum elevans illud coram Domino de ariete consecrationis in partem suam, sicut praeceperat Dominus Moysi. ³⁰Assumensque de unguento et sanguine, qui erat in altari, aspersit super Aaron et vestimenta eius et super filios illius ac vestes eorum. ³¹Cumque sanctificasset eos in vestitu suo, praecepit eis dicens: «Coquite carnes ante fores tabernaculi et ibi comedite eas; panes quoque consecrationis edite, qui positi sunt in canistro, sicut mihi praeceptum est: 'Aaron et filii eius comedent eos; ³²quidquid autem reliquum fuerit de carne et panibus, ignis absumet'. ³³De ostio quoque tabernaculi conventus non exibitis septem diebus usque ad diem, quo complebitur tempus consecrationis vestrae; septem enim diebus finitur consecratio. ³⁴Sicut et impraesentiarum factum est, praecepit Dominus, ut fieret in expiationem eorum. ³⁵Die ac nocte manebitis in ostio tabernaculi conventus observantes observationem Domini, ne moriamini: sic enim mihi praeceptum est». ³⁶Feceruntque Aaron et filii eius cuncta, quae locutus est Dominus per manum Moysi. ¹Facto autem octavo die, vocavit Moyses Aaron et filios eius ac maiores natu Israel

1 Kings 12:31
2 Chron 13:9ff
Heb 7:26–27

The priests and their functions

9 ¹On the eighth day Moses called Aaron and his sons and the elders of Israel; ²and he said to Aaron, "Take a bull calf for a sin offering, and a ram for a burnt offering, both without blemish, and offer them before the LORD. ³And say to the people of Israel, 'Take a male goat for a sin offering, and a calf and a lamb, both a year old without blemish, for a burnt offering, ⁴and an ox and a ram for peace offerings, to sacrifice before the LORD, and a cereal offering mixed with oil; for today the LORD will appear to you.'" ⁵And they brought what Moses commanded before the tent of meeting; and all the congregation drew near and stood before the LORD. ⁶And Moses said, "This is the thing which the Lord commanded you to do; and the glory of the LORD will appear to you." ⁷Then Moses said to Aaron, "Draw near to the altar, and offer your sin offering and your burnt offering, and make atonement for yourself and for the people; and bring the offering of the people, and make atonement for them; as the LORD has commanded."

Ex 24:16

Heb 5:1–5;
7:27

⁸So Aaron drew near to the altar, and killed the calf of the sin offering, which was for himself. ⁹And the sons of Aaron presented the blood to him, and he dipped his finger in the blood and put it on the horns of the altar, and poured out the blood at the base of the altar; ¹⁰but the fat and the kidneys and the appendage of the liver from the sin offering he burned upon the altar, as the LORD commanded Moses. ¹¹The flesh and the skin he burned with fire outside the camp.

9:1–14. After being consecrated, the priests begin to exercise their ministry. First, they make offerings for their own sins, and then for those of the people. Under Moses' supervision they perform the rites which are exclusive to priests (cf. 1 Kings 12:31; 2 Chron 13:9ff). The Letter to the Hebrews refers to this passage when it distinguishes the priests of the Old Testament from Jesus Christ, who "has no need, like those high priests, to offer sacrifices daily, first for his own sins and then for those of the people; he did this once for all when he offered up himself" (Heb 7:27).

---

dixitque ad Aaron: ²«Tolle de armento vitulum pro peccato et arietem in holocaustum, utrumque immaculatum, et affer illos coram Domino. ³Et ad filios Israel loqueris: 'Tollite hircum pro peccato et vitulum atque agnum anniculos et sine macula in holocaustum, ⁴bovem et arietem pro pacificis, et immolate eos coram Domino, et sacrificium similae oleo conspersae: hodie enim Dominus apparebit vobis'». ⁵Tulerunt ergo cuncta, quae iusserat Moyses, ad ostium tabernaculi conventus; ubi, cum omnis coetus accessisset et staret coram Domino, ⁶ait Moyses: «Iste est sermo, quem praecepit Dominus: facite et apparebit vobis gloria eius». ⁷Dixit et ad Aaron: «Accede ad altare et immola pro peccato tuo; offer holocaustum et expia te et populum. Et fac hostiam populi et expia eum, sicut praecepit Dominus». ⁸Statimque Aaron accedens ad altare immolavit vitulum pro peccato suo, ⁹cuius sanguinem obtulerunt ei filii sui; in quo tinguens digitum tetigit cornua altaris et fudit residuum ad basim eius. ¹⁰Adipemque et renunculos ac reticulum iecoris, quae sunt de sacrificio pro peccato, adolevit super altare, sicut praeceperat Dominus Moysi. ¹¹Carnes vero et pellem eius extra castra combussit igni.

¹²And he killed the burnt offering; and Aaron's sons delivered to him the blood, and he threw it on the altar round about. ¹³And they delivered the burnt offering to him, piece by piece, and the head; and he burned them upon the altar. ¹⁴And he washed the entrails and the legs, and burned them with the burnt offering on the altar.

Lev 4:13–21   ¹⁵Then he presented the people's offering, and took the goat of the sin offering which was for the people, and killed it, and Lev 1:2–13 offered it for sin, like the first sin offering. ¹⁶And he presented the Lev 2:1–3 burnt offering, and offered it according to the ordinance. ¹⁷And he presented the cereal offering, and filled his hand from it, and burned it upon the altar, besides the burnt offering of the morning.

¹⁸He killed the ox also and the ram, the sacrifice of peace offerings for the people; and Aaron's sons delivered to him the blood, which he threw upon the altar round about, ¹⁹and the fat of the ox and of the ram, the fat tail, and that which covers the entrails, and the kidneys, and the appendage of the liver; ²⁰and they put the fat upon the breasts, and he burned the fat upon the altar, ²¹but the breasts and the right thigh Aaron waved for a wave offering before the LORD; as Moses commanded.

Ex 16:10; 24:16   ²²Then Aaron lifted up his hands toward the people and Num 16:4f blessed them; and he came down from offering the sin offering Is 35:2; 60:1 and the burnt offering and the peace offerings. ²³And Moses and Aaron went into the tent of meeting; and when they came out they

---

9:15–24. The rules about sacrifices or offerings on behalf of the people were given previously. The first offering is a sin offering (cf. 4:13–21); this is followed by a burnt offering (cf. 1:2–13) and then a peace offering (cf. 2:1–3). Aaron enters the tent of meeting with Moses (v. 23); this shows that the new high priest shares in the same intimacy with God as Moses

has; the fact that he joins in blessing the people also shows his new status.

No sooner have the people been blessed than God demonstrates his approval of the priesthood by making his glory manifest; and this is complemented by the fire that comes down on the altar (as happened on other occasions too: cf. Judg 6:21; 1 Kings 18:38; etc.).

---

¹²Immolavit et holocausti victimam; obtuleruntque ei filii sui sanguinem eius, quem fudit per altaris circuitum. ¹³Ipsam etiam hostiam in frusta concisam cum capite ei obtulerunt, quae omnia super altare cremavit igni; ¹⁴lavit quoque aqua intestina cruraque et adolevit super holocausto in altari. ¹⁵Et applicavit oblationem populi sumensque hircum pro peccato populi mactavit et obtulit in expiationem sicut priorem; ¹⁶fecit quoque holocaustum secundum ritum ¹⁷et addens sacrificium similae implevit manum ex illa et adolevit super altare praeter holocaustum matutinum. ¹⁸Immolavit et bovem atque arietem, hostias pacificas populi; obtuleruntque ei filii sui sanguinem, quem fudit super altare in circuitu. ¹⁹Adipes autem bovis et caudam arietis renunculosque cum adipibus suis et reticulum iecoris ²⁰posuerunt super pectora; cumque cremati essent adipes in altari, ²¹pectora eorum et armos dextros Aaron elevavit coram Domino, sicut praeceperat Moyses. ²²Et elevans Aaron manus ad populum benedixit eis. Sicque, completis hostiis pro peccato et holocaustis et pacificis, descendit. ²³Ingressi

blessed the people, and the glory of the LORD appeared to all the people. ²⁴And fire came forth from before the LORD and consumed the burnt offering and the fat upon the altar; and when all the people saw it, they shouted, and fell on their faces.

Judg 6:21
1 Kings 18:38

Punishment for ritual irregularity

Ex 16:10; 24:1
Num 3:4; 16:4ff
Is 35:2; 60:1

10 ¹Now Nadab and Abihu, the sons of Aaron, each took his censer, and put fire in it, and laid incense on it, and offered unholy fire before the LORD, such as he had not commanded them. ²And fire came forth from the presence of the LORD and devoured them, and they died before the LORD. ³Then Moses said to Aaron, "This is what the LORD has said, 'I will show myself holy among those who are near me, and before all the people I will be glorified.'" And Aaron held his peace.

Rules for officiating priests

⁴And Moses called Misha-el and Elzaphan, the sons of Uzziel the uncle of Aaron, and said to them, "Draw near, carry your brethren from before the sanctuary out of the camp." ⁵So they drew near, and carried them in their coats out of the camp, as Moses had said. ⁶And Moses said to Aaron and to Eleazar and Ithamar, his sons, "Do not let the hair of your heads hang loose, and do not rend your clothes, lest you die, and lest wrath come upon all the congregation; but your brethren, the whole house of Israel, may bewail the

Ex 6:18–22
Acts 5:6, 10

Mt 26:65

10:1–3. We do not know the exact nature of these priests' infringement. Apparently they used a fire other than that from the altar of holocaust. Some scholars, on the basis of the rules that follow (vv. 8–11), think that maybe in the meal held after the ordination these two sons of Aaron drank to excess and were not quite aware of what they were doing. Anyway, they infringed the rules on worship laid down

by Moses. The episode shows that God prefers obedience to sacrifice (cf. 1 Sam 15:22–23; Hos 6:6).

On the use of censers cf. the note on Num 16:6–7.

10:4–20. The other sons of Aaron were not allowed to take part in the burial of the dead priests because that would have rendered them unclean; that was why

---

autem Moyses et Aaron tabernaculum conventus et deinceps egressi benedixerunt populo. Apparuitque gloria Domini omni populo; ²⁴et ecce egressus ignis a Domino devoravit holocaustum et adipes, qui erant super altare. Quod cum vidissent turbae, exultaverunt ruentes in facies suas. ¹Arreptisque Nadab et Abiu filii Aaron turibulis, posuerunt ignem et incensum desuper offerentes coram Domino ignem alienum, qui eis praeceptus non erat. ²Egressusque ignis a Domino devoravit eos, et mortui sunt coram Domino. ³Dixitque Moyses ad Aaron: «Hoc est, quod locutus est Dominus: 'Sanctificabor in his, qui appropinquant mihi, et in conspectu omnis populi glorificabor'». Quod audiens tacuit Aaron. ⁴Vocatis autem Moyses Misael et Elisaphan filiis Oziel patrui Aaron, ait ad eos: «Ite et tollite fratres vestros de conspectu sanctuarii et asportate extra castra». ⁵Confestimque pergentes tulerunt eos, sicut iacebant vestitos subuculis suis, foras, ut sibi fuerat imperatum. ⁶Locutus est Moyses ad Aaron et ad Eleazar

burning which the LORD has kindled. [7]And do not go out from the door of the tent of meeting, lest you die; for the anointing oil of the LORD is upon you." And they did according to the word of Moses.

Ezek 44:21
Lk 1:15 [8]And the LORD spoke to Aaron, saying, [9]"Drink no wine nor strong drink, you nor your sons with you, when you go into the tent of meeting, lest you die; it shall be a statute forever throughout your generations. [10]You are to distinguish between the holy and the common, and between the unclean and the clean; [11]and you are to teach the people of Israel all the statutes which the LORD has spoken to them by Moses."

[12]And Moses said to Aaron and to Eleazar and Ithamar, his sons who were left, "Take the cereal offering that remains of the offerings by fire to the LORD, and eat it unleavened beside the altar, for it is most holy; [13]you shall eat it in a holy place, because it is your due and your sons' due, from the offerings by fire to the LORD; for so I am commanded. [14]But the breast that is waved and the thigh that is offered you shall eat in any clean place, you and your sons and your daughters with you; for they are given as your due and your sons' due, from the sacrifices of the peace offerings of the people of Israel. [15]The thigh that is offered and the breast that is waved they shall bring with the offerings by fire of the fat, to wave

---

other close relatives took charge (cf. Exod 6:18, 22). Nor were they to engage in mourning after the style of the time; that was not considered proper in those who served at the sanctuary. A priest should remember his sacred status, even if that meant keeping a rein on his feelings.

The reason why alcohol was banned was obviously because priests should be completely lucid all the time—not only to be able to perform their liturgical ministry but also because they were the people's teachers, especially as regards the laws of ritual purity.

Verses 12–20 contains rules (some already known: cf. chap. 9) about how and where meat from sacrifices should be eaten. Moses takes Aaron to task (vv. 16ff) for not having obeyed the rules about the sacred meal after the sin offering. The high priest makes his excuse and explains that the reason why they did not eat the offering was that they were afraid of incurring a further punishment. Moses accepts his explanation.

---

atque Ithamar filios eius: «Comas vestras nolite excutere et vestimenta nolite scindere, ne moriamini, et super omnem coetum oriatur indignatio. Fratres vestri, omnis domus Israel, plangant incendium, quod Dominus suscitavit. [7]Vos autem non egredimini fores tabernaculi conventus, alioquin peribitis; oleum quippe unctionis Domini est super vos». Qui fecerunt omnia iuxta praeceptum Moysi. [8]Dixit quoque Dominus ad Aaron: [9]«Vinum et omne, quod inebriare potest, non bibetis tu et filii tui, quando intratis tabernaculum conventus, ne moriamini—praeceptum est sempiternum in generationes vestras— [10]et ut habeatis scientiam discernendi inter sanctum et profanum, inter pollutum et mundum, [11]doceatisque filios Israel omnia legitima mea, quae locutus est Dominus ad eos per manum Moysi». [12]Locutusque est Moyses ad Aaron et ad Eleazar atque Ithamar filios eius, qui residui erant: «Tollite oblationem similae, quae remansit de incensis Domini, et comedite illam absque fermento iuxta altare,

for a wave offering before the LORD, and it shall be yours, and your sons' with you, as a due for ever; as the LORD has commanded." ¹⁶Now Moses diligently inquired about the goat of the sin offering, and behold, it was burned! And he was angry with Eleazar and Ithamar, the sons of Aaron who were left, saying, ¹⁷"Why have you not eaten the sin offering in the place of the sanctuary, since it is a thing most holy and has been given to you that you may bear the iniquity of the congregation, to make atonement for them before the LORD? ¹⁸Behold, its blood was not brought into the inner part of the sanctuary. You certainly ought to have eaten it in the sanctuary, as I commanded." ¹⁹And Aaron said to Moses, "Behold, today they have offered their sin offering and their burnt offering before the LORD; and yet such things as these have befallen me! If I had eaten the sin offering today, would it have been acceptable in the sight of the LORD?" ²⁰And when Moses heard that, he was content.

Lev 6:19

PART THREE

Rules concerning the Clean and the Unclean*

Gen 7:2
Lev 20:25–26
Deut 14:3–21
Mt 15:10–20
Acts 10:9–16;
11:1–18
Heb 9:10

Clean and unclean animals

11 ¹*And the LORD said to Moses and Aaron, ²"Say to the people of Israel, These are the living things which you may eat among all the beasts that are on the earth. ³Whatever

---

11:1—16:34. These chapters about ritual cleanness form the third part of the book of Leviticus; they identify which animals are regarded as unclean and the various reasons why they fall within that category. Chapter 16 is a special section to do

quia sanctum sanctorum est. ¹³Comedetis autem in loco sancto, quia data est tibi et filiis tuis de incensis Domini, sicut praeceptum est mihi. ¹⁴Pectusculum quoque elationis et armum donationis edetis in loco mundissimo, tu et filii tui ac filiae tuae tecum; tibi enim ac liberis tuis reposita sunt de hostiis pacificis filiorum Israel. ¹⁵Armum et pectus cum incensis adipum afferent ad elationem coram Domino, et pertineant ad te et ad filios tuos lege perpetua, sicut praecepit Dominus». ¹⁶De hirco autem pro peccato cum quaereret Moyses, exustum repperit; iratusque contra Eleazar et Ithamar filios Aaron, qui remanserant, ait: ¹⁷«Cur non comedistis sacrificium pro peccato in loco sancto? Quod sanctum sanctorum est, et datum vobis, ut portetis iniquitatem coetus in expiaionem eorum in conspectu Domini; ¹⁸praesertim cum de sanguine illius non sit illatum intra sancta, comedere eam debuistis in sanctuario, sicut praeceptum est mihi». ¹⁹Respondit Aaron: «Oblata est hodie victima pro peccato et holocaustum

parts the hoof and is cloven-footed and chews the cud, among
Mt 23:24 the animals, you may eat. ⁴Nevertheless among those that chew
the cud or part the hoof, you shall not eat these: The camel,
because it chews the cud but does not part the hoof, is unclean
to you. ⁵And the rock badger, because it chews the cud but does
not part the hoof, is unclean to you. ⁶And the hare, because it
chews the cud but does not part the hoof, is unclean to you.
⁷And the swine, because it parts the hoof and is cloven-footed
but does not chew the cud, is unclean to you. ⁸Of their flesh you
shall not eat, and their carcasses you shall not touch; they are
unclean to you.

⁹"These you may eat, of all that are in the waters. Everything
in the waters that has fins and scales, whether in the seas or in the
rivers, you may eat. ¹⁰But anything in the seas or the rivers that
has not fins and scales, of the swarming creatures in the waters

---

with the ceremonies on the day of atonement, Yom Kippur, when purification is prescribed for the entire people.

Uncleanness came from four main sources—animals, dead bodies, leprosy and improper use of sex. This does not mean that it is easy to see exactly why things were classified as unclean: the reason for some of the taboos is lost in antiquity; sometimes an animal might be classified as unclean just because it looked repugnant. Apropos of the rules given here, Novatian teaches that the forbidden foods were banned not because they particularly deserved to be but simply as a way of rendering homage to God: thus, it is a good thing to be frugal in eating and drinking, it fits in well with being a religious person, and it is almost essential for someone whose ministry it

is to worship God; in the same way insobriety and the self-indulgence it causes are enemies of holiness (cf. *De cibis iudaicis,* 4).

The uncleanness caused was normally something external; it did not mean that the person had committed a moral fault; that was why the uncleanness was removed by means of an external rite. God's holiness and purity have always led men to avoid anything unworthy of God, especially when they are worshipping him or petitioning him. Sometimes the uncleanness of an animal has to do with how neighbouring peoples regarded that animal (they may have made it an object of worship or reserved it as something untouchable in honour of a god: the pig, for example, was used for sacrifices to the Babylonian god Tammuz.

---

eorum coram Domino; mihi autem accidit, quod vides. Quomodo potui comedere eam et placere Domino?». ²⁰Quod cum audisset Moyses, recepit satisfactionem. ¹Locutus est Dominus ad Moysen et Aaron dicens: ²«Dicite filiis Israel: Haec sunt animalia, quae comedere debetis de cunctis animantibus terrae. ³Omne, quod habet plene divisam ungulam et ruminat in pecoribus, comedetis. ⁴Haec autem non comedetis ex ruminantibus vel dividentibus ungulam: camelum, quia ruminat quidem, sed non dividit ungulam, inter immunda reputabis; ⁵hyracem, qui ruminat ungulamque non dividit, immundus est; ⁶leporem quoque, nam et ipse ruminat, sed ungulam non dividit; ⁷et suem, qui, cum ungulam plene dividat, non ruminat. ⁸Horum carnibus non vescemini nec cadavera contingetis, quia immunda sunt vobis. ⁹Haec sunt, quae gignuntur in aquis et vesci licitum est: omne, quod habet pinnulas et squamas,

and of the living creatures that are in the waters, is an abomination to you. [11]They shall remain an abomination to you; of their flesh you shall not eat, and their carcasses you shall have in abomination. [12]Everything in the waters that has not fins and scales is an abomination to you.

[13]"And these you shall have in abomination among the birds, they shall not be eaten, they are an abomination: the eagle, the vulture, the osprey, [14]the kite, the falcon according to its kind, [15]every raven according to its kind, [16]the ostrich, the nighthawk, the sea gull, the hawk according to its kind, [17]the owl, the cormorant, the ibis, [18]the water hen, the pelican, the carrion vulture, [19]the stork, the heron according to its kind, the hoopoe, and the bat.

[20]"All winged insects that go upon all fours are an abomination to you. [21]Yet among the winged insects that go on all fours you may eat those which have legs above their feet, with which to

Mt 3:4
Mk 1:6

11:1–46. This division of animals into groups is reminiscent of the Creation account in the book of Genesis. First came the quadrupeds (vv. 3–8), followed by fish (vv. 9–12), birds (vv. 13–19) and insects (vv. 20–23), with reptiles last (vv. 29–30). Of the four-footed animals those are clean (that is, eatable) which are cloven-hoofed and chew the cud. The reason why the passage says that the "rock badger" (J.B. "hyrax", which OED explains as "rock-rabbit or rock-badger") chews the cud is that its nose moves when it eats, but in fact it is a rodent, not a ruminant. As regards fish, those which have no fins or scales are unclean—perhaps because they look like snakes (as is the case with eels).

The birds listed as unclean normally feed on carrion or reptiles—which is what makes them unclean. However, it has to be said that it is not always easy to identify the birds (and some of the animals) mentioned in the Bible, because sometimes they are mentioned only once and their distinguishing features are not given.

As regards insects, only the different kinds of land locusts or grasshoppers are clean. Most Westerners would not think of eating them, but we do know that St John the Baptist lived off them (cf. Mt 3:4) and the Bedouin still eat them.

Contact with the carcasses of animals (clean or unclean, it did not matter) caused uncleanness (vv. 24–40).

---

tam in mari quam in fluminibus et torrentibus, comedetis. [10]Quidquid autem pinnulas et squamas non habet, reptilium vel quorumlibet aliorum animalium, quae in aquis moventur, abominabile vobis [11]et execrandum erit; carnes eorum non comedetis et morticina vitabitis. [12]Cuncta, quae non habent pinnulas et squamas in aquis, polluta erunt vobis. [13]Haec sunt, quae de avibus comedere non debetis, et vitanda sunt vobis: aquilam et grypem et haliaeetum, [14]milvum ac vultu rem iuxta genus suum [15]et omne corvini generis, [16]struthionem et noctuam et larum et accipitrem iuxta genus suum, [17]bubonem et mergulum et ibin, [18]cycnum et nyctocoracem et porphyrionem, [19]erodionem et charadrion iuxta genus suum, upupam quoque et vespertilionem. [20]Omne de volucribus, quod reptat super quattuor pedes, abominabile erit vobis. [21]Quidquid autem ambulat quidem super quattuor pedes, sed habet longiora retro crura, per quae salit super terram, [22]comedere debetis; ut est bruchus in genere suo et atta-

leap on the earth. ²²Of them you may eat: the locust according to its kind, the bald locust according to its kind, the cricket according to its kind, and the grasshopper according to its kind. ²³But all other winged insects which have four feet are an abomination to you.

²⁴"And by these you shall become unclean; whoever touches their carcass shall be unclean until the evening, ²⁵and whoever carries any part of their carcass shall wash his clothes and be unclean until the evening. ²⁶Every animal which parts the hoof but is not cloven-footed or does not chew the cud is unclean to you; every one who touches them shall be unclean. ²⁷And all that go on their paws, among the animals that go on all fours, are unclean to you; whoever touches their carcass shall be unclean until the evening, ²⁸and he who carries their carcass shall wash his clothes and be unclean until the evening; they are unclean to you.

²⁹"And these are unclean to you among the swarming things that swarm upon the earth: the weasel, the mouse, the great lizard according to its kind, ³⁰the gecko, the land crocodile, the lizard, the sand lizard, and the chameleon. ³¹These are unclean to you among all that swarm; whoever touches them when they are dead shall be unclean until the evening. ³²And anything upon which any of them falls when they are dead shall be unclean, whether it is an article of wood or a garment or a skin or a sack, any vessel that is used for any purpose; it must be put into water, and it shall be unclean until the evening; then it shall be clean. ³³And if any of them falls into any earthen vessel, all that is in it shall be unclean, and you shall break it. ³⁴Any food in it which may be eaten, upon which water may come, shall be unclean; and all drink which may

---

cus atque ophiomachus ac locusta, singula iuxta genus suum. ²³Quidquid autem ex volucribus reptantibus quattuor tantum habet pedes, execrabile erit vobis. ²⁴Et quicumque morticina eorum tetigerit, polluetur et erit immundus usque ad vesperum. ²⁵Et si necesse fuerit, ut portet quippiam horum mortuum, lavabit vestimenta sua et immundus erit usque ad solis occasum. ²⁶Omne animal, quod habet quidem ungulam, sed non dividit eam nec ruminat, immundum erit vobis; et qui tetigerit illud, contaminabitur. ²⁷Quod ambulat super plantas pedum ex cunctis animantibus, quae incedunt quadrupedia, immundum erit; qui tetigerit morticina eorum, polluetur usque ad vesperum. ²⁸Et qui portaverit huiuscemodi cadavera, lavabit vestimenta sua et immundus erit usque ad vesperum; quia omnia haec immunda sunt vobis. ²⁹Haec quoque inter polluta reputabuntur de his, quae reptant in terra: mustela et mus et lacerta iuxta genus suum, ³⁰mygale et testudo et stellio et talpa et chamaeleon: ³¹omnia haec immunda sunt. Qui tetigerit morticina eorum, immundus erit usque ad vesperum; ³²et super quod ceciderit quidquam de morticinis eorum, polluetur tam vas ligneum et vestimentum quam pelles et cilicia, et in quocumque fit opus; tinguentur aqua et polluta erunt usque ad vesperum et postea munda. ³³Vas autem fictile, in quo horum quidquam intro ceciderit, polluetur et frangendum est. ³⁴Omnis cibus, quem comedetis, si fusa fuerit exinde super eum aqua, immundus erit; et omne liquens, quod bibitur de tali vase, immundum erit. ³⁵Et quidquid de morticinis istiusmodi ceciderit super illud, immundum erit; sive

be drunk from every such vessel shall be unclean. [35]And everything upon which any part of their carcass falls shall be unclean; whether oven or stove, it shall be broken in pieces; they are unclean, and shall be unclean to you. [36]Nevertheless a spring or a cistern holding water shall be clean; but whatever touches their carcass shall be unclean. [37]And if any part of their carcass falls upon any seed for sowing that is to be sown, it is clean; [38]but if water is put on the seed and any part of their carcass falls on it, it is unclean to you.

[39]"And if any animal of which you may eat dies, he who touches its carcass shall be unclean until the evening, [40]and he who eats of its carcass shall wash his clothes and be unclean until the evening; he also who carries the carcass shall wash his clothes and be unclean until the evening.

[41]"Every swarming thing that swarms upon the earth is an abomination; it shall not be eaten. [42]Whatever goes on its belly, and whatever goes on all fours, or whatever has many feet, all the swarming things that swarm upon the earth, you shall not eat; for they are an abomination. [43]You shall not make yourselves abominable with any swarming thing that swarms; and you shall not defile yourselves with them, lest you become unclean. [44]For I am the LORD your God; consecrate yourselves therefore, and be holy, for I am holy. You shall not defile yourselves with any swarming thing that crawls upon the earth. [45]For I am the LORD who brought you up out of the land of Egypt, to be your God; you shall therefore be holy, for I am holy."

[46]This is the law pertaining to beast and bird and every living creature that moves through the waters and every creature that swarms upon the earth, [47]to make a distinction between the unclean and the clean and between the living creature that may be eaten and the living creature that may not be eaten.

Lev 17:1

Lev 17:1;
19:2; 22:33
Mt 5:48
1 Pet 1:16
1 Jn 3:3

---

clibani sive chytropodes destruentur: immundi sunt et immundi erunt vobis. [36]Fontes tamen et cisternae et omnis aquarum congregatio munda erit. Qui vero morticinum eorum tetigerit, polluetur. [37]Si ceciderint super sementem, non polluent eam; [38]sin autem quispiam aqua sementem perfuderit, et postea morticinis tacta fuerit, immunda erit vobis. [39]Si mortuum fuerit animal, quod licet vobis comedere, qui cadaver eius tetigerit, immundus erit usque ad vesperum; [40]et qui comederit ex eo quippiam sive portaverit cadaver eius, lavabit vestimenta sua et immundus erit usque ad vesperum. [41]Omne, quod reptat super terram, abominabile erit nec assumetur in cibum. [42]Quidquid super pectus et quidquid quadrupes graditur, vel multos habet pedes sive per humum trahitur, non comedetis, quia abominabile est. [43]Nolite contaminare animas vestras nec tangatis quidquam eorum, ne immundi sitis. [44]Ego enim sum Dominus Deus vester; sanctificamini et sancti estote, quoniam et ego sanctus sum. Ne polluatis animas vestras in omni reptili, quod movetur super terram. [45]Ego enim sum Dominus, qui eduxi vos de terra Aegypti, ut essem vobis in Deum: sancti eritis, quia et ego sanctus sum. [46]Ista est lex animantium et volucrum et omnis animae viventis, quae movetur in aqua et reptat in terra, [47]ut differentias noveritis mundi et immundi, et sciatis quid comedere et quid respuere debeatis». [1]Locutus est Dominus ad

Purification of a woman after childbirth

Lev 15:19
Lk 2:22

12 ¹The LORD said to Moses, ²"Say to the people of Israel, If a woman conceives, and bears a male child, then she shall be unclean seven days; as at the time of her menstruation, she shall

Gen 17:10–14
Lk 1:59; 2:2–38
Jn 7:22

be unclean. ³And on the eighth day the flesh of his foreskin shall be circumcised. ⁴Then she shall continue for thirty-three days in the blood of her purifying; she shall not touch any hallowed thing, nor come into the sanctuary, until the days of her purifying are completed. ⁵But if she bears a female child, then she shall be unclean two weeks, as in her menstruation; and she shall continue in the blood of her purifying for sixty-six days.

12:1–4. Rules about uncleanness deriving from childbearing and allied subjects (touched on here) will be dealt with further in chapter 15.

As regards the precept of circumcision (v. 3), this already came up in Genesis 17:10–14. The *Catechism of the Catholic Church* sees circumcision as prefiguring Baptism (cf. no. 527); and the *Catechism of the Council of Trent* sees the fact that circumcision was done on the eighth day after birth as being a figure for the baptism of children: "Circumcision, which is a figure of Baptism, affords a strong argument in proof of this practice. That children were circumcised on the eighth day is universally known. If then circumcision, made by hand, in despoiling of the body of the flesh, was profitable to children, it is clear that Baptism, which is the circumcision of Christ, not made by hand, is also profitable to them" (2, 2, 32).

From very ancient times, it was common for people to regard sex and generative faculties as something sacred. The coming to birth of a new being is always a sign of God's blessing. Besides, God himself commanded the first human

couple to increase and multiply (cf. Gen 1:28). The sacredness of human generation was what led some ancient peoples to associate sexual practices with divine worship: hence so-called "sacred prostitution"; in fact the moral fault in some sexual irregularities was compounded by their connexion with idolatry.

It was also the case that man's abuse of his reproductive faculties (his search for mere pleasure, a pursuit at odds with the very nature of sex) gave him a sense of rejection because he (quite rightly) saw his behaviour as shameful. Feelings of this sort gave rise to purification rules and to high regard for virginity and continence, especially as regards anything to do with divine worship; hence the regulations which prohibit conjugal relations when a person is involved in something holy (cf. 1 Sam 21:5–7). Besides, man has an instinctive modesty as regards sex. The Genesis account about Adam and Eve's nakedness (cf. Gen 2:25; 3:7) before and then after they commit sin bears this out; and the same point is made by St Paul when he says that "those parts of the body that we think less honourable we invest with the greatest

---

Moysen dicens: ²«Loquere filiis Israel et dices ad eos: Mulier, si, suscepto semine, pepererit masculum, immunda erit septem diebus iuxta dies separationis menstruae, ³et die octavo circumcidetur infantulus; ⁴ipsa vero triginta tribus diebus manebit in sanguine purificationis suae; omne sanctum non tanget nec ingredietur sanctuarium, donec impleantur dies purificationis eius. ⁵Sin autem feminam

⁶"And when the days of her purifying are completed, whether for a son or for a daughter, she shall bring to the priest at the door of the tent of meeting a lamb a year old for a burnt offering, and a young pigeon or a turtledove for a sin offering, ⁷and he shall offer it before the LORD, and make atonement for her; then she shall be clean from the flow of her blood. This is the law for her who bears a child, either male or female. ⁸And if she cannot afford a lamb, *Lk 2:24* then she shall take two turtledoves or two young pigeons, one for a burnt offering and the other for a sin offering; and the priest shall make atonement for her, and she shall be clean."

---

honour" (1 Cor 12:23). So, among ancient peoples (Israel included) everything connected with human generation was wrapped in mystery; we find a mixture of veneration (even idolatry) and a sometimes irrational rejection of sex. Hence the advantage of rules and regulations on the subject.

12:5–8. The different kinds of purification of a mother depending on whether her new child was a boy or a girl, was due, partly, to a belief at the time that the pregnancy for a female child was more severe on the mother and therefore (as one can read in Hippocrates) a long convalescence was needed. Also, it is well known that many ancient peoples had the conviction that women were inferior to men. This was an opinion held in Israel also at that time—possibly due to a misinterpretation of the account of the first sin, in which Eve sinned first and then induced Adam to sin (cf. Gen 3:1–7). Yet, even so, by comparison with other cultures of the time, Israel did hold womankind in higher regard. Even the

Creation account clearly shows the essential equality of man and woman when it says: "God created man in his own image, in the image of God he created him; male and female he created them" (Gen 1:27).

There are passages in the New Testament which some have misinterpreted to mean that women are inferior to men. However, it needs to be said that when there is mention simply of "man", that means both man and woman. Besides, as St Paul teaches, after the Redemption " in Christ Jesus you are all sons of God, through faith. [. . .] There is neither slave nor free, there is neither male nor female" (Gal 3:26, 28). John Paul II defends the dignity of women and their essential equality with men as something deriving from the very word "woman": "In biblical language this name indicates her essential identity with regard to man—*'is-'issab*—something which unfortunately modern languages in general are unable to express: 'She shall be called woman (*'issah*) because she was taken out of man (*'is*): Gen 2:33" (*Mulieris dignitatem*, 6). The Pope

pepererit, immunda erit duabus hebdomadibus iuxta ritum fluxus menstrui, et sexaginta ac sex diebus manebit in sanguine purificationis suae. ⁶Cumque expleti fuerint dies purificationis suae pro filio sive pro filia, deferet agnum anniculum in holocaustum et pullum columbae sive turturem pro peccato ad ostium tabernaculi conventus et tradet sacerdoti. ⁷Qui offeret illa coram Domino et expiabit eam; et sic mundabitur a profluvio sanguinis sui: ista est lex parientis masculum aut feminam. ⁸Quod si non invenerit manus eius, nec potuerit offerre agnum, sumet duos turtures vel duos pullos columbae, unum in holocaustum et alterum pro peccato; expiabitque eam sacerdos, et sic mundabitur». ¹Locutus est

459

Num 5:2;
12:10–15
Deut 24:8–9

Tests for leprosy*

13 [1]The LORD said to Moses and Aaron, [2]"When a man has on the skin of his body a swelling or an eruption or a spot, and it turns into a leprous disease on the skin of his body, then he shall be brought to Aaron the priest or to one of his sons the priests, [3]and the priest shall examine the diseased spot on the skin of his body; and if the hair in the diseased spot has turned white and the disease appears to be deeper than the skin of his body, it is a leprous disease; when the priest has examined him he shall pronounce him unclean. [4]But if the spot is white in the skin of his body, and appears no deeper than the skin, and the hair in it has not turned white, the priest shall shut up the diseased person for seven days; [5]and the priest shall examine him on the seventh day, and if in his eyes the disease is checked and the disease has not spread in the skin, then the priest shall shut him up seven days more; [6]and the priest shall examine him again on the seventh day, and if the diseased spot is dim and the disease has not spread in the skin, then the priest shall pronounce him clean; it is only an eruption; and he shall wash his clothes, and be clean. [7]But if the

---

focuses particularly on the sublime figure of Mary, for she "is 'the new beginning' of the *dignity and vocation of women*, of each and every woman" (ibid., 11).

***13:1—14:57.** These chapters contain the regulations to do with leprosy, its treatment, and purification after contact with the disease. They cover leprosy in persons (13:1–46; 14:1–32), in clothing and in accommodation (13:47–59; 14:33–53); the cleansing of the poor is specially facilitated (14:21–32). The section ends by looking at the different kinds of leprosy (14:54–57).

13:1–59. According to the state of knowledge at the time, there were various indications for this terrible disease. Although some of the data given here may be of interest to historians of medicine, there was generally confusion between leprosy and other skin diseases. However, the fact that people suffering from these diseases are unsightly was sufficient reason to declare them unclean.

Because leprosy was an infectious disease, every effort had to be made to keep it from spreading. It was widely held as being a punishment for some sin. Indeed, in the case of Miriam, who was leprous for a while, we are told that she

---

Dominus ad Moysen et Aaron dicens: [2]«Homo, in cuius carne et cute ortus fuerit tumor sive pustula aut quasi lucens quippiam, id est plaga leprae, adducetur ad Aaron sacerdotem vel ad unum quemlibet filiorum eius sacerdotum. [3]Qui cum viderit plagam in cute et pilos in album mutatos colorem ipsamque speciem plagae humiliorem cute et carne reliqua: plaga leprae est; quod cum viderit sacerdos, eum immundum esse decernet. [4]Sin autem lucens candor fuerit in cute, nec humilior carne reliqua, et pili coloris pristini, recludet eum sacerdos septem diebus. [5]Et considerabit eum die septimo: et, siquidem plaga ultra non creverit nec transierit in cute priores terminos, rursum recludet eum septem diebus aliis. [6]Et die septimo contemplabitur eum iterum: si obscurior fuerit plaga et non creverit in cute, eum mundum esse decernet, quia scabies est. Lavabitque homo vestimenta sua et mundus erit. [7]Quod si,

eruption spreads in the skin, after he has shown himself to the priest for his cleansing, he shall appear again before the priest; [8]and the priest shall make an examination, and if the eruption has spread in the skin, then the priest shall pronounce him unclean; it is leprosy.

[9]"When a man is afflicted with leprosy, he shall be brought to the priest; [10]and the priest shall make an examination, and if there is a white swelling in the skin, which has turned the hair white, and there is quick raw flesh in the swelling, [11]it is a chronic leprosy in the skin of his body, and the priest shall pronounce him unclean; he shall not shut him up, for he is unclean. [12]And if the leprosy breaks out in the skin, so that the leprosy covers all the skin of the diseased person from head to foot, so far as the priest can see, [13]then the priest shall make an examination, and if the leprosy has covered all his body, he shall pronounce him clean of the disease; it has all turned white, and he is clean. [14]But when raw flesh appears on him, he shall be unclean. [15]And the priest shall examine the raw flesh, and pronounce him unclean; raw flesh is unclean, for it is leprosy. [16]But if the raw flesh turns again

---

got the disease because she had been murmuring against her brother Moses (cf. Num 12:1–10). Also, the suffering servant of Yahweh is portrayed as having leprosy, an affliction God sent him on account of our sins (cf. Is 53:4). And Job, who had something like leprosy, was accused by his friends of having committed some terrible, hidden sin: it was the only explanation they could think of for his sorry state.

Life was very different for a person with leprosy. He had to live in settlements or camps away from towns. When travelling about, he had to warn people he was coming by shouting to show he was unclean; he wore his clothes torn and hair uncombed: all this was meant to make him stand out, so that people could avoid him easily. We often come across wretched lepers in the Gospels, on whom Jesus has compassion and whom he makes clean (cf. Mt 8:2–3; Lk 17:12–14): the curing of lepers was one of the signs of the messianic times prophesied in the Old Testament (cf. Mt 11:5). And our Lord gives the apostles power to cure lepers (cf. Mt 10:8).

The New Vulgate abbreviates the original Hebrew text, especially 13:52–53.

---

postquam a sacerdote visus est et redditus munditiae, iterum scabies creverit, adducetur ad eum; [8]et si viderit ita esse, immunditiae condemnabitur: est lepra. [9]Plaga leprae si fuerit in homine, adducetur ad sacerdotem, [10]et videbit eum. Cumque tumor albus in cute fuerit et capillorum mutaverit aspectum in album, caro quoque viva creverit in tumore, [11]lepra vetustissima iudicabitur atque inolita cuti. Contaminabit itaque eum sacerdos et non recludet, quia perspicue immunditia est. [12]Sin autem effloruerit discurrens lepra in cute et operuerit omnem cutem a capite usque ad pedes, quidquid sub aspectu oculorum cadit, [13]considerabit eum sacerdos et teneri lepra mundissima iudicabit, eo quod omnis in candorem versa sit, et idcirco homo mundus erit. [14]Quando vero caro vivens in eo apparuerit, immundus erit. [15]Quod cum sacerdos viderit, inter immundos reputabit; caro enim viva immunda est: lepra est. [16]Quod si rursum versa fuerit in alborem, veniet ad sacerdotem, [17]qui cum hoc consideraverit,

and is changed to white, then he shall come to the priest, [17]and the priest shall examine him, and if the disease has turned white, then the priest shall pronounce the diseased person clean; he is clean.

[18]"And when there is in the skin of one's body a boil that has healed, [19]and in the place of the boil there comes a white swelling or a reddish-white spot, then it shall be shown to the priest; [20]and the priest shall make an examination, and if it appears deeper than the skin and its hair has turned white, then the priest shall pronounce him unclean; it is the disease of leprosy, it has broken out in the boil. [21]But if the priest examines it, and the hair on it is not white and it is not deeper than the skin, but is dim, then the priest shall shut him up seven days; [22]and if it spreads in the skin, then the priest shall pronounce him unclean; it is diseased. [23]But if the spot remains in one place and does not spread, it is the scar of the boil; and the priest shall pronounce him clean.

[24]"Or, when the body has a burn on its skin and the raw flesh of the burn becomes a spot, reddish-white or white, [25]the priest shall examine it, and if the hair in the spot has turned white and it appears deeper than the skin, then it is leprosy; it has broken out in the burn, and the priest shall pronounce him unclean; it is a leprous disease. [26]But if the priest examines it, and the hair in the spot is not white and it is no deeper than the skin, but is dim, the priest shall shut him up seven days, [27]and the priest shall examine him the seventh day; if it is spreading in the skin, then the priest shall pronounce him unclean; it is a leprous disease. [28]But if the spot remains in one place and does not spread in the skin, but is dim, it is a swelling from the burn, and the priest shall pronounce him clean; for it is the scar of the burn.

[29]"When a man or woman has a disease on the head or the beard, [30]the priest shall examine the disease; and if it appears

---

eum mundum esse decernet. [18]Caro et cutis, in qua ulcus natum est et sanatum [19]et in loco ulceris tumor apparuerit albus sive macula subrufa, ostendet se homo sacerdoti. [20]Qui cum viderit locum maculae humiliorem carne reliqua et pilos versos in candorem, contaminabit eum: plaga enim leprae orta est in ulcere. [21]Quod si pilus coloris est pristini et cicatrix subobscura et vicina carne non est humilior, recludet eum septem diebus. [22]Et, siquidem creverit, adiudicabit eum leprae; [23]sin autem steterit in loco suo macula nec creverit, ulceris est cicatrix, et sacerdos eum mundum esse decernet. [24]Vel si alicuius cutem ignis exusserit, et locus exustionis subrufam sive albam habuerit maculam, [25]considerabit eam sacerdos; et ecce pilus versus est in alborem et locus eius reliqua cute humilior, contaminabit eum, quia plaga leprae in cicatrice orta est. [26]Quod si pilorum color non fuerit immutatus, nec humilior macula carne reliqua, et ipsa leprae species fuerit subobscura, recludet eum septem diebus. [27]Et die septimo contemplabitur eum; si creverit in cute macula, contaminabit eum: plaga est leprae; [28]sin autem in loco suo macula steterit non satis clara, tumor combustionis est, et idcirco mundabit eum, quia cicatrix est combusturae. [29]Vir sive mulier, in cuius capite vel barba germinarit plaga, videbit eam sacerdos. [30]Et,

deeper than the skin, and the hair in it is yellow and thin, then the priest shall pronounce him unclean; it is an itch, a leprosy of the head or the beard. [31]And if the priest examines the itching disease, and it appears no deeper than the skin and there is no black hair in it, then the priest shall shut up the person with the itching disease for seven days, [32]and on the seventh day the priest shall examine the disease; and if the itch has not spread, and there is in it no yellow hair, and the itch appears to be no deeper than the skin, [33]then he shall shave himself, but the itch he shall not shave; and the priest shall shut up the person with the itching disease for seven days more; [34]and on the seventh day the priest shall examine the itch, and if the itch has not spread in the skin and it appears to be no deeper than the skin, then the priest shall pronounce him clean; and he shall wash his clothes, and be clean. [35]But if the itch spreads in the skin after his cleansing, [36]then the priest shall examine him, and if the itch has spread in the skin, the priest need not seek for the yellow hair; he is unclean. [37]But if in his eyes the itch is checked, and black hair has grown in it, the itch is healed, he is clean; and the priest shall pronounce him clean.

[38]"When a man or a woman has spots on the skin of the body, white spots, [39]the priest shall make an examination, and if the spots on the skin of the body are of a dull white, it is tetter that has broken out in the skin; he is clean.

[40]"If a man's hair has fallen from his head, he is bald but he is clean. [41]And if a man's hair has fallen from his forehead and temples, he has baldness of the forehead but he is clean. [42]But if there is on the bald head or the bald forehead a reddish-white diseased spot, it is leprosy breaking out on his bald head or his bald forehead. [43]Then the priest shall examine him, and if the diseased swelling is reddish-white on his bald head or on his bald forehead, like the appearance of leprosy in the skin of the body, [44]he is a

siquidem humilior fuerit locus carne reliqua et capillus flavus solitoque subtilior, contaminabit eos, quia scabies est, lepra capitis vel barbae. [31]Sin autem viderit plagam scabiei aequalem vicinae carni, nec capillum nigrum in ea, recludet eos septem diebus. [32]Et die septimo intuebitur plagam: si non creverit scabies, nec capillus flavus fuerit in ea, et locus plagae carni reliquae aequalis, [33]radetur homo absque loco maculae, et includet eum sacerdos septem diebus aliis. [34]Si die septimo visa fuerit stetisse plaga in loco suo nec humilior carne reliqua, mundabit eum sacerdos; lotisque vestibus mundus erit. [35]Sin autem post emundationem rursus creverit scabies in cute, [36]non quaeret amplius utrum capillus in flavum colorem sit commutatus, quia aperte immundus est. [37]Porro si steterit macula, et capilli nigri fuerint, noverit hominem esse sanatum et confidenter eum pronuntiet mundum. [38]Vir et mulier, in cuius cute maculae, maculae albae apparuerint, [39]intuebitur eos sacerdos. Si deprehenderit subobscurum alborem lucere in cute, sciat impetiginem ortam esse in cute; mundus est. [40]Vir, de cuius capite capilli fluunt, calvus ac mundus est; [41]et, si a fronte ceciderint pili, recalvaster et mundus est. [42]Sin autem in calvitio sive in recalvatione plaga alba vel subrufa fuerit exorta, lepra est capitis. [43]Sacerdos eum

leprous man, he is unclean; the priest must pronounce him unclean; his disease is on his head.

Lk 17:12   ⁴⁵"The leper who has the disease shall wear torn clothes and let the hair of his head hang loose, and he shall cover his upper lip and cry, 'Unclean, unclean.' ⁴⁶He shall remain unclean as long as he has the disease; he is unclean; he shall dwell alone in a habitation outside the camp.

Leprosy in clothes

⁴⁷"When there is a leprous disease in a garment, whether a woolen or a linen garment, ⁴⁸in warp or woof of linen or wool, or in a skin or in anything made of skin, ⁴⁹if the disease shows greenish or reddish in the garment, whether in warp or woof or in skin or in anything made of skin, it is a leprous disease and shall be shown to the priest. ⁵⁰And the priest shall examine the disease, and shut up that which has the disease for seven days; ⁵¹then he shall examine the disease on the seventh day. If the disease has spread in the garment, in warp or woof, or in the skin, whatever be the use of the skin, the disease is a malignant leprosy; it is unclean. ⁵²And he shall burn the garment, whether diseased in warp or woof, woollen or linen, or anything of skin, for it is a malignant leprosy; it shall be burned in the fire.

⁵³"And if the priest examines, and the disease has not spread in the garment in warp or woof or in anything of skin, ⁵⁴then the priest shall command that they wash the thing in which is the disease, and he shall shut it up seven days more; ⁵⁵and the priest shall examine the diseased thing after it has been washed. And if the diseased spot has not changed colour, though the disease has not spread, it is unclean; you shall burn it in the fire, whether the leprous spot is on the back or on the front.

⁵⁶"But if the priest examines, and the disease is dim after it is washed, he shall tear the spot out of the garment or the skin or

---

videbit, et ecce tumor plagae subrufus secundum aspectum leprae cutis carnis. ⁴⁴Vir maculatus est lepra, et sacerdos omnino decernet eum esse immundum; plaga est in capite eius. ⁴⁵Leprosus hac plaga percussus habebit vestimenta dissuta, comam capitis excussam, barbam contectam; clamabit: 'Immundus! Immundus!'. ⁴⁶Omni tempore, quo leprosus est immundus, immundus est et solus habitabit extra castra. ⁴⁷Si in veste lanea sive linea lepra fuerit, ⁴⁸in stamine sive subtemine lineo vel laneo aut in pelle vel quolibet ex pelle confecto, ⁴⁹si macula pallida aut rufa fuerit, lepra reputabitur ostendeturque sacerdoti. ⁵⁰Qui considerabit macula infectum et recludet septem diebus, ⁵¹et die septimo rursus aspiciens, si crevisse deprehenderit, lepra maligna est; pollutum iudicabit vestimentum et omne, in quo fuerit inventa, ⁵²et idcirco comburetur flammis. ⁵³Quod si eam viderit non crevisse, ⁵⁴praecipiet, et lavabunt id, in quo plaga est; recludetque illud septem diebus aliis. ⁵⁵Et cum viderit post lavationem faciem quidem pristinam non mutatam, nec tamen crevisse plagam, immunda est res, et igne combures eam, eo quod infusa sit plaga in superficie rei vel in parte aversa. ⁵⁶Sin autem obscurior fuerit locus plagae, postquam res est lota, sacerdos abrumpet eum et a solido dividet. ⁵⁷Quod si macula ultra

the warp or woof; [57]then if it appears again in the garment, in warp or woof, or in anything of skin, it is spreading; you shall burn with fire that in which is the disease. [58]But the garment, warp or woof, or anything of skin from which the disease departs when you have washed it, shall then be washed a second time, and be clean."

[59]This is the law for a leprous disease in a garment of wool or linen, either in warp or woof, or in anything of skin, to decide whether it is clean or unclean.

Cleansing of leprosy

Mt 8:4
Mk 1:44
Lk 5:14; 17:14

14 [1]The LORD said to Moses, [2]"This shall be the law of the leper for the day of his cleansing. He shall be brought to the priest; [3]and the priest shall go out of the camp, and the priest shall make an examination. Then, if the leprous disease is healed in the leper, [4]the priest shall command them to take for him who is to be cleansed two living clean birds and cedarwood and scarlet stuff and hyssop; [5]and the priest shall command them to kill

Heb 9:19

14:1–57. In ancient times leprosy was incurable. However, because there were skin diseases which had symptoms similar to those of leprosy, rules are given here for the cleansing of "lepers". Once a leper was cleansed, he had to be certified by a priest: this makes sense if we bear in mind the theoratic nature of the people of Israel and also the conviction that divine intervention was responsible both for a person getting leprosy and for him being cured of it. Our Lord recognized the validity of these rules, as can be seen from the fact that he told lepers he cured to show themselves to the priest (cf. Lk 17:14).

The whole ceremony is very rich in symbolism. The cedar tree was the symbol of eternity because it was so long-lived and it had various medicinal qualities. Hyssop was thought to have cleansing properties. The scarlet fabric symbolizes blood which like running water always flowed like life itself. The bird which takes flight symbolizes freedom the newly cured leper obtains at that moment. In the language of liturgy a "tenth" was a tenth of an ephah of flour (cf. 15:11; 6:13), that is a tenth of the capacity of a receptacle that could hold about 21 kilos or 46 pounds (cf. the note on Exodus 16:32–36). A "log" (this is the only chapter in the Bible where the word appears) was a measure used for offertory wine; all we know is that it was very small, perhaps a third of a litre, less than a pint.

---

apparuerit in his rebus, quae prius immaculata erant, lepra volatilis et vaga, igne combures illas. [58]Quas vero laveris et a quibus cessaverit plaga, illas lavabis secundo, et mundae erunt. [59]Ista est lex leprae vestimenti lanei et linei, staminis atque subteminis, omnisque supellectilis pelliceae, quomodo mundari debeat vel contaminari» [1]Locutusque est Dominus ad Moysen dicens: [2]«Hic est ritus leprosi, quando mundandus est: adducetur ad sacerdotem, [3]qui egressus e castris, cum invenerit lepram esse sanatam, [4]praecipiet, ut sumant pro eo, qui purificatur, duas aves vivas, mundas et lignum cedrinum vermiculumque et hyssopum. [5]Et unam ex avibus immolari iubebit in vase fictili super aquas viventes. [6]Aliam

one of the birds in an earthen vessel over running water. [6]He shall take the living bird with the cedarwood and the scarlet stuff and the hyssop, and dip them and the living bird in the blood of the bird that was killed over the running water; [7]and he shall sprinkle it seven times upon him who is to be cleansed of leprosy; then he shall pronounce him clean, and shall let the living bird go into the open field. [8]And he who is to be cleansed shall wash his clothes, and shave off all his hair, and bathe himself in water, and he shall be clean; and after that he shall come into the camp, but shall dwell outside his tent seven days. [9]And on the seventh day he shall shave all his hair off his head; he shall shave off his beard and his eyebrows, all his hair. Then he shall wash his clothes, and bathe his body in water, and he shall be clean.

Num 19:6–18
Ps 51:7

[10]"And on the eighth day he shall take two male lambs without blemish, and one ewe lamb a year old without blemish, and a cereal offering of three tenths of an ephah of fine flour mixed with oil, and one log of oil. [11]And the priest who cleanses him shall set the man who is to be cleansed and these things before the LORD, at the door of the tent of meeting. [12]And the priest shall take one of the male lambs, and offer it for a guilt offering, along with the log of oil, and wave them for a wave offering before the LORD; [13]and he shall kill the lamb in the place where they kill the sin offering and the burnt offering, in the holy place; for the guilt offering, like the sin offering, belongs to the priest; it is most holy. [14]The priest shall take some of the blood of the guilt offering, and the priest shall put it on the tip of the right ear of him who is to be cleansed, and on the thumb of his right hand, and on the great toe of his right foot. [15]Then the priest shall take some of the log of oil, and pour it into the palm of his own left hand, [16]and dip his right finger in the oil that is in his left hand,

autem vivam cum ligno cedrino et cocco et hyssopo tinguet in sanguine avis super aquas viventes immolatae, [7]quo asperget illum, qui a lepra mundandus est, septies, ut iure purgetur; et dimittet avem vivam, ut in agrum avolet. [8]Cumque laverit homo vestimenta sua, radet omnes pilos corporis, et lavabitur aqua; purificatusque ingredietur castra, ita dumtaxat ut maneat extra tabernaculum suum septem diebus. [9]Et die septimo radet capillos capitis, barbamque et supercilia ac totius corporis pilos et lavabit vestimenta carnemque suam aqua, et mundus erit. [10]Die octavo assumet duos agnos immaculatos et ovem anniculam absque macula et tres decimas ephi similae in sacrificium, quae conspersa sit oleo, et log olei. [11]Cumque sacerdos purificans hominem statuerit eum et haec omnia coram Domino in ostio tabernaculi conventus, [12]tollet agnum unum et offeret eum in sacrificium pro delicto, oleique log et, elevatis ante Dominum omnibus, [13]immolabit agnum, ubi immolari solet hostia pro peccato et holocaustum, id est in loco sancto. Sicut enim pro peccato ita et pro delicto ad sacerdotem pertinet sacrificium: sanctum sanctorum est. [14]Assumensque sacerdos de sanguine hostiae pro delicto ponet super extremum auriculae dextrae eius, qui mundatur, et super pollices manus dextrae et pedis; [15]et de olei log mittet in manum suam sinistram [16]tinguetque digitum dextrum in eo et asperget septies coram

and sprinkle some oil with his finger seven times before the LORD. [17]And some of the oil that remains in his hand the priest shall put on the tip of the right ear of him who is to be cleansed, and on the thumb of his right hand, and on the great toe of his right foot, upon the blood of the guilt offering; [18]and the rest of the oil that is in the priest's hand he shall put on the head of him who is to be cleansed. Then the priest shall make atonement for him before the LORD. [19]The priest shall offer the sin offering, to make atonement for him who is to be cleansed from his uncleanness. And afterward he shall kill the burnt offering; [20]and the priest shall offer the burnt offering and the cereal offering on the altar. Thus the priest shall make atonement for him, and he shall be clean.

[21]"But if he is poor and cannot afford so much, then he shall take one male lamb for a guilt offering to be waved, to make atonement for him, and a tenth of an ephah of fine flour mixed with oil for a cereal offering, and a log of oil; [22]also two turtledoves or two young pigeons, such as he can afford; the one shall be a sin offering and the other a burnt offering. [23]And on the eighth day he shall bring them for his cleansing to the priest, to the door of the tent of meeting, before the LORD; [24]and the priest shall take the lamb of the guilt offering, and the log of oil, and the priest shall wave them for a wave offering before the LORD. [25]And he shall kill the lamb of the guilt offering; and the priest shall take some of the blood of the guilt offering, and put it on the tip of the right ear of him who is to be cleansed, and on the thumb of his right hand, and on the great toe of his right foot. [26]And the priest shall pour some of the oil into the palm of his own left hand; [27]and shall sprinkle with his right finger some of the oil that is in his left hand seven times before the LORD; [28]and the priest shall put some of the oil that is in his hand on the tip of the right ear of him who is to be cleansed, and on the thumb

Lev 5:7–13; 12:8

Domino. [17]Quod autem reliquum est olei in laeva manu, fundet super extremum auriculae dextrae eius, qui mundatur, et super pollices manus ac pedis dextri et super sanguinem sacrificii pro delicto [18]et super caput eius, qui mundatur; expiabitque eum coram Domino [19]et faciet sacrificium pro peccato. Tunc immolabit holocaustum [20]et ponet illud in altari cum sacrificio similae, et homo rite mundabitur. [21]Quod si pauper est, et non potest manus eius invenire, quae dicta sunt, assumet agnum pro delicto ad elationem, ut expiet eum sacerdos, decimamque partem similae conspersae oleo in sacrificium et olei log [22]duosque turtures sive duos pullos columbae, quos manus eius invenire poterit, unum pro peccato et alterum in holocaustum. [23]Offeretque ea die octavo purificationis suae sacerdoti ad ostium tabernaculi conventus coram Domino. [24]Qui suscipiens agnum pro delicto et log olei levabit simul coram Domino; [25]immolatoque agno pro delicto, de sanguine eius ponet super extremum auriculae dextrae illius, qui mundatur, et super pollices manus ac pedis dextri; [26]olei vero partem mittet in manum suam sinistram. [27]In quo tinguens digitum dextrae manus asperget septies coram Domino; [28]tangetque extremum auriculae dextrae illius, qui mundatur, et pollices manus ac pedis dextri super locum san-

of his right hand, and the great toe of his right foot, in the place where the blood of the guilt offering was put; [29]and the rest of the oil that is in the priest's hand he shall put on the head of him who is to be cleansed, to make atonement for him before the LORD. [30]And he shall offer, of the turtledoves or young pigeons such as he can afford, [31]one[x] for a sin offering and the other for a burnt offering, along with a cereal offering; and the priest shall make atonement before the LORD for him who is being cleansed. [32]This is the law for him in whom is a leprous disease, who cannot afford the offerings for his cleansing."

Cleaning of houses infected by leprosy
[33]The LORD said to Moses and Aaron, [34]"When you come into the land of Canaan, which I give you for a possession, and I put a leprous disease in a house in the land of your possession, [35]then he who owns the house shall come and tell the priest, 'There seems to me to be some sort of disease in my house.' [36]Then the priest shall command that they empty the house before the priest goes to examine the disease, lest all that is in the house be declared unclean; and afterward the priest shall go in to see the house. [37]And he shall examine the disease; and if the disease is in the walls of the house with greenish or reddish spots, and if it appears to be deeper than the surface, [38]then the priest shall go out of the house to the door of the house, and shut up the house seven days. [39]And the priest shall come again on the seventh day, and look; and if the disease has spread in the walls of the house, [40]then the priest shall command that they take out the stones in which is the disease and throw them into an unclean place outside the city; [41]and he shall cause the inside of the house to be scraped round about, and the plaster that they scrape off they shall pour into an

---

guinis, qui effusus est pro delicto. [29]Reliquam autem partem olei, quae est in sinistra manu, mittet super caput hominis, qui purificatur, in expiationem eius coram Domino; [30]et turtures sive pullos columbae, quos manus illius invenerit, offeret, [31]unum pro delicto et alterum in holocaustum cum sacrificio similae, et sic expiabit eum sacerdos coram Domino. [32]Hoc est sacrificium leprosi, qui habere non potest omnia in emundationem sui». [33]Locutus est Dominus ad Moysen et Aaron dicens: [34]«Cum ingressi fueritis terram Chanaan, quam ego dabo vobis in possessionem, si fuerit plaga leprae in aedibus terrae possessionis vestrae, [35]ibit, cuius est domus, nuntians sacerdoti et dicet: 'Quasi plaga videtur mihi esse in domo mea'. [36]At ille praecipiet, ut efferant universa de domo, priusquam ingrediatur eam, et videat plagam, ne immunda fiant omnia, quae in domo sunt. Intrabitque postea, ut consideret domum; [37]et, cum viderit in parietibus illius quasi valliculas pallore sive rubore deformes et humiliores superficie reliqua, [38]egredietur ostium domus et statim claudet eam septem diebus. [39]Reversusque die septimo considerabit eam; si invenerit crevisse plagam, [40]iubebit erui lapides, in quibus plaga est, et proici eos extra civitatem in loco immundo; [41]domum autem ipsam radi intrinsecus per circuitum et spargi pul-

x. Gk Syr: Heb *afford*, [31]*such as he can afford, one*

unclean place outside the city; ⁴²then they shall take other stones and put them in the place of those stones, and he shall take other plaster and plaster the house.

⁴³"If the disease breaks out again in the house, after he has taken out the stones and scraped the house and plastered it, ⁴⁴then the priest shall go and look; and if the disease has spread in the house, it is a malignant leprosy in the house; it is unclean. ⁴⁵And he shall break down the house, its stones and timber and all the plaster of the house; and he shall carry them forth out of the city to an unclean place. ⁴⁶Moreover he who enters the house while it is shut up shall be unclean until the evening; ⁴⁷and he who lies down in the house shall wash his clothes; and he who eats in the house shall wash his clothes.

⁴⁸"But if the priest comes and makes an examination, and the disease has not spread in the house after the house was plastered, then the priest shall pronounce the house clean, for the disease is healed. ⁴⁹And for the cleansing of the house he shall take two small birds, with cedarwood and scarlet stuff and hyssop, ⁵⁰and shall kill one of the birds in an earthen vessel over running water, ⁵¹and shall take the cedarwood and the hyssop and the scarlet stuff, along with the living bird, and dip them in the blood of the bird that was killed and in the running water, and sprinkle the house seven times. ⁵²Thus he shall cleanse the house with the blood of the bird, and with the running water, and with the living bird, and with the cedarwood and hyssop and scarlet stuff; ⁵³and he shall let the living bird go out of the city into the open field; so he shall make atonement for the house, and it shall be clean."

⁵⁴This is the law for any leprous disease: for an itch, ⁵⁵for leprosy in a garment or in a house, ⁵⁶and for a swelling or an eruption or a spot, ⁵⁷to show when it is unclean and when it is clean. This is the law for leprosy.

verem rasurae extra urbem in locum immundum ⁴²lapidesque alios reponi pro his, qui ablati fuerint, et luto alio liniri domum. ⁴³Sin autem plaga rursum effloruerit in domo, postquam eruti sunt lapides et pulvis erasus et alia terra lita, ⁴⁴et ingressus sacerdos viderit crevisse plagam in domo: lepra est maligna et domus immunda. ⁴⁵Quam statim destruent et lapides eius ac ligna atque universum pulverem domus proicient extra oppidum in loco immundo. ⁴⁶Qui intraverit domum, quando clausa est, immundus erit usque ad vesperum; ⁴⁷et, qui dormierit in ea vel comederit quippiam, lavabit vestimenta sua. ⁴⁸Quod si introiens sacerdos viderit plagam non crevisse in domo, postquam denuo lita est, mundam eam esse decernet, reddita sanitate. ⁴⁹Et in purificationem eius sumet duas aves lignumque cedrinum et vermiculum atque hyssopum ⁵⁰et, immolata una avi in vase fictili super aquas vivas, ⁵¹tollet lignum cedrinum et hyssopum et coccum et avem vivam et intinguet omnia in sanguine avis immolatae atque in aquis viventibus et asperget domum septies; ⁵²purificabitque eam tam in sanguine avis quam in aquis viventibus et in avi viva lignoque cedrino et hyssopo atque vermiculo; ⁵³cumque dimiserit avem avolare extra urbem in agrum libere, expiabit domum, et erit munda. ⁵⁴Ista est lex omnis leprae et scabiei, ⁵⁵leprae vestium et domorum, ⁵⁶tumoris et pustulae et lucentis maculae, ⁵⁷ut possit sciri quo tempore immundum quid vel mundum sit». ¹Locutus est Dominus ad Moysen et Aaron dicens:

Male uncleanness*

^{Num 5:2} **15** [1]The L<small>ORD</small> said to Moses and Aaron, [2]"Say to the people of Israel, When any man has a discharge from his body, his discharge is unclean. [3]And this is the law of his uncleanness for a discharge: whether his body runs with his discharge, or his body is stopped from discharge, it is uncleanness in him. [4]Every bed on which he who has the discharge lies shall be unclean; and everything on which he sits shall be unclean. [5]And any one who touches his bed shall wash his clothes, and bathe himself in water, and be unclean until the evening. [6]And whoever sits on anything on which he who has the discharge has sat shall wash his clothes, and bathe himself in water, and be unclean until the evening. [7]And whoever touches the body of him who has the discharge shall wash his clothes, and bathe himself in water, and be unclean until the evening. [8]And if he who has the discharge spits on one who is clean, then he shall wash his clothes, and bathe himself in water, and be unclean until the evening. [9]And any saddle on which he who has the discharge rides shall be unclean. [10]And whoever touches anything that was under him shall be unclean until the evening; and he who carries such a thing shall wash his clothes, and bathe himself in water, and be unclean until the evening. [11]Any one whom he that has the discharge touches without having rinsed his hands in water shall wash his clothes, and bathe himself

---

*15:1–33. We have already noticed, in connexion with chapter 12, how ancient peoples saw anything to do with reproduction as being very mysterious—and how sexual irregularities were regarded as impure and obscene. This attitude was not exclusive to Israel; but in Israel a high ethical and moral sense in things sexual was developed.

In the case of males there was a rule that no one should have any contact with a woman when on active service. In the last analysis war against pagans was regarded as something holy, and an unclean man could not fight in the holy name of God (cf. 1 Sam 21:5–7). Although this sort of thing sounds shocking to people nowadays, the opposite would have been the case at that time.

---

[2]«Loquimini filiis Israel et dicite eis: Vir, si patitur fluxum seminis, immundus erit. [3]Et tunc iudicabitur huic vitio subiacere: sive emiserit caro eius fluxum suum vel occluserit se a fluxu. [4]Omne stratum, in quo iacuerit, immundum erit, et ubicumque sederit. [5]Si quis hominum tetigerit lectum eius, lavabit vestimenta sua, et ipse lotus aqua immundus erit usque ad vesperum. [6]Si sederit, ubi ille sederat, et ipse lavabit vestimenta sua et lotus aqua immundus erit usque ad vesperum. [7]Qui tetigerit carnem eius, lavabit vestimenta sua et ipse lotus aqua immundus erit usque ad vesperum. [8]Si salivam huiuscemodi homo iecerit super eum, qui mundus est, hic lavabit vestem suam et lotus aqua immundus erit usque ad vesperum. [9]Sagma, super quo sederit, immundum erit; [10]et quicumque tetigerit omne, quod sub eo fuerit, qui fluxum seminis patitur, pollutus erit usque ad vesperum. Qui portaverit horum aliquid, lavabit vestem suam et ipse lotus aqua immundus erit usque ad vesperum. [11]Omnis, quem tetigerit, qui fluxum patitur, non lotis ante manibus, lavabit vestimenta sua et lotus aqua immundus erit usque ad vesperum. [12]Vas fictile, quod tetigerit, confringetur; vas autem ligneum lavabitur aqua. [13]Si sanatus

in water, and be unclean until the evening. ¹²And the earthen vessel which he who has the discharge touches shall be broken; and every vessel of wood shall be rinsed in water.

¹³"And when he who has a discharge is cleansed of his discharge, then he shall count for himself seven days for his cleansing, and wash his clothes; and he shall bathe his body in running water, and shall be clean. ¹⁴And on the eighth day he shall take two turtledoves or two young pigeons, and come before the LORD to the door of the tent of meeting, and give them to the priest; ¹⁵and the priest shall offer them, one for a sin offering and the other for a burnt offering; and the priest shall make atonement for him before the LORD for his discharge.

¹⁶"And if a man has an emission of semen, he shall bathe his whole body in water, and be unclean until the evening. ¹⁷And every garment and every skin on which the semen comes shall be washed with water, and be unclean until the evening. ¹⁸If a man lies with a woman and has an emission of semen, both of them shall bathe themselves in water, and be unclean until the evening.

Heb 9:10

Female uncleanness

¹⁹"When a woman has a discharge of blood which is her regular discharge from her body, she shall be in her impurity for seven days, and whoever touches her shall be unclean until the evening. ²⁰And everything upon which she lies during her impurity shall be unclean; everything also upon which she sits shall be unclean. ²¹And whoever touches her bed shall wash his clothes, and bathe himself in water, and be unclean until the evening. ²²And whoever touches anything upon which she sits shall wash his clothes, and bathe himself in water, and be unclean until the evening; ²³whether it is the bed or anything upon which she sits, when he touches it he shall be unclean until the evening. ²⁴And if any

fuerit, qui huiuscemodi sustinet passionem, numerabit septem dies ad emundationem sui et, lotis vestibus ac toto corpore in aquis viventibus, erit mundus. ¹⁴Die autem octavo sumet duos turtures aut duos pullos columbae et veniet in conspectu Domini ad ostium tabernaculi conventus dabitque eos sacerdoti. ¹⁵Qui faciet unum in sacrificium pro peccato et alterum in holocaustum; expiabitque eum coram Domino et emundabitur a fluxu seminis sui. ¹⁶Vir, de quo egreditur semen, lavabit aqua omne corpus suum et immundus erit usque ad vesperum. ¹⁷Vestem et pellem, super quam fuerit semen effusum, lavabitur aqua et immunda erit usque ad vesperum. ¹⁸Si cum muliere coierit vir, lavabunt se aqua et immundi erunt usque ad vesperum. ¹⁹Mulier, quae redeunte mense patitur fluxum sanguinis, septem diebus separabitur. Omnis, qui tetigerit eam, immundus erit usque ad vesperum; ²⁰et in quo iacuerit vel sederit diebus separationis suae, polluetur. ²¹Qui tetigerit lectum eius, lavabit vestimenta sua et ipse lotus aqua immundus erit usque ad vesperum. ²²Omne vas, super quo illa sederit, quisquis attigerit, lavabit vestimenta sua et ipse lotus aqua pollutus erit usque ad vesperum. ²³Et quicumque tetigerit omne, quod fuerit super lectum vel supellectilem, in qua illa sederit, immundus erit usque ad vesperum. ²⁴Si coierit cum ea vir tempore sanguinis menstrualis, immundus erit septem diebus, et omne stratum, in quo dormierit, polluetur. ²⁵Mulier, quae patitur multis diebus fluxum sanguinis non in tempore

man lies with her, and her impurity is on him, he shall be unclean seven days; and every bed on which he lies shall be unclean.

Mt 9:20 ²⁵"If a woman has a discharge of blood for many days, not at the time of her impurity, or if she has a discharge beyond the time of her impurity, all the days of the discharge she shall continue in uncleanness; as in the days of her impurity, she shall be unclean. ²⁶Every bed on which she lies, all the days of her discharge, shall be to her as the bed of her impurity; and everything on which she sits shall be unclean, as in the uncleanness of her impurity. ²⁷And whoever touches these things shall be unclean, and shall wash his clothes, and bathe himself in water, and be unclean until the evening. ²⁸But if she is cleansed of her discharge, she shall count for herself seven days, and after that she shall be clean. ²⁹And on the eighth day she shall take two turtledoves or two young pigeons, and bring them to the priest, to the door of the tent of meeting. ³⁰And the priest shall offer one for a sin offering and the other for a burnt offering; and the priest shall make atonement for her before the LORD for her unclean discharge.

³¹"Thus you shall keep the people of Israel separate from their uncleanness, lest they die in their uncleanness by defiling my tabernacle that is in their midst."

³²This is the law for him who has a discharge and for him who has an emission of semen, becoming unclean thereby; ³³also for her who is sick with her impurity; that is, for any one, male or female, who has a discharge, and for the man who lies with a
Lev 23:26–32 woman who is unclean.
Num 29:7–11
Heb 9:6–14
Rom 8:3 **The day of atonement***

Lev 10:1–3 **16** ¹The LORD spoke to Moses, after the death of the two sons of Aaron, when they drew near before the LORD and died;

---

*16:1–34. Due to the connexion between this chapter and chapter 10, and also the

later description in 23:26ff, some scholars have thought that this passage was

menstruali vel quae post menstruum sanguinem fluere non cessat, quamdiu huic subiacet passioni, immunda erit quasi sit in tempore menstruo. ²⁶Omne stratum, in quo dormierit, et vas, in quo sederit, pollutum erit. ²⁷Quicumque tetigerit ea, polluetur; lavabit vestimenta sua et ipse lotus aqua immundus erit usque ad vesperum. ²⁸Si steterit sanguis et fluere cessarit, numerabit septem dies et deinde munda erit. ²⁹Et octavo die assumet pro se duos turtures vel duos pullos columbae afferetque sacerdoti ad ostium tabernaculi conventus. ³⁰Qui unum faciet in sacrificium pro peccato et alterum in holocaustum; expiabitque eam coram Domino a fluxu immunditiae eius. ³¹Docebitis ergo filios Israel, ut caveant immunditiam, ne moriantur in sordibus suis, cum polluerint habitaculum meum, quod est inter eos. ³²Ista est lex eius, qui patitur fluxum seminis et de quo egreditur semen, et polluitur, ³³et quae menstruis temporibus separatur vel quae iugi fluit sanguine, et hominis, qui dormierit cum immunda».

²and the LORD said to Moses, "Tell Aaron your brother not to come at all times into the holy place within the veil, before the mercy seat which is upon the ark, lest he die; for I will appear in the cloud upon the mercy seat. ³But thus shall Aaron come into the holy place: with a young bull for a sin offering and a ram for a burnt offering. ⁴He shall put on the holy linen coat, and shall have the linen breeches on his body, be girded with the linen girdle, and wear the linen turban; these are the holy garments. He shall bathe his body in water, and then put them on. ⁵And he shall take from the congregation of the people of Israel two male goats for a sin offering, and one ram for a burnt offering.

⁶"And Aaron shall offer the bull as a sin offering for himself, and shall make atonement for himself and for his house. ⁷Then he shall take the two goats, and set them before the LORD at the door of the tent of meeting; ⁸and Aaron shall cast lots upon the two goats, one lot for the LORD and the other lot for Azazel. ⁹And Aaron shall present the goat on which the lot fell for the LORD, and offer it as a sin offering; ¹⁰but the goat on which the lot fell

Ex 19:12;
25:17
Heb 10:22

Heb 5:3; 7:27

---

made up of fragments assembled at a later period, perhaps during the reforms led by Ezekiel. However, after the exile in Babylon there was no Ark of the Covenant, no mercy seat—essential elements in the ceremonies on the day of atonement. Also, when Ezra speaks about the post-exilic Jewish institutions around the year 450 BC, he does not mention this feast. So, it may well be that what we have here is some early material elaborated on later. This theory is supported by the fact that there were feasts very like the day of atonement in very early civilizations such as that of Babylonia. Rome

and Athens also had similar customs. In the capital of Imperial Rome, for example, every five years a "lustre" was held (hence the verb "to lustre", to clean or polish): that is, sins were officially expiated to "clean" the people.

Given Israel's elaborate legislation on matters to do with worship, it was quite easy to infringe a rule, so there were lots of ritual transgressions on top of all the other sins that needed to be atoned for.

Certainly, the day of atonement came to occupy a pre-eminent place in the Jewish calendar. It was called "the big day", Yoma rabbá, as well as Yom

---

¹Locutusque est Dominus ad Moysen post mortem duum filiorum Aaron, quando appropinquantes in conspectu Domini interfecti sunt, ²et praecepit ei dicens: «Loquere ad Aaron fratrem tuum, ne omni tempore ingrediatur sanctuarium, quod est intra velum coram propitiatorio, quo tegitur arca, ut non moriatur, quia in nube apparebo super propitiatorium; ³sed hoc modo ingrediatur: vitulum offeret pro peccato et arietem in holocaustum; ⁴subucula linea sancta vestietur, feminalibus lineis verecunda celabit, accingetur zona linea, cidarim lineam imponet capiti. Haec enim vestimenta sunt sancta, quibus cunctis, cum lotus fuerit, induetur. ⁵Suscipietque a coetu filiorum Israel duos hircos in sacrificium pro peccato et unum arietem in holocaustum. ⁶Cumque obtulerit vitulum in sacrificium suum pro peccato et expiaverit se et domum suam, ⁷duos hircos stare faciet coram Domino in ostio tabernaculi conventus, ⁸mittens super utrumque sortem, unam Domino et alteram Azazel. ⁹Cuius sors exierit Domino, offeret illum pro peccato; ¹⁰cuius autem in Azazel, statuet eum vivum coram Domino in expiationem,

for Azazel shall be presented alive before the LORD to make atonement over it, that it may be sent away into the wilderness to Azazel.

Heb 7:27; 9:7   ¹¹"Aaron shall present the bull as a sin offering for himself, and shall make atonement for himself and for his house; he shall Heb 6:19 kill the bull as a sin offering for himself. ¹²And he shall take a Rev 8:5 censer full of coals of fire from the altar before the LORD, and two handfuls of sweet incense beaten small; and he shall bring it Ex 25:17 within the veil ¹³and put the incense on the fire before the LORD, that the cloud of the incense may cover the mercy seat which is Ex 33:20 upon the testimony, lest he die; ¹⁴and he shall take some of the Heb 9:7 blood of the bull, and sprinkle it with his finger on the front of the mercy seat, and before the mercy seat he shall sprinkle the blood with his finger seven times.

Ezek 45:18–20   ¹⁵"Then he shall kill the goat of the sin offering which is for Rom 3:25 the people, and bring its blood within the veil, and do with its

---

Kippur. It was celebrated with great fervour by all the people, in hope of winning God's forgiveness. It was held on the tenth day of the seventh month, Tishri, at the start of autumn, five days before the feast of Tabernacles.

16:10. This is the only place where "Azazel" appears. It is not easy to identify him. In fact, according to some early translations such as the Septuagint, Symmachus and Aquila, the name refers to the animal which is sent out into the wilderness. That is also the interpretation given by the Vulgate, which speaks of the "caprum emmissarium", the he-goat cast out. The New Vulgate [and the RSV] speak of "Azazel", respecting the Hebrew proper name. So, what we have here is someone who is an enemy of the Lord— according to some scholars, a kind of demon or fallen angel—who appears also

in the apocryphal book of Enoch as one of the leaders of the rebellious angels who is eventually shackled by the archangel Raphael. There were some who said that this demon was an object of worship in Israel: such was people's fear of him that they sought to appease him. St Cyril of Alexandria protested against that interpretation on the grounds that it was unthinkable that a rival of the Lord should be venerated (cf. *Contra Iulianem*, 8, 3). This name may also refer to the evil spirit of the desert whom Raphael bound (cf. Tob 8:3), but without there being any element of cult involved. Rather, the fact that the he-goat laden with the people's sins is sent out to Azazel indicates that he is someone despised, not worshipped.

16:15–16. The *Catechism of the Catholic Church* describes as follows the signification of the rite of purification on Yom

---

ut emittat illum ad Azazel in solitudinem. ¹¹Afferet ergo Aaron vitulum pro peccato et expians se et domum suam immolabit eum; ¹²assumptoque turibulo, quod de prunis altaris coram Domino impleverit, et hauriens manu compositum thymiama in incensum ultra velum intrabit in sancta, ¹³ut, positis super agnem aromatibus coram Domino, nebula eorum et vapor operiat propitiatorium, quod est super testimonium, et non moriatur. ¹⁴Tollet quoque de sanguine vituli et asperget digito septies contra frontem propitiatorii. ¹⁵Cumque mactaverit hircum pro peccato populi, inferet sanguinem eius

blood as he did with the blood of the bull, sprinkling it upon the mercy seat and before the mercy seat; [16]thus he shall make atonement for the holy place, because of the uncleannesses of the people of Israel, and because of their transgressions, all their sins; and so he shall do for the tent of meeting, which abides with them in the midst of their uncleannesses. [17]There shall be no man in the tent of meeting when he enters to make atonement in the holy place until he comes out and has made atonement for himself and for his house and for all the assembly of Israel. [18]Then he shall go out to the altar which is before the LORD and make atonement for it, and shall take some of the blood of the bull and of the blood of the goat, and put it on the horns of the altar round about. [19]And he shall sprinkle some of the blood upon it with his finger seven times, and cleanse it and hallow it from the uncleannesses of the people of Israel.

Deut 4:7

Heb 9:7

[20]"And when he has made an end of atoning for the holy place and the tent of meeting and the altar, he shall present the live goat; [21]and Aaron shall lay both his hands upon the head of the live goat, and confess over him all the iniquities of the people of Israel, and all their transgressions, all their sins; and he shall put them upon the head of the goat, and send him away into the wilderness by the hand of a man who is in readiness. [22]The goat shall bear all their iniquities upon him to a solitary land; and he shall let the goat go in the wilderness.

Kippur: "The name of the Saviour God was invoked only once in the year by the high priest in atonement for the sins of Israel, after he had sprinkled the mercy seat in the Holy of Holies with the sacrificial blood. The mercy seat was the place of God's presence (cf. Ex 25:22; Lev 16:2, 15–16; Num 7:89; Sir 50:20; Heb 9:5–7). When St Paul speaks of Jesus whom 'God put forward as an expiation by his blood' (Rom 3:25), he means that in Christ's humanity 'God was in Christ reconciling the world to himself' (2 Cor 5:19)" (no. 433).

intra velum, sicut praeceptum est de sanguine vituli, ut aspergat e regione propitiatorii [16]et expiet sanctuarium ab immunditiis filiorum Israel et a praevaricationibus eorum cunctisque peccatis. Iuxta hunc ritum faciet tabernaculo conventus, quod fixum est inter eos in medio sordium habitationis eorum. [17]Nullus hominum sit in tabernaculo conventus, quando pontifex ingreditur sanctuarium, ut expiet se et domum suam et universam congregationem Israel, donec egrediatur. [18]Cum autem exierit ad altare, quod coram Domino est, expiabit illud et sumptum sanguinem vituli atque hirci fundet super cornua eius per gyrum; [19]aspergensque de sanguine digito septies mundabit sanctificabitque illud ab immunditiis filiorum Israel. [20]Et postquam compleverit expiationem sanctuarii et tabernaculi conventus et altaris, tunc afferat hircum viventem; [21]et, posita utraque manu super caput eius, confiteatur Aaron super eum omnes iniquitates filiorum Israel et universa delicta atque peccata eorum; quae ponens super caput eius emittet illum per hominem paratum in desertum. [22]Cumque portaverit hircus super se omnes iniquitates eorum in terram solitariam et dimissus fuerit in desertum, [23]ingredietur Aaron in tabernaculum conventus; et, depositis vestibus lineis, quibus prius indutus erat, cum intraret sanctuarium, relic-

²³"Then Aaron shall come into the tent of meeting, and shall put off the linen garments which he put on when he went into the holy place, and shall leave them there; ²⁴and he shall bathe his body in water in a holy place, and put on his garments, and come forth, and offer his burnt offering and the burnt offering of the people, and make atonement for himself and for the people. ²⁵And the fat of the sin offering he shall burn upon the altar. ²⁶And he who lets the goat go to Azazel shall wash his clothes and bathe his

Heb 13:11 body in water, and afterward he may come into the camp. ²⁷And the bull for the sin offering and the goat for the sin offering, whose blood was brought in to make atonement in the holy place, shall be carried forth outside the camp; their skin and their flesh and their dung shall be burned with fire. ²⁸And he who burns them shall wash his clothes and bathe his body in water, and afterward he may come into the camp.

Acts 27:9   ²⁹"And it shall be a statute to you for ever that in the seventh month, on the tenth day of the month, you shall afflict your-selves, and shall do no work, either the native or the stranger who sojourns among you; ³⁰for on this day shall atonement be made for you, to cleanse you; from all your sins you shall be clean before the LORD. ³¹It is a sabbath of solemn rest to you, and you shall afflict yourselves; it is a statute for ever. ³²And the priest who is anointed and consecrated as priest in his father's place shall make atonement, wearing the holy linen garments; ³³he shall make atonement for the sanctuary, and he shall make atonement for the tent of meeting and for the altar, and he shall make atonement for the priests and for all the people of the

Heb 10:3 assembly. ³⁴And this shall be an everlasting statute for you, that atonement may be made for the people of Israel once in the year because of all their sins." And Moses did as the LORD com-manded him.

---

tisque ibi, ²⁴lavabit carnem suam aqua in loco sancto indueturque vestimentis suis. Et postquam egres-sus obtulerit holocaustum suum ac plebis, expiabit se et populum; ²⁵et adipem sacrificii pro peccato adolebit super altare. ²⁶Ille vero, qui dimiserit caprum emissarium ad Azazel, lavabit vestimenta sua et corpus aqua et postea ingredietur in castra. ²⁷Vitulum autem et hircum, qui pro peccato fuerant immo-lati et quorum sanguis illatus est, ut in sanctuario expiatio compleretur, asportabunt foras castra et com-burent igni tam pelles quam carnes eorum et fimum; ²⁸et quicumque combusserit ea, lavabit vestimenta sua et carnem aqua et postea ingredietur in castra. ²⁹Eritque hoc vobis legitimum sempiternum: mense septimo, decima die mensis affligetis animas vestras nullumque facietis opus sive indigena sive advena, qui peregrinatur inter vos. ³⁰In hac die expiatio erit vestri atque mundatio; ab omnibus peccatis vestris coram Domino mundabimini. ³¹Sabbatum requietionis est vobis, et affligetis animas vestras religione perpetua. ³²Expiabit autem sacerdos, qui unctus fuerit et cuius initiatae manus, ut sacerdotio fungatur pro patre suo; indueturque vestimentis lineis, vestibus sanctis, ³³et expiabit sanctuarium sanc-tissimum et tabernaculum conventus atque altare sacerdotes quoque et universum populum congrega-tionis. ³⁴Eritque hoc vobis legitimum sempiternum, ut expietis filios Israel a cunctis peccatis eorum

PART FOUR

The Law of Holiness*

The place of sacrifice and the eating of blood   Deut 12:4–28

17 ¹*And the LORD said to Moses, ²"Say to Aaron and his sons, and to all the people of Israel, This is the thing which the LORD has commanded. ³If any man of the house of Israel kills an

---

*17:1—26:46. These chapters make up what is usually referred to as the "Law of Holiness" or "Code of Holiness", a very important part of the book of Leviticus. The "Law of Holiness" has marked similarity to the liturgical regulations given in the book of Ezekiel. Although it is not easy for scholarship to prove that it was the case, it seems reasonable to think that when the life of Israel was being reconstructed after the Exile (as described in the book of Ezekiel) the inspiration for that renewal must have come from the legislation assembled in Leviticus.

Throughout the entire Bible, holiness is one of the essential attributes of God; even though Leviticus is not entirely focused on this subject, it does perhaps give it special emphasis (cf. 11:44–45; 19:2; 21:8, 15; 22:32: cf. Is 1:4; 5:19, 24). The main aspects of God's holiness include his transcendence and inaccessibility, which inspire man with religious fear and respect (cf. Exod 19:12; 2 Sam 6:7). Other persons share in that holiness (cf. Ex 19:6), particularly priests (Lev 21:6), and also some times and places (cf. Ex 16:23).

Alongside the idea of holiness we find that of ritual cleanness on account of

its close connexion with divine worship. Thus, the "Law of Holiness" also becomes a "law of cleanness". As Old Testament revelation increased, the holy or sacred becomes separated from the profane insofar as the profane involves distance from God, drawing away from him, something connected with sin, whereas the sacred means drawing closer to God, moral sanctification through ritual purification.

So, the kind of moral obligation envisaged in the chapters on the Law of Holiness puts the emphasis primarily on ritual cleanness in offerings, persons, institutions and (especially) priests; all of this is designed to promote a more interior moral perfection: the Most Holy God must be treated in a holy way.

Through the Incarnation, the Word of God fully assumed a human nature with all its limitations, thereby rising above and transcending the tension between the sacred and the profane. Jesus has interiorized the Law by going right to its root—love for God and love for others. And so St Paul can say, "Whatever you do, in word or deed, do everything in the name of the Lord Jesus, giving thanks to God the Father through him" (Col 3:17);

---

semel in anno». Fecit igitur, sicut praeceperat Dominus Moysi. ¹Et locutus est Dominus ad Moysen dicens: ²«Loquere Aaron et filiis eius et cunctis filiis Israel et dices ad eos: Iste est sermo, quem mandavit Dominus dicens: ³Homo quilibet de domo Israel, si occiderit bovem aut ovem sive capram in cas-

477

Lev 1:5 ox or a lamb or a goat in the camp, or kills it outside the camp, [4]and does not bring it to the door of the tent of meeting, to offer it as a gift to the LORD before the tabernacle of the LORD, bloodguilt shall be imputed to that man; he has shed blood; and that man shall be cut off from among his people. [5]This is to the end that the people of Israel may bring their sacrifices which they slay in the open field, that they may bring them to the LORD, to the priest at the door of the tent of meeting, and slay them as sacrifices of peace offerings to the LORD; [6]and the priest shall sprinkle the blood on the altar of the LORD at the door of the tent of meeting, and burn the fat for a

Lev 16:8 pleasing odor to the LORD. [7]So they shall no more slay their sacri-
Is 13:21; fices for satyrs, after whom they play the harlot. This shall be a
34:12–14
1 Cor 10:20 statute for ever to them throughout their generations.

[8]"And you shall say to them, Any man of the house of Israel, or of the strangers that sojourn among them, who offers a burnt offering or sacrifice, [9]and does not bring it to the door of the tent of meeting, to sacrifice it to the LORD; that man shall be cut off

Gen 9:4 from his people.
1 Sam 14:33ff   [10]"If any man of the house of Israel or of the strangers that
Jn 6:53
Acts 15:13ff sojourn among them eats any blood, I will set my face against that

---

"so, whether you eat or drink, or whatever you do, do all for the glory of God" (1 Cor 10:31).

17:1–9. We can notice here an evolution in the rules about animal sacrifices. In the early period these offerings could be made in any place which in some way or other was connected with God (cf. Ex 20:24). Later, after the conquest of the promised land, all sacrifices had to take place in the sanctuary and on its altar; but an animal could be slaughtered anywhere, provided that it was not being offered as a sacrifice to God (cf. Deut 12:4–28). This passage seems to refer not

to any ordinary immolation of an animal for all to eat, but rather to a sacrifice being specially offered to God. The latter had to take place in the sanctuary, to avoid any possible idolatry cult in honour of the devil-gods of the desert (this seems to be what v. 7 implies). The Hebrew word translated here as "satyr" means literally a "he-goat", but it was also used to refer to the little gods in animal form who were thought to live in the wilderness (cf. Is 34:14). Azazel may have been one of those.

17:10–16. The commandment not to eat blood is a very old one (cf. Gen 9:4).

---

tris vel extra castra [4]et non attulerit ad ostium tabernaculi conventus in oblationem Domino coram habitaculo Domini, sanguinis reus erit; sanguinem fudit et peribit de medio populi sui. [5]Ideo offerre debent sacerdoti filii Israel hostias suas, quas occidunt in agro, ut afferant Domino ante ostium tabernaculi conventus et immolent eas hostias pacificas Domino. [6]Fundetque sacerdos sanguinem super altare Domini ad ostium tabernaculi conventus et adolebit adipem in odorem suavitatis Domino; [7]et nequaquam ultra immolabunt hostias suas daemonibus, cum quibus fornicati sunt: legitimum sempiternum erit hoc illis et posteris eorum». [8]Et ad ipsos dices: «Homo de domo Israel et de advenis, qui

person who eats blood, and will cut him off from among his people. ¹¹For the life of the flesh is in the blood; and I have given it for you upon the altar to make atonement for your souls; for it is the blood that makes atonement, by reason of the life. ¹²Therefore I have said to the people of Israel, No person among you shall eat blood, neither shall any stranger who sojourns among you eat blood. ¹³Any man also of the people of Israel, or of the strangers that sojourn among them, who takes in hunting any beast or bird that may be eaten shall pour out its blood and cover it with dust.

¹⁴"For the life of every creature is the blood of it;ᵉ therefore I have said to the people of Israel, You shall not eat the blood of any creature, for the life of every creature is its blood; whoever eats it shall be cut off. ¹⁵And every person that eats what dies of itself or what is torn by beasts, whether he is a native or a sojourner, shall wash his clothes, and bathe himself in water, and be unclean until the evening; then he shall be clean. ¹⁶But if he does not wash them or bathe his flesh, he shall bear his iniquity."

Heb 9:7–21

Ex 22:30
Deut 14:21
Ezra 4:14

Eating blood was regarded as an offence against God (cf. 1 Sam 14:33ff), because blood was thought to be the source of life (cf. note on Lev 1:5–9) and therefore something belonging to God. Hence also its atonement value: the blood shed by a sacrificed animal took the place of the offerer, who thereby was cleansed of his sin. Also, this commandment helped to keep Jews away from pagan cults in which the blood of an animal was sometimes drunk in the belief that the life of the victim thereby passed into the person who drank the blood.

From the New Testament we learn that the Jews kept up this practice—even Jews who had become Christians. Some Jews, indeed, were scandalized by the fact that Christians of Gentile background did eat blood. To prevent this scandal, which pained some, the council held in Jerusalem prudently laid down the temporary ruling that Christians were to abstain from blood (cf. Acts 15:13ff).

The cleansing quality of blood is recognized in the Letter to the Hebrews, which puts such stress on the redemptive value of Christ's blood: "how much more shall the blood of Christ, who through the eternal Spirit offered himself without blemish to God, purify your conscience from dead works to serve the living God" (Heb 9:14).

peregrinantur apud vos, qui obtulerit holocaustum sive sacrificium ⁹et ad ostium tabernaculi conventus non adduxerit victimam, ut offeratur Domino, interibit de populo suo. ¹⁰Homo quilibet de domo Israel et de advenis, qui peregrinantur inter eos, si comederit sanguinem, confirmabo faciem meam contra talem animam et disperdam eam de populo suo. ¹¹Quia anima carnis in sanguine est, et ego dedi illum vobis, ut super altare in eo expietis pro animabus vestris, quia sanguis ipse per animam expiat. ¹²Idcirco dixi filiis Israel: Omnis anima ex vobis non comedet sanguinem, nec ex advenis, qui peregrinantur inter vos. ¹³Homo quicumque de filiis Israel et de advenis, qui peregrinantur apud vos, si

e. Gk Syr Compare Vg: Heb *for the life of all flesh, its blood is in its life*

Lev 20:8–21 **Rules concerning marriage and chastity**

Ex 23:23–24
Ezra 20:7–8

18 [1]And the LORD said to Moses, [2]"Say to the people of Israel, I am the LORD your God. [3]You shall not do as they do in the land of Egypt, where you dwelt, and you shall not do as they do in the land of Canaan, to which I am bringing you. You shall not walk in their statutes. [4]You shall do my ordinances and keep my

Deut 4:1; 5:29; statutes and walk in them. I am the LORD your God. [5]You shall
6:24; 8:1 therefore keep my statutes and my ordinances, by doing which a
Ezek 20:11
Neh 9:29 man shall live: I am the LORD.
Rom 10:5; [6]"None of you shall approach any one near of kin to him to
2:26; 7:10
Gal 3:12 uncover nakedness. I am the LORD. [7]You shall not uncover the
Lk 10:28 nakedness of your father, which is the nakedness of your mother;
Deut 23:1; she is your mother, you shall not uncover her nakedness. [8]You
27:20 shall not uncover the nakedness of your father's wife; it is your
1 Cor 5:1 father's nakedness. [9]You shall not uncover the nakedness of your sister, the daughter of your father or the daughter of your mother, whether born at home or born abroad. [10]You shall not uncover the nakedness of your son's daughter or of your daughter's daughter, for their nakedness is your own nakedness. [11]You shall not uncover the nakedness of your father's wife's daughter, begotten by your father, since she is your sister. [12]You shall not uncover the nakedness of your father's sister; she is your father's near kinswoman. [13]You shall not uncover the nakedness of your mother's sister, for she is your mother's near kinswoman. [14]You shall not uncover the nakedness of your father's brother, that is, you shall not approach his wife; she is your aunt. [15]You shall not uncover the nakedness of your daughter-in-law; she is your son's wife, you shall not uncover her nakedness. [16]You shall not

venatione ceperit feram vel avem, quibus vesci licitum est, fundat sanguinem eius et operiat illum terra. [14]Anima enim omnis carnis, sanguis est anima eius, unde dixi filiis Israel: Sanguinem universae carnis non comedetis, quia anima omnis carnis sanguis eius est; et, quicumque comederit illum, interibit. [15]Anima, quae comederit morticinum vel captum a bestia, tam de indigenis quam de advenis, lavabit vestes suas et semetipsum aqua, et contaminatus erit usque ad vesperum; et hoc ordine mundus fiet. [16]Quod si non laverit vestimenta sua nec corpus, portabit iniquitatem suam». [1]Locutus est Dominus ad Moysen dicens: [2]«Loquere filiis Israel et dices ad eos: Ego Dominus Deus vester. [3]Iuxta consuetudinem terrae Aegypti, in qua habitastis, non facietis; et iuxta morem regionis Chanaan, ad quam ego introducturus sum vos, non agetis nec in legitimis eorum ambulabitis. [4]Facietis iudicia mea et praecepta mea servabitis et ambulabitis in eis. Ego Dominus Deus vester. [5]Custodite leges meas atque iudicia; quae faciens homo vivet in eis. Ego Dominus. [6]Omnis homo ad consanguineum suum non accedet, ut revelet turpitudinem eius. Ego Dominus. [7]Turpitudinem patris et turpitudinem matris tuae non discooperies: mater tua est, non revelabis turpitudinem eius. [8]Turpitudinem uxoris patris tui non discooperies, turpitudo enim patris tui est. [9]Turpitudinem sororis tuae ex patre sive ex matre, quae domi vel foris genita est, non revelabis. [10]Turpitudinem filiae filii tui vel neptis ex filia non revelabis, quia turpitudo tua est. [11]Turpitudinem filiae uxoris patris tui, quam peperit patri tuo et est soror tua, non revelabis. [12]Turpitudinem sororis patris tui non discooperies, quia caro est patris tui. [13]Turpitudinem sororis matris tuae non revelabis, eo quod caro sit matris tuae. [14]Turpitudinem patrui tui non revelabis nec accedes ad uxorem eius, quae tibi affinitate coniungitur. [15]Turpitudinem nurus tuae non revelabis, quia

uncover the nakedness of your brother's wife; she is your brother's nakedness. [17]You shall not uncover the nakedness of a woman and of her daughter, and you shall not take her son's daughter or her daughter's daughter to uncover her nakedness; they are your near[f] kinswomen; it is wickedness. [18]And you shall not take a woman as a rival wife to her sister, uncovering her nakedness while her sister is yet alive.

[19]"You shall not approach a woman to uncover her nakedness while she is in her menstrual uncleanness. [20]And you shall not lie carnally with your neighbour's wife, and defile yourself with her. [21]You shall not give any of your children to devote them by fire to Molech, and so profane the name of your God: I am the LORD. [22]You shall not lie with a male as with a woman; it is an abomination. [23]And you shall not lie with any beast and defile yourself

Mt 14:4
Mk 6:17f

Ex 20:14
Gen 22:1
Deut 12:31; 18:10
2 Kings 16:3;
21:6; 23:10
Jer 7:31; 19:5
Gen 19:5
Rom 1:27
Ex 22:18

18:21. One case for which Leviticus legislates is the sacrifice of children to Moloch. Archeological diggings at Gezer have revealed traces of such sacrifices. In Jerusalem these sacrifices were held in the valley of Ben-Hinnom (cf. 2 Kings 16:3; 21:6; 23:10; Jer 7:31; 19:5; etc.), later cursed with a permanently burning rubbish dump (called Gehenna), which became a symbol of the literal fires of hell (cf. Mt 5:22; 10:28; Mk 9:42–50; Lk 12:5; etc.).

The Jews needed to be protected from the influence of the peoples on its borders, whose cultures contained much immorality even to the extent of sexual perversions such as sacred prostitution, homosexuality, incest and bestiality. For example, in Egypt it was normal for a pharaoh to marry his own sister; in Greece the laws of Solon permitted the marriage of people who shared the same

father. In spite of the precepts given here, Israel did at times fall into the same abominable behaviour (cf. Gen 19:1–38; Judg 19:22; 2 Sam 13:14; etc.). The early Church always condemned incestuous unions of this kind (cf. 1 Cor 5:1-8). The same holds for cults of the goddess of fertility, Astarte, in which male prostitution also was encouraged. In the time of the Roman empire similar aberrations were in vogue, as St Paul laments in his Letter to the Romans (cf. Rom 1:18ff).

As regards homosexuality, the Church continues to describe it as a sin against nature, even though homosexual orientation is a disorder, not a sin; thus, the Church is openly at odds with the opinions of those who regard homosexual activity as normal; it says that such actions violate the order willed by God (cf. the note on Gen 19:4–5).

---

uxor filii tui est, nec discooperies ignominiam eius. [16]Turpitudinem uxoris fratris tui non revelabis, quia turpitudo fratris tui est. [17]Turpitudinem mulieris et filiae eius non revelabis. Filiam filii eius et filiam filiae illius non sumes, ut reveles ignominiam eius, quia caro illius sunt: nefas est. [18]Sororem uxoris tuae aemulam illius non accipies nec revelabis turpitudinem eius, adhuc illa vivente. [19]Ad mulierem, quae patitur menstrua, non accedes nec revelabis foeditatem eius. [20]Cum uxore proximi tui non coibis nec seminis commixtione maculaberis. [21]De semine tuo non dabis, ut consecretur idolo Moloch, nec pollues nomen Dei tui. Ego Dominus. [22]Cum masculo non commisceberis coitu femineo: abominatio

f. Gk: Heb lacks *your*

with it, neither shall any woman give herself to a beast to lie with it: it is perversion.

²⁴"Do not defile yourselves by any of these things, for by all these the nations I am casting out before you defiled themselves; ²⁵and the land became defiled, so that I punished its iniquity, and the land vomited out its inhabitants. ²⁶But you shall keep my statutes and my ordinances and do none of these abominations, either the native or the stranger who sojourns among you ²⁷(for all of these abominations the men of the land did, who were before you, so that the land became defiled); ²⁸lest the land vomit you out, when you defile it, as it vomited out the nation that was before you. ²⁹For whoever shall do any of these abominations, the persons that do them shall be cut off from among their people. ³⁰So keep my charge never to practise any of these abominable customs which were practised before you, and never to defile yourselves by them: I am the LORD your God."

Acts 15:20 (margin)

Moral and religious duties*

Ex 19:6
Lev 11:44–45;
17:1–20; 16
Mt 5:48
1 Pet 1:16

19 ¹And the LORD said to Moses, ²"Say to all the congregation of the people of Israel, You shall be holy; for I the LORD

---

*19:1–37. The holiness asked of the Israelites is much more than merely ritual holiness. As in 20:26, the exhortation made to them is based on the highest possible reason—the fact that the Lord is holy. The injunction to honour parents, as also the obligation to keep the sabbath and the prohibition on idolatry, are commandments of the Decalogue already spelt out in Exodus 20:3–4, 12; 21:15, 17. The rules about peace offerings were covered in Leviticus 7:11–15, and the rules to protect the weaker members of society are repeated

on a number of occasions (cf. 23:22; Deut 24:19:22).

Verse 2 ("You shall be holy, for I the Lord your God am holy": cf. also 20:26) and v. 18 ("you shall love your neighbour as yourself: I am the Lord": cf. also 19:33–34) sum up the entire ethic of Leviticus and indeed of the whole Law of God. Jesus himself says this, as reported in Matthew 22:34–40 (parallel texts in Mk 12:28–31 and Luke 10:25–28): "When the Pharisees heard that he had silenced the Sadducees, they came together. And one of them, a lawyer, asked him a question,

---

est. ²³Cum omni pecore non coibis nec maculaberis cum eo. Mulier non succumbet iumento nec miscebitur ei, quia scelus est. ²⁴Ne polluamini in omnibus his, quibus contaminatae sunt universae gentes, quas ego eiciam ante conspectum vestrum ²⁵et quibus polluta est terra, cuius ego scelera visitavi, et evomuit habitatores suos. ²⁶Vos autem custodite legitima mea atque iudicia et non faciatis ex omnibus abominationibus istis tam indigena quam colonus, qui peregrinatur apud vos. ²⁷Omnes enim execrationes istas fecerunt accolae terrae, qui fuerunt ante vos, et polluerunt eam. ²⁸Cavete ergo, ne et vos similiter evomat, cum pollueritis eam, sicut evomuit gentem, quae fuit ante vos. ²⁹Omnis enim anima, quae fecerit de abominationibus his quippiam, peribit de medio populi sui. ³⁰Custodite mandata mea. Nolite facere legitima abominabilia, quae fecerunt hi, qui fuerunt ante vos, et ne polluamini in eis. Ego Dominus Deus vester». ¹Locutus est Dominus ad Moysen dicens: ²«Loquere ad omnem coetum filio-

your God am holy. [3]Every one of you shall revere his mother and ~~Ex 20:12~~ Ex 20:12
his father, and you shall keep my sabbaths: I am the LORD your Lev 19:30; 23:3; 26:2
God. [4]Do not turn to idols or make for yourselves molten gods: I Ex 20:4
am the Lord your God.

[5]"When you offer a sacrifice of peace offerings to the LORD,
you shall offer it so that you may be accepted. [6]It shall be eaten
the same day you offer it, or on the morrow; and anything left
over until the third day shall be burned with fire. [7]If it is eaten at
all on the third day, it is an abomination; it will not be accepted,
[8]and every one who eats it shall bear his iniquity, because he has
profaned a holy thing of the LORD; and that person shall be cut off
from his people.

[9]"When you reap the harvest of your land, you shall not reap Lev 23:22
your field to its very border, neither shall you gather the gleanings Deut 24:19–22
after your harvest. [10]And you shall not strip your vineyard bare,
neither shall you gather the fallen grapes of your vineyard; you
shall leave them for the poor and for the sojourner: I am the LORD
your God.

---

to test him. 'Teacher, which is the great
commandment in the law?' And he said to
him, 'You shall love the Lord your God
with all your heart, and with all your soul,
and with all your mind. This is the great
and first commandment. And a second is
like it, You shall love your neighbour as
yourself. On these two commandments
depend all the law and the prophets' " (Mt
22:34–40).

19:11–18. Our Lord refers to the criteria
about perjury in his Sermon on the Mount,
in which he rejects the prevalent abuse of
swearing by holy things such as heaven,
earth or the holy city for no good reason
(cf. Mt 5:33–37). Jesus' teaching on this
point is that all one need do is simply tell

the truth, without any oath to back up
one's words. St James reminds Christians
of that same teaching (cf. Jas 5:12).

The blind and the deaf (v. 14) are to
be respected out of fear of the Lord: any
harm done them he regards as done to
himself.

Fraternal correction is a practice
which Jesus will put on a higher plane
(cf. Mt 18:15f). He does the same for
love of neighbour. For one thing, one's
neighbour is not just members of the
Jewish people or sojourners in Judea: for
Christ everyone we meet is our neighbour, irrespective of his religion or race.
And it is not just a matter of loving
others as oneself, but of loving them as
Christ loved us (cf. Jn 15:12).

---

rum Israel et dices ad eos: Sancti estote, quia sanctus sum ego, Dominus Deus vester. [3]Unusquisque
matrem et patrem suum timeat. Sabbata mea custodite. Ego Dominus Deus vester. [4]Nolite converti ad
idola nec deos conflatiles faciatis vobis. Ego Dominus Deus vester. [5]Si immolaveritis hostiam pacificorum Domino, immolabitis eam ita ut sit vobis placabilis. [6]Eo die, quo fuerit immolata, comedetur et
die altero; quidquid autem residuum fuerit in diem tertium, igne comburetur. [7]Si quid post biduum
comestum fuerit, profanum erit neque acceptabile. [8]Qui manducaverit illud, portabit iniquitatem suam,
quia sanctum Domini polluit, et peribit anima illa de populo suo. [9]Cum messueris segetes terrae tuae,
non tondebis usque ad marginem agri tui nec remanentes spicas colliges. [10]Neque in vinea tua racemos

Ex 20:15
Deut 5:19;
19:16–21;
24:7; 25:13
Ex 20:16
Mt 5:33
Deut 24:14–15
Mt 20:8
Heb 9:10
Jas 5:4
Ex 23:2
Deut 1:17
Acts 23:3
Jas 2:9
Jude 16
Ex 23:1
Lk 10:29
Ezek 33:1–9
Sir 10:6
Mt 18:15ff
Lk 17:3

¹¹"You shall not steal, nor deal falsely, nor lie to one another. ¹²And you shall not swear by my name falsely, and so profane the name of your God: I am the LORD. ¹³"You shall not oppress your neighbor or rob him. The wages of a hired servant shall not remain with you all night until the morning. ¹⁴You shall not curse the deaf or put a stumbling block before the blind, but you shall fear your God: I am the LORD. ¹⁵"You shall do no injustice in judgment; you shall not be partial to the poor or defer to the great, but in righteousness shall you judge your neighbor. ¹⁶You shall not go up and down as a slanderer among your people, and you shall not stand forth against the life^g of your neighbour: I am the LORD. ¹⁷"You shall not hate your brother in your heart, but you shall reason with your neighbour, lest you bear sin because of him. ¹⁸You

---

19:13. The social teaching of the Church, which is part of moral theology and is based on Revelation and on reason enlightened by faith, is summed up on the subject of the just wage by the *Catechism of the Catholic Church*: "A *just wage* is the legitimate fruit of work. To refuse or withhold it can be a grave injustice (cf. Lev 19:13; Deut 24:14–15; Jas 5:4). In determining fair pay both the needs and the contributions of each person must be taken into account. 'Remuneration for work should guarantee man the opportunity to provide a dignified livelihood for himself and his family on the material, social, cultural and spiritual level, taking into account the role and the productivity of each, the state of the business, and the common good' (*Gaudium et spes*, 67). Agreement between the parties is not sufficient to justify morally the amount to be received in wages" (no. 2434).

19:15. "Justice is the moral virtue that consists in the constant and firm will to give their due to God and neighbour. Justice toward God is called the 'virtue of religion'. Justice toward men disposes one to respect the rights of each and to establish in human relationships the harmony that promotes equity with regard to persons and to the common good. The just man, often mentioned in the Sacred Scriptures, is distinguished by habitual right thinking and the uprightness of his conduct toward his neighbour. 'You shall not be partial to the poor or defer to the great, but in righteousness shall you judge your neighbour' (Lev 19:15)" (*Catechism of the Catholic Church*, 1807).

---

et grana decidentia congregabis, sed pauperibus et peregrinis carpenda dimittes. Ego Dominus Deus vester. ¹¹Non facietis furtum. Non mentiemini, nec decipiet unusquisque proximum suum. ¹²Non periurabis in nomine meo nec pollues nomen Dei tui. Ego Dominus. ¹³Non facies calumniam proximo tuo nec spoliabis eum. Non morabitur merces mercennarii apud te usque mane. ¹⁴Non maledices surdo nec coram caeco pones offendiculum; sed timebis Deum tuum. Ego Dominus. ¹⁵Non facietis, quod iniquum est in iudicio. Non consideres personam pauperis nec honores vultum potentis. Iuste iudica proximo tuo. ¹⁶Non eris criminator et susurro in populo tuo. Non stabis contra sanguinem proximi tui. Ego

g. Heb *blood*

484

shall not take vengeance or bear any grudge against the sons of
your own people, but you shall love your neighbour as yourself: I
am the Lord. ¹⁹"You shall keep my statutes. You shall not let your cattle
breed with a different kind; you shall not sow your field with two
kinds of seed; nor shall there come upon you a garment of cloth
made of two kinds of stuff.
²⁰"If a man lies carnally with a woman who is a slave,
betrothed to another man and not yet ransomed or given her freedom, an inquiry shall be held. They shall not be put to death,
because she was not free; ²¹but he shall bring a guilt offering for
himself to the LORD, to the door of the tent of meeting, a ram for a

Rom 12:19
Mt 5:43;
19:19; 22:39
Mk 12:31, 33
Lk 10:27
Rom 12:19;
13:9
Gal 5:14
Jas 2:8
Deut 22:10

19:19–37. The regulations about the mating of animals of different species or about sowing with mixed seed or wearing garments of mixed textiles, seem to have been directed against pagan customs involving belief in magic: hence the prohibition. Also, the rules about abuses against slaves stem from circumstances and customs of the time. Behind all these rules and regulations lies respect for one's neighbour and the need to make atonement to God for offences committed. The criteria given here were designed to prevent the Jews' being affected by the superstitions and magical practices prevalent at the time. Yet despite this we know from the Bible that there are instances of the Jews' having recourse to various kinds of magic, such as summoning up the dead (cf. Deut 18:11; Is 19:3; 1 Sam 28:7), marking one's skin with cuts or tattoos (cf. 1 Kings 18:28; Is 44:5). The reference to making one's daughter a harlot probably has to do with Canaanite fertility rites and the cult of Astarte.

Honouring old people, who deserve respect for their experience (cf. Job 11:12), is a teaching to be found in many passages of the Bible. The book of Proverbs, for example, puts it this way: "A hoary head is a crown of glory" (Prov 16:31).

Regard for foreigners who are working away from home is also often instilled by the Bible (cf. Ex 22:20; Deut 10:19; 24:17); these, along with orphans and widows, were under God's special protection.

In the Gospel we see that Christ has similar concern for the weak and needy, such as children (cf. Mt 9:36; Lk 18:16–17) or sinners, whom society looked down on (cf. Mt 9:11; Lk 7:34), or the poor and infirm (cf. Mt 8:2ff; Lk 5:12–14; etc.). In his encyclical *Solicitudo rei socialis* John Paul II says apropos of the *option* or *love of preference* for the poor: "This is an option, or a *special form* of primacy in the exercise of Christian charity, to which the whole tradition of the Church bears witness' (no. 42).

Dominus. ¹⁷Ne oderis fratrem tuum in corde tuo; argue eum, ne habeas super illo peccatum. ¹⁸Non quaeres ultionem nec irasceris civibus tuis. Diliges proximum tuum sicut teipsum. Ego Dominus. ¹⁹Leges meas custodite. Iumenta tua non facies coire cum alterius generis animantibus. Agrum tuum non saeres diverso semine. Veste, quae ex duobus texta est, non indueris. ²⁰Homo, si dormierit cum muliere coitu seminis, quae sit ancilla destinata viro et tamen pretio non redempta nec libertate donata, vapulabunt ambo et non morientur, quia non fuit libera. ²¹Et in sacrificium suum pro delicto offeret

guilt offering. ²²And the priest shall make atonement for him with the ram of the guilt offering before the LORD for his sin which he has committed; and the sin which he has committed shall be for-

Gen 17:10
Lk 13:7

given him. ²³"When you come into the land and plant all kinds of trees for food, then you shall count their fruit as forbidden;ʰ three years it shall be forbidden to you, it must not be eaten. ²⁴And in the fourth year all their fruit shall be holy, an offering of praise to the LORD. ²⁵But in the fifth year you may eat of their fruit, that they may yield more richly for you: I am the LORD your God.

Lev 1:5

²⁶"You shall not eat any flesh with the blood in it. You shall not practice augury or witchcraft. ²⁷You shall not round off the hair on

Deut 14:1
1 Kings 18:28
Is 44:5

your temples or mar the edges of your beard. ²⁸You shall not make any cuttings in your flesh on account of the dead or tattoo any marks upon you: I am the LORD.

²⁹"Do not profane your daughter by making her a harlot, lest the land fall into harlotry and the land become full of wickedness.

Ex 20:8

³⁰You shall keep my sabbaths and reverence my sanctuary: I am the LORD.

Lev 19:26
Deut 18:10
1 Sam 28:7

³¹"Do not turn to mediums or wizards; do not seek them out, to be defiled by them: I am the LORD your God.

Job 11:12
Prov 16:31

³²"You shall rise up before the hoary head, and honour the face of an old man, and you shall fear your God: I am the LORD.

Ex 22:20
Deut 10:19;
24:19–22
Lk 10:29
Mt 4:44; 22:29

³³"When a stranger sojourns with you in your land, you shall not do him wrong. ³⁴The stranger who sojourns with you shall be to you as the native among you, and you shall love him as yourself; for you were strangers in the land of Egypt: I am the LORD your God.

Deut 25:13–16

³⁵"You shall do no wrong in judgment, in measures of length or weight or quantity. ³⁶You shall have just balances, just weights, a just ephah, and a just hin: I am the LORD your God, who brought you out of the land of Egypt. ³⁷And you shall observe all my statutes and all my ordinances, and do them: I am the LORD."

Domino ad ostium tabernaculi conventus arietem; ²²expiabitque eum sacerdos ariete a peccato eius coram Domino, et dimittetur ei peccatum, quod peccavit. ²³Quando ingressi fueritis terram et plantaveritis omnimoda ligna pomifera, non auferetis praeputia eorum, id est poma, quae germinant; tribus annis erunt vobis immunda ut praeputia, nec edetis ex eis. ²⁴Quarto anno omnis fructus eorum sanctificabitur laudabilis Domino. ²⁵Quinto autem anno comedetis fructus eorum, ut augeatur vobis proventus eorum. Ego Dominus Deus vester. ²⁶Non comedetis cum sanguine. Non augurabimini nec observabitis omina. ²⁷Neque in rotundum attondebitis marginem comae nec truncabis barbam. ²⁸Et super mortuo non incidetis carnem vestram neque figuras aliquas in cute incidetis vobis. Ego Dominus. ²⁹Ne polluas et prostituas filiam tuam, ne contaminetur terra et impleatur piaculo. ³⁰Sabbata mea custodite et sanctuarium meum metuite. Ego Dominus. ³¹Non declinetis ad pythones nec ab hariolis aliquid sciscitemini, ut polluamini per eos. Ego Dominus Deus vester. ³²Coram cano capite consurge et honora personam senis; et time Deum tuum. Ego Dominus. ³³Si habitaverit tecum advena in terra

h. Heb *their uncircumcision*

Penalties for offences against true worship

20 ¹The LORD said to Moses, ²"Say to the people of Israel, Any man of the people of Israel, or of the strangers that sojourn in Israel, who gives any of his children to Molech shall be put to death; the people of the land shall stone him with stones. ³I myself will set my face against that man, and will cut him off from among his people, because he has given one of his children to Molech, defiling my sanctuary and profaning my holy name. ⁴And if the people of the land do at all hide their eyes from that man, when he gives one of his children to Molech, and do not put him to death, ⁵then I will set my face against that man and against his family, and will cut them off from among their people, him and all who follow him in playing the harlot after Molech.

⁶"If a person turns to mediums and wizards, playing the harlot after them, I will set my face against that person, and will cut him off from among his people. ⁷Consecrate yourselves therefore, and be holy; for I am the LORD your God. ⁸Keep my statutes, and do them; I am the LORD who sanctify you.

Lev 18:21

Ex 34:15–16
Deut 31:16
1 Kings 11:7

Ex 22:17
Lev 19:31

Lev 11:44ff;
17:1
1 Pet 1:16

20:1–6. The text refers first to the idolatrous cult of Moloch (cf. 18:21). Here, as in other passages, idolatry is seen as a form of prostitution (cf. 17:7; Hos 1:2; 4:12–14; etc.), partly because the ceremonies involved sexual acts (as, for example, in the case of "sacred prostitution") and also because the love of God is seen as a spousal love and therefore to reject it and adore other gods amounted to a form of adultery (cf. Hos 2:4–15; 3:1; Deut 13:1–19). The punishment extended to the family of the sinner because acts of this type were regarded as tainting close relatives. In later times more emphasis will be put on personal responsibility for sin and its consequences, so the punishment will apply only to the true culprit (cf. Ezek 18). Calling up the spirits of the dead also implied disrespect for God.

20:7–21. Because the Lord is the Holy One, everything to do with the chosen people should also be holy. Holiness lies in keeping his commandments (v. 8). The

---

vestra, non opprimetis eum; ³⁴sed sit inter vos quasi indigena, et diliges eum sicut teipsum: fuistis enim et vos advenae in terra Aegypti. Ego Dominus Deus vester. ³⁵Nolite facere iniquum aliquid in iudicio, in regula, in pondere, in mensura. ³⁶Statera iusta, aequa pondera, iustum ephi aequumque hin sint vobis. Ego Dominus Deus vester, qui eduxi vos de terra Aegypti. ³⁷Custodite omnia praecepta mea et universa iudicia et facite ea. Ego Dominus». ¹Locutusque est Dominus ad Moysen dicens: ²«Haec loqueris filiis Israel: Homo de filiis Israel et de advenis, qui habitant in Israel, si dederit de semine suo idolo Moloch, morte moriatur: populus terrae lapidabit eum. ³Et ego ponam faciem meam contra illum; succidamque eum de medio populi sui, eo quod dederit de semine suo Moloch et contaminaverit sanctuarium meum ac polluerit nomen sanctum meum. ⁴Quod si clauserit populus terrae oculos suos, ne videat hominem illum, qui dederit de semine suo Moloch, nec voluerit eum occidere, ⁵ponam ego faciem meam super hominem illum et cognationem eius succidamque et ipsum et omnes, qui consenserunt ei, ut fornicarentur cum Moloch, de medio populi sui. ⁶Anima, quae declinaverit ad pythones et hariolos et fornicata fuerit cum eis, ponam faciem meam contra eam et interficiam illam de medio populi sui.

Lev 18 **Penalties for moral faults**

Ex 21:17
Deut 27:16 ⁹For every one who curses his father or his mother shall be put to
Prov 19:26 death; he has cursed his father or his mother, his blood is upon
Sir 3:11 him.
Mt 15:4
Mk 7:10 ¹⁰"If a man commits adultery with the wife ofⁱ his neighbor, both
Ex 20:14 the adulterer and the adulteress shall be put to death. ¹¹The man who
Deut 5:18; 22:20
Jn 8:5 lies with his father's wife has uncovered his father's nakedness; both
of them shall be put to death, their blood is upon them. ¹²If a man
lies with his daughter-in-law, both of them shall be put to death;
Gen 19:5 they have committed incest, their blood is upon them. ¹³If a man lies
Rom 1:27 with a male as with a woman, both of them have committed an
abomination; they shall be put to death, their blood is upon them.
¹⁴If a man takes a wife and her mother also, it is wickedness; they
shall be burned with fire, both he and they, that there may be no
wickedness among you. ¹⁵If a man lies with a beast, he shall be put

---

lifestyle, the morality, of the people of God must be on a higher plane than that of other peoples. Jesus says the same thing, but more clearly and directly: if we love him we will keep his commandments (cf. Jn 14:15). Therefore, someone who keeps his commandments abides in his love, just as Christ keeps the Father's commands and abides in his love (cf. Jn 15:10).

Love for one's parents is stressed (cf. Ex 21:17; Deut 27:16; Sir 3:11–16; Prov 19:26; etc.). Jesus will quote this passage to remind people of the importance of the precept, against some Pharisees who had distorted its application by bringing in new rules (cf. Mt 15:4–7).

In many passages of the Bible "neighbour" (v. 10) means a person who belongs to the people of Israel.

John the Baptist used the rule of v. 21 to accuse Herod Antipas, telling him in no uncertain terms that it was unlawful for him to marry his brother's wife (cf. Mt 14:4; Mk 6:18).

The penalties imposed for these various offences today seems to be disproportionate and draconian. However, that is not the case if they are set beside other laws and customs of the period: the Code of Hammurabi, for example, imposes heavier penalties. We also need to bear in mind that these penalties were designed to act as a severe deterrent (ancient peoples went in for that style of law).

To be childless (vv. 20–21) was regarded as a punishment, because fertility was esteemed as a gift from God (cf. Ps 127).

---

⁷Sanctificamini et estote sancti, quia ego Dominus Deus vester. ⁸Custodite praecepta mea et facite ea. Ego Dominus, qui sanctifico vos. ⁹Qui maledixerit patri suo et matri, morte moriatur; qui patri matrique maledixit, sanguis eius sit super eum. ¹⁰Si moechatus quis fuerit cum uxore alterius et adulterium perpetrarit cum coniuge proximi sui, morte moriantur et moechus et adultera. ¹¹Qui dormierit cum noverca sua et revelaverit ignominiam patris sui, morte moriantur ambo: sanguis eorum sit super eos. ¹²Si quis dormierit cum nuru sua, uterque moriatur, quia scelus operati sunt: sanguis eorum sit super eos. ¹³Qui dormierit cum masculo coitu femineo, uterque operatus est nefas, morte moriantur: sit sanguis eorum super eos. ¹⁴Qui supra uxorem filiam duxerit matrem eius, scelus operatus est: vivus ardebit cum eis,

---

i. Heb repeats *if a man commits adultery with the wife of*

to death; and you shall kill the beast. [16]If a woman approaches any beast and lies with it, you shall kill the woman and the beast; they shall be put to death, their blood is upon them.

[17]"If a man takes his sister, a daughter of his father or a daughter of his mother, and sees her nakedness, and she sees his nakedness, it is a shameful thing, and they shall be cut off in the sight of the children of their people; he has uncovered his sister's nakedness, he shall bear his iniquity. [18]If a man lies with a woman having her sickness, and uncovers her nakedness, he has made naked her fountain, and she has uncovered the fountain of her blood; both of them shall be cut off from among their people. [19]You shall not uncover the nakedness of your mother's sister or of your father's sister, for that is to make naked one's near kin; they shall bear their iniquity. [20]If a man lies with his uncle's wife, he has uncovered his uncle's nakedness; they shall bear their sin, they shall die childless. [21]If a man takes his brother's wife, it is impurity; he has uncovered his brother's nakedness, they shall be childless.

Ex 3:8
Mt 14:4
Mk 6:18

An exhortation to holiness

[22]"You shall therefore keep all my statutes and all my ordinances, and do them; that the land where I am bringing you to dwell may not vomit you out. [23]And you shall not walk in the customs of the nation which I am casting out before you; for they did all these things, and therefore I abhorred them. [24]But I have said to you, 'You shall inherit their land, and I will give it to you to possess, a land flowing with milk and honey.' I am the LORD your God, who have separated you from the peoples. [25]You shall therefore make a distinction between the clean beast and the unclean, and between the unclean bird and the clean; you shall not make yourselves abominable by beast or by bird or by anything with which

nec permanebit tantum nefas in medio vestri. [15]Qui cum iumento et pecore coierit, morte moriatur; pecus quoque occidite. [16]Mulier, quae succubuerit cuilibet iumento, simul interficies illam cum eo, morte moriantur: sanguis eorum sit super eos. [17]Qui acceperit sororem suam filiam patris sui vel filiam matris suae et viderit turpitudinem eius, illaque conspexerit fratris ignominiam, nefaria res est; occidentur in conspectu populi sui, eo quod turpitudinem sororis suae revelaverit, portabit iniquitatem suam. [18]Qui coierit cum muliere in fluxu menstruo et revelaverit turpitudinem eius—fontem eius nudavit, ipsaque aperuit fontem sanguinis sui—interficientur ambo de medio populi sui. [19]Turpitudinem materterae et amitae tuae non discooperies; qui hoc fecerit ignominiam carnis suae nudavit; portabunt ambo iniquitatem suam. [20]Qui coierit cum uxore patrui vel avunculi sui et revelaverit ignominiam cognationis suae, portabunt ambo peccatum suum: absque liberis morientur. [21]Qui duxerit uxorem fratris sui, immunditia est, turpitudinem fratris sui revelavit: absque liberis erunt. [22]Custodite omnes leges meas atque omnia iudicia et facite ea, ne et vos evomat terra, quam intraturi estis et habitaturi. [23]Nolite ambulare in legitimis nationum, quas ego expulsurus sum ante vos. Omnia enim haec fecerunt, et abominatus sum eas [24]locutusque sum vobis: Vos possidebitis terram eorum et ego dabo eam vobis in hereditatem, terram fluentem lacte et melle. Ego Dominus Deus vester, qui se-

Lev 11:44ff;
17:1
1 Pet:1:16 the ground teems, which I have set apart for you to hold unclean. ²⁶You shall be holy to me; for I the LORD am holy, and have separated you from the peoples, that you should be mine.

Ex 22:17 ²⁷"A man or a woman who is a medium or a wizard shall be put to death; they shall be stoned with stones, their blood shall be upon them."

The holiness of priests*

Num 19:11 **21** ¹And the LORD said to Moses, "Speak to the priests, the sons of Aaron, and say to them that none of them shall defile himself for the dead among his people, ²except for his nearest of kin, his mother, his father, his son, his daughter, his brother, ³or his virgin sister (who is near to him because she has had no

---

20:26. This verse, like 19:2, which we have already commented on, sums up the whole Law. St Cyprian of Carthage, writing from a Christian theological perspective, comments on this passage as follows: " 'Be holy because I am holy': we pray that, sanctified by Baptism, we persevere in what we have begun to be. And we pray for this every day because every day we commit faults and we should be cleansed of our sins by constant sanctification. [. . .] We have recourse to prayer, therefore, to ensure that this holiness stay in us" (*De oratione dominica*, 12).

*21:1—22:33. Within the Law of Holiness, chapters 21–22 deal with the holiness of priests (chap. 21) and with that of offerings (chap. 22). Once again we can see that the closer a person is to God, the greater the requirement of cleanness and holiness. And more is demanded of the high priest than of other priests.

The high priest was not allowed to perform his ministry if he was in mourning; he could not even be involved in the burial of his father or mother. The reference to hair being ungroomed and clothes rent has to do with burial rites; similarly, when it says that he shall stay in the sanctuary that means that he is not to get involved in funeral ceremonies. As regards marriage, he must choose a virgin—which shows that even in the Old Testament virginity was held in high regard. There is in some sense a recognition that virginity has a sacredness about it, a prelude to being "like angels in heaven" which Jesus speaks about in the Gospel (cf. Mt 19:12 and 22:30).

Finally, there are rules which denote respect and concern for divine worship: its dignity and decorum called for, as they still do, special dispositions in ministers—even in their demeanour. The rules about physical defects do not imply disrespect for people with physi-

---

paravi vos a ceteris populis. ²⁵Separate ergo et vos iumentum mundum ab immundo et avem immundam a munda, ne polluatis animas vestras in pecore et in avibus et cunctis, quae moventur in terra, et quae vobis separavi tamquam immunda. ²⁶Eritis mihi sancti, quia sanctus sum ego Dominus et separavi vos a ceteris populis, ut essetis mei. ²⁷Vir sive mulier, in quibus pythonicus vel divinationis fuerit spiritus, morte moriantur; lapidibus obruent eos: sanguis eorum sit super illos». ¹Dixit quoque Dominus ad Moysen: «Loquere ad sacerdotes filios Aaron et dices eis: Ne contaminetur sacerdos in mortibus civium suorum, ²nisi tantum in consanguineis propinquis, id est super matre et patre et filio

husband; for her he may defile himself). ⁴He shall not defile himself as a husband among his people and so profane himself. ⁵They shall not make tonsures upon their heads, nor shave off the edges of their beards, nor make any cuttings in their flesh. ⁶They shall be holy to their God, and not profane the name of their God; for they offer the offerings by fire to the LORD, the bread of their God; therefore they shall be holy. ⁷They shall not marry a harlot or a woman who has been defiled; neither shall they marry a woman divorced from her husband; for the priest is holy to his God. ⁸You shall consecrate him, for he offers the bread of your God; he shall be holy to you; for I the LORD, who sanctify you, am holy. ⁹And the daughter of any priest, if she profanes herself by playing the harlot, profanes her father; she shall be burned with fire.

Lev 1:9

Lev 11:44;17:1

The holiness of the high priest
¹⁰"The priest who is chief among his brethren, upon whose head the anointing oil is poured, and who has been consecrated to wear the garments, shall not let the hair of his head hang loose, nor rend his clothes; ¹¹he shall not go in to any dead body, nor defile himself, even for his father or for his mother; ¹²neither shall he go out of the sanctuary, nor profane the sanctuary of his God; for the consecration of the anointing oil of his God is upon him: I am the LORD. ¹³And he shall take a wife in her virginity. ¹⁴A widow, or one divorced, or a woman who has been defiled, or a harlot, these he shall not marry; but he shall take to wife a virgin of his own

Lev 8:7–12
Mt 26:65

cal disability; they aim, rather, to offer the very best to God, in all senses. Sons of Levi who did have a physical defect were held in high esteem, as can be seen from the fact that they enjoyed the same benefits and advantages as their brethren.

21:4. "As a husband": it is not easy to work out what is meant. The Hebrew text differs from the Greek and Latin versions. Anyway, the point being made is that the high priest has a special position, and extreme ritual cleanness is demanded of him.

ac filia, fratre quoque ³et sorore virgine propinqua, quae non est nupta viro; in ipsa contaminabitur. ⁴Non contaminabitur ut maritus in cognatis suis, ne profanetur. ⁵Non radent caput nec barbam, neque in carne sua facient incisuras. ⁶Sancti erunt Deo suo et non polluent nomen eius: incensa enim Domini et panem Dei sui offerunt et ideo sancti erunt. ⁷Scortum et oppressam non ducent uxorem, nec eam, quae repudiata est a marito, quia consecratus est Deo suo. ⁸Et sanctificabis eum, quia panem Dei sui offert. Sit ergo sanctus tibi, quia ego sanctus sum, Dominus, qui sanctifico vos. ⁹Sacerdotis filia, si profanaverit se stupro, profanat nomen patris sui; flammis exuretur. ¹⁰Sacerdos maximus inter fratres suos, super cuius caput fusum est unctionis oleum et cuius manus in sacerdotio consecratae sunt vestitusque est sanctis vestibus, comam suam non excutiet, vestimenta non scindet ¹¹et ad omnem mortuum non ingredietur omnino; super patre quoque suo et matre non contaminabitur. ¹²Nec egredietur de sanctuario, ne polluat sanctuarium Domini, quia consecratus est oleo unctionis Dei sui. Ego Dominus. ¹³Virginem ducet uxorem; ¹⁴viduam et repudiatam et oppressam atque meretricem non accipiet, sed vir-

people, [15]that he may not profane his children among his people; for I am the Lord who sanctify him."

Impediments to the priesthood

[16]And the Lord said to Moses, [17]"Say to Aaron, None of your descendants throughout their generations who has a blemish may approach to offer the bread of his God. [18]For no one who has a blemish shall draw near, a man blind or lame, or one who has a mutilated face or a limb too long, [19]or a man who has an injured foot or an injured hand, [20]or a hunchback, or a dwarf, or a man with a defect in his sight or an itching disease or scabs or crushed testicles; [21]no man of the descendants of Aaron the priest who has a blemish shall come near to offer the Lord's offerings by fire; since he has a blemish, he shall not come near to offer the bread of his God. [22]He may eat the bread of his God, both of the most holy and of the holy things, [23]but he shall not come near the veil or approach the altar, because he has a blemish, that he may not profane my sanctuaries; for I am the Lord who sanctify them." [24]So Moses spoke to Aaron and to his sons and to all the people of Israel.

Priests partaking of the sacred meal

22 [1]And the Lord said to Moses, [2]"Tell Aaron and his sons to keep away from the holy things of the people of Israel, which they dedicate to me, so that they may not profane my holy name; I am the Lord. [3]Say to them, 'If any one of all your des-

---

22:1–16. The sacred nature of the offerings entailed the holiness and purity of those who ate them, whether they were priests or lay people. In the case of priests there is first a general precept and then the text moves on to particular cases (these came up earlier: cf. 13:1ff; 15:2, 16, 18; 21:16–23). As regards lay people, even if they were guests of priests they were not to eat food which was offered in sacrifices.

ginem de cognatis suis ducet uxorem. [15]Ne profanet stirpem suam inter cognatos suos, quia ego Dominus, qui sanctifico eum». [16]Locutusque est Dominus ad Moysen dicens: [17]«Loquere ad Aaron: Homo de semine tuo in generationibus suis, qui habuerit maculam, non accedet, ut offerat panem Dei sui; [18]quia quicumque habuerit maculam, non accedet: si caecus fuerit vel claudus, si mutilo naso vel deformis, [19]si fracto pede vel manu, [20]si gibbus, si pusillus, si albuginem habens in oculo, si iugem scabiem, si impetiginem in corpore vel contritos testiculos. [21]Omnis, qui habuerit maculam de semine Aaron sacerdotis, non accedet offerre incensa Domini nec panem Dei sui. [22]Vescetur tamen pane Dei sui de sanctissimis et de sanctis. [23]Sed ad velum non ingrediatur, nec accedat ad altare, quia maculam habet et contaminare non debet sanctuaria mea, quia ego Dominus, qui sanctifico ea». [24]Locutus est ergo Moyses ad Aaron et filios eius et ad omnem Israel. [1]Locutus quoque est Dominus ad Moysen dicens: [2]«Loquere ad Aaron et ad filios eius, ut caveant ab his, quae ipsi offerunt mihi. Ego Dominus. [3]Dic ad eos pro posteris vestris: omnis homo, qui accesserit de omni stirpe vestra ad sancta, quae consecraverunt filii Israel

cendants throughout your generations approaches the holy things, which the people of Israel dedicate to the LORD, while he has an uncleanness, that person shall be cut off from my presence: I am the LORD. ⁴None of the line of Aaron who is a leper or suffers a Lev 15:2, 16, discharge may eat of the holy things until he is clean. Whoever 18 touches anything that is unclean through contact with the dead or a man who has had an emission of semen, ⁵and whoever touches a creeping thing by which he may be made unclean or a man from whom he may take uncleanness, whatever his uncleanness may be—⁶the person who touches any such shall be unclean until the evening and shall not eat of the holy things unless he has bathed his body in water. ⁷When the sun is down he shall be clean; and afterward he may eat of the holy things, because such are his food. ⁸That which dies of itself or is torn by beasts he shall not eat, defiling himself by it: I am the LORD.' ⁹They shall therefore keep my charge, lest they bear sin for it and die thereby when they profane it: I am the LORD who sanctify them.

Others partaking of the sacred meal

¹⁰"An outsider shall not eat of a holy thing. A sojourner of the Mt 7:6 priest's or a hired servant shall not eat of a holy thing; ¹¹but if a priest buys a slave as his property for money, the slave may eat of it; and those that are born in his house may eat of his food. ¹²If a priest's daughter is married to an outsider she shall not eat of the offering of the holy things. ¹³But if a priest's daughter is a widow or divorced, and has no child, and returns to her father's house, as in her youth, she may eat of her father's food; yet no outsider shall eat of it. ¹⁴And if a man eats of a holy thing unwittingly, he shall add the fifth of its value to it, and give the holy thing to the priest. ¹⁵The priests shall not profane the holy things of the people of Israel, which they offer to the LORD, ¹⁶and so cause them to

---

Domino, in immunditia sua, peribit coram me. Ego Dominus. ⁴Homo de semine Aaron, qui fuerit leprosus aut patiens fluxum, non vescetur de his, quae sanctificata sunt, donec sanetur. Qui tetigerit omne, quod immundum est ex mortuo, vel vir, ex quo egreditur semen, ⁵et qui tangit reptile, quo polluitur, vel hominem, quo polluitur qualibet immunditia illius, ⁶immundus erit usque ad vesperum et non vescetur his, quae sanctificata sunt; sed cum laverit carnem suam aqua ⁷et occubuerit sol, tunc mundatus vescetur de sanctificatis, quia cibus illius est. ⁸Morticinum et dilaceratum a bestia non comedent, nec polluentur in eis. Ego Dominus. ⁹Custodient praeceptum meum, ut non habeant super illo peccatum et propterea moriantur, cum polluerint illud; ego Dominus qui sanctifico eos. ¹⁰Omnis alienigena non comedet de sanctificatis, inquilinus sacerdotis et mercennarius non vescentur ex eis. ¹¹Quem autem sacerdos emerit et qui vernaculus domus eius fuerit, hi comedent ex eis. ¹²Si filia sacerdotis cuilibet ex populo nupta fuerit, de muneribus, quae sanctificata sunt, non vescetur; ¹³sin autem vidua vel repudiata et absque liberis reversa fuerit ad domum patris sui, sicut puella consueverat, aletur cibo patris sui. Omnis alienigena comedendi ex eo non habet potestatem. ¹⁴Qui comederit de sanctificatis per ignorantiam, addet quintam partem cum eo, quod comedit, et dabit sacerdoti sanctificatum. ¹⁵Nec contami-

bear iniquity and guilt, by eating their holy things: for I am the LORD who sanctify them."

Victims to be unblemished

[17]And the LORD said to Moses, [18]"Say to Aaron and his sons and all the people of Israel, When any one of the house of Israel or of the sojourners in Israel presents his offering, whether in payment of a vow or as a freewill offering which is offered to the LORD as a burnt offering, [19]to be accepted you shall offer a male without blemish, of the bulls or the sheep or the goats. [20]You shall not offer anything that has a blemish, for it will not be acceptable for you. [21]And when any one offers a sacrifice of peace offerings to the LORD, to fulfil a vow or as a freewill offering, from the herd or from the flock, to be accepted it must be perfect; there shall be no blemish in it. [22]Animals blind or disabled or mutilated or having a discharge or an itch or scabs, you shall not offer to the LORD or make of them an offering by fire upon the altar to the LORD. [23]A bull or a lamb which has a part too long or too short you may present for a freewill offering; but for a votive offering it cannot be accepted. [24]Any animal which has its testicles bruised or crushed or torn or cut, you shall not offer to the LORD or sacrifice within your land; [25]neither shall

Deut 17:1

22:17–28. The rule about the age of the animal offered suggests that anything that could not be used as food could not be sacrificed to God either. The rule about not killing the mother and her offspring on the same day seems to be designed to avoid certain idolatrous practices, though some have interpreted it as indicating a kind of respect and compassion towards the animal being sacrificed.

The requirement that victims should be unblemished reminds the Christian of his duty to offer the Lord the "spiritual sacrifice" (cf. 1 Pet 2:5) of work done with human and supernatural perfection. "It is no good offering to God something that is less perfect than our poor human limitations permit. The work that we offer must be without blemish and it must be done as carefully as possible, even in its smallest details, for God will not accept shoddy workmanship. 'You shall not offer anything that has a blemish,' Holy Scripture warns us, 'for it will

---

nabunt sanctificata filiorum Israel, quae tamquam munus offerunt Domino, [16]ne inducant super eos iniquitatem delicti, cum illi sanctificata sua comederint. Ego Dominus, qui sanctifico». [17]Locutus est Dominus ad Moysen dicens: [18]«Loquere ad Aaron et filios eius et ad omnes filios Israel dicesque ad eos: Homo de domo Israel et de advenis, qui habitant apud vos, qui obtulerit oblationem suam vel vota solvens vel sponte offerens, quidquid illud obtulerit in holocaustum Domino, [19]in beneplacitum pro vobis offeratur masculus immaculatus ex bobus et ex ovibus et ex capris; [20]si maculam habuerit, non offeretis, quia non erit vobis acceptabile. [21]Homo, qui obtulerit victimam pacificorum Domino, vel vota solvens vel sponte offerens tam de bobus quam de ovibus immaculatum offeret, ut acceptabile sit; omnis macula non erit in eo. [22]Si caecum fuerit, si fractum, si mutilum, si verrucam habens aut scabiem vel impetiginem, non offeretis ea Domino, nec in incensum dabitis ex eis super altare Domino. [23]Bovem et ovem deformem et debilem voluntarie offerre potes; votum autem ex his solvi non potest.

you offer as the bread of your God any such animals gotten from a foreigner. Since there is a blemish in them, because of their mutilation, they will not be accepted for you."

²⁶And the LORD said to Moses, ²⁷"When a bull or sheep or goat is born, it shall remain seven days with its mother; and from the eighth day on it shall be acceptable as an offering by fire to the LORD. ²⁸And whether the mother is a cow or a ewe, you shall not kill both her and her young in one day. ²⁹And when you sacrifice a sacrifice of thanksgiving to the LORD, you shall sacrifice it so that you may be accepted. ³⁰It shall be eaten on the same day, you shall leave none of it until morning: I am the LORD.

Exhortation to obedience

³¹"So you shall keep my commandments and do them: I am the LORD. ³²And you shall not profane my holy name, but I will be hallowed among the people of Israel; I am the LORD who sanctify you, ³³who brought you out of the land of Egypt to be your God: I am the LORD."

Celebration of the sabbath

23 ¹The LORD said to Moses, ²"Say to the people of Israel, The appointed feasts of the LORD which you shall proclaim as holy convocations, my appointed feasts, are these. ³Six

Ex 20:8–11; 23:12; 34:21
Num 28:1–31

---

not be acceptable for you' (Lev 22:20). For that reason, the work of each one of us, the activities that take up our time and energy, must be an offering worthy of our Creator. It must be *operatio Dei*, a work of God that is done *for* God: in short, a task that is complete and faultless" (St Josemaría Escrivá, *Friends of God*, 55).

23:1–4. Some of the feasts mentioned in this calendar are also to be found in other

books (cf. Ex 23:14–19; 34:18–26; Deut 16:1). It deals first with the sabbath, which becomes the paradigm for all the other feasts, especially as far as rest is concerned. Such importance was given to what could or could not be done on the sabbath that all sorts of absurd and formalistic exaggerations developed. More than once Jesus criticized the severe interpretations devised by the scribes—a complicated and intolerable casuistry (cf. Mt 15:1–9; 23:4l; Acts 15:10).

²⁴Omne animal, quod vel contritis vel tusis vel sectis ablatisque testiculis est, non offeretis Domino, et in terra vestra hoc omnino ne faciatis. ²⁵De manu alienigenae non offeretis cibum Dei vestri ex omnibus his animalibus, quia corrupta et maculata sunt omnia; non erunt in beneplacitum pro vobis». ²⁶Locutusque est Dominus ad Moysen dicens: ²⁷«Bos, ovis et capra, cum genita fuerint, septem diebus erunt sub ubere matris suae; die autem octavo et deinceps erunt acceptabile munus incensi Domino. ²⁸Sive illa bos sive ovis non immolabuntur una die cum fetibus suis. ²⁹Si sacrificaveritis hostiam pro gratiarum actione Domino, sacrificabitis, ut possit esse placabilis. ³⁰Eodem die comedetis eam; non remanebit quidquam in mane alterius diei. Ego Dominus. ³¹Custodite mandata mea et facite ea. Ego Dominus. ³²Ne polluatis nomen meum sanctum, ut sanctificer in medio filiorum Israel. Ego Dominus,

days shall work be done; but on the seventh day is a sabbath of solemn rest, a holy convocation; you shall do no work; it is a sabbath to the LORD in all your dwellings.

[4]"These are the appointed feasts of the LORD, the holy convocations, which you shall proclaim at the time appointed for them.

Ex 12:1–14, 21–28; 13:3–10; 23:15; 34:18 Num 28:16–25 Deut 16:1ff

Celebration of the Passover and the feast of the unleavened bread
[5]In the first month, on the fourteenth day of the month in the evening,[j] is the LORD'S passover. [6]And on the fifteenth day of the same month is the feast of unleavened bread to the LORD; seven days you shall eat unleavened bread. [7]On the first day you shall

Lk 23:58

have a holy convocation; you shall do no laborious work. [8]But you shall present an offering by fire to the LORD seven days; on the seventh day is a holy convocation; you shall do no laborious work."

Celebration of the first fruits
[9]And the LORD said to Moses, [10]"Say to the people of Israel, When you come into the land which I give you and reap its harvest, you

---

23:5–8. The Passover is also dealt with in Exodus 12:1–14, 21–28 and 13:3–10. The first month was called Nisan; earlier on it was called Abib, "spring" or "ears (of grain)". The feast began at sundown. Here it is depicted as a preparation for the feast of the unleavened bread, which began the following day, 15 Nisan, and lasted seven days, during which bread was eaten unleavened. The religious assembly took place on the first day and the last. During these assemblies various sacrifices were offered and a sacred meal took place. We recall that it was during this feast that Jesus instituted the

Eucharist, doing so in the context of the Passover supper. And it was during the Passover that Jesus was sacrificed on the altar of the cross. St John tells us that the sacrifice of Christ began at the sixth hour on the day of Preparation, the exact time that the passover lambs were sacrificed. This makes the beginning of a new Passover, in which a new victim is sacrificed, the Lamb of God who takes away the sin of the world (cf. Jn 1:29, 36; 19:14).

23:9–14. The feast of the first fruits, although the date is not a fixed one, is

---

qui sanctifico vos [33]et eduxi de terra Aegypti, ut essem vobis in Deum. Ego Dominus». [1]Locutus est Dominus ad Moysen dicens: [2]«Loquere filiis Israel et dices ad eos: Hae sunt feriae Domini, quas vocabitis conventus sanctos; hae sunt feriae meae. [3]Sex diebus facietis opus; dies septimus sabbatum requiei est, conventus sanctus; omne opus non facietis; sabbatum est Domino in cunctis habitationibus vestris. [4]Hae sunt ergo feriae Domini, conventus sancti, quas celebrare debetis temporibus suis. [5]Mense primo, quarta decima die mensis ad vesperum Pascha Domini est. [6]Et quinta decima die mensis huius sollemnitas Azymorum Domini est. Septem diebus azyma comedetis. [7]Die primo erit vobis conventus sanctus; omne opus servile non facietis in eo, [8]sed offeretis incensum Domino septem diebus. Die

j. Heb *between the two evenings*

shall bring the sheaf of the first fruits of your harvest to the priest; [11]and he shall wave the sheaf before the LORD, that you may find acceptance; on the morrow after the sabbath the priest shall wave it. [12]And on the day when you wave the sheaf, you shall offer a male lamb a year old without blemish as a burnt offering to the LORD. [13]And the cereal offering with it shall be two tenths of an ephah of fine flour mixed with oil, to be offered by fire to the LORD, a pleasing odour; and the drink offering with it shall be of wine, a fourth of a hin. [14]And you shall eat neither bread nor grain parched or fresh until this same day, until you have brought the offering of your God: it is a statute for ever throughout your generations in all your dwellings.

Ex 29:24

Ex 23:14
Num 28:26–31
Deut 16:9ff

Celebration of the feast of Weeks

[15]"And you shall count from the morrow after the sabbath, from the day that you brought the sheaf of the wave offering; seven full weeks shall they be, [16]counting fifty days to the morrow after the seventh sabbath; then you shall present a cereal offering of new grain to the LORD. [17]You shall bring from your dwellings two

Acts 2:1

---

connected with the Passover. In the Jordan valley grain was already ripe for harvest by this time (cf. Num 28:26–31). The offering of first fruits is based on the conviction that everything comes from God. In recognition of that divine sovereignty the first sheaf to ripen was offered in sacrifice—a tradition which developed to the point that no one could eat the crop without first making this offering to God. The "morrow" after the sabbath was thought by some to have been the first sabbath after 14 Nisan. Other scholars think that the sabbath was 15 Nisan and then the offering of the first fruits took

place on 16 Nisan. The "morrow" was the base day for reckoning the start of the feast of Pentecost, seven weeks later. The offering of the first sheaves was accompanied by the sacrifice of a year-old lamb and two tenths of an ephah of flour (cf. the note on Ex 29:38–46), that is, approximately 4.2 litres, and a quarter of a hin of wine (approximately one litre or two pints).

23:15–22. This feast, too, has elements connected with the grain harvest. Later on it became linked with the giving of the Law at Sinai. It was called Pentecost

---

autem septimo erit conventus sanctus, nullumque servile opus facietis in eo». [9]Locutusque est Dominus ad Moysen dicens: [10]«Loquere filiis Israel et dices ad eos: Cum ingressi fueritis terram, quam ego dabo vobis, et messueritis segetem, feretis manipulum spicarum primitias messis vestrae ad sacerdotem, [11]qui elevabit fasciculum coram Domino, ut acceptabile sit pro vobis; altero die sabbati sanctificabit illum. [12]Atque in eodem die, quo manipulum consecrabitis, facietis agnum immaculatum anniculum in holocaustum Domino, [13]et oblationem cum eo duas decimas similae conspersae oleo in incensum Domino odoremque suavissimum et libamentum eius vini quartam partem hin. [14]Panem et grana tosta farrem recentem non comedetis ex segete usque ad diem, qua offeretis ex ea munus Deo vestro. Praeceptum est sempiternum generationibus vestris in cunctis habitaculis vestris. [15]Numerabitis vobis ab altero die sabbati, in quo obtulistis manipulum elationis septem hebdomadas plenas, [16]usque ad

loaves of bread to be waved, made of two tenths of an ephah; they shall be of fine flour, they shall be baked with leaven, as first fruits to the LORD. [18]And you shall present with the bread seven lambs a year old without blemish, and one young bull, and two rams; they shall be a burnt offering to the LORD, with their cereal offering and their drink offerings, an offering by fire, a pleasing odour to the LORD. [19]And you shall offer one male goat for a sin offering, and two male lambs a year old as a sacrifice of peace offerings. [20]And the priest shall wave them with the bread of the first fruits as a wave offering before the LORD, with the two lambs; they shall be holy to the LORD for the priest. [21]And you shall make proclamation on the same day; you shall hold a holy convocation; you shall do no laborious work: it is a statute for ever in all your dwellings throughout your generations.

Lev 19:9–10   [22]"And when you reap the harvest of your land, you shall not reap your field to its very border, nor shall you gather the gleanings after your harvest; you shall leave them for the poor and for the stranger: I am the LORD your God."

---

because it came fifty days after the Passover. In Hebrew it was called Aseret, the "great convocation" or assembly. Another name for it is the feast of Weeks (a reference to the seven weeks which had passed since the Passover). The offering of the loaves of bread made from the first sheaf expressed thanksgiving and joy for the harvest recently completed. The various sacrifices were also offered as a sign of repentance for sins and as an act of adoration for the greatness of God who had blessed the work of his people.

From a Christian point of view, it is interesting that it was on the feast of Pentecost that the Holy Spirit came down on the apostles. For one thing, that Pentecost marked the start of a new stage with another Law, a much more perfect one, written not on stones but in the depths of men's hearts (cf. 2 Cor 3:3). For another, because it also seems significant that it was at the moment when the fruits of the earth were being harvested that the Church should receive the most precious fruit of Christ's death on the cross, the strength of the Spirit who purifies and sanctifies men with his divine grace.

alteram diem expletionis hebdomadae septimae, id est quinquaginta dies; et sic offeretis oblationem novam Domino [17]ex habitaculis vestris panes elationis duos de duabus decimis similae fermentatae, quos coquetis in primitias Domino; [18]offeretisque cum panibus septem agnos immaculatos anniculos et vitulum de armento unum et arietes duos et erunt holocaustum Domino cum oblatione similae et libamentis suis in odorem suavissimum Domino. [19]Facietis et hircum in sacrificium pro peccato duosque agnos anniculos, hostias pacificorum. [20]Cumque elevaverit eos sacerdos cum panibus primitiarum coram Domino, cum duobus agnis sanctum erunt Domino in usum sacerdotis. [21]Et vocabitis hoc ipso die conventum, conventus sanctus erit vobis; omne opus servile non facietis in eo. Legitimum sempiternum erit in cunctis habitaculis generationibus vestris. [22]Cum autem metatis segetem terrae vestrae, non secabis eam usque ad oram agri, nec remanentes spicas colliges, sed pauperibus et peregrinis dimittes eas. Ego Dominus Deus vester». [23]Locutusque est Dominus ad Moysen dicens: [24]«Loquere

Celebration of the New Year

²³And the LORD said to Moses, ²⁴"Say to the people of Israel, In the seventh month, on the first day of the month, you shall observe a day of solemn rest, a memorial proclaimed with blast of trumpets, a holy convocation. ²⁵You shall do no laborious work; and you shall present an offering by fire to the LORD."

Celebration of the day of atonement

Lev 16
Num 29:7–11

²⁶And the LORD said to Moses, ²⁷"On the tenth day of this seventh month is the day of atonement; it shall be for you a time of holy convocation, and you shall afflict yourselves and present an offering by fire to the LORD. ²⁸And you shall do no work on this same day; for it is a day of atonement, to make atonement for you before the LORD your God. ²⁹For whoever is not afflicted on this *Acts 3:23* same day shall be cut off from his people. ³⁰And whoever does any work on this same day, that person I will destroy from among his people. ³¹You shall do no work: it is a statute for ever throughout your generations in all your dwellings. ³²It shall be to you a

---

23:23–44. In the Bible the number seven had a sacred character, symbolizing in some way the perfection of God. Therefore the seventh month, as also the seventh year, had special significance in Israel. Thus, in the seventh month (in Hebrew, Tishre) three feasts were held. The first was the feast of Trumpets, which took place on the seventh day. It began with the sounding of trumpets; hence its name. Trumpets were also used to greet the appearance of the new moon. These details probably reflect traces of astral cults; however, by becoming incorporated into the liturgy, they became purified and raised to a new plane, to express at different times and different ways a deep feeling of attachment to the Creator of heaven and earth.

On the tenth of the same month the day of atonement was celebrated—Yom Kippur. It was a day of penance and expiation. It began at sundown, with the start of the sabbath rest. The grave penalties imposed for transgressions show the importance this day had, and still has today, in Jewish liturgy.

The other great feast is that of Tabernacles, celebrated over seven days, beginning on 15 Tishre. In the Code of the Covenant it is called the feast of ingathering (cf. Ex 23:16). The last of the harvest was saved around this time, particularly the grape harvest. The feast marked the close of the agricultural year; it was a most joyful feast. It was also regarded as preparation for the new period which would start immediately with the new

---

filiis Israel: Mense septimo, prima die mensis, erit vobis requies, memoriale, clangentibus tubis, conventus sanctus. ²⁵Omne opus servile non facietis in eo et offeretis incensum Domino». ²⁶Locutusque est Dominus ad Moysen dicens: ²⁷«Attamen decimo die mensis huius septimi dies Expiationum est, conventus sanctus erit vobis; affligetisque animas vestras in eo et offeretis incensum Domino. ²⁸Omne opus non facietis in tempore diei huius, quia dies expiationum est in expiationem vestram coram Domino Deo vestro. ²⁹Omnis anima, quae afflicta non fuerit die hoc, peribit de populis suis; ³⁰et, quae

sabbath of solemn rest, and you shall afflict yourselves; on the ninth day of the month beginning at evening, from evening to evening shall you keep your sabbath."

Ex 23:14
Num 29:12–39
Deut 16:13–17

Celebration of the feast of Tabernacles

Jn 7:2 [33]And the Lord said to Moses, [34]"Say to the people of Israel, On the fifteenth day of this seventh month and for seven days is the feast of booths[k] to the Lord. [35]On the first day shall be a holy con-
Jn 7:37 vocation; you shall do no laborious work. [36]Seven days you shall present offerings by fire to the Lord; on the eighth day you shall hold a holy convocation and present an offering by fire to the Lord; it is a solemn assembly; you shall do no laborious work.

[37]"These are the appointed feasts of the Lord, which you shall proclaim as times of holy convocation, for presenting to the Lord offerings by fire, burnt offerings and cereal offerings, sacrifices and drink offerings, each on its proper day; [38]besides the sabbaths of the Lord, and besides your gifts, and besides all your votive offerings, and besides all your freewill offerings, which you give to the Lord.

---

sowing. Prayers were offered for early rains, which were so crucial to starting the work. This was why the rite of water was so much to the fore. Water was borne in procession from the pool of Siloe and then poured round the altar of the temple. In Jesus' time a bunch of myrtle and acacia branches (from trees growing on the river bank) was shaken during the procession, thereby invoking the divine blessing of rain. In the times of Ezra and Nehemiah, in the middle of the 5th century BC, huts made from branches of trees were set up on the terraces of houses or in the countryside, and the people camped in

them over the days of the feast, in memory of the pilgrimage of the people of Israel in the desert, when they lived in tents. This custom still survives in the Jewish religion.

The Gospel of St John has much to say about this feast and about Jesus' activity in connexion with it (cf. Jn 7:2ff), including the important revelations our Lord made apropos of its rites: it was on this feast that Jesus proclaimed that from his heart rivers of living water would flow, a reference to "the Spirit, which those who believed in him were to receive" (Jn 7:39).

---

operis quippiam fecerit die hac, delebo eam de populo suo. [31]Nihil ergo operis facietis in eo: legitimum sempiternum erit vestris generationibus in cunctis habitationibus vestris. [32]Sabbatum requietionis est vobis, et affligetis animas vestras; die nono mensis a vespero usque ad vesperum servabitis sabbatum vestrum». [33]Et locutus est Dominus ad Moysen dicens: [34]«Loquere filiis Israel: Quinto decimo die mensis huius septimi erit festum Tabernaculorum septem diebus Domino. [35]Die primo conventus sanctus, omne opus servile non facietis in eo; [36]septem diebus offeretis incensum Domino. Die octavo conventus sanctus erit vobis et offeretis incensum Domino; est enim coetus: omne opus servile non facietis. [37]Hae sunt feriae Domini, quas vocabitis conventus sanctos, offeretisque in eis incensum

k. Or *tabernacles*

[39]"On the fifteenth day of the seventh month, when you have gathered in the produce of the land, you shall keep the feast of the LORD seven days; on the first day shall be a solemn rest, and on the eighth day shall be a solemn rest. [40]And you shall take on the first day the fruit of goodly trees, branches of palm trees, and boughs of leafy trees, and willows of the brook; and you shall rejoice before the LORD your God seven days. [41]You shall keep it as a feast to the LORD seven days in the year; it is a statute for ever throughout your generations; you shall keep it in the seventh month. [42]You shall dwell in booths for seven days; all that are native in Israel shall dwell in booths, [43]that your generations may know that I made the people of Israel dwell in booths when I brought them out of the land of Egypt: I am the LORD your God."

[44]Thus Moses declared to the people of Israel the appointed feasts of the LORD.

Jn 12:13
Rev 7:9

Rev 7:9

Rules about lighting the sanctuary

24 [1]The LORD said to Moses, [2]"Command the people of Israel to bring you pure oil from beaten olives for the lamp, that a light may be kept burning continually. [3]Outside the veil of the testimony, in the tent of meeting, Aaron shall keep it in order from evening to morning before the LORD continually; it shall be a statute for ever throughout your generations. [4]He shall keep the lamps in order upon the lampstand of pure gold before the LORD continually.

Ex 25:31–40;
27:20–21
Lev 6:5–6
Num 8:2

Rules about the offertory bread

[5]"And you shall take fine flour, and bake twelve cakes of it; two tenths of an ephah shall be in each cake. [6]And you shall set them

Ex 25:23–30
1 Sam 21:1–6
Mt 12:4
Mk 2:6

24:1–4. The seven-branch lampstand, the *menoráh*, was located in the Holy, in front of the curtain or veil which divided off the Holy of Holies in the temple. Exodus 25:31–40, also, describes the features of this candelabra. Here detailed

instructions are given to ensure that it always stayed lit; it was a sign of Israel's unceasing adoration of God.

24:5–9. The offertory bread is also dealt with in Exodus (25:23–30). These loaves,

Domino, holocausta et oblationes similae, sacrificia et libamenta iuxta ritum uniuscuiusque diei; [38]praeter sabbata Domini donaque vestra et omnia, quae offeretis ex voto vel quae sponte tribuetis Domino. [39]Sed quinto decimo die mensis septimi, quando congregaveritis omnes fructus terrae, celebrabitis festum Domini septem diebus; die primo et die octavo erit requies. [40]Sumetisque vobis die primo fructus arboris pulcherrimos spatulasque palmarum et ramos ligni densarum frondium et salices de torrente et laetabimini coram Domino Deo vestro. [41]Celebrabitisque sollemnitatem eius septem diebus per annum: legitimum sempiternum erit generationibus vestris. Mense septimo festum celebrabitis [42]et habitabitis in umbraculis septem diebus; omnis, qui de genere est Israel, manebit in tabernaculis, [43]ut discant posteri vestri quod in tabernaculis habitare fecerim filios Israel, cum educerem eos de terra Aegypti. Ego Dominus Deus vester». [44]Locutusque est Moyses super sollemnitatibus Domini

Lk 6:4 in two rows, six in a row, upon the table of pure gold. [7]And you
1 Cor 11:24 shall put pure frankincense with each row, that it may go with the
bread as a memorial portion to be offered by fire to the LORD.
[8]Every sabbath day Aaron shall set it in order before the LORD
continually on behalf of the people of Israel as a covenant for
ever. [9]And it shall be for Aaron and his sons, and they shall eat it
in a holy place, since it is for him a most holy portion out of the
offerings by fire to the LORD, a perpetual due."

Rules for blasphemy

[10]Now an Israelite woman's son, whose father was an Egyptian,
went out among the people of Israel; and the Israelite woman's
son and a man of Israel quarrelled in the camp, [11]and the Israelite
woman's son blasphemed the Name, and cursed. And they
brought him to Moses. His mother's name was Shelomith, the
daughter of Dibri, of the tribe of Dan. [12]And they put him in custody, till the will of the Lord should be declared to them.

[13]And the LORD said to Moses, [14]"Bring out of the camp him
Acts 7:58   who cursed; and let all who heard him lay their hands upon his
Heb 13:13

---

replaced each week, became a symbol of
Israel's permanent offering to God. Some
grains of incense were placed on top of the
loaves; the incense was later burned on the
altar of holocaust, whereas the bread was
eaten by the priests in a holy place. In 1
Samuel 21:1–7 we find an exception to
this rule. Ahimelech the priest gave the
loaves to David and his men, on condition
that they were ritually clean. Our Lord
used that incident to reject the rigorism of
Pharisees who accused Christ's disciples
of not keeping the sabbath (cf. Mt 12:4).

24:10–16. Blasphemy was punishable
by death because it was a grave sin.
The case recounted here is of a prose-
lyte, that is, the son of a pagan father
and a Hebrew mother. The implication
is that blasphemy was inconceivable on
the lips of a Hebrew. This makes it
easier to understand the malice
involved in accusing Jesus of blasphemy (cf. Jn 10:33; 19:7); the same
charge was laid against St Stephen (cf.
Acts 7:51–58).

---

ad filios Israel. ¹Et locutus est Dominus ad Moysen dicens: ²«Praecipe filiis Israel, ut afferant tibi oleum
de olivis purissimum ac lucidum ad concinnandas lucernas candelabri iugiter. ³Extra velum testimonii
in tabernaculo conventus parabit illud Aaron a vespere usque ad mane coram Domino iugiter, ritu perpetuo in generationibus vestris. ⁴Super candelabro mundissimo parabit lucernas semper in conspectu
Domini. ⁵Accipies quoque similam et coques ex ea duodecim panes, qui singuli habebunt duas decimas, ⁶quorum senos altrinsecus super mensam purissimam coram Domino statues. ⁷Et pones super
ambas strues tus lucidissimum, ut sit panis in memoriale, incensum Domino. ⁸Per singula sabbata
mutabuntur coram Domino suscepti a filiis Israel; foedus sempiternum. ⁹Eruntque Aaron et filiorum
eius, ut comedant eos in loco sancto, quia sanctum sanctorum est ei de incensis Domini; iure perpetuo». ¹⁰Ecce autem egressus filius mulieris Israelitis, quem pepererat de viro Aegyptio inter filios
Israel, iurgatus est in castris cum viro Israelita. ¹¹Cumque blasphemasset nomen et maledixisset ei,
adductus est ad Moysen; vocabatur autem mater eius Salomith filia Dabri de tribu Dan. ¹²Miseruntque

head, and let all the congregation stone him. ¹⁵And say to the Ex 22:27
people of Israel, Whoever curses his God shall bear his sin. ¹⁶He Mt 26:66
who blasphemes the name of the LORD shall be put to death; all Mk 14:64
Jn 10:33; 19:7
the congregation shall stone him; the sojourner as well as the 2 Tim 2:9
native, when he blasphemes the Name, shall be put to death.

Ex 21:12ff,
23–25

The law of retaliation Deut 19:21

¹⁷He who kills a man shall be put to death. ¹⁸He who kills a beast Mt 5:21
shall make it good, life for life. ¹⁹When a man causes a disfigure-
ment in his neighbour, as he has done it shall be done to him,
²⁰fracture for fracture, eye for eye, tooth for tooth; as he has dis- *Mt 5:38*
figured a man, he shall be disfigured. ²¹He who kills a beast shall
make it good; and he who kills a man shall be put to death. ²²You
shall have one law for the sojourner and for the native; for I am
the LORD your God." ²³So Moses spoke to the people of Israel;
and they brought him who had cursed out of the camp, and stoned
him with stones. Thus the people of Israel did as the LORD commanded Moses.

Ex 23:10–11
Lev 25:20–22

Rules about the sabbatical year Deut 15:1–11

25 ¹The LORD said to Moses on Mount Sinai, ²"Say to the
people of Israel, When you come into the land which I give

24:17–23. This passage stipulates penalties for various offences, already included
in the Code of the Covenant of Exodus
21. They apply to both Israelites and foreigners in Israel, and they evidence a
higher ethic than that of other cultures of
the time.

On the law of retaliation, see the note
on Dt 19:21.

25:1–7. Here we can see concern for the
conservation of land, trying to ensure that

short-term productivity is not obtained at
the cost of deterioration in the long term.
It is always made clear that the earth is a
gift from God: therefore, God's sovereignty over the land has to be periodi-
cally acknowledged. This is the primary
reason for these rules about allowing the
land to lie fallow.

Exodus 23:10–11 also talks about the
sabbatical year, but here there is reference
to additional reasons for it, to do with the
welfare of the under-privileged. These

---

eum in custodiam, donec nossent quid iuberet Dominus. ¹³Qui locutus est ad Moysen dicens: ¹⁴«Educ
blasphemum extra castra, et ponant omnes, qui audierunt, manus suas super caput eius, et lapidet eum
coetus universus. ¹⁵Et ad filios Israel loqueris: Homo, qui maledixerit Deo suo, portabit peccatum
suum; ¹⁶et, qui blasphemaverit nomen Domini, morte moriatur: lapidibus opprimet eum omnis coetus,
sive ille peregrinus sive civis fuerit. Qui blasphemaverit nomen Domini, morte moriatur. ¹⁷Qui percusserit et occiderit hominem, morte moriatur. ¹⁸Qui percusserit animal, reddet vicarium, id est animam
pro anima. ¹⁹Qui irrogaverit maculam cuilibet civium suorum, sicut fecit, sic fiet ei: ²⁰fracturam pro
fractura, oculum pro oculo, dentem pro dente restituet; qualem inflixerit maculam, talem sustinere
cogetur. ²¹Qui percusserit iumentum, reddet aliud. Qui percusserit hominem, morietur. ²²Aequum iudicium sit inter vos, sive peregrinus sive civis peccaverit; quia ego sum Dominus Deus vester».

you, the land shall keep a sabbath to the LORD. [3]Six years you shall sow your field, and six years you shall prune your vineyard, and gather in its fruits; [4]but in the seventh year there shall be a sabbath of solemn rest for the land, a sabbath to the LORD; you shall not sow your field or prune your vineyard. [5]What grows of itself in your harvest you shall not reap, and the grapes of your undressed vine you shall not gather; it shall be a year of solemn rest for the land. [6]The sabbath of the land shall provide food for you, for yourself and for your male and female slaves and for your hired servant and the sojourner who lives with you; [7]for your cattle also and for the beasts that are in your land all its yield shall be for food.

Rules about the jubilee year

[8]"And you shall count seven weeks[1] of years, seven times seven years, so that the time of the seven weeks of years shall be to you forty-nine years. [9]Then you shall send abroad the loud trumpet on the tenth day of the seventh month; on the day of atonement you shall send abroad the trumpet throughout all your land. [10]And you shall hallow the fiftieth year, and proclaim liberty throughout the land to all its inhabitants; it shall be a jubilee for you, when each

Ex 21:2–11
Deut 15:12–18
Lk 4:19

---

rules did not all have to be put into effect at the same time, because that might have created a huge problem of generalized idleness. In the book of Maccabees, for example, there are references to difficulties that arose at that time due to one sabbatical year (cf. 1 Mac 6:49).

25:8–22. Here again the number seven, by being applied to the calendar, creates a special situation. Now we have seven weeks of years, that is a run of forty-nine

years; and this leads to the following year, the fiftieth, being a jubilee year. The rules about letting the land lie fallow are applied to the jubilee year; special clauses are added, such as that to do with the redemption of property. So, in the jubilee year, land acquired had to be returned to its original owner. This custom meant that what in fact was sold was the usufruct of the land and its price would be a function of the number of years' use the buyer was getting.

[23]Locutusque est Moyses ad filios Israel, et eduxerunt eum, qui blasphemaverat, extra castra, ac lapidibus oppresserunt. Feceruntque filii Israel, sicut praeceperat Dominus Moysi. [1]Locutusque est Dominus ad Moysen in monte Sinai dicens: [2]«Loquere filiis Israel et dices ad eos: Quando ingressi fueritis terram, quam ego dabo vobis, sabbatizet terra sabbatum Domino. [3]Sex annis seres agrum tuum et sex annis putabis vineam tuam colligesque fructus eius; [4]septimo autem anno, sabbatum requietionis erit terrae, sabbatum Domino: agrum tuum non seres et vineam tuam non putabis. [5]Quae sponte gignit humus, non metes et uvas vineae tuae non putatae non colliges quasi vindemiam; annus enim requietionis erit terrae. [6]Et erit sabbatum terrae vobis in cibum: tibi et servo tuo, ancillae et mercennario tuo et advenis, qui peregrinantur apud te, [7]iumentis tuis et animalibus, quae in terra tua sunt, omnia, quae nascuntur, praebebunt cibum. [8]Numerabis quoque tibi septem hebdomadas annorum, id est septem septies, quae simul faciunt annos quadraginta novem; [9]et clanges bucina mense septimo,

l. Or *sabbaths*

of you shall return to his property and each of you shall return to his family. [11]A jubilee shall that fiftieth year be to you; in it you shall neither sow, nor reap what grows of itself, nor gather the grapes from the undressed vines. [12]For it is a jubilee; it shall be holy to you; you shall eat what it yields out of the field.

[13]"In this year of jubilee each of you shall return to his property. [14]And if you sell to your neighbour or buy from your neighbour, you shall not wrong one another. [15]According to the number of years after the jubilee, you shall buy from your neighbour, and according to the number of years for crops he shall sell to you. [16]If the years are many you shall increase the price, and if the years are few you shall diminish the price, for it is the number of the crops that he is selling to you. [17]You shall not wrong one another, but you shall fear your God; for I am the LORD your God.

[18]"Therefore you shall do my statutes, and keep my ordinances and perform them; so you will dwell in the land securely. [19]The land will yield its fruit, and you will eat your fill, and dwell in it securely. [20]And if you say, 'What shall we eat in the seventh year,

Jer 34:8–22
Is 61:1–3

Again, underlying this is the idea that the land is a divine gift which ought always to revert to those to whom the Lord originally granted it. Even so, these regulations were not obeyed very well. Thus, we find the prophets vigorously denouncing the way some people built up land holdings to the detriment of others. The basic reason for their complaint was not just a fine sense of social justice but the fact that God's rules were being violated (cf. Is 5:8; Mic 2:2).

Verses 14–15 here are [as in the Spanish edition, which is also in line with most modern vernacular transla-

tions] divided differently from the New Vulgate division.

Verses 18–22 round off the previous passage and introduce what follows. They remind people about the promises God makes to those who are faithful to his commandments, and they are meant to encourage those who might be tempted to think that God will not look after them if they have to face three years without harvest (the sabbatical year, the jubilee year and the year after it, at the *end* of which a harvest would be reaped). A provident God will ensure that those who stay true to him will experience no want.

---

decima die mensis expiationis die clangetis tuba in universa terra vestra. [10]Sanctificabitisque annum quinquagesimum et vocabitis remissionem in terra cunctis habitatoribus eius: ipse est enim iobeleus. Revertemini unusquisque ad possessionem suam, et unusquisque rediet ad familiam pristinam. [11]Iobeleus erit vobis quinquagesimus annus. Non seretis neque metetis sponte in agro nascentia neque vineas non putatas vindemiabitis [12]ob sanctificationem iobelei; sed de agro statim ablatas comedetis fruges. [13]Hoc anno iobelei rediet unusquisque vestrum ad possessionem suam. [14]Quando vendes quippiam civi tuo vel emes ab eo, ne contristet unusquisque fratrem suum; sed iuxta numerum annorum post iobeleum emes ab eo, [15]et iuxta supputationem annorum frugum vendet tibi. [16]Quanto plures anni remanserint post iobeleum, tanto crescet et pretium; et quanto minus temporis numeraveris, tanto minoris et emptio constabit: tempus enim frugum vendet tibi. [17]Nolite affligere contribules vestros, sed timeas Deum tuum, quia ego Dominus Deus vester. [18]Facite praecepta mea et iudicia, custodite et implete ea, ut habitare possitis in terra absque ullo pavore, [19]et gignat vobis humus fructus suos, quibus

if we may not sow or gather in our crop?' [21]I will command my blessing upon you in the sixth year, so that it will bring forth fruit for three years. [22]When you sow in the eighth year, you will be eating old produce; until the ninth year, when its produce comes in, you shall eat the old.

Rules about redeeming landed property

[23]The land shall not be sold in perpetuity, for the land is mine; for you are strangers and sojourners with me. [24]And in all the country you possess, you shall grant a redemption of the land.

Lev 25:47
Num 35:19
Ruth 3:13;
4:1–10

[25]"If your brother becomes poor, and sells part of his property, then his next of kin shall come and redeem what his brother has sold. [26]If a man has no one to redeem it, and then himself becomes prosperous and finds sufficient means to redeem it, [27]let him reckon the years since he sold it and pay back the overpayment to the man to whom he sold it; and he shall return to his property. [28]But if he has not sufficient means to get it back for

---

25:23–34. Keeping the rules about letting the land lie fallow and about its redemption gave rise to further consequences. The basic idea being stressed is that the land is a gift from God and therefore it must not be sold outright. So, the seller will always have the option to redeem the ownership of land which he sold and which his family had received from the Lord. If that seller could not afford to recover the property by paying back the price he sold it for, he could have a near relative help him to do so. That helper is called a *goel*, "deliverer, redeemer"; the word occurs often in the Old Testament; sometimes it is used for an "avenger of blood" (cf. Num 35:19), sometimes for a man who raises up offspring for his dead brother by mar-

rying his widow (cf. Ruth 3:13; 4:1–10), or someone who liberates a slave (cf. Lev 25:47). In this sense of "deliverer" the word *goel* is also applied to God, because he delivered his people from bondage (cf. Ex 6:6; Deut 5:15; Is 41:14).

Where the property sold is a house, the conditions for redemption vary, depending on whether it is in a walled town or in the countryside. In the case of a dwelling house belonging to a Levite, the right of redemption endures for ever. The reason for this is that Levites' houses are, in a special way, the sacred property of God which he has granted to his priests and Levites; the same applies to the fields adjoining these in some way sacred properties.

---

vescamini usque ad saturitatem, et habitabitis super terram, nullius impetum formidantes. [20]Quod si dixeritis: 'Quid comedemus anno septimo, si non seruerimus neque collegerimus fruges nostras?'. [21]Dabo benedictionem meam vobis anno sexto, et faciet fructus trium annorum, [22]seretisque anno octavo et comedetis veteres fruges usque ad nonum annum; donec nova nascantur, edetis vetera. [23]Terra quoque non veniet in perpetuum, quia mea est, et vos advenae et coloni mei estis. [24]Unde cuncta regio possessionis vestrae sub redemptionis condicione a vobis vendetur. [25]Si attenuatus frater tuus vendiderit partem possessionis suae, veniet ut redemptor propinquus eius, et redimet, quod ille vendiderat. [26]Sin autem non habuerit redemptorem et ipse pretium ad redimendum potuerit invenire, [27]computabuntur fructus ex eo tempore, quo vendidit; et quod reliquum est, reddet emptori sicque recipiet possessionem

himself, then what he sold shall remain in the hand of him who bought it until the year of jubilee; in the jubilee it shall be released, and he shall return to his property.

²⁹"If a man sells a dwelling house in a walled city, he may redeem it within a whole year after its sale; for a full year he shall have the right of redemption. ³⁰If it is not redeemed within a full year, then the house that is in the walled city shall be made sure in perpetuity to him who bought it, throughout his generations; it shall not be released in the jubilee. ³¹But the houses of the villages which have no wall around them shall be reckoned with the fields of the country; they may be redeemed, and they shall be released in the jubilee. ³²Nevertheless the cities of the Levites, the houses in the cities of their possession, the Levites may redeem at any time. ³³And if one of the Levites does not exercise^m his right of redemption, then the house that was sold in a city of their possession shall be released in the jubilee; for the houses in the cities of the Levites are their possession among the people of Israel. ³⁴But the fields of common land belonging to their cities may not be sold; for that is their perpetual possession.

Rules about loans

³⁵"And if your brother becomes poor, and cannot maintain himself

Ex 22:26
Deut 23:20–21
Neh 5:1–11
Lk 6:33

25:35–55. If God takes an interest in the earth, he takes much more interest in those who live on it, especially if they are descendants of Abraham. This is why special criteria apply to the children of Israel. They must not be charged any interest on loans, nor should they be treated as no better than slaves. At the very least an Israelite should be a day labourer, and in a jubilee year he must be relieved of any debt or charge. The episode recounted by Nehemiah about

the favourable treatment given to impoverished Israelites shows how these rules were put into practice (cf. Neh 5:1–11); cf. also Ex 22:26 and Deut 23:20–21. The Code of the Covenant even lays down that an Israelite has to be set free from serfdom after six years' indenture (cf. Ex 21:1–6). Also, Deuteronomy 15:13–14 specifies that a liberated slave has to be given certain goods, to ensure he is able to survive. The duty to help a brother in need is a further indication

---

suam. ²⁸Quod si non invenerit manus eius, ut reddat pretium, habebit emptor, quod emerat, usque ad annum iobeleum. In ipso enim omnis venditio rediet ad dominum et ad possessorem pristinum. ²⁹Qui vendiderit domum intra urbis muros, habebit licentiam redimendi, donec unus impleatur annus. ³⁰Si non redemerit, et anni circulus fuerit evolutus, emptor possidebit eam et posteri eius in perpetuum; et redimi non poterit, etiam in iobeleo. ³¹Sin autem in villa fuerit domus, quae muros non habet, agrorum iure vendetur: potest redimi et in iobeleo revertetur ad dominum. ³²Aedes Levitarum, quae in urbibus possessionis eorum sunt, semper possunt ab eis redimi. ³³Si autem quis redemerit a Levitis, domus et urbs in iobeleo revertentur ad dominos; quia domus urbium leviticarum pro possessionibus eorum sunt

m. Compare Vg: Heb *exercises*

with you, you shall maintain him; as a stranger and a sojourner he shall live with you. ³⁶Take no interest from him or increase, but fear your God; that your brother may live beside you. ³⁷You shall not lend him your money at interest, nor give him your food for profit. ³⁸I am the LORD your God, who brought you forth out of the land of Egypt to give you the land of Canaan, and to be your God.

Lev 22:33

Rules about slaves

Lev 25:25
Ex 21:1–11
Deut 15:12–18
Jer 34:8–22

³⁹"And if your brother becomes poor beside you, and sells himself to you, you shall not make him serve as a slave: ⁴⁰he shall be with you as a hired servant and as a sojourner. He shall serve with you

Ex 21:1–6
Deut 15:13–14

until the year of the jubilee; ⁴¹then he shall go out from you, he and his children with him, and go back to his own family, and return to the possession of his fathers. ⁴²For they are my servants, whom I brought forth out of the land of Egypt; they shall not be

---

that temporal goods have a social purpose. "If anyone has the world's goods and sees his brother in need, yet closes his heart against him, how does God's love abide in him?" (1 Jn 3:17). The Fathers of the Church were very specific about the proper attitudes of the haves to the have-nots: "It is not part of your property," St Ambrose says, "that you are giving to the poor person; what you give him belongs to him. For what has been given for the use of everyone, you have appropriated to yourself. The earth has been given to everyone, not just to the well-to-do" (St Ambrose, *De Nabuthae historia*, 12, 53). In other words, no one has an unconditional and absolute right to private property. There is no justification for keeping for oneself something one does not need if other people lack

the basics for living (cf. Paul VI, *Populorum progressio*, 23).

It is permissible for strangers to be enslaved, and there is no requirement that they be set free in a jubilee year. However, if an Israelite fell into the hands of a sojourner who became wealthy in the land of Israel, it was possible for him to be redeemed at any time, and when a jubilee came round he had to be set free. The reason for this always lies in God's sovereignty over his people. Because all Israelites belong to him, no one is allowed to own an Israelite in perpetuity. However, it must be admitted that these just criteria were often a dead letter. When that happened, the prophets protested and threatened punishment to make people take the Lord's laws to heart (cf. Jer 32:7; Ezek 46:17).

---

inter filios Israel. ³⁴Suburbana autem pascua eorum non venient, quia possessio sempiterna est eis. ³⁵Si attenuatus fuerit frater tuus et infirma manus eius apud te, suscipies eum quasi advenam et peregrinum, et vivet tecum. ³⁶Ne accipias usuras ab eo, nec amplius quam dedisti: time Deum tuum, ut vivere possit frater tuus apud te. ³⁷Pecuniam tuam non dabis ei ad usuram, nec plus aequo exiges pro cibo tuo. ³⁸Ego Dominus Deus vester, qui eduxi vos de terra Aegypti, ut darem vobis terram Chanaan et essem vester Deus. ³⁹Si paupertate compulsus vendiderit se tibi frater tuus, non eum opprimes servitute servorum, ⁴⁰sed quasi mercennarius et colonus erit tecum. Usque ad annum iobeleum operabitur apud te ⁴¹et postea egredietur cum liberis suis et revertetur ad cognationem suam et ad possessionem patrum suorum. ⁴²Mei enim servi sunt, et ego eduxi eos de terra Aegypti: non venient condicione servorum;

sold as slaves. ⁴³You shall not rule over him with harshness, but Eph 6:9
Col 4:1
shall fear your God. ⁴⁴As for your male and female slaves whom
you may have: you may buy male and female slaves from among
the nations that are round about you. ⁴⁵You may also buy from
among the strangers who sojourn with you and their families that
are with you, who have been born in your land; and they may be
your property. ⁴⁶You may bequeath them to your sons after you, to
inherit as a possession for ever; you may make slaves of them, but
over your brethren the people of Israel you shall not rule, one over
another, with harshness.

⁴⁷"If a stranger or sojourner with you becomes rich, and your
brother beside him becomes poor and sells himself to the stranger
or sojourner with you, or to a member of the stranger's family,
⁴⁸then after he is sold he may be redeemed; one of his brothers
may redeem him, ⁴⁹or his uncle, or his cousin may redeem him, or
a near kinsman belonging to his family may redeem him; or if he
grows rich he may redeem himself. ⁵⁰He shall reckon with him
who bought him from the year when he sold himself to him until
the year of jubilee, and the price of his release shall be according
to the number of years; the time he was with his owner shall be
rated as the time of a hired servant. ⁵¹If there are still many years,
according to them he shall refund out of the price paid for him the
price for his redemption. ⁵²If there remain but a few years until the
year of jubilee, he shall make a reckoning with him; according to
the years of service due from him he shall refund the money for
his redemption. ⁵³As a servant hired year by year shall he be with
him; he shall not rule with harshness over him in your sight. ⁵⁴And
if he is not redeemed by these means, then he shall be released in
the year of jubilee, he and his children with him. ⁵⁵For to me the
people of Israel are servants, they are my servants whom I brought
forth out of the land of Egypt: I am the LORD your God.

⁴³ne affligas eum per potentiam, sed metuito Deum tuum. ⁴⁴Servus et ancilla sint tibi de nationibus,
quae in circuitu vestro sunt; de illis emetis servum et ancillam. ⁴⁵De filiis quoque advenarum, qui peregrinantur apud vos, emetis et de cognatione eorum, quae est apud vos et quam genuerint in terra vestra,
hos habebitis in possessionem ⁴⁶et hereditario iure transmittetis ad posteros ac possidebitis in aeternum
ut servos; fratres autem vestros filios Israel ne opprimatis cum potentia. ⁴⁷Si invaluerit apud vos manus
advenae atque peregrini, et attenuatus frater tuus vendiderit se ei aut cuiquam de stirpe eius, ⁴⁸post ven-
ditionem potest redimi. Unus ex fratribus suis redimet eum ⁴⁹et patruus et patruelis et consanguineus
et affinis. Sin autem et ipse potuerit, redimat se, ⁵⁰supputatis dumtaxat cum emptore annis a tempore
venditionis suae usque ad annum iobeleum, et pecunia, qua venditus fuerat, iuxta annorum numerum
et rationem mercennarii supputata. ⁵¹Si plures fuerint anni, qui remanent usque ad iobeleum, secundum
hos reddet et pretium redemptionis de pecunia emptionis; ⁵²si pauci, ponet rationem cum eo; iuxta
annorum numerum reddet emptori, quod reliquum est annorum, ⁵³quibus ante servivit, mercedibus
mercennarii imputatis. Non affliget eum violenter in conspectu tuo. ⁵⁴Quod si per haec redimi non
potuerit, anno iobeleo egredietur cum liberis suis: ⁵⁵mei sunt enim servi filii Israel, quos eduxi de terra

Ex 23:20–23
Deut 28 **Blessings for observing the Law***

Ex 20:14
Deut 5:8
Lev 17:1

26 [1]"You shall make for yourselves no idols and erect no graven image or pillar, and you shall not set up a figured stone in your land, to bow down to them; for I am the LORD your

Lev 19:30 God. [2]You shall keep my sabbaths and reverence my sanctuary: I
Jer 17:17–19
Ezek 20:12–13 am the LORD.

Deut 11:13–14 [3]"If you walk in my statutes and observe my commandments

Is 1:19 and do them, [4]then I will give you your rains in their season, and
Ezek 34:26–27 the land shall yield its increase, and the trees of the field shall
Acts 14:17 yield their fruit. [5]And your threshing shall last to the time of vintage, and the vintage shall last to the time for sowing; and you shall eat your bread to the full, and dwell in your land securely. [6]And I will give peace in the land, and you shall lie down, and none shall make you afraid; and I will remove evil beasts from the land, and the sword shall not go through your land. [7]And you shall chase your enemies, and they shall fall before you by the sword. [8]Five of you shall chase a hundred, and a hundred of you shall chase ten thousand; and your enemies shall fall before you by the sword. [9]And I will have regard for you and make you fruit-

---

*26:1–46. This is really the concluding chapter of Leviticus, though there is a further chapter (27) by way of appendix. The present chapter is an exhortation encouraging the fulfilment of all the rules and regulations laid down; it promises blessings on those who are faithful to God's will and threatens punishment on those who fail to obey his laws. It is reminiscent of the end of the Code of the Covenant (in Ex 23:20–23); and we find a similar passage in Deuteronomy 28. All these texts are reminders that God's justice will apply to each according to his deeds. This same truth is taught in the New Testament, albeit in different ways. Thus, in addition to the reference to the

last judgment (cf. Mt 25:31–46) it speaks of the book of life (cf. Rev 3:5; 13:8; 17:8; 20:12) in which are written the names of the elect, because the consequences of what man does during his earthly life will follow him beyond the grave (cf. Rev 14:13).

The promises are prefaced by verses about idolatry which repeat the second commandment; and there are many other passages in the Pentateuch which repeat the same teaching (cf. Ex 20:4; Deut 5:8; etc.). It was essential to hammer home this point because the polytheism and idolatry of neighbouring peoples were always a temptation for Israel.

Aegypti. Ego Dominus Deus vester. [1]Non facietis vobis idolum et sculptile, nec lapidem erigetis, nec imaginem sculptam in petra ponetis in terra vestra, ut adoretis eam. Ego enim sum Dominus Deus vester. [2]Custodite sabbata mea et pavete sanctuarium meum. Ego Dominus. [3]Si in praeceptis meis ambulaveritis et mandata mea custodieritis et feceritis ea, [4]dabo vobis pluvias temporibus suis, et terra gignet germen suum, et pomis arbores replebuntur. [5]Apprehendet messium tritura vindemiam, et vindemia occupabit sementem; et comedetis panem vestrum in saturitatem et absque pavore habitabitis in terra vestra. [6]Dabo pacem in finibus vestris, dormietis, et non erit qui exterreat. Auferam malas bestias, et gladius non transibit per terminos vestros. [7]Persequemini inimicos vestros, et corruent coram vobis

ful and multiply you, and will confirm my covenant with you. [10]And you shall eat old store long kept, and you shall clear out the old to make way for the new. [11]And I will make my abode among you, and my soul shall not abhor you. [12]And I will walk among you, and will be your God, and you shall be my people. [13]I am the LORD your God, who brought you forth out of the land of Egypt, that you should not be their slaves; and I have broken the bars of your yoke and made you walk erect.

Deut 4:7
2 Cor 6:16
Ezek 48:35
Jn 1:14
Rev 21:3, 7
Lev 22:33
Rev 21:3

Curses for disobedience

[14]"But if you will not hearken to me, and will not do all these commandments, [15]if you spurn my statutes, and if your soul abhors my ordinances, so that you will not do all my commandments, but break my covenant, [16]I will do this to you: I will appoint over you sudden terror, consumption, and fever that waste the eyes and cause life to pine away. And you shall sow your seed in vain, for your enemies shall eat it; [17]I will set my face against you, and you shall be smitten before your enemies; those who hate you shall rule over you, and you shall flee when none pursues you. [18]And if in spite of this you will not hearken to me, then

Deut 28:15–68
Amos 4:6–12
Jer 26:4–6

26:12. Throughout the Bible one finds a crescendo which runs from the goods and circumstances of this life to those of eternal beatitude. In this verse we can see once again this gradual raising of sights. In his masterpiece, *The City of God*, St Augustine, taking his cue from this very passage, puts it this way: "Perfect peace will reign [in heaven], since nothing in ourselves or in any others could disturb the peace. The promised reward of virtue will be the best and the greatest of all possible prizes—the very Giver of virtue Himself, for that is what the Prophet meant: 'I will be your God and you shall be my people.' [. . .] He will be the consummation of all our desiring—the object of our unending vision, of our unlessening love, of our unwearying praise. And in this gift of vision, this response of love, this paean of praise, all alike will share, as all will share in everlasting life" (*De civitate Dei*, 22, 30).

26:14–46. The punishments are not listed in any particular order, which makes it

---

gladio. [8]Persequentur quinque de vestris centum alienos et centum ex vobis decem milia; cadent inimici vestri in conspectu vestro gladio. [9]Respiciam vos et crescere faciam; multiplicabimini, et firmabo pactum meum vobiscum. [10]Comedetis vetusta congregata priorum messium; et vetera, novis supervenientibus, proicietis. [11]Ponam habitaculum meum in medio vestri, et non abominabitur vos anima mea. [12]Ambulabo inter vos et ero vester Deus, vosque eritis populus meus. [13]Ego Dominus Deus vester, qui eduxi vos de terra Aegyptiorum, ne serviretis eis, et qui confregi vectes iugi vestri, ut incederetis erecti. [14]Quod si non audieritis me nec feceritis omnia mandata haec, [15]si spreveritis leges meas, et iudicia mea contempserit anima vestra, ut non faciatis omnia, quae a me constituta sunt, et ad irritum perducatis pactum meum, [16]ego quoque haec faciam vobis: visitabo vos in terrore repentino, in tabe et ardore, qui conficiant oculos et consumant animam, frustra seretis sementem, quae ab hostibus devorabitur. [17]Ponam faciem meam contra vos, et corruetis coram hostibus vestris et subiciemini his,

I will chastise you again sevenfold for your sins, [19]and I will break the pride of your power, and I will make your heavens like iron and your earth like brass; [20]and your strength shall be spent in vain, for your land shall not yield its increase, and the trees of the land shall not yield their fruit.

Rev 15:1–6 [21]"Then if you walk contrary to me, and will not hearken to me, I will bring more plagues upon you, sevenfold as many as your sins. [22]And I will let loose the wild beasts among you, which shall rob you of your children, and destroy your cattle, and make you few in number, so that your ways shall become desolate.

[23]"And if by this discipline you are not turned to me, but walk contrary to me, [24]then I also will walk contrary to you, and I myself will smite you sevenfold for your sins. [25]And I will bring a sword upon you, that shall execute vengeance for the covenant; and if you gather within your cities I will send pestilence among you, and you shall be delivered into the hand of the enemy. [26]When I break your staff of bread, ten women shall bake your bread in one oven, and shall deliver your bread again by weight; and you shall eat, and not be satisfied.

[27]"And if in spite of this you will not hearken to me, but walk contrary to me, [28]then I will walk contrary to you in fury, and chas-

---

difficult to see any penalty "structure". Many, if not all, aspects of life can be affected by the wrath of God. So, the land will become unproductive, health will be undermined even unto death, implacable and cruel enemies will beset the people, hunger will force people even to eat the flesh of their children. In this connexion we cannot but remember Flavius Josephus' description of the siege of Jerusalem in the year 70 AD which led to the destruction of the temple. One of the horrors he reported was of a woman so crazed by hunger that she ate her own son (cf. Josephus, *De bello Iudaico*, 7, 8).

But the people will admit their sins, confess their faults, and realize they have deserved those terrible punishments; and the Lord, once again, will have compassion on them, remembering the Covenant he made with the three great patriarchs— Abraham, Isaac and Jacob.

---

qui oderunt vos, et fugietis, nemine persequente. [18]Sin autem nec sic oboedieritis mihi, addam correptiones vestras septuplum propter peccata vestra [19]et conteram superbiam duritiae vestrae. Daboque caelum vobis desuper sicut ferrum et terram aeneam. [20]Consumetur incassum robur vestrum: non proferet terra germen, nec arbores poma praebebunt. [21]Si ambulaveritis ex adverso mihi nec volueritis audire me, addam plagas vestras usque in septuplum propter peccata vestra; [22]emittamque in vos bestias agri, quae absque liberis vos faciant et deleant pecora vestra et ad paucitatem vos redigant, desertaeque fiant viae vestrae. [23]Quod si nec sic volueritis recipere disciplinam, sed ambulaveritis ex adverso mihi, [24]ego quoque contra vos adversus incedam et percutiam vos septies propter peccata vestra [25]inducamque super vos gladium ultorem foederis mei; cumque confugeritis in urbes vestras, mittam pestilentiam in medio vestri, et trademini hostium manibus. [26]Postquam confregero vobis baculum panis, coquent decem mulieres in uno clibano panem vestrum et reddent eum ad pondus, et comedetis et non saturabimini. [27]Sin autem nec per haec audieritis me, sed ambulaveritis contra me, [28]et ego incedam adversus vos in furore contrario; et corripiam vos septem plagis propter peccata vestra, [29]ita ut come-

Deut 28:53
2 Kings 6:26–29
Jer 19:9
Lam 2:20;
4:1–10
Ezek 5:10

tise you myself sevenfold for your sins. [29]You shall eat the flesh of your sons, and you shall eat the flesh of your daughters. [30]And I will destroy your high places, and cut down your incense altars, and cast your dead bodies upon the dead bodies of your idols; and my soul will abhor you. [31]And I will lay your cities waste, and will make your sanctuaries desolate, and I will not smell your pleasing odors. [32]And I will devastate the land, so that your enemies who settle in it shall be astonished at it. [33]And I will scatter you among the nations, and I will unsheathe the sword after you; and your land shall be a desolation, and your cities shall be a waste.

[34]"Then the land shall enjoy[n] its sabbaths as long as it lies desolate, while you are in your enemies' land; then the land shall rest, and enjoy its sabbaths. [35]As long as it lies desolate it shall have rest, the rest which it had not in your sabbaths when you dwelt upon it. [36]And as for those of you that are left, I will send faintness into their hearts in the lands of their enemies; the sound of a driven leaf shall put them to flight, and they shall flee as one flees from the sword, and they shall fall when none pursues. [37]They shall stumble over one another, as if to escape a sword, though none pursues; and you shall have no power to stand before your enemies. [38]And you shall perish among the nations, and the land of your enemies shall eat you up. [39]And those of you that are left shall pine away in your enemies' lands because of their iniquity; and also because of the iniquities of their fathers they shall pine away like them.

[40]"But if they confess their iniquity and the iniquity of their fathers in their treachery which they committed against me, and also in walking contrary to me, [41]so that I walked contrary to them and brought them into the land of their enemies; if then their uncircumcised heart is humbled and they make amends for their

Deut 30:1–14

Ezek 16:60;
20:9
Jer 4:4
Acts 7:51

datis carnes filiorum et filiarum vestrarum. [30]Destruam excelsa vestra et thymiamateria confringam et ponam cadavera vestra super cadavera idolorum vestrorum, et abominabitur vos anima mea, [31]in tantum ut urbes vestras redigam in solitudinem et deserta faciam sanctuaria vestra, nec recipiam ultra odorem suavissimum. [32]Disperdamque terram vestram; et stupebunt super ea inimici vestri, cum habitatores illius fuerint. [33]Vos autem dispergam in gentes et evaginabo post vos gladium; eritque terra vestra deserta et civitates dirutae. [34]Tunc placebunt terrae sabbata sua cunctis diebus solitudinis suae; quando fueritis in terra hostili, sabbatizabit et sabbata sua supplebit. [35]Cunctis diebus solitudinis sabbatizabit, eo quod non requieverit in sabbatis vestris, quando habitabatis in ea. [36]Et qui de vobis remanserint, dabo pavorem in cordibus eorum in regionibus hostium; terrebit eos sonitus folii volantis, et ita fugient quasi gladium; cadent, nullo persequente. [37]Et corruent singuli super fratres suos quasi bella fugientes, nemine persequente. Nemo vestrum inimicis audebit resistere. [38]Peribitis inter gentes, et hostilis vos terra consumet. [39]Quod si et de vobis aliqui remanserint, tabescent in iniquitatibus suis in terris inimicorum vestrorum, et propter peccata patrum suorum cum ipsis tabescent. [40]Et confitebuntur iniquitates suas et maiorum suorum, quibus praevaricati sunt in me et ambulaverunt ex adverso mihi, [41]ut et ego ambularem contra eos et inducerem illos in terram hostilem; vel tunc humiliabitur

n. Or *pay for*

Lk 1:72   iniquity; [42]then I will remember my covenant with Jacob, and I will remember my covenant with Isaac and my covenant with Abraham, and I will remember the land. [43]But the land shall be left by them, and enjoy[n] its sabbaths while it lies desolate without them; and they shall make amends for their iniquity, because they

Deut 4:29–31   spurned my ordinances, and their soul abhorred my statutes. [44]Yet for all that, when they are in the land of their enemies, I will not spurn them, neither will I abhor them so as to destroy them utterly and break my covenant with them; for I am the LORD their God;

Lev 22:33   [45]but I will for their sake remember the covenant with their forefathers, whom I brought forth out of the land of Egypt in the sight of the nations, that I might be their God: I am the LORD."

Gal 3:19   [46]These are the statutes and ordinances and laws which the LORD made between him and the people of Israel on Mount Sinai by Moses.

Appendix*

Num 30:2–17   **The discharge of vows**

27 [1]The LORD said to Moses, [2]"Say to the people of Israel, When a man makes a special vow of persons to the LORD at your valuation, [3]then your valuation of a male from twenty

---

*27:1–34. This chapter is an appendix which rounds off all the laws and regulations that have gone before it; it focuses mainly on vows (vv. 1–29) and on the question of tithes (vv. 30–34).

A vow could be made to consecrate to God a person over whom one had authority—as, for example, the vow Hannah made to dedicate Samuel to God (1 Sam 1:24–28).

---

incircumcisum cor eorum, et tunc expiabunt pro impietatibus suis. [42]Et recordabor foederis mei, quod pepigi cum Iacob et Isaac et Abraham. Terrae quoque memor ero, [43]quae, cum relicta fuerit ab eis, complacebit sibi in sabbatis suis patiens solitudinem propter illos. Ipsi vero expiabunt pro peccatis suis, eo quod abiecerint iudicia mea et leges meas despexerint. [44]Et tamen, etiam cum essent in terra hostili, non penitus abieci eos neque sic despexi, ut consumerentur, et irritum facerem pactum meum cum eis. Ego enim sum Dominus Deus eorum. [45]Et recordabor eis foederis cum maioribus, quos eduxi de terra Aegypti in conspectu gentium, ut essem Deus eorum. Ego Dominus». [46]Haec sunt iudicia atque praecepta et leges, quas dedit Dominus inter se et inter filios Israel in monte Sinai per manum Moysi. [1]Locutusque est Dominus ad Moysen dicens: [2]«Loquere filiis Israel et dices ad eos: Homo, qui votum fecerit et spoponderit Deo animas, sub aestimatione dabit pretium: [3]si fuerit masculus a vicesimo usque

n. Or *pay for*

years old up to sixty years old shall be fifty shekels of silver, according to the shekel of the sanctuary. [4]If the person is a female, your valuation shall be thirty shekels. [5]If the person is from five years old up to twenty years old, your valuation shall be for a male twenty shekels, and for a female ten shekels. [6]If the person is from a month old up to five years old, your valuation shall be for a male five shekels of silver, and for a female your valuation shall be three shekels of silver. [7]And if the person is sixty years old and upward, then your valuation for a male shall be fifteen shekels, and for a female ten shekels. [8]And if a man is too poor to pay your valuation, then he shall bring the person before the priest, and the priest shall value him; according to the ability of him who vowed the priest shall value him.

Evaluation of an animal offered to the Lord

[9]"If it is an animal such as men offer as an offering to the LORD, all of such that any man gives to the LORD is holy. [10]He shall not substitute anything for it or exchange it, a good for a bad, or a bad for a good; and if he makes any exchange of beast for beast, then both it and that for which it is exchanged shall be holy. [11]And if it is an unclean animal such as is not offered as an offering to the LORD, then the man shall bring the animal before the priest, [12]and the priest shall value it as either good or bad; as you, the priest, value it, so it shall be. [13]But if he wishes to redeem it, he shall add a fifth to the valuation.

Evaluation of landed property offered to the Lord

[14]"When a man dedicates his house to be holy to the LORD, the priest shall value it as either good or bad; as the priest values it, so it shall stand. [15]And if he who dedicates it wishes to redeem his house, he shall add a fifth of the valuation in money to it, and it shall be his.

ad sexagesimum annum, dabit quinquaginta siclos argenti ad mensuram sanctuarii; [4]si mulier, triginta. [5]A quinto autem anno usque ad vicesimum masculus dabit viginti siclos, femina decem; [6]ab uno mense usque ad annum quintum pro masculo dabuntur quinque sicli, pro femina tres; [7]sexagenarius et ultra masculus dabit quindecim siclos, femina decem. [8]Si pauper fuerit et aestimationem reddere non valebit, sistet eum coram sacerdote, et quantum ille aestimaverit et viderit posse reddere, tantum dabit. [9]Animal autem, quod immolari potest Domino, si quis voverit, sanctum erit [10]et mutari non poterit, id est nec melius malo nec peius bono. Quod si mutaverit, et ipsum quod mutatum est et illud pro quo mutatum est, consecratum erit Domino. [11]Animal immundum, quod immolari Domino non potest, si quis voverit, adducetur ante sacerdotem, [12]qui diiudicans utrum bonum an malum sit, sicut statuet pretium, sic erit. [13]Quod si redimere illud voluerit is qui offert, addet supra aestimationem quintam partem. [14]Homo si voverit domum suam et sanctificaverit Domino, considerabit eam sacerdos utrum bona an mala sit, et iuxta pretium, quod ab eo fuerit constitutum, stabit. [15]Sin autem ille, qui voverat, voluerit redimere eam, dabit quintam partem aestimationis supra et habebit domum. [16]Quod si agrum posses-

¹⁶"If a man dedicates to the LORD part of the land which is his by inheritance, then your valuation shall be according to the seed for it; a sowing of a homer of barley shall be valued at fifty shekels of silver. ¹⁷If he dedicates his field from the year of jubilee, it shall stand at your full valuation; ¹⁸but if he dedicates his field after the jubilee, then the priest shall compute the money-value for it according to the years that remain until the year of jubilee, and a deduction shall be made from your valuation. ¹⁹And if he who dedicates the field wishes to redeem it, then he shall add a fifth of the valuation in money to it, and it shall remain his. ²⁰But if he does not wish to redeem the field, or if he has sold the field to another

Lev 27:28   man, it shall not be redeemed any more; ²¹but the field, when it is released in the jubilee, shall be holy to the LORD, as a field that has been devoted; the priest shall be in possession of it. ²²If he dedicates to the LORD a field which he has bought, which is not a part of his possession by inheritance, ²³then the priest shall compute the valuation for it up to the year of jubilee, and the man shall give the amount of the valuation on that day as a holy thing to the LORD. ²⁴In the year of jubilee the field shall return to him from whom it was bought, to whom the land belongs as a possession by inheritance. ²⁵Every valuation shall be according to the shekel of the sanctuary: twenty gerahs shall make a shekel.

Compensation for the redemption of persons

Ex 13:11   ²⁶"But a firstling of animals, which as a firstling belongs to the LORD, no man may dedicate; whether ox or sheep, it is the LORD'S. ²⁷And if it is an unclean animal, then he shall buy it back at your valuation, and add a fifth to it; or, if it is not redeemed, it shall be sold at your valuation.

27:16. A "homer" meant literally an ass' burden but it was also used as a measure of grain (cf. Ezek 45:13; Hos 13:2), the equivalent of 210 litres (46 gallons).

sionis suae voverit et consecraverit Domino, iuxta mensuram sementis aestimabitur pretium: si triginta homer hordei seritur terra, quinquaginta siclis aestimabitur argenti. ¹⁷Si statim ab anno iobelei voverit agrum, quanto valere potest, tanto aestimabitur. ¹⁸Sin autem post aliquantum temporis, supputabit ei sacerdos pecuniam iuxta annorum, qui reliqui sunt, numerum usque ad iobeleum, et detrahetur ex pretio. ¹⁹Quod si voluerit redimere agrum ille, qui voverat, addet quintam partem aestimatae pecuniae et possidebit eum. ²⁰Sin autem noluerit redimere, sed alteri cuilibet vendiderit, ultra redimi non poterit; ²¹sed, cum iobelei venerit dies, sanctum erit Domino sicut ager anathematis; sacerdotis erit possessio eius. ²²Quod si agrum emptum, qui non est de possessione maiorum, sanctificare voluerit Domino, ²³supputabit ei sacerdos iuxta annorum numerum usque ad iobeleum pretium, quod dabit ille, qui voverat, in ipso die ut sanctum Domino. ²⁴In anno autem iobelei revertetur ager ad priorem dominum, qui vendiderat eum et habuerat in sortem possessionis suae. ²⁵Omnis aestimatio siclo sanctuarii ponderabitur; siclus viginti gera habet. ²⁶Primogenita, quae de animalibus ad Dominum pertinent, nemo sanctificare poterit et vovere: sive bos sive ovis fuerit, Domini sunt. ²⁷Quod si immundum est animal,

²⁸"But no devoted thing that a man devotes to the LORD, of anything that he has, whether of man or beast, or of his inherited field, shall be sold or redeemed; every devoted thing is most holy to the LORD. ²⁹No one devoted, who is to be utterly destroyed from among men, shall be ransomed; he shall be put to death.

Deut 7:26

Num 31
1 Sam 15

Rules about tithing

Num 18:26–32
Deut 14:22
Mt 23:23

³⁰"All the tithe of the land, whether of the seed of the land or of the fruit of the trees, is the LORD's; it is holy to the LORD. ³¹If a man wishes to redeem any of his tithe, he shall add a fifth to it. ³²And all the tithe of herds and flocks, every tenth animal of all that pass under the herdsman's staff, shall be holy to the LORD. ³³A man shall not inquire whether it is good or bad, neither shall he exchange it; and if he exchanges it, then both it and that for which it is exchanged shall be holy; it shall not be redeemed."

³⁴These are the commandments which the LORD commanded Moses for the people of Israel on Mount Sinai.

27:28–29. "Devoting something to the Lord", as the RSV puts it, translates the Hebrew *jérem*, which means "separating something off for the Lord's exclusive use". When applied to war, it involved destroying all booty in honour of God; this had the effect of making Israel less keen to invade weak peoples purely for the purpose of enriching itself at the expense of those it defeated (cf. the notes on Ex 22:18–31; Num 21:3; Deut 2:24–27).

The Jerusalem Bible translates the RSV's "devoted" as "laid under ban". When applied to divine worship this "ban" or "anathema" means an offering made because of a vow; once offered, the thing can no longer be used to one's own advantage (vv. 21–28) because it is a very holy thing. In the sphere of judicial sanctions, "laid under ban" applies to every condemned wrongdoer (and in biblical law to be condemned means to be sentenced to death). Therefore, a person condemned to death was "laid under law" and could not be used as a slave or put to forced labour. The prescription in v. 29 helped lessen any desire to accuse or condemn one's neighbour in order to benefit the community or its leaders. All these rules contained imperfections which became very clear in the light of the New Testament's precept of love of God and neighbour.

redimet, qui obtulit, iuxta aestimationem et addet quintam partem pretii; si redimere noluerit, vendetur quanto fuerit. ²⁸Omne anathema, quod aliquis vir consecrat Domino de omni possessione sua, sive homo fuerit sive animal sive ager, non veniet, nec redimi poterit; quidquid semel fuerit consecratum, sanctum sanctorum erit Domino. ²⁹Et omnis homo, qui ut anathema offertur, non redimetur, sed morte morietur. ³⁰Omnes decimae terrae sive de frugibus sive de pomis arborum Domini sunt, sanctum Domino. ³¹Si quis autem voluerit redimere aliquid de decimis suis, addet quintam partem. ³²Omnes decimae boves et oves et caprae, quae sub pastoris virga transeunt, quidquid decimum venerit, erit sanctum Domino. ³³Non discernetur inter bonum et malum, nec altero commutabitur; si quis mutaverit, et quod mutatum est et pro quo mutatum est, sanctum erit et non redimetur». ³⁴Haec sunt praecepta, quae mandavit Dominus Moysi ad filios Israel in monte Sinai.

NUMBERS

Introduction

The name of this book, *Numbers*, comes from the Greek translation of the Pentateuch (*c.*2nd century BC) which called it *aritmoí* "numbers" on account of the census of the people which is covered in the first chapter. The Jewish name for the book is *Bemidbar* ("in the desert") because this is the opening word of the book and it denotes its theme—the time the people of Israel made their pilgrimage through the desert, where God manifested himself to them.

1. STRUCTURE AND CONTENT

The book has a varied subject matter and literary style. It contains many narrative passages alongside quite extensive legal texts and short poetic pieces. Although for the most part it contains material different from that in the rest of the Pentateuch, there are also many passages (both narrative and legal) which repeat what appears elsewhere. For example, the people's complaints and the miracle of the quails recounted in chapter 11 are practically a repeat of Exodus 16; and Numbers 20:1–9 about the water from the rock is very similar to a passage in Exodus 17; etc.

The book divides into four parts based on scenarios that occur as the people of Israel make their way through the wilderness.

PART ONE: THE PEOPLE IN THE SINAI DESERT (1:1—10:10). Here we see it in its full numerical strength and structured as a religious community, preparing to set out on its march.

In this scenario (which is the same as that found in the second part of the book of Exodus and in Leviticus) we are given a detailed description of the people of the Covenant. The sacred writer must have thought it important to provide, before the journey begins, a tribe by tribe count of the male Israelites of military age (cf. 1:2–46) and a description of where they were positioned in the camp (2:1–34), because these were the men who made up the army of the Lord. But the tribe of Levi held a special place and therefore its status and functions called for special treatment (3:1—4:49); so the description of it gives rise to detailing various laws about cleanness (5:1–4), restitution etc. (5:5–31), the Nazarite vow (6:1–22), the wording of a blessing (6:23–27), offerings (7:1–89), the design of the lampstand (8:1–4), the presentation of Levites to the Lord (8:5–56) and the celebration of the Passover (9:1–14). Before they set

out on their pilgrimage we are once more told about the meaning and purpose of the cloud that accompanies them (9:15–23; even though this was already covered in Exodus 40:34–38) and about how trumpets are to be sounded to assemble the people (10:1–10). Once all this is done everything is in place for the departure from Sinai.

PART TWO: THE PEOPLE IN KADESH (10:11—20:21). This place was between the desert of Paran and that of Sin. Here the people rebelled against the Lord and experienced the bitterness of divine punishment, the effectiveness of Moses' prayer, and the mercy of God, who pardons time and time again.

Very little space is given to the journey to Kadesh (10:11): the narrative focuses immediately on what occurred at Kadesh itself. However, it does stress that the cloud led them to the desert of Paran, and that as they walked they kept to their order of camp (10:13–34). There are a number of episodes connected with Kadesh, all of which have to do basically with the people's complaints, Moses' intercession and the manifestation of divine anger and pardon. These episodes include the fire at Taberah (11:1–3), the protest about the manna and Moses' difficulties in controlling the people, God's reply with the appointment of the judges (11:24–30) and the sending of the quails (11:31–35), Aaron and Miriam grumbling against Moses (12:1–15). In the same context we are told about the reconnoitring of Canaan and the people's refusal to fight their way into the Land (13:1—14:38), and also their defeat when they eventually do decide to enter the Land without relying on God's help (14:39–45).

And then, out of the blue, as it were, come various laws about sacrifice, offerings, expiation, keeping the sabbath and the Law (15:1–41), all specifically designed for when they will eventually reach the Land. These laws, therefore, are meant to keep the Israelites' hope alive during these difficult times in the desert, and they help the reader to see that, despite all that has happened, God remains true to his promise (but see the note on Num 15:1—19:22). The rebellion of Korah, Moses' and Aaron's cousin (16:1–35), which is the next thing dealt with, provides a suitable framework for expounding the priestly role of Aaron's family (17:16–26), the rights and functions of priests and Levites (17:27—18:32), and the rites of atonement (19:1–22). After describing these laws the text goes back to Kadeh, this time with a view to leaving that place; once more it touches on the Israelites' arrival there (it is now called the wilderness of Sin: 20:1), and again we meet the basic theme of the book, the complaining of the people, this time over the shortage of water (20:1–13). At this point an explanation is given for why they have to take an unforeseen route: Edom has blocked their way (20:1–13). And so the scene of the action changes and becomes the journey to Moab.

PART THREE: FROM KADESH TO MOAB (20:22—21:35). At various stages in this journey the people of Israel continue to experience God's punishment and

his mercy—but most of all his mercy, in the form of Israel's first victories over its enemies.

More important than the actual itinerary is what happens in this new scenario—the death of Aaron (20:22–29); the taking of Hormah, which confirms that God is on their side (21:1–3); the constant grumbling of the people, culminating in the episode of the bronze serpent (21:4–9); memories of specific places, recorded in poems and songs (21:10–20); and finally passages celebrating the victories over Sihon and Og (21:21–35) which open up to Israel the plains of Moab, where the last scene in this book is set.

PART FOUR: ISRAEL ON THE PLAINS OF MOAB (22:1—36:13). This is the last place the Israelites spend some time in prior to entering the promised land. Here God continues to protect them from powerful enemies, and he enables them to gain further victories which already allow some tribes to settle in the Transjordan.

Being the last scene in the book the sacred writer uses it not just to give an account of what happened there but also to provide an over-view of the whole desert period and of the preparations for the occupation of the promised land. So, with all these subjects vying for attention, the narrative looks rather untidy. It begins with the account of Balaam's oracles (22:2—24:25) which exalt the greatness and glorious future of Israel, and it goes on to deal with the infidelity of the people at Peor (25:1–18). At the end of the desert journey and all its vicissitudes, a new census of the people is described (26:1–65) with a view to the division of the Land. In this context the question of daughters' inheritance is brought up (28:1–11), and the appointment of Joshua as Moses' successor is reported (27:17–23). Also, various laws are recorded which have to do with sacrifices, feasts, and vows which the people must undertake to carry out when they gain possession of the promised land (28:1—30:17).

The theme of the conquest of the promised land and how it is shared out forms the background of this last part of the book; already we have the waging of war against Midian and the division of the booty (31:1–54) and the allocation of Transjordan to some tribes (32:1–42). This invites a glance backward to the whole itinerary from Egypt to Canaan, followed by the plan for the carving up of Canaan (33:50–56), its boundaries (34:1–29), the cities where the Levites are to live (25:1–8), the special cities of refuge (35:9–34), and the regulations about the marriage of women of property, to ensure that each tribe's landholding is not eroded (36:1–12). This means that practically everything is in place for making the great move on Jericho, the gateway to the promised land. However, there is still a need for God to give Israel the Law a second time: this is what the book of Deuteronomy deals with (and the setting for that book is still the plains of Moab).

2. HISTORICAL BACKGROUND: ISRAEL IN THE DESERT

No archaeological evidence has been found of the Israelites' stay in the desert. This is not surprising, given, on the one hand, the conditions that obtain in a desert, and on the other the type of nomadic life the people of Israel led there. However, this stage in their history left a profound mark on the culture and the very make-up of the people of Israel. We can see this in their form of speech, where, for example, "tent" is equivalent to "house"; in certain customs, such as vengeance by blood and the importance of hospitality; in the very fact that the nation is made up of tribes; and, most especially, in its religion which hinges on the worship of Yahweh. Besides, many of the stories told in the book reveal a desert background—shortage of water, manna as a plant secretion; quails which arrive exhausted from the sea; the serpent made of bronze in the mining region of Eslon Gueber; the basic geography; and the information about the peoples living in that area. So, the testimony of Exodus and Numbers about Israel's having come from the desert seems to be well-founded.

Yet, for all that, the Numbers account of Israel's journey does not provide details of the route followed, the various stages, or even the external and internal difficulties the Israelites encountered. Instead it offers an interpretation of the meaning of that time as seen from a later perspective—the life and history of a people that has never quite decided whether to be unfaithful to God, and then take its punishment, or to serve that God by means of temple worship and thereby experience his mercy. The book records ancient memories that go back to the time Israel spent in the desert; but often these are anecdotal memories that have in some way become detached from the group that was responsible for their transmission and have been given a general application to the entire people. It is not surprising, therefore, that Numbers leaves some things unclear from the historical point of view: for example, it does not tell us exactly what route was followed from Sinai to Moab; it does not say exactly how long the crossing of the desert took or even whether there was just one expedition led of Moses or whether there were a number of groups which made their way to the promised land at different times and by different routes.

3. COMPOSITION

As we already pointed out in the "Introduction to the Pentateuch" (above), one of the most important of Israel's traditions is that which records accounts of the people's stay in the desert. The prophets bear witness to the survival of these traditions. Thus, in the book of Amos, God tells his people, "I brought you up out of the land of Egypt, and led you forty years in the wilderness to possess the land of the Amorite" (Amos 2:10). In fact this crossing of the

desert is interpreted as a moment of crucial importance in the relationship between God and Israel, a relationship in which manifestations of God's goodness, and infidelity on the part of the people, recur all the time: "Like grapes in the wilderness, I found Israel. Like the first fruit on the fig tree, in its first season, I saw your fathers. But they came to Baal-peor, and consecrated themselves to Baal and became detestable like the thing they loved" (Hos 9:10).

Oral traditions about this time in the desert were passed on from parents to children as something to be learned and pondered. Other, stray bits of stories would become attached to those traditions until a fairly substantial narrative was in place, big enough to provide the framework for lots of legal texts. The redaction process of the book of Numbers did not differ much from that of Genesis and the first part of Exodus: there a similar interweaving of the great threads of the literary tradition presents in the text (cf. "Introduction to the Pentateuch", pp. 19-21 above).

It is the Priestly tradition that has been conserved most vigorously and extensively in the book of Numbers. Moreover, the final redaction of the book keeps largely to the spirit of that tradition, which it takes, by preference, from Exodus 25. Most of the present text of Numbers is probably taken from that tradition. There is also good reason to think that when Numbers came to be included in the Pentateuch it underwent some retouching, perhaps near the end of the book or in the parts dealing with the death of Moses, thereby leaving the Moab section open to allow the Deuteronomy legislation to be inserted into it. In any event, the unity of the overall content of Numbers is plain to see: it covers the pilgrimage of the people of God in the desert from the mountain of the Lord, Sinai, to the plains of Moab facing Jericho, the gateway to the promised land.

4. MESSAGE

The book of Numbers has its own way of describing how God acts towards men and, specifically, towards the people whom he chose to be his own— Israel. This special feature lies in the fact that God is depicted as the one who guides his people through the desert, en route to the promised land. In the book of Numbers the people are no longer the shapeless crowd they were when they left Egypt; they are a holy community (which can be the subject of a detailed census), a community that is the outcome of the Covenant (cf. pp. 240–243 above). The desert here is a place of transit, involving all kinds of difficulties; this tempts the people to be disheartened and to rebel against God, who has led them here; but the desert is also the place where they experience at first hand the forgiveness and mercy of God. In spite of their rebelliousness, God puts into action his plan to lead them to the promised land.

God's mysterious presence among his people as they make their pilgrim way is symbolized by the cloud; and the cloud is also what shows them the way to follow. It is God himself who leads the people this way and that as he so chooses, even though sometimes they cannot see the sense of it all. Two things show their recognition of God's presence—the tent of meeting (which is where they meet God) and the ark of the Covenant which houses the tables of the Law. These things form the centre around which the camp is pitched, and around which the life of the people turns. However, God also manifests his presence through events—adverse events which are a form of chastisement, such as disease, fire, military defeats etc., and favourable events which are a form of forgiveness and salvation, such as water, food, curing of disease, victories etc. God expects his people to be docile to his plans, but they seldom prove to be so; and yet he continues to lead them forward. Indeed, the people's complaints and grumbling actually provide the occasion for God to manifest his holiness and his glory, not only by punishing them but above all by granting them new gifts—water from the rock, quails, sharing his spirit with the seventy elders, the bronze serpent, etc.

During this desert pilgrimage, God keeps on purifying his people through a series of tests or trials—the external difficulties they encounter and, for the most part, fail to cope with: instead, they complain and rebel. The punishment which follows these rebellions is also meant to purify them and bring about their conversion. The entire generation which left Egypt, including Moses and Aaron, proved rebellious, and therefore God purified the people by letting that generation die in the desert, before bringing the Israelites into the promised land. But God does not wipe out his people; the people which will enter the Land will be a people renewed.

God looks after his people and guides them by showing them not only the route to take but also the way to live their lives and serve him; this he does through intermediaries whom he himself appoints. These are Moses, the head of the community, and Aaron, its priest. And because these two men will end their days while still in the desert, God himself singles out and consecrates their successors—Joshua and Eleazar. They too will be his representatives.

The time Israel spent on its desert pilgrimage survived in the folk memory as a golden age of its relationship with God, in sharp contrast with its comfort-loving and easy-going lifestyle in later times. The prophets will recall those years as a time when God was worshipped with sincerity of heart, even though that liturgy was quite poor compared with the splendour of the liturgy to come (cf. Hos 5:25). Reacting against Israel's idolatrous infidelity in Canaan, the prophet Hosea proclaims that God will lead his people out into the desert a second time; there he will speak to its heart, to revive the love it had in its days of youth (cf. Hos 2:16; Jer 2:2–3). So too, in order to draw closer to God and gain strength from his mission, the prophet Elijah will make his way into the wilderness, to Mount Horeb or Sinai in fact (cf. 1 Kings 19).

The Psalms, too, will sing of the wonders worked by God in the desert —
particularly the fact that in his mercy he did not destroy his people despite its
rebellions (cf. Ps 78:15–24; 106:7–11). Recalling the events of the desert, the
Psalms appeal for conversion to God at the very moment they are being
recited—today (cf. Ps 95:7–11). The crossing of the desert, like the Exodus,
will also become a symbol of the joyous return of the Jews exiled in Babylon,
with the wilderness turning into a fruitful field (cf. Is 32:15; 35:1).

Drawing on Israel's happy memories, the book of Numbers gathers up the
traditions of the desert to show the meaning of Israel's pilgrimage through the
centuries. The features of this book recur again and again in Israel's history—
hope of better times, or the establishment of the Kingdom of God; the trials
and infidelities of the people, as also its liturgical worship of God; and, over
and above everything else, the merciful God who is always calling men to a
change of heart and who will bring his plans to fruition despite human weakness and wavering.

5. NUMBERS IN THE LIGHT OF THE NEW TESTAMENT

Before beginning his public ministry Jesus was led by the Spirit into the
desert, where he was tempted. But, unlike the people of Israel, Jesus came out
victorious (cf. Mt 4:1–11 and par.). He went on to work miracles similar to
those God worked in the desert—the multiplication of the loaves, for example
(cf. Mt 14:13–21 and par.)—and he proclaimed that in him were fulfilled the
divine gifts prefigured during that stage in Israel's history: he is the living
water (cf. Jn 4:7), the true bread comes down from heaven (cf. Jn 6), the way
(cf. Jn 14:6); like the bronze serpent bringing healing and salvation (cf. Jn
3:14–16); he is truly the place to find God (cf. Jn 14:8). If we live in communion with Christ during our pilgrimage in this world, that means we are
advancing steadily towards the goal of our everlasting home.

The Gospels also portray Jesus as "actualizing" features of that desert
experience. His virginal conception in Mary's womb is brought about by an
action of God that can be likened to God's presence in the cloud in the desert
(cf. Lk 1:38). Christ's life among men is interpreted as being like the presence
of the tent of meeting in the Israelites' camp, the place where they meet God
(cf. Jn 1:14; cf. the note on Num 2:1–34).

If the book of Numbers meant for the Israelites not just a reminder of
things past but also, so to speak, a model epitomizing their entire history, for
Christians that model is Jesus Christ in whom the words of this book find their
fulfilment, and who has become our way and our guide, showing us how to go
forward in our lives, how to deal with the same sort of trials and difficulties as
the Israelites met in the desert. Thus, the Letter to the Hebrews exhorts us to
keep going forward and not let our hearts be seduced by sin; since "we have a

Numbers

great high priest who has passed through the heavens, Jesus, the Son of God, let us hold fast to our confession" (Heb 4:14). If we do that, we shall reach our eternal rest. The Church itself is making its way through history amid all kinds of trials, yet confident in God's protection, just as the ancient people of Israel were in the desert (cf. Rev 12:6, 14): "As Israel according to the flesh which wandered in the desert was already called the Church of God, so too, the new Israel, which advances in this present era in search of a future and permanent city, is called also the Church of Christ. It is Christ indeed who had purchased it with his own blood; he has filled it with his Spirit; he has provided means adapted to its visible and social union. [. . .] Advancing through trials and tribulations, the Church is strengthened by God's grace, promised to her by the Lord so that she may not waver from perfect fidelity"[3] (Vatican II, *Lumen gentium*, 9). In the general context of Holy Scripture, what the book of Numbers does, therefore, is show the Word of God encouraging us to make our way forward, at the pace set by him, to strive manfully in the midst of difficulties and to serve the Lord with sincere worship.

In interpreting the book of Numbers, and following the line of interpretation given it in the New Testament, the Tradition of the Church has identified many symbols referring both to Jesus Christ and to the Church itself and Christian life. In the commentary that follows we give some examples of that interpretation and of ways in which the teaching contained in Numbers can find application today.

The People of Israel in the Sinai Desert*

1. THE COMMUNITY OF ISRAEL

The census of the tribes

Num 10:13–
28; 26:1–51
2 Sam 24
Rev 7:5–8

1 ¹The LORD spoke to Moses in the wilderness of Sinai, in the
tent of meeting, on the first day of the second month, in the
second year after they had come out of the land of Egypt, saying,
²"Take a census of all the congregation of the people of Israel, by
families, by fathers' houses, according to the number of names,
every male, head by head; ³from twenty years old and upward, all
in Israel who are able to go forth to war, you and Aaron shall
number them, company by company. ⁴And there shall be with you
a man from each tribe, each man being the head of the house of
his fathers. ⁵And these are the names of the men who shall attend

Ex 7:4

---

*1:1—10:36. The first ten chapters of the
book of Numbers extend and complete
the narrative contained in the last chapters of Exodus about the Israelites' stay
in the Sinai desert after God made the
Covenant with the people and before they
set out again on their journey. Here we
see them preparing to move out. They
form a holy community, perfectly organized and congregated around the tent of
meeting, where the Levites perform their
ministry with care and dedication.

1:2–46. God calls for the census to show
that Israel belongs to him. A count is
made of all the men capable of bearing
arms. However, in the context of the
Pentateuch this military census is seen as

having a religious dimension, given that
the people constitute the army of the
Lord (cf. Ex 7:4). We already saw in
Exodus 38:25–26 that the overall result
of this census was taken account of when
it came to calculating the contribution
each person should make to the cost of
building the tabernacle.

The figures reflect the people's
memory of the relative strength of the
tribes. The tribe of Judah is depicted as
being the largest. The place where this
census is put in the final redaction of the
Pentateuch has significance: it comes at
the point when Israel is making its pilgrimage through the desert to the
promised land. The high total number
suggests that of the two promises the

---

¹Locutusque est Dominus ad Moysen in deserto Sinai in tabernaculo conventus, prima die mensis
secundi, anno altero egressionis eorum ex Aegypto, dicens: ²«Tollite summam universae congregationis filiorum Israel per cognationes et domos suas et nomina singulorum, quidquid sexus est masculini
³a vicesimo anno et supra omnium ex Israel, qui possunt ad bella procedere, et numerabitis eos per
turmas suas, tu et Aaron. ⁴Eritque vobiscum vir per tribum, princeps domus patrum suorum, ⁵quorum
ista sunt nomina: de Ruben Elisur filius Sedeur; ⁶de Simeon Salamiel filius Surisaddai; ⁷de Iuda

529

you. From Reuben, Elizur the son of Shedeur; [6]from Simeon, Shelumi-el the son of Zurishaddai; [7]from Judah, Nahshon the son of Amminadab; [8]from Issachar, Nethanel the son of Zuar; [9]from Zebulun, Eliab the son of Helon; [10]from the sons of Joseph, from Ephraim, Elishama the son of Ammihud, and from Manasseh, Gamaliel the son of Pedahzur; [11]from Benjamin, Abidan the son of Gideoni; [12]from Dan, Ahiezer the son of Ammishaddai; [13]from Asher, Pagiel the son of Ochran; [14]from Gad, Eliasaph the son of Deuel; [15]from Naphtali, Ahira the son of Enan." [16]These were the ones chosen from the congregation, the leaders of their ancestral tribes, the heads of the clans of Israel.

[17]Moses and Aaron took these men who have been named, [18]and on the first day of the second month, they assembled the whole congregation together, who registered themselves by families, by fathers' houses, according to the number of names from twenty years old and upward, head by head, [19]as the LORD commanded Moses. So he numbered them in the wilderness of Sinai.

[20]The people of Reuben, Israel's first-born, their generations, by their families, by their fathers' houses, according to the number of names, head by head, every male from twenty years old and upward, all who were able to go forth to war: [21]the number of the tribe of Reuben was forty-six thousand five hundred.

Lord made to Jacob (to give him the Land and numerous descendants: cf. Gen 28:13–14), the second has already come about, and the first is about to happen.

The Jewish reader of this passage can see the splendid unity and diversity of the chosen people, while at the same time identifying with the particular group to which family tradition tells him he belongs.

The Christian reader sees in that people of the twelve tribes a prefiguring of the Church which was founded by Christ on the twelve apostles (cf. Mt 19:28) and which is the new people of God. In view of this, neither the Church nor the Christian can feel a stranger to that people, whose census in the wilderness proclaims the symbolic "census" of those who are saved by the blood of Christ (cf. Rev 7:5–8).

Naasson filius Aminadab; [8]de Issachar Nathanael filius Suar; [9]de Zabulon Eliab filius Helon. [10]Filiorum autem Ioseph: de Ephraim Elisama filius Ammiud; de Manasse Gamaliel filius Phadassur. [11]De Beniamin Abidan filius Gedeonis; [12]de Dan Ahiezer filius Ammisaddai; [13]de Aser Phegiel filius Ochran; [14]de Gad Eliasaph filius Deuel; [15]de Nephthali Ahira filius Enan». [16]Hi viri nobilissimi congregationis principes tribuum patrum suorum et capita milium Israel. [17]Quos tulerunt Moyses et Aaron nominatim designatos [18]et omnem congregationem congregaverunt primo die mensis secundi recensentes eos per cognationes et domos patrum eorum, per nomina singulorum a vicesimo anno et supra per capita, [19]sicut praeceperat Dominus Moysi. Numeratique sunt in deserto Sinai. [20]De Ruben primogenito Israelis generationes per familias ac domos patrum suorum, per nomina capitum singulorum omne quod sexus est masculini a vicesimo anno et supra procedentium ad bellum. [21]Recensiti tribus Ruben quadraginta sex milia quingenti. [22]De filiis Simeon generationes per familias ac domos cognationum

²²Of the people of Simeon, their generations, by their families, by their fathers' houses, those of them that were numbered, according to the number of names, head by head, every male from twenty years old and upward, all who were able to go forth to war: ²³the number of the tribe of Simeon was fifty-nine thousand three hundred.

²⁴Of the people of Gad, their generations, by their families, by their fathers' houses, according to the number of the names, from twenty years old and upward, all who were able to go forth to war: ²⁵the number of the tribe of Gad was forty-five thousand six hundred and fifty.

²⁶Of the people of Judah, their generations, by their families, by their fathers' houses, according to the number of names, from twenty years old and upward, every man able to go forth to war: ²⁷the number of the tribe of Judah was seventy-four thousand six hundred.

²⁸Of the people of Issachar, their generations, by their families, by their fathers' houses, according to the number of names, from twenty years old and upward, every man able to go forth to war: ²⁹the number of the tribe of Issachar was fifty-four thousand four hundred.

³⁰Of the people of Zebulun, their generations, by their families, by their fathers' houses, according to the number of names, from twenty years old and upward, every man able to go forth to war: ³¹the number of the tribe of Zebulun was fifty-seven thousand four hundred.

³²Of the people of Joseph, namely, of the people of Ephraim, their generations, by their families, by their fathers' houses, according to the number of names, from twenty years old and upward, every man able to go forth to war: ³³the number of the tribe of Ephraim was forty thousand five hundred.

---

suarum recensiti sunt per nomina et capita singulorum omne quod sexus est masculini a vicesimo anno et supra procedentium ad bellum. ²³Recensiti tribus Simeon quinquaginta novem milia trecenti. ²⁴De filiis Gad generationes per familias ac domos cognationum suarum recensiti sunt per nomina singulorum a viginti annis et supra omnes, qui ad bella procederent, ²⁵quadraginta quinque milia sexcenti quinquaginta. ²⁶De filiis Iudae generationes per familias ac domos cognationum suarum per nomina singulorum a vicesimo anno et supra omnes, qui poterant ad bella procedere, ²⁷recensiti sunt septuaginta quattuor milia sexcenti. ²⁸De filiis Issachar generationes per familias ac domos cognationum suarum per nomina singulorum a vicesimo anno et supra omnes, qui ad bella procederent, ²⁹recensiti sunt quinquaginta quattuor milia quadringenti. ³⁰De filiis Zabulon generationes per familias ac domos cognationum suarum recensiti sunt per nomina singulorum a vicesimo anno et supra omnes, qui poterant ad bella procedere, ³¹quinquaginta septem milia quadringenti. ³²De filiis Ioseph filiorum Ephraim generationes per familias ac domos cognationum suarum recensiti sunt per nomina singulorum a vicesimo anno et supra omnes, qui poterant ad bella procedere, ³³quadraginta milia quingenti. ³⁴Porro filiorum Manasse generationes per familias ac domos cognationum suarum recensiti sunt per nomina

³⁴Of the people of Manasseh, their generations, by their families, by their fathers' houses, according to the number of names, from twenty years old and upward, every man able to go forth to war: ³⁵the number of the tribe of Manasseh was thirty-two thousand two hundred.

³⁶Of the people of Benjamin, their generations, by their families, by their fathers' houses, according to the number of names, from twenty years old and upward, every man able to go forth to war: ³⁷the number of the tribe of Benjamin was thirty-five thousand four hundred.

³⁸Of the people of Dan, their generations, by their families, by their fathers' houses, according to the number of names, from twenty years old and upward, every man able to go forth to war: ³⁹the number of the tribe of Dan was sixty-two thousand seven hundred.

⁴⁰Of the people of Asher, their generations, by their families, by their fathers' houses, according to the number of names, from twenty years old and upward, every man able to go forth to war: ⁴¹the number of the tribe of Asher was forty-one thousand five hundred.

⁴²Of the people of Naphtali, their generations, by their families, by their fathers' houses, according to the number of names, from twenty years old and upward, every man able to go forth to war: ⁴³the number of the tribe of Naphtali was fifty-three thousand four hundred.

⁴⁴These are those who were numbered, whom Moses and Aaron numbered with the help of the leaders of Israel, twelve men, each representing his fathers' house. ⁴⁵So the whole number of the people of Israel, by their fathers' houses, from twenty years old and upward, every man able to go forth to war in Israel— ⁴⁶their whole number was six hundred and three thousand five hundred and fifty.

Ex 12:37; 38:26 Num 26:51

singulorum a viginti annis et supra omnes, qui poterant ad bella procedere, ³⁵triginta duo milia ducenti. ³⁶De filiis Beniamin generationes per familias ac domos cognationum suarum recensiti sunt nominibus singulorum a vicesimo anno et supra omnes, qui poterant ad bella procedere, ³⁷triginta quinque milia quadringenti. ³⁸De filiis Dan generationes per familias ac domos cognationum suarum recensiti sunt nominibus singulorum a vicesimo anno et supra omnes, qui poterant ad bella procedere, ³⁹sexaginta duo milia septingenti. ⁴⁰De filiis Aser generationes per familias ac domos cognationum suarum recensiti sunt per nomina singulorum a vicesimo anno et supra omnes, qui poterant ad bella procedere, ⁴¹quadraginta milia et mille quingenti. ⁴²De filiis Nephthali generationes per familias ac domos cognationum suarum recensiti sunt nominibus singulorum a vicesimo anno et supra omnes, qui poterant ad bella procedere, ⁴³quinquaginta tria milia quadringenti. ⁴⁴Hi sunt quos numeraverunt Moyses et Aaron et duodecim principes Israel, singuli per domos patrum suorum. ⁴⁵Fueruntque omnis numerus filiorum Israel per domos patrum suorum a vicesimo anno et supra, qui poterant ad bella procedere, ⁴⁶sexcenta tria milia virorum quingenti quinquaginta. ⁴⁷Levitae autem in tribu patrum suorum non sunt numerati

A special statute for the tribe of Levi

[47]But the Levites were not numbered by their ancestral tribe along with them. [48]For the LORD said to Moses, [49]"Only the tribe of Levi you shall not number, and you shall not take a census of them among the people of Israel; [50]but appoint the Levites over the tabernacle of the testimony, and over all its furnishings, and over all that belongs to it; they are to carry the tabernacle and all its furnishings, and they shall tend it, and shall encamp around the tabernacle. [51]When the tabernacle is to set out, the Levites shall take it down; and when the tabernacle is to be pitched, the Levites shall set it up. And if any one else comes near, he shall be put to death. [52]The people of Israel shall pitch their tents by their companies, every man by his own camp and every man by his own standard; [53]but the Levites shall encamp around the tabernacle of the testimony, that there may be no wrath upon the congregation

---

1:47–54. The members of the tribe of Levi are not included in the census of the children of Israel. The census had a military purpose, and the Levites, whose role it was to perform functions directly connected with the sanctuary, were not allowed to engage in other activities so that contact with profane things would not render them unclean. The tribe of Levi was set aside to be exclusively at the service of the tabernacle.

Liturgical functions to be carried out by the Levites in the sanctuary and particularly in the temple of Jerusalem have their roots in the Covenant; that is why the text recalls the fact that those functions began at the time when Israel was in the desert.

Extraordinary importance is given to the care of the tabernacle, such that, according to the sacred text, an entire tribe was allocated to looking after all its equipment and attending to its service.

The text even points out that this watchfulness redounds to the benefit of all because it ensures that the wrath of God will not fall "upon the congregation of the people of Israel" (v. 53).

This passage is an invitation to reflect on the care that should be given to everything having to do with worship. The tabernacle in the desert was a sign of God's presence among his people. Christians use the same word, "tabernacle", to refer to that sacred place of the "real presence", where Jesus Christ, the Son of God, is present under the sacramental species. The care that the Levites took of that earlier tabernacle is an example for Christians of the veneration they should have for the tabernacle of the Real Presence. "The dignity, placing and security of the Eucharistic tabernacle should foster adoration before the Lord really present in the Blessed Sacrament of the altar" (*Catechism of the Catholic Church*, 1183).

cum eis. [48]Locutusque est Dominus ad Moysen dicens: [49]«Tribum Levi noli numerare neque pones summam eorum cum filiis Israel, [50]sed constitue eos super habitaculum testimonii et cuncta vasa eius et quidquid ad caeremonias pertinet. Ipsi portabunt habitaculum et omnia utensilia eius et erunt in ministerio ac per gyrum habituli metabuntur. [51]Cum proficiscendum fuerit, deponent Levitae habitaculum; cum castrametandum, erigent; quisquis externorum accesserit, occidetur. [52]Metabuntur autem castra filii Israel, unusquisque per turmas et cuneos atque exercitum suum. [53]Porro Levitae per gyrum

of the people of Israel; and the Levites shall keep charge of the tabernacle of the testimony." ⁵⁴Thus did the people of Israel; they did according to all that the LORD commanded Moses.

Ezek 48:30–35
Rev 21:12–13

The order of the tribes in the camp

2 ¹The LORD said to Moses and Aaron, ²"The people of Israel shall encamp each by his own standard, with the ensigns of their fathers' houses; they shall encamp facing the tent of meeting on every side. ³Those to encamp on the east side toward the sunrise shall be of the standard of the camp of Judah by their companies, the leader of the people of Judah being Nahshon the son of Amminadab, ⁴his host as numbered being seventy-four thousand six hundred. ⁵Those to encamp next to him shall be the tribe of Issachar, the leader of the people of Issachar being Nethanel the son of Zuar, ⁶his host as numbered being fifty-four thousand four hundred. ⁷Then the tribe of Zebulun, the leader of the people of Zebulun being Eliab the son of Helon, ⁸his host as numbered being fifty-seven thousand four hundred. ⁹The whole number of the camp of Judah, by their companies, is a hundred and eighty-six thousand four hundred. They shall set out first on the march.

¹⁰"On the south side shall be the standard of the camp of Reuben by their companies, the leader of the people of Reuben being Elizur the son of Shedeur, ¹¹his host as numbered being

---

2:1–34. The people are described as being drawn up in formation around the tabernacle, a holy people, in perfect array, encamped in the desert, and on the move, united to their Lord. Whether encamped or on the march, the twelve tribes keep this formation, in the shape of a square. There are three tribes on each of the four sides and at the centre are the Levites, surrounding the tent. The city of Jerusalem is depicted in the same kind of way by the prophet Ezekiel (cf. Ezek 48:30–35), and the heavenly Jerusalem by the book of Revelation (cf. Rev 21:12–13). The passage contains a key teaching: God is always present in the midst of his people; there he has his dwelling.

---

habitaculi testimonii figent tentoria, ne fiat indignatio super congregationem filiorum Israel, et excubabunt in custodiis habitaculi testimonii». ⁵⁴Fecerunt ergo filii Israel iuxta omnia, quae praeceperat Dominus Moysi. ¹Locutusque est Dominus ad Moysen et Aaron dicens: ²«Singuli per turmas, signa atque vexilla et domos patrum suorum castrametabuntur filii Israel per gyrum tabernaculi conventus. ³Ad orientem Iudae figet tentoria per turmas exercitus sui, fuitque princeps filiorum eius Naasson filius Aminadab; ⁴et eius summa pugnantium septuaginta quattuor milia sexcenti. ⁵Iuxta eum castrametabuntur de tribu Issachar, quorum princeps fuit Nathanael filius Suar; ⁶et omnis numerus pugnatorum eius quinquaginta quattuor milia quadringenti. ⁷In tribu Zabulon princeps fuit Eliab filius Helon; ⁸et numerus exercitus pugnatorum eius quinquaginta septem milia quadringenti. ⁹Universi, qui in castris Iudae annumerati sunt, fuerunt centum octoginta sex milia quadringenti, et per turmas suas primi egredientur. ¹⁰Vexillum castrorum Ruben ad meridianam plagam erit, secundum exercitus eorum; princeps Elisur filius Sedeur; ¹¹et cunctus exercitus pugnatorum eius, qui numerati sunt, quadraginta sex

forty-six thousand five hundred. [12]And those to encamp next to him shall be the tribe of Simeon, the leader of the people of Simeon being Shelumi-el the son of Zurishaddai, [13]his host as numbered being fifty-nine thousand three hundred. [14]Then the tribe of Gad, the leader of the people of Gad being Eliasaph the son of Reuel, [15]his host as numbered being forty-five thousand six hundred and fifty. [16]The whole number of the camp of Reuben, by their companies, is a hundred and fifty-one thousand four hundred and fifty. They shall set out second.

[17]"Then the tent of meeting shall set out, with the camp of the Levites in the midst of the camps; as they encamp, so shall they set out, each in position, standard by standard.

[18]"On the west side shall be the standard of the camp of Ephraim by their companies, the leader of the people of Ephraim being Elishama the son of Ammihud, [19]his host as numbered being forty thousand five hundred. [20]And next to him shall be the tribe of Manasseh, the leader of the people of Manasseh being Gamaliel the son of Pedahzur, [21]his host as numbered being thirty-two thousand two hundred. [22]Then the tribe of Benjamin, the leader of the people of Benjamin being Abidan the son of Gideoni, [23]his host as numbered being thirty-five thousand four hundred. [24]The whole number of the camp of Ephraim, by their companies, is a hundred and eight thousand one hundred. They shall set out third on the march.

In the prologue to his Gospel St John says: "And the Word became flesh and dwelt [literally, "camped"] among us" (Jn 1:14). Jesus, perfect God and perfect man, brings into full effect something which is just hinted at in this passage—the fact that

"The God of our faith is not a distant being who contemplates indifferently the fate of men—their desires, their struggles, their sufferings. He is a Father who loves his children so much that he sends the Word" (St J. Escrivá, *Christ Is Passing By*, 84).

---

milia quingenti. [12]Iuxta eum castrametabuntur de tribu Simeon, quorum princeps fuit Salamiel filius Surisaddai; [13]et cunctus exercitus pugnatorum eius, qui numerati sunt, quinquaginta novem milia trecenti. [14]In tribu Gad princeps fuit Eliasaph filius Deuel; [15]et cunctus exercitus pugnatorum eius, qui numerati sunt, quadraginta quinque milia sexcenti quinquaginta. [16]omnes, qui recensiti sunt in castris Ruben, centum quinquaginta milia et mille quadringenti quinquaginta, per turmas suas in secundo loco proficiscentur. [17]Levabitur deinde tabernaculum conventus, castra Levitarum in medio castrorum, quomodo erigetur ita et deponetur; singuli per loca et vexilla sua proficiscentur. [18]Ad occidentalem plagam erit vexillum castrorum filiorum Ephraim per turmas suas, quorum princeps fuit Elisama filius Ammiud; [19]cunctus exercitus pugnatorum eius, qui numerati sunt, quadraginta milia quingenti. [20]Et cum eis tribus filiorum Manasse, quorum princeps fuit Gamaliel filius Phadassur; [21]cunctusque exercitus pugnatorum eius, qui numerati sunt, triginta duo milia ducenti. [22]In tribu filiorum Beniamin princeps fuit Abidan filius Gedeonis; [23]et cunctus exercitus pugnatorum eius, qui recensiti sunt, triginta quinque milia quadringenti. [24]Omnes, qui numerati sunt in castris Ephraim, centum octo milia centum, per turmas suas tertii proficiscentur. [25]Ad aquilonis partem stabit vexillum castrorum filiorum Dan

²⁵"On the north side shall be the standard of the camp of Dan by their companies, the leader of the people of Dan being Ahiezer the son of Ammishaddai, ²⁶his host as numbered being sixty-two thousand seven hundred. ²⁷And those to encamp next to him shall be the tribe of Asher, the leader of the people of Asher being Pagiel the son of Ochran, ²⁸his host as numbered being forty-one thousand five hundred. ²⁹Then the tribe of Naphtali, the leader of the people of Naphtali being Ahira the son of Enan, ³⁰his host as numbered being fifty-three thousand four hundred. ³¹The whole number of the camp of Dan is a hundred and fifty-seven thousand six hundred. They shall set out last, standard by standard."

³²These are the people of Israel as numbered by their fathers' houses; all in the camps who were numbered by their companies were six hundred and three thousand five hundred and fifty. ³³But the Levites were not numbered among the people of Israel, as the LORD commanded Moses.

³⁴Thus did the people of Israel. According to all that the LORD commanded Moses, so they encamped by their standards, and so they set out, every one in his family, according to his fathers' house.

Num 1:46

The tribe of Levi

3 ¹These are the generations of Aaron and Moses at the time when the LORD spoke with Moses on Mount Sinai.

Num 26:59–61

The priests

²These are the names of the sons of Aaron: Nadab the first-born, and Abihu, Eleazar, and Ithamar; ³these are the names of the sons

Lev 8–9
Ex 30:22

3:2–4 These verses show how the lawful priesthood came to be assigned to the family of Eleazar, from which will come Zadok (the priest whose line exclusively exercised the priesthood in the temple of Jerusalem down to the time of the Exile) and the family of Ithamar, from which will come Abiathar (a priest who was Zadok's contemporary—cf. 2 Sam 8:17 —and whose line shared the priestly ministry with the Zadokites after the Exile: cf. 1 Chron 24:1–6).

secundum exercitus suos, quorum princeps fuit Ahiezer filius Ammisaddai; ²⁶cunctus exercitus pugnatorum eius, qui numerati sunt, sexaginta duo milia septingenti. ²⁷Iuxta eum figet tentoria tribus Aser, quorum princeps fuit Phegiel filius Ochran; ²⁸cunctus exercitus pugnatorum eius, qui numerati sunt, quadraginta milia et mille quingenti. ²⁹De tribu filiorum Nephthali princeps fuit Ahira filius Enan; ³⁰cunctus exercitus pugnatorum eius quinquaginta tria milia quadringenti. ³¹Omnes, qui numerati sunt in castris Dan, fuerunt centum quinquaginta septem milia sexcenti, et novissimi proficiscentur secundum vexilla sua». ³²Hic numerus filiorum Israel, per domos patrum suorum omnes recensiti secundum exercitus suos, sexcenta tria milia quingenti. ³³Levitae autem non sunt numerati inter filios Israel; sic enim praeceperat Dominus Moysi. ³⁴Feceruntque filii Israel iuxta omnia, quae mandaverat Dominus: castrametati sunt per vexilla sua et profecti per tribus ad domos patrum suorum. ¹Hae sunt generationes Aaron et Moysi, in die, qua locutus est Dominus ad Moysen in monte Sinai. ²Et haec

of Aaron, the anointed priests, whom he ordained to minister in the priest's office. [4]But Nadab and Abihu died before the LORD when they offered unholy fire before the LORD in the wilderness of Sinai; and they had no children. So Eleazar and Ithamar served as priests in the lifetime of Aaron their father.

Lev 10:1–7

The Levites

Num 18:1–7

[5]And the LORD said to Moses, [6]"Bring the tribe of Levi near, and set them before Aaron the priest, that they may minister to him. [7]They shall perform duties for him and for the whole congregation before the tent of meeting, as they minister at the tabernacle; [8]they shall have charge of all the furnishings of the tent of meeting, and attend to the duties for the people of Israel as they minister at the tabernacle. [9]And you shall give the Levites to Aaron and his sons; they are wholly given to him from among the people of Israel. [10]And you shall appoint Aaron and his sons, and they shall attend to their priesthood; but if any one else comes near, he shall be put to death."

Num 8:14–19
Ezra 2:43

Like other offices, the priesthood in ancient Israel was hereditary. The words "whom he ordained" (v. 3) is literally "whose hand he filled", a very early wording for the investiture of someone as a priest. Apparently, it was not until much later, after the Exile, that the rite of anointing came to be used in the sense of equipping someone to perform sacred functions (cf. Ex 40:12–15). Originally only a king was anointed, and when this rite was transferred to the priest, it not only served to underline the fact that he was a sacred person but also to prepare the way for people to see that the Anointed *par excellence*, the Messiah (a title that originally applied only to kingship), would also be the only true priest.

3:5–10. This passage provides the basis for the differentiation of priests and Levites (this will be gone into in more detail in 18:1–7). On the one hand, we can see that priests and Levites share the same origin: they are all descendants of Levi and therefore are all of equal dignity; and, on the other, the difference between their functions goes right back to the very constitution of the people at Sinai. The Levites, the text tells us, are of lower rank because God chose "to give them" to Aaron and his sons (cf. 3:9) to minister to them; by performing their functions, humble though they be, they are doing what the Lord commanded Moses to do, that is, obeying the Law of God.

nomina filiorum Aaron: primogenitus eius Nadab, deinde Abiu et Eleazar et Ithamar. [3]Haec nomina filiorum Aaron sacerdotum, qui uncti sunt et quorum repletae manus, ut sacerdotio fungerentur. [4]Mortui sunt enim Nadab et Abiu, cum offerrent ignem alienum in conspectu Domini in deserto Sinai, absque liberis; functique sunt sacerdotio Eleazar et Ithamar coram Aaron patre suo. [5]Locutusque est Dominus ad Moysen dicens: [6]«Applica tribum Levi et fac stare in conspectu Aaron sacerdotis, ut ministrent ei [7]et observent, quidquid ad eum pertinet et ad totam congregationem coram tabernaculo conventus, servientes in ministerio habituli, [8]et custodiant vasa tabernaculi conventus explentes officia filiorum Israel, servientes in ministerio habituli. [9]Dabisque dono Levitas Aaron et filiis eius, quibus traditi

Ex 13:1, 14–15
Num 8:17

¹¹And the LORD said to Moses, ¹²"Behold, I have taken the Levites from among the people of Israel instead of every first-born that opens the womb among the people of Israel. The Levites

Ex 13:11
Num 3:40–51

shall be mine, ¹³for all the first-born are mine; on the day that I slew all the first-born in the land of Egypt, I consecrated for my own all the first-born in Israel, both of man and of beast; they shall be mine: I am the LORD."

Num 26:57–62

The census of the Levites
¹⁴And the LORD said to Moses in the wilderness of Sinai, ¹⁵"Number the sons of Levi, by fathers' houses and by families; every male from a month old and upward you shall number." ¹⁶So Moses numbered them according to the word of the LORD, as he

Gen 46:11
Ex 6:16–19

was commanded. ¹⁷And these were the sons of Levi by their names: Gershon and Kohath and Merari. ¹⁸And these are the names of the sons of Gershon by their families: Libni and Shimei. ¹⁹And the sons of Kohath by their families: Amram, Izhar,

---

3:11–13. The end of chapter 1 (cf. 1:49–53) spoke of the distinction between the Levites and the rest of the children of Israel. The Levites were set apart to devote themselves to the service of the tabernacle. Here another feature of their special calling is underlined: God has taken them as a ransom for the first-born sons of the whole people. As we should remember, all first-born (of men as well as livestock) had to be offered to God (cf. Ex 13:1). Moreover, the first-born of the sons of Israel belong to the Lord in a special way because he preserved them from death during the tenth plague that beset Egypt (cf. Ex 13:14–15; Num 8:17). In exchange for these first-

born the Lord took the Levites into his service. So, it is made very plain that they are the Lord's possession (just as the first-born are), and they minister to the whole community, insofar as they also have this vicarious role of taking the place of others.

3:14–39. This passage specifies how the various Levite families are to be positioned within the camp. Pride of place (on the east, in front of the entrance to the sanctuary) are Moses, Aaron and his sons, the priests. Other Levite families are ranged around the other sides of the sanctuary. Each of them is given a specific part of the tabernacle to look after.

---

sunt a filiis Israel; ¹⁰Aaron autem et filios eius constitues super cultum sacerdotii. Externus, qui ad ministrandum accesserit, morietur». ¹¹Locutusque est Dominus ad Moysen dicens: ¹²«Ecce ego tuli Levitas a filiis Israel pro omni primogenito, qui aperit vulvam in filiis Israel; eruntque Levitae mei. ¹³Meum est enim omne primogenitum: ex quo percussi omnes primogenitos in terra Aegypti, sanctificavi mihi, quidquid primum nascitur in Israel ab homine usque ad pecus; mei sunt. Ego Dominus». ¹⁴Locutusque est Dominus ad Moysen in deserto Sinai dicens: ¹⁵«Numera filios Levi per domos patrum suorum et familias omnem masculum ab uno mense et supra». ¹⁶Numeravit eos Moyses, ut praeceperat Dominus, ¹⁷et inventi sunt filii Levi per nomina sua Gerson et Caath et Merari. ¹⁸Haec sunt nomina filiorum Gerson secundum familias suas: Lobni et Semei; ¹⁹filii Caath secundum familias suas: Amram et Isaar, Hebron et Oziel; ²⁰filii Merari secundum familias suas: Moholi et Musi. Hae sunt familiae Levi per

Hebron, and Uzziel. [20]And the sons of Merari by their families: Mahli and Mushi. These are the families of the Levites, by their fathers' houses.

[21]Of Gershon were the family of the Libnites and the family of the Shime-ites; these were the families of the Gershonites. [22]Their number according to the number of all the males from a month old and upward was[a] seven thousand five hundred. [23]The families of the Gershonites were to encamp behind the tabernacle on the west, [24]with Eliasaph, the son of Lael as head of the fathers' house of the Gershonites. [25]And the charge of the sons of Gershon in the tent of meeting was to be the tabernacle, the tent with its covering, the screen for the door of the tent of meeting, [26]the hangings of the court, the screen for the door of the court which is around the tabernacle and the altar, and its cords; all the service pertaining to these.   Ex 26–27

[27]Of Kohath were the family of the Amramites, and the family of the Izharites, and the family of the Hebronites, and the family of the Uzzielites; these are the families of the Kohathites. [28]According to the number of all the males, from a month old and upward, there were eight thousand six hundred, attending to the duties of the sanctuary. [29]The families of the sons of Kohath were to encamp on the south side of the tabernacle, [30]with Elizaphan the son of Uzziel as head of the fathers' house of the families of the Kohathites. [31]And their charge was to be the ark, the table, the lampstand, the altars, the vessels of the sanctuary with which the priests minister, and the screen; all the service pertaining to these.   Ex 25:10–40; 27:1–8; 30:1–10
[32]And Eleazar the son of Aaron the priest was to be chief over the leaders of the Levites, and to have oversight of those who had charge of the sanctuary.

[33]Of Merari were the family of the Mahlites and the family of the Mushites: these are the families of Merari. [34]Their number

domos patrum suorum. [21]De Gerson fuere familiae duae Lobnitica et Semeitica, [22]quarum numeratus est omnis populus sexus masculini ab uno mense et supra septem milia quingenti. [23]Hi post habitaculum metabantur ad occidentem [24]sub principe Eliasaph filio Lael; [25]et habebant excubias in tabernaculo conventus, ipsum habitaculum et tabernaculum, operimentum eius, velum, quod trahitur ante fores tabernaculi conventus, [26]et cortinas atrii, velum quoque, quod appenditur in introitu atrii, quod est circa habitaculum et circa altare, et funes ad omne opus eius. [27]Caath habet familias: Amramitas et Isaaritas et Hebronitas et Ozielitas; hae sunt familiae Caathitarum. [28]Omnes generis masculini ab uno mense et supra octo milia sexcenti habebant excubias sanctuarii. [29]Familiae filiorum Caath castrametabantur ad latus habitaculi ad meridianam plagam, [30]princepsque eorum erat Elisaphan filius Oziel. [31]Et custodiebant arcam mensamque et candelabrum, altaria et vasa sanctuarii, in quibus ministratur, et velum cunctamque huiuscemodi supellectilem. [32]Princeps autem principum Levitarum Eleazar filius Aaron sacerdotis erat super excubitores custodiae sanctuarii. [33]At vero de Merari erant familiae Moholitae et Musitae. [34]Omnes generis masculini ab uno mense et supra sex milia ducenti; [35]princeps familiarum

a. Heb *their number was*

according to the number of all the males from a month old and upward was six thousand two hundred. ³⁵And the head of the fathers' house of the families of Merari was Zuriel the son of Abihail; they were to encamp on the north side of the tabernacle. ³⁶And the appointed charge of the sons of Merari was to be the frames of the tabernacle, the bars, the pillars, the bases, and all their accessories; all the service pertaining to these; ³⁷also the pillars of the court round about, with their bases and pegs and cords.

³⁸And those to encamp before the tabernacle on the east, before the tent of meeting toward the sunrise, were Moses and Aaron and his sons, having charge of the rites within the sanctuary, whatever had to be done for the people of Israel; and any one else who came near was to be put to death. ³⁹All who were numbered of the Levites, whom Moses and Aaron numbered at the commandment of the LORD, by families, all the males from a month old and upward, were twenty-two thousand.

Redeeming the first-born of Israel

⁴⁰And the LORD said to Moses, "Number all the first-born males of the people of Israel, from a month old and upward, taking their number by names. ⁴¹And you shall take the Levites for me—I am the LORD—instead of all the first-born among the people of Israel, and the cattle of the Levites instead of all the firstlings among the cattle of the people of Israel." ⁴²So Moses numbered all the first-born among the people of Israel, as the LORD commanded him. ⁴³And all the first-born males, according to the number of names, from a month old and upward as numbered were twenty-two thousand two hundred and seventy-three.

⁴⁴And the LORD said to Moses, ⁴⁵"Take the Levites instead of all the first-born among the people of Israel, and the cattle of the

Num 3:12–13
Ex 13:11

3:40–51. See the note on 3:11–13.

Merari Suriel filius Abihail. In plaga septentrionali ad latus habitaculi castrametabantur; ³⁶erant sub custodia eorum tabulae habitaculi et vectes et columnae ac bases earum et cuncta vasa eius et omnia, quae ad cultum huiuscemodi pertinent, ³⁷columnaeque atrii per circuitum cum basibus suis et paxilli cum funibus. ³⁸Castrametabantur ante habitaculum, ad orientalem plagam ante tabernaculum conventus ad orientem, Moyses et Aaron cum filiis suis habentes custodiam sanctuarii in medio filiorum Israel. Quisquis alienus accesserit, morietur. ³⁹Omnes Levitae, quos numeravit Moyses iuxta praeceptum Domini per familias suas in genere masculino a mense uno et supra, fuerunt viginti duo milia. ⁴⁰Et ait Dominus ad Moysen: «Numera omnes primogenitos sexus masculini de filiis Israel ab uno mense et supra et habebis summam eorum; ⁴¹tollesque Levitas mihi pro omni primogenito filiorum Israel— ego sum Dominus—et pecora eorum pro universis primogenitis pecorum filiorum Israel». ⁴²Recensuit Moyses, sicut praeceperat Dominus, omnes primogenitos filiorum Israel, ⁴³et fuerunt omnes masculi per nomina sua a mense uno et supra viginti duo milia ducenti septuaginta tres. ⁴⁴Locutusque est Dominus ad Moysen dicens: ⁴⁵«Tolle Levitas pro omnibus primogenitis filiorum Israel et pecora

Levites instead of their cattle; and the Levites shall be mine: I am the LORD. ⁴⁶And for the redemption of the two hundred and seventy- Ex 13:11 three of the first-born of the people of Israel, over and above the number of the male Levites, ⁴⁷you shall take five shekels apiece; Lev 5:15 reckoning by the shekel of the sanctuary, the shekel of twenty gerahs, you shall take them, ⁴⁸and give the money by which the excess number of them is redeemed to Aaron and his sons." ⁴⁹So Moses took the redemption money from those who were over and above those redeemed by the Levites; ⁵⁰from the first-born of the people of Israel he took the money, one thousand three hundred and sixty-five shekels, reckoned by the shekel of the sanctuary; ⁵¹and Moses gave the redemption money to Aaron and his sons, according to the word of the LORD, as the LORD commanded Moses.

The Kohathites

4 ¹The LORD said to Moses and Aaron, ²"Take a census of the sons of Kohath from among the sons of Levi, by their families and their fathers' houses, ³from thirty years old up to fifty years old, all who can enter the service, to do the work in the tent

---

4:1–49. Whereas in the general census which counted males aged twenty and more, in the census of Levites there is an upper and lower age limit. This is a way of showing the importance of their ministry: they have to be of mature age and in the fullness of their health.

One cannot help noticing how detailed the text is as regards the respect owed to liturgical objects; and it points out that this is the will of God. The Fathers of the Church point out that there is even more reason to look after objects to do with eucharistic worship. St Jerome, for example says that "the testi-

monies borne by the Holy Scriptures show the veneration that should be given to holy things and to those things which are used in the ministry of the altar. For the sacred vessels, the sacred linens and everything else to do with the liturgy of the Lord's Passion should not be regarded as ordinary everyday objects which have no holiness attaching to them: on account of their being in contact with the Body and Blood of the Lord they should be venerated with the same respect as is shown his Body and his Blood" (*Epistle* 114, 2).

Levitarum pro pecoribus eorum; eruntque Levitae mei. Ego sum Dominus. ⁴⁶In pretio autem ducentorum septuaginta trium, qui excedunt numerum Levitarum de primogenitis filiorum Israel, ⁴⁷accipies quinque siclos per singula capita, ad mensuram sanctuarii. Siclus habet viginti obolos. ⁴⁸Dabisque pecuniam Aaron et filiis eius pretium eorum, qui supra sunt». ⁴⁹Tulit igitur Moyses pecuniam eorum, qui excesserant numerum eorum, qui redempti erant a Levitis; ⁵⁰a primogenitis filiorum Israel tulit pecuniam mille trecentorum sexaginta quinque siclorum iuxta pondus sanctuarii. ⁵¹Et dedit eam Aaron et filiis eius iuxta verbum, quod praeceperat sibi Dominus. ¹Locutusque est Dominus ad Moysen et Aaron dicens: ²«Tolle summam filiorum Caath de medio Levitarum per familias et domos suas ³a tri-

of meeting. [4]This is the service of the sons of Kohath in the tent

Ex 26:31–37;
35:12; 39:34
2 Sam 6:7
of meeting: the most holy things. [5]When the camp is to set out, Aaron and his sons shall go in and take down the veil of the screen, and cover the ark of the testimony with it; [6]then they shall put on it a covering of goatskin, and spread over that a cloth all of

Ex 25:23
blue, and shall put in its poles. [7]And over the table of the bread of the Presence they shall spread a cloth of blue, and put upon it the plates, the dishes for incense, the bowls, and the flagons for the drink offering; the continual bread also shall be on it; [8]then they shall spread over them a cloth of scarlet, and cover the same with a covering of goatskin, and shall put in its poles. [9]And they shall take a cloth of blue, and cover the lampstand for the light, with its lamps, its snuffers, its trays, and all the vessels for oil with which it is supplied: [10]and they shall put it with all its utensils in a cov-

Ex 30:1–6
ering of goatskin and put it upon the carrying frame. [11]And over the golden altar they shall spread a cloth of blue, and cover it with a covering of goatskin, and shall put in its poles; [12]and they shall take all the vessels of the service which are used in the sanctuary, and put them in a cloth of blue, and cover them with a covering of goatskin, and put them on the carrying frame. [13]And they shall take away the ashes from the altar, and spread a purple cloth over it; [14]and they shall put on it all the utensils of the altar, which are used for the service there, the firepans, the forks, the shovels, and the basins, all the utensils of the altar; and they shall spread upon

2 Sam 6:7
Lev 17:1
it a covering of goatskin, and shall put in its poles. [15]And when Aaron and his sons have finished covering the sanctuary and all the furnishings of the sanctuary, as the camp sets out, after that the sons of Kohath shall come to carry these, but they must not touch the holy things, lest they die. These are the things of the tent of meeting which the sons of Kohath are to carry.

cesimo anno et supra usque ad quinquagesimum annum omnium, qui ingrediuntur, ut stent et ministrent in tabernaculo conventus. [4]Hic est cultus filiorum Caath in tabernaculo conventus: sanctum sanctorum. [5]Ingredientur Aaron et filii eius, quando movenda sunt castra, et deponent velum, quod pendet ante fores, involventque eo arcam testimonii; [6]et operient rursum velamine pellium delphini extendentque desuper pallium totum hyacinthinum et inducent vectes. [7]Mensam quoque propositionis involvent hyacinthino pallio et ponent cum ea acetabula et phialas, cyathos et crateras ad liba fundenda; panes semper in ea erunt. [8]Extendentque desuper pallium coccineum, quod rursum operient velamento pellium delphini et inducent vectes. [9]Sument et pallium hyacinthinum, quo operient candelabrum cum lucernis et forcipibus suis et emunctoriis et cunctis vasis olei, quae ad concinnandas lucernas necessaria sunt; [10]et super omnia ponent operimentum pellium delphini et ponent super feretrum. [11]Nec non et altare aureum involvent hyacinthino vestimento et extendent desuper operimentum pellium delphini et inducent vectes. [12]omnia vasa, quibus ministratur in sanctuario, involvent hyacinthino pallio; et extendent desuper operimentum pellium delphini ponentque super feretrum. [13]Sed et altare mundabunt cinere et involvent illud purpureo vestimento; [14]ponentque super illud omnia vasa, quibus in ministerio eius utuntur, id est ignium receptacula, fuscinulas ac vatilla et pateras. Cuncta vasa altaris operient simul velamine pellium delphini et inducent vectes. [15]Cumque involverint Aaron et filii eius sanctua-

¹⁶"And Eleazar the son of Aaron the priest shall have charge of the oil for the light, the fragrant incense, the continual cereal offering, and the anointing oil, with the oversight of all the tabernacle and all that is in it, of the sanctuary and its vessels."

¹⁷The LORD said to Moses and Aaron, ¹⁸"Let not the tribe of the families of the Kohathites be destroyed from among the Levites; ¹⁹but deal thus with them, that they may live and not die when they come near to the most holy things: Aaron and his sons shall go in and appoint them each to his task and to his burden, ²⁰but they shall not go in to look upon the holy things even for a moment, lest they die."

The Gershonites

²¹The LORD said to Moses, ²²"Take a census of the sons of Gershon also, by their families and their fathers' houses; ²³from thirty years old up to fifty years old, you shall number them, all who can enter for service, to do the work in the tent of meeting. ²⁴This is the service of the families of the Gershonites, in serving and bearing burdens: ²⁵they shall carry the curtains of the tabernacle, and the tent of meeting with its covering, and the covering of goatskin that is on top of it, and the screen for the door of the tent of meeting, ²⁶and the hangings of the court, and the screen for the entrance of the gate of the court which is around the tabernacle and the altar, and their cords, and all the equipment for their service; and they shall do all that needs to be done with regard to them. ²⁷All the service of the sons of the Gershonites shall be at the command of Aaron and his sons, in all that they are to carry, and in all that they have to do; and you shall assign to their charge all that they are to carry. ²⁸This is the service of

rium et omnia vasa eius in commotione castrorum, tunc intrabunt filii Caath, ut portent involuta et non tangent sanctuarium, ne moriantur. Ista sunt onera filiorum Caath in tabernaculo conventus. ¹⁶Ad curam Eleazari filii Aaron sacerdotis pertinet oleum ad concinnandas lucernas et gratissimum incensum, et oblatio, quae semper offertur, et oleum unctionis et, quidquid ad cultum habituli pertinet omniumque vasorum, quae in sanctuario sunt». ¹⁷Locutusque est Dominus ad Moysen et Aaron dicens: ¹⁸«Nolite perdere populum Caath de medio Levitarum, ¹⁹sed hoc facite eis, ut vivant et non moriantur, quando appropinquant ad sancta sanctorum: Aaron et filii eius intrabunt ipsique disponent opera singulorum et divident quid portare quis debeat. ²⁰Non intrabunt ad videndum, nec puncto quidem, sanctuarium; alioquin morientur». ²¹Locutusque est Dominus ad Moysen dicens: ²²«Tolle summam etiam filiorum Gerson per domos ac familias et cognationes suas; ²³a triginta annis et supra usque ad annos quinquaginta numera omnes, qui ingrediuntur et ministrant in tabernaculo conventus. ²⁴Hoc est officium familiarum Gersonitarum, ²⁵ut portent cortinas habitaculi, tabernaculum conventus, operimentum eius et super illud velamen delphini velumque, quod pendet in introitu tabernaculi conventus, ²⁶cortinas atrii et velum in introitu atrii, quod est circa habitaculum et altare, funiculos et vasa ministerii, omnia quae facta sunt, ut eis laborent. ²⁷Iubente Aaron et filiis eius, portabunt filii Gerson, et scient singuli cui debeant oneri mancipari. ²⁸Hic est cultus familiarum Gersonitarum in tabernaculo conventus; eruntque sub manu Ithamar filii Aaron sacerdotis. ²⁹Filios quoque Merari per familias et domos patrum suorum

the families of the sons of the Gershonites in the tent of meeting, and their work is to be under the oversight of Ithamar the son of Aaron the priest.

The Merarites

[29]"As for the sons of Merari, you shall number them by their families and their fathers' houses; [30]from thirty years old up to fifty years old, you shall number them, every one that can enter the service, to do the work of the tent of meeting. [31]And this is what they are charged to carry, as the whole of their service in the tent of meeting: the frames of the tabernacle, with its bars, pillars, and bases, [32]and the pillars of the court round about with their bases, pegs, and cords, with all their equipment and all their accessories; and you shall assign by name the objects which they are required to carry. [33]This is the service of the families of the sons of Merari, the whole of their service in the tent of meeting, under the hand of Ithamar the son of Aaron the priest."

The result of the census of the Levites

[34]And Moses and Aaron and the leaders of the congregation numbered the sons of the Kohathites, by their families and their fathers' houses, [35]from thirty years old up to fifty years old, every one that could enter the service, for work in the tent of meeting; [36]and their number by families was two thousand seven hundred and fifty. [37]This was the number of the families of the Kohathites, all who served in the tent of meeting, whom Moses and Aaron numbered according to the commandment of the LORD by Moses.

[39]The number of the sons of Gershon, by their families and their fathers' houses, [39]from thirty years old up to fifty years old, every one that could enter the service for work in the tent of meeting—[40]their number by their families and their fathers' houses was two thousand six hundred and thirty. [41]This was the number of the families of the sons of Gershon, all who served in the tent

recensebis [30]a triginta annis et supra usque ad annos quinquaginta, omnes, qui ingrediuntur ad officium ministerii sui et cultum tabernaculi conventus. [31]Haec sunt onera eorum: portabunt tabulas habitaculi et vectes eius, columnas ac bases earum, [32]columnas quoque atrii per circuitum cum basibus et paxillis et funibus suis; omnia vasa et supellectilem ad numerum accipient sicque portabunt. [33]Hoc est officium familiarum Meraritarum et ministerium in tabernaculo conventus eruntque sub manu Ithamar filii Aaron sacerdotis». [34]Recensuerunt igitur Moyses et Aaron et principes synagogae filios Caath per cognationes et domos patrum suorum [35]a triginta annis et supra usque ad annum quinquagesimum, omnes, qui ingrediuntur ad ministerium tabernaculi conventus; [36]et inventi sunt duo milia septingenti quinquaginta. [37]Hic est numerus familiarum Caath, qui ministrant in tabernaculo conventus: hos numeravit Moyses et Aaron iuxta sermonem Domini per manum Moysi. [38]Numerati sunt et filii Gerson per cognationes et domos patrum suorum [39]a triginta annis et supra usque ad quinquagesimum annum, omnes, qui ingrediuntur, ut ministrent in tabernaculo conventus; [40]et inventi sunt secundum familias et domos

of meeting, whom Moses and Aaron numbered according to the commandment of the LORD.

⁴²The number of the families of the sons of Merari, by their families and their fathers' houses, ⁴³from thirty years old up to fifty years old, every one that could enter the service, for work in the tent of meeting—⁴⁴their number by families was three thousand two hundred. ⁴⁵These are those who were numbered of the families of the sons of Merari, whom Moses and Aaron numbered according to the commandment of the LORD by Moses.

⁴⁶All those who were numbered of the Levites, whom Moses and Aaron and the leaders of Israel numbered, by their families and their fathers' houses, ⁴⁷from thirty years old up to fifty years old, every one that could enter to do the work of service and the work of bearing burdens in the tent of meeting, ⁴⁸those who were numbered of them were eight thousand five hundred and eighty. ⁴⁹According to the commandment of the LORD through Moses they were appointed, each to his task of serving or carrying; thus they were numbered by him, as the LORD commanded Moses.

2. LAWS ABOUT RITUAL UNCLEANNESS

Expulsion of the unclean

Deut 23:10–15

5 ¹The LORD said to Moses, ²"Command the people of Israel that they put out of the camp every leper, and every one having a discharge, and every one that is unclean through contact with the dead; ³you shall put out both male and female, putting them outside the camp, that they may not defile their camp, in the midst of

Lev 13;
15:1–18; 21:1
Num 19:11–16

1 Cor 5:7–13
2 Cor 6:16–18
Rev 21:27

5:1–4. The first legislative section of the book begins at this point. This is the first of a series of dispositions about the ritual cleanness required of individuals in gen-

eral. The message is clear: where God is present, everything has to be clean. Because God dwells in the camp, every effort must be made to ensure that it is

patrum suorum duo milia sexcenti triginta. ⁴¹Hic est numerus Gersonitarum, omnes, qui ministrant in tabernaculo conventus, quos numeraverunt Moyses et Aaron iuxta verbum Domini. ⁴²Numeratae sunt et familiae filiorum Merari per cognationes et domos patrum suorum ⁴³a triginta annis et supra usque ad annum quinquagesimum, omnes, qui ingrediuntur ad explendos ritus tabernaculi conventus; ⁴⁴et inventi sunt tria milia ducenti. ⁴⁵Hic est numerus familiarum filiorum Merari, quos recensuerunt Moyses et Aaron iuxta imperium Domini per manum Moysi. ⁴⁶Omnes, qui recensiti sunt de Levitis et quos recenseri fecit ad nomen Moyses et Aaron et principes Israel per cognationes et domos patrum suorum ⁴⁷a triginta annis et supra usque ad annum quinquagesimum ingredientes ad ministerium tabernaculi et onera portanda in tabernaculo conventus, ⁴⁸fuerunt simul octo milia quingenti octoginta. ⁴⁹Iuxta verbum Domini per manum Moysi recensuit eos unumquemque iuxta officium et onera sua, sicut praeceperat ei Dominus. ¹Locutusque est Dominus ad Moysen dicens: ²«Praecipe filiis Israel, ut eiciant de castris omnem leprosum et qui semine fluit pollutusque est super mortuo. ³Tam masculum

which I dwell." ⁴And the people of Israel did so, and drove them outside the camp; as the LORD said to Moses, so the people of Israel did.

Lev 5:20–26 **Restitution**

Lk 19:8 ⁵And the LORD said to Moses, ⁶"Say to the people of Israel, When a man or woman commits any of the sins that men commit by breaking faith with the LORD, and that person is guilty, ⁷he shall Num 5:5 confess his sin which he has committed; and he shall make full restitution for his wrong, adding a fifth to it, and giving it to him to whom he did the wrong. ⁸But if the man has no kinsman to whom restitution may be made for the wrong, the restitution for wrong shall go to the LORD for the priest, in addition to the ram of atonement with which atonement is made for him. ⁹And every offering, all the holy things of the people of Israel, which they bring to the priest, shall be his; ¹⁰and every man's holy things shall be his; whatever any man gives to the priest shall be his."

---

clean. Therefore, any sin or uncleanness (even if only external) must be removed.

At that time the view was that the following were to be put out of the camp— a leper (cf. Lev 13), anyone who had a seminal discharge (cf. Lev 15:1–18) or had touched a corpse (cf. 21:1; Num 19:11–16), probably because of the danger of contagion involved.

Like many others in the Pentateuch, the rule about the expulsion of the unclean was a temporary one. Jesus Christ, who brought the Law to perfection, welcomed lepers and made them clean (cf. Mk 1:40–42); he taught that the only things which made men unclean were evil thoughts which arose in their hearts (cf. Mt 25:18–19); and filled with compassion he approached the dead (cf.

Mt 9:25; Lk 7:14). However, the teaching underlying these rules, that is, the need for purity if one is to draw near to the Lord, has enduring value (cf. Mt 5:8).

5:5–8. More important than ritual cleanness (vv. 1–4) is moral purity in one's relationships with others. And so now come instructions about the ownership of material things, and about fidelity in marriage (vv. 11–31).

Leviticus 5:20–26 gives a more elaborate account of the law about the unjust taking of others' property. This passage specifies that when making restitution one needs to give back not only what one stole but a fifth more (twenty per cent); this goes to the injured party or, in his absence, to his *goel* (the relative respon-

---

quam feminam eicite de castris, ne contaminent ea, cum habitaverim cum eis». ⁴Feceruntque ita filii Israel et eiecerunt eos extra castra, sicut locutus erat Dominus Moysi. ⁵Locutusque est Dominus ad Moysen dicens: ⁶«Loquere ad filios Israel: Vir sive mulier, cum fecerint ex omnibus peccatis, quae solent hominibus accidere, et fraude transgressi fuerint mandatum Domini, ille homo reus erit; ⁷et confitebuntur peccatum suum et reddent ipsum caput quintamque partem desuper ei, in quem peccaverint. ⁸Sin autem non fuerit, qui recipiat, dabunt Domino, et erit sacerdotis, praeter arietem, qui offertur pro expiatione, ut sit placabilis hostia. ⁹Omnis quoque praelibatio rerum sacrarum, quas offerunt filii Israel, ad sacerdotem pertinet; ¹⁰et quidquid in sanctuarium offertur a singulis et traditur manibus sacerdotis,

Offering in cases of jealousy

[11]And the LORD said to Moses, [12]"Say to the people of Israel, If Jn 8:3
any man's wife goes astray and acts unfaithfully against him, [13]if
a man lies with her carnally, and it is hidden from the eyes of her
husband, and she is undetected though she has defiled herself, and
there is no witness against her, since she was not taken in the act;
[14]and if the spirit of jealousy comes upon him, and he is jealous of
his wife who has defiled herself; or if the spirit of jealousy comes
upon him, and he is jealous of his wife, though she has not defiled
herself; [15]then the man shall bring his wife to the priest, and bring Heb 10:3
the offering required of her, a tenth of an ephah of barley meal; he
shall pour no oil upon it and put no frankincense on it, for it is a
cereal offering of jealousy, a cereal offering of remembrance,
bringing iniquity to remembrance.

[16]"And the priest shall bring her near, and set her before the
LORD; [17]and the priest shall take holy water in an earthen vessel,
and take some of the dust that is on the floor of the tabernacle and

---

sible for asserting the rights of a dead
person) and, if there is no *goel*, to the
priest. Offences against a neighbour were
severely punished; also, they also put a
person in the Lord's debt and therefore
he was obliged to make a guilt offering
(cf. the note on Lev 5:14–26).

The detail the text goes into is important: the man who wrongs his neighbour
not only sins against him but is also
guilty of "breaking faith with the Lord"
(v. 6).

5:11–31. The people's cleanness also
entails marital fidelity. Adultery is a very
serious offence (cf. the note on Ex
20:14); if proven, the guilty parties were
condemned to death (cf. Lev 20:10). The
particular rite described here was estab-

lished in the case where a husband had a
reasonable doubt about his wife's faithfulness but had no evidence against her.
The ceremonies prescribed are reminiscent of the rites of ordeals or magical
tests used in an attempt to expose the
guilt or innocence of a suspect against
whom there was no clear evidence.
Among Israel's neighbours, a women
under suspicion might be thrown into a
river to see if she survived; so, this rite
was relatively mild: in addition to listening to the terrible curses calling on God
to make her barren forever if she had
been unfaithful, the only thing she was
obliged to do was drink water mixed
with a little dust and some scraps of the
papers on which the curses had been
written.

---

ipsius erit». [11]Locutusque est Dominus ad Moysen dicens: [12]«Loquere ad filios Israel et dices ad eos:
Vir, cuius uxor erraverit maritumque decipiens [13]dormierit cum altero viro, et hoc maritus deprehen-
dere non quiverit, sed latet quod impuram se reddiderit et testibus argui non potest, quia non est inventa
in stupro, [14]si spiritus zelotypiae concitaverit virum contra uxorem suam, quae vel polluta est vel falsa
suspicione appetitur, [15]adducet eam ad sacerdotem et offeret oblationem pro illa decimam partem ephi
farinae hordeaceae. Non fundet super eam oleum, nec imponet tus, quia sacrificium zelotypiae est et
oblatio investigans adulterium. [16]Afferet igitur eam sacerdos et statuet coram Domino; [17]assumetque
aquam sanctam in vase fictili et pauxillum terrae de pavimento habitaculi mittet in eam. [18]Cumque

put it into the water. [18]And the priest shall set the woman before the Lord, and unbind the hair of the woman's head, and place in her hands the cereal offering of remembrance, which is the cereal offering of jealousy. And in his hand the priest shall have the water of bitterness that brings the curse. [19]Then the priest shall make her take an oath, saying, 'If no man has lain with you, and if you have not turned aside to uncleanness, while you were under your husband's authority, be free from this water of bitterness that brings the curse. [20]But if you have gone astray, though you are under your husband's authority, and if you have defiled yourself, and some man other than your husband has lain with you, [21]then' (let the priest make the woman take the oath of the curse, and say to the woman) 'the LORD make you an execration and an oath among your people, when the LORD makes your thigh fall away and your body swell; [22]may this water that brings the curse pass into your bowels and make your body swell and your thigh fall away.' And the woman shall say, 'Amen, Amen.'

[23]"Then the priest shall write these curses in a book, and wash them off into the water of bitterness; [24]and he shall make the woman drink the water of bitterness that brings the curse, and the water that brings the curse shall enter into her and cause bitter pain. [25]And the priest shall take the cereal offering of jealousy out of the woman's hand, and shall wave the cereal offering before the LORD and bring it to the altar; [26]and the priest shall take a handful of the cereal offering, as its memorial portion, and burn it upon the altar, and afterward shall make the woman drink the water. [27]And when he has made her drink the water, then, if she has defiled herself and has acted unfaithfully against her husband, the water that brings the curse shall enter into her and cause bitter pain, and her body shall swell, and her thigh shall fall away, and the woman shall become an execration among her people. [28]But if

posuerit sacerdos mulierem in conspectu Domini, discooperiet caput eius et ponet super manus illius sacrificium recordationis, oblationem zelotypiae; ipse autem tenebit aquas amarissimas, in quibus cum exsecratione maledicta congessit. [19]Adiurabitque eam et dicet: 'Si non dormivit vir alienus tecum, et si non declinasti a viro tuo et non polluta es, deserto mariti toro, non te nocebunt aquae istae amarissimae, in quas maledicta congessi. [20]Sin autem declinasti a viro tuo atque polluta es et concubuisti cum altero viro', [21]adiurabit eam sacerdos iuramento maledictionis: 'Det te Dominus in maledictionem, iuramentum in medio populi tui; putrescere faciat femur tuum, et tumens uterus tuus disrumpatur; [22]ingrediantur aquae maledictae in ventrem tuum, et utero tumescente putrescat femur!' Et respondebit mulier: 'Amen, amen'. [23]Scribetque sacerdos in libello ista maledicta et delebit ea aquis amarissimis [24]et dabit ei bibere aquas amaras, in quas maledicta congessit, et ingredientur in eam aquae maledictionis, quae amarae fient; [25]tollet sacerdos de manu eius sacrificium zelotypiae et agitabit illud coram Domino imponetque illud super altare; [26]pugillum sacrificii tollat de eo, quod offertur in memoriale, et incendat super altare; et deinde potum det mulieri aquas amarissimas. [27]Quas cum biberit, si polluta est et, contempto viro, adulterii rea, pertransibunt eam aquae maledictionis et, inflato ventre, computrescet

the woman has not defiled herself and is clean, then she shall be free and shall conceive children.

²⁹"This is the law in cases of jealousy, when a wife, though under her husband's authority, goes astray and defiles herself, ³⁰or when the spirit of jealousy comes upon a man and he is jealous of his wife; then he shall set the woman before the LORD, and the priest shall execute upon her all this law. ³¹The man shall be free from iniquity, but the woman shall bear her iniquity."

The Nazirite

6 ¹And the LORD said to Moses, ²"Say to the people of Israel, When either a man or a woman makes a special vow, the vow of a Nazirite,ᵇ to separate himself to the LORD, ³he shall separate himself from wine and strong drink; he shall drink no vinegar made from wine or strong drink, and shall not drink any juice of grapes or eat grapes, fresh or dried. ⁴All the days of his separationᶜ he shall eat nothing that is produced by the grapevine, not even the seeds or the skins.

Acts 18:18

Lk 1:15

Judg 13:5; 16:17
Jer 35:3–6
Amos 2:12

6:1–21. The Nazirite vow spoken about here was practised from very early on. Samson was a Nazirite for life (cf. Judg 13:2–7) and Samuel may have been also (cf. 1 Sam 1:28); there were Nazirites in the time of Amos (Amos 2:11) and in that of the Maccabees (1 Mac 3:49–50). It is probable that some Jewish converts to Christianity had taken this vow (cf. Acts 21:24) and perhaps even St Paul himself took it (cf. Acts 18:18). If someone took the vow, it meant he was consecrated to God, at least for a period of time.

The Nazirite committed himself to three things—to let his hair grow, to abstain from all alcohol, and to avoid contact with dead bodies. Of these, the

most specific was the one about not cutting his hair, which is always mentioned when there is reference to a Nazirite; the term even enters into profane vocabulary in the Bible, which in Hebrew describes undressed vines (cf. Lev 25:5) as 'Nazarite' vines. It is not quite clear what the significance was of letting one's hair grow long; perhaps it was a sign of strength (cf. Judg 5:2) or of closeness to God, because there are some passages which imply that priests wore long hair (Lev 21:5). Abstinence from alcoholic drinks does not imply that it was considered sinful to drink wine, since it is permissible to drink wine during the sacred meal which marks the end of the Nazirite

---

femur; eritque mulier in maledictionem omni populo eius. ²⁸Quod si polluta non fuerit, sed munda, erit innoxia et faciet liberos». ²⁹Ista est lex zelotypiae, si declinaverit mulier a viro suo et si polluta fuerit, ³⁰maritusque zelotypiae spiritu concitatus adduxerit eam in conspectu Domini, et fecerit ei sacerdos iuxta omnia, quae scripta sunt; ³¹maritus absque culpa erit, et illa recipiet iniquitatem suam. ¹Locutusque est Dominus ad Moysen dicens: ²«Loquere ad filios Israel et dices ad eos: Vir sive mulier cum fecerint votum, ut sanctificentur et se voluerint Domino consecrare, ³a vino et omni quod inebriare potest abstinebunt; acetum ex vino et ex qualibet alia potione et, quidquid de uva exprimitur, non

b. That is *one separated* or *one consecrated* **c.** Or *Naziriteship*

549

⁵"All the days of his vow of separation no razor shall come upon his head; until the time is completed for which he separates himself to the LORD, he shall be holy; he shall let the locks of hair of his head grow long.

Lev 21:1 ⁶"All the days that he separates himself to the LORD he shall not go near a dead body. ⁷Neither for his father nor for his mother, nor for brother or sister, if they die, shall he make himself Lev 21:12 unclean; because his separation to God is upon his head. ⁸All the Acts 21:23–26 days of his separation he is holy to the Lord.

⁹"And if any man dies very suddenly beside him, and he defiles his consecrated head, then he shall shave his head on the day of his cleansing; on the seventh day he shall shave it. ¹⁰On the eighth day he shall bring two turtledoves or two young pigeons to the priest to the door of the tent of meeting, ¹¹and the priest shall offer one for a sin offering and the other for a burnt offering, and make atonement for him, because he sinned by reason of the dead body. And he shall consecrate his head that same day, ¹²and separate himself to the LORD for the days of his separation, and bring a male lamb a year old for a guilt offering; but the former time shall be void, because his separation was defiled.

¹³"And this is the law for the Nazirite, when the time of his separation has been completed: he shall be brought to the door of the tent of meeting, ¹⁴and he shall offer his gift to the LORD, one

---

ceremony; it is probably meant to show that the consecrated person does without unessential earthly things in order to devote him to the things of God. It was, undoubtedly, a sign of dedicating oneself entirely to God. The requirement to avoid contact with dead bodies was one that applied also to priests (cf. Lev 21:1) and

it protected the person from falling into ritual uncleanness.

The ceremonies that mark the end of the vow are particularly solemn and reflect the joy of someone who has tried to be closer to God. The priests and the man's friends join with him in his communion offering and in his joy.

---

bibent; uvas recentes siccasque non comedent ⁴cunctis diebus, quibus ex voto Domino consecrantur: quidquid ex vinea esse potest ab uva acerba usque ad pellicula non comedent. ⁵omni tempore separationis suae novacula non transibit per caput eius usque ad completum tempus, quo Domino consecratur; sanctus erit crescente caesarie capitis eius. ⁶Omni tempore consecrationis suae ad mortuum non ingredietur; ⁷nec super patris quidem et matris et fratris sororisque funere contaminabitur, quia consecratio Dei sui super caput eius est. ⁸Omnibus diebus separationis suae sanctus erit Domino. ⁹Sin autem mortuus fuerit subito quispiam coram eo, polluetur caput consecrationis eius; quod radet ilico in eadem die purgationis suae, id est die septima. ¹⁰In octava autem die offeret duos turtures vel duos pullos columbae sacerdoti in introitu tabernaculi conventus, ¹¹facietque sacerdos unum pro peccato et alterum in holocaustum et expiabit pro eo, quia peccavit super mortuo, sanctificabitque caput eius in die illo ¹²et consecrabit Domino dies separationis suae offerens agnum anniculum pro delicto; ita tamen, ut dies priores irriti fiant, quoniam polluta est consecratio eius. ¹³Ista est lex consecrationis, cum dies, quos ex voto decreverat, complebuntur: adducent eum ad ostium tabernaculi conventus, ¹⁴et offeret oblationem

male lamb a year old without blemish for a burnt offering, and one ewe lamb a year old without blemish as a sin offering, and one ram without blemish as a peace offering, [15]and a basket of unleavened bread, cakes of fine flour mixed with oil, and unleavened wafers spread with oil, and their cereal offering and their drink offerings. [16]And the priest shall present them before the LORD and offer his sin offering and his burnt offering, [17]and he shall offer the ram as a sacrifice of peace offering to the LORD, with the basket of unleavened bread; the priest shall offer also its cereal offering and its drink offering. [18]And the Nazirite shall shave his consecrated head at the door of the tent of meeting, and shall take the hair from his consecrated head and put it on the fire which is under the sacrifice of the peace offering. [19]And the priest shall take the shoulder of the ram, when it is boiled, and one unleavened cake out of the basket, and one unleavened wafer, and shall put them upon the hands of the Nazirite, after he has shaven the hair of his consecration, [20]and the priest shall wave them for a wave offering before the LORD; they are a holy portion for the priest, together with the breast that is waved and the thigh that is offered; and after that the Nazirite may drink wine.

Lev 7:34; 10:14

[21]"This is the law for the Nazirite who takes a vow. His offering to the LORD shall be according to his vow as a Nazirite, apart from what else he can afford; in accordance with the vow which he takes, so shall he do according to the law for his separation as a Nazirite."

Blessing by priests

[22]The LORD said to Moses, [23]"Say to Aaron and his sons, Thus you shall bless the people of Israel: you shall say to them,

Ps 121:7–8

6:23–27. This is one of the earliest blessing formulae that the Bible has conserved for us. It is referred to in some psalms (cf. Ps 31:16; 67:1; etc.) and it was used by priests in the temple liturgy. It consists of three petitions, each beginning with

suam Domino agnum anniculum immaculatum in holocaustum et ovem anniculam immaculatam pro peccato et arietem immaculatum hostiam pacificam, [15]canistrum quoque panum azymorum, qui permixti sint oleo, et lagana absque fermento uncta oleo ac oblationem et libamina singulorum. [16]Quae offeret sacerdos coram Domino et faciet tam pro peccato quam in holocaustum; [17]arietem vero immolabit hostiam pacificam Domino offerens simul canistrum azymorum; facietque oblationem eius et libamenta. [18]Tunc radet nazaraeus ante ostium tabernaculi conventus caesariem consecrationis suae tolletque capillos suos et ponet super ignem, qui est suppositus sacrificio pacificorum, [19]et sumet sacerdos armum coctum arietis tortamque absque fermento unam de canistro et laganum azymum unum et tradet in manus nazaraei, postquam rasum fuerit caput eius; [20]et agitabit in conspectu Domini, et sanctificata sacerdotis erunt sicut pectusculum, quod agitari, et femur, quod praelevari iussum est. Post haec potest bibere nazaraeus vinum». [21]Ista est lex nazaraei, cum voverit oblationem suam Domino tempore consecrationis suae, exceptis his, quae invenerit manus eius. Iuxta quod devoverat, ita faciet secundum legem consecrationis suae. [22]Locutusque est Dominus ad Moysen dicens: [23]«Loquere Aaron et filiis

Ps 4:6; 31:16; 67:1

Deut 28:10

[24]The LORD bless you and keep you:
[25]The LORD make his face to shine upon you, and be gracious to you:
[26]The LORD lift up his countenance upon you, and give you peace. [27]"So shall they put my name upon the people of Israel, and I will bless them."

3. OFFERINGS AT THE CONSECRATION OF THE SANCTUARY*

Presentation of offerings

Ex 40:9–15

7 [1]On the day when Moses had finished setting up the tabernacle, and had anointed and consecrated it with all its furnishings, and had anointed and consecrated the altar with all its utensils, [2]the leaders of Israel, heads of their fathers' houses, the leaders of the tribes, who were over those who were numbered, [3]offered and brought their offerings before the LORD, six covered wagons and twelve oxen, a wagon for every two of the leaders, and for each one an ox; they offered them before the tabernacle. [4]Then the LORD said to Moses, [5]"Accept these from them, that they may be used in doing the service of the tent of meeting, and give them to the Levites, to each man according to his service." [6]So Moses took the wagons and the oxen, and gave them to the Levites. [7]Two wagons and four oxen he gave to the sons of Gershon, according to

---

the name of the Lord. Some ancient authors saw in this triple invocation an advance announcement of the Blessed Trinity. It goes on to pray for protection, grace and peace—three gifts which sum up man's aspirations and which God alone can provide in all their fullness.

The Church carries on the tradition of blessing the faithful during liturgical ceremonies, especially at the end of the

eucharistic celebration, beseeching God to show them his favour. The Roman Missal includes this text as one of the optional blessings the priest can use at the end of Mass.

*7:1–88. In the Pentateuch there are two ways of conveying the rules that are to govern the life of the people—one, in legalistic terms (as in the two preceding

---

eius: Sic benedicetis filiis Israel et dicetis eis: [24]'Benedicat tibi Dominus et custodiat te! / [25]Illuminet Dominus faciem suam super te et misereatur tui! / [26]Convertat Dominus vultum suum ad te et det tibi pacem!'. [27]Invocabuntque nomen meum super filios Israel, et ego benedicam eis». [1]Factum est autem in die, qua complevit Moyses habitaculum et erexit illud unxitque et sanctificavit cum omnibus vasis suis, altare similiter et omnia vasa eius, [2]obtulerunt principes Israel et capita familiarum, qui erant per singulas tribus praefecti eorum, qui numerati fuerant, [3]munera coram Domino sex plaustra tecta cum duodecim bobus. Unum plaustrum obtulere duo duces et unum bovem singuli; obtuleruntque ea in conspectu habitaculi. [4]Ait autem Dominus ad Moysen: [5]«Suscipe ab eis, ut serviant in ministerio taberna-

their service; [8]and four wagons and eight oxen he gave to the sons of Merari, according to their service, under the direction of Ithamar the son of Aaron the priest. [9]But to the sons of Kohath he gave none, because they were charged with the care of the holy things which had to be carried on the shoulder.

Offerings of leaders

[10]And the leaders offered offerings for the dedication of the altar on the day it was anointed; and the leaders offered their offering before the altar. [11]And the LORD said to Moses, "They shall offer their offerings, one leader each day, for the dedication of the altar."

[12]He who offered his offering the first day was Nahshon the son of Amminadab, of the tribe of Judah; [13]and his offering was one silver plate whose weight was a hundred and thirty shekels, one silver basin of seventy shekels, according to the shekel of the sanctuary, both of them full of fine flour mixed with oil for a cereal offering; [14]one golden dish of ten shekels, full of incense; [15]one young bull, one ram, one male lamb a year old, for a burnt offering; [16]one male goat for a sin offering; [17]and for the sacrifice of peace offerings, two oxen, five rams, five male goats, and five male lambs a year old. This was the offering of Nahshon the son of Amminadab.

[18]On the second day Nethanel the son of Zuar, the leader of Issachar, made an offering; [19]he offered for his offering one silver

---

chapters); the other, by means of narratives about what the people did in their pilgrimage through the desert (as in this section, which recounts the events of the day when the sanctuary was built and dedicated: cf. Ex 40). Once the Israelites settle down in Canaan they will always look back to their ancestors, in order to imitate them; in this particular case, to emulate their generosity in divine worship and the refinement with which they brought their offerings to the Lord in the temple.

culi conventus, et trades ea Levitis iuxta ordinem ministerii sui». [6]Itaque cum suscepisset Moyses plaustra et boves, tradidit eos Levitis. [7]Duo plaustra et quattuor boves dedit filiis Gerson, iuxta id quod habebant necessarium. [8]Quattuor alia plaustra et octo boves dedit filiis Merari, secundum officia sua sub manu Ithamar filii Aaron sacerdotis. [9]Filiis autem Caath non dedit plaustra et boves, quia in sanctuario serviunt et onera propriis portant umeris. [10]Igitur obtulerunt duces in dedicationem altaris, die qua unctum est, oblationem suam ante altare. [11]Dixitque Dominus ad Moysen: «Singuli duces per singulos dies offerant munera in dedicationem altaris». [12]Primo die obtulit oblationem suam Naasson filius Aminadab de tribu Iudae. [13]Fueruntque in ea scutula argentea pondo centum triginta siclorum, phiala argentea habens septuaginta siclos iuxta pondus sanctuarii, utraque plena simila conspersa oleo in sacrificium, [14]acetabulum ex decem siclis aureis plenum incenso, [15]bos de armento et aries et agnus anniculus in holocaustum [16]hircusque pro peccato; [17]et in sacrificio pacificorum boves duo, arietes quinque, hirci quinque, agni anniculi quinque: haec est oblatio Naasson filii Aminadab. [18]Secundo die obtulit Nathanael filius Suar dux de tribu Issachar [19]scutulam argenteam appendentem centum triginta

plate, whose weight was a hundred and thirty shekels, one silver basin of seventy shekels, according to the shekel of the sanctuary, both of them full of fine flour mixed with oil for a cereal offering; [20]one golden dish of ten shekels, full of incense: [21]one young bull, one ram, one male lamb a year old, for a burnt offering; [22]one male goat for a sin offering; [23]and for the sacrifice of peace offerings, two oxen, five rams, five male goats, and five male lambs a year old. This was the offering of Nethanel the son of Zuar.

[24]On the third day Eliab the son of Helon, the leader of the men of Zebulun: [25]his offering was one silver plate, whose weight was a hundred and thirty shekels, one silver basin of seventy shekels, according to the shekel of the sanctuary, both of them full of fine flour mixed with oil for a cereal offering; [26]one golden dish of ten shekels, full of incense; [27]one young bull, one ram, one male lamb a year old, for a burnt offering; [28]one male goat for a sin offering; [29]and for the sacrifice of peace offerings, two oxen, five rams, five male goats, and five male lambs a year old. This was the offering of Eliab the son of Helon.

[30]On the fourth day Elizur the son of Shedeur, the leader of the men of Reuben: [31]his offering was one silver plate whose weight was a hundred and thirty shekels, one silver basin of seventy shekels, according to the shekel of the sanctuary, both of them full of fine flour mixed with oil for a cereal offering; [32]one golden dish of ten shekels, full of incense; [33]one young bull, one ram, one male lamb a year old, for a burnt offering; [34]one male goat for a sin offering; [35]and for the sacrifice of peace offerings, two oxen, five rams, five male goats, and five male lambs a year old. This was the offering of Elizur the son of Shedeur.

[36]On the fifth day Shelumi-el the son of Zurishaddai, the leader of the men of Simeon: [37]his offering was one silver plate,

siclos, phialam argenteam habentem septuaginta siclos iuxta pondus sanctuarii, utramque plenam simila conspersa oleo in sacrificium, [20]acetabulum aureum habens decem siclos plenum incenso, [21]bovem de armento et arietem et agnum anniculum in holocaustum [22]hircumque pro peccato; [23]et in sacrificio pacificorum boves duos, arietes quinque, hircos quinque, agnos anniculos quinque: haec fuit oblatio Nathanael filii Suar. [24]Tertio die princeps filiorum Zabulon Eliab filius Helon [25]obtulit scutulam argenteam appendentem centum triginta siclos, phialam argenteam habentem septuaginta siclos ad pondus sanctuarii, utramque plenam simila conspersa oleo in sacrificium, [26]acetabulum aureum appendens decem siclos plenum incenso, [27]bovem de armento et arietem et agnum anniculum in holocaustum [28]hircumque pro peccato; [29]et in sacrificio pacificorum boves duos, arietes quinque, hircos quinque, agnos anniculos quinque: haec est oblatio Eliab filii Helon. [30]Die quarto princeps filiorum Ruben Elisur filius Sedeur [31]obtulit scutulam argenteam appendentem centum triginta siclos, phialam argenteam habentem septuaginta siclos ad pondus sanctuarii, utramque plenam simila conspersa oleo in sacrificium, [32]acetabulum aureum appendens decem siclos plenum incenso, [33]bovem de armento et arietem et agnum anniculum in holocaustum [34]hircumque pro peccato; [35]et in hostias pacificorum boves duos, arietes quinque, hircos quinque, agnos anniculos quinque: haec fuit oblatio Elisur filii Sedeur. [36]Die quinto princeps filiorum Simeon Salamiel filius Surisaddai [37]obtulit scutulam argenteam appen-

whose weight was a hundred and thirty shekels, one silver basin of seventy shekels, according to the shekel of the sanctuary, both of them full of fine flour mixed with oil for a cereal offering; [38]one golden dish of ten shekels, full of incense; [39]one young bull, one ram, one male lamb a year old, for a burnt offering; [40]one male goat for a sin offering; [41]and for the sacrifice of peace offerings, two oxen, five rams, five male goats, and five male lambs a year old. This was the offering of Shelumi-el the son of Zuri-shaddai.

[42]On the sixth day Eliasaph the son of Deuel, the leader of the men of Gad: [43]his offering was one silver plate, whose weight was a hundred and thirty shekels, one silver basin of seventy shekels, according to the shekel of the sanctuary, both of them full of fine flour mixed with oil for a cereal offering; [44]one golden dish of ten shekels, full of incense; [45]one young bull, one ram, one male lamb a year old, for a burnt offering; [46]one male goat for a sin offering; [47]and for the sacrifice of peace offerings, two oxen, five rams, five male goats, and five male lambs a year old. This was the offering of Eliasaph the son of Deuel.

[48]On the seventh day Elishama the son of Ammihud, the leader of the men of Ephraim: [49]his offering was one silver plate, whose weight was a hundred and thirty shekels, one silver basin of seventy shekels, according to the shekel of the sanctuary, both of them full of fine flour mixed with oil for a cereal offering; [50]one golden dish of ten shekels, full of incense; [51]one young bull, one ram, one male lamb a year old, for a burnt offering; [52]one male goat for a sin offering; [53]and for the sacrifice of peace offerings, two oxen, five rams, five male goats, and five male lambs a year old. This was the offering of Elishama the son of Ammihud.

dentem centum triginta siclos, phialam argenteam habentem septuaginta siclos ad pondus sanctuarii, utramque plenam simila conspersa oleo in sacrificium, [38]acetabulum aureum appendens decem siclos plenum incenso, [39]bovem de armento et arietem et agnum anniculum in holocaustum, [40]hircumque pro peccato; [41]et in hostias pacificorum boves duos, arietes quinque, hircos quinque, agnos anniculos quinque: haec fuit oblatio Salamiel filii Surisaddai. [42]Die sexto princeps filiorum Gad Eliasaph filius Deuel [43]obtulit scutulam argenteam appendentem centum triginta siclos, phialam argenteam habentem septuaginta siclos ad pondus sanctuarii, utramque plenam simila conspersa oleo in sacrificium, [44]acetabulum aureum appendens decem siclos plenum incenso, [45]bovem de armento et arietem et agnum anniculum in holocaustum, [46]hircumque pro peccato; [47]et in hostias pacificorum boves duos, arietes quinque, hircos quinque, agnos anniculos quinque: haec fuit oblatio Eliasaph filii Deuel. [48]Die septimo princeps filiorum Ephraim Elisama filius Ammiud [49]obtulit scutulam argenteam appendentem centum triginta siclos, phialam argenteam habentem septuaginta siclos ad pondus sanctuarii, utramque plenam simila conspersa oleo in sacrificium, [50]acetabulum aureum appendens decem siclos plenum incenso, [51]bovem de armento et arietem et agnum anniculum in holocaustum, [52]hircumque pro peccato; [53]et in hostias pacificorum boves duos, arietes quinque, hircos quinque, agnos anniculos quinque: haec fuit oblatio Elisama filii Ammiud. [54]Die octavo princeps filiorum Manasse Gamaliel filius Phadassur

⁵⁴On the eighth day Gamaliel the son of Pedahzur, the leader of the men of Manasseh: ⁵⁵his offering was one silver plate, whose weight was a hundred and thirty shekels, one silver basin of seventy shekels, according to the shekel of the sanctuary, both of them full of fine flour mixed with oil for a cereal offering; ⁵⁶one golden dish of ten shekels, full of incense; ⁵⁷one young bull, one ram, one male lamb a year old, for a burnt offering; ⁵⁸one male goat for a sin offering; ⁵⁹and for the sacrifice of peace offerings, two oxen, five rams, five male goats, and five male lambs a year old. This was the offering of Gamaliel the son of Pedahzur.

⁶⁰On the ninth day Abidan the son of Gideoni, the leader of the men of Benjamin: ⁶¹his offering was one silver plate, whose weight was a hundred and thirty shekels, one silver basin of seventy shekels, according to the shekel of the sanctuary, both of them full of fine flour mixed with oil for a cereal offering; ⁶²one golden dish of ten shekels, full of incense; ⁶³one young bull, one ram, one male lamb a year old, for a burnt offering; ⁶⁴one male goat for a sin offering; ⁶⁵and for the sacrifice of peace offerings, two oxen, five rams, five male goats, and five male lambs a year old. This was the offering of Abidan the son of Gideoni.

⁶⁶On the tenth day Ahiezer the son of Ammishaddai, the leader of the men of Dan: ⁶⁷his offering was one silver plate, whose weight was a hundred and thirty shekels, one silver basin of seventy shekels, according to the shekel of the sanctuary, both of them full of fine flour mixed with oil for a cereal offering; ⁶⁸one golden dish of ten shekels, full of incense; ⁶⁹one young bull, one ram, one male lamb a year old, for a burnt offering; ⁷⁰one male goat for a sin offering; ⁷¹and for the sacrifice of peace offerings, two oxen, five rams, five male goats, and five male lambs a year old. This was the offering of Ahiezer the son of Ammishaddai.

⁵⁵obtulit scutulam argenteam appendentem centum triginta siclos, phialam argenteam habentem septuaginta siclos ad pondus sanctuarii, utramque plenam simila conspersa oleo in sacrificium, ⁵⁶acetabulum aureum appendens decem siclos plenum incenso, ⁵⁷bovem de armento et arietem et agnum anniculum in holocaustum ⁵⁸hircumque pro peccato; ⁵⁹et in hostias pacificorum boves duos, arietes quinque, hircos quinque, agnos anniculos quinque: haec fuit oblatio Gamaliel filii Phadassur. ⁶⁰Die nono princeps filiorum Beniamin Abidan filius Gedeonis ⁶¹obtulit scutulam argenteam appendentem centum triginta siclos, phialam argenteam habentem septuaginta siclos ad pondus sanctuarii, utramque plenam simila conspersa oleo in sacrificium, ⁶²et acetabulum aureum appendens decem siclos plenum incenso, ⁶³bovem de armento et arietem et agnum anniculum in holocaustum ⁶⁴hircumque pro peccato; ⁶⁵et in hostias pacificorum boves duos, arietes quinque, hircos quinque, agnos anniculos quinque: haec fuit oblatio Abidan filii Gedeonis. ⁶⁶Die decimo princeps filiorum Dan Ahiezer filius Ammisaddai ⁶⁷obtulit scutulam argenteam appendentem centum triginta siclos, phialam argenteam habentem septuaginta siclos ad pondus sanctuarii, utramque plenam simila conspersa oleo in sacrificium, ⁶⁸acetabulum aureum appendens decem siclos plenum incenso, ⁶⁹bovem de armento et arietem et agnum anniculum in holocaustum ⁷⁰hircumque pro peccato; ⁷¹et in hostias pacificorum boves duos, arietes quinque, hircos quinque, agnos anniculos quinque: haec fuit oblatio Ahiezer filii Ammisaddai. ⁷²Die

⁷²On the eleventh day Pagiel the son of Ochran, the leader of the men of Asher: ⁷³his offering was one silver plate, whose weight was a hundred and thirty shekels, one silver basin of seventy shekels, according to the shekel of the sanctuary, both of them full of fine flour mixed with oil for a cereal offering; ⁷⁴one golden dish of ten shekels, full of incense; ⁷⁵one young bull, one ram, one male lamb a year old, for a burnt offering; ⁷⁶one male goat for a sin offering; ⁷⁷and for the sacrifice of peace offerings, two oxen, five rams, five male goats, and five male lambs a year old. This was the offering of Pagiel the son of Ochran.

⁷⁸On the twelfth day Ahira the son of Enan, the leader of the men of Naphtali: ⁷⁹his offering was one silver plate, whose weight was a hundred and thirty shekels, one silver basin of seventy shekels, according to the shekel of the sanctuary, both of them full of fine flour mixed with oil for a cereal offering; ⁸⁰one golden dish of ten shekels, full of incense; ⁸¹one young bull, one ram, one male lamb a year old, for a burnt offering; ⁸²one male goat for a sin offering; ⁸³and for the sacrifice of peace offerings, two oxen, five rams, five male goats, and five male lambs a year old. This was the offering of Ahira the son of Enan.

⁸⁴This was the dedication offering for the altar, on the day when it was anointed, from the leaders of Israel: twelve silver plates, twelve silver basins, twelve golden dishes, ⁸⁵each silver plate weighing a hundred and thirty shekels and each basin seventy, all the silver of the vessels two thousand four hundred shekels according to the shekel of the sanctuary, ⁸⁶the twelve golden dishes, full of incense, weighing ten shekels apiece according to the shekel of the sanctuary, all the gold of the dishes being a hundred and twenty shekels; ⁸⁷all the cattle for the burnt offering

undecimo princeps filiorum Aser Phegiel filius Ochran ⁷³obtulit scutulam argenteam appendentem centum triginta siclos, phialam argenteam habentem septuaginta siclos ad pondus sanctuarii, utramque plenam simila conspersa oleo in sacrificium, ⁷⁴acetabulum aureum appendens decem siclos plenum incenso, ⁷⁵bovem de armento et arietem et agnum anniculum in holocaustum ⁷⁶hircumque pro peccato; ⁷⁷et in hostias pacificorum boves duos, arietes quinque, hircos quinque, agnos anniculos quinque: haec fuit oblatio Phegiel filii Ochran. ⁷⁸Die duodecimo princeps filiorum Nephthali Ahira filius Enan ⁷⁹obtulit scutulam argenteam appendentem centum triginta siclos, phialam argenteam habentem septuaginta siclos ad pondus sanctuarii, utramque plenam simila oleo conspersa in sacrificium, ⁸⁰acetabulum aureum appendens decem siclos plenum incenso, ⁸¹bovem de armento et arietem et agnum anniculum in holocaustum ⁸²hircumque pro peccato; ⁸³et in hostias pacificorum boves duos, arietes quinque, hircos quinque, agnos anniculos quinque: haec fuit oblatio Ahira filii Enan. ⁸⁴Haec in dedicatione altaris oblata sunt a principibus Israel, in die qua consecratum est: scutulae argenteae duodecim, phialae argenteae duodecim, acetabula duodecim, ⁸⁵ita ut centum triginta siclos argenti haberet una scutella, et septuaginta siclos haberet una phiala, id est in commune vasorum omnium ex argento sicli duo milia quadringenti pondere sanctuarii; ⁸⁶acetabula aurea duodecim plena incenso denos siclos appendentia pondere sanctuarii, id est simul auri sicli centum viginti; ⁸⁷omnes boves de armento in holocaustum duodecim, arietes duodecim, agni anniculi duodecim et libamenta eorum; hirci

twelve bulls, twelve rams, twelve male lambs a year old, with their cereal offering; and twelve male goats for a sin offering; [88]and all the cattle for the sacrifice of peace offerings twenty-four bulls, the rams sixty, the male goats sixty, the male lambs a year old sixty. This was the dedication offering for the altar, after it was anointed.

Conversations between Moses and the Lord

[89]And when Moses went into the tent of meeting to speak with the LORD, he heard the voice speaking to him from above the mercy seat that was upon the ark of the testimony, from between the two cherubim; and it spoke to him.

Ex 25:31–40

The golden lampstand

Lev 24:2–4

8 [1]Now the LORD said to Moses, [2]"Say to Aaron, When you set up the lamps, the seven lamps shall give light in front of the lampstand." [3]And Aaron did so; he set up its lamps to give light in front of the lampstand, as the LORD commanded Moses. [4]And this was the workmanship of the lampstand, hammered work of gold; from its base to its flowers, it was hammered work; according to the pattern which the LORD had shown Moses, so he made the lampstand.

8:1–4. The lampstand or *menoráh* was a rich golden artifact (cf. Ex 25:31–40) placed beside the table of the offertory bread. Although the exact meaning of this candelabra is unclear, it was obviously a very important feature of divine worship, given that the lamps had to be kept burning all the time (cf. Lev 24:2–4). The fact that the arms were seven in number indicates completeness. Flavius Josephus comments that the lampstand symbolized the creative power of God because the seven branches stood for the moon and the planets (cf. *Antiquitates Iudaicae*, 3, 144–6). In the tradition of the Church, the lamps are said to typify Christ. Clement of Alexandria comments: "The golden lampstand has another symbolic meaning—that of being a sign of Christ [. . .] not because of its unique nature but because it provides light 'in many and various ways' (Heb 1:1) to those who believe and hope in him" (*Stromata*, 5, 6, 35). For his part, Rabanus Maurus says that "the seven lamps are the seven gifts of the Holy Spirit, which abide forever in the Lord, our Redeemer, and in his members, that is, in all those chosen in keeping with his will" (*Commentarium in Numeros*, 14).

---

duodecim pro peccato. [88]In hostias pacificorum omnes boves viginti quattuor, arietes sexaginta, hirci sexaginta, agni anniculi sexaginta: haec oblata sunt in dedicatione altaris, quando unctum est. [89]Cumque ingrederetur Moyses tabernaculum testimonii, ut consuleret oraculum, audiebat vocem loquentis ad se de propitiatorio, quod erat super arcam testimonii inter duos cherubim, unde et loquebatur ei. [1] Locutusque est Dominus ad Moysen dicens: [2]«Loquere Aaron et dices ad eum: Cum posueris lucernas, contra eam partem, quam candelabrum respicit, lucere debebunt septem lucernae». [3]Fecitque sic Aaron et posuit lucernas super candelabrum, ut praeceperat Dominus Moysi. [4]Haec autem erat factura candelabri: ex auro ductili, tam medius stipes quam flores eius. Iuxta exemplum, quod ostendit Dominus Moysi, ita operatus est candelabrum. [5]Et locutus est Dominus ad Moysen dicens: [6]«Tolle

The purification and offering of the Levites Lev 8

[5]And the LORD said to Moses, [6]"Take the Levites from among the people of Israel, and cleanse them. [7]And thus you shall do to Num 19:1–10
Lev 14:8–9
Ezek 36:25 them, to cleanse them: sprinkle the water of expiation upon them, and let them go with a razor over all their body, and wash their clothes and cleanse themselves. [8]Then let them take a young bull and its cereal offering of fine flour mixed with oil, and you shall take another young bull for a sin offering. [9]And you shall present the Levites before the tent of meeting, and assemble the whole congregation of the people of Israel. [10]When you present the Levites before the LORD, the people of Israel shall lay their hands upon the Levites, [11]and Aaron shall offer the Levites before the LORD as a wave offering from the people of Israel, that it may be theirs to do the service of the LORD. [12]Then the Levites shall lay their hands upon the heads of the bulls; and you shall offer the one for a sin offering and the other for a burnt offering to the LORD, to make atonement for the Levites. [13]And you shall cause Ex 29:24 the Levites to attend Aaron and his sons, and shall offer them as a wave offering to the LORD.

8:5–22. The ceremony of the dedication of the Levites is in many ways similar to that of priests (cf. Lev 8), with this difference—that priests are consecrated (cf. Lev 8:12) whereas Levites are only cleansed (v. 6). Levites were held in high regard. Levi is a son of Leah, like Judah and Simeon. In the episode of the golden calf, the Levites stayed loyal to Moses in his confrontation with the idolators (cf. Ex 32:25–29). They were co-operators of the priests, but the functions they performed in the temple were secondary ones (cf. Num 3:6–9 and Ezek 44:11–31). Due to their special status they were omitted from the census (cf. Num 1:47–49; 4:1–49) and no territory was allocated to them when the land was distributed (cf. Josh 14:3–4); instead, their income consisted in tithes from the other tribes (cf. Num 18:21–24). Because of their dedication to the service of the Lord, they had to be very scrupulous about ritual cleanness, as can be seen from this very detailed ceremony. The water of expiation (literally, "water of sin": v. 7) may have been a kind of lustral water, water used for the purification of persons or objects, similar to that whose preparation is described in 19:1–10. There were probably different ways of preparing the water, depending on the type of ablution

---

Levitas de medio filiorum Israel et purificabis eos [7]iuxta hunc ritum. Aspergantur aqua lustrationis et radant omnes pilos carnis suae, lavabunt vestimenta sua et mundabunt se. [8]Tollent bovem de armentis et oblationem eius similam oleo conspersam; bovem autem alterum de armento tu accipies pro peccato [9]et applicabis Levitas coram tabernaculo conventus, convocata omni multitudine filiorum Israel. [10]Cumque Levitae fuerint coram Domino, ponent filii Israel manus suas super eos, [11]et agitabit Aaron Levitas munus in conspectu Domini a filiis Israel, ut serviant in ministerio eius. [12]Levitae quoque ponent manus suas super capita boum, e quibus unum facies pro peccato et alterum in holocaustum Domini, ut expies eos. [13]Statuesque Levitas in conspectu Aaron et filiorum eius et agitabis eos Domino [14]ac separabis de medio filiorum Israel, ut sint mei; [15]et postea ingredientur, ut serviant tabernaculo con-

¹⁴"Thus you shall separate the Levites from among the people of Israel, and the Levites shall be mine. ¹⁵And after that the Levites shall go in to do service at the tent of meeting, when you have cleansed them and offered them as a wave offering. ¹⁶For they are wholly given to me from among the people of Israel; instead of all that open the womb, the first-born of all the people of Israel, I have taken them for myself. ¹⁷For all the first-born among the people of Israel are mine, both of man and of beast; on the day that I slew all the first-born in the land of Egypt I consecrated them for myself, ¹⁸and I have taken the Levites instead of all the first-born among the people of Israel. ¹⁹And I have given the Levites as a gift to Aaron and his sons from among the people of Israel, to do the service for the people of Israel at the tent of meeting, and to make atonement for the people of Israel, that there may be no plague among the people of Israel in case the people of Israel should come near the sanctuary."

²⁰Thus did Moses and Aaron and all the congregation of the people of Israel to the Levites; according to all that the LORD com-

Ex 13:11
Num 3:40–51;
18:15

(cf. 31:23) and the people involved in them. The detailed rules about the cleansing of Levites prior to starting their ministry in divine worship has given the Church food for thought. What type of cleansing is called for when the liturgy is no longer one of shadows and figure but has as its victim Christ himself? "What should the purity not be of him who offers so great a sacrifice," St John Chrysostom asks. "Ought not the hand which cuts the victim be more splendid than the sun? And what of the mouth, which is filled with this spiritual fire, and the tongue, which is reddened by such precious blood?" (*Homiliae in Matthaeum*, 82, 5).

The laying-on of hands showed that the offering being made to God was the property of the offerer: the children of Israel were transferring to God their ownership of the Levites (v. 10), just as the Levites did with the young bulls (v. 12).

"Aaron shall offer the Levites before the Lord as a wave offering" (vv. 11, 13, 15). Once a wave offering was presented before the Lord, what was offered became the property of the priests (cf. Ex 29:24–28). In the present case the same system of waving as applied when cereals or animals were being offered was not used. Anyway, what this ceremony showed was that the Levites would always be at the service of the priests. It made it clear that they were a gift that all Israel was making to the Lord in place of the first-born (v. 18; cf. 3:12–13).

---

ventus. Sicque purificabis et agitabis eos, ¹⁶quoniam dono donati sunt mihi e medio filiorum Israel; pro primogenitis, quae aperiunt omnem vulvam in Israel, accepi eos. ¹⁷Mea sunt enim omnia primogenita filiorum Israel, tam ex hominibus quam ex iumentis. Ex die, quo percussi omne primogenitum in terra Aegypti, sanctificavi eos mihi. ¹⁸Et tuli Levitas pro cunctis primogenitis filiorum Israel ¹⁹tradidique eos dono Aaron et filiis eius de medio filiorum Israel, ut serviant mihi pro Israel in tabernaculo conventus et expient pro eis, ne sit in populo plaga, si ausi fuerint accedere ad sanctuarium». ²⁰Feceruntque Moyses et Aaron et omnis congregatio filiorum Israel super Levitis, quae praeceperat Dominus Moysi.

manded Moses concerning the Levites, the people of Israel did to them. ²¹And the Levites purified themselves from sin, and washed their clothes; and Aaron offered them as a wave offering before the LORD, and Aaron made atonement for them to cleanse them. ²²And after that the Levites went in to do their service in the tent of meeting in attendance upon Aaron and his sons; as the LORD had commanded Moses concerning the Levites, so they did to them.

²³And the LORD said to Moses, ²⁴"This is what pertains to the Levites: from twenty-five years old and upward they shall go in to perform the work in the service of the tent of meeting; ²⁵and from the age of fifty years they shall withdraw from the work of the service and serve no more, ²⁶but minister to their brethren in the tent of meeting, to keep the charge, and they shall do no service. Thus shall you do to the Levites in assigning their duties."

4. PREPARATION FOR THE DEPARTURE

The second celebration of the Passover*   Ex 12:1–14

9 ¹And the LORD spoke to Moses in the wilderness of Sinai, in the first month of the second year after they had come out of the land of Egypt, saying, ²"Let the people of Israel keep the   Ex 12:6 passover at its appointed time. ³On the fourteenth day of this month, in the evening, you shall keep it at its appointed time;

---

*9:1–14. This account of the second celebration of the Passover includes rules to be followed when a person is unable to celebrate the feast at the right time either because he has contracted uncleanness through contact with a dead body, or because he is travelling on the day. These rulings seem to particularly fit the circumstances Israel found itself in after it was sent into exile—when the Passover was held in scattered communities and it

was difficult to meet together for the feast. According to the book of Chronicles (2 Chron 3), Hezekiah applied these rules when re-establishing the Passover in the temple as part of his religious reform.

The Passover was the most specific of Israel's feasts: if someone was able to take part in it and failed to do so, he was regarded as excluded from the people; on the other hand, strangers who took part in

---

²¹Purificatique sunt et laverunt vestimenta sua, agitavitque eos Aaron in conspectu Domini et expiavit eos, ut purificati ²²ingrederentur ad officia sua in tabernaculo conventus coram Aaron et filiis eius; sicut praeceperat Dominus Moysi de Levitis, ita factum est. ²³Locutusque est Dominus ad Moysen dicens: ²⁴«Haec est lex Levitarum: a viginti quinque annis et supra ingredientur, ut ministrent in tabernaculo conventus; ²⁵cumque quinquagesimum annum aetatis impleverint, servire cessabunt ²⁶eruntque ministri fratrum suorum in tabernaculo conventus, ut custodiant, quae sibi fuerint commendata; opera autem ipsa non faciant. Sic dispones Levitis in custodiis suis». ¹Locutus est Dominus ad Moysen in deserto Sinai anno seccundo, postquam egressi sunt de terra Aegypti, mense primo dicens: ²«Faciant filii Israel Pascha in tempore suo ³quarta decima die mensis huius ad vesperam iuxta omnia praecepta

according to all its statutes and all its ordinances you shall keep it." ⁴So Moses told the people of Israel that they should keep the passover. ⁵And they kept the passover in the first month, on the fourteenth day of the month, in the evening, in the wilderness of Sinai; according to all that the LORD commanded Moses, so the people of Israel did.

2 Chron 30:2ff **Individual cases**
Num, 5:2;
19:11 ⁶And there were certain men who were unclean through touching the dead body of a man, so that they could not keep the passover on that day; and they came before Moses and Aaron on that day; ⁷and those men said to him, "We are unclean through touching the dead body of a man; why are we kept from offering the LORD's offering at its appointed time among the people of Israel?" ⁸And Moses said to them, "Wait, that I may hear what the LORD will command concerning you."

⁹The LORD said to Moses, ¹⁰"Say to the people of Israel, If any man of you or of your descendants is unclean through touching a dead body, or is afar off on a journey, he shall still keep the passover to the LORD. ¹¹In the second month on the fourteenth day in the evening they shall keep it; they shall eat it with unleavened
Ex 12:46 bread and bitter herbs. ¹²They shall leave none of it until the
Jn 19:36
1 Cor 5:7 morning, nor break a bone of it; according to all the statute for the

---

it were considered fellow citizens. This feast means a great deal to the chosen people: it is the memorial of their deliverance from bondage in Egypt; every time it is celebrated it reminds them how God came to his people's rescue; each member of the community tailors his life to the events of the first Passover (cf. also the notes on Ex 23:14–17; Lev 23:5–8; and Deut 16:1–8).

Therefore, just as it was essential for the Israelites to take part in the Passover in order to recall how God intervened on their behalf, the Church now, following a apostolic tradition, has laid it down that Christians should take part at least on Sundays in the re-enactment of the paschal mystery which takes place in the Eucharist (cf. *Code of Canon Law*, can. 1246, 1).

---

et iustificationes eius». ⁴Praecepitque Moyses filiis Israel, ut facerent Pascha. ⁵Qui fecerunt tempore suo quarta decima die mensis ad vesperam in deserto Sinai; iuxta omnia, quae mandaverat Dominus Moysi, fecerunt filii Israel. ⁶Ecce autem quidam immundi super animam hominis, qui non poterant facere Pascha in die illo, accedentes ad Moysen et Aaron ⁷dixerunt ei: «Immundi sumus super animam hominis; quare fraudamur, ut non valeamus oblationem offerre Domino in tempore suo inter filios Israel?». ⁸Quibus respondit Moyses: «State, ut consulam quid praecipiat Dominus de vobis». ⁹Locutusque est Dominus ad Moysen dicens: ¹⁰«Loquere filiis Israel: Homo, qui fuerit immundus super anima, sive in via procul in gente vestra, faciat Pascha Domino ¹¹in mense secundo quarta decima die mensis ad vesperam; cum azymis et lactucis agrestibus comedent illud, ¹²non relinquent ex eo quippiam usque mane et os eius non confringent: omnem ritum Pascha observabunt. ¹³Si quis autem et

passover they shall keep it. [13]But the man who is clean and is not on a journey, yet refrains from keeping the passover, that person shall be cut off from his people, because he did not offer the LORD's offering at its appointed time; that man shall bear his sin. [14]And if a stranger sojourns among you, and will keep the passover to the Lord, according to the statute of the passover and according to its ordinance, so shall he do; you shall have one statute, both for the sojourner and for the native." Ex 12:48

The cloud covers the tabernacle
[15]On the day that the tabernacle was set up, the cloud covered the tabernacle, the tent of the testimony; and at evening it was over the tabernacle like the appearance of fire until morning. [16]So it was continually; the cloud covered it by day,[d] and the appearance of fire by night. [17]And whenever the cloud was taken up from over the tent, after that the people of Israel set out; and in the place where the cloud settled down, there the people of Israel encamped. [18]At the command of the LORD the people of Israel set out, and at the command of the LORD they encamped; as long as the cloud rested over the tabernacle, they remained in camp. [19]Even when the cloud continued over the tabernacle many days, the people of Israel kept the charge of the LORD, and did not set out. [20]Sometimes the cloud was a few days over the tabernacle, and according

Ex 13:22;
40:34–38

9:15–23. The cloud which at night took on the appearance of fire and which stayed with the Israelites on their journey through the desert, symbolizes the protective presence of the Lord and, at the same time, his transcendence. The children of Israel were convinced that God's constant protection was what mattered most—more than just shielding them from the torrid heat of the desert. As well as this, the cloud is a sign of the Supreme Being, whom no one on this earth can see face to face.

Here we see how Holy Scripture shows that God uses ordinary visible things as signs to manifest invisible

mundus est et in itinere non fuit et tamen non fecit Pascha, exterminabitur anima illa de populis suis, quia sacrificium Domino non obtulit tempore suo: peccatum suum ipse portabit. [14]Peregrinus quoque et advena, si fuerint apud vos, facient Pascha Domino iuxta praecepta et iustificationes eius; praeceptum idem erit apud vos tam advenae quam indigenae». [15]Igitur die qua erectum est habitaculum, operuit nubes habitaculum, tabernaculum testimonii; a vespere autem super habitaculum erat quasi species ignis usque mane. [16]Sic fiebat iugiter: per diem operiebat illud nubes, et per noctem quasi species ignis. [17]Cumque ablata fuisset nubes, quae tabernaculum protegebat, tunc proficiscebantur filii Israel; et in loco, ubi stetisset nubes, ibi castrametabantur. [18]Ad imperium Domini proficiscebantur et ad imperium illius castrametabantur. Cunctis diebus, quibus stabat nubes super habitaculum, manebant in eodem loco. [19]Et si evenisset ut multo tempore maneret super illud, erant filii Israel in excubiis Domini et non proficiscebantur; [20]si diebus paucis fuisset nubes super habitaculum, ad imperium Domini erigebant

d. Gk Syr Vg: Heb lacks *by day*

to the command of the Lord they remained in camp; then according to the command of the Lord they set out. [21]And sometimes the cloud remained from evening until morning; and when the cloud was taken up in the morning, they set out, or if it continued for a day and a night, when the cloud was taken up they set out. [22]Whether it was two days, or a month, or a longer time, that the cloud continued over the tabernacle, abiding there, the people of Israel remained in camp and did not set out; but when it was taken up they set out. [23]At the command of the Lord they encamped, and at the command of the Lord they set out; they kept the charge of the Lord, at the command of the Lord by Moses.

Joel 2:1, 15ff
1 Thess 4:16ff
1 Cor 15:52

The silver trumpets

10 [1]The Lord said to Moses, [2]"Make two silver trumpets; of hammered work you shall make them; and you shall use them for summoning the congregation, and for breaking camp. [3]And when both are blown, all the congregation shall gather themselves to you at the entrance of the tent of meeting. [4]But if they blow only one, then the leaders, the heads of the tribes of Israel, shall gather themselves to you. [5]When you blow an alarm,

---

supernatural realities: the cloud which shelters the people from the sun manifests God's presence among them, his providential guidance and his care and protection. The people of God do not walk alone nor do they wander aimlessly, for God accompanies them and guides them.

The archangel Gabriel seems to allude to the symbolism of the cloud when he announces to Mary that she is to be the mother of the Messiah through the action of God: "The Holy Spirit will come upon you, and the power of the Most High will overshadow you; therefore the child to be born will be called

holy, the Son of God" (Lk 1:35). In the person of Jesus we can see the sign of the tabernacle in all its fullness: he is the Word, who establishes his home among men (cf. Jn 1:14). Like the people of Israel, the Church does not walk alone: the presence of God stays in her midst protecting her and guiding her on her pilgrimage in this world.

10:1–10. These silver trumpets were used to summon the assembly and as an element in divine worship; but they were also used to call people to arms. They took the form of a long pipe opening out

---

tentoria et ad imperium illius deponebant. [21]Si fuisset nubes a vespere usque mane et statim diluculo habitaculum reliquisset, proficiscebantur; et si post diem et noctem recessisset, dissipabant tentoria. [22]Si vero biduo aut uno mense vel longiore tempore fuisset super habitaculum, manebant filii Israel in eodem loco et non proficiscebantur. Statim autem ut recessisset, movebant castra. [23]Per verbum Domini figebant tentoria et per verbum illius proficiscebantur; erantque in excubiis Domini iuxta imperium eius per manum Moysi. [1] Locutusque est Dominus ad Moysen dicens: [2]«Fac tibi duas tubas argenteas ductiles, quibus convocare possis congregationem, quando movenda sunt castra. [3]Cumque increpueris tubis, congregabitur ad te omnis turba ad ostium tabernaculi conventus. [4]Si semel clangueris, venient ad te principes et capita congregationis Israel; [5]si autem prolixior clangor increpuerit, movebunt castra

the camps that are on the east side shall set out. [6]And when you blow an alarm the second time, the camps that are on the south side shall set out. An alarm is to be blown whenever they are to set out. [7]But when the assembly is to be gathered together, you shall blow, but you shall not sound an alarm. [8]And the sons of Aaron, the priests, shall blow the trumpets. The trumpets shall be to you for a perpetual statute throughout your generations. [9]And when you go to war in your land against the adversary who oppresses you, then you shall sound an alarm with the trumpets, that you may be remembered before the LORD your God, and you shall be saved from your enemies. [10]On the day of your gladness Lev 17:1 also, and at your appointed feasts, and at the beginnings of your months, you shall blow the trumpets over your burnt offerings and over the sacrifices of your peace offerings; they shall serve you for remembrance before your God: I am the LORD your God."

PART TWO

The People in Kadesh

5. THE MARCH THROUGH THE DESERT

Departure from Sinai*
[11]In the second year, in the second month, on the twentieth day of the month, the cloud was taken up from over the tabernacle of the

---

at the end. The sound of alarm (vv. 5, 7) was a sharp, penetrating noise which could be heard at a distance or above the noise of battle.

But, most of all, the trumpets were a call to God, an appeal to him to come to the aid of his people. They were designed to remind them that God was always with them and would give them victory (v. 10).

*10:11–28. The Israelites have been at the foot of Mount Sinai for almost a year

primi, qui sunt ad orientalem plagam; [6]in secundo autem sonitu et pari ululatu tubae levabunt tentoria, qui habitant ad meridiem, et iuxta hunc modum reliqui facient, ululantibus tubis in profectionem. [7]Quando autem congregandus est populus, simplex tubarum clangor erit, et non ululabunt. [8]Filii autem Aaron sacerdotes clangent tubis. Eritque hoc vobis legitimum sempiternum in generationibus vestris. [9]Si exieritis ad bellum in terra vestra contra hostes, qui dimicant adversum vos, clangetis ululantibus tubis; et erit recordatio vestri coram Domino Deo vestro, ut eruamini de manibus inimicorum vestrorum. [10]Si quando habebitis epulum et dies festos et calendas, canetis tubis super holocaustis vestris et pacificis victimis, ut sint vobis in recordationem Dei vestri. Ego Dominus Deus vester». [11]Anno

testimony, [12]and the people of Israel set out by stages from the wilderness of Sinai; and the cloud settled down in the wilderness of Paran.

Num 2:1–34 **The order of the march**
[13]They set out for the first time at the command of the LORD by Moses. [14]The standard of the camp of the men of Judah set out first by their companies; and over their host was Nahshon the son of Amminadab. [15]And over the host of the tribe of the men of Issachar was Nethanel the son of Zuar. [16]And over the host of the tribe of the men of Zebulun was Eliab the son of Helon.

[17]And when the tabernacle was taken down, the sons of Gershon and the sons of Merari, who carried the tabernacle, set out. [18]And the standard of the camp of Reuben set out by their companies; and over their host was Elizur the son of Shedeur. [19]And over the host of the tribe of the men of Simeon was Shelumi-el the son of Zurishaddai. [20]And over the host of the tribe of the men of Gad was Eliasaph the son of Deuel.

(cf. Ex 19:1). Now they set out again, heading for the wilderness of Paran, in the north-east of the Sinai peninsula, to the south of the Negeb. The text makes it clear that the initiative lies with the Lord, his presence symbolized by the cloud. The Lord himself is the one who guides them to their destination. The caravan, which has features of a liturgical procession, keeps the order of the camp described in chapter 2, but with the special feature that the Levites, whose responsibility it is to carry the tabernacle, are divided into two groups. Thus, at the head of the march go the tribes that formed the eastern wing of the camp, and

these are followed by part of the tribe of Levi carrying the tent of meeting. Then come those who made up the southern wing, and then the rest of the tribe of Levi with the ark and the sacred furniture. In this way, when the people carrying the ark reach the stopping point they find the tent already set up. This was a clever way of complying with the Lord's instructions in 2:17 about where the tent should be during the journey, while avoiding any need to leave the ark in the open air when the tent was being set up. The rest of the caravan was made up of those who formed the northern and western wings of the camp.

---

secundo, mense secundo, vicesima die mensis elevata est nubes de habitaculo testimonii; [12]profectique sunt filii Israel per migrationes suas de deserto Sinai, et recubuit nubes in solitudine Pharan. [13]Moveruntque castra prima vice, iuxta imperium Domini in manu Moysi. [14]Elevatum est primum vexillum castrorum filiorum Iudae per turmas suas, quorum princeps erat Naasson filius Aminadab; [15] et super turmam tribus filiorum Issachar fuit princeps Nathanael filius Suar; [16]et super turmam tribus Zabulon erat princeps Eliab filius Helon. [17]Depositumque est habitaculum, quod portantes egressi sunt filii Gerson et Merari. [18]Profectum est vexillum castrorum filiorum Ruben per turmas suas, et super turbam suam princeps erat Elisur filius Sedeur. [19]Super turmam autem tribus filiorum Simeon princeps fuit Salamiel filius Surisaddai. [20]Porro super turmam tribus filiorum Gad erat princeps Eliasaph filius Deuel. [21]Profectique sunt et Caathitae portantes sanctuarium. Et erectum est habitaculum, antequam

²¹Then the Kohathites set out, carrying the holy things, and the tabernacle was set up before their arrival. ²²And the standard of the camp of the men of Ephraim set out by their companies; and over their host was Elishama the son of Ammihud. ²³And over the host of the tribe of the men of Manasseh was Gamaliel the son of Pedahzur. ²⁴And over the host of the tribe of the men of Benjamin was Abidan the son of Gideoni.

²⁵Then the standard of the camp of the men of Dan, acting as the rearguard of all the camps, set out by their companies; and over their host was Ahiezer the son of Ammishaddai. ²⁶And over the host of the tribe of the men of Asher was Pagiel the son of Ochran. ²⁷And over the host of the tribe of the men of Naphtali was Ahira the son of Enan. ²⁸This was the order of march of the people of Israel according to their hosts, when they set out.

Moses' proposal to Hobab

²⁹And Moses said to Hobab the son of Reuel the Midianite, Moses' father-in-law, "We are setting out for the place of which the LORD said, 'I will give it to you'; come with us, and we will do you good; for the LORD has promised good to Israel." ³⁰But he said to him, "I will not go; I will depart to my own land and to my kindred." ³¹And he said, "Do not leave us, I pray you, for you know how we are to encamp in the wilderness, and you will serve as eyes for us. ³²And if you go with us, whatever good the LORD will do to us, the same will we do to you."

³³So they set out from the mount of the LORD three days' journey; and the ark of the covenant of the Lord went before them

Gen 12:2
Ex 2:18; 3:1;
4:18; 18:1ff

10:33–36. The people of Israel were given special divine protection against their enemies. Later, when they were in the promised land and things were particularly difficult, they carried the ark onto the field of battle and acclaimed the Lord to implore his help and to offer him thanks. Moses' acclamations (10:35–36) are two very ancient poetic pieces which were probably used in the early liturgy of the ark and which inspired Psalm 132 (c. v. 8), which was written to praise the Lord at commemorations of the transfer of the ark to the temple of Jerusalem.

---

venirent. ²²Elevatum est vexillum castrorum filiorum Ephraim per turmas suas, in quorum exercitu princeps erat Elisama filius Ammiud. ²³Et super turmam tribus filiorum Manasse princeps fuit Gamaliel filius Phadassur; ²⁴et super turmam tribus filiorum Beniamin erat dux Abidan filius Gedeonis. ²⁵Novissime elevatum est vexillum castrorum filiorum Dan per turmas suas, in quorum exercitu princeps fuit Ahiezer filius Ammisaddai. ²⁶Et super turmam tribus filiorum Aser erat princeps Phegiel filius Ochran; ²⁷et super turmam tribus filiorum Nephthali princeps fuit Ahira filius Enan. ²⁸Hae sunt profectiones filiorum Israel per turmas suas, quando egrediebantur. ²⁹Dixitque Moyses Hobab filio Raguel Madianitae cognato suo: «Proficiscimur ad locum, quem Dominus daturus est nobis; veni nobiscum, ut benefaciamus tibi, quia Dominus bona promisit Israeli». ³⁰Cui ille respondit: «Non vadam tecum,

three days' journey, to seek out a resting place for them. ³⁴And the cloud of the LORD was over them by day, whenever they set out from the camp.

Ps 68:1; 132:8 ³⁵And whenever the ark set out, Moses said, "Arise, O LORD, and let thy enemies be scattered; and let them that hate thee flee before thee." ³⁶And when it rested, he said, "Return, O LORD, to the ten thousand thousands of Israel."

6. REBELLIONS*

The fire at Taberah

Deut 9:22
Ex 14:11 **11** ¹And the people complained in the hearing of the LORD about their misfortunes; and when the LORD heard it, his

---

*11:1—12:16. Rather than being a description of the journey through the desert from Sinai to Kadesh (cf. 13:26), these chapters tell us things of great importance regarding the relationship between God and his people—the repeated protest and rebellion of the Israelites over the difficulties of the long journey, the punishments God sends them, and finally the forgiveness they receive as a result of Moses' intercession.

These accounts incorporate memories of various events—the quails and the manna (cf. Ex 16), the appointment of the seventy elders (cf. Ez 18:13–26; Ex 24:9), the case of the prophets Eldad and Medad, and the grumbling of Aaron and Miriam against Moses. The chain of events is as follows: the people complain about having no meat to eat and about the manna; they wear Moses out and he turns to the Lord; and the Lord replies by doing

two things: he gives Moses seventy elders to aid him in governing the people, and he sends quails to satisfy their hunger.

When the people were on the march they were described as maintaining a perfect order, almost like an army keeping formation; there is no sign of that now, when they feel beset by hunger and are under the influence of hangers-on who had joined them. A "rabble" (cf. v. 4), stirs them to rebel. Their protest arises from their sense of insecurity: What are God's real intentions? (cf. Ex 16:3); and they express their feelings by bemoaning the fact that they ever left Egypt; they want to retrace their steps and return to bondage (cf. v. 4). Their great sin is to give in to this temptation.

The experiences of the people of God during their desert pilgrimage help us to understand the life of the new people of God: "Advancing through trials and

---

sed revertar in terram meam, in qua natus sum». ³¹Et ille: «Noli, inquit, nos relinquere; tu enim nosti in quibus locis per desertum castra ponere debeamus, et eris ductor noster. ³²Cumque nobiscum veneris, quidquid optimum fuerit ex opibus, quas nobis traditurus est Dominus, dabimus tibi». ³³Profecti sunt ergo de monte Domini viam trium dierum; arcaque foederis Domini praecedebat eos per dies tres providens castrorum locum. ³⁴Nubes quoque Domini super eos erat per diem, cum incederent. ³⁵Cumque elevaretur arca, dicebat Moyses: «Surge, Domine, et dissipentur inimici tui, et fugiant qui oderunt te a facie tua». ³⁶Cum autem deponeretur, aiebat: «Revertere, Domine, ad multitudinem exercitus Israel». ¹Ortum est murmur populi, quasi dolentium pro labore, contra Dominum. Quod cum audisset

anger was kindled, and the fire of the LORD burned among them, and consumed some outlying parts of the camp. ²Then the people cried to Moses; and Moses prayed to the LORD, and the fire abated. ³So the name of that place was called Taberah,ᵉ because Ex 32:11 the fire of the LORD burned among them.

Craving for Egyptian food

Ex 16

⁴Now the rabble that was among them had a strong craving; and 1 Cor 10:6 the people of Israel also wept again, and said, "O that we had meat to eat! ⁵We remember the fish we ate in Egypt for nothing, the cucumbers, the melons, the leeks, the onions, and the garlic; ⁶but now our strength is dried up, and there is nothing at all but this manna to look at."

⁷Now the manna was like coriander seed, and its appearance like that of bdellium. ⁸The people went about and gathered it, and

---

tribulations, the Church is stenghened by God's grace, promised to her by the Lord so that she may not waver from perfect fidelity" (Vatican II, *Lumen gentium*, 9).

11:1–3. *Teberah* in Hebrew means "fire, blaze". In the traditions of Israel Taberah always evokes the complaint of the people when they were disheartened on their journey, and how it provoked the Lord's anger. What the passage highlights is the absolute sovereignty of God and his plans (which man should go along with, no matter what the cost). It also stresses Moses' role as mediator. No particular reason is given for the people's complaints other than what it says immediately after this (v. 4); but they are clearly tired out and have lost their enthusiasm since they left Egypt.

As the children of God make their way through life, they can sometimes feel the temptation to discouragement. That should not alarm them. "After initial enthusiasm, the doubts, hesitations and anxieties have begun. You are worried about your studies, your family, your financial situation, and, above all, the thought that you are not up to it, that perhaps you are of no use, that you lack experience in life. I will give you a sure means of overcoming such fears, which are temptations coming from the devil or from your lack of generosity! *Despise them*: remove those recollections from your memory. The Master already poignantly preached this twenty centuries ago: 'No one who looks behind him . . .' " (St J. Escrivá, *Furrow*, 133).

11:7–9. The people dream of the sort of food they had in Egypt. The manna was a

---

Dominus, iratus est, et accensus in eos ignis Domini devoravit extremam castrorum partem. ²Cumque clamasset populus ad Moysen, oravit Moyses ad Dominum, et absorptus est ignis. ³Vocaverunt nomen loci illius Tabera, eo quod incensus fuisset contra eos ignis Domini. ⁴Vulgus autem promiscuum, quod erat in medio eius, flagravit desiderio, et sedentes fleverunt pariter filii Israel et dixerunt: «Quis dabit nobis ad vescendum carnes? ⁵Recordamur piscium, quos comedebamus in Aegypto gratis; in mentem nobis veniunt cucumeres et pepones porrique et cepae et alia. ⁶Guttur nostrum aridum est; nihil aliud

e. That is *Burning*

ground it in mills or beat it in mortars, and boiled it in pots, and made cakes of it; and the taste of it was like the taste of cakes baked with oil. ⁹When the dew fell upon the camp in the night, the manna fell with it.

Moses' prayer

Ex 32:11

1 Thess
2:7–11

Mt 15:33
Jn 6:5

Ex 18:18
Deut 1:9
1 Kings 3:9
1 Kings 19:4

¹⁰Moses heard the people weeping throughout their families, every man at the door of his tent; and the anger of the LORD blazed hotly, and Moses was displeased. ¹¹Moses said to the LORD, "Why hast thou dealt ill with thy servant? And why have I not found favour in thy sight, that thou dost lay the burden of all this people upon me? ¹²Did I conceive all this people? Did I bring them forth, that thou shouldst say to me, 'Carry them in your bosom, as a nurse carries the sucking child, to the land which thou didst swear to give their fathers?' ¹³Where am I to get meat to give to all this people? For they weep before me and say, 'Give us meat, that we may eat.' ¹⁴I am not able to carry all this people alone, the burden is too heavy for me. ¹⁵If thou wilt deal thus with me, kill me at once, if I find favour in thy sight, that I may not see my wretchedness."

---

sign of the providence of God, who supplied his people with food in the arid desert. Therefore, their lack of appreciation for the manna, and on top of that their protest against God, show their blindness, their inability to appreciate the gifts God is giving them. Regarding the manna, cf. the note on Exodus 16:1–36.

11:10–15. Despite the tone of complaint, in Moses' words we can glimpse God's relationship to his people: he is their father, he made them into a people. And the passage also shows the heavy responsibility he put on Moses' shoulders—to the point that he feels unable to carry it any longer.

The imagery used here to describe God's concern for his people will later be used by St Paul when he speaks of his concern for all the Christian communities which grew from his preaching and which he has to guide towards Christ (cf. 1 Thess 2:7–11).

---

respiciunt oculi nostri nisi man». ⁷Erat autem man quasi semen coriandri aspectus bdellii. ⁸Circuibatque populus et colligens illud frangebat mola sive terebat in mortario coquens in olla et faciens ex eo tortulas saporis quasi panis oleati. ⁹Cumque descenderet nocte super castra ros, descendebat pariter et man. ¹⁰Audivit ergo Moyses flentem populum per familias, singulos per ostia tentorii sui. Iratusque est furor Domini valde; quod Moysi intoleranda res visa est, ¹¹et ait ad Dominum: «Cur afflixisti servum tuum? Quare non invenio gratiam coram te? Et cur imposuisti pondus universi populi huius super me? ¹²Numquid ego concepi omnem hunc populum vel genui eum, ut dicas mihi: 'Porta eum in sinu tuo, sicut portare solet nutrix infantulum, et defer in terram, pro qua iurasti patribus eorum?' ¹³Unde mihi carnes, ut dem universo populo isti? Flent contra me dicentes: 'Da nobis carnes, ut comedamus!' ¹⁴Non possum ego solus sustinere omnem hunc populum, quia nimis gravis est mihi. ¹⁵Si hoc modo agis mecum, obsecro ut interficias me, si inveni gratiam in oculis tuis, ne videam amplius mala mea!». ¹⁶Et dixit Dominus ad Moysen: «Congrega mihi septuaginta viros de senibus Israel, quos tu nosti quod

[16]And the LORD said to Moses, "Gather for me seventy men of   Lk 10:1
the elders of Israel, whom you know to be the elders of the people
and officers over them; and bring them to the tent of meeting, and
let them take their stand there with you. [17]And I will come down
and talk with you there; and I will take some of the spirit which is
upon you and put it upon them; and they shall bear the burden of
the people with you, that you may not bear it yourself alone.
[18]And say to the people, 'Consecrate yourselves for tomorrow,
and you shall eat meat; for you have wept in the hearing of the
LORD, saying, "Who will give us meat to eat? For it was well with
us in Egypt. "Therefore the LORD will give you meat, and you
shall eat. [19]You shall not eat one day, or two days, or five days, or
ten days, or twenty days, [20]but a whole month, until it comes out
at your nostrils and becomes loathsome to you, because you have
rejected the LORD who is among you, and have wept before him,
saying, "Why did we come forth out of Egypt?"'" [21]But Moses   Num 1:46
said, "The people among whom I am number six hundred thousand on foot; and thou hast said, 'I will give them meat, that they
may eat a whole month!' [22]Shall flocks and herds be slaughtered
for them, to suffice them? Or shall all the fish of the sea be gath-

---

11:16–23. We already saw in Exodus
18:13–27 how Moses needed help in
governing the people. There he gathered
able men around him, on the advice of
Jethro; but here it is God himself who
tells him to choose seventy elders, or
heads of family, and he passes to them
some of the spirit that was Moses'. We
already heard about the seventy in
Exodus 24:9, but now the point is made
that Moses had the spirit of prophecy to
such a degree that even a share of it given
to someone else causes that person to fall
into a prophetic trance. In Deuteronomy

18:18 Moses will be portrayed as a great
prophet, and in Numbers 12 his special
relationship with God is what is highlighted. In this way the tradition of Israel
builds up its profile of the greatness of
Moses. However, the passage we are discussing makes it clear that the people can
be governed only through the spirit of
God.

"Is the Lord's hand shortened?" (v.
23). This is an expression that the Bible
often uses to show that God is almighty
and magnanimous (cf. Is 50:2; 59:1).
When Moses meets an apparently insu-

---

senes populi sint ac magistri, et duces eos ad ostium tabernaculi conventus, stabuntque ibi tecum. [17]Et
descendam et loquar tibi et auferam de spiritu tuo tradamque eis, ut sustentent tecum onus populi, et
non tu solus graveris. [18]Populo quoque dices: Sanctificamini, cras comedetis carnes; ego enim audivi
vos flere: 'Quis dabit nobis escas carnium? Bene nobis erat in Aegypto'. Et dabit vobis Dominus carnes
et comedetis [19]non uno die nec duobus vel quinque aut decem nec viginti quidem, [20]sed usque ad
mensem dierum, donec exeat per nares vestras et vertatur in nauseam, eo quod reppuleritis Dominum,
qui in medio vestri est, et fleveritis coram eo dicentes: 'Quare egressi sumus ex Aegypto?'». [21]Et ait
Moyses: «Populus, in cuius medio sum, sexcenta milia peditum sunt, et tu dicis: 'Dabo eis esum
carnium mense integro!'. [22]Numquid ovium et boum multitudo caedetur, ut possit sufficere ad cibum?
Vel omnes pisces maris in unum congregabuntur, ut eos satient?». [23]Cui respondit Dominus: «Numquid

Is 50:2; 59:1 ered together for them, to suffice them?" ²³And the LORD said to Moses, "Is the LORD's hand shortened? Now you shall see whether my word will come true for you or not."

Ex 18:13–26; 24:9 **The appointment of the seventy elders**

²⁴So Moses went out and told the people the words of the LORD; and he gathered seventy men of the elders of the people, and

Num 12:17 placed them roundabout the tent. ²⁵Then the LORD came down in

Acts 2:3 the cloud and spoke to him, and took some of the spirit that was upon him and put it upon the seventy elders; and when the spirit rested upon them, they prophesied. But they did so no more.

Mk 9:38 ²⁶Now two men remained in the camp, one named Eldad, and

1 Thess 5:19 the other named Medad, and the spirit rested upon them; they were among those registered, but they had not gone out to the tent, and so they prophesied in the camp. ²⁷And a young man ran and told Moses, "Eldad and Medad are prophesying in the camp."

Lk 9:49 ²⁸And Joshua the son of Nun, the minister of Moses, one of his

Joel 3:1–2 chosen men, said, "My lord Moses, forbid them." ²⁹But Moses

Acts 2:18
1 Cor 14:5 said to him, "Are you jealous for my sake? Would that all the

---

perable obstacle, God calms him down by making him realize that nothing is impossible for God. We too should keep calm, because " 'The arm of the Lord has not been shortened' (Is 59:1). God is no less powerful today than he was in other times; his love for man is no less true" (St J. Escrivá, *Christ Is Passing By*, 130).

11:24–30. God himself is the source of the spirit and he can give it to whomever he chooses, irrespective of human qualifications. Moses, for his part, has absolutely the right attitude: he has no desire to monopolize the spirit or to be its only channel; he seeks only the people's

welfare and is delighted to see signs of the spirit in other people; indeed, he would like all the Israelites to have it.

Commenting on this passage, St Cyril of Jerusalem teaches: "there is a hint here of what happened at Pentecost among us" (*Catechesis ad illuminandos*, 16, 26). God did indeed promise the spirit to all the people (cf. Joel 3:1–2) and the day came when that promise was fulfilled through Jesus Christ who, after his ascension into heaven, sent the Holy Spirit to the Church (cf. Acts 1:13). Therefore, the Church, "the holy people of God shares also in Christ's prophetic office: it spreads abroad a living witness to him especially by a life of faith and

---

manus Domini abbreviata est? Iam nunc videbis utrum meus sermo opere compleatur an non». ²⁴Venit igitur Moyses et narravit populo verba Domini congregans septuaginta viros de senibus Israel, quos stare fecit circa tabernaculum. ²⁵Descenditque Dominus per nubem et locutus est ad eum auferens de spiritu, qui erat in Moyse, et dans septuaginta viris senibus. Cumque requievisset in eis spiritus, prophetaverunt nec ultra fecerunt. ²⁶Remanserant autem in castris duo viri, quorum unus vocabatur Eldad et alter Medad, super quos requievit spiritus; nam et ipsi descripti fuerant et non exierant ad tabernaculum. Cumque prophetarent in castris, ²⁷cucurrit puer et nuntiavit Moysi dicens: «Eldad et

LORD'S people were prophets, that the LORD would put his spirit upon them!" [30]And Moses and the elders of Israel returned to the camp.*

The quails

Ex 16:13ff

[31]And there went forth a wind from the LORD, and it brought quails from the sea, and let them fall beside the camp, about a day's journey on this side and a day's journey on the other side, round about the camp, and about two cubits above the face of the earth. [32]And the people rose all that day, and all night, and all the next day, and gathered the quails; he who gathered least gathered ten homers; and they spread them out for themselves all around the camp. [33]While the meat was yet between their teeth, before it Rev 16:21 was consumed, the anger of the LORD was kindled against the people, and the LORD smote the people with a very great plague. [34]Therefore the name of that place was called Kibroth-hattaavah,[f] 1 Cor 10:6 because there they buried the people who had the craving. [35]From Kibroth-hattaavah the people journeyed to Hazeroth; and they remained at Hazeroth.

---

love [. . .]. It is not only through the sacraments and the ministrations of the Church that the Holy Spirit makes holy the people, leads them and enriches them with his virtues. Allotting his gifts according as he wills (cf. Cor 12:11), he also distributes special graces among the faithful of every rank. By these gifts he makes them fit and ready to undertake various tasks and offices for the renewal and building up of the Church" (Vatican II, *Lumen gentium*, 12).

11:31–34. In recounting this episode, what is highlighted is the care that God

takes of his own. In the present context God's care is in sharp contrast with the rebellious and sinful attitude of the people, whose greed is such that what is a gift from God becomes a form of punishment.

The name of the place—Kibroth-hattavah means "graves of greed"—links the episode of the quails to the way the people were punished for their gluttony and hardness of heart.

A homer (v. 32) was a donkey's load (cf. the note on Lev 27:16). The text shows that the Israelites gathered an enormous amount of meat.

Medad prophetant in castris». [28]Statim Iosue filius Nun minister Moysi et electus eius a iuventute sua ait: «Domine mi Moyses, prohibe eos!». [29]At ille: «Quid, inquit, aemularis pro me? Quis tribuat, ut omnis populus prophetet, et det eis Dominus spiritum suum?». [30]Reversusque est Moyses et maiores natu Israel in castra. [31]Ventus autem egrediens a Domino arreptas trans mare coturnices detulit et demisit in castra itinere, quantum uno die confici potest, ex omni parte castrorum per circuitum; volabantque in aere duobus cubitis altitudine super terram. [32]Surgens ergo populus toto die illo et nocte ac die altero congregavit coturnicum, qui parum, decem choros; et extenderunt eas per gyrum castrorum. [33]Adhuc carnes erant in dentibus eorum, nec defecerat huiuscemodi cibus, et ecce furor Domini conci-

f. That is *Graves of craving*

The complaint of Miriam and Aaron against Moses*

Ex 15:20
Num 20:1
Deut 24:8–9

Jn 9:29

Ex 3:11; 4:10–11
Sir 45:4
Mt 11:29

Ex 13:22

Heb 3:2–5
Rev 15:3

Ex 33:11

Jn 9:29
1 Cor 13:12
Heb 11:27

12 [1]Miriam and Aaron spoke against Moses because of the Cushite woman whom he had married, for he had married a Cushite woman; [2]and they said, "Has the LORD indeed spoken only through Moses? Has he not spoken through us also?" And the LORD heard it. [3]Now the man Moses was very meek, more than all men that were on the face of the earth. [4]And suddenly the LORD said to Moses and to Aaron and Miriam, "Come out, you three, to the tent of meeting." And the three of them came out. [5]And the LORD came down in a pillar of cloud, and stood at the door of the tent, and called Aaron and Miriam; and they both came forward. [6]And he said, "Hear my words: If there is a prophet among you, I the LORD make myself known to him in a vision, I speak with him in a dream. [7]Not so with my servant Moses; he is entrusted with all my house. [8]With him I speak mouth to mouth, clearly, and not in dark speech; and he beholds the form of the LORD. Why then were you not afraid to speak against my servant Moses?"

***12:1–16.** Aaron and Miriam's complaints about Moses begin with the subject of his marriage to a foreigner. (The Hebrew text says "Cushite", which means "from Ethiopia", but if we look at Habakkuk 3:7, which links Cushan to the Midianites, perhaps we can read this passage as referring to Zipporoah: cf. Ex 2:16–21.) But their complaints are really aimed at something much deeper— Moses' unique authority as intermediary between God and his people. He is not the only prophet, they say; however, unlike Moses, they have not the humility to see that prophecy is a charism, a gift to be exercised *on behalf of* the people; rather, they see it as a privilege from which they can gain advantage. This negative feature of Aaron, along with what Exodus 32 has to tell about him, seems to suggest that his place in folk memory is less positive than might appear at first sight.

The passage really shows what a unique personality Moses was in the history of Israel. He was the one who most put his trust in the Lord (perhaps that is the meaning of the Hebrew word *anaw*, here translated as "meek": v. 3). Such was his trust that he became the most long-suffering of men; and it brought God to his defence. The severity of Miriam's punishment and the swiftness of her cure at Moses' interces-

---

tatus in populum percussit eum plaga magna nimis. [34]Vocatusque est ille locus Cibrottaava; ibi enim sepelierunt populum, qui desideraverat. [35]Egressi autem de Cibrottaava, venerunt in Aseroth et manserunt ibi. [1]Locutaque est Maria et Aaron contra Moysen propter uxorem eius Aethiopissam [2]et dixerunt: «Num per solum Moysen locutus est Dominus? Nonne et per nos similiter est locutus?». Quod cum audisset Dominus—[3]erat enim Moyses vir humillimus super omnes homines, qui morabantur in terra—[4]statim locutus est ad eum et ad Aaron et Mariam: «Egredimini vos tantum tres ad tabernaculum conventus». Cumque fuissent egressi, [5]descendit Dominus in columna nubis et stetit in introitu tabernaculi vocans Aaron et Mariam. Qui cum issent, [6]dixit ad eos: «Audite sermones meos! / Si quis fuerit inter vos propheta Domini, / in visione apparebo ei, / vel per somnium loquar ad illum. / [7]At non talis servus meus Moyses, / qui in omni domo mea fidelissimus est! / [8]Ore enim ad os loquor

⁹And the anger of the LORD was kindled against them, and he departed; ¹⁰and when the cloud removed from over the tent, behold, Miriam was leprous, as white as snow. And Aaron turned towards Miriam, and behold, she was leprous. ¹¹And Aaron said to Moses, "Oh, my lord, do not[g] punish us because we have done foolishly and have sinned. ¹²Let her not be as one dead, of whom the flesh is half consumed when he comes out of his mother's womb."

2 Jn 12
3 Jn 14
Ex 32:11
Mt 8:2

Moses intercedes

¹³And Moses cried to the LORD, "Heal her, O God, I beseech thee." ¹⁴But the LORD said to Moses, "If her father had but spit in her face, should she not be shamed seven days? Let her be shut up outside the camp seven days, and after that she may be brought in again." ¹⁵So Miriam was shut up outside the camp seven days; and the people did not set out on the march till Miriam was brought in again. ¹⁶After that the people set out from Hazeroth, and encamped in the wilderness of Paran.

Lev 12:4–6

sion, serve to show how great Moses is. What really makes him great is the fact that God speaks directly to him and not through visions or dreams as in the case of the prophets. So, Moses is greater than the prophets. According to the Hebrew text, Moses saw the "form" of the Lord (v. 8); the Greek translation (presumably because of the spiritual nature of God and his transcendence) says that Moses saw "the glory of the Lord". Similarly St John will say that "no one has ever seen God" (Jn 1:18), in order then to go on and stress that only Jesus Christ, the Son of God and himself true God, could reveal to us all the truth about God.

However, God's spirituality and transcendence does not mean we cannot enter into direct conversation with him through prayer. "Moses' prayer is characteristic of contemplative prayer by which God's servant remains faithful to his mission. Moses converses with God often and at length, climbing the mountain to hear and entreat him and coming down to the people to repeat the words of his God for their guidance. Moses 'is entrusted with all my house. With him I speak face to face, clearly, not in riddles', for 'Moses was very humble, more so than everyone else on the face of the earth' (Num 12:3, 7–8)' " (*Catechism of the Catholic Church*, 2576).

ei, / et palam et non per aenigmata et figuras / Dominum videt! / Quare ergo non timuistis detrahere / servo meo Moysi?». ⁹Iratusque contra eos abiit, ¹⁰nubes quoque recessit, quae erat super tabernaculum; et ecce Maria apparuit candens lepra quasi nix. Cumque respexisset eam Aaron et vidisset perfusam lepra, ¹¹ait ad Moysen: «Obsecro, domine mi, ne imponas nobis hoc peccatum, quod stulte commisimus, ¹²ne fiat haec quasi mortua et ut abortivum, quod proicitur de vulva matris suae; ecce iam medium carnis eius devoratum est a lepra». ¹³Clamavitque Moyses ad Dominum dicens: «Deus, obsecro, sana eam!». ¹⁴Cui respondit Dominus: «Si pater eius spuisset in faciem illius, nonne debuerat saltem septem diebus rubore suffundi? Separetur septem diebus extra castra et postea revocabitur».

g. Heb *lay not sin upon us*

_{Deut 1:20–29} **Reconnoitring the promised land***

13 ¹The L<small>ORD</small> said to Moses, ²"Send men to spy out the land of Canaan, which I give to the people of Israel; from each tribe of their fathers shall you send a man, everyone a leader among them." ³So Moses sent them from the wilderness of Paran, according to the command of the L<small>ORD</small>, all of them men who were heads of the people of Israel. ⁴And these were their names: From the tribe of Reuben, Shammu-a the son of Zaccur; ⁵from the tribe of Simeon, Shaphat the son of Hori; ⁶from the tribe of Judah, Caleb the son of Jephunneh; ⁷from the tribe of Issachar, Igal the son of Joseph; ⁸from the tribe of Ephraim, Hoshea the son of Nun; ⁹from the tribe of Benjamin, Palti the son of Raphu; ¹⁰from the tribe of Zebulun, Gaddiel the son of Sodi; ¹¹from the tribe of Joseph (that is from the tribe of Manasseh), Gaddithe son of Susi; ¹²from the tribe of Dan, Ammiel the son of Gemalli; ¹³from the tribe of Asher, Sethur the son of Michael; ¹⁴from the tribe of Naphtali, Nahbi the son of Vophsi; ¹⁵from the tribe of Gad, Geuel _{Ex 17:9–12} the son of Machi. ¹⁶These were the names of the men whom _{Josh 1:1} Moses sent to spy out the land. And Moses called Hoshea the son of Nun Joshua.

---

*13:1—14:45. The general background of the people's rebelliousness, and God's forgiveness (chapters 13 and 14) helps to explain why the Israelites did not enter the promised land immediately from Kadesh, but had to make a detour and enter via Transjordan. The cause for this detour was, basically, their faltering obedience to the Lord, their disdain for the promised land and their nostalgia for Egypt. In the account given here we find memories that go back to the earliest times, such as, for example, the leadership shown by Caleb (from the tribe of Judah), a reconnoitring of the Land which does not extend beyond the zone of Hebron, and a failed attempt to enter it via the Negeb (cf. 14:39–45).

13:16. The name Joshua means "Yahweh saves". The fact that it is Moses who confers this name on him gives a hint of his future mission: acting on God's behalf, Joshua will save the people as he

---

¹⁵Exclusa est itaque Maria extra castra septem diebus, et populus non est motus de loco illo, donec revocata est Maria. ¹⁶Profectusque est populus de Aseroth, fixis tentoriis in deserto Pharan. ¹Ibi locutus est Dominus ad Moysen dicens: ²«Mitte viros, qui considerent terram Chanaan, quam daturus sum filiis Israel, singulos de singulis tribubus ex principibus». ³Fecit Moyses quod Dominus imperaverat, de deserto Pharan mittens principes viros, quorum ista sunt nomina: ⁴de tribu Ruben Sammua filium Zacchur, ⁵de tribu Simeon Saphat filium Hori, ⁶de tribu Iudae Chaleb filium Iephonne, ⁷de tribu Issachar Igal filium Ioseph, ⁸de tribu Ephraim Osee filium Nun, ⁹de tribu Beniamin Phalti filium Raphu, ¹⁰de tribu Zabulon Geddiel filium Sodi, ¹¹de tribu Ioseph, tribu Manasse, Gaddi filium Susi, ¹²de tribu Dan Ammiel filium Gemalli, ¹³de tribu Aser Sthur filium Michael, ¹⁴de tribu Nephthali Nahabi filium Vaphsi, ¹⁵de tribu Gad Guel filium Machi. ¹⁶Haec sunt nomina virorum, quos misit Moyses ad considerandam terram. Vocavitque Osee filium Nun Iosue. ¹⁷Misit ergo eos Moyses ad considerandam terram Chanaan et dixit ad eos: «Ascendite per Nageb. Cumque veneritis ad montes, ¹⁸con-

¹⁷Moses sent them to spy out the land of Canaan, and said to them, "Go up into the Negeb yonder, and go up into the hill country, ¹⁸and see what the land is, and whether the people who dwell in it are strong or weak, whether they are few or many, ¹⁹and whether the land that they dwell in is good or bad, and whether the cities that they dwell in are camps or strongholds, ²⁰and whether the land is rich or poor, and whether there is wood in it or not. Be of good courage, and bring some of the fruit of the land." "Now the time was the season of the first ripe grapes.

²¹So they went up and spied out the land from the wilderness of Zin to Rehob, near the entrance of Hamath. ²²They went up into the Negeb, and came to Hebron; and Ahiman, Sheshai, and Talmai, the descendants of Anak, were there. (Hebron was built seven years before Zoan in Egypt.) ²³And they came to the Valley of Eshcol, and cut down from there a branch with a single cluster of grapes, and they carried it on a pole between two of them; they brought also some pomegranates and figs. ²⁴That place was called the Valley of Eshcol,^h because of the cluster which the men of Israel cut down from there.

---

had already done in the battle against the Amalekites according to Exodus 17:9–13. Joshua's name and his mission to lead the people into the Land gave the Fathers of the Church grounds for seeing in him an advance announcement of Christ, whose name, Jesus, means the same as Joshua (cf. Mt 1:21; Lk 1:31).

13:24. The "Valley of Eschol", literally "Torrent of the Cluster", is located near Hebron.

Some Fathers gave an allegorical interpretation to this: the cluster of grapes grown in the promised land stands for Jesus Christ, born of the Virgin Mary. And its being hung on a pole stands for Christ hung from the cross. "The two bearers", St Caesarius of Arles comments, "are the two Testaments—the Jews lead the way, the Christians come behind; the latter can see salvation in front of them [. . .]. We, who come behind, have merited to adore and to bear the Lord Jesus. [. . .] Let us work as best we can with his help; let us not try to shed such a sweet burden" (*Sermons*, 107, 3).

---

siderate terram, qualis sit, et populum, qui habitator est eius, utrum fortis sit an infirmus, si pauci numero an plures; ¹⁹ipsa terra bona an mala, urbes quales, absque muris an muratae; ²⁰humus pinguis an sterilis, nemorosa an absque arboribus. Confortamini et afferte nobis de fructibus terrae». Erat autem tempus, quando iam praecoquae uvae vesci possunt. ²¹Cumque ascendissent, exploraverunt terram a deserto Sin usque Rohob in introitu Emath. ²²Ascenderuntque ad Nageb et venerunt in Hebron, ubi erant Ahiman et Sesai et Tholmai filii Enac. Nam Hebron septem annis ante Tanim urbem Aegypti condita est. ²³Pergentesque usque ad Nehelescol absciderunt palmitem cum uva sua, quem portaverunt in vecte duo viri. De malis quoque granatis et de ficis loci illius tulerunt, ²⁴qui appellatus est Nehelescol, eo quod botrum portassent inde filii Israel. ²⁵Reversique exploratores terrae post quadraginta dies, omni

---

h. That is *Cluster*

Deut 1:25ff **The spies return**

^{25}At the end of forty days they returned from spying out the land.

^{26}And they came to Moses and Aaron and to all the congregation
Gen 15:19–21
Ex 3:8; 3:17; of the people of Israel in the wilderness of Paran, at Kadesh; they
13:5; 23:23, brought back word to them and to all the congregation, and
28; 23:2; 34:11
Lev 20:24 showed them the fruit of the land. ^{27}And they told him, "We came
Deut 7:1; 26:9,5 to the land to which you sent us; it flows with milk and honey,
Jer 11:5; 32:22 and this is its fruit. ^{28}Yet the people who dwell in the land are
Ezek 20:15
Gen 6:1–4 strong, and the cities are fortified and very large; and besides, we
Ex 17:8–16 saw the descendants of Anak there. ^{29}The Amalekites dwell in the
land of the Negeb; the Hittites, the Jebusites, and the Amorites
dwell in the hill country; and the Canaanites dwell by the sea, and
along the Jordan."

^{30}But Caleb quieted the people before Moses, and said, "Let us
go up at once, and occupy it; for we are well able to overcome it."

^{31}Then the men who had gone up with him said, "We are not able

---

13:27–29. The spies' report confirms all God promised about the Land (cf. Ex 3:8). In stressing the strength of the peoples who live there, God's own strength is being highlighted, as also his love for his people, because he will be the one who uproots the present occupiers (cf. Deut 7;1); and, besides, it gives the background to the protests the text goes on to describe.

The descendants of Anak (v. 28) are the giants who, according to Israelite tradition, occupy the southern part of Canaan; an explanation of their origin is given in Genesis 6:1–4.

The Amalekites were a semi-nomadic people who moved to the south of the Negeb; the Israelites fought with them more than once (cf. Ex 17:8–6). The Hittites had ruled a huge empire in the

14th century BC, and the Amorites occupied the Tigris and Euphrates valleys. The Jebusites were earlier occupiers of Jerusalem. The description given of where each of these peoples lived in the Land is a very sketchy one.

13:30–33. There are two opposed attitudes here—that of Caleb, who is influenced by faith, and that of the other scouts who, when they come up against obstacles, fail to count on God and in fact question the value of the gift God has promised, the gift of the Land. This last point is what provokes their open rebellion against God and Moses.

It is often easy to see the obstacles to any human or supernatural project. The way to deal with these difficulties is not to close one's eyes but to fight bravely

---

regione circuita, ^{26}venerunt ad Moysen et Aaron et ad omnem coetum filiorum Israel in desertum Pharan, quod est in Cades. Locutique eis et omni congregationi ostenderunt fructus terrae ^{27}et narraverunt dicentes: «Venimus in terram, ad quam misisti nos, quae re vera fluit lacte et melle, ut ex his fructibus cognosci potest. ^{28}Sed cultores fortissimos habet et urbes grandes atque muratas. Stirpem Enac vidimus ibi; ^{29}Amalec habitat in Nageb, Hetthaeus et Iebusaeus et Amorraeus in montanis, Chananaeus vero moratur iuxta mare et circa fluenta Iordanis». ^{30}Inter haec Chaleb compescens murmur populi, qui oriebatur contra Moysen, ait: «Ascendamus et possideamus terram, quoniam poterimus obtinere eam». ^{31}Alii vero, qui fuerant cum eo, dicebant: «Nequaquam ad hunc populum valemus

to go up against the people; for they are stronger than we." ³²So they brought to the people of Israel an evil report of the land which they had spied out, saying, "The land, through which we have gone, to spy it out, is a land that devours its inhabitants; and all the people that we saw in it are men of great stature. ³³And there we saw the Nephilim (the sons of Anak, who come from the Nephilim); and we seemed to ourselves like grasshoppers, and so we seemed to them."

Gen 6:4
Deut 2:10
Bar 3:26–28

The rebellion of Israel

Deut 1:26–32

14 ¹Then all the congregation raised a loud cry; and the people wept that night. ²And all the people of Israel murmured against Moses and Aaron; the whole congregation said to them, "Would that we had died in the land of Egypt! Or would

Ex 14:11
1 Cor 10:10

---

and faithfully to overcome them. The Israelites were filled with fear at the prospect of having to conquer the Land (because their enemies were so powerful); so frightened were they that some came to reject and disparage the Land itself. Something similar happens to a Christian when fearfulness makes him go into reverse in his efforts to attain perfection. "I know that the moment we talk about fighting we recall our weakness and we foresee falls and mistakes. God takes this into account. As we walk along, it is inevitable that we will raise dust; we are creatures and full of defects. I would almost say that we will always *need* defects. They are the shadow which shows up the light of God's grace and our resolve to respond to God's kindness. And this *chiaroscuro* will make us human, humble, understanding and generous" (St Josemaría Escrivá, *Christ Is Passing By*, 76).

14:1–25. The rebellion reaches its

climax; the people want to replace Moses with someone else, return to Egypt and stone those who encourage trust in God. We see Aaron backing up Moses, and Joshua sharing Caleb's enthusiasm (vv. 5–6). However, it will be the glory and might of God that sorts things out: he threatens punishment and (the most terrible thing of all) to disinherit the people: he is ready to create a new people, starting with Moses (vv. 11–12). But once more Moses pleads on the people's behalf; this time he uses the strongest argument he can find—the very reputation of Yahweh among the nations, and his gracious and merciful nature (according to his own description: cf. Ex 34:6–7). And God in fact does forgive his people yet another time; he does not destroy them; but he has to act in a just way, distinguishing between those who put their trust in him (like Caleb) and those who rebelled against him as many as "ten times" (v. 22), that is, totally and deliberately.

---

ascendere, quia fortior nobis est». ³²Detraxeruntque terrae, quam inspexerant, apud filios Israel dicentes: «Terra, quam lustravimus, devorat habitatores suos; populus, quem aspeximus, procerae staturae est; ³³ibi vidimus gigantes, filios Enac de genere giganteo, quibus comparati quasi locustae videbamur». ¹Igitur vociferans omnis turba flevit nocte illa, ²et murmurati sunt contra Moysen et Aaron

Acts 7:39 that we had died in this wilderness! ³Why does the LORD bring us into this land, to fall by the sword? Our wives and our little ones will become a prey; would it not be better for us to go back to Egypt?"

⁴And they said to one another, "Let us choose a captain, and go back to Egypt." ⁵Then Moses and Aaron fell on their faces before all the assembly of the congregation of the people of Israel. ⁶And Joshua the son of Nun and Caleb the son of Jephunneh, who were among those who had spied out the land, rent their clothes, ⁷and said to all the congregation of the people of Israel, "The land, which we passed through to spy it out, is an exceedingly good land. ⁸If the LORD delights in us, he will bring us into this land and give it to us, a land which flows with milk and honey. ⁹Only, do not rebel against the LORD; and do not fear the people of the land, for they are bread for us; their protection is removed from them, and the LORD is with us; do not fear them."

Ex 32:7–14 **God's threat and Moses' appeal**
¹⁰But all the congregation said to stone them with stones.

Then the glory of the LORD appeared at the tent of meeting to all the people of Israel. ¹¹And the LORD said to Moses, "How long will this people despise me? And how long will they not believe in me, in spite of all the signs which I have wrought among them? ¹²I will strike them with the pestilence and disinherit them, and I will make of you a nation greater and mightier than they."

¹³But Moses said to the LORD, "Then the Egyptians will hear of it, for thou didst bring up this people in thy might from among them, ¹⁴and they will tell the inhabitants of this land. They have heard that thou, O LORD, art in the midst of this people; for thou, O LORD, art seen face to face, and thy cloud stands over them and

cuncti filii Israel dicentes: «Utinam mortui essemus in Aegypto vel in hac vasta solitudine! ³Cur inducit nos Dominus in terram istam, ut cadamus gladio, et uxores ac liberi nostri ducantur captivi? Nonne melius est reverti in Aegyptum?». ⁴Dixeruntque alter ad alterum: «Constituamus nobis ducem et revertamur in Aegyptum!». ⁵Quo audito, Moyses et Aaron ceciderunt proni in terram coram omni congregatione filiorum Israel. ⁶At vero Iosue filius Nun et Chaleb filius Iephonne, qui et ipsi lustraverant terram, sciderunt vestimenta sua ⁷et ad omnem congregationem filiorum Israel locuti sunt: «Terra, quam circuivimus, valde bona est. ⁸Si propitius fuerit Dominus, inducet nos in eam et tradet humum lacte et melle manantem. ⁹Nolite rebelles esse contra Dominum neque timeatis populum terrae huius, quia sicut panem ita eos possumus devorare. Recessit ab eis omne praesidium; Dominus nobiscum est, nolite metuere». ¹⁰Cumque clamaret omnis congregatio et lapidibus eos vellet opprimere, apparuit gloria Domini super tabernaculum conventus cunctis filiis Israel, ¹¹et dixit Dominus ad Moysen: «Usquequo detrahet mihi populus iste? Quousque non credent mihi in omnibus signis, quae feci coram eis? ¹²Feriam igitur eos pestilentia atque consumam; te autem faciam in gentem magnam et fortiorem quam haec est». ¹³Et ait Moyses ad Dominum: «Audient Aegyptii, de quorum medio eduxisti populum istum in virtute tua, ¹⁴et dicent ad habitatores terrae huius, quia audierunt quod tu, Domine, in populo

thou goest before them, in a pillar of cloud by day and in a pillar
of fire by night. [15]Now if thou dost kill this people as one man,
then the nations who have heard thy fame will say, [16]'Because the   1 Cor 10:5
LORD was not able to bring this people into the land which he
swore to give to them, therefore he has slain them in the wilderness.' [17]And now, I pray thee, let the power of the LORD be great
as thou hast promised, saying, [18]'The LORD is slow to anger, and   Ex 34:6–7
abounding in steadfast love, forgiving iniquity and transgression,
but he will by no means clear the guilty, visiting the iniquity of
fathers upon children, upon the third and upon the fourth generation.' [19]Pardon the iniquity of this people, I pray thee, according to
the greatness of thy steadfast love, and according as thou hast forgiven this people, from Egypt even until now."

   [20]Then the LORD said, "I have pardoned, according to your   Ex 24:16
word; [21]but truly, as I live, and as all the earth shall be filled with   Deut 1:34
the glory of the LORD, [22]none of the men who have seen my glory   Heb 3:16–19
and my signs which I wrought in Egypt and in the wilderness,
and yet have put me to the proof these ten times and have not
hearkened to my voice, [23]shall see the land which I swore to give   Jn 6:49
to their fathers; and none of those who despised me shall see it.
[24]But my servant Caleb, because he has a different spirit and has
followed me fully, I will bring into the land into which he went,
and his descendants shall possess it. [25]Now, since the Amalekites
and the Canaanites dwell in the valleys, turn tomorrow and set out
for the wilderness by the way to the Red Sea."

God's new reply   Deut 1:34–40
[26]And the LORD said to Moses and to Aaron, [27]"How long shall
this wicked congregation murmur against me? I have heard the

14:26–38. Once again the text mentions   and low spirits, and we are told about the
God's reaction to the people's complaints   punishment, which takes into account the

isto sis et facie videaris ad faciem, et nubes tua protegat illos, et in columna nubis praecedas eos per
diem et in columna ignis per noctem. [15]Et occidisti hunc populum quasi unum hominem, et dicent
gentes, quae audierunt auditum tuum: [16]'Non poterat Dominus introducere populum in terram, pro qua
iuraverat, idcirco occidit eos in solitudine!'. [17]Magnificetur ergo fortitudo Domini, sicut iurasti dicens:
[18]'Dominus patiens et multae misericordiae, auferens iniquitatem et scelera nullumque innoxium dere-
linquens, qui visitas peccata patrum in filios in tertiam et quartam generationem.' [19]Dimitte obsecro
peccatum populi huius secundum magnitudinem misericordiae tuae, sicut propitius fuisti populo huic
de Aegypto usque ad locum istum». [20]Dixitque Dominus: «Dimisi iuxta verbum tuum. [21]Vivo ego, et
implebit gloria Domini universam terram! [22]Attamen omnes homines, qui viderunt maiestatem meam
et signa, quae feci in Aegypto et in solitudine, et tentaverunt me iam per decem vices nec oboedierunt
voci meae, [23]non videbunt terram, pro qua iuravi patribus eorum; nec quisquam ex illis, qui detraxit
mihi, intuebitur eam. [24]Servum meum Chaleb, qui plenus alio spiritu secutus est me, inducam in terram
hanc, quam circuivit, et semen eius possidebit eam. [25]Quoniam Amalecites et Chananaeus habitant in

murmurings of the people of Israel, which they murmur against me. ²⁸Say to them, 'As I live,' says the LORD, 'what you have said

Heb 3:17
Jude 5

in my hearing I will do to you: ²⁹your dead bodies shall fall in this wilderness; and of all your number, numbered from twenty years old and upward, who have murmured against me, ³⁰not one shall come into the land where I swore that I would make you dwell, except Caleb the son of Jephunneh and Joshua the son of Nun. ³¹But your little ones, who you said would become a prey, I will bring in, and they shall know the land which you have despised. ³²But as for you, your dead bodies shall fall in this wilderness.

Acts 7:36;
13:18

³³And your children shall be shepherds in the wilderness forty years, and shall suffer for your faithlessness, until the last of your dead bodies lies in the wilderness. ³⁴According to the number of the days in which you spied out the land, forty days, for every day a year, you shall bear your iniquity, forty years, and you shall know my displeasure.' ³⁵I, the LORD, have spoken; surely this will I do to all this wicked congregation that are gathered together against me: in this wilderness they shall come to a full end, and there they shall die."

1 Cor 10:10

³⁶And the men whom Moses sent to spy out the land, and who returned and made all the congregation to murmur against him by bringing up an evil report against the land, ³⁷the men who

---

census held previously: except for Caleb and Joshua, no one over twenty will escape the wrath of God. The forty years' pilgrimage in the desert is going to start now, and it corresponds to the forty days it took them to spy out the Land: so it is a severe punishment and it is at the same time proportionate to the crime. The first to receive this punishment were those who, although they had the good fortune to actually see the Land, undermined the morale of the others and instigated their protest—that is, those who, although they in some way experienced the gift of God, failed to appreciate it out of cowardice and even discredited it to others.

---

vallibus, cras movete castra et revertimini in solitudinem per viam maris Rubri». ²⁶Locutusque est Dominus ad Moysen et Aaron dicens: ²⁷«Usquequo congregatio haec pessima murmurat contra me ? Querelas filiorum Israel audivi. ²⁸Dic ergo eis: Vivo ego, ait Dominus, sicut locuti estis, audiente me, sic faciam vobis! ²⁹In solitudine hac iacebunt cadavera vestra. Omnes, qui numerati estis a viginti annis et supra et murmurastis contra me, ³⁰non intrabitis terram, super quam levavi manum meam, ut habitare vos facerem, praeter Chaleb filium Iephonne et Iosue filium Nun. ³¹Parvulos autem vestros, de quibus dixistis quod praedae hostibus forent, introducam, ut videant terram, quae vobis displicuit. ³²Vestra cadavera iacebunt in solitudine hac; ³³filii vestri erunt pastores in deserto annis quadraginta et portabunt fornicationem vestram, donec consumantur cadavera vestra in deserto. ³⁴Iuxta numerum quadraginta dierum, quibus considerastis terram—annus pro die imputabitur—quadraginta annis portabitis iniquitates vestras et scietis ultionem meam. ³⁵Ego Dominus locutus sum, ita faciam omni congregationi huic pessimae, quae consurrexit adversum me: in solitudine hac deficiet et morietur». ³⁶Igitur omnes viri, quos miserat Moyses ad contemplandam terram et qui reversi murmurare fecerant contra eum omnem congregationem detrahentes terrae quod esset mala, ³⁷mortui sunt atque percussi in conspectu Domini.

brought up an evil report of the land, died by plague before the Lord. ³⁸But Joshua the son of Nun and Caleb the son of Jephunneh remained alive, of those men who went to spy out the land.

A frustrated attempt to enter the promised land

Deut 1:41–45
Num 20:12

³⁹And Moses told these words to all the people of Israel, and the people mourned greatly. ⁴⁰And they rose early in the morning, and went up to the heights of the hill country, saying, "See, we are here, we will go up to the place which the LORD has promised; for we have sinned." ⁴¹But Moses said, "Why now are you transgressing the command of the Lord, for that will not succeed? ⁴²Do not go up lest you be struck down before your enemies, for the LORD is not among you. ⁴³For there the Amalekites and the Canaanites are before you, and you shall fall by the sword; because you have turned back from following the LORD, the LORD will not be with you." ⁴⁴But they presumed to go up to the heights of the hill country, although neither the ark of the covenant of the LORD, nor Moses, departed out of the camp. ⁴⁵Then the Amalekites and the Canaanites who dwelt in that hill country came down, and defeated them and pursued them, even to Hormah.

Ex 17:8

14:39–45. Hormah is a Hebrew word meaning "destruction".

Behind this account there seems to lie a memory of a failed attempt to enter Canaan from the Negeb. The reason behind the failure was primarily religious: the people repented, but not soon enough; their basic attitude continued to be one of disobedience to the Lord; they would not listen to Moses; in fact, they did not want to be dependent on God,

Moses or the Covenant but to rely on their own resources. As things turned out, they made a big mistake—which can be a lesson to us: "Without the Lord you will not be able to take one sure step forward. This conviction that you need his help will lead you to be more united to him, with a strong, enduring confidence, accompanied by joy and peace, even if the road might become hard and steep" (St J. Escrivá, *Furrow*, 770).

³⁸Iosue autem filius Nun et Chaleb filius Iephonne vixerunt ex omnibus, qui perrexerant ad considerandam terram. ³⁹Locutusque est Moyses universa verba haec ad omnes filios Israel, et luxit populus nimis. ⁴⁰Et ecce mane primo surgentes ascenderunt verticem montis atque dixerunt: «Parati sumus ascendere ad locum, de quo Dominus locutus est, quia peccavimus». ⁴¹Quibus Moyses: «Cur, inquit, transgredimini verbum Domini, quod vobis non cedet in prosperum? ⁴²Nolite ascendere, non enim est Dominus vobiscum, ne corruatis coram inimicis vestris! ⁴³Amalecites et Chananaeus ante vos sunt, quorum gladio corruetis, eo quod nolueritis acquiescere Domino, nec erit Dominus vobiscum». ⁴⁴At illi contenebrati ascenderunt in verticem montis; arca autem foederis Domini et Moyses non recesserunt de castris. ⁴⁵Descenditque Amalecites et Chananaeus, qui habitabat in monte, et percutiens eos atque concidens persecutus est eos usque Horma. ¹Locutus est Dominus ad Moysen dicens:

7. LAWS FOR PRIESTS AND LEVITES*

Rules about offerings

15 ¹The LORD said to Moses, ²"Say to the people of Israel, When you come into the land you are to inhabit, which I give you, ³and you offer to the LORD from the herd or from the flock an offering by fire or a burnt offering or a sacrifice, to fulfil a vow or as a freewill offering or at your appointed feasts, to make a pleasing odour to the LORD, ⁴then he who brings his offering shall offer to the LORD a cereal offering of a tenth of an ephah of fine flour, mixed with a fourth of a hin of oil; ⁵and wine for the drink offering, a fourth of a hin, you shall prepare with the burnt offering, or for the sacrifice, for each lamb. ⁶Or for a ram, you shall prepare for a cereal offering two tenths of an ephah of fine flour mixed with a third of a hin of oil; ⁷and for the drink offering you shall offer a third of a hin of wine, a pleasing odour to the LORD. ⁸And when you prepare a bull for a burnt offering, or for a sacrifice, to fulfil a vow, or for peace offerings to the LORD, ⁹then one shall offer with the bull a cereal offering of three tenths of an

---

*****15:1—19:22.** The narrative is interrupted again to give a series of prescriptions, most of them to do with religious worship. As on other occasions, ordinances to do with the temple during the monarchy period (v. 2) and particularly after the return from exile, are attributed to Moses, to give them maximum authority.

15:1–16. This section specifies which cereal offerings and libations are to accompany offerings of animals. The latter were of two kinds—burnt offerings (holocausts) in which the victims were burned, and peace offerings (where the

offerers and the priests share the offerings, as explained in the Leviticus ritual (Lev 1–7). Both kinds were offered for three possible reasons (v. 3)—to fulfil a vow; as a freewill offering; or in thanksgiving (particularly on feast days).

Cereal and drink offerings go very far back in Israelite tradition, though it is possible that many details may have been borrowed from Canaanite rites. The basic idea is that the offering/sacrifice is the sacred meal in which God and the offerers share, thereby entering into communion. Although some expressions, like "a pleasing odour to the Lord" (v. 3), are

---

²«Loquere ad filios Israel et dices ad eos: Cum ingressi fueritis terram habitationis vestrae, quam ego dabo vobis, ³et feceritis oblationem Domino in holocaustum aut victimam vota solventes vel sponte offerentes munera aut in sollemnitatibus vestris adolentes odorem suavitatis Domino de bobus sive de ovibus, ⁴offeret, quicumque immolaverit victimam, sacrificium similae decimam partem ephi conspersae oleo, quod mensuram habebit quartam partem hin, ⁵et vinum ad liba fundenda eiusdem mensurae dabit in holocaustum sive in victimam per agnos singulos. ⁶Per arietes erit sacrificium similae duarum decimarum, quae conspersa sit oleo tertiae partis hin; ⁷et vinum ad libamentum tertiae partis eiusdem mensurae offeret in odorem suavitatis Domino. ⁸Quando vero de bobus feceris holocaustum aut hostiam, ut impleas votum vel pacificas victimas, ⁹dabis per singulos boves similae tres decimas

ephah of fine flour, mixed with half a hin of oil, [10]and you shall offer for the drink offering half a hin of wine, as an offering by fire, a pleasing odour to the LORD.
[11]"Thus it shall be done for each bull or ram, or for each of the male lambs or the kids. [12]According to the number that you prepare, so shall you do with everyone according to their number. [13]All who are native shall do these things in this way, in offering an offering by fire, a pleasing odour to the LORD. [14]And if a stranger is sojourning with you, or any one is among you throughout your generations, and he wishes to offer an offering by fire, a pleasing odour to the LORD, he shall do as you do. [15]For the assembly, there shall be one statute for you and for the stranger who sojourns with you, a perpetual statute throughout your generations; as you are, so shall the sojourner be before the LORD. [16]One law and one ordinance shall be for you and for the stranger who sojourns with you."
[17]The LORD said to Moses, [18]"Say to the people of Israel, When you come into the land to which I bring you [19]and when you eat of the food of the land, you shall present an offering to the LORD. [20]Of the first of your coarse meal you shall present a cake

Ex 12:48

Lev 24:22
Num 9:14;
15:29

Rom 11:16

---

very anthropomorphic (as if God needed to smell it), the Old Testament again and again takes issue with that way of thinking: it teaches that sacrifices are not designed to satisfy any need on God's part; they are, rather, an acknowledgment by man of God's sovereignty, covenant, reconciliation, friendship etc. But sacrifices are not merely external affairs: they should come from the heart, as the prophets reminded the Jews and as Jesus stressed: "I desire mercy, and not sacrifice" (Mt 9:13 and note).

The "tenth" (v. 4) of an ephah: an ephah was about 21 litres (4.6 gallons): see the note on Ex 16:32–36. A hin was a liquid measure—approximately 3.5 litres (just under a gallon).

15:17–21. The "present" or tribute of the first fruits was very much a religious affair: we find the same word being used in liturgical terminology. It is an acknowledgment of the sovereignty and absolute dominion of God: he is given a share in the first and best of the crop, in recognition of the fact that it is thanks to him that men enjoy the good things of the earth.

---

conspersae oleo, quod habeat medium mensurae hin, [10]et vinum ad liba fundenda eiusdem mensurae in oblationem suavissimi odoris Domino. [11]Sic facies per singulos boves et arietes et agnos et capras. [12]Secundum numerum victimarum quas offeretis, ita facietis singulis secundum numerum earum. [13]Omnis indigena eodem ritu offeret sacrificium ignis in odorem suavitatis Domino. [14]Et omnis peregrinus, qui habitat vobiscum vel qui commoratur in medio vestri in omnibus generationibus vestris, offeret sacrificium ignis in odorem suavitatis Domino eodem modo sicut et vos. [15]Unum praeceptum erit tam vobis quam advenis pro omnibus generationibus vestris coram Domino. [16]Una lex erit atque unum iudicium tam vobis quam advenis, qui vobiscum commorantur». [17]Locutus est Dominus ad Moysen dicens: [18]«Loquere filiis Israel et dices ad eos: Cum veneritis in terram, quam dabo vobis, [19]et comederitis de panibus regionis illius, separabitis donaria Domino [20]de pulmento placentam. Sicut de areis donaria separatis, [21]ita et de pulmentis dabitis ea Domino. [22]Quod si per ignorantiam praeterieri-

as an offering; as an offering from the threshing floor, so shall you present it. [21]Of the first of your coarse meal you shall give to the LORD an offering throughout your generations.

Lev 4 **Atonement for faults of inadvertence**

[22]"But if you err, and do not observe all these commandments which the LORD has spoken to Moses, [23]all that the LORD has commanded you by Moses, from the day that the LORD gave commandment, and onward throughout your generations, [24]then if it was done unwittingly without the knowledge of the congregation, all the congregation shall offer one young bull for a burnt offering, a pleasing odour to the LORD, with its cereal offering and its drink offering, according to the ordinance, and one male goat for a sin offering. [25]And the priest shall make atonement for all the congregation of the people of Israel, and they shall be forgiven; because it was an error, and they have brought their offering, an offering by fire to the LORD, and their sin offering before the LORD, for their error. [26]And all the congregation of the people of Israel shall be forgiven, and the stranger who sojourns among them, because the whole population was involved in the error.

[27]"If one person sins unwittingly, he shall offer a female goat a year old for a sin offering. [28]And the priest shall make atone-

---

15:22–31. What is said here about offerings to atone for sins committed unwittingly (by the community or by an individual) needs to be complemented by Leviticus 4–5. It is worth noting the importance that awareness of a sin has when it comes to deciding its gravity. If a sin is committed unwittingly, remission can be obtained by making the prescribed offerings; but if the action is a deliberate one, ritual offerings are incapable of bringing about forgiveness, and anyone who commits such a sin is excluded from the community.

Something which the New Testament will make clear is already being implied here—that not all sins are of equal gravity. Thus, the *Catechism of the Catholic Church* distinguishes mortal from venial sins: "*Mortal sin* destroys charity in the heart of man by a grave violation of God's law; it turns man away from God, who is his ultimate end and his beatitude, by preferring an inferior good to him.

---

tis quidquam horum, quae locutus est Dominus ad Moysen [23]et mandavit per eum ad vos, a die, qua coepit iubere et ultra ad generationes vestras, [24]si longe ab oculis congregationis, offeret congregatio vitulum de armento, holocaustum in odorem placabilem Domino et oblationem ac liba eius, ut caeremoniae postulant, hircumque pro peccato. [25]Et expiabit sacerdos pro omni congregatione filiorum Israel, et dimittetur eis, quoniam non sponte peccaverunt, nihilominus offerentes sacrificium ignis Domino pro se et pro peccato atque errore suo. [26]Et dimittetur universae plebi filiorum Israel et advenis, qui peregrinantur inter eos, quoniam culpa est omnis populi per ignorantiam. [27]Quod si anima una nesciens peccaverit, offeret capram anniculam pro peccato suo. [28]Et expiabit pro ea sacerdos, quod inscia peccaverit coram Domino; expiabit pro ea, et dimittetur illi. [29]Tam indigenis quam advenis una

ment before the Lord for the person who commits an error, when he sins unwittingly, to make atonement for him; and he shall be forgiven. ²⁹You shall have one law for him who does anything unwittingly, for him who is native among the people of Israel, and for the stranger who sojourns among them. ³⁰But the person who does anything with a high hand, whether he is native or a sojourner, reviles the LORD, and that person shall be cut off from among his people. ³¹Because he has despised the word of the LORD, and has broken his commandment, that person shall be utterly cut off; his iniquity shall be upon him."

Penalty for breaking the sabbath
³²While the people of Israel were in the wilderness, they found a man gathering sticks on the sabbath day. ³³And those who found him gathering sticks brought him to Moses and Aaron, and to all the congregation. ³⁴They put him in custody, because it had not been made plain what should be done to him. ³⁵And the LORD said to Moses, "The man shall be put to death; all the congregation shall stone him with stones outside the camp." ³⁶And all the congregation brought him outside the camp, and stoned him to death with stones, as the LORD commanded Moses.

Ex 31:12–17; 20:8

Heb 13:13
Acts 7:58

Venial sin allows charity to subsist, even though it offends and wounds it" (no. 1855). It also establishes that "For a *sin* to be *mortal*, three conditions must together be met: 'Mortal sin is sin whose object is grave matter and which is also committed with full knowledge and deliberate consent' (*Reconciliatio et poenitentia*, 17)" (no. 1837); whereas, "one commits *venial sin* when, in a less serious matter, one does not observe the standard prescribed by the moral law, or when one disobeys the moral law in a

grave matter, but without full knowledge or without complete consent" (no. 1862).

15:32–36. This section deals with a sin committed deliberately, and where the matter is serious (as can be seen from the fact that the death penalty applies: cf. Ex 31:14–15). In this particular case the method of executing the sentence is specified—by stoning, the usual method in ancient Judaism. The harshness of the penalty helps to show how grave an offence against God a mortal sin is.

---

lex erit omnium, qui peccaverint ignorantes. ³⁰Anima vero, quae per superbiam aliquid commiserit, sive civis sit ille sive peregrinus, quoniam adversus Dominum rebellis fuit, peribit de populo suo. ³¹Verbum enim Domini contempsit et praeceptum illius fecit irritum; idcirco delebitur et portabit iniquitatem suam». ³²Factum est autem, cum essent filii Israel in solitudine et invenissent hominem colligentem ligna in die sabbati, ³³obtulerunt eum Moysi et Aaron et universae congregationi, ³⁴qui recluserunt eum in carcerem nescientes quid super eo facere deberent. ³⁵Dixitque Dominus ad Moysen: «Morte moriatur homo iste; obruat eum lapidibus omnis turba extra castra». ³⁶Cumque eduxissent eum foras, obruerunt lapidibus; et mortuus est, sicut praeceperat Dominus. ³⁷Dixit quoque Dominus ad Moysen: ³⁸«Loquere filiis Israel et dices ad eos, ut faciant sibi fimbrias per angulos palliorum ponentes

Deut 22:12 **Tassels on garments**

Mt 9:20; 23:5
Mk 6:56
Lk 8:44

[37]The LORD said to Moses, [38]"Speak to the people of Israel, and bid them to make tassels on the corners of their garments throughout their generations, and to put upon the tassel of each corner a cord of blue; [39]and it shall be to you a tassel to look upon and remember all the commandments of the LORD, to do them, not to follow after your own heart and your own eyes, which you are inclined to go after wantonly. [40]So you shall remember and do all my commandments, and be holy to your God. [41]I am the LORD your God, who brought you out of the land of Egypt, to be your God: I am the LORD your God."

Lev 10:1–3
Deut 11:6–7
Ps 106:16–18
Sir 45:18–20
Jude 11

The rebellion of Korah, Dathan and Abiram; their punishment*

16 [1]Now Korah the son of Izhar, son of Kohath, son of Levi, and Dathan and Abiram the sons of Eliab, and On the son

---

15:37–41. Here is another instance of the sacred text giving a religious explanation for customs of the period—this time the use of tassels on the fringes of clothes. These coloured tassels will act as a reminder to the Israelites that they are different from all other nations, and they will be a sign of their resolve to faithfully obey the precepts of the Law, unafraid of being seen to be different. Jesus himself probably used them: this seems to be implied in the episode of the woman with the hemorrhage (cf. Mt 9:20); but he criticized people who hypocritically wore them only for show (cf. Mt 23:5).

***16:1–35.** This section interweaves accounts of the rebellion of the Levites, led by Korah, and that of the Reubenites, laymen, led by Dathan and Abiram. It carries a lesson that the Israelites will never forget: only those who are docile to the will of God will stay on the path that leads to the promised land. It makes it crystal clear that Moses is the pre-eminent leader of the people, put by God in that position; that worship is the priests' prerogative; and that the Levites' role in worship is secondary to that of priests.

The Levites' grievance seems to be twofold—on the one hand, against Moses and Aaron whose privilege it is to approach the sanctuary (v. 3), even though the entire congregation of Israel is also sanctified by the presence of God (cf. Ex 19:16); and, on the other, against the priests who perform functions to which the Levites feel they have a right (v. 10). The fact that the rebels were "two hundred and fifty well-known men" from among the leaders of the congregation shows the seriousness of the incident. They will all receive the same punishment (16:35).

Moses justifies his mission on the grounds that he has been chosen for it,

---

in eis vittas hyacinthinas. [39]Quas cum videbitis, recordabimini omnium mandatorum Domini eaque facietis nec sequamini cogitationes vestras et oculos per res varias fornicantes, [40]sed magis me, mores omnium praeceptorum meorum faciatis ea sitisque sancti Deo vestro. [41]Ego Dominus Deus vester, qui eduxi vos de terra Aegypti, ut essem Deus vester. Ego Dominus Deus vester». [1]Ecce autem Core filius Isaar filii Caath filii Levi et Dathan atque Abiram filii Eliab, Hon quoque filius Pheleth de filiis Ruben

of Peleth, sons of Reuben, [2]took men; and they rose up before Moses, with a number of the people of Israel, two hundred and fifty leaders of the congregation, chosen from the assembly, well-known men; [3]and they assembled themselves together against Moses and against Aaron, and said to them, "You have gone too far! For all the congregation are holy, every one of them, and the LORD is among them; why then do you exalt yourselves above the assembly of the LORD?" [4]When Moses heard it, he fell on his face; [5]and he said to Korah and all his company, "In the morning the LORD will show who is his, and who is holy, and will cause him to come near to him; him whom he will choose he will cause to come near to him. [6]Do this: take censers, Korah and all his

Ex 19:6

2 Tim 2:19

---

and he proposes to the rebels that they offer incense (v. 7; cf. vv. 17–19). The offering of incense was regarded as being the exclusive prerogative of priests; therefore, Moses' proposal is a bold one because it leaves it up to God himself to decide whether to accept or reject these men as priests. It turns out that he rejects them (v. 35).

The mutiny of the Reubenites is recounted with all its aggravating details: they refuse to attend the meeting called by Moses (v. 12); they describe Egypt as a "land flowing with milk and honey"— words that apply to the promised land (v. 13); they despair of inheriting fields and vineyards (v. 14). So, their attack on Moses' leadership is a frontal one. And they will pay heavily for it: not even Moses' intercession can save them (v. 22), just as Abraham failed to prevent the destruction of Sodom (cf. Gen 18:16–33); the punishment extends to the families and property of the ringleaders (vv. 26, 32), and it means not just death but annihilation (vv. 31–32). This underscores the

message contained in this account: the penalty imposed is a terrible one because rebellion against God's plans is a most grievous offence.

"God of the spirits of all flesh " (v. 22) is a circumlocution found only here and in 27:16; it graphically conveys the idea that God is the only one who has power over the life (spirit) of all men (flesh). That is, he is the Creator and he is Providence.

The overall message of the chapter is that God chooses whomsoever he wishes, and he allots each person his or her role. All should be faithful to their designated roles. However, ambition for power or love of the limelight can lead people to claim a right to positions to which they are not called. Rebelliousness against the order established by God is a serious matter; so the text makes it clear that there are severe penalties for it.

16:6–7 Censers were used in religious worship. However, censers hanging from chains, of the type used nowadays, were

---

[2]surrexerunt contra Moysen aliique filiorum Israel ducenti quinquaginta viri proceres synagogae vocati ad concilium, viri famosi. [3]Cumque stetissent adversum Moysen et Aaron, dixerunt: «Sufficiat vobis quia omnis congregatio sanctorum est, et in ipsis est Dominus! Cur elevamini super congregationem Domini?». [4]Quod cum audisset Moyses, cecidit pronus in faciem [5]locutusque ad Core et ad omne concilium: «Mane, inquit, notum faciet Dominus qui ad se pertineant et qui sint sancti, et sanctos applicabit sibi; et, quos elegerit, appropinquare sibi faciet. [6]Hoc igitur facite: tollat unusquisque turibulum

company; ⁷put fire in them and put incense upon them before the
LORD tomorrow, and the man whom the LORD chooses shall be
the holy one. You have gone too far, sons of Levi!" ⁸And Moses
said to Korah, "Hear now, you sons of Levi: ⁹is it too small a thing
for you that the God of Israel has separated you from the congregation of Israel, to bring you near to himself, to do service in the
tabernacle of the LORD, and to stand before the congregation to
minister to them; ¹⁰and that he has brought you near him, and all
your brethren the sons of Levi with you? And would you seek the
priesthood also? ¹¹Therefore it is against the LORD that you and all
your company have gathered together; what is Aaron that you
murmur against him?"

¹²And Moses sent to call Dathan and Abiram the sons of Eliab;
and they said, "We will not come up. ¹³Is it a small thing that you
have brought us up out of a land flowing with milk and honey, to
kill us in the wilderness, that you must also make yourself a
prince over us? ¹⁴Moreover you have not brought us into a land
flowing with milk and honey, nor given us inheritance of fields
and vineyards. Will you put out the eyes of these men? We will
not come up."

¹⁵And Moses was very angry, and said to the LORD, "Do not
respect their offering. I have not taken one ass from them, and I
have not harmed one of them." ¹⁶And Moses said to Korah, "Be
present, you and all your company, before the LORD, you and they,
and Aaron, tomorrow; ¹⁷and let every one of you take his censer,
and put incense upon it, and every one of you bring before the
LORD his censer, two hundred and fifty censers; you also, and
Aaron, each his censer." ¹⁸So every man took his censer, and they
put fire in them and laid incense upon them, and they stood at the
entrance of the tent of meeting with Moses and Aaron. ¹⁹Then

Num 3:45;
8:14–19

1 Cor 10:10

Ex 38

1 Sam 12:3–5

suum, tu, Core, et omne concilium tuum; ⁷et hausto cras igne, ponite desuper thymiama coram
Domino; et, quemcumque elegerit, ipse erit sanctus. Sufficiat vobis, filii Levi!». ⁸Dixitque rursum ad
Core: «Audite, filii Levi. ⁹Num parum vobis est quod separavit vos Deus Israel ab omni congregatione
et iunxit sibi, ut serviretis ei in cultu habitaculi Domini et staretis coram frequentia populi et minis-
traretis pro ea? ¹⁰Idcirco ad se fecit accedere te et omnes fratres tuos filios Levi, ut vobis etiam sacerdotium vindicetis, ¹¹et omne concilium tuum stet contra Dominum? Quid est enim Aaron, ut
murmuretis contra eum?». ¹²Misit ergo Moyses, ut vocaret Dathan et Abiram filios Eliab, qui responderunt: «Non venimus! ¹³Numquid parum est tibi quod eduxisti nos de terra, quae lacte et melle ma-
nabat, ut occideres in deserto, nisi et dominatus fueris nostri? ¹⁴Revera non induxisti nos in terram,
quae fluit rivis lactis et mellis, nec dedisti nobis possessiones agrorum et vinearum! An et oculos illorum hominum vis eruere? Non venimus!». ¹⁵Iratusque Moyses valde ait ad Dominum: «Ne respicias
sacrificia eorum; tu scis quod ne asellum quidem umquam acceperim ab eis, nec afflixerim quempiam
eorum». ¹⁶Dixitque ad Core: «Tu et omne concilium tuum state seorsum coram Domino, et Aaron die
crastino separatim. ¹⁷Tollite singuli turibula vestra et ponite super ea incensum offerentes Domino
ducenta quinquaginta turibula; tu et Aaron teneatis unusquisque turibulum suum». ¹⁸Quod cum fecis-
sent, stantibus Moyse et Aaron, ¹⁹et coacervasset Core adversum eos omne concilium ad ostium taber-

Korah assembled all the congregation against them at the entrance of the tent of meeting. And the glory of the LORD appeared to all the congregation. ²⁰And the LORD said to Moses and to Aaron, ²¹"Separate yourselves from among this congregation, that I may consume them in a moment." ²²And they fell on their faces, and said, "O God, the God of the spirits of all flesh, shall one man sin, and wilt thou be angry with all the congregation?" ²³And the LORD said to Moses, ²⁴"Say to the congregation, Get away from about the dwelling of Korah, Dathan, and Abiram."

Then Moses rose and went to Dathan and Abiram; and the elders of Israel followed him. ²⁶And he said to the congregation, "Depart, I pray you, from the tents of these wicked men, and touch nothing of theirs, lest you be swept away with all their sins." ²⁷So they got away from about the dwelling of Korah, Dathan, and Abiram; and Dathan and Abiram came out and stood at the door of their tents, together with their wives, their sons, and their little ones. ²⁸And Moses said, "Hereby you shall know that the LORD has sent me to do all these works, and that it has not been of my own accord. ²⁹If these men die the common death of all men, or if they are visited by the fate of all men, then the LORD has not sent me. ³⁰But if the LORD creates something new, and the ground opens its mouth, and swallows them up, with all that belongs to them, and they go down alive into Sheol, then you shall know that these men have despised the LORD."

³¹And as he finished speaking all these words, the ground under them split asunder; ³²and the earth opened its mouth and swallowed them up, with their households and all the men that belonged to Korah and all their goods. ³³So they and all that belonged to them went down alive into Sheol; and the earth closed

Margin references: Num 27:16; Job 12:10; Heb 12:9; Rev 22:6; Ex 3:12; 4:30–31; Jn 5:30; 7:17; Rev 12:16; Rev 19:20

naculi conventus, apparuit cunctis gloria Domini. ²⁰Locutusque Dominus ad Moysen et Aaron ait: ²¹«Separamini de medio congregationis huius, ut eos repente disperdam». ²²Qui ceciderunt proni in faciem atque dixerunt: «Deus, Deus spirituum universae carnis; num, uno peccante, contra omnes ira tua desaeviet?». ²³Et ait Dominus ad Moysen: ²⁴«Praecipe universo populo, ut separetur ab habitaculis Core et Dathan et Abiram». ²⁵Surrexitque Moyses et abiit ad Dathan et Abiram et, sequentibus eum senioribus Israel, ²⁶dixit ad turbam: «Recedite ab habitaculis hominum impiorum et nolite tangere, quae ad eos pertinent, ne involvamini in peccatis eorum». ²⁷Cumque recessissent a tentoriis eorum per circuitum, Dathan et Abiram egressi stabant in introitu papilionum suorum cum uxoribus et filiis et parvulis. ²⁸Et ait Moyses: «In hoc scietis quod Dominus miserit me, ut facerem universa, quae cernitis, et non ex proprio ea corde protulerim: ²⁹Si consueta hominum morte interierint, et visitaverit eos plaga, qua et ceteri visitari solent, non misit me Dominus. ³⁰Sin autem novam rem fecerit Dominus, ut aperiens terra os suum deglutiat eos et omnia, quae ad illos pertinent, descenderintque viventes in infernum, scietis quod blasphemaverint Dominum». ³¹Confestim igitur, ut cessavit loqui, dirupta est terra sub pedibus eorum ³²et aperiens os suum devoravit illos cum domibus suis et omnibus hominibus Core et universa substantia eorum; ³³descenderuntque vivi in infernum operti humo et perierunt de medio congregationis. ³⁴At vero omnis Israel, qui stabat per gyrum, fugit ad clamorem pereuntium dicens:

over them, and they perished from the midst of the assembly. [34]And all Israel that were round about them fled at their cry; for they said, "Lest the earth swallow us up!" [35]And fire came forth from the LORD, and consumed the two hundred and fifty men offering the incense.

Recovering the altar

Ex 27:2

[36i]Then the LORD said to Moses, [37]"Tell Eleazar the son of Aaron the priest to take up the censers out of the blaze; then scatter the fire far and wide. For they are holy, [38]the censers of these men who have sinned at the cost of their lives; so let them be made into hammered plates as a covering for the altar, for they offered them before the LORD; therefore they are holy. Thus they shall be a sign to the people of Israel." [39]So Eleazar the priest took the bronze censers, which those who were burned had offered; and they were hammered out as a covering for the altar, [40]to be a reminder to the people of Israel, so that no one who is not a priest, who is not of the descendants of Aaron, should draw near to burn incense before the LORD, lest he become as Korah and as his company— as the LORD said to Eleazar through Moses.

Hb 12:3

Num 1:51

[41]But on the morrow all the congregation of the people of Israel murmured against Moses and against Aaron, saying, "You have killed the people of the LORD."

---

unknown: at that period the censer was a simple metal bowl or basin with hot embers in it, on to which incense was put; archaeological excavations have yielded various primitive censers of this type.

16:36–41 This short account explains why the altar for burnt offerings had a metal covering (cf. Ex 27:2): on this altar the expiation offerings were made, and

therefore even the material of which the sheeting was made ("the censers of these men who have sinned": v. 38) should reflect its purpose; besides, this sheeting would remind people that no one other than a priest should in the future approach the altar (v. 40), to make sure that no one suffered the same fate as these Levites.

«Ne forte et nos terra deglutiat». [35]Sed et ignis egressus a Domino interfecit ducentos quinquaginta viros, qui offerebant incensum. [1]Locutusque est Dominus ad Moysen dicens: [2]«Praecipe Eleazaro filio Aaron sacerdoti, ut tollat turibula, quae iacent in incendio, et ignem huc illucque dispergat, quoniam sanctificata sunt [3]in mortibus peccatorum; producatque ea in laminas et affigat altari, eo quod attulerunt ea Domino et sanctificata sunt, ut sint pro signo filiis Israel». [4]Tulit ergo Eleazar sacerdos turibula aenea, in quibus obtulerant hi quos incendium devoravit, et produxit ea in laminas affigens altari, [5]ut haberent postea filii Israel, quibus commonerentur, ne quis accedat alienigena et, qui non est de semine Aaron, ad offerendum incensum Domino, ne patiatur sicut passus est Core et omnis congregatio eius, loquente Domino ad Moysen. [6]Murmuravit autem omnis congregatio filiorum Israel sequenti die contra

i. Ch 17:1 in Heb [and in New Vulgate]

The people complain and are punished

Wis 18:20–25

[42]And when the congregation had assembled against Moses and against Aaron, they turned toward the tent of meeting; and behold, the cloud covered it, and the glory of the LORD appeared. [43]And Moses and Aaron came to the front of the tent of meeting, [44]and the LORD said to Moses, [45]"Get away from the midst of this congregation, that I may consume them in a moment." And they fell on their faces. [46]And Moses said to Aaron, "Take your censer, and put fire therein from off the altar, and lay incense on it, and carry it quickly to the congregation, and make atonement for them; for wrath has gone forth from the LORD, the plague has begun." [47]So Aaron took it as Moses said, and ran into the midst of the assembly; and behold, the plague had already begun among the people; and he put on the incense, and made atonement for the people. [48]And he stood between the dead and the living; and the plague was stopped. [49]Now those who died by the plague were fourteen thousand seven hundred, besides those who died in the affair of Korah. [50]And Aaron returned to Moses at the entrance of the tent of meeting, when the plague was stopped.

Aaron's rod

17 [1j]The LORD said to Moses, [2]"Speak to the people of Israel, and get from them rods, one for each fathers' house, from

---

16:42–51. One of the functions reserved to priests was to perform atonement rites, as this episode makes plain. We are told here about a mutiny, although its punishment is not described in detail: there is just a mention of a "plague", that is, a misfortune which, like the plagues of Egypt, would show the Lord's dominion over created beings and how he intervenes in the history of the Israelites.

However, the passage goes into detail about the offering of incense (vv. 46–48), to make the point that the primary function of a priest is to perform the rite of atonement for the people's sins. The book of Wisdom (cf. Wis 18:20–25) refers to this fact, underlining the figure and role of the Aaronic priesthood.

17:1–10. The prodigy of the sprouting

Moysen et Aaron dicens: «Vos interfecistis populum Domini». [7]Cumque oriretur seditio contra Moysen et Aaron, converterunt se ad tabernaculum conventus; quod operuit nubes et apparuit gloria Domini. [8]Moyses et Aaron venerunt ante tabernaculum conventus. [9]Dixitque Dominus ad Moysen: [10]«Recedite de medio congregationis huius, nam extemplo delebo eos». Et ceciderunt in faciem suam. [11]Dixit Moyses ad Aaron: «Tolle turibulum et, hausto igne de altari, mitte incensum desuper pergens cito ad populum, ut expies pro eis; iam enim egressa est ira a Domino, et plaga desaevit». [12]Quod cum fecisset Aaron et cucurrisset ad mediam congregationem, quam iam vastabat plaga, obtulit thymiama et expiavit pro populo; [13]et stetit inter mortuos ac viventes, et plaga cessavit. [14]Fuerunt autem, qui percussi sunt, quattuordecim milia hominum et septingenti, absque his, qui perierant in seditione Core. [15]Reversusque est Aaron ad Moysen ad ostium tabernaculi conventus, postquam quievit interitus. [16]Et

j. Ch 17:16 in Heb [and in New Vulgate]

all their leaders according to their fathers' houses, twelve rods. Write each man's name upon his rod, [3]and write Aaron's name upon the rod of Levi. For there shall be one rod for the head of each fathers' house. [4]Then you shall deposit them in the tent of meeting before the testimony, where I meet with you. [5]And the rod of the man whom I choose shall sprout; thus I will make to cease from me the murmurings of the people of Israel, which they murmur against you." [6]Moses spoke to the people of Israel; and all their leaders gave him rods, one for each leader, according to their fathers' houses, twelve rods; and the rod of Aaron was among their rods. [7]And Moses deposited the rods before the LORD in the tent of the testimony.

[8]And on the morrow Moses went into the tent of the testimony; and behold, the rod of Aaron for the house of Levi had sprouted and put forth buds, and produced blossoms, and it bore ripe almonds. [9]Then Moses brought out all the rods from before the LORD to all the people of Israel; and they looked, and each man took his rod. [10]And the LORD said to Moses, "Put back the

Heb 9:4

---

rod demonstrates the pre-eminence of the tribe of Aaron. However, the rod does not sprout because it was any different from the other rods (vv. 2–3), but because God singled it out gratuitously. Flowering and bearing fruit symbolize vitality and divine blessing (cf. Gen 1:11, 22, 28).

This account is a beautiful paradigm of divine vocation; thus, an ancient apocryphal text tells of St Joseph's rod flowering as Aaron's did (*Protoevangelium Iacobi*, 9). This has passed into Christian iconography, as can be seen from depictions of St Joseph. Church tradition also

applies this idea to the Blessed Virgin: "The rod, which is neither planted nor cultivated, flourishes; it bears fruit and, as the Prophet said, it grows out of the root of Jesse and produces a flower on which rests the septiform spirit of the Lord. Who, then, is that rod if not the Royal Virgin of the line of David, who, according to evangelical faith, without the action of man gave unto us Christ, the true flower and glory of mankind, in whom all the fullness of divinity dwells bodily?" (Rupert of Deutz, *Commentarium in Numeros*, 2, 4).

---

locutus est Dominus ad Moysen dicens: [17]«Loquere ad filios Israel et accipe ab eis virgas singulas per cognationes suas, a cunctis principibus tribuum virgas duodecim, et uniuscuiusque nomen superscribes virgae suae. [18]Nomen autem Aaron scribes in virga Levi, et una virga cunctas seorsum familias continebit. [19]Ponesque eas in tabernaculo conventus coram testimonio, ubi conveniam cum vobis. [20]Quem ex his elegero, germinabit virga eius; et cohibebo a me querimonias filiorum Israel, quibus contra vos murmurant». [21]Locutusque est Moyses ad filios Israel, et dederunt ei omnes principes virgas per singulas tribus; fueruntque virgae duodecim, et virga Aaron in medio earum. [22]Quas cum posuisset Moyses coram Domino in tabernaculo testimonii, [23]sequenti die regressus invenit germinasse virgam Aaron in domo Levi; et turgentibus gemmis eruperant flores, qui, foliis dilatatis, in amygdalas deformati sunt. [24]Protulit ergo Moyses omnes virgas de conspectu Domini ad cunctos filios Israel; videruntque et receperunt singuli virgas suas. [25]Dixitque Dominus ad Moysen: «Refer virgam Aaron coram testimonio, ut servetur ibi in signum rebellium filiorum Israel, et quiescant querelae eorum a me, ne

rod of Aaron before the testimony, to be kept as a sign for the rebels, that you may make an end of their murmurings against me, lest they die." [11]Thus did Moses; as the LORD commanded him, so he did.

[12]And the people of Israel said to Moses, "Behold, we perish, we are undone, we are all undone. [13]Every one who comes near, who comes near to the tabernacle of the Lord, shall die. Are we all to perish?"

Priests and Levites

Num 3:1–13
Deut 18:1–8
Heb 7:25–28

18 [1]So the Lord said to Aaron, "You and your sons and your fathers' house with you shall bear iniquity in connection with the sanctuary; and you and your sons with you shall bear iniquity in connection with your priesthood. [2]And with you bring your brethren also, the tribe of Levi, the tribe of your father, that they may join you, and minister to you while you and your sons with you are before the tent of the testimony. [3]They shall attend you and attend to all duties of the tent; but shall not come near to the vessels of the sanctuary or to the altar, lest they, and you, die. [4]They shall join you, and attend to the tent of meeting, for all the service of the tent; and no one else shall come near you. [5]And you shall attend to the duties of the sanctuary and the duties of

Heb 9:6

17:12–13. As a tail-piece to these two chapters, the sacred writer records the moral the people have drawn: no one other than a priest may approach the altar. The language is blunt because the rule is an important one. It should be remembered that many of these prescriptions to do with worship have a pedagogical purpose—to teach people the transcendence of God; this lesson will ensure that no one thinks he can use religious cult to manipulate the Lord to his own advantage.

18:1–7. The message contained in narrative form in the previous two chapters is now spelt out in the form of regulations about the rights and duties of priests and Levites. This section specifies the roles of each: priests exercise a ministry which has greater dignity—to do with the altar and the holy of holies (v. 7); Levites are at the service of priests, to whom they have been given as a "gift" (vv. 2–6). These rules are handed down directly to Aaron and not, as is normally the case, to Moses.

See also the note on Num 3:5–10.

moriantur». [26]Fecitque Moyses, sicut praeceperat Dominus. [27]Dixerunt autem filii Israel ad Moysen: «Ecce consumpti sumus, perimus, omnes perimus! [28]Quicumque accedit ad habitaculum Domini, moritur. Num usque ad internecionem cuncti delendi sumus?». [1]Dixitque Dominus ad Aaron: «Tu et filii tui et domus patris tui tecum portabitis iniquitatem sanctuarii; et tu et filii tui simul sustinebitis peccata sacerdotii vestri. [2]Sed et fratres tuos de tribu Levi, tribum patris tui sume tecum, praestoque sint et ministrent tibi; tu autem et filii tui ministrabitis in tabernaculo testimonii. [3]Excubabuntque Levitae ad praecepta tua et ad cuncta opera tabernaculi, ita dumtaxat ut ad vasa sanctuarii et ad altare non accedant, ne et illi moriantur, et vos pereatis simul. [4]Sint autem tecum et excubent in custodiis

the altar, that there be wrath no more upon the people of Israel.
Ezra 2:43 [6]And behold, I have taken your brethren the Levites from among
the people of Israel; they are a gift to you, given to the LORD, to
Num 1:51 do the service of the tent of meeting. [7]And you and your sons
with you shall attend to your priesthood for all that concerns the
altar and that is within the veil; and you shall serve. I give your
priesthood as a gift,[k] and any one else who comes near shall be
put to death."

Lev 6–7
Deut 18:3–5
Ezek 44:29–31 **Tithes and portions**
1 Cor 9:13 [8]Then the LORD said to Aaron, "And behold, I have given you
whatever is kept of the offerings made to me, all the consecrated
things of the people of Israel; I have given them to you as a portion, and to your sons as a perpetual due. [9]This shall be yours of
the most holy things, reserved from the fire; every offering of
theirs, every cereal offering of theirs and every sin offering of

---

18:8–32. The rights of priests are spelled
out in detail (vv. 8–19) and then those of
the Levites (vv. 21–32). Priests always get
their upkeep from their share in the
people's sacrifices and offerings, as specified in various texts (cf. Deut 18:3–5; Lev
6–7; Ezek 44:29–31). The shares allocated
here are very advantageous to priests.
Levites, for their part, receive only the
tithes specified. Priests are regarded as
being a "gift" to God in place of the first-
born (cf. 3:12; 8:16). Underlying these
regulations is the idea that service in the
temple redounds to the benefit of the
whole community, and therefore the community has a duty to ensure that ministers
have a suitably dignified standard of

living. St Paul makes the same point: without going into detail he tells Christians
that they should help meet church
expenses (cf. 1 Cor 9:8–14).

"A covenant of salt" (v. 19): a
covenant sealed with salt was permanent
and inviolable. Salt was a very precious
commodity in desert life because it prevented dehydration; sharing a meal and
using the same salt was the way pacts
between individuals were sealed. Salt
was also used in offerings (cf. Lev 2:13)
because, given its preservative properties, it acted as a symbol of permanence
and fidelity. Our Lord used salt as a
metaphor with this same meaning (cf.
Mt 5:13).

---

tabernaculi conventus et in omni ministerio eius; alienigena non miscebitur vobis. [5]Excubate in ministerio sanctuarii et in ministerio altaris, ne oriatur amplius indignatio super filios Israel. [6]Ego sumpsi
fratres vestros Levitas de medio filiorum Israel et tradidi donum Domino, ut serviant in ministeriis
tabernaculi conventus. [7]Tu autem et filii tui custodite sacerdotium vestrum et omnia, quae ad cultum
altaris pertinent et intra velum sunt, administrabitis. Ministerium do vobis sacerdotium in donum; si
quis externus accesserit, occidetur». [8]Locutusque est Dominus ad Aaron: «Ecce dedi tibi custodiam
praelibationum mearum. Omnia, quae sanctificantur a filiis Israel, tradidi tibi et filiis tuis pro officio
sacerdotali, legitima sempiterna. [9]Haec ergo accipies de sanctis sanctorum, exceptis his quae combu-
runtur: omnis oblatio et sacrificium pro peccato atque delicto, quod redditur mihi, sanctum sanctorum

k. Heb *service of gift*

theirs and every guilt offering of theirs, which they render to me, shall be most holy to you and to your sons. [10]In a most holy place shall you eat of it; every male may eat of it; it is holy to you. [11]This also is yours, the offering of their gift, all the wave offerings of the people of Israel; I have given them to you, and to your sons and daughters with you, as a perpetual due; every one who is clean in your house may eat of it. [12]All the best of the oil, and all the best of the wine and of the grain, the first fruits of what they give to the LORD, I give to you. [13]The first ripe fruits of all that is in their land, which they bring to the LORD, shall be yours; every one who is clean in your house may eat of it. [14]Every devoted thing in Israel shall be yours. [15]Everything that opens the womb of all flesh, whether man or beast, which they offer to the LORD, shall be yours; nevertheless the first-born of man you shall redeem, and the firstling of unclean beasts you shall redeem. [16]And their redemption price (at a month old you shall redeem them) you shall fix at five shekels in silver, according to the shekel of the sanctuary, which is twenty gerahs. [17]But the firstling of a cow, or the firstling of a sheep, or the firstling of a goat, you shall not redeem; they are holy. You shall sprinkle their blood upon the altar, and shall burn their fat as an offering by fire, a pleasing odor to the LORD; [18]but their flesh shall be yours, as the breast that is waved and as the right thigh are yours. [19]All the holy offerings which the people of Israel present to the LORD I give to you, and to your sons and daughters with you, as a perpetual due; it is a covenant of salt for ever before the LORD for you and for your offspring with you." [20]And the LORD said to Aaron, "You shall have no inheritance in their land, neither shall you have any portion among them; I am your portion and your inheritance among the people of Israel.

Ex 29:24

Deut 26:1

Ex 13:11
Num 3:11–13,
40–51; 8:16–18

Lev 2:13

tuum erit et filiorum tuorum. [10]In sanctuario comedes illud; mares tantum edent ex eo, quia consecratum est tibi. [11]Praelibationem donorum, quae elevando obtulerint filii Israel, tibi dedi et filiis tuis ac filiabus tuis iure perpetuo: qui mundus est in domo tua, vescetur eis. [12]Omnem medullam olei et vini ac frumenti quidquid offerunt primitiarum Domino, tibi dedi. [13]Universa frugum initia, quas gignit humus et Domino deportantur, cedent in usus tuos: qui mundus est in domo tua, vescetur eis. [14]omne, quod ex voto reddiderint filii Israel, tuum erit. [15]Quidquid primum erumpit e vulva cunctae carnis, quod offerunt Domino, sive ex hominibus sive de pecoribus fuerit, tui iuris erit; ita dumtaxat, ut hominis primogenitum et omne animal, quod immundum est, redimi facias. [16]Cuius redemptio erit post unum mensem siclis argenti quinque pondere sanctuarii. Siclus viginti obolos habet. [17]Primogenitum autem bovis vel ovis vel caprae non facies redimi, quia sanctificata sunt Domino; sanguinem tantum eorum fundes super altare, et adipes adolebis in suavissimum odorem Domino. [18]Carnes vero eorum in usum tuum cedent, sicut pectusculum elevatum et armus dexter tua erunt. [19]Omnes praelibationes sanctas, quas offerunt filii Israel Domino, tibi dedi et filiis ac filiabus tuis iure perpetuo: pactum salis est sempiternum coram Domino tibi ac filiis tuis». [20]Dixitque Dominus ad Aaron: «In terra eorum nihil possidebitis, nec habebitis partem inter eos: Ego pars et hereditas tua in medio filiorum Israel. [21]Filiis autem Levi dedi omnes decimas Israelis in possessionem pro ministerio, quo serviunt mihi in taber-

Deut 14:22
Heb 7:5

²¹"To the Levites I have given every tithe in Israel for an inheritance, in return for their service which they serve, their service in

Ex 19:12 the tent of meeting. ²²And henceforth the people of Israel shall not come near the tent of meeting, lest they bear sin and die. ²³But the Levites shall do the service of the tent of meeting, and they shall bear their iniquity; it shall be a perpetual statute throughout your generations; and among the people of Israel they shall have no

Deut 14:22 inheritance. ²⁴For the tithe of the people of Israel, which they present as an offering to the LORD, I have given to the Levites for an inheritance; therefore I have said of them that they shall have no inheritance among the people of Israel."

²⁵And the LORD said to Moses, ²⁶"Moreover you shall say to the Levites, 'When you take from the people of Israel the tithe which I have given you from them for your inheritance, then you shall present an offering from it to the LORD, a tithe of the tithe. ²⁷And your offering shall be reckoned to you as though it were the grain of the threshing floor, and as the fulness of the wine press. ²⁸So shall you also present an offering to the LORD from all your tithes, which you receive from the people of Israel; and from it you shall give the LORD's offering to Aaron the priest. ²⁹Out of all the gifts to you, you shall present every offering due to the LORD, from all the best of them, giving the hallowed part from them.' ³⁰Therefore you shall say to them, 'When you have offered from it the best of it, then the rest shall be reckoned to the Levites as

Mt 10:11 produce of the threshing floor, and as produce of the wine press;
Lk 10:7 ³¹and you may eat it in any place, you and your households; for it
1 Cor 9:13 is your reward in return for your service in the tent of meeting.
1 Tim 5:18 ³²And you shall bear no sin by reason of it, when you have offered the best of it. And you shall not profane the holy things of the people of Israel, lest you die.'"

naculo conventus, ²²ut non accedant ultra filii Israel ad tabernaculum conventus, nec committant peccatum mortiferum. ²³Solis filiis Levi mihi in tabernaculo conventus servientibus et portantibus peccata populi; legitimum sempiternum erit in generationibus vestris, et in medio filiorum Israel nihil aliud possidebunt. ²⁴Decimas, quas filii Israel in praelibationem elevant Domino, dedi Levitis in possessionem. Propterea dixi eis: In medio filiorum Israel non habebitis possessionem». ²⁵Locutusque est Dominus ad Moysen dicens: ²⁶«Praecipe Levitis atque denuntia: Cum acceperitis a filiis Israel decimas, quas dedi vobis, praelibationem earum elevabitis Domino, id est decimam partem decimae, ²⁷ut reputetur vobis in praelibationem tam de areis quam de torcularibus. ²⁸Sic de universis, quorum accipitis primitias a filiis Israel, elevate Domino: date Aaron sacerdoti. ²⁹Omnia, quae offeretis ex decimis, in donaria Domini separabitis: optima et electa erunt. ³⁰Dicesque ad eos: Si praeclara et meliora quaeque obtuleritis ex decimis, reputabitur vobis quasi de area et torculari dederitis fructus; ³¹et comedetis eas in omnibus locis vestris, tam vos quam familiae vestrae, quia pretium est pro ministerio, quo servitis in tabernaculo conventus. ³²Et non peccabitis super hoc egregia vobis et pinguia reservantes, ne polluatis oblationes filiorum Israel et moriamini». ¹Locutusque est Dominus ad Moysen et Aaron dicens: ²«Ista est religio legis, quam constituit Dominus. Praecipe filiis Israel, ut adducant ad te

Num 31:23
Heb 9:13

The rite of the red heifer

19 ¹Now the LORD said to Moses and to Aaron, ²"This is the Deut 21:3
statute of the law which the LORD has commanded: Tell the
people of Israel to bring you a red heifer without defect, in which
there is no blemish, and upon which a yoke has never come. Heb 13:12
³And you shall give her to Eleazar the priest, and she shall be Lev 4:12
taken outside the camp and slaughtered before him; ⁴and Eleazar
the priest shall take some of her blood with his finger, and sprinkle some of her blood toward the front of the tent of meetings
even times. ⁵And the heifer shall be burned in his sight; her skin,
her flesh, and her blood, with her dung, shall be burned; ⁶and the Ex 12:22
priest shall take cedarwood and hyssop and scarlet stuff, and cast Lev 14:6–9
Heb 9:19
them into the midst of the burning of the heifer. ⁷Then the priest
shall wash his clothes and bathe his body in water, and afterwards he shall come into the camp; and the priest shall be
unclean until evening. ⁸He who burns the heifer shall wash his
clothes in water and bathe his body in water, and shall be unclean Lev 4:11–12
until evening. ⁹And a man who is clean shall gather up the ashes Heb 9:13
of the heifer, and deposit them outside the camp in a clean place;
and they shall be kept for the congregation of the people of Israel

---

19:1–10 The common thread in this
chapter is ceremonies having to do with
ritual cleansing; it contains three sections—the ashes of the red heifer (vv.
1–10); rules for various types of ritual
cleansing (vv. 11–16); the preparation
and use of lustral water (vv. 17–22).

The rite of the red heifer contains elements so old that their meaning is not
entirely clear; however, the notion of protection is dominant throughout: the colour
red symbolized the absence of evil, and
the cedarwood, hyssop and red dye were
regarded as medicinal. The heifer had to
be slaughtered with great care—outside
the camp, by a layman in the presence of
a priest, burned so that it was reduced to
ashes, etc. This may have been originally
a pagan rite but one which, when brought
into use in Israel, was divested of any
magical element; it is mentioned only in
two places—here, and in connexion with
the cleansing of war booty (cf. 31:23).
The heifer was killed "outside the camp"
(v. 3). Some Fathers see this immolation
which is part of an atonement rite as a
prefiguring of the sacrifice of Jesus who
"also suffered outside the gate in order to
sanctify the people through his own
blood" (Heb 13:12).

---

vaccam rufam aetatis integrae, in qua nulla sit macula, nec portaverit iugum. ³Tradetisque eam
Eleazaro sacerdoti, quae educta extra castra mactabitur in conspectu eius; ⁴et tinguens digitum in sanguine eius asperget contra fores tabernaculi conventus septem vicibus, ⁵combureturque in conspectu
eius, tam pelle et carnibus eius quam sanguine et fimo flammae traditis. ⁶Lignum quoque cedrinum et
hyssopum coccumque sacerdos mittet in flammam, quae vaccam vorat. ⁷Et tunc demum, lotis vestibus
et corpore suo, ingredietur in castra, commaculatusque erit usque ad vesperum. ⁸Sed et ille, qui combusserit eam, lavabit vestimenta sua et corpus, et immundus erit usque ad vesperum. ⁹Colliget autem
vir mundus cineres vaccae et effundet eos extra castra in loco purissimo, ut sint congregationi filiorum

for the water for impurity, for the removal of sin. ¹⁰And he who gathers the ashes of the heifer shall wash his clothes, and be unclean until evening. And this shall be to the people of Israel, and to the stranger who sojourns among them, a perpetual statute.

Purification with water

Lev 21:1
Hag 2:13

¹¹"He who touches the dead body of any person shall be unclean seven days; ¹²he shall cleanse himself with the water on the third day and on the seventh day, and so be clean; but if he does not cleanse himself on the third day and on the seventh day, he will not become clean. ¹³Whoever touches a dead person, the body of any man who has died, and does not cleanse himself, defiles the tabernacle of the LORD, and that person shall be cut off from Israel; because the water for impurity was not thrown upon him, he shall be unclean; his uncleanness is still on him.

¹⁴"This is the law when a man dies in a tent: every one who comes into the tent, and every one who is in the tent, shall be unclean seven days. ¹⁵And every open vessel, which has no cover fastened upon it, is unclean. ¹⁶Whoever in the open field touches

---

19:11–16. Contact with a dead body was regarded as a serious uncleanness and it called for two washings with lustral water ("water for impurity") prior to entering the sanctuary (vv. 12–13). The Nazarite (cf. 6:9–11) and the priest (cf. Lev 21:1–4) were forbidden to touch a dead body, and the high priest was not even allowed to go near his own father's body (cf. Lev 21:11). Regulations of this sort show the deep respect people had at that time for anything to do with life or death: both come from God, but he alone is the author of life. Therefore, even those who had touched a dead body out of family piety or because it was a duty of their office, had to be carefully purified before approaching the altar of God. It is very likely that the background to all this was a desire to avoid contagion; like other peoples of antiquity, the Hebrews may well have had a taboo about contact with bodies of the dead. However, over and above that, the rules laid down in the Bible are really designed with religious worship in mind (rather than any possible contagion etc.): its dignity was such that people needed to be cleansed of anything that in the popular mind implied contamination, even though there was no scientific basis for it.

Israel in custodiam pro aqua aspersionis. ¹⁰Cumque laverit, qui vaccae portaverat cineres, vestimenta sua, immundus erit usque ad vesperum. Habebunt hoc filii Israel et advenae, qui habitant inter eos, sanctum iure perpetuo. ¹¹Qui tetigerit cadaver hominis et propter hoc septem diebus fuerit immundus, ¹²aspergetur ex hac aqua die tertio et septimo et sic mundabitur. Si die tertio aspersus non fuerit, septimo non erit mundus. ¹³Omnis, qui tetigerit humanae animae morticinum et aspersus hac commixtione non fuerit, polluet habitaculum Domini et peribit ex Israel, quia aqua expiationis non est aspersus: immundus erit, et manebit spurcitia eius super eum. ¹⁴Ista est lex hominis, qui moritur in tabernaculo: omnes, qui ingrediuntur tentorium illius, et universa vasa, quae ibi sunt, polluta erunt septem diebus. ¹⁵Vas, quod non habuerit operculum nec ligaturam desuper, immundum erit. ¹⁶Si quis in agro tetigerit

one who is slain with a sword, or a dead body, or a bone of a man, or a grave, shall be unclean seven days. ¹⁷For the unclean they Heb 9:13 shall take some ashes of the burnt sin offering, and running water shall be added in a vessel; ¹⁸then a clean person shall take hyssop, and dip it in the water, and sprinkle it upon the tent, and upon all the furnishings, and upon the persons who were there, and upon him who touched the bone, or the slain, or the dead, or the grave; ¹⁹and the clean person shall sprinkle upon the unclean on the third day and on the seventh day; thus on the seventh day he shall cleanse him, and he shall wash his clothes and bathe himself in water, and at evening he shall be clean.

²⁰"But the man who is unclean and does not cleanse himself, that person shall be cut off from the midst of the assembly, since he has defiled the sanctuary of the LORD; because the water for impurity has not been thrown upon him, he is unclean. ²¹And it shall be a perpetual statute for them. He who sprinkles the water for impurity shall wash his clothes; and he who touches the water for impurity shall be unclean until evening. ²²And whatever the unclean person touches shall be unclean; and any one who touches it shall be unclean until evening."

8. VARIOUS EVENTS IN KADESH*

Moses brings water from the rock
Ex 17:1–7
Deut 33:8ff

20 ¹And the people of Israel, the whole congregation, came into the wilderness of Zin in the first month, and the

---

*20:1–19. When the spies sent to explore the land of Canaan returned to base, the people of Israel were in the desert of Paran, in Kadesh (13:26). The desert of Zin, which is referred to here, and which is different from that of a very similar

name (Sin) mentioned in Exodus 16:1 and 17:1, was the north-west part of the wilderness of Paran, to which the cloud had led the Israelites from Sinai (cf. 10:12). Kadesh was not really a town but an area containing leafy oases. It was a

cadaver hominis gladio occisi aut per se mortui sive os illius vel sepulcrum, immundus erit septem diebus. ¹⁷Tollentque de cineribus combustionis peccati et mittent aquas vivas super eos in vas; ¹⁸in quibus cum homo mundus tinxerit hyssopum, asperget ex eo omne tentorium et cunctam supellectilem et homines, qui ibi fuerint, et super eum, qui tetigerit ossa vel occisum hominem aut per se mortuum aut sepultum. ¹⁹Atque hoc modo mundus lustrabit immundum tertio et septimo die; expiatusque die septimo lavabit et se et vestimenta sua et mundus erit ad vesperum. ²⁰Si quis hoc ritu non fuerit expiatus, peribit anima illius de medio ecclesiae, quia sanctuarium Domini polluit et non est aqua lustrationis aspersus; immundus est. ²¹Erit vobis praeceptum legitimum sempiternum. Ipse quoque, qui aspergit aqua lustrali, lavabit vestimenta sua; omnis, qui tetigerit aquas expiationis, immundus erit usque ad vesperum. ²²Quidquid tetigerit immundus, immundum erit, et anima, quae horum quippiam tetigerit, immunda erit usque ad vesperum». ¹Veneruntque filii Israel et omnis congregatio in desertum Sin

601

people stayed in Kadesh; and Miriam died there, and was buried there.

Ex 14:11   ²Now there was no water for the congregation; and they assembled themselves together against Moses and against Aaron. ³And the people contended with Moses, and said, "Would that we had died when our brethren died before the LORD! ⁴Why have you brought the assembly of the LORD into this wilderness, that we should die here, both we and our cattle? ⁵And why have you made us come up out of Egypt, to bring us to this evil place? It is no place for grain, or figs, or vines, or pomegranates; and there is no water to drink." ⁶Then Moses and Aaron went from the presence of the assembly to the door of the tent of meeting, and fell on their faces. And the glory of the LORD appeared to them, ⁷and the LORD

1 Cor 10:4–5   said to Moses, ⁸"Take the rod, and assemble the congregation, you and Aaron your brother, and tell the rock before their eyes to yield its water; so you shall bring water out of the rock for them; so you shall give drink to the congregation and their cattle." ⁹And Moses took the rod from before the LORD, as he commanded him.

---

key point of reference for the people of Israel's route towards Canaan. From Kadesh they will leave for the plains of Moab (cf. 22:1). Kadesh marks the end of the desert trek (cf. chaps. 33–38); from now on the land is inhabited and the Israelites will have contact with those who live there.

As they make their way, the people encounter both external and internal difficulties, but that does not stop their advance to the promised Land, because God is their guide and he is helping them. In this sense the people of Israel prefigures the Church, for "as Israel according to the flesh which wandered in the desert was already called the Church

of God (cf. Num 20:4; etc.), so too, the new Israel which advances in this present era in search of a future and permanent city (cf. Heb 13:14), is called also the Church of Christ (cf. Mt 16:18). It is Christ indeed who had purchased it with his own blood (cf. Acts 20:28); he has filled it with his Spirit; he has provided means adapted to its visible and social union" (Vatican II, *Lumen gentium*, 9).

20:2–13. Unlike Exodus 17:1–17, here it is Aaron who accompanies Moses, so that both of them share in the sin of mistrusting God (cf. v. 12). The text does not say what their sin was exactly: presumably it was because they struck the rock

---

mense primo, et mansit populus in Cades. Mortuaque est ibi Maria et sepulta in eodem loco. ²Cumque indigeret aqua populus, convenerunt adversum Moysen et Aaron ³et versi in seditionem dixerunt: «Utinam perissemus inter fratres nostros coram Domino! ⁴Cur eduxistis ecclesiam Domini in solitudinem, ut et nos et nostra iumenta moriamur? ⁵Quare nos fecistis ascendere de Aegypto et adduxistis in locum istum pessimum, qui seri non potest, qui nec ficum gignit nec vineas nec malogranata, insuper et aquam non habet ad bibendum?». ⁶Venitque Moyses et Aaron, relicta congregatione, ad introitum tabernaculi conventus corrueruntque proni in terram, et apparuit gloria Domini super eos. ⁷Locutusque est Dominus ad Moysen dicens: ⁸«Tolle virgam et congrega populum, tu et Aaron frater

¹⁰And Moses and Aaron gathered the assembly together before the rock, and he said to them, "Hear now, you rebels; shall we bring forth water for you out of this rock?" ¹¹And Moses lifted up his hand and struck the rock with his rod twice; and water came forth abundantly, and the congregation drank, and their cattle. ¹²And the LORD said to Moses and Aaron, "Because you did not believe in me, to sanctify me in the eyes of the people of Israel, therefore you shall not bring this assembly into the land which I have given them." ¹³These are the waters of Meribah,¹ where the people of Israel contended with the LORD, and he showed himself holy among them.

1 Cor 10:4

Deut 1:37;
32:52
Ps 106:32:33

Edom refuses right of way

Deut 2:4–7
Judg 11:17

¹⁴Moses sent messengers from Kadesh to the king of Edom, "Thus says your brother Israel: You know all the adversity that

twice due to lack of faith, instead of once (cf. vv. 11–12) or in the fact that they struck the rock whereas God had told them to speak to the rock (cf. v. 8)—although in Exodus 17:6 Moses was in fact told to hit it. In v. 24 we are told it was a sin of rebellion, and in Psalm 106:32–33 it says that Moses "spoke words that were rash". In Deuteronomy 1:37 and elsewhere, the punishment inflicted on Moses is, however, attributed to the people's disobedience. At any event, the event is recounted here, just before the narrating of the death of Aaron (as it will also be mentioned in Deuteronomy 32:51 before the account of Moses' death). Here the episode is connected with two place-names—Kadesh, which means in fact "holiness" and which would remind people of the

holiness of God (cf. v. 13), and Meribah, which means "rebellion" and would evoke Moses' sin. The two names appear linked (Meri-bath-kadesh) in Deuteronomy 32:51 and Exodus 47:19.

This rock prefigured Christ, according to 1 Corinthians 10:4–5. The Fathers gave an allegorical interpretation: the rock is Jesus, and the water the grace which flows from the open side of our Lord; the double strike stands for the two beams of the cross. Moses stands for the Jews, because just as Moses doubted and struck the rock, the Jewish people crucified Christ, not believing that he was the Son of God (cf. St Augustine, *Contra Faustum*, 16, 15; *Questiones in Heptateuchum*, 35).

20:14–21. Chapters 13–14 already

tuus; et loquimini ad petram coram eis, et illa dabit aquas. Cumque eduxeris aquam de petra, potabit congregationem et iumenta eius» ⁹Tulit igitur Moyses virgam, quae erat in conspectu Domini, sicut praeceperat ei. ¹⁰Et congregaverunt Moyses et Aaron populum ante petram, dixitque eis: «Audite, rebelles; num de petra hac vobis aquam poterimus eicere?». ¹¹Cumque elevasset Moyses manum percutiens virga bis silicem, egressae sunt aquae largissimae, ita ut populus biberet et iumenta. ¹²Dixitque Dominus ad Moysen et Aaron: «Quia non credidistis mihi, ut sanctificaretis me coram filiis Israel, non introducetis hos populos in terram, quam dabo eis». ¹³Haec sunt aquae Meriba, ubi iurgati sunt filii

l. That is *Contention*

has befallen us: [15]how our fathers went down to Egypt, and we
dwelt in Egypt a long time; and the Egyptians dealt harshly with
Ex 23:20 us and our fathers; [16]and when we cried to the LORD, he heard our
voice, and sent an angel and brought us forth out of Egypt; and
here we are in Kadesh, a city on the edge of your territory. [17]Now
let us pass through your land. We will not pass through field or
vineyard, neither will we drink water from a well; we will go
along the King's Highway, we will not turn aside to the right hand
or to the left, until we have passed through your territory." [18]But
Edom said to him, "You shall not pass through, lest I come out
with the sword against you." [19]And the people of Israel said to
him, "We will go up by the highway; and if we drink of your
water, I and my cattle, then I will pay for it; let me only pass
through on foot, nothing more." [20]But he said, "You shall not pass
through." And Edom came out against them with many men, and
with a strong force. [21]Thus Edom refused to give Israel passage
through his territory; so Israel turned away from him.

explained why the Israelites did not enter
Canaan directly by following the route
from Egypt to Beer-sheba and Hebron
(cf. 14:26–38). Another difficulty is mentioned here which forced them yet again
to avoid the shortest route. Because
Edom blocked their way, they had to skirt
the country of the Edomites, going south
again, towards the gulf of Akabah (cf.
21:4), so as to enter the Land from the
other side of the Jordan.

Edom was the nation descended from
Esau, just as Israel came from Jacob. So,
they were brother nations; but there was
a traditional enmity between them, as can

be seen even in the story of their ancestors (cf. Gen 32). To Edom Israel depicts
its own history as a "history of salvation"
(cf. vv. 15–16), but Edom will not listen
and refuses to open a corridor. Israel,
however, keeps on going, but by another
route, undeterred by difficulty.

20:22–29. It is not possible to say exactly
where Aaron died (the place-name given
in Deuteronomy is Moserah). However,
the main thing in this passage is the fact
that God passes Aaron's priesthood to his
son through the rite of the transfer of garments (cf. Deut 10:6).

Israel contra Dominum, et sanctificatus est in eis. [14]Misit nuntios Moyses de Cades ad regem Edom,
qui dicerent: «Haec mandat frater tuus Israel: Nosti omnem laborem, qui apprehendit nos, [15]quomodo
descenderint patres nostri in Aegyptum, et habitaverimus ibi multo tempore, afflixerintque nos Aegyptii
et patres nostros, [16]et quomodo clamaverimus ad Dominum, et exaudierit nos miseritque angelum, qui
eduxerit nos de Aegypto. Ecce nos in urbe Cades, quae est in extremis finibus tuis, positi [17]obsecramus,
ut nobis transire liceat per terram tuam: non ibimus per agros nec per vineas, non bibemus aquas de
puteis tuis; sed gradiemur via regia, nec ad dexteram nec ad sinistram declinantes, donec transeamus
terminos tuos». [18]Cui respondit Edom: «Non transibis per me, alioquin armatus occurram tibi».
[19]Dixeruntque filii Israel: «Per tritam gradiemur viam et, si biberimus aquas tuas ego et pecora mea,
dabo, quod iustum est: nulla erit in pretio difficultas; tantum velociter transeamus». [20]At ille respondit:
«Non transibis!». Statimque egressus est obvius cum infinita multitudine et manu forti, [21]nec voluit
acquiescere Israeli, ut concederet transitum per fines suos; quam ob rem divertit ab eo Israel. [22]Cumque

PART THREE

From Kadesh to Moab

The death of Aaron
Num 33:38–39
Deut 10:6

²²And they journeyed from Kadesh, and the people of Israel, the whole congregation, came to Mount Hor. ²³And the LORD said to Moses and Aaron at Mount Hor, on the border of the land of Edom, ²⁴"Aaron shall be gathered to his people; for he shall not enter the land which I have given to the people of Israel, because you rebelled against my command at the waters of Meribah. ²⁵Take Aaron and Eleazar his son, and bring them up to Mount Hor; ²⁶and strip Aaron of his garments, and put them upon Eleazar his son; and Aaron shall be gathered to his people, and shall die there." ²⁷Moses did as the LORD commanded; and they went up Mount Hor in the sight of all the congregation. ²⁸And Moses [Deut 10:6] stripped Aaron of his garments, and put them upon Eleazar his son; and Aaron died there on the top of the mountain. Then Moses and Eleazar came down from the mountain. ²⁹And when all the congregation saw that Aaron was dead, all the house of Israel wept for Aaron thirty days.

The destruction of the Aradites
Num 31:1–53
Judg 1:16–17

21 ¹When the Canaanite, the king of Arad, who dwelt in the Negeb, heard that Israel was coming by the way of

---

21:1–3. On top of grief at losing one of its leaders comes this attack from an outsider; but Israel seeks the Lord's help and comes out victorious. The capture of this city takes on special significance: it is the first-fruits of the victory over the Canaanites, and it comes prior to the long trek to Moab.

The name of the city, Hormah, is linked to the custom of the anathema (in Hebrew, *jerem*). (Regarding the anathema cf. 31:1–53.) It has to do with the

---

castra movissent de Cades, venerunt in montem Hor, ²³ubi locutus est Dominus ad Moysen et Aaron in monte Hor, qui est in finibus terrae Edom: ²⁴«Congregabitur, inquit, Aaron ad populum suum. Non enim intrabit terram, quam dedi filiis Israel, eo quod rebelles fuistis ori meo ad aquas Meriba. ²⁵Tolle Aaron et Eleazarum filium eius cum eo et duces eos in montem Hor. ²⁶Cumque nudaveris patrem veste sua, indues ea Eleazarum filium eius: Aaron colligetur et morietur ibi». ²⁷Fecit Moyses, ut praeceperat Dominus, et ascenderunt in montem Hor coram omni congregatione. ²⁸Cumque Aaron spoliasset vestibus suis, induit eis Eleazarum filium eius. Illo mortuo in montis supercilio, descendit cum Eleazaro. ²⁹Omnis autem congregatio videns occubuisse Aaron flevit super eo triginta diebus tota domus Israel. ¹Quod cum audisset Chananaeus rex Arad, qui habitabat in Nageb, venisse scilicet Israel per viam Atarim, pugnavit contra illum et duxit ex eo captivos. ²At Israel voto se Domino obligans ait:

Atharim, he fought against Israel, and took some of them captive.
Josh 6:17 ²And Israel vowed a vow to the LORD, and said, "If thou wilt
indeed give this people into my hand, then I will utterly destroy
1 Cor 12:3 their cities." ³And the LORD hearkened to the voice of Israel, and
gave over the Canaanites; and they utterly destroyed them and
their cities; so the name of the place was called Hormah.ᵐ

Wis 16:5–12
Jn 3:14–15 **The bronze serpent**
⁴From Mount Hor they set out by the way to the Red Sea, to go
around the land of Edom; and the people became impatient on the
Ex 14:11 way. ⁵And the people spoke against God and against Moses,
1 Cor 19:9 "Why have you brought us up out of Egypt to die in the wilderness? For there is no food and no water, and we loathe this worth-
Deut 8:15 less food." ⁶Then the LORD sent fiery serpents among the people,
1 Cor 10:9 and they bit the people, so that many people of Israel died. ⁷And
Ex 32:11 the people came to Moses, and said, "We have sinned, for we

---

idea that war booty belongs to God and
therefore must not benefit the victors: it
should be destroyed to show that it is
dedicated to the Lord.

21:4–9. The people continue to complain
against Moses, this time because they
have to go right around Edom. But their
protest is also directed against God.
When they are punished, Moses once
again intercedes on their behalf. The
events covered in this account may have
taken place in the region of Araba, where
copper mines existed from the 13th century BC onwards. In the town now called
Timna, an Egyptian shrine has been
unearthed which contained a copper serpent, indicating that some sort of magical
power was attributed to these serpents.

This passage in Numbers is interpreted in Wisdom 16:5–12, where the
point is emphasized that it was not the
bronze serpent that cured them but the
mercy of God; the serpent was a sign of
the salvation which God offers all men.
The bronze serpent is mentioned later, in
the Gospel, as typifying Christ raised up
on the cross, the cause of salvation for
those who look at him with faith: "As
Moses lifted up the serpent in the
wilderness, so must the Son of man be
lifted up; that whosoever believes in him
may have eternal life" (Jn 3:14–15).
When Christ is raised above all human
things, he draws them towards himself;
so his glorification is the means whereby
all mankind obtain healing for ever
more.

«Si tradideris populum istum in manu mea, delebo urbes eius». ³Exaudivitque Dominus preces Israel
et tradidit Chananaeum, quem ille interfecit, subversis urbibus eius, et vocavit nomen loci illius Horma.
⁴Profecti sunt autem et de monte Hor per viam, quae ducit ad mare Rubrum, ut circumirent terram
Edom. Et taedere coepit populus itineris. ⁵Locutusque contra Deum et Moysen ait: «Cur eduxisti nos
de Aegypto, ut moreremur in solitudine? Deest panis, non sunt aquae; anima nostra iam nauseat super
cibo isto levissimo». ⁶Quam ob rem misit Dominus in populum ignitos serpentes, qui mordebant populum, et mortuus est populus multus ex Israel. ⁷Et venerunt ad Moysen atque dixerunt: «Peccavimus,

m. Heb *Destruction*

have spoken against the LORD and against you; pray to the LORD, that he take away the serpents from us." So Moses prayed for the people. ⁸And the LORD said to Moses, "Make a fiery serpent, and set it on a pole; and every one who is bitten, when he sees it, shall live." ⁹So Moses made a bronze serpent, and set it on a pole; and if a serpent bit any man, he would look at the bronze serpent and live.*

2 Kings 18:4
Wis 16:5ff
Jn 3:14ff

Movements in the region of Moab

¹⁰And the people of Israel set out, and encamped in Oboth. ¹¹And they set out from Oboth, and encamped at Iye-abarim, in the wilderness which is opposite Moab, toward the sunrise. ¹²From there they set out, and encamped in the Valley of Zered. ¹³From there they set out, and encamped on the other side of the Arnon, which is in the wilderness, that extends from the boundary of the Amorites; for the Arnon is the boundary of Moab, between Moab and the Amorites. ¹⁴Wherefore it is said in the Book of the Wars of the LORD,

Num 20:23

> "Waheb in Suphah,
> and the valleys of the Arnon,
> ¹⁵and the slope of the valleys
> that extends to the seat of Ar,
> and leans to the border of Moab."

21:10–20. Nomadic shepherds had the custom of celebrating a newly dug water-hole. The lyrical tone the text takes on here evidences the joy the people feel as they near the promised land. *Beer* (v. 16) means "well"; the song shows the people's joy at having all the water they need.

It is not possible to say exactly what route they took, or how much time they spent, on the way from Kadesh to the plains of Moab. According to Deuteronomy 2:14, they spend thirty-eight years on this journey; that figure does not seem to include the time spent going from Sinai to Kadesh. On this, see the "Introduction" (pp. 521ff above). It seems reasonable to suppose that during this period they lived the life of nomadic shepherds.

---

quia locuti sumus contra Dominum et te; ora, ut tollat a nobis serpentes». Oravitque Moyses pro populo. ⁸Et locutus est Dominus ad eum: «Fac serpentem ignitum et pone eum pro signo: qui percussus aspexerit eum, vivet». ⁹Fecit ergo Moyses serpentem aeneum et posuit eum pro signo; quem cum percussi aspicerent, sanabantur. ¹⁰Profectique filii Israel castrametati sunt in Oboth, ¹¹unde egressi fixere tentoria in Ieabarim, in solitudine, quae respicit Moab contra orientalem plagam. ¹²Et inde moventes venerunt ad torrentem Zared; ¹³quem relinquentes castrametati sunt ultra Arnon, qui est in deserto, quod prominet de finibus Amorraei. Siquidem Arnon terminus est Moab dividens Moabitas et Amorraeos. ¹⁴Unde dicitur in libro bellorum Domini: «Vaheb in Supha et torrentes Arnon. / ¹⁵Scopuli torrentium inclinati sunt / in habitationem Ar / et recumbunt in finibus Moabitarum». ¹⁶Ex eo loco in Beer. Hic est puteus, super quo locutus est Dominus ad Moysen: «Congrega populum, et dabo ei

¹⁶And from there they continued to Beer;[n] that is the well of which the LORD said to Moses, "Gather the people together, and I Jn 4:1 will give them water." ¹⁷Then Israel sang this song:

"Spring up, O well!—Sing to it!—
¹⁸the well which the princes dug,
which the nobles of the people
delved with the scepter and with their staves."

And from the wilderness they went on to Mattanah, ¹⁹and from Mattanah to Nahaliel, and from Nahaliel to Bamoth, ²⁰and from Bamoth to the valley lying in the region of Moab by the top of Pisgah which looks down upon the desert.[o]

Deut 2:26–3:11
Judg 11:19–20 **Sihon and Og defeated**

²¹Then Israel sent messengers to Sihon king of the Amorites, saying, ²²"Let me pass through your land; we will not turn aside into field or vineyard; we will not drink the water of a well; we will go by the King's Highway, until we have passed through your territory." ²³But Sihon would not allow Israel to pass through his territory. He gathered all his men together, and went out against Israel to the wilderness, and came to Jahaz, and Num 20:23 fought against Israel. ²⁴And Israel slew him with the edge of the sword, and took possession of his land from the Arnon to the Jabbok, as far as to the Ammonites; for Jazer was the boundary

---

21:21–35. This small Canaanite kingdom, to the north of Arnon, in Transjordan, was the first territory the Israelites captured, a kind of foretaste of their conquest of the promised Land. Hence the importance that this victory over Sihon, king of the Amorites, will take on in biblical traditions. The conquered territory was occupied by the

tribes of Reuben and Gad (cf. chap. 32). After this victory, we are told about the victory over Og, the king of Bashan (referred to in Deuteronomy 2:26—3:11). The scale of these victories was God's response to the obstinacy these kingdoms showed by putting obstacles in the way of his plan (for Israel to enter the promised land).

---

aquam». ¹⁷Tunc cecinit Israel carmen istud: «Ascendat puteus. Concinite ei. / ¹⁸Puteus, quem foderunt principes / et paraverunt duces populi / in sceptris et in baculis suis». De solitudine in Matthana; ¹⁹de Matthana in Nahaliel; de Nahaliel in Bamoth; ²⁰de Bamoth in vallem, quae est in regione Moab in vertice Phasga, qui respicit contra desertum. ²¹Misit autem Israel nuntios ad Sehon regem Amorraeorum dicens: ²²«Obsecro, ut transire mihi liceat per terram tuam: non declinabimus in agros et vineas, non bibemus aquas ex puteis. Via regia gradiemur, donec transeamus terminos tuos». ²³Qui concedere noluit, ut transiret Israel per fines suos; quin potius, populo congregato, egressus est obviam in desertum et venit in Iasa pugnavitque contra Israel. ²⁴A quo percussus est in ore gladii, et possessa est terra eius ab Arnon usque Iaboc et filios Ammon; quia forti praesidio tenebantur termini Ammonitarum. ²⁵Tulit ergo Israel omnes civitates eius et habitavit in urbibus Amorraei, in Hesebon scilicet et viculis

n. That is *Well* **o.** Or *Jeshimon*

608

of the Ammonites.ᵖ ²⁵And Israel took all these cities, and Israel settled in all the cities of the Amorites, in Heshbon, and in all its villages. ²⁶For Heshbon was the city of Sihon the king of the Amorites, who had fought against the former king of Moab and taken all his land out of his hand, as far as the Arnon. Therefore the ballad singers say,

²⁷"Come to Heshbon, let it be built,
    let the city of Sihon be established.
²⁸For fire went forth from Heshbon,
    flame from the city of Sihon.
It devoured Ar of Moab,
    the lords of the heights of the Arnon.
²⁹Woe to you, O Moab!
    You are undone, O people of Chemosh!
He has made his sons fugitives,
    and his daughters captives,
    to an Amorite king, Sihon.
³⁰So their posterity perished from Heshbon,�q
    as far as Dibon, and we laid waste until fire spread to
    Medeba."ʳ

³¹Thus Israel dwelt in the land of the Amorites. ³²And Moses sent to spy out Jazer; and they took its villages, and dispossessed the Amorites that were there. ³³Then they turned and went up by the way to Bashan; and Og the king of Bashan came out against them, he and all his people, to battle at Edre-i. ³⁴But the LORD said to Moses, "Do not fear him; for I have given him into your hand, and all his people, and his land; and you shall do to him as you did to Sihon king of the Amorites, who dwelt at Heshbon." ³⁵So they slew him, and his sons, and all his people, until there was not one survivor left to him; and they possessed his land.

Deut 3:1–17

eius. ²⁶Hesebon enim erat urbs Sehon regis Amorraei, qui pugnavit contra primum regem Moab et tulit omnem terram, quae dicionis illius fuerat usque Arnon. ²⁷Idcirco dicitur in proverbio: «Venite in Hesebon! / Aedificetur et construatur civitas Sehon! / ²⁸Ignis egressus est de Hesebon, / flamma de oppido Sehon / et devoravit Ar Moabitarum / et deglutivit excelsa Arnon. / ²⁹Vae tibi, Moab, / peristi, popule Chamos! / Dedit filios eius in fugam / et filias in captivitatem / regi Amorraeorum Sehon. / ³⁰Iecimus sagittas in eos, / disperiit Hesebon usque Dibon. / Vastavimus usque Nophe / et usque Medaba». ³¹Habitavit itaque Israel in terra Amorraei. ³²Misitque Moyses, qui explorarent Iazer, cuius ceperunt viculos et expulerunt Amorraeos, qui erant ibi. ³³Verteruntque se et ascenderunt per viam Basan, et occurrit eis Og rex Basan cum omni populo suo pugnaturus in Edrai. ³⁴Dixitque Dominus ad Moysen: «Ne timeas eum, quia in manu tua tradidi illum et omnem populum ac terram eius, faciesque illi, sicut fecisti Sehon regi Amorraeorum habitatori Hesebon». ³⁵Percusserunt igitur et hunc cum filiis suis universumque populum eius usque ad internectionem; et possederunt terram illius. ¹Profectique

p. Gk: Heb *the boundary of the Ammonites was strong* **q.** Gk: Heb *we have shot at them. Heshbon has perished* **r.** Compare Sam and Gk: Heb *we have laid waste to Mophah which to Medebah*

PART FOUR

Israel on the Plains of Moab*

Deut 23:5–6
Josh 24:9–10
2 Pet 2:15–16
Jude 11
Rev 2:14

9. THE STORY OF BALAAM*

Balak calls in Balaam

22 [1]Then the people of Israel set out, and encamped in the plains of Moab beyond the Jordan at Jericho. [2]And Balak the son of Zippor saw all that Israel had done to the Amorites. [3]And Moab was in great dread of the people, because they were Ex 2:15 many; Moab was overcome with fear of the people of Israel. [4]And

---

*22:1—36:13. The rest of the book of Numbers and all of Deuteronomy is taken up with accounts of events on the plains of Moab, in front of Jericho, a city which would be the gateway to the promised land. Taken together, they describe at length the detailed preparations the Israelites made prior to crossing the Jordan.

*22:1—24:25. The account of Israel's stay in Moab begins with the oracles of Balaam, in which its glorious future is painted. The editor has produced an extensive narrative which is an important piece of the Bible.

Joyful acknowledgment of God's special love for his people underlies the whole story of Balaam. That the initiative comes from God is emphasized by the fact that he chooses a soothsayer who is not an Israelite and that he causes Balaam to make prophecies which, contrary to what one would have expected, are increasingly favourable to Israel.

Balaam is typical of the soothsayers and utterers of curses for which Mesopot-

amia was famous (that was where the king of Moab's messengers went to obtain his services: cf. 22:5). It is surprising that he should know the God of Israel, Yahweh, and speak with him; but this detail serves to highlight that the God of Israel is also the Lord of pagan magi and can use even them to make his plans known. Besides, the story of Balaam taken as a whole shows that God saves his people from both foreign armies and from the dark forces of magic.

The main thing about the passage is the four oracles spoken by Balaam in which Israel's glorious future is linked to the fact that God is its special protector— oracles in which we can glimpse the figure of the Messiah King. These oracles, which are couched in the form of poetry, may have originally come from an ancient collection of oracles against Moab; they are very similar to a literary style developed later by the prophets.

22:4. Midian was a group of nomadic tribes which moved around the south of Moab and around Edom, but which also

---

castrametati sunt filii Israel in campestribus Moab, ubi trans Iordanem Iericho sita est. [2]Videns autem Balac filius Sephor omnia, quae fecerat Israel Amorraeo, [3]valde metuit Moab populum, quia multus

Moab said to the elders of Midian, "This horde will now lick up all that is round about us, as the ox licks up the grass of the field. "So Balak the son of Zippor, who was king of Moab at that time, ⁵sent messengers to Balaam the son of Beor at Pethor, which is near the River, in the land of Amaw to call him, saying, "Behold, a people has come out of Egypt; they cover the face of the earth, and they are dwelling opposite me. ⁶Come now, curse this people for me, since they are too mighty for me; perhaps I shall be able to defeat them and drive them from the land; for I know that he whom you bless is blessed, and he whom you curse is cursed."

⁷So the elders of Moab and the elders of Midian departed with the fees for divination in their hand; and they came to Balaam, and gave him Balak's message. ⁸And he said to them, "Lodge here this night, and I will bring back word to you, as the LORD speaks to me"; so the princes of Moab stayed with Balaam. ⁹And God came to Balaam and said, "Who are these men with you?" ¹⁰And Balaam said to God, "Balak the son of Zippor, king of Moab, has sent to me, saying, ¹¹'Behold, a people has come out of Egypt, and it covers the face of the earth; now come, curse them for me; perhaps I shall be able to fight against them and drive them out.'" ¹²God said to Balaam, "You shall not go with them; you shall not curse the people, for they are blessed." ¹³So Balaam rose in the morning, and said to the princes of Balak, "Go to your

1 Sam 9:7

---

made incursions further north (cf. Judg 6:1–6): this explains their presence at this place. It was to a group of Midianite traders that Joseph was sold (cf. Gen 37:28), and it was with Midianites that Moses lived after he fled from the pharaoh (cf. Ex 2:11–22). Later on, the Midianites will settle to the east of the gulf of Akabah.

22:6. In the cultural context of the ancient Middle East a curse or a blessing was considered to take instant effect, especially when it came from someone in authority, as for example from the father of a family (cf. Gen 27:37). In the case of Balaam his words were thought to be exceptionally effective.

erat. Et cum pertimeret Moab filios Israel, ⁴dixit ad maiores natu Madian: «Nunc carpet haec congregatio omnem regionem per circuitum, quomodo solet bos herbas campi carpere». Balac filius Sephor erat eo tempore rex in Moab. ⁵Misit ergo nuntios ad Balaam filium Beor in Phethor, quae est super flumen in terra filiorum Ammau, ut vocarent eum et dicerent: «Ecce egressus est populus ex Aegypto, qui operuit superficiem terrae sedens contra me. ⁶Veni igitur et maledic populo huic, quia fortior me est; si quo modo possim percutere et eicere eum de terra mea. Novi enim quod benedictus sit, cui benedixeris, et maledictus, in quem maledicta congesseris». ⁷Perrexeruntque seniores Moab et maiores natu Madian habentes divinationis pretium in manibus. Cumque venissent ad Balaam et narrassent ei omnia verba Balac, ⁸ille respondit: «Manete hic nocte, et respondebo quidquid mihi dixerit Dominus». Manentibus illis apud Balaam, ⁹venit Deus et ait ad eum: «Quid sibi volunt homines isti apud te?». ¹⁰Respondit: «Balac filius Sephor rex Moabitarum misit ad me ¹¹dicens: 'Ecce populus, qui egressus est de Aegypto, operuit superficiem terrae; veni et maledic ei pro me, si quo modo possim pugnans abigere eum'». ¹²Dixitque Deus ad Balaam: «Noli ire cum eis, neque maledicas populo, quia benedic-

own land; for the LORD has refused to let me go with you." ¹⁴So the princes of Moab rose and went to Balak, and said, "Balaam refuses to come with us."

¹⁵Once again Balak sent princes, more in number and more Acts 9:38 honorable than they. ¹⁶And they came to Balaam and said to him, "Thus says Balak the son of Zippor: 'Let nothing hinder you from coming to me; ¹⁷for I will surely do you great honor, and whatever you say to me I will do; come, curse this people for me.'" ¹⁸But Balaam answered and said to the servants of Balak, "Though Balak were to give me his house full of silver and gold, I could not go beyond the command of the LORD my God, to do less or more. ¹⁹Pray, now, tarry here this night also, that I may know what more the LORD will say to me." ²⁰And God came to Balaam at night and said to him, "If the men have come to call you, rise, go with them; but only what I bid you, that shall you do."

²¹So Balaam rose in the morning, and saddled his ass, and went with the princes of Moab.

Balaam's ass

²²But God's anger was kindled because he went; and the angel of the LORD took his stand in the way as his adversary. Now he was riding on the ass, and his two servants were with him. ²³And the ass saw the angel of the Lord standing in the road, with a drawn sword in his hand; and the ass turned aside out of the road, and went into the field; and Balaam struck the ass, to turn her into the road. ²⁴Then the angel of the LORD stood in a narrow path between

---

22:20. Earlier, in v. 12, God forbade Balaam to curse Israel as Balak had asked him to do. Now, however, God tells him to go with Barak's messengers, thus using him to further his own (God's) plans, not those of Balaam himself (who is interested only in money) or those of Balak.

---

tus est». ¹³Qui mane consurgens dixit ad principes: «Ite in terram vestram, quia prohibuit me Dominus venire vobiscum». ¹⁴Reversi principes dixerunt ad Balac: «Noluit Balaam venire nobiscum». ¹⁵Rursum ille multo plures et nobiliores, quam ante miserat, misit. ¹⁶Qui, cum venissent ad Balaam, dixerunt: «Sic dicit Balac filius Sephor: 'Ne cuncteris venire ad me; ¹⁷paratus sum honorare te et, quidquid volueris, dabo tibi. Veni et maledic pro me populo isti'».¹⁸Respondit Balaam: «Si dederit mihi Balac plenam domum suam argenti et auri, non potero transgredi verbum Domini Dei mei, ut vel plus vel minus loquar. ¹⁹Obsecro, ut hic maneatis etiam hac nocte, et scire queam quid mihi rursum respondeat Dominus». ²⁰Venit ergo Deus ad Balaam nocte et ait ei: «Si vocare te venerunt homines isti, surge et vade cum eis, ita dumtaxat, ut, quod tibi praecepero, facias». ²¹Surrexit Balaam mane et, strata asina sua, profectus est cum eis. ²²Et iratus est Deus, cum profectus esset; stetitque angelus Domini in via contra Balaam, ut adversaretur ei, qui insidebat asinae et duos pueros habebat secum. ²³Cernens asina angelum Domini stantem in via, evaginato gladio in manu sua, avertit se de itinere et ibat per agrum. Quam cum verberaret Balaam et vellet ad semitam reducere, ²⁴stetit angelus Domini in angustiis duarum maceriarum, quibus vineae cingebantur. ²⁵Quem videns asina iunxit se parieti et attrivit seden-

the vineyards, with a wall on either side. ²⁵And when the ass saw the angel of the LORD, she pushed against the wall, and pressed Balaam's foot against the wall; so he struck her again. ²⁶Then the angel of the LORD went ahead, and stood in a narrow place, where there was no way to turn either to the right or to the left. ²⁷When the ass saw the angel of the LORD, she lay down under Balaam; and Balaam's anger was kindled, and he struck the ass with his staff. ²⁸Then the LORD opened the mouth of the ass, and she said to Balaam, "What have I done to you, that you have struck me these three times?" ²⁹And Balaam said to the ass, "Because you have made sport of me. I wish I had a sword in my hand, for then I would kill you." ³⁰And the ass said to Balaam, "Am I not your ass, upon which you have ridden all your life long to this day? Was I ever accustomed to do so to you?" And he said, "No."

²Pet 2:16

³¹Then the LORD opened the eyes of Balaam, and he saw the angel of the LORD standing in the way, with his drawn sword in his hand; and he bowed his head, and fell on his face. ³²And the angel of the LORD said to him, "Why have you struck your ass these three times? Behold, I have come forth to withstand you, because your way is perverse before me; ³³and the ass saw me, and turned aside before me these three times. If she had not turned aside from me, surely just now I would have slain you and let her live." ³⁴Then Balaam said to the angel of the LORD, "I have sinned, for I did not know that thou didst stand in the road against me. Now therefore, if it is evil in thy sight, I will go back again." ³⁵And the angel of the LORD said to Balaam, "Go with the men; but only the

---

22:31–33. The ass seems to have more sense than Balaam. There is an implied dismissiveness here towards the power of magic. Just as in the rest of the account, the point is plainly made that God is the one who guides events. It makes no sense to try to put into effect plans which run contrary to God's: any such attempt is bound to fail.

---

tis pedem. At ille iterum verberabat eam; ²⁶et angelus Domini iterum transiens ad locum angustum, ubi nec ad dexteram nec ad sinistram poterat deviare, obvius stetit. ²⁷Cumque vidisset asina stantem angelum Domini, concidit sub pedibus sedentis; qui iratus vehementius caedebat fuste latera eius. ²⁸Aperuitque Dominus os asinae, et locuta est: «Quid feci tibi? Cur percutis me ecce iam tertio?». ²⁹Respondit Balaam: «Quia illusisti mihi. Utinam haberem gladium, ut te interficerem!». ³⁰Dixit asina: «Nonne animal tuum sum, cui semper sedere consuevisti usque in praesentem diem? Dic quid simile umquam fecerim tibi». At ille ait: «Numquam». ³¹Protinus aperuit Dominus oculos Balaam, et vidit angelum Domini stantem in via, evaginato gladio in manu eius; adoravitque eum pronus in terram. ³²Cui angelus Domini: «Cur, inquit, tertio verberas asinam tuam? Ego veni, ut adversarer tibi, quia perversa est via tua mihique contraria. ³³Et videns me asina declinavit ter a me; nisi declinasset, te occidissem et illam vivam reliquissem». ³⁴Dixit Balaam: «Peccavi nesciens quod tu stares contra me in via; et nunc, si displicet tibi, revertar». ³⁵Ait angelus Domini: «Vade cum istis et cave, ne aliud, quam praecepero tibi, loquaris». Ivit igitur cum principibus Balac. ³⁶Quod cum audisset Balac, venisse scilicet

word which I bid you, that shall you speak." So Balaam went on with the princes of Balak.*

³⁶When Balak heard that Balaam had come, he went out to meet him at the city of Moab, on the boundary formed by the Arnon, at the extremity of the boundary· ³⁷And Balak said to Balaam, "Did I not send to you to call you? Why did you not come to me? Am I not able to honour you?" ³⁸Balaam said to Balak, "Lo, I have come to you! Have I now any power at all to speak anything? The word that God puts in my mouth, that must I speak." ³⁹Then Balaam went with Balak, and they came to Kiriath-huzoth· ⁴⁰And Balak sacrificed oxen and sheep, and sent to Balaam and to the princes who were with him.

⁴¹And on the morrow Balak took Balaam and brought him up to Bamoth-baal; and from there he saw the nearest of the people.

Balaam's first oracle

23 ¹And Balaam said to Balak, "Build for me here seven altars, and provide for me here seven bulls and seven rams." ²Balak did as Balaam had said; and Balak and Balaam offered on each altar a bull and a ram. ³And Balaam said to Balak, "Stand beside your burnt offering, and I will go; perhaps the LORD will come to meet me; and whatever he shows me I will tell you." And he went to a bare height. ⁴And God met Balaam; and Balaam said to him, "I have prepared the seven altars, and I have offered upon each altar a bull and a ram." ⁵And the LORD put a word in Balaam's mouth, and said, "Return to Balak, and thus you shall speak." ⁶And he returned to him, and lo, he and all the princes of Moab were standing beside his burnt offering. ⁷And Balaam took up his discourse, and said,

---

22:40. This sacrifice was offered with a view to a communion meal between Balaam and Balak. However, the sacrifice that the text goes on to mention (cf. 23:2) is a burnt offering which prepares the way for God to make himself manifest.

23:7–10. Balaam will make three attempts to curse Israel, each time taking

Balaam, egressus est in occursum eius in Irmoab, quod situm est in extremis finibus Arnon; ³⁷dixitque ad Balaam: «Nonne misi nuntios, ut vocarem te? Cur non statim venisti ad me? An quia honorare te nequeo?». ³⁸Cui ille respondit: «Ecce adsum; numquid loqui potero aliud, nisi quod Deus posuerit in ore meo?». ³⁹Perrexerunt ergo simul et venerunt in Cariathusoth. ⁴⁰Cumque occidisset Balac boves et oves, misit ad Balaam et principes, qui cum eo erant. ⁴¹Mane autem facto, duxit eum ad excelsa Baal et intuitus est extremam partem populi. ¹Dixitque Balaam ad Balac: «Aedifica mihi hic septem aras et para totidem vitulos eiusdemque numeri arietes». ²Cumque fecisset iuxta sermonem Balaam, imposuerunt vitulum et arietem super aram. ³Dixitque Balaam ad Balac: «Sta paulisper iuxta holocaustum tuum, donec vadam, si forte occurrat mihi Dominus; et, quodcumque imperaverit, loquar tibi».

"From Aram Balak has brought me,
   the king of Moab from the eastern mountains:
'Come, curse Jacob for me,
   and come, denounce Israel!'
[8]How can I curse whom God has not cursed?
   How can I denounce whom the LORD has not denounced?
[9]For from the top of the mountains I see him,
   from the hills I behold him;
lo, a people dwelling alone,
   and not reckoning itself among the nations!
[10]Who can count the dust of Jacob,
   or number the fourth part[s] of Israel?
Let me die the death of the righteous,
   and let my end be like his!"
[11]And Balak said to Balaam, "What have you done to me? I took you to curse my enemies, and behold, you have done nothing but bless them." [12]And he answered, "Must I not take heed to speak what the LORD puts in my mouth?"

Ex 19:5
Deut 33:28

Gen 13:16;
15:5

Balaam's second oracle
[13]And Balak said to him, "Come with me to another place, from which you may see them; you shall see only the nearest of them, and shall not see them all; then curse them for me from there." [14]And he took him to the field of Zophim, to the top of Pisgah,

---

a different vantage-point so he can see as many of the people as possible. But in fact he pronounces three blessings, not curses. The first oracle, which begins with a reference to the background, high-lights Israel's status as God's chosen people, different from other nations (cf. Ex 19:5), and in which God's promise of fruitfulness to Abraham has become a reality (cf. Gen 15:5).

Cumque abiisset in collem nudum, [4]occurrit illi Deus. Locutusque ad eum Balaam: «Septem, inquit, aras erexi et imposui vitulum et arietem desuper». [5]Dominus autem posuit verbum in ore eius et ait: «Revertere ad Balac et haec loqueris». [6]Reversus invenit stantem Balac iuxta holocaustum suum et omnes principes Moabitarum; [7]assumptaque parabola sua, dixit: «De Aram adduxit me Balac, / rex Moabitarum de montibus orientis: / 'Veni, inquit, et maledic pro me Iacob; / propera et detestare Israel!'. / [8]Quomodo maledicam, cui non maledixit Deus? / Qua ratione detester, quem Dominus non detestatur? / [9]De summis silicibus video eum / et de collibus considero illum: / populus solus habitabit / et inter gentes non reputabitur. / [10]Et quis dinumerare possit pulverem Iacob / et quis numeravit arenam Israel? / Moriatur anima mea morte iustorum, / et fiant novissima mea horum similia». [11]Dixitque Balac ad Balaam: «Quid est hoc, quod agis? Ut malediceres inimicis meis, vocavi te, et tu e contrario benedicis eis!». [12]Cui ille respondit: «Num aliud possum loqui, nisi quod iusserit Dominus?». [13]Dixit ergo Balac: «Veni mecum in alterum locum, unde partem Israel videas et totum videre non possis; inde male, dicito ei». [14]Cumque duxisset eum in campum speculatorum super verticem montis Phasga, aedificavit septem aras imposuitque supra vitulum atque arietem. [15]Et dixit

s. Or *dust clouds*

615

and built seven altars, and offered a bull and a ram on each altar. ¹⁵Balaam said to Balak, "Stand here beside your burnt offering, while I meet the LORD yonder." ¹⁶And the LORD met Balaam, and put a word in his mouth, and said, "Return to Balak, and thus shall you speak." ¹⁷And he came to him, and, lo, he was standing beside his burnt offering, and the princes of Moab with him. And Balak said to him, "What has the LORD spoken?" ¹⁸And Balaam took up his discourse, and said,

"Rise, Balak, and hear;
    hearken to me, O son of Zippor:

1 Sam 15:29
Mal 3:6
Rom 11:29
Heb 6:18
Tit 1:2
Jas 1:17

¹⁹God is not man, that he should lie,
    or a son of man, that he should repent.
Has he said, and will he not do it?
    Or has he spoken, and will he not fulfil it?
²⁰Behold, I received a command to bless:
    he has blessed, and I cannot revoke it.
²¹He has not beheld misfortune in Jacob;
    nor has he seen trouble in Israel.
The LORD their God is with them,
    and the shout of a king is among them.

Mt 2:15

²²God brings them out of Egypt;
    they have as it were the horns of the wild ox.
²³For there is no enchantment against Jacob,
    no divination against Israel;
now it shall be said of Jacob and Israel,
    'What has God wrought!'

Gen 49:9

²⁴Behold, a people! As a lioness it rises up
    and as a lion it lifts itself;
it does not lie down till it devours the prey,
    and drinks the blood of the slain."

23:18–34. The second poem recalls the Covenant and Israel's deliverance from Egypt. The lion imagery presages Israel's future victories.

Balaam ad Balac: «Sta hic iuxta holocaustum tuum, donec ego obvius pergam». ¹⁶Cui cum Dominus occurrisset posuissetque verbum in ore eius, ait: «Revertere ad Balac et haec loqueris ei». ¹⁷Reversus invenit eum stantem iuxta holocaustum suum et principes Moabitarum cum eo. Ad quem Balac: «Quid, inquit, locutus est Dominus?». ¹⁸At ille, assumpta parabola sua, ait: «Surge, Balac, et ausculta; / audi, fili Sephor. / ¹⁹Non est Deus quasi homo, ut mentiatur, / nec ut filius hominis, ut mutetur. / Numquid dixit et non faciet? / Locutus est et non implebit? / ²⁰Ad benedicendum adductus sum, / benedictionem prohibere non valeo. / ²¹Non conspicitur malum in Iacob, / nec videtur calamitas in Israel. / Dominus Deus eius cum eo est, / et clangor regis in illo. / ²²Deus eduxit illum de Aegypto, / sicut cornua bubali' est ei. / ²³Non est augurium in Iacob / nec divinatio in Israel. / Temporibus suis dicetur Iacob et Israeli / quid operatus sit Deus. / ²⁴Ecce populus ut leaena consurget, / et quasi leo erigetur; / non accubabit, donec devoret praedam / et occisorum sanguinem bibat». ²⁵Dixitque Balac ad Balaam: «Nec maledi-

²⁵And Balak said to Balaam, "Neither curse them at all, nor bless them at all." ²⁶But Balaam answered Balak, "Did I not tell you, 'All that the LORD says, that I must do'?" ²⁷And Balak said to Balaam, "Come now, I will take you to another place; perhaps it will please God that you may curse them for me from there." ²⁸So Balak took Balaam to the top of Peor, that overlooks the desert.ᵗ ²⁹And Balaam said to Balak, "Build for me here seven altars, and provide for me here seven bulls and seven rams." ³⁰And Balak did as Balaam had said, and offered a bull and a ram on each altar.

Balaam's third oracle

24 ¹When Balaam saw that it pleased the LORD to bless Israel, he did not go, as at other times, to look for omens, but set his face toward the wilderness. ²And Balaam lifted up his eyes, and saw Israel encamping tribe by tribe. And the Spirit of God came upon him, ³and he took up his discourse, and said,

"The oracle of Balaam the son of Beor,
the oracle of the man whose eye is opened,ᵘ
⁴the oracle of him who hears the words of God,   Gen 17:1
who sees the vision of the Almighty,
falling down, but having his eyes uncovered:
⁵how fair are your tents, O Jacob,
your encampments, O Israel!
⁶Like valleys that stretch afar,   Heb 8:2
like gardens beside a river,   Mt 2:15
like aloes that the LORD has planted,
like cedar trees beside the waters.

24:3–9. This third oracle consists not so much in words placed by God on Balaam's lips, as in the vision given to him, which shows the splendour of Israel (expressed in images of luxuriant scenery); it also alludes to a victorious king and recalls, once more, deliverance from Egypt.

cas ei, nec benedicas!». ²⁶Et ille ait: «Nonne dixi tibi quod, quidquid mihi Dominus imperaret, hoc facerem?». ²⁷Et ait Balac ad eum: «Veni, et ducam te ad alium locum, si forte placeat Deo, ut inde maledicas ei». ²⁸Cumque duxisset eum super verticem montis Phegor, qui respicit solitudinem, ²⁹dixit ei Balaam: «Aedifica mihi hic septem aras et para totidem vitulos eiusdemque numeri arietes». ³⁰Fecit Balac, ut Balaam dixerat, imposuitque vitulos et arietes per singulas aras. ¹Cumque vidisset Balaam quod placeret Domino, ut benediceret Israeli, nequaquem abiit, ut ante perrexerat, ut augurium quaereret; sed dirigens contra desertum vultum suum ²et elevans oculos vidit Israel commorantem per tribus suas et, irruente in se spiritu Dei, ³assumpta parabola sua, ait: «Dixit Balaam filius Beor, / dixit homo, cuius apertus est oculus, / ⁴dixit auditor sermonum Dei, / qui visionem omnipotentis intuitus est, / qui cadit, et sic aperiuntur oculi eius. / ⁵Quam pulchra tabernacula tua, Iacob, / et tentoria tua, Israel! / ⁶Ut valles dilatantur, / ut horti iuxta fluvios irrigui, / ut aloe, quam plantavit Dominus, / quasi cedri prope

t. Or *Heshimon* **u.** Or *closed* or *perfect*

Mt 2:15

Gen 49:9

⁷Water shall flow from his buckets,
and his seed shall be in many waters,
his king shall be higher than Agag,
and his kingdom shall be exalted.
⁸God brings him out of Egypt;
he has as it were the horns of the wild ox,
he shall eat up the nations his adversaries,
and shall break their bones in pieces,
and pierce them through with his arrows.
⁹He couched, he lay down like a lion,
and like a lioness; who will rouse him up?
Blessed be every one who blesses you,
and cursed be every one who curses you."

Balaam's fourth oracle

¹⁰And Balak's anger was kindled against Balaam, and he struck his hands together; and Balak said to Balaam, "I called you to curse my enemies, and behold, you have blessed them these three times. ¹¹Therefore now flee to your place; I said, 'I will certainly honor you,' but the LORD has held you back from honor." ¹²And Balaam said to Balak, "Did I not tell your messengers whom you sent to me, ¹³'If Balak should give me his house full of silver and gold, I would not be able to go beyond the word of the LORD, to do either good or bad of my own will; what the LORD speaks, that will I speak'? ¹⁴And now, behold, I am going to my people; come, I will let you know what this people will do to your people in the latter days." ¹⁵And he took up his discourse, and said,

24:15–24. The three blessings are now followed by four oracles about nations—Israel, Amalek, the Kainites and Asshur. The first tells about the coming of a king, symbolized by a star and a sceptre (v. 17). In the ancient East stars were considered to be gods and goddesses. This passage of Numbers may contain a reference to David and his star: in fact, from very early on this text was given a messianic interpretation; Jewish traditions link the coming of the Messiah with the

aquas. ⁷Fluet aqua de situlis eius, / et semen illius erit in aquis multis. / Extolletur super Agag rex eius, / et elevabitur regnum illius. / ⁸Deus eduxit illum de Aegypto, / sicut cornua bubali est ei. / Devorabit gentes, hostes suos, / ossaque eorum confringet / et perforabit sagittis. ⁹Accubans dormit ut leo, / et quasi leaena, quis suscitare illum audebit? / Qui benedixerit tibi, erit et ipse benedictus; / qui maledixerit tibi, maledictus erit!». ¹⁰Iratusque Balac contra Balaam, complosis manibus, ait: «Ad maledicendum inimicis meis vocavi te, quibus iam tertio benedixisti! ¹¹Revertere nunc ad locum tuum! Decreveram quidem magnifice honorare te, sed Dominus privavit te honore disposito». ¹²Respondit Balaam ad Balac: «Nonne iam nuntiis tuis, quos misisti ad me, dixi: ¹³Si dederit mihi Balac plenam domum suam argenti et auri, non potero praeterire sermonem Domini, ut vel boni quid vel mali proferam ex corde meo, sed, quidquid Dominus dixerit, hoc loquar? ¹⁴Et nunc, pergens ad populum meum dabo consilium, quid populus hic populo tuo faciat extremo tempore». ¹⁵Sumpta igitur parabola sua,

"The oracle of Balaam the son of Beor,
   the oracle of the man whose eye is opened,[v]
[16]the oracle of him who hears the words of God,
   and knows the knowledge of the Most High,
who sees the vision of the Almighty,
   falling down, but having his eyes uncovered:
[17]I see him, but not now;
   I behold him, but not nigh:
a star shall come forth out of Jacob,
   and a sceptre shall rise out of Israel;
it shall crush the forehead[w] of Moab,
   and break down all the sons of Sheth.
[18]Edom shall be dispossessed,
   Seir also, his enemies, shall be dispossessed,
   while Israel does valiantly.
[19]By Jacob shall dominion be exercised,
   and the survivors of cities be destroyed!"
[20]Then he looked on Amalek, and took up his discourse, and said,
   "Amalek was the first of the nations,
   but in the end he shall come to destruction."
[21]And he looked on the Kenite, and took up his discourse, and
said,

Gen 49:10
Mt 2:2
Rev 22:16

Num 20:23
Gen 25:23;
27:39

Ex 17:8

---

appearing of a star—cf. some Aramaic translations (*targumin*) of this text. In St Matthew's Gospel there is mention of a star in the episode of the Magi who came to adore Jesus (cf. Mt 2:1–12). And in the second Jewish revolt against Rome (132–135 AD), a famous Jewish teacher, Rabbi Akiba, changed the name of the Jewish leader of the rebellion from Ben Kosheba, to Bar Kokheba, that is, "son of the star"—another indication of the connexion between the star and the expected Messiah.

The Fathers interpreted the star that Balaam speaks about, as being the one the Magi saw. From this they went on to deduce that the Wise Men came from Mesopotamia, which was where Balaam came from.

24:21–22. In the Hebrew this prophecy involves a play on words. The Kainite capital was Kain, a word which in Hebrew means "nest", and thus, before the name of the city is given, there is mention of the "nest" (Kain) being

rursum ait: «Dixit Balaam filius Beor, / dixit homo, cuius apertus est oculus, / [16]dixit auditor sermonum Dei, / qui novit doctrinam Altissimi / et visiones Omnipotentis videt, / qui cadens apertos habet oculos. / [17]Video eum, sed non modo; / intueor illum, sed non prope. / Oritur stella ex Iacob, / et consurgit virga de Israel; / et percutit tempora Moab / et verticem omnium filiorurn Seth. / [18]Et erit Idumaea possessio eius / et hereditas eius Seir, inimicus eius; / Israel vero fortiter aget. / [19]De Iacob erit, qui dominetur / et perdat reliquias civitatis». [20]Cumque vidisset Amalec, assumens parabolam suam ait: «Principium gentium Amalec, / cuius extrema perdentur». [21]Vidit quoque Cinaeum et, assumpta parabola sua, ait:

v. Or *closed* or *perfect*   **w.** Heb *corners* (of the head)

"Enduring is your dwelling place,
and your nest is set in the rock;
Gen 4:17;
15:19
²²nevertheless Kain shall be wasted.
How long shall Asshur take you away captive?"
²³And he took up his discourse, and said,
"Alas, who shall live when God does this?
Dan 11:30
²⁴But ships shall come from Kittim
and shall afflict Asshur and Eber;
and he also shall come to destruction."
²⁵Then Balaam rose, and went back to his place; and Balak
also went his way.

Num 31:16
Ps 106:28–31
1 Cor 10:8
Rev 2:14

Israel's idolatry is punished*

25 ¹While Israel dwelt in Shittim the people began to play the harlot with the daughters of Moab. ²These invited the people to the sacrifices of their gods, and the people ate, and bowed down to their gods. ³So Israel yoked himself to Baal of
Deut 4:3
Peor. And the anger of the LORD was kindled against Israel; ⁴and the LORD said to Moses, "Take all the chiefs of the people, and hang them in the sun before the LORD, that the fierce anger of the
Ex 18:25ff
LORD may turn away from Israel." ⁵And Moses said to the judges of Israel, "Every one of you slay his men who have yoked themselves to Baal of Peor."

---

solidly built on rock. Yet despite this the city will be destroyed and its inhabitants sold into slavery.

*25:1–18 Israel had proved victorious over enemy armies (cf. 21:21–35) and it had also been freed from the powers of magic (cf. chaps. 22–24); now it has to face another enemy, whom there is even more reason to fear—seduction by idolatrous cults. The text deals with two

accounts which show Israel's reaction to contamination by pagan cults: the first tells how the Israelites prostituted themselves with the Moabites both in a physical sense (by fornication) and in a spiritual one (by adoring their idols): cf. 25:1–4; the second, on the other hand, acclaims the punishment meted out to an Israelite man for marrying a Midianite woman (cf. 25:6–15). Both stories are a stern warning against taking part in

«Robustum quidem est habitaculum tuum, / et in petra positus nidus tuus. / ²²Erit in combustionem Cain, / donec Assur capiat te». ²³Assumptaque parabola sua, iterum locutus est: «Heu! Quis vivet, / quando ista faciet Deus? / ²⁴Venient naves de Cetthim, / superabunt Assyrios vastabuntque Heber; / et ad extremum etiam ipsi peribunt». ²⁵Surrexitque Balaam et reversus est in locum suum; Balac quoque via, qua venerat, rediit. ¹Morabatur autem Israel in Settim, et incepit populus fornicari cum filiabus Moab, ²quae vocaverunt populum ad sacrificia deorum suorum. Et illi comederunt et adoraverunt deos earum; ³et adhaesit Israel Baalphegor. Et iratus Dominus ⁴ait ad Moysen: «Tolle cunctos principes populi et suspende eos coram Domino contra solem in patibulis, ut avertatur furor meus ab Israel». ⁵Dixitque Moyses ad iudices Israel: «Occidat unusquisque proximos suos, qui adhaeserunt Baalphegor». ⁶Et ecce unus de filiis Israel intravit coram fratribus suis ad scortum Madianitidem,

620

Phinehas' jealousy

⁶And behold, one of the people of Israel came and brought a Ex 2:15
Midianite woman to his family, in the sight of Moses and in the
sight of the whole congregation of the people of Israel, while they
were weeping at the door of the tent of meeting. ⁷When Phinehas Ex 6:25
the son of Eleazar, son of Aaron the priest, saw it, he rose and left
the congregation, and took a spear in his hand ⁸and went after the
man of Israel into the inner room, and pierced both of them, the
man of Israel and the woman, through her body. Thus the plague
was stayed from the people of Israel. ⁹Nevertheless those that died 1 Cor 10:8
by the plague were twenty-four thousand.

¹⁰And the LORD said to Moses, ¹¹"Phinehas the son of Eleazar,
son of Aaron the priest, has turned back my wrath from the people
of Israel, in that he was jealous with my jealousy among them, so
that I did not consume the people of Israel in my jealousy.
¹²Therefore say, 'Behold, I give to him my covenant of peace; Deut 4:24
¹³and it shall be to him, and to his descendants after him, the Ex 32:25–29
covenant of a perpetual priesthood, because he was jealous for his Lev 1:7
God, and made atonement for the people of Israel.'" Deut 33:8–11
2 Sam 8:17
¹⁴The name of the slain man of Israel, who was slain with the 1 Chron 5:30–34
Ezra 7:1–5
Midianite woman, was Zimri the son of Salu, head of a fathers' Ezek 44:15
house belonging to the Simeonites. ¹⁵And the name of the Sir 45:23–26
Midianite woman who was slain was Cozbi the daughter of Zur,
who was the head of the people of a fathers' house in Midian.

Canaanite rites (a constant temptation to the Israelites).

Phinehas' action is depicted as something very fine and as meriting a divine promise in his favour. Allowances must be made for the way things were done at that time, but the biblical message is designed to explain why a house of the tribe of Levi, the Zadokites or descendants of Zadok, a priest of the temple at Jerusalem in the time of David and Solomon (cf. 2 Sam 8:17), held legitimate priesthood (cf. Ezek 44:15): the reason was that they were descended from Phinehas, with whom God had made a priestly covenant (cf. 1 Chron 5:30–34; Ezra 7:1–5). It also made the point that the basis for that legitimate priesthood was zeal for Yahweh. On priestly families, cf. Num 3:1–4.

---

vidente Moyse et omni turba filiorum Israel, qui flebant ante fores tabernaculi conventus. ⁷Quod cum vidisset Phinees filius Eleazari filii Aaron sacerdotis, surrexit de medio congregationis et, arrepta lancea, ⁸ingressus est post virum Israelitem in cubiculum et perfodit ambos simul, virum scilicet et mulierem, in locis genitalibus; cessavitque plaga a filiis Israel. ⁹Et occisi sunt viginti quattuor milia hominum. ¹⁰Dixitque Dominus ad Moysen: ¹¹«Phinees filius Eleazari filii Aaron sacerdotis avertit iram meam a filiis Israel, quia zelo meo commotus est in medio eorum, ut non ipse delerem filios Israel in zelo meo. ¹²Idcirco loquere ad eum: Ecce do ei pacem foederis mei, ¹³et erit tam ipsi quam semini eius pactum sacerdotii sempiternum, quia zelatus est pro Deo suo et expiavit scelus filiorum Israel». ¹⁴Erat autem nomen viri Israelitae, qui occisus est cum Madianitide, Zamri filius Salu dux de cognatione et tribu Simeonis; ¹⁵porro mulier Madianitis, quae pariter interfecta est, vocabatur Cozbi filia Sur principis tribus in

¹⁶And the LORD said to Moses, ¹⁷"Harass the Midianites, and smite them; ¹⁸for they have harassed you with their wiles, with which they beguiled you in the matter of Peor, and in the matter of Cozbi, the daughter of the prince of Midian, their sister, who was slain on the day of the plague on account of Peor."

10. FURTHER LEGISLATION

Gen 46:8ff **The census on the plains of Moab**

26 ¹After the plague the LORD said to Moses and to Eleazar the son of Aaron, the priest, ²"Take a census of all the congregation of the people of Israel, from twenty years old and upward, by their fathers' houses, all in Israel who are able to go forth to war." ³And Moses and Eleazar the priest spoke with them in the plains of Moab by the Jordan at Jericho, saying, ⁴"Take a census of the people,ˣ from twenty years old and upward," as the LORD commanded Moses. The people of Israel, who came forth out of the land of Egypt, were:

Mt 2:13–15
Acts 7:14

⁵Reuben, the first-born of Israel; the sons of Reuben: of Hanoch, the family of the Hanochites; of Pallu, the family of the Palluites; ⁶of Hezron, the family of the Hezronites; of Carmi, the family of the Carmites. ⁷These are the families of the Reubenites;

26:1–56. The census held at the start of the great desert journey (cf. chaps. 1–4) needed to be updated forty years on, with a view to the partition of the Land, because the previous generation had died in the desert on account of its sin (cf. chaps. 13–14). This new census is designed to show that God kept the promise he made in Kadesh after that sin (cf. 14:30–31). Strictly speaking it was a military census, like the previous one, and it depicts Eleazar as carrying out the functions previously discharged by Aaron. One prominent feature is the considerable reduction in the numbers belonging to the tribe of Simeon, and the increase in the tribe of Manasseh—possibly a reflection of the later history of those tribes.

Madian. ¹⁶Locutusque est Dominus ad Moysen dicens: ¹⁷«Pugnate contra Madianitas et percutite eos, ¹⁸quia ipsi hostiliter egerunt contra vos et decepere insidiis per idolum Phegor et in negotio Cozbi filiae ducis Madian sororis eorum, quae percussa est in die plagae pro sacrilegio Phegor». ¹Post hanc plagam dixit Dominus ad Moysen et Eleazarum filium Aaron sacerdotem: ²«Numerate summam totius congregationis filiorum Israel a viginti annis et supra per domos et cognationes suas, cunctos, qui possunt ad bella procedere». ³Locuti sunt itaque Moyses et Eleazar sacerdos in campestribus Moab super Iordanem contra Iericho ad eos, qui erant ⁴ a viginti annis et supra, sicut Dominus imperaverat Moysi. Filiorum Israel, qui egressi sunt de terra Aegypti, iste est numerus. ⁵Ruben primogenitus Israel. Huius filius Henoch, a quo familia Henochitarum, et Phallu, a quo familia Phalluitarum, ⁶et Hesron, a quo familia Hesronitarum, et Charmi, a quo familia Charmitarum. ⁷Hae sunt familiae de stirpe Ruben,

x. Supplying *take a census of the people.* Compare verse 2

and their number was forty-three thousand seven hundred and thirty. [8]And the sons of Pallu: Eliab. [9]The sons of Eliab: Nemuel, Num 16:1–35 Dathan, and Abiram. These are the Dathan and Abiram, chosen from the congregation, who contended against Moses and Aaron in the company of Korah, when they contended against the Lord, [10]and the earth opened its mouth and swallowed them up together with Korah, when that company died, when the fire devoured two hundred and fifty men; and they became a warning. [11]Notwithstanding, the sons of Korah did not die.

[12]The sons of Simeon according to their families: of Nemuel, the family of the Nemuelites; of Jamin, the family of the Jaminites; of Jachin, the family of the Jachinites; [13]of Zerah, the family of the Zerahites; of Shaul, the family of the Shaulites. [14]These are the families of the Simeonites, twenty-two thousand two hundred.

[15]The sons of Gad according to their families: of Zephon, the family of the Zephonites; of Haggi, the family of the Haggites; of Shuni, the family of the Shunites; [16]of Ozni, the family of the Oznites; of Eri, the family of the Erites; [17]of Arod, the family of the Arodites; of Areli, the family of the Arelites. [18]These are the families of the sons of Gad according to their number, forty thousand five hundred.

[19]The sons of Judah were Er and Onan; and Er and Onan died in the land of Canaan. [20]And the sons of Judah according to their families were: of Shelah, the family of the Shelanites; of Perez, the family of the Perezites; of Zerah, the family of the Zerahites. [21]And the sons of Perez were: of Hezron, the family of the Hezronites; of Hamul, the family of the Hamulites. [22]These are the families of Judah according to their number, seventy-six thousand five hundred.

quarum numerus inventus est quadraginta tria milia et septingenti triginta. [8]Filius Phallu: Eliab. [9]Huius filii: Namuel et Dathan et Abiram. Isti sunt Dathan et Abiram principes populi, qui surrexerunt contra Moysen et Aaron in seditione Core, quando adversus Dominum rebellaverunt, [10]et aperiens terra os suum devoravit eos et Core, morientibus plurimis, quando combussit ignis ducentos quinquaginta viros; et facti sunt in signum. [11]Core pereunte, filii illius non perierunt. [12]Filii Simeon per cognationes suas: Namuel, ab hoc familia Namuelitarum; Iamin, ab hoc familia Iaminitarum; Iachin, ab hoc familia Iachinitarum; [13]Zara, ab hoc familia Zaraitarum; Saul, ab hoc familia Saulitarum. [14]Hae sunt familiae de stirpe Simeon, quarum omnis numerus fuit viginti duo milia ducenti. [15]Filii Gad per cognationes suas: Sephon, ab hoc familia Sephonitarum; Haggi, ab hoc familia Haggitarum; Suni, ab hoc familia Sunitarum; [16]Ozni, ab hoc familia Oznitarum; Heri, ab hoc familia Heritarum; [17]Arodi, ab hoc familia Aroditarum; Areli, ab hoc familia Arelitarum. [18]Istae sunt familiae Gad, quarum omnis numerus fuit quadraginta milia quingenti. [19]Filii Iudae Her et Onan, qui ambo mortui sunt in terra Chanaan. [20]Fueruntque filii Iudae per cognationes suas: Sela, a quo familia Selanitarum; Phares, a quo familia Pharesitarum; Zara, a quo familia Zaraitarum. [21]Porro filii Phares: Esrom, a quo familia Esromitarum; et Hamul, a quo familia Hamulitarum. [22]Istae sunt familiae Iudae, quarum omnis numerus fuit septuaginta sex milia quingenti. [23]Filii Issachar per cognationes suas: Thola, a quo familia Tholaitarum;

²³The sons of Issachar according to their families: of Tola, the family of the Tolaites; of Puvah, the family of the Punites; ²⁴of Jashub, the family of the Jashubites; of Shimron, the family of the Shimronites. ²⁵These are the families of Issachar according to their number, sixty-four thousand three hundred.

²⁶The sons of Zebulun, according to their families: of Sered, the family of the Seredites; of Elon, the family of the Elonites; of Jahleel, the family of the Jahleelites. ²⁷These are the families of the Zebulunites according to their number, sixty thousand five hundred.

²⁸The sons of Joseph according to their families: Manasseh and Ephraim. ²⁹The sons of Manasseh: of Machir, the family of the Machirites; and Machir was the father of Gilead; of Gilead, the family of the Gileadites. ³⁰These are the sons of Gilead: of Iezer, the family of the Iezerites; of Helek, the family of the Helekites; ³¹and of Asriel, the family of the Asrielites; and of Shechem, the family of the Shechemites; ³²and of Shemida, the family of the Shemidaites; and of Hepher, the family of the Hepherites. ³³Now Zelophehad the son of Hepher had no sons, but daughters: and the names of the daughters of Zelophehad were Mahlah, Noah, Hoglah, Milcah, and Tirzah. ³⁴These are the families of Manasseh; and their number was fifty-two thousand seven hundred.

³⁵These are the sons of Ephraim according to their families: of Shuthelah, the family of the Shuthelahites; of Becher, the family of the Becherites; of Tahan, the family of the Tahanites. ³⁶And these are the sons of Shuthelah: of Eran, the family of the Eranites. ³⁷These are the families of the sons of Ephraim according to their number, thirty-two thousand five hundred. These are the sons of Joseph according to their families.

³⁸The sons of Benjamin according to their families: of Bela, the family of the Bela-ites; of Ashbel, the family of the Ashbelites; of

Marginal references: Josh 17:1; Judg 5:14; 1 Chron 7:14–19; Num 27:1–11

<hr>

Phua, a quo familia Phuaitarum; ²⁴Iasub, a quo familia Iasubitarum; Semron, a quo familia Semronitarum. ²⁵Hae sunt cognationes Issachar, quarum numerus fuit sexaginta quattuor milia trecenti. ²⁶Filii Zabulon per cognationes suas: Sared, a quo familia Sareditarum; Elon, a quo familia Elonitarum; Iahelel, a quo familia Iahelelitarum. ²⁷Hae sunt cognationes Zabulon, quarum numerus fuit sexaginta milia quingenti. ²⁸Filii Ioseph per cognationes suas: Manasse et Ephraim. ²⁹De Manasse ortus est Machir, a quo familia Machiritarum; Machir genuit Galaad, a quo familia Galaaditarum. ³⁰Galaad habuit filios: Iezer, a quo familia Iezeritarum; et Helec, a quo familia Helecitarum; ³¹et Asriel, a quo familia Asrielitarum; et Sechem, a quo familia Sechemitarum; ³²et Semida, a quo familia Semidaitarum; et Hepher, a quo familia Hepheritarum. ³³Fuit autem Hepher pater Salphaad, qui filios non habebat sed tantum filias, quarum ista sunt nomina: Maala et Noa et Hegla et Melcha et Thersa. ³⁴Hae sunt familiae Manasse, et numerus earum quinquaginta duo milia septingenti. ³⁵Filii autem Ephraim per cognationes suas fuerunt hi: Suthala, a quo familia Suthalaitarum; Becher, a quo familia Becheritarum; Thehen, a quo familia Thehenitarum. ³⁶Porro filius Suthala fuit Heran, a quo familia Heranitarum. ³⁷Hae sunt cognationes filiorum Ephraim, quarum numerus fuit triginta duo milia quingenti. Isti sunt filii Ioseph per familias suas. ³⁸Filii Beniamin in cognationibus suis: Bela, a quo familia Belaitarum; Asbel, a quo familia Asbelitarum; Ahiram, a quo familia Ahiramitarum; ³⁹Supham, a quo

Ahiram, the family of the Ahiramites; [39]of Shephupham, the family of the Shuphamites; of Hupham, the family of the Huphamites. [40]And the sons of Bela were Ard and Naaman: of Ard, the family of the Ardites; of Naaman, the family of the Naamites. [41]These are the sons of Benjamin according to their families; and their number was forty-five thousand six hundred.

[42]These are the sons of Dan according to their families: of Shuham, the family of the Shuhamites. These are the families of Dan according to their families. [43]All the families of the Shuhamites, according to their number, were sixty-four thousand four hundred.

[44]The sons of Asher according to their families: of Imnah, the family of the Imnites; of Ishvi, the family of the Ishvites; of Beriah, the family of the Beriites. [45]Of the sons of Beriah: of Heber, the family of the Heberites; of Malchi-el, the family of the Malchi-elites. [46]And the name of the daughter of Asher was Serah. [47]These are the families of the sons of Asher according to their number, fifty-three thousand four hundred.

[48]The sons of Naphtali according to their families: of Jahzeel, the family of the Jahzeelites; of Guni, the family of the Gunites; [49]of Jezer, the family of the Jezerites; of Shillem, the family of the Shillemites. [50]These are the families of Naphtali according to their families; and their number was forty-five thousand four hundred.

[51]This was the number of the people of Israel, six hundred and one thousand seven hundred and thirty. Ex 12:37 / Num 1:46

[52]The LORD said to Moses: [53]"To these the land shall be divided for inheritance according to the number of names. [54]To a large tribe you shall give a large inheritance, and to a small tribe you shall give a small inheritance; every tribe shall be given its inheritance according to its numbers. [55]But the land shall be

---

familia Suphamitarum; Hupham, a quo familia Huphamitarum. [40]Filii Bela: Ared et Naaman; de Ared familia Areditarum, de Naaman familia Naamanitarum. [41]Hi sunt filii Beniamin per cognationes suas, quorum numerus fuit quadraginta quinque milia sexcenti. [42]Filii Dan per cognationes suas: Suham, a quo familia Suhamitarum. Hae sunt cognationes Dan per familias suas: [43]omnes fuere Suhamitae, quorum numerus erat sexaginta quattuor milia quadringenti. [44]Filii Aser per cognationes suas: Iemna, a quo familia Iemnaitarum; Isui, a quo familia Isuitarum; Beria, a quo familia Beriaitarum. [45]Filii Beria: Heber, a quo familia Heberitarum, et Melchiel a quo familia Melchielitarum. [46]Nomen autem filiae Aser fuit Sara. [47]Hae cognationes filiorum Aser, et numerus eorum quinquaginta tria milia quadringenti. [48]Filii Nephthali per cognationes suas: Iasiel, a quo familia Iasielitarum; Guni, a quo familia Gunitarum; [49]Ieser, a quo familia Ieseritarum; Sellem, a quo familia Sellemitarum. [50]Hae sunt cognationes filiorum Nephthali per familias suas, quorum numerus quadraginta quinque milia quadringenti. [51]Ista est summa filiorum Israel qui recensiti sunt: sexcenta milia et mille septingenti triginta. [52]Locutusque est Dominus ad Moysen dicens: [53]«Istis dividetur terra iuxta numerum vocabulorum in possessiones suas. [54]Pluribus maiorem partem dabis et paucioribus minorem: singulis, sicut nunc recensiti sunt, tradetur possessio; [55]ita dumtaxat, ut sors terram dividat. Secundum numerum tribuum patrum

divided by lot; according to the names of the tribes of their fathers they shall inherit. [56]Their inheritance shall be divided according to lot between the larger and the smaller."

Gen 46:11
Ex 6:16–23
1 Chron
6:1–15
[57]These are the Levites as numbered according to their families: of Gershon, the family of the Gershonites; of Kohath, the family of the Kohathites; of Merari, the family of the Merarites. [58]These are the families of Levi: the family of the Libnites, the family of the Hebronites, the family of the Mahlites, the family of the Mushites, the family of the Korahites. And Kohath was the father of Amram. Ex 6:20 [59]The name of Amram's wife was Jochebed the daughter of Levi, who was born to Levi in Egypt; and she bore to Amram Aaron and Moses and Miriam their sister. [60]And to Aaron were born Nadab, Abihu, Eleazar and Ithamar. [61]But Nadab and 1 Cor 10:8 Abihu died when they offered unholy fire before the LORD. [62]And those numbered of them were twenty-three thousand, every male from a month old and upward; for they were not numbered among the people of Israel, because there was no inheritance given to them among the people of Israel.

[63]These were those numbered by Moses and Eleazar the priest, who numbered the people of Israel in the plains of Moab by the Jordan at Jericho. [64]But among these there was not a man of those numbered by Moses and Aaron the priest, who had numbered the people of Israel in the wilderness of Sinai. [65]For the LORD had said of them, "They shall die in the wilderness." There was not left a man of them, except Caleb the son of Jephunneh and Joshua the son of Nun.

Num 26:33
Josh 17:34
The inheritance of daughters

27 [1]Then drew near the daughters of Zelophehad the son of Hepher, son of Gilead, son of Machir, son of Manasseh, from the families of Manasseh the son of Joseph. The names of his daughters were: Mahlah, Noah, Hoglah, Milcah, and Tirzah.

2And they stood before Moses, and before Eleazar the priest, and before the leaders and all the congregation, at the door of the tent of meeting, saying, 3"Our father died in the wilderness; he was not among the company of those who gathered themselves together against the LORD in the company of Korah, but died for his own sin; and he had no sons. 4Why should the name of our father be taken away from his family, because he had no son? Give to us a possession among our father's brethren."

5Moses brought their case before the Lord. 6And the LORD said to Moses, 7"The daughters of Zelophehad are right; you shall give them possession of an inheritance among their father's brethren and cause the inheritance of their father to pass to them. 8And you shall say to the people of Israel, 'If a man dies, and has no son, then you shall cause his inheritance to pass to his daughter. 9And if he has no daughter, then you shall give his inheritance to his brothers. 10And if he has no brothers, then you shall give his inheritance to his father's brothers. 11And if his father has no brothers, then you shall give his inheritance to his kinsman that is next to him of his family, and he shall possess it. And it shall be to the people of Israel a statute and ordinance, as the LORD commanded Moses.'"

27:1–11. This deals with a particular incident and with Moses' decision, after consulting the Lord, about the inheritance laws that will apply in the Land. Because it is a gift from God, their part of the Land must continue to be owned by the same family or by the same tribe. This aim is furthered by the law which allows a daughter to inherit when there is no son, provided of course that she marries within her father's tribe (cf. chap. 36). That was also the idea behind the law concerning the jubilee (cf. Lev 25), the levirite law (cf. Deut 25:5–10), and the right of the nearest relative to acquire land if it had to be sold. All this conspired to maintain a social structure in which everyone shared in the great gift God had given his people—the Land. This idea is applicable by analogy to all human beings as regards the goods of the earth: everyone has a right to obtain what he or she needs for personal development: in the beginning God gave the earth to all mankind (cf. Gen 1:18).

Hegla et Melcha et Thersa. 2Steteruntque coram Moyse et Eleazaro sacerdote et principibus et cuncta congregatione ad ostium tabernaculi conventus atque dixerunt: 3«Pater noster mortuus est in deserto, nec fuit in seditione, quae concitata est contra Dominum sub Core, sed in peccato suo mortuus est; hic non habuit mares filios. 4Cur tollitur nomen illius de familia sua, quia non habuit filium? Date nobis possessionem inter fratres patris nostri». 5Rettulitque Moyses causam earum ad iudicium Domini, 6qui dixit ad eum: 7«Iustam rem postulant filiae Salphaad. Da eis possessionem inter fratres patris sui, et ei in hereditatem succedant. 8Ad filios autem Israel loqueris haec: Homo cum mortuus fuerit absque filio, ad filiam eius transibit hereditas; 9si filiam non habuerit, habebit successores fratres suos. 10Quod si et fratres non fuerint, dabitis hereditatem fratribus patris eius. 11Sin autem nec patruos habuerit, dabitur hereditas illi, qui ei proximus est e cognatione sua; possidebitque eam. Eritque hoc filiis Israel sanc-

Deut 31:1–8 **Moses' successor**

[12]The LORD said to Moses, "Go up into this mountain of Abarim, and see the land which I have given to the people of Israel. [13]And when you have seen it, you also shall be gathered to your people, Num 20:12 as your brother Aaron was gathered, [14]because you rebelled against Acts 7:51 my word in the wilderness of Zin during the strife of the congregation, to sanctify me at the waters before their eyes." (These are Acts 6:3 the waters of Meribah of Kadesh in the wilderness of Zin.) Heb 12:9 [15]Moses said to the LORD, [16]"Let the LORD, the God of the spirits Rev 22:6 of all flesh, appoint a man over the congregation, [17]who shall go *Mt 9:36* out before them and come in before them, who shall lead them out *Mk 6:34* Jn 10:9 and bring them in; that the congregation of the LORD may not be Deut 34:9 as sheep which have no shepherd." [18]And the LORD said to Moses, 1 Kings 22:17 "Take Joshua the son of Nun, a man in whom is the spirit, and lay Josh 1:1 Ezek 34:5 your hand upon him; [19]cause him to stand before Eleazar the priest *Mt 9:36* and all the congregation, and you shall commission him in their Acts 6:6 2 Kings 2:9–15 sight. [20]You shall invest him with some of your authority, that all Josh 1:16–17 the congregation of the people of Israel may obey. [21]And he shall Ex 28:30 stand before Eleazar the priest, who shall inquire for him by the

---

27:17–23. Like the entire generation of those who came out of Egypt (except for Caleb and Joshua), Moses too will die before entering the promised land. However, unlike Aaron, God gives him the very special grace of being able to set his eyes on the Land from a distance before he dies. But Moses' thoughts are on the people and, as a result of his mediation, God gives them a new leader, so that even though they lose Moses the promise will be kept.

Joshua already possesses the spirit, that is, the ability to act with the strength of God, a superhuman strength. Now, by laying his hands on Joshua, Moses will give him part of his authority, to equip him to lead the people. Yet Joshua does not receive all the authority that is Moses', for Moses is someone quite unique, the only man who spoke face to face with God (cf. 12:6–8).

In addition to Eleazar's being a special witness, he performs the rite of the Urim (cf. Ex 28:30 and Lev 8:8) by which God confirms what he personally instructed Moses to do.

Moses and Joshua are the key protagonists in the events of the Exodus and the conquest of the Land. For the Christian reader, Moses represents a first step on the road to salvation, because of his close

tum lege perpetua, sicut praecepit Dominus Moysi». [12]Dixit quoque Dominus ad Moysen: «Ascende in montem istum Abarim et contemplare inde terram, quam daturus sum filiis Israel. [13]Cumque videris eam, ibis et tu ad populum tuum, sicut ivit frater tuus Aaron, [14]quia offendistis me in deserto Sin in contradictione congregationis, nec sanctificare me voluistis coram ea super aquas». Hae sunt aquae Meribathcades deserti Sin. [15]Cui respondit Moyses: [16]«Provideat Dominus, Deus spirituum omnis carnis, hominem, qui sit super congregationem hanc [17]et possit exire et intrare ante eos et educere eos vel introducere, ne sit populus Domini sicut oves absque pastore». [18]Dixitque Dominus ad eum: «Tolle Iosue filium Nun, virum in quo est spiritus; et pone manum tuam super eum, [19]quem statues coram Eleazaro sacerdote et omni congregatione et dabis ei praecepta, cunctis videntibus, [20]et partem gloriae

judgment of the Urim before the LORD; at his word they shall go out, and at his word they shall come in, both he and all the people of Israel with him, the whole congregation." ²²And Moses did as the LORD commanded him; he took Joshua and caused him to stand before Eleazar the priest and the whole congregation, ²³and he laid his hands upon him, and commissioned him as the LORD directed through Moses.

Lev 8:8
Deut 33:8
1 Sam 14:41
Jn 11:51

Acts 6:6

Rules about sacrifices*

Ex 23:14
Lev 23

28 ¹The LORD said to Moses, ²"Command the people of Israel, and say to them, 'My offering, my food for my offerings by fire, my pleasing odour, you shall take heed to offer to me in its due season.'

Ex 29:18

Daily sacrifices
³And you shall say to them, This is the offering by fire which you shall offer to the LORD: two male lambs a year old without blemish, day by day, as a continual offering. ⁴The one lamb you shall

Lev 6:2
Ezek 46:13–15
Heb 7:27

---

connexion with the Law—and the Law was, as it were, a teacher which led mankind to Christ; Joshua, for his part, is also a precursor of Christ, who, by his victory over death, opens up for us the path that leads to the rest we are promised in eternal life (cf. 13:1–24).

*28:1—29:39. The death of Moses is not going to be recounted here, at the point where God announces it (whereas Aaron's death was, after *its* announcement) or after he names his successor: it won't be covered until the end of Deuteronomy (cf. Deut 34). This creates a literary space where Moses can continue to be portrayed as a legislator who

makes regulations about divine worship and about the application of the Law just prior to the entry into the Land.

Chapters 28 and 29 provide a liturgical calendar very much on the lines of that given in Leviticus 23; but this time it goes into detail about what offerings were to be made to the Lord daily and on the occasion of each feast. Unlike the calendar in Leviticus 23, this one prescribes a monthly feast, on the day of the new moon which marks the start of each month; however, it does not include the feast of the offering of the first sheaf (cf. Lev 23:9–14). On the meaning of these feasts cf. the note on Leviticus 23.

---

tuae, ut audiat eum omnis synagoga filiorum Israel. ²¹Stabit coram Eleazaro sacerdote, qui pro eo iudicium Urim consulet Dominum. Ad verbum eius egredietur et ingredietur ipse et omnes filii Israel cum eo, cuncta congregatio». ²²Fecit Moyses, ut praeceperat Dominus. Cumque tulisset Iosue, statuit eum coram Eleazaro sacerdote et omni frequentia populi; ²³et, impositis capiti eius manibus, constituit eum, sicut mandaverat Dominus per manum Moysi. ¹Dixit quoque Dominus ad Moysen: ²«Praecipe filiis Israel et dices ad eos: oblationem meam et panem meum, sacrificium ignis in odorem suavissimum offerte per tempora sua. ³Hoc est sacrificium ignis, quod offerre debetis: agnos anniculos immaculatos duos cotidie in holocaustum sempiternum; ⁴unum offeretis mane et alterum ad vesperam; ⁵decimam

offer in the morning, and the other lamb you shall offer in the evening; [5]also a tenth of an ephah of fine flour for a cereal offering, mixed with a fourth of a hin of beaten oil. [6]It is a continual burnt offering, which was ordained at Mount Sinai for a pleasing odour, an offering by fire to the LORD. [7]Its drink offering shall be a fourth of a hin for each lamb; in the holy place you shall pour out a drink offering of strong drink to the LORD. [8]The other lamb you shall offer in the evening; like the cereal offering of the morning, and like its drink offering, you shall offer it as an offering by fire, a pleasing odour to the LORDd.

Lev 23:3
Ezek 46:4–5
Mt 12:5

Sabbath sacrifices

[9]"On the sabbath day two male lambs a year old without blemish, and two tenths of an ephah of fine flour for a cereal offering, mixed with oil, and its drink offering: [10]this is the burnt offering of every sabbath, besides the continual burnt offering and its drink offering.

Ezek 46:6–7
Amos 8:5

The feast of the new moon

[11]"At the beginnings of your months you shall offer a burnt offering to the LORD: two young bulls, one ram, seven male lambs a year old without blemish; [12]also three tenths of an ephah of fine flour for a cereal offering, mixed with oil, for each bull; and two tenths of fine flour for a cereal offering, mixed with oil, for the one ram; [13]and a tenth of fine flour mixed with oil as a cereal offering for every lamb; for a burnt offering of pleasing odour, an offering by fire to the LORD. [14]Their drink offerings shall be half a hin of wine for a bull, a third of a hin for a ram, and a fourth of a hin for a lamb; this is the burnt offering of each month throughout the months of the year. [15]Also one male goat for a sin offering to the LORD; it shall be offered besides the continual burnt offering and its drink offering.

partem ephi similae in oblationem, quae conspersa sit oleo purissimo et habeat quartam partem hin. [6]Holocaustum iuge est, quod obtulistis in monte Sinai in odorem suavissimum, sacrificium ignis Domino; [7]et libabitis vini quartam partem hin per agnos singulos; in sanctuario effundetis libamen potus inebriantis Domino. [8]Alterumque agnum similiter offeretis ad vesperam, iuxta ritum sacrificii matutini: sacrificium ignis in odorem suavissimum Domino. [9]Die autem sabbati offeretis duos agnos anniculos immaculatos et duas decimas similae oleo conspersae et libamentum eius. [10]Est holocaustum sabbati per singula sabbata, praeter holocaustum sempiternum et libamentum eius. [11]In calendis autem offeretis holocaustum Domino vitulos de armento duos, arietem unum, agnos anniculos septem immaculatos [12]et tres decimas similae oleo conspersae in oblatione per singulos vitulos et duas decimas similae oleo conspersae per singulos arietes, [13]et decimam unam similae oleo conspersae in oblatione per agnos singulos: holocaustum in odorem suavissimum, sacrificium ignis Domino. [14]Libamenta autem eorum ista erunt: media pars hin vini per singulos vitulos, tertia per arietem, quarta per agnum. Hoc erit holocaustum per omnes menses, qui sibi anno vertente succedunt. [15]Hircus quoque offeretur

Ex 12
Lev 23:5–8
Deut 16:1–8
Ezek 45:21–24

The feast of the unleavened bread

[16]"On the fourteenth day of the first month is the LORD's passover. [17]And on the fifteenth day of this month is a feast; seven days shall unleavened bread be eaten. [18]On the first day there shall be a holy convocation: you shall do no laborious work, [19]but offer an offering by fire, a burnt offering to the LORD: two young bulls, one ram, and seven male lambs a year old; see that they are without blemish; [20]also their cereal offering of fine flour mixed with oil; three tenths of an ephah shall you offer for a bull, and two tenths for a ram; [21]a tenth shall you offer for each of the seven lambs; [22]also one male goat for a sin offering, to make atonement for you. [23]You shall offer these besides the burnt offering of the morning, which is for a continual burnt offering. [24]In the same way you shall offer daily, for seven days, the food of an offering by fire, a pleasing odour to the LORD; it shall be offered besides the continual burnt offering and its drink offering. [25]And on the seventh day you shall have a holy convocation; you shall do no laborious work.

Ex 23:14
Lev 23:15–21
Deut 16:9–12

The feast of Weeks

[26]"On the day of the first fruits, when you offer a cereal offering of new grain to the LORD at your feast of weeks, you shall have a holy convocation; you shall do no laborious work, [27]but offer a burnt offering, a pleasing odour to the LORD; two young bulls, one ram, seven male lambs a year old; [28]also their cereal offering of fine flour mixed with oil, three tenths of an ephah for each bull, two tenths for one ram, [29]a tenth for each of the seven lambs; [30]with one male goat, to make atonement for you. [31]Besides the continual burnt offering and its cereal offering, you shall offer them and their drink offering. See that they are without blemish.

Domino pro peccato, praeter holocaustum sempiternum cum libamentis suis. [16]Mense autem primo, quarta decima die mensis Pascha Domini erit, [17]et quinta decima die sollemnitas. Septem diebus vescemini azymis, [18]quarum die prima conventus sanctus erit; omne opus servile non facietis in ea. [19]Offeretisque sacrificium ignis, holocaustum Domino: vitulos de armento duos, arietem unum, agnos anniculos immaculatos septem; [20]et oblationem singulorum ex simila, quae conspersa sit oleo, tres decimas per singulos vitulos et duas decimas per arietem [21]et decimam unam per agnos singulos, id est per septem agnos; [22]et hircum pro peccato unum, ut expietur pro vobis, [23]praeter holocaustum matutinum, quod semper offeretis. [24]Ita facietis per singulos dies septem dierum: panem, sacrificium ignis in odorem suavissimum Domino praeter holocaustum iuge et libationem eius. [25]Die quoque septimo conventus sanctus erit vobis; omne opus servile non facietis in eo. [26]Die etiam primitivorum, quando offeretis oblationem novam Domino, in sollemnitate Hebdomadarum, conventus sanctus erit vobis; omne opus servile non facietis in ea. [27]Offeretisque holocaustum in odorem suavissimum Domino: vitulos de armento duos, arietem unum et agnos anniculos immaculatos septem, [28]atque in oblatione eorum similae oleo conspersae, tres decimas per singulos vitulos, per arietem duas, [29]per agnos decimam unam, qui simul sunt agni septem; [30]hircum quoque, qui mactatur pro expiatione, [31]praeter holocaustum sempiternum et oblationem eius. Immaculata offeretis omnia cum libationibus suis. [1]Mensis etiam septimi

631

Lev 23:24
Num 10:10 **The day to blow the trumpet**

29 [1]"On the first day of the seventh month you shall have a holy convocation; you shall do no laborious work. It is a day for you to blow the trumpets, [2]and you shall offer a burnt offering, a pleasing odour to the LORD: one young bull, one ram, seven male lambs a year old without blemish; [3]also their cereal offering of fine flour mixed with oil, three tenths of an ephah for the bull, two tenths for the ram, [4]and one tenth for each of the seven lambs; [5]with one male goat for a sin offering, to make atonement for you; [6]besides the burnt offering of the new moon, and its cereal offering, and the continual burnt offering and its cereal offering, and their drink offering, according to the ordinance for them, a pleasing odour, an offering by fire to the LORD.

Lev 16: 23:26–32
Ezek 45:18–20 **The day of atonement**

[7]"On the tenth day of this seventh month you shall have a holy convocation, and afflict yourselves; you shall do no work, [8]but you shall offer a burnt offering to the LORD, a pleasing odor: one young bull, one ram, seven male lambs a year old; they shall be to you without blemish; [9]and their cereal offering of fine flour mixed with oil, three tenths of an ephah for the bull, two tenths for the one ram, [10]a tenth for each of the seven lambs: [11]also one male goat for a sin offering, besides the sin offering of atonement, and the continual Ex 23:14
Lev 23:33–43 burnt offering and its cereal offering, and their drink offerings.

Deut 16:13–15
Ezek 45:25
Jn 7:2 **The feast of Tabernacles**

[12]"On the fifteenth day of the seventh month you shall have a holy convocation; you shall do no laborious work, and you shall keep a feast to the LORD seven days; [13]and you shall offer a burnt offering, an offering by fire, a pleasing odour to the LORD, thirteen young bulls, two rams, fourteen male lambs a year old; they shall

prima die conventus sanctus erit vobis; omne opus servile non facietis in ea, quia dies clangoris est et tubarum. [2]Offeretisque holocaustum in odorem suavissimum Domino: vitulum de armento unum, arietem unum et agnos anniculos immaculatos septem; [3]et in oblationibus eorum similae oleo conspersae tres decimas per vitulum, duas decimas per arietem, [4]unam decimam per agnum, qui simul sunt agni septem; [5]et hircum pro peccato, qui offertur in expiationem vestram, [6]praeter holocaustum calendarum cum oblatione et holocaustum sempiternum cum oblatione et libationibus solitis in odorem suavissimum, sacrificium ignis Domino. [7]Decima quoque die mensis huius septimi erit vobis conventus sanctus, et affligetis animas vestras; omne opus servile non facietis. [8]Offeretisque holocaustum Domino in odorem suavissimum: vitulum de armento unum, arietem unum, agnos anniculos immaculatos septem; [9]et in oblatione eorum similae oleo conspersae tres decimas per vitulum, duas decimas per arietem, [10]decimam unam per agnos singulos, qui sunt simul septem agni; [11]et hircum pro peccato, absque his, quae offerri pro delicto solent in expiationem et holocaustum sempiternum cum oblatione et libaminibus eorum. [12]Quinta decima vero die mensis septimi conventus sanctus erit; omne opus servile non facietis in ea, sed celebrabitis sollemnitatem Domino septem diebus [13]offeretisque holocaustum in odorem suavissimum Domino: vitulos de armento tredecim, arietes duos, agnos anniculos immaculatos quattuordecim; [14]et in oblatione eorum similae oleo conspersae tres decimas per vitulos singulos,

be without blemish; [14]and their cereal offering of fine flour mixed with oil, three tenths of an ephah for each of the thirteen bulls, two tenths for each of the two rams, [15]and a tenth for each of the fourteen lambs; [16]also one male goat for a sin offering, besides the continual burnt offering, its cereal offering and its drink offering.

[17]"On the second day twelve young bulls, two rams, fourteen male lambs a year old without blemish, [18]with the cereal offering and the drink offerings for the bulls, for the rams, and for the lambs, by number, according to the ordinance; [19]also one male goat for a sin offering, besides the continual burnt offering and its cereal offering, and their drink offerings.

[20]"On the third day eleven bulls, two rams, fourteen male lambs a year old without blemish, [21]with the cereal offering and the drink offerings for the bulls, for the rams, and for the lambs, by number, according to the ordinance; [22]also one male goat for a sin offering, besides the continual burnt offering and its cereal offering and its drink offering.

[23]"On the fourth day ten bulls, two rams, fourteen male lambs a year old without blemish, [24]with the cereal offering and the drink offerings for the bulls, for the rams, and for the lambs, by number, according to the ordinance; [25]also one male goat for a sin offering, besides the continual burnt offering, its cereal offering and its drink offering.

[26]"On the fifth day nine bulls, two rams, fourteen male lambs a year old without blemish, [27]with the cereal offering and the drink offerings for the bulls, for the rams, and for the lambs, by number, according to the ordinance; [28]also one male goat for a sin offering; besides the continual burnt offering and its cereal offering and its drink offering.

[29]"On the sixth day eight bulls, two rams, fourteen male lambs a year old without blemish, [30]with the cereal offering and the

qui sunt simul vituli tredecim, et duas decimas arieti uno, id est simul arietibus duobus, [15]et decimam unam agnis singulis, qui sunt simul agni quattuordecim; [16]et hircum pro peccato absque holocausto sempiterno et oblatione et libamine eius. [17]In die altero offeretis vitulos de armento duodecim, arietes duos, agnos anniculos immaculatos quattuordecim; [18]oblationemque et libamina singulorum per vitulos et arietes et agnos iuxta numerum eorum rite celebrabitis, [19]et hircum pro peccato absque holocausto sempiterno oblationeque et libamine eorum. [20]Die tertio offeretis vitulos undecim, arietes duos, agnos anniculos immaculatos quattuordecim, [21]oblationem et libamina singulorum per vitulos et arietes et agnos iuxta numerum eorum rite celebrabitis, [22]et hircum pro peccato absque holocausto sempiterno oblationeque et libamine eius. [23]Die quarto offeretis vitulos decem, arietes duos, agnos anniculos immaculatos quattuordecim, [24]oblationem et libamina singulorum per vitulos et arietes et agnos iuxta numerum eorum rite celebrabitis, [25]et hircum pro peccato absque holocausto sempiterno, oblatione eius et libamine. [26]Die quinto offeretis vitulos novem, arietes duos, agnos anniculos immaculatos quattuordecim, [27]oblationem et libamina singulorum per vitulos et arietes et agnos iuxta numerum eorum rite celebrabitis, [28]et hircum pro peccato absque holocausto sempiterno, oblatione eius et libamine. [29]Die sexto offeretis vitulos octo, arietes duos, agnos anniculos immaculatos quat-

drink offerings for the bulls, for the rams, and for the lambs, by number, according to the ordinance; [31]also one male goat for a sin offering; besides the continual burnt offering, its cereal offering, and its drink offerings.

[32]"On the seventh day seven bulls, two rams, fourteen male lambs a year old without blemish, [33]with the cereal offering and the drink offerings for the bulls, for the rams, and for the lambs, by number, according to the ordinance; [34]also one male goat for a sin offering; besides the continual burnt offering, its cereal offering, and its drink offering.

[35]"On the eighth day you shall have a solemn assembly: you shall do no laborious work, [36]but you shall offer a burnt offering, an offering by fire, a pleasing odour to the LORD: one bull, one ram, seven male lambs a year old without blemish, [37]and the cereal offering and the drink offerings for the bull, for the ram, and for the lambs, by number, according to the ordinance; [38]also one male goat for a sin offering; besides the continual burnt offering and its cereal offering and its drink offering.

[39]"These you shall offer to the LORD at your appointed feasts, in addition to your votive offerings and your freewill offerings, for your burnt offerings, and for your cereal offerings, and for your drink offerings, and for your peace offerings."

Lev 27
Num 6 **Laws concerning vows**

[40][y]And Moses told the people of Israel everything just as the LORD had commanded Moses.

30 [1]Moses said to the heads of the tribes of the people of Israel, "This is what the LORD has commanded. [2]When a

---

30:1–16. On vows in general cf. Lev 27; Num 6; Deut 23:22–27. This is the only

passage which specifically deals with vows made by women. Underlying it is

tuordecim, [30]oblationem et libamina singulorum per vitulos et arietes et agnos iuxta numerum eorum rite celebrabitis, [31]et hircum pro peccato absque holocausto sempiterno, oblatione eius et libamine. [32]Die septimo offeretis vitulos septem et arietes duos, agnos anniculos immaculatos quattuordecim, [33]oblationem et libamina singulorum per vitulos et arietes et agnos iuxta numerum eorum rite celebrabitis, [34]et hircum pro peccato absque holocausto sempiterno, oblatione eius et libamine. [35]Die octavo erit conventus sollemnis, omne opus servile non facietis [36]offerentes holocaustum in odorem suavissimum Domino: vitulum unum, arietem unum, agnos anniculos immaculatos septem, [37]oblationem et libamina singulorum per vitulum et arietem et agnos iuxta numerum eorum rite celebrabitis, [38]et hircum pro peccato absque holocausto sempiterno, oblatione eius et libamine. [39]Haec offeretis Domino in sollemnitatibus vestris, praeter vota et oblationes spontaneas in holocaustis, in oblationibus, in libaminibus et in hostiis pacificis». [1]Narravitque Moyses filiis Israel omnia, quae ei Dominus imperarat, [2]et locutus est ad principes tribuum filiorum Israel: «Iste est sermo, quem praecepit Dominus: [3]Si

y. Ch 30:1 in Heb [and New Vulgate]

man vows a vow to the LORD, or swears an oath to bind himself by a pledge, he shall not break his word; he shall do according to all that proceeds out of his mouth. ³Or when a woman vows a vow to the LORD, and binds herself by a pledge, while within her father's house, in her youth, ⁴and her father hears of her vow and of her pledge by which she has bound herself, and says nothing to her; then all her vows shall stand, and every pledge by which she has bound herself shall stand. ⁵But if her father expresses disapproval to her on the day that he hears of it, no vow of hers, no pledge by which she has bound herself, shall stand; and the LORD will forgive her, because her father opposed her. ⁶And if she is married to a husband, while under her vows or any thoughtless utterance of her lips by which she has bound herself, ⁷and her husband hears of it, and says nothing to her on the day that he hears; then her vows shall stand, and her pledges by which she has bound herself shall stand. ⁸But if, on the day that her husband comes to hear of it, he expresses disapproval, then he shall make void her vow which was on her, and the thoughtless utterance of her lips, by which she bound herself; and the LORD will forgive her. ⁹But any vow of a widow or of a divorced woman, anything by which she has bound herself, shall stand against her. ¹⁰And if she vowed in her husband's house, or bound herself by a pledge with an oath, ¹¹and her husband heard of it, and said nothing to her, and did not oppose her; then all her vows shall stand, and every pledge by which she bound herself shall stand. ¹²But if her husband makes them null

Deut 23:22–24
Judg 11:30–40
Eccles 5:3–4
Ps 50:14
Mt 5:55

Lev 5:4

---

the idea that an unmarried woman comes under the authority of her father, and a married woman under that of her husband; this is true even in matters to do with God when these involve offering something external (as by a vow) which belonged by right to the father or the husband. So a widow or a repudiated wife was seen as having the same responsibility as a man as far as fulfilment of vows was concerned. The discrimination which this custom might imply was not discrimination against women as such; it stemmed from the familial position of women in a specific socio-cultural setting.

---

quis virorum votum Domino voverit aut se constrinxerit iuramento, non faciet irritum verbum suum, sed omne, quod promisit, implebit. ⁴Mulier, si quippiam voverit Domino aut se constrinxerit iuramento, quae est in domo patris sui et in aetate adhuc puellari, ⁵Si cognoverit pater votum, quod pollicita est, aut iuramentum, quo ligavit animam suam, et tacuerit, voti rea erit; quidquid pollicita est aut iuravit, opere complebit. ⁶Sin autem, quo die audierit contradixerit pater, et vota et iuramenta eius irrita erunt; et propitius erit ei Dominus, eo quod contradixerit pater. ⁷Si maritum habuerit et voverit aliquid, aut semel de ore eius verbum egrediens animam eius ligaverit iuramento, ⁸quo die audierit vir eius et non contradixerit, voti rea erit reddetque, quodcumque promiserat. ⁹Sin autem, quo die audierit contradixerit, irritas facit pollicitationes eius verbaque, quibus obstrinxerit animam suam et propitius erit ei Dominus. ¹⁰Vidua et repudiata, quidquid voverint, reddent. ¹¹Uxor in domo viri cum se voto constrinxerit aut iuramento, ¹²si audierit vir et tacuerit nec contradixerit sponsioni, reddet, quodcumque

and void on the day that he hears them, then whatever proceeds out of her lips concerning her vows, or concerning her pledge of herself, shall not stand: her husband has made them void, and the LORD will forgive her. [13]Any vow and any binding oath to afflict herself, her husband may establish, or her husband may make void. [14]But if her husband says nothing to her from day to day, then he establishes all her vows, or all her pledges, that are upon her; he has established them, because he said nothing to her on the day that he heard of them. [15]But if he makes them null and void after he has heard of them, then he shall bear her iniquity."

[16]These are the statutes which the LORD commanded Moses, as between a man and his wife, and between a father and his daughter, while in her youth, within her father's house.

11. PREPARATIONS FOR ENTERING THE PROMISED LAND

Deut 20:1–21: 14 **Vengeance on Midian; division of the booty**

Ex 2:15
Josh 6:17
1 Sam 15:1–33

31 [1]The LORD said to Moses, [2]"Avenge the people of Israel on the Midianites; afterward you shall be gathered to your

---

31:1–54. This chapter continues the narrative of chapter 25 which was interrupted to cover the military census, the appointment of Joshua and the rules about worship, which reflect of the holiness of Israel. Now we see the Israelites, in response to God's command, taking action to eradicate something which represented an occasion of sin.

The sacred text, which has been constructed on folk-memories, epic in style, talks about the rules for holy war and division of booty, specifying what should go to priests. The passage must have to do with the victory of some Hebrew group over the Midianites, Israel's declared enemies during the conquest of the Land (cf. Judg 6–8); that is why the encounter has the nature of a holy war, a war ordered by God for the annihilation of Midian. Only young women who are still virgins are spared: to ensure that Midian will have offspring no more. Unlike the anathema dealt with in 21:1–3, in this instance part of the booty is reserved (after being cleansed) for the

---

promiserat. [13]Sin autem extemplo contradixerit, non tenebitur promissionis rea, quia maritus contradixit, et Dominus ei propitius erit. [14]Si voverit aut iuramento se constrinxerit, ut per ieiunium affligat animam suam, in arbitrio viri erit, ut faciat sive non faciat. [15]Quod si audiens vir tacuerit et de die in diem distulerit sententiam, quidquid voverat atque promiserat, reddet, quia, quo die audierat, tacuit. [16]Sin autem contradixerit, postquam rescivit, portabit ipse iniquitatem eius». [17]Istae sunt leges, quas constituit Dominus Moysi inter virum et uxorem, inter patrem et filiam, quae in puellari adhuc aetate manet in parentis domo. [1]Locutusque est Dominus ad Moysen dicens: [2]«Ulciscere filios Israel de Madianitis et sic colligeris ad populum tuum». [3]Statimque Moyses: «Armate, inquit, ex vobis viros ad pugnam, qui possint ultionem Domini expetere de Madianitis. [4]Mille viri de singulis tribubus eligantur ex Israel, qui mittantur ad bellum». [5]Dederuntque millenos de singulis tribubus, id est duodecim

people." ³And Moses said to the people, "Arm men from among you for the war, that they may go against Midian, to execute the LORD'S vengeance on Midian. ⁴You shall send a thousand from each of the tribes of Israel to the war." ⁵So there were provided, out of the thousands of Israel, a thousand from each tribe, twelve thousand armed for war. ⁶And Moses sent them to the war, a thousand from each tribe, together with Phinehas the son of Eleazar the priest, with the vessels of the sanctuary and the trumpets for the alarm in his hand. ⁷They warred against Midian, as the LORD commanded Moses, and slew every male. ⁸They slew the kings of Midian with the rest of their slain, Evi, Rekem, Zur, Hur, and Reba, the five kings of Midian; and they also slew Balaam the son of Beor with the sword. ⁹And the people of Israel took captive the women of Midian and their little ones; and they took as booty all their cattle, their flocks, and all their goods. ¹⁰All their cities in the places where they dwelt, and all their encampments, they burned with fire, ¹¹and took all the spoil and all the booty, both of man and of beast. ¹²Then they brought the captives and the booty and the spoil to Moses, and to Eleazar the priest, and to the congrega-

---

sanctuary, and the rest is distributed among the army, the community and the priests.

The notion of holy war as found in this passage and elsewhere (cf., e.g., the note on Lev 27:28–29) in the Bible derives from the idea that those against whom the Israelites were fighting were enemies of God who sought to frustrate his plans. Thus, the war was seen as obedience to a divine decree, and the final outcome was annihilation of the enemy, to show the strength of the wrath of God. This interpretation of war, adding a religious dimension to an already existing phenomenon, will gradually be corrected as time goes on until eventually, in the New Testament it no longer holds any

meaning: the New Testament does speak of war, not against men (who are all children of the same Father), but against sin and evil. In the light of that teaching the Church regards war as something caused by sin, and the Second Vatican Council "proposes to outline the true and noble nature of peace, to condemn the savagery of war, and earnestly to exhort Christians to cooperate with all in securing a peace based on justice and charity and in promoting the means necessary to attain it, under the help of Christ, author of peace" (*Gaudium et spes*, 77).

31:6. This verse has given rise to a beautiful allegorical interpretation: the holy vessels are the angels who encourage and

milia expeditorum ad pugnam, ⁶quos misit Moyses cum Phinees filio Eleazari sacerdotis. Vasa quoque sancta et tubas ad clangendum tradidit ei. ⁷Cumque pugnassent contra Madianitas, sicut praeceperat Dominus Moysi, omnes mares occiderunt ⁸et reges eorum Evi et Recem et Sur et Hur et Rebe, quinque principes gentis, Balaam quoque filium Beor interfecerunt gladio; ⁹ceperuntque mulieres eorum et parvulos. Omniaque pecora et cuncta supellectilem, quidquid habere potuerant, depopulati sunt: ¹⁰tam urbes quam viculos et castra flamma consumpsit; ¹¹et tulerunt praedam et universa, quae ceperant, tam ex hominibus quam ex iumentis, ¹²et adduxerunt captivos, spolia et praedam ad Moysen et

tion of the people of Israel, at the camp on the plains of Moab by the Jordan at Jericho. [13]Moses, and Eleazar the priest, and all the leaders of the congregation, went forth to meet them outside the camp. [14]And Moses was angry with the officers of the army, the commanders of thousands and the commanders of hundreds, who had come from service in the war. [15]Moses said to them, "Have you let all the women live? [16]Behold, these caused the people of Israel, by the counsel of Balaam, to act treacherously against the LORD in the matter of Peor, and so the plague came among the congregation of the LORD. [17]Now therefore, kill every male among the little ones, and kill every woman who has known man by lying with him. [18]But all the young girls who have not known man by lying with him, keep alive for yourselves. [19]Encamp outside the camp seven days; whoever of you has killed any person, and whoever has touched any slain, purify yourselves and your captives on the third day and on the seventh day. [20]You shall purify every garment, every article of skin, all work of goats' hair, and every article of wood."

[21]And Eleazar the priest said to the men of war who had gone to battle: "This is the statute of the law which the LORD has commanded Moses: [22]only the gold, the silver, the bronze, the iron, the tin, and the lead, [23]everything that can stand the fire, you shall pass through the fire, and it shall be clean. Nevertheless it shall also be purified with the water of impurity; and whatever cannot

2 Pet 2:15
Rev 2:14

---

help upright and devout people in their struggle against demons and sins; the trumpets are the preaching and exhortations of the apostles sent out by Jesus; Phinehas the priest is Christ, the leader and captain in this war. Similarly the ark of the Covenant, which contains the manna, Christ, is interpreted as standing for the Blessed Virgin, who brings us victory over the devil.

Eleazarum sacerdotem et ad omnem congregationem filiorum Israel ad castra in campestribus Moab iuxta Iordanem contra Iericho. [13]Egressi sunt autem Moyses et Eleazar sacerdos et omnes principes synagogae in occursum eorum extra castra. [14]Iratusque Moyses principibus exercitus, tribunis et centurionibus, qui venerant de bello, [15]ait: «Cur omnes feminas reservastis? [16]Nonne istae sunt, quae deceperunt filios Israel ad suggestionem Balaam et praevaricari vos fecerunt in Dominum super peccato Phegor, unde et percussus est populus Domini? [17]Ergo cunctos interficite parvulos generis masculini et omnes mulieres, quae noverunt viros in coitu, iugulate; [18]puellas autem et omnes feminas virgines reservate vobis. [19]Et vos manete extra castra septem diebus; qui occiderit hominem vel occisum tetigerit, lustrabitur die tertio et septimo, vos et captivi vestri. [20]Et de omni praeda, sive vestimentum fuerit sive aliquid in utensilia praeparatum de caprarum pellibus et pilis et ligno, lustrabitis». [21]Eleazar quoque sacerdos ad viros exercitus, qui pugnaverant, sic locutus est: «Hoc est praeceptum legis, quod mandavit Dominus Moysi: [22]Aurum et argentum et aes et ferrum et stannum et plumbum, [23]omne, quod potest transire per flammas, igne purgabitur; quidquid autem ignem non potest sustinere, aqua expiationis sanctificabitur. [24]Et lavabitis vestimenta vestra die septimo, et purificati postea castra

stand the fire, you shall pass through the water. [24]You must wash your clothes on the seventh day, and you shall be clean; and afterward you shall come into the camp."

[25]The LORD said to Moses, [26]"Take the count of the booty that was taken, both of man and of beast, you and Eleazar the priest and the heads of the fathers' houses of the congregation; [27]and divide the booty into two parts, between the warriors who went out to battle and all the congregation. [28]And levy for the LORD a tribute from the men of war who went out to battle, one out of five hundred, of the persons and of the oxen and of the asses and of the flocks; [29]take it from their half, and give it to Eleazar the priest as an offering to the LORD. [30]And from the people of Israel's half you shall take one drawn out of every fifty, of the persons, of the oxen, of the asses, and of the flocks, of all the cattle, and give them to the Levites who have charge of the tabernacle of the LORD." [31]And Moses and Eleazar the priest did as the LORD commanded Moses.

[32]Now the booty remaining of the spoil that the men of war took was: six hundred and seventy-five thousand sheep, [33]seventy-two thousand cattle, [34]sixty-one thousand asses, [35]and thirty-two thousand persons in all, women who had not known man by lying with him. [36]And the half, the portion of those who had gone out to war, was in number three hundred and thirty-seven thousand five hundred sheep, [37]and the LORD's tribute of sheep was six hundred and seventy-five. [38]The cattle were thirty-six thousand, of which the LORD's tribute was seventy-two. [39]The asses were thirty thousand five hundred, of which the LORD's tribute was sixty-one. [40]The persons were sixteen thousand, of which the LORD's tribute was thirty-two persons. [41]And Moses gave the tribute, which was the offering for the LORD, to Eleazar the priest, as the LORD commanded Moses.

intrabitis». [25]Dixit quoque Dominus ad Moysen: [26]«Tollite summam eorum, quae capta sunt, ab homine usque ad pecus, tu et Eleazar sacerdos et principes familiarum; [27]dividesque ex aequo praedam inter eos, qui pugnaverunt egressique sunt ad bellum, et inter omnem congregationem. [28]Et separabis partem Domino ab his, qui pugnaverunt et fuerunt in bello, unam animam de quingentis tam ex hominibus quam ex bobus et asinis et ovibus [29]et dabis eam Eleazaro sacerdoti, quia praelibatio Domini sunt. [30]Ex media quoque parte filiorum Israel accipies quinquagesimum caput hominum et boum et asinorum et ovium cunctorum animantium et dabis ea Levitis, qui excubant in custodiis habitaculi Domini». [31]Feceruntque Moyses et Eleazar sacerdos, sicut praeceperat Dominus. [32]Fuit autem praeda, quae supererat, quam exercitus ceperat, ovium sexcenta septuaginta quinque milia, [33]boum septuaginta duo milia, [34]asinorum sexaginta milia et mille, [35]animae hominum sexus feminei, quae non cognoverant viros, triginta duo milia. [36]Dataque est media pars his, qui in proelio fuerant, ovium trecenta triginta septem milia quingentae, [37]e quibus in partem Domini supputatae sunt oves sexcentae septuaginta quinque, [38]et de bobus triginta sex milibus, boves septuaginta et duo, [39]de asinis triginta milibus quingentis, asini sexaginta unus, [40]de animabus hominum sedecim milibus, cesserunt in partem Domini triginta duae animae. [41]Tradiditque Moyses tributum praelibationis Domini Elcazaro sacerdoti, sicut fuerat ei impe-

⁴²From the people of Israel's half, which Moses separated from that of the men who had gone to war—⁴³now the congregation's half was three hundred and thirty-seven thousand five hundred sheep, ⁴⁴thirty-six thousand cattle, ⁴⁵and thirty thousand five hundred asses, ⁴⁶and sixteen thousand persons—⁴⁷from the people of Israel's half Moses took one of every fifty, both of persons and of beasts, and gave them to the Levites who had charge of the tabernacle of the LORD; as the LORD commanded Moses.

⁴⁸Then the officers who were over the thousands of the army, the captains of thousands and the captains of hundreds, came near to Moses, ⁴⁹and said to Moses, "Your servants have counted the men of war who are under our command, and there is not a man missing from us. ⁵⁰And we have brought the LORD's offering, what each man found, articles of gold, armlets and bracelets, signet rings, earrings, and beads, to make atonement for ourselves before the LORD." ⁵¹And Moses and Eleazar the priest received from them the gold, all wrought articles. ⁵²And all the gold of the offering that they offered to the LORD, from the commanders of thousands and the commanders of hundreds, was sixteen thousand seven hundred and fifty shekels. ⁵³(The men of war had taken booty, every man for himself.) ⁵⁴And Moses and Eleazar the priest received the gold from the commanders of thousands and of hundreds, and brought it into the tent of meeting, as a memorial for the people of Israel before the LORD.

Num 21:24ff
Deut 3:12–20
Josh 1:12–18;
13:8–32

The tribes of Transjordania

32 ¹Now the sons of Reuben and the sons of Gad had a very great multitude of cattle; and they saw the land of Jazer

---

32:1–42. Chapter 32 taken as a whole is designed to show that the tribes of the Transjordan and therefore that whole area also belong to Israel, even though the Jordan might normally be seen as the eastern frontier of the promised land. The

text also wants to underline (as the book of Joshua does) that all twelve tribes play their part in the conquest of the Land, for all have a share in this gift from God to his people.

---

ratum. ⁴²Ex media vero parte filiorum Israel, quam separaverat a parte eorum, qui in proelio fuerant, ⁴³de hac media parte, quae contigerat congregationi, id est de ovibus trecentis triginta septem milibus quingentis ⁴⁴et de bobus triginta sex milibus ⁴⁵et de asinis triginta milibus quingentis ⁴⁶de hominibus sedecim milibus, ⁴⁷tulit Moyses quinquagesimum caput et dedit Levitis, qui excubabant in habitaculo Domini, sicut praeceperat Dominus. ⁴⁸Cumque accessissent principes exercitus ad Moysen, tribuni centurionesque, dixerunt: ⁴⁹«Nos servi tui recensuimus numerum pugnatorum, quos habuimus sub manu nostra, et ne unus quidem defuit. ⁵⁰Ob hanc causam offerimus in donariis Domini singuli, quod auri potuimus invenire, periscelidas et armillas, anulos et inaures ac muraenulas, ad placandum pro nobis Dominum». ⁵¹Susceperuntque Moyses et Eleazar sacerdos aurum in diversis speciebus; ⁵²omne aurum, quod elevaverunt Domino, pondo sedecim milia septingentos quinquaginta siclos, a tribunis et centu-

and the land of Gilead, and behold, the place was a place for cattle. [2]So the sons of Gad and the sons of Reuben came and said to Moses and to Eleazar the priest and to the leaders of the congregation, [3]"Ataroth, Dibon, Jazer, Nimrah, Heshbon, Elealeh, Sebam, Nebo, and Beon, [4]the land which the LORD smote before the congregation of Israel, is a land for cattle; and your servants have cattle." [5]And they said, "If we have found favour in your sight, let this land be given to your servants for a possession; do not take us across the Jordan."

[6]But Moses said to the sons of Gad and to the sons of Reuben, "Shall your brethren go to the war while you sit here? [7]Why will you discourage the heart of the people of Israel from going over into the land which the LORD has given them? [8]Thus did your fathers, when I sent them from Kadesh-barnea to see the land. [9]For when they went up to the Valley of Eshcol, and saw the land, they discouraged the heart of the people of Israel from going into the land which the LORD had given them. [10]And the LORD's anger was kindled on that day, and he swore, saying, [11]'Surely none of the men who came up out of Egypt, from twenty years old and upward, shall see the land which I swore to give to Abraham, to Isaac, and to Jacob, because they have not wholly followed me; [12]none except Caleb the son of Jephunneh the Kenizzite and Joshua the son of Nun, for they have wholly followed the Lord.' [13]And the LORD's anger was kindled against Israel, and he made them wander in the wilderness forty years, until all the generation that had done evil in the sight of the LORD was consumed. [14]And behold, you have risen in your fathers' stead, a brood of sinful men, to increase still more

---

rionibus. [53]Unusquisque enim, quod in praeda rapuerat, suum erat. [54]Et susceptum intulerunt in tabernaculum conventus in monumentum filiorum Israel coram Domino. [1]Filii autem Ruben et Gad habebant pecora multa, et erat illis in iumentis infinita substantia. Cumque vidissent Iazer et Galaad aptas animalibus alendis terras, [2]venerunt ad Moysen et ad Eleazarum sacerdotem et principes congregationis atque dixerunt: [3]«Ataroth et Dibon et Iazer et Nemra, Hesebon et Eleale et Sabam et Nabo et Beon, [4]terra, quam percussit Dominus in conspectu congregationis Israel, regio uberrima est ad pastum animalium, et nos servi tui habemus iumenta plurima». [5]Dixeruntque: «Si invenimus gratiam coram te, detur haec terra famulis tuis in possessionem, nec facias nos transire Iordanem». [6]Quibus respondit Moyses: «Numquid fratres vestri ibunt ad pugnam, et vos hic sedebitis? [7]Cur subvertitis mentes filiorum Israel, ne transire audeant in terram, quam eis daturus est Dominus? [8]Nonne ita egerunt patres vestri, quando misi de Cadesbarne ad explorandam terram? [9]Cumque venissent usque ad Nehelescol, lustrata omni regione, subverterunt cor filiorum Israel, ut non intrarent terram, quam eis Dominus dedit. [10]Qui iratus iuravit dicens: [11]'Non videbunt homines isti, qui ascenderunt ex Aegypto, a viginti annis et supra, terram, quam sub iuramento pollicitus sum Abraham, Isaac et Iacob; nam noluerunt sequi me, [12]praeter Chaleb filium Iephonne Cenezaeum et Iosue filium Nun: isti secuti sunt Dominum!'. [13]Iratusque Dominus adversum Israel circumduxit eum per desertum quadraginta annis, donec consumeretur universa generatio, quae fecerat malum in conspectu eius. [14]Et ecce, inquit, vos surrexistis pro patribus vestris progenies hominum peccatorum, ut augeretis furorem irae Domini contra Israel. [15]Quod si nolueritis sequi eum, in solitudine iterum populum hunc circumducet, et vos

the fierce anger of the LORD against Israel! ¹⁵For if you turn away from following him, he will again abandon them in the wilderness; and you will destroy all this people."

¹⁶Then they came near to him, and said, "We will build sheepfolds here for our flocks, and cities for our little ones, ¹⁷but we will take up arms, ready to go before the people of Israel, until we have brought them to their place; and our little ones shall live in the fortified cities because of the inhabitants of the land. ¹⁸We will not return to our homes until the people of Israel have inherited each his inheritance. ¹⁹For we will not inherit with them on the other side of the Jordan and beyond; because our inheritance has come to us on this side of the Jordan to the east." ²⁰So Moses said to them, "If you will do this, if you will take up arms to go before the LORD for the war, ²¹and every armed man of you will pass over the Jordan before the LORD, until he has driven out his enemies from before him ²²and the land is subdued before the LORD; then after that you shall return and be free of obligation to the LORD and to Israel; and this land shall be your possession before the LORD. ²³But if you will not do so, behold, you have sinned against the LORD; and be sure your sin will find you out. ²⁴Build cities for your little ones, and folds for your sheep; and do what you have promised." ²⁵And the sons of Gad and the sons of Reuben said to Moses, "Your servants will do as my lord commands. ²⁶Our little ones, our wives, our flocks, and all our cattle, shall remain there in the cities of Gilead; ²⁷but your servants will pass over, every man who is armed for war, before the LORD to battle, as my lord orders."

²⁸So Moses gave command concerning them to Eleazar the priest, and to Joshua the son of Nun, and to the heads of the fathers' houses of the tribes of the people of Israel. ²⁹And Moses said to them, "If the sons of Gad and the sons of Reuben, every

causa eritis necis omnium». ¹⁶At illi prope accedentes dixerunt: «Caulas ovium fabricabimus pro iumentis nostris, parvulis quoque nostris urbes; ¹⁷nos autem ipsi armati et accincti pergemus ad proelium ante filios Israel, donec introducamus eos ad loca sua. Parvuli nostri erunt in urbibus muratis propter habitatorum insidias. ¹⁸Non revertemur in domos nostras usque dum possideant filii Israel hereditatem suam; ¹⁹nec quidquam quaeremus trans Iordanem et ultra, quia iam habemus nostram hereditatem in orientali eius plaga». ²⁰Quibus Moyses ait: «Si feceritis quod promittitis, si expediti perrexeritis coram Domino ad pugnam, ²¹et omnis vir bellator armatus Iordanem transierit, donec expulerit Dominus inimicos suos ante se, ²²et subiecta ei omni terra redieritis in terram hanc, tunc eritis inculpabiles apud Dominum et apud Israel et obtinebitis terram hanc in hereditatem coram Domino. ²³Sin autem, quod dicitis, non feceritis, nulli dubium est quin peccetis in Dominum et scitote quoniam peccatum vestrum apprehendet vos. ²⁴Aedificate ergo urbes parvulis vestris et caulas ovibus et, quod polliciti estis, implete». ²⁵Dixeruntque filii Gad et Ruben ad Moysen: «Servi tui sumus, faciemus, quod iubet dominus noster: ²⁶parvulos nostros, mulieres, pecora ac iumenta remanebunt ibi in urbibus Galaad; ²⁷famuli autem tui, omnes expediti pergent coram Domino ad bellum, sicut tu, domine, loqueris». ²⁸Praecepit ergo Moyses Eleazaro sacerdoti et Iosue filio Nun et principibus familiarum per tribus filiorum Israel et dixit ad eos: ²⁹«Si transierint filii Gad et filii Ruben vobiscum Iordanem omnes

man who is armed to battle before the Lord, will pass with you over the Jordan and the land shall be subdued before you, then you shall give them the land of Gilead for a possession; [30]but if they will not pass over with you armed, they shall have possessions among you in the land of Canaan." [31]And the sons of Gad and the sons of Reuben answered, "As the Lord has said to your servants, so we will do. [32]We will pass over armed before the Lord into the land of Canaan, and the possession of our inheritance shall remain with us beyond the Jordan."

[33]And Moses gave to them, to the sons of Gad and to the sons of Reuben and to the half-tribe of Manasseh the son of Joseph, the kingdom of Sihon king of the Amorites and the kingdom of Og king of Bashan, the land and its cities with their territories, the cities of the land throughout the country. [34]And the sons of Gad built Dibon, Ataroth, Aroer, [35]Atroth-shophan, Jazer, Jogbehah, [36]Beth-nimrah and Beth-haran, fortified cities, and folds for sheep. [37]And the sons of Reuben built Heshbon, Elealeh, Kiriathaim, [38]Nebo, and Baal-meon (their names to be changed), and Sibmah; and they gave other names to the cities which they built. [39]And the sons of Machir the son of Manasseh went to Gilead and took it, and dispossessed the Amorites who were in it. [40]And Moses gave Gilead to Machir the son of Manasseh, and he settled in it. [41]And Jair the son of Manasseh went and took their villages, and called them Havvoth-jair.[z] [42]And Nobah went and took Kenath and its villages, and called it Nobah, after his own name. Deut 3:14

The stages of Israel's journey

33 [1]These are the stages of the people of Israel, when they went forth out of the land of Egypt by their hosts under

---

33:1–49. The journey through the wilderness to the promised Land was a vitally important folk memory for Israel. God used Moses to guide them stage by stage

---

armati ad bellum coram Domino, et vobis fuerit terra subiecta, date eis Galaad in possessionem. [30]Sin autem noluerint transire armati vobiscum in terram Chanaan, inter vos habitandi accipiant loca». [31]Responderuntque filii Gad et filii Ruben: «Sicut locutus est Dominus servis suis, ita faciemus. [32]Ipsi armati pergemus coram Domino in terram Chanaan; et possidebimus hereditatem nostram trans Iordanem». [33]Dedit itaque Moyses filiis Gad et Ruben et dimidiae tribui Manasse filii Ioseph regnum Sehon regis Amorraei et regnum Og regis Basan, terram cum urbibus suis et terminis, urbes terrae per circuitum. [34]Igitur exstruxerunt filii Gad Dibon et Ataroth et Aroer [35]et Atrothsophan et Iazer et Iegbaa [36]et Bethnemra et Betharan, urbes munitas, et caulas pecoribus suis. [37]Filii vero Ruben aedificaverunt Hesebon et Eleale et Cariathaim [38]et Nabo et Baalmeon, versis nominibus, Sabama quoque, imponentes vocabula urbibus, quas exstruxerant. [39]Porro filii Machir filii Manasse perrexerunt in Galaad et ceperunt eam, expulso Amorraeo habitatore eius. [40]Dedit ergo Moyses terram Galaad Machir filio Manasse,

z. That is *the villages of Jair*

the leadership of Moses and Aaron. ²Moses wrote down their starting places, stage by stage, by command of the LORD; and these are their stages according to their starting places. ³They set out from Rameses in the first month, on the fifteenth day of the first month; on the day after the passover the people of Israel

Ex 12:12 went out triumphantly in the sight of all the Egyptians, ⁴while the Egyptians were burying all their first-born, whom the LORD had struck down among them; upon their gods also the LORD executed judgments.

Ex 12:37; 13:20; 19:2 ⁵So the people of Israel set out from Rameses, and encamped at Succoth. ⁶And they set out from Succoth, and encamped at Etham, which is on the edge of the wilderness. ⁷And they set out from Etham, and turned back to Pi-hahiroth, which is east of Baal-zephon; and they encamped before Migdol. ⁸And they set out from before Hahiroth, and passed through the midst of the sea into the wilderness, and they went a three days' journey in the wilderness of Etham, and encamped at Marah. ⁹And they set out from Marah, and came to Elim; at Elim there were twelve springs of water and seventy palm trees, and they encamped there. ¹⁰And they set out from Elim, and encamped by the Red

---

over a period of forty years, making forty-two stops. It made sense to list all these stages as a testimony to God's and Israel's great adventure: that is the purpose of this chapter. To reconstruct the stages of that journey, the redaction of Numbers drew on material to be found in ancient traditional accounts. Thus, to begin with (vv. 5–15) the redactor gives the names which appeared in Exodus 12:37—19:2 (except for the two new

names given in v. 13); later (vv. 16–36) he mentions places which for the most part we have never heard of; and then (vv. 37-38) he slots in names previously mentioned in Numbers 20:22–29. However, in the last two stages (vv. 41–49), that is, in the journey from Kadesh to Moab, he recalls how Israel crossed through Edom and Moab without making any mention of the detour via the south of the Araba referred to in 20:14–21 (the

---

qui habitavit in ea. ⁴¹Iair autem filius Manasse abiit et occupavit vicos eius, quos appellavit Havoth Iair (*id est villas Iair*). ⁴²Nobe quoque perrexit et apprehendit Canath cum viculis suis vocavitque eam ex nomine suo Nobe. ¹Hae sunt mansiones filiorum Israel, qui egressi sunt de Aegypto per turmas suas in manu Moysi et Aaron, ²quas descripsit Moyses iuxta castrorum loca, quae Domini iussione mutabant. ³Profecti igitur de Ramesse mense primo, quinta decima die mensis primi, altera die Paschae, filii Israel in manu excelsa, videntibus cunctis Aegyptiis ⁴et sepelientibus primogenitos, quos percusserat Dominus, nam et in diis eorum exercuerat ultionem, ⁵castrametati sunt in Succoth. ⁶Et de Succoth venerunt in Etham, quae est in extremis finibus solitudinis. ⁷Inde egressi venerunt contra Phihahiroth, quae respicit Beelsephon, et castrametati sunt ante Magdolum. ⁸Profectique de Phihahiroth transierunt per medium mare in solitudinem, et ambulantes tribus diebus per desertum Etham castrametati sunt in Mara. ⁹Profectique de Mara venerunt in Elim, ubi erant duodecim fontes aquarum et palmae septuaginta; ibique castrametati sunt. ¹⁰Sed et inde egressi fixerunt tentoria super mare Rubrum. Profectique de mari Rubro ¹¹castrametati sunt in deserto Sin; ¹²unde egressi venerunt in Daphca. ¹³Profectique de

Sea. [11]And they set out from the Red Sea, and encamped in the wilderness of Sin. [12]And they set out from the wilderness of Sin, and encamped at Dophkah. [13]And they set out from Dophkah, and encamped at Alush. [14]And they set out from Alush, and Ex 17:1–7 encamped at Rephidim, where there was no water for the people to drink. [15]And they set out from Rephidim, and encamped in the wilderness of Sinai. [16]And they set out from the wilderness of Sinai, and encamped at Kibroth-hattaavah. [17]And they set out from Kibroth-hattaavah, and encamped at Hazeroth. [18]And they set out from Hazeroth, and encamped at Rithmah. [19]And they set out from Rithmah, and encamped at Rimmon-perez. [20]And they set out from Rimmon-perez, and encamped at Libnah. [21]And they set out from Libnah, and encamped at Rissah. [22]And they set out from Rissah, and encamped at Kehelathah. [23]And they set out from Kehelathah, and encamped at Mount Shepher. [24]And they set out from Mount Shepher, and encamped at Haradah. [25]And they set out from Haradah, and encamped at Makheloth. [26]And they set out from Makheloth, and encamped at Tahath. [27]And they set out from Tahath, and encamped at Terah. [28]And they set out from Terah, and encamped at Mithkah. [29]And they set out from Mithkah, and encamped at Hashmonah. [30]And they

---

Araba is a low-lying desert, covering the whole area from the Dead Sea to the gulf of Akaba).

The stages in Israel's journey through the desert were interpreted by some Fathers such as St Ambrose and by other Christian writers such as Tertullian as prefiguring the forty days of the Lenten fast, en route to the resurrection of the Lord. St Jerome, going further with this line of interpretation, saw each of the forty-two names of these stopping places in the desert as one of the forty-two points or virtues along the Christian's way to heaven. Thus, Rameses or "the joy of thunder" stands for the joy of conversion through listening to preaching; Marah or "bitterness" stands for penance; Sinai or "bramble" means the difficulties ones meets which are in fact an indication of the will of God; Kadesh or "holy", where God punished Moses and Aaron, reminds us that we all have to die on account of sin; etc. (cf. St Peter Damian, *De XLII Hebraeorum mansionibus*).

Daphca castrametati sunt in Alus. [14]Egressique de Alus in Raphidim fixere tentoria, ubi populo defuit aqua ad bibendum; [15]profectique de Raphidim castrametati sunt in deserto Sinai. [16]Sed et de solitudine Sinai egressi venerunt ad Cibrottaava; [17]profectique de Cibrottaava castrametati sunt in Aseroth. [18]Et de Aseroth venerunt in Rethma; [19]profectique de Rethma castrametati sunt in Remmonphares. [20]Unde egressi venerunt in Lebna; [21]de Lebna castrametati sunt in Ressa; [22]egressique de Ressa venerunt in Ceelatha, [23]unde profecti castrametati sunt in monte Sepher. [24]Egressi de monte Sepher venerunt in Arada; [25]inde proficiscentes castrametati sunt in Maceloth; [26]profectique de Maceloth venerunt in Thahath; [27]de Thahath castrametati sunt in Thare. [28]Unde egressi fixere tentoria in Methca [29]et de Methca castrametati sunt in Hesmona; [30]profectique de Hesmona venerunt in Moseroth. [31]Et de Moseroth castrametati sunt in Beneiacam; [32]profectique de Beneiacan venerunt in montem Gadgad;

set out from Hashmonah, and encamped at Moseroth. ³¹And they set out from Moseroth, and encamped at Bene-jaakan. ³²And they set out from Bene-jaakan, and encamped at Hor-haggidgad.

Deut 10:6 ³³And they set out from Hor-haggidgad, and encamped at Jotbathah. ³⁴And they set out from Jotbathah, and encamped at Deut 2:1–8 1 Kings 9:26 Abronah. ³⁵And they set out from Abronah, and encamped at Ezion-geber. ³⁶And they set out from Ezion-geber, and Num 20:22–29 encamped in the wilderness of Zin (that is, Kadesh). ³⁷And they set out from Kadesh, and encamped at Mount Hor, on the edge of the land of Edom.

³⁸And Aaron the priest went up Mount Hor at the command of the LORD, and died there, in the fortieth year after the people of Israel had come out of the land of Egypt, on the first day of the fifth month. ³⁹And Aaron was a hundred and twenty-three years old when he died on Mount Hor.

⁴⁰And the Canaanite, the king of Arad, who dwelt in the Negeb in the land of Canaan, heard of the coming of the people of Israel.

⁴¹And they set out from Mount Hor, and encamped at Zalmonah. ⁴²And they set out from Zalmonah, and encamped at Punon. ⁴³And they set out from Punon, and encamped at Oboth. ⁴⁴And they set out from Oboth, and encamped at Iye-abarim, in the territory of Moab. ⁴⁵And they set out from Iyim, and encamped at Dibon-gad. ⁴⁶And they set out from Dibon-gad, and encamped at Almon-diblathaim. ⁴⁷And they set out from Almon-diblathaim, and encamped in the mountains of Abarim, before Num 22:1 Nebo. ⁴⁸And they set out from the mountains of Abarim, and encamped in the plains of Moab by the Jordan at Jericho; ⁴⁹they encamped by the Jordan from Beth-jeshimoth as far as Abel-shit-timin the plains of Moab.

³³unde profecti castrametati sunt in Ietebatha. ³⁴Et de Ietebatha venerunt in Ebrona; ³⁵egressique de Ebrona castrametati sunt in Asiongaber. ³⁶Inde profecti venerunt in desertum Sin, hoc est Cades. ³⁷Egressique de Cades castrametati sunt in monte Hor in extremis finibus terrae Edom. ³⁸Ascenditque Aaron sacerdos in montem Hor, iubente Domino, et ibi mortuus est anno quadragesimo egressionis filiorum Israel ex Aegypto, mense quinto, prima die mensis, ³⁹cum esset annorum centum viginti trium. ⁴⁰Audivitque Chananaeus rex Arad, qui habitabat in Nageb, in terra Chanaan, venisse filios Israel. ⁴¹Et profecti de monte Hor castrametati sunt in Salmona; ⁴²unde egressi venerunt in Phinon. ⁴³Profectique de Phinon castrametati sunt in Oboth; ⁴⁴et de Oboth venerunt in Ieabarim, quae est in finibus Moabitarum. ⁴⁵Profectique de Ieabarim fixere tentoria in Dibongad; ⁴⁶unde egressi castrametati sunt in Elmondeblathaim. ⁴⁷Egressique de Elmondeblathaim venerunt ad montes Abarim contra Nabo. ⁴⁸Profectique de montibus Abarim transierunt ad campestria Moab supra Iordanem contra Iericho; ⁴⁹ibique castrametati sunt de Bethiesimoth usque ad Abelsettim in campestribus Moab. ⁵⁰Ubi locutus est Dominus ad Moysen: ⁵¹«Praecipe filiis Israel et dic ad eos: Quando transieritis Iordanem intrantes terram Chanaan, ⁵²disperdite cunctos habitatores terrae ante vos, confringite omnes imagines eorum et omnes statuas comminuite atque omnia excelsa vastate. ⁵³Possidebitis terram et habitabitis in ea. Ego

Lev 26
Deut 7:1–6;
12:2–3

The Lord's orders to drive out the Canaanites

[50]And the LORD said to Moses in the plains of Moab by the Jordan at Jericho, [51]"Say to the people of Israel, When you pass over the Jordan into the land of Canaan, [52]then you shall drive out all the inhabitants of the land from before you, and destroy all their figured stones, and destroy all their molten images, and demolish all their high places; [53]and you shall take possession of the land and settle in it, for I have given the land to you to possess it. [54]You shall inherit the land by lot according to your families; to a large tribe you shall give a large inheritance, and to a small tribe you shall give a small inheritance; wherever the lot falls to any man, that shall be his; according to the tribes of your fathers you shall inherit. [55]But if you do not drive out the inhabitants of the land from before you, then those of them whom you let remain shall be as pricks in your eyes and thorns in your sides, and they shall trouble you in the land where you dwell. [56]And I will do to you as I thought to do to them."

1 Sam 9:12

2 Cor 12:7

The boundaries of the promised land

Josh 14–19
Judg 20:1
Ezra 47:13–21

34 [1]The LORD said to Moses, [2]"Command the people of Israel, and say to them, When you enter the land of Canaan (this is the land that shall fall to you for an inheritance,

---

33:50–56. By passing through these stages the people reach the promised land. So, by recalling them, the people are also reminded of the conditions God imposed for obtaining the Land and dwelling there in peace: the people are required to be absolutely faithful to God, and to uproot anything which might draw them away from him—in particular, idols and places where Canaanite religious ceremonies took place. In some way the underlying tone of these verses is that the opposite was what really happened—that Israel often took part in idolatrous practices.

The distribution of land by lot shows that, since Canaan was God's gift to Israel, all the people had a share in it, each possessing the portion assigned by lot. This sharing by all in the promised land is in a way an application of the fact that the earth and all it contains were given to mankind (cf. the note on Num 27:1–11).

34:1–15. The Lord himself fixes the frontiers of the Land; this shows that he is the One who gives Israel its inheritance. In this passage, not all the borders are easy to identify. Some places, especially on the

---

enim dedi vobis illam in possessionem, [54]quam dividetis inter tribus vestras. Maiori dabitis latiorem et minori angustiorem; singulis, ut sors ceciderit, ita tribuetur hereditas; per tribus et familias possessio dividetur. [55]Sin autem nolueritis expellere habitatores terrae, qui remanserint, erunt vobis quasi spinae in oculis vestris et sudes in lateribus, et adversabuntur vobis in terra habitationis vestrae; [56]et, quidquid illis cogitaveram facere, vobis faciam». [1]Locutusque est Dominus ad Moysen dicens: [2]«Praecipe filiis Israel et dices ad eos: Cum ingressi fueritis terram hanc Chanaan, et in possessionem vobis sorte

the land of Canaan in its full extent), [3]your south side shall be from the wilderness of Zin along the side of Edom, and your southern boundary shall be from the end of the Salt Sea on the east; [4]and your boundary shall turn south of the ascent of Akrabbim, and cross to Zin, and its end shall be south of Kadesh-barnea; then it shall go on to Hazar-addar, and pass along to Azmon; [5]and the boundary shall turn from Azmon to the Brook of Egypt, and its termination shall be at the sea.

[6]"For the western boundary, you shall have the Great Sea and its[a] coast; this shall be your western boundary.

[7]"This shall be your northern boundary: from the Great Sea you shall mark out your line to Mount Hor; [8]from Mount Hor you shall mark it out to the entrance of Hamath, and the end of the boundary shall be at Zeded; [9]then the boundary shall extend to Ziphron, and its end shall be at Hazar-enan; this shall be your northern boundary.

[10]"You shall mark out your eastern boundary from Hazar-enan to Shepham; [11]and the boundary shall go down from Shepham to Riblah on the east side of Ain; and the boundary shall go down, and reach to the shoulder of the sea of Chinnereth on the east; [12]and the boundary shall go down to the Jordan, and its end shall be at the Salt Sea. This shall be your land with its boundaries all round."

[13]Moses commanded the people of Israel, saying, "This is the land which you shall inherit by lot, which the LORD has com-

---

northern border, we cannot identify at all. Mount Hor, different from the mountain of the same name in 20:22, seems to be the northern massif of Lebanon. Basic-ally, these frontiers are those of the Egyptian province of Canaan around the end of the 13th century BC, as remembered by later generations of Israelites.

---

ceciderit, his finibus terminabitur. [3]Pars meridiana incipiet a solitudine Sin, quae est iuxta Edom, et habebit terminos contra orientem mare Salsissimum. [4]Qui circuibunt australem plagam per ascensum Acrabbim (*id est Scorpionum*), ita ut transeant in Sin et perveniant ad meridiem Cadesbarne, unde egredientur ad Asaraddar et tendent usque ad Asemona. [5]Ibitque per gyrum terminus ab Asemona usque ad torrentem Aegypti, et maris Magni litore finietur. [6]Plaga autem occidentalis a mari Magno incipiet et ipso fine claudetur. [7]Porro ad septentrionalem plagam a mari Magno termini incipient per-venientes usque ad montem Hor, [8]a quo venient in introitum Emath usque ad terminos Sedada. [9]Ibuntque confinia usque ad Zephrona et Asarenon. Hi erunt termini in parte aquilonis. [10]Inde metabun-tur fines contra orientalem plagam de Asarenon usque Sephama; [11]et de Sephama descendent termini in Rebla ad orientem Ain; inde descendent et pervenient ad latus maris Chenereth in oriente [12]et ten-dent usque ad Iordanem, et ad ultimum Salsissimo claudentur mari. Hanc habebitis terram per fines suos in circuitu». [13]Praecepitque Moyses filiis Israel dicens: «Haec erit terra, quam possidebitis sorte et quam iussit Dominus dari novem tribubus et dimidiae tribui. [14]Tribus enim filiorum Ruben per fami-

a. Syr: Heb lacks *its*

manded to give to the nine tribes and to the half-tribe; [14]for the tribe of the sons of Reuben by fathers' houses and the tribe of the sons of Gad by their fathers' houses have received their inheritance, and also the half-tribe of Manasseh; [15]the two tribes and the half-tribe have received their inheritance beyond the Jordan at Jericho eastward, toward the sunrise."

The leaders in charge of allocating the land

[16]The LORD said to Moses, [17]"These are the names of the men who shall divide the land to you for inheritance: Eleazar the priest and Joshua the son of Nun. [18]You shall take one leader of every tribe, to divide the land for inheritance. [19]These are the names of the men: Of the tribe of Judah, Caleb the son of Jephunneh. [20]Of the tribe of the sons of Simeon, Shemuel the son of Ammihud. [21]Of the tribe of Benjamin, Elidad the son of Chislon. [22]Of the tribe of the sons of Dan a leader, Bukki the son of Jogli. [23]Of the sons of Joseph: of the tribe of the sons of Manasseh a leader, Hanniel the son of Ephod. [24]And of the tribe of the sons of Ephraim a leader, Kemuel the son of Shiphtan. [25]Of the tribe of the sons of Zebulun a leader, Eli-zaphan the son of Parnach. [26]Of the tribe of the sons of Issachar a leader, Paltiel the son of Azzan. [27]And of the tribe of the sons of Asher a leader, Ahihud the son of Shelomi. [28]Of the tribe of the sons of Naphtali a leader, Pedahel the son of Ammihud. [29]These are the men whom the LORD commanded to divide the inheritance for the people of Israel in the land of Canaan."

34:16–29. Of all the names on this list, only those of Joshua and Caleb have appeared before (cf. 14:30). The others are new, for the very good reason that this is a different generation from that which set out on the great journey. The previous generation has already died out due to its rebellion against God or, as the Letter to

the Hebrews tells us, due to its unbelief (Heb 3:19). In that Letter we are told that the promised land was a symbol for eternal rest, and what happened in the wilderness is an encouragement to us not to falter, as the Hebrews did; if we stay true, we will be able to enter that everlasting rest: God's promise still holds (Heb 3–4).

---

lias suas et tribus filiorum Gad iuxta cognationum numerum media quoque tribus Manasse, [15]id est duae semis tribus, acceperunt partem suam trans Iordanem contra Iericho ad orientalem plagam». [16]Et ait Dominus ad Moysen: [17]«Haec sunt nomina virorum, qui terram vobis divident: Eleazar sacerdos et Iosue filius Nun [18]et singuli principes de tribubus singulis, [19]quorum ista sunt vocabula: de tribu Iudae Chaleb filius Iephonne; [20]de tribu Simeon Samuel filius Ammiud; [21]de tribu Beniamin Elidad filius Chaselon; [22]de tribu filiorum Dan Bocci filius Iogli. [23]Filiorum Ioseph: de tribu Manasse Hanniel filius Ephod, [24]de tribu Ephraim Camuel filius Sephtan. [25]De tribu Zabulon Elisaphan filius Pharnach; [26]de tribu Issachar dux Phaltiel filius Ozan; [27]de tribu Aser Ahiud filius Salomi; [28]de tribu Nephthali Phedael filius Ammiud». [29]Hi sunt, quibus praecepit Dominus, ut dividerent filiis Israel terram Chanaan. [1]Haec

Num 18:20-24
Josh 20–21 **Cities for the Levites**
Ezek 48:13

35 [1]The LORD said to Moses in the plains of Moab by the Jordan at Jericho, [2]"Command the people of Israel, that they give to the Levites, from the inheritance of their possession, cities to dwell in; and you shall give to the Levites pasture lands round about the cities. [3]The cities shall be theirs to dwell in, and their pasture lands shall be for their cattle and for their livestock and for all their beasts. [4]The pasture lands of the cities, which you shall give to the Levites, shall reach from the wall of the city outward a thousand cubits all round. [5]And you shall measure, outside the city, for the east side two thousand cubits, and for the south side two thousand cubits, and for the west side two thousand cubits, and for the north side two thousand cubits, the city being in the middle; this shall

Deut 4:41–43 belong to them as pasture land for their cities. [6]The cities which you give to the Levites shall be the six cities of refuge, where you shall permit the manslayer to flee, and in addition to them you shall give forty-two cities. [7]All the cities which you give to the Levites shall be forty-eight, with their pasture lands. [8]And as for the cities which you shall give from the possession of the people of Israel, from the larger tribes you shall take many, and from the smaller tribes you shall take few; each, in proportion to the inheritance which it inherits, shall give of its cities to the Levites."

Ex 21:13
Deut 19:1–13 **Cities of refuge**
[9]And the LORD said to Moses, [10]"Say to the people of Israel, When you cross the Jordan into the land of Canaan, [11]then you

---

35:1–8. Once again we can see here concern for the material needs of the Levites: they are the responsibility of all the tribes, so much so that they are to be given part of what the other tribes inherit.

35:9–34. It is God himself, through

Moses, who decides how the people of Israel are to be organized in the promised land, and the kinds of cities they are to have. This passage deals with cities of refuge; later when the distribution of the land is reported, it is specified which cities these are to be (cf. Josh 20:7–8).

---

quoque locutus est Dominus ad Moysen in campestribus Moab supra Iordanem contra Iericho: [2]«Praecipe filiis Israel, ut dent Levitis de possessionibus suis urbes ad habitandum et suburbana earum per circuitum, [3]ut ipsi in oppidis maneant, et suburbana sint pecoribus ac substantiae et omnibus animalibus eorum; [4]quae a muris civitatum forinsecus per circuitum mille cubitos spatio tendentur. [5]Et mensurabitis extra civitatem contra orientem duo milia cubitorum, et contra meridiem similiter duo milia, ad mare quoque, quod respicit ad occidentem, eadem mensura erit, et septentrionalis plaga aequali termino finietur; eruntque urbes in medio et foris suburbana. [6]De ipsis autem oppidis, quae Levitis dabitis, sex erunt in fugitivorum auxilia separata, ut fugiat ad ea, qui nesciens fuderit sanguinem; et, exceptis his, alia quadraginta duo oppida dabitis, [7]id est simul quadraginta octo cum suburbanis suis. [8]Ipsaeque urbes, quas dabitis de possessionibus filiorum Israel, ab his, qui plus habent, plures auferetis, et, qui minus, pauciores; singuli iuxta mensuram hereditatis suae dabunt oppida

650

shall select cities to be cities of refuge for you, that the manslayer who kills any person without intent may flee there. [12]The cities shall be for you a refuge from the avenger, that the manslayer may not die until he stands before the congregation for judgment. [13]And the cities which you give shall be your six cities of refuge. [14]You shall give three cities beyond the Jordan, and three cities in the land of Canaan, to be cities of refuge. [15]These six cities shall be for refuge for the people of Israel, and for the stranger and for the sojourner among them, that any one who kills any person without intent may flee there.

[16]"But if he struck him down with an instrument of iron, so that he died, he is a murderer; the murderer shall be put to death. [17]And if he struck him down with a stone in the hand, by which a man may die, and he died, he is a murderer; the murderer shall be put to death. [18]Or if he struck him down with a weapon of wood in the hand, by which a man may die, and he died, he is a murderer; the murderer shall be put to death. [19]The avenger of blood shall himself put the murderer to death; when he meets him, he shall put him to death. [20]And if he stabbed him from hatred, or hurled at him, lying in wait, so that he died, [21]or in enmity struck him down with his hand, so that he died, then he who struck the blow shall be put to death; he is a murderer; the avenger of blood shall put the murderer to death, when he meets him.

Heb 10:28

[22]"But if he stabbed him suddenly without enmity, or hurled anything on him without lying in wait, [23]or used a stone, by which a man may die, and without seeing him cast it upon him, so that

---

The purpose of these cities is linked to what it says in Exodus 21:13; it establishes a limit on the law of vengeance for violent death which laid down that a man who died violently was to be avenged by his nearest male relative. In the Exodus text referred to, it was God who protected the avenger; here it is the community designated by God to act as protector.

Levitis». [9]Ait Dominus ad Moysen: [10]«Loquere filiis Israel et dices ad eos: Quando transgressi fueritis Iordanem in terram Chanaan, [11]eligetis urbes, quae esse debeant in praesidia fugitivorum, qui nolentes sanguinem fuderint; [12]erunt vobis urbes refugii contra ultorem, et occisor non morietur, donec stet in conspectu congregationis, et causa illius iudicetur. [13]De ipsis autem sex urbibus, quae ad fugitivorum subsidia separantur, [14]tres erunt trans Iordanem et tres in terra Chanaan, [15]tam filiis Israel quam advenis atque peregrinis, ut confugiat ad eas sex, qui nolens sanguinem fuderit. [16]Si quis ferro percusserit, et mortuus fuerit, qui percussus est, reus erit homicidii et ipse morietur. [17]Si lapidem mortiferum iecerit, et ictus occiderit, similiter punietur. [18]Si ligno mortifero percusserit eum et interfecerit, homicida est; ipse morte punietur. [19]Ultor sanguinis homicidam interficiet: statim ut apprehenderit eum, interficiet. [20]Si per odium quis hominem impulerit vel iecerit quippiam in eum per insidias [21]aut, cum esset inimicus, manu percusserit, et ille mortuus fuerit, percussor homicidii reus erit: ultor sanguinis statim ut invenerit eum, iugulabit. [22]Quod si fortuito et absque odio eum percusserit vel quidpiam in eum iecerit absque insidiis, [23]vel quemlibet lapidem mortiferum in eum devolverit, cum eum non vidisset, et ille mortuus est, quamvis eum non oderit nec quaesierit ei malum, [24]iudicabit congregatio inter percus-

he died, though he was not his enemy, and did not seek his harm; ²⁴then the congregation shall judge between the manslayer and the avenger of blood, in accordance with these ordinances; ²⁵and the congregation shall rescue the manslayer from the hand of the avenger of blood, and the congregation shall restore him to his city of refuge, to which he had fled, and he shall live in it until the death of the high priest who was anointed with the holy oil. ²⁶But if the manslayer shall at any time go beyond the bounds of his city of refuge to which he fled, ²⁷and the avenger of blood finds him outside the bounds of his city of refuge, and the avenger of blood slays the manslayer, he shall not be guilty of blood. ²⁸For the man must remain in his city of refuge until the death of the high priest; but after the death of the high priest the manslayer may return to the land of his possession.

²⁹"And these things shall be for a statute and ordinance to you throughout your generations in all your dwellings. ³⁰If any one kills a person, the murderer shall be put to death on the evidence of witnesses; but no person shall be put to death on the testimony of one witness. ³¹Moreover you shall accept no ransom for the life of a murderer, who is guilty of death; but he shall be put to death. ³²And you shall accept no ransom for him who has fled to his city of refuge, that he may return to dwell in the land before the death of the high priest. ³³You shall not thus pollute the land in which you live; for blood pollutes the land, and no expiation can be made for the land, for the blood that is shed in it, except by the blood of him who shed it. ³⁴You shall not defile the land in which you live, in the midst of which I dwell; for I the LORD dwell in the midst of the people of Israel."

Num 27:1–11 **Laws about wives' inheritance**

36 ¹The heads of the fathers' houses of the families of the sons of Gilead the son of Machir, son of Manasseh, of the

---

36:1–2. This passage marks a development in the law of inheritance as applied to women (cf. 27:1–11). This specific case is used to make a rule about the

sorem et ultorem sanguinis secundum has regulas ²⁵et liberabit occisorem de manu ultoris sanguinis et reducet in civitatem refugii, ad quam confugerat, manebitque ibi, donec sacerdos magnus, qui oleo sancto unctus est, moriatur. ²⁶Si interfector extra fines civitatis refugii, in quam confugerat, exierit, ²⁷et invenerit eum ultor sanguinis ibi et interfecerit, absque noxa erit, qui eum occiderit; ²⁸debuerat enim profugus usque ad mortem pontificis in civitate refugii residere. Postquam autem ille obierit, homicida revertetur in terram suam. ²⁹Haec erunt vobis in legitima iudicii pro generationibus vestris, in cunctis habitationibus vestris. ³⁰Homicida sub testibus occidetur; ad unius testimonium nullus ad mortem condemnabitur. ³¹Non accipietis pretium pro eo, qui reus est sanguinis, sed morietur. ³²Neque accipietis pretium, ut fugiat in civitatem refugii sui, ut revertatur et habitet in terra ante mortem sacerdotis. ³³Non polluetis terram habitationis vestrae, quia sanguis polluit terram, nec aliter expiari potest nisi per eius

fathers' houses of the sons of Joseph, came near and spoke before Moses and before the leaders, the heads of the fathers' houses of the people of Israel; ²they said, "The LORD commanded my lord to give the land for inheritance by lot to the people of Israel; and my lord was commanded by the LORD to give the inheritance of Zelophehad our brother to his daughters. ³But if they are married to any of the sons of the other tribes of the people of Israel then their inheritance will be taken from the inheritance of our fathers, and added to the inheritance of the tribe to which they belong; so it will be taken away from the lot of our inheritance. ⁴And when the jubilee of the people of Israel comes, then their inheritance will be added to the inheritance of the tribe to which they belong; and their inheritance will be taken from the inheritance of the tribe of our fathers."

Lev 25:1

⁵And Moses commanded the people of Israel according to the word of the LORD, saying, "The tribe of the sons of Joseph is right. ⁶This is what the LORD commands concerning the daughters of Zelophehad, 'Let them marry whom they think best; only, they shall marry within the family of the tribe of their father. ⁷The inheritance of the people of Israel shall not be transferred from one tribe to another; for every one of the people of Israel shall cleave to the inheritance of the tribe of his fathers. ⁸And every daughter who possesses an inheritance in any tribe of the people of Israel shall be wife to one of the family of the tribe of her father, so that every one of the people of Israel may possess the inheritance of his fathers. ⁹So no inheritance shall be transferred

---

marriage of a daughter who has inheritance rights, a rule designed to ensure that that ownership of the Land does not pass to another tribe. Once again it reflects belief in the fact that the Land is a gift from God, not to the people in general but to each family and each individual. It follows that the portion allotted to each has to be carefully looked after as a gift from God.

---

sanguinem, qui alterius sanguinem fuderit. ³⁴Non maculabitis terram habitationis vestrae, me commorante vobiscum. Ego enim sum Dominus, qui habito inter filios Israel». ¹Accesserunt autem et principes familiarum tribus filiorum Galaad filii Machir filii Manasse de stirpe filiorum Ioseph, locutique sunt Moysi coram principibus familiarum Israel ²atque dixerunt: «Tibi domino nostro praecepit Dominus, ut terram sorte divideres filiis Israel et ut filiabus Salphaad fratris nostri dares hereditatem debitam patri; ³quas si alterius tribus homines uxores acceperint, sequetur possessio sua, et translata ad aliam tribum de nostra hereditate minuetur. ⁴Atque ita fiet, ut cum iobeleus advenerit, addetur possessio earum possessioni tribus, ad quam pertinent, et a possessione tribus patrum nostrorum auferetur». ⁵Respondit Moyses filiis Israel et, Domino praecipiente, ait: «Recte tribus filiorum Ioseph locuta est, ⁶et haec lex super filiabus Salphaad a Domino promulgata est: Nubant, quibus volunt, tantum ut suae tribus hominibus, ⁷ne commisceatur possessio filiorum Israel de tribu in tribum; filii Israel adhaerebunt possessioni tribus patrum suorum, ⁸et cunctae filiae heredes e filiis Israel maritos e cognatione tribus patrum suorum accipient, ut hereditas permaneat in familiis, ⁹nec commisceatur possessio de tribu in

from one tribe to another; for each of the tribes of the people of Israel shall cleave to its own inheritance.'"

[10]The daughters of Zelophehad did as the LORD commanded Moses; [11]for Mahlah, Tirzah, Hoglah, Milcah, and Noah, the daughters of Zelophehad, were married to sons of their father's brothers. [12]They were married into the families of the sons of Manasseh the son of Joseph, and their inheritance remained in the tribe of the family of their father.

[13]These are the commandments and the ordinances which the LORD commanded by Moses to the people of Israel in the plains of Moab by the Jordan at Jericho.

---

tribum alteram, sed filii Israel adhaerebunt possessioni tribuum suarum». [10]Sicut mandavit Dominus Moysi, sic fecerunt filiae Salphaad [11]et nupserunt Maala et Thersa et Hegla et Melcha et Noa filiis patruorum suorum [12]de familiis Manasse, qui fuit filius Ioseph; et possessio, quae illis fuerat attributa, mansit in tribu et familia patris earum. [13]Haec sunt mandata atque iudicia, quae mandavit Dominus per manum Moysi ad filios Israel in campestribus Moab supra Iordanem contra Iericho.

DEUTERONOMY

Introduction

Deuteronomy is the title commonly given by the Christian Church to the fifth book of the Pentateuch. The name comes from the Septuagint Greek translation of Deuteronomy 17:18; instead of translating "he shall write for himself in a book *a copy of this law,*" the translators put *this second law* (= *to deuteronómion toúto*). However, the title is not inappropriate, because the book includes, along with historical accounts, long discourses, exhortations etc., a second body of laws similar in content (with more or less substantial differences, depending on the case) found in the book of Exodus (and, sometimes, in Leviticus). In Judaism this book is known by its opening words: '*Elleh ha-debarim* ("These are the words") or, simply, *Debarim* ("Words").

1. STRUCTURE AND CONTENT

Deuteronomy recounts the main events at the end of the forty years the Israelites spent wandering in the desert under the leadership of Moses: they are encamped in the lands of Moab, east of the Dead Sea, within sight of the promised land which extends westwards from the Dead Sea and the river Jordan. The people are about to embark on the conquest of the land the Lord is going to give them, and Moses will now address them in farewell addresses which contain his last will and tell them the rule of behaviour they should keep. To this end, he reminds them of the main events that occurred during the Exodus and he urges them to keep the main Law of the Covenant or the Decalogue (promulgated also in Exodus 20:2–17); he makes a number of exhortative speeches, promulgates groupings of laws and rounds off his farewell discourses with a long canticle and various blessings.

The structure of Deuteronomy as it now stands can be viewed in a number of ways. Many commentators like to see the book as consisting basically of three great discourses attributed to Moses, with a short introduction and a long epilogue made up of a number of separate pieces. From a descriptive point of view this is a useful way to divide up the book; it works out as follows:

INTRODUCTION (1:1–5)

PART ONE: THE FIRST DISCOURSE OF MOSES: HISTORICAL INTRODUCTION (1:6—4:43). To the fore here is an account of the Exodus from the time of the

revelation at Horeb up to when Israel finds itself encamped on the plains of Moab. The people are exhorted to be grateful to God for the great deeds he has done in their favour.

The discourse begins by recalling how the expedition set out from Mount Horeb (Deut 1:6–18), the events at Kadesh (1:19–46), the arrival and settlement in Transjordan (2:1—3:29), and the people's unfaithfulness at Baal-peor when they were almost on the threshold of the promised land (4:1–8). The address ends by stipulating what the covenant of Mount Horeb entails and outlining possible punishment, the threat of which helps to convert the people to the Lord (4:9–40).

PART TWO: THE SECOND DISCOURSE OF MOSES: THE LAW (4:44—28:68). This is the main part of the book.

It begins with the proclamation of the Ten Commandments (5:1–22), followed by a call to be faithful to God: this starts with a profession of faith in the one God—the *Shemá* (6:1–9)—and it then reminds people that they are the object of God's special election, which endows them with special strength (6:10—7:26). The pilgrimage in the desert, and all that it involved in terms of the people's infidelities and the punishment meted out to them by God, and also the victories he won for them—all this is seen as a model of what can happen once they reach the promised land (8:1—11:31).

The central part of the discourse is taken up with the Deuteronomic Code or the Covenant of Moab (chaps. 12–26), a lengthy reworking of various legal and moral traditions. The first part of this deals with various religious regulations built around the key theme of there being only One God, and that there should be only one place where lawful worship is to be rendered to him (12:2—18:22). After this come prescriptions about specific matters—the law of retaliation (19:1—21:9), family and marriage (21:10—23:15) and protection of the weak (23:16—25:19). It ends with some ritual rules about first fruits and tithes (26:1–15).

There is a long conclusion to this second discourse, much of which is devoted to blessings and curses which apply to those who fail to fulfil what is laid down (26:16—28:69).

PART THREE: THE THIRD DISCOURSE OF MOSES: THE COVENANT OF MOAB (28:69—30:20). This repeats the exhortations to be faithful to the Covenant.

The discourse begins by recalling the escape from Egypt and the Covenant made with God (29:1–12)—the purpose being to remind future generations of their duty to stay true to that Covenant (29:13–27). It ends with an urgent call to opt for fidelity to God (= choosing life) rather than straying from his paths (= choosing death): cf. 29:28—30:20.

HISTORICAL CONCLUSION (31:1—34:12). This section records the last acts of Moses.

It begins by recounting the choice of Joshua as Moses' successor (31:1–8); this is followed by the famous song or canticle of Moses (32:1–43) and his Blessings on each of the tribes (33:1–29). Finally, it narrates the death of Israel's great deliverer and lawgiver (34:1–12).

In line with this thematic structure, the Deuteronomic laws are set within the framework of a generally historical account of events and various moral exhortations rich in religious meaning. Thus, the sacred writer manages to avoid the dryness of a purely legal-moral text. It all flows together nicely and is interesting to read.

Another possible approach to the structure of Deuteronomy is to follow what seem to be headings provided by the book itself. These are:

I. 1:1 *"These are the words* that Moses spoke to all Israel beyond the Jordan."

II. 4:44: *"This is the law* which Moses set before the children of Israel."

III. 6:1: *"Now this is the commandment, the statutes and the ordinances* which the Lord your God commanded me to teach you, that you may do them in the land to which you are going over, to possess it."

IV. 12:1: *"These are the statutes and ordinances* which you shall be careful to do in the land which the Lord, the God of your fathers, has given you to possess."

V. 29:1: *"These are the words* of the covenant which the Lord commanded Moses to make with the people of Israel in the land of Moab."

VI. 33:1: *"This is the blessing* with which Moses the man of God blessed the children of Israel before his death."

These headings serve to introduce (or perhaps to conclude, in the case of 6:1 and 29:1) the various parts which we have more or less indicated in our division of the book into the three great discourses of Moses.

2. THE DEUTERONOMIC TRADITION: A THEOLOGY OF HISTORY

The theological, literary, stylistic and other features which scholars have identified as common to Deuteronomy and the books of Joshua, Judges, Samuel and Kings have led them to believe that all these books are the (impressive) outcome of the work of a tradition or school which can be described as

"Deuteronomic". This tradition worked on a heritage left by previous generations[1] and was aided by the inspiration of the Holy Spirit who was educating
his people by enlightening them (and chastising them when necessary); it
developed the first great theology of the history of the people of Israel from
the time when they settled in the land of Canaan around the end of the second
millennium BC up to the time of the Babylonian captivity (6th century BC). The
providence of God and Israel's deep conviction of its being a chosen people
create the greatest history ever written.

According to this interpretation, the book of Deuteronomy acts as a prologue to this great theological explanation of history developed with the
"Deuteronomic" tradition. In compiling this great work, the authors did not
start from scratch: they had available to them earlier historical and legal material and ancient traditions of the people. In the details of this history we can
see the active role played by prophets at key moments: Nathan with David at
the point when the monarchy is being consolidated; Elijah confronting the
danger of polytheism at the time of Ahab, etc. This history also highlights the
presence of important personalities—Moses, to whom the Law was given;
Joshua, who led the conquest of the promised land; David, who brought the
monarchy to its zenith; Solomon, who built the temple; Josiah, who centralized religious worship. From time to time this history records important
speeches by key figures which help to explain the meaning of the main
events.

All this combines to teach the people that the promise of the Land was
never an absolute one: it was conditional on their doing what they undertook
to do in the Covenant. The following text from Deuteronomy (30:15–20) is a
good example of this: "See, I have set before you this day life and good,
death and evil. If you obey the commandments of the Lord your God which
I command you this day, by loving the Lord your God, by walking in his way,
and by keeping his commandments and his statutes and his ordinances, then
you shall live and multiply, and the Lord your God will bless you in the land
which you are entering to take possession of it. But if your heart turns away,
and you will not hear, but are drawn away to worship other gods and serve
them, I declare to you this day, that you shall perish; you shall not live long
in the land which you are going over the Jordan to enter and possess. I call
heaven and earth to witness against you this day, that I have set before you
life and death, blessing and curse; therefore choose life, that you and your
descendants may live, loving the Lord your God, obeying his voice, and
cleaving to him; for that means life to you and length of days, that you may
dwell in the land which the Lord swore to your fathers, to Abraham, to Isaac,
and to Jacob, to give them."

The words of this passage establish a correlation between faithfulness to
the Covenant and settlement on the Land; and between infidelity and exile.
This will be the key used to interpret the events that occur in the course of

this history. The conclusion is crystal clear: Israel cannot blame God for not keeping his promises; Israel's sins were what brought about the Exile. God has been ever patient and merciful, in the hope that his people will mend their ways. The cycle of rebellion-punishment-repentance-salvation will occur again and again; yet despite that the people never learn the clear lesson.

3. COMPOSITION

Apparently the Israelite tribes that occupied the Northern regions of the promised land (more numerous than those in the South) conserved memories of the period prior to the Davidic monarchy, and their religious life underwent a degree of development in connexion with certain holy places and feasts. The ceremony of renewing the Covenant seems to have been better maintained in the North than in the South. Thus, in Joshua 8:30–35 there is a mention of a religious assembly near Shechem (in the Samaria region). There are grounds for thinking that at assemblies of this sort an account was read of the main episodes of the deliverance from Egypt, of the ten commandments given to Israel through Moses and of the lists of blessings and curses designed to encourage the people to obey those commandments which upheld their pact with God. Joshua 24:25 reports a ceremony of covenant renewal that took place at Shechem, and 1 Samuel 12:7ff reports a renewal ceremony at Gilgal.

The renewal of the Covenant was probably one of the key occasions when people were reminded about the Mosaic laws and took them to heart: this must have been the origin of the core of Deuteronomy (chaps 5–26). Some of the traditions must have developed among the Northern tribes (the Elohistic tradition) and been brought to Jerusalem after Samaria fell to the Assyrians (722–721 BC). The fusion of these Elohistic elements with the tradition which had been taking shape in Jerusalem circles over the course of the Davidic monarchy must have been what led to the Deuteronomic tradition, the tradition to which the core chapters of Deuteronomy is ascribed; the text must have attained a form very close to that of our present text around the 6th century BC.

This text, as we said, may have originally acted as a prologue to a history of Israel from the time of settlement in Canaan up to the Exile; but it would have been edited slightly to become the concluding book of the Pentateuch, which is how it has come down to us in the canon of Holy Scripture. The suite of five books would have been completed to coincide nicely with the return from exile around the end of the 5th century BC. This function of the book of Deuteronomy—to act as the conclusion of the Pentateuch (though that is still just a theory)—does seem consistent with its position not only in the Pentateuch but also in Old Testament history as a whole: it rounds off the first stage, when Israel is within sight of the promised land, and it opens the way to

the book of Joshua (dealing with the conquest of the Land) and the so-called historical books of the Old Testament up to the Exile (that is, Joshua itself and Judges, Samuel and Kings).

In any case, irrespective of how the book came to be written, Deuteronomy is a majestic book containing key theological and moral teaching concerning the history of Revelation and human thought. Its message is built up on the concepts of the election of the people of Israel by God, and the Covenant: God for his own good reasons chose the children of Israel and made them his own property, offering them a Covenant whereby they committed themselves to acknowledge and worship Yahweh (the Lord) as their only Elohim (God). In addition to making the Covenant with them, God promised them a land of their own. Deuteronomy, really, marks the transition from the prehistory of Israel (patriarchs and Exodus) to the history of the people of the Covenant and of the Prophets.

4. MESSAGE

The basic theological message contained in Deuteronomy can be summed up as: one God, one people, one temple, one land, one law.

The unicity of God is formally proclaimed in Deuteronomy 6:4: "Hear, O Israel: The Lord our God is one Lord". This "one" means not only that there is no such thing as a number of different gods; it also proclaims the inner unity of God: God is undivided. Therefore, love for him should also be undivided, not shared with other gods or other loves in one's heart which do not lead to him. "You shall love the Lord your God with all your heart, and with all your soul, and with all your might" (6:5).

Given that there is only one God, the worship offered to him is to take place in only one sanctuary—the temple of Jerusalem (Deut 12).

This one and only God has chosen one people and made his covenant with that people. It is a people that must have no diversity of cult or social class, no discrimination of any kind. Unlike the Priestly tradition, the Deuteronomic tradition does not distinguish the people as being made up of different tribes or families. Its ideal is that the entire people, from the highest to the lowest, should be brothers and sisters. It is no ordinary people, but the People of God.

The land of Israel is a gift from God to his people, a magnificent endowment, but it contains within it a danger that cannot be gainsaid—a tendency on Israel's part to enjoy its benefits as if it had a perfect right to them, forgetting that they are a gift which God has entrusted to men to manage wisely (8:7ff).

Finally, the Law is an expression of God's will which shows his people the paths that they should follow.

When Deuteronomy was composed, the situation of Israelite society was certainly not that described above. But that was the ideal God set before them:

they were to strive to change their present situation and make it fit the model; that model in turn sheds light on concrete historical circumstances and provides fixed markers.

5. DEUTERONOMY IN THE LIGHT OF THE NEW TESTAMENT

The great theme of Deuteronomy, that of unity, finds its fulfilment in Christ, the Only Son of God, who calls all mankind to share in divine nature through grace: "that they may all be one; even as thou, Father, art in me, and I in thee, that they also may be in us" (Jn 17:21).

The rule of conduct that Jesus proposes to his disciples reduces to just one law—that of love, which takes in the two basic precepts: "The first is, 'Hear, O Israel: The Lord our God, the Lord is one; and you shall love the Lord your God with all your heart, and with all your soul, and with all your mind, and with all your strength.' The second is this, 'You shall love your neighbour as yourself'" (Mk 12:29–31).

In the new Covenant there is only one supreme act of worship—the redemptive sacrifice of Jesus on the cross; it has a universal value and it is constantly being re-presented in the Church in a sacramental way. This sacrifice has done away with enmity between God and man and has made all humankind into one people, the people of God (cf. Eph 2:11–22). Each and every member of that people has to make his or her pilgrim way on earth, through this world which they have been given as a gift from God; they must be detached from earthly things as they head for their ultimate homeland.

Introduction

1 ¹These are the words that Moses spoke to all Israel beyond the Jordan in the wilderness, in the Arabah over against Suph, between Paran and Tophel, Laban, Hazeroth, and Di-zahab. ²It is eleven days' journey from Horeb by the way of Mount Seir to Kadesh-barnea. ³And in the fortieth year, on the first day of the eleventh month, Moses spoke to the people of Israel according to all that the LORD had given him in commandment to them, ⁴after he had defeated Sihon the king of the Amorites, who lived in Heshbon, and Og the king of Bashan, who lived in Ashtaroth and in Edre-i. ⁵Beyond the Jordan, in the land of Moab, Moses undertook to explain this law, saying,

Deut 2:30–35;
3:12–17; 29:6;
31:4
Ps 135:10–12;
136:17–22
Num 21:21–35

1:1–5. The opening verses act as an introduction (fixing the time and place) to the discourses of Moses, which are basically the subject matter of Deuteronomy. The sacred writer sets the scene on the plains of Moab (v. 5; 34:1) on the north-east of the Dead Sea; the time is the last year of Israel's pilgrimage to the promised land, a little before the conquest, which will be led by Joshua.

Throughout the book (2:30–35; 3:12–17; 29:6; 31:4) the Israelites will be reminded about victories over Sihon and Og (v. 4) to encourage them to trust in the Lord's help in the approaching battles. These victories are also extolled in certain psalms (cf. Ps 135:10–12; 136:17–22).

*1:6—4:43. Strictly speaking, the "First Discourse of Moses" starts here (v. 6) and it continues to 4:43 (there are a few comments or asides, which break the flow). What we have here is a summary of events in Israel's journey from the time of its long stay at Mount Horeb (Sinai) until it reached the mountainous area above the left bank of the Jordan where it flows into the Dead Sea. Here and there, we are given summaries of episodes which for the most part are covered more extensively in Exodus and Numbers; but they are re-worked here perhaps with more theological depth; the perspective always has to do with the way divine Providence impinges on human history; the unmerited election of Israel by God; the divine gift of the promised land.

Thus, this first discourse acts as a kind of general introduction to everything that falls within "Deuteronomic

---

¹Haec sunt verba, quae locutus est Moyses ad omnem Israel trans Iordanem in solitudine, in Araba contra Suph, inter Pharan et Thophel et Laban et Aseroth et Dizahab. ²Undecim dies de Horeb per viam montis Seir usque Cadesbarne. ³Quadragesimo anno, undecimo mense, prima die mensis locutus est Moyses ad filios Israel omnia, quae praeceperat illi Dominus ut diceret eis. ⁴Postquam percussit Sehon regem Amorraeorum, qui habitavit in Hesebon, et Og regem Basan, qui mansit in Astharoth et in Edrai,

PART ONE

The First Discourse of Moses: Historical Introduction*

1. HISTORICAL SUMMARY OF THE EXODUS

Departure from Horeb-Sinai

[6]"The LORD our God said to us in Horeb, 'You have stayed long enough at this mountain; [7]turn and take your journey, and go to the hill country of the Amorites, and to all their neighbors in the Arabah, in the hill country and in the lowland, and in the Negeb, and by the seacoast, the land of the Canaanites, and Lebanon, as far as the great river, the river Euphrates. [8]Behold, I have set the

Rev 9:14

Gen 12:7; 15; 26:2–5; 28:13–15

history", an ambitious historical theological text which surveys the salvation history of Israel from the point where it is getting ready to enter Canaan under the leadership of Joshua (c.1200 BC) up to the time of the deportation to Babylon (587–586 BC). This history covers more than six centuries and comprises this book and also Joshua, Judges, 1 and 2 Samuel and 1 and 2 Kings.

Moses' first discourse consists of two separate parts: the first (chaps. 1–3) gives a summary of the Exodus, stressing Yahweh's special protection of his people; in the second (chap. 4) the Israelites are exhorted to be faithful to God's commandments.

Christian tradition has often applied the years the Israelites spent on their pilgrimage to the life of the Church in this world: "These forty years", St Isidore of Seville comments, "stand for all the time of this world, in which the Church makes

its way through trials and dangerous temptations, hoping patiently for what it cannot see, until it reaches the promised land of eternal happiness" (*Quaestiones in Deuteronomium, 2*).

1:6. In Deuteronomy we can see a certain continuity with the Elohistic tradition (cf. "Introduction to the Pentateuch", above). For example, both traditions (the Elohistic and the Deuteronomic) speak of Horeb rather than Sinai (the latter is preponderant in the Yahwistic and Priestly traditions); from the information available to us we know that the two names refer to the same mountain, although some scholars think that Horeb is the name of the whole mountain block and Sinai refers to just one of its peaks. The massif is crowned by two peaks which are close to one another—Djébel Mûsa and Djébel Serbal. Jewish and Christian tradition identifies the former as being

[5]trans Iordanem in terra Moab coepitque Moyses explanare legem hanc et dicere: [6]«Dominus Deus noster locutus est ad nos in Horeb dicens: 'Sufficit vobis quod in hoc monte mansistis; [7]convertimini et proficiscimini et venite ad montem Amorraeorum et ad omnes vicinos eius: in Araba atque monta-

land before you; go in and take possession of the land which the
LORD swore to your fathers, to Abraham, to Isaac, and to Jacob, to
give to them and to their descendants after them.'

Ex 18:13–27
Num 11:11–17 **Appointment of judges**

Heb 11:12 ⁹"At that time I said to you, 'I am not able alone to bear you; ¹⁰the
LORD your God has multiplied you, and behold, you are this day
Gen 15:5; as the stars of heaven for multitude. ¹¹May the LORD, the God of
22:17 your fathers, make you a thousand times as many as you are, and
bless you, as he has promised you! ¹²How can I bear alone the
Num 11:16–17 weight and burden of you and your strife? ¹³Choose wise, understanding, and experienced men, according to your tribes, and I
will appoint them as your heads.' ¹⁴And you answered me, 'The
thing that you have spoken is good for us to do.' ¹⁵So I took the
heads of your tribes, wise and experienced men, and set them as
heads over you, commanders of thousands, commanders of hundreds, commanders of fifties, commanders of tens, and officers,
Jn 5:51 throughout your tribes. ¹⁶And I charged your judges at that time,
'Hear the cases between your brethren, and judge righteously
Lev 19:15 between a man and his brother or the alien that is with him. ¹⁷You
shall not be partial in judgment; you shall hear the small and the
great alike; you shall not be afraid of the face of man, for the

---

the peak to which Moses ascended (cf.
also the note on Ex 16:1).

"The Lord our God": this expression
(and similar ones such as "Your God")
occur often in Deuteronomy, underlining
the close relationship between Yahweh
(the Lord) and his people, based on the
Covenant.

1:9–18. The institution of the judges,
which Moses establishes here to help him
in his work of government, is recounted in
Exodus 18:13–27. In Exodus, however, the
idea is attributed to Jethro, Moses' father-
in-law (cf. the notes to Ex 18:13–27). The
basic principle established here for the
administration of justice is impartiality:
everyone is equal before the law.

nis et in Sephela et in Nageb et iuxta litus maris, in terram Chananaeorum et in Libanum usque ad
flumen magnum Euphraten. ⁸En, inquit, tradidi vobis terram: ingredimini et possidete eam, super qua
iuravit Dominus patribus vestris Abraham, Isaac et Iacob ut daret illam eis et semini eorum post eos.
⁹Dixique vobis illo in tempore: Non possum solus sustinere vos; ¹⁰Dominus Deus vester multiplicavit
vos, et estis hodie sicut stellae caeli plurimi. ¹¹Dominus, Deus patrum vestrorum, addat ad hunc
numerum multa milia et benedicat vobis, sicut locutus est vobis. ¹²Non valeo solus vestra negotia
sustinere et pondus ac iurgia; ¹³date vobis viros sapientes et gnaros, et quorum conversatio sit probata
in tribubus vestris, ut ponam eos vobis principes. ¹⁴Tunc respondistis mihi: 'Bona res est, quam vis
facere'. ¹⁵Tulique principes de tribubus vestris viros sapientes et probatos et constitui eos principes
super vos: tribunos et centuriones et quinquagenarios ac decanos et praefectos operum pro tribubus
vestris. ¹⁶Praecepique iudicibus vestris in tempore illo: Audite causam fratrum vestrorum et, quod
iustum est, iudicate, sive civis sit ille sive peregrinus. ¹⁷Non accipietis personam in iudicio; ita parvum
audietis ut magnum nec timebitis cuiusquam personam, quia Dei iudicium est. Quod si difficile vobis
aliquid visum fuerit, referte ad me, et ego audiam. ¹⁸Praecepique vobis in tempore illo omnia, quae

judgment is God's; and the case that is too hard for you, you shall bring to me, and I will hear it.' [18]And I commanded you at that time all the things that you should do.

The rebellion and punishment of the people*

[19]"And we set out from Horeb, and went through all that great and terrible wilderness which you saw, on the way to the hill country of the Amorites, as the LORD our God commanded us; and we came to Kadesh-barnea. [20]And I said to you, 'You have come to the hill country of the Amorites, which the LORD our God gives us. [21]Behold, the LORD your God has set the land before you; go up, take possession, as the LORD, the God of your fathers, has told you; do not fear or be dismayed.' [22]Then all of you came near me, and said, 'Let us send men before us, that they may explore the land for us, and bring us word again of the way by which we must go up and the cities into which we shall come.' [23]The thing seemed good to me, and I took twelve men of you, one man for each tribe; [24]and they turned and went up into the hill country, and came to the Valley of Eshcol and spied it out. [25]And they took in their hands some of the fruit of the land and brought it down to us, and brought us word again, and said, 'It is a good land which the LORD our God gives us.'

Num 13:1; 14:9

Josh 1:6–9

---

*1:19–46. The people's rebellion against the Lord's plans and the punishment they receive are covered more extensively in Numbers 13–14, where there is mention of Joshua's exhortation not to lose heart in the face of the superiority of the inhabitants of Canaan. In recalling the punishment Israel suffers, reference is also made to Moses (v. 37) although his punishment is more directly connected with what happened at Meribah (cf. Num 20:1–13). Neither the present passage nor the one in Numbers makes it clear what precise offence Moses and Aaron committed. In Deuteronomy 1:19–46 it seems that the reason why all the people (Moses and Aaron included), were punished, was because they refused to conquer the land of Canaan (this refusal occurred early on in the Exodus and both leaders went along with it). Certainly, the passages in Numbers and Deuteronomy do attribute some degree of responsibility to Moses and Aaron in connexion with the people's sin.

facere deberetis. [19]Profecti autem de Horeb transivimus per totam illam eremum maximam et terribilem, quam vidistis, per viam montis Amorraei, sicut praeceperat Dominus Deus noster nobis. Cumque venissemus in Cadesbarne, [20]dixi vobis: Venistis ad montem Amorraei, quem Dominus Deus noster daturus est nobis. [21]Vide terram, quam Dominus Deus tuus dat tibi: ascende et posside eam, sicut locutus est tibi Dominus, Deus patrum tuorum; noli metuere, nec quidquam paveas. [22]Et accessistis ad me vos omnes atque dixistis: 'Mittamus viros ante nos, qui considerent terram et renuntient de itinere, per quod debeamus ascendere, et de civitatibus, ad quas pergere'. [23]Cumque mihi sermo placuisset, misi ex vobis duodecim viros singulos de tribubus suis. [24]Qui cum perrexissent et ascendissent in montana, venerunt usque ad Nehelescol et, considerata terra, [25]sumentes de fructibus eius attulerunt ad nos

26"Yet you would not go up, but rebelled against the command of the LORD your God; 27and you murmured in your tents, and said, 'Because the LORD hated us he has brought us forth out of the land of Egypt, to give us into the hand of the Amorites, to destroy us. 28Whither are we going up? Our brethren have made our hearts melt, saying, "The people are greater and taller than we; the cities are great and fortified up to heaven; and moreover we have seen the sons of the Anakim there."' 29Then I said to you, 'Do not be in dread or afraid of them. 30The LORD your God who goes before you will himself fight for you, just as he did for you in Egypt before your eyes, 31and in the wilderness, where you have seen how the LORD your God bore you, as a man bears his son, in all the way that you went until you came to this place.' 32Yet in spite of this word you did not believe the LORD your God, 33who went before you in the way to seek you out a place to pitch your tents, in fire by night, to show you by what way you should go, and in the cloud by day.

34"And the LORD heard your words, and was angered, and he swore, 35'Not one of these men of this evil generation shall see the good land which I swore to give to your fathers, 36except Caleb the son of Jephunneh; he shall see it, and to him and to his children I will give the land upon which he has trodden, because he has wholly followed the LORD!' 37The LORD was angry with me also on your account, and said, 'You also shall not go in there; 38Joshua the son of Nun, who stands before you, he shall enter;

Num 13:27
Deut 2:10

Deut 32:9–11
Is 46:3–4
Hos 11:3
Acts 13:18
Deut 4:1; 7:6;
32:6

Num 14:21–35

Jn 6:49

Num 20:12

1:28. "Sons of the Anakim": descendants of Anak, a name which designates both a race and a particular individual; in Arabic it can mean "long-necked men" which would explain why the parallel passage of Numbers speaks of them as being giants (cf. Num 13:27–29 and note).

Other scholars think that Anakim means "men of the neck bands". In Joshua 15:13; 21:11; etc. Anak is referred to as a specific person.

1:31. The metaphor of the Lord carrying the people of Israel "as a man bears his

atque dixerunt: 'Bona est terra, quam Dominus Deus noster daturus est nobis'. 26Et noluistis ascendere, sed increduli ad sermonem Domini Dei vestri 27murmurastis in tabernaculis vestris atque dixistis: 'Odit nos Dominus et idcirco eduxit nos de terra Aegypti, ut traderet nos in manu Amorraei atque deleret. 28Quo ascendemus? Fratres nostri terruerunt cor nostrum dicentes: Maxima multitudo est et nobis in statura procerior; urbes magnae et ad caelum usque munitae; etiam filios Enacim vidimus ibi'. 29Et dixi vobis: Nolite metuere nec timeatis eos. 30 Dominus Deus, qui ductor est vester, ipse pro vobis pugnabit, sicut fecit in Aegypto, vobis videntibus. 31Et in solitudine—ipse vidisti—portavit te Dominus Deus tuus, ut solet homo gestare parvulum filium suum, in omni via, per quam ambulastis, donec veniretis ad locum istum. 32Et nec sic quidem credidistis Domino Deo vestro, 33qui praecessit vos in via, et metatus est locum, in quo tentoria figere deberetis, nocte ostendens vobis iter per ignem et die per columnam nubis. 34Cumque audisset Dominus vocem sermonum vestrorum, iratus iuravit et ait: 35"Non videbit quispiam de viris generationis huius pessimae terram bonam, quam sub iuramento pollicitus sum patribus vestris, 36praeter Chaleb filium Iephonne: ipse enim videbit eam, et ipsi dabo terram,

encourage him, for he shall cause Israel to inherit it. [39]Moreover your little ones, who you said would become a prey, and your children, who this day have no knowledge of good or evil, shall go in there, and to them I will give it, and they shall possess it. [40]But as for you, turn, and journey into the wilderness in the direction of the Red Sea.'

[41]"Then you answered me, 'We have sinned against the LORD;   Num 14:39–45 we will go up and fight, just as the LORD our God commanded us.' And every man of you girded on his weapons of war, and thought it easy to go up into the hill country. [42]And the LORD said to me, 'Say to them, Do not go up or fight, for I am not in the midst of you; lest you be defeated before your enemies.' [43]So I spoke to you, and you would not hearken; but you rebelled against the command of the LORD, and were presumptuous and went up into the hill country. [44]Then the Amorites who lived in that hill country came out against you and chased you as bees do and beat you down in Seir as far as Hormah. [45]And you returned and wept before the LORD; but the LORD did not hearken to your voice or give ear to you. [46]So you remained at Kadesh many days, the days that you remained there.

From Kadesh to Transjordania

2 [1]"Then we turned, and journeyed into the wilderness in the direction of the Red Sea, as the LORD told me; and for many

---

son" depicts God as the people's father who ensures that no harm will come to them. The same imagery occurs elsewhere in the Old Testament (cf., e.g., Deut 32:9–11; Is 46:3–4; Hos 11:3). Once our Lord Jesus Christ comes, the personal meaning of divine sonship will become plain to see: not only is the New

Israel as a whole the son of God, but each Christian (by virtue of Baptism, which identifies him or her with Christ), has been made a son or daughter of God (cf. Rom 8:14–30; 1 Jn 3:1–2).

2:1. "Red Sea": This seems to refer to the eastern arm, either the gulf of Akaba or

quam calcavit, et filiis eius, quia adimplevit ut sequeretur Dominum'. [37]Mihi quoque iratus Dominus propter vos dixit: 'Nec tu ingredieris illuc; [38]sed Iosue filius Nun minister tuus ipse intrabit illuc. Hunc robora, et ipse terram sorte dividat Israeli. [39]Parvuli vestri, de quibus dixistis quod captivi ducerentur, et filii, qui hodie boni ac mali ignorant distantiam, ipsi ingredientur; et ipsis dabo terram, et possidebunt eam. [40]Vos autem revertimini et abite in solitudinem per viam maris Rubri'. [41]Et respondistis mihi: 'Peccavimus Domino; nos ascendemus atque pugnabimus, sicut praecepit nobis Dominus Deus noster'. Cumque instructi armis pergeretis in montem, [42]ait mihi Dominus: 'Dic ad eos: Nolite ascendere neque pugnetis, non enim sum vobiscum, ne cadatis coram inimicis vestris'. [43]Locutus sum et non audistis, sed adversantes imperio Domini et tumentes superbia ascendistis in montem. [44]Itaque egressus Amorraeus, qui habitat in monte illo, obviam vobis, persecutus est vos, sicut solent apes persequi, et cecidit vos de Seir usque Horma. [45]Cumque reversi ploraretis coram Domino, non audivit vos nec voci vestrae voluit acquiescere. [46]Sedistis ergo in Cades multo illo tempore, dum ibi mansistis. [1]Profectique inde venimus in solitudinem per viam maris Rubri, sicut mihi dixerat Dominus; et cir-

days we went about Mount Seir. ²Then the Lord said to me, ³'You have been going about this mountain country long enough; turn northward. ⁴And command the people, You are about to pass through the territory of your brethren the sons of Esau, who live in Seir; and they will be afraid of you. So take good heed; ⁵do not contend with them; for I will not give you any of their land, no, not so much as for the sole of the foot to tread on, because I have given Mount Seir to Esau as a possession. ⁶You shall purchase food from them for money, that you may eat; and you shall also buy water of them for money, that you may drink. ⁷For the LORD your God has blessed you in all the work of your hands; he knows your going through this great wilderness; these forty years the LORD your God has been with you; you have lacked nothing.' ⁸So we went on, away from our brethren the sons of Esau who live in Seir, away from the Arabah road from Elath and Ezion-geber.

"And we turned and went in the direction of the wilderness of Moab. ⁹And the LORD said to me, 'Do not harass Moab or contend with them in battle, for I will not give you any of their land for a

Side references:
Num 20:14–21
Is 34–35
Ezek25:12–14
Ps 137:7
Gen 36:8
Acts 7:5
Ex 33:14, 16;
34:9–10
Deut 8:2ff;
29:5
Neh 9:20–21
Num 21:10–20

---

the gulf of Elan. The text indicates that the Israelites turned south.

2:4–5. The territory of the sons of Esau was the kingdom of Edom (cf. Gen 36:30)—Idumea in Greco-Roman times —which extended south from the Dead Sea to the gulf of Akaba, on the Red Sea. The mountains of Seir lie in this region, and the Bible sometimes gives the name Seir to all that region.

In the parallel passage in Numbers (20:14–21) the rest of the story is told: the king of Edom refused to let the Israelites pass through, and this meant they had to make a long detour (cf. Deut 2:8). The king's refusal is recalled many

times in the Old Testament as a symbol of opposition to God's plans, which will deserve punishment (cf. Is 34–35; Ezek 25:12–14; Ps 137:7).

2:9. The Moabites, like the Ammonites (vv. 18–19), were descendants of Lot, Abraham's nephew (cf. Gen 19:30–38), and their territory was located on the eastern fringe of the Dead Sea. Ar was their main city, although here the name describes the entire region.

The Israelites went northwards through the wilderness of Moab (cf. Num 21:11) which was the eastern border of the Moabite lands.

---

cuivimus montem Seir longo tempore. ²Dixitque Dominus ad me: ³'Sufficit vobis circuire montem istum; ite contra aquilonem. ⁴Et populo praecipe dicens: Transibitis per terminos fratrum vestrorum filiorum Esau, qui habitant in Seir, et timebunt vos. ⁵Cavete ergo diligenter, ne moveamini contra eos; neque enim dabo vobis de terra eorum, quantum potest unius pedis calcare vestigium, quia in possessionem Esau dedi montem Seir. ⁶Cibos emetis ab eis pecunia et comedetis; etiam aquam emptam haurietis et bibetis. ⁷Dominus Deus tuus benedixit tibi in omni opere manuum tuarum; novit iter tuum, quomodo transieris solitudinem hanc magnam per quadraginta annos habitans tecum Dominus Deus tuus, et nihil tibi defuit'. ⁸Cumque transissemus fratres nostros filios Esau, qui habitabant in Seir, per viam Arabae de Ailath et de Asiongaber, vertimus nos et venimus per iter, quod ducit in desertum

possession, because I have given Ar to the sons of Lot for a possession.' ¹⁰(The Emim formerly lived there, a people great and Gen 14:5
Deut 2:10
many, and tall as the Anakim; ¹¹like the Anakim they are also 2 Sam 21:18–20
known as Rephaim, but the Moabites call them Emim. ¹²The Gen 36:20
Horites also lived in Seir formerly, but the sons of Esau dispossessed them, and destroyed them from before them, and settled in
their stead; as Israel did to the land of their possession, which the
LORD gave to them.) ¹³'Now rise up, and go over the brook
Zered.' So we went over the brook Zered. ¹⁴And the time from our Jn 5:5
leaving Kadesh-barnea until we crossed the brook Zered was
thirty-eight years, until the entire generation, that is, the men of
war, had perished from the camp, as the LORD had sworn to them.
¹⁵For indeed the hand of the LORD was against them, to destroy
them from the camp, until they had perished.

¹⁶"So when all the men of war had perished and were dead
from among the people, ¹⁷the LORD said to me, ¹⁸'This day you
are to pass over the boundary of Moab at Ar; ¹⁹and when you
approach the frontier of the sons of Ammon, do not harass them
or contend with them, for I will not give you any of the land of the
sons of Ammon as a possession, because I have given it to the
sons of Lot for a possession.' ²⁰(That also is known as a land of

---

2:10–12. These verses—and vv. 20–23—
are a kind of explanatory note which
records ancient traditions about the previous inhabitants of these lands.

On the Anakim, see the note on 1:28.
The Rephaim or Rephaites were a warlike people, tall in stature (cf. Gen 14:5;
2 Sam 21:18–20), who lived in
Transjordan and had enclaves in the land
of Canaan.

The Horites must have been a non-
Semitic people, established in the south
of Palestine; in Genesis 36:20 there is
mention of the descendants of Seir the
Horite living in that region. Apparently
they were a very small group which was
quickly absorbed by others. It is not clear
whether they are the same as the Hurrites
mentioned in cuneiform documents.

Moab. ⁹Dixitque Dominus ad me: 'Non pugnes contra Moabitas, nec ineas adversus eos proelium; non
enim dabo tibi quidquam de terra eorum, quia filiis Lot tradidi Ar in possessionem. ¹⁰—Emim primi
fuerunt habitatores eius, populus magnus et multus et tam excelsus ut Enacim; ¹¹ipsi quoque Raphaim
reputabantur sicut Enacim; denique Moabitae appellant eos Emim. ¹²In Seir autem prius habitaverunt
Horim; quibus expulsis atque deletis, habitaverunt filii Esau pro eis, sicut fecit Israel in terra possessionis suae, quam dedit eis Dominus—. ¹³Surgite ergo et transite torrentem Zared'. Et transivimus torrentem Zared. ¹⁴Tempus autem, quo ambulavimus de Cadesbarne usque ad transitum torrentis Zared,
triginta octo annorum fuit, donec consumeretur omnis generatio hominum bellatorum de castris, sicut
iuraverat eis Dominus, ¹⁵cuius manus fuit adversum eos, ut interirent de castrorum medio. ¹⁶Postquam
autem universi ceciderunt pugnatores de medio populi, ¹⁷locutus est Dominus ad me dicens: ¹⁸'Tu transibis hodie terminos Moab, urbem nomine Ar; ¹⁹et accedens in vicina filiorum Ammon, cave, ne
pugnes contra eos nec movearis ad proelium; non enim dabo tibi de terra filiorum Ammon, quia filiis
Lot dedi eam in possessionem. ²⁰—Terra Raphaim reputata est et ipsa olim habitaverunt Raphaim in
ea, quos Ammonitae vocant Zomzommim, ²¹populus magnus et multus et procerae longitudinis sicut

Rephaim; Rephaim formerly lived there, but the Ammonites call them Zamzummim, [21]a people great and many, and tall as the Anakim; but the LORD destroyed them before them; and they dispossessed them, and settled in their stead; [22]as he did for the sons of Esau, who live in Seir, when he destroyed the Horites before them, and they dispossessed them, and settled in their stead even to this day. [23]As for the Avvim, who lived in villages as far as Gaza, the Caphtorim, who came from Caphtor, destroyed them and settled in their stead.)

Josh 13:2

Num 21:21–25
Judg 11:19–22 **Victory over Sihon**

[24]'Rise up, take your journey, and go over the valley of the Arnon; behold, I have given into your hand Sihon the Amorite, king of Heshbon, and his land; begin to take possession, and contend with him in battle. [25]This day I will begin to put the dread and fear of you upon the peoples that are under the whole heaven, who shall hear the report of you and shall tremble and be in anguish because of you.'

Acts 2:5

[26]"So I sent messengers from the wilderness of Kedemoth to Sihon the king of Heshbon, with words of peace, saying, [27]'Let me pass through your land; I will go only by the road, I will turn aside neither to the right nor to the left. [28]You shall sell me food

---

2:23. The Avvim must also have been a non-Semitic people, scattered in small settlements in the south of Palestine. Caphtorim is the name given to "the peoples of the sea", which included the Philistines, who settled as far as the coastal area of the Nile delta but were expelled from there and moved up to the southern coastal area of Palestine. Caphtor must be the island of Crete, which was one of the stages on the emigration from other parts (it is not clear where). The Philistines contended with

the Israelites for centuries over possession of the land of Canaan.

2:24–37. The sacred writer recalls the victory over the Amorites, recounted in Numbers (21:21–31), and the occupation of their lands between the Arnon river (which flowed in to the Dead Sea half way up) and the Jabbok, a tributary of the Jordan. Gilead (v. 36) may mean the area comprising the Jabbok basin and its mountains. This account keeps stressing the key role of the Lord in the Israelites'

Enacim, quos delevit Dominus a facie eorum et fecit illos habitare pro eis, [22]sicut fecerat filiis Esau, qui habitant in Seir, delens Horim et terram eorum illis tradens, quam possident usque in praesens. [23]Hevaeos quoque, qui habitabant in villis usque Gazam, Caphtorim, qui egressi de Caphtor deleverunt eos et habitaverunt pro illis—. [24]Surgite! Proficiscimini et transite torrentem Arnon: ecce tradidi in manu tua Sehon regem Hesebon Amorraeum; et terram eius incipe possidere et committe adversus eum proelium. [25]Hodie incipiam mittere terrorem atque formidinem tuam in populos, qui habitant sub omni caelo, ut, audito nomine tuo, paveant et contremiscant coram te'. [26]Misi ergo nuntios de solitudine Cademoth ad Sehon regem Hesebon verbis pacificis dicens: [27]Transibo per terram tuam, publica gradiar via, non declinabo neque ad dexteram neque ad sinistram; [28]alimenta pretio vende mihi, ut vescar,

for money, that I may eat, and give me water for money, that I may drink; only let me pass through on foot, [29]as the sons of Esau who live in Seir and the Moabites who live in Ar did for me, until I go over the Jordan into the land which the LORD our God gives to us.' [30]But Sihon the king of Heshbon would not let us pass by him; for the LORD your God hardened his spirit and made his heart obstinate, that he might give him into your hand, as at this day. [31]And the LORD said to me, 'Behold, I have begun to give Sihon and his land over to you; begin to take possession, that you may occupy his land.' [32]Then Sihon came out against us, he and all his people, to battle at Jahaz. [33]And the LORD our God gave him over to us; and we defeated him and his sons and all his people. [34]And we captured all his cities at that time and utterly destroyed every city, men, women, and children; we left none remaining; [35]only the cattle we took as spoil for ourselves, with the booty of the cities which we captured. [36]From Aroer, which is on the edge of the valley of the Arnon, and from the city that is in the valley, as far as Gilead, there was not a city too high for us; the LORD our God gave all into our hands. [37]Only to the land of the sons of Ammon you did not draw near, that is, to all the banks of the river Jabbok and the cities of the hill country, and wherever the LORD our God forbade us.

Num 20:18–21

Josh 6:17

---

victory, thereby underlining God's special provident care of the chosen people.

It is typical of Old Testament style to attribute to God not only the good things he does or expressly wills but also the evils he permits to happen out of respect for the freedom of men: when it says that the Lord hardened Sihon's heart (v. 30), one needs to interpret the statement in the light of that fact.

The custom of the anathema (the *jerem* of the Jews; cf. the note on Lev 27:28–29), common among the peoples of the ancient East, involved the total destruction (v. 34) of the enemy and all he possessed, though it did admit of degrees: here the Israelites kept the cattle and the booty (vv. 34–35). To our modern mentality it seems quite ferocious and inhuman; in the case of the Israelites it

---

aquam pecunia tribue mihi et sic bibam; tantum est ut mihi concedas transitum, [29]sicut fecerunt mihi filii Esau, qui habitant in Seir, et Moabitae, qui morantur in Ar, donec veniam ad Iordanem et transeam in terram, quam Dominus Deus noster daturus est nobis. [30]Noluitque Sehon rex Hesebon dare nobis transitum, quia induraverat Dominus Deus tuus spiritum eius et obfirmaverat cor illius, ut traderetur in manus tuas, sicut est in praesenti die. [31]Dixitque Dominus ad me: 'Ecce coepi tradere tibi Sehon et terram eius. Incipe possidere eam !' [32]Egressusque est Sehon obviam nobis cum omni populo suo ad proelium in Iasa, [33]et tradidit eum Dominus Deus noster nobis; percussimusque eum cum filiis suis et omni populo suo. [34]Cunctasque urbes eius in tempore illo cepimus et percussimus anathemate singulas civitates cum viris ac mulieribus et parvulis; neminem reliquimus in eis superstitem, [35]absque iumentis, quae in partem venere praedantium, et spoliis urbium, quas cepimus. [36]Ab Aroer, quae est super ripam torrentis Arnon, et oppido, quod in valle situm est, usque Galaad non fuit civitas, quae nostras effugeret manus: omnia tradidit Dominus Deus noster nobis, [37]absque terra filiorum Ammon, ad

Num
21:33–35

Victory over Og

3 [1]"Then we turned and went up the way to Bashan; and Og the king of Bashan came out against us, he and all his people, to battle at Edre-i. [2]But the LORD said to me, 'Do not fear him; for I have given him and all his people and his land into your hand; and you shall do to him as you did to Sihon the king of the Amorites, who dwelt at Heshbon.' [3]So the LORD our God gave into our hand Og also, the king of Bashan, and all his people; and we smote him until no survivor was left to him. [4]And we took all his cities at that time—there was not a city which we did not take from them—sixty cities, the whole region of Argob, the kingdom of Og in Bashan. [5]All these were cities fortified with high walls, gates, and bars, besides very many unwalled villages. [6]And we utterly destroyed them, as we did to Sihon the king of Heshbon, destroying every city, men, women, and children. [7]But all the cattle and the spoil of the cities we took as our booty. [8]So we took the land at that time out of the hand of the two kings of the Amorites who were beyond the Jordan, from the valley of the Arnon to Mount Hermon [9](the Sidonians call Hermon Sirion,

---

also had a religious motive behind it—the need to avoid the possible contamination of idolatry, to which they were strongly inclined during the early period.

3:1–11. This passage recalls the conquest of Bashan, another Amorite kingdom, situated in the north of the region of Ammon. The land was of volcanic origin, famous for its fertility (cf. Jer 50:19; Ps 68:15). By this victory the Israelites gained control of the eastern side of the Jordan, from the river Arnon to Mount Hermon. The size of the bedstead of King Og (some translate it as "sarcophagus"), about four and a half metres by two (15 feet by 7 feet) according to the text, comes from a tradition about the physical size of this survivor of the Rephaim giants. Rabbah of the Ammonites (called Philadelphia later by Greeks and Romans), situated in the valley of the Jabbok, is present-day Amman, the capital of Jordan.

---

quam non accessisti, cunctis, quae adiacent torrenti Iaboc, et urbibus montanis universisque locis, a quibus nos prohibuit Dominus Deus noster. [1]Itaque conversi ascendimus per iter Basan; egressusque est Og rex Basan in occursum nobis cum omni populo suo ad bellandum in Edrai. [2]Dixitque Dominus ad me: 'Ne timeas eum, quia in manu tua tradidi eum cum omni populo ac terra sua; faciesque ei, sicut fecisti Sehon regi Amorraeorum, qui habitavit in Hesebon'. [3]Tradidit ergo Dominus Deus noster in manibus nostris etiam Og regem Basan et universum populum eius; percussimusque eos usque ad internecionem. [4]Et cepimus cunctas civitates eius in illo tempore. Non fuit oppidum, quod nos effugeret: sexaginta urbes, omnem regionem Argob, regnum Og in Basan. [5]Cunctae urbes erant munitae muris altissimis portisque et vectibus, absque oppidis innumeris, quae non habebant muros. [6]Et percussimus eos anathemate, sicut feceramus Sehon regi Hesebon, disperdentes omnem civitatem virosque ac mulieres et parvulos; [7]iumenta autem et spolia urbium diripuimus. [8]Tulimusque illo in tempore terram de manu duorum regum Amorraeorum, qui erant trans Iordanem, a torrente Arnon usque ad montem Hermon [9]—Sidonii vocant Hermon Sarion et Amorraei Sanir—[10]omnes civitates, quae sitae

while the Amorites call it Senir), [10]all the cities of the tableland and all Gilead and all Bashan, as far as Salecah and Edre-i, cities of the kingdom of Og in Bashan. [11](For only Og the king of Bashan was left of the remnant of the Rephaim; behold, his bedstead was a bedstead of iron; is it not in Rabbah of the Ammonites? Nine cubits was its length, and four cubits its breadth, according to the common cubit.[a])

Deut 2:10
Rev 21:17

Num 32
Deut 34
Josh 1:1–51

The allocation of Transjordania

[12]"When we took possession of this land at that time, I gave to the Reubenites and the Gadites the territory beginning at Aroer, which is on the edge of the valley of the Arnon, and half the hill country of Gilead with its cities; [13]the rest of Gilead, and all Bashan, the kingdom of Og, that is, all the region of Argob, I gave to the half-tribe of Manasseh. (The whole of that Bashan is called the land of Rephaim. [14]Jair the Manassite took all the region of Argob, that is, Bashan, as far as the border of the Geshurites and the Ma-acathites, and called the villages after his own name, Havvoth-jair, as it is to this day.) [15]To Machir I gave Gilead, [16]and to the Reubenites and the Gadites I gave the territory from Gilead as far as the valley of the Arnon, with the middle of the valley as a boundary, as far over as the river Jabbok, the boundary of the Ammonites; [17]the Arabah also, with the Jordan as the

Num 32:41

3:12–22. This passage deals with the division of the conquered Transjordan territories among the tribes of Reuben, Gad and the half-tribe of Manasseh—Machir (v. 15)—and Jair (v. 14) belonged to that tribe (cf. the note on Num 32:1–42)—and the duty incumbent on them to help their brothers in the conquest of the lands on the other side of the Jordan.

The second half of v. 13 and v. 14 seems to be an explanatory gloss. The sea of Arabah or Salt Sea (v. 17) is the Dead Sea.

The passage should be read in conjunction with Deuteronomy 34 and Joshua 1:1.

---

sunt in planitie, et universam terram Galaad et Basan usque Salcha et Edrai, civitates regni Og in Basan. [11]—Solus quippe Og rex Basan remanserat de residuis Raphaim. Monstratur lectus eius ferreus. Nonne est in Rabba filiorum Ammon? Novem cubitos habet longitudinis et quattuor latitudinis ad mensuram cubiti virilis manus—. [12]Terramque hanc possedimus in tempore illo ab Aroer, quae est super ripam torrentis Arnon, usque ad mediam partem montis Galaad; et civitates illius dedi Ruben et Gad. [13]Reliquam autem partem Galaad et omnem Basan, regnum Og, tradidi mediae tribui Manasse, omnem regionem Argob. Cuncta Basan vocatur terra Raphaim. [14]Iair filius Manasse possedit omnem regionem Argob usque ad terminos Gesuri et Maachathi; vocavitque ea ex nomine suo Basan Havoth Iair (id est villas Iair), usque in praesentem diem. [15]Machir quoque dedi Galaad. [16]Et tribubus Ruben et Gad dedi de terra Galaad usque ad torrentem Arnon, medium torrentis et confinium usque ad torrentem Iaboc, qui est terminus filiorum Ammon; [17]et Arabam atque Iordanem et terminos a Chenereth usque ad mare

a. Heb *cubit of a man*

boundary, from Chinnereth as far as the sea of the Arabah, the Salt Sea, under the slopes of Pisgah on the east.

[18]"And I commanded you at that time, saying, 'The LORD your God has given you this land to possess; all your men of valor shall pass over armed before your brethren the people of Israel. [19]But your wives, your little ones, and your cattle (I know that you have many cattle) shall remain in the cities which I have given you, [20]until the LORD gives rest to your brethren, as to you, and they also occupy the land which the LORD your God gives them beyond the Jordan; then you shall return every man to his possession which I have given you.'

Moses' exhortation to Joshua

Josh 1:1 [21]And I commanded Joshua at that time, 'Your eyes have seen all that the LORD your God has done to these two kings; so will the LORD do to all the kingdoms into which you are going over. [22]You shall not fear them; for it is the LORD your God who fights for you.'

Moses' plea

[23]"And I besought the LORD at that time, saying, [24]'O LORD God, thou hast only begun to show thy servant thy greatness and thy

---

3:23–29. Moses' fervent prayer is in sharp contrast with the Lord's harsh reply. Here we come up against the mysteries of divine Wisdom—its rejection of the pleadings of the greatest of the prophets, "whom the Lord knew face to face" (34:10). The passage also reminds us of the need *always* to be faithful to God, and of the fact that God's elect will often find themselves in painful situations in this life. See the note on 1:19–46.

The Pisgah is a section of the Abarim mountains, whose highest peak is Mount Nebo (cf. 34:1).

Beth-peor (or Beth-Fogor) was situated in the Abarim mountains. It had a temple where the Moabites rendered an obscene cult to Baál-Peor; many Israelites were seduced by this idolatry, for which they suffered severe punishment (cf. Num 25:1–18).

Arabae, quod est mare Salis, ad radices montis Phasga contra orientem. [18]Praecepique vobis in tempore illo dicens: Dominus Deus vester dedit vobis terram hanc in hereditatem; expediti praecedite fratres vestros filios Israel, omnes viri robusti, [19]absque uxoribus et parvulis ac iumentis. Novi enim quod plura habeatis pecora, et in urbibus remanere debebunt, quas tradidi vobis, [20]donec requiem tribuat Dominus fratribus vestris, sicut vobis tribuit, et possideant etiam ipsi terram, quam Dominus Deus vester daturus est eis trans Iordanem; tunc revertetur unusquisque in possessionem suam, quam dedi vobis. [21]Iosue quoque in tempore illo praecepi dicens: oculi tui viderunt, quae fecit Dominus Deus vester duobus his regibus; sic faciet omnibus regnis, ad quae transiturus es. [22]Ne timeas eos: Dominus enim Deus vester pugnabit pro vobis. [23]Precatusque sum Dominum in tempore illo dicens: [24]Domine Deus, tu coepisti ostendere servo tuo magnitudinem tuam manumque fortissimam; neque enim est alius

mighty hand; for what god is there in heaven or on earth who can do such works and mighty acts as thine? ²⁵Let me go over, I pray, and see the good land beyond the Jordan, that goodly hill country, and Lebanon.' ²⁶But the LORD was angry with me on your account, and would not hearken to me; and the LORD said to me, 'Let it suffice you; speak no more to me of this matter. ²⁷Go up to the top of Pisgah, and lift up your eyes westward and northward and southward and eastward, and behold it with your eyes; for you shall not go over this Jordan. ²⁸But charge Joshua, and encourage and strengthen him; for he shall go over at the head of this people, and he shall put them in possession of the land which you shall see.' ²⁹So we remained in the valley opposite Beth-peor.

Num 20:12
Lk 22:38

Num 25:1–8

2. EXHORTATION TO KEEP THE LAW

Faithfulness to the Law: God's closeness to his people

4 ¹"And now, O Israel, give heed to the statutes and the ordi-
nances which I teach you, and do them; that you may live, and go in and take possession of the land which the LORD, the God of your fathers, gives you. ²You shall not add to the word which I command you, nor take from it; that you may keep the commandments of the LORD your God which I command you. ³Your eyes

Lev 18:5

Rev 22:18f

Num 25:1–18

4:1–8. Having recalled the main events in Israel's journey from Sinai-Horeb onwards, in which God's special providence was evident, the text now stresses the privileged position of the Hebrew people, chosen as they are by God from among all the nations of the earth, and enabled to draw near to him in a close relationship quite beyond the experience of the Gentiles.

The passage acts as an advance exhortation to fidelity to the Law, the core of which will be recorded later on (5:1–6; 6; 12:1—28:68); it may have been inserted in the course of a revision of the book. The main argument it makes in favour of keeping the Law is the fact that God is so near his people and so accessible to them (vv. 7–8).

Deus vel in caelo vel in terra, qui possit facere opera tua et comparari fortitudini tuae. ²⁵Transeam igitur et videam terram hanc optimam trans Iordanem et montem istum egregium et Libanum. ²⁶Iratusque est Dominus mihi propter vos, nec exaudivit me, sed dixit mihi: 'Sufficit tibi; nequaquam ultra loquaris de hac re ad me. ²⁷Ascende cacumen Phasgae et oculos tuos circumfer ad occidentem et aquilonem austrumque et orientem et aspice; nec enim transibis Iordanem istum. ²⁸Praecipe Iosue et corrobora eum atque conforta, quia ipse praecedet populum istum et dividet eis terram, quam visurus es'. ²⁹Mansimusque in valle contra Bethphegor. ¹Et nunc, Israel, audi praecepta et iudicia, quae ego doceo vos, ut facientes ea vivatis et ingredientes possideatis terram, quam Dominus, Deus patrum vestrorum, daturus est vobis. ²Non addetis ad verbum, quod vobis loquor, neque auferetis ex eo; custodite mandata Domini Dei vestri, quae ego praecipio vobis. ³oculi vestri viderunt omnia, quae fecit Dominus

677

have seen what the LORD did at Baal-peor; for the LORD your God destroyed from among you all the men who followed the Baal of Peor; [4]but you who held fast to the LORD your God are all alive this day. [5]Behold, I have taught you statutes and ordinances, as the LORD my God commanded me, that you should do them in the land which you are entering to take possession of it. [6]Keep them and do them; for that will be your wisdom and your understanding in the sight of the peoples, who, when they hear all these statutes, will say, 'Surely this great nation is a wise and understanding people.' [7]For what great nation is there that has a god so near to it as the LORD our God is to us, whenever we call upon him? [8]And what great nation is there, that has statutes and ordinances so righteous as all this law which I set before you this day?

Job 28:28
Ps 19:7
Sir 1:14–16
Prov 1:7; 9:10

Rom 3:1

The revelation at Horeb

[9]"Only take heed, and keep your soul diligently, lest you forget the things which your eyes have seen, and lest they depart from your heart all the days of your life; make them known to your children and your children's children—[10]how on the day that you

---

4:6–8. The theme of these verses is typical of Wisdom writing. The very life of Israel, shaped as it is by obedience to the Law, will be an eloquent lesson for all other nations. This message, open and out-reaching, implies a universal mission for the chosen people, a message which looks far ahead and will find its fulfilment in the future spread of the Church throughout the world.

4:9–14. This section concentrates on a line of teaching found throughout Holy Scripture: salvation history is based on the will of God who on his own initiative offers a Covenant to the chosen people.

The key points in this Covenant have to do with Abraham (Gen 17:1–14) and Moses (Ex 19–24) and they culminate in the future New Covenant in Jesus Christ (Mt 26:28; Mk 14:24; Lk 22:20; 1 Cor 11:25). The promulgation of the Law on Sinai-Horeb is a product of the Covenant: God promises the people of Israel protection, a land of their own, etc. Because a covenant or pact is involved, certain things are laid down that the people must do: these are contained in the precepts of the Law. God will be true to the promises he makes, but the people never quite decide whether to be faithful or unfaithful. According to this passage

---

contra Baalphegor, quomodo contriverit omnes cultores eius de medio vestri; [4]vos autem, qui adhaeretis Domino Deo vestro, vivitis universi usque in praesentem diem. [5]En docui vos praecepta atque iudicia, sicut mandavit mihi Dominus Deus meus, ut faceretis ea in terra, quam possessuri estis, [6]et observaretis et impleretis opere. Haec est enim vestra sapientia et intellectus coram populis, ut audientes universa praecepta haec dicant: 'En populus sapiens et intellegens, gens magna haec!'. [7]Quae est enim alia natio tam grandis, quae habeat deos appropinquantes sibi, sicut Dominus Deus noster adest cunctis obsecrationibus nostris? [8]Et quae est alia gens sic inclita, ut habeat praecepta iustaque iudicia, sicut est universa lex haec, quam ego proponam hodie ante oculos vestros? [9]Custodi igitur temetipsum et animam tuam sollicite, ne obliviscaris verborum, quae viderunt oculi tui, et ne excidant de corde tuo

stood before the Lord your God at Horeb, the Lord said to me, 'Gather the people to me, that I may let them hear my words, so that they may learn to fear me all the days that they live upon the earth, and that they may teach their children so.' [11]And you came near and stood at the foot of the mountain, while the mountain burned with fire to the heart of heaven, wrapped in darkness, cloud, and gloom. [12]Then the Lord spoke to you out of the midst of the fire; you heard the sound of words, but saw no form; there was only a voice. [13]And he declared to you his covenant, which he commanded you to perform, that is, the ten commandments;[b] and he wrote them upon two tables of stone. [14]And the Lord commanded me at that time to teach you statutes and ordinances, that you might do them in the land which you are going over to possess.

Ex 19:16–20
Acts 7:38

Heb 12:18

Jn 5:37
Acts 9:7
Heb 12:19

Deut 10:4
Ex 20:1;
34:28

Condemnation and punishment of idolatry*

Deut 5:6–10
Ex 20:3–6
Rom 1:23

[15]"Therefore take good heed to yourselves. Since you saw no form on the day that the Lord spoke to you at Horeb out of the midst of the fire, [16]beware lest you act corruptly by making a

Ex 20:4–5

---

the Law consists in the Ten Commandments (v. 13).

On the events of Baal-Peor, cf. Num 25:1–18.

***4:15–31.** This is a kind of explanatory elaboration of the first prescriptions of the Decalogue (cf. 5:6–10; Ex 20:3–6): it stresses the outright rejection of the idolatry (worship of graven images of divinities) which was such a feature of the cultures that surrounded the Hebrews. In their ignorance people confused sculpted (and pictorial) images with the divinity they represented. Hence the prohibition

on graven images of God whether these were in human form (vv. 15–16) or in the form of animals (vv. 17–18), as well as on the cult of heavenly bodies (v. 19), very common in Babylonia and among other Eastern peoples.

This passage (together with 5:6–10, Ex 20:3–6 and others) was influential much later on in the Iconoclastic movements in the provinces of the Byzantine empire which rejected the Christian use of images in the 7th to 10th centuries AD.

The *Catechism of the Catholic Church* explains: "The Christian veneration of images is not contrary to the first com-

---

cunctis diebus vitae tuae. Docebis ea filios ac nepotes tuos [10]die, in quo stetisti coram Domino Deo tuo in Horeb, quando Dominus locutus est mihi: 'Congrega ad me populum, ut audiant sermones meos et discant timere me omni tempore, quo vivunt in terra, doceantque filios suos'. [11]Et accessistis et stetistis ad radices montis, qui ardebat usque ad caelum, erantque in eo tenebrae, nubes et caligo. [12]Locutusque est Dominus ad vos de medio ignis; vocem verborum audistis et formam penitus non vidistis. [13]Et ostendit vobis pactum suum, quod praecepit ut faceretis, et decem verba, quae scripsit in duabus tabulis lapideis. [14]Mihique mandavit in illo tempore, ut docerem vos praecepta et iudicia, quae facere deberetis in terra, quam possessuri estis. [15]Custodite igitur sollicite animas vestras. Non vidistis aliquam similitudinem in die, qua locutus est vobis Dominus in Horeb de medio ignis; [16]ne forte cor-

b. Heb *words*

graven image for yourselves, in the form of any figure, the likeness of male or female, [17]the likeness of any beast that is on the earth, the likeness of any winged bird that flies in the air, [18]the likeness of anything that creeps on the ground, the likeness of any fish that is in the water under the earth. [19]And beware lest you lift up your eyes to heaven, and when you see the sun and the moon and the stars, all the host of heaven, you be drawn away and worship them and serve them, things which the LORD your God has

Jer 11:4
1 Kings 8:51
Deut 7:6

allotted to all the peoples under the whole heaven. [20]But the LORD has taken you, and brought you forth out of the iron furnace, out of Egypt, to be a people of his own possession, as at this day.

Num 20:12

[21]Furthermore the LORD was angry with me on your account, and he swore that I should not cross the Jordan, and that I should not enter the good land which the LORD your God gives you for an inheritance. [22]For I must die in this land, I must not go over the Jordan; but you shall go over and take possession of that good land. [23]Take heed to yourselves, lest you forget the covenant of the

---

mandment, which proscribes idols. Indeed, 'the honour rendered to an image passes to its prototype' (St Basil, *De Spiritu Sancto*, 18, 45), and 'whoever venerates an image venerates the person portrayed in it' (Second Council of Nicea, *De sacris imaginibus*). The honour paid to sacred images is a 'respectful veneration', not the adoration due to God alone" (no. 2132).

"Religion", says St Thomas Aquinas, "does not offer worship to images considered as mere things in themselves, but as images drawing us to God incarnate. Motion to an image does not stop there at the image, but goes on towards the thing it represents" (*Summa theologiae*, 2-2, 81, 3 ad 3).

Verses 25–31 paint a picture which fits the calamities which would overtake the people of Israel during the exile in

Babylon (587 BC and the years following). The threats contained in these verses were a frequent theme in writings attributed to the Deuteronomic tradition (cf., e.g., chaps. 28–29; Josh 23:16) and the Priestly tradition (cf. Lev 26:14–42). They contain an exhortation to fidelity to the Covenant with God; failure will bring retribution: the sin of infidelity, in the form of idolatry and following Canaanite cults, would be an ever-present threat to the purity of Israelite religion. Unlike those idols (v. 28), the God of Israel is a living God (cf. 2 Kings 19:4), able to render help; he is not like "other gods", the gods of other nations, who have no life in them and who are utterly powerless (cf. Is 37:19; Hab 2:18; Ps 115:3–7).

4:19–20. The text declares that the heavenly bodies are a God-given heritage

---

rupti faciatis vobis sculptam similitudinem, imaginem masculi vel feminae, [17]similitudinem omnium iumentorum, quae sunt super terram, vel avium sub caelo volantium [18]atque reptilium, quae moventur in terra, sive piscium, qui sub terra morantur in aquis; [19]et ne forte oculis elevatis ad caelum videas solem et lunam et astra, omnem exercitum caeli, et errore deceptus adores ea et colas, quae attribuit Dominus Deus tuus cunctis gentibus, quae sub caelo sunt. [20]Vos autem tulit Dominus et eduxit de fornace ferrea Aegypti, ut haberet populum hereditarium, sicut est in praesenti die. [21]Iratusque est

LORD your God, which he made with you, and make a graven image in the form of anything which the LORD your God has forbidden you. ²⁴For the LORD your God is a devouring fire, a jealous God. Ex 13:22; 20:5
Is 33:14
Zeph 1:18
Heb 12:29

²⁵"When you beget children and children's children, and have grown old in the land, if you act corruptly by making a graven image in the form of anything, and by doing what is evil in the sight of the LORD your God, so as to provoke him to anger, ²⁶I call heaven and earth to witness against you this day, that you will soon utterly perish from the land which you are going over the Jordan to possess; you will not live long upon it, but will be utterly destroyed. ²⁷And the LORD will scatter you among the peoples, and you will be left few in number among the nations where the LORD will drive you. ²⁸And there you will serve gods of wood and stone, the work of men's hands, that neither see, nor hear, nor eat, nor smell. ²⁹But from there you will seek the LORD your God, and you will find him, if you search after him Deut 28:29
Josh 23:16

Is 1:2

Is 4:3

Acts 7:41;
17:29

Acts 7:27

---

belonging to all nations, whereas he has chosen to make Israel his own portion, to be a people who will render him worship. Some ancient peoples regarded the sun, moon and stars not as inanimate heavenly bodies but as living beings (cf. 17:3; Job 38:7; Wis 13:2) whose activity impacted on nature and on man.

The sacred writer demythologizes beliefs of this sort which constituted a danger for true religion. The passage seeks to stress God's special providence towards his chosen people.

The *Catechism of the Catholic Church* has this to say: "This state of division into many nations (cf. Acts 17:26–27), each entrusted by divine providence to the guardianship of angels, is at once cosmic, social and religious (cf. Deut 4:19; Deut [LXX] 32:8). It is intended to limit the pride of fallen humanity (cf. Wis 10:5), united only in its perverse ambition to forge its own unity as at Babel (cf. Gen 11:4–6). But, because of sin (cf. Rom 1:18–25), both polytheism and the idolatry of the nation and of its rulers constantly threaten this provisional economy with the perversion of paganism" (no. 57).

Dominus contra me propter sermones vestros et iuravit, ut non transirem Iordanem nec ingrederer terram optimam, quam Dominus Deus tuus daturus est tibi in haereditatem. ²²Ecce morior in hac humo, non transibo Iordanem; vos transibitis et possidebitis terram egregiam hanc. ²³Cavete, ne quando obliviscamini pacti Domini Dei vestri, quod pepigit vobiscum, et faciatis vobis sculptam similitudinem omnium, quae fieri Dominus Deus tuus prohibuit; ²⁴quia Dominus Deus tuus ignis consumens est, Deus aemulator. ²⁵Si genueris filios ac nepotes, et morati fueritis in terra corruptique feceritis aliquam similitudinem sculptam patrantes malum coram Domino Deo tuo, ut eum ad iracundiam provocetis, ²⁶testes invoco contra vos hodie caelum et terram, cito perituros vos esse de terra, quam, transito Iordane, possessuri estis: non habitabitis in ea longo tempore, sed delebit vos Dominus ²⁷atque disperget in gentes, et remanebitis pauci in nationibus, ad quas vos ducturus est Dominus. ²⁸Ibique servietis diis, qui hominum manu fabricati sunt, ligno et lapidi, qui non vident nec audiunt nec comedunt nec odorantur. ²⁹Cumque quaesieris ibi Dominum Deum tuum, invenies eum, si tamen toto corde quaesieris eum et tota anima tua. ³⁰Postquam in tribulatione tua te invenerint omnia, quae praedicta sunt, novis-

with all your heart and with all your soul. [30]When you are in tribulation, and all these things come upon you in the latter days, you will return to the LORD your God and obey his voice, [31]for the LORD your God is a merciful God; he will not fail you or destroy you or forget the covenant with your fathers which he swore to them.

The Lord's special providence towards his people

Mk 13:19 [32]"For ask now of the days that are past, which were before you, since the day that God created man upon the earth, and ask from one end of heaven to the other, whether such a great thing as this Deut 4:7 has ever happened or was ever heard of. [33]Did any people ever Ex 33:20 hear the voice of a god speaking out of the midst of the fire, as you have heard, and still live? [34]Or has any god ever attempted to Deut 7:6 go and take a nation for himself from the midst of another nation, Acts 13:17 by trials, by signs, by wonders, and by war, by a mighty hand and an outstretched arm, and by great terrors, according to all that the

---

4:32–40. The end of this first discourse carries an important theological message: the profound notion of one God (monotheism); the election of Israel as God's specific people; his special and kindly providence towards this people; the might of God, as manifested in the prodigious works he does in favour of the chosen people; and the consequence of all this—Israel's duty to be faithful to the one and only God, keeping his commandments and offering due cult only to him; by so doing, Israel will continue to enjoy his protection.

Reading this and other passages in the sacred books shows the efforts the inspired writers made to update the teaching of religious traditions and apply it to the situation and needs of Israelites in later periods; this is perhaps the reason for the frequent calls to fidelity to the Covenant. "In the course of its history, Israel was able to discover that God had only one reason to reveal himself to them, a single motive for choosing them from among all peoples as his special possession: his sheer gratuitous love (cf. Deut 4:37; 7:8; 10:15). And thanks to the prophets Israel understood that it was again out of love that God never stopped saving them (cf. Is 43:1–7) and pardoning their unfaithfulness and sins (cf. Hos 2)" (*Catechism of the Catholic Church*, 218).

The Deuteronomic formula of "the Lord is God [*ha-Elohim*, that is, the only God] and there is no other besides him" (v. 35), which occurs often (cf. 4:39; 6:4;

---

simo tempore reverteris ad Dominum Deum tuum et audies vocem eius; [31]quia Deus misericors Dominus Deus tuus est, non dimittet te nec omnino delebit neque obliviscetur pacti, in quo iuravit patribus tuis. [32]Interroga de diebus antiquis, qui fuerunt ante te ex die, quo creavit Deus hominem super terram, et a summo caeli usque ad summum eius, si facta est aliquando huiuscemodi res magna, aut umquam cognitum est, [33]num audivit populus vocem Dei loquentis de medio ignis, sicut tu audisti et vixisti? [34]Aut tentavit Deus, ut ingrederetur et tolleret sibi gentem de medio nationis per tentationes, signa atque portenta, per pugnam et robustam manum extentumque brachium et terrores magnos, iuxta omnia, quae fecit pro vobis Dominus Deus vester in Aegypto, videntibus oculis tuis? [35]Tibi monstra-

LORD your God did for you in Egypt before your eyes? ³⁵To you it was shown, that you might know that the LORD is God; there is no other besides him. ³⁶Out of heaven he let you hear his voice, that he might discipline you; and on earth he let you see his great fire, and you heard his words out of the midst of the fire. ³⁷And because he loved your fathers and chose their descendants after them, and brought you out of Egypt with his own presence, by his great power, ³⁸driving out before you nations greater and mightier than yourselves, to bring you in, to give you their land for an inheritance, as at this day; ³⁹know therefore this day, and lay it to your heart, that the LORD is God in heaven above and on the earth beneath; there is no other. ⁴⁰Therefore you shall keep his statutes and his commandments, which I command you this day, that it may go well with you, and with your children after you, and that you may prolong your days in the land which the LORD your God gives you for ever."*

Deut 4:39; 6:4; 32:9
Jer 2:11–33
Is 41:2–29; 43:10–13; 44:6; 46:9
Mk 12:32
Acts 13:17

Mt 5:5

Lk 1:6

32:39; etc.) is also the essence of the Prophets' message (cf. Jer 2:11–33; Is 41:2–29; 44:6; 46:9). The Prophets strove to draw Israel towards or maintain it in fidelity to the One and Only God who revealed himself to the patriarchs and to Moses, and helped to develop and deepen an appreciation of monotheism, of the universality of the power of Yahweh, of his moral demands, etc. But the core of all this teaching is to be found expounded, profoundly and very specifically, in the book of Deuteronomy. This teaching builds up the notion of the Lord as a "jealous God" (cf. Ex 20:5) who requires his adherents to be totally obedient to him; it is a notion incompatible with worshipping the divinities adored by other peoples (cf. Ex 20:3).

Being good, obeying the commandments of the Law of God, brings life (v. 40), initially understood as longevity; whereas sin often brings with it misfortune or death, as a punishment from God (cf. Ezek 18:10–13, 19–20; etc.). The fact that God is just in his treatment of man, rewarding him or punishing, sooner or later, for the good or the evil he does, is a message that runs right through the Old and New Testaments. In ancient texts, the accent is on reward or punishment in this present life. In the New Testament more emphasis is put on divine retribution in the future life. It is not surprising that there should be this line of development in the biblical ethic: God takes account of time and grace to lead men to the fullness of truth.

tum est, ut scires quoniam Dominus ipse est Deus, et non est alius praeter eum. ³⁶De caelo te fecit audire vocem suam, ut doceret te, et in terra ostendit tibi ignem suum maximum; et audisti verba illius de medio ignis, ³⁷quia dilexit patres tuos et elegit semen eorum post eos. Eduxitque te vultu suo in virtute sua magna ex Aegypto, ³⁸ut expelleret nationes maiores et fortiores te in introitu tuo et introduceret te daretque tibi terram earum in possessionem, sicut cernis in praesenti die. ³⁹Scito ergo hodie et cogitato in corde tuo quod Dominus ipse sit Deus in caelo sursum et in terra deorsum, et non sit alius. ⁴⁰Custodi praecepta eius atque mandata, quae ego praecipio tibi hodie, ut bene sit tibi et filiis tuis post te, et permaneas multo tempore super terram, quam Dominus Deus tuus daturus est tibi». ⁴¹Tunc se-

Deut 19:1–13 **Cities of refuge**

Ex 21:13 41*Then Moses set apart three cities in the east beyond the Jordan, 42that the manslayer might flee there, who kills his neighbor unintentionally, without being at enmity with him in time past, and that by fleeing to one of these cities he might save his life: 43Bezer in the wilderness on the tableland for the Reubenites, and Ramoth in Gilead for the Gadites, and Golan in Bashan for the Manassites.

PART TWO

The Second Discourse of Moses: The Law*

Its time and place

44This is the law which Moses set before the children of Israel; 45these are the testimonies, the statutes, and the ordinances, which Moses spoke to the children of Israel when they came out of

4:41–43. It is a little surprising to find at the end of this discourse so early a mention of the cities of refuge (cf., further on, 19:1–13). The setting up of these cities was a humanitarian move to alleviate the effects of the age-old custom of seeking vengeance, a custom widespread among nomadic tribes of this zone: since there was no political authority that could protect people who committed involuntary and accidental offences, the best that could be done was to set up a sanctuary system.

***4:44—26:15.** Verse 44 marks the start of the "Second Discourse of Moses", the

longest one in Deuteronomy (almost 22 chapters) and the essence and most important part of the book. It includes, among other texts, the Decalogue (5:1–33), an ancient rendering of the *Shemá* (6:4–9) and the Deuteronomic Code (12:1—26:19).

Nowadays there is a consensus that this second discourse constitutes, in its general lines and main passages, the basic "great text" of the entire book; the preceding chapters (1:1—4:43) and the ones which come after it (26:16—34:12) act as the frame of this central nucleus.

This part of Deuteronomy accounts

paravit Moyses tres civitates trans Iordanem ad orientalem plagam, 42ut confugiat ad eas, qui occiderit nolens proximum suum, nec fuerit inimicus ante unum et alterum diem, et ad harum aliquam urbium possit evadere et vivat: 43 Bosor in solitudine, quae sita est in terra campestri, pro tribu Ruben, et Ramoth in Galaad pro tribu Gad et Golan in Basan pro tribu Manasse. 44Ista est lex, quam proposuit Moyses coram filiis Israel; 45haec testimonia et praecepta atque iudicia, quae locutus est ad filios Israel, quando egressi sunt de Aegypto, 46trans Iordanem in valle contra Bethphegor, in terra Sehon regis

Egypt, ⁴⁶beyond the Jordan in the valley opposite Beth-peor, in the land of Sihon the king of the Amorites, who lived at Heshbon, whom Moses and the children of Israel defeated when they came out of Egypt. ⁴⁷And they took possession of his land and the land of Og the king of Bashan, the two kings of the Amorites, who lived to the east beyond the Jordan; ⁴⁸from Aroer, which is on the edge of the valley of the Arnon, as far as Mount Sirionᶜ (that is, Hermon), ⁴⁹together with all the Arabah on the east side of the Jordan as far as the Sea of the Arabah, under the slopes of Pisgah.

3. THE TEN COMMANDMENTS*

Ex 20:2–17

5 ¹And Moses summoned all Israel, and said to them, "Hear, O Israel, the statutes and the ordinances which I speak in your

---

for a large part of the basic cultic and legal text of Jewish life—the Law or *Toráh* pondered in the heart, and kept before people's minds as constantly as possible. It speaks of the centralizing of worship in the temple of Jerusalem, of the conviction that Yahweh, the Only God and Saviour of Israel, is the best of fathers to his people, the God who has come so close that it is possible to speak to him and who continues to take care of Israel with special providence and love. These are the key ideas that run through the second discourse of Moses. In a way they are a summary of Old Testament revelation and life.

4:44–49. These verses are clearly an

introductory note. "Law" in Hebrew (*Toráh*) has a wider meaning than in modern languages, because it has a didactic and sapiential connotation as well as a legal one. Therefore, *Toráh* has to be read as Law-teaching-wisdom, and it is useful to notice which dimension is to the fore at any one point. The modern reader of the Old Testament should bear this in mind in order the better to understand the overall meaning of the "Law of Moses", as the entire Pentateuch is often called.

***5:1—11:32.** After some verses by way of prologue (4:44–49), at 5:1 a section begins which we might call the "Introduction to the Deuteronomic Code" and which will go on as far as 11:32. These

---

Amorraei, qui habitavit in Hesebon, quem percussit Moyses et filii Israel egressi ex Aegypto. ⁴⁷Et possederunt terram eius et terram Og regis Basan, duorum regum Amorraeorum, qui erant trans Iordanem ad solis ortum, ⁴⁸ab Aroer, quae sita est super ripam torrentis Arnon, usque ad montem Sion, qui est Hermon, ⁴⁹omnem Arabam trans Iordanem ad orientalem plagam usque ad mare Arabae et usque ad radices montis Phasga. ¹Vocavitque Moyses omnem Israelem et dixit ad eos: «Audi, Israel, praecepta atque iudicia, quae ego loquor in auribus vestris hodie; discite ea et opere complete. ²Dominus Deus noster pepigit nobiscum foedus in Horeb. ³Non cum patribus nostris iniit pactum hoc

c. Syr: Heb *Sion*

Deut 4:10–13 hearing this day, and you shall learn them and be careful to do them. ²The LORD our God made a covenant with us in Horeb. ³Not with our fathers did the LORD make this covenant, but with us, who are all of us here alive this day. ⁴The LORD spoke with you

---

seven chapters are particularly important for understanding the mind of Old Testament legislation: in a specific yet profound way the Law provides the structure for man's relationship with God. Deuteronomy underscores the social dimension of life: the accent falls on Israel as a people, without that in any way excluding individual moral responsibility. In the prophetical books (especially from Ezekiel onwards) the accent will shift to personal responsibility, and yet the social dimension remains. Right judgment in moral decisions always involves taking account of both the personal and the social dimensions.

5:1–22. The discourse begins by recalling the promulgation on Horeb (Sinai) of the central theme of the Covenant—the "Ten Words" (4:13; 10:4; Ex 20:1; 34:28)— *déka lógoi* in Greek, hence the name "Decalogue". The book of Exodus recounts the theophany at Sinai and it also gives the wording of these Ten Commandments (Ex 20:1–17): the essential content is the same but there are slight variations in the reasons given for the sabbath rest (Ex:10–11 and Deut 5:14–15), and in the place where the wife is mentioned in the prohibition about covetousness (Ex 20:17 and Deut 5:21). It may be that the text on the two tables of stone (v. 22) was couched very succinctly: some sacred editor may very well have added the short explanations which are given in some commandments, which would explain the small variations between the wording in Exodus and Deuteronomy. Cf. the notes on Ex 20:1–17.

We do know that some peoples in the ancient East had legal codes; the most famous of these is the code of Hammurabi, king of Babylon around the 18th century BC; however, no earlier text has been discovered whose overall content coincides with the Decalogue in Deuteronomy and Exodus, nor do any of the great literatures of antiquity contain anything that parallels the biblical text. This fact makes it more remarkable and surprising that a people such as the Israelites, which was so dependent in all aspects (cultural, agricultural, technical etc.) on the cultures round about it (Egyptian, Mesopotamian, Canaanite, Assyrian etc.) should produce such an amount of material—and material with much deeper theological and ethical content than its neighbours'. This is an historical enigma; scholarship has been unable to explain it; a special divine providence must have been at work.

"The commandments of the Decalogue, although accessible to reason alone, have been revealed. To attain a complete and certain understanding of the requirements of the natural law, sinful humanity needed this revelation: 'A full explanation of the commandments of the Decalogue became necessary in the state of sin because the light of reason was obscured and the will had gone astray' (St Bonaventure, *In IV Sent.* 37, 13). We know God's commandments through the divine revelation proposed to us in the Church, and through the voice of moral conscience" (*Catechism of the Catholic Church*, 2017).

In the Decalogue the Lord is the ulti-

---

sed nobiscum, qui in praesentiarum hic sumus, omnibus nobis, qui vivimus. ⁴Facie ad faciem locutus

face to face at the mountain, out of the midst of the fire, [5]while I Gal 3:19 stood between the LORD and you at that time, to declare to you the word of the LORD; for you were afraid because of the fire, and you did not go up into the mountain. He said:

---

mate source of the Law, and it is he who gives it its obligatory character; so, any infraction of the Law is in the last analysis an offence against God. The Hebrew religion is unique in that God requires a high standard of moral holiness: this is not the case in the religions of neighbouring peoples, nor in Greek religion.

"Since they express man's fundamental duties towards God and towards his neighbour, the Ten Commandments reveal, in their primordial content, *grave* obligations. They are fundamentally immutable, and they oblige always and everywhere. No one can dispense from them. The Ten Commandments are engraved by God in the human heart" (ibid., 2072).

This page of the Bible is so important that, over the course of the centuries and even today, it continues to be the basis of human morality and a perfect expression of the natural moral law that is inscribed by God on the conscience of every human being. In the Sermon on the Mount Jesus gives it its most perfect formulation (Mt 5:17–19).

5:1–5. The special relevance of the Decalogue, which is the very core of the Law, is highlighted by these verses which act as a kind of portico. The solemn nature of what follows is signalled by the words of warning: "Hear, O Israel" (repeated also at 6:4 and 9:1). In the thinking of the rabbis, for whom the Law was the expression *par excellence* of the "Word of God", the Law is eternal; it always existed in the divine mind, but

only in time, through Moses, was it communicated to the people of Israel.

5:3. The change of person—"our fathers", "us"—has importance in the message and theology of Deuteronomy: the Covenant is not only something that happened in the past; it is present and active from generation to generation; it is something that is current for everyone who reads the book. By virtue of God's fidelity to the Covenant offered in bygone days, every generation and every believer retains faith in the protection and providence of God and hopes to be forgiven his or her sins and to be able to begin anew. The Covenant was sealed between God and our forebears and it continues to apply in every generation.

In this connexion, St Irenaeus commented: "Through the Decalogue God prepared man to be his friend and to be of one heart with his neighbour. [. . .] The words of the Decalogue continue to apply among us [Christians]. Far from being abolished, they have been expanded and developed by the fact of the Lord coming in the flesh" (*Adversus haereses*, 4, 16, 3–4).

5:6–15. The "first table" of the commandments "calls us to acknowledge God as the one Lord of all and to worship him alone for his infinite holiness (cf. Ex 20:2–11; Deut 5:6–15) [. . .] *Acknowledging the Lord as God is the very core, the heart of the Law,* from which the particular precepts flow and towards which they are ordered. In the morality

---

est vobis in monte de medio ignis; [5]ego sequester et medius fui inter Dominum et vos in tempore illo, ut annuntiarem vobis verba eius; timuistis enim ignem et non ascendistis in montem. Et ait: [6]'Ego

Ex 20:2 ⁶"'I am the LORD your God, who brought you out of the land of Egypt, out of the house of bondage.

Rev 5:3 ⁷"'You shall have no other gods before^d me.

⁸"'You shall not make for yourself a graven image, or any likeness of anything that is in heaven above, or that is on the earth

Deut 4:24 beneath, or that is in the water under the earth; ⁹you shall not bow down to them or serve them; for I the LORD your God am a jealous God, visiting the iniquity of the fathers upon the children to

---

of the commandments the fact that the people of Israel belongs to the Lord is made evident [. . .]. Such is the witness of Sacred Scripture, imbued in every one of its pages with a lively perception of God's absolute holiness: 'Holy, holy, holy is the Lord of hosts' (Is 6:3)" (John Paul II, *Veritatis splendor*, 11).

Origen points out that, just as punishment for sin involved the step from the paradise of freedom to the servitude of this world, so it is that the first words of the Decalogue, the first word of the commandments of God, refer to freedom: "I am the Lord your God, who brought you out of the land of Egypt, out of the house of bondage" (Ex 20:2; Deut 5:6): cf. *Homiliae in Exodum*, 8, 10.

5:6–10. There are two aspects to the first commandment: it states that there is only one God and it forbids making images to represent him. This outright declaration of monotheism is very remarkable, given the polytheism of Eastern peoples of that period. Isaiah 44:6 gives a short and profound explanation of the first part of this commandment: "I am the first and the last; besides me there is no god."

The ban on making images is design-

ed to underline the spiritual nature of God and his immateriality. However, some imagery by way of ornamentation is permitted, as for example the cherubim of the mercy seat (cf. Ex 25:18–20) or the bulls of the sea of bronze in the temple (1 Kings 7:25; cf. the note on 4:15–31).

In Christian teaching, the wording of the first commandment—You shall love God above all things—echoes the wording in Deuteronomy which Jesus identifies in the Gospel (Mt 22:37) as being the main commandment: "You shall love the Lord your God with all your heart, and with all your soul, and with all your mind."

5:8–10. In the Old Testament idolatry was seen as a kind of adultery. This is the reason why God's wrath is described as "jealousy".

To understand the threat to punish children for the sins of their fathers, one needs to bear in mind that in the Eastern culture of the time each person had a strong sense of solidarity with his family and his people. Many episodes are to be found in the Bible (even in the New Testament) which reflect this outlook (cf., e.g., 2 Sam 21:1–14; Jn 9:1–2).

Dominus Deus tuus, qui eduxi te de terra Aegypti, de domo servitutis. ⁷Non habebis deos alienos in conspectu meo. ⁸Non facies tibi sculptile nec similitudinem omnium, quae in caelo sunt desuper et quae in terra deorsum et quae versantur in aquis sub terra. ⁹Non adorabis ea et non coles: Ego enim

d. Or *besides*

the third and fourth generation of those who hate me, ¹⁰but showing steadfast love to thousands of those who love me and keep my
commandments.

¹¹"'You shall not take the name of the LORD your God in vain:
for the Lord will not hold him guiltless who takes his name in
vain.

¹²"'Observe the sabbath day, to keep it holy, as the LORD your
God commanded you. ¹³Six days you shall labour, and do all your   Lk 13:14

However, even the notion of personal
responsibility comes across quite clearly:
"The fathers shall not be put to death for
the children, nor should the children be
put to death for the fathers; every man
shall be put to death for his own sin"
(24:16). This in turn does not exclude the
tremendously negative way the sins of
parents can impact on their children by
depriving them of spiritual benefits
through the Communion of Saints and by
giving them bad example.

5:11. This verse contains the second
commandment of the Decalogue as
found in the Christian catechism (the
third, in the Hebrew Decalogue).

In the cultural and religious context
of the Hebrew people and neighbouring
peoples, a name was a symbol and
expression of the person named. The prohibition on using the name of God in
vain (that is, falsely) means that it should
always be used with due reverence (an
extreme case of transgressing this commandment is a sin of blasphemy) and it
should never be used to call on God to
witness something untrue. It is not prohibited to swear an oath (cf. 6:13): Holy
Scripture praises such action in the right
conditions (cf. Jer 4:2). However, in

Jesus' time, the practice of swearing
oaths had become an almost ridiculous
abuse because it happened so often and a
whole casuistry had built up around the
practice. In the Sermon on the Mount our
Lord establishes the moral principles that
should govern uprightness and sincerity
in speech and fidelity to one's word (cf.
Mt 5:33–37). The Church teaches that it
is lawful and even honourable to take an
oath when necessary and when it is done
truthfully and justly (cf. the notes on Mt
5:33–37 and Jas 5:12).

5:12–15. Ancient peoples had their festivals dedicated to their gods, and to rest
and relaxation; but there is no evidence
of their having a regular custom of sabbath rest of the sort found in the Mosaic
Law. The humanitarian reason given
here (to allow family, servants and animals to have a break), recalling the times
of bondage in Egypt, is different from
the theological reason given in Exodus
(recalling God's work of creation and his
rest on the seventh day: cf. Gen 2:2–3):
these two aspects are complementary
and they point to the fact that the sabbath
should be devoted to God and to rest.

Casuistry and rigorism were later
responsible for turning the sabbath rest

sum Dominus Deus tuus, Deus aemulator, reddens iniquitatem patrum super filios in tertiam et quartam generationem his, qui oderunt me, ¹⁰et faciens misericordiam in multa milia diligentibus me et cus-
todientibus praecepta mea. ¹¹Non usurpabis nomen Domini Dei tui frustra, quia non erit impunitus, qui
super re vana nomen eius assumpserit. ¹²Observa diem sabbati, ut sanctifices eum, sicut praecepit tibi
Dominus Deus tuus. ¹³Sex diebus operaberis et facies omnia opera tua. ¹⁴Septimus dies sabbatum est

Gen 2:2–3 work; [14]but the seventh day is a sabbath to the LORD your God; in
Mt 12:1
Mk 2:27 it you shall not do any work, you, or your son, or your daughter,
or your manservant, or your maidservant, or your ox, or your ass,
or any of your cattle, or the sojourner who is within your gates,
that your manservant and your maidservant may rest as well as
you. [15]You shall remember that you were a servant in the land of
Egypt, and the LORD your God brought you out thence with a

---

into something very burdensome for the
Jews: our Lord criticized this in the
Gospel (cf., e.g. Mt 12:1–13; Lk
13:10–17).

Ever since the apostolic age, the
Church has celebrated Sunday instead of
Saturday as this day; and apropos of
Sunday observance it teaches: "The institution of the Lord's Day helps everyone
enjoy adequate rest and leisure to cultivate their familial, cultural, social and
religious lives" (*Catechism of the Catholic Church*, 2184). On that day, moreover, the faithful have a grave obligation
to keep the precept of attendance at Sunday Mass, because "the Sunday Eucharist
is the foundation and confirmation of all
Christian practice" (ibid., 2181). See also
John Paul II, Apostolic Letter, *Dies
Domini* (31 May 1998).

"To keep it holy": the semi-official
Jewish commentary on the book of
Exodus, called the *Mekhilta*, makes the
point that to be able to keep the precept
of rest on the seventh day, one is obliged
to work on the preceding six days. If
someone does not have work to do, one
should look for it: if one has a property in
need of repair, one should repair it; a
field needing attention should be cultivated. And traditional Jewish teaching
says that, during the six days of the
week, Israelites are cooperators with God

in creation and they should cooperate by
improving and enhancing the things that
God has created. And, as a parallel to
this, on the seventh day they should rest
along with the Almighty and proclaim
that he is the Lord.

5:16–21. Now come the commandments
to do with one's neighbour. Some ideas
similar to what is here are also to be
found in other Eastern codes, as might be
expected, because they stem from the
basic exigences of the natural law.
However, in this area also the Mosaic
code is original in that it links these precepts with those that have direct reference to God: they are all part of a suite,
inseparable from one another, as will
become even plainer in the New
Testament (cf., e.g., Mt 25:31–46; 1 Jn
4:20–21).

John Paul II in his explanation of the
Decalogue based on Jesus' conversation
with the rich young man teaches: "Jesus
does not intend to list each and every one
of the commandments required in order
to 'enter into life', but rather wishes to
draw the young man's attention to the
'*centrality*' *of the Decalogue* with regard
to every other precept inasmuch as it is
the interpretation of what the words 'I am
the Lord your God' mean for man. Nevertheless we cannot fail to notice which

---

Domino Deo tuo. Non facies in eo quidquam operis tu et filius tuus et filia, servus et ancilla et bos et
asinus et omne iumentum tuum et peregrinus tuus, qui est intra portas tuas, ut requiescat servus tuus et
ancilla tua sicut et tu. [15]Memento quod et ipse servieris in Aegypto, et eduxerit te inde Dominus Deus
tuus in manu forti et brachio extento: idcirco praecepit tibi, ut observares diem sabbati. [16]Honora

mighty hand and an outstretched arm; therefore the LORD your God commanded you to keep the sabbath day.

¹⁶"'Honour your father and your mother, as the LORD your God commanded you; that your days may be prolonged, and that it may go well with you, in the land which the LORD your God gives you.

¹⁷"'You shall not kill.

Sir 3:1–16;
7:27–28; Mt
1:4; 19:18ff
Mk 7:10;
10:19
Lk 18:20
Eph 6:2
Mt 5:21
Rom 13:9
Jas 2:1

---

commandments of the Law the Lord recalls to the young man. They are some of the commandments belonging to the so-called 'second tablet' of the Decalogue, the summary (cf. Rom 13:8–10) and foundation of which is *the commandment of love of neighbour*: 'You shall love your neighbour as yourself' (Mt 19:19; cf. Mk 12:31). In this commandment we find a precise expression of *the singular dignity of the human person*, 'the only creature that God has wanted for its own sake' (*Gaudium et spes*, 24)" (*Veritatis splendor*, 13).

5:16. The commandment to honour parents is the only one in the series which is couched in positive terms, and also the only one whose wording includes a reward for its observance. This reward—a long and happy life—seems to do with the present life only: as Revelation unfolds, God will gradually reveal a reward which transcends this life (cf. the notes on 4:32–40; 28:1–69). In this precept are included duties towards all those whom we should respect as we respect parents, on account of their dignity, authority or office—teachers, authorities in general, priests, etc.

5:17. Life is the most basic good that should be respected in our neighbour. The fifth commandment has to do with the dignity of the human person, who is

created in the image and likeness of God. Therefore, this offence is a kind of attack on the divine, a forgetting that only God is the Lord of life and death. Even in the very first chapters of Genesis God severely reproved the murder of Abel by Cain (Gen 4:8–15), and in Genesis 9:6 he adds: "Whoever sheds the blood of man, by man shall his blood be shed; for God made man in his own image." In the Sermon on the Mount, Jesus perfected the meaning of this precept (which is not confined to the simple act of killing), teaching that any unjust action, word or thought against others is evil; moreover, he identified the duties which charity involves and which extend even to love for one's enemies (cf. Mt 5:21–26, 43–48). In this way Jesus sets human relations on a higher level than previously—beyond the already high level of relations between persons to that of relations between children of the same (and only) heavenly Father.

In the contemporary world the Church has often had to denounce many crimes against human life, such as "murder, genocide, abortion, euthanasia and wilful suicide" (Vatican II, *Gaudium et spes*, 27).

"It needs to be vigorously restated that nothing and no one may authorize the death of an innocent human being, whether foetus or embryo, child or adult, old, incurably sick or dying. Nor may

---

patrem tuum et matrem, sicut praecepit tibi Dominus Deus tuus, ut longo vivas tempore et bene sit tibi in terra, quam Dominus Deus tuus daturus est tibi. ¹⁷Non occides. ¹⁸Neque moechaberis. ¹⁹Furtumque

Lev 20:10
Deut 22:22
Mt 5:27

Ex 20:15
Lev 19:11–13

Rom 7:7

Ex 24:16
Deut 4:12–13
Heb 12:18

18"'Neither shall you commit adultery. 19"'Neither shall you steal. 20"'Neither shall you bear false witness against your neighbour. 21"'Neither shall you covet your neighbor's wife; and you shall not desire your neighbour's house, his field, or his manservant, or his maidservant, his ox, or his ass, or anything that is your neighbour's.'

22"These words the LORD spoke to all your assembly at the mountain out of the midst of the fire, the cloud, and the thick darkness, with a loud voice; and he added no more. And he wrote them upon two tables of stone, and gave them to me. 23And when

---

anyone request this homicidal action for himself or for others entrusted to his care [. . .]. No one in authority can lawfully impose or permit such action. For it is a violation of the divine law, an offence against the dignity of the human person, a crime against life, an attack on mankind" (Congregation for the Doctrine of the Faith, *Iura et bona,* 2).

5:18. In the Mosaic Law adultery was punishable by death (cf. Lev 20:10; Deut 22:22). However, because polygamy was so widespread at the time the position and rights of man and woman in marriage differed: a wife's unfaithfulness was always adultery; in the case of a husband, only sexual intercourse with a married woman was adulterous.

As the centuries went by, Israel became more conscious of the implications of this very succinctly couched commandment; witness, for example, the Wisdom books, where this precept is extended to cover various kinds of immodest acts and licentious sexual behaviour (cf., e.g., Sir 23:19; Job 31:1, 9–11).

In the New Testament Jesus restores its original meaning to marriage (one and

indissoluble: Mt 19:1–9) and perfects this precept by pointing to the evil of looking lustfully at a woman, be she married or not (Mt 5:27–30). Setting aside the casuistic distinctions made by scribes, Jesus teaches that the precept applies not only to external actions that have taken place but also to one's intentions, one's heart, which is where external actions begin. The Mosaic Law imposed penalties for the act of adultery or for externalized adulterous intentions; but Jesus, going to the root of moral behaviour, puts the emphasis on the internal act: that, even without an external act, can exclude a person from the Kingdom of heaven.

5:19. The prohibition on stealing is expressed in very general terms. This precept is aimed at protecting the property of one's neighbour (normally the product of his work) especially when he needs it to develop his personality and maintain himself and his family.

5:20. "Bear false witness": the Hebrew verb, with its preposition, means "to speak badly about someone" (Deut 19:18; 2 Sam 1:16). From the wording it seems to refer mainly to evidence given

---

non facies. 20Nec loqueris contra proximum tuum falsum testimonium. 21Nec concupisces uxorem proximi tui. Nec desiderabis domum proximi tui, non agrum, non servum, non ancillam, non bovem, non asinum et universa, quae illius sunt'. 22Haec verba locutus est Dominus ad omnem multitudinem

you heard the voice out of the midst of the darkness, while the mountain was burning with fire, you came near to me, all the heads of your tribes, and your elders; ²⁴and you said, 'Behold, the LORD our God has shown us his glory and greatness, and we have heard his voice out of the midst of the fire; we have this day seen God speak with man and man still live. ²⁵Now therefore why should we die? For this great fire will consume us; if we hear the voice of the LORD our God any more, we shall die. ²⁶For who is there of all flesh, that has heard the voice of the living God speaking out of the midst of fire, as we have, and has still lived? ²⁷Go near, and hear all that the LORD our God will say; and speak to us

Ex 19:16

Ex 19:21; 33:20
Judg 13:22
Is 6:5

---

by witnesses at lawsuits, although other types of testimony are not excluded. The administration of justice is something basic to the defence of human rights and the establishment of a peaceful society; that is why the truthfulness of witnesses is so essential.

This commandment is the eighth precept of the catechism, where the prohibition on bearing false witness is linked to that on lying: "Thou shalt not bear false witness against thy neighbour" (cf. *Catechism of the Catholic Church*, 2475–2487).

5:21. This wording varies slightly from that in Exodus 20:17. Whereas in Exodus a woman looks as if she were just part of man's property, here in Deuteronomy she clearly is different from the rest of one's neighbour's possessions; she holds first place. This variant clearly marks a moral advance.

In Christian catechisms the two parts of the verse are usually broken down to form the ninth and tenth commandments of the Decalogue. The first part is worded: "Thou shalt not covet thy neighbour's wife", thereby filling out the more external and physical content of the sixth commandment and stressing temperance in the sense of controlling one's sexual appetite; it encourages the practice of the virtue of chastity, according to each person's state (married or single).

The second part forms our tenth commandment: "Thou shalt not covet thy neighbour's goods." In parallel to the first part, it fills out the seventh commandment by stressing temperance in the ownership of material things, by getting to the root of a disordered desire for them.

5:23–31. The Hebrews had the conviction that it was impossible to see God and still live. This idea comes up often in the Old Testament (cf., e.g., Ex 19:21; Judg 13:22; Is 6:5). The passage brilliantly manages to underline both the transcendence of God and his closeness to his people through his word and his Law.

vestram in monte, de medio ignis et nubis et caliginis voce magna nihil addens amplius; et scripsit ea in duabus tabulis lapideis, quas tradidit mihi. ²³Vos autem, postquam audistis vocem de medio tenebrarum et montem ardere vidistis, accessistis ad me omnes principes tribuum et maiores natu ²⁴atque dixistis: 'Ecce ostendit nobis Dominus Deus noster maiestatem et magnitudinem suam; vocem eius audivimus de medio ignis et probavimus hodie quod, loquente Deo cum homine, vixerit homo. ²⁵Nunc autem cur moriemur, et devorabit nos ignis hic maximus? Si enim audierimus ultra vocem Domini Dei nostri, moriemur. ²⁶Quid est omnis caro, ut audiat vocem Dei viventis, qui de medio ignis loquitur, sicut nos audivimus, et possit vivere? ²⁷Tu magis accede et audi cuncta, quae dixerit Dominus Deus noster,

all that the Lord our God will speak to you; and we will hear and do it.'

²⁸"And the Lord heard your words, when you spoke to me; and the Lord said to me, 'I have heard the words of this people, which they have spoken to you; they have rightly said all that they have spoken. ²⁹Oh that they had such a mind as this always, to fear me and to keep all my commandments, that it might go well with them and with their children for ever! ³⁰Go and say to them, "Return to your tents." ³¹But you, stand here by me, and I will tell you all the commandment and the statutes and the ordinances which you shall teach them, that they may do them in the land which I give them to possess.' ³²You shall be careful to do therefore as the Lord your God has commanded you; you shall not turn aside to the right hand or to the left. ³³You shall walk in all the way which the Lord your God has commanded you, that you may live, and that it may go well with you, and that you may live long in the land which you shall possess.

The Lord is the only God*

6 ¹"Now this is the commandment, the statutes and the ordinances which the Lord your God commanded me to teach

*6:1—11:32. Chapters 6–11 form the main part of the introduction to the Deuteronomic Code (chaps. 12–26) to which we already referred in the note to 5:1—11:32. They begin with the confession of the Only God (the *Shema*, 6:1–9) and end with a passage about Israel seen as a great nation which is going to settle in the promised land (11:10–25), a land for it to enjoy or lose: what it freely chooses to do will bring down upon it God's blessing or his curse (11:26–32). These chapters reveal an historical-theo-logical scheme of things involving three protagonists—God, people and land. In a way what we have here is a kind of fore-taste of and a response to a three-fold theme—God, man, world. And we say "response" because the sacred author provides us with the key: salvation has been brought about by God. It began with the people getting out of Egypt and it is furthered by God's gift of the Law (the written Word of God which antici-pates and prefigures the Incarnate Word of God, Jesus Christ), which will guide

et tu loqueris ad nos cuncta, quae dixerit Dominus Deus noster tibi, et nos audientes faciemus ea'. ²⁸Quod cum audisset Dominus, ait ad me: 'Audivi vocem verborum populi huius, quae locuti sunt tibi: bene omnia sunt locuti. ²⁹Quis det talem eos habere mentem, ut timeant me et custodiant universa man-data mea in omni tempore, ut bene sit eis et filiis eorum in sempiternum? ³⁰Vade et dic eis: Revertimini in tentoria vestra. ³¹Tu vero, hic sta mecum, et loquar tibi omnia mandata et praecepta atque iudicia, quae docebis eos, ut faciant ea in terra, quam dabo illis in possessionem'. ³²Custodite igitur et facite, quae praecepit Dominus Deus vester vobis; non declinabitis neque ad dexteram neque ad sinistram, ³³sed per totam viam, quam praecepit Dominus Deus vester, ambulabitis, ut vivatis, et bene sit vobis, et protelentur dies in terra possessionis vestrae. ¹Haec sunt mandata et praecepta atque iudicia, quae

you, that you may do them in the land to which you are going over, to possess it; ²that you may fear the LORD your God, you and your son and your son's son, by keeping all his statutes and his commandments, which I command you, all the days of your life; and that your days may be prolonged. ³Hear therefore, O Israel, and be careful to do them; that it may go well with you, and that you may multiply greatly, as the LORD, the God of your fathers, has promised you, in a land flowing with milk and honey.

Lk 11:28

Deut 4:25
Mk 12:29, 32
1 Cor 8:4
Jas 2:19

The Shema*

⁴"Hear, O Israel: The LORD our God is one LORD;ᵉ ⁵and you shall love the LORD your God with all your heart, and with all your

Deut 10:12–13
Hos 2:21–22; 6:6

---

the people and each individual member of it to the promised land, itself a figure of eternal beatitude in heaven.

*6:1–9. This is a very moving text and one of special importance for the faith and life of the chosen people. The high-point comes at v. 5, which is reminiscent of other pages of the Old Testament (Deut 10:12; Hos 2:21–22; 6:6). The love which God seeks from Israel is preceded by God's love for Israel (cf. Deut 5:32–33). Here we touch one of the central points of God's revelation to mankind, both in the Old and in the New Testament: over and above everything else, God is love (cf., e.g., 1 Jn 4:8–16).

Verse 4 is a clear, solemn profession of monotheism, which is a distinctive feature of Israel that marks it out from the nations round about (cf. the note on 5:6–10). The first Hebrew word of v. 4 (*shema*: "Hear") has given its name to the famous prayer which the Israelites recited over the centuries and which is made up largely of 6:4–9; 11:18–21 and

Numbers 15:37–41. Pious Jews still say it today, every morning and evening. In the Catholic Church, vv. 4–7 are said at Compline after first vespers on Sundays and solemnities in the Liturgy of Hours.

The exhortations in vv. 8–9 were given a literal interpretation by the Jews: this is the origin of phylacteries and of the *mezuzah*. Phylacteries were short tassels or tapes which were attached to the forehead and to the left arm, and each tassel held a tiny box containing a biblical text, the two Deuteronomy texts of the *Shemá* plus Exodus 3:1–10, 11–16; in our Lord's time the Pharisees wore wider tassels to give the impression that they were particularly observant of the Law (cf. Mt 23:5). The *mezuzah* is a small box, attached to the doorposts of houses, which contains a parchment or piece of paper inscribed with the two texts from Deuteronomy referred to; Jews touch the *mezuzah* with their fingers, which they then kiss, on entering or leaving the house.

6:5. God asks Israel for all its love. Yet, is

---

mandavit Dominus Deus vester, ut docerem vos, et faciatis ea in terra, ad quam transgredimini possidendam; ²ut timeas Dominum Deum tuum et custodias omnia praecepta et mandata eius, quae ego praecipio tibi et filiis ac nepotibus tuis, cunctis diebus vitae tuae, ut prolongentur dies tui. ³Audi, Israel, et observa, ut facias, et bene sit tibi, et multipliceris amplius, sicut pollicitus est Dominus, Deus patrum tuorum, tibi terram lacte et melle manantem. ⁴Audi, Israel: Dominus Deus noster Dominus unus est. ⁵Diliges Dominum Deum tuum ex toto corde tuo et ex tota anima tua et ex tota fortitudine tua.

e. Or *the LORD our God, the LORD is one*. Or *the LORD is our God, the LORD is one*. Or *the LORD is our God, the LORD alone*

Mt 22:37
Mk 12:30, 33
Lk 10:27

Mt 23:5

soul, and with all your might. [6]And these words which I command you this day shall be upon your heart; [7]and you shall teach them diligently to your children, and shall talk of them when you sit in your house, and when you walk by the way, and when you lie down, and when you rise. [8]And you shall bind them as a sign upon your hand, and they shall be as frontlets between your eyes. [9]And you shall write them on the doorposts of your house and on your gates.*

An appeal for faithfulness

[10]"And when the LORD your God brings you into the land which he swore to your fathers, to Abraham, to Isaac, and to Jacob, to give you, with great and goodly cities, which you did not build, [11]and houses full of all good things, which you did not fill, and cisterns hewn out, which you did not hew, and vineyards and olive trees, which you did not plant, and when you eat and are full, [12]then take heed lest you forget the LORD, who brought you

---

love something that can be made the subject of a commandment? What God asks of Israel, and of each of us, is not a mere feeling which man cannot control; it is something that has to do with the will. It is an affection which can and should be cultivated by taking to heart, evermore profoundly, our filial relationship with our Father; as the New Testament (1 Jn 4:10, 19) will later put it: "In this is love, not that we loved God but that he loved us and sent his Son to be the expiation for our sins.[...] We love, because he first loved us." That is why God can indeed promulgate the precept of love; as he does in this verse of Deuteronomy (6:5) and further on in 10:12–13.

"With all your heart, and with all your soul, and with all your might" (v. 5): the wording shows that love for God

should be total. Our Lord will quote these verses (4–5), which were so familiar to his listeners, when identifying the first and most important of the commandments (cf. Mt 12:29–30).

"When someone asks him, 'Which commandment in the Law is the greatest?' (Mt 22:36), Jesus replies: 'You shall love the Lord your God with all your heart, and with all your soul, and with all your mind. This is the greatest and first commandment. And a second is like it: You shall love your neighbour as yourself. On these two commandments hang all the Law and the prophets' (Mt 22:37–40; cf. Deut 6:5; Lev 19:18). The Decalogue must be interpreted in light of this twofold yet single commandment of love, the fullness of the Law" (*Catechism of the Catholic Church*, 2055).

---

[6]Eruntque verba haec, quae ego praecipio tibi hodie, in corde tuo, [7]et inculcabis ea filiis tuis et loqueris ea sedens in domo tua et ambulans in itinere, decumbens atque consurgens; [8]et ligabis ea quasi signum in manu tua, eruntque quasi appensum quid inter oculos tuos, [9]scribesque ea in postibus domus tuae et in portis tuis. [10]Cumque introduxerit te Dominus Deus tuus in terram, pro qua iuravit patribus tuis Abraham, Isaac et Iacob, ut daret tibi, civitates magnas et optimas, quas non aedificasti, [11]domos plenas cunctarum opum, quas non implevisti, cisternas, quas non fodisti, vineta et oliveta, quae non plantasti, et comederis et saturatus fueris, [12]cave diligenter, ne obliviscaris Domini, qui eduxit te de terra Aegypti,

out of the land of Egypt, out of the house of bondage. [13]You shall
fear the LORD your God; you shall serve him, and swear by his
name. [14]You shall not go after other gods, of the gods of the peoples who are round about you; [15]for the LORD your God in the
midst of you is a jealous God; lest the anger of the LORD your
God be kindled against you, and he destroy you from off the face
of the earth.

Jer 4:2
Mt 4:10
Lk 4:8

Deut 4:24

[16]"You shall not put the LORD your God to the test, as you
tested him at Massah. [17]You shall diligently keep the commandments of the LORD your God, and his testimonies, and his statutes,
which he has commanded you. [18]And you shall do what is right
and good in the sight of the LORD, that it may go well with you,
and that you may go in and take possession of the good land
which the LORD swore to give to your fathers [19]by thrusting out all
your enemies from before you, as the Lord has promised.

Mt 4:7
Lk 4:12
Heb 3:9

[20]"When your son asks you in time to come, 'What is the
meaning of the testimonies and the statutes and the ordinances

---

6:13. The exhortation to fear of the Lord
is to be found often in Deuteronomy and
in the entire Old Testament. It does not
mean an irrational fear or terror in regard
to Yahweh. Fear of the Lord is, rather, a
rule of behaviour, equivalent to being
faithful to the Covenant, obeying the
commandments, walking in the way of
the Lord, serving him with all one's heart
(cf. 10:12); it is a fear which means that
one fears nothing else—enemies or strange
gods (cf., e.g., 5:7; 6:14; 11:16). In practice, a "God-fearing" Jew is a devout Jew
(cf., e.g., 1 Kings 18:3; Lk 1:50).

6:16. "*Tempting God* consists in putting
his goodness and almighty power to the
test by word or deed. Thus Satan tried to
induce Jesus to throw himself down from

the Temple and, by this gesture, force
God to act (cf. Lk 4:9). Jesus opposed
Satan with the word of God: 'You shall
not put the Lord your God to the test'
(Deut 6:16). The challenge contained in
such tempting of God wounds the respect
and trust we owe our Creator and Lord. It
always harbours doubt about his love, his
providence and his power (cf. 1 Cor 10:9;
Ex 17:2–7; Ps 95:9)" (*Catechism of the
Catholic Church*, 2119).

6:20–25. This passage shows the important place tradition held in Hebrew culture: although they had the *Toráh* or
written Law, the basis of teaching
(including religious teaching) was oral—
passed on by word of mouth from one
generation to the next.

---

de domo servitutis: [13]Dominum Deum tuum timebis et ipsi servies ac per nomen illius iurabis. [14]Non
ibitis post deos alienos, de diis gentium, quae in circuitu vestro sunt, [15]quoniam Deus aemulator
Dominus Deus tuus in medio tui; ne quando irascatur furor Domini Dei tui contra te et auferat te de
superficie terrae. [16]Non tentabitis Dominum Deum vestrum, sicut tentastis in Massa. [17]Custodite mandata Domini Dei vestri ac testimonia et praecepta, quae praecepit tibi; [18]et fac, quod rectum est et
bonum in conspectu Domini, ut bene sit tibi, et ingressus possideas terram optimam, de qua iuravit
Dominus patribus tuis, [19]ut deleret omnes inimicos tuos coram te, sicut locutus est Dominus. [20]Cumque
interrogaverit te filius tuus cras dicens: 'Quid sibi volunt testimonia haec et praecepta atque iudicia,

which the LORD our God has commanded you?' ²¹then you shall say to your son, 'We were Pharaoh's slaves in Egypt; and the LORD brought us out of Egypt with a mighty hand; ²²and the LORD showed signs and wonders, great and grievous, against Egypt and against Pharaoh and all his household, before our eyes; ²³and he brought us out from there, that he might bring us in and give us the land which he swore to give to our fathers. ²⁴And the LORD commanded us to do all these statutes, to fear the LORD our God, for our good always, that he might preserve us alive, as at this day. ²⁵And it will be righteousness for us, if we are careful to do all this commandment before the LORD our God, as he has commanded us.'

The reply of the father to the son contains the basic rationale of the Old Law: God, who delivered Israel from bondage in Egypt, by mighty and prodigious deeds, has given it the Law, which it has an obligation to obey. Just as the reason why God intervened in the history of Israel was to save it, so too the Law that he lays down is, first and foremost, designed to bring salvation.

"*The commandments*," John Paul II points out, "*are linked to a promise*. In the Old Covenant the object of the promise was the possession of a land where the people would be able to live in freedom and in accordance with righteousness (cf. Deut 6:20–25). In the New Covenant the object of the promise is the 'Kingdom of Heaven', as Jesus declares at the beginning of the 'Sermon on the Mount'—a sermon which contains the fullest and most complete formulation of the New Law (cf. Mt 5–7), clearly linked to the Decalogue entrusted by God to Moses on Mount Sinai. This same reality of the Kingdom is referred to in the expression 'eternal life', which is a participation in the very life of God. It is attained in its perfection only after death, but in faith it is even now a light of truth, a source of meaning for life, an inchoate share in the full following of Christ" (*Veritatis splendor*, 12).

The picture of the boy asking his father about the basics of his faith is a very touching one. It reminds us of the great responsibility parents have for the religious education of their children. In this connexion John Paul II said: "by praying with their children, by reading the word of God with them and by introducing them deeply through Christian initiation into the Body of Christ—both the Eucharistic and the ecclesial Body—they become fully parents, in that they are begetters not only of bodily life but also of the life that through the Spirit's renewal flows from the Cross and Resurrection of Christ" (*Familiaris consortio*, 39).

The concept of righteousness or justice (v. 25) in Holy Scripture is essen-

quae praecepit Dominus Deus noster vobis?', ²¹dices ei: 'Servi eramus pharaonis in Aegypto, et eduxit nos Dominus de Aegypto in manu forti ²²fecitque signa atque prodigia magna et pessima in Aegypto contra pharaonem et omnem domum illius in conspectu nostro; ²³et eduxit nos inde, ut introductis daret terram, super qua iuravit patribus nostris. ²⁴Praecepitque nobis Dominus, ut faciamus omnia praecepta haec et timeamus Dominum Deum nostrum, et bene sit nobis cunctis diebus vitae nostrae, sicut est hodie. ²⁵Eritque iustitia nobis, si custodierimus et fecerimus omnia mandata haec coram Domino Deo

4. ISRAEL, A PEOPLE HOLY TO THE LORD*

The Canaanites to be driven out

Ex 34:11–17
Ps 106:34–39

7 ¹"When the LORD your God brings you into the land which you are entering to take possession of it, and clears away many nations before you, the Hittites, the Girgashites, the Amorites, the Canaanites, the Perizzites, the Hivites, and the Jebusites, seven nations greater and mightier than yourselves, ²and when the LORD your God gives them over to you, and you defeat them; then you must utterly destroy them; you shall make no covenant with them, and show no mercy to them. ³You shall not make marriages with them, giving your daughters to their sons or taking their daughters for your sons. ⁴For they would turn away your sons from following me, to serve other gods; then the anger of the LORD would be kindled against you, and he would destroy you quickly. ⁵But thus shall you deal with them: you shall break down their altars, and dash in pieces their pillars, and hew down their Asherim, and burn their graven images with fire.

Deut 4:38
Acts 13:9

Mt 5:43

Ex 34:12–16

Ex 34:13

---

tially a religious one. A righteous person is someone who lives in accord with God's will, who keeps his commandments. Righteousness in the Bible is usually what we would now call holiness or saintliness (cf. the note on Mt 3:15).

*7:1–16. These instructions are aimed at defending the religion of Israel from contamination by cults of the neighbouring peoples. During those centuries when Israel's institutions were taking shape, there was need also to make sure the people were well grounded in the true faith. The measures described here seem very harsh to us nowadays, but they were thought necessary at the time. Hence the

rigid prohibition on dealings with those peoples (cf. in this connexion 14:1–2 and 32:8–9). In the New Testament the scene will change radically, and the new people of God, the Church, relying on the strength of Christ's grace, will open herself to all nations and will offer them the energy and salvific resources with which God has endowed her.

The "pillars" (v. 5)—*massebot*—were tall tapering stones stood upright on the ground, erected in honour of Canaanite gods. The Asherim ("maypoles" or memorial stones) were tree trunks commonly set near Canaanite altars.

On the custom of "utter destruction" (*anathema*), cf. the note on 2:24–37.

nostro, sicut mandavit nobis'. ¹Cum introduxerit te Dominus Deus tuus in terram, quam possessurus ingredieris, et deleverit gentes multas coram te, Hetthaeum et Gergesaeum et Amorraeum, Chananaeum et Pherezaeum et Hevaeum et Iebusaeum, septem gentes multo maioris numeri quam tu es et robustiores te, ²tradideritque eas Dominus Deus tuus tibi, percuties eas usque ad internecionem. Non inibis cum eis foedus, nec misereberis earum ³neque sociabis cum eis coniugia; filiam tuam non dabis filio eius, nec filiam illius accipies filio tuo, ⁴quia seducet filium tuum, ne sequatur me et ut serviat diis alienis, irasceturque furor Domini contra vos et delebit te cito. ⁵Quin potius haec facietis eis: aras eorum subvertite et confringite lapides et palos lucosque succidite et sculptilia comburite;

^{Ex 19:6}
^{Deut 14:2;}
^{32:8-9}
^{Tit 2:14}

⁶"For you are a people holy to the LORD your God; the LORD your God has chosen you to be a people for his own possession, out of all the peoples that are on the face of the earth.

God's election of Israel

^{Rom 9:4-5} ⁷It was not because you were more in number than any other people that the LORD set his love upon you and chose you, for you were the fewest of all peoples; ⁸but it is because the LORD loves you, and is keeping the oath which he swore to your fathers, that the LORD has brought you out with a mighty hand, and redeemed you from the house of bondage, from the hand of Pharaoh king of Egypt. ⁹Know therefore that the LORD your God is God, the faithful God who keeps covenant and steadfast love with those who love him and keep his commandments, to a thousand generations,

^{Deut 4:35}
^{1 Cor 10:13}
^{2 Cor 1:18}

7:6–16. It is fair to say that Deuteronomy 7:6–7 is the classic passage in Old Testament revelation on God's special election of Israel. That election, and the love which it evidences, are themes basic to this book; it keeps on stressing them (cf., e.g., 4:20, 34; 9:5). God makes his choice first—quite independently of the qualities or merits of the people or of individuals. The only reason for his choice is pure love and (in the case of the Israelites) the promises he made to their ancestors (cf. the note on Ex 1:8–14). Consciousness of this election, awareness that Israel is God's special possession, runs right through Holy Scripture. The New Testament upholds this privilege that belongs to Israel: John 1:11 ("He came to his own home") must be interpreted in the first instance as meaning that the Word comes specially to his people Israel; in the second instance he comes to all mankind. Romans 9:4–5 carries the same message: "They are Israelites, and to them belong the sonship, the glory, the covenants, the giving of the law, the worship, and the promise, and of their race, according to the flesh, is the Christ [. . .]."

Verses 7–8 give the theological explanation of this election: God's pure love, his predilection, is totally unmerited by Israel; this means that God is sovereignly free to choose whomever he wishes for the mission he has in mind; and no one has any right to be chosen specially by God.

What happens in the collectivity of the people of Israel also applies when God singles out individuals for special assignments. In the New Testament, it says apropos of the apostles, that "he called to him those whom he desired" (Mt 3:13); and the case of St Paul is particularly apposite: Jesus called him though he "had blasphemed and persecuted and insulted him [Christ]" (1 Tim 1:13).

⁶quia populus sanctus es Domino Deo tuo. Te elegit Dominus Deus tuus, ut sis ei populus peculiaris de cunctis populis, qui sunt super terram. ⁷Non quia cunctas gentes numero vincebatis, vobis iunctus est Dominus et elegit vos, cum omnibus sitis populis pauciores, ⁸sed quia dilexit vos Dominus et custodivit iuramentum, quod iuravit patribus vestris, eduxit vos in manu forti et redemit te de domo servitutis, de manu pharaonis regis Aegypti. ⁹Et scies quia Dominus Deus tuus ipse est Deus, Deus fidelis, custodiens pactum et misericordiam diligentibus se et his, qui custodiunt mandata eius, in mille genera-

Deut 24:16
Ezek 14:12

¹⁰and requites to their face those who hate him, by destroying them; he will not be slack with him who hates him, he will requite him to his face. ¹¹You shall therefore be careful to do the commandment, and the statutes, and the ordinances, which I command you this day.

¹²"And because you hearken to these ordinances, and keep and do them, the LORD your God will keep with you the covenant and the steadfast love which he swore to your fathers to keep; ¹³he will love you, bless you, and multiply you; he will also bless the fruit of your body and the fruit of your ground, your grain and your wine and your oil, the increase of your cattle and the young of your flock, in the land which he swore to your fathers to give you. ¹⁴You shall be blessed above all peoples; there shall not be male or female barren among you, or among your cattle. ¹⁵And the

"Vocation comes first," St Josemaría Escrivá reminds us. "God loves us before we even know how to go toward him, and he places in us the love with which we can respond to his call. God's fatherly goodness comes out to meet us. The Lord is not only just. He is much more: he is merciful. He does not wait for us to go to him. He takes the initiative, with the unmistakable signs of paternal affection" (*Christ Is Passing By*, 33).

7:10. This verse touches on something very important as regards human behaviour: God rewards those who do good and punishes those who do evil. Everyday experience does not always seem to bear this out: evil people enjoy success whereas good people are mistreated and despised. Men have always asked themselves how God's justice can be compatible with these facts.

The prophet Jeremiah will ask the Lord: "Why does the way of the wicked prosper? Why do all who are treacherous thrive?" (Jer 12:1). Many psalms echo the same idea (cf. Ps 37; 38; 29; 49; 73; 92). But the place where the matter is dealt with most dramatically is the book of Job. The Wisdom books of the Old Testament do a lot to provide an answer to this question, but it will not be until the fullness of Revelations in the New Testament that it is fully solved. Throughout the New Testament reward or punishment is not depicted as a mathematical calculation, to produce instant recompense in this life; rather, the way a person behaves in this life decides his or her fate in the next life. If the wicked are successful in this life, that is something very short-lived; whereas the joy of the righteous will reach its fullness in eternal beatitude. Prior to that, the righteous often suffer

tiones ¹⁰et reddens odientibus se protinus, ita ut disperdat eos et ultra non differat, protinus eis restituens, quod merentur. ¹¹Custodi ergo mandata et praecepta atque iudicia, quae ego mando tibi hodie, ut facias. ¹²Si audieritis haec iudicia et custodieritis ea et feceritis, custodiet et Dominus Deus tuus tibi pactum et misericordiam, quam iuravit patribus tuis, ¹³et diliget te et benedicet tibi ac multiplicabit te benedicetque fructui ventris tui et fructui terrae tuae, frumento tuo atque vindemiae, oleo et partui armentorum et incremento ovium tuarum super terram, pro qua iuravit patribus tuis, ut daret eam tibi. ¹⁴Benedictus eris prae omnibus populis. Non erit apud te sterilis utriusque sexus, tam in hominibus quam in gregibus tuis. ¹⁵Auferet Dominus a te omnem languorem; et infirmitates Aegypti pessimas,

LORD will take away from you all sickness; and none of the evil diseases of Egypt, which you knew, will he inflict upon you, but he will lay them upon all who hate you. [16]And you shall destroy all the peoples that the LORD your God will give over to you, your eye shall not pity them; neither shall you serve their gods, for that would be a snare to you.

Trust in God

[17]"If you say in your heart, 'These nations are greater than I; how can I dispossess them?' [18]you shall not be afraid of them, but you shall remember what the LORD your God did to Pharaoh and to all Egypt, [19]the great trials which your eyes saw, the signs, the wonders, the mighty hand, and the outstretched arm, by which the Lord your God brought you out; so will the LORD your God do to all the peoples of whom you are afraid. [20]Moreover the LORD your God will send hornets among them, until those who are left and hide themselves from you are destroyed. [21]You shall not be in dread of them; for the LORD your God is in the midst of you, a great and terrible God. [22]The LORD your God will clear away these nations before you little by little; you may not make an end of them at once,[f] lest the wild beasts grow too numerous for you.

Ex 23:28
Josh 24:12

---

contradiction, pain and sorrow: it purifies their lives and gives them an increase of divine grace.

7:17–26. There is nothing fickle about God's choice; God is faithful, with a fidelity that endures forever (cf. 2 Tim 2:13). Therefore, the Israelites have nothing to fear as long as they stay true to the Covenant: the Lord always keeps his promises, and the people of Israel will conquer the promised land despite being heavily outnumbered. St Bede applies v. 22 to the Christian's struggle against the enemies of the soul: "It shows us the care we must take, not that the sins of our flesh may be expelled, or overcome quickly, so that the spiritual beasts [demons] like boastfulness or pride or vainglory may come, which require greater strength in order to be rooted out than the bodily vices" (*Commentaria in Pentateuchum*, 5, 7–13).

quas novisti, non inferet tibi, sed cunctis hostibus tuis. [16]Devorabis omnes populos, quos Dominus Deus tuus daturus est tibi; non parcet eis oculus tuus, nec servies diis eorum, ne sint in ruinam tui. [17]Si dixeris in corde tuo: 'Plures sunt gentes istae quam ego; quomodo potero delere eas?', [18]noli metuere eas, sed recordare, quae fecerit Dominus Deus tuus pharaoni et cunctis Aegyptiis, [19]plagas maximas, quas viderunt oculi tui, et signa atque portenta manumque robustam et extentum brachium, ut educeret te Dominus Deus tuus; sic faciet cunctis populis, quos metuis. [20]Insuper et crabrones mittet Dominus Deus tuus in eos, donec deleat omnes atque disperdat, qui te fugerint et latere potuerint. [21]Non timebis eos, quia Dominus Deus tuus in medio tui est, Deus magnus et terribilis. [22]Ipse consumet nationes has in conspectu tuo paulatim atque per partes. Non poteris delere eas cito, ne multiplicentur contra te bes-

f. Or *quickly*

²³But the L<small>ORD</small> your God will give them over to you, and throw Judg 2:6 them into great confusion, until they are destroyed. ²⁴And he will give their kings into your hand, and you shall make their name perish from under heaven; not a man shall be able to stand against you, until you have destroyed them. ²⁵The graven images of their gods you shall burn with fire; you shall not covet the silver or the gold that is on them, or take it for yourselves, lest you be ensnared by it; for it is an abomination to the Lord your God. ²⁶And you Lev 27:28 shall not bring an abominable thing into your house, and become accursed like it; you shall utterly detest and abhor it; for it is an accursed thing.

5. THE GIFT OF THE PROMISED LAND

Israel's character forged in the desert

8 ¹"All the commandment which I command you this day you shall be careful to do, that you may live and multiply, and go in and possess the land which the L<small>ORD</small> swore to give to your fathers. ²And you shall remember all the way which the L<small>ORD</small> your God has led you these forty years in the wilderness, that he might humble you, testing you to know what was in your heart,

---

8:1–6. The Israelites are reminded about the way they were tested in the wilderness and how God gave them special protection and fatherly care; and they are once again exhorted to fidelity. This context needs to be borne in mind when considering v. 4: it need not be taken literally as some rabbinical fables did, which took it to mean that in those desert years the Israelites' clothes did not wear out and their children's clothes increased in size as they grew up.

"Man does not live by bread alone" (v. 3): Jesus will quote these words when rejecting Satan's first temptation in the desert (cf. Mt 4:4).

The relationship between Israel and God, which is compared to that of father and son (v. 5) was central to Jesus' thinking and teaching. Some other Old Testament passages, though not many, speak of this relationship (cf., e.g., Hos 11:1); a greater number of passages apply this idea to the relationship between the Lord and the King (cf., e.g., 2 Sam 7:14–15; Ps 2:7; 89:27).

tiae terrae. ²³Dabitque eos Dominus Deus tuus in conspectu tuo et conturbabit illos conturbatione magna, donec penitus deleantur. ²⁴Tradetque reges eorum in manus tuas, et disperdes nomina eorum sub caelo; nullus poterit resistere tibi, donec conteras eos. ²⁵Sculptilia eorum igne combures; non concupisces argentum et aurum, quibus vestita sunt, neque assumes ex eis tibi quidquam, ne offendas propterea, quia abominatio est Domini Dei tui. ²⁶Nec inferes abominationem in domum tuam, ne fias anathema sicut et illa est; quasi spurcitiam detestaberis et velut inquinamentum ac sordes abominationi habebis, quia anathema est. ¹Omne mandatum, quod ego praecipio tibi hodie, cave diligenter ut facias, ut possitis vivere et multiplicemini ingressique possideatis terram, pro qua iuravit Dominus patribus vestris. ²Et recordaberis cuncti itineris, per quod adduxit te Dominus Deus tuus his quadraginta annis

Mt 4:4
Lk 4:4
1 Cor 10:3 whether you would keep his commandments, or not. ³And he humbled you and let you hunger and fed you with manna, which you did not know, nor did your fathers know; that he might make you know that man does not live by bread alone, but that man lives by everything that proceeds out of the mouth of the LORD. ⁴Your clothing did not wear out upon you, and your foot did not

Heb 12:5f swell, these forty years. ⁵Know then in your heart that, as a man disciplines his son, the LORD your God disciplines you. ⁶So you shall keep the commandments of the LORD your God, by walking in his ways and by fearing him.

God not to be forgotten in the time of plenty
⁷For the LORD your God is bringing you into a good land, a land of brooks of water, of fountains and springs, flowing forth in valleys and hills, ⁸a land of wheat and barley, of vines and fig trees and pomegranates, a land of olive trees and honey, ⁹a land in which you will eat bread without scarcity, in which you will lack

---

8:7–20. This passage is more profound than might appear at first reading, because the sacred writer is using the theme of the Land to show the salvific dimension of God's actions. Israel's *departure from Egypt* marked the beginning of God's salvific action on behalf of his chosen people. The *wilderness*, described as "terrible", helped to make that people realize that they needed God and helped them to hope in him. The *promised land*, a "good land", particularly when compared with the wilderness, shows God's kindness towards Israel: in it they will find rest, peace and happiness. The only thing they need to guard against is glorying in it, as if they merited this good fortune. If ever they

did give in to that temptation, they would be lost. Clearly, this theological-moral lesson should be taken to heart by everyone in his relations with God, whatever his or her circumstances.

The Canaanites went in for coarse and disgusting fertility rites to win the favour of the gods that protected agriculture and livestock. The Israelites must do no such thing. They should show their gratitude to the Lord who sends rain, sun and dew, by offering sober and sensible sacrifices from field and flock. The Deuteronomic Code (chaps. 12–26) in fact deals with agriculture-based festivals such as "Weeks" (Deut 16:9–12), "unleavened bread" (16:3–4), "tithes" (14:22–29), etc. It is through this, and

---

per desertum, ut affligeret te atque tentaret, et nota fierent, quae in tuo animo versabantur, utrum custodires mandata illius an non. ³Afflixit te penuria et dedit tibi cibum manna, quem ignorabas tu et patres tui, ut ostenderet tibi quod non in solo pane vivat homo, sed in omni verbo, quod egreditur de ore Domini. ⁴Vestimentum tuum, quo operiebaris, nequaquam defecit, et pes tuus non intumuit his quadraginta annis. ⁵Recogites ergo in corde tuo quia, sicut erudit homo filium suum, sic Dominus Deus tuus erudivit te, ⁶ut custodias mandata Domini Dei tui et ambules in viis eius et timeas eum. ⁷Dominus enim Deus tuus introducet te in terram bonam, terram rivorum aquarum et fontium, in cuius campis et montibus erumpunt fluviorum abyssi, ⁸terram frumenti, hordei ac vinearum, in qua ficus et malogranata et oliveta nascuntur, terram olei ac mellis, ⁹ubi absque ulla penuria comedes panem tuum et rerum

nothing, a land whose stones are iron, and out of whose hills you can dig copper. [10]And you shall eat and be full, and you shall bless the LORD your God for the good land he has given you.

[11]"Take heed lest you forget the LORD your God, by not keeping his commandments and his ordinances and his statutes, which I command you this day: [12]lest, when you have eaten and are full, and have built goodly houses and live in them, [13]and when your herds and flocks multiply, and your silver and gold is multiplied, and all that you have is multiplied, [14]then your heart be lifted up, and you forget the LORD your God, who brought you out of the land of Egypt, out of the house of bondage, [15]who led you through the great and terrible wilderness, with its fiery serpents and scorpions and thirsty ground where there was no water, who brought you water out of the flinty rock, [16]who fed you in the wilderness with manna which your fathers did not know, that he might humble you and test you, to do you good in the end. [17]Beware lest you say in your heart, 'My power and the might of my hand have

Num 21:6

---

above all, though living up to the moral demands of the Law, that Israel will show its fidelity to Yahweh.

The ease with which men (and nations) forget God once they become rich and prosperous is something readily proved from history. And when that happens the threat contained in Deuteronomy in vv. 19–20 inevitably becomes a reality, for "without a creator there can be no creature. [. . .] Besides, once God is forgotten, the creature is lost sight of as well" (Vatican II, *Gaudium et spes*, 36); hence the need not to put one's heart on material things. "You need to realize," St Gregory of Nyssa urges, "the origin of your life, your mind, your wisdom and, what is more important still, the fact that you know God, your hope in the kingdom

of heaven and your expectation of seeing God [. . .], being a son of God, a co-heir of Christ and (dare I say it) becoming divinized: where do all these things come from; who causes them to happen?" (*De pauperum amore*, 23).

Christian writers often apply the benefits the Israelites received during the Exodus to the graces of Baptism and the Eucharist (cf., e.g., 1 Cor 10:1–11). And the Church's liturgy, after recalling the pillar of fire, the voice of Moses on Sinai, the manna and the water that flowed from the rock, prays that our Lord should be for us, through his Resurrection, the light of life, the word and bread of life (cf. Liturgy of the Hours, Prayer, Lauds, Tuesday of Week 6, Eastertide).

---

omnium abundantia perfrueris; cuius lapides ferrum sunt et de montibus eius aeris metalla fodiuntur; [10]ut, cum comederis et satiatus fueris, benedicas Domino Deo tuo pro terra optima, quam dedit tibi. [11]Observa et cave, ne quando obliviscaris Domini Dei tui et neglegas mandata eius atque iudicia et praecepta, quae ego praecipio tibi hodie; [12]ne, postquam comederis et satiatus fueris, domos pulchras aedificaveris et habitaveris in eis [13]habuerisque armenta et ovium greges multos, argenti et auri cunctarumque rerum copiam, [14]elevetur cor tuum et obliviscaris Domini Dei tui, qui eduxit te de terra Aegypti, de domo servitutis, [15]et ductor tuus fuit in solitudine magna atque terribili, in qua erat serpens adurens et scorpio ac terra arida et nullae omnino aquae; qui eduxit tibi rivos de petra durissima [16]et

705

gotten me this wealth.' [18]You shall remember the LORD your God, for it is he who gives you power to get wealth; that he may confirm his covenant which he swore to your fathers, as at this day. [19]And if you forget the LORD your God and go after other gods and serve them and worship them, I solemnly warn you this day

Deut 4:26 that you shall surely perish. [20]Like the nations that the LORD makes to perish before you, so shall you perish, because you would not obey the voice of the LORD your God.

Victory comes from the Lord*

Deut 4:38   **9** [1]"Hear, O Israel; you are to pass over the Jordan this day, to go into dispossess nations greater and mightier than your-
Deut 2:10   selves, cities great and fortified up to heaven, [2]a people great and tall, the sons of the Anakim, whom you know, and of whom you have heard it said, 'Who can stand before the sons of Anak?'
Deut 7:22   [3]Know therefore this day that he who goes over before you as a
Heb 12:29   devouring fire is the LORD your God; he will destroy them and subdue them before you; so you shall drive them out, and make them perish quickly, as the LORD has promised you.

---

*9:1–29. Entry into the promised land and conquest over its inhabitants could easily make the chosen people feel absurdly proud—as if all this were the outcome of their "righteousness" (vv. 4 and 6), that is, their holiness (the meaning is the same: cf. the notes on 6:20–25; Mt 1:19; 5:6). That is why the sacred writer reminds them of the real reasons for their success: the wickedness of the Canaanite tribes, their idolatry, meant that they deserved to be swept away; moreover, God's merciful love had forgiven Israel's infidelities so many times.

The prophet reminds them of the worst instance of their unfaithfulness: at the very time when Moses was on Mount Horeb receiving the tables of the Covenant which God had just sealed with the people, they were sinning against that Covenant by adoring an idol (cf. Ex 32–34). The sin of the golden calf will remain engraved on the conscience of the chosen people as one of Israel's worst acts of unfaithfulness. It was later referred to by St Stephen the martyr (Acts 7:39ff) and St Paul (1 Cor 10:7). However, Jeroboam (10th century BC) will repeat the very same sin by erecting golden calves in Dan and Bethel (cf. 1 Kings 12–13).

---

cibavit te manna in solitudine, quod nescierunt patres tui, et, postquam afflixit ac probavit te, ad extremum misertus est tui, [17]ne diceres in corde tuo: 'Fortitudo mea et robur manus meae haec mihi omnia praestiterunt'; [18]sed recorderis Domini Dei tui, quod ipse vires tibi praebuerit, ut consequereris prosperitatem, ut impleret pactum suum, super quo iuravit patribus tuis, sicut praesens indicat dies. [19]Sin autem oblitus Domini Dei tui secutus fueris deos alienos coluerisque illos et adoraveris, ecce nunc testificor vobis quod omnino dispereatis: [20]sicut gentes, quas delevit Dominus in introitu vestro, ita et vos peribitis, si inoboedientes fueritis voci Domini Dei vestri. [1]Audi, Israel: Tu transgredieris hodie Iordanem, ut possideas nationes maximas et fortiores te, civitates ingentes et ad caelum usque muratas, [2]populum magnum atque sublimem, filios Enacim, quos ipse nosti et audisti, quibus nullus potest ex adverso resistere. [3]Scies ergo hodie quod Dominus Deus tuus ipse transibit ante te ignis devorans, qui

4"Do not say in your heart, after the LORD your God has thrust them out before you, 'It is because of my righteousness that the LORD has brought me in to possess this land'; whereas it is because of the wickedness of these nations that the LORD is driving them out before you. 5Not because of your righteousness or the uprightness of your heart are you going in to possess their land; but because of the wickedness of these nations the LORD your God is driving them out from before you, and that he may confirm the word which the LORD swore to your fathers, to Abraham, to Isaac, and to Jacob.

6"Know therefore, that the Lord your God is not giving you this good land to possess because of your righteousness; for you are a stubborn people.

Rom 10:6
Deut 8:17

Tit 3:5

Ex 32:9
Is 48:4
Jer 7:26

Isreals' unfaithfulness. Moses intercedes

7Remember and do not forget how you provoked the LORD your God to wrath in the wilderness; from the day you came out of the land of Egypt, until you came to this place, you have been rebellious against the LORD. 8Even at Horeb you provoked the LORD to

Ex 32
Acts 7:39ff

Moses' repentance and his prayer succeed in getting God not to vent his anger on the people. "Prayer alone conquers God. [. . .] Prayer forgives sins, keeps temptation at bay, snuffs out persecution [. . .], raises up those who have fallen, supports those who are about to fall, strengthens those who stand their ground" (Tertullian, *De oratione*, 29). Scripture will cite Moses as a model of prayer (cf. Ps 99:6; Jer 15:1; *Catechism of the Catholic Church*, 2574).

This passage shows how big-hearted and well-meaning Moses was: even though the Lord offered to start again and make him the father of a stronger nation, Moses preferred to save his people.

9:6. "A stubborn people": literally a stiff-necked people—a metaphor fairly often used in the Bible to describe Israel's obstinacy—rebellious like a beast of burden which stiffens its neck against the yoke (cf., e.g., Ex 32:9; Is 48:4; Jer 7:26).

---

conteret eos atque subiciet ante faciem tuam, ut velociter expellas et deleas eos, sicut locutus est tibi. 4Ne dicas in corde tuo, cum deleverit eos Dominus Deus tuus in conspectu tuo: 'Propter iustitiam meam introduxit me Dominus, ut terram hanc possiderem', cum propter impietates nationum istarum expellat eas Dominus ante te. 5Neque enim propter iustitiam tuam et aequitatem cordis tui ingredieris, ut possideas terras earum, sed quia illae egerunt impie, introeunte te, Dominus Deus tuus expellet eos ante te, et ut compleat verbum suum Dominus, quod sub iuramento pollicitus est patribus tuis Abraham, Isaac et Iacob. 6Scito igitur quod non propter iustitiam tuam Dominus Deus tuus dederit tibi terram hanc optimam in possessionem, cum durissimae cervicis sis populus. 7Memento et ne obliviscaris quomodo ad iracundiam provocaveris Dominum Deum tuum in solitudine; ex eo die, quo egressus es ex Aegypto, usque ad locum istum adversum Dominum contendistis. 8Nam et in Horeb provocastis eum, et iratus delere vos voluit, 9quando ascendi in montem, ut acciperem tabulas lapideas, tabulas pacti, quod pepigit vobiscum Dominus, et perseveravi in monte quadraginta diebus ac noctibus panem non comedens et aquam non bibens. 10Deditque mihi Dominus duas tabulas lapideas scriptas

wrath, and the LORD was so angry with you that he was ready to
Mt 4:2 destroy you. [9]When I went up the mountain to receive the tables
Heb 9:4 of stone, the tables of the covenant which the LORD made with
you, I remained on the mountain forty days and forty nights; I nei-
Acts 7:38 ther ate bread nor drank water. [10]And the LORD gave me the two
2 Cor 3:3 tables of stone written with the finger of God; and on them were
all the words which the LORD had spoken with you on the mountain out of the midst of the fire on the day of the assembly. [11]And
at the end of forty days and forty nights the LORD gave me the two
tables of stone, the tables of the covenant. [12]Then the LORD said to
me, 'Arise, go down quickly from here; for your people whom
you have brought from Egypt have acted corruptly; they have
turned aside quickly out of the way which I commanded them;
they have made themselves a molten image.'

[13]"Furthermore the LORD said to me, 'I have seen this people,
Ex 32:10 and behold, it is a stubborn people; [14]let me alone, that I may
destroy them and blot out their name from under heaven; and I
will make of you a nation mightier and greater than they.' [15]So I
turned and came down from the mountain, and the mountain was
burning with fire; and the two tables of the covenant were in my
Acts 1:25 two hands. [16]And I looked, and behold, you had sinned against the
LORD your God; you had made yourselves a molten calf; you had
turned aside quickly from the way which the LORD had commanded you. [17]So I took hold of the two tables, and cast them out

---

9:10. "The day of the assembly": this is
the way the sacred texts usually refer to
the day on which the people congregated
to renew the Covenant. The assembly
(*qahal* in Hebrew) was an act of worship,
a partly religious, partly political institution; an act of a people who, precisely
because it was originally constituted by a
religious event, was an essentially "theocratic" society, as the Jewish historian
Flavius Josephus defined it. In Deuteron-

omy, the term *qahal* has a technical and
religious meaning: the *qahal* or *qehal
Yahweh* (assembly of the Lord) shows
that the people of Israel (or its lawful representatives) are convoked and meet
together as God's people to ratify the
Covenant, to render God worship and to
take important decisions (cf., e.g., Deut
4:10; 10:4; Num 16:3). Elsewhere in the
Old Testament the word also means "all
the people of Israel" even though they

digito Dei et continentes omnia verba, quae vobis locutus est in monte de medio ignis, quando contio
populi congregata est. [11]Cumque transissent quadraginta dies et totidem noctes, dedit mihi Dominus
duas tabulas lapideas, tabulas foederis, [12]dixitque mihi: 'Surge et descende hinc cito, quia peccavit populus tuus, quem eduxisti de Aegypto: deseruerunt velociter viam, quam praecepi eis, feceruntque sibi
conflatile'. [13]Rursumque ait Dominus ad me: 'Cerno quod populus iste durae cervicis sit; [14]dimitte me,
ut conteram eos et deleam nomen eorum sub caelo et faciam te in gentem, quae hac fortior et maior
sit'. [15]Cumque reversus de monte ardente descenderem et duas tabulas foederis utraque tenerem manu
[16]vidissemque vos peccasse Domino Deo vestro et fecisse vobis vitulum conflatilem ac deseruisse
velociter viam eius, quam Dominus vobis praeceperat, [17]arripui duas tabulas et proieci eas de manibus

of my two hands, and broke them before your eyes. [18]Then I lay prostrate before the LORD as before, forty days and forty nights; I neither ate bread nor drank water, because of all the sin which you had committed, in doing what was evil in the sight of the LORD, to provoke him to anger. [19]For I was afraid of the anger and hot displeasure which the LORD bore against you, so that he was ready to destroy you. But the LORD hearkened to me that time also. [20]And the LORD was so angry with Aaron that he was ready to destroy him; and I prayed for Aaron also at the same time. [21]Then I took the sinful thing, the calf which you had made, and burned it with fire and crushed it, grinding it very small, until it was as fine as dust; and I threw the dust of it into the brook that descended out of the mountain.

[22]"At Taberah also, and at Massah, and at Kibroth-hattaavah, you provoked the LORD to wrath. [23]And when the LORD sent you from Kadesh-barnea, saying, 'Go up and take possession of the land which I have given you,' then you rebelled against the commandment of the LORD your God, and did not believe him or obey his voice. [24]You have been rebellious against the LORD from the day that I knew you.

[25]"So I lay prostrate before the LORD for these forty days and forty nights, because the LORD had said he would destroy you. [26]And I prayed to the LORD, 'O LORD God, destroy not thy people

Heb 12:21

Ex 17:1–7
Num 11:4–34
Deut 1:19–46

Ex 32:11–14

Acts 13:17

---

may not actually be meeting in one place (cf., e.g., Ezra 2:64; Neh 7:66).

The word and notion of *Church* in the New Testament has its origin in this Hebrew word, *qahal*, and its Greek translation, *ekklesia*.

9:22–24. This reminder about episodes of unfaithfulness highlights the recurring

rebellions in Israel's history (cf. Deut 9:7). On Taberah: cf. Num 11:1–31; Massah: Ex 17:1–7; Kibroth-hattavah: Num 11:4–34; Kadesh-barnea: Deut 1:19–46.

9:26. The verbs "to rescue, ransom, redeem", hence "redemption", have to do with a key concept in salvation history.

---

meis confregique eas in conspectu vestro; [18]et procidi ante Dominum, sicut prius quadraginta diebus et noctibus panem non comedens et aquam non bibens propter omnia peccata vestra, quae gessistis contra Dominum et eum ad iracundiam provocastis; [19]timui enim indignationem et iram illius, qua adversum vos concitatus delere vos voluit. Et exaudivit me Dominus etiam hac vice. [20]Adversum Aaron quoque vehementer iratus voluit eum conterere; et pro illo similiter tunc deprecatus sum. [21]Peccatum autem vestrum, quod feceratis, id est vitulum, arripiens igne combussi et in frusta comminuens omninoque in pulverem redigens proieci in torrentem, qui de monte descendit. [22]In Tabera quoque et in Massa et in Cibrottaava provocastis Dominum; [23]et quando misit Dominus vos de Cadesbarne dicens: 'Ascendite et possidete terram, quam dedi vobis', contempsistis imperium Domini Dei vestri et non credidistis ei neque vocem eius audire voluistis; [24]semper fuistis rebelles contra Dominum a die, qua nosse vos coepi. [25]Et iacui coram Domino quadraginta diebus ac noctibus, quibus eum suppliciter deprecabar, ne deleret vos, ut fuerat comminatus. [26]Et orans dixi: Domine Deus, ne dis-

and thy heritage, whom thou hast redeemed through thy great-ness, whom thou hast brought out of Egypt with a mighty hand.

Rom 2:5 ²⁷Remember thy servants, Abraham, Isaac, and Jacob; do not regard the stubbornness of this people, or their wickedness, or their sin, ²⁸lest the land from which thou didst bring us say, "Because the LORD was not able to bring them into the land which he promised them, and because he hated them, he has brought

Acts 13:17 them out to slay them in the wilderness." ²⁹For they are thy people and thy heritage, whom thou didst bring out by thy great power and by thy outstretched arm.'

Ex 34:1ff **Historical insertion: the ark of the covenant and the choice of Levi**

10 ¹"At that time the Lord said to me, 'Hew two tables of stone like the first, and come up to me on the mountain, and make an ark of wood. ²And I will write on the tables the words that were on the first tables which you broke, and you shall put

Ex 25:10–16;
37:1–9 them in the ark.' ³So I made an ark of acacia wood, and hewed two tables of stone like the first, and went up the mountain with the two tables in my hand. ⁴And he wrote on the tables, as at the first writing, the ten commandments^g which the LORD had spoken to you on the mountain out of the midst of the fire on the day of

---

Over the course of the Old Testament one can see the concept of redemption-liber-ation developing bit by bit. First, God sets people free from temporal misfor-tune, bondage and danger: we see this in the passages in Exodus and Deuteron-omy having to do with deliverance from Egypt—a prototype for any instance of God's liberating action. In the Prophets, attention spreads to deliverance from spiritual misfortunes and from sin. In this

way the notion of redemption becomes linked to that of the salvation which the Messiah will bring as we can see when the angel proclaims to St Joseph that Mary's son "will save his people from their sins" (Mt 20:28).

10:1–9. Some scholars regard these verses as a parenthesis or note, set into Moses' discourse, to provide a few pieces of his-torical information. On the building of the

---

perdas populum tuum et hereditatem tuam, quam redemisti in magnitudine tua, quos eduxisti de Aegypto in manu forti. ²⁷Recordare servorum tuorum Abraham, Isaac et Iacob; ne aspicias duritiam populi huius et impietatem atque peccatum, ²⁸ne forte dicant habitatores terrae, de qua eduxisti nos: 'Non poterat Dominus introducere eos in terram, quam pollicitus est eis, et oderat illos; idcirco eduxit, ut interficeret eos in solitudine'. ²⁹Attamen ipsi sunt populus tuus et hereditas tua, quos eduxisti in for-titudine tua magna et in brachio tuo extento. ¹In tempore illo dixit Dominus ad me: 'Dola tibi duas ta-bulas lapideas, sicut priores fuerunt, et ascende ad me in montem faciesque tibi arcam ligneam. ²Et scribam in tabulis verba, quae fuerunt in his, quas ante confregisti, ponesque eas in arca'. ³Feci igitur arcam de lignis acaciae; cumque dolassem duas tabulas lapideas instar priorum, ascendi in montem

g. Heb *words*

the assembly; and the LORD gave them to me. [5]Then I turned and came down from the mountain, and put the tables in the ark which I had made; and there they are, as the LORD commanded me.

[6](The people of Israel journeyed from Be-eroth Bene-jaakan[h] to Moserah. There Aaron died, and there he was buried; and his son Eleazar ministered as priest in his stead. [7]From there they journeyed to Gudgodah, and from Gudgodah to Jotbathah, a land with brooks of water. [8]At that time the LORD set apart the tribe of Levi to carry the ark of the covenant of the LORD, to stand before the Lord to minister to him and to bless in his name, to this day. [9]Therefore Levi has no portion or inheritance with his brothers; the Lord is his inheritance, as the LORD your God said to him.)

[10]"I stayed on the mountain, as at the first time, forty days and forty nights, and the LORD hearkened to me that time also; the LORD was unwilling to destroy you. [11]And the LORD said to me, 'Arise, go on your journey at the head of the people, that they may go in and possess the land, which I swore to their fathers to give them.'

Num 33:31–38

Num 1:48–53; 3:1–10; 4:1–33 Heb 10:11

A further call to faithfulness

[12]"And now, Israel, what does the LORD your God require of you, but to fear the LORD your God, to walk in all his ways, to love

Deut 6:5
Lk 10:27

---

ark, cf., e.g., Ex 25:10–16; 37:1–9; on the election of the tribe of Levi, cf. Num 3:4.

The information about the route (vv. 6–7) differs somewhat from that in Numbers 33:30ff—most noticeably apropos of the death of Aaron, which in Numbers takes place on Mount Hor. The name Moseroth (or Moserot) seems to refer to the area around Mount Hor, to the north-east of Kadesh and to the south of the land of Canaan.

10:10–11. These verses mark the end of the first discourse of Moses (which began at 9:1), in which the Israelites were reminded of their awful infidelity at Horeb (Sinai). God forgives them (he tells them to set out again on their journey), thanks to Moses' pleading. There now follows a further exhortation to be faithful to the Covenant (10:12—11:32).

10:12–16. With divine teaching skill, the

---

habens eas in manibus. [4]Scripsitque in tabulis iuxta id, quod prius scripserat, verba decem, quae locutus est Dominus ad vos in monte de medio ignis, quando populus congregatus est, et dedit eas mihi. [5]Reversusque de monte descendi et posui tabulas in arcam, quam feceram; quae hucusque ibi sunt, sicut mihi praecepit Dominus. [6]Filii autem Israel castra moverunt ex Berothbeneiacan in Mosera, ubi Aaron mortuus ac sepultus est; pro quo sacerdotio functus est Eleazar filius eius. [7]Inde venerunt in Gadgad; de quo loco profecti castrametati sunt in Ietebatha, in terra torrentium aquarum. [8]Eo tempore separavit Dominus tribum Levi, ut portaret arcam foederis Domini et staret coram eo in ministerio ac benediceret in nomine illius usque in praesentem diem. [9]Quam ob rem non habuit Levi partem neque hereditatem cum fratribus suis, quia ipse Dominus hereditas eius est, sicut promisit ei Dominus Deus tuus. [10]Ego autem steti in monte sicut prius quadraginta diebus ac noctibus, exaudivitque me Dominus etiam hac vice et te perdere noluit. [11]Dixitque mihi: 'Surge, vade et praecede populum, ut ingrediatur

h. Or *the wells of Bene-jaakan*

him, to serve the LORD your God with all your heart and with all your soul, [13]and to keep the commandments and statutes of the LORD, which I command you this day for your good? [14]Behold, to the LORD your God belong heaven and the heaven of heavens, the earth with all that is in it; [15]yet the LORD set his heart in love upon your fathers and chose their descendants after them, you above all peoples, as at this day. [16]Circumcise therefore the foreskin of your heart, and be no longer stubborn. [17]For the LORD your God is God of gods and Lord of lords, the great, the mighty, and the terrible God, who is not partial and takes no bribe. [18]He executes justice for the fatherless and the widow, and loves the sojourner, giving him food and clothing. [19]Love the sojourner therefore; for you were sojourners in the land of Egypt. [20]You shall fear the LORD your God; you shall serve him and cleave to him, and by his name you shall swear. [21]He is your praise; he is your God, who has done for you these great and terrible things which your eyes have seen. [22]Your fathers went down to Egypt seventy persons; and now the LORD your God has made you as the stars of heaven for multitude.

Deut 7:6
Acts 13:17
Deut 9:13; 30:6
Jer 4:4
Acts 7:51
Rom 2:29
Rom 2:11
Gal 2:6
Acts 10:34
Rev 17:14; 19:16
Deut 14:29;
16:11–14
Gen 46:27
Mt 4:10
Lk 4:8
1 Cor 6:7
Lk 1:49
Heb 11:12

sacred writer emphasizes the special love the Lord is showing Israel: the Lord of heaven and earth has "set his heart in love" on them (v. 15; cf. 7:7). It would be difficult to express more tenderly God's love for his people (cf. the note on 7:7–16).

An uncircumcised heart (v. 16) is a hard heart, insensitive to God's calls because it is closed in on itself. This is an image often used in both Old and New Testaments (cf., e.g., 30:6; Jer 4:4; Acts 7:51; Rom 2:29). Christian tradition sees circumcision of the heart as a figure of Baptism: "Now those whose hearts are circumcised live and are circumcised by

the new Jordan, which is the baptism of forgiveness of sins. [. . .] Jesus our Saviour worked this circumcision a second time through circumcision of heart of all those who believe in Him and are cleansed in baptism. [. . .] Joshua, the son of Nun, led the people into the promised land; Jesus, our Saviour, promised the land of life to all those who were ready to cross the true Jordan, who believed and who allowed the foreskin of their heart to be circumcised" (Aphraates, *Demonstrationes*, 11).

10:17–22. It is easy to appreciate the beauty and majesty of this passage; it is

et possideat terram, quam iuravi patribus eorum, ut traderem eis'. [12]Et nunc, Israel, quid Dominus Deus tuus petit a te, nisi ut timeas Dominum Deum tuum et ambules in viis eius et diligas eum ac servias Domino Deo tuo in toto corde tuo et in tota anima tua [13]custodiasque mandata Domini et praecepta eius, quae ego hodie praecipio, ut bene sit tibi? [14]En Domini Dei tui caelum est et caelum caeli, terra et omnia, quae in ea sunt; [15]et tamen patribus tuis conglutinatus est Dominus et amavit eos elegitque semen eorum post eos, id est vos, de cunctis gentibus, sicut hodie comprobatur. [16]Circumcidite igitur praeputium cordis vestri et cervicem vestram, ne induretis amplius, [17]quia Dominus Deus vester ipse est Deus deorum et Dominus dominantium, Deus magnus, potens et terribilis, qui personam non accipit nec munera, [18]facit iudicium pupillo et viduae, amat peregrinum et dat ei victum atque vestitum. [19]Et vos ergo, amate peregrinos, quia et ipsi fuistis advenae in terra Aegypti. [20]Dominum Deum tuum time-

A further evocation of the Exodus

Ex 7–15
Num 16

11 [1]"You shall therefore love the LORD your God, and keep his charge, his statutes, his ordinances, and his commandments always. [2]And consider this day (since I am not speaking to your children who have not known or seen it), consider the discipline[i] of the LORD your God, his greatness, his mighty hand and his outstretched arm, [3]his signs and his deeds which he did in Egypt to Pharaoh the king of Egypt and to all his land; [4]and what he did to the army of Egypt, to their horses and to their chariots; how he made the water of the Red Sea overflow them as they pursued after you, and how the LORD has destroyed them to this day; [5]and what he did to you in the wilderness, until you came to this place; [6]and what he did to Dathan and Abiram the sons of Eliab, Rev 12:16 son of Reuben; how the earth opened its mouth and swallowed them up, with their households, their tents, and every living thing that followed them, in the midst of all Israel; [7]for your eyes have seen all the great work of the LORD which he did.

The promised land

[8]"You shall therefore keep all the commandment which I command you this day, that you may be strong, and go in and take

---

filled with profound respect for the greatness of God and with tenderness towards the needy. Deuteronomy makes many appeals (e.g., 14:29; 16:11, 14) on behalf of orphans, widows and strangers (vv. 18–19). This concern for the weak is a recurring theme in Holy Scripture (cf., e.g., Mal 3:5; Jas 1:26–27).

11:1–7. The sacred writer is addressing the survivors of the Exodus. They have experienced the Lord's singular protec-

tion; their children have not seen the wonders worked by God but they should believe in them on the word of their ancestors. The episodes mentioned here are recounted in detail elsewhere in the Pentateuch: cf. Ex 7–15 and Num 16.

11:8–25. Faithfulness to the Covenant brings with it not just the conquest of the promised land but the fertility of that country, which God himself tends (v. 12) by sending rains when needed. After the

---

bis et ei servies, ipsi adhaerebis iurabisque in nomine illius. [21]Ipse est laus tua et Deus tuus, qui fecit tibi haec magnalia et terribilia, quae viderunt oculi tui. [22]In septuaginta animabus descenderunt patres tui in Aegyptum; et ecce nunc multiplicavit te Dominus Deus tuus sicut astra caeli. [1]Ama itaque Dominum Deum tuum et custodi observationem eius et praecepta, iudicia atque mandata omni tempore. [2]Cognoscite hodie, quae ignorant filii vestri, qui non viderunt disciplinam Domini Dei vestri, magnalia eius et robustam manum extentumque brachium, [3]signa et opera, quae fecit in medio Aegypti pharaoni regi et universae terrae eius [4]omnique exercitui Aegyptiorum et equis ac curribus; quomodo operuerint eos aquae maris Rubri, cum vos persequerentur, et deleverit eos Dominus usque in praesentem diem; [5]vobisque, quae fecerit in solitudine, donec veniretis ad hunc locum; [6]et Dathan atque Abiram filiis Eliab, qui fuit filius Ruben, quos aperto ore suo terra absorbuit cum domibus et taberna-

i. Or *instruction*

713

possession of the land which you are going over to possess, ⁹and that you may live long in the land which the LORD swore to your fathers to give to them and to their descendants, a land flowing with milk and honey. ¹⁰For the land which you are entering to take possession of it is not like the land of Egypt, from which you have come, where you sowed your seed and watered it with your feet,

Heb 6:7 like a garden of vegetables; ¹¹but the land which you are going over to possess is a land of hills and valleys, which drinks water by the rain from heaven, ¹²a land which the LORD your God cares for; the eyes of the LORD your God are always upon it, from the beginning of the year to the end of the year.

Rom 1:9   ¹³"And if you will obey my commandments which I command you this day, to love the LORD your God, and to serve him with all

Jer 5:24 your heart and with all your soul, ¹⁴heʲ will give the rain for your
Joel 2:19, 23ff land in its season, the early rain and the later rain, that you may
Jas 5:7 gather in your grain and your wine and your oil. ¹⁵And heʲ will give grass in your fields for your cattle, and you shall eat and be full. ¹⁶Take heed lest your heart be deceived, and you turn aside and serve other gods and worship them, ¹⁷and the anger of the LORD be kindled against you, and he shut up the heavens, so that there be no rain, and the land yield no fruit, and you perish quickly off the good land which the LORD gives you.

---

years spent wandering in the desert, not to mention the harshness of their life as farm labourers in Egypt, these promises of the rains must have been very consoling and appealing to the Israelites. Drought (vv. 16–17), sometimes extremely severe (like that which occurred in the time of the prophet Elijah: cf. 1 Kings 17–18) will be interpreted as a punishment for Israel's infidelities.

Israelite territory will never extend as far as the borders mentioned here (v. 24). Addressing himself figuratively to Israel, St Jerome reminds it that "all this land was promised you, but not given, on condition that you kept the commandments of almighty God and walked in his precepts, if in place of almighty God you did not worship Beelphegor and Baal, Beelzebub and Chemosh. But because

---

culis et universa substantia eorum, quam habebant in medio Israel. ⁷Oculi vestri viderunt omnia opera Domini magna, quae fecit, ⁸ut custodiatis universa mandata, quae ego hodie praecipio vobis, ut roboremini et possitis introire et possidere terram, ad quam ingredimini, ⁹multoque in ea vivatis tempore, quam sub iuramento pollicitus est Dominus patribus vestris et semini eorum, lacte et melle manantem. ¹⁰Terra enim, ad quam ingredieris possidendam, non est sicut terra Aegypti, de qua existis, ubi, iacto semine, in hortorum morem aquae pede ducuntur irriguae; ¹¹sed montuosa est et campestris, de caelo exspectans pluvias, ¹²quam Dominus Deus tuus semper invisit, et oculi illius in ea sunt a principio anni usque ad finem eius. ¹³Si ergo oboedieritis mandatis meis, quae hodie praecipio vobis, ut diligatis Dominum Deum vestrum et serviatis ei in toto corde vestro et in tota anima vestra, ¹⁴dabo pluviam terrae vestrae temporaneam et serotinam in tempore suo, ut colligas frumentum et vinum et oleum, ¹⁵et dabit fenum ex agris ad pascenda iumenta, et ut ipse comedas ac satureris. ¹⁶Cavete, ne

j. Sam Gk Vg: Heb *I*

A further exhortation

Deut 6:6–9
Mt 23:5

[18]"You shall therefore lay up these words of mine in your heart and in your soul; and you shall bind them as a sign upon your hand, and they shall be as frontlets between your eyes. [19]And you shall teach them to your children, talking of them when you are sitting in your house, and when you are walking by the way, and when you lie down, and when you rise. [20]And you shall write them upon the doorposts of your house and upon your gates, [21]that your days and the days of your children may be multiplied in the land which the LORD swore to your fathers to give them, as long as the heavens are above the earth. [22]For if you will be careful to do all this commandment which I command you to do, loving the LORD your God, walking in all his ways, and cleaving to him, [23]then the LORD will drive out all these nations before you, and you will dispossess nations greater and mightier than yourselves. [24]Every place on which the sole of your foot treads shall be yours; Josh 1:3–5 your territory shall be from the wilderness and Lebanon and from the River, the river Euphrates, to the western sea. [25]No man shall be able to stand against you; the Lord your God will lay the fear of you and the dread of you upon all the land that you shall tread, as he promised you.

A blessing and a curse

Deut 27–28
Josh 8:30-35

[26]"Behold, I set before you this day a blessing and a curse: [27]the blessing, if you obey the commandments of the LORD your God,

---

you preferred them to God, you lost everything you were promised" (*Epistulae* 129, 5).

11:26–32. The ceremony of blessing and cursing will be explained fully in chap-

ters 27–28; and Joshua will in due course perform it (cf. Josh 8:30–35). It does not consist so much in blessing or cursing as in proclaiming a summary of God's commandments and ordinances in terms like "Cursed be he who does not do them",

---

decipiatur cor vestrum, et recedatis a Domino serviatisque diis alienis et adoretis eos, [17]iratusque Dominus contra vos claudat caelum, et pluviae non descendant, nec terra det fructum suum, pereatisque velociter de terra optima, quam Dominus daturus est vobis. [18]Ponite haec verba mea in cordibus et in animis vestris et ligate ea pro signo in manibus et inter oculos vestros collocate quasi appensum quid. [19]Docete ea filios vestros, de illis loquendo, quando sederis in domo tua et ambulaveris in via et accubueris atque surrexeris. [20]Scribes ea super postes domus tuae et portas tuas, [21]ut multiplicentur dies tui et filiorum tuorum in terra, quam iuravit Dominus patribus tuis, ut daret eis, quamdiu caelum imminet terrae. [22]Si enim custodieritis omnia mandata haec, quae ego praecipio vobis, et feceritis ea, ut diligatis Dominum Deum vestrum et ambu, letis in omnibus viis eius adhaerentes ei, [23]disperdet Dominus omnes gentes istas ante faciem vestram et possidebitis eas, quae maiores et fortiores vobis sunt; [24]omnis locus, quem calcaverit pes vester, vester erit. A deserto et a Libano, a flumine magno Euphrate usque ad mare occidentale erunt termini vestri. [25]Nullus stabit contra vos; terrorem vestrum et formidinem dabit Dominus Deus vester super omnem terram, quam calcaturi estis, sicut

Josh 8:33
Jn 4:20

Josh 4:19

which I command you this day, [28]and the curse, if you do not obey the commandments of the LORD your God, but turn aside from the way which I command you this day, to go after other gods which you have not known. [29]And when the LORD your God brings you into the land which you are entering to take possession of it, you shall set the blessing on Mount Gerizim and the curse on Mount Ebal. [30]Are they not beyond the Jordan, west of the road, toward the going down of the sun, in the land of the Canaanites who live in the Arabah, over against Gilgal, beside the oak[k] of Moreh? [31]For you are to pass over the Jordan to go in to take possession of the land which the LORD your God gives you; and when you possess it and live in it, [32]you shall be careful to do all the statutes and the ordinances which I set before you this day.

Ex 20:22–2;
23:19

6. THE DEUTERONOMIC CODE*

1. DUTIES TOWARDS GOD*

There is to be only one sanctuary

12 [1]"These are the statutes and ordinances which you shall be careful to do in the land which the LORD, the God of your fathers, has given you to possess, all the days that you live upon

---

"Blessed be he who obeys them." Mount Gerizim and Mount Ebal are situated to the south-west and north-east respectively of the Samaritan city of Shechem and are separated by a narrow valley. In later times the Samaritans will come to regard Gerizim as a holy mountain, building a temple there when the Jews came back from Babylon (537 BC), to rival the temple of Jerusalem; although

the temple was destroyed towards the end of the 2nd century BC, the Samaritans continued to see this mountain as a place of worship and sacrifice. The Samaritan woman mentions it in her conversation with our Lord (cf. Jn 4:20).

***12:1—26:15.** These chapters contain what is called the "Deuteronomic code". Some of the penalties it lays down seem

---

locutus est vobis. [26]En propono in conspectu vestro hodie benedictionem et maledictionem: [27]benedictionem, si oboedieritis mandatis Domini Dei vestri, quae ego hodie praecipio vobis; [28]maledictionem, si non oboedieritis mandatis Domini Dei vestri, sed recesseritis de via, quam ego nunc ostendo vobis, et ambulaveritis post deos alienos, quos ignoratis. [29]Cum introduxerit te Dominus Deus tuus in terram, ad quam pergis habitandam, pones benedictionem super montem Garizim, maledictionem super montem Hebal, [30]qui sunt trans Iordanem, post viam quae vergit ad solis occubitum in terra Chananaei, qui habitat in Araba contra Galgalam, quae est iuxta Quercus Moreh. [31]Vos enim transibitis Iordanem, ut possideatis terram, quam Dominus Deus vester daturus est vobis, et habitetis in illa. [32]Videte ergo ut impleatis omnia praecepta atque iudicia, quae ego hodie ponam in conspectu vestro. [1]Haec sunt prae-

k. Gk Syr See Gen 12:6: Heb *oaks* or *terebinths*

the earth. [2]*You shall surely destroy all the places where the ⟨Deut 7:5, 25⟩ nations whom you shall dispossess served their gods, upon the high mountains and upon the hills and under every green tree; [3]you shall tear down their altars, and dash in pieces their pillars, ⟨Ex 23:24; and burn their Asherim with fire; you shall hew down the graven 34:13⟩ images of their gods, and destroy their name out of that place. ⟨Ex 20:24 [4]You shall not do so to the LORD your God. [5]But you shall seek ⟨Jn 4:20⟩

to us nowadays to be terribly harsh; they need to be seen in context—in the context of their time and culture and in the light of Israel's having become the "people of God". This new nature of Israel implied special demands in terms of moral holiness. The severity of the penalties was designed to act as a deterrent, but it was mainly aimed at educating a fairly uncivilized people who had contact with the evil customs of other peoples.

As often happens with legal codes, there is a tendency to incorporate into them earlier laws, some of which may go back a very long time. The Deuteronomic Code, in the form that it has come down to us, also contains passages which envisage the people being settled down (rather than nomadic), engaged in trade and having a more developed social structure with kings, priests, elders, etc.; and it contains precepts about there being only one sanctuary, about the altar, about tithes etc. There are many references to the heart, to the need for morality to be more an interior thing. The overall tone quite often changes from an imperative one to become more exhortative; one could say that what we have here are "preached" ordinances, rather than codified ones.

Their having been put in writing is attributed to the "Deuteronomic tradition" which, as we have said, gathers up many very ancient legal traditions.

More or less half of the Deuteronomic Code parallels the Code of the Covenant in Exodus 20:22—23:19.

Generally speaking one can say that there are three sections to it: 1) duties towards God (12:1—16:17); 2) institutions of Israel (16:18—18:22); 3) rights and duties of people towards one another, that is, social rules (chaps. 19–26). This structure is somewhat reminiscent of that of the Ten Commandments, but too much should not be made of that. The third section contains within it an extensive section dealing with a range of moral and legal rules (20:1—26:15), which is followed by an appendix (not part of the Deuteronomic Code) on faithfulness and on renewal of the Covenant (27:1—28:68).

*12:1–31. The promised land is a key theme in Deuteronomy: Israel is given the Land on the basis of its election by God, and the Land is the foundation for fulfilment of the Law. In 12:1 land and law are clearly linked; but the same linkage is to be found in many other passages

cepta atque iudicia, quae facere debetis in terra, quam Dominus, Deus patrum tuorum, daturus est tibi, ut possideas eam cunctis diebus, quibus super humum gradieris. [2]Subvertite omnia loca, in quibus coluerunt gentes, quas possessuri estis, deos suos super montes excelsos et colles et subter omne lignum frondosum. [3]Dissipate aras eorum et confringite lapides, palos igne comburite et idola comminuite, disperdite nomina eorum de locis illis. [4]Non facietis ita Domino Deo vestro. [5]Sed ad locum, quem elegerit Dominus Deus vester de cunctis tribubus vestris, ut ponat nomen suum ibi et habitet in eo, venietis [6]et offeretis in illo loco holocausta et victimas vestras, decimas et donaria manuum ves-

the place which the LORD your God will choose out of all your tribes to put his name and make his habitation there; thither you Lev 1–3 shall go, ⁶and thither you shall bring your burnt offerings and Deut 14:22 your sacrifices, your tithes and the offering that you present, your votive offerings, your freewill offerings, and the firstlings of your herd and of your flock; ⁷and there you shall eat before the LORD your God, and you shall rejoice, you and your households, in all that you undertake, in which the LORD your God has blessed you. ⁸You shall not do according to all that we are doing here this day, every man doing whatever is right in his own eyes; ⁹for you have not as yet come to the rest and to the inheritance which the LORD your God gives you. ¹⁰But when you go over the Jordan, and live in the land which the LORD your God gives you to inherit, and when he gives you rest from all your enemies round about, so that you live in safety, ¹¹then to the place which the LORD your God will choose, to make his named well there, thither you shall

---

also—e.g., 6:10–13; 8:7–18; 11:10–12; 16:1–16; 26:1–15; etc.

The laws about religion include some measures aimed at ensuring that Israel keeps a firm grip on monotheism and renders proper cult to the Lord—the destruction of everything connected with places where other gods are worshiped (vv. 2–3; cf. 7:5, 25), and particularly the law about there being only one sanctuary (vv. 4–28), a characteristic feature of Deuteronomic legislation.

"The place which the Lord your God will choose" (cf. v. 5): here the Lord will put his name that is, it will be where he dwells, his dwelling-place *par excellence*. That is where the Israelites should gather to offer their sacrifices and hold their sacred meals, in connexion with the various feasts (cf. chap. 16). From the

time of Solomon (970–930 BC), when Jerusalem will have its temple, worship will be centralized there. However, the concentration of worship in Jerusalem did not really happen until the reform by King Josiah (622 BC). In the New Covenant, with the institution of the Eucharist God does not confine himself to dwelling in only one church building; the miracle of the Eucharist means that he is really present in all tabernacles.

The apparent contrast between this law and other rules in the Law of Moses (cf. Ex 20:22–26; Lev 17:1–7), and also the fact that this law had been ignored for centuries leads one to think that this passage is a gloss, designed to endorse the religious reform focused on there being only one temple, only one place of worship. The long text that follows (chaps.

---

trarum et vota atque dona, primogenita boum et ovium. ⁷Et comedetis ibi in conspectu Domini Dei vestri ac laetabimini in cunctis, ad quae miseritis manum vos et domus vestrae, in quibus benedixerit vobis Dominus Deus vester. ⁸Non facietis secundum omnia, quae nos hic facimus hodie, singuli, quod sibi rectum videtur; ⁹neque enim usque in praesens tempus venistis ad requiem et possessionem, quam Dominus Deus vester daturus est vobis. ¹⁰Transibitis Iordanem et habitabitis in terra, quam Dominus Deus vester daturus est vobis, ut requiescatis a cunctis hostibus per circuitum et absque ullo timore habitetis ¹¹in loco, quem elegerit Dominus Deus vester, ut habitet nomen eius in eo. Illuc omnia, quae praecipio conferetis: holocausta et hostias ac decimas et donaria manuum vestrarum et, quidquid prae-

bring all that I command you: your burnt offerings and your sacrifices, your tithes and the offering that you present, and all your votive offerings which you vow to the LORD. [12]And you shall rejoice before the LORD your God, you and your sons and your daughters, your menservants and your maidservants, and the Levite that is within your towns, since he has no portion or inheritance with you.

Ex 32:25–29
Acts 8:21

Regulations concerning sacrifice

Lev 17:1–9

[13]Take heed that you do not offer your burnt offerings at every place that you see; [14]but at the place which the LORD will choose in one of your tribes, there you shall offer your burnt offerings, and there you shall do all that I am commanding you.

[15]"However, you may slaughter and eat flesh within any of your towns, as much as you desire, according to the blessing of the LORD your God which he has given you; the unclean and the

---

12–26) seems to combine various bodies of laws from different sources (it is not easy to work out exactly what the order is): see the possible structure we outlined at the end of the previous note. It may be that some laws originated in the Northern tribes and made their way into Judah after the fall of the Northern kingdom to the Assyrians (721 BC).

The last verses of this chapter (vv. 29–31) take issue with an idea widespread among pagan peoples at that time: it was essential to do homage to the gods of the places one entered (whether as an invader or as someone who had been defeated and transported to some new place): otherwise they would take umbrage. Israel should not act in that way, and Israelites must give no heed to other gods.

12:11–12. There was good reason to insist on duties towards Levites (vv. 18–19); because they belonged to the tribe God had singled out for the priesthood, they had no territory of their own (cf. Ex 32:25–29). The book of Judges speaks of the precarious position in which some of them found themselves (cf. Judg 17:7–12). There also seem to have been Levites in the Northern kingdom. After it fell, some Levitical families must have emigrated to Jerusalem.

"The offering that you present": a technical term (in Hebrew, *terumáh*), indicating the part of the victim reserved to the priests (cf. 18:3). No one else was allowed to eat this portion (cf. 12:17). The rite of these offerings consisted in waving them, swinging them with one's hands (*tenufáh*). Later on, both terms were used for the religious tax every family was required to pay.

---

cipuum est in muneribus, quae vovebitis Domino. [12]Ibi laetabimini coram Domino Deo vestro vos, filii ac filiae vestrae, famuli et famulae atque Levites, qui in urbibus vestris commoratur; neque enim habet partem et possessionem inter vos. [13]Cave, ne offeras holocausta tua in omni loco, quem videris, [14]sed in eo, quem elegerit Dominus in una tribuum tuarum, offeres holocausta et ibi facies quaecumque praecipio tibi. [15]Sin autem comedere volueris, et te esus carnium delectaverit, occide et comede carnem iuxta benedictionem Domini Dei tui, quam dedit tibi in omnibus urbibus tuis; sive immundus sive mundus comedet illam, sicut capream et cervum, [16]absque esu dumtaxat sanguinis, quem super terram

Lev 1:5 clean may eat of it, as of the gazelle and as of the hart. [16]Only you shall not eat the blood; you shall pour it out upon the earth like water. [17]You may not eat within your towns the tithe of your grain Deut 14:22 or of your wine or of your oil, or the firstlings of your herd or of your flock, or any of your votive offerings which you vow, or your freewill offerings, or the offering that you present; [18]but you shall eat them before the LORD your God in the place which the LORD your God will choose, you and your son and your daughter, your manservant and your maidservant, and the Levite who is within your towns; and you shall rejoice before the LORD your God in all that you undertake. [19]Take heed that you do not forsake the Levite as long as you live in your land.

[20]"When the LORD your God enlarges your territory, as he has promised you, and you say, 'I will eat flesh,' because you crave flesh, you may eat as much flesh as you desire. [21]If the place which the LORD your God will choose to put his name there is too far from you, then you may kill any of your herd or your flock, which the LORD has given you, as I have commanded you; and you may eat within your towns as much as you desire. [22]Just as the gazelle or the hart is eaten, so you may eat of it; the unclean and the clean alike may eat of it. [23]Only be sure that you Lev 1:5 do not eat the blood; for the blood is the life, and you shall not eat the life with the flesh. [24]You shall not eat it; you shall pour it

---

12:20–25. These verses are an explanation of vv. 15–16. Leviticus (17:1–9) laid down that any killing of an animal had something sacred about it and that it had to be done in front of the Lord's dwelling; this may have been a way of avoiding sacrifices carried out elsewhere, thereby leading to idolatrous practices. This ordinance must have been repealed once worship became centralized in one place only, in such a way that it would no longer be necessary (or possible, on account of the distances involved) to bring to the temple animals which needed to be slaughtered for food. The mention of the gazelle and the deer (vv. 15, 22), animals which were clean and which could be eaten, but which were not used in sacrifices, helps to high-

---

quasi aquam effundes. [17]Non poteris comedere in oppidis tuis decimam frumenti et vini et olei tui, primogenita armentorum et pecorum et omnia, quae voveris et sponte offerre volueris, et primitiva manuum tuarum. [18]Sed coram Domino Deo tuo comedes ea in loco, quem elegerit Dominus Deus tuus, tu et filius tuus ac filia tua, servus et famula atque Levites, qui manet in urbibus tuis; et laetaberis coram Domino Deo tuo in cunctis, ad quae extenderis manum tuam. [19]Cave, ne derelinquas Levitem omni tempore, quo versaris in terra tua. [20]Quando dilataverit Dominus Deus tuus terminos tuos, sicut locutus est tibi, et volueris vesci carnibus, quas desiderat anima tua, comedes carnem secundum omne desiderium animae tuae; [21]locus autem, quem elegerit Dominus Deus tuus, ut sit nomen eius ibi, si procul fuerit, occides de armentis et pecoribus, quae dederit tibi Dominus, sicut praecepi tibi, et comedes in oppidis tuis, ut tibi placet. [22]Sicut comeditur caprea et cervus, ita vesceris eis; et mundus et immundus in commune vescentur. [23]Hoc solum cave, ne sanguinem comedas; sanguis enim eorum anima est, et idcirco non debes animam comedere cum carnibus. [24]Non comedes eum, sed super terram fundes quasi aquam; [25]non comedes eum, ut bene sit tibi et filiis tuis post te, cum feceris, quod placet

out upon the earth like water. [25]You shall not eat it; that all may go well with you and with your children after you, when you do what is right in the sight of the LORD. [26]But the holy things which are due from you, and your votive offerings, you shall take, and you shall go to the place which the LORD will choose, [27]and offer your burnt offerings, the flesh and the blood, on the altar of the LORD your God; the blood of your sacrifices shall be poured out on the altar of the LORD your God, but the flesh you may eat. [28]Be careful to heed all these words which I command you, that it may go well with you and with your children after you for ever, when you do what is good and right in the sight of the LORD your God.

Against Canaanite cults

[29]"When the LORD your God cuts off before you the nations whom you go in to dispossess, and you dispossess them and dwell in their land, [30]take heed that you be not ensnared to follow them, after they have been destroyed before you, and that you do not inquire about their gods, saying, 'How did these nations serve their gods?—that I also may do likewise.' [31]You shall not do so to the LORD your God; for every abominable thing which the LORD hates they have done for their gods; for they even burn their sons and their daughters in the fire to their gods.

Lev 18:21

---

light the difference between sacred offerings and the mere slaughter of an animal for food: in the latter case they could be eaten even by people who had some uncleanness in them, whereas those who took part in sacred meals had to conform to the requirements of ritual cleanness (cf. Lev 7:19–21).

There existed a strong conviction among those peoples that blood was the seat and source of life. Hence the insistence on the prohibition against eating it (vv. 16, 23–25; cf. Lev 17:14): life belongs to God, and he alone may dispose of it. This idea was so deep-rooted among the Israelites, that the council of Jerusalem (c. AD 49) laid it down that Christians of Gentile background should abstain from blood, in order to avoid scandalizing Jewish Christians.

---

in conspectu Domini. [26]Quae autem sanctificaveris et voveris Domino, tolles et venies ad locum, quem elegerit Dominus, [27]et offeres holocausta tua, carnem et sanguinem super altare Domini Dei tui; sanguis hostiarum tuarum fundetur in altari, carnibus autem ipse vesceris. [28]Observa et audi omnia, quae ego praecipio tibi, ut bene sit tibi et filiis tuis post te in sempiternum, cum feceris, quod bonum est et placitum in conspectu Domini Dei tui. [29]Quando disperdiderit Dominus Deus tuus ante faciem tuam gentes, ad quas ingredieris possidendas, et possederis eas atque habitaveris in terra earum, [30]cave, ne irretiaris per eas, postquam te fuerint introeunte subversae, et requiras caeremonias earum dicens: 'Sicut coluerunt gentes istae deos suos, ita et ego colam'. [31]Non facies similiter Domino Deo tuo; omnes enim abominationes, quas aversatur Dominus, fecerunt diis suis offerentes etiam filios et filias et comburentes igne. [1]Quod praecipio vobis, hoc custodite et facite, nec addas quidquam nec minuas.

Deut 17:2–7;
18:20–21 **Against those who promote idolatry**

Rev 22:18f ³²¹"Everything that I command you you shall be careful to do; you shall not add to it or take from it.

Mk 13:22
Mt 24:24 **13** ¹"If a prophet arises among you, or a dreamer of dreams, and gives you a sign or a wonder, ²and the sign or wonder which he tells you comes to pass, and if he says, 'Let us go after other gods,' which you have not known, 'and let us serve them,' ³you shall not listen to the words of that prophet or to that dreamer of dreams; for the LORD your God is testing you, to know whether you love the LORD your God with all your heart and with all your soul. ⁴You shall walk after the LORD your God and fear him, and keep his commandments and obey his voice, and you shall serve Deut 18:21
1 Cor 5:13 him and cleave to him. ⁵But that prophet or that dreamer of dreams shall be put to death, because he has taught rebellion against the LORD your God, who brought you out of the land of Egypt and redeemed you out of the house of bondage, to make you leave the

---

12:32—13:18. This passage is a kind of expansion of the ordinances contained in 12:29–31; it spells out what should be done against those who promote the worship of other gods—whether they be false prophets (a temptation religious in origin: vv. 2–7) or members of one's own family (vv. 8–13). It also looks at the case of an entire city that has given in to the temptation of practising an idolatrous cult (a temptation social in origin). The harshness and exemplary nature of the penalties helps to make it clear that faithfulness to the Lord is something more important than family or racial loyalties.

The New Testament does not rely on the penalties specified here but it asks people for the same radicalism in following Christ. Thus, St Paul tells the Galatians: "Even if we, or an angel from heaven, should preach to you a gospel contrary to that which we preached to you, let him be accursed [anathema]" (Gal 1:8). And our Lord had said: "He who loves father or mother more than me is not worthy of me; and he who loves son or daughter more than me is not worthy of me" (Mt 10:37). These teachings show how decisively and promptly one should reject anything that could separate one from God: "Take away from me, Lord, all those things which take me away from you," St Teresa prayed.

12:32. We can see here the respect of the people the Old Testament had for the word of God. There is a similar warning in Revelation 22:18–19.

---

²Si surrexerit in medio tui prophetes aut, qui somnium vidisse se dicat, et dederit tibi signum vel portentum, ³et evenerit, quod locutus est, et dixerit tibi: 'Eamus et sequamur deos alienos, quos ignoras, et serviamus eis', ⁴non audies verba prophetae illius aut somniatoris, quia tentat vos Dominus Deus vester, ut sciat utrum diligatis eum an non in toto corde et in tota anima vestra. ⁵Dominum Deum vestrum sequimini et ipsum timete et mandata illius custodite et audite vocem eius; ipsi servietis et ipsi adhaerebitis. ⁶Propheta autem ille aut fictor somniorum interficietur, quia locutus est, ut vos averteret

l. Ch 13:1 in Heb [and New Vulgate]

way in which the LORD your God commanded you to walk. So you shall purge the evil from the midst of you.

⁶"If your brother, the son of your mother, or your son, or your daughter, or the wife of your bosom, or your friend who is as your own soul, entices you secretly, saying, 'Let us go and serve other gods, 'which neither you nor your fathers have known, ⁷some of the gods of the peoples that are round about you, whether near you or far off from you, from the one end of the earth to the other, ⁸you shall not yield to him or listen to him, nor shall your eye pity him, nor shall you spare him, nor shall you conceal him; ⁹but you shall kill him; your hand shall be first against him to put him to death, and afterwards the hand of all the people. ¹⁰You shall stone him to death with stones, because he sought to draw you away from the LORD your God, who brought you out of the land of Egypt, out of the house of bondage. ¹¹And all Israel shall hear, and fear, and never again do any such wickedness as this among you.

¹²"If you hear in one of your cities, which the LORD your God gives you to dwell there, ¹³that certain base fellows have gone out among you and have drawn away the inhabitants of the city, saying, 'Let us go and serve other gods, 'which you have not known, ¹⁴then you shall inquire and make search and ask diligently; and behold, if it be true and certain that such an abominable thing has been done among you, ¹⁵you shall surely put the Josh 6:17 inhabitants of that city to the sword, destroying it utterly, all who

---

13:13. "Certain base fellows", literally "sons of Belial"; it is not clear what "Belial" means; it may be a compound of *beli*, the Hebrew for "sin", and *al*, perhaps originally *ol*, meaning "law, ordinance"; in which case Belial would be the same as "Law-less", hence its frequent application to the devil: cf. 2 Cor 6:15. It is also frequently found in Jewish literature immediately prior to and contemporary with the New Testament.

---

a Domino Deo vestro, qui eduxit vos de terra Aegypti et redemit te de domo servitutis; ut errare te faceret de via, quam tibi praecepit Dominus Deus tuus; et auferes malum de medio tui. ⁷Si tibi voluerit persuadere frater tuus filius matris tuae aut filius tuus vel filia sive uxor, quae est in sinu tuo, aut amicus, quem diligis ut animam tuam, clam dicens: 'Eamus et serviamus diis alienis', quos ignorasti tu et patres tui, ⁸de diis cunctarum in circuitu gentium, quae iuxta vel procul sunt ab initio usque ad finem terrae, ⁹non acquiescas ei nec audias, neque parcat ei oculus tuus, ut miserearis et occultes eum, ¹⁰sed interficies. Sit primum manus tua super eum, et postea omnis populus mittat manum: ¹¹lapidibus obrutus necabitur, quia voluit te abstrahere a Domino Deo tuo, qui eduxit te de terra Aegypti, de domo servitutis, ¹²ut omnis Israel audiens timeat, et nequaquam ultra faciat quippiam huius rei simile in medio tui. ¹³Si audieris in una urbium tuarum, quas Dominus Deus tuus dabit tibi ad habitandum, dicentes aliquos: ¹⁴'Egressi sunt filii Belial de medio tui et averterunt habitatores urbis suae atque dixerunt: Eamus et serviamus diis alienis', quos ignorastis, ¹⁵quaere sollicite et, diligenter rei veritate perspecta, si inveneris certum esse, quod dicitur, et abominationem hanc opere perpetratam in medio

are in it and its cattle, with the edge of the sword. [16]You shall gather all its spoil into the midst of its open square, and burn the city and all its spoil with fire, as a whole burnt offering to the LORD your God; it shall be a heap for ever, it shall not be built again. [17]None of the devoted things shall cleave to your hand; that the LORD may turn from the fierceness of his anger, and show you mercy, and have compassion on you, and multiply you, as he swore to your fathers, [18]if you obey the voice of the LORD your God, keeping all his commandments which I command you this day, and doing what is right in the sight of the LORD your God.

Lev 19:28
Rom 8:14; 9:4
Ex 19:6
Deut 7:6

A ban on certain funeral rites

14 [1]"You are the sons of the LORD your God; you shall not cut yourselves or make any baldness on your foreheads for the dead. [2]For you are a people holy to the LORD your God, and the LORD has chosen you to be a people for his own possession, out of all the peoples that are on the face of the earth.

Lev 11
Acts 15:14
Tit 2:4

Clean and unclean animals

[3]"You shall not eat any abominable thing. [4]These are the animals you may eat: the ox, the sheep, the goat, [5]the hart, the gazelle, the roebuck, the wild goat, the ibex, the antelope, and the mountain-sheep. [6]Every animal that parts the hoof and has the hoof cloven

---

14:1–21. After the measures stipulated in the previous chapter for preventing and punishing idolatry, further practices are prohibited here which have some sort of connexion with idolatry. The ban on certain funeral rites (v. 1) may be connected with similar customs in neighbouring countries which had idolatrous elements

mixed in with them (cf. a similar rite in 1 Kings 18:28).

We cannot say exactly what criteria applied in the distinction between clean and unclean animals (cf. in Leviticus 11 a similar list, and the note on same); it may be that these rules derive from popular notions and natural repugnance and

---

tui, [16]percuties habitatores urbis illius in ore gladii et delebis eam ac omnia, quae in illa sunt. [17]Quidquid etiam supellectilis fuerit, congregabis in medio platearum eius et cum ipsa civitate succendes, ita ut universa consumas Domino Deo tuo, et sit tumulus sempiternus: non aedificabitur amplius. [18]Et non adhaerebit de illo anathemate quidquam in manu tua, ut avertatur Dominus ab ira furoris sui et misereatur tui multiplicetque te, sicut iuravit patribus tuis, [19]quando audieris vocem Domini Dei tui custodiens omnia mandata eius, quae ego praecipio tibi hodie, ut facias quod placitum est in conspectu Domini Dei tui. [1]Filii estote Domini Dei vestri; non vos incidetis nec facietis calvitium inter oculos vestros super mortuo, [2]quoniam populus sanctus es Domino Deo tuo, et te elegit, ut sis ei in populum peculiarem de cunctis gentibus, quae sunt super terram. [3]Ne comedatis quidquid abominabile est. [4]Hoc est animal, quod comedere potestis: bovem et ovem et capram, [5]cervum et capream, bubalum, tragelaphum, pygargum, orygem, rupicapram. [6]Omne animal inter pecora, quod findit ungulam plene in duas partes et ruminat, comedetis; [7]de his autem, quae ruminant et ungulam non findunt, haec

in two, and chews the cud, among the animals, you may eat. [7]Yet of those that chew the cud or have the hoof cloven you shall not eat these: the camel, the hare, and the rock badger, because they chew the cud but do not part the hoof, are unclean for you. [8]And the swine, because it parts the hoof but does not chew the cud, is unclean for you. Their flesh you shall not eat, and their carcasses you shall not touch.

[9]"Of all that are in the waters you may eat these: whatever has fins and scales you may eat. [10]And whatever does not have fins and scales you shall not eat; it is unclean for you.

[11]"You may eat all clean birds. [12]But these are the ones which you shall not eat: the eagle, the vulture, the osprey, [13]the buzzard, the kite, after their kinds; [14]every raven after its kind; [15]the ostrich, the nighthawk, the sea gull, the hawk, after their kinds; [16]the little owl and the great owl, the water hen [17]and the pelican, the carrion vulture and the cormorant, [18]the stork, the heron, after their kinds; the hoopoe and the bat. [19]And all winged insects are unclean for you; they shall not be eaten. [20]All clean winged things you may eat.

[21]"You shall not eat anything that dies of itself; you may give   Lev 17:15
it to the alien who is within your towns, that he may eat it, or you may sell it to a foreigner; for you are a people holy to the LORD your God.

"You shall not boil a kid in its mother's milk.

---

from the fact that some of these animals (pigs, for example), were used by pagans in their sacred sacrifices.

In any event, it is twice pointed out (vv. 2 and 21) that the reason for these prescriptions goes back to the fact that Israel is a people consecrated to the Lord: having been chosen by God, it is a holy people, separated out from other peoples and from anything which could have any connexion with the worship of their gods.

In the New Testament our Lord will abolish this distinction between clean and unclean food (cf. Mk 7:18–19; Acts 10:9–16).

---

comedere non debetis: camelum, leporem, hyracem, quia ruminant et non dividunt ungulam, immunda erunt vobis. [8]Sus quoque, quoniam dividit ungulam et non ruminat, immunda erit vobis: carnibus eorum non vescemini et cadavera non tangetis. [9]Haec comedetis ex omnibus, quae morantur in aquis: quae habent pinnulas et squamas comedite; [10]quae absque pinnulis et squamis sunt, ne comedatis, quia immunda sunt vobis. [11]Omnes aves mundas comedite; [12]has autem ne comedatis: aquilam scilicet et grypem et alietum, [13]ixon et vulturem ac milvum iuxta genus suum [14]et omne corvini generis, [15]struthionem ac noctuam et larum atque accipitrem iuxta genus suum, [16]bubonem ac cycnum et ibin [17]ac mergulum, porphyrionem et nycticoracem, [18]erodium et charadrium, singula in genere suo, upupam quoque et vespertilionem. [19]Et omne, quod reptat et pinnulas habet, immundum erit vobis, nec comedetur. [20]Omne volatile, quod mundum est, comedite. [21]Quidquid morticinum est, ne vescamini ex eo; advenae, qui intra portas tuas est, da, ut comedat, aut vende peregrino: quia tu populus sanctus es Domino Deo tuo. Non coques haedum in lacte matris suae. [22]Decimam partem separabis de cunctis

Lev 27:30–33
Num 18:20–32
Mt 23:23
Lk 18:18 **The annual tithe**

²²"You shall tithe all the yield of your seed, which comes forth from the field year by year. ²³And before the LORD your God, in the place which he will choose, to make his name dwell there, you shall eat the tithe of your grain, of your wine, and of your oil, and the firstlings of your herd and flock; that you may learn to fear the LORD your God always. ²⁴And if the way is too long for you, so that you are not able to bring the tithe, when the LORD your God blesses you, because the place is too far from you, which the Lord your God chooses, to set his name there, ²⁵then you shall turn it into money, and bind up the money in your hand, and go to the place which the LORD your God chooses, ²⁶and spend the money for whatever you desire, oxen, or sheep, or wine or strong drink, whatever your appetite craves; and you shall eat there before the

---

14:22–29. Tithes are an institution found also in other ancient religions. They are a way of acknowledging that the land belongs to God and thereby showing him due gratitude; they are also a way of contributing to the cost of religious worship and the maintenance of priests. Thus, Abraham gives a tenth of all he has to Melchizedek, priest and king of Salem (cf. Gen 14:20), and Jacob promises to give God a tenth of anything he gains with God's help (cf. Gen 28:22). The other books of the Pentateuch also have things to say about tithes, about what they apply to and to whom they go, and they differ to some degree from what is said here: for example, in Leviticus (27:30–33) it says that they are to go to the Lord, that is, they are to be spent on religious worship in the temple, and on priests; in Numbers (18:20–32) it specifies that they are for the upkeep of the

Levites, who in turn will give a tithe of what they receive to the Lord. Scholars explain these differences as being applications of the law at different times over the course of history. In all cases, the offerers enjoy themselves and rejoice before the Lord, showing that the custom (of tithes) has a religious origin.

Only Deuteronomy mentions the three-year tithes (cf. also 26:12–15); these have a charitable purpose—concern for those in need, about which the book makes numerous exhortations (cf. the note on 10:12–22); here the custom also envisages caring for Levites (cf. the note on 12:12).

The spirit behind this ancient custom of tithing continues to apply in the Church. The *Code of Canon Law*, in canon 222, reminds us that "Christ's faithful have the obligation to provide for the needs of the Church, so that the

---

frugibus seminis tui, quae nascuntur in terra per annos singulos; ²³et comedes in conspectu Domini Dei tui in loco, quem elegerit, ut in eo nomen illius habitet, decimam frumenti tui et vini et olei et primogenita de armentis et ovibus tuis, ut discas timere Dominum Deum tuum omni tempore. ²⁴Cum autem longior fuerit tibi via et locus, quem elegerit Dominus Deus tuus, ut ponat nomen suum ibi tibique benedixerit, nec potueris ad eum haec cuncta portare, ²⁵vendes omnia et in pretium rediges; portabisque manu tua et proficisceris ad locum, quem elegerit Dominus Deus tuus, ²⁶et emes ex eadem pecunia, quidquid tibi placuerit, sive ex armentis sive ex ovibus, vinum quoque et siceram et omne, quod desiderat anima tua; et comedes ibi coram Domino Deo tuo et epulaberis tu et domus tua ²⁷et Levites,

LORD your God and rejoice, you and your household. ²⁷And you shall not forsake the Levite who is within your towns, for he has no portion or inheritance with you.

²⁸"At the end of every three years you shall bring forth all the tithe of your produce in the same year, and lay it up within your towns; ²⁹and the Levite, because he has no portion or inheritance with you, and the sojourner, the fatherless, and the widow, who are within your towns, shall come and eat and be filled; that the LORD your God may bless you in all the work of your hands that you do.

The sabbatical year

15 ¹"At the end of every seven years you shall grant a release. ²And this is the manner of the release: every creditor shall

Acts 8:21
Deut 26:12–15
Lk 14:13
Acts 8:21
Ex 23:10–12
Lev 25:1–7, 20–22

Church has available to it those things which are necessary for divine worship, for works of the apostolate and of charity and for the worthy support of its ministers. They are also obliged to promote social justice and, mindful of the Lord's precept, to help the poor from their own resources."

15:1–11. Two further measures are described here which have to do with alleviating those most in need—the remission of debts and the liberation of bondsmen. The remission of debts every seven years automatically involved release from bondage.

The institution of the sabbatical year is also covered elsewhere in the Pentateuch (Ex 23:10–12; Lev 25:1–7, 20–22) and prescribes that land shall be left fallow every seven years. Here it also lays down that debts are also to be remitted in a sabbatical year. It is not quite clear what the scope of this law was: did

it involve the total write-off of what was owed to creditors, or was it simply that no payment was required or no interest charged during that year? The appeals in vv. 9–10 seem to suggest that it involved total remission (which shows the humanitarian purpose of these rules), but this could have led to the system being abused by debtors, so it may have been quite a complicated matter to put this law into effect. The complaints about usury in the time of Nehemiah (5th century BC) suggest that it had fallen into abeyance by then (cf. Neh 5:1–13).

The apparent contradictions between vv. 4, 7 and 11 (were there poor people in Israel, or were there not?) can be explained if vv. 4–5 are taken as describing the ideal situation which could come about if everyone kept to the commandments of Yahweh. However, the fact is that there were poor people. That fact is an indictment, and therefore the believer should take to heart his duty to look after

qui intra portas tuas est: cave, ne derelinquas eum, quia non habet partem nec possessionem tecum. ²⁸Anno tertio separabis aliam decimam ex omnibus, quae nascuntur tibi eo tempore, et repones intra portas tuas; ²⁹venietque Levites, qui non habet partem nec possessionem tecum, et peregrinus ac pupillus ac vidua, qui intra portas tuas sunt, et comedent et saturabuntur, ut benedicat tibi Dominus Deus tuus in cunctis operibus manuum tuarum, quae feceris. ¹Septimo anno facies remissionem, ²quae hoc ordine celebrabitur: cui debetur aliquid a proximo ac fratre suo, repetere non poterit, quia annus remis-

release what he has lent to his neighbour; he shall not exact it of his neighbour, his brother, because the LORD's release has been proclaimed. ³Of a foreigner you may exact it; but whatever of yours

Acts 4:24 is with your brother your hand shall release. ⁴But there will be no poor among you (for the Lord will bless you in the land which the LORD your God gives you for an inheritance to possess), ⁵if only you will obey the voice of the LORD your God, being careful to do all this commandment which I command you this day. ⁶For the LORD your God will bless you, as he promised you, and you shall lend to many nations, but you shall not borrow; and you shall rule over many nations, but they shall not rule over you.

Mt 5:42 ⁷"If there is among you a poor man, one of your brethren, in
2 Cor 8:1–9:15 any of your towns within your land which the LORD your God
Jas 2:15–16
1 Jn 3:17 gives you, you shall not harden your heart or shut your hand against your poor brother, ⁸but you shall open your hand to him,

Mt 6:23 and lend him sufficient for his need, whatever it may be. ⁹Take heed lest there be a base thought in your heart, and you say, 'The seventh year, the year of release is near,' and your eye be hostile to your poor brother, and you give him nothing, and he cry to the LORD against you, and it be sin in you. ¹⁰You shall give to him freely, and your heart shall not be grudging when you give to him; because for this the LORD your God will bless you in all your work and in all that you undertake. ¹¹For the poor will never

those in need. This marks a social and humanitarian advance on the part of Old Testament law as compared with that of nations in the Mesopotamian basin. And it constitutes a legacy and a message for all times.

This moving appeal for generosity towards one's brother in need (vv. 7–8) is echoed in many New Testament passages (cf., e.g., 2 Cor 8–9; Jas 2:15–16; 1 Jn

3:17). "Practise earthly mercy", St Caesarius of Arles exhorted, "and you will receive heavenly mercy. The poor man makes his petition to you, and you make yours to God: he asks for a mouthful of food, you ask for eternal life. Give to the needy and you will merit to receive from Christ; listen to what he says: 'Give, and it will be given to you' (Lk 6:38)" (*Sermones*, 25, 1).

sionis est Domino. ³A peregrino exiges; civem et propinquum repetendi, quod tuum est, non habebis potestatem. ⁴Sed omnino indigens non erit apud te, quia benedicet tibi Dominus Deus tuus in terra, quam traditurus est tibi in possessionem, ⁵Si tamen audieris vocem Domini Dei tui et custodieris universum mandatum hoc, quod ego hodie praecipio tibi, ⁶quia Dominus Deus tuus benedicet tibi, ut pollicitus est. Fenerabis gentibus multis et ipse a nullo accipies mutuum; dominaberis nationibus plurimis, et tui nemo dominabitur. ⁷Si unus de fratribus tuis, qui morantur in una civitatum tuarum in terra, quam Dominus Deus tuus daturus est tibi, ad paupertatem venerit, non obdurabis cor tuum, nec contrahes manum; ⁸sed aperies eam pauperi fratri tuo et dabis mutuum, quod eum indigere perspexeris. ⁹Cave, ne forte subrepat tibi impia cogitatio, et dicas in corde tuo: 'Appropinquat septimus annus remissionis', et avertas oculos tuos a paupere fratre tuo nolens ei, quod postulat, mutuum commodare, ne clamet contra te ad Dominum, et fiat tibi in peccatum. ¹⁰Sed dabis ei, nec contristabitur cor tuum in

cease out of the land; therefore I command you, You shall open wide your hand to your brother, to the needy and to the poor, in the land.

Mt 26:11
Mk 14:7
Jn 12:8

Slaves

Ex 21:1–11
Lev 25:25, 39–53

[12]"If your brother, a Hebrew man, or a Hebrew woman, is sold to you, he shall serve you six years, and in the seventh year you shall let him go free from you. [13]And when you let him go free from you, you shall not let him go empty-handed; [14]you shall furnish him liberally out of your flock, out of your threshing floor, and out of your wine press; as the LORD your God has blessed you, you shall give to him. [15]You shall remember that you were a slave in the land of Egypt, and the LORD your God redeemed you; therefore I command you this today. [16]But if he says to you, 'I will not go out from you,' because he loves you and your household, since he fares well with you, [17]then you shall take an awl, and thrust it through his ear into the door, and he shall be your bondman for ever. And to your bondwoman you shall do likewise. [18]It shall not seem hard to you, when you let him go free from you; for at half the cost of a hired servant he has served you six years. So the LORD your God will bless you in all that you do.

Ex 21:2–4
Lev 25:8

Jer 34:14

Lev 25:8ff

Ex 21:5–6

15:12–18. Other passages in the Pentateuch give similar instructions designed to improve the position of Hebrews who were forced through need to become bondsmen of fellow Hebrews (cf. Ex 21:2–6; Lev 25:39–53). The discrepancies between different bodies of laws can probably be explained by the fact that the system became more humanitarian as time went by. Only Deuteronomy stipulates that a bondsman should not be let go "empty-handed" (vv. 13–14). The reminder about the slavery the Israelites endured in Egypt should encourage them to be generous towards their brethren (v. 15). The motive for alleviating or abolishing slavery is primarily a religious one.

The rite of punching a hole in the ear with an awl against the door (v. 17)—widespread among other peoples—must have been designed to show that the person was one's property; it may also have symbolized the obedience to which that person was now subject. The connexion between obedience and the ear is

eius necessitatibus sublevandis, nam propter hoc benedicet tibi Dominus Deus tuus in omni opere tuo et in cunctis, ad quae manum miseris. [11]Non deerunt pauperes in terra habitationis tuae; idcirco ego praecipio tibi, ut aperias manum fratri tuo egeno et pauperi, qui tecum versatur in terra tua. [12]Cum tibi venditus fuerit frater tuus Hebraeus aut Hebraea et sex annis servierit tibi, in septimo anno dimittes eum liberum; [13]et quem libertate donaveris, nequaquam vacuum abire patieris. [14]Sed dabis ei viaticum de gregibus et de area et torculari tuo, quibus Dominus Deus tuus benedixerit tibi. [15]Memento quod et ipse servieris in terra Aegypti, et liberaverit te Dominus Deus tuus; idcirco ego nunc hoc praecipio tibi. [16]Sin autem dixerit: 'Nolo egredi', eo quod diligat te et domum tuam et bene sibi apud te esse sentiat, [17]assumes subulam et perforabis aurem eius in ianua domus tuae, et serviet tibi usque in aeternum. Ancillae quoque similiter facies. [18]Non sit durum in oculis tuis dimittere eum liberum, quoniam iuxta

729

Ex 13:2; **First-born livestock**
13:11–16 [19]"All the firstling males that are born of your herd and flock you shall consecrate to the LORD your God; you shall do no work with the firstling of your herd, nor shear the firstling of your flock. [20]You shall eat it, you and your household, before the LORD your God year by year at the place which the LORD will choose. [21]But if it has any blemish, if it is lame or blind, or has any serious blemish whatever, you shall not sacrifice it to the LORD your God. [22]You shall eat it within your towns; the unclean and the clean alike may eat it, as though it were a gazelle or a hart. [23]Only you shall not eat its blood; you shall pour it out on the ground like water.

The three great feasts*

Ex 12:1ff *The Passover*
Lev 23:5–8

16 [1]"Observe the month of Abib, and keep the passover to the LORD your God; for in the month of Abib the LORD your

---

to be found elsewhere in Scripture (cf. Ps 40:6–8; Is 50:4–5). In some languages there is a linguistic connexion between hearing and obeying: in Hebrew the same verb, *sharma*, means both actions. This equivalence between hearing/listening and obeying applies to passages in which God tells Israel: "Hear": cf. Deut 4:1; 5:1; 6:4; 9:1; 15:5; 18:15; 28:1; 30:10.

15:19–23. The offering of the male first-born of animals is one of the most ancient sacrifices we know of; it implies a profound conviction that it is God who bestows fertility. For the Israelites it also meant a reminder of their miraculous deliverance from Egypt, with the death of the Egyptian first-born. Exodus 22:29 stipulated that the sacrifice should take

place on the eighth day (something quite easy to do during the pilgrimage through the wilderness); now, in view of the fact that the Israelites will be established in Canaan and have only one holy place (v. 20) it made sense to extend the period of one year. The gift of these first-born to priests (cf. Num 18:15–18) is a further nuance found in the law.

The rule about not offering God any blemished first-born (vv. 21–23) derived from the reverence and respect due to him, and is a reminder of the need always to give him the very best, avoiding any kind of niggardliness. Applying this teaching to ordinary life, St Josemaría Escrivá says, "You cannot sanctify work which humanly speaking is slapdash, for we must not offer God badly-done jobs" (*Furrow*, 493).

---

mercedem mercennarii per sex annos servivit tibi, et benedicet tibi Dominus Deus tuus in cunctis operibus, quae egeris. [19]De primogenitis, quae nascuntur in armentis et ovibus tuis, quidquid sexus est masculini, sanctificabis Domino Deo tuo; non operaberis in primogenito bovis et non tondebis primogenita ovium. [20]In conspectu Domini Dei tui comedes ea per annos singulos in loco, quem elegerit Dominus, tu et domus tua. [21]Sin autem habuerit maculam et vel claudum fuerit vel caecum aut in aliqua parte deforme vel debile, non immolabis illud Domino Deo tuo, [22]sed intra portas tuas comedes illud; tam mundus quam immundus similiter vescentur eis, quasi caprea et cervo. [23]Solum sanguinem eorum non comedes, sed effundes in terram quasi aquam. [1]Observa mensem Abib, ut facias Pascha Domino

God brought you out of Egypt by night. [2]And you shall offer the Mk 14:12 passover sacrifice to the LORD your God, from the flock or the herd, at the place which the LORD will choose, to make his name dwell there. [3]You shall eat no leavened bread with it; seven days Lk 22:19 you shall eat it with unleavened bread, the bread of affliction—for you came out of the land of Egypt in hurried flight—that all the days of your life you may remember the day when you came out of the land of Egypt. [4]No leaven shall be seen with you in all your territory for seven days; nor shall any of the flesh which you sacrifice on the evening of the first day remain all night until morning. [5]You may not offer the passover sacrifice within any of your towns which the LORD your God gives you; [6]but at the place which the LORD your God will choose, to make his name dwell in it, there you shall offer the passover sacrifice, in the evening at the going down of the sun, at the time you came out of Egypt. [7]And you shall boil it and eat it at the place which the LORD your God

---

*16:1–17. This passage covers ordinances about how to celebrate the three main Jewish feasts: the Passover and the unleavened bread; Weeks; and Tabernacles (booths). The main thing that Deuteronomy stresses (unlike what is handed down in other books of the Pentateuch: cf. Ex 23:14–17; Lev 23) is that they are to be celebrated "at the place which the Lord will choose", that is, in the temple, where religious worship will be centralized.

In this connexion, it stipulates the duty that all male Hebrews have to go there on pilgrimage for these feasts (vv. 16–17). Women were under no such obligations, but they were not excluded: in point of fact, Hannah (Samuel's mother) and the Blessed Virgin accompany their husbands on such occasions (cf. 1 Sam 1:2; Lk 2:41).

16:1–8. The Passover was the main feast of the Jews, instituted in memory of deliverance from Egypt, when the Angel passed over, killing the first-born of the Egyptians (cf. Ex 12:1—13:16 and the notes on same). It was celebrated in "the month of Abib", the month of spring or of the ears of grain, not only because that was when wheat began to ripen but because, according to ancient traditions, it was the time of year when the Exodus took place; later on, the name given to this month was "Nisan", which was more or less our April. The Passover is regulated here in the same breath as is the feast of the unleavened bread which had

---

Deo tuo; quoniam in isto mense Abib eduxit te Dominus Deus tuus de Aegypto nocte. [2]Immolabisque Pascha Domino Deo tuo de ovibus et de bobus in loco, quem elegerit Dominus Deus tuus, ut habitet nomen eius ibi. [3]Non comedes cum eo panem fermentatum; septem diebus comedes absque fermento afflictionis panem, quoniam festinanter egressus es de Aegypto, ut memineris diei egressionis tuae de Aegypto omnibus diebus vitae tuae. [4]Non apparebit fermentum in omnibus terminis tuis septem diebus; et non manebit de carnibus eius, quod immolatum est vespere in die primo, usque mane. [5]Non poteris immolare Pascha in qualibet urbium tuarum, quas Dominus Deus tuus daturus est tibi, [6]sed in loco, quem elegerit Dominus Deus tuus, ut habitet nomen eius ibi, immolabis Pascha vespere ad solis occasum, quando egressus es de Aegypto. [7]Et coques et comedes in loco, quem elegerit Dominus Deus

will choose; and in the morning you shall turn and go to your tents. [8]For six days you shall eat unleavened bread; and on the seventh day there shall be a solemn assembly to the LORD your God; you shall do no work on it.

Lev 23:15–21
Num 28:26–31
Ex 23:14

The feast of Weeks

[9]"You shall count seven weeks; begin to count the seven weeks from the time you first put the sickle to the standing grain. [10]Then you shall keep the feast of weeks to the LORD your God with the tribute of a freewill offering from your hand, which you shall give as the LORD your God blesses you; [11]and you shall rejoice before the LORD your God, you and your son and your daughter, your manservant and your maidservant, the Levite who is within

---

to be held on the seven days following, during which bread had to be eaten unleavened. It is called "bread of affliction" (v. 3) in memory of the sudden departure from Egypt on the night of the Hebrews' deliverance, when they did not have time to leaven dough (cf. Ex 12:34).

In Jesus' time, the sacrifice of the animal was carried out in the temple, but the Passover meal was held in private houses (cf. Mk 14:12ff).

The Passover supper would be the moment chosen by Jesus to institute the Eucharist, the sacrifice of the New Covenant which would take the place of the Old Testament sacrifices (cf. Lk 22:14–20). The Passover victim, whose blood saved from death the first-born of the Israelites in Egypt (cf. Ex 12:7–13), is a promise and figure of the Sacrifice of Jesus on Calvary for the salvation of all mankind: Christ, "our paschal lamb, has been sacrificed" (1 Cor 5:7).

Bishop Melitus of Sardes (2nd century) taught: "The sacrifice of the lamb,

the rite of the Passover and the letter of the Law reached their climax in Christ Jesus, on whose account everything happened in the Old Law, and even more so in the new economy. Thus, the Law has become the Word, and the old has changed to the new (both came out of Zion and Jesus Christ); commandment has become grace, figure has become reality; the lamb is now the Son, and the sheep man, and man God" (*De Pascha*, 6–7).

16:9–12. The feast of Weeks was held in thanksgiving to God for the first fruits of the fields; it was also called the feast of harvest or the feast of first fruits (cf. Ex 23:16; Num 28:26), and, later on, Pentecost, because it fell *fifty* days after Passover (cf. Lev 23:15–16; Tob 2:1; 2 Mac 12:32). Deuteronomy stresses the humanitarian dimension of the feast: those most in need were to be part of it (v. 11). Later on, around the 2nd century AD, the Jews will link the feast to the

---

tuus, maneque consurgens vades in tabernacula tua. [8]Sex diebus comedes azyma et in die septimo, quia collecta est Domino Deo tuo, non facies opus. [9]Septem hebdomadas numerabis tibi ab ea die, qua falcem in segetem miseris, [10]et celebrabis diem festum Hebdomadarum Domino Deo tuo, oblationem spontaneam manus tuae, quam offeres iuxta benedictionem Domini Dei tui. [11]Et epulaberis coram Domino Deo tuo tu, filius tuus et filia tua, servus tuus et ancilla tua et Levites, qui est intra portas tuas, advena ac pupillus et vidua, qui morantur tecum, in loco quem elegerit Dominus Deus tuus, ut habitet

your towns, the sojourner, the fatherless, and the widow who are among you, at the place which the LORD your God will choose, to make his name dwell there. [12]You shall remember that you were a slave in Egypt; and you shall be careful to observe these statutes.

The feast of Tabernacles

Lev 23:33–43
Num 29:12–39

[13]"You shall keep the feast of booths seven days, when you make your ingathering from your threshing floor and your wine press; [14]you shall rejoice in your feast, you and your son and your daughter, your manservant and your maidservant, the Levite, the sojourner, the fatherless, and the widow who are within your towns. [15]For seven days you shall keep the feast to the LORD your

---

memory of Moses' being given the Law on Mount Sinai.

This was the feast that God chose for sending the Holy Spirit: the material harvest which it celebrated became the symbol of the spiritual harvest which the apostles began to reap on that day (cf. Acts 2).

16:13–15. This feast was held at the beginning of autumn, to mark the end of work in the fields (hence its other name, Ingathering: cf. Ex 23:16), to give thanks to God for the harvest won. The name Tabernacles (tents, booths) comes from the fact that during the days of the feast the Israelites lived in tents or shelters, recalling their lifestyle during their years in the wilderness (cf. Lev 23:41–43). In some places in the Old Testament it is called simply "the Feast", maybe because of the special joy that marked those days, which would have made it particularly popular (v. 15; cf. Judg 21:19–21; 1

Kings 8:2; Ezek 45:25; Hos 9:1–5).

As time went by, the Israelites added on ceremonies to make this feast more solemn; our Lord took advantage of some of these in his preaching. The *Succoth* treatise 4, 9, of the *Mishnáh*, for example, tells us that, on each of the eight days of the feast, water in a golden receptacle was brought in procession from the pool of Siloam to the temple, where it was sprinkled on the altar, asking God to send rain in plenty. Jesus may have had this in mind when he taught: "If any one thirst, let him come to me and drink" (Jn 7:37), portraying himself as the one who could meet all the yearnings of the human heart. Also, four large lampstands were lit in the temple, shedding light that could be seen all over Jerusalem, recalling the pillar of fire which guided the Israelites through the desert: it was probably on this occasion that our Lord depicted himself as the "light of the world" (Jn 8:12).

---

nomen eius ibi; [12]et recordaberis quoniam servus fueris in Aegypto custodiesque ac facies, quae praecepta sunt. [13]Sollemnitatem quoque Tabernaculorum celebrabis per septem dies, quando collegeris de area et torculari fruges tuas; [14]et epulaberis in festivitate tua tu, filius tuus et filia, servus tuus et ancilla, Levites quoque et advena, pupillus ac vidua, qui intra portas tuas sunt. [15]Septem diebus Domino Deo tuo festa celebrabis in loco, quem elegerit Dominus, quia benedicet tibi Dominus Deus tuus in cunctis

God at the place which the LORD will choose; because the LORD your God will bless you in all your produce and in all the work of your hands, so that you will be altogether joyful.

Lk 2:41
Jn 7:2

[16]"Three times a year all your males shall appear before the LORD your God at the place which he will choose: at the feast of unleavened bread, at the feast of weeks, and at the feast of booths. They shall not appear before the LORD empty-handed; [17]every man shall give as he is able, according to the blessing of the LORD your God which he has given you.

2. INSTITUTIONS OF ISRAEL*

Ex 23:1–3, 6–
8; 18:13–27
Deut 1:9–18

Judges

[18]"You shall appoint judges and officers in all your towns which the LORD your God gives you, according to your tribes; and they shall judge the people with righteous judgment. [19]You shall not pervert justice; you shall not show partiality; and you shall not take a bribe, for a bribe blinds the eyes of the wise and subverts

Rom 9:31

the cause of the righteous. [20]Justice, and only justice, you shall follow, that you may live and inherit the land which the LORD your God gives you.

---

*16:18—18:22. A new section begins at 16:18 which goes on up to chapter 18 inclusive; it regulates the rights of judges, kings, Levites and prophets.

The institution of the judges, established according to Exodus and Deuteronomy to help Moses to deal with lawsuits between Israelites (cf. Ex 18:13–27; Deut 1:9–18), is extended here to each city of Israel (16:18); also, a kind of supreme court is established, for the resolution of more difficult cases (17:8–13). Elsewhere in Holy Scripture we see Samuel and his sons exercising

this office (1 Sam 8:1–2; 12:2–4), and King Josaphat (9th century BC) appointed the judges and tribunals specified in this passage of Deuteronomy (2 Chron 19:4–11). The exhortations to honesty and impartiality addressed to the judges sometimes fell on deaf ears, as can be seen from complaints about arbitrary decisions (cf., e.g., Is 1:23; 5:23; Ezek 22:12; Prov 17:23).

Verses 16:21—17:7 seem to be connected more with chapter 13. However, in 17:2–7 there is reference to a possible legal process against idolators.

---

frugibus tuis et in omni opere manuum tuarum, erisque totus in laetitia. [16]Tribus vicibus per annum apparebit omne masculinum tuum in conspectu Domini Dei tui in loco, quem elegerit: in sollemnitate Azymorum et in sollemnitate Hebdomadarum et in sollemnitate Tabernaculorum. Non apparebit ante Dominum vacuus, [17]sed offeret unusquisque secundum quod habuerit, iuxta benedictionem Domini Dei tui, quam dederit tibi. [18]Iudices et praefectos operum constitues in omnibus portis tuis, quas Dominus Deus tuus dederit tibi per singulas tribus tuas, ut iudicent populum iusto iudicio. [19]Non declinabis iudicium. Non accipies personam nec munera, quia munera excaecant oculos sapientum et mutant causas iustorum. [20]Iustitiam, iustitiam persequeris, ut vivas et possideas terram, quam Dominus Deus tuus dederit tibi. [21]Non plantabis tibi palum, omnem arborem iuxta altare Domini Dei tui, quod

²¹"You shall not plant any tree as an Asherah beside the altar Ex 34:13
of the LORD your God which you shall make. ²² And you shall not Ex 23:24
set up a pillar, which the LORD your God hates.

17 ¹"You shall not sacrifice to the LORD your God an ox or a Lev 22:20–25
sheep in which is a blemish, any defect whatever; for that
is an abomination to the LORD your God.

²"If there is found among you, within any of your towns which
the Lord your God gives you, a man or woman who does what is
evil in the sight of the LORD your God, in transgressing his
covenant, ³and has gone and served other gods and worshiped
them, or the sun or the moon or any of the host of heaven, which
I have forbidden, ⁴and it is told you and you hear of it; then you
shall inquire diligently, and if it is true and certain that such an
abominable thing has been done in Israel, ⁵then you shall bring
forth to your gates that man or woman who has done this evil
thing, and you shall stone that man or woman to death with Deut 19:15
stones. ⁶On the evidence of two witnesses or of three witnesses he Mk 14:56
that is to die shall be put to death; a person shall not be put to Jn 8:7
Heb 10:28
death on the evidence of one witness. ⁷The hand of the witnesses Jn 8:7
shall be first against him to put him to death, and afterward the Acts 7:58
1 Cor 5:13
hand of all the people. So you shall purge the evil from the midst
of you.

⁸"If any case arises requiring decision between one kind of Mt 5:22
homicide and another, one kind of legal right and another, or one
kind of assault and another, any case within your towns which is
too difficult for you, then you shall arise and go up to the place
which the LORD your God will choose, ⁹and coming to the
Levitical priests, and to the judge who is in office in those days,
you shall consult them, and they shall declare to you the decision.
¹⁰Then you shall do according to what they declare to you from

feceris tibi. ²²Neque constitues lapidem, quem odit Dominus Deus tuus. ¹Non immolabis Domino Deo
tuo ovem et bovem, in quo est macula aut quippiam vitii, quia abominatio est Domino Deo tuo. ²Cum
reperti fuerint apud te intra unam portarum tuarum, quas Dominus Deus tuus dabit tibi, vir aut mulier,
qui faciant, quod malum est in conspectu Domini Dei tui, et transgrediantur pactum illius, ³ut vadant
et serviant diis alienis et adorent eos, solem vel lunam vel omnem militiam caeli, quae non praecepi,
⁴et hoc tibi fuerit nuntiatum, audiensque inquisieris diligenter et verum esse reppereris, et abominatio
haec facta est in Israel, ⁵educes virum vel mulierem, qui hanc rem sceleratissimam perpetrarunt, ad
portas civitatis tuae, et lapidibus obruentur. ⁶In ore duorum aut trium testium peribit, qui interficietur;
nemo occidatur uno contra se dicente testimonium. ⁷Manus testium prima erit ad interficiendum eum,
et manus reliqui populi extrema mittetur, ut auferas malum de medio tui. ⁸Si intra portas tuas in litibus
difficile et ambiguum apud te iudicium esse perspexeris inter sanguinem et sanguinem, causam et
causam, plagam et plagam, surge et ascende ad locum, quem elegerit Dominus Deus tuus, ⁹veniesque
ad sacerdotes levitici generis et ad iudicem, qui fuerit illo tempore; quaeresque ab eis, qui indicabunt
tibi iudicii sententiam. ¹⁰Et facies quodcumque dixerint tibi de loco, quem elegerit Dominus, et obser-

that place which the LORD will choose; and you shall be careful to do according to all that they direct you; [11]according to the instructions which they give you, and according to the decision which they pronounce to you, you shall do; you shall not turn aside from the verdict which they declare to you, either to the right hand or to the left. [12]The man who acts presumptuously, by not obeying the priest who stands to minister there before the LORD your God, or the judge, that man shall die; so you shall purge the evil from Israel. [13]And all the people shall hear, and fear, and not act presumptuously again.

1 Sam 8–10 **Kings**

[14]"When you come to the land which the LORD your God gives you, and you possess it and dwell in it, and then say, 'I will set a king over me, like all the nations that are round about me'; [15]you may indeed set as king over you him whom the LORD your God will choose. One from among your brethren you shall set as king over you; you may not put a foreigner over you, who is not your brother. [16]Only he must not multiply horses for himself, or cause

---

17:14–20. Here we have some ordinances to do with monarchy in Israel. The rules given make reference to the danger that a desire to copy the military power (based mainly on cavalry) of other eastern courts, and their wealth and high-living, might get the better of the king and lead him to be unfaithful to the Lord and to act like a despot.

The powers of the king as described here seem to be more circumscribed than in fact they generally were.

"A copy of this law" (v. 18): the Greek translation of this passage made by the Septuagint (2nd century BC)—*deuteronomion* (in the sense of a recapit-

ulation of the law or a *second law*—was taken straight into the Latin translation of the Vulgate, and it gave its name to this book, which was given as a "Second Law" to the Levites (cf. 31:9, 26). The New Vulgate prefers to speak of an *exemplar legis*, "copy of the law": cf. the "Introduction", p. 657 above).

The exhortation to read this law "all the days of his life" (v. 19) is a reminder of how important it is to know Holy Scripture well so as to be able to live in accordance with it. In later Judaism all Jews will be asked to read and study the *Torah*, at least on the sabbath.

In Christianity, from the early cen-

---

vabis, ut facias omnia quae docuerint te [11]iuxta mandatum, quod mandaverunt, et iuxta sententiam, quam dixerint tibi. Nec declinabis ad dexteram vel ad sinistram. [12]Qui autem superbierit nolens oboedire sacerdotis imperio, qui eo tempore ministrat Domino Deo tuo, aut decreto iudicis, morietur homo ille, et auferes malum de Israel; [13]cunctusque populus audiens timebit, ut nullus deinceps intumescat superbia. [14]Cum ingressus fueris terram, quam Dominus Deus tuus dabit tibi, et possederis eam habitaverisque in illa et dixeris: 'Constituam super me regem, sicut habent omnes per circuitum nationes', [15]eum constitues super te regem, quem Dominus Deus tuus elegerit de numero fratrum tuorum. Non poteris alterius gentis hominem regem facere, qui non sit frater tuus. [16]Tantummodo non multiplicabit sibi equos nec reducet populum in Aegyptum, ut equitatus numerum augeat, praesertim

the people to return to Egypt in order to multiply horses, since the LORD has said to you, 'You shall never return that way again.' [17]And he shall not multiply wives for himself, lest his heart turn away; nor shall he greatly multiply for himself silver and gold.

[18]"And when he sits on the throne of his kingdom, he shall write for himself in a book a copy of this law, from that which is in the charge of the Levitical priests; [19]and it shall be with him, and he shall read in it all the days of his life, that he may learn to fear the LORD his God, by keeping all the words of this law and these statutes, and doing them; [20]that his heart may not be lifted up above his brethren, and that he may not turn aside from the commandment, either to the right hand or to the left; so that he may continue long in his kingdom, he and his children, in Israel.

Acts 1:25

Priests

18 [1]"The Levitical priests, that is, all the tribe of Levi, shall have no portion or inheritance with Israel; they shall eat

Num 18

1 Cor 9:13

---

turies, the reading of the Holy Scripture was an important element in the education of pastors and of the faithful in general. For example, St Jerome exhorted the priest Nepotian as follows: "Read the divine Scriptures frequently; indeed, never let them out of your hands" (*Epistulae*, 52:7). And in the prologue to his *Commentarium in Isaiam* he wrote: "Ignorance of the Scriptures is ignorance of Christ."

The Second Vatican Council encourages the faithful to "go gladly to the sacred text itself, whether in the sacred liturgy, which is full of the divine words, or in devout reading, or in such suitable exercises and various other helps which, with the approval and guidance of the pastors of the Church, are happily

spreading everywhere in our day" (*Dei Verbum*, 25).

18:1–8. Even though the book has already called on the people several times to look after the needs of the Levites, it specifies here what portion they should be given of offerings and first fruits, so as to make sure they can worthily devote themselves to their duties in regard to divine worship.

Apropos of this passage, there are those who point out that no distinction is made in Deuteronomy between priests (descendants of Aaron) and Levites (a broader group, all the male descendants of Levi). This distinction, which is clearly to be seen elsewhere in the Penta-

---

cum Dominus praeceperit vobis, ut nequaquam amplius per hanc viam revertamini. [17]Neque habebit uxores plurimas, ne declinet cor eius, neque argenti et auri immensa pondera. [18]Postquam autem sederit in solio regni sui, describet sibi exemplar legis huius in volumine accipiens illam a sacerdotibus leviticae tribus; [19]et habebit secum legetque illud omnibus diebus vitae suae, ut discat timere Dominum Deum suum et custodire verba legis huius et praecepta ista et quae in lege praecepta sunt. [20]Nec elevetur cor eius in superbiam super fratres suos neque declinet a mandatis in partem dexteram vel sinistram, ut longo tempore regnet ipse et filii eius in medio Israel. [1]Non habebunt sacerdotes levitae, omnis tribus Levi, partem et hereditatem cum reliquo Israel; de sacrificiis Domini et hereditate eius comedent [2]et nihil accipient de possessione fratrum suorum: Dominus enim ipse est hereditas eorum, sicut locu-

the offerings by fire to the LORD, and his rightful dues. [2]They shall have no inheritance among their brethren; the LORD is their inheritance, as he promised them. [3]And this shall be the priests' due from the people, from those offering a sacrifice, whether it be ox or sheep: they shall give to the priest the shoulder and the two cheeks and the stomach. [4]The first fruits of your grain, of your wine and of your oil, and the first of the fleece of your sheep, you shall give him. [5]For the LORD your God has chosen him out of all your tribes, to stand and minister in the name of the LORD, him and his sons for ever.

2 Kings 23:9

[6]"And if a Levite comes from any of your towns out of all Israel, where he lives—and he may come when he desires—to the

Heb 10:11

place which the LORD will choose, [7]then he may minister in the name of the LORD his God, like all his fellow-Levites who stand to minister there before the LORD. [8]They shall have equal portions to eat, besides what he receives from the sale of his patrimony.[m]

Prophets

[9]"When you come into the land which the LORD your God gives you, you shall not learn to follow the abominable practices of

---

teuch (cf., e.g., Num 18) may be something that emerged at a stage in Israel's history when the institution of priesthood had evolved somewhat.

Other commentators, however, in addition to stressing that Deuteronomy is aware of the privileged position held by Aaron's descendants (cf. 10:6), make the point that the expressions "the Levitical priests" and "all the tribe of Levi" (v. 1) do not mean the same thing; rather, the former means the priests, the latter the rest of the Levites. In this passage where instructions are being given as to what the people should do for those who dedicate themselves to religious worship, there is

no need to go into any further detail.

The instructions given in vv. 6-8 may be connected with the need to centralize worship in line with the law about there being only one sanctuary; however, it is not quite clear whether the Levite is relocating temporarily or permanently.

The New Testament, too, speaks of how important it is for the faithful to contribute to the sustenance of ministers of religion, to free them from other concerns so they can devote themselves to their ministry (cf. 1 Cor 9:1–14).

18:9–22. This is a key text as regards the institution of the prophethood in Israel,

---

tus est illis. [3]Hoc erit ius sacerdotum a populo, ab his qui offerunt victimas: sive bovem sive ovem immolaverint, dabunt sacerdoti armum et duas maxillas ac ventriculum, [4]primitias frumenti, vini et olei et lanarum ex ovium tonsione. [5]Ipsum enim elegit Dominus Deus tuus de cunctis tribubus tuis, ut stet et ministret in nomine Domini ipse et filii eius in sempiternum. [6]Si exierit Levites de una urbium tuarum ex omni Israel, in qua ut advena habitat, et voluerit venire desiderans locum, quem elegerit Dominus, [7]ministrabit in nomine Domini Dei sui, sicut omnes fratres eius levitae, qui stabunt ibi coram

m. Heb obscure

those nations. [10]There shall not be found among you any one who
burns his son or his daughter as an offering,[n] any one who practices divination, a soothsayer, or an augur, or a sorcerer, [11]or a
charmer, or a medium, or a wizard, or a necromancer. [12]For whoever does these things is an abomination to the LORD; and because
of these abominable practices the LORD your God is driving them
out before you. [13]You shall be blameless before the LORD your
God. [14]For these nations, which you are about to dispossess, give
heed to soothsayers and to diviners; but as for you, the LORD your
God has not allowed you so to do.

Lev 18:21; 19:31
2 Kings 21:6
Acts 19:19

Mt 5:48

---

and even for the notion of Messiah.
Together with the king and the priest, the
prophet is one of the great institutions of
Israel; the prophet has a very important
religious position and special moral
authority. In the Deuteronomic tradition
(cf. 34:10–12) Moses is seen not only as
the one who delivered Israel from
bondage in Egypt, not only as a lawgiver,
but also as the first prophet and the outstanding model for all future prophets.

The fundamental role of the prophet
is to speak in the name of the Lord and
proclaim the meaning and scope of past,
present and future events: the Israelites
would never have any need, therefore, of
wizards, magi or necromancers (people
who call up the spirits of the dead), who
were closely linked to idolatry and super-
stition. However, the fact was that they
often fell into this temptation—even the
horrendous sacrificial burning of children
(cf. 2 Kings 21:6), repeatedly condemned
in the Old Testament (cf., e.g., Jer 7:31;
Ezek 16:20–21).

Tradition has shown the messianic
meaning of vv. 15 and 18. In the New

Testament St Paul identifies the
"prophet" who will be raised up as being
Jesus Christ (cf. Acts 3:22–23 which
actually quotes Deuteronomy 18:18; cf.
also Jn 1:21, 45; 6:14; 7:40).

Foremost among the evidence of Jewish tradition in Jesus' time, giving a
strongly messianic interpretation to this
passage, is that from the Qumran manuscripts (cf. 1 QS 9) which add to this passage that of Deuteronomy 5:28–29 and the
references to the star of Jacob (Num 24:17)
and the sceptre of Israel (Gen 49:10); and
they link 18:9–22 to 33:8–11 through the
reference to the priest-Messiah.

The possible collective meaning of
what Moses announces here (the fact that
it can be interpreted as referring to the
many prophets that God will arise up
over time) is perfectly compatible with
its achieving its fullest expression in
Jesus Christ, the greatest of all the
prophets (cf. Heb 1:4).

18:13. In the Sermon on the Mount our
Lord evokes the words of this verse (very
like those of Leviticus 19:2, too) when

Domino. [8]Partem ciborum eandem accipiet quam et ceteri, excepto eo, quod ex paterna ei successione
debetur. [9]Quando ingressus fueris terram, quam Dominus Deus tuus dabit tibi, cave, ne imitari velis
abominationes illarum gentium. [10]Nec inveniatur in te, qui filium suum aut filiam traducat per ignem,
aut qui sortes sciscitetur et observet nubes atque auguria, nec sit maleficus [11]nec incantator, nec qui
pythones consulat nec divinos, aut quaerat a mortuis veritatem; [12]omnia enim haec abominatur
Dominus et propter istiusmodi scelera expellet eos in introitu tuo. [13]Perfectus eris et absque macula

---

n. Heb *makes his son or his daughter pass through the fire*

Mt 12:6
Mk 9:4, 7
Lk 7:39; 9:35
Jn 1:21; 5:46
Acts 3:22–23;
7:37

Acts 3:22; 7:37
Jn 1:21;
12:49–50
Ex 4:12

[15]"The LORD your God will raise up for you a prophet like me from among you, from your brethren—him you shall heed—[16]just as you desired of the LORD your God at Horeb on the day of the assembly, when you said, 'Let me not hear again the voice of the LORD my God, or see this great fire any more, lest I die.' [17]And the LORD said to me, 'They have rightly said all that they have spoken. [18]I will raise up for them a prophet* like you from among their brethren; and I will put my words in his mouth, and he shall speak to them all that I command him. [19]And whoever will not give heed to my words which he shall speak in my name, I myself will require it of him. [20]But the prophet who presumes to speak a word in my name which I have not commanded him to speak, or who speaks in the name of other gods, that same prophet shall die.' [21]And if you say in your heart, 'How may we know the word which the LORD has not spoken?'—[22]when a prophet speaks in the name of the LORD, if the word does not come to pass or come true, that is a word which the LORD has not spoken; the prophet has spoken it presumptuously, you need not be afraid of him.

Ex 21:12–14
Num 35:9–34
Deut 4:41–43

3. SOCIAL RIGHTS*

Cities of refuge

19 [1]"When the LORD your God cuts off the nations whose land the LORD your God gives you, and you dispossess them and dwell in their cities and in their houses, [2]you shall set apart three

---

summing up the first part of his discourse: "You, therefore, must be perfect, as your heavenly Father is perfect" (Mt 5:48).

*19:1–21. After specifying the rules designed to support Israel's religious life and

theocratic structure, there now begins (it takes us to the end of the second discourse: 26:19) a section consisting of miscellaneous ordinances aimed at defending the rights of the individual, family and society.

---

cum Domino Deo tuo. [14]Gentes istae, quarum possidebis terram, augures et divinos audiunt; tu autem a Domino Deo tuo aliter institutus es. [15]Prophetam de gente tua et de fratribus tuis sicut me suscitabit tibi Dominus Deus tuus; ipsum audietis, [16]ut petiisti a Domino Deo tuo in Horeb, quando contio congregata est, atque dixisti: 'Ultra non audiam vocem Domini Dei mei et ignem hunc maximum amplius non videbo, ne moriar'. [17]Et ait Dominus mihi: 'Bene omnia sunt locuti; [18]prophetam suscitabo eis de medio fratrum suorum similem tui et ponam verba mea in ore eius, loqueturque ad eos omnia, quae praecepero illi. [19]Qui autem verba mea, quae loquetur in nomine meo, audire noluerit, ego ultor exsistam. [20]Propheta autem qui, arrogantia depravatus, voluerit loqui in nomine meo, quae ego non praecepi illi ut diceret, aut ex nomine alienorum deorum, interficietur'. [21]Quod si tacita cogitatione responderis: 'Quomodo possum intellegere verbum, quod Dominus non est locutus?', [22]hoc habebis signum: quod in nomine Domini propheta ille praedixerit, et non evenerit, hoc Dominus non est locutus, sed per tumorem animi sui propheta confinxit; et idcirco non timebis eum. [1]Cum disperderit Dominus Deus tuus gentes, quarum tibi traditurus est terram, et possederis eam habitaverisque in urbibus eius et in

cities for you in the land which the LORD your God gives you to possess. ³You shall prepare the roads, and divide into three parts the area of the land which the LORD your God gives you as a possession, so that any manslayer can flee to them.

⁴"This is the provision for the manslayer, who by fleeing there may save his life. If any one kills his neighbour unintentionally without having been at enmity with him in time past—⁵as when a man goes into the forest with his neighbour to cut wood, and his hand swings the axe to cut down a tree, and the head slips from the handle and strikes his neighbour so that he dies—he may flee to one of these cities and save his life; ⁶lest the avenger of blood in hot anger pursue the manslayer and overtake him, because the way is long, and wound him mortally, though the man did not deserve to die, since he was not at enmity with his neighbour in time past. ⁷Therefore I command you, You shall set apart three cities. ⁸And if the LORD your God enlarges your border, as he has sworn to your fathers, and gives you all the land which he promised to give to your fathers—⁹provided you are careful to keep all this commandment, which I command you this day, by loving the LORD your God and by walking ever in his ways—then you shall add three other cities to these three, ¹⁰lest innocent blood be shed in your land which the LORD your God gives you for an inheritance, and so the guilt of bloodshed be upon you.

This chapter deals mainly with the cities of refuge (already dealt with in detail in Num 35:9–34: cf. the note on same and also Ex 21:12–14 and Deut 4:41–43), property boundaries and qualifications for witnesses. Verse 15 (on witnesses) will be referred to in the New Testament (cf., e.g., Jn 8:17–18; 1 Tim 5:19). The background to all this legislation is not only the notion of the sacredness of human life but also the sacredness of the land. The shedding of innocent blood cries to heaven, but so too does the fraudulent shifting of landmarks

---

aedibus, ²tres civitates separabis tibi in medio terrae, quam Dominus Deus tuus dabit tibi in possessionem ³sternens diligenter viam; et in tres aequaliter partes totam terrae tuae provinciam divides, ut habeat e vicino, qui propter homicidium profugus est, quo possit evadere. ⁴Haec erit lex homicidae fugientis, cuius vita servanda est: qui percusserit proximum suum nesciens et qui heri et nudiustertius nullum contra eum habuisse odium comprobatur, ⁵sed abiisse cum eo simpliciter in silvam ad ligna caedenda, et in succisione lignorum securis fugerit manu, ferrumque lapsum de manubrio amicum eius percusserit et occiderit, hic ad unam supradictarum urbium confugiet et vivet; ⁶ne forsitan ultor sanguinis cordis calore stimulatus persequatur et apprehendat eum, si longior via fuerit, et percutiat eum, et moriatur, qui non est reus mortis, quia nullum contra eum, qui occisus est, odium prius habuisse monstratur. ⁷Idcirco praecipio tibi, ut tres civitates aequalis inter se spatii dividas. ⁸Cum autem dilataverit Dominus Deus tuus terminos tuos, sicut iuravit patribus tuis, et dederit tibi cunctam terram, quam eis pollicitus est ⁹—si tamen custodieris omne mandatum hoc et feceris, quae hodie praecipio tibi, ut diligas Dominum Deum tuum et ambules in viis eius omni tempore—addes tibi tres alias civitates et supradictarum trium urbium numerum duplicabis, ¹⁰ut non effundatur sanguis innoxius in

¹¹"But if any man hates his neighbour, and lies in wait for him, and attacks him, and wounds him mortally so that he dies, and the man flees into one of these cities, ¹²then the elders of his city shall send and fetch him from there, and hand him over to the avenger of blood, so that he may die. ¹³Your eye shall not pity him, but you shall purge the guilt of innocent blood° from Israel, so that it may be well with you.

Deut 27:17 **Boundaries of properties**

¹⁴"In the inheritance which you will hold in the land that the LORD your God gives you to possess, you shall not remove your neighbour's landmark, which the men of old have set.

Deut 17:2–7
Mt 18:16 **Witnesses**
Mk 14:56
Jn 8:16–17 ¹⁵"A single witness shall not prevail against a man for any crime
2 Cor 13:1 or for any wrong in connection with any offence that he has com-
1 Tim 5:19 mitted; only on the evidence of two witnesses, or of three wit-
Heb 10:28 nesses, shall a charge be sustained. ¹⁶If a malicious witness rises against any man to accuse him of wrongdoing, ¹⁷then both parties

---

and boundaries (it goes against the division of land devised by God himself).

The law of retaliation (v. 21)—also dealt with elsewhere in the Pentateuch (cf. Ex 21:23–25; Lev 24:17–23)— occurs in other ancient Eastern codes, such as that of Hammurabi (*c.*1700 BC) although in that code it is not spelt out exactly (cf., e.g., arts. 196, 197, 200). The law of retaliation seems harsh to the modern mind, but it marked a considerable ethical and legal advance when first promulgated. It sought to temper a desire for revenge (very common among desert tribesmen—homicide was a commonplace: cf., e.g., Gen 4:23) by setting limits to the punishment that could be inflicted; this present passage refers to sentences handed down by courts). In the New Testament, our Lord will establish other criteria for settling disputes by stressing that justice should always be imbued with forgiveness and charity (cf. Mt 5:38–42). The law of forgiveness promulgated by Christ is a reflection of God's attitude towards humankind; man should imitate God in this regard: cf. the Our Father.

---

medio terrae, quam Dominus Deus tuus dabit tibi possidendam, nec sis sanguinis reus. ¹¹Si quis autem odio habens proximum suum insidiatus fuerit vitae eius surgensque percusserit illum, et mortuus fuerit, fugeritque ad unam de supradictis urbibus, ¹²mittent seniores civitatis eius et arripient eum de loco effugii tradentque in manu ultoris sanguinis, et morietur: ¹³non misereberis eius et auferes innoxium sanguinem de Israel, ut bene sit tibi. ¹⁴Non transferes terminos proximi tui, quos fixerunt priores in possessione tua, quam acceperis in terra, quam Dominus Deus tuus dabit tibi possidendam. ¹⁵Non stabit testis unus contra aliquem, quidquid illius peccatum vel facinus fuerit; sed in ore duorum aut trium testium stabit omne verbum. ¹⁶Si steterit testis mendax contra hominem accusans eum praevaricationis, ¹⁷stabunt ambo, quorum causa est, ante Dominum in conspectu sacerdotum et iudicum, qui fuerint in diebus illis. ¹⁸Cumque diligentissime perscrutantes iudices invenerint falsum testem dixisse contra

o. Or *the blood of the innocent*

to the dispute shall appear before the Lord, before the priests and the judges who are in office in those days; [18]the judges shall inquire diligently, and if the witness is a false witness and has accused his brother falsely, [19]then you shall do to him as he had meant to do to his brother; so you shall purge the evil from the midst of you. [20]And the rest shall hear, and fear, and shall never again commit any such evil among you. [21]Your eye shall not pity; Jn 7:51

The law of retaliation

it shall be life for life, eye for eye, tooth for tooth, hand for hand, foot for foot.

Ex 21:23–25
Lev 24:17–23
Mt 5:38

4. MORAL AND LEGAL RULES*

Laws of war

20 [1]"When you go forth to war against your enemies, and see horses and chariots and an army larger than your own, you shall not be afraid of them; for the Lord your God is with you, who brought you up out of the land of Egypt. [2]And when you draw near to the battle, the priest shall come forward and speak to the people, [3]and shall say to them, 'Hear, O Israel, you draw near this day to battle against your enemies: let not your heart faint; do not fear, or tremble, or be in dread of them; [4]for the Lord your God is he that goes with you, to fight for you against your ene-

Heb 12:3

---

*20:1–20. This set of laws about war (not found elsewhere in the Pentateuch) is typical of the humanitarian feelings which are such a feature of Deuteronomy. Although some of the ordinances given here can seem to us harsh and brutal (cf. 10–18), one needs to remember that they were a very considerable advance for their time; cf. what the prophets have to say in criticism of the cruel practices of neighbouring peoples:

e.g. Amos 1:13; 2 Kings 8:12.

The reason for different criteria applying to Canaanites as distinct from other peoples in the country is that they represented a threat to the Israelites' faithfulness to Yahweh (cf. note on 2:23–37).

On Israelite marriage (v. 7) and its two phases (betrothal and bringing the betrothed woman to her husband's house) cf. the note on Mt 1:18.

fratrem suum mendacium, [19]reddent ei, sicut fratri suo facere cogitavit, et auferes malum de medio tui, [20]ut audientes ceteri timorem habeant et nequaquam ultra talia audeant facere in medio tui. [21]Non misereberis eius, sed animam pro anima, oculum pro oculo, dentem pro dente, manum pro manu, pedem pro pede exiges. [1]Si exieris ad bellum contra hostes tuos et videris equitatus et currus et maiorem, quam tu habes, adversarii exercitus multitudinem, non timebis eos, quia Dominus Deus tuus tecum est, qui eduxit te de terra Aegypti. [2]Appropinquante autem iam proelio, stabit sacerdos ante aciem et sic loquetur ad populum: [3]'Audi, Israel: Vos hodie contra inimicos vestros pugnam committitis; non pertimescat cor vestrum, nolite metuere, nolite cedere nec formidetis eos, [4]quia Dominus Deus vester incedit vobis-

1 Mac 3:56
1 Cor 9:7 mies, to give you the victory.' ⁵Then the officers shall speak to the people, saying, 'What man is there that has built a new house and has not dedicated it? Let him go back to his house, lest he die in the battle and another man dedicate it. ⁶And what man is there that has planted a vineyard and has not enjoyed its fruit? Let him go back to his house, lest he die in the battle and another man Deut 24:5 enjoy its fruit. ⁷And what man is there that has betrothed a wife and has not taken her? Let him go back to his house, lest he die in the battle and another man take her.' ⁸And the officers shall speak further to the people, and say, 'What man is there that is fearful and fainthearted? Let him go back to his house, lest the heart of his fellows melt as his heart.' ⁹And when the officers have made an end of speaking to the people, then commanders shall be appointed at the head of the people.

¹⁰"When you draw near to a city to fight against it, offer terms of peace to it. ¹¹And if its answer to you is peace and it opens to you, then all the people who are found in it shall do forced labor for you and shall serve you. ¹²But if it makes no peace with you, but makes war against you, then you shall besiege it; ¹³and when the Lᴏʀᴅ your God gives it into your hand you shall put all its males to the sword, ¹⁴but the women and the little ones, the cattle, and everything else in the city, all its spoil, you shall take as booty for yourselves; and you shall enjoy the spoil of your enemies, which the Lᴏʀᴅ your God has given you. ¹⁵Thus you shall do to all the cities which are very far from you, which are not cities of the nations here. ¹⁶But in the cities of these peoples that the Lᴏʀᴅ your God gives you for an inheritance, you shall save alive nothing that breathes, ¹⁷but you shall utterly destroy them, the Hittites

---

cum et pro vobis contra adversarios vestros dimicabit, ut eruat vos de periculo'. ⁵Praefecti quoque per singulas turmas, audiente exercitu, proclamabunt: 'Quis est homo, qui aedificavit domum novam et non dedicavit eam? Vadat et revertatur in domum suam, ne forte moriatur in bello, et alius dedicet illam. ⁶Quis est homo, qui plantavit vineam et necdum vindemiavit eam? Vadat et revertatur in domum suam, ne forte moriatur in bello, et alius homo vindemiet illam. ⁷Quis est homo, qui despondit uxorem et non accepit eam? Vadat et revertatur in domum suam, ne forte moriatur in bello, et alius homo accipiat eam'. ⁸His dictis, addent reliqua et loquentur ad populum: 'Quis est homo formidulosus et corde pavido? Vadat et revertatur in domum suam, ne pavere faciat corda fratrum suorum, sicut ipse timore perterritus est'. ⁹Cumque praefecti finem loquendi ad populum fecerint, constituantur duces exercitus in capite populi. ¹⁰Si quando accesseris ad expugnandam civitatem, offeres ei primum pacem; ¹¹si receperit et aperuerit tibi portas, cunctus populus, qui in ea est, serviet tibi sub tributo. ¹²Sin autem foedus inire noluerit et coeperit contra te bellum, oppugnabis eam. ¹³Cumque tradiderit Dominus Deus tuus illam in manu tua, percuties omne, quod in ea generis masculini est, in ore gladii ¹⁴absque mulieribus et infantibus, iumentis et ceteris, quae in civitate sunt. Omnem praedam hanc diripies tibi et comedes de spoliis hostium tuorum, quae Dominus Deus tuus dederit tibi. ¹⁵Sic facies cunctis civitatibus, quae a te procul valde sunt et non sunt de gentium istarum urbibus, quas in possessionem accepturus es. ¹⁶De his autem civitatibus, quae dabuntur tibi, nullum omnino permittes vivere, ¹⁷sed interficies in ore gladii, Hetthaeum videlicet et Amorraeum et Chananaeum, Pherezaeum et Hevaeum

and the Amorites, the Canaanites and the Perizzites, the Hivites and the Jebusites, as the LORD your God has commanded; [18]that they may not teach you to do according to all their abominable practices which they have done in the service of their gods, and so to sin against the LORD your God.

[19]"When you besiege a city for a long time, making war against it in order to take it, you shall not destroy its trees by wielding an axe against them; for you may eat of them, but you shall not cut them down. Are the trees in the field men that they should be besieged by you? [20]Only the trees which you know are not trees for food you may destroy and cut down that you may build siege works against the city that makes war with you, until it falls.

Atonement for murder by a person unknown

21 [1]"If in the land which the LORD your God gives you to possess, any one is found slain, lying in the open country, and it is not known who killed him, [2]then your elders and your judges shall come forth, and they shall measure the distance to the cities which are around him that is slain; [3]and the elders of the city which is nearest to the slain man shall take a heifer which has never been worked and which has not pulled in the yoke. [4]And

---

21:1–23. The main part of this chapter consists of laws to do with the family (vv. 10–21); other laws on the same subject will be found in later chapters. The first section (vv. 10–14), which perhaps has more to do with the content of chapter 20 (on the laws of war), refers to marriage with a woman who is a prisoner of war—presumably not a Canaanite, since marriage to Canaanites was strictly forbidden (cf. 7:16). The ceremonies described in vv. 12–13 seem to have to do with her leaving her nation of origin

and becoming apart of Israel. Once again the humanitarian spirit of Deuteronomy can be seen: cf. the warning against possible abuses on the part of victors (v. 14).

The purification prescribed for a dead person killed by an unknown hand (vv. 1–9) derives from the fact that bloodshed cries for vengeance (cf. Gen 4:10); since it cannot be expiated by the blood of the culprit, the blood of a heifer is substituted, to cleanse Israel of the crime in the eyes of God. This law too is in line with the idea that both the chosen people and

---

et Iebusaeum, sicut praecepit tibi Dominus Deus tuus, [18]ne forte doceant vos facere cunctas abominationes, quas ipsi operati sunt diis suis, et peccetis in Dominum Deum vestrum. [19]Quando obsederis civitatem multo tempore et munitionibus circumdederis, ut expugnes eam, non immittes securim in arbores eius, de quibus vesci potes, nec succidas eas. Numquid homo est arbor campi, ut eam obsideas? [20]Si qua autem ligna non sunt pomifera, succide illa et exstrue machinas, donec capias civitatem, quae contra te dimicat. [1]Quando inventum fuerit in terra, quam Dominus Deus tuus daturus est tibi, hominis cadaver occisi, et ignoratur caedis reus, [2]egredientur maiores natu et iudices tui et metientur a loco cadaveris singularum per circuitum spatia civitatum [3]et, quam viciniorem ceteris esse perspexerint, seniores civitatis illius tollent vitulam de armento, quae non traxit iugum, nec terram scidit vomere, [4]et

the elders of that city shall bring the heifer down to a valley with running water, which is neither plowed nor sown, and shall break _{Deut 17:8–12} the heifer's neck there in the valley. ⁵And the priests the sons of Levi shall come forward, for the LORD your God has chosen them to minister to him and to bless in the name of the LORD, and by _{Mt 27:24} their word every dispute and every assault shall be settled. ⁶And all the elders of that city nearest to the slain man shall wash their hands over the heifer whose neck was broken in the valley; ⁷and they shall testify, 'Our hands did not shed this blood, neither did our eyes see it shed. ⁸Forgive, O LORD, thy people Israel, whom thou hast redeemed, and set not the guilt of innocent blood in the midst of thy people Israel; but let the guilt of blood be forgiven them.' ⁹So you shall purge the guilt of innocent blood from your midst, when you do what is right in the sight of the LORD.

Women taken in war

¹⁰"When you go forth to war against your enemies, and the LORD your God gives them into your hands, and you take them captive, ¹¹and see among the captives a beautiful woman, and you have desire for her and would take her for yourself as wife, ¹²then you shall bring her home to your house, and she shall shave her head and pare her nails. ¹³And she shall put off her captive's garb, and shall remain in your house and bewail her father and her mother a

---

their land must not lose their sacredness, which derives from the fact that they belong to God in a special way. Hence the need for cleansing whenever any grave sin is committed.

The law forbidding the body of a criminal to be left hanging overnight (vv. 22–23) was probably in the mind of the Jewish authorities when they asked Pilate to have Jesus' legs broken when he was on the cross, to make him die more quickly so that he could be buried before nightfall (Jn 19:31); or they may have feared that the city would be at the risk of legal uncleanness (which might have prevented the celebration of the Passover). St Paul linked this passage to our Lord on the cross (cf. Gal 3:13–14): by taking upon himself the curse of the Law, which rightfully was mankind's, he won for us salvation.

---

ducent eam ad torrentem perennem, ubi numquam aratum est nec seminatum, et caedent apud eum cervices vitulae; ⁵accedentque sacerdotes filii Levi, quos elegerit Dominus Deus tuus, ut ministrent ei et benedicant in nomine eius, et ad verbum eorum omnis causa et omnis percussio iudicetur. ⁶Et omnes maiores natu civitatis illius, qui prope interfectum sunt, lavabunt manus suas super vitulam, quae apud torrentem percussa est, ⁷et dicent: 'Manus nostrae non effuderunt hunc sanguinem, nec oculi nostri viderunt; ⁸propitius esto populo tuo Israel, quem redemisti, Domine, et non reputes sanguinem innocentem in medio populi tui Israel'. Et auferetur ab eis reatus sanguinis. ⁹Tu autem removebis innocentem cruorem, cum feceris, quod rectum est in oculis Domini. ¹⁰Si egressus fueris ad pugnam contra inimicos tuos, et tradiderit eos Dominus Deus tuus in manu tua, captivosque duxeris ¹¹et videris in numero captivorum mulierem pulchram et adamaveris eam voluerisque habere uxorem, ¹²introduces eam in domum tuam. Quae radet caesariem et circumcidet ungues ¹³et deponet vestem captivitatis

full month; after that you may go in to her, and be her husband, and she shall be your wife. [14]Then, if you have no delight in her, you shall let her go where she will; but you shall not sell her for money, you shall not treat her as a slave, since you have humiliated her.

Birthright

Gen 29:30–31

[15]"If a man has two wives, the one loved and the other disliked, and they have borne him children, both the loved and the disliked, and if the first-born son is hers that is disliked, [16]then on the day when he assigns his possessions as an inheritance to his sons, he may not treat the son of the loved as the first-born in preference to the son of the disliked, who is the first-born, [17]but he shall acknowledge the first-born, the son of the disliked, by giving him a double portion of all that he has, for he is the first issue of his strength; the right of the first-born is his.

The rebellious son

[18]"If a man has a stubborn and rebellious son, who will not obey   Mt 5:22
the voice of his father or the voice of his mother, and, though they chastise him, will not give heed to them, [19]then his father and his mother shall take hold of him and bring him out to the elders of his city at the gate of the place where he lives, [20]and they shall say   Mt 11:19
to the elders of his city, 'This our son is stubborn and rebellious, he will not obey our voice; he is a glutton and a drunkard.' [21]Then all the men of the city shall stone him to death with stones; so you shall purge the evil from your midst; and all Israel shall hear, and fear.

Mt 27:58
Mk 15:42
The body of an executed person   Lk 23:53

[22]"And if a man has committed a crime punishable by death and   Acts 5:30
he is put to death, and you hang him on a tree, [23]his body shall

---

sedensque in domo tua flebit patrem et matrem suam uno mense; et postea intrabis ad eam sociaberisque illi, et erit uxor tua. [14]Sin autem postea non sederit animo tuo, dimittes eam liberam; nec vendere poteris pecunia nec opprimere per potentiam, quia humiliasti eam. [15]Si habuerit homo uxores duas, unam dilectam et alteram odiosam, genuerintque ei liberos, et fuerit filius odiosae primogenitus, [16]volueritque substantiam inter filios suos dividere, non poterit filium dilectae facere primogenitum et praeferre filio odiosae, [17]sed filium odiosae agnoscet primogenitum dabitque ei de cunctis, quae habuerit, duplicia; iste est enim principium roboris eius, et huic debentur primogenita. [18]Si genuerit homo filium contumacem et protervum, qui non audiat patris aut matris imperium et coercitus oboedire contempserit, [19]apprehendent eum et ducent ad seniores civitatis suae et ad portam iudicii [20]dicentque ad eos: 'Filius noster iste protervus et contumax est: monita nostra audire contemnit, comissationibus vacat et luxuriae atque conviviis potatorum'. [21]Lapidibus eum obruent viri civitatis, et morietur, ut auferatis malum de medio vestri, et universus Israel audiens pertimescat. [22]Quando peccaverit homo, quod morte plectendum est, et occisum appenderis in patibulo, [23]non permanebit cadaver eius in ligno;

Jn 19:31
Gal 3:13
not remain all night upon the tree, but you shall bury him the same day, for a hanged man is accursed by God; you shall not defile your land which the LORD your God gives you for an inheritance.

Ex 23:4-5 **Various rulings**

22 ¹"You shall not see your brother's ox or his sheep go astray, and withhold your help[p] from them; you shall take them back to your brother. ²And if he is not near you, or if you do not know him, you shall bring it home to your house, and it shall be with you until your brother seeks it; then you shall restore it to him. ³And so you shall do with his ass; so you shall do with his garment; so you shall do with any lost thing of your brother's, which he loses and you find; you may not withhold your help.[p]

Lk 14:5 ⁴You shall not see your brother's ass or his ox fallen down by the way, and withhold your help[p] from them; you shall help him to lift them up again.

⁵"A woman shall not wear anything that pertains to a man, nor shall a man put on a woman's garment; for whoever does these things is an abomination to the LORD your God.

22:1–12. In some of these ordinances on miscellaneous subjects, the aim is clearly humanitarian and in line with common sense (vv. 1–14, 6–80; the reason behind others is more difficult to see.

The prohibition in v. 5, as well as being for reasons of modesty, may have had to do with pagan cults (or even sacred prostitution: cf. 23:18–19), which involved these practices. Various explanations have been put forward for the prohibitions on mixing and mingling (vv. 9–11); maybe the background idea is to be found in the first chapter of Genesis,

where God imposes an order on things by means of separations and distinctions: he separates light from darkness, land from sea, etc. Thus mixing can often imply the destruction of created order, causing confusion. Other scholars think it may be connected with pagan cults or superstitions; still others suggest that it may be a symbolic way of showing the aversion the Israelites had to marriages with foreign women (cf. 7:1–6). The tassels on cloaks (v. 12) were meant to remind people to be faithful to the commandments of Yahweh (cf. Num 15:37–41).

---

sed in eadem die sepelietur, quia maledictus a Deo est, qui pendet in ligno; et nequaquam contaminabis terram tuam, quam Dominus Deus tuus dederit tibi in possessionem. ¹Non videbis bovem fratris tui aut ovem errantem et praeteribis, sed reduces fratri tuo; ²Si autem non est prope frater tuus nec nosti eum, duces in domum tuam, et erunt apud te quamdiu quaerat ea frater tuus et recipiat. ³Similiter facies de asino et de vestimento et de omni re fratris tui, quae perierit: si inveneris eam, ne subtrahas te. ⁴Si videris asinum fratris tui aut bovem cecidisse in via, non subtrahes te, sed sublevabis cum eo. ⁵Non induetur mulier veste virili, nec vir utetur veste feminea: abominabilis enim apud Dominum Deum tuum est omnis, qui facit haec. ⁶Si ambulans per viam, in arbore vel in terra nidum avis inveneris et

p. Heb *hide yourself*

⁶"If you chance to come upon a bird's nest, in any tree or on the ground, with young ones or eggs and the mother sitting upon the young or upon the eggs, you shall not take the mother with the young; ⁷you shall let the mother go, but the young you may take to yourself; that it may go well with you, and that you may live long.

⁸"When you build a new house, you shall make a parapet for your roof, that you may not bring the guilt of blood upon your house, if any one fall from it.

⁹"You shall not sow your vineyard with two kinds of seed, lest the whole yield be forfeited to the sanctuary,q the crop which you have sown and the yield of the vineyard. ¹⁰You shall not plow with an ox and an ass together. ¹¹You shall not wear a mingled stuff, wool and linen together.

¹²"You shall make yourself tassels on the four corners of your cloak with which you cover yourself.

Lev 19:19

Num 15:37–41
Mt 9:20

Laws about marriage

¹³"If any man takes a wife, and goes in to her, and then spurns her, ¹⁴and charges her with shameful conduct, and brings an evil name

22:13–30. Various offences against marriage are severely condemned here. In the first offence (vv. 13–21) one cannot help noticing that the sanction applied to a woman (stoning) is different from that for a man: he is subject to a lashing (possibly thirty-nine lashes: cf. 25:3) and a fine; in line with what was said about false witnesses (cf. 19:18–19), one would have expected a lying husband to be punishable by stoning. The different treatment may be due to differences of status in that society, where a husband, the head of a family clan, could have had a number of wives and where a wife's position was clearly inferior. These laws designed to protect aggrieved wives (cf. also vv. 28–29) were an advance in defence of women's rights compared with other ancient civilizations. The New Testament will restore the natural and original order of things: "There is [. . .] neither male nor female; for you are all one in Christ Jesus" (Gal 3:28).

A "betrothed" woman (v. 23), even though she was not yet living with her husband (that is, before her "conduction", *nissuim*, to her husband's house: cf. the

matrem pullis vel ovis desuper incubantem, non sumes eam de filiis, ⁷sed abire patieris matrem tenens filios, ut bene sit tibi, et longo vivas tempore. ⁸Cum aedificaveris domum novam, facies murum tecto tuo per circuitum, ne adducas sanguinem super domum tuam et sis reus, labente aliquo in praeceps ruente. ⁹Non seres vineam tuam altero semine, ne et sementis, quam sevisti, et quae nascuntur ex vinea, pariter sanctificentur. ¹⁰Non arabis in bove simul et asino. ¹¹Non indueris vestimento, quod ex lana linoque contextum est. ¹²Funiculos facies per quattuor angulos pallii tui, quo operieris. ¹³Si duxerit vir uxorem et intraverit ad eam et postea odio habuerit eam ¹⁴imputaveritque ei obiciens ei nomen pessimum et dixerit: 'Uxorem hanc accepi et ingressus ad eam non inveni virginem', ¹⁵tollent pater et mater

q. Heb *become holy*

upon her, saying, 'I took this woman, and when I came near her, I did not find in her the tokens of virginity,' [15]then the father of the young woman and her mother shall take and bring out the tokens of her virginity to the elders of the city in the gate; [16]and the father of the young woman shall say to the elders, 'I gave my daughter to this man to wife, and he spurns her; [17]and lo, he has made shameful charges against her, saying, "I did not find in your daughter the tokens of virginity." And yet these are the tokens of my daughter's virginity.' And they shall spread the garment before the elders of the city. [18]Then the elders of that city shall take the man and whip him; [19]and they shall fine him a hundred shekels of silver, and give them to the father of the young woman, because he has brought an evil name upon a virgin of Israel; and she shall be his wife; he may not put her away all his days. [20]But if the thing is true, that the tokens of virginity were not found in the young woman, [21]then they shall bring out the young woman to the door of her father's house, and the men of her city shall stone her to death with stones, because she has wrought folly in Israel by playing the harlot in her father's house; so you shall purge the evil from the midst of you.

Ex 20:14
Lev 20:10
Deut 5:18
Jn 8:5

[22]"If a man is found lying with the wife of another man, both of them shall die, the man who lay with the woman, and the woman; so you shall purge the evil from Israel.

[23]"If there is a betrothed virgin, and a man meets her in the city and lies with her, [24]then you shall bring them both out to the gate of that city, and you shall stone them to death with stones, the young woman because she did not cry for help though she was in

---

note on Deut 20:1–20) already had the same obligations to faithfulness as a wife. That is why her sin is seen as adultery and is punishable by stoning (vv. 23–24).

All these precepts show the high regard in which virginity was held in ancient Israel.

eius et ferent secum signa virginitatis eius ad seniores urbis, qui in porta sunt, [16]et dicet pater: 'Filiam meam dedi huic uxorem, quam, quia odit, [17]imponit ei nomen pessimum, ut dicat: Non inveni filiam tuam virginem; et ecce haec sunt signa virginitatis filiae meae'. Expandent vestimentum coram senioribus civitatis. [18]Apprehendentque senes urbis illius virum et verberabunt illum [19]condemnantes insuper centum siclis argenti, quos dabunt patri puellae, quoniam diffamavit nomen pessimum super virginem Israel; habebitque eam uxorem et non poterit dimittere eam omnibus diebus vitae suae. [20]Quod si verum est, quod obicit, et non est in puella inventa virginitas, [21]educent eam ad fores domus patris sui et lapidibus obruent viri civitatis eius, et morietur, quoniam fecit nefas in Israel, ut forni-caretur in domo patris sui; et auferes malum de medio tui. [22]Si inventus fuerit vir dormiens cum uxore alterius, uterque morietur, id est adulter et adultera; et auferes malum de Israel. [23]Si puellam virginem desponsatam viro invenerit aliquis in civitate et concubuerit cum illa, [24]educetis utrumque ad portam civitatis illius et lapidibus obruetis, et morientur: puella quia non clamavit, cum esset in civitate, vir quia humiliavit uxorem proximi sui; et auferes malum de medio tui. [25]Sin autem in agro reppererit vir

the city, and the man because he violated his neighbor's wife; so you shall purge the evil from the midst of you.

²⁵"But if in the open country a man meets a young woman who is betrothed, and the man seizes her and lies with her, then only the man who lay with her shall die. ²⁶But to the young woman you shall do nothing; in the young woman there is no offence punishable by death, for this case is like that of a man attacking and murdering his neighbour; ²⁷because he came upon her in the open country, and though the betrothed young woman cried for help there was no one to rescue her.

²⁸"If a man meets a virgin who is not betrothed, and seizes her and lies with her, and they are found, ²⁹then the man who lay with her shall give to the father of the young woman fifty shekels of silver, and she shall be his wife, because he has violated her; he may not put her away all his days.

³⁰ʳ"A man shall not take his father's wife, nor shall he uncover her who is his father's.ˢ

Acts 8:27

Exclusion from public worship

23 ¹"He whose testicles are crushed or whose male member is cut off shall not enter the assembly of the LORD.

Is 56:3–5
Neh 13:1–3
Gal 5:12

23:1–14. "Assembly of the Lord": see the note on 9:10.

The exclusion of eunuchs from the chosen people (v. 1) derived, according to some scholars, from the fact that they were incompatible with the natural order of things willed by God and were unable to contribute to the growth of Israel. Others think that this rule was a way of showing rejection of certain pagan practices: mutilation of this kind was practised in some pagan cults and also in Eastern courts in connexion with harems (practices which some kings of Israel would imitate: cf., e.g., 1 Kings 22:9; 2 Kings 8:6). The prophet Isaiah will revoke this ban, saying that the messianic kingdom is open to all (Is 56:3–5).

Although none of these peoples (vv. 3–8) had come to Israel's aid during the Exodus (cf. Deut 2:1–19 and the notes on same), the Idumeans were, however, descendants of Esau, Jacob's brother; and the Egyptians had accommodated the Israelites when they were at risk from famine during Jacob's last years.

Once again there is a reminder of Yahweh's special presence in the midst

---

puellam, quae desponsata est, et apprehendens concubuerit cum illa, ipse morietur solus; ²⁶puella nihil patietur nec est rea mortis, quoniam sicut vir consurgit contra fratrem suum et occidit eum, ita et puella perpessa est: ²⁷sola erat in agro, clamavit puella desponsata, et nullus affuit, qui liberaret eam. ²⁸Si invenerit vir puellam virginem, quae non habet sponsum, et apprehendens concubuerit cum ea, et res ad iudicium venerit, ²⁹dabit, qui dormivit cum ea, patri puellae quinquaginta siclos argenti et habebit eam uxorem, quia humiliavit illam: non poterit dimittere eam cunctis diebus vitae suae. ¹Non accipiet

r. Ch 23:1 in Heb [and New Vulgate]   **s.** Heb *uncover his father's skirt*

Mt 5:43

Num
22:2–24:25

Pet 2:15

²"No bastard shall enter the assembly of the L<small>ORD</small>; even to the tenth generation none of his descendants shall enter the assembly of the L<small>ORD</small>. ³"No Ammonite or Moabite shall enter the assembly of the L<small>ORD</small>; even to the tenth generation none belonging to them shall enter the assembly of the L<small>ORD</small> for ever; ⁴because they did not meet you with bread and with water on the way, when you came forth out of Egypt, and because they hired against you Balaam the son of Beor from Pethor of Mesopotamia, to curse you. ⁵Nevertheless the L<small>ORD</small> your God would not hearken to Balaam; but the L<small>ORD</small> your God turned the curse into a blessing for you, because the L<small>ORD</small> your God loved you. ⁶You shall not seek their peace or their prosperity all your days forever.

Mt 5:43

⁷"You shall not abhor an Edomite, for he is your brother; you shall not abhor an Egyptian, because you were a sojourner in his land. ⁸The children of the third generation that are born to them may enter the assembly of the L<small>ORD</small>.

Num 5:1–4 **The camp and legal purity**

⁹"When you go forth against your enemies and are in camp, then you shall keep yourself from every evil thing.

¹⁰"If there is among you any man who is not clean by reason of what chances to him by night, then he shall go outside the camp, he shall not come within the camp; ¹¹but when evening comes on,

---

of his people (v. 14) and various things are pointed out which, without being sinful, are inappropriate, given the seemliness and respect his presence deserves (vv. 9–13). St Cyril of Alexandria explained that Christ, too, "dwells and walks among us, and when he sees something indecent and unseemly he moves away. [. . .] But if he finds us clean and

washed, and free from unclean affections, then he will quickly make his abode and will deliver us from the hand of enemies" (*Glaphyra in Deuteronomium,* 23, 2–15).

23:4–6. But more specifically it was the king of Moab who hired Balaam. Cf. Num 22:2—24:25.

---

homo uxorem patris sui nec revelabit operimentum eius. ²Non intrabit eunuchus, attritis vel amputatis testiculis et absciso veretro, ecclesiam Domini. ³Non ingredietur mamzer in ecclesiam Domini neque decima generatione. ⁴Ammonites et Moabites etiam in decima generatione non intrabunt ecclesiam Domini in aeternum, ⁵quia noluerunt vobis occurrere cum pane et aqua in via, quando egressi estis de Aegypto, et quia conduxerunt contra te Balaam filium Beor de Phethor in Aramnaharaim, ut malediceret tibi; ⁶et noluit Dominus Deus tuus audire Balaam vertitque tibi maledictionem eius in benedictionem, eo quod diligeret te. ⁷Non facies cum eis pacem, nec quaeres eis bona cunctis diebus vitae tuae in sempiternum. ⁸Non abominaberis Idumaeum, quia frater tuus est, nec Aegyptium, quia advena fuisti in terra eius: ⁹qui nati fuerint ex eis tertia generatione, intrabunt ecclesiam Domini. ¹⁰Quando egressus fueris adversus hostes tuos in pugnam, custodies te ab omni re mala. ¹¹'Si fuerit

he shall bathe himself in water, and when the sun is down, he may come within the camp. [12]"You shall have a place outside the camp and you shall go out to it; [13]and you shall have a stick with your weapons; and when you sit down outside, you shall dig a hole with it, and turn back and cover up your excrement. [14]Because the LORD your God walks in the midst of your camp, to save you and to give up your enemies before you, therefore your camp must be holy, that he may not see anything indecent among you, and turn away from you.

Other rulings

[15]"You shall not give up to his master a slave who has escaped from his master to you; [16]he shall dwell with you, in your midst, in the place which he shall choose within one of your towns, where it pleases him best; you shall not oppress him.

[17]"There shall be no cult prostitute of the daughters of Israel, Mt 27:6 neither shall there be a cult prostitute of the sons of Israel. [18]You shall not bring the hire of a harlot, or the wages of a dog,[s] into the house of the LORD your God in payment for any vow; for both of these are an abomination to the LORD your God.

[19]"You shall not lend upon interest to your brother, interest on money, interest on victuals, interest on anything that is lent for interest. [20]To a foreigner you may lend upon interest, but to your Acts 5:4

23:17–18. Sacred prostitution was an institution that developed in some places connected with pagan cult in the ancient East; it was thought that this practice would bring the gods to bestow blessings and fertility; all or part of the fees or gain obtained from this prostitution was spent on the cult of the particular god(s). This aberration was not confined to some peoples of the East; it was also to be found, for example, in Corinth and (in the 1st century AD) in connexion with the cult of Aphrodite.

The Bible's rejection of such practices is based on the fact that it is from Yahweh that life and death come, and fertility and barrenness—whether of human beings or other creatures. The

---

apud te homo, qui nocturno pollutus sit somnio, egredietur extra castra et non revertetur, [12]priusquam ad vesperam lavetur aqua; et ad solis occasum regredietur in castra. [13]Habebis locum extra castra, ad quem egrediaris ad requisita naturae [14]gerens paxillum in balteo; cumque sederis foris, fodies foveam et egesta humo operies. [15]Dominus enim Deus tuus ambulat in medio castrorum tuorum, ut eruat te et tradat tibi inimicos tuos; sint castra tua sancta, et nihil in eis videat foeditatis nec derelinquat te. [16]Non trades servum domino suo, qui ad te confugerit: [17]habitabit tecum in medio tui in loco, quem elegerit in una urbium tuarum, quae placuerit ei, nec contristes eum. [18]Non erit prostibulum sacrum de filiabus Israel, nec scortator sacer de filiis Israel. [19]Non offeres mercedem prostibuli nec pretium canis in domo

t. Or *sodomite*

brother you shall not lend upon interest; that the LORD your God may bless you in all that you undertake in the land which you are entering to take possession of it.

Mt 5:33
Jas 4:17 [21]"When you make a vow to the LORD your God, you shall not be slack to pay it; for the LORD your God will surely require it of you, and it would be sin in you. [22]But if you refrain from vowing, it shall be no sin in you. [23]You shall be careful to perform what has passed your lips, for you have voluntarily vowed to the LORD your God what you have promised with your mouth.

[24]"When you go into your neighbour's vineyard, you may eat your fill of grapes, as many as you wish, but you shall not put any Mt 12:1
Mk 2:33
Lk 6:1 in your vessel. [25]When you go into your neighbour's standing grain, you may pluck the ears with your hand, but you shall not put a sickle to your neighbour's standing grain.

The bill of divorce

Mt 5:31; 19:7
Mk 10:4 **24** [1]*"When a man takes a wife and marries her, if then she finds no favour in his eyes because he has found some indecency in her, and he writes her a bill of divorce and puts it in her

---

description of a male sacred prostitute as a "dog" shows the writer's sense of horror.

In spite of these laws, aberrations of this kind did find their way into Israel and even into Jerusalem on occasions (cf., e.g., 1 Kings 14:24; 2 Kings 23:7). Canaanite agricultural fertility cults may have been responsible for this: the Israelites learned from Canaanite agricultural methods much superior to their own (they had originally been a pastoral people); but the Israelites were not always able to distinguish agricultural methods from the religious rites associated with them.

23:25. In the Gospel we will see the apostles availing themselves of this right to use grains of someone else's wheat to assuage their hunger.

24:1–4. The writing of a bill of divorce or repudiation was a very ancient practice; it was to be found among other ancient peoples of the East, but there were notable differences from one culture to another. Given the temporary nature of some precepts of the Old Law, one should not be surprised to find morally imperfect social customs reflected in these laws, particularly when

---

Domini Dei tui, quidquid illud est, quod voveris, quia abominatio est utrumque apud Dominum Deum tuum. [20]Non fenerabis fratri tuo ad usuram pecuniam, nec alimenta nec quamlibet aliam rem, [21]sed alieno fenerabis. Fratri autem tuo absque usura id, quo indiget, commodabis, ut benedicat tibi Dominus Deus tuus in omni opere tuo in terra, ad quam ingredieris possidendam. [22]Cum voveris votum Domino Deo tuo, non tardabis reddere; quia requiret illud Dominus Deus tuus a te, et reputabitur tibi in peccatum. [23]Si nolueris polliceri, absque peccato eris; [24]quod autem egressum est de labiis tuis, observabis et facies, sicut promisisti Domino Deo tuo: propria voluntate et ore tuo locutus es. [25]Ingressus vineam proximi tui comede uvas, quantum tibi placuerit; in sporta autem ne efferas tecum. [26]Si intraveris in segetem amici tui, franges spicas manu; falce autem non metes. [1]Si acceperit homo uxorem et habuerit

hand and sends her out of his house, and she departs out of his house, [2]and if she goes and becomes another man's wife, [3]and the latter husband dislikes her and writes her a bill of divorce and puts it in her hand and sends her out of his house, or if the latter husband dies, who took her to be his wife, [4]then her former husband, who sent her away, may not take her again to be his wife, after she has been defiled; for that is an abomination before the LORD, and you shall not bring guilt upon the land which the LORD your God gives you for an inheritance.

---

they are set alongside New Testament teaching. Although this passage does not *prescribe* divorce via a bill of divorce but only *permits* it, that permission represents a compromise with social customs and the historical context in which Israel found itself at that time. Whatever translation is used for the first two verses, Deuteronomy 24:1–4 allows divorce on more restrictive conditions than those which applied in neighbouring cultures.

A bill of repudiation imposed on the husband an impediment (unknown among the Arabs, for example) to the effect that he could not marry again a wife he had repudiated; maybe this measure, which prevented a woman being regarded as a mere commodity, would help reduce the incidence of repudiation. Also, in an early society such as Israel's it was not a little troublesome to have to write a public document such as a bill of divorce—so this was another reason why a man would not easily seek divorce. That having been said, it is very obvious that a woman had a lower status than a man: only the husband had a right to repudiate; it seems that in later times a wife could take the initiative in a divorce (cf. Mk 10:12).

Our Lord, who says that Moses allowed divorce "for your hardness of heart", re-establishes marriage's original indissolubility: "Have you not read that he who made them from the beginning made them male and female, and said, 'For this reason a man shall leave his father and mother and be joined to his wife, and the two shall become one'? What therefore God has joined together, let no man put asunder" (Mt 19:4–6). On the indissolubility of marriage, cf. Mt 19:1–9; Mk 10:1–12 and the notes on same.

It must be said that even in the Old Testament one finds a line of thought against the dissolution of marriage. Malachi 2:13–16 is the clearest and most forceful Old Testament passage to condemn divorce, on the grounds of the religious character of marriage: it is something which is similar to God's Covenant with Israel; and of course the main passage to show that God desires marriage to be stable is Genesis 2:24 ("and they become one flesh"). Here is the text from Malachi: "And this again you do. You cover the Lord's altar with tears, with weeping and groaning because he no longer regards the offering or accepts it with the favour of your hand. You ask, 'Why does he not [accept

eam, et non invenerit gratiam ante oculos eius propter aliquam foeditatem, et scripserit libellum repudii dederitque in manu illius et dimiserit eam de domo sua, [2]cumque egressa alterius uxor facta fuerit, [3]et ille quoque oderit eam dederitque ei libellum repudii et dimiserit de domo sua, vel mortuus fuerit, [4]non poterit prior maritus recipere eam in uxorem, quia polluta est; hoc esset abominatio coram Domino.

Humanitarian measures

Lk 14:20   ⁵"When a man is newly married, he shall not go out with the army or be charged with any business; he shall be free at home one year, to be happy with his wife whom he has taken.

⁶"No man shall take a mill or an upper millstone in pledge; for he would be taking a life in pledge.

Ex:21:16   ⁷"If a man is found stealing one of his brethren, the people of Israel, and if he treats him as a slave or sells him, then that thief shall die; so you shall purge the evil from the midst of you.

⁸"Take heed, in an attack of leprosy, to be very careful to do according to all that the Levitical priests shall direct you; as I commanded them, so you shall be careful to do. ⁹Remember what the LORD your God did to Miriam on the way as you came forth out of Egypt.

Num 12:1–5

¹⁰"When you make your neighbour a loan of any sort, you shall not go into his house to fetch his pledge. ¹¹You shall stand outside, and the man to whom you make the loan shall bring the pledge

---

it]?' Because the Lord was witness to the covenant between you and the wife of your youth, to whom you have been faithless, though she is your companion and your wife by covenant. Has not the one God made and sustained for us the spirit of life? And what does he desire? Godly offspring. So take heed to yourselves and let none be faithless to the wife of his youth. 'For I hate divorce', says the Lord the God of Israel [. . .]. So take heed to yourselves and do not be faithless'."

24:5—25:4. In these rules we can see, once again, the compassionate spirit of Deuteronomic law. The insistence on caring for strangers, orphans and widows

(vv. 17–21) makes this plainer still; even domestic animals claim attention (v. 25:4). Through this regulation about oxen, St John Chrysostom comments, "God had in mind a much greater and higher purpose; by means of it he wanted to accustom the Jews, a rough people, to have more refined feelings towards their fellow men" (*Homiliae in 1 Corinthios*, 21, 3).

On two occasions St Paul mentions the last rule given in this section, "You shall not muzzle an ox when it treads out the grain", applying it to the duty of the faithful to support the clergy (1 Cor 9:9; cf. 1 Tim 5:18).

The two-stone hand-mill (v. 6), worked by a wife (cf. Mt 24:41), was an

---

Ne peccare facias terram tuam, quam Dominus Deus tuus tradiderit tibi possidendam. ⁵Cum acceperit homo nuper uxorem, non procedet ad bellum, nec ei quippiam necessitatis iniungetur publicae, sed vacabit liber domui suae, ut uno anno laetetur cum uxore sua. ⁶Non accipies loco pignoris molam vel superiorem lapidem molarem, quia animam suam apposuit tibi. ⁷Si deprehensus fuerit homo rapiens unum de fratribus suis de filiis Israel et, vendito eo, accipiens pretium, interficietur; et auferes malum de medio tui. ⁸Observa diligenter, si incurras plagam leprae, quaecumque docuerint vos sacerdotes levitici generis; quod praecepi eis, implete sollicite. ⁹Memento, quae fecerit Dominus Deus tuus Mariae in via, cum egrederemini de Aegypto. ¹⁰Cum mutuam dabis proximo tuo rem aliquam, non ingredieris domum eius, ut pignus auferas, ¹¹sed stabis foris, et ille tibi pignus proferet, quod habuerit. ¹²Sin autem

out to you. [12]And if he is a poor man, you shall not sleep in his pledge; [13]when the sun goes down, you shall restore to him the pledge that he may sleep in his cloak and bless you; and it shall be righteousness to you before the LORD your God.

[14]"You shall not oppress a hired servant who is poor and needy, whether he is one of your brethren or one of the sojourners who are in your land within your towns; [15]you shall give him his hire on the day he earns it, before the sun goes down (for he is poor, and sets his heart upon it); lest he cry against you to the LORD, and it be sin in you.

Mt 20:8
Mk 10:19
Jas 5:4
Eph 4:26
Jas 4:17

[16]"The fathers shall not be put to death for the children, nor shall the children be put to death for the fathers; every man shall be put to death for his own sin.

Gen 18:24
2 Kings 14:6
Jer 31:29ff
Ezek 14:12

[17]"You shall not pervert the justice due to the sojourner or to the fatherless, or take a widow's garment in pledge; [18]but you shall remember that you were a slave in Egypt and the LORD your God redeemed you from there; therefore I command you to do this.

Jn 8:21

---

appliance no family could be without; the upper millstone was very small and it could be easily taken as a pledge or pawn—which meant that no milling could be done until it was redeemed.

Silent mills were a sign of death and desolation (cf. Jer 25:10; Rev 18:22).

God punished Miriam (v. 9), Moses' sister, with leprosy and temporary expulsion from the camp, because of her murmuring against Moses (cf. Num 12:1–15).

The explanation of day labourers and cheating them of their due (vv. 14–15) is one of the sins that cries to heaven for vengeance. Scripture puts it in the same category as homicide (Gen 4:10), sodomy (Gen 18:20–21) and oppression of widows and children (Ex 22:21–23).

The prohibition on punishing one member of a family for the sins of another (v. 16) might seem to contradict what was said in 5:9–10: cf. the note on that passage; moreover it should be borne in mind that what is being spoken of here is human justice, whereas there divine justice was involved. The prophets (especially Ezekiel, at chapter 18) will insist on personal responsibility before God—and the corresponding retribution, also personal.

As regards punishment by the lash (25:1–3), later rabbinical tradition specified that the maximum number of stripes was thirty-nine, to ensure that the number of forty was not exceeded. "Five times I have received at the hands of the Jews the forty lashes less one" (2 Cor 11:24).

---

pauper est, non pernoctabit apud te pignus, [13]sed statim reddes ei ad solis occasum, ut dormiens in vestimento suo benedicat tibi, et habeas iustitiam coram Domino Deo tuo. [14]Non negabis mercedem indigentis et pauperis ex fratribus tuis sive advenis, qui tecum morantur in terra intra portas tuas, [15]sed eadem die reddes ei pretium laboris sui ante solis occasum, quia pauper est, et illud desiderat anima sua; ne clamet contra te ad Dominum, et reputetur tibi in peccatum. [16]Non occidentur patres pro filiis, nec filii pro patribus, sed unusquisque pro peccato suo morietur. [17]Non pervertes iudicium advenae et pupilli nec auferes pignoris loco viduae vestimentum. [18]Memento quod servieris in Aegypto, et eruerit te Dominus Deus tuus inde; idcirco praecipio tibi, ut facias hanc rem. [19]Quando messueris segetem in

Lev 19:9ff ¹⁹"When you reap your harvest in your field, and have forgotten a sheaf in the field, you shall not go back to get it; it shall be for the sojourner, the fatherless, and the widow; that the LORD your God may bless you in all the work of your hands. ²⁰When you beat your olive trees, you shall not go over the boughs again; it shall be for the sojourner, the fatherless, and the widow. ²¹When you gather the grapes of your vineyard, you shall not glean it afterward; it shall be for the sojourner, the fatherless, and the widow. ²²You shall remember that you were a slave in the land of Egypt; therefore I command you to do this.

25 ¹"If there is a dispute between men, and they come into court, and the judges decide between them, acquitting the innocent and condemning the guilty, ²then if the guilty man deserves to be beaten, the judge shall cause him to lie down and be beaten in his presence with a number of stripes in proportion 2 Cor 11:24 to his offense. ³Forty stripes may be given him, but not more; lest, if one should go onto beat him with more stripes than these, your brother be degraded in your sight.

1 Cor 9:9
1 Tim 5:18 ⁴"You shall not muzzle an ox when it treads out the grain.

Gen 38
Ruth 4 **The levirate law**

Mt 22:24
Mk 12:19
Lk 20:28 ⁵"If brothers dwell together, and one of them dies and has no son, the wife of the dead shall not be married outside the family to a

---

25:5–19. The levirate law (from Latin *levir*, brother-in-law) was practised among the Jews from patriarchal times onwards (cf. Gen 38), its purpose being to avoid any branch of the family becoming extinct—something that was regarded as a great disgrace (vv. 5–10). In keeping with this law, the first son of the new marriage was regarded as the son of the dead husband in the eyes of the law. Similar customs obtained in other Eastern peoples, such as the Assyrians and the Hittites. The gesture of handing over a sandal symbolized giving up one's rights over a piece of property (cf. Ruth 4:7); the way it is done here implied great humiliation for the brother-in-law.

---

agro tuo et oblitus manipulum reliqueris, non reverteris, ut tollas eum, sed advenam et pupillum et viduam auferre patieris, ut benedicat tibi Dominus Deus tuus in omni opere manuum tuarum. ²⁰Si fruges collegeris olivarum, quidquid remanserit in arboribus, non reverteris, ut colligas, sed relinques advenae, pupillo ac viduae. ²¹Si vindemiaveris vineam tuam, non colliges remanentes racemos, sed cedent in usus advenae, pupilli ac viduae. ²²Memento quod et tu servieris in Aegypto; et idcirco praecipio tibi, ut facias hanc rem. ¹Si fuerit causa inter aliquos, et interpellaverint iudices, quem iustum esse perspexerint, illi iustitiae palmam dabunt; quem impium, condemnabunt impietatis. ²Sin autem iudex eum, qui peccavit, dignum viderit plagis, prosternet et coram se faciet verberari; pro mensura peccati erit et plagarum modus, ³ita dumtaxat, ut quadragenarium numerum non excedant, ne ultra percussus plagis multis et foede laceratus ante oculos tuos abeat frater tuus. ⁴Non ligabis os bovis terentis in area fruges tuas. ⁵Quando habitaverint fratres simul, et unus ex eis absque filio mortuus fuerit, uxor defuncti

stranger; her husband's brother shall go in to her, and take her as his wife, and perform the duty of a husband's brother to her. [6]And the first son whom she bears shall succeed to the name of his brother who is dead, that his name may not be blotted out of Israel. [7]And if the man does not wish to take his brother's wife, then his brother's wife shall go up to the gate to the elders, and say, 'My husband's brother refuses to perpetuate his brother's name in Israel; he will not perform the duty of a husband's brother to me.' [8]Then the elders of his city shall call him, and speak to him: and if he persists, saying, 'I do not wish to take her,' [9]then his brother's Ruth 4:7 wife shall go up to him in the presence of the elders, and pull his sandal off his foot, and spit in his face; and she shall answer and say, 'So shall it be done to the man who does not build up his brother's house.' [10]And the name of his house[u] shall be called in Israel, The house of him that had his sandal pulled off.

Honesty and uprightness

[11]"When men fight with one another, and the wife of the one draws near to rescue her husband from the hand of him who is beating him, and puts out her hand and seizes him by the private parts, [12]then you shall cut off her hand; your eye shall have no pity.

[13]"You shall not have in your bag two kinds of weights, a large Lev 19:35–36 and a small. [14]You shall not have in your house two kinds of mea-

---

The cunning question the Sadducees put to our Lord in connexion with this law—the hypothetical case of a woman who married seven brothers in turn (Mt 22:23–33)—shows that it was still in force in our Lord's time, although we have no evidence as to the extent to which it was actually applied.

The reason for the special harshness to be dealt out to the Amalekites (vv. 17–19) was the reprehensible way they behaved towards the Israelites during the Exodus (Ex 17:8–16); desert customs required that the needy should be helped with the hospitality proverbial among desert peoples.

25:14–15. On the ephah, see the notes on Lev 5:7–13 and Ex 29:38–46.

---

non nubet foras alteri, sed accipiet eam frater eius uxorem et suscitabit semen fratris sui; [6]et primogenitum ex ea filium nomine illius appellabit, ut non deleatur nomen eius ex Israel. [7]Sin autem noluerit accipere uxorem fratris sui, quae ei lege debetur, perget mulier ad portam civitatis et interpellabit maiores natu dicetque: 'Non vult frater viri mei suscitare nomen fratris sui in Israel nec me in coniugium sumere'; [8]statimque accersiri eum facient et interrogabunt. Si responderit: 'Nolo eam uxorem accipere', [9]accedet mulier ad eum coram senioribus et tollet calceamentum de pede eius spuetque in faciem illius et dicet: 'Sic fit homini, qui non aedificat domum fratris sui'. [10]Et vocabitur nomen illius in Israel: 'Domus discalceati'. [11]Si habuerint inter se iurgium viri, et unus contra alterum rixari coeperit, volensque uxor alterius eruere virum suum de manu fortioris, miserit manum et apprehenderit verenda

u. Heb *its name*

sures, a large and a small. [15]A full and just weight you shall have, a full and just measure you shall have; that your days may be prolonged in the land which the LORD your God gives you. [16]For all who do such things, all who act dishonestly, are an abomination to the LORD your God.

Ex 17:8–16 **The Amalekites**

[17]"Remember what Amalek did to you on the way as you came out of Egypt, [18]how he attacked you on the way, when you were faint and weary, and cut off at your rear all who lagged behind you; and he did not fear God. [19]Therefore when the LORD your God has given you rest from all your enemies round about, in the land which the LORD your God gives you for an inheritance to possess, you shall blot out the remembrance of Amalek from under heaven; you shall not forget.

First fruits

26 [1]"When you come into the land which the LORD your God gives you for an inheritance, and have taken possession of it, and live in it, [2]you shall take some of the first of all the fruit of the ground, which you harvest from your land that the LORD your God gives you, and you shall put it in a basket, and you shall go

---

26:1–11. The Deuteronomic Code, which began by specifying that there should be only one sanctuary (cf. chap. 12), concludes by giving the prayers that were to be said in that sanctuary in connexion with the offering of the first fruits.

The offering of the first fruits was an appropriate way for Israel to express gratitude for the great deeds done by God, the *magnalia Dei*, the wonders he worked in

liberating the people from bondage and establishing them in the promised land.

The prayer that is said on this occasion (vv. 5–9) is a kind of historical-religious Creed, a very important one, which takes in all the main features of Old Testament faith. It is a summary of the history of Israel, centred on its deliverance from Egypt and settlement in the promised land. These two saving actions

---

eius, [12]abscides manum illius nec flecteris super eam ulla misericordia. [13]Non habebis in sacculo tuo diversa pondera maius et minus; [14]nec erit in domo tua ephi maius et minus. [15]Pondus habebis iustum et verum, et ephi iustum et verum erit tibi, ut multo vivas tempore super terram, quam Dominus Deus tuus dederit tibi. [16]Abominatur enim Dominus tuus eum, qui facit haec, et aversatur omnem iniustitiam. [17]Memento quae fecerit tibi Amalec in via, quando egrediebaris ex Aegypto; [18]quomodo occurrerit tibi et omnes extremos agminis tui, qui lassi residebant, ceciderit, quando tu eras fame et labore confectus, et non timuerit Deum. [19]Cum ergo Dominus Deus tuus dederit tibi requiem a cunctis per circuitum inimicis tuis in terra, quam tibi daturus est, delebis nomen Amalec sub caelo: cave, ne obliviscaris! [1]Cumque intraveris terram, quam Dominus Deus tuus tibi daturus est possidendam, et obtinueris eam atque habitaveris in illa, [2]tolles primitias de cunctis frugibus agri, quas collegeris de terra tua, quam Dominus Deus tuus dabit tibi, et pones in cartallo pergesque ad locum, quem Dominus Deus tuus elegerit, ut ibi habitet nomen eius, [3]accedesque ad sacerdotem, qui fuerit in diebus illis, et dices ad eum:

to the place which the LORD your God will choose, to make his name to dwell there. ³And you shall go to the priest who is in office at that time, and say to him, 'I declare this day to the LORD your God that I have come into the land which the LORD swore to our fathers to give us.' ⁴Then the priest shall take the basket from your hand, and set it down before the altar of the LORD your God.

⁵"And you shall make response before the LORD your God, 'A wandering Aramean was my father; and he went down into Egypt and sojourned there, few in number; and there he became a nation, great, mighty, and populous. ⁶And the Egyptians treated us harshly, and afflicted us, and laid upon us hard bondage. ⁷Then we cried to the LORD the God of our fathers, and the LORD heard our voice, and saw our affliction, our toil, and our oppression; ⁸and the LORD brought us out of Egypt with a mighty hand and an outstretched arm, with great terror, with signs and wonders; ⁹and he brought us into this place and gave us this land, a land flowing with milk and honey. ¹⁰And behold, now I bring the first of the fruit of the ground, which thou, O Lord, hast given me.' And you shall set it down before the LORD your God, and worship before the LORD your God; ¹¹and you shall rejoice in all the good which the LORD your God has given to you and to your house, you, and the Levite, and the sojourner who is among you.

Deut 6:20–23
Josh 24:1–13
Neh 9:4ff
Jer 32:16–25
Ps 136
Acts 7:15

---

form a paradigm: they are the hinges on which this "creed" (vv. 8–9) turns. Other Old Testament passages containing similar "professions of faith" are to be found in Deut 6:20–23; Josh 24:1–13; Neh 9:4ff; Jer 32:16–25 and Ps 136.

Jacob is portrayed as a key figure in the early history of the people of Israel; he personifies the patriarchal era. The reference to him not by name but as a "wandering Aramaean" (v. 5) underlines the contrast between the miserable circumstances of Israel earlier and settlement in the promised land. Jacob could be called an Aramaean because Abraham may have been connected with the migrations of Aramaean tribes. Moreover, one must bear in mind the long years Jacob spent in north-eastern Mesopotamia, and his Aramaean wives (Gen 29–30). The prayer at the first-fruits offering heightens the contrast between the poverty of the homeless, landless Aramaean and the prosperity of the rich landowner enjoying his freedom in a land flowing with milk and honey.

'Profiteor hodie coram Domino Deo tuo quod ingressus sim terram, pro qua iuravit patribus nostris, ut daret eam nobis'. ⁴Suscipiensque sacerdos cartallum de manu tua ponet ante altare Domini Dei tui, ⁵et loqueris in conspectu Domini Dei tui: 'Syrus vagus erat pater meus et descendit in Aegyptum et ibi peregrinatus est in paucissimo numero; crevitque in gentem magnam ac robustam et infinitae multitudinis. ⁶Afflixeruntque nos Aegyptii et persecuti sunt imponentes onera gravissima. ⁷Et clamavimus ad Dominum, Deum patrum nostrorum, qui exaudivit nos et respexit humilitatem nostram et laborem atque angustias, ⁸et eduxit nos Dominus de Aegypto in manu forti et brachio extento, in ingenti pavore, in signis atque portentis, ⁹et introduxit ad locum istum et tradidit nobis terram hanc lacte et melle manantem. ¹⁰Et ecce nunc attuli primitias frugum terrae, quam dedisti mihi, Domine'. Et

Deut 14:28–29   **The three-year tithe**

Deut 14:22   ¹²"When you have finished paying all the tithe of your produce in
Ex 12:48   the third year, which is the year of tithing, giving it to the Levite, the sojourner, the fatherless, and the widow, that they may eat within your towns and be filled, ¹³then you shall say before the LORD your God, 'I have removed the sacred portion out of my house, and moreover I have given it to the Levite, the sojourner, the fatherless, and the widow, according to all thy commandment which thou hast commanded me; I have not transgressed any of thy commandments, neither have I forgotten them; ¹⁴I have not eaten of the tithe while I was mourning, or removed any of it while I was unclean, or offered any of it to the dead; I have obeyed the voice of the LORD my God, I have done according to all that thou hast commanded me. ¹⁵Look down from thy holy habitation, from heaven, and bless thy people Israel and the ground which thou hast given us, as thou didst swear to our fathers, a land flowing with milk and honey.'

26:12–15. Now, just after acknowledging the good things received from God (26:5–10), is the right time to imitate the generosity of God and share one's wealth with the needy—the Levite (to whom no land has been allotted), the sojourner (who hires himself out to the Israelite), the orphan and the widow. In other words, life in the promised land should be happy for everyone, even for those who are less well off: we have here an "earthly" ideal which prefigures the future eschatological state of affairs in the heavenly fatherland.

Tithes were covered already in 14:22–29. The first part of v. 14 is open to diverse translations and interpretations: most commentators think that that

"mourning" caused uncleanness because it involved contact with a dead body (cf. Lev 22:4; Num 19:4); perhaps the verse is referring to the funeral meals held in connexion with a bereavement. "I have not offered any of it to the dead" may refer to Egyptian ceremonies in which food was offered to the dead at their tombs in the belief that they needed it, or else to Canaanite superstitions which annually commemorated the death of the fertility god (Baal).

26:16–19. The main part of Moses' second discourse (chaps. 5-26) ends with a new, solemn proclamation of the Covenant between the Lord and his people, on which their mutual relation-

---

dimittes eas in conspectu Domini Dei tui et adorato Domino Deo tuo. ¹¹Et epulaberis in omnibus bonis, quae Dominus Deus tuus dederit tibi et domui tuae, tu et Levites et advena, qui tecum est. ¹²Quando compleveris decimam cunctarum frugum tuarum, anno tertio, anno decimarum, et dederis Levitae et advenae et pupillo et viduae, ut comedant intra portas tuas et saturentur, ¹³loqueris in conspectu Domini Dei tui: 'Abstuli, quod sanctificatum est, de domo mea et dedi illud Levitae et advenae, pupillo ac viduae, sicut iussisti mihi; non praeterivi mandata tua nec sum oblitus imperii tui, ¹⁴non comedi ex eis in luctu meo nec separavi ex eis in qualibet immunditia nec expendi ex his quidquam mortuo: oboedivi voci Domini Dei mei et feci omnia, sicut praecepisti mihi. ¹⁵Respice de habitaculo sancto tuo, de caelo, et benedic populo tuo Israel et terrae, quam dedisti nobis, sicut iurasti patribus nostris, terrae

Israel, the people of the Lord

[16]"This day the LORD your God commands you to do these statutes and ordinances; you shall therefore be careful to do them with all your heart and with all your soul. [17]You have declared this day concerning the Lord that he is your God, and that you will walk in his ways, and keep his statutes and his commandments and his ordinances, and will obey his voice; [18]and the LORD has declared this day concerning you that you are a people for his own possession, as he has promised you, and that you are to keep all his commandments, [19]that he will set you high above all nations that he has made, in praise and in fame and in honour, and that you shall be a people holy to the LORD your God, as he has spoken."

7. CONCLUDING DISCOURSES.
ISRAEL, THE PEOPLE OF GOD*

Instructions regarding the law and worship

27 [1]Now Moses and the elders of Israel commanded the people, saying, "Keep all the commandment which I com-

ship is based. Israel is the people-property of God, chosen by him from among all nations. And the Lord, for his part, is the God and Lord of Israel, whom he has solemnly promised to protect.

Verses 17 and 18 begin with turns of phrase typical of the language of contacts and pacts: one contracting party has the other declare or swear something. This gives the passage great beauty and strength: through the wording of the Covenant, Israel makes the Lord undertake to be its God and protector, while God calls on Israel to testify that it will be faithful to his commandments. The wording of the Covenant is extolled in other passages of the Old Testament.

Thus, Hosea 2:25 uses the imagery of love to express the dialogue between God and Israel: "You are my people. [. . .] Thou art my God."

By treating man in this way, God shows himself to be both near to man and far above him. The mutual commitment of God and men in the Covenant is not a simple business-like transaction; it is something enduring, something which is being renewed all the time: for man, and particularly for the Christian, every day is a renewal of the Covenant, a new beginning (cf. Is 43:19). St J. Escrivá writes "Committed. How much I like that word! We children of God freely put ourselves under an obligation to live a life of

lacte et melle mananti'. [16]Hodie Dominus Deus tuus mandavit tibi, ut facias praecepta haec atque iudicia et custodias et impleas illa ex toto corde tuo et ex tota anima tua. [17]Dominum elegisti hodie, ut sit tibi Deus, et ambules in viis eius et custodias praecepta illius et mandata atque iudicia et oboedias eius imperio; [18]et Dominus elegit te hodie, ut sis ei populus peculiaris, sicut locutus est tibi, et custodias omnia mandata illius, [19]et faciat te excelsiorem cunctis gentibus, quas creavit in laudem et nomen et gloriam suam, ut sis populus sanctus Domini Dei tui, sicut locutus est». [1]Praecepit autem Moyses et

Josh 8:32 mand you this day. ²And on the day you pass over the Jordan to the land which the LORD your God gives you, you shall set up large stones, and plaster them with plaster; ³and you shall write upon them all the words of this law, when you pass over to enter the land which the LORD your God gives you, a land flowing with milk and honey, as the LORD, the God of your fathers, has Deut 11:29–30 promised you. ⁴And when you have passed over the Jordan, you shall set up these stones, concerning which I command you this day, on Mount Ebal, and you shall plaster them with plaster. ⁵And there you shall build an altar to the LORD your God, an altar of Ex 20:24ff stones; you shall lift up no iron tool upon them. ⁶You shall build an altar to the LORD your God of unhewnᵛ stones; and you shall offer burnt offerings on it to the LORD your God; ⁷and you shall sacrifice peace offerings, and shall eat there; and you shall rejoice

---

dedication to God, striving that He may have complete and absolute sovereignty over our lives" (*The Forge*, 855).

As regards the structure of Deuteronomy in its present form, vv. 16–19 act as both a summing up of Moses' second discourse and as a preparation for chapter 28, the end of that discourse, consisting of "Blessings and Curses" exhorting Israel to be faithful to the Covenant it has made with the Lord.

*27:1–26. This chapter seems to consist of complementary fragments, set in between chapters 26 and 28. The material seems to have come from three different traditions: the first (vv. 1–8) and the third (vv. 11–26), passages regulating divine worship, seem to have to do with the sanctuary at Shechem, where the Covenant may have been renewed on a

number of occasions (cf. Josh 24). The second part (vv. 9–10) could be linked to the end of chapter 26. So, the previous career of the text seems to have been quite complicated. In any event, the chapter does elaborate on the very bold instruction in 11:29–30 about the ceremony of blessing and cursing. The book of Joshua reports on how this instruction was eventually carried out (cf. 8:30–35). These elaborate ceremonies signified Israel's solemn acceptance of the Covenant with Yahweh.

As regards how the ceremony actually worked, Eusebius of Caesarea and St Jerome, who were very familiar with the topography of the region, made the point that Mount Ebal and Mount Gerizim were too far apart for either group to hear the other. Some scholars solve this difficulty by suggesting that the people

---

seniores Israel populo dicentes: «Custodite omne mandatum, quod praecipio vobis hodie. ²Cumque transieritis Iordanem in terram, quam Dominus Deus tuus dabit tibi, eriges ingentes lapides et calce obduces eos, ³ut possis in eis scribere omnia verba legis huius, Iordane transmisso, ut introeas terram, quam Dominus Deus tuus dabit tibi, terram lacte et melle manantem, sicut locutus est Dominus, Deus patrum tuorum, tibi. ⁴Quando ergo transieritis Iordanem, erigite istos lapides, sicut ego hodie praecipio vobis, in monte Hebal, et obduces eos calce; ⁵et aedificabis ibi altare Domino Deo tuo de lapidibus, quos ferrum non tetigit, ⁶de saxis impolitis, et offeres super eo holocausta Domino Deo tuo. ⁷Et immolabis hostias pacificas comedesque ibi et epulaberis coram Domino Deo tuo; ⁸et scribes super lapides

v. Heb *whole*

before the LORD your God. [8]And you shall write upon the stones all the words of this law very plainly."

[9]And Moses and the Levitical priests said to all Israel, "Keep silence and hear, O Israel: this day you have become the people of the LORD your God. [10]You shall therefore obey the voice of the LORD your God, keeping his commandments and his statutes, which I command you this day."

[11]And Moses charged the people the same day, saying, Jn 4:20 [12]"When you have passed over the Jordan, these shall stand upon Mount Gerizim to bless the people: Simeon, Levi, Judah, Issachar, Joseph, and Benjamin. [13]And these shall stand upon Mount Ebal for the curse: Reuben, Gad, Asher, Zebulun, Dan, and Naphtali.

Curses for unfaithfulness

[14]And the Levites shall declare to all the men of Israel with a loud voice:

---

were spread up the sides of their respective mountains—so that the mountains were like two amphitheatres facing into the narrow valley running between them in which were the ark and the Levites, who were charged with pronouncing the blessings and curses.

Nothing is said about the position each tribe should take up on the two hills (vv. 12–13). We might mention that on Ebal (the hill more to the north) are mainly tribes which will occupy the northern part of Palestine, and on Gerizim are those who will take over the southern part. Also on the mount of the blessings are the sons of the two lawful wives of Jacob (Leah and Rachel) and on the other the four sons of his slave wives, plus Reuben (maybe due to his misconduct: cf. Gen 35:21–22; 49:4) and Zabulon, the last of Leah's sons.

This chapter gives only the text of the curses (vv. 15–26). The blessings are recorded later, in 28:1–14.

27:1–10. It was a custom among peoples of antiquity to write on stones covered with plaster or chalk.

27:14–26. The twelve curses are punishment for transgression of a number of precepts of the Law. It is not clear what criterion the sacred writer is using in this selection: the sins condemned are not those that we would regard as the gravest. There are sins against God (v. 15), parent (v. 10), justice and charity (vv. 17–19), and lust and homicide (vv. 20–25).

Verse 26 is quoted by St Paul in Galatians 3:10 to illustrate his teaching about justification through the works of the Mosaic Law belonging to a divine disposition for the period prior to the Redemption wrought by Christ.

---

omnia verba legis huius plane et lucide». [9]Dixeruntque Moyses et sacerdotes levitici generis ad omnem Israelem: «Attende et audi, Israel: hodie factus es populus Domino Deo tuo; [10]audies vocem eius et facies mandata atque praecepta, quae ego praecipio tibi». [11]Praecepitque Moyses populo in die illo dicens: [12]«Hi stabunt ad benedicendum populo super montem Garizim, Iordane transmisso: Simeon, Levi, Iudas, Issachar, Ioseph et Beniamin. [13]Et e regione isti stabunt ad maledicendum in monte Hebal: Ruben, Gad et Aser et Zabulon, Dan et Nephthali. [14]Et pronunciabunt Levitae dicentque ad omnes viros

Ex 20:4   ¹⁵"'Cursed be the man who makes a graven or molten image, an abomination to the LORD, a thing made by the hands of a craftsman, and sets it up in secret.' And all the people shall answer and say, 'Amen.'

Ex 21:17   ¹⁶"'Cursed be he who dishonours his father or his mother.' And all the people shall say, 'Amen.'

¹⁷"'Cursed be he who removes his neighbour's landmark.' And all the people shall say, 'Amen.'

¹⁸"'Cursed be he who misleads a blind man on the road.' And all the people shall say, 'Amen.'

Ex 22:20ff   ¹⁹"'Cursed be he who perverts the justice due to the sojourner, the fatherless, and the widow.' And all the people shall say, 'Amen.'

²⁰"'Cursed be he who lies with his father's wife, because he has uncovered her who is his father's.'ʷ And all the people shall say, 'Amen.'

Ex 22:18   ²¹"'Cursed be he who lies with any kind of beast.' And all the people shall say, 'Amen.'

²²"'Cursed be he who lies with his sister, whether the daughter of his father or the daughter of his mother.' And all the people shall say, 'Amen.'

²³"'Cursed be he who lies with his mother-in-law.' And all the people shall say, 'Amen.'

²⁴"'Cursed be he who slays his neighbour in secret.' And all the people shall say, 'Amen.'

Mk 27:4   ²⁵"'Cursed be he who takes a bribe to slay an innocent person.' And all the people shall say, 'Amen.'

Jn 7:49
2 Cor 3:9
Gal 3:10–13   ²⁶"'Cursed be he who does not confirm the words of this law by doing them.' And all the people shall say, 'Amen.'

Israel excelsa voce: ¹⁵'Maledictus homo, qui facit sculptile et conflatile, abominationem Domini, opus manuum artificum, ponetque illud in abscondito'. Et respondebit omnis populus et dicet: 'Amen'. ¹⁶'Maledictus, qui contemnit patrem suum et matrem'. Et dicet omnis populus: 'Amen'. ¹⁷'Maledictus, qui transfert terminos proximi sui'. Et dicet omnis populus: ' Amen'. ¹⁸'Maledictus, qui errare facit caecum in itinere'. Et dicet omnis populus: 'Amen'. ¹⁹'Maledictus, qui pervertit iudicium advenae, pupilli et viduae'. Et dicet omnis populus: 'Amen'. ²⁰'Maledictus, qui dormit cum uxore patris sui, quia revelat operimentum lectuli eius'. Et dicet omnis populus: 'Amen'. ²¹'Maledictus, qui dormit cum omni iumento'. Et dicet omnis populus: 'Amen'. ²²'Maledictus, qui dormit cum sorore sua, filia patris sui sive matris suae'. Et dicet omnis populus: 'Amen'. ²³'Maledictus, qui dormit cum socru sua'. Et dicet omnis populus: 'Amen'. ²⁴'Maledictus, qui clam percusserit proximum suum'. Et dicet omnis populus: 'Amen'. ²⁵'Maledictus, qui accipit munera, ut percutiat sanguinem innocentem'. Et dicet omnis populus: 'Amen'. ²⁶'Maledictus, qui non permanet in sermonibus legis huius, nec eos opere perficit'. Et dicet omnis populus: 'Amen'. ¹Sin audieris vocem Domini Dei tui, ut facias atque custodias omnia mandata eius, quae ego praecipio tibi hodie, faciet te Dominus Deus tuus excelsiorem cunctis gentibus, quae versantur in terra, ²venientque super te universae benedictiones istae et apprehendent te, si tamen

w. Heb *uncovered his father's skirt*

Blessings for faithfulness*

28 [1]"And if you obey the voice of the LORD your God, being careful to do all his commandments which I command you this day, the LORD your God will set you high above all the nations of the earth. [2]And all these blessings shall come upon you and overtake you, if you obey the voice of the LORD your God. [3]Blessed shall you be in the city, and blessed shall you be in the field. [4]Blessed shall be the fruit of your body, and the fruit of your ground, and the fruit of your beasts, the increase of your cattle, and the young of your flock. [5]Blessed shall be your basket and your kneading-trough. [6]Blessed shall you be when you come in, and blessed shall you be when you go out.

Deut 11:10–15
Gen 49:25–26

Lk 1:42

---

*28:1–69. This chapter links up with the end of chapter 26 (and 27:9–10): the "Blessings" and the "Curses" are in line with a model found in other documents of the ancient East designed to reinforce and solemnize pacts or covenants; but in Deuteronomy they take on special moral qualities consistent with the type of exhortations made by the prophets of Israel.

The sacred author teaches that the Covenant brings with it blessings and curses depending on whether Israel is faithful or unfaithful to its precepts. There are similar passages elsewhere in the Pentateuch: in the book of Exodus, various promises of blessing ratify the Code of the Covenant (23:20–23); in Leviticus, blessings and curses mark the end of the Law of Holiness (chap. 26).

There is a remarkable imbalance between the curses (vv. 15–68) and the blessings (which take up only fourteen verses: vv. 1–14).

The rewards and punishments have to do with material things only. This is another example of God's teaching method and of the way he accommodated

himself to the mentality and culture of those people; prosperity and power on the one hand, and wretchedness and slavery on the other were, for them, proofs of fidelity or infidelity to the Covenant with the Lord. As Revelation gradually unfolded, God would show the chosen people that there was a reward or punishment that would not come until the next life (cf. the note on 4:32–40). Jesus brought out this teaching fully, and the Beatitudes (Mt 5:1–12) completely changed the perspective: worldly prosperity or misfortune cease to be indications of God's blessing or punishment.

28:1–14. This series of blessings contains promises of great prosperity—fruitfulness in the form of children, good harvests, increase in livestock, power over other nations. They will be successful in everything they do. The promises are meant to cover all aspects of life, as we can see from expressions like "when you come in . . .", "when you go out . . ." (v. 6), "city and field" (v. 3), human offspring and increase in livestock and in harvests (v. 4), in basket and kneading-

---

vocem Domini Dei tui audieris. [3]Benedictus tu in civitate et benedictus in agro. [4]Benedictus fructus ventris tui et fructus terrae tuae fructusque iumentorum tuorum, partus armentorum tuorum et incrementum ovium tuarum. [5]Benedictum canistrum et pistrinum tuum. [6]Benedictus eris et ingrediens et egrediens. [7]Dabit Dominus inimicos tuos, qui consurgunt adversum te, corruentes in conspectu tuo; per

[7]"The LORD will cause your enemies who rise against you to be defeated before you; they shall come out against you one way, and flee before you seven ways. [8]The LORD will command the blessing upon you in your barns, and in all that you undertake; and he will bless you in the land which the LORD your God gives you. [9]The LORD will establish you as a people holy to himself, as he has sworn to you, if you keep the commandments of the LORD

Jas 2:7   your God, and walk in his ways. [10]And all the peoples of the earth shall see that you are called by the name of the LORD; and they shall be afraid of you. [11]And the LORD will make you abound in prosperity, in the fruit of your body, and in the fruit of your cattle, and in the fruit of your ground, within the land which the LORD swore to your fathers to give you. [12]The LORD will open to you his good treasury the heavens, to give the rain of your land in its season and to bless all the work of your hands; and you shall lend to many nations, but you shall not borrow. [13]And the LORD will make you the head, and not the tail; and you shall tend upward only, and not downward; if you obey the commandments of the LORD your God, which I command you this day, being careful to do them, [14]and if you do not turn aside from any of the words which I command you this day, to the right hand or to the left, to go after other gods to serve them.

Other curses

Lev 26:14–39   [15]"But if you will not obey the voice of the LORD your God or be
Jer 26:4–6
Amos 4:6–12   careful to do all his commandments and his statutes which I com-

---

trough (v. 5), etc. All of this will come about through obedience to the precepts of the Covenant and fidelity to the Lord.

Even when the promises have to do with material prosperity, Israel's happiness will not come from that alone; it must also come from God's special pres-

ence in the midst of his people (cf. Lev 26:11–12).

28:15–68. This very full list of curses is a warning to the people of Israel about the terrible punishments they can expect if they are unfaithful to the Covenant.

---

unam viam venient contra te et per septem fugient a facie tua. [8]Emittet Dominus benedictionem super cellaria tua et super omnia opera manuum tuarum; benedicetque tibi in terra, quam Dominus Deus tuus dabit tibi. [9]Suscitabit te Dominus sibi in populum sanctum, sicut iuravit tibi, si custodieris mandata Domini Dei tui et ambulaveris in viis eius. [10]Videbuntque omnes terrarum populi quod nomen Domini invocatum sit super te, et timebunt te. [11]Abundare te faciet Dominus omnibus bonis, fructu uteri tui et fructu iumentorum tuorum, fructu terrae tuae, quam iuravit Dominus patribus tuis, ut daret tibi. [12]Aperiet Dominus tibi thesaurum suum optimum, caelum, ut tribuat pluviam terrae tuae in tempore suo; benedicatque cunctis operibus manuum tuarum; et fenerabis gentibus multis et ipse a nullo fenus accipies. [13]Constituet te Dominus in caput et non in caudam, et eris semper supra et non subter, si audieris mandata Domini Dei tui, quae ego praecipio tibi hodie, et custodieris et feceris [14]ac non de-

mand you this day, then all these curses shall come upon you and overtake you. [16]Cursed shall you be in the city, and cursed shall you be in the field. [17]Cursed shall be your basket and your kneading-trough. [18]Cursed shall be the fruit of your body, and the fruit of your ground, the increase of your cattle, and the young of your flock. [19]Cursed shall you be when you come in, and cursed shall you be when you go out.

[20]"The Lord will send upon you curses, confusion, and frustration, in all that you undertake to do, until you are destroyed and perish quickly, on account of the evil of your doings, because you have forsaken me. [21]The LORD will make the pestilence cleave to you until he has consumed you off the land which you are entering to take possession of it. [22]The LORD will smite you with con- Acts 23:3 sumption, and with fever, inflammation, and fiery heat, and with drought,[x] and with blasting, and with mildew; they shall pursue you until you perish. [23]And the heavens over your head shall be brass, and the earth under you shall be iron. [24]The LORD will make the rain of your land powder and dust; from heaven it shall come down upon you until you are destroyed.

[25]"The LORD will cause you to be defeated before your enemies; you shall go out one way against them, and flee seven ways

---

The list begins in parallel with the previous list of blessings (cf. vv. 16–19 and vv. 3–6), but after this the order changes; the same subjects are dealt with, but more is said about them: crops and livestock will be hit hard; and the Israelites themselves, who will suffer all kinds of sickness, will be reduced in number and will find themselves at the mercy of their enemies, their cities destroyed and they themselves sent into exile. Over the course of Israel's history, all these adverse circumstances will arise until eventually Jerusalem is destroyed in AD 70 and the Jewish people are scattered.

As regards the wording of these curses, they fall into two clearly distinct categories—vv. 15–46 and vv. 47–68.

---

clinaveris a verbis, quae ego praecipio vobis hodie, nec ad dexteram nec ad sinistram, nec secutus fueris deos alienos neque colueris eos. [15]Quod si audire nolueris vocem Domini Dei tui, ut custodias et facias omnia mandata eius et praecepta, quae ego praecipio tibi hodie, venient super te omnes maledictiones istae et apprehendent te: [16]Maledictus eris in civitate, maledictus in agro. [17]Maledictum canistrum et pistrinum tuum. [18]Maledictus fructus ventris tui et fructus terrae tuae, partus armentorum tuorum et incrementum ovium tuarum. [19]Maledictus eris ingrediens et maledictus egrediens. [20]Mittet Dominus super te maledictionem et conturbationem et increpationem in omnia opera tua, quae facies, donec conterat te et perdat velociter propter adinventiones tuas pessimas, in quibus reliquisti me. [21]Adiunget Dominus tibi pestilentiam, donec consumat te de terra, ad quam ingredieris possidendam. [22]Percutiet te Dominus consumptione, febri et inflammatione, ardore et aestu, uredine ac aurugine, et persequentur te, donec pereas. [23]Et erit caelum, quod est supra caput tuum, aeneum, et terra, quam calcas, ferrea. [24]Convertet Dominus imbrem terrae tuae in pulverem, et de caelo descendet super te cinis, donec conteraris. [25]Tradet te Dominus corruentem ante hostes tuos: per unam viam egredieris contra eos et per

---

x. Another reading is *sword*

before them; and you shall be a horror to all the kingdoms of the earth. ²⁶And your dead body shall be food for all birds of the air, and for the beasts of the earth; and there shall be no one to frighten them away. ²⁷The LORD will smite you with the boils of Egypt, and with the ulcers and the scurvy and the itch, of which you cannot be healed. ²⁸The LORD will smite you with madness and blindness and confusion of mind; ²⁹and you shall grope at noonday, as the blind grope in darkness, and you shall not prosper in your ways; and you shall be only oppressed and robbed continually, and there shall be no one to help you. ³⁰You shall betroth a wife, and another man shall lie with her; you shall build a house, and you shall not dwell in it; you shall plant a vineyard, and you shall not use the fruit of it. ³¹Your ox shall be slain before your eyes, and you shall not eat of it; your ass shall be violently taken away before your face, and shall not be restored to you; your sheep shall be given to your enemies, and there shall be no one to help you. ³²Your sons and your daughters shall be given to another people, while your eyes look on and fail with longing for them all the day; and it shall not be in the power of your hand to prevent it. ³³A nation which you have not known shall eat up the fruit of your ground and of all your labours; and you shall be only oppressed and crushed continually; ³⁴so that you shall be driven mad by the sight which your eyes shall see. ³⁵The LORD will smite you on the knees and on the legs with grievous boils of which you cannot be healed, from the sole of your foot to the crown of your head.

³⁶"The LORD will bring you, and your king whom you set over you, to a nation that neither you nor your fathers have known; and there you shall serve other gods, of wood and stone. ³⁷And you shall become a horror, a proverb, and a byword, among all the peoples where the LORD will lead you away. ³⁸You shall carry

Marginal references:
Acts 22:11
2 Pet 1:9

Is 62:8–9
Amos 5:11
Mic 6:15
Deut 20:5–7

Rev 16:2

2 Kings 17:4–6;
25:7–11
Lk 19:41–44

---

septem fugies et eris in terrorem omnibus regnis terrae. ²⁶Eritque cadaver tuum in escam cunctis volatilibus caeli et bestiis terrae, et non erit qui abigat. ²⁷Percutiet te Dominus ulcere Aegypti et tumore, scabie quoque et prurigine, ita ut curari nequeas. ²⁸Percutiet te Dominus amentia et caecitate ac stupore mentis; ²⁹et palpabis in meridie, sicut palpare solet caecus in tenebris, et non diriges vias tuas. Omnique tempore eris oppressus et exspoliatus nec habebis, qui liberet te. ³⁰Uxorem accipies, et alius dormiet cum ea. Domum aedificabis et non habitabis in ea. Plantabis vineam et non vindemiabis eam. ³¹Bos tuus mactabitur coram te, et non comedes ex eo. Asinus tuus rapietur in conspectu tuo et non reddetur tibi. Oves tuae dabuntur inimicis tuis, et non erit qui te adiuvet. ³²Filii tui et filiae tuae tradentur alteri populo, videntibus oculis tuis et deficientibus ad conspectum eorum tota die, et non erit fortitudo in manu tua. ³³Fructus terrae tuae et omnes labores tuos comedet populus, quem ignoras, et eris semper oppressus et confractus cunctis diebus ³⁴et insanies in aspectu eorum, quae videbunt oculi tui. ³⁵Percutiet te Dominus ulcere pessimo in genibus et in suris, sanarique non poteris a planta pedis usque ad verticem tuum. ³⁶Ducet te Dominus et regem tuum, quem constitueris super te, in gentem, quam ignorasti tu et patres tui, et servies ibi diis alienis, ligno et lapidi; ³⁷et eris in stuporem et in proverbium ac fabulam omnibus populis, ad quos te introduxerit Dominus. ³⁸Sementem multam iacies in terram et modicum congregabis, quia locustae devorabunt omnia. ³⁹Vineas plantabis et coles et vinum non bibes,

much seed into the field, and shall gather little in; for the locust shall consume it. [39]You shall plant vineyards and dress them, but you shall neither drink of the wine nor gather the grapes; for the worm shall eat them. [40]You shall have olive trees throughout all your territory, but you shall not anoint yourself with the oil; for your olives shall drop off. [41]You shall beget sons and daughters, but they shall not be yours; for they shall go into captivity. [42]All your trees and the fruit of your ground the locust shall possess. [43]The sojourner who is among you shall mount above you higher and higher; and you shall come down lower and lower. [44]He shall lend to you, and you shall not lend to him; he shall be the head, and you shall be the tail. [45]All these curses shall come upon you

---

28:45–68. The change in literary style, the references to invasion by a foreign power, and similarities with 8th- and 7th-century BC prophetical writing (cf., e.g., Hos 8–9) lead one to think that these verses may have been added by a later writer. The description of the invading nation could fit either the Assyrians (who conquered the Northern kingdom that is, Samaria, in 721 BC) or the Babylonians (who defeated Judah and destroyed Jerusalem in 587 BC); in both cases, many of the Israelites who survived were sent into exile.

The contrast between the joy that comes from serving God and the misfortune of having to serve his enemies (vv. 47–48) continues to be a universal experience. When a person rejects the gentle yoke of the Lord (cf. Mt 11:28–30), he ends up wearing the "iron yoke" of his own wretchedness. "We will be slaves either way," St J. Escrivá explains; "since we must serve anyway, for whether we like it or not this is our lot as men, then there is nothing better than recognising

that Love has made us slaves of God. From the moment we recognise this we cease being slaves and become friends, sons" (*Friends of God*, 35).

The hair-raising picture of people under siege (vv., 53–57) became a reality for Israel at the time of the siege of Samaria (2 Kings 6:26–29). The book of Lamentations describes similar scenes in Jerusalem (cf., e.g., Lam 2:20; 4:1–10).

The forced return to Egypt (v. 68), the worst-possible scenario, is the severest of all these threats. Going back to the country where they had lived in bondage would mean that all the sufferings of the Exodus and the entire conquest of the promised land would have been to no avail: it would spell utter failure; and they would be worse off than ever they were: previously they had been slaves, which at least meant they could survive; now they would not even be accepted as slaves, so their wretchedness would know no limits. And, worst of all, a return to Egypt would mean writing-off all the salvific acts that God had done in their regard.

---

nec colliges ex ea quippiam, quoniam vastabitur vermibus. [40]olivas habebis in omnibus terminis tuis et non ungeris oleo, quia defluent et peribunt. [41]Filios generabis et filias et non frueris eis, quoniam ducentur in captivitatem. [42]Omnes arbores tuas et fruges terrae tuae locusta consumet. [43]Advena, qui tecum versatur in terra, ascendet super te eritque sublimior; tu autem descendes et eris inferior. [44]Ipse fenerabit tibi, et tu non fenerabis ei; ipse erit in caput, et tu eris in caudam. [45]Et venient super te omnes maledictiones istae et persequentes apprehendent te, donec intereas, quia non audisti vocem Domini

and pursue you and overtake you, till you are destroyed, because you did not obey the voice of the LORD your God, to keep his commandments and his statutes which he commanded you. ⁴⁶They shall be upon you as a sign and a wonder, and upon your descendants for ever.

Jer 5:19

⁴⁷"Because you did not serve the LORD your God with joyfulness and gladness of heart, by reason of the abundance of all things, ⁴⁸therefore you shall serve your enemies whom the Lord

Is 5:26; 33:19
Jer 5:15
Bar 4:15

will send against you, in hunger and thirst, in nakedness, and in want of all things; and he will put a yoke of iron upon your neck, until he has destroyed you. ⁴⁹The LORD will bring a nation against you from afar, from the end of the earth, as swift as the eagle flies, a nation whose language you do not understand, ⁵⁰a nation of stern countenance, who shall not regard the person of the old or show favour to the young, ⁵¹and shall eat the offspring of your cattle and the fruit of your ground, until you are destroyed; who also shall not leave you grain, wine, or oil, the increase of your cattle or the young of your flock, until they have caused you to perish. ⁵²They shall besiege you in all your towns, until your high and fortified walls, in which you trusted, come down throughout all your land; and they shall besiege you in all

2 Kings 6:26–29
Lam 2:20; 4:1–10
Jer 19:9
Lev 26:29
Ezek 5:10
Rom 2:9

your towns throughout all your land, which the LORD your God has given you. ⁵³And you shall eat the offspring of your own body, the flesh of your sons and daughters, whom the LORD your God has given you, in the siege and in the distress with which your enemies shall distress you. ⁵⁴The man who is the most

---

Given that the Old Testament taken as a whole is a figure and anticipation of the New, one needs to realize that its prophecies are also in some way applicable to the people brought into being by the New Covenant in Jesus Christ.

Indeed, since Christians have been favoured with infinitely more proofs of divine love and mercy, it behoves us to think of the consequences of our own infidelities to the love of God.

Dei tui nec servasti mandata eius et praecepta, quae praecepit tibi. ⁴⁶Et erunt in te signa atque prodigia et in semine tuo usque in sempiternum. ⁴⁷Eo quod non servieris Domino Deo tuo in gaudio cordisque laetitia propter rerum omnium abundantiam, ⁴⁸servies inimico tuo, quem immittet Dominus tibi, in fame et siti et nuditate et omnium penuria, et ponet iugum ferreum super cervicem tuam, donec te conterat. ⁴⁹Adducet Dominus super te gentem de longinquo et de extremis finibus terrae in similitudinem aquilae volantis cum impetu, cuius linguam intellegere non possis: ⁵⁰gentem procacissimam, quae non deferat seni nec misereatur parvulo; ⁵¹et devoret fructum iumentorum tuorum ac fruges terrae tuae, donec intereas, et non relinquat tibi triticum, vinum et oleum, partum armentorum et incrementum ovium, donec te disperdat ⁵²et obsideat te in cunctis urbibus tuis, donec destruantur muri tui firmi atque sublimes, in quibus habebas fiduciam in omni terra tua. Obsideberis intra portas tuas in omni terra tua, quam dabit tibi Dominus Deus tuus, ⁵³et comedes fructum uteri tui, carnes filiorum tuorum et filiarum tuarum, quas dederit tibi Dominus Deus tuus, in obsidione et angustia, qua opprimet te hostis tuus.

tender and delicately bred among you will grudge food to his brother, to the wife of his bosom, and to the last of the children who remain to him; [55]so that he will not give to any of them any of the flesh of his children whom he is eating, because he has nothing left him, in the siege and in the distress with which your enemy shall distress you in all your towns. [56]The most tender and delicately bred woman among you, who would not venture to set the sole of her foot upon the ground because she is so delicate and tender, will grudge to the husband of her bosom, to her son and to her daughter, [57]her afterbirth that comes out from between her feet and her children whom she bears, because she will eat them secretly, for want of all things, in the siege and in the distress with which your enemy shall distress you in your towns.

[58]"If you are not careful to do all the words of this law which are written in this book, that you may fear this glorious and awful name, the LORD your God, [59]then the LORD will bring on you and your offspring extraordinary afflictions, afflictions severe and lasting, and sicknesses grievous and lasting. [60]And he will bring upon you again all the diseases of Egypt, which you were afraid of; and they shall cleave to you. [61]Every sickness also, and every affliction which is not recorded in the book of this law, the LORD will bring upon you, until you are destroyed. [62]Whereas you were as the stars of heaven for multitude, you shall be left few in number; because you did not obey the voice of the LORD your God. [63]And as the LORD took delight in doing you good and multiplying you, so the LORD will take delight in bringing ruin upon you and destroying you; and you shall be plucked off the land which you are entering to take possession of it. [64]And the LORD will scatter you among all peoples, from one end of the earth to the other; and there you shall serve other gods, of wood and stone,

Gal 3:10

Lk 21:24

[54]Homo tener in te et delicatus valde invidebit fratri suo et uxori, quae cubat in sinu suo, et residuis filiis suis, quos reservaverit, [55]ne det uni ex eis de carnibus filiorum suorum, quas comedet, eo quod nihil aliud habeat in obsidione et angustia, qua oppresserit te inimicus tuus intra omnes portas tuas. [56]Tenera mulier in te et delicata, quae non tentabat pedis vestigium figere in terram propter mollitiem et teneritudinem nimiam, invidebit viro suo, qui cubat in sinu eius, filio et filiae [57]et illuviei secundarum, quae egrediuntur de medio feminum eius, et liberis, qui eadem hora nati sunt; comedet enim eos clam propter rerum omnium penuriam in obsidione et angustia, qua opprimet te inimicus tuus intra portas tuas. [58]Nisi custodieris et feceris omnia verba legis huius, quae scripta sunt in hoc volumine, et timueris nomen gloriosum et terribile hoc, Dominum Deum tuum, [59]augebit ultra modum Dominus plagas tuas et plagas seminis tui, plagas magnas et perseverantes, infirmitates pessimas et perpetuas, [60]et convertet in te omnes afflictiones Aegypti, quas timuisti, et adhaerebunt tibi. [61]Insuper universos languores et plagas, quae non sunt scriptae in volumine legis huius, inducet Dominus super te, donec te conterat; [62]et remanebitis pauci numero, qui prius eratis sicut astra caeli prae multitudine, quoniam non audisti vocem Domini Dei tui. [63]Et sicut ante laetatus est Dominus super vos bene vobis faciens vosque multiplicans, sic laetabitur super vos disperdens vos atque subvertens, ut auferamini de terra, ad quam ingredieris possidendam. [64]Disperget te Dominus in omnes populos a summitate terrae usque

which neither you nor your fathers have known. [65]And among these nations you shall find no ease, and there shall be no rest for the sole of your foot; but the LORD will give you there a trembling heart, and failing eyes, and a languishing soul; [66]your life shall hang in doubt before you; night and day you shall be in dread, and have no assurance of your life. [67]In the morning you shall say, 'Would it were evening!' and at evening you shall say, 'Would it were morning!' because of the dread which your heart shall fear, and the sights which your eyes shall see. [68]And the LORD will bring you back in ships to Egypt, a journey which I promised that you should never make again; and there you shall offer yourselves for sale to your enemies as male and female slaves, but no man will buy you.'"

Hos 8:13

PART THREE

The Third Discourse of Moses:
The Covenant of Moab*

29 [1y]These are the words of the covenant which the LORD commanded Moses to make with the people of Israel in the land of Moab, besides the covenant which he had made with them at Horeb.

---

*29:1—30:20. The "Third Discourse of Moses" covers chapters 29 and 30; it has been given the name of "The Covenant of Moab". Deuteronomy is the only book to speak of this Covenant made in Moab, a text which repeats and completes that

ad terminos eius, et servies ibi diis alienis, quos et tu ignorasti et patres tui, lignis et lapidibus. [65]In gentibus quoque illis non quiesces, neque erit requies vestigio pedis tui; dabit enim tibi Dominus ibi cor pavidum et deficientes oculos et animam consumptam maerore. [66]Et erit vita tua quasi pendens ante te; timebis nocte et die et non credes vitae tuae. [67]Mane dices: 'Quis mihi det vesperum?'; et vespere: 'Quis mihi det mane?', propter cordis tui formidinem, qua terreberis, et propter ea, quae tuis videbis oculis. [68]Reducet te Dominus classibus in Aegyptum per viam, de qua dixi tibi, ut eam amplius non videres; ibi vendetis vos inimicis vestris in servos et ancillas, et non erit qui emat». [69]Haec sunt verba foederis, quod praecepit Dominus Moysi, ut feriret cum filiis Israel in terra Moab, praeter illud foedus, quod cum eis pepigit in Horeb. [1]Vocavitque Moyses omnem Israel et dixit ad eos: «Vos vidistis uni-

y. Ch 28:69 in Heb [and New Vulgate]

The Exodus recalled

[22z]And Moses summoned all Israel and said to them: "You have seen all that the LORD did before your eyes in the land of Egypt, to Pharaoh and to all his servants and to all his land, [3]the great trials which your eyes saw, the signs, and those great wonders; [4]but to this day the LORD has not given you a mind to understand, or eyes to see, or ears to hear. [5]I have led you forty years in the wilderness; your clothes have not worn out upon you, and your sandals have not worn off your feet; [6]you have not eaten bread, and you have not drunk wine or strong drink; that you may know that I am the LORD your God. [7]And when you came to this place,

Is 29:10
Rom 11:8

---

of the Covenant made at Horeb (Sinai). It is possible that the sacred writer who gave the final editorial touch to this text was conscious of the repetition the passage implied and therefore added in the last words of 29:1 ("besides the covenant which he had made with them at Horeb"). Both the content of this third discourse and its introductory verse (29:1) seem to reinforce the Deuteronomic Code (12:1—26:15).

The third discourse has all the essential formal features of every Eastern covenant or pact; after an historical introduction (29:2–9) it describes what could be called the preamble of the Covenant (29:10–15); there follows an exhortation on the obligation to keep the Covenant (29:16–21); and the blessings and curses which were normally attached to such documents (30:15–20). In between the last two parts comes a passage (29:22—30:10) assembling miscellaneous small pieces which form a sort of extension of

the exhortatory section that precedes it; it seems to be a text later than the main body of the third discourse.

The figure of Moses is very much to the fore in these two chapters: the sacred text stresses the exceptionally important mission that was Moses' as the mediator of the Covenant between the Lord and his people.

29:1. It is not clear whether this verse marks the end of the previous discourse or the start of the third discourse attributed to Moses. The Hebrew Masoretic text, which the New Vulgate goes along with, seems to favour the former interpretation, whereas the Vulgate (in the Sixto-Clementine edition) and many commentators are inclined towards the latter.

29:2–9. This passage recalls again the very special way God protected his people during the Exodus; however, they have failed to appreciate those salvific

---

versa, quae fecit Dominus coram vobis in terra Aegypti, pharaoni et omnibus servis eius universaeque terrae illius, [2]tentationes magnas, quas viderunt oculi tui, signa illa portentaque ingentia; [3]et non dedit Dominus vobis cor intellegens et oculos videntes et aures, quae possint audire, usque in praesentem diem. [4]Adduxi vos quadraginta annis per desertum; non sunt attrita vestimenta vestra, nec calceamenta pedum tuorum vetustate consumpta sunt, [5]panem non comedistis, vinum et siceram non bibistis, ut sciretis quia ego sum Dominus Deus vester. [6]Et venistis ad hunc locum, egressusque est Sehon rex Hesebon et Og rex Basan occurrentes nobis ad pugnam, et percussimus eos. [7]Et tulimus terram eorum ac tradidimus possidendam Ruben et Gad et dimidiae tribui Manasse. [8]Custodite ergo verba pacti huius

z. Ch 29:1 in Heb [and New Vulgate]

Deut 2:30–35;
3:12–16 Sihon the king of Heshbon and Og the king of Bashan came out against us to battle, but we defeated them; [8]we took their land, and gave it for an inheritance to the Reubenites, the Gadites, and the half-tribe of the Manassites. [9]Therefore be careful to do the words of this covenant, that you may prosper[a] in all that you do.

The Covenant and generations to come

[10]"You stand this day all of you before the LORD your God; the heads of your tribes,[b] your elders, and your officers, all the men of Israel, [11]your little ones, your wives, and the sojourner who is in your camp, both he who hews your wood and he who draws your water, [12]that you may enter into the sworn covenant of the LORD your God, which the LORD your God makes with you this day; [13]that he may establish you this day as his people, and that he may be your God, as he promised you, and as he swore to your fathers, to Abraham, to Isaac, and to Jacob. [14]Nor is it with you only that I make this sworn covenant, [15]but with him who is not here with us this day as well as with him who stands here with us this day before the LORD our God.

[16]"You know how we dwelt in the land of Egypt, and how we came through the midst of the nations through which you passed;

---

actions of God's, and have not been faithful to him (v. 4). The Israelites' hardness of heart cannot be imputed to God (although the style of Old Testament language is such that it is attributed to him); they are completely free to choose between good and evil (cf. 30:15–20), and their obduracy is due to their bad dispositions. St Augustine comments in this connexion that Moses would not upbraid them for their hardness of heart if they were free from guilt (cf. *Quaestionum in Heptateuchum*, 5, 50).

Verse 4, along with Isaiah 29:10, is quoted by St Paul in Romans 11:8. The Apostle interprets both Old Testament texts as prophetic and uses them to justify his criticism of a considerable part of Israel for their failure to accept the Messiah.

29:10–21. The Covenant between the Lord and Israel—"to establish you this day as his people and to be your God" (v. 13)—is made not only with the present generation but also with future ones, with

---

et implete ea, ut prosperemini in universis, quae facitis. [9]Vos statis hodie cuncti coram Domino Deo vestro, principes vestri ac tribus et maiores natu atque praefecti, omnis vir Israel, [10]liberi et uxores vestrae et advena tuus, qui tecum moratur in castris, a lignorum caesoribus usque ad hos, qui hauriunt aquas tuas, [11]ut transeas in foedere Domini Dei tui et in iure iurando, quod hodie Dominus Deus tuus percutit tecum, [12]ut suscitet te sibi hodie in populum, et ipse sit Deus tuus, sicut locutus est tibi et sicut iuravit patribus tuis Abraham, Isaac et Iacob. [13]Nec vobis solis ego hoc foedus ferio et haec iuramenta confirmo, [14]sed cunctis hic nobiscum hodie praesentibus coram Domino Deo nostro et illis, qui hodie hic nobiscum non adsunt. [15]Vos enim nostis quomodo habitaverimus in terra Aegypti et quomodo tran-

a. Or *deal wisely*   **b.** Gk Syr: Heb *your heads, your tribes*

¹⁷and you have seen their detestable things, their idols of wood and stone, of silver and gold, which were among them. ¹⁸Beware lest there be among you a man or woman or family or tribe, *Heb 12:15* whose heart turns away this day from the LORD our God to go and serve the gods of those nations; lest there be among you a root bearing poisonous and bitter fruit, ¹⁹one who, when he hears the words of this sworn covenant, blesses himself in his heart, saying, 'I shall be safe, though I walk in the stubbornness of my heart.' This would lead to the sweeping away of moist and dry alike. ²⁰The LORD would not pardon him, but rather the anger of the *Rev 22:18* LORD and his jealousy would smoke against that man, and the curses written in this book would settle upon him, and the LORD would blot out his name from under heaven. ²¹And the LORD would single him out from all the tribes of Israel for calamity, in accordance with all the curses of the covenant written in this book of the law.

Threats of exile

²²And the generation to come, your children who rise up after *Gen 14:2;*
19:24–25 you, and the foreigner who comes from a far land, would say, *Hos 11:8* when they see the afflictions of that land and the sicknesses with

---

the whole people, from the foremost men of the tribes to the humblest members of society, like hewers of wood and drawers of water, jobs usually done by outsiders working for the Israelites (cf. Josh 9:27).

Once more, stress is put on the need to avoid idolatry (vv. 16–21), and a warning is issued to anyone who disobeys this injunction, thinking he can get away with it. The proverbial expression, "This would lead to the sweeping away of moist and dry alike" (v. 19)—it is not clear how it should be translated—indicates the scope

of the punishment and, perhaps, the social repercussion of the sin.

"Sworn covenant" (vv. 12, 14, 19): another possible translation is "solemn covenant". Covenants were usually accompanied by oaths, whereby the contracting parties called down curses on anyone who did not keep to what was agreed (cf. 27:14–26; 28:15–68).

29:22–29. Admah and Zeboiim (v. 23) were two cities situated to the south of the Dead Sea, close to Sodom and

---

sierimus per medium nationum, quas transeuntes ¹⁶vidistis abominationes et idola eorum, lignum et lapidem, argentum et aurum, quae colebant. ¹⁷Ne forte sit inter vos vir aut mulier, familia aut tribus, cuius cor aversum est hodie a Domino Deo nostro, ut vadat et serviat diis illarum gentium, et sit inter vos radix germinans fel et absinthium; ¹⁸cumque audierit verba iuramenti huius, benedicat sibi in corde suo dicens: 'Pax erit mihi, etsi ambulabo in pravitate cordis mei', et absumat terram irriguam et sitientem. ¹⁹Dominus non ignoscet ei, sed tunc quam maxime furor eius fumabit et zelus contra hominem illum, et sedebunt super eum omnia maledicta, quae scripta sunt in hoc volumine, et delebit Dominus nomen eius sub caelo ²⁰et consumet eum in perditionem ex omnibus tribubus Israel, iuxta maledictiones foederis, quae in hoc libro legis scriptae sunt. ²¹Dicetque sequens generatio, filii vestri, qui nascentur deinceps, et peregrini, qui de longe venerint, videntes plagas terrae illius et infirmitates,

which the LORD has made it sick—[23]the whole land brimstone and salt, and a burnt-out waste, unsown, and growing nothing, where no grass can sprout, an overthrow like that of Sodom and Gomorrah, Admah and Zeboiim, which the LORD overthrew in his anger and wrath—[24]yea, all the nations would say, 'Why has the LORD done thus to this land? What means the heat of this great anger?' [25]Then men would say, 'It is because they forsook the covenant of the LORD, the God of their fathers, which he made with them when he brought them out of the land of Egypt, [26]and went and served other gods and worshiped them, gods whom they had not known and whom he had not allotted to them; [27]therefore the anger of the LORD was kindled against this land, bringing upon it all the curses written in this book; [28]and the LORD uprooted them from their land in anger and fury and great wrath, and cast them into another land, as at this day.'

[29]"The secret things belong to the LORD our God; but the things that are revealed belong to us and to our children for ever, that we may do all the words of this law.

Lev 26:40–45 **Restoration after repentance**

30 [1]"And when all these things come upon you, the blessing and the curse, which I have set before you, and you call

---

Gomorrah (cf. Gen 14:2), and which must have perished along with them (Gen 19:24–25). The prophet Hosea also recalls this punishment (Hos 11:8).

30:1–10. This passage shows God's faithfulness to his word: even when Israel's transgression of the Covenant provokes the extreme punishment of exile, the Lord will forgive the people if they repent, and will bring them home again. Even more than that, he will take

delight in them, as he did in their forebears (v. 9); the passage is reminiscent of the forgiveness shown and the joy felt by the father when the prodigal son repents (cf. Lk 15:20–24). The sacred writer plays with the word "return, restore", linking conversion (turning away from sin) with repatriation (returning from exile, leaving punishment behind).

In the Old Testament, God's loving mercy, *hésed*, is very much linked to faithfulness, *émet*. And in turn God's

---

quibus eam afflixerit Dominus, [22]sulphur et salem: combusta est omnis humus eius, ita ut ultra non seratur, nec virens quippiam germinet in exemplum subversionis Sodomae et Gomorrae, Adamae et Seboim, quas subvertit Dominus in ira et furore suo. [23]Et dicent omnes gentes: 'Quare sic fecit Dominus terrae huic? Quae est haec ira furoris immensa?'. [24]Et respondebunt: 'Quia dereliquerunt pactum Domini, Dei patrum suorum, quod pepigit cum eis, quando eduxit eos de terra Aegypti, [25]et servierunt diis alienis et adoraverunt eos, quos nesciebant et quibus non fuerant attributi; [26]idcirco iratus est furor Domini contra terram istam, ut induceret super eam omnia maledicta, quae in hoc volumine scripta sunt, [27]et eiecit eos de terra eorum in ira et furore et indignatione maxima proiecitque in terram alienam, sicut hodie comprobatur'. [28]Abscondita Domino Deo nostro, manifesta autem nobis et filiis nostris usque in sempiternum, ut faciamus universa verba legis huius. [1]Cum ergo venerint super te

them to mind among all the nations where the LORD your God has driven you, [2]and return to the LORD your God, you and your children, and obey his voice in all that I command you this day, with all your heart and with all your soul; [3]then the LORD your God will restore your fortunes, and have compassion upon you, and he will gather you again from all the peoples where the LORD your God has scattered you. [4]If your outcasts are in the uttermost parts of heaven, from there the LORD your God will gather you, and from there he will fetch you; [5]and the LORD your God will bring you into the land which your fathers possessed, that you may possess it; and he will make you more prosperous and numerous than your fathers. [6]And the LORD your God will circumcise your heart and the heart of your offspring, so that you will love the LORD your God with all your heart and with all your soul, that you may live. [7]And the LORD your God will put all these curses upon your foes and enemies who persecuted you. [8]And you shall again obey the voice of the LORD, and keep all his commandments which I command you this day. [9]The LORD your God will make you abundantly prosperous in all the work of your hand, in the fruit of your body, and in the fruit of your

Mt 24:31
Mk 13:27

Deut 10:16
Rom 2:29

---

mercy is linked to the Covenant (which is a gift and a grace for Israel) and it involves, in some way, legal obligations. "The juridical commitment on God's part," John Paul II teaches, "ceased to oblige whenever Israel broke the covenant and did not respect its conditions. But precisely at this point, *hesed*, in ceasing to be a juridical obligation, revealed its deeper aspect: it showed itself as what it was at the beginning, that is, as love that gives, love more powerful than betrayal, grace stronger than sin"

(*Dives in misericordia*, 28, note 52). Christian piety often invokes God "to whom it is proper always to be merciful and to forgive".

"The uttermost parts of heaven" (v. 4): this expression reflects the thinking of the time, according to which the vault of heaven rested on the edges of the earth.

30:6–10. The Mosaic Law showed the moral path to follow. Its teaching was clear and encouraging. Yet, in itself, it did not provide man with the strength he

---

omnes sermones isti, benedictio et maledictio, quas proposui in conspectu tuo, et ductus paenitudine cordis tui in universis gentibus, in quas disperserit te Dominus Deus tuus, [2]et reversus fueris ad eum et oboedieris eius imperiis secundum omnia, quae ego hodie praecipio tibi, cum filiis tuis in toto corde tuo et in tota anima tua, [3]reducet Dominus Deus tuus captivitatem tuam ac miserebitur tui et rursum congregabit te de cunctis populis, in quos te ante dispersit. [4]Si ad cardines caeli fueris dissipatus, inde te retrahet Dominus Deus tuus et assumet [5]atque introducet in terram, quam possederunt patres tui, et obtinebis eam; et feliciorem et maioris numeri esse te faciet quam fuerunt patres tui. [6]Circumcidet Dominus Deus tuus cor tuum et cor seminis tui, ut diligas Dominum Deum tuum in toto corde tuo et in tota anima tua, ut possis vivere. [7]Omnes autem maledictiones has convertet super inimicos tuos et eos, qui oderunt te et persequuntur. [8]Tu autem reverteris et audies vocem Domini faciesque universa mandata, quae ego praecipio tibi hodie; [9]et abundare te faciet Dominus Deus tuus in cunctis operibus

779

cattle, and in the fruit of your ground; for the LORD will again take delight in prospering you, as he took delight in your fathers, ^{Gal 3:10} ¹⁰if you obey the voice of the LORD your God, to keep his commandments and his statutes which are written in this book of the law, if you turn to the LORD your God with all your heart and with all your soul.

^{Rom 10:6–8}
^{1 Jn 5:3} **The Law of God is accessible to all**
¹¹"For this commandment which I command you this day is not ^{Jn 3:13} too hard for you, neither is it far off. ¹²It is not in heaven, that you ^{Rom 10:6} should say, 'Who will go up for us to heaven, and bring it to us, that we may hear it and do it?' ¹³Neither is it beyond the sea, that you should say, 'Who will go over the sea for us, and bring it to

---

needed to keep to it; only the grace of Jesus Christ could do that. Referring to the Letter to the Romans (8:2–4), John Paul II says that "the Apostle Paul invites us to consider in the perspective of the history of salvation, which reaches its fulfilment in Christ, *the relationship between the* (Old) *Law and grace* (the New Law). He recognizes the pedagogic function of the Law, which, by enabling sinful man to take stock of his own powerlessness and by stripping him of the presumption of his self-sufficiency, leads him to ask for and to receive 'life in the Spirit'. Only in this new life is it possible to carry out God's commandments. Indeed, it is through faith in Christ that we have been made righteous (cf. Rom 3:28): the 'righteousness' which the Law demands, but is unable to give, is found by every believer to be revealed and granted by the Lord Jesus. Once again it is St Augustine who admirably sums up

this Pauline dialectic of law and grace: 'The law was given that grace might be sought; and grace was given, that the law might be fulfilled' (*De spiritu et littera*, 19, 34)" (*Veritatis splendor*, 23).

30:11–14. What this passage directly refers to is how privileged Israel was to have the Law. The sacred writer puts it very beautifully, by using two nice metaphors in a passage that has a certain poetic rhythm to it. St Paul, in his Letter to the Romans (10:6–8), uses this passage, applying it not to knowledge of the Law but to "the word of faith" that is preached by the apostles: it is now that word (as previously it was the Law) that makes manifest the precepts and commandments of God and (like the Law in its time, too) it should be constantly on our lips and in our heart. Theodoret of Cyrrhus (commenting on the Greek Septuagint version, which adds in v. 14

---

manuum tuarum, in subole uteri tui et in fructu iumentorum tuorum et in ubertate terrae tuae, in rerum omnium largitate; revertetur enim Dominus, ut gaudeat super te in omnibus bonis, sicut gavisus est in patribus tuis. ¹⁰Si tamen audieris vocem Domini Dei tui et custodieris mandata eius et praecepta, quae in hac lege conscripta sunt, et revertaris ad Dominum Deum tuum in toto corde tuo et in tota anima tua. ¹¹Mandatum hoc, quod ego praecipio tibi hodie, non supra te est neque procul positum ¹²nec in caelo situm, ut possis dicere: 'Quis nobis ad caelum valet ascendere, ut deferat illud ad nos, et audiamus atque opere compleamus?'. ¹³Neque trans mare positum, ut causeris et dicas: 'Quis nobis transfretare poterit mare et illud ad nos usque deferre, ut possimus audire et facere quod praeceptum est?'. ¹⁴Sed

us, that we may hear it and do it?' [14]But the word is very near you; *Rom 10:8*
it is in your mouth and in your heart, so that you can do it.

Deut 11:26–28
Ps 1
Rom 6:21–23

Israel facing life and death: the two ways
[15]"See, I have set before you this day life and good, death and
evil. [16]If you obey the commandments of the LORD your God[c] Rom 2:26
which I command you this day, by loving the LORD your God, by
walking in his ways, and by keeping his commandments and his
statutes and his ordinances, then you shall live and multiply, and
the LORD your God will bless you in the land which you are entering to take possession of it. [17]But if your heart turns away, and
you will not hear, but are drawn away to worship other gods and
serve them, [18]I declare to you this day, that you shall perish; you

---

"and in your hands") says: "The mouth
stands for meditation on the divine
words; the heart, readiness of spirit; the
hands for doing what is commanded"
(*Quaestiones in Octateuchum*, 38).

The Christian people, who possess
the New Law and the New Covenant, are
in an even better position than the people
of old, for they have been given the grace
of Christ. And so the Council of Trent
teaches that "God does not command
impossible things; when he makes a
commandment he is telling you to do
what you can and to ask (his help) as
regards what is beyond you, and he helps
you to fulfil it" (*De iustificatione*, 11). In
the Old Law, even though the Israelites
did not have available to them the grace
won by Christ, divine Providence helped
them to do what was required of them in
anticipation of that grace.

30:15–20. The last verses of the dis-

course addresses a touching and solemn
appeal to Israel, spelling out what its
responsibilities are: it is completely free
to choose between good and evil; but
depending on whether it is faithful or
unfaithful, it will be blessed or punished
by the Lord.

The concluding exhortation (vv.
19–20) is particularly moving: "choose
life", loving the Lord, for "that means
life". In the New Testament we find passages which echo the same ideas: "I am
the life," our Lord will say (Jn 14:6); and
St Paul: "It is no longer I who live, but
Christ who lives in me" (Gal 2:20); "for
to me to live is Christ, and to die is gain"
(Phil 1:21).

Cf. RSV footnote to v. 16: this follows the (fuller) Septuagint Greek (as do
the New Vulgate and the Spanish). The
words "If you obey the commandments
of the Lord your God" do help to stress
the contrast with what it says in v. 17.

---

iuxta te est sermo valde in ore tuo et in corde tuo, ut facias illum. [15]Considera quod hodie proposuerim
in conspectu tuo vitam et bonum, et e contrario mortem et malum. [16]Si oboedieris mandatis Domini
Dei tui, quae ego praecipio tibi hodie, ut diligas Dominum Deum tuum et ambules in viis eius et custodias mandata illius et praecepta atque iudicia, vives; ac multiplicabit te benedicetque tibi in terra, ad
quam ingredieris possidendam. [17]Sin autem aversum fuerit cor tuum, et audire nolueris atque errore
deceptus adoraveris deos alienos et servieris eis, [18]praedico vobis hodie quod pereatis et parvo tempore

c. Gk: Heb lacks *If you obey the commandments of the Lord your God*

shall not live long in the land which you are going over the Jordan to enter and possess. [19]I call heaven and earth to witness against you this day, that I have set before you life and death, blessing and curse; therefore choose life, that you and your descendants may live, [20]loving the LORD your God, obeying his voice, and cleaving to him; for that means life to you and length of days, that you may dwell in the land which the LORD swore to your fathers, to Abraham, to Isaac, and to Jacob, to give them."

Mt 26:1

Historical Conclusion*

Joshua and his mission

31 [1]So Moses continued to speak these words to all Israel. [2]And he said to them, "I am a hundred and twenty years old this day; I am no longer able to go out and come in. The LORD has said to me, 'You shall not go over this Jordan.' [3]The LORD your God himself will go over before you; he will destroy these nations before you, so that you shall dispossess them; and Joshua will go

---

*31:1—34:12. These chapters form a conclusion which seems to refer not just to Deuteronomy but to the entire Pentateuch. The last editor of the text has availed himself of material from earlier traditions (more from some than from others).

The predominant type of material here is what we might call "historical", including (as is common to both Eastern and Classical history writing) a number of poetic pieces, notably the "Song of Moses" (32:1–43) and the "Blessing of Moses" (33:2–29). The narrative sections cover the last days of Moses, and the appointment of Joshua and his mission (31:1–9, 14–15), the ceremonial reading of the Law (31:9–13) and the death of the great deliverer of Israel (chap. 34).

31:1–8. Joshua will take over the leadership of Israel from Moses (cf. also vv. 14, 23) and will bring about the conquest of the promised land.

The one hundred and twenty years of Moses' life are divided into three periods

---

moremini in terra, ad quam, Iordane transmisso, ingredieris possidendam. [19]Testes invoco hodie contra vos caelum et terram quod proposuerim vobis vitam et mortem, benedictionem et maledictionem. Elige ergo vitam, ut et tu vivas et semen tuum [20]et diligas Dominum Deum tuum atque oboedias voci eius et illi adhaereas—ipse est enim vita tua et longitudo dierum tuorum—ut habites in terra, pro qua iuravit Dominus patribus tuis Abraham, Isaac et Iacob, ut daret eam illis». [1]Abiit itaque Moyses et locutus est omnia verba haec ad universum Israel [2]et dixit ad eos: «Centum viginti annorum sum hodie, non possum ultra egredi et ingredi, praesertim cum et Dominus dixerit mihi: 'Non transibis Iordanem istum'. [3]Dominus Deus tuus ipse transibit ante te; ipse delebit gentes has in conspectu tuo, et possidebis eas, et Iosue transibit ante te, sicut locutus est Dominus. [4]Facietque Dominus eis, sicut fecit Sehon

over at your head, as the LORD has spoken. ⁴And the LORD will do to them as he did to Sihon and Og, the kings of the Amorites, and to their land, when he destroyed them. ⁵And the LORD will give them over to you, and you shall do to them according to all the commandment which I have commanded you. ⁶Be strong and of good courage, do not fear or be in dread of them: for it is the Lord your God who goes with you; he will not fail you or forsake you." *Heb 13:5*

⁷Then Moses summoned Joshua, and said to him in the sight of all Israel, "Be strong and of good courage; for you shall go with this people into the land which the LORD has sworn to their fathers to give them; and you shall put them in possession of it. ⁸It is the LORD who goes before you; he will be with you, he will not fail you or forsake you; do not fear or be dismayed." *Heb 4:8* *Heb 13:5*

The ritual reading of the Law

⁹And Moses wrote this law, and gave it to the priests the sons of Levi, who carried the ark of the covenant of the LORD, and to all the elders of Israel. ¹⁰And Moses commanded them, "At the end of every seven years, at the set time of the year of release, at the feast of booths, ¹¹when all Israel comes to appear before the LORD your God at the place which he will choose, you shall read this law before all Israel in their hearing. ¹²Assemble the people, men, *2 Kings 23:1ff* *Ex 17:14; 34:27*

---

of forty years each—in Egypt (Acts 7:28), in Midian (Ex 7:7) and in the desert. It could be that the number forty is meant to indicate a generation; but it is not easy to say exactly what the hagiographer had in mind. Anyway, the three phases in the great lawgiver's life are fairly clear to see. In each of them God made manifest his power and his choice of Moses, and at every stage Moses proved docile and effective.

31:9–13. This passage prescribes a periodic reading out of the Law in the year of Release (cf. 15:1–18); all the inhabitants of Israel are to be present, not just the men, whose duty it was to attend on the feast of Tabernacles as a matter of course (cf. 16:16). This reading would help people to know and be familiar with the commandments of the Lord (cf. 30:11–14). The rule about all meeting in the one place was more suited to the early times

---

et Og regibus Amorraeorum et terrae eorum delevitque eos. ⁵Cum ergo et hos tradiderit vobis, similiter facietis eis, sicut praecepi vobis. ⁶ Viriliter agite et confortamini; nolite timere nec paveatis a conspectu eorum, quia Dominus Deus tuus ipse est ductor tuus et non dimittet nec derelinquet te». ⁷Vocavitque Moyses Iosue et dixit ei coram omni Israel: «Confortare et esto robustus; tu enim introduces populum istum in terram, quam daturum se patribus eorum iuravit Dominus, et tu eam sorte divides eis. ⁸Et Dominus, qui ductor tuus est, ipse erit tecum, non dimittet nec derelinquet te: noli timere nec paveas». ⁹Et scripsit Moyses legem hanc et tradidit eam sacerdotibus filiis Levi, qui portabant arcam foederis Domini, et cunctis senioribus Israel; ¹⁰praecepitque eis dicens: «Post septem annos, anno remissionis, in sollemnitate Tabernaculorum, ¹¹convenientibus cunctis ex Israel, ut appareant in conspectu Domini Dei tui in loco, quem elegerit, leges verba legis huius coram omni Israel, audientibus eis; ¹²congrega populum tam viros quam mulieres, parvulos et advenas, qui sunt intra portas tuas, ut audientes discant

women, and little ones, and the sojourner within your towns, that they may hear and learn to fear the LORD your God, and be careful to do all the words of this law, [13]and that their children, who have not known it, may hear and learn to fear the LORD your God, as long as you live in the land which you are going over the Jordan to possess."

Israel's future apostasy

Ex 25:22   [14]And the LORD said to Moses, "Behold, the days approach when you must die; call Joshua, and present yourselves in the tent of meeting, that I may commission him." And Moses and Joshua went and presented themselves in the tent of meeting. [15]And the LORD appeared in the tent in a pillar of cloud; and the pillar of cloud stood by the door of the tent.

Ex 34:15–16   [16]And the LORD said to Moses, "Behold, you are about to
Lev 20:5   sleep with your fathers; then this people will rise and play the harlot after the strange gods of the land, where they go to be

---

when Israel was still a small people; it helps underline the fact that it is one people, with one faith and one code of conduct.

Applying this to the New Testament, Pope John Paul II wrote: "Within the unity of the Church, promoting and preserving the faith and the moral life is the task entrusted by Jesus to the Apostles (cf. Mt 28:19–20), a task which continues in the ministry of their successors. This is apparent from the *living Tradition*, whereby—as the Second Vatican Council teaches—'the Church, in her teaching, life and worship, perpetuates and hands on to every generation all that she is and all that she believes. This Tradition which comes from the Apostles, progresses in the Church under the assistance of the Holy Spirit' (*Dei Verbum*, 8) [. . .]. Within Trad-

ition, *the authentic interpretation* of the Lord's law develops, with the help of the Holy Spirit. The same Spirit who is at the origin of the Revelation of Jesus' commandments and teachings guarantees that they will be reverently preserved, faithfully expounded and correctly applied in different times and places. This constant 'putting into practice' of the commandments is the sign and fruit of a deeper insight into Revelation and of an understanding in the light of faith of new historical and cultural situations" (*Veritatis splendor*, 27).

31:14–30. Once again the sacred writer refers to the infidelities of the people of Israel, which bring down terrible retribution. The Song of Moses bears witness to this unfaithfulness (v. 19).

et timeant Dominum Deum vestrum et custodiant impleantque omnes sermones legis huius; [13]filii quoque eorum, qui nunc ignorant, audiant et discant timere Dominum Deum vestrum cunctis diebus, quibus versamini in terra, ad quam vos, Iordane transmisso, pergitis obtinendam». [14]Et ait Dominus ad Moysen: «Ecce prope sunt dies mortis tuae; voca Iosue, et state in tabernaculo conventus, ut praecipiam ei». Abierunt ergo Moyses et Iosue et steterunt in tabernaculo conventus; [15]apparuitque Dominus ibi in columna nubis, quae stetit in introitu tabernaculi. [16]Dixitque Dominus ad Moysen: «Ecce tu dormies cum patribus tuis, et populus iste consurgens fornicabitur post deos alienos terrae, ad quam

among them, and they will forsake me and break my covenant which I have made with them. [17]Then my anger will be kindled against them in that day, and I will forsake them and hide my face from them, and they will be devoured; and many evils and troubles will come upon them, so that they will say in that day, 'Have not these evils come upon us because our God is not among us?' [18]And I will surely hide my face in that day on account of all the evil which they have done, because they have turned to other gods.

The song of witness

[19]Now therefore write this song, and teach it to the people of   Deut 8:7–20
Israel; put it in their mouths, that this song may be a witness for me against the people of Israel. [20]For when I have brought them into the land flowing with milk and honey, which I swore to give to their fathers, and they have eaten and are full and grown fat, they will turn to other gods and serve them, and despise me and

---

Abundance of worldly wealth is often a danger to the holiness of individuals and nations (cf. 8:7–20). This passage prophesies to that effect, as does the prophet Hosea: "It was I who knew you in the wilderness, in the land of drought; but when they were fed to the full, they were filled, and their heart was lifted up; therefore they forgot me" (Hos 13:5–6). In fact, there were many in salvation history who were righteous and devout until wealth and power led them astray, as happened to King Solomon (cf. 1 Kings 10–11).

Moreover, the sad experience of the chosen people is being repeated endlessly in human history, with people who are well aware of all God's gifts (the Incarnation; the death of Jesus on the

cross; the Sacraments . . .) and yet they turn their backs on him and are unfaithful to him. Hence the *Roman Catechism's* exhortation and prayer that "we yield not to evil desires, and be not wearied in enduring temptation; that we deviate not from the way of the Lord (Deut 31:29); that in adversity, as in prosperity, we preserve equanimity and fortitude; and that God may never deprive us of his protection" (4, 15, 15).

Israel's apostasy is depicted as a kind of prostitution (v. 16); the same imagery is used elsewhere in the Pentateuch (cf., e.g., Ex 34:15–16; Lev 20:5), because the Covenant between the Lord and his people is seen as a kind of marriage. The prophet Hosea will use this simile extensively.

---

ingredietur; ibi derelinquet me et irritum faciet foedus, quod pepigi cum eo. [17]Et irascetur furor meus contra eum in die illo, et derelinquam eos et abscondam faciem meam ab eis, et erit in devorationem; invenient eum mala multa et afflictiones, ita ut dicat in illo die: 'Vere, quia non est Deus mecum, invenerunt me haec mala'. [18]Ego autem abscondam et celabo faciem meam in die illo, propter omnia mala, quae fecit, quia secutus est deos alienos. [19]Nunc itaque scribite vobis canticum istud, et doce filios Israel, ut memoriter teneant et ore decantent, ut sit mihi carmen istud pro testimonio inter filios Israel. [20]Introducam enim eum in terram, pro qua iuravi patribus eius, lacte et melle manantem. Cumque comederit et saturatus crassusque fuerit, avertetur ad deos alienos, et servient eis detrahentque

break my covenant. ²¹And when many evils and troubles have come upon them, this song shall confront them as a witness (for it will live unforgotten in the mouths of their descendants); for I know the purposes which they are already forming, before I have brought them into the land that I swore to give." ²²So Moses wrote this song the same day, and taught it to the people of Israel.

²³And the LORD commissioned Joshua the son of Nun and said, "Be strong and of good courage; for you shall bring the children of Israel into the land which I swore to give them: I will be with you."

The Law placed beside the ark

²⁴When Moses had finished writing the words of this law in a book, to the very end, ²⁵Moses commanded the Levites who carried the ark of the covenant of the LORD, ²⁶"Take this book of the law, and put it by the side of the ark of the covenant of the LORD your God, that it may be there for a witness against you. ²⁷For I know how rebellious and stubborn you are; behold, while I am yet alive with you, today you have been rebellious against the LORD; how much more after my death! ²⁸Assemble to me all the elders of your tribes, and your officers, that I may speak these words in their ears and call heaven and earth to witness against them. ²⁹For I know that after my death you will surely act corruptly, and turn aside from the way which I have commanded you; and in the days to come evil will befall you, because you will do what is evil in the sight of the LORD, provoking him to anger through the work of your hands."

³⁰Then Moses spoke the words of this song until they were finished, in the ears of all the assembly of Israel:

Mt 10:18
Jn 5:45f

---

mihi et irritum facient pactum meum. ²¹Postquam invenerint eum mala multa et afflictiones, respondebit ei canticum istud pro testimonio, quod nulla delebit oblivio ex ore seminis sui; scio enim cogitationes eius, quae facit hodie, antequam introducam eum in terram, quam ei pollicitus sum». ²²Scripsit ergo Moyses canticum istud in die illo et docuit filios Israel. ²³Praecepitque Dominus Iosue filio Nun et ait: «Confortare et esto robustus; tu enim introduces filios Israel in terram, quam eis pollicitus sum, et ego ero tecum». ²⁴Postquam ergo scripsit Moyses verba legis huius in volumine atque complevit, ²⁵praecepit Levitis, qui portabant arcam foederis Domini, dicens: ²⁶«Tollite librum legis istum et ponite eum in latere arcae foederis Domini Dei vestri, ut sit ibi contra te in testimonium. ²⁷Ego enim scio contentionem tuam et cervicem tuam durissimam. Adhuc vivente me vobiscum, semper contentiose egistis contra Dominum; quanto magis cum mortuus fuero? ²⁸Congregate ad me omnes maiores natu per tribus vestras atque praefectos vestros, et loquar audientibus eis sermones istos et invocabo contra eos caelum et terram. ²⁹Novi enim quod post mortem meam inique agetis et declinabitis de via, quam praecepi vobis, et occurrent vobis mala in extremo tempore, quando feceritis malum in conspectu Domini, ut irritetis eum per opera manuum vestrarum». ³⁰Locutus est ergo Moyses, audiente universo coetu Israel, verba carminis huius et ad finem usque complevit: ¹«Audite,

The song of Moses*

32 [1]"Give ear, O heavens, and I will speak;   _{Is 55:10}
and let the earth hear the words of my mouth.
[2]May my teaching drop as the rain,
my speech distil as the dew,
as the gentle rain upon the tender grass,
and as the showers upon the herb.
[3]For I will proclaim the name of the LORD.
Ascribe greatness to our God!

[4]"The Rock, his work is perfect;
for all his ways are justice.
A God of faithfulness and without iniquity,
just and right is he.

Gen 1:31
Is 44:8; 17:10
Ps 89:26; 18:31
Rom 9:14
1 Jn 1:9
Rev 15:3–4;
16:5

---

*32:1–52. The Song of Moses is a sublime poetic description of the Covenant. It elaborates on the very different ways the two protagonists of the Covenant behave in its regard: on the one hand, there is God's unwavering fidelity; on the other, Israel's disloyalty. It begins by recalling all the wonderful benefits God has showered on his people (vv. 1–14) and their incredible ingratitude (vv. 15–18). It goes on to describe God's natural irritation and how he allows Israel to fall into the hands of its enemies (vv. 19–25). But the arrogance of Israel's oppressors and God's fidelity and mercy will eventually bring him to pardon his people and deliver them (vv. 26–43). The Song, filled with great epic force, paints a panoramic picture of the history of Israel, similar to that found in some of the Psalms (cf., e.g., Ps 78; 105; 106) and in passages in the book of the prophet Ezekiel (cf., e.g., chaps. 16 and 20). In many stanzas we can see the profound ideas about God which underlie the thinking of the poem, such as the fact that he is Father and Creator (v. 6) and the God who lives eternally (v. 40).

This poem contains features which have all the appearance of deriving from very early traditions, as well as others whose concepts and style are closer to those of Wisdom literature and to certain later prophetical texts. All this suggests that this is a text developed over a long period of time rather than one written at a given time: at least there are reasonable grounds for thinking so.

32:1–14. These verses very movingly and poetically recall the goodness of God to his people. We see him spreading the nations over the face of the earth and keeping Israel for himself, to be his chosen portion, even seeing to the very number of his people (vv. 8–9). Instead of "sons of Israel" (v. 8), the Septuagint has "angels of God"—which is more or less the same as the "sons of God" found in some Hebrew manuscripts, and which would mean that God gives charge of each nation to one of his angels (cf. Deut 10:13, 20–21), but in the case of Israel he himself looks after it. Verses 10–11 are a particularly touching

---

caeli, quae loquor; / audiat terra verba oris mei! / [2]Stillet ut pluvia doctrina mea, / fluat ut ros eloquium meum / quasi imber super herbam / et quasi stillae super gramina. / [3]Quia nomen Domini invocabo: / date magnificentiam Deo nostro! / [4]Petra, perfecta sunt opera eius, / quia omnes viae eius iustitia. /

^{Mt 12:39;}
^{17:17}
^{Acts 2:40}
^{Phil 2:15}

⁵They have dealt corruptly with him,
they are no longer his children because of their blemish;
they are a perverse and crooked generation.

^{Jer 31:9}
^{Prov 3:11–12}
^{Ps 88}
^{Sir 23:1–4}
^{Wis 2:16; 14:3}
^{Deut 1:31}

⁶Do you thus requite the LORD,
you foolish and senseless people?
Is not he your father, who created you,
who made you and established you?
⁷Remember the days of old,
consider the years of many generations;
ask your father, and he will show you;
your elders, and they will tell you.

^{Gen 10}
^{Acts 17:26}
^{Heb 2:5}

⁸When the Most High gave to the nations their inheritance,
when he separated the sons of men,
he fixed the bounds of the peoples
according to the number of the sons of God.ᵈ

---

instance of a description of God's maternal care for Israel.

The name "the Rock" (v. 5) used to describe the Lord (which recurs throughout the poem) underlines his loyalty to the Covenant. It is found in some other places in the Old Testament, such as Psalm 89:26: "He shall cry to me, 'Thou art my Father, my God, and the Rock of my salvation' " or Isaiah 44:8b: "And you are my witnesses! Is there a God besides me! There is no Rock; I know not any!" (cf. also Ps 18:31; Is 17:10). In the New Testament, this name is applied to Christ, thus indicating his divinity (cf. 1 Cor 10:4 and the note on same).

In the entire Old Testament God is called "Father" more than twenty times. This description is linked to his absolute dominion or the fact that he is the Creator of heaven and earth, or is the Founder of Israel. The present verse is a key one where this description occurs. Other important relevant passages are,

for example, Exodus 4:22–33, Hosea 11:1–4 and Deuteronomy 1:31. In the Old Testament God's fatherhood has to do mostly with his relationship with Israel as a whole. Some fifty times the Old Testament refers to the relationship between God and Israel as being one of father and son. A father gives his son life and sustenance and all kinds of consolations (cf. Jer 31:9), and he also corrects him (cf. Prov 3:11–12). God's fatherhood is to be seen at its most intimate and profound in the prayers of the just man in the Psalms (cf. Ps 88) and the Wisdom books (cf. Sir 23:1, 4; Wis 2:16; 14:3).

However, the personal piety of the Israelite never managed to express itself in the terms used by Jesus and in the way he taught his disciples. We could say that, recourse to God as Father, in personal piety, was a revelation from Jesus received by the early Christian community.

32:8–9. In these two verses we see the

Deus fidelis et absque ulla iniquitate, / iustus et rectus. / ⁵Peccaverunt ei non filii eius in sordibus suis, / generatio prava atque perversa. / ⁶Haeccine redditis Domino, / popule stulte et insipiens? / Numquid non ipse est pater tuus, qui possedit te, / ipse fecit et stabilivit te? / ⁷Memento dierum antiquorum, /

d. Compare Gk: Heb *Israel*

⁹For the LORD's portion is his people,
  Jacob his allotted heritage.

Deut 7:6

¹⁰"He found him in a desert land,
  and in the howling waste of the wilderness;
he encircled him, he cared for him,
  he kept him as the apple of his eye.
¹¹Like an eagle that stirs up its nest,
  that flutters over its young,
spreading out its wings, catching them,
  bearing them on its pinions,
¹²the LORD alone did lead him,
  and there was no foreign god with him.
¹³He made him ride on the high places of the earth,
  and he ate the produce of the field;
and he made him suck honey out of the rock,
  and oil out of the flinty rock.
¹⁴Curds from the herd, and milk from the flock,
  with fat of lambs and rams,
  herds of Bashan and goats,
with the finest of the wheat—
  and of the blood of the grape you drank wine.

Jer 2:6
2 Cor 6:14

Ps 17:8
Lk 13:34

¹⁵"But Jeshurun waxed fat, and kicked;
  you waxed fat, you grew thick, you became sleek;

Deut 33:5–26
Is 44:2
Eph 1:6

theme of the land God gives his people expressed in very poetic and sapiential language. Over the centuries the Hebrews were very conscious of the fact that they were the chosen people and had been promised a Land as a sheer gift from God.

However, in salvation history the "promised land" gradually acquires dimensions which transcend the mere geographical meaning of "land of Israel" until it becomes the "heavenly fatherland"—heaven and eternal blessedness.

32:15–18. Despite everything done for them, the chosen people prove ungrateful to God and go after strange gods. The sacred writer (possibly in view of the

cogita generationes singulas; / interroga patrem tuum, et annuntiabit tibi, / maiores tuos, et dicent tibi. / ⁸Quando dividebat Altissimus gentes, / quando separabat filios Adam, / constituit terminos populorum / iuxta numerum filiorum Israel; / ⁹pars autem Domini populus eius, / Iacob funiculus hereditatis eius. / ¹⁰Invenit eum in terra deserta, / in loco horroris et ululatu solitudinis, / circumdedit eum et attendit / et custodivit quasi pupillam oculi sui. / ¹¹Sicut aquila provocans ad volandum pullos suos / et super eos volitans expandit alas suas / et assumpsit eum / atque portavit super pennas suas. / ¹²Dominus solus dux eius fuit, / et non erat cum eo deus alienus. / ¹³Constituit eum super excelsam terram, / ut comederet fructus agrorum, / ut sugeret mel de petra / oleumque de saxo durissimo, / ¹⁴butyrum de armento et lac de ovibus, / cum adipe agnorum et arietum / filiorum Basan et hircorum, / cum medulla tritici, / et sanguinem uvae biberet meracissimum. / ¹⁵Incrassatus est dilectus et recalcitravit; / incrassatus, impinguatus, dilatatus / dereliquit Deum factorem suum / et recessit a Petra salutari suo. /

then he forsook God who made him,
and scoffed at the Rock of his salvation.

^{Deut 4:24} ¹⁶They stirred him to jealousy with strange gods;
with abominable practices they provoked him to anger.

^{1 Cor 10:20}
^{Rev 9:20} ¹⁷They sacrificed to demons which were no gods,
to gods they had never known,
to new gods that had come in of late,
whom your fathers had never dreaded.

^{Is 17:10} ¹⁸You were unmindful of the Rock that begot[e] you,
and you forgot the God who gave you birth.

¹⁹"The LORD saw it, and spurned them,
because of the provocation of his sons and his daughters.

^{Mt 17:17} ²⁰And he said, 'I will hide my face from them,
I will see what their end will be,
for they are a perverse generation,
children in whom is no faithfulness.

^{Rom 10:19}
^{1 Cor 10:22} ²¹They have stirred me to jealousy with what is no god;
they have provoked me with their idols.

---

similarity of the consonants) calls Israel "Jeshurun" (v. 15: this is an honorific title, equivalent to "upright" or "just", and it is to be found in only three other places in the Bible (33:5, 26; Is 44:2); in the context of Israel's unfaithfulness, it is a bitter irony to describe it in this way. The references to Israel's growing fat are reminiscent of the earlier warnings about the danger that in times of prosperity the Israelites will forget about God (cf., e.g. 31:20).

In v. 18 we see once more the father/mother imagery: "the Rock begot you", "the God who gave you birth".

The chosen people's ingratitude and infidelity is repeated by mankind down the centuries. The benefits God has show-

ered on men through the Redemption are immensely greater than those that he gave Israel. In this connexion St John Chrysostom teaches, apropos of Baptism: "The Jews could see miracles taking place. You too will see them, even greater miracles, more spectacular ones than the Jews experienced when they left Egypt. You do not see the pharoah and his armies drowning, but you have seen the demon and his ilk being overwhelmed. The Jews crossed the sea; you have crossed over death. They were set free from the Egyptians; you have seen yourself set free from demons. They escaped a savage slavery; you have escaped the bondage of sin, a much worse and terrible bondage" (*Ad illuminados catecheses*, 3, 24).

---

¹⁶Provocaverunt eum in diis alienis / et in abominationibus ad iracundiam concitaverunt. / ¹⁷Immolaverunt daemonibus et non Deo, / diis, quos ignorabant; / novi recentesque venerunt, / quos non coluerunt patres vestri. / ¹⁸Petram, quae te genuit, dereliquisti, / et oblitus es Domini creatoris tui. / ¹⁹Vidit Dominus et sprevit, / quia provocaverunt eum filii sui et filiae. / ²⁰Et ait: 'Abscondam faciem meam ab eis / et considerabo novissima eorum; / generatio enim perversa est, / et infideles filii. / ²¹Ipsi

e. Or *bore*

So I will stir them to jealousy with those who are no people;
I will provoke them with a foolish nation.
²²For a fire is kindled by my anger,
and it burns to the depths of Sheol,
devours the earth and its increase,
and sets on fire the foundations of the mountains.

²³"'And I will heap evils upon them;
I will spend my arrows upon them;
²⁴ they shall be wasted with hunger,
and devoured with burning heat
and poisonous pestilence;
and I will send the teeth of beasts against them,
with venom of crawling things of the dust.
²⁵In the open the sword shall bereave,
and in the chambers shall be terror,
destroying both young man and virgin,
the sucking child with the man of gray hairs.
²⁶I would have said, "I will scatter them afar,
I will make the remembrance of them cease from among
men,"
²⁷had I not feared provocation by the enemy,
lest their adversaries should judge amiss,

Ex 32:7–14
Deut 9:25–29

32:19–33. The Lord's understandable indignation leads to Israel's punishment. Because the Israelites have gone over to idols ("what is no god"), God is going to allow them be made vassals of "those who are no people" (v. 21).

There is even a danger of his permitting the chosen people to disappear altogether (v. 26); but the foolishness and arrogance of their oppressors (they attribute to their own might what is really a retribution inflicted by God) will prevent this happening (vv. 26–33): this is an argument similar to that used by Moses after the episode of the golden calf when the Lord talks about possibly destroying his people (9:25–29; Ex 32:7–14).

In his Letter to the Romans St Paul will apply v. 21 to the conversion of the Gentiles, contrasting that with the unfaithfulness of Israel (cf. Rom 10:19).

---

me provocaverunt in eo, / qui non erat Deus, / et irritaverunt in vanitatibus suis; / et ego provocabo eos in eo, / qui non est populus, / et in gente stulta irritabo illos. / ²²Ignis succensus est in furore meo / et ardebit usque ad inferni profundissima; / devorabitque terram cum germine suo / et montium fundamenta comburet. / ²³Congregabo super eos mala / et sagittas meas complebo in eis. / ²⁴Consumentur fame et devorabuntur febri / et peste amarissima; / dentes bestiarum immittam in eos, / cum veneno serpentium in pulvere. / ²⁵Foris vastabit eos gladius / et intus pavor: / iuvenem simul ac virginem, / lactantem cum homine sene. ²⁶Dixi: Disperdam eos, / cessare faciam ex hominibus memoriam eorum!, / ²⁷ sed arrogantiam inimicorum timui, / ne superbirent hostes eorum / et dicerent: "Manus nostra excelsa, / et non Dominus fecit haec omnia!" / ²⁸Gens enim absque consilio est / et sine prudentia. / ²⁹Utinam saperent et intellegerent haec / ac novissima sua providerent! / ³⁰Quomodo persequatur unus

lest they should say, "Our hand is triumphant,
the LORD has not wrought all this."'

Lk 19:42

²⁸"For they are a nation void of counsel,
and there is no understanding in them.
²⁹If they were wise, they would understand this,
they would discern their latter end!
³⁰How should one chase a thousand,
and two put ten thousand to flight,
unless their Rock had sold them,
and the LORD had given them up?
³¹For their rock is not as our Rock,
even our enemies themselves being judges.
³²For their vine comes from the vine of Sodom,
and from the fields of Gomorrah;
their grapes are grapes of poison,
their clusters are bitter;
³³their wine is the poison of serpents,
and the cruel venom of asps.

³⁴"Is not this laid up in store with me,
sealed up in my treasuries?

Lk 21:22
Rom 12:19
Heb 10:30

³⁵Vengeance is mine, and recompense,
for the time when their foot shall slip;
for the day of their calamity is at hand,
and their doom comes swiftly.

Heb 10:30

³⁶For the LORD will vindicate his people
and have compassion on his servants,
when he sees that their power is gone,
and there is none remaining, bond or free.

32:34–43. In the end, the mercy of God prevails and he restores Israel and sets it free from its enemies. The words God addresses to his people are a new and radical assertion of the monotheism that is expected of them (cf. especially v. 39), clearly differentiating him from the false gods of the pagans: as against all these non-gods, he is the only God there is; as against their weakness and powerlessness, he is the almighty Lord of life and death.

---

mille, / et duo fugent decem milia? / Nonne ideo, quia Petra eorum vendidit eos, / et Dominus tradidit illos?'. / ³¹Non enim est petra eorum ut Petra nostra, / et inimici nostri sunt iudices. / ³²Vere de vinea Sodomorum vinea eorum / et de suburbanis Gomorrae; / uva eorum uva fellis / et botri amarissimi; / ³³fel draconum vinum eorum / et venenum aspidum insanabile. / ³⁴Nonne haec condita sunt apud me / et signata in thesauris meis? / ³⁵Mea est ultio, et ego retribuam in tempore, / in quo labetur pes eorum! / Iuxta est dies perditionis, / et adesse festinat sors eorum. / ³⁶Iudicabit Dominus populum suum / et in servis suis miserebitur; / videbit quod infirmata sit manus, / et defecerint clausi ac liberati. / ³⁷Et dicet:

³⁷Then he will say, 'Where are their gods,
the rock in which they took refuge,
³⁸who ate the fat of their sacrifices,
and drank the wine of their drink offering?
Let them rise up and help you,
let them be your protection!

³⁹"'See now that I, even I, am he,
and there is no god beside me;
I kill and I make alive;
I wound and I heal;
and there is none that can deliver out of my hand.
⁴⁰For I lift up my hand to heaven,
and swear, As I live for ever,
⁴¹if I whet my glittering sword,^f
and my hand takes hold on judgment,
I will take vengeance on my adversaries,
and will requite those who hate me.
⁴²I will make my arrows drunk with blood,
and my sword shall devour flesh—
with the blood of the slain and the captives,
from the long-haired heads of the enemy.'

⁴³"Praise his people, O you nations;
for he avenges the blood of his servants,
and takes vengeance on his adversaries,
and makes expiation for the land of his people."^g

⁴⁴Moses came and recited all the words of this song in the hearing of the people, he and Joshua^h the son of Nun.

The Law, the source of life

⁴⁵And when Moses had finished speaking all these words to all Israel, ⁴⁶he said to them, "Lay to heart all the words which I

Is 19:22; 34:10, 3; 41:4 Jn 5:21

Rev 1:18; 10:5f

Jer 46:10

Mt 4:10; 25:31 *Rom 15:10* *Heb 1:6* Rev 6:10; 12:12; 19:2

'Ubi sunt dii eorum, / petra, in qua habebant fiduciam, / ³⁸de quorum victimis comedebant adipes, / et bibebant vinum libaminum? / Surgant et opitulentur vobis / et in necessitate vos protegant! / ³⁹Videte nunc quod ego sim solus, / et non sit Deus praeter me. / Ego occidam et ego vivere faciam; / percutiam et ego sanabo; / et non est qui de manu mea possit eruere. / ⁴⁰Levabo ad caelum manum meam / et dicam: Vivo ego in aeternum! / ⁴¹Si acuero ut fulgur gladium meum, / et arripuerit iudicium manus mea, / reddam ultionem hostibus meis / et his, qui oderunt me, retribuam. / ⁴²Inebriabo sagittas meas sanguine, / et gladius meus devorabit carnes, / de cruore occisorum et captivorum, / de capite ducum inimici!' / ⁴³Laudate, gentes, populum eius, / quia sanguinem servorum suorum ulciscetur, / et vindictam retribuet in hostes suos / et propitius erit terrae populi sui». ⁴⁴Venit ergo Moyses et locutus est omnia verba cantici huius in auribus populi ipse et Iosue filius Nun; ⁴⁵complevitque omnes sermones

f. Heb *the lightning of my sword*   **g.** Gk Vg: Heb *his land his people*   **h.** Gk Syr Vg: Heb *Hoshea*

enjoin upon you this day, that you may command them to your children, that they may be careful to do all the words of this law.
Acts 7:38 ⁴⁷For it is no trifle for you, but it is your life, and thereby you shall live long in the land which you are going over the Jordan to possess."

Moses' death foretold

⁴⁸And the LORD said to Moses that very day, ⁴⁹"Ascend this mountain of the Abarim, Mount Nebo, which is in the land of Moab, opposite Jericho; and view the land of Canaan, which I give to the people of Israel for a possession; ⁵⁰and die on the mountain which you ascend, and be gathered to your people, as Aaron your brother died in Mount Hor and was gathered to his people;
Num 20:12 ⁵¹because you broke faith with me in the midst of the people of Israel at the waters of Meri-bath-kadesh, in the wilderness of Zin; because you did not revere me as holy in the midst of the people of Israel. ⁵²For you shall see the land before you; but you shall not go there, into the land which I give to the people of Israel."

Acts 7:45 (margin, Moses' death foretold paragraph)

Gen 49 **Moses' blessing for Israel***

33 ¹This is the blessing with which Moses the man of God blessed the children of Israel before his death. ²He said,

---

32:48–53. Theodoret of Cyrrhus comments that "the Lord is teaching us, by these things, that he requires the height of virtue from the perfect: and whereas with other men he is very forebearing, he does not show that indulgence towards the saints. The Wise Man also said this: 'The lowliest man may be pardoned in mercy, but mighty men will be mightily tested' (Wis 6:6)" (*Quaestiones in Octateuchum*, 43). Jesus' words are clearer still: "Every

one to whom much is given, of him will much be required; and of him to whom men commit much they will demand the more" (Lk 12:48).

***33:1–29.** Just as Genesis tells about Jacob blessing his sons at the end of his life (Gen 49), so too Deuteronomy says that Moses, when he was on the point of death, blessed the tribes of Israel one by one. Whereas Jacob mixed blessings with

---

istos loquens ad universum Israel. ⁴⁶Et dixit ad eos: «Ponite corda vestra in omnia verba, quae ego testificor vobis hodie, ut mandetis ea filiis vestris custodire et facere et implere universa verba legis huius; ⁴⁷quia verbum non incassum vobis, sed est vita vestra: et in verbo hoc longo perseverabitis tempore in terra, ad quam, Iordane transmisso, ingredimini possidendam». ⁴⁸Locutusque est Dominus ad Moysen in eadem die dicens: ⁴⁹«Ascende in montem istum Abarim, in montem Nabo, qui est in terra Moab contra Iericho, et vide terram Chanaan, quam ego tradam filiis Israel obtinendam. ⁵⁰Et morere in monte, quem conscendens iungeris populo tuo, sicut mortuus est Aaron frater tuus in monte Hor et appositus populo suo. ⁵¹Quia praevaricati estis contra me in medio filiorum Israel ad aquas Meribathcades deserti Sin, quia non sanctificastis me inter filios Israel». ⁵²E contra videbis terram et non ingredieris in eam, quam ego dabo filiis Israel». ¹ Haec est benedictio, qua benedixit Moyses homo Dei filiis Israel ante mortem suam. ²Et ait: «Dominus de Sinai venit / et de Seir ortus est eis; / apparuit de monte Pharan /

"The LORD came from Sinai,
and dawned from Seir upon us;[i]
he shone forth from Mount Paran,
he came from the ten thousands of holy ones,
with flaming fire[j] at his right hand.
[3]Yea, he loved his people;[k]
all those consecrated to him were in his[x] hand;
so they followed[j] in thy steps,
receiving direction from thee,
[4]when Moses commanded us a law,
as a possession for the assembly of Jacob.
[5]Thus the LORD became king in Jeshurun,
when the heads of the people were gathered,
all the tribes of Israel together.

Ex 19:1
Mt 25:31
Acts 7:53
Jude 14

Acts 7:38;
20:32

Deut 32:15
Eph 1:6

reproaches, Moses speaks only blessings. The tribe of Simeon is not mentioned, maybe because it very quickly becomes absorbed into that of Judah. This little detail leads one to think that those verses may date from the time of the monarchy (10th–9th centuries BC).

The chapter divides into three parts: the blessings make up the central part (vv. 6–25), with an introduction (vv. 2–5) and an epilogue which describes the peace and happiness Israel experiences under the protection of God (vv. 26–29).

The blessings contain fairly definite references to a period when the tribes were already settled in their respective territories: this would lead one to think that this section dates from a later period. Also, the fact that the text comes in stanzas may indicate that this passage is different in origin from its context.

33:1–5. God is depicted in great majesty,

set at the head of his people; thus, he moves out from Sinai (note that here it is not called Horeb) to the various different places of the Exodus. The splendour with which the Lord's protection is described is reminiscent of other Old Testament passages, such as the introduction to the Song of Deborah (Judg 5:4–5) or Psalm 68 (vv. 8–9).

It is really very difficult to translate these verses; they are open to various interpretations, especially the last two lines of v. 2 and all v. 3, where the Hebrew text is so difficult that versions (both ancient and modern) interpret it in different ways (cf., e.g., the RSV's own notes).

The Law (v. 4) is regarded by the Israelites as the supreme divine gift; cf. what St John says in the prologue to his Gospel: "The law was given through Moses; grace and truth came through Jesus Christ" (Jn 1:17).

et venit in Meribathcades / de meridie eius in Asedoth. / [3]Vere diligit populos / omnes sancti eius in manu illius sunt, / et, qui appropinquant pedibus tuis, / accipient de doctrina tua. / [4]Legem praecepit nobis Moyses, / hereditatem multitudinis Iacob. / [5]Et factus est apud dilectum rex, / congregatis principibus populi / cum tribubus Israel». / [6]«Vivat Ruben et non moriatur, / et sit parvus in numero». [7]Haec

i. Gk Syr Vg: Heb *them* **j.** The meaning of the Hebrew word is uncertain **k.** Gk: Heb *peoples* **x.** Heb *thy*

⁶"Let Reuben live, and not die,
nor let his men be few."

⁷And this he said of Judah:
"Hear, O LORD, the voice of Judah,
and bring him in to his people.
With thy hands contend¹ for him,
and be a help against his adversaries."

Ex 17:17   ⁸And of Levi he said,
Num 20:1–13   "Give to Leviᵐ thy Thummim,
and thy Urim to thy godly one,
whom thou didst test at Massah,
with whom thou didst strive at the waters of Meribah;
Ex 32:25–29   ⁹who said of his father and mother,
Mt 10:37   'I regard them not';
Lk 14:26   he disowned his brothers,
and ignored his children.

33:6–7. The reference to the tribe of Reuben, Jacob's first-born, seems to imply that it is going through difficult times, and is in danger of disappearing. In fact, its territory (situated in the southern part of Transjordan) will soon fall to the Moabites, and this tribe will have no importance in the future history of Israel. This painful situation (particularly painful, in view of the fact that it is the tribe of the first-born) may be connected with the grave sin recounted in Genesis 35:21–22 (cf. also Gen 49:4).

The plea for Judah leads one also to think that this tribe too is in difficult circumstances: maybe the reference here is to its struggle to gain control of the part of Canaan allocated to it, where there were peoples who cut it off somewhat

from the other tribes: this would explain the petition in the third line of v. 7: "bring him in to his people". These circumstances would suggest the first period of the Judges (1200–1100 BC).

33:8–11. The blessing for the tribe of Levi is (with that of Joseph) the longest. This was the tribe of Moses and Aaron and maybe the mention of Massah and Meribah refers more to them than to the tribe as a whole (v. 8; cf. Ex 17:7; Num 20:1–13). The Levites' faithfulness to the Lord is asserted, a faithfulness over and above family loyalties (v. 9), by recalling the episode of the golden calf, when the sons of Levi slaughtered a considerable number of Israelites in punishment for their idolatry (cf. Ex 32:25–29). There is

---

est Iudae benedictio: «Audi, Domine, vocem Iudae, / et ad populum suum introduc eum. / Manus eius pugnabunt pro eo, / et adiutor illius contra adversarios eius eris». ⁸De Levi quoque ait: «Tummim et Urim tui / viro sancto tuo, / quem probasti in Massa / et cum quo litigasti ad aquas Meriba. / ⁹Qui dixit de patre suo et matre sua: / 'Nescio vos'; / et fratres suos ignoravit / et filios suos nescivit. / Quia custodierunt eloquium tuum / et pactum tuum servaverunt. / ¹⁰Docebunt iudicia tua Iacob / et legem tuam

---

l. Cn: Heb *with his hands he contended*   m. Gk: Heb lacks *Give to Levi*

For they observed thy word,
    and kept thy covenant.
[10]They shall teach Jacob thy ordinances,
    and Israel thy law;
they shall put incense before thee,
    and whole burnt offering upon thy altar.
[11]Bless, O LORD, his substance,
    and accept the work of his hands;
crush the loins of his adversaries,
    of those that hate him, that they rise not again."

[12]Of Benjamin he said,   2 Thess 2:13
    "The beloved of the LORD,
        he dwells in safety by him;
    he encompasses him all the day long,
        and makes his dwelling between his shoulders."

[13]And of Joseph he said,
    "Blessed by the LORD be his land,
        with the choicest gifts of heaven above,[n]
        and of the deep that couches beneath,

---

also mention of their priestly role—to teach the Law and attend to divine worship (v. 10).

The Urim and Thummim were small objects used for casting lots (thought to disclose the divine will: cf. 1 Sam 14:41). According to Exodus 28:30 and Leviticus 8:8, the high priests carried the Urim and Thummim; it was his function to consult God.

33:12. "And makes his dwelling between his shoulders": it is not clear what this means. The subject may be Benjamin, whom God lovingly bears upon his shoulders. But the subject could be God himself; in which case the dwelling could

mean Jerusalem, located on the border of the territories of Benjamin and Judah; or, more likely, Bethlehem, where the ark of the Covenant had previously been kept (Judg 20:27). The word translated as "shoulders" could mean "hills".

33:13–17. The elaborate blessing for Joseph is reminiscent of the corresponding blessing given by Jacob in Genesis 49:22–26. It includes Ephraim and Manasseh, who were treated as two different tribes in the allotting of the promised land. It makes mention of the fertility of their lands, situated in the central part of Canaan on either side of the Jordan. It also refers to their warlike zeal

---

Israel; / ponent thymiama in naribus tuis / et holocaustum super altare tuum. / [11]Benedic, Domine, fortitudini eius / et opera manuum illius suscipe. / Percute lumbos inimicorum eius; / et, qui oderunt eum, non consurgant». [12]De Beniamin ait: «Amantissimus Domini habitabit confidenter in eo; / Altissimus proteget eum tota die, et inter umeros illius requiescet». [13]De Ioseph quoque ait: «Benedicta a Domino terra eius: / donis caeli, rore / atque abysso subiacente, / [14]fructibus solis / et donis mensium, / [15]pri-

n. Two Heb Mss and Tg: Heb *with the dew*

Gen 49:26

Acts 7:35

¹⁴with the choicest fruits of the sun,
and the rich yield of the months,
¹⁵with the finest produce of the ancient mountains,
and the abundance of the everlasting hills,
¹⁶with the best gifts of the earth and its fulness,
and the favour of him that dwelt in the bush.
Let these come upon the head of Joseph,
and upon the crown of the head of him that is prince
among his brothers.
¹⁷His firstling bull has majesty,
and his horns are the horns of a wild ox;
with them he shall push the peoples,
all of them, to the ends of the earth;
such are the ten thousands of Ephraim,
and such are the thousands of Manasseh."

¹⁸And of Zebulun he said,
"Rejoice, Zebulun, in your going out;
and Issachar, in your tents.
¹⁹They shall call peoples to their mountain;
there they offer right sacrifices;
for they suck the affluence of the seas
and the hidden treasures of the sand."

(v. 17). The tribe of Ephraim will have a key role in the future history of Israel: on the death of Solomon (931 BC), when the country is divided into two kingdoms, the Ephraimite chief Jeroboam will become the leader and guide of the Northern tribes (cf. 1 Kings 12).

33:18–19. The blessings of these tribes contain references to their geographical location and their lifestyles. Issachar occupied the fertile plan of Esdraelon, to the north of the mountains of Carmel, from the mountains of southern Galilee to the Mediterranean. Zebulun, to the

north-east of Issachar, was in direct contact with Phoenician peoples (famous seafarers and traders), with whom they maintained trading contact.

"The hidden treasures of the sand": some interpret this as reference to purple, which was extracted from a small mollusc; others apply it to glass-making.

The two first lines of v. 19 may refer to the tribes of Israel assembled to offer sacrifices to God on Mount Carmel or on Tabor, which are located in the territories of these two tribes. In the Septuagint Greek they are translated differently—along these lines: "They will

mitiis antiquorum montium / et donis collium aeternorum, / ¹⁶frugibus terrae et plenitudine eius. / Benedictio illius, qui apparuit in rubo, / veniat super caput Ioseph / et super verticem nazaraei inter fratres suos; / ¹⁷quasi primogeniti tauri pulchritudo eius, / cornua unicornis cornua illus, / in ipsis ventilabit gentes / usque ad terminos terrae. / Hae sunt multitudines Ephraim, / et hae milia Manasse». ¹⁸De Zabulon ait: «Laetare, Zabulon, in exitu tuo, / et Issachar, in tabernaculis tuis! / ¹⁹Populos ad montem vocabunt, / ibi immolabunt victimas iustitiae. / Qui inundationem maris, quasi lac, sugent, / et thesauros

²⁰And of Gad he said,
"Blessed be he who enlarges Gad!
Gad couches like a lion,
he tears the arm, and the crown of the head.
²¹He chose the best of the land for himself,
for there a commander's portion was reserved;
and he came to the heads of the people,
with Israel he executed the commands
and just decrees of the LORD."

Josh 4:12
Num 32

²² And of Dan he said,
"Dan is a lion's whelp,
that leaps forth from Bashan."

Judg 18

²³And of Naphtali he said,
"O Naphtali, satisfied with favour,
and full of the blessing of the LORD,
possess the lake and the south."

²⁴And of Asher he said,
"Blessed above sons be Asher;
let him be the favourite of his brothers,
and let him dip his foot in oil.

---

wipe out peoples, and you will be invoked."

33:20–21. There is a reference here to the valour and warlike character of the tribe of Gad who (having shared in the first allocation of land, in Transjordan) later came to the aid of the other tribes in their conquests (cf. Josh 4:12), as they had promised they would (cf. Num 32). The words "he executed the just decrees of the Lord" may be a reference to their fidelity to the religion of the Lord, as shown in the episode recounted in Joshua 22:9–34.

33:22–23. The blessings of Dan seems to be a reference to their journey from the region originally assigned to them (in central Canaan, to the west of Benjamin) to become the most northerly of the tribes; in the north they conquered Laish, which means "lion", an area thereafter known as "Dan" (cf. Judg 18). In ancient times Bashan was a hilly region, well wooded and with wild animals, situated on the opposite bank of the Jordan, to the east of Lake Gennesaret.

The tribe of Naphtali occupied the most fertile part of Galilee, from Lake Gennesaret to the Lebanon.

33:24–25. Asher occupied the north-east part of Palestine, a territory rich in olive groves (v. 25).

absconditos arenarum». ²⁰De Gad ait: «Benedictus, qui dilatat Gad! / Quasi leo requiescit / dilaceratque brachium et verticem. / ²¹Et vidit primitias sibi, / quia ibi pars ducis erat reposita; / qui fuit cum principibus populi et fecit iustitiam Domini / et iudicia sua cum Israel». ²²De Dan quoque ait: «Dan catulus leonis / prosiliet largiter de Basan». ²³De Nephthali dixit: «Nephthali satiabatur bene- placito, / et plenus erit benedictione Domini: / mari et meridiem possidebit». ²⁴De Aser quoque ait:

Deut 32:15
Ps 68:5
Eph 1:6

^{25}Your bars shall be iron and bronze;
and as your days, so shall your strength be.

^{26}"There is none like God, O Jeshurun,
who rides through the heavens to your help,
and in his majesty through the skies.
^{27}The eternal God is your dwelling place,
and underneath are the everlasting arms.
And he thrust out the enemy before you,
and said, Destroy.
^{28}So Israel dwelt in safety,
the fountain of Jacob alone,
a land of grain and wine;
yea, his heavens drop down dew.
^{29}Happy are you, O Israel! Who is like you,
a people saved by the Lord,
the shield of your help,
and the sword of your triumph!
Your enemies shall come fawning to you;
and you shall tread upon their high places."

The death of Moses*

Num 22:1
Mt 4:8

34 ^{1}And Moses went up from the plains of Moab to Mount Nebo, to the top of Pisgah, which is opposite Jericho. And the LORD showed him all the land, Gilead as far as Dan, ^{2}all

---

*34:1–12. Before he dies, Moses looks down on the promised land, and its main regions (Transjordan), Galilee (Naphtali), Samaria (Ephraim and Manasseh) and Judea. However, if one looks out from Mount Nebo it is not possible to see all this panorama: only God could make Moses see all these territories. Zoar may have been to the south-east of the Dead Sea.

"He buried him" (v. 6): the Hebrew construction does not allow us to say who the subject of the verb is, but from the context it must be God.

The book of Sirach provides a short summary of the life of this man of God (cf. Sir 45:1–5).

The Jewish scholar Philo of Alexandria (15 BC–AD 45) also praises his virtues, and at length: he was the friend

---

«Benedictus prae filiis Aser! / Sit placens fratibus suis, / et tingat in oleo pedem suum. / ^{25}Ferrum et aes serae tuae, / sicut dies tui robur tuum». / ^{26}«Non est ut Deus Iesurun, / qui ascendit super caelos ad auxilium tuum / et in magnificentia sua super nubes. / ^{27}Habitaculum Deus antiquus, / et subter brachia sempiterna. / Eiciet a facie tua inimicum dicetque: 'Conterere!'. / ^{28}Habitabit Israel confidenter, / et fons Iacob solus; / stillabunt in terra frumenti et vini, / caelique rorem. / ^{29}Beatus tu, Israel! Quis similis tui, / popule, qui salvaris in Domino? / Ipse est scutum auxilii tui / et gladius gloriae tuae. / Blandientur tibi inimici tui, et tu eorum altitudines calcabis». ^{1}Ascendit ergo Moyses de campestribus Moab super montem Nabo in verticem Phasga contra Iericho; ostenditque ei Dominus omnem terram Galaad usque Dan ^{2}et universum Nephthali terramque Ephraim et Manasse et omnem terram Iudae

Naphtali, the land of Ephraim and Manasseh, all the land of Judah as far as the Western Sea, ³the Negeb, and the Plain, that is, the valley of Jericho the city of palm trees, as far as Zoar. ⁴And the LORD said to him, "This is the land of which I swore to Abraham, to Isaac, and to Jacob, 'I will give it to your descendants. 'I have let you see it with your eyes, but you shall not go over there." ⁵So Moses the servant of the LORD died there in the land of Moab, according to the word of the LORD, ⁶and he buried him in the valley in the land of Moab opposite Beth-peor; but no man knows the place of his burial to this day. ⁷Moses was a hundred and twenty years old when he died; his eye was not dim, nor his natural force abated. ⁸And the people of Israel wept for Moses in the plains of Moab thirty days; then the days of weeping and mourning for Moses were ended.

Rev 15:3

⁹And Joshua the son of Nun was full of the spirit of wisdom, for Moses had laid his hands upon him; so the people of Israel obeyed him, and did as the LORD had commanded Moses.

Num 27:18–23
Acts 6:6

---

and disciple of God, who taught him "face to face"; he was "a man of God", able to work wonders and signs; he was greater than the patriarchs Abraham, Isaac, Jacob and Joseph in his intimacy with God and his grasp of the divine Word, which inspired him and guided him as a leader, lawgiver, prophet, wonder-worker, ascetic and thinker (cf. *De vita Mosis*, 1, 80, 154, 158; 2, 187–292; 3, 1–186).

St Gregory of Nyssa, one of the greatest Greek Fathers, praised Moses in the following terms: "Our brief discourse has offered you, man of God, these things concerning the perfection of the virtuous life, by describing to you the life of the great Moses as a visible model of goodness, so that each of us, by imitating

his actions, may himself acquire the features of the beauty we have described. And to know that Moses attained all possible perfection, what more worthy testimony can we find than the divine word, when it says, "I know you by name" (Ex 33:12, 17)? Also (there is) the fact that he was called the friend of God by God himself (cf. Ex 33:11), and the fact that, having chosen to perish with the others unless God in his kindness overlooked the offence they had done him, he checked God's wrath against the Israelites, getting him to change his mind so as not to grieve his friend (cf. Ex 32:7–14). All these testimonies are a clear proof that in his life Moses attained the height of perfection" (*De vita Mosis*, 2, 319).

---

usque ad mare occidentale ³et Nageb et latitudinem campi Iericho civitatis palmarum usque Segor. ⁴Dixitque Dominus ad eum: «Haec est terra, pro qua iuravi Abraham, Isaac et Iacob, dicens: Semini tuo dabo eam. Vidisti eam oculis tuis et non transibis ad illam». ⁵Mortuusque est ibi Moyses servus Domini in terra Moab, iubente Domino. ⁶Et sepelivit eum in valle in terra Moab contra Bethphegor; et non cognovit homo sepulcrum eius usque in praesentem diem. ⁷Moyses centum et viginti annorum erat, quando mortuus est; non caligavit oculus eius, nec robur illius defecit. ⁸Fleveruntque eum filii Israel in campestribus Moab triginta diebus; et completi sunt dies planctus lugentium Moysen. ⁹Iosue

A eulogy of Moses

Ex 33:11;
33:20 [10]And there has not arisen a prophet since in Israel like Moses, whom the LORD knew face to face, [11]none like him for all the signs and the wonders which the LORD sent him to do in the land of Egypt, to Pharaoh and to all his servants and to all his land, [12]and for all the mighty power and all the great and terrible deeds which Moses wrought in the sight of all Israel.

34:10. "Face to face" conversation with God means a very intimate relationship, but it does not have to be taken literally. The visions that the patriarchs—Abraham, Moses himself, Elijah, Isaiah etc.—had of God in this world were indirect ones; what they saw were various manifestations of the divine glory, the splendour of his greatness. These Old Testament theophanies were surpassed by the *epiphany* of Jesus Christ; God could reveal himself to man in no more perfect way than in the Incarnation of his eternal Word: "No one has ever seen God; the only Son, who is in the bosom of the Father, he has made him

known" (Jn 1:18).

Comparing the mission of Moses with that of Jesus, St Cyril of Alexandria taught: "Our Lord Jesus Christ set the world free from its ancient offences; for He is the truth and is holy by his very nature; he sanctifies those who have believed through his blood, and he sets them above death, and he will bring them into his own kingdom of heaven, into the land that is truly holy and desirable—to the loftier mansions, to the heavenly city, to the Church of the first-born, whose maker and creator is God" (*Glaphyra in Deuteronomium*, 34:10).

vero filius Nun repletus est spiritu sapientiae, quia Moyses posuit super eum manus suas; et oboedierunt ei filii Israel fecerunt que, sicut praecepit Dominus Moysi. [10]Et non surrexit ultra propheta in Israel sicut Moyses, quem nosset Dominus facie ad faciem, [11]in omnibus signis atque portentis, quae misit per eum, ut faceret in terra Aegypti pharaoni et omnibus servis eius universaeque terrae illius, [12]et in cuncta manu robusta magnisque mirabilibus, quae fecit Moyses coram universo Israel.

Explanatory Notes

(N.B. In these notes Vulgate additions are quoted in the Douay Version.)

GENESIS

1:1–2:4a: The aim of this narrative is not to present a scientific picture but to teach religious truth, especially the dependence of all creation on God and its consecration to him through the homage rendered by man, who is the climax of creation. Hence its strong liturgical character and the concluding emphasis on the sabbath. It serves as a prologue to the whole of the Old Testament.

2:4b ff: This account of the state of the world at the beginning, which introduces the story of the first sin, comes from a different and earlier source and is composed in a very different style. There is nothing in these early chapters that commits us to any particular scientific view of the origins of the world or man, or that would exclude the evolution hypothesis.

3:15, *he shall bruise your head*: i.e., the seed of the woman, that is, mankind descended from Eve, will eventually gain the victory over the powers of evil. This victory will, of course, be gained through the work of the Messiah who is *par excellence* the seed of the woman.

The Latin Vulgate has the reading *ipsa conteret*, "she shall bruise". Some Old Latin manuscripts have this reading and it occurs also in St Augustine, *De Genesi contra Manichaeos*, 2, which is earlier than St Jerome's translation. It could be due originally to a copyist's mistake, which was then seen to contain a genuine meaning—namely, that Mary, too, would have her share in the victory, inasmuch as she was mother of the Saviour.

4:1: The story of Cain and Abel has the purpose of showing the effects of sin within society, the fratricide of Cain leading to the vengeance of Lamech and so to the Flood. We are, however, no longer in the first age of humanity as can be seen from verses 14, 17, etc.

4:26: *Seth* takes the place of the murdered Abel and is the ancestor of Noah. In Ex 3:14 and 6:2–3 we find another account of the origins of Yahwism.

5:1, *generations*: It should be noted that these genealogies are selective and schematic, and the numbers, as often in the Old Testament, are symbolic.

6:2, *sons of God*: could mean simply "divine beings", as elsewhere in the Old Testament. The writer, however, may be using an old story or myth to point out the progressive degradation of mankind before the Flood and to warn against the evil effects of intermarriage either of the descendants of Seth with Kenites or, more probably, of the Israelites with the native population of Canaan.

6:11: Here begins the Flood narrative formed of two almost parallel accounts. This fact explains the existence of repetitions and discrepancies. It is, in places, remarkably similar to other Flood stories from the ancient Near East.

10:1, *generations*: This "table of the nations" makes use of old material to show how all the nations of the world as then known have descended from the generation that survived the Flood. It was from this world that Abraham was called to be the father of the chosen people.

11:1–9: The tower of Babel (= Babylon) is taken as a symbol of political power, empire-building and the civilization that opposes God's plan. The tower was probably a ziggurat, i.e. (Babylonian) temple mound.

12:1–3: With Abraham's call, sacred history in the strict sense begins. The promise-theme runs through the whole patriarchal history, e.g., 18:18, 28:14.

14:18: *Melchizedek* was later taken as a Messianic figure (Ps 110:4) and interpreted in the New Testament as foreshadowing Christ, whose priesthood (including the offering of bread and wine) exceeds that of the Old Testament; cf. Heb 7:1–7.

15:1: The Vulgate has, "I am thy protector, and thy reward exceeding great." There was, however, at this stage, no idea of a reward in a future life.

16:1–4: The practice suggested by Sarai, involving as it did polygamy, was in accord with the moral standards at the time and is referred to in legal codes of the period.

Explanatory Notes

19:1: The Sodom episode, so often referred to in the Old and New Testaments, expresses the abhorrence of the true Israelite for unnatural sin and the violation of the sacred duty of hospitality; cf. Judg 19:11–30.

22:1–19: The sacrifice of Isaac, while reprobating the practice of human sacrifice then in use among the Canaanites, gives a magnificent example of Abraham's faith and obedience, as also does 18:1–15; cf. Rom 4 and Heb 11:8–12.

22:6: Isaac, carrying the wood up the mountain for the sacrifice, has often be seen as a figure of Christ carrying his cross to die on Golgotha.

25:19: With the birth of Easu and Jacob we enter a new narrative cycle. Jacob, renamed Israel, is represented as the ancestor of the twelve tribes and, therefore, of the whole people; cf. Deut 26:5.

28:10–22: This narrative explains and justifies the use of what had formerly been a Canaanite sanctuary, Bethel. The ladder seems to represent the ziggurat, which was a temple with steps leading to a platform at the top.

32:24–32: The meaning of this, one of the oldest and most mysterious narratives in Genesis, remains obscure. It is intended to explain the place name Penuel which means "face of God".

37:2: From this point the book of Genesis is chiefly concerned with the Joseph story, which is full of the sense of divine providence. It has, as might be expected, a markedly Egyptian character.

49:1–27: In their present form these "Oracles of Jacob", blessings pronounced upon his sons as epitomizing the twelve tribes, date from the period of the early monarchy.

EXODUS

This book, made up of various traditions of different dates, deals with two events: the deliverance from Egypt and the Sinai covenant, which, closely linked together, form the basis of Old Testament faith. It is dominated by the personality of Moses.

3:14: This translation is uncertain: it is, therefore, difficult to decide whether this is a refusal to disclose the name or an explanation of the divine title Yahweh revealed immediately afterwards.

7:14: Here begins the story of the ten plagues. Again the narrative is composite and originally different traditions knew of different numbers of plagues. All, however, lead up to the climax of the death of the first-born. Some of the plagues correspond to natural phenomena that are known to occur, or to have occurred in the past, in Egypt.

12:1: The feast of the Passover, the regulations for which are given here, commemorates the deliverance from Egypt. The feast of unleavened bread would probably have been added only after the entry into Canaan. The Passover foreshadows the sacrifice of Jesus (1 Cor 5:7).

16:14: The mysterious manna may have been a substance secreted by the tamarisk or perhaps an insect that feeds on its leaves and is edible. In the New Testament it is a type of the Eucharist: cf. Jn 6:31–35, 48–51.

19:3: The covenant makes Israel the people of God and binds them to the fulfilment of the commandments; it is concluded in chapter 24.

20:1–17: The Ten Commandments, in their original form even briefer than here, are found in a different version in Deut 5:6–21.

40:34, *the cloud* and the fire, that is, the *glory*, are ways of representing at the same time the presence and the transcendence of God.

LEVITICUS

As the name suggests, this book is almost exclusively concerned with the regulation of the religious life of Israel by the Levitical priesthood. Although its underlying concept of Israel as a holy people contains an element of permanent importance, the law as such, except for those parts that Christ expressly sanctioned, is not binding on Christians.

11:1: These regulations concerning what is ritually pure or impure depend, for the most part, on circumstances peculiar to that time; e.g., animals, such as the pig, used in pagan sacrifices. Some correspond to ancient taboos.

Explanatory Notes

17:1: The so-called "Code of Holiness" (chapters 17–26) implies an exalted idea of the holiness and otherness of the God of Israel.

NUMBERS

The title of this book is explained by the census with which it opens. It is composed of both history and legislation and, though edited finally by the priests after the Exile, it contains much ancient material.

11:16–30: The account of the election of the seventy elders emphasizes the charismatic or prophetic basis of authority in the community.

21:4–9: The bronze serpent may have been the standard or symbol of the tribe of Levi, to which Moses and Aaron belonged. In Jn 3:14 it becomes a type of the saving cross of Christ.

22:21–35: The story of Balaam and his ass is of popular origin. The oracles of this foreign seer, especially the fourth (24:15–19), refer to the Messianic king of the future, of whom David is the type.

DEUTERONOMY

The title comes from the mistranslation of 17:18 in the Greek version (the Septuagint) and really means "a second copy of the law". The book comprises the so-called "Deuteronomic Code of Law" (chapters 12–26) edited within the framework of two discourses attributed to Moses represented as a prophet and lawgiver. The whole is rounded off with a third discourse, a psalm, and an account of Moses' death and burial. The central theme of Deuteronomy is the election of Israel as the people of God by means of the covenant.

4:32–40: This passage gives the clearest and most eloquent expression of Israel's consciousness of its election as the people of God.

4:41: The beginning of the second discourse of Moses containing the Deuteronomic version of the Ten Commandments; cf. Ex 20:1–17.

6:4–9: The recital thrice daily of this text, plus two others, is the principal practice of piety of the religious Jew; it is called the Shema ("Hear"). It contains the greatest commandment of the law, that is, the love of the covenant-God (cf. Mt 22:37), and a clear statement of monotheism.

12:2: This law, enforcing one single place of worship, connects Deuteronomy historically with the religious reform of Josiah just before the Exile, in the opinion of many scholars; cf. 2 Kings 22–23.

18:18: The prophet like Moses mentioned here refers either to the prophetic movement as a whole or to an individual, either Joshua, successor of Moses, or Samuel. The New Testament sees here a reference to the Messiah; cf. Jn 1:21; Acts 3:22; 7:37.

24:1: Divorce was permitted in Old Testament times on account of "hardness of heart"; Jesus, however, insists that it was not in the original plan of God (Mt 19:7–9).

Sources Quoted in the Commentary

1. DOCUMENTS OF THE CHURCH

Nicea, Second Council of
De sacris imaginibus: Actio VII: *Definitio de sacris imaginibus*, 13 October 787, DS 600–603.
Lateran, Fourth Council of the
De fide catholica: Capitulum I: *De fide catholica. Definitio contra Albigenses et Catharos*, 11–30 November 1215, DS 800–802.
Vienne, Council of
Fidei catholicae: Sessio III: *Constitutio Fidei catholicae*, 6 May 1312, DS 900–904.
Trent, Council of
De peccato originali: Sessio V: *Decretum de peccato originali*, 17 June 1546, DS 1510–1516.
De iustificatione: Session VI: *Decretum de iustificatione*, 13 January 1547, DS 1520–1583.
Vatican, Second Council of the
Sacrosanctum Concilium: Constitution on the Sacred Liturgy, 4 December 1963, AAS 56 (1964) 97–138.
Lumen gentium: Dogmatic Constitution on the Church, 21 November 1964, AAS 57 (1965) 5–71.
Dei Verbum: Dogmatic Constitution on Divine Revelation, 18 November 1965, AAS 58 (1966) 817–835.
Apostolicam actuositatem: Decree on the apostolate of lay people, 18 November 1965, AAS 58 (1966) 837–864.
Presbyterorum ordinis: Decree on the ministry and life of priests, 7 December 1965, AAS 58 (1966) 991–1024.
Gaudium et spes: Pastoral Constitution on the Church in the modern world, 7 December 1965, AAS 58 (1966) 1025–1120.
Paul VI
Populorum Progressio: Encyclical Letter on the development of peoples, 26 March 1967, AAS 59 (1967) 257–299.
John Paul II
Dives in misericordia: Encyclical Letter on the mercy of God, 30 November 1980, AAS (1980) 1177–1232.
Laborem exercens: Encyclical Letter on human work, 14 September 1981, AAS 73 (1981) 577–647.
Familiaris consortio: Apostolic Exhortation on the duties of the Christian family, 22 November 1981, AAS 73 (1981) 81–191.
Reconciliatio et paenitentia: Apostolic Exhortation on reconciliation and penance, 2 December 1984, AAS 77 (1985) 185–275.
Dominum et Vivificantem: Encyclical Letter on the Holy Spirit in the life of the Church and of the world, 18 May 1986, AAS 78 (1986) 809–900.
Sollicitudo rei socialis: Encyclical Letter on the twentieth anniversary of *Populorum Progressio*, 30 November 1987, AAS 80 (1988) 513–586.
Mulieris dignitatem: Apostolic Letter on the dignity and vocation of women, 15 August 1988, AAS 80 (1988) 1653–1729.
Veritatis splendor: Apostolic Letter on certain fundamental questions of the Church's moral teaching, 6 August 1993, AAS 85 (1993) 1133–1228.
Evangelium vitae: Apostolic Letter on the value and inviolability of human life, 25 March 1995, AAS 87 (1995) 401–522.
Dominicae Cenae: Letter on the mystery and worship of the Blessed Eucharist, 24 February 1980, AAS 72 (1980) 113–148.
General Audience: on 14 November 1979, *Insegnamenti di Giovannni Paolo II*, II, 2 (1979) 1153–1157.

Sources Quoted in the Commentary

Address to the UN Special Committee against Apartheid, 7 August 1984, *Insegnamenti di Giovanni Paolo II*, VII, 2 (1984) 35–39.

OTHER

Catechism of the Catholic Church, New York, 1994.
Code of Canon Law: *Codex Iuris Canonici auctoritate Ioannis Pauli PP II promulgatus*, Vatican City, 1983; English edition, London, 1983.
Catechism of the Council of Trent, trs. by McHugh and Callan, reprinted Manila, 1974.
Congregation for the Doctrine of the Faith
Persona humana: Declaration on sexual ethics, 29 December 1975, AAS 68 (1976) 77–96.
Iura et bona: Declaration on euthanasia, 5 May 1980, AAS 72 (1980) 542–552.
Libertatis conscientia: Instruction on Christian freedom and liberation, 22 March 1986, AAS 79 (1987) 554–599.
Pontifical Biblical Commission
The Interpretation of the Bible in the Church, Ottawa, 1994.

2. LITURGICAL TEXTS

Roman Missal: *Missale Romanum*, editio typica altera, Vatican City, 1975.
The Divine Office, London, Sydney, Dublin, 1974.

3. THE FATHERS, ECCLESIASTICAL WRITERS AND OTHER AUTHORS

Aphraates
Demonstrationes: *Aphraatis Sapientis Persae Demonstrationes,* PS 1, 1–2, 489.
Augustine, St
Contra Faustum manichaeum libri XXXIII, PL 42, 207–518.
De civitate Dei libri XII, PL 41, 13–804.
De spiritu et littera: De spiritu et littera ad Marcellinum liber I, PL 44, 201–246.
Enarrationes in Psalmos, PL 36–37.
Quaestiones in Heptateuchum, PL 34, 547–824.
Sermones, PL 38–39.
Alcuin
Interrogationes et responsiones in Genesim, PL 100, 515–566.
Ambrose, St
De Abraham libri II, PL 14, 441–524.
De Iacob et vita beata, PL 14, 627–670.
De Ioseph patriarcha, PL 14, 673–704.
De benedictionibus patriarcharum, PL 14, 707–728.
De Nabuthae historia, PL 14, 765–792.
De Noe et arca, PL 14, 381–438.
De sacramentis, PL 15, 435–482.
Basil, St
Adversus Eunomium, PG 29, 497–774.
Regulae morales, PG 31, 699–870.
De Spiritu Sancto, PG 32, 67–218.
Bede, St
Hexaemeron sive libri quattuor in principium Genesis, PL 91, 9–190.
Commentaria in Pentateuchum, PL 91, 189–394.
Bernard, St
Homiliae super Missus est, PL 183, 55–88.

Sources Quoted in the Commentary

Sermo ad Beatam Virginem Deiparam, PL 184, 1009–1022.
Sermones de diversis, PL 183, 537–743.
Bonaventure, St
Commentaria in quatuor libros sententiarum Magistri Petri Lombardi, Florence: 1934–1949.
Caesarus of Arles, St
Sermones, CCL 103–104 (1953).
Cyprian, St
De oratione dominica, PL 4, 535–562.
Ad Quirinum: Testimoniorum adversus Iudaeos libri III, PL 4, 703–810.
Cyril of Alexandria, St
Contra Iulianum: Adversus libros athei Iuliani, PG 76, 509–1058.
De adoratione et cultu in spiritu et veritate, PG 68, 133–1126.
Glaphyra in Genesim libri VII, PG 69, 13–385.
Glaphyrorum in Exodum libri III, PG 69, 386–538.
Glaphyrorum in Deuteronomium liber I, PG 69, 643–678.
Clement of Alexandria
Paedagogus, PG 8, 247–684.
Stromata, PG 8, 685–9, 602.
Philo of Alexandria
De vita Mosis: L. Cohn (ed.), *Philonis Alexandrini opera quae supersunt*, vol. 4, Berlin, 1986, 119–268.
Flavius Josephus
Antiquitates Iudaicae: B. Niese (ed.), *Flavii Iosephi opera*, vols. 1–4, Berlin, 1887–1890.
De bello Iudaico: B. Niese (ed.), *Flavii Iosephi opera*, vol. 6, Berlin, 1895.
Glossa ordinaria
Glossa ordinaria in Exodum, PL 113, 183–296.
Gregory of Nyssa, St
De vita Mosis, PG 44, 297–430.
Gregory the Great, St
Expositio in librum Beati Iob sive Moralium libri, PL 75, 509–76, 782.
Homiliarum in Ezechielem Prophetam libri II, PL 76, 785–1072.
Gregory of Nazianzen, St
De pauperum amore (Oratio 14), PG 35, 857–910.
Irenaeus, St
Adversus haereses: A. Rousseau et al. (eds.), *Irénée de Lyon, Contre les hérésies* (SC 211, 100, 153) Paris, 1965–1974.
Isidore of Seville, St
Quaestiones in Vetus Testamentum. In Exodum, PL 83, 287–322.
Quaestiones in Vetus Testamentum. In Deuteronomium, PL 83, 359–370.
Jerome, St
Commentariorum in Isaiam prophetam libri XVIII, PL 24, 9–678.
Epistulae, Pl 22, 325–1224.
Josemaría Escrivá, Blessed
Friends of God, London, New Rochelle and Dublin, 1988.
The Way, Dublin, 1985.
Christ Is Passing By, Dublin, St Peter's (N.S.W.) and New Rochelle, 1982.
The Forge, London and New Rochelle, 1988.
Furrow, London, New Rochelle and Manila, 1987.
S. Bernal, *Monsignor Josemaría Escrivá de Balaguer*, London 1982.
John Cassian
Collationes XXIV, PL 49, 477–1328.
John of the Cross, St
Spiritual Canticle: E. Allison Peers (trs. and ed.), *Complete Works,* vol. II, London, 1947.
John Chrysostom, St
Homiliae in Epistolam primam ad Corinthios, PG 61, 9–382.
Homiliae in Genesim, PG 53, 21–386.
Homiliae in Matthaeum, PG 57, 13–472.

Sources Quoted in the Commentary

Melito of Sardes
De Pascha: J. Ibáñez and F. Mendoza (eds.), *Melitón de Sardes. Homilia sobre la Pascua*, Pamplona, 1975.

Novatian
De cibis iudaicis, PL 3, 981–992.

Origen
Homiliae in Genesim: H. de Lubac and L. Doutreleau (eds.), *Origène. Homélies sur la Genèse* (SC 7bis), Paris, 1976.

Homiliae in Exodum: P. Fortier and H. de Lubac (eds.), *Origène. Homélies sur l'Exode* (SC 16), Paris, 1947.

Homiliae in Jeremiam: P. Nautin (ed.), *Origène. Homélies sur Jérémie*, vol. I (SC 232), Paris, 1976.

Peter Damien, St
De Quadragesima et de quadragintaduabus Hebraeorum mansionibus (Ad Hildebrandum, Epistula II, 7), Pl 145, 543–560.

Protoevangelio de Santiago: A. de Santos Otero, *Los Evangelios Apócrifos*, Madrid, 1975.

Quodvultdeus
De promissionibus et praedictionibus Dei, PL 51, 733–858.

Rabanus Maurus
Enarrationes in Numeros libri quatuor, PL 108, 587–838.

Rupert of Deutz
De Trinitate et operibus eius libri XLII. Commentarium in Genesim, PL 167, 199–566.

De Trinitate et operibus eius libri XLII. Commentarium in Numeros, PL 167, 837–918.

Theodoret of Cyrrhus
Quaestiones in Octateuchum, PG 80, 75–528.

Tertullian
Adversus Marcionem libri V, PL 2, 239–524.

De oratione, Pl 1, 1249–1304.

De poenitentia, Pl 1, 1335–1360.

Thomas Aquinas, St
Summa theologiae: T. McDermott (ed.), London 1964.

Headings Added to the Biblical Text

GENESIS

Part One
The creation and the first age of mankind

1. THE ORIGIN OF HEAVEN AND EARTH 1:1
The Creation account 1:1
The creation of Adam 2:4
Man in paradise 2:8
The creation of Eve 2:18
Temptation and the first sin 3:1
Adam and Eve are expelled from paradise 3:21
The first children of Adam and Eve 4:1
Cain and Abel 4:3
The descendants of Cain 4:17
The birth of Seth 4:25

2. ADAM'S DESCENDANTS. FROM SETH TO NOAH 5:1
The increase of the human race 5:1
The spread of wickedness 6:1

3. THE STORY OF NOAH. HIS DESCENDANTS 6:9
The announcement of the flood 6:13
Boarding the ark 7:5
The flood 7:11
The flood subsides 8:1
Leaving the ark 8:15
God's covenant with Noah 9:1
A curse on Canaan, a blessing on Shem 9:18

4. THE ORIGIN OF PEOPLES. THE TOWER OF
   BABEL 10:1
The descendants of Japheth 10:2
The descendants of Ham 10:6
The descendants of Shem 10:21
Babel: the confusion of language 11:1

5. THE SEMITES 11:10

Part Two
The origin and formation of the chosen people

6. THE STORY OF ABRAHAM 11:27
The call of Abram and God's promise to him 12:1
Abram in Egypt 12:10
Abram in Bethel 13:1
Abram and Lot separate 13:8
A new promise to Abram 13:14
Lot is captured 14:1
Lot is set free 14:13
Melchizedek blesses Abram 14:17
God's Covenant with Abram 15:1
The birth of Ishmael 16:1
The renewal of the Covenant: Abram's name is
   changed 17:1
The commandment of circumcision 17:9
Sarai's name is changed and Abraham is promised a
   son 17:15
Circumcision 17:23
The apparition of God at Mamre 18:1
Isaac's birth is promised 18:9
Abraham intercedes for Sodom 18:16
The sin of the inhabitants of Sodom 19:1
The flight of Lot and his family 19:15
The destruction of Sodom and Gomorrah 19:23
The children of Lot: the origin of the Moabites and
   Ammonites 19:30
Abraham and Sarah in Gerar: the meeting with
   Abimelech 20:1

The birth and circumcision of Isaac 21:1
Hagar and Ismael are sent away 21:8
Abraham and Abimelech make a pact 21:22
The sacrifice of Isaac and the renewal of the promise
   22:1
The descendants of Nahor 22:20
Abraham buys the cave of Mach-pelah 23:1
The marriage of Isaac 24:1
Rebekah at the well 24:15
Abraham's servant is welcomed to Rebekah's home
   24:29
The meeting between Rebekah and Isaac 24:54
Other descendants of Abraham 25:1
The death and burial of Abraham 25:7

7. THE DESCENDANTS OF ISHMAEL 25:12

8. THE DESCENDANTS OF ISAAC. THE STORY OF
   JACOB 25:19
The birth of Esau and Jacob 25:19
Esau sells his birthright 25:27
Isaac at Gerar: his meeting with Abimelech 26:1
Disputes over wells 26:15
God appears to Isaac 26:23
Isaac's pact with the inhabitants of Canaan 26:26
Jacob obtains Isaac's blessing by cunning 27:1
Esau's reaction 27:34

Headings Added to the Biblical Text

Jacob leaves for Haran 27:46
Jacob's dream 28:10
Jacob and Laban meet 29:1
Jacob marries Leah and Rachel 29:15
The sons of Jacob in Paddan-aram 29:31
Jacob plans to leave Laban 30:25
How Jacob becomes rich 30:37
Jacob's flight 31:1
Laban overtakes Jacob 31:22
A pact between Laban and Jacob 31:43
Jacob prepares for his meeting with Esau 32:3
Jacob wrestles with the angel of the Lord 32:21
Jacob's meeting with Esau 33:1
Jacob in Shechem 33:16
Dinah is dishonoured by Shechem 34:1
The sons of Jacob take revenge 34:13
Jacob returns to Bethel 35:1
The birth of Benjamin and the death of Rachel 35:16
Reuben's sin 35:21
Jacob reaches Hebron. The death of Isaac 35:22

9. THE DESCENDANTS OF ESAU 36:1

10. THE DESCENDANTS OF JACOB. THE STORY OF JOSEPH 37:2
Joseph and his brothers 37:2
Joseph's dreams 37:5
Joseph is sold to Egyptians as a slave 37:12
The story of Judah and Tamar 38:1

The sin of Onan 38:9
Tamar deceives Judah 38:12
The birth of Perez, David's ancestor 38:27
Joseph in Egypt, in the house of Potiphar 39:1
Joseph in prison 39:21
Joseph, the interpreter of dreams 40:1
The pharaoh's dreams 41:1
Joseph's promotion 41:37
Joseph, the pharaoh's administrator 41:45
The sons of Jacob go down to Egypt 42:1
Joseph tests his brothers by keeping Simeon in Egypt 42:8
The sons of Jacob return to Egypt, bringing Benjamin with them 43:1
Joseph puts his brother to the test again 44:1
Judah's reaction 44:18
Joseph makes himself known 45:1
Jacob journeys to Egypt 46:1
Israel settles in the land of Goshen 47:1
Joseph administers Egypt to the pharaoh's advantage 47:13
Jacob blesses Joseph's sons 47:27
Jacob adopts and blesses Manasseh and Ephraim 48:1
Jacob's blessings on his twelve sons 49:1
The death of Jacob 49:29
Jacob's funeral 50:1
After the death of Jacob 50:15
The death of Joseph 50:24

EXODUS

Part One
The departure from Egypt

1. THE SONS OF ISRAEL IN EGYPT 1:1
The prosperity of the sons of Israel in Egypt 1:1
The sons of Israel are oppressed 1:8

2. THE CALL OF MOSES 2:1
The birth and early years of Moses 2:1
Moses in Midian 2:11
God appears to Moses in the burning bush 3:1
The divine name is revealed 3:11
The mission of Moses 3:16
Moses is granted miraculous powers 4:1
Aaron, the mouthpiece of Moses 4:10
Moses returns to Egypt 4:18
Moses' son is circumcised 4:24
Moses meets Aaron 4:27
Moses' first audience with the pharaoh 5.1
The Hebrews' work is made heavier 5:6
Moses intercedes with the pharaoh 5:19
A new call to Moses 6:2
The genealogy of Aaron and Moses 6:14
The announcement of the plagues 6:28

3. THE PLAGUES 7:8
Moses' miraculous rod 7:8
The first plague: the water turns to blood 7:14
The second plague: the frogs 7:25

The third plague: the gnats 8:16
The fourth plague: the flies 8:20
The fifth plague: the livestock epidemic 9:1
The sixth plague: the boils 9:8
The seventh plague: the hail 9:13
The eighth plague: the locusts 10:1
The ninth plague: the darkness 10:21
The tenth plague is announced 11:1

4. PASSOVER 12:1
The institution of the Passover 12:1
The feast of the unleavened bread 12:15
Instructions relating to the Passover 12:21
The tenth plague: death of the first-born 12:29
Provisions for the Exodus 12:33
The sons of Israel leave Egypt 12:37
Further instructions about the Passover 12:43
The law about the first-born 13:1
Instructions about the feast of the unleavened bread 13:3
Instructions about redeeming the first-born 13:11

5. THE DEPARTURE FROM EGYPT 13:17
A roundabout way 13:17
The Lord shapes events 14:1
The Egyptians in pursuit 14:5

Headings Added to the Biblical Text

Crossing the Red Sea 14:15
Song of victory 15:1

6. ISRAEL IN THE DESERT 15:22
The bitter water of Marah 15:22

The manna and the quails 16:1
The water from the rock 17:1
A battle against the Amalekites 17:8
The meeting of Jethro and Moses 18:1
The appointment of judges 18:13

Part Two
The people of Israel

7. IN THE DESERT OF SINAI 19:1
The Israelites arrive in Sinai 19:1
God promises a Covenant 19:3
The theophany on Sinai 19:10
The ten commandments 20:1

8. THE BOOK OF THE COVENANT 20:22
Laws concerning worship 20:22
Laws concerning slaves 21:1
Laws concerning homicide 21:12
Laws concerning violence 21:18
Laws concerning restitution 21:33
Violation of a virgin 22:16
Social laws 22:18
Duties of justice 23:1
The sabbatical year and the sabbath 23:10
The great feasts 23:14
Warnings and promises 23:20

9. THE COVENANT IS RATIFIED 24:1
A sacred meal and sprinkling with blood 24:1
Moses spends forty days on the mountain 24:12

10. INSTRUCTIONS FOR THE SANCTUARY 25:1
Contributions for the sanctuary 25:1
The ark 25:10
The table for the offertory bread 25:23
The lampstand 25:31
The tabernacle 26:1
The framework for the tabernacle 26:15
The veil 26:31
The screen at the entrance 26:36
The altar of holocaust 27:1
The court of the tabernacle 27:9
The oil for the lamps 27:20
The priests' vestments 28:1
The ephod 28:6
The breastpiece 28:15
The robe 28:31
The tiara or turban 28:36
The vestments of the priests 28:40
The ordination of priests 29:1
Sacrifices at ordination 29:10
The sacred meal 29:31
The consecration of the altar 29:35
The daily burnt offering 29:38
The altar of incense 30:1
The half-shekel tax 30:11

The bronze basin 30:17
The oil for anointing 30:22
The incense 30:34
The craftsmen for the sanctuary 31:1
The sabbath rest 31:12
The tables of the Law 31:18

11. ISRAEL'S APOSTASY 32:1
The golden calf 32:1
The Lord's ire 32:7
Moses' prayer for Israel 32:11
The golden calf is destroyed 32:15
The zeal of the Levites 32:25
Moses intercedes again 32:30
The order to pull out. An angel will lead the way 33:1
The tent of meeting 33:7
God agrees to stay with his people 33:12
Moses sees the glory of God 33:18

12. THE COVENANT IS RENEWED 34:1
God appears 34:6
The Covenant 34:10
The Ritual Decalogue 34:14
Moses' shining face 34:29

13. BUILDING THE SANCTUARY 35:1
The sabbath rest 35:1
Generous contributions 35:4
The craftsmen chosen 35:30
Building the tabernacle 36:8
The framework for the tabernacle 36:20
The veil 36:35
The ark 37:1
The table for the offertory bread 37:10
The golden lampstand 37:17
The altar of incense 37:25
The altar of holocaust 38:1
The court of the sanctuary 38:9
Materials used 38:21
The priestly vestments 39:1
The ephod 39:2
The breastpiece 39:8
The robe 39:22
Other vestments 39:27
The tiara or turban 39:30
The finished work is presented to Moses 39:33
The sanctuary is consecrated 40:1
Moses' obedience to God's commands 40:16
The glory of God fills the tabernacle 40:34

Headings Added to the Biblical Text

LEVITICUS

Part One
Rules concerning sacrifice

Burnt offerings (holocaust) 1:1
Cereal offerings 2:1
Peace offerings (communion offerings) 3:1
Sin offerings 4:1
Offerings for sins of a priest 4:3
Offerings for sins of the people 4:13
Offerings for sins of a ruler 4:22
Offerings for sins of a private individual 4:27
Other sin offerings 5:1
Offerings for sins of poor people 5:7

Guilt offerings 5:14
The priest and burnt offerings 6:1
The priest and cereal offerings 6:14
The priest and sin offerings 6:24
The priest and guilt offerings 7:1
The priest and peace offerings 7:11
Rules concerning victims 7:19
The priest's portion 7:28
Conclusion 7:36

Part Two
The ordination of priests

Ordination rites 8:1
The priests and their functions 9:1

Punishment for ritual irregularity 10:1
Rules for officiating priests 10:4

Part Three
Rules concerning the clean and the unclean

Clean and unclean animals 11:1
Purification of a woman after childbirth 12:1
Tests for leprosy 13:1
Leprosy in clothes 13:47
Cleansing of leprosy 14:1

Cleansing of houses infected by leprosy 14:33
Male uncleanness 15:1
Female uncleanness 15:19
The day of atonement 16:1

Part Four
The law of holiness

The place of sacrifice and the eating of blood 17:1
Rules concerning marriage and chastity 18:1
Moral and religious duties 19:1
Penalties for offences against true worship 20:1
Penalties for moral faults 20:9
An exhortation to holiness 20:22
The holiness of priests 21:1
The holiness of the high priest 21:10
Impediments to the priesthood 21:16
Priests partaking of the sacred meal 22:1
Others partaking of the sacred meal 22:10
Victims to be unblemished 22:17
Exhortation to obedience 22:31
Celebration of the sabbath 23:1
Celebration of the Passover and the feast of the unleavened bread 23:5
Celebration of the first fruits 23:9
Celebration of the feast of Weeks 23:15
Celebration of the New Year 23:23
Celebration of the day of atonement 23:26

Celebration of the feast of Tabernacles 23:33
Rules about lighting the sanctuary 24:1
Rules about the offertory bread 24:5
Punishment for blasphemy 24:10
The law of retaliation 24:17
Rules about the sabbatical year 25:1
Rules about the jubilee year 25:8
Rules about redeeming landed property 25:23
Rules about loans 25:35
Rules about slaves 25:39
Blessings for observing the law 26:1
Curses for disobedience 26:14

APPENDIX 27:1
The discharge of vows 27:1
Evaluation of an animal offered to the Lord 27:9
Evaluation of landed property offered to the Lord 27:14
Compensation for the redemption of persons 27:26
Rules about tithing 27:30

Headings Added to the Biblical Text

NUMBERS

Part One
The people of Israel in the Sinai desert

1. THE COMMUNITY OF ISRAEL 1:1
The census of the tribes 1:1
A special statute for the tribe of Levi 1:47
The order of the tribes in the camp 2:1
The tribe of Levi 3:1
The priests 3:2
The Levites 3:5
The census of the Levites 3:14
Redeeming the first-born of Israel 3:40
The Kohathites 4:1
The Gershonites 4:21
The Merarites 4:29
The result of the census of the Levites 4:34

2. LAWS ABOUT RITUAL UNCLEANNESS 5:1
Expulsion of the unclean 5:1
Restitution 5:5

Offering in cases of jealousy 5:11
The Nazirite 6:1
Blessing by priests 6:22

3. OFFERINGS AT THE CONSECRATION OF THE
SANCTUARY 7:1
Presentation of offerings 7:1
Offerings of leaders 7:10
Conversations between Moses and the Lord 7:89
The golden lampstand 8:1
The purification and offering of the Levites 8:5

4. PREPARATION FOR THE DEPARTURE 9:1
The second celebration of the Passover 9:1
Individual cases 9:6
The cloud covers the tabernacle 9:15
The silver trumpets 10.1

Part Two
The people in Kadesh

5. THE MARCH THROUGH THE DESERT 10:11
Departure from Sinai 10:11
The order of the march 10:13
Moses's proposal to Hobab 10:29

6. REBELLIONS 11:1
The fire at Taberah 11:1
Craving for Egyptian food 11:4
Moses' prayer 11:10
The appointment of the seventy elders 11:24
The quails 11:31
The complaint of Miriam and Aaron against Moses 12:1
Moses intercedes 12:13
The reconnoitring the promised land 13:1
The spies return 13:25
The rebellion of Israel 14:1
God's threat and Moses' appeal 14:10
God's new reply 14:26
A frustrated attempt to enter the promised land 14:39

7. LAWS FOR PRIESTS AND LEVITES 15:1
Rules about offerings 15:1
Atonement for faults of inadvertence 15:22
Penalty for breaking the sabbath 15:32
Tassels on garments 15:37
The rebellion of Korah and Abiram; their punishment
16:1
Recovering the altar 16:36
The people complain and are punished 16:42
Aaron's rod 17:1
Priests and Levites 18:1
Tithes and portions 18:8
The rite of the red heifer 19:1
Purification with water 19:11

8. VARIOUS EVENTS IN KADESH 20:1
Moses brings water from the rock 20:1
Edom refuses right of way 20:14

Part Three
From Kadesh to Moab

The death of Aaron 20:22
The destruction of the Aradites 21:1
The bronze serpent 21:4

Movements in the region of Moab 21:10
Sihon and Og defeated 21:21

Part Four
Israel on the plains of Moab*

9. THE STORY OF BALAAM 22:1
Balak calls in Balaam 22:1
Balaam's ass 22:22

Balaam's first oracle 23:1
Balaam's second oracle 23:13
Balaam's third oracle 24:1

Headings Added to the Biblical Text

Balaam's fourth oracle 24:10
Israel's idolatry is punished 25:1
Phinehas's jealousy 25:6

10. FURTHER LEGISLATION 26:1
The census on the plains of Moab 26:1
The inheritance of daughters 27:1
Moses' successor 27:12
Rules about sacrifices 28:1
Daily sacrifices 28:3
Sabbath sacrifices 28:9
The feast of the new moon 28:11
The feast of the unleavened bread 28:16
The feast of Weeks 28:26
The day to blow the trumpet 29:1

The day of atonement 29:7
The feast of Tabernacles 29:12
Laws concerning vows 29:40

11. PREPARATIONS FOR ENTERING THE PROMISED
    LAND 31:1
Vengeance on Midian; division of the booty 31:1
The tribes of Transjordania 32:1
The stages of Israel's journey 33:1
The Lord's order to drive out the Canaanites 33:50
The boundaries of the promised land 34:1
The leaders in charge of allocating the land 34:16
Cities for the Levites 35:1
Cities of refuge 35:9
Laws about wives' inheritance 36:1

DEUTERONOMY

Introduction 1:1

Part One
The first discourse of Moses: historical introduction

1. HISTORICAL SUMMARY OF THE EXODUS 1:6
Departure from Horeb-Sinai 1:6
Appointment of judges 1:9
The rebellion and punishment of the people 1:19
From Kadesh to Transjordania 2:1
Victory over Sihon 2:24
Victory over Og 3:1
The allocation of Transjordania 3:12
Moses' exhortation to Joshua 3:21
Moses' plea 3:23

2. EXHORTATION TO KEEP THE LAW 4:1
Faithfulness to the law. God's closeness to his people
    4:1
The revelation at Horeb 4:9
Condemnation and punishment of idolatry 4:15
The Lord's special providence towards his people 4:32
Cities of refuge 4:41

Part Two
The second discourse of Moses: the law

Its time and place 4:44

3. THE TEN COMMANDMENTS 5:1
The Lord is the only God 6:1
The Shema 6:4
An appeal for faithfulness 6:10

4. ISRAEL, A PEOPLE HOLY TO THE LORD 7:1
The Canaanites to be driven out 7:1
God's election of Israel 7:7
Trust in God 7:17

5. THE GIFT OF THE PROMISED LAND 8:1
Israel's character forged in the desert 8:1
God not to be forgotten in the time of plenty 8:7
Victory comes from the Lord 9:1
Israel's unfaithfulness. Moses intercedes 9:7
Historical insertion: the ark of the covenant and the
    choice of Levi 10:1
A further call to faithfulness 10:12
A further evocation of the Exodus 11:1

The promised land 11:8
A further exhortation 11:18
A blessing and a curse 11:26

6. THE DEUTERONOMIC CODE 12:1
1. Duties towards God
There is to be only one sanctuary 12:1
Regulations concerning sacrifice 12:13
Against Canaanite cults 12:29
Against those who promote idolatry 12:32
A ban on certain funeral rites 14:1
Clean and unclean animals 14:3
The annual tithe 14:22
The sabbatical year 15:1
Slaves 15:12
First-born livestock 15:19
The three great feasts
    The Passover 16:1
    The feast of Weeks 16:9
    The feast of Tabernacles 16:13

Headings Added to the Biblical Text

2. Institutions of Israel 16:18
Judges 16:18
Kings 17:14
Priests 18:1
Prophets 18:9

3. Social rights 19:1
Cities of refuge 19:1
Boundaries of properties 19:14
Witnesses 19:15
The law of retaliation 19:21

4. Moral and legal rules 20:1
Laws of war 20:1
Atonement for murder by a person unknown 21:1
Women taken in war 21:10
Birthright 21:15
The rebellious son 21:18
The body of an executed person 21:22
Various rulings 22:1

Laws about marriage 22:13
Exclusion from public worship 23:1
The camp and legal purity 23:9
Other rulings 23:15
The bill of divorce 24:1
Humanitarian measures 24:5
The levirate law 25:5
Honesty and uprightness 25:11
The Amalekites 25:17
First-fruits 26:1
The three-year tithe 26:12
Israel, the people of the Lord 26:16

7. CONCLUDING DISCOURSES. ISRAEL, THE PEOPLE OF GOD 27:1
Instructions regarding the law and worship 27:1
Curses for unfaithfulness 27:14
Blessings for faithfulness 28:1
Other curses 28:15

Part Three
The third discourse of Moses: the covenant of Moab

The Exodus recalled 29:2
The Covenant and generations to come 29:10
Threats of exile 29:22

Restoration after repentance 30:1
The Law of God is accessible to all 30:11
Israel facing life and death: the two ways 30:15

Historical conclusion

Joshua and his mission 31:1
The ritual reading of the law 31:9
Israel's future apostasy 31:14
The song of witness 31:19
The Law placed beside the ark 31:34
The song of Moses 32:1

The Law, the source of life 32:45
Moses' death foretold 32:48
Moses' blessing for Israel 33:1
The death of Moses 34:1
A eulogy of Moses 34:10

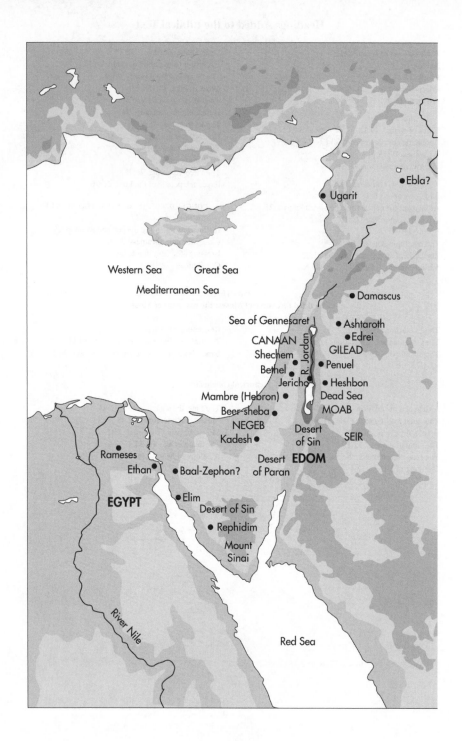

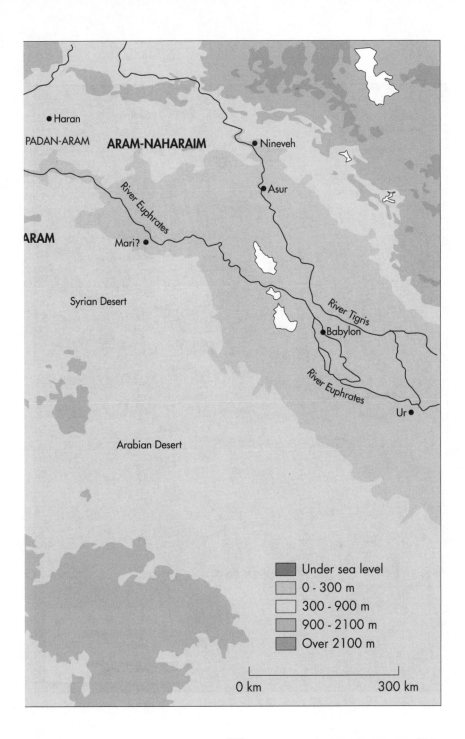

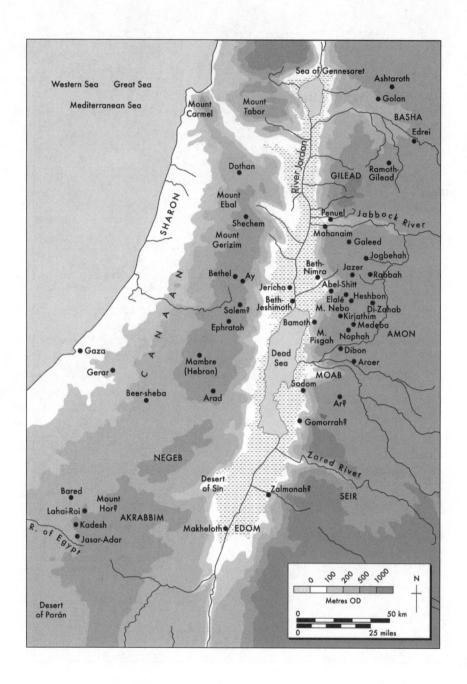